FOOD, ETHICS, AND SOCIETY

An Introductory Text with Readings

Anne Barnhill

Mark Budolfson

Tyler Doggett

New York   Oxford

OXFORD UNIVERSITY PRESS

Oxford University Press is a department of the University of Oxford.
It furthers the University's objective of excellence in research,
scholarship, and education by publishing worldwide. Oxford is a
registered trade mark of Oxford University Press in the UK and
certain other countries.

Published in the United States of America by
Oxford University Press
198 Madison Avenue, New York, NY 10016
http://www.oup.com

For titles covered by Section 112 of the US Higher Education
Opportunity Act, please visit www.oup.com/us/he for the
latest information about pricing and alternate formats.

Library of Congress Cataloging-in-Publication Data

Names: Barnhill, Anne, editor.
Title: Food, ethics, and society: an introductory text with readings /
   [edited by] Anne Barnhill, Mark Budolfson, Tyler Doggett.
Description: New York : Oxford University Press, 2016.
Identifiers: LCCN 2016021921 | ISBN 9780199321742 (pbk.)
Subjects: LCSH: Food--Moral and ethical aspects.
Classification: LCC TX357 .F6393 2016 | DDC 178--dc23 LC record
available at https://lccn.loc.gov/2016021921

9 8 7 6 5 4 3 2 1
Printed by R.R. Donnelley, United States of America

Contents

PREFACE

When we started teaching food ethics courses several years ago, we were struck by three things: first, that there was a lot of interest in the topic from our students; second, that there was a wealth of interesting work that had to do with food ethics from all sorts of academic disciplines, as well as from policymakers, advocates, and citizens; and third, that despite the wealth of interesting work on food, there were no textbooks we could use for our courses. This book fills that gap.

About This Book

As we have been working on the book, there has been steadily growing a subfield of philosophy, food ethics, that has roots in and incorporates some philosophical work on animal ethics, agricultural ethics, environmental ethics, and the philosophy of food. This book is not meant to represent these discourses in their entirety, but to introduce students to some of the real-world ethical issues that are at the forefront of discussion. We have selected scholarly works and popular works that present these topics, and the ethical issues surrounding them, in a compelling and approachable way.

This book covers:

- Hunger
- Food justice
- Consumer ethics
- Food and identity
- Food and religion
- Raising animals for food
- Raising plants for food
- Food workers
- Overconsumption and obesity
- Paternalism

Each of these topics gets at least one chapter. Raising animals and plants for food get two each. And some issues, such as food justice, recur throughout the book. Discussion of them is not limited to one chapter.

How to Use This Book

Each chapter has the following structure. First, there is a chapter introduction, written by us, that explains and analyzes the main issues in the chapter. At the end of each of those chapter introductions, there is a short bibliography of further readings on the topic and some discussion of further issues that the introduction and readings in the chapter bring up. Next, there are selected readings on the chapter's topic. Each reading comes with, at the start, a very short introduction by us and then, at the end, some questions about the reading. The questions are designed to help students understand the reading, understand issues the reading engages with, and understand how the reading fits with other readings and topics in the book.

The introductions to Chapters 2 through 4 not only summarize the main issues in those chapters but also do more general work: explaining key philosophical and ethical ideas, explaining some philosophical methodology, explaining some big-picture issues in food ethics. Because of this, it might be helpful to read those three chapters first and in order. But each chapter can be read independently of the others. The book is not written so that each chapter builds on the previous one, although the chapters, like various aspects of the food system, are interconnected.

Acknowledgments

We received a great deal of help with this book and are deeply grateful to all those who helped. Oxford University Press furnished us with many useful referee reports. For those reports and many other helpful comments, we thank an anonymous referee, as well as Andrew Chignell, Harold Gamble, Matthew C. Halteman, Lisa Heldke, Jessica Hellmann, David Kaplan, Shen-yi Liao, Marion Nestle, David Plunkett, Tisha Rajendra, Timothy Roufs, Jeff Sebo, Chris Schlottman, and Paul B. Thompson. We especially thank Jeff Sebo for his extensive feedback and suggestions. Matthew Halteman's help with the religion chapter was so extensive that we have added him as a co-author.

Anne and Tyler are especially grateful to one referee, Mark Budolfson, who first gave us extraordinarily good comments and then joined on as a co-editor and co-author.

For additional help, advice, and commentary along the way, we thank Terence Cuneo, Helena de Bres, Maria Deloso, Priya Fielding-Singh, Sally Haslanger, Elizabeth Harman, Arthur Kuflik, R. J. Leland, Rachel Licker, Eliot Michaelson, Tristram McPherson, Alison Nihart, Rob Reich, Yashar Saghai, Dave Schmidtz, Dan Shahar, Seana Shiffrin, Dean Spears, Tony Singh, Amy Trubek, Ian Werkheiser, and Kyle Powys Whyte. For their help as research assistants, we thank Kathryn Barth, Jesse Mazar, and Eric Temmel.

For editorial guidance, patience, and support, we thank Kaitlin Coats, Emily Krupin, Kristin Maffei, Robert Miller, and Alyssa Palazzo of Oxford University Press.

For funding to secure permissions and for administrative support, we thank Rutgers University, the Department of Medical Ethics and Health Policy at the University of Pennsylvania, the University of Vermont Food Initiative, and the University of Vermont Philosophy Department. We are especially grateful to Doug Lantagne and Alison Nihart.

For their assiduous work securing permissions, we thank Will Fleisher and Chris Weaver.

1 〉Introduction: The Ethically Troubling Food System

To eat, some hermit crabs simply stick out their claws and shovel aquatic detritus into their mouths.

To eat, some sea anenomes, attached to the backs of those hermit crabs, suck up leftover bits of detritus.

And some of that detritus itself—algae, kelp—"eats" simply by absorbing sunlight.

Things are more complicated for us. We have to get food. Some of us don't get it or don't get enough. Those of us who do get food might get it from a store or a restaurant. That store or restaurant has to get food. It might get it from a farm. On that farm, it's picked or processed by workers or taken from an animal.

Unlike eating or breathing or other things we have to do to stay alive, feeding ourselves is a highly involved, ethically fraught business. This book explains why.

In doing so, it explains the situation in the food system: What are we eating? How are we getting it? Can we keep getting it in that way? Who's *we* anyway? These are not themselves ethical questions. But the answers to these questions might well have ethical implications.

For example, billions of animals are given painful, short lives and then killed to be eaten. Is that ethically permissible? What, if anything, should be done about it?

Nearly a billion people worldwide are malnourished. Is that ethically permissible? What, if anything, should be done about it?

Large numbers of badly paid agricultural workers work back-breaking, tenuous jobs so that much better-off people can enjoy cheap produce. Is that ethically permissible? What, if anything, should be done about it?

These workers and the food they produce for industrialized countries are part of an economic framework that stretches all over the globe with effects on both the best-off and the worst-off. Indeed, food policy in America operates within that framework and also puts huge amounts of dollars here, withholding huge amounts of dollars there. Is that framework just? What, if anything, should be done about it? Who should be doing it?

In this book, we start to answer these questions.

WHAT IS ETHICS?

In this chapter, you will read about the suffering of animals in animal agriculture. You will read about the back-breaking, poorly paid work of agricultural workers. You will read about how consumption patterns in the United States are causing illness.

One might ask various *ethical* questions about the facts and situations described in those readings: Are these *ethically good* states of affairs? *Bad*? Are people in them acting *wrongly*? (Are things other than individual people—governments, corporations, collectives—acting wrongly?) How does an action being wrong differ from a state of affairs being bad? If an action is wrong, why is it wrong? Because it involves *injustice*? *Cruelty*? *Oppression*? Or something else? Are agents who perform some of these actions *blameworthy*? Are other agents performing other actions *praiseworthy*?

The readings in this chapter do not dispassionately present information. They are written from an ethical point of view. The authors of the readings are not only presenting information about what the world is like—People are hungry! Animals are farmed! Workers are paid low wages!—but are also suggesting answers to the ethical questions that arise given these facts—It's *bad* that people are hungry! It's *wrong* that animals are farmed! It's *unjust* that workers are treated as they are!

These might be the correct answers. Or they might not be. But before we evaluate that, we should think more about the nature of these ethical questions.

When you learn that billions of animals are annually killed for us to eat, you can ask, "Was that okay? Should they be killed? Was killing them wrong?" Similarly, when you jaywalk, you can ask, "Was that okay? Should I jaywalk? Was it wrong to do so?" When you talk with food in your mouth, you can ask, "Is this okay? Should I do this? Is it wrong?" and when you sleep too late, you can ask, "Was that okay? Should I have done this? Was it wrong?"

Not all of these *shoulds, okays,* and *wrongs* are about *ethics* or *morality* (we use those last two words and their cognates interchangeably). Instead, the jaywalking questions are naturally understood as questions about *law*, the talking questions about *manners*, and the sleeping questions about *prudence*. In this book, when we ask whether it is okay—permissible—to kill chickens for food or whether it is permissible that some people are hungry while others have too much food, we should be understood as asking *ethical* questions, the sort of questions we are asking when we ask whether lying is permissible or whether targeting civilians in war is permissible. They are ethical questions we are asking when we ask whether capitalism is exploitative or hunger in the United States is an injustice or when we ask whether it is permissible to eat chicken or to buy organic food.

To help answer these questions about permissibility, we can try to identify the *moral reasons for* actions and states of affairs, and *moral reasons against* them. What are the reasons in favor of lying? The reasons against lying? When you wonder whether it is permissible to lie to your friend about something important, it could be that a reason to do so is that it will make her feel better. A reason not to do it might be that it is manipulative or disrespectful. A reason to do it might be that everyone will be happier as a result. A reason not to do it might be that, in doing so, you'll be being a bad friend. These reasons combine to make it the case that your action is permissible or impermissible or morally required.

Ethicists use a wide range of these and other ethical concepts to articulate *general ethical theories* that aim to identify and explain the ethical reasons we actually have, and to do so in the most fundamental and unified way possible——just as general theories in chemistry and physics attempt to explain the basic physical mechanisms of the world in the most fundamental and unified way possible. We will introduce some core ethical concepts and theories in the following three chapters in connection with a few central issues in food ethics. Then, in later chapters, we will build on and go beyond these while discussing other central issues about ethics and food.

ABOUT THIS BOOK

Scholars from many disciplines, as well as policymakers and advocates and citizens, research and debate ethical issues pertaining to the food system. Sometimes they call the topic of this research and debate "ethics" or "food ethics" but not always. There is also a growing subfield of philosophy, food ethics, that has roots in and incorporates some philosophical work on animal ethics, agricultural ethics, environmental ethics, and the philosophy of food. This book is not meant to represent these discourses in their entirety, but to introduce students to some of the real-world ethical issues that are at the forefront of discussion. We have selected scholarly works and popular works that present these topics, and the ethical issues surrounding them, in a compelling and approachable way.

In food ethics, ethical conclusions often rest on empirical premises. A good empirical ground is important to reaching ethical conclusions. Yet that ground is often unstable and the premises that grow from it are often complicated, with lots of unknowns, and disagreement about their truth. We flag these issues at places and sometimes weigh in, but in this book, we don't get into the weeds about these empirical issues or disagreements.

With some topics we do not dig deeply. On every topic we discuss, we had to leave out many important works because there is only space to include a fraction of the important work. And many important ethical topics pertaining to the food system are not discussed in this book or are just barely touched on. As just a few examples:

- Eating disorders
- Food and character
- Food and gender
- Food and race
- Gluttony
- Seafood

That we don't include these topics is no reflection on their importance, but just a sign of limits on how much can go into one book.

FURTHER ISSUES

1. *Duties to the Poor and Hungry*
What kind of moral obligations do we have (or not have) to improve the situation of those who are poor and hungry? Some foods are out of reach for many people because they cost

too much money. For example, we can't afford to buy the limited edition Gout de Diamants champagne that cost £1.2 million. There is nothing morally wrong with that. (Whether there is something wrong with making a champagne that costs so much money is different. Our point is that there is nothing objectionable in the mere fact that *we* can't afford a certain luxury product.) But others, discussed by Ken Weiss in his reading in this chapter, face significantly more serious problems, such as being unable to secure adequate nutrition for themselves and their families because they cannot afford to buy staple foods. Is it unjust when some people cannot afford to buy staple foods but others can? Is it unjust when someone cannot afford to buy staple foods, never mind if anyone else can? When some people cannot afford to buy staple foods, do wealthier people have a moral obligation to help them get enough food? If so, is this because everyone has a right to food? If wealthier people have these moral obligations, why? Because they have a moral obligation toward other individuals to relieve their suffering if they can do so at relatively little cost to themselves? Because all people have a right to food and so wealthier people have a moral obligation to make sure they get enough food? Because poverty and food insecurity are injustices? Or is it because wealthier people are, in some way, implicated in or responsible for the bad situation of the poor, such that the wealthier people are obligated to help fix it?

We discuss related issues in more detail in Chapter 2, "Global Hunger," and Chapter 3, "Food Justice."

2. *Nutrition in Developing Countries*

If we want to improve nutrition in developing countries, how should we do this? Through private charities and aid organizations? Through nutrition programs run by governments and international organizations such as the United Nations? Through economic development that helps developing countries become incorporated into the global economy, so that the poor in those countries are more likely to have jobs and money to buy food? Or is the structure of the global economy the underlying cause of much poverty and food insecurity, such that efforts to incorporate the poor into the global economy are the wrong approach?

We discuss related issues in more detail in Chapter 2, "Global Hunger," and Chapter 3, "Food Justice."

3. *Working Conditions*

What ethical reasons do we have (or not have) to improve working conditions in our food system? Consider the agricultural workers Barry Estabrook discusses in his reading in this chapter. There is no doubt that their treatment is bad, that it's regrettable, and that there is something awful about the characters of some of their bosses. From all that, though, it does not follow that their treatment is wrong.

To see this, think about babysitters. When we pick babysitters, we not only pick those who'll take good care of our children, but we also pick those who charge us a reasonable rate. If we have a choice between a 25-year-old and a 15-year-old, the latter will typically charge less than the former. Is it permissible to hire the latter? If we know the latter is hard up for money, may we ask her to take a pay cut? Is that just permissible hard-bargaining? Or impermissible exploitation?

Or think about NFL players. NFL players routinely subject themselves to a sizeable risk of terrible injury and a non-negligible risk of death. They routinely subject themselves to activities that might well disfigure them for the rest of their lives. These risks come from the violence of the hits players are subjected to. Everyone knows there is a straightforward way to reduce these risks: Move from tackle football to touch football. Does the NFL do wrong by not doing so?

Of course, NFL players are very well paid. But the vast majority of football players in the United States are kids who don't get paid at all but are still subject to terrible risks. Is that permissible? If it is permissible to treat babysitters as we do or permissible to treat football players as the NFL and organizations do, is it permissible to treat workers in the way Estabrook describes?

We discuss related issues in more detail in Chapter 11, "Workers."

4. *Relieving Hunger*
The questions of whether it is permissible to subject workers to awful conditions are harder than they might first appear.

How does this compare to "Is it permissible to let millions of people starve?" Is that a hard question? What sort of moral monster says "yes" to that? And yet think about the money you paid for this textbook. Was it permissible for you to spend that money? Just in the minutes you've been reading this introduction, several children around the world have died from hunger-related conditions. Instead of spending the money on the textbook, you could have used it to buy food to feed these children. Was it permissible for you to buy the book? This illustrates that ethical questions that may initially appear easy are sometimes much harder than they might first look.

We discuss related issues in more detail in Chapter 2, "Global Hunger," Chapter 3, "Food Justice," and Chapter 7, "Industrial Animal Agriculture."

5. *Hurting and Killing Animals*
What ethical reasons do we have (or not have) to hurt or kill animals? Consider the animals Jonathan Safran Foer discusses in his reading in this chapter. Everyone might agree that *hurting* sentient creatures is *bad*. They might agree that someone who delights in hurting things has *bad character* or is *blameworthy* for what he does.

Yet it does not *follow* that hurting those animals is wrong, in the sense that someone could agree with those initial judgments that hurting is bad, so on, but yet quite consistently disagree with the further claim that hurting is wrong in this particular case. Sometimes hurting is permissible. We know, for example, that it can be permissible to end a romantic relationship with someone even when doing so will lead to much heartache. We know it is permissible to forcibly, painfully restrain persons if that is the only way to prevent them from assaulting an innocent victim. In each of these cases, inflicting pain is permissible because it is justified. A question for food ethics is whether the infliction of pain on animals on farms is like the infliction of pain in the cases just listed.

Similarly, everyone might agree that *killing* animals is *bad* or that someone who delights in doing so has *bad character* or is *blameworthy* for doing so. Yet it does not follow that killing animals is wrong. Killing living things is sometimes permissible. We know, for example, that it is permissible to kill bacteria with antibiotics, to kill weeds by uprooting them, to kill mosquitos by crushing them as they try to suck our blood. We know it is permissible to kill humans sometimes as in some cases of soldiers killing other soldiers in war or in cases of justified self-defense. Another question for food ethics, then, is whether the infliction of death on animals on farms is like the infliction of death in the cases just listed.

We discuss related issues in more detail throughout the book, particularly in Chapter 7, "Industrial Animal Agriculture."

6. *Consumption*

If a food is produced in a way that is wrong, is it wrong for you to consume it? Consider next the individual consumer that Grace Boey discusses in her reading in this chapter. Suppose—only for the sake of argument—that someone becomes convinced that, for example, factory-farmed pork chops are produced in a way that is wrong. Does it follow from what they believe that it is wrong to eat factory-farmed pork chops? What if the nature of the problem is systemic—is caused by the large complex political-economic-social-food system in the background, which results in pork chops coming from factory farms rather than small farmers as in an earlier age—and as a single consumer your purchases have no influence on that system? How does the systemic nature of these issues complicate questions about what you have ethical reason to do as an individual person? If most social and political problems are systems problems in this sense—both within the domain of food and outside—what does this imply about what you as a single individual have reason to do about the world's problems?

We discuss related issues in more detail in Chapter 4, "Consumer Ethics."

7. *Control over the Food System*

Do the agricultural and food industries exert too much control over the food system? As Raj Patel describes in his reading in this chapter, large agricultural and food companies exert a powerful influence over the structure of the global agricultural and food system. These companies include large agribusiness companies such as Monsanto; large food manufacturers such as Kraft, Coca-Cola, and Nestlé; restaurant chains such as McDonald's and Starbucks; and large food retailers such as Kroger and Walmart. These companies influence food and agricultural policy by influencing the political process. They influence agricultural practices by setting standards that farmers, distributors, and others along the supply chain must meet, as described by Patel: "By virtue of its size, Nestlé can dictate the terms of supply to its growers, millers, exporters and importers, and each is being squeezed dry." They control significant amounts of land in both developing and developed countries, and they control seeds and many other technologies used in modern farming. The food industry also influences consumer tastes and expectations, as Patel describes: "[T]he food industry adds tens of thousands of new products to the shelves every year, some of which become indispensable fixtures which, after a generation, make life unimaginable without them."

Is it ethically problematic that companies have this much influence over the structure of the food system and over consumers? If it is ethically problematic, why? Because the policies and practices that industry promotes have bad results—for example, bad for the environment, bad for workers, or bad for human health? What if companies used their influence and power to bring about good outcomes? For example, Estabrook describes how the Campaign for Fair Food got fast food and grocery chains to pay more for tomatoes, such that the wages of tomato pickers would increase to a livable wage. What if companies made such changes of their own accord? Would it still be ethically problematic for private interests to have so much influence? If so, why? Because it is undemocratic? Because communities have a right to decide for themselves how their land is used, how their food is grown, and what kind of food choices they have?

We discuss related issues in more detail in Chapter 3, "Food Justice," and Chapter 12, "Overconsumption and Obesity."

8. *Race, Class, Gender, and the Food System*
How do people's experiences of food and the food system vary based on race, class, gender, and membership in other social groups, and which of these differences are ethically problematic? People's experiences of food and the food system—their experience as eaters, cooks, workers, activists—differ to some extent depending upon their gender, class, race, ethnicity, and membership in other social groups. How do they differ? Which of these differences are ethically problematic, and which are not? Eating particular foods is a way of expressing our group identities: for example, eating kimchi expresses Korean identity and drinking vodka expresses Russian identity. It does not seem inherently ethically problematic for groups to have different food traditions and food practices. But other differences between groups do seem ethically problematic, or potentially so. For example, as we discuss in Chapter 11, "Workers," the food system workers who have low-paying, hard, and disgusting jobs are disproportionately people of color. And more women than men tend to occupy lower-paying jobs in the food system. Are these differences ethically problematic? If so, why? Are they injustices—that is, instances of people being treated unfairly and not being given what they're due from society?

We discuss related issues in more detail in Chapter 3, "Food Justice," and Chapter 11, "Workers."

9. *Do We Need a Food Movement? What Should It Be Like?*
In the reading "The Food Movement, Rising," Michael Pollan speaks favorably of food movements—a variety of social movements that aim to change how food is produced and consumed. As we discuss in Chapter 3, "Food Justice," some critics of the alternative food movement in the United States see it as elitist and exclusionary—made up of mostly white, middle-class people and reflecting their experience and interests. Does the alternative food movement reflect the values of some groups but not others? Does the alternative food movement focus too much on meeting the needs of relatively privileged people—for example, creating farmer's markets in wealthy areas that offer many varieties of kale, rather than helping low-income people who have little access to fresh food because their neighborhoods have no grocery stores? Has the alternative food movement been effective in changing the food system, or has it just created niche products for affluent people? Will it be a movement that predictably serves the elite rather than actually benefits society?

We discuss these issues in more detail in Chapter 3, "Food Justice," and Chapter 10, "Alternatives to Industrial Plant Agriculture."

FURTHER READING

Kaplan, David. n.d. *The Philosophy of Food Project.* http://www.food.unt.edu.
Sandler, Ronald L. 2014. *Food Ethics: The Basics.* New York: Routledge.
Singer, Peter, and Jim Mason. 2007. *The Ethics of What We Eat.* Emmaus, PA: Rodale.
Thompson, Paul B., and David Kaplan, eds. 2014. *Encyclopedia of Food and Agricultural Ethics.* Dordrecht: Springer.

KENNETH R. WEISS

As the World's Population Grows, Hunger Persists on a Massive Scale

In this article, originally published in the *Los Angeles Times*, journalist Ken Weiss describes the scope and human toll of hunger. The article raises questions and describes problems that are taken up in Chapter 2, "Global Hunger," and Chapter 3, "Food Justice."

DADAAB, Kenya—His rib cage rose and fell with tight, rapid breaths.

Saad Siyat looked shrunken beneath the hospital blanket. His wide-set eyes rolled up into his head, and his body burned with fever.

The boy was unconscious and convulsing when his aunt brought him to the hospital at Ifo camp, one of five massive camps in eastern Kenya filled with Somali refugees. The family had arrived months earlier after a nearly 300-mile journey across the desert.

Saad was suffering from pneumonia and chronic undernourishment—in particular, a protein deficiency known as kwashiorkor. The name derives from a West African term for "rejected one," a child pushed from his mother's breast to make way for a newborn.

Saad was 2½ years old. He weighed 18 pounds.

"This child has been sick a very long time," Dr. Ibtisam Salim said as she made her rounds in the hospital's stabilization center, a concrete building filled with emaciated children lying on squeaky metal beds.

She felt Saad's forehead and questioned his aunt, who was shooing away flies and using a soiled rag to wipe mucus from his oxygen and feeding tubes. The boy's mother was at home, tending to her seven other children.

Salim gently held up one of his feet, to show the swelling, a classic symptom of protein deficiency.

"Malnutrition opens up a very big window for infection," Salim said. "It destroys their defenses."

She heard a gasp and stiffened.

"Excuse me," she said, wheeling around on her heels and digging in her bag. She pulled out a stethoscope and held it to the boy's chest.

With the tips of three fingers, she began pumping rapidly on his frail torso.

Around the world, population is rising most rapidly in places where life is most precarious.

Across Africa and in parts of South Asia and Latin America, hundreds of millions of people live on the edge of starvation. A drought, flood or outbreak of violence can push them over the brink.

Many end up on the march, crossing borders in search of relief. Some arrive in places like Dadaab, famished and desperately ill. Millions more are displaced within their own countries.

They represent one face of hunger in a world that, on paper at least, produces enough food to feed all 7 billion inhabitants.

Somalia, a nation of 10 million, has one of the highest birthrates in the world, averaging 6.4 children per woman. Runaway population growth, food scarcity and political strife have combined to cause a mass exodus. One-fourth of Somalis have fled their homes.

Last year, during the worst of a three-year drought, shortage turned to famine. Forty percent of Somali children who reached the refugee camps in Dadaab were malnourished. Despite emergency feeding and medical treatment, many died within 24 hours.

More commonly, children live on tenuously, the effects of chronic malnutrition masked by the swelling caused by kwashiorkor. By the time their parents realize how sick they are and take them to the camp hospital, it can be too late.

It has been four decades since advances in agriculture known as the Green Revolution seemed to promise relief from this kind of mass suffering.

An American plant breeder named Norman Borlaug won the Nobel Peace Prize in 1970 for helping to develop high-yield, disease-resistant varieties of wheat and other grains, making it possible to triple harvests around the world.

Mankind finally seemed to be gaining ground on its longtime nemesis: pervasive hunger.

Yet Borlaug cautioned against hubris: "The frightening power of human reproduction must also be curbed," he said. "Otherwise, the success of the Green Revolution will be ephemeral only."

Today, with nearly twice as many people on the planet, his words seem sadly prescient.

Nearly 1 billion people are malnourished, according to the U.N. Food and Agriculture Organization. At least 8 million die every year of hunger-related diarrhea, pneumonia and other illnesses—more than succumb to AIDS, malaria and tuberculosis combined. A child dies of hunger every 11 seconds.

In raw volume, the world's farmers produce enough food for everyone. People go hungry in developing countries because they can't afford to buy food and can't grow enough on their own. Inadequate transportation and storage aggravate shortages.

By midcentury, global food production could simply be insufficient. There will be at least 2 billion more mouths to feed, and an expanding middle class will consume more grain-fed beef, pork and other meats.

To meet the demand, the world's farmers will have to double their crop production by 2050, according to researchers' calculations.

Jonathan Foley, a University of Minnesota climatologist, says it's the challenge of the 21st century: "How will we feed 9 billion people without destroying the planet?"

Most of Earth's best farmland is already under cultivation, and prime acreage is being lost every year to expanding cities and deserts, contamination from agricultural chemicals and other causes.

Carving large new tracts of farmland out of the world's remaining forests and grasslands would exact a heavy toll, destroying wildlife and unleashing climate-warming gases now locked in soils and vegetation.

Complicating the problem is that rivers and aquifers are running dry, and heat waves and droughts associated with global warming are withering crops. Pests and diseases thought to have been vanquished are bedeviling farmers again, often in more virulent forms.

Major international research projects are underway to develop hybrid crops to withstand these challenges. But such efforts take decades, and there is no guarantee of success.

"The easy things have been done," said Nina V. Fedoroff, a biotechnology expert at Pennsylvania State University. "The problems that are left are hard."

The traditional low-tech solution to hunger—mass migration—is increasingly impractical on a crowded planet.

The looming crisis is expected to be most severe in Africa, where birthrates are high and where the Green Revolution never took hold. By midcentury, the continent's population is expected to double—to 2 billion.

Africa already is home to nearly 30% of the planet's chronically hungry. About 400 million people in sub-Saharan Africa live on less than $1.25 a day, most of which is spent on food.

Increasingly, they are competing with the appetites of wealthier nations, which are snapping up some of Africa's best rain-fed farmland to secure long-term food supplies. The U.S., China and other countries are also using more grain to fatten livestock and make ethanol, pushing up prices.

All of this leaves more and more people on the edge.

When it opened in 1991, the camp complex in Dadaab was intended as a temporary shelter for 90,000 Somalis. It now holds the world's largest concentration of refugees: 472,000 and counting.

On a blistering morning, more than 1,000 new arrivals massed outside the fence. Most had trudged through the desert for days or weeks.

Guards bellowed at the mob with bullhorns and swatted men with switches to herd them into lines. Lone refugees were rare; the lines contained families of eight, 10 or more.

Nearly all the newcomers were skinny, some skeletal. As they shuffled through processing stations, workers measured their outstretched arms for body fat. Children were immunized against measles and polio and given a squirt of vitamin A.

Clutching her ration card in one hand and cradling a 2-month-old girl with the other, Shamsa Adow Hassan said she had fled her riverbank farm in Somalia with her husband and four children.

"The farms have dried up," said Hassan, 32. "Some people had died of starvation."

She decided to leave when a rocket struck and killed her father.

At the center of one camp, the new arrivals joined other refugees lining up with empty sacks, plastic jugs and tins to receive two-week rations of food staples. To keep women from being trampled, security officers in white coats put the men in separate lines.

After some jostling and a sprint to the entrance, the refugees made their way through large tunnels similar to cattle chutes, fashioned from barbed wire, chain-link fencing and corrugated metal. Through openings at various intervals, aid workers scooped wheat flour, cornmeal, dried peas, soy protein powder and salt into the refugees' gunnysacks.

Thousands of tons of food are distributed in these camps every year by the U.N.'s World Food Program and other aid organizations. The U.S. government pays most of the cost. Worldwide, the U.N. program feeds an average of 90 million people per year.

On this day, not far from the chutes, Mohamed Abdi Yussuf was holding forth, encircled by some of the camps' younger leaders. They were talking about crowding, the lack of water and a shortage of flour.

Even so, Yussuf said he wanted to have as many children as possible.

At 26, with three children, he is just getting started.

How many does he want? "Seventy," he said. "Sixty boys and 10 girls."

This brought some tittering from his fellow youth leaders. He didn't crack a smile.

"I think these guys will support me," Yussuf said. "Our elders, our fathers, had many children. It's a common idea."

He hadn't consulted his 21-year-old wife and said he planned to divorce her before she turns 40.

"When she stops breeding, I will jump to another young lady."

Asked how he would provide for all those children, Yussuf shrugged.

"I don't worry what the children will feed on," he said. "They have their own fate. They have their own mouths, teeth. God knows what to put in there."

James Mukunga worries every day about how to feed his children.

Outside Dadaab, across the arid expanses of East Africa, farmers like him are struggling to provide for large families. Once-fertile grasslands have been overgrazed and trampled by herds of goats and cows.

Mukunga lives with his wife and 12 children, 27 goats and one donkey on a small farm 200 miles from the refugee camps.

The skinny Kenyan farmer wore tattered clothes and kicked at a shriveled patch of millet with sandals fashioned from car tires. Stunted stalks of corn, sorghum and other plants poked through sun-baked clay.

This year, like the one before, his crop had failed because of drought. "Since 2004, we have not had a reasonable harvest," Mukunga said.

The family chopped down their few remaining trees to make charcoal to sell. Otherwise, they subsist on donated food from the United States. Their small granary is empty but for a few spent cans of vegetable oil labeled "USAID."

Mukunga wonders if his goats, a source of meat and milk, will survive another dry year.

The family gets its water from a village borehole four miles away. It was a mob scene on this hot day. Dozens of women toting jerrycans waited in the shade of an acacia tree, next to herds of scrawny goats and cattle. A cow licked an empty spigot.

The water pump had run out of diesel fuel, and a few men had gone off to find some.

Hours passed as the thirsty waited for relief.

At the hospital at Ifo camp in Dadaab, Dr. Salim used her fingers to spread Saad's upper and lower eyelids and shined a light into a pupil. Then she went back to work, compressing his chest.

Somali women covered head to toe in brightly colored scarves and dresses crowded around the bed.

A nurse squeezed through with a syringe of adrenaline.

"He's gasping," Salim said, tilting Saad's head back to open his airways.

The boy's aunt, with large frightened eyes, climbed onto the bed, squatting on her haunches. She poured water into his mouth from a red plastic cup.

"Mama, please, please, please . . . Mama, *please*," Salim said, gently moving the woman's arm out of the way.

The doctor continued the chest compressions, faster now.

An assistant brought a hand-pumped respirator. Salim placed a clear plastic mask over the boy's nose and mouth and began squeezing the bag.

As she pumped air into his lungs, she handed her stethoscope to a nurse and said: "Listen—listen to the heart."

She watched as the nurse leaned over the child.

"Is there any heartbeat?"

The nurse met her gaze with a weary expression that left no doubt.

"There isn't," Salim said.

The doctor stepped away from the bed, leaned against the wall and silently wept.

QUESTIONS

1. What are the causes of starvation that Weiss either asserts or hints at?
2. What is the Green Revolution? Why was it supposed to solve the problem of starvation? Why, according to Norman Borlaug, can't it do so on its own?
3. Is the main cause of hunger that not enough food is produced? If so, then why don't people just grow more crops? What are the costs of doing so and obstacles to doing so that are articulated in the paragraphs that mention Jonathan Foley, Nina Fedoroff, and James Mukunga? If that is not the main cause of hunger, then what are the main causes?

BARRY ESTABROOK

The Price of Tomatoes

This is a groundbreaking article about the treatment of workers in Florida tomato fields: the abuse they are subjected to by bosses, the harshness of the work, and the lack of legal

Barry Estabrook, "Politics of the Plate: The Price of Tomatoes," in *Gourmet*, March 2, 2009. http://www.gourmet.com/magazine/2000s/2009/03/politics-of-the-plate-the-price-of-tomatoes.html protection against this treatment. See Chapter 11, "Workers," for more discussion of the treatment of agricultural workers and Chapter 9, "Industrial Plant Agriculture," for more discussion of the sort of agriculture Estabrook describes.

Arriving from Naples, Florida, the nation's second-wealthiest metropolitan area, to Immokalee takes less than an hour on a straight road. You pass houses that sell for an average of $1.4 million, shopping malls anchored by Tiffany's and Saks Fifth Avenue, manicured golf courses. Eventually, gated communities with names like Monaco Beach Club and Imperial Golf Estates give way to modest ranches, and the highway shrivels from six lanes to two. Through the scruffy palmettos, you glimpse flat, sandy tomato fields shimmering in the broiling sun. Rounding a long curve, you enter Immokalee. The heart of town is a nine-block grid of dusty, potholed streets lined by boarded-up bars and bodegas, peeling shacks, and sagging, mildew-streaked house trailers. Mongrel dogs snooze in the shade, scrawny chickens peck in yards. Just off the main drag, vultures squabble over roadkill. Immokalee's population is 70 percent Latino. Per capita income is only $8,500 a year. One third of the families in this city of nearly 25,000 live below the poverty line. Over one third of the children drop out before graduating from high school.

Immokalee is the tomato capital of the United States. Between December and May, as much as 90 percent of the fresh domestic tomatoes we eat come from south Florida, and Immokalee is home to one of the area's largest communities of farmworkers. According to Douglas Molloy, the chief assistant U.S. attorney based in Fort Myers, Immokalee has another claim to fame: It is "ground zero for modern slavery."

The beige stucco house at 209 South Seventh Street is remarkable only because it is in better repair than most Immokalee dwellings. For two and a half years, beginning in April 2005, Mariano Lucas Domingo, along with several other men, was held as a slave at that address. At first, the deal must have seemed reasonable. Lucas, a Guatemalan in his thirties, had slipped across the border to make money to send home for the care of an ailing parent. He expected to earn about $200 a week in the fields. Cesar

Navarrete, then a 23-year-old illegal immigrant from Mexico, agreed to provide room and board at his family's home on South Seventh Street and extend credit to cover the periods when there were no tomatoes to pick.

Lucas's "room" turned out to be the back of a box truck in the junk-strewn yard, shared with two or three other workers. It lacked running water and a toilet, so occupants urinated and defecated in a corner. For that, Navarrete docked Lucas's pay by $20 a week. According to court papers, he also charged Lucas for two meager meals a day: eggs, beans, rice, tortillas, and, occasionally, some sort of meat. Cold showers from a garden hose in the backyard were $5 each. Everything had a price. Lucas was soon $300 in debt. After a month of ten-hour workdays, he figured he should have paid that debt off.

But when Lucas—slightly built and standing less than five and a half feet tall—inquired about the balance, Navarrete threatened to beat him should he ever try to leave. Instead of providing an accounting, Navarrete took Lucas's paychecks, cashed them, and randomly doled out pocket money, $20 some weeks, other weeks $50. Over the years, Navarrete and members of his extended family deprived Lucas of $55,000.

Taking a day off was not an option. If Lucas became ill or was too exhausted to work, he was kicked in the head, beaten, and locked in the back of the truck. Other members of Navarrete's dozen-man crew were slashed with knives, tied to posts, and shackled in chains. On November 18, 2007, Lucas was again locked inside the truck. As dawn broke, he noticed a faint light shining through a hole in the roof. Jumping up, he secured a hand hold and punched himself through. He was free.

What happened at Navarrete's home would have been horrific enough if it were an isolated case. Unfortunately, involuntary servitude—slavery—is alive and well in Florida. Since 1997, law-enforcement officials have freed more than 1,000 men and women in seven different cases. And those are only the instances that resulted in convictions. Frightened, undocumented, mistrustful of the police, and speaking little or no English, most slaves refuse to testify, which means their captors cannot be tried. "Unlike victims of other crimes, slaves don't report themselves," said Molloy, who was one of the prosecutors on the Navarrete case. "They hide from us in plain sight."

And for what? Supermarket produce sections overflow with bins of perfect red-orange tomatoes even during the coldest months—never mind that they are all but tasteless. Large packers, which ship nearly $500 million worth of tomatoes annually to major restaurants and grocery retailers nationwide, own or lease the land upon which the workers toil. But the harvesting is often done by independent contractors called crew bosses, who bear responsibility for hiring and overseeing pickers. Said Reggie Brown, executive vice president of the Florida Tomato Growers Exchange, "We abhor slavery and do everything we can to prevent it. We want to make sure that we always foster a work environment free from hazard, intimidation, harassment, and violence." Growers, he said, cooperated with law-enforcement officers in the Navarette case.

But when asked if it is reasonable to assume that an American who has eaten a fresh tomato from a grocery store or food-service company during the winter has eaten fruit picked by the hand of a slave, Molloy said, "It is not an assumption. It is a fact."

Gerardo Reyes, a former picker who is now an employee of the Coalition of Immokalee Workers (CIW), a 4,000-member organization that provides the only voice for the field hands, agrees. Far from being an anomaly, Reyes told me, slavery is a symptom of a vast system of labor abuses. Involuntary servitude represents just one rung on a grim ladder of exploitation. Reyes said that the victims of this system come to Florida for one reason—to send money to their families back home. "But when they get here, it's all they can do to keep themselves alive with rent, transportation, food. Poverty and misery are the perfect recipe for slavery."

Tomato harvesting involves rummaging through staked vines until you have filled a bushel basket to the brim with hard, green fruits. You hoist the basket over your shoulder, trot across the field, and heave it overhead to a worker in an open trailer the size of the bed of a gravel truck. For every 32-pound basket you pick, you receive a token typically worth about 45 cents—almost the same rate you would have gotten 30 years ago. Working at breakneck speed, you might be able to pick a ton of tomatoes on a good day, netting about $50. But a lot can go wrong. If it rains, you can't pick. If the dew is heavy, you sit and wait until it evaporates. If trucks aren't available to transport the harvest, you're out of luck. You receive neither overtime nor benefits. If you are injured (a common occurrence, given the pace of the job), you have to pay for your own medical care.

Leaning against the railing of an unpainted wooden stoop in front of a putty-colored trailer, a tired Juan Dominguez told an all-too-familiar story. He had left for the fields that morning at six o'clock and returned at three. But he worked for only two of those nine hours because the seedlings he was to plant had been delivered late. His total earnings: $13.76.

I asked him for a look inside his home. He shrugged and gestured for me to come in. In one ten-foot-square space there were five mattresses, three directly on the floor, two suspended above on sheets of flimsy plywood. The room was littered with T-shirts, jeans, running shoes, cheap suitcases. The kitchen consisted of a table, four plastic chairs, an apartment-size stove, a sink with a dripping faucet, and a rusty refrigerator whose door wouldn't close. Bare lightbulbs hung from fixtures, and a couple of fans put up a noisy, futile effort against the stale heat and humidity. In a region where temperatures regularly climb into the nineties, there were no air conditioners. One tiny, dank bathroom served ten men. The rent was $2,000 a month—as much as you would pay for a clean little condo near Naples.

Most tomato workers, however, have no choice but to live like Dominguez. Lacking vehicles, they must reside within walking distance of the football-field-size parking lot in front of La Fiesta, a combination grocery store, taqueria, and check-cashing office. During the predawn hours, the lot hosts a daily hiring fair. I arrived a little before 5 a.m. The parking lot was filled with more than a dozen former school buses. Outside each bus stood a silent scrum of 40 or 50 would-be pickers. The driver, or crew boss, selected one worker at a time, choosing young, fit-looking men first. Once full, the bus pulled away.

Later that day, I encountered some of the men and women who had not been picked when I put in a shift at the Guadalupe Center of Immokalee's soup kitchen. Tricia Yeggy, the director of the kitchen, explained that it runs on two simple rules: People can eat as much as they want, and no one is turned away hungry. This means serving between 250 and 300 people a day, 44 per sitting, beginning at eleven o'clock. Cheerful retirees volunteer as servers, and the "guests" are unabashedly appreciative. The day's selection—turkey and rice soup with squash, corn, and a vigorous sprinkle of cumin—was both hearty and tasty. You could almost forget the irony: Workers who pick the food we eat can't afford to feed themselves.

The CIW has been working to ease the migrants' plight since 1993, when a few field hands began meeting sporadically in a church hall. Lucas Benitez, one of the coalition's main spokespeople, came to the group in its early years. Back then, the challenge was taking small steps, often for individual workers. To make the point, Benitez unfolded a crumpled shirt covered in dried blood. "This is Edgar's shirt," he said.

One day in 1996, a 16-year-old Guatemalan boy named Edgar briefly stopped working in the field for a drink of water. His crew boss bludgeoned him. Edgar fled and arrived at the coalition's door, bleeding. In response to the CIW's call for action, over 500 workers assembled and marched to the boss's house. The next morning, no one would get on his bus. "That was the last report of a worker being beaten by his boss in the field," said Benitez. The shirt is kept as a reminder that by banding together, progress is possible.

Even though the CIW has been responsible for bringing police attention to a half dozen slavery prosecutions, Benitez feels that slavery will persist until overall conditions for field workers improve. The group has made progress on that front by securing better pay. Between the early 1980s and the mid-1990s, the rate for a basket of tomatoes remained 40 cents—meaning that workers' real wages dropped as inflation rose. Work stoppages, demonstrations, and a hunger strike helped raise it to 45 cents on average, but the packers complained that competition for customers prevented them from paying more. One grower refused to enter a dialogue with CIW hunger strikers because, in his words, "a tractor doesn't tell the farmer how to run the farm." The CIW decided to try an end run around the growers by going directly to the biggest customers and asking them to pay one cent more per pound directly to the workers. Small change to supermarket chains and fast-food corporations, but it would add about twenty dollars to the fifty a picker makes on a good day, the difference between barely scraping by and earning a livable wage.

The Campaign for Fair Food, as it is called, first took aim at Yum! Brands, owner of Taco Bell, Pizza Hut, KFC, Long John Silver's, and A&W. After four years of pressure, Yum! agreed to the one-cent raise in 2005 and, importantly, pledged to make sure that no worker who picked its tomatoes was being exploited. McDonald's came aboard in 2007, and in 2008 Burger King, Whole Foods Market, and Subway followed, with more expected to join up this year. But the program faces a major obstacle. Claiming that the farmers are not party to the arrangement, the Florida Tomato Growers Exchange, an agricultural cooperative that represents some 90 percent of the state's producers, has refused to be a conduit for the raise, citing legal concerns.

When the Navarrete case came to light, there were no howls of outrage from growers. Or from Florida government circles. When Cesar Navarrete, who pleaded guilty, was sentenced to 12 years in prison this past December, Terence McElroy of the Florida Department of Agriculture and Consumer Services offered his perspective on the crime: "Any legitimate grower certainly does not engage in that activity. But you're talking about maybe a case a year."

Charlie Frost, the Collier County Sheriff's Office detective who investigated and arrested Navarrete, disagrees. With one case wrapped up, he and prosecutor Molloy turned to several other active slavery cases. Sitting in his Naples office and pointing his index finger east, toward the fields of Immokalee, he said, "It's happening out there right now."

Lucas, who received a temporary visa for his testimony, is now back in the fields, still chasing the dream of making a little money to send back home.

BUYING SLAVE-FREE FRUITS

In the warm months, the best solution is to follow that old mantra: buy seasonal, local, and small-scale. But what about in winter? So far, Whole Foods is the only grocery chain that has signed on to the Coalition of Immokalee Workers (CIW) Campaign for Fair Food, which means that it has promised not to deal with growers who tolerate serious worker abuses and, when buying tomatoes, to a pay price that supports a living wage. When shopping elsewhere, you can take advantage of the fact that fruits and vegetables must be labeled with their country of origin. Most of the fresh tomatoes in supermarkets during winter months come from Florida, where labor conditions are dismal for field workers, or from Mexico, where they are worse, according to a CIW spokesman. One option during these months is to buy locally produced hydroponic greenhouse tomatoes, including cluster tomatoes still attached to the vine.

Greenhouse tomatoes are also imported from Mexico, however, so check signage or consult the little stickers often seen on the fruits themselves to determine their source. You can also visit the CIW's information-packed website (ciw-online.org) if you are interested in becoming part of the coalition's efforts.

QUESTIONS

1. Let's separate cases of slavery from the other cases Estabrook discusses, cases in which workers are treated harshly, have limited choice, are pressured to do this or that, but are also free to leave their jobs. These latter cases are *limited option cases*. First, focus on the slavery cases. What is wrong with slavery? Do the reasons it is wrong to enslave people *also* explain what it is wrong with treatment of workers in limited option cases?

2. Are the limited options cases—cases in which workers are treated harshly, have limited choice, are pressured to do this or that, but are also free to leave their jobs—wrong? If so, which ones? Why?

3. Sometimes people say: The workers could be treated much better than they are and at little cost to their employers. That's true. But it is also true, for most of you, that your professors could be paid more than they are currently being paid and at little cost to their employers. Is it wrong for your professors to not get a raise?

4. Estabrook reports that Yum! Brands, the company that owns Taco Bell, pledged to ensure that no one who picks tomatoes for it is exploited. Using the account of exploitation in the Liberto reading in Chapter 11, "Workers," how could a company ensure its workers are not exploited?

5. Estabrook thinks *you* are *complicit* in slavery if you buy Floridian tomatoes. What does he mean? Why does he think it's true? Is he right?

6. Conditions in Florida's tomato fields have improved since Estabrook wrote this article. As the Coalition of Immolakee Workers reports, 90% of Floridian tomato farms now participate in the CIW's Fair Food Program, a program designed to improve pay and working conditions. But the Estabrook reading is still timely since a full 10% of farms haven't signed on and since what is wrong on the farms might still be going on even if the situations there have *improved*. (Compare: You can imagine situations that are wrongful being improved so that they are much *better* while still being *wrong*. If, for example, you are lying to your brother while also punching him, that's wrong. If you keep lying but at least stop punching him, that's better! But what you do is still wrong.) Research the Fair Food Program. Which wrongful conditions does the program ameliorate? Which does it eliminate?

Jonathan Safran Foer

The Truth about Eating Animals

In this excerpt from his nonfiction book *Eating Animals*, novelist Jonathan Safran Foer discusses the treatment of cows in industrial animal agriculture, otherwise known as *factory farming*. In graphic detail, Foer describes what happens to cows in slaughterhouses and describes the deliberate cruel treatment of animals by slaughterhouse workers, using quotes from the workers themselves. See Chapter 7, "Industrial Animal Agriculture," for more discussion of animal welfare and the ethics of animal agriculture.

TAKE A DEEP BREATH

Virtually all cows come to the same end: the final trip to the kill floor. Cattle raised for beef are still adolescents when they meet their end. While early American ranchers kept cattle on the range for four or five years, today they are slaughtered at twelve to fourteen months. Though we could not be more intimate with the end product of this journey (it's in our homes and mouths, our children's mouths . . .), for most of us, the journey itself is unfelt and invisible.

Cattle seem to experience the trip as a series of distinct stresses: scientists have identified a different set of hormonal stress reactions to handling, transport, and slaughter itself. If the kill floor is working optimally, the initial "stress" of handling, as indicated by hormone levels, can actually be greater than that of either transport or slaughter.

Although acute pain is fairly easy to recognize, what counts as a good life for animals is not obvious until you know the species—even the herd, even the individual animal—in question. Slaughter might be ugliest to contemporary urbanites, but if you consider the cow's-eye view, it's not hard to imagine how after a life in cow communities, interactions with strange, loud, pain-inflicting, upright creatures might be more frightening than a controlled moment of death.

When I wandered among Bill's herd, I developed some sense of why this is so. If I stayed a good distance from the grazing cattle, they seemed unaware I was even there. Not so: Cows have nearly 360-degree vision and keep a vigilant watch on their environs. They know the other animals around them, select leaders, and will defend their herd. Whenever I approached an animal just shy of the reach of an outstretched arm, it was as if I had crossed some invisible boundary and the cow quickly jerked away. As a rule, cattle have a heavy dose of a prey-species flight instinct, and many common handling procedures—roping, shouting, tail twisting, shocking with electric prods, and hitting—terrify the animals.

One way or another, they are herded onto trucks or trains. Once aboard, cattle face a journey of up to forty-eight hours, during which they are deprived of water and food. As a result, virtually all of them lose weight and many show signs of dehydration. They are often exposed to extremes of heat and cold. A number of animals will die from the conditions or arrive at the slaughterhouse too sick to be considered fit for human consumption.

I couldn't get near the inside of a large slaughter facility. Just about the only way for someone outside the industry to see industrial cattle slaughter is to go undercover, and that is not only a project that takes half a year or more, it can be life-threatening work. So the description of slaughter I will provide here comes from eyewitness accounts and the industry's own statistics. I'm going to try to let workers on the kill floor speak the realities in their own words as much as possible.

In his bestselling book *The Omnivore's Dilemma,* Michael Pollan traces the life of an industry-raised beef cow, #534, which he personally purchased. Pollan provides a rich and thorough account of the raising of cattle but stops short of any serious probing into slaughter, discussing its ethics from a safely abstract distance, signaling a fundamental failure of his often clear-eyed and revelatory journey.

"Slaughter," Pollan reports, was "the one event in his [#534's] life I was not allowed to witness or even learn anything about, save its likely date. This didn't exactly surprise me: The meat industry understands that the more people know about what happens on the kill floor, the less meat they're likely to eat." Well said.

But, Pollan continues, "that's not because slaughter is necessarily inhumane, but because most of us would simply rather not be reminded of exactly what meat is or what it takes to bring it to our plates." This strikes me as somewhere between a half-truth and an evasion. As Pollan explains, "Eating industrial meat takes an almost heroic act of not knowing, or, now, forgetting." That heroism is needed precisely because one has to forget a lot more than the mere *fact* of animal deaths: one has to forget not only *that* animals are killed, but *how.*

Even among writers who deserve great praise for bringing factory farming into public view, there is often an insipid disavowal of the real horror we inflict. In his provocative and often brilliant review of

The Omnivore's Dilemma, B. R. Myers explains this accepted intellectual fashion:

> The technique goes like this: One debates the other side in a rational manner until pushed into a corner. Then one simply drops the argument and slips away, pretending that one has not fallen short of reason but instead *transcended* it. The irreconcilability of one's belief with reason is then held up as a great mystery, the humble readiness to live with which puts one above lesser minds and their cheap certainties.

There is one other rule to this game: never, absolutely never, emphasize that virtually all of the time one's choice is between cruelty and ecological destruction, and ceasing to eat animals.

It isn't hard to figure out why the beef industry won't let even an enthusiastic carnivore near its slaughter facilities. Even in abattoirs where most cattle die quickly, it's hard to imagine that any day passes in which several animals (tens, hundreds?) don't meet an end of the most horrifying kind. A meat industry that follows the ethics most of us hold (providing a good life and an easy death for animals, little waste) is not a fantasy, but it cannot deliver the immense amount of cheap meat per capita we currently enjoy.

At a typical slaughter facility, cattle are led through a chute into a knocking box—usually a large cylindrical hold through which the head pokes. The stun operator, or "knocker," presses a large pneumatic gun between the cow's eyes. A steel bolt shoots into the cow's skull and then retracts back into the gun, usually rendering the animal unconscious or causing death. Sometimes the bolt only dazes the animal, which either remains conscious or later wakes up as it is being "processed." The effectiveness of the knocking gun depends on its manufacture and maintenance, and the skill of its application—a small hose leak or firing the gun before pressure sufficiently builds up again can reduce the force with which the bolt is released and leave animals grotesquely punctured but painfully conscious.

The effectiveness of knocking is also reduced because some plant managers believe that animals can become "too dead" and therefore, because their hearts are not pumping, bleed out too slowly or insufficiently. (It's "important" for plants to have a quick bleed-out time for basic efficiency and because blood left in the meat promotes bacterial growth and reduces shelf life.) As a result, some plants deliberately choose less-effective knocking methods. The side effect is that a higher percentage of animals require multiple knocks, remain conscious, or wake up in processing.

No jokes here, and no turning away. Let's say what we mean: animals are bled, skinned, and dismembered while conscious. It happens all the time, and the industry and the government know it. Several plants cited for bleeding or skinning or dismembering live animals have defended their actions as common in the industry and asked, perhaps rightly, why they were being singled out.

When Temple Grandin conducted an industry-wide audit in 1996, her studies revealed that the vast majority of cattle slaughter-houses were unable to regularly render cattle unconscious with a single blow. The USDA, the federal agency charged with enforcing humane slaughter, responded to these numbers not by stepping up enforcement, but by changing its policy to cease tracking the number of humane slaughter violations and removing any mention of humane slaughter from its list of rotating tasks for inspectors. The situation has improved since then, which Grandin attributes largely to audits demanded by fast-food companies (which these companies demanded after being targeted by animal rights groups) but remains disturbing. Grandin's most recent estimates—which optimistically rely on data from announced audits—still found one in four cattle slaughter-houses unable to reliably render animals unconscious on the first blow. For smaller facilities, there are virtually no statistics available, and experts agree that these slaughter-houses can be significantly worse in their treatment of cattle. No one is spotless.

Cattle at the far end of the lines leading to the kill floor do not appear to understand what's coming, but if they survive the first knock, they sure as hell appear to know they are fighting for their lives. Recalls one worker, "Their heads are up in the air; they're looking around, trying to hide. They've already been hit before by this thing, and they're not going to let it get at them again."

The combination of line speeds that have increased as much as 800 percent in the past hundred years and poorly trained workers laboring under nightmarish conditions guarantees mistakes. (Slaughterhouse workers have the highest injury rate of any job—27 percent annually—and receive low pay to kill as many as 2,050 cattle a shift.)

Temple Grandin has argued that ordinary people can become sadistic from the dehumanizing work of constant slaughter. This is a persistent problem, she reports, that management must guard against. Sometimes animals are not knocked *at all*. At one plant, a secret video was made by workers (not animal activists) and given to the *Washington Post*. The tape revealed conscious animals going down the processing line, and an incident where an electric prod was jammed into a steer's mouth. According to the *Post*, "More than twenty workers signed affidavits alleging that the violations shown on the tape are commonplace and that supervisors are aware of them." In one affidavit, a worker explained, "I've seen thousands and thousands of cows go through the slaughter process alive. . . . The cows can get seven minutes down the line and still be alive. I've been in the side puller where they're still alive. All the hide is stripped out down the neck there." And when workers who complain are listened to at all, they often get fired.

> I'd come home and be in a bad mood. . . . Go right downstairs and go to sleep. Yell at the kids, stuff like that. One time I got really upset—[my wife] knows about this. A three-year-old heifer was walking up through the kill alley. And she was having a calf right there, it was half in and half out. I knew she was going to die, so I pulled the calf out. Wow, did my boss get mad. . . . They call these calves "slunks." They use the blood for cancer research. And he wanted that calf. What they usually do is when the cow's guts fall onto the gut table, the workers go along and rip the uterus open and pull these calves out. It's nothing to have a cow hanging up in front of you and see the calf inside kicking, trying to get out. . . . My boss wanted that calf, but I sent it back down to the stockyards. . . . [I complained] to the foremen, the inspectors, the kill floor superintendent. Even the superintendent over at the

beef division. We had a long talk one day in the cafeteria about this crap that was going on. I've gotten so mad, some days I'd go and pound on the wall because they won't do anything about it. . . . I've never seen a [USDA] vet near the knocking pen. Nobody wants to come back there. See, I'm an ex-Marine. The blood and guts don't bother me. It's the inhumane treatment. There's just so much of it.

In twelve seconds or less, the knocked cow— unconscious, semiconscious, fully conscious, or dead— moves down the line to arrive at the "shackler," who attaches a chain around one of the hind legs and hoists the animal into the air.

From the shackler, the animal, now dangling from a leg, is mechanically moved to a "sticker," who cuts the carotid arteries and a jugular vein in the neck. The animal is again mechanically moved to a "bleed rail" and drained of blood for several minutes. A cow has in the neighborhood of five and a half gallons of blood, so this takes some time. Cutting the flow of blood to the animal's brain will kill it, but not instantly (which is why the animals are supposed to be unconscious). If the animal is partially conscious or improperly cut, this can restrict the flow of blood, prolonging consciousness further. "They'd be blinking and stretching their necks from side to side, looking around, really frantic," explained one line worker.

The cow should now be carcass, which will move along the line to a "head-skinner," which is exactly what it sounds like—a stop where the skin is peeled off the head of the animal. The percentage of cattle still conscious at this stage is low but not zero. At some plants it is a regular problem—so much so that there are informal standards about how to deal with these animals. Explains a worker familiar with such practices, "A lot of times the skinner finds out an animal is still conscious when he slices the side of its head and it starts kicking wildly. If that happens, or if a cow is already kicking when it arrives at their station, the skinners shove a knife into the back of its head to cut the spinal cord."

This practice, it turns out, immobilizes the animal but does not render it insensible. I can't tell you how many animals this happens to, as no one is allowed to properly investigate. We only know that it is an

inevitable by-product of the present slaughter system and that it will continue to happen.

After the head-skinner, the carcass (or cow) proceeds to the "leggers," who cut off the lower portions of the animal's legs. "As far as the ones that come back to life," says a line worker, "it looks like they're trying to climb the walls. . . . And when they get to the leggers, well, the leggers don't want to wait to start working on the cow until somebody gets down there to reknock it. So they just cut off the bottom part of the leg with the clippers. When they do that, the cattle go wild, just kicking in every direction."

The animal then proceeds to be completely skinned, eviscerated, and cut in half, at which point it finally looks like the stereotyped image of beef— hanging in freezers with eerie stillness. . . .

THE TRUTH ABOUT EATING ANIMALS

Since 2000—*after* Temple Grandin reported improvement in slaughterhouse conditions—workers have been documented using poles like baseball bats to hit baby turkeys, stomping on chickens to watch them "pop," beating lame pigs with metal pipes, and knowingly dismembering fully conscious cattle. One needn't rely on undercover videos by animal rights organizations to know of these atrocities—although they are plentiful and sufficient. I could have filled several books—an encyclopedia of cruelty—with worker testimonials.

Gail Eisnitz comes close to creating such an encyclopedia in her book *Slaughterhouse*. Researched over a ten-year period, it is filled with interviews with workers who, combined, represent more than two million hours of slaughterhouse experience; no work of investigative journalism on the topic is as comprehensive.

One time the knocking gun was broke all day, they were taking a knife and cutting the back of the cow's neck open while he's still standing up. They would just fall down and be a-shaking. And they stab cows in the butt to make 'em move. Break their tails. They beat them so bad. . . . And the cow be crying with its tongue stuck out.

This is hard to talk about. You're under all this stress, all this pressure. And it really sounds mean, but I've taken [electric] prods and stuck them in their eyes. And held them there.

Down in the blood pit they say that the smell of blood makes you aggressive. And it does. You get an attitude that if that hog kicks at me, I'm going to get even. You're already going to kill the hog, but that's not enough. It has to suffer. . . . You go in hard, push hard, blow the windpipe, make it drown in its own blood. Split its nose. A live hog would be running around the pit. It would just be looking up at me and I'd be sticking, and I would just take my knife and—eerk—cut its eye out while it was just sitting there. And this hog would just scream. One time I took my knife—it's sharp enough—and I sliced off the end of a hog's nose, just like a piece of bologna. The hog went crazy for a few seconds. Then it just sat there looking kind of stupid. So I took a handful of salt brine and ground it into his nose. Now that hog really went nuts, pushing its nose all over the place. I still had a bunch of salt left on my hand—I was wearing a rubber glove—and I stuck the salt right up the hog's ass. The poor hog didn't know whether to shit or go blind. . . . I wasn't the only guy doing this kind of stuff. One guy I work with actually chases hogs into the scalding tank. And everybody—hog drivers, shacklers, utility men—uses lead pipes on hogs. Everybody knows it, all of it.

These statements are disturbingly representative of what Eisnitz discovered in interviews. The events described are not sanctioned by industry, but they should not be regarded as uncommon.

Undercover investigations have consistently revealed that farmworkers, laboring under what Human Rights Watch describes as "systematic human rights violations," have often let their frustrations loose on farmed animals or simply succumbed to the demands of supervisors to keep slaughter lines moving at all costs and without second thoughts. Some workers clearly are sadistic in the literal sense of that term. But I never met such a person. The several dozen workers I met were good people, smart and honest people doing their best in an impossible situation. The responsibility lies with the mentality of the meat industry that treats both animals and

"human capital" like machines. One worker put it this way:

The worst thing, worse than the physical danger, is the emotional toll. If you work in the stick pit for any period of time, you develop an attitude that lets you kill things but doesn't let you care. You may look a hog in the eye that's walking around down in the blood pit with you and think, God, that really isn't a bad-looking animal. You may want to pet it. Pigs down on the kill floor have come up and nuzzled me like a puppy. Two minutes later I had to kill them—beat them to death with a pipe. . . . When I worked upstairs taking hogs' guts out, I could cop an attitude that I was working on a production line, helping to feed people. But down in the stick pit I wasn't feeding people. I was killing things.

Just how common do such savageries have to be for a decent person to be unable to overlook them? If you knew that one in one thousand food animals suffered actions like those described above, would you continue to eat animals? One in one hundred? One in ten? Toward the end of *The Omnivore's Dilemma*, Michael Pollan writes, "I have to say there is a part of me that envies the moral clarity of the vegetarian. . . . Yet part of me pities him, too. Dreams of innocence are just that; they usually depend on a denial of reality that can be its own form of hubris." He's right that emotional responses can lead us to an arrogant disconnect. But is the person who makes an effort to act on the dream of innocence really the one to be pitied? And who, in this case, is denying reality?

When Temple Grandin first began to quantify the scale of abuse in slaughterhouses, she reported witnessing "deliberate acts of cruelty occurring on a regular basis" at 32 percent of the plants she surveyed during announced visits in the United States. It's such a shocking statistic I had to read it three times. *Deliberate* acts, occurring on a *regular* basis, witnessed by an *auditor*—witnessed during *announced* audits that gave the slaughterhouse time to clean up the worst problems. What about cruelties that weren't witnessed? And what about accidents, which must have been far more common? . . .

It might sound naive to suggest that whether you order a chicken patty or a veggie burger is a profoundly important decision. Then again, it certainly would have sounded fantastic if in the 1950s you were told that where you sat in a restaurant or on a bus could begin to uproot racism. It would have sounded equally fantastic if you were told in the early 1970s, before César Chávez's workers' rights campaigns, that refusing to eat grapes could begin to free farmworkers from slave-like conditions. It might sound fantastic, but when we bother to look, it's hard to deny that our day-to-day choices shape the world. When America's early settlers decided to throw a tea party in Boston, forces powerful enough to create a nation were released. Deciding what to eat (and what to toss overboard) is the founding act of production and consumption that shapes all others. Choosing leaf or flesh, factory farm or family farm, does not in itself change the world, but teaching ourselves, our children, our local communities, and our nation to choose conscience over ease can. One of the greatest opportunities to live our values—or betray them—lies in the food we put on our plates. And we will live or betray our values not only as individuals, but as nations.

We have grander legacies than the quest for cheap products. Martin Luther King Jr. wrote passionately about the time when "one must take a position that is neither safe, nor politic, nor popular." Sometimes we simply have to make a decision because "one's conscience tells one that it is right." These famous words of King's, and the efforts of Chávez's United Farm Workers, are also our legacy. We might want to say that these social-justice movements have nothing to do with the situation of the factory farm. Human oppression is not animal abuse. King and Chávez were moved by a concern for suffering humanity, not suffering chickens or global warming. Fair enough. One can certainly quibble with, or even become enraged by, the comparison implicit in invoking them here, but it is worth nothing that César Chávez and King's wife, Coretta Scott King, were vegans, as is King's son Dexter. We interpret the Chavez and King legacies—we interpret America's legacy—too narrowly if we assume in advance that they cannot speak against the oppression of the factory farm.

QUESTIONS

1. Foer writes that "virtually all of the time one's choice is between cruelty and ecological destruction [from factory farming], and ceasing to eat animals." What does he mean? Do you agree?
2. It is a frequent occurrence in slaughterhouses that cows get slaughtered alive, according to Foer's account. Why does this happen?
3. Foer quotes Michael Pollan: "I have to say there is a part of me that envies the moral clarity of the vegetarian. . . . Yet part of me pities him, too. Dreams of innocence are just that; they usually depend on a denial of reality that can be its own form of hubris." Foer is critical of Pollan's sentiment that vegetarians are arrogant or pitiable for thinking that they are innocent of the wrong involved in meat-eating. What is Pollan's point, exactly? What do you think?

GRACE BOEY

Eating Animals and Personal Guilt: The Individualization of Responsibility for Factory Farming

Boey details some common personal and interpersonal challenges faced by people who decide to be vegans for ethical reasons, and she outlines a number of common responses to veganism that are given by non-vegans. She focuses on one objection to being a vegan that she believes may have important merit, which is, roughly, that choosing to be vegan is a pointless and perhaps even irrational way to try to reduce animal suffering, and that such a choice might also involve a misunderstanding of the best way of reducing suffering within food systems. She concludes with what she takes to be a good reason to choose not to eat animals—but where these reasons may not make it *morally wrong* to continue to eat animals.

Last year, I decided to stop eating animal products and meat, apart from some seafood. I'd felt uncomfortable about the facts of animal cruelty in factory farming for quite some time, and finally resolved to take the plunge. Having enjoyed meat, eggs and dairy for all my life, it was initially a challenge adjusting to my new diet—while cutting meat was surprisingly easy, I mourned the loss of scrambled eggs for breakfast for at least a month. I still sometimes find it hard to resist certain desserts made with eggs, butter and milk. It helps, though, that I carry pictures depicting factory farm conditions on my phone. The bright yellow hue of a lemon tart that comes from egg yolks doesn't seem so appealing anymore after I call up pictures of filthy hens squished together in cages. I slip up sometimes, but on the whole, I've been pretty good about sticking to my diet.

The tougher challenge for me was, and still is, talking to others about my abstention. Ideally, I'd proudly announce my decision, and freely share my reasons for making it. But in reality, I avoid talking about it as much as possible. I almost never proactively tell anyone about my diet, and I don't mention it unless circumstances make it necessary. There are few things that make me more physically uncomfortable than having my personal business suddenly put on the spot. I'm also hopeless at expressing myself verbally. And bringing up animal abstention tends to open up a conversational can of worms of the most squirmish kind. Okay, so I'm making my abstention public here— but it's not too often I get to kick off a conversation by explaining myself in a couple thousand words, in my medium of choice, before the other party gets to respond.

Before I began abstaining from animals, I'd heard about the legendary amount of snark and hostility experienced by others who did. I've since gotten my fair share of this ugliness, which usually goes like this: someone will wrangle information about my diet out of me, and then proceed, entirely unsolicited, to say something f!#@ing rude about it. I've gradually learned to let idiotic comments like—*for every steak you don't eat, I'm going to eat three*—slide. I'm still wondering how to respond to those who make a show of delightedly biting into chicken wings, right after I sincerely express my sadness over animals being tortured in factory farms.

Such crassness is tiresome, but what genuinely troubles me more are remarks like—*I know I should do it, but it tastes so good*—or—*I know it's wrong, but what difference are you making by stopping? Is it just something that helps you sleep better at night?* To me, they represent a bunch of concerns that I myself have mixed feelings about. And the fact that people feel the need to proactively justify themselves says this—that they, in some way, perceive that I'm judging them. Once, as I was munching on vegan cookies in the subway, my partner confessed they sometimes worried I thought they were a bad person for eating meat.

The truth is: judgment doesn't even enter my mind until others bring it up themselves. I know how hard it is to give up food you've grown up eating all your life. I also know how pointless it seems, in the grand scheme of things, for one person out of billions to abstain from meat, milk and eggs. I also get how hard it is not to eat the stuff, when it's everywhere in innocent-looking forms. I know that we're rarely physically confronted with the reality of how it's all produced. I may be a philosophy grad student, but I'm also a human being who was still eating meat not too long ago. I'm wholly capable of stepping outside my little box of moral reasoning to identify with the phenomenology driving human behaviour.

Unfortunately, I've yet to figure out how to verbally communicate this in a way that doesn't make me sound like a condescending prick (for some reason, I suspect "I don't judge you, because I'm stepping outside my philosophical box of moral reasoning to empathize with humanity" just doesn't cut

it). It also raises the question: why exactly am *I* abstaining, and why on earth do I carry pictures of battery cages on my phone? For the moment, let's put that question on hold; I'll answer it later. I'm interested in first examining this troubling phenomenon of guilt, pointlessness and self-conscious indifference that so many of us have experienced at least once in our lives. How many of us have been traumatized after watching a PETA video, and resolved to go vegetarian . . . only to give in to a cheeseburger one day later? We know there's something terribly wrong about the way we treat and eat animals, but for various reasons it seems too hard and too pointless to give it up. How has it come to this, and how should we view abstinence in light of it?

PROBLEMS WITH INDIVIDUALIZING RESPONSIBILITY

It's helpful to first take a brief step back from the issue of animal rights, and look to a parallel discussion in another field: environmental degradation. Earth's resources are quickly depleting, and we as citizens of the planet are constantly told that we can save the environment with our individual choices. We should recycle, "buy green," eat organic, and ride bikes or walk instead of driving. Singapore, my home country, isn't too big on recycling. But since I've shifted to New York, where recycling is mandatory, I've become fairly dutiful about sorting out my trash. I felt bad last week when I accidentally condemned a glass jar of pasta sauce to the landfill—every little bit counts, and this little bit could have been recycled or re-used (to store my homemade vegan lemon curd, perhaps).

In his influential 2001 paper *Individualization. Plant a Tree, Ride a Bike, Save the World?*, Michael Maniates refers to this mindset as the "individualization of responsibility":

> [The individualization of responsibility] understands environmental degradation as the product of *individual* shortcomings . . . best countered by action that is

staunchly *individual* and typically *consumer-based* . . . It embraces the notion that knotty issues of consumption, consumerism, power and responsibility can be resolved neatly and cleanly through enlightened, uncoordinated consumer choice . . . Call this response the *individualization of responsibility.*

The problem with this kind of thinking, though, is that it diverts our attention from the major structural and institutional factors at play:

When responsibility for environmental problems is individualized, there is little room to ponder institutions, the nature and exercise of political power, or ways of collectively changing the distribution of power and influence in society—to, in other words, "think institutionally." . . . Individualization, by implying that any action beyond the private and the consumptive is irrelevant, insulates people from the empowering experiences and political lessons of *collective* struggle for social change and reinforces corrosive myths about the difficulties of public life. By legitimating notions of consumer sovereignty and a self-balancing and autonomous market, it also diverts attention from political arenas that matter.

Individualization, ironically, affects the individual in a way that is ultimately disempowering:

In the end, individualizing responsibility does not work—you can't plant a tree to save the world—and as citizens and consumers slowly come to discover this fact their cynicism about social change will only grow: "you mean after fifteen years of washing out these crummy jars and recycling them, environmental problems are still getting worse—geesh, what's the use?"

Well, I don't feel so bad about trashing that glass jar now.

Why doesn't individualizing responsibility work well to curb environmental degradation? There are several reasons for this. First, as Maniates argues, the very structure of society makes it difficult—if not impossible—for the individual to make any real choice; anything we do against the backdrop of this industrial, consumerist society is going to have some kind of deleterious effect on the environment. Second, given the billions of people on Earth, any change that any one individual makes is simply going to be negligible in the grand scheme of things. Third, the fragmentation of agency involved in pollution and resource depletion leads to the classic Prisoner's Dilemma. In *A Perfect Moral Storm*, philosopher Stephen Gardiner summarizes the structure of the Prisoner's Dilemma in the following way:

Suppose that a number of distinct agents are trying to decide whether or not to engage in a polluting activity, and that their situation is characterized by the following two claims:

(PD1) It is *collectively rational* to cooperate and restrict overall pollution: each agent prefers the outcome produced by everyone restricting their individual pollution over the outcome produced by no one doing so.

(PD2) It is *individually rational* not to restrict one's own pollution: when each agent has the power to decide whether or not she will restrict her pollution, each (rationally) prefers not to do so, whatever the others do.

Agents in such a situation find themselves in a paradoxical position. On the one hand, given (PD1), they understand that it would be better for everyone if every agent cooperated; but, on the other hand, given (PD2), they also know that they should all choose to defect.

The three reasons above make it hard, pointless and even irrational (!) for individuals to try and save the environment by changing their personal patterns of consumption. It's no wonder, then, that the problem of environmental degradation looms bigger than ever.

It's easy to see how some of this relates to animal rights and dietary abstinence. We are often told that if we want horrific animal suffering to stop, it is *our* responsibility to vote with our dollars and simply stop consuming what the factory farms produce. As consumers, *we* are responsible for generating the demand for the products we buy. This boycott is the primary course of action that ethicist Peter Singer advocates in his animal rights classic, *Animal Liberation*:

Becoming a vegetarian is a highly practical and effective step one can take toward ending both the killing of nonhuman animals and the infliction of suffering upon them. . . . So long as people are prepared to buy the products of intensive farming, the usual forms of protest and political action will never bring about a major reform. . . . The people who profit by exploiting large numbers of animals do not need our approval. They need our money. The purchase of the corpses of the animals they rear is the main support the factory farmers ask from the public. . . . This is not to say that the normal channels of protest and political action are useless and should be abandoned. On the contrary, they are a necessary part of the overall struggle for effective change in the treatment of animals. But in themselves, these methods are not enough.

Animal Liberation will always have a spot on my bookshelf; the facts and arguments it presents were instrumental in getting me to care more about animal welfare. But I cannot help but think that, in advocating individualistic boycott as the primary course of remedy to his readers, Singer is being much too naïve.

Assume, like Singer does as a utilitarian, that what we're concerned with is reducing or eliminating the total amount of animal suffering in factory farms. If this is the case, then the last two out of the three of reasons why individualization fails for environmental degradation apply here as well. To recap: given the billions of people on Earth, any change that any one individual makes is going to be negligible in the grand scheme of things; and, the fragmentation of agency involved leads to the Prisoner's Dilemma. From our individualistic and utilitarian perspective, it seems pointless and even irrational for any one person to start abstaining from animals, given that they like eating meat.

There are those who will challenge the legitimacy of applying the negligibility premise to animal abstention. Surely the individual can make *some* impact, however small. Again, here is Singer:

> I believe we do achieve something by our individual acts, even if the boycott as a whole should not succeed. George Bernard Shaw once said that he would be followed to his grave by numerous sheep, cattle, pigs, chickens, and a whole shoal of fish, all grateful at having been spared from slaughter because of his vegetarian diet. Although we cannot identify any individual animals whom we have benefitted by becoming a vegetarian, we can assume that our diet, together with that of the many others who are already avoiding meat, will have some impact on the number of animals raised

in factory farms and slaughtered for food. This assumption is reasonable because the number of animals raised and slaughtered depends on the profitability of this process, and this profit depends in part on the demand for the product. The smaller the demand, the lower the price and the lower the profit. The lower the profit, the fewer the animals that will be raised and slaughtered.

There are some problems with Singer's attempt at persuasion here. For sure, I think that sparing the suffering of just *one* animal is something worth doing. But, realistically, it's doubtful that even this could be achieved by one person acting within the system—the food market is simply too enormous to sense the choice of one single consumer. Sadly, we as individuals actually *can't* assume that our diet will have *any* impact at all on the number of animals raised in factory farms. In all likelihood, the massive number of animals processed by factory farms over the course of my lifetime will remain exactly the same, whether I boycott or not. Singer appeals to the impact of an *aggregate* of boycotts, but what he hasn't done is to give a very convincing reason for any *individual* reader to give up meat *independently* of anyone else. For one person looking to make a real difference, abstinence still seems hopeless. Maybe a group of one hundred is enough to send a minute signal to the market, but one person is probably not.

One might respond by saying that our actions could influence others to abstain, which *would* make a difference. But for one, we don't all have the influence of Peter Singer. Also, if influencing others is what we're concerned with, there are arguably better ways to go about doing this than abstaining from meat (like campaigning for systemic change, which I'll get to in a moment). Abstaining from meat yourself isn't necessary for influencing others to abstain—to take things to an extreme, one could very well persuade five hundred people to go meatless by pretending to be vegetarian while really eating meat in private, and make just as much difference to animal suffering as someone else who did the same without lying.

Independent abstinence would also be more compelling for the individual utilitarian if we, and not the market, were directly responsible for rearing and killing our own meat; unfortunately, this doesn't go through against the backdrop of factory farms.

I've argued so far that, for any one person concerned about reducing the amount of animal suffering in factory farms, abstaining from animals understandably seems pointless and even irrational. This assumes, however, that the individual *will* keep on eating meat as much as possible—regardless of its source—as long as she doesn't see much practical, utilitarian point in stopping. This is getting us closer to one of the reasons why *I* chose to stop eating meat. But before I directly address that, I want to raise the question: what gives us this intense desire to consume meat? Why is it so *hard* to stop? How is it that we can watch gross PETA videos but go back to eating hamburgers within the hour? What gives rise to the sentiment—*I know I should stop eating meat, but I just can't*—that I've heard from at least two thirds of my friends?

I've gotten flak from a lot of vegans for saying this, but I will stick to my guns: I think there is some legitimacy to this excuse. Sure, we should definitely feel awful about our food when we are confronted with the reality of how it's farmed; I *would* judge someone who denied that there was any problem at all with this. But the reality is, the system acts in a way that aggressively shields us from the facts of farming and simultaneously stokes our desire for animal products at every turn. Meat and animal products, in their final form, are *everywhere*. From infanthood, we are raised eating meat, eggs and milk; we are taken to McDonald's as a treat, and normalized to the sight of raw, red beef in supermarkets. *Meat, milk and eggs are everywhere.* Ice cream is everywhere. Burgers are everywhere. But what goes on inside factory farms is *not*. Factory farms don't have glass walls, and those who run them are doing everything they can to keep us out.[1] I don't even know where the one nearest to my house *is*. For most people, there is a deep psychological disconnect between the meat they see in supermarkets, and the live animals they see in pictures and documentaries. Whether or not this is a theoretically legitimate moral excuse, in reality, this makes it very

hard for most to bridge the gap between morals and actions.

Whose fault is this? I'm not really sure how to answer this question, nor am I sure that it's a terribly productive one to ask. I think it's safe to say that *no one* wants billions of animals to live and die in such suffering, and almost everyone thinks it's morally reprehensible. Just try taking a poll of people right after watching a documentary that accurately depicts factory farm conditions. Animal consumption didn't historically start out that way; it's just that industrialization and capitalism eventually gave rise to a system where producing the most food at the lowest price depends on doing so. Judge all you want, but in some sense, consumers *and producers* (and middlemen too) are stuck in a deadlock, where it's both incredibly difficult and not in our interests to step back from a system we nonetheless know to be inherently based on dirty fundamentals. No wonder we've become so cynical.

I think it's clear by now that the only way out of this is reform on an institutional and legal level. The way out of the Prisoner's Dilemma is to change the rules of the game, such that collectively rational action converges with individually rational action. And the way out of systemic blindness is to push for constant education and exposure—even mandate it. It's going to be hard, but nothing's going to change until this happens. One possible path out of society's indifference towards what goes on in factory farms is to require graphic and factual information about our food *wherever* it is bought and consumed; although this is a controversial method, I myself am all for it. We must ensure that the walls of these farms remain effectively transparent, to everyone, for good. Once this is done, people will no longer be able to ignore the facts of intensive farming. I believe it will then be clear to everyone that what goes on in there cannot be allowed to continue. And the natural way out of exploiting the welfare of animals for the sake of cost and efficiency is to pass and *enforce* laws that make it unattractive or ideally *illegal* for producers to do so. By this I mean laws that *really* matter—not like current cage-free labelling farce that does little other than to make money off well-intentioned customers.[2] At least guarantee farm animals the same legal rights we already accord to pets. That's right—in many jurisdictions, including the USA, anti-cruelty laws that cover "companion animals" don't apply to farm animals.[3] If this drives up prices or even collapses the market, so be it; this will only motivate society to seriously search for other ways to feed everyone cheaply and nutritiously.[4]

Peter Singer may be pessimistic about the institutional tactic for eliminating animal suffering, but I am even more pessimistic about the prospects of persuading individual consumers to give up animals. It is not realistic to think we will achieve an overhaul of tastes this way: all this will do is saddle society with a massive guilt trip, while achieving little else towards our collective cause. The current context means that it is not at all productive, nor entirely fair, to charge individual consumers with the suffering of animals. Stop calling people monsters for eating steak. I think we can do better. Understand the forces that push them to participate in the system, and work strategically from there.

INDIVIDUAL ABSTINENCE AND INTEGRITY

Now it's time for me to fulfill my promise, and answer this question: why did *I* stop eating most animals? This may put a big, ethical crosshair on my forehead, but I'm actually not entirely certain that I'm morally required to stop eating factory-farmed meat as a small cog in a large wheel. Though I'm pretty certain, I believe there's still a small chance I'm acting beyond what moral duty calls for. I'm just being intellectually honest here, and I've yet to work the uncertainty out. I'm also thinking of cutting the seafood, and pondering over my boyfriend's offer to carefully shoot a duck for me in the wild and roast it. I haven't made up my mind, and all these things make for a whole bunch of other questions.

So while moral concerns brought me to my decision, what gave me the final push was really this: I just felt *sad* every time I looked down at my plate. The reason why I started feeling so sad was because work had seen me meticulously poring through animal rights books and academic papers for months; so much of this information had seeped into my brain that I could no longer live with eating the stuff I knew to be produced in this way. That's why giving up meat was so easy for me: where I used to see a pork chop on a plate, I now see a tail-less, crusty-eyed, psychotic sow. And it's important to me that I keep this aversion going: I have no wish to remain in a system I don't believe in, even if it should make no utilitarian impact.

For me, this is what animal abstinence in a broken system boils down to: integrity. Emotion and some cognition may have been the spark, but the desire for integrity is what really keeps this flame going. And this is why I keep pictures of battery cages in my phone, even though I don't spontaneously visualize miserable hens when peeking into patisseries. When I opt out, I act in accordance with my own values about how the world should be—which is, free of the system. Whether or not the "virtue" of such integrity makes for a strict moral requirement, it's certainly important to my own project of self-integration and identity that I pursue it.

Abstention from the system is a legitimate and desirable reflection of my own values, and it is largely for *this* reason that I would encourage others to join me. It's none of my business if they don't, but I'm happy for those who do: I think it helps them achieve a more cohesive identity, helps them live better with themselves, and helps them break out of their indifference in general to animal welfare. For me, abstention is something that keeps me motivated towards my goal of being in a position to influence this cause in a substantial way. Perhaps there's nothing theoretically incoherent about someone who lobbies against the system, while continuing to eat factory-farmed meat. Good for anyone who can do that, I suppose. But I can't, and I suspect the same is true of most others. In reality, continuing to participate in a system we disapprove of in our heads tends to push it further towards the back of our minds.

NOTES

1. In 2014, Idaho passed a controversial "Agricultural Security Act" (commonly known as the "ag gag law") that imposes jail time and fines on activists who covertly film animal rights violations in the state's industrial farms. Cody Carlson discusses the ag gag law in The Atlantic article *The Ag Gag Laws: Hiding Factory Farm Abuses From Public Scrutiny.*

2. Contrary to marketing and popular perception, most hens raised in "cage-free" environments unfortunately do not lead lives that are much better (or better at all) than hens raised in battery cages. Like battery hens, cage-free chickens still have their beaks forcibly cut to prevent them from harming each other in tight spaces. Hens are still crowded by the thousands into tiny, dark buildings, and their waste exposes them to concentrated levels of toxic gases. For more information, visit http://www.humanemyth.org/cagefree.htm.

3. In a 2011 New York Times opinion piece *Some Animals are More Equal than Others*, Mark Bittman notes that American law "protects 'companion animals' like hamsters while largely ignoring what amounts to the torture of chickens and cows and pigs." Common Farming Exemptions allow for many anti-animal-cruelty requirements to be waived in the case of farm animals raised for consumption.

4. Laboratory-grown meat, for example, has been gaining traction.

BIBLIOGRAPHY

Bittman, M. (2013, March 15). Some Animals are More Equal than Others. Retrieved 2015, from http://opinionator.blogs.nytimes.com/2011/03/15/some-animals-are-more-equal-than-others

Carlson, C. (2012, March 20). The Ag Gag Laws: Hiding Factory Farm Abuses from Public Scrutiny. Retrieved 2015, from http://www.theatlantic.com/health/archive/2012/03/the-ag-gag-laws-hiding-factory-farm-abuses-from-public-scrutiny/254674/

Gardiner, S. (2011). *A Perfect Moral Storm: The Ethical Tragedy of Climate Change.* New York: Oxford University Press.

Maniates, M. (2001). *Individualization: Plant a Tree, Buy a Bike, Save the World?* Global Environmental Politics, 1(3), 31–52.

Singer, P. (2001). *Animal Liberation.* Revised edition. HarperCollins.

QUESTIONS

1. Boey seems to think, roughly, that trying to give everyone in society a guilt trip about a general problem in society they are only tangentially responsible for—such as the suffering of animals on factory farms—may not be the best way of solving every such problem in society. What does she think is a better way of solving the problem of animal suffering? Make a list of other society-wide problems, now or in the past, for which you can easily imagine someone giving the same analysis that Boey gives the problem of animal suffering. Is the sort of analysis that Boey gives more plausible in some of these cases than others? Why?

2. What is the prisoner's dilemma? Building off your answer to the previous set of questions, what does Boey argue is the best way out of the prisoner's dilemma in connection to animal suffering? (Use the concept of the prisoner's dilemma in explaining your answer this time.) Can you think of reasons why someone else might disagree with Boey's analysis in terms of the prisoner's dilemma? What are those reasons exactly? Explain.

3. In everyday ethical thought and talk, it is common to indicate that we think someone is doing something wrong in some specific cases by saying, "But what if everyone did that?" Give two examples where this kind of ethical criticism seems on the right track. Now imagine someone who is thinking of becoming a doctor, and consider the question "But what if everyone did that?" Would it be a disaster if every single person in society became a medical doctor, and so no one did any of the other incredibly diverse and sometimes specialized things that people in fact do? What should we say about the "But what if everyone did that?" test in light of this and the fact that sometimes that question seems to be on the right track?

4. In a prisoner's dilemma, is every person better off if each person acts on the belief that s/he is morally required to choose the collectively rational option? Are there reasons to think that this shows

that choosing the collectively rational option is in fact morally required? What is the best example you can think of that could be used to argue against this last idea?

5. What does Boey ultimately say is her reason for not eating most animals? Does she think that she would be doing something morally wrong if she were to eat animals? Can you think of other choices that we sometimes face where we might be attracted to thinking something similar to what Boey thinks? Give a number of different examples from different areas of life, such as business, family, friends, dating, and so on. What is "integrity" in the sense that Boey uses that term? Does integrity in Boey's sense correspond to how you'd use the term in your own life?

RAJ PATEL

Stuffed and Starved

In this excerpt from his book *Stuffed and Starved*, food scholar and activist Raj Patel describes how the array of consumer "choices" presented to us in supermarkets distracts us from thinking about the global food system—how food is produced, who is harmed and who benefits, who has the power to determine what happens—and from examining our own role in perpetuating this system. See Chapter 3, "Food Justice," for more discussion of injustices in the global food system and proposed responses.

As consumers, we're encouraged to think that an economic system based on individual choice will save us from the collective ills of hunger and obesity. Yet it is precisely "freedom of choice" that has incubated these ills. Those of us able to head to the supermarket can boggle at the possibility of choosing from fifty brands of sugared cereals, from half a dozen kinds of milk that all taste like chalk, from shelves of bread so sopped in chemicals that they will never go bad, from aisles of products in which the principal ingredient is sugar. For instance, of the myriad branded breakfast cereals marketed directly to children in Britain, around 88% are high in sugar, 13% were high in salt, and 10% were high in saturated fat. Some cereals have the same amount of sugar as a candy bar, and others are over 50% sugar by weight. What's more, this information is deliberately hidden from consumers and parents. There are 23 names for added sugar on ingredients labels that companies may use to avoid writing "sugar" as the

Raj Patel, *Stuffed and Starved: The Hidden Battle for the World Food System*, 11–19. Reprinted by permission of Melville House Publishing, Brooklyn, NY.

first and most prevalent ingredient on the list.[1] It's hardly surprising, then, that one in three children between the ages of two and fifteen in the UK are obese or overweight.[2] The breakfast cereal story is a sign of a wider systemic feature: there's every incentive for food producing corporations to sell food that has undergone processing which renders it more profitable, if less nutritious. Incidentally, this also helps explain why there are so many more varieties of breakfast cereals on sale than varieties of apples.

There are natural limits to our choices. There are, for instance, only so many naturally occurring fruits, vegetables and animals that people are prepared to eat. But even here, a little advertising can persuade us to expand the ambit of our choices. Think of the kiwi fruit, once known as the Chinese gooseberry, but rebranded to accommodate Cold War prejudices by the New Zealand food company that sold it to the world at the end of the 1950s. It's a taste no-one had grown up with, but which now seems as if it has always been there. And while new natural foods are slowly added to our menus, the food industry adds tens of thousands of new products to the shelves every year, some of which become indispensable fixtures which, after a generation, make life unimaginable without them. It's a sign of how limited our gastronomic imaginations can be. And also a sign that we're not altogether sure how or where or why certain foods end up on our plate.

ARCADIA LOST

Old Macdonald had a farm, E-I-E-I-O,
And on his farm he had a cow, E-I-E-I-O,
With a "moo-moo" here and a "moo-moo" there,
Here a "moo," there a "moo,"
Everywhere a "moo-moo,"
Old Macdonald had a farm, E-I-E-I-O.
Traditional

The story of food production to which most of us can admit, almost as a reflex, owes more to fairy tales and children's television programming than anything else. Without a reason to revisit the creation myths of food we learned when young, we carry around unquestioned our received opinions of pastoral bliss, of farmers planting the seeds in the ground, watering them and hoping that the sun will come out so that the plants can grow big and strong. This is certainly one description of how food is grown. It's just one that glosses over the most important parts. The tales we tell about farming stuff a sock into the mouths of the world's rural poor. When food's provenance is reduced to a single line on a label, there's much we don't understand, nor even understand that we should ask.

Who, for example, is the central character in our story of food—the farmer? What is her life like? What can she afford to eat? If only we asked, we'd know: the majority of the world's farmers are suffering. Some are selling off their lands to become labourers on their family plots. Some migrate to the cities, or even overseas. A few, too many, resort to suicide.

The questions continue. What, for example, does a farmer plant? Most farmers' choice of crop is tightly circumscribed by the kinds of land they own, the climate, their access to markets, credit and a range of visible and invisible ingredients in the production of food. There is no moment of sucking a finger, holding it to the wind and deciding what it'd be nice to eat next year. If they're hoping to sell their crops for cash rather than eat them themselves, most farmers have few options, particularly those in the Global South (the term I use in this book to refer to the world's poorer countries).[3] They will have to grow the crops that the market demands.

The business of farming is, at the end of the day, constrained by the playing-field of the market. What this language hides, though, is that the terrain of the market isn't so much a playing-field as a razor's edge. If there's room to make planting choices at all, they are tough decisions based on optimizing multiple parameters, with little room for error. The market punishes poor choices with penury. For farmers who are already highly indebted, this means bankruptcy. Banks and grain distributors have developed novel ways for dealing with the subsequent insolvency.

Contract farming or land rental arrangements, for example, reduce farmers to providing raw labour on what used to be their own land. Old MacDonald now rents his farm. Yet farmers are willing to subject themselves to these new farming arrangements because they have so little choice. With banks wielding the threat of foreclosure, any kind of farming, even the kind of farming that asset-strips the soil, is preferable to no farming at all.

As the farmer is forced into "choosing" among these alternatives, other options are removed as possibilities. And at the same time as the set of choices for farmers is winnowed down, others—powerful groups, corporations, governments—expand the empire of their options. At every stage of the story of food, choices are made over a wide range of issues, from the obvious to the esoteric. Who chooses the safe levels of pesticides, and how is "safe" defined? Who chooses what should be sourced from where in making your meal? Who decides what to pay the farmers who grow the food, or the farm workers who work for farmers? Who decides that the processing techniques used in bringing the meal together are safe? Who makes money from the additives in food and decides they do more good than harm? Who makes sure there is plenty of cheap energy to transport and assemble the ingredients from all around the world?

These choices may seem impossibly distant, so removed from our experience as food shoppers that they might as well happen on Mars. Yet the very same forces that shape farmers' choices also reach to the stacked aisles of the supermarket. Who, after all, fixes the range of items that fill the aisles in the supermarket? Who chooses how much it costs? Who spends millions of dollars to find out that the smell of baking bread and the wail of Annie Lennox in the aisles might make people buy more? Who decides that the prices in the market are higher than the poorest can afford?

Here lies the crux. The narrow abundance of the aisles, the apparently low prices at the checkout and the almost constant availability of foods, these things are our sop. "Convenience" anaesthetizes us as consumers. We are dissuaded from asking hard

questions, not only about how our individual tastes and preferences are manipulated, but about how our choices at the checkout take away the choices of those who grow our food.

ABOUT JOE

A recent report from Oxfam provides fodder for thinking about where the power lies along the chain of food production. Consider the case of Lawrence Seguya, a coffee-grower in Uganda. He puts it like this: "I'd like you to tell people in your place that the drink they are now drinking is the cause of all our problems."[4] His assessment is widely shared. Salome Kafuluzi lives on a coffee-farm with her thirteen children, and she has this to say: "We're broke. We're not happy. We're failing in everything. We can't buy essentials. We can't have meat, fish, rice, just sweet potatoes, beans and *matoke* [a kind of green banana mash] . . . We can't send the children to school." Salome's husband, Peter, links their situation quite directly to the price of coffee: "I remember when *kiboko* [the local term for sun-dried coffee cherry] sold for 69 cents/kg. We slept without worries. We could support our families. For me, I'd need to see a price of at least 34 cents/kg. Even at 29 cents/kg we can't look after the land."[5] The price at the moment is around 14 cents per kilo.

The laws of supply and demand would suggest that coffee-growers would move out of the market and do something else. This would presuppose that there *is* something else they can do. Too often, there isn't. The immediate result of low farm income—and this is a law to which anyone living on the breadline can attest—is a panicked self-exploitation. Rather than throwing in the towel and moving to the cities, or trying to grow something else, farmers grow *more* coffee, working themselves to exhaustion and scraping together whatever they can to be able to maintain some sort of standard of living, and sometimes, reluctantly, hurting the natural environment in a desperate bid to survive. This has resulted in a global coffee surplus of 900 million kilos. You'd think that with all that coffee floating around, we'd see the end-price of coffee go down. But there are a good few steps along the way from the fields to the bottom of the cup.

Lawrence and his family live in an area well suited to coffee—it's high-altitude, hilly terrain. This means that their land is unsuited to anything else. The choice that faces them is this: grow coffee or leave. With little else to go to, they grow coffee.

They sell to a local middleman at around 14 cents per kilo, who then takes the bag to the mill and sells it for 19 cents. The mill will process it for an additional 5 cents per kilo—which is barely enough to keep the mill going. Mary Goreti runs the mill in Kituntu to which the coffee is brought. "The profit margins are so small right now," she says, "and the electricity is so high . . . We have so few people bringing *kiboko*. Some farmers are just keeping it at home because the prices are so low. If the prices stay low, the business will fail. You can't open a factory to process ten bags."[6] But she can't choose to do anything else with the mill but process coffee. So, for the moment, Mary chooses to keep the mill open, and the coffee is processed.

The coffee is bagged and, with a 2 cent per kilo freight cost, sent to Kampala, by which time the price has reached 26 cents. Yet the vast profits aren't being made here either. Hannington Karuhanga, a manager with Ugacof, one of the larger Ugandan coffee exporters, is happy to be making a profit of US$10 a ton, or 1 cent on the kilo. And that's on the quality coffee—"Some of these grades we have are not worth transporting. It would be cheaper to destroy them." Yet transport them he does, as part of the complex dance of sorting, grading, insuring and shipping the coffee to a roaster. By the time this kilo of coffee lands up in, say, West London, where Nestlé has a coffee-processing facility, it'll cost US$1.64 per kilo. Already, at the gates of the Nescafé factory, the cost per bag is well over ten times what the Kafuluzis or the Seguyas received for it. But here comes the big jump. By the time the coffee rolls out of the other side, the price is US$26.40 per kilo, or nearly 200 times the cost of a kilo in Uganda.

While coffee farmers there are living off their savings, Nestlé's profits seem unstoppable. In 2005, they sold over US$70 billion in food and beverages. With high levels of brand loyalty, and with such market dominance, Nestlé is in a position to raise the price that its growers receive. But why would it choose to do that? Nestlé isn't a charity—it's a corporation in a world of other corporations, guided by the cardinal rule of market capitalism: "buy cheap, sell dear." By virtue of its size, Nestlé can dictate the terms of supply to its growers, millers, exporters and importers, and each is being squeezed dry. If the coffee industry in Uganda goes belly up, that's OK. Vietnam has been brought into the world market by the World Bank, and they're turning out bags of coffee cheaper than anyone else. So wherever coffee is grown, farmers are struggling, pitted against one another across vast distances by the international market in coffee, with few if any choices about the future. Meanwhile, farmers who try to increase their share of the price find themselves facing the might of the food industry. Ethiopian farmers recently applied to turn their signature coffee bean names—Sidamo, Harar and Yirgacheffe—into trademarks, a move that might increase their share of the revenue by 25 per cent. They were opposed almost instantly by Starbucks, a company with an annual turnover equal to three-quarters that of Ethiopia.[7]

Large corporations are very reluctant to cede their control over the food system. Yet, Nestlé, Starbucks and every other food system corporation have a rock-solid alibi: us. In the name of consumers, and "consumer freedom," wages are kept low and opportunities for farmers to increase their income are stymied. And, the thing is, it works.

NOTES

1. Harvard School of Public Health, 2011. How to Spot Added Sugar on Food Labels. Harvard University [cited 17 June 2011]. Online at http://www.hsph.harvard.edu/nutritionsource/healthy-drinks/added-sugar-on-food-labels/index.html

2. NHS Information Centre, 2010. National Child Measurement Programme: England, 2009/10 school year. Leeds: The NHS Information Centre, Lifestyles Statistics.

3. This is a term much to be preferred to "Third World" or to the depoliticized "developing countries," and certainly better than the increasingly out of date division of the world into "the West" and everyone else.

4. Gresser, Charis and Sophia Tickell 2002. *Mugged: Poverty in Your Coffee Cup.* Oxford: Oxfam International: 6.

5. op. cit.: 22.

6. op. cit.: 23.

7. Seager 2006. Starbucks, the Coffee Beans and the Copyright Row that Cost Ethiopia £47m. *Guardian,* 26 October. Klein 2000 (*No Logo: No Space, No Choice, No Jobs, Taking Aim at the Brand Bullies.* London, Flamingo) has made public the ruthlessness of their marketing practices.

QUESTIONS

1. Patel notes that there are a lot of consumer options at supermarkets—"fifty brands of sugared cereals"—but he suggests that virtually none of them are good options. Given this, do we have "freedom of choice"?

2. As Patel describes it, farmers have limited options and little power over what they grow and how they grow it. Why?

3. Patel says that "'Convenience' anaesthetizes us as consumers." What does this mean? Do you agree?

4. Patel describes how coffee grown in Uganda, which the farmers sell for 14 cents per kilogram, ends up being sold in developed countries for $26.40 per kilogram. What are all the steps in the supply chain, in between the farmer and consumer? Is profit shared equally along this chain? If not, who profits most?

MICHAEL POLLAN

The Food Movement, Rising

Journalist Michael Pollan is known for his book *The Omnivore's Dilemma* and many other influential articles and books on the food system. In this excerpt, he discusses some of the costs of cheap food, including environmental degradation and increasing rates of diet-related illness.

. . .

FOOD MADE VISIBLE

It might sound odd to say this about something people deal with at least three times a day, but food in America has been more or less invisible, politically speaking, until very recently. At least until the early 1970s, when a bout of food price inflation and the appearance of books critical of industrial agriculture (by Wendell Berry, Francis Moore Lappé, and Barry Commoner, among others) threatened to propel the subject to the top of the national agenda, Americans have not had to think very hard about where their food comes from, or what it is doing to the planet, their bodies, and their society.

Most people count this a blessing. Americans spend a smaller percentage of their income on food than any people in history—slightly less than 10 percent—and a smaller amount of their time preparing it: a mere thirty-one minutes a day on average, including clean-up. The supermarkets brim with produce summoned from every corner of the globe, a steady stream of novel food products (17,000 new ones each year) crowds the middle aisles, and in the freezer case you can find "home meal replacements" in every conceivable ethnic stripe, demanding nothing more of the eater than opening the package and waiting for the microwave to chirp. Considered in the long sweep of human history, in which getting food dominated not just daily life but economic and political life as well, having to worry about food as little as we do, or did, seems almost a kind of dream.

The dream that the age-old "food problem" had been largely solved for most Americans was sustained by the tremendous postwar increases in the productivity of American farmers, made possible by cheap fossil fuel (the key ingredient in both chemical fertilizers and pesticides) and changes in agricultural policies. Asked by President Nixon to try to drive down the cost of food after it had spiked in the early 1970s, Agriculture Secretary Earl Butz shifted the historical focus of federal farm policy from supporting prices for farmers to boosting yields of a small handful of commodity crops (corn and soy especially) at any cost.

The administration's cheap food policy worked almost too well: crop prices fell, forcing farmers to produce still more simply to break even. This led to a deep depression in the farm belt in the 1980s followed by a brutal wave of consolidation. Most importantly, the price of food came down, or at least the price of the kinds of foods that could be made from corn and soy: processed foods and sweetened beverages and feedlot meat. (Prices for fresh produce have increased since the 1980s.) Washington had succeeded in eliminating food as a political issue—an objective dear to most governments at least since the time of the French Revolution.

But although cheap food is good politics, it turns out there are significant costs—to the environment, to public health, to the public purse, even to the culture—and as these became impossible to ignore in recent years, food has come back into view. Beginning in the late 1980s, a series of food safety scandals opened people's eyes to the way their food was being produced, each one drawing the curtain back a little further on a food system that had changed beyond recognition. When BSE, or mad cow disease, surfaced in England in 1986, Americans learned that cattle, which are herbivores, were routinely being fed the flesh of other cattle; the practice helped keep meat cheap but at the risk of a hideous brain-wasting disease.

The 1993 deaths of four children in Washington State who had eaten hamburgers from Jack in the Box were traced to meat contaminated with *E.coli* 0157:H7, a mutant strain of the common intestinal bacteria first identified in feedlot cattle in 1982. Since then, repeated outbreaks of food-borne illness linked to new antibiotic-resistant strains of bacteria (campylobacter, salmonella, MRSA) have turned a bright light on the shortsighted practice of routinely administering antibiotics to food animals, not to treat disease but simply to speed their growth and allow them to withstand the filthy and stressful conditions in which they live.

In the wake of these food safety scandals, the conversation about food politics that briefly flourished in the 1970s was picked up again in a series of books, articles, and movies about the consequences of industrial food production. Beginning in 2001 with the publication of Eric Schlosser's *Fast Food Nation*, a surprise best-seller, and, the following year, Marion Nestle's *Food Politics*, the food journalism of the last decade has succeeded in making clear and telling connections between the methods of industrial food production, agricultural policy, food-borne illness, childhood obesity, the decline of the family meal as an institution, and, notably, the decline of family income beginning in the 1970s.

Besides drawing women into the work force, falling wages made fast food both cheap to produce and a welcome, if not indispensible, option for pinched and harried families. The picture of the food economy Schlosser painted resembles an upside-down version of the social compact sometimes referred to as "Fordism": instead of paying workers well enough to allow them to buy things like cars, as Henry Ford proposed to do, companies like Wal-Mart and McDonald's pay their workers so poorly that they can afford *only* the cheap, low-quality food these companies sell, creating a kind of nonvirtuous circle driving down both wages and the quality of food. The advent of fast food (and cheap food in general) has, in effect, subsidized the decline of family incomes in America.

FOOD POLITICS

Cheap food has become an indispensable pillar of the modern economy. But it is no longer an invisible or uncontested one. One of the most interesting social movements to emerge in the last few years is the "food movement," or perhaps I should say "movements," since it is unified as yet by little more than the recognition that industrial food production is in need of reform because its social/environmental/public health/animal welfare/gastronomic costs are too high.

As that list suggests, the critics are coming at the issue from a great many different directions. Where many social movements tend to splinter as time goes on, breaking into various factions representing divergent concerns or tactics, the food movement starts out splintered. Among the many threads of advocacy that can be lumped together under that rubric we can include school lunch reform; the campaign for animal rights and welfare; the campaign against genetically modified crops; the rise of organic and locally produced food; efforts to combat obesity and type 2 diabetes; "food sovereignty" (the principle that nations should be allowed to decide their agricultural policies rather than submit to free trade regimes); farm bill reform; food safety regulation; farmland preservation; student organizing around food issues on campus; efforts to promote urban agriculture and ensure that communities have access to healthy food; initiatives to create gardens and cooking classes in schools; farm worker rights; nutrition labeling; feedlot pollution; and the various efforts to regulate food ingredients and marketing, especially to kids.

QUESTIONS

1. According to Pollan, food is cheap in the United States. People spend less of their income on food and less time preparing food than at any point in human history. Why is food cheap? What are the policies and societal changes that brought about cheap food?
2. Many people consider cheap food to be a blessing. But Pollan thinks cheap food comes at a cost. What are some of the costs of cheap food? Who pays these costs?
3. Pollan lists a number of distinct "food movements" that arose to develop specific problems with the food system. What are some of these movements?

2 〉Global Hunger

In this chapter, we introduce ethical arguments about whether people in richer "developed nations" like the United States have an ethical duty to make financial sacrifices to help the world's poorest and most malnourished people. We also introduce related arguments about whether our planet is overpopulated, and whether there is a basic human right to proper nutrition.

In his reading in Chapter 1, Kenneth Weiss provides a summary of the current state of global hunger:

> Around the world, population is rising most rapidly in places where life is most precarious. Across Africa and in parts of South Asia and Latin America, hundreds of millions of people live on the edge of starvation. A drought, flood or outbreak of violence can push them over the brink. . . . Nearly 1 billion people are malnourished, according to the U.N. Food and Agriculture Organization. At least 8 million die every year of hunger-related diarrhea, pneumonia and other illnesses—more than succumb to AIDS, malaria and tuberculosis combined. A child dies of hunger every 11 seconds.[1]

The rest of Weiss's article makes vivid that this suffering and death is happening right now, as you read this. Furthermore, in 40 to 50 years, the world is also projected to have at least two billion *more* people, which means that we will likely need to produce *twice* as much food as we produce now in order to feed everyone. That is because people in poorer countries in the future will be much wealthier than their counterparts are now, and thus will likely consume much more meat than their counterparts do presently. And because it is less efficient to feed people with meat than with plants, disproportionately more crops will therefore need to be grown in the future so that all of those animals can be fed before being eaten by humans.[2]

Taken together, all of this raises a number of pressing questions, which we can divide into two interrelated categories:

Food Systems, Animal Agriculture, and the Challenge of Feeding the World without Destroying It

How feasible is it to feed 9 billion people by 2050? And if global population doubles to 14 billion by 2150, will it then even be *possible* to feed all those people? Is global population growth unsustainable? What costs would be involved in feeding that many people? For example, in order to feed everyone, would we then have to cut down most of the world's rainforests, and destroy the planet with environmental pollution, including greenhouse gas emissions? Is it sometimes worth harming the environment and making other tradeoffs in order to feed a larger population? Or should we instead adopt public policies to reduce population growth? If global population were reduced, how much less burdensome would the costs of feeding the world be? In light of that, do we have an ethical obligation to reduce population? What if the only way of reducing population is to interfere with people's procreation decisions? Does everyone have a fundamental right to procreate? To have as many children as they would like? How much less burdensome would the costs of a growing population be if we all stopped eating meat? In light of this, do we have an ethical obligation to stop eating meat?

Hunger, Global Justice, and Basic Human Rights

Does everyone have a fundamental right to food? And if the earth is overpopulated with people, how does that complicate the answer to all of the preceding questions? If future people are born into the world's poorest and most densely populated nations, do we in richer nations have an ethical obligation to ensure that they are well fed, even if we have to make financial sacrifices to feed them? What if, in order to feed them, we also have to pay costs that are not merely financial but that involve, for example, degradation of our own environment, which negatively impacts our own health and well-being? More generally, what do people in richer nations owe to the global poor, and why?

The first set of questions are discussed more in other chapters, which focus on contemporary food systems, including the challenge of feeding the world without destroying it (Chapters 7–10). This chapter focuses on the last set of questions, and also introduces some of the questions about human population along the way.

SINGER'S ARGUMENT THAT WE HAVE DEMANDING DUTIES TO ASSIST THE GLOBAL POOR

In his reading for this chapter, Peter Singer argues that you are ethically required either to give away most of your wealth to help those who are suffering in lesser-developed countries, or else to do something of comparable ethical significance instead. One way of understanding his main argument is that given the circumstances you always find yourself in, unless you do something of such significance, you are morally no different from a person who refuses to save a drowning child when it is easy, riskless, but merely financially costly to do so. If he is right, then your actions are almost always immoral, because you almost never do anything of such significance. More generally, if he is right, then most of our actions within our affluent society are wrong. In particular, it is wrong for us to spend our lives spending large amounts of resources on inessential consumer goods given that there are people starving and suffering in other ways throughout the world from afflictions that could be alleviated at comparatively low cost.

Singer's argument can be understood as relying on only two controversial premises. The first of these premises is what we might call "Singer's Ethical Premise"; it is the claim that there is *no morally relevant difference* between two situations you could find yourself in, in the sense that there is no difference that makes for a difference in what it is right and wrong to do in these two cases:

POND

You can easily, risklessly, and with great probability of success save a child from drowning; but you do not save the child, merely because doing so would require a significant financial sacrifice.

CHARITY

You decide not to give away a significant amount of your wealth, when giving away that wealth would have reduced the number of innocent people who die from easily treatable afflictions.

So, the first controversial premise in Singer's argument is that there is no morally relevant difference between POND and CHARITY. The other controversial premise of Singer's argument is what we might call the "Empirical Premise"; it is that you are always in the CHARITY case. In other words, the claim of this premise is that CHARITY is not just an imaginary scenario that you *could* find yourself in; rather, it describes the situation that you are *actually* in right now as you read this, and it is the situation that you are *always* in as a person who is affluent enough to be reading this book: The way the world *actually* is, people well-off enough to be reading this book *always* are in a position to reduce the number of people who die from easily treatable conditions and, instead, we do things like read books.

From these premises, and the obvious premise that it would be wrong not to save the child in POND, the conclusion that Singer draws is striking: namely, that you are morally required either to give away most of your wealth to help those who are suffering in lesser-developed countries, or else to do something of comparable moral significance instead. Here is this argument in "standard form" with the premises numbered in an order that helps explain the logical structure of the reasoning:

1. It would be seriously wrong not to save the child in POND.
2. *Singer's Ethical Premise*: There is no morally relevant difference between POND and CHARITY.

Thus, it would be seriously wrong not to give in CHARITY.

3. *Empirical Premise*: CHARITY is a situation that we always find ourselves in, because it is always possible for each of us to give to effective charities that would then save additional lives that would not otherwise be saved.

Thus, it is seriously morally wrong for us not to give away most of our wealth to effective charities, or else to do something of comparable ethical significance instead.

This is one possible representation of Singer's main *argument* in "Famine, Affluence, and Morality"—in other words, it is a way of representing the main *reasons* he gives the reader for accepting his main conclusion, and it is a way of representing how those reasons are supposed to work together to establish the truth of that conclusion. This is what we mean by the term "argument" here and in the rest of this book.

Note that Singer's conclusion is very *demanding*—it says not only that we must give *some* to others, and not only that we must give *a lot*, but that we must give away *most* of what we conventionally think of as our own, all the way to the point at which giving away more would reduce our well-being by more than the amount of additional well-being we could secure for others by giving to them.

It appears that Singer's argument is *valid* in the sense that philosophers use that term, according to which an argument is valid if and only if there is no possible way all the premises could be true but the conclusion false. And if an argument is valid in that sense *and* it also has all true premises, then we say that it is a *sound* argument, which implies that it must also have a true conclusion. So, what should we make of Singer's argument? Is it sound?

INITIAL OBJECTIONS TO SINGER'S MAIN ETHICAL PREMISE, AND A REPLY

The initial reaction that many people have to Singer's argument is to think that the argument is unsound because the main ethical premise is dubious at best—namely, that there is no morally relevant difference between POND and CHARITY. This initial reaction is driven by the fact that there are so many *obvious* differences between POND and CHARITY. For example, here are some obvious differences that you may have already identified:

A List of Some Obvious Differences between POND and CHARITY

The extent to which there are other people (or institutions) who:

- are able to offer much more efficacious and/or efficient aid to those in need
- are much closer physically to those in need
- are much closer socially to those in need
- have a special responsibility for the existence of the need
- have a special responsibility for helping those in need

The extent to which this problem is:

- a recurring problem
- caused by background factors that you can do nothing about
- caused by factors for which you are blameless, and so on

However, it is important to see that the fact that there are a lot of obvious differences between POND and CHARITY is *not* itself a good objection to Singer's Argument. (Here and in the rest of this book we use "objection" to mean a reason or an argument someone could give to think that an argument is *unsound*, i.e., is either invalid or has one or more false premises). In order to be a *good* objection to Singer's argument, the fact that there are a lot of obvious differences between POND and CHARITY would have to be a *good* reason for thinking that Singer's argument is invalid or has one or more false premises. But the mere existence of these differences is *not* a good reason for thinking that Singer's argument is defective in either of those ways. That is because Singer's argument does not depend on the claim that there is *no difference* between POND and CHARITY. Instead, it depends only on the claim that there is *no morally relevant difference* between POND and CHARITY—that is to say, it depends only on the claim that there is no difference between POND and CHARITY that makes a difference in what it is right and wrong to do in those two cases.

To see why this subtle point is so important, let's begin by considering one particular difference between POND and CHARITY: namely, the *physical distance* between the person who is in need and the person who is in a position to provide aid. This is an obvious difference between those cases. But, in reply to an objection that claims that this makes for a morally relevant difference between those cases, Singer might ask us to imagine an example in which it is 100% certain that a child in a pond far away will drown unless you make a financial sacrifice to activate a rescue machine, in which case the child will be saved and will live happily ever after. If all of this is certain to you, and you are just standing there, perfectly capable of activating the rescue machine and saving the child, doesn't it seem that it would be wrong to let the child drown in that case just as it would be wrong to let the child drown in POND? And doesn't that seem to show that a difference in physical distance does not by itself make for a morally relevant difference between cases? Similarly, Singer might ask us to imagine a variation on POND in which dozens of callous people are watching the child drown from the shore of the pond, and you are 100% sure that none of them will save the child if you do not. Doesn't it seem that it would be just as wrong to do nothing and let the child drown in this case as in POND? And doesn't that seem to show that a difference in the number of other people who could help in CHARITY is not itself the sort of thing that could make for a morally relevant difference to POND? With these replies on behalf of Singer in mind, can you anticipate now how he might respond to all of the differences listed earlier?[3] (For each of the differences listed previously in bullet points, can you construct a similar argument on behalf of Singer using an imaginary case that differs from POND in the relevant way, but does not differ regarding what is the right and wrong thing to do?)

If you are like many people, you'll find that even if Singer's argument *initially* seems difficult to believe, it gains great power the more you try to articulate what could possibly be a morally relevant difference between POND and CHARITY—because it is difficult to identify anything that would make for a genuine morally relevant difference between those cases. For each thing that initially seems like it might make a difference, upon reflection it seems that Singer can offer a fairly simple and compelling reply analogous to those stated earlier that that difference itself does not make for an ethically relevant difference. If upon reflection you find each step in this reasoning convincing, then that might increase your confidence in the intuitive general principle that Singer defends:

Principle of Preventing Bad Occurrences (Strong Version)

If it is in our power to prevent something bad from happening, without thereby sacrificing anything of comparable moral significance, we ought, morally, to do it.

This is the more fundamental ethical principle that Singer believes explains the truth of premises such as that there is no ethically relevant difference between POND and CHARITY. And, even more fundamentally, Singer takes this principle to imply (and, most fundamentally, to be explained by) the truth of the general ethical theory called *utilitarianism*, as he explains in a later part of his reading. Utilitarianism is a *general ethical theory* in the sense that it attempts to explain what it is right and wrong to do in all possible circumstances. Utilitarianism claims that a person's action is morally permissible if and only if that action is, among all the actions it is possible for that person to perform, the one that results in the most well-being in the world. (Utilitarianism is discussed at greater length in Chapter 4, "Consumer Ethics.")

Although Singer's conclusions and general ethical theory utilitarianism might initially seem implausible to some readers, as you continue to consider Singer's argument that there is no morally relevant difference between cases like POND and CHARITY, you may ultimately find yourself drawn more strongly to his conclusions and utilitarianism than you initially expected, as many others have been drawn to them before. And insofar as you are drawn to those conclusions, Singer would say that you should find yourself drawn to a life of *effective altruism* rather than a life of typical consumerism—in other words, drawn to a life of doing as much good for others as you can, regardless of whether those others are strangers or family and friends.[4]

ONE POSSIBLE OBJECTION TO SINGER'S ETHICAL PRINCIPLES: ADDING UP THE DIFFERENCES BETWEEN POND AND CHARITY

In response to all of the obvious differences between POND and CHARITY noted in the previous section, we saw a "recipe" that Singer might use to argue that those differences are not morally relevant differences: Namely, for each such difference between POND and CHARITY, provide a carefully constructed case derived from POND, where POND is modified only by introducing that difference while holding the other factors in POND constant; then, when we reflect carefully on the resulting case, Singer thinks we will agree that that difference in isolation does not make for a difference in what it is permissible to do.

One thing to note is that this recipe relies heavily on our *ethical intuitions* about examples in a way that seems analogous to how a simple natural science experiment relies on our *visual perception*. In other words, in a simple science experiment we might hold fixed as many things as we can in a number of trials, in order to *observe* what the effect is of changing one particular thing that we want to study in more detail. Similarly, in the kind of recipe outlined here, we hold fixed as many things as we can, in order to "observe" what the effect is of introducing one difference. Thus, we must rely on our *ethical intuition* of the moral facts about what is right and wrong in hypothetical examples in a way that seems analogous to how we rely on our *perceptual observation* of what the empirical facts are in many natural science experiments. But is this legitimate? Can we "see" moral facts in such a way?

This leads into a number of important questions in the branch of philosophy called *metaethics* about the nature of ethical facts and our knowledge of them. These are important questions worth pursuing in further study, but they are outside of our focus here: Just as we will not focus here on further questions about the nature of *empirical* facts and how we know them, so too we will not focus here on further questions about the nature of *ethical* facts and how we know them. We will simply assume here the natural view that there are indeed facts about right and wrong just as there are facts about deaths and pains, and that it is often possible to have knowledge of both of these kinds of facts. For example, we will assume that it is unproblematic that we can know that it would be seriously wrong not to save the child from drowning in POND.[5]

Returning then to Singer's recipe described in the first paragraph of this section for replying to alleged morally relevant differences between POND and CHARITY, we might understand that recipe as itself constituting an argument for Singer's crucial premise that there is no morally relevant difference between those cases. In particular, we might understand this background argument as follows:

1. *Stipulation*: Let D1, D2, . . . D*n* refer to *all* of the *individual* differences between POND and CHARITY.
2. None of D1, D2, . . . D*n* in isolation can make a difference in what you are required to do.

Therefore, there is no morally relevant difference between POND and CHARITY, just as Singer's Ethical Premise claims.

Therefore, none of the differences between POND and CHARITY give rise to a good objection to Singer's Principle of Preventing Bad Occurrences, even on the strongest version of that principle that implies utilitarianism.

As noted at the end of the previous section, this argument can seem decisive, partly because the second premise can seem difficult to deny upon reflection.

But someone might worry that this argument is *invalid*, which is to say, again, that even if the premises were all true, the conclusion *could* be false, and so the truth of all the premises of the argument could not give one logically decisive reason to believe the conclusion. The reason this particular argument might seem invalid is that it might appear to commit the "fallacy of composition," which is a fancy name for the observation that: from the fact that each individual difference lacks a particular property (here, the property of not making a difference in what it is permissible to do), it does not follow that the *conjunction* of those differences lacks that property. To illustrate why that does not follow, suppose that when taken individually each of D1, D2, . . . D*n* slightly undermines the strength of an obligation to provide aid without making it the case that one lacks that obligation; from that supposition, it does not follow that *the large combination* of D1 & D2 . . . & D*n* does not make it the case that one lacks an obligation to provide aid. Instead, if each factor individually slightly undermines the force of such an obligation, we might well expect that the combination of very many such factors could be sufficient to remove the *obligation* to provide aid itself, and instead make it the case that providing aid is merely *supererogatory*, which is a word philosophers use for permissible action that is "above and beyond the call of duty."[6]

To see how this might then lead to an alternative substantive view, it could be argued that, contrary to Singer's claim that you have an obligation to make large sacrifices to aid others in developing nations, when a need exists that is *far away* from you in both physical and social distance, *and* when some other society or institutions have a special responsibility for the *existence* of that need, *and* when they also have a special responsibility to help *satisfy* that need, then all of those things *together* are sufficient to undermine the claim that you have a duty to provide that aid. And this is consistent with the claim that none of those things *in isolation* would be sufficient to undermine the claim that you have a duty to provide aid, and thus is consistent with also endorsing the truth of premise 2 that "None of D1, D2, . . . D*n* in isolation can make a difference in what you are required to do."[7]

So, the possible objection to Singer's argument in this section is that when we add up all the individual differences between POND and a real-world version of a case like CHARITY, this could arguably give rise to a morally relevant difference between those cases, contrary to what is claimed by Singer's Ethical Premise. The more substantive proposal outlined in the last paragraph is that there are many dimensions along which each of us is separated from the global poor, where those dimensions of separation do not exist in POND, and when all of those differences are taken in combination, they could arguably make for a morally relevant difference between POND and CHARITY.

If one were to agree with this kind of objection to Singer's argument, and thus agree that there is a morally relevant difference between POND and CHARITY, this would also provide an objection to Singer's Strong Version of the Principle of Preventing Bad Occurrences and the utilitarian general ethical theory that Singer endorses.

RECIPROCITY AS AN ALTERNATIVE ETHICAL FOUNDATION FOR DUTIES TO ASSIST THE POOR, AND THE IMPORTANCE OF GLOBALIZATION

Some philosophers argue that the separateness of societies matters in a more specific way, based on their general ethical theory that obligations to others can only arise from actual interactions and relationships with others. One influential idea along these lines is that people who are in a society together are in some important sense *engaged in a cooperative venture for mutual benefit*, which is an idea often summarized by saying that such people have relations of cooperation and *reciprocity* with one another. Some philosophers argue that actual relations of reciprocity of this type are what fundamentally explain facts about what obligations we have to others, in combination with other obligations we explicitly undertake such as by making explicit promises to do things for others.[8] Among other things, these philosophers take relations of reciprocity within our own society to show that the rich *owe* some support to those who are poor as a matter of *justice*, rather than merely for ethical reasons of *beneficence* that Singer invokes which allegedly arise simply from the amount of good the rich could do for the poor. We can understand the following ethical principle as the key difference between the reciprocity-based view and Singer's view:

> *Ethical Premise about Reciprocity*: You have an obligation to give resources to help a poor person if and only if: you stand in relations of reciprocity with that poor person, and you are rich enough to help (or if you explicitly take on an obligation by promising to help them).

From this principle, it is possible to argue for a conclusion in the direction of Singer's by adding the premise that the global poor stand in relations of reciprocity with us and we are rich enough to help. However, that premise is controversial, and some philosophers deny that it is true on the grounds that the world's most desperately poor people in lesser developed nations do not stand in relations of reciprocity with us because they are not part of our society and do not cooperate with us in the relevant ways—and of course we also haven't explicitly promised to do anything for them. If one combines this claim about the *lack* of reciprocity with the global poor with the Ethical Premise about Reciprocity, it then seems to follow that we do not have any obligations to the world's poorest people, even if we do have important obligations to poor people within our nations who do actually stand in relations of reciprocity with us.[9] Here is how that argument can be represented in standard form:

1. People in our own society stand in relations of reciprocity with us, but the world's most desperately poor people in lesser developed nations do not stand in relations of reciprocity with us—and we have not promised to help the global poor.
2. *Ethical Premise about Reciprocity*: You have an obligation to give resources to help a poor person if and only if: you stand in relations of reciprocity with that poor person, and you are rich enough to help (or if you explicitly take on an obligation by promising to help them).

Thus, richer people in our society have an obligation to transfer resources to poorer people in our society, but people in our society do not have an obligation to transfer resources to the global poor.

Thus, Singer's conclusions about our obligations to aid the poor are incorrect.

It is worth noting that there is some irony in a theory of justice that has the implication that we must make sacrifices for poor people in our society, but not for the global poor, since poor people in our developed nations are very rich compared to the poorest people in the world.[10] For this reason, and on the basis of his more general arguments for utilitarianism, Singer would reject this alternative view.

But it is worth wondering what we should make of such an argument if, unlike Singer, we find ourselves attracted to the general ethical theory that the argument invokes, namely that actual relations of reciprocity are what fundamentally explain all of the facts about what obligations we have to others, beyond things like explicit promises that we might make. From that ethical theory, note that one must add the crucial premise 1 (namely, that we do not actually stand in relations of reciprocity with the world's poorest people) in order to get an argument against Singer's conclusion about an obligation to help the global poor. However, many people reject that premise on the grounds that in a globalized economy, that premise is false, even if it may have been true at an earlier time in human history. Here is how Charles Beitz puts this objection to that premise:

> [I]f evidence of global economic and political interdependence shows the existence of a global scheme of social cooperation, we should not view national boundaries as having fundamental moral significance. Since boundaries are not coextensive with the scope of social cooperation, they do not mark the limits of social obligation. . . . [Principles of justice that describe our obligations to the poor] will therefore apply globally [and not merely domestically].[11]

Beitz's point is strengthened when we note that the World Trade Organization (WTO) and other international institutions create overwhelming incentives for nations of the world to comply with the neoliberal global economic order that they have created, which emphasizes minimally regulated global free trade. The result is an increasingly pervasive scheme of global cooperation that is arguably sufficient to create relations of reciprocity between everyone in the world.

The WTO is particularly important in this story, and it is of great importance in connection with other more general issues of global justice both within and outside the domain of food. The WTO arose historically from a club of nations who saw it as in their interest to jointly reduce tariffs and to create incentives for other nations to do so as well, and the WTO was arguably disproportionately influenced in its current design by the United States and its allies. Given the existence of the WTO, nations face a "take it or leave it" choice of either signing on and complying with *all* of its trade rules and other provisions, or else missing out on all of the very substantial economic benefits of membership. As a result, many poor nations are compelled by these incentives (despite not being directly coerced by force) to join the WTO, because on balance doing so makes their nation much better off, even though doing so often seriously harms some *parts* of their economy and citizenry. For example, many experts argue that WTO rules make farmers in poor nations worse off, and put those farmers in a position where they are easily exploited and dominated by large, multinational corporations. In addition, many experts argue that agricultural trade under the WTO is distorted so as to benefit agribusiness in rich nations like the United States at the expense of farmers in poor nations.[12] For example, Thomas Pogge writes,

> I see the appalling trajectory of world poverty and global inequality since the end of the Cold War as a shocking indictment of one particular, especially brutal path of economic globalization that our governments have chosen to impose.... Our governments ... cannot justify foreseeable harms the WTO Agreement does to some among the global poor by appeal to larger benefits it brings to others. This is so, because our governments could have avoided most of those harms, without losing these benefits, by making the WTO Agreement less burdensome on the poor countries and their citizens. They could have agreed that tariffs on manufacturing imports faced by poor countries should be no higher than those faced by rich countries, rather than four times as high. They could have agreed to open their markets to agricultural, textile, and footwear imports from the poor countries. They could have agreed to reduce their agricultural subsidies— which in 2005 amounted to $300 billion. And they could have left access by the world's poor to vital generic medicines undisturbed. Our governments did not do this because they sought to maximize our gains from the treaty. But our material gains cannot justify the harm either.[13]

Although it may initially seem surprising that the WTO could have these regrettable properties, this may not be as difficult to believe as you learn more about the history and purpose of the WTO, the fact that nations often pursue their own interests in the international realm, and the fact that there is no "world government" or other source of power that stops nations from doing things that are deeply *unfair* but do not involve the use of coercive force against other nations.

In any event, the important upshot for our purposes in this section is that, partly because of the WTO and related global agreements, we now live in a world in which globalized trade is the norm rather than the exception. Arguably, this makes everyone on the planet into citizens of one world in a philosophically deep sense that makes for relations of reciprocity between everyone on the planet: We are now all engaged together in a coordinated venture, whereas at an earlier time our ventures with others tended to be confined to the borders of our nation if they even extended that far. If this is correct, then the crucial premise 1 is incorrect in the argument displayed previously for the conclusion that we do not have obligations to the world's poorest people.

If we imagine removing premise 1 and replacing it with the premise that everyone in the world now stands in relations of reciprocity with each other, the resulting argument is roughly the one that would be offered by philosophers such as Beitz who argue that we have substantial obligations to aid those who have the misfortune of being the world's poorest people, just as (they would argue) we have substantial obligations to aid those who have the misfortune of being the poorest people in our own nations, all on the basis of considerations of reciprocity and the obligations that allegedly follow from it. Thus, theorists such as Beitz arrive at conclusions that are in the same direction as Singer's, but are not quite as *demanding* in the sense that they might not require as great of sacrifices on behalf of others. They are also based on different arguments premised on the kind of reciprocity-based general ethical theory described earlier, rather than premised on anything like utilitarian ethical theory, in contrast to Singer's arguments.

THE DUTY TO AVOID HARMING OTHERS AND TO COMPENSATE THEM FOR HARM AS AN ALTERNATIVE ETHICAL FOUNDATION FOR DUTIES TO ASSIST THE POOR

A different perspective on global poverty, reciprocity arguments, and Singer's argument is that both arguments miss the most important reasons we have to assist the global poor, because as citizens of developed nations the most important fact of all (according to the new line of argument outlined in this section) is that we are currently *harming* the world's poorest people through the WTO and related international institutions such as the World Bank and International Monetary Fund, and this harm is so extreme that it rises to the level of violations of fundamental human rights. So, according to this line of argument from philosophers like Thomas Pogge, the most important point is not whether we agree with Singer and Beitz's arguments that we have strong *positive* duties *to provide* aid to the global poor. Rather, according to this response, the more important and more obvious ethical principle is that we have *negative* duties *not to violate* people's most fundamental human rights—and if we do violate them, then we must *compensate* them for those violations, as well as doing what is necessary to make those violations stop. Pogge demonstrates this basic idea and its connection to the global poor and the WTO with the following analogy:

> The moral point is obvious in small-scale contexts: suppose you can do something that would gain you $10,000 while foreseeably saving three and killing two innocent persons. It would be clearly impermissible to do this if instead you could do something else that would gain you $5,000 while foreseeably saving three and killing no innocent persons. The case of introducing *this* WTO Agreement rather than a less burdensome alternative is analogous.[14]

On the basis of this kind of argument, together with descriptions (such as one quoted further previously) of the ways in which he claims that the WTO and other institutions harm the world's poor, Pogge reaches the following conclusion:

> . . . we are involved in harming—and, more specifically, in massively violating the human rights of—the global poor. . . . This does not mean that we must become hermits or emigrants. We can compensate for our contribution to collective harm also by contributing to efforts toward institutional reform or toward protecting the victims of present institutional injustice. Focusing on negative duties alone, I limit such compensatory duties to the amount of harm one is responsible for by cooperating in the imposition of an unjust institutional order.[15]

So, Pogge also reaches a conclusion that is in the direction of Singer's, although one that is not as demanding as the Strong Version of Singer's Principle of Preventing Bad Occurrences, because it does not require that we give away our wealth until giving away more would reduce our well-being by more than the amount of additional well-being we could secure for others. Pogge's argument might be represented as follows:

1. We are involved in killing some of the global poor merely for our own financial gain, because that is the effect of trade agreements that our powerful nation could easily make less harmful.
2. *Ethical Premise about Harm*: It is wrong to harm others in serious ways merely for our own financial gain; if one does so, one must pay compensation to those who are harmed.

Thus, our actual trade agreements are wrong, we should change them, and in the meantime you must pay compensation to the global poor who are harmed by them.

Pogge's argument is important because it does not rely on controversial ethical principles that are in tension with commonsense morality or that imply that morality is highly demanding. Instead, Pogge's argument relies only on the widely accepted Ethical Premise about Harm, together with the claim of premise 1 that, when we pay careful attention to the workings of the actual world order under the current rules of the WTO, we are harming the world's poor to an extent that rises to the level of a serious rights violation.[16]

In response, some argue that the WTO actually benefits the global poor and does not harm them, contrary to Pogge's premise 1. Some argue that although Pogge is correct that the WTO makes many of the global poor worse off than they would be with a better international trade regime, for more subtle philosophical reasons this does not mean that we are violating a canonical ethical constraint against harming people in the way that premise 2, the Ethical Premise about Harm, suggests, or this does not mean that *you as a single individual* are involved in harming people. (Pogge's arguments are discussed further in Chapter 3, "Food Justice," and issues about the ethical obligations of individual people are discussed further in Chapter 4, "Consumer Ethics.")

This section and the preceding sections have outlined the most influential arguments that it would be wrong for us not to assist the global poor by making financial sacrifices for them. It is important to note that it is consistent to believe that we have (or fail to have) any combination of the types of duties to assist the global poor discussed thus far in this chapter— which, again, include positive duties of beneficence simply because of the good we can do by assisting (as Singer claims), reciprocity-based positive duties of justice to assist (as Beitz claims), and negative duties of justice not to harm them unjustly and compensate them for the harm they are suffering at our hands by assisting (as Pogge claims). Many philosophers take one of these sources of reasons to be most important, but it is clearly possible to think that more than one applies and gives us reasons to help the global poor.

AN OBJECTION TO ETHICAL ARGUMENTS FOR ASSISTING THE GLOBAL POOR: PERVERSE INCENTIVES, SUSTAINABILITY, AND THE TRAGEDY OF THE COMMONS

A common objection to the ethical arguments noted previously for assisting the global poor focuses on the *incentives* that would be created if we acted in accord with those ethical principles, and argues that creating those incentives would actually make the world much worse—from which it is then taken to follow that acting in accord with those principles is not genuinely ethically required. For an example of this kind of objection, and to better understand the notion of incentives, consider this example from David Schmidtz:

TRAGIC COMMONS

A baby is drowning in the pool beside you. You can save the baby by a process that involves giving its family $100. If you do not save it, it will die. You save the baby. A crowd begins to gather. Seeing what you have done, two onlookers throw their babies into the pool. The babies will drown unless you give each of their families $100. More onlookers begin to gather, waiting to see what you do.

Commenting on this example, Schmidtz writes, "I am not saying our world is like TRAGIC COMMONS. I would say, though, that TRAGIC COMMONS is a world we have no good reason to want to live in. And one way to make our world more like TRAGIC COMMONS is to embrace [Singer's Principle of Preventing Bad Occurrences]."[17] In connection with Singer's Ethical Premise, Schmidtz's objection is that the difference in incentives that would be created by assisting the people in need in POND vs. CHARITY constitutes a morally relevant difference between those cases.

The title Schmidtz gives to his case is inspired by a widely discussed example called "the tragedy of the commons," which illustrates the way in which a bad outcome for everyone can sometimes be brought about by the perverse incentives each of us has when there are valuable resources that everyone shares control over together, and thus that no individual has the right to prevent anyone from using.[18] Here is one of Garrett Hardin's examples of the tragedy of the commons:

If a pasture becomes a commons open to all, the right of each to use it may not be matched by a corresponding responsibility to protect it. Asking everyone to use it with discretion will hardly do, for the considerate herdsman who refrains from overloading the commons suffers more than a selfish one who says his needs are greater. If everyone would restrain himself, all would be well; but it takes only one less than everyone to ruin a system of voluntary restraint. In a crowded world of less-than-perfect human beings, mutual ruin is inevitable if there are no controls. This is the tragedy of the commons. . . . Only the replacement of [our actual] system of the commons with a responsible system of control will save [our] land, air, water, and oceanic fisheries.[19]

With the "perverse incentives" that lead to the tragedy of the commons in mind, Hardin goes on to argue not only that the ethical arguments discussed earlier are unsound, but that it would in fact be wrong to help people who are starving:

Only rich countries have anything in the way of food reserves set aside, and even they do not have as much as they should. Poor countries have none. If poor countries received no food from the outside, the rate of population growth would be periodically checked by crop failures and famines. But if they can always draw on a world food bank in time of need, their population can continue to grow unchecked, and so will their "need" for aid. . . . Without some system of worldwide food sharing, the proportion of people in the rich and poor nations might eventually stabilize. . . . But with a well-meaning system of sharing, such as a world food bank, the growth differential between the rich and the poor countries will not only persist, it will increase. . . . A world food bank is thus a commons in disguise. People will have more motivation to draw from it than to add to any common store. The less provident and less able will multiply at the expense of the abler and more provident, bringing eventual ruin upon all. . . .[20]

Hardin's conclusions are disturbing. But even if one disagrees with them, it is important to consider his arguments carefully, in part because they reflect an influential and recurring thought over the last several hundred years that a fundamental global problem is that human population growth is out of control and must be curtailed, through coercive means when necessary—and that as a consequence it would be a mistake to assist the global poor and thereby create incentives for even more people to exist.

Hardin argues that coercive population policies are justified, and that it would be a mistake to think that individuals have a fundamental right to procreate:

> Our society is deeply committed to the welfare state, and hence is confronted with another aspect of the tragedy of the commons. . . . To couple the concept of freedom to breed with the belief that everyone born has an equal right to the commons is to lock the world into a tragic course of action. Unfortunately this is just the course of action that is being pursued by the United Nations. In late 1967, some 30 nations agreed to the following: "The Universal Declaration of Human Rights describes the family as the natural and fundamental unit of society. It follows that any choice and decision with regard to the size of the family must irrevocably rest with the family itself, and cannot be made by anyone else." . . . If we love the truth we must openly deny the validity of the Universal Declaration of Human Rights, even though it is promoted by the United Nations.[21]

Hardin continues:

> Coercion is a dirty word to most liberals now, but it need not forever be so. . . . The only kind of coercion I recommend is mutual coercion, mutually agreed upon by the majority of the people affected. To say that we mutually agree to coercion is not to say that we are required to enjoy it, or even to pretend we enjoy it. Who enjoys taxes? We all grumble about them. But we accept compulsory taxes because we recognize that voluntary taxes would favor the conscienceless. We institute and (grumblingly) support taxes and other coercive devices to escape the horror of the commons. . . . The most important aspect of necessity that we must now recognize, is the necessity of abandoning the commons in breeding. . . . The only way we can preserve and nurture other and more precious freedoms is by relinquishing the freedom to breed, and that very soon. "Freedom is the recognition of necessity"—and it is the role of education to reveal to all the necessity of abandoning the freedom to breed.[22]

So, Hardin's view is that we should all favor coercive policies to reduce population growth. One important objection to Hardin's arguments is that they overlook the possibility that economic development, subsidization of birth control, and increases in education, especially for women, might be as effective at reducing population growth as more coercive policies, and of course would not come at such a dramatic cost along the dimension of coercion. Many experts believe that these non-coercive population policies are actually more effective in many places, or at least are better, all things considered, because they are nearly as effective and do not require the problematic forms of coercion that Hardin's policies would require.[23] Further, population growth has already essentially stopped in the developed world, and so the coercion that Hardin recommends would have to be imposed entirely on the developing world, perhaps at the behest of developed nations, which might seem extremely unjust. In light of all this, in his reading for this chapter Paul Ehrlich advocates policies for population reduction that are far less coercive than more Hardin-like measures that Ehrlich himself previously endorsed in the 1960s.[24]

Another important worry about Hardin's view arises from the fact that most people do not actually favor the coercive policies that he recommends. So, there is not actually the kind of democratic support for those policies that Hardin seems to think would be ideally best given his slogan of "mutual coercion, mutually agreed upon." So, what does Hardin's view say we should actually do in light of this? From the tone of Hardin's comments here and elsewhere, one gets the idea that in a non-ideal case where people do not support the best policy, nonetheless the best policy should still be imposed on them with the justification that it is the policy they would all agree upon if they were "more rational." But this raises the pressing question of who gets to decide this and then impose this policy on everyone else? Who decides when everyone is wrong about what is best for them?

In light of this, on Hardin's view there is a worry about "who will watch the watchers." In other words, even if we agree that the tragedy of the commons shows that leaving people free in an unbridled way can have consequences that are really bad by everyone's lights, Hardin's solution to this problem is controversial, because it assumes that people should then be put in charge to coercively change everyone's behavior. But if the essence of the problem is that people respond to incentives, and when people are unconstrained this can lead to disastrous results, shouldn't we worry that putting people in charge and giving them coercive power will lead to even larger problems via the same mechanisms, since the people in charge are, after all, *people*—and the essence of the problem, again, is that people respond to incentives, and when people are unconstrained this can lead to disastrous results? Putting people in charge with coercive power arguably creates a situation where those people have even worse incentives and even more unbridled power than in the problematic situations such as the tragedy of the commons that we are initially concerned with. So, perhaps government is not the solution, but is merely a way of making the problem worse?[25]

On the other hand, before we go too far in the other direction and decide to get rid of all regulations of all kinds, it is important to keep in mind that it is an empirical question how well regulation of specific kinds work in specific situations, and the evidence indicates that although the answer to this question is highly variable, regulation is sometimes a clear improvement over no regulation when it is well designed. In light of this, most experts now think that there is an important need for *some* substantial government regulations in society—for example, to regulate the levels of cyanide in our drinking water, to cite a fairly uncontroversial example. But at the same time, there is appreciation that just as free markets do not necessarily ensure optimal outcomes, so too government intervention to try to correct the suboptimal consequences of free markets does not necessarily ensure an improvement either. Sometimes government intervention makes things worse rather than better, especially when policy-makers are driven by an over-application of metaphors such as the tragedy of the commons and an overly simplistic view that "solutions" to such problems must be imposed by a privileged group of decision-makers, as Elinor Ostrom and others have pointed out in response to Hardin's arguments. (Ostrom was awarded the Nobel Prize in Economics for her work on these issues and her contribution to understanding of how to promote sustainable use of resources.[26])

MALTHUSIAN ARGUMENTS AND FOOD SUPPLY

Hardin's argument that unchecked population growth should be expected to lead to societal collapse echoes an extremely influential argument made by Thomas Malthus in 1798, which has been used by many people since then to argue for conclusions like Hardin's, including by Ehrlich. The basic argument is that the earth's arable land is finite (where "arable" means "suitable for growing crops"), and so as global population continues to increase by billions of people, we should expect the *food supply* per capita to begin to decline soon in a way that will lead to mass starvation.[27] (The term "food supply" means the total amount of crops produced that are devoted to human consumption, and so the food supply per capita is the total food supply divided by the total population. Sen in his reading for this chapter uses the term "food output" and "food availability" in a way that means roughly the same thing as "food supply." Sometimes it is useful to focus on a nation's *domestic* food supply, or on some more *local* food supply [e.g., for purposes of analyzing a famine that occurs in a particular area].)

Experts now agree that one crucial variable overlooked by this argument is the rate of increase in *crop yields*, which represent the amount of food produced per acre under cultivation. To see why this is a crucial additional variable, note that if population increases by $x\%$ per year, but yields increase by more than $x\%$ per year, then food supply per capita will continue to increase even without increasing the amount of land under cultivation. In fact, contrary to Malthus's predictions, global food supply per capita has grown on average since his argument in 1798, and it has continued to grow since Hardin and Ehrlich endorsed Malthusian arguments in the 1960s. World population has gone from 1 billion in 1798 to 2 billion in 1930 to 3 billion in 1960 to over 7 billion today, and over that time food supply per capita has increased due to increases in crop yields, as well as increases in the percentage of arable land under cultivation.[28] Yield increases have been driven primarily by the development of higher-yielding seeds, and by technological improvements such as mechanization and fertilizer and water application techniques, all of which have squeezed more and more production out of each cultivated acre. (Yield increases are discussed in more detail in Chapter 9, "Industrial Plant Agriculture.")

So, our actual experience has shown why the following argument is invalid, and it has also shown that the first premise presented here has been false in some recent decades:

1. If population increases, so does the quantity of arable land needed to feed that population.
2. There is a finite quantity of arable land.

Hence, there must be some number of people such that once that number is reached, then food supply per capita will decrease.

The problem with the argument, as explained already, is that it overlooks the possibility that yield growth will exceed population growth even holding cultivated land fixed.

However, some experts believe that we should still have worries about our ultimate ability to support an increasingly affluent (and meat-consuming) human population that may still double in the next 100 years, partly because of diminishing returns on investments in yield increases.[29] Or, at the very least, many experts think we should worry about the extreme costs that might be involved in supporting such a population, as we may need to cut down rainforests and thus accelerate climate change in order to create enough agricultural land to meet demand—and accelerating climate change will itself reduce yields even further (because the changes in weather have already made growing conditions for many staple crops worse, and will do so even more as climate change gets worse and worse), which means the need for more land, which means feeding people becomes even more costly and climate change gets worse, which means . . . you get the idea.[30]

Another factor overlooked by Malthusian arguments is that global population might peak and then start to decline. This variable was not part of Malthus's own conceptualization of these issues in 1798, as he instead saw population growth as exponentially increasing until some external shock or constraint (such as total arable land) forced reductions in population. This variable of population peak and eventual decline seems to be ignored by the Malthusian analyses of Hardin and Ehrlich as well. But current United Nations population projections (based on the work of leading *demographers*, the experts who study population dynamics) indicate that we should expect world population to peak in around 100 years at around 12 billion, with an 80% chance that the peak will occur within the following range: peaking at around 10 billion near the end of this century or peaking at around 14 billion later next century.[31] The reasons why experts predict population to peak in the foreseeable future are complex, but the main reason is that when people become more affluent and educated, especially women, they tend to reproduce at a lower rate, which is why developed nations now tend to have negative population growth, bracketing immigration. As the world becomes increasingly affluent, we should thus expect global population to peak at some point and then decline. This phenomenon was not part of Malthus's thinking for understandable reasons, because the average person is about 30 times as rich today than in 1798,[32] and thus people in Malthus's day were very far from the level of affluence at which an important reduction in birth rates would begin, and so Malthus was unable to anticipate such a phenomenon for understandable reasons. But we are past the relevant threshold today in developed nations, and so we have many decades of rich evidence of declining birth rates that we must take into proper account in population projections. In addition to explaining why we should not think that unregulated reproduction must necessarily lead to mass starvation, this also provides a somewhat more detailed explanation of why many experts today believe that policies that promote economic growth and education in developing nations, especially for women, are the most effective policies for reducing population growth rates—contrary to what appear to be Hardin's recommendations for more coercive population policies presented earlier.[33] The upshot of all of this is that contrary to the predictions of Malthus and Hardin, declining global food supply has not been a primary driver of hunger. However, as we noted previously, there is arguably reason to worry that global food supply *could* still become a problem in the future.

FOOD ENTITLEMENTS, FOOD SECURITY, AND THE RIGHT TO FOOD

Amartya Sen, in his reading for this chapter, also emphasizes that global food supply is *not* the main worry now or in the recent past in connection with global hunger. He notes, counterintuitively, that many cases of mass starvation in the twentieth century happened *without* a reduction even in the *local* food supply, and that most contemporary cases of malnutrition occur in nations with more than enough domestic food supply for everyone. Sen argues that therefore the best explanation of most current cases of malnutrition is not inadequate food supply, but rather inadequate *food entitlements*, where an individual person's food entitlement is, roughly, the food that that person *actually has the ability to acquire*, given the facts about them and the legal, economic, and social situation in which they find themselves. So, in rough terms, the problem is not that there is not enough food *produced*; rather, the problem is that some people nevertheless don't have the *ability* to get the food that they need even though enough has been produced.

To better illustrate this notion of food entitlements and its explanatory power, let's imagine a simplified example that highlights some of the mechanisms in Sen's analysis, which he uses to explain actual famines such as the Bengal Famine of 1943.[34] Imagine that a nation's domestic food supply is more than enough to feed everyone, but nonetheless lots of its people starve. How could that happen? Here is one way: Suppose that in a relatively poor nation the wealthiest 50% of people suddenly become much wealthier because of some unforeseen event—for example, suppose those particular people own a resource that suddenly becomes much more valuable in the global marketplace. As a result, they suddenly have a lot more money and affluence, and as a result they eat a lot more food, which starts to drive up the price of food, and drives up the price of food to an extent that the poorer 50% of people start to become a little worried about the trajectory of food prices. As a result, there is a chain reaction of worry whereby people start to buy a little extra food to hedge against future price increases and "just in case," which increases prices even more, leading to more worry, and pretty soon everyone who can afford it is buying extra food for the now-more-uncertain future, including the richest 50% who have the purchasing power to hoard far more food than the large amount they are already consuming. As a result, even if food supply per capita for this nation is larger than ever and beyond levels that have historically been sufficient for proper nutrition for all, many people could starve in this scenario if as a result of the spike in food prices they are then unable to afford enough food.

In this story and in other actual situations where malnutrition threatens, an analysis in terms of food entitlements provides a particularly compelling explanation of why the people who are most at risk for malnutrition are the people who are likely to end up having the lowest *food entitlements*, which may be different from the people who are the *poorest*. For example, suppose that the poorest people in the story above (as in the actual Bengal Famine of 1943) are people who are subsistence farmers who control just enough land so that they can farm it and barely meet their basic needs. Meanwhile, a group with slightly more material wealth than the subsistence farmers are tradespeople. In the scenario described, after the price spike, it is easy to see why the subsistence farmers might be expected to have greater food entitlements than the tradespeople even though the former have less material wealth than the latter, because the subsistence farmers directly control enough food to feed themselves—they have more *direct entitlements* to food—whereas the latter group have only more fragile *exchange entitlements* to food in the sense that they depend on people's ability to exchange their labor and wealth for food and are thus highly contingent on the prevailing prices in the external marketplace, and in the scenario described these entitlements are sharply reduced by the price spike, below the level of entitlements necessary for them to ensure proper nutrition. So, insofar as the poorest would have greater food entitlements than others in a famine scenario, we should expect them to starve less than those with more wealth but who would have lesser food entitlements. All of these facts are explained elegantly by Sen's analysis and cannot be explained by an analysis in terms of food supply and wealth alone.

At a more general level, Sen's analysis explains why it is important to consider what *entitlements* people have to the things they need to live a healthy life, and to consider how reliable those entitlements are given various possible setbacks that a person could suffer (such as getting sick, breaking a leg, becoming unemployed, etc.), and given possible external events (e.g., events that change that person's purchasing power). For many people, the fragile nature of their entitlements is a constant and pressing matter of life and death, and for many more (at least a billion people in the world in total) entitlements to proper nutrition for themselves and their children are constantly in peril and are a constant source of stress and uncertainty. Note that it is highly implausible that most of these people bear any personal responsibility for their plight, as they simply lack any real opportunity to rise out of that poverty. (And even if they were held responsible to some extent for some reason, it would not be plausible to hold their very young children responsible.)

In light of these troubling facts together with analyses like Sen's that reveal the fundamental importance of entitlements in this sense, much emphasis in food policy is now placed on facts about *food security* rather than mere facts about food supply, where food security is understood primarily as a matter of how *reliably* people have the actual ability—*physically* and *economically*—to acquire *proper nutrition*.[35]

In light of Sen's analysis of the importance of what *entitlements* people have, a natural thought is that people's actual entitlements in a society should correspond to the fundamental *ethical entitlements* that they have to food and other basic necessities of life (such as clean air, water, and so on). In other words, in connection with food, a common thought is that:

1. People have a fundamental human right to adequate nutrition.

Therefore, we have an obligation to ensure that people have reliable *entitlements* to adequate nutrition in Sen's sense and in the food security sense of *reliably having physical and economic access to proper nutrition*.

The idea here is that people have a fundamental right to sufficient food, which is to say that there is a fundamental ethical entitlement to sufficient food; so, we have an obligation to ensure that people are *food secure* in the sense of reliably having actual entitlements (in Sen's sense) to sufficient food. This is roughly the sense in which many people argue (or take it for granted) that everyone has a basic "right to food," and it is the sense in which the United Nations currently understands the right to food. (The United Nations' definition of the right to food is discussed more in the next section.)

RIGHTS: WHAT THEY ARE, WHICH WE HAVE, WHAT THEY IMPLY

It is important to note that in the preceding argument, the right to food is understood as a fundamental *positive* right, in the sense that it is a fundamental right each person has against other people to *be provided with* something (in this case, food, or at least the actual ability to have enough of it). As such, it is arguably different from *negative* rights, such as the right to life, which is roughly the right each person has against other people *not* to do something (in this case, kill them). The general difference is that fundamental *negative* rights only imply that everyone has an obligation *not* to do particular things to each other, whereas fundamental *positive* rights would imply that everyone has an obligation *to do* particular things *for* each other.

With this intuitive difference in mind, some philosophers argue that there is no such thing as fundamental positive rights, such as the right to food in this sense, on the grounds that *fundamental* rights are rights one has simply in virtue of existing as the sort of being that one is, and if one avoids violating anyone's fundamental negative rights, then there is no good sense in which one might nonetheless have violated anyone's fundamental rights in some other way.[36] In contrast, other philosophers argue that fundamental positive rights do exist. Arguments for these opposing views might be supported by a number of different general ethical theories. As one example of how a positive right to food might be supported by an argument based on a particular general ethical theory, Onora O'Neill argues for such a right to food (and other rights) on the basis of *Kantian ethics*, which takes autonomy to be a fundamental ethical value that takes priority over other values:

> If we are not indifferent or neglectful of the requirements for sustaining others' autonomy we will, I suggest, find ourselves committed not only to justice but to various further principles in our action toward the poor and vulnerable. First we will be committed to material help that sustains agency, by helping people over the threshold of poverty below which possibilities for autonomous action are absent or meager. Since sustained and systematic help is needed if vulnerability and dependence are not to recur endlessly, this implies a commitment to development policies as well as to emergency food aid.[37]

So, there are arguments for and against the existence of fundamental positive rights to things that are necessary for a healthy life, such as food. But what are *rights* exactly, and what do they imply in ethical practice? What is the correct way of thinking about rights?

In 1920, the United States adopted a law permitting women across the country to vote. Before then, it was illegal in some parts of the country for women to vote. In those parts of the country, women had no legal right to vote. In some parts of the country today, there is a law that requires cities or towns to pick up recycling. In those parts of the country, citizens have a legal right to have their recycling picked up.

So there are *legal rights*. But there also are *moral rights*, at least according to ethicists who endorse the existence of fundamental moral rights. In the voting case, their idea is not only that women have a legal right to vote, but they also have a fundamental moral right to vote: If they are not allowed to vote, they are done a moral wrong. The movement to give women legal rights to vote was fueled, in part, by the conviction that they had a moral right to vote and that the state, by depriving them of that right, was doing something morally wrong. In the recycling case, it is less plausible that there are any moral rights in play. In parts of the country where there is no law about recycling and so the state does not pick up citizens' recycling, the state is not doing a moral wrong. So moral and legal rights can go together—as in the voting case—or they can come apart—as in the recycling case.

If you have a right to something—a moral or legal right—others have (at least) a corresponding obligation not to take that thing away from you. For example, if you have a right to vote, then others have (at least) a corresponding obligation to allow you to vote. If people stop you from voting, they are treating you *unjustly* (more on injustice in the next chapter). Even theorists who believe only in fundamental negative rights agree with this.

Theorists who believe in positive rights go even further than this idea that a person *A*'s right to *x* obligates each other person *not to take* x *away from* A (which is sometimes called the view that rights have correlative duties to be *respected*). Going further, these theorists who believe in positive rights to *x* tend to also believe that *A*'s right to *x* also implies that others have an obligation to ensure that *A* actually has the ability to get *x*, or even that *A* be provided with *x* (which is sometimes called the view that a right has a correlative duty to be *fulfilled*). They might also believe that *A*'s right to *x* also implies that each other person has an obligation to ensure that other people also respect *A*'s right to *x* (which is sometimes called the view that a right has a correlative duty to be *protected*).

With that in mind, we can now see that those who reject the right to food, in the sense articulated before, likely have a different theory of the nature of fundamental human rights than those who accept the right to food. Those who reject the right to food may reject it because they believe that there are only fundamental negative rights. Whereas those who endorse the right may believe that if there is a basic human right to something (e.g., food), then others have duties to respect, protect, and fulfill that right. The latter view, unlike the former, is a view on which human rights imply positive rights to a range of related things. For example, the United Nations Committee on Economic, Social and Cultural Rights understands the right to food in the following way:

> The right to adequate food, like any other human right, imposes three types or levels of obligations on States parties: the obligations to respect, to protect and to fulfil. In turn, the obligation to fulfil incorporates both an obligation to facilitate and an obligation to provide. The obligation to respect existing access to adequate food requires States parties not to take any measures that result in preventing such access. The obligation to protect requires measures by the State to ensure that enterprises or individuals do not deprive individuals of their access to adequate food. The obligation to fulfil (facilitate) means the State must proactively engage in activities intended to strengthen people's access to and utilization of resources and means to ensure their livelihood, including food security. Finally, whenever an individual or group is unable, for reasons beyond their control, to enjoy the right to adequate food by the means at their disposal, States have the obligation to fulfil (provide) that right directly.[38]

Again, some philosophers reject the view that human rights, such as the alleged human right to food, have all of these implications, especially the implication of positive rights to be provided with things. These critics believe instead that discourse about rights such as this from the UN is rhetoric that effectively promotes a particular set of goals, but that the rights enumerated do not correspond to moral rights. Instead, these philosophers are apt to understand a fundamental right to food as merely implying that others have an obligation not to take food away from those who have it, need it, and have acquired it in a way that respects other's rights (i.e., they understand it merely in the sense of a duty to respect, in the sense defined earlier).

Which rights do we have? The legal ones are much easier to enumerate since we can simply look them up. Looking for the moral ones is harder. It is relatively uncontroversial in our society that citizens of all genders, races and ethnicities, and socioeconomic groups have a moral right to vote. It is relatively uncontroversial in our society that people have a moral right to life. In the political debate about health care reform undertaken by the Obama Administration, there was much discussion about whether people have a moral right to healthcare. In this book, an important question is whether people have a moral right to food.

It might seem like this is a totally obvious question. If people have a right to life, then, since they need food to live, of course they have a right to food. But as we've seen, things are actually not so obvious, including for reasons related to the controversy over positive and negative rights outlined previously. The healthcare example provides an opportunity to make a further wrinkle clear. There are cases where the only way to save a person's life is for a certain surgeon to perform a certain procedure. Does the surgeon do something wrong if she refuses? Maybe. If she were in the room next door, watching TV, it is plausible she should have done the surgery and violates the patient's rights and thereby treats her unjustly if she does not. If, instead, she is halfway across the world, it is much less clear that she does wrong if she refuses to fly to the patient to save her. Generally, it is not obviously true that if you have a right to something, then you have a right to anything you need to acquire that thing.[39] So just because a person has a right to life, it does not immediately follow that s/he has a right to food in the sense endorsed by the argument at the end of the last section.

To summarize the discussion in this section, we've seen that the following intuitive argument relies on two ethically controversial ideas:

1. People have a fundamental right to life.

Therefore, people have a fundamental right to adequate nutrition.

Therefore, we have an obligation to ensure that people have reliable *entitlements* to adequate nutrition in Sen's sense and in the food security sense of *reliably having physical and economic access to proper nutrition.*

Even if we agree with the initial premise that people have a fundamental right to life, it could be argued that it does not follow that people have a fundamental right to adequate nutrition, on the grounds that from the fact that someone has a fundamental human right to x, and the fact that they need y for x, it does not follow that they have a fundamental right to y, contrary to what the argument seems to assume. And even if we agree that people have a fundamental right to adequate nutrition, it could be argued that the second conclusion does not follow that we have an obligation to ensure that everyone has adequate nutrition in the food security sense of ensuring that they actually have (access to) adequate nutrition. Instead, if one believes that the only fundamental human rights are negative rights, this second conclusion might be rejected on that basis. However, many others will be happy to add the UN's premise that "any . . . human right imposes three types or levels of obligations. . . : the obligations to respect, to protect and to fulfil." If one adds that premise to the argument, then the second conclusion follows from the first.

OBJECTIONS TO THE EMPIRICAL PREMISES IN ARGUMENTS FOR ASSISTING THE GLOBAL POOR: DOES AID TO THE WORLD'S POOR ACTUALLY HELP?

The preceding sections covered a lot of ground and outlined many of the most prominent debates regarding global hunger and global justice: Singer's very influential argument was articulated for the conclusion that it would be wrong for you not to provide large amounts of aid to the global poor, several objections were identified to its main ethical premise, replies to those objections were considered, alternative justice-based arguments were explained for less demanding conclusions about our obligations to assist the global poor, and related issues were summarized connected to population, the tragedy of the commons, and coercive public policy.

Instead of objecting to the *ethical* premises in Singer's and others' arguments, one might object to non-ethical premises. This section notes objections to the non-ethical premises in ethical arguments for assisting the global poor—namely, their empirical premises that claim, roughly, that we have the ability to dramatically help the global poor by investing a relatively small fraction of our wealth for their benefit. In the case of Singer's argument, this empirical premise is the claim that CHARITY is a situation that we always find ourselves in, because it is always possible for each of us to give to effective charities that would then save additional lives that would not otherwise be saved. Objections to this premise in Singer's argument also translate into objections to the empirical assumptions of many of the approaches to global hunger and global justice that are most naturally suggested by the preceding arguments. In this way, Singer's argument is exemplary of others in the book: It contains an ethical component that one might accept or reject and a non-ethical component that one might accept or reject. These components are independent in that someone might agree with Singer about the ethics and disagree about the non-ethical claim or vice versa.

In Singer's case, the main objection to these empirical premises is straightforward and is outlined by Angus Deaton in his reading for this chapter. The objection is that, contrary to these empirical premises, it is actually very difficult to help the world's poor, and it is naïve and mistaken to think that sending $100 in an envelope to OXFAM will really make any difference in the outcome for anyone in need, and it is just as naïve and mistaken to think that sending $100,000 in aid would do much good either.[40] This is a highly empirical disagreement with Singer, and Deaton outlines some of the empirical arguments for his position in his reading for this chapter, which he articulates in more detail in the last chapter of his book *The Great Escape: Health, Wealth, and the Origins of Inequality* (Princeton University Press, 2013).

In response to Deaton, Bill Gates in his reading for this chapter argues for a less pessimistic view and provides some examples of areas in which he thinks we can reliably do a lot of good with philanthropy. In their reading for this chapter, Abhijit Banerjee and Esther Duflo provide a number of further dimensions along which the problem of global hunger is more complicated than it initially appears. Banerjee, Duflo, and Deaton argue that global hunger and global poverty are much more complicated than is assumed by theorists such as Singer and Pogge, and that the truth is very far from, for example, Pogge's claim that the eradication of world poverty is fairly straightforward and would require redistribution of no more than 1% of global wealth.[41]

Among the objections that Deaton raises to optimists about aid, such as Singer and Pogge, the following is particularly striking:

> In today's Rwanda, President Paul Kagame has discovered how to use Singer's utilitarian calculus against his own people. By providing health care for Rwandan mothers and children, he has become one of the darlings of the industry and a favorite recipient of aid. Essentially, he is "farming" Rwandan children, allowing more of them to live in exchange for support for his undemocratic and oppressive rule. Large aid flows to Africa sometimes help the intended beneficiaries, but they also help create dictators and provide them with the means to insulate themselves from the needs and wishes of their people.

Beyond the disturbing dynamics of this particular example involving Kagame and Rwanda, Deaton is making a number of more general points. If we believe that everyone in the world has a right to food, a right to health, and so on—or even if we don't believe in those rights, but we at least genuinely care about those people and want to help them—then it can seem obvious that the way of making things better is to try to have those rights enshrined in the law and to try to help those people in the most direct way possible. But Deaton is pointing out that doing so can have *unintended consequences*, and those unintended consequences can be so severe that our well-intentioned aid can actually make things worse rather than better along the dimensions that we care about. The most straightforward worries along these lines are that aid might be funneled to support dictators, or that aid might not actually have the beneficial effects that we anticipate, but might succeed in destroying local markets and incentives to make things better. For example, if there is hunger and poverty in a region, and we deluge that region with free food and other goods, then that could bankrupt everyone in that region who is in the business of growing food and producing other goods, and it could remove any perceived incentive for anyone else there to engage in food-growing or other wealth-creating activities. This could transform that region's crisis from a temporary one into a permanent one. If crises were repeatedly responded to in such a way, that could be the crucial factor that explains why those regions are never ultimately able to rise out of poverty or able to create sustainable societies.

A more subtle worry is that if we believe that people have a fundamental right to food, health, and so on, then it can seem obvious that trying to get those rights enshrined in the law as formal legal entitlements is the way of solving the problems of food security (and health security more generally) to which Sen's analysis draws our attention. However, it does not actually follow that enshrining a right to x in the law will actually help people get x who do not already have the ability to get x, because there might be a lack of government capacity to enforce that law—a point that is particularly relevant in connection with developing nations. More subtly, enshrining a right to x in the law and funding the additional bureaucratic structure involved with that right takes resources, and those resources might better invested elsewhere to yield greater gains in people's actual entitlements to x—and more worrisome, creating additional bureaucratic structure might increase corruption and the power of corrupt agents of the government, which could make things even worse for the people we care about helping. More subtle still is a situation along the lines that Deaton describes, where a corrupt government is incentivized to enshrine a legal right to x without any intention of generally enforcing that law beyond the subset of citizens that are its constituents, so as to reap the benefits of foreign aid and thus become a more firmly entrenched dictatorship, which might then result in a situation in which things are made worse with respect to x for the overall population. In such a case, a more effective way of helping people might be to work to benefit them in a much more indirect way, such as reducing inequities in global trade policy (such as described previously in connection with the WTO) and promoting economic growth in the developing world in other ways. (These issues are discussed in more detail in Chapter 3, "Food Justice.")

If we care about people, and if we care about justice, then it is important to go beyond a thin veneer of empiricism, and instead ask seriously and honestly what actually works to help people, and what actually bends the arc toward justice. These are difficult empirical questions, and it would be surprising if the answers were obvious—as Deaton puts it, "If it were so simple, the world would already be a much better place."

At the same time, many argue that there are *some* things that we can reliably do to help, even if they are empirically difficult to identify, or politically difficult to enact—for example, Gates claims that "programs that are actually designed to improve human welfare—especially health and agriculture—are some of the best spending that a rich country can do on behalf of the poor."

FURTHER READING

The Ethics of Assistance to the Global Poor

Arneson, Richard. 2004. "Moral Limits on the Demands of Beneficence?" in Deen Chatterjee, ed., *The Ethics of Assistance*. Cambridge, MA: Cambridge University Press.

Ashford, Elizabeth. 2011. "The Alleged Dichotomy between Positive and Negative Duties of Justice", in Beitz and Goodin 2011.

Beitz, Charles and Robert Goodin eds. 2011. *Global Basic Rights*. Oxford University Press.

Blake, Michael, and Patrick Taylor Smith. 2013. "International Distributive Justice." *Stanford Encyclopedia of Philosophy*.

Cohen, Joshua. 2010. "Philosophy, Social Science, Global Poverty," in Alison Jaggar, ed., *Thomas Pogge and His Critics*. Cambridge, MA: Cambridge University Press

Nussbaum, Martha. 2013. *Creating Capabilities*. Cambridge, MA: Harvard University Press.

Øverland, Gerhard, and Christian Barry. forthcoming. *The Responsibilities of the Affluent to the Poor*. Cambridge, MA: Cambridge University Press.

Pogge, Thomas. 2014. "Are We Violating the Rights of the World's Poor?" *Yale Human Rights and Development Law Journal* 14 (2):1–33.

Pogge, Thomas, and Keith Horton, eds. 2008. *Global Ethics*. St. Paul, MN: Paragon.

Pogge, Thomas, and Darrel Moellendorf, eds. 2008. *Global Justice*. St. Paul, MN: Paragon.

Singer, Peter. 2009. *The Life You Can Save*. New York: Random House.

Thompson, Paul B. 1992. *The Ethics of Aid and Trade*. Cambridge, MA: Cambridge University Press.

Unger, Peter. 1996. *Living High and Letting Die*. New York: Oxford University Press.

The Empirics and Economics of Assistance to the Global Poor

Banerjee, Abhijit, and Esther Duflo. 2012. *Poor Economics: A Radical Rethinking of the Way to Fight Global Poverty*. PublicAffairs.

Cartwright, Nancy. 2012. "Will this Policy work for You? Predicting Effectiveness Better: How Philosophy Helps" *Philosophy of Science*, 79 (5) pp. 973–989.

Deaton, Angus. 2013. *The Great Escape: Health, Wealth, and the Origins of Inequality*. Princeton, NJ: Princeton University Press.

GiveDirectly. "Operating Model and Evidence on Cash Transfers." www.givedirectly.com.

GiveWell. "Process and Reports on Top Charities." www.givewell.com.

Mullainathan, Sendhil, and Eldar Shafir. 2013. *Scarcity: Why Having Too Little Means So Much*. Picador.

Sen, Amartya. 1999. *Development as Freedom*. Anchor.

Food Security and Feeding the World

Conway, Gordon. 2012. *One Billion Hungry: Can We Feed the World?* Cornell University Press.

Naylor, Rosamond. 2014. "The Many Faces of Food Security," in *The Evolving Sphere of Food Security*. Oxford University Press.

Paarlberg, Robert. 2013. *Food Politics: What Everyone Needs to Know*, 2nd ed. Oxford University Press.

Sustainability and the Tragedy of the Commons

Hilborn, Ray, and Hilborn, Ulrike. 2012. *Overfishing: What Everyone Needs to Know*. Oxford University Press.
Ostrom, Elinor, et al. 1999. "Revisiting the Commons." *Science* 284: 278–282.

NOTES

1. Kenneth Weiss, "As the World's Population Grows, Hunger Persists on a Massive Scale," *Los Angeles Times*, July 22, 2012, reprinted in Chapter 1 and online at: http://www.latimes.com/world/population/la-fg-population-matters3-20120726-html-htmlstory.html.

2. For further explanation and discussion of the claims in this paragraph, see the discussion in Chapter 9 and David Tilman et al., "Global Food Demand and the Sustainable Intensification of Agriculture," *Proceedings of the National Academy of Sciences* 108 (2011): 20260–20264, and for an accessible summary, see the graphic "A World Demanding More" in Jonathan Foley, "A Five-Step Plan to Feed the World," *National Geographic*, online at: http://www.nationalgeographic.com/foodfeatures/feeding-9-billion.

3. See Peter Singer, *The Life You Can Save* (Random House, 2009), for discussion of these differences and responses to other objections.

4. For more on effective altruism, which is roughly the idea that we try to do the most good we can based on careful study of the evidence on what really works in practice, see Peter Singer, "The Logic of Effective Altruism," *Boston Review*, July 6, 2015, online at: http://bostonreview.net/forum/peter-singer-logic-effective-altruism. The selection from Angus Deaton in this chapter is a reply to this essay on effective altruism by Singer.

5. To get a taste of one important further objection along these lines: There is some evidence that our intuitions are subject to important, systematic, and worrisome biases. In light of that, might we worry about our ability to have reliable intuitions about the examples Singer describes? It is worth noting that Singer has argued that when we closely examine the empirical evidence about biasing factors and moral intuitions, this ultimately supports utilitarianism over alternative ethical theories, because among ethical theories only utilitarianism is driven by psychological responses that plausibly track the ethical truth rather than irrelevant emotional factors. See Peter Singer, "Ethics and Intuitions," *Journal of Ethics* 9 (2005): 331–352. Unsurprisingly, many non-utilitarian philosophers disagree with Singer's arguments here.

6. Peter Unger briefly considers something like this kind of objection in his book *Living High and Letting Die* (Oxford University Press, 1996), pp. 53–54 and 73–75.

7. For more on the objection described here based on the fallacy of composition, and an evaluation of Unger's attempt at a reply, see Mark Budolfson, "Global Ethics and the Problem with Singer and Unger's Argument for an Extreme Duty to Provide Aid."

8. For influential views that are along these simplified lines, see Thomas Scanlon, *What We Owe to Each Other* (Harvard University Press, 2000), and John Rawls, *A Theory of Justice* (Harvard University Press, 1971).

9. John Rawls, *The Law of Peoples* (Harvard University Press, 2001), argues for a slightly different view than this, which involves a number of additional principles that are listed but not supported with extensive arguments. In rough terms, Rawls's idea seems to be that rich nations should help poor nations become more just domestically, but rich nations do not have obligations to transfer resources to poor nations beyond that, and Rawls thinks that resource transfers will not generally be a significant part of how rich nations can best help poor nations become more just domestically either.

10. Peter Singer, *The Life You Can Save* (Random House, 2009), makes this point and discusses its implications at length, arguing that we should reject ethical and political theories that have such implications.

11. Charles Beitz, "Bounded Morality: Justice and the State in World Politics," *International Organization* 33 (Summer 1979): 151. See also Charles Beitz, "Justice and International Relations," *Philosophy & Public Affairs* 4, no. 4 (Summer, 1975): 360–389, especially section III, Joshua Cohen and Charles Sabel (2006), "Extram Republicam Nulla Justitia?" *Philosophy & Public Affairs* 34, no. 2 (March 2006): 147–175.

12. For example, see Duncan Green and Matthew Griffin (2002), "Dumping on the Poor: The Common Agricultural Policy, the WTO, and International Development." http://www.iatp.org/documents/dumping-on-the-poor-the-common-agricultural-policy-the-wto-and-international-development, and Joseph Stiglitz and Andrew Carlton (2007), *Fair Trade for All* (Oxford: Oxford University Press).

13. Thomas Pogge, *World Poverty and Human Rights*, 2nd ed. (Polity, 2008), 18–22.

14. Ibid., 22, italics in the original.

15. Ibid., 26.

16. For some objections or complications relevant to Pogge's argument, see Joshua Cohen, "Philosophy, Social Science, Global Poverty," in *Thomas Pogge and His Critics*, ed. Alison Jaggar (Cambridge, UK: Polity Press, 2010), 18–45, and Gerhard Øverland and Christian Barry (forthcoming), *The Responsibilities of the Affluent to the Poor* (Cambridge University Press).

17. David Schmidtz, "Separateness, Suffering, and Moral Theory," in *Person, Polis, Planet* (Oxford University Press, 2008), 148.

18. Many situations that fall under the rubric of the tragedy of the commons can be understood as having the incentive structure of a *Prisoner's Dilemma*, which Grace Boey explains in her reading in Chapter 1. The Prisoner's Dilemma and the tragedy of the commons are enormously influential in discussions of individual freedom, the failure of free markets to ensure optimal outcomes, and public policy.

19. Garrett Hardin, "Lifeboat Ethics: The Case against Helping the Poor", *Psychology Today* 8 (September 1974): 38–43.

20. Ibid.

21. Garrett Hardin, "The Tragedy of the Commons," *Science* 162, no. 3859 (1968): 1243–1248. The UN Universal Declaration of Human Rights is online at: http://www.un.org/en/documents/udhr.

22. Ibid.

23. See Amartya Sen, "Population: Delusion and Reality," *New York Review of Books*, September 22, 1994, and Elizabeth Willott, "Recent Population Trends," in *Environmental Ethics*, 2nd ed., eds. David Schmidtz and Elizabeth Willott (Oxford University Press, 2012).

24. See Paul Ehrlich and Anne Ehrlich, *The Population Bomb: Population Control or the Race to Oblivion* (Ballantine Books, 1968).

25. See, e.g., James Buchanan, "Politics without Romance," reprinted in *Collected Works of James M. Buchanan*, Vol. 1 (Liberty Fund, 1979). See also Dennis Mueller, ed., *Public Choice III* (Cambridge University Press, 2003). A further and central question in political philosophy is what are the conditions under which government is *justified* in imposing coercive policies, even when they are known to make things better from a societal point of view? For further discussion of this question, see the *Stanford Encyclopedia of Philosophy* articles on "Political Legitimacy," "Liberalism," "Public Reason," "Legal Obligation and Authority," and related topics linked within those articles, available online at: http://plato.stanford.edu/index.html.

26. See Elinor Ostrom et al., "Revisiting the Commons," *Science* 284 (1999): 278–282, and Elinor Ostrom, *Governing the Commons* (Cambridge University Press, 1990).

27. Thomas Malthus, "Essay on the Principle of Population" (1798), online at: http://www.esp.org/books/malthus/population/malthus.pdf. Malthus's actual argument is more sophisticated than this argument, as it may arguably acknowledge the relevance of crop yield improvements. Basically, Malthus's argument is that unchecked human population growth is geometric (i.e., is compounded at a positive rate each time period), whereas the growth in food supply is arithmetic (i.e., increases by a

fixed quantity each time period) even taking into account yield increases and increases in land under cultivation. These premises imply that if unchecked, population will inevitably outgrow the capacity of food supply to feed everyone. This argument by Malthus (who was an early economist) inspired the title "the dismal science" for economics. On any interpretation, the ultimate problem with Malthus's argument has been that food supply per capita has continued to grow despite population doubling three times since Malthus's writing, primarily as a result of yield increases that have outpaced population growth, contrary to Malthus's premises.

28. Robert Paarlberg, *Food Politics: What Everyone Needs to Know*, 2nd ed., ch. 2 (Oxford University Press, 2013); U.S. Census Bureau world population data, online at: https://www.census.gov/population/international/data/worldpop/table_history.php.

29. Patricio Grassini, Kent Eskridge, and Kenneth Cassman, "Distinguishing between Yield Advances and Yield Plateaus in Historical Crop Production Trends," *Nature Communications* 4 (2013), DOI: 10.1038/ncomms3918.

30. For climate change and yield decreases, see J. Porter et al., "Food Security and Food Production Systems," in *Climate Change 2014: Impacts, Adaptation, and Vulnerability*, ed. Intergovernmental Panel on Climate Change, WG2 (Cambridge University Press, 2014), Chapter 7; D. Lobell et al., "Climate Trends and Global Crop Production Since 1980," *Science* 333 (2011): 616–620.

31. United Nations (2015), *World Population Prospects: The 2015 Revision*, Key Findings and Advance Tables, available online (with data also available) at http://esa.un.org/unpd/wpp.

32. See Brad DeLong, "Estimates of World GDP, One Million B.C.–Present," online at: http://delong.typepad.com/print/20061012_LRWGDP.pdf. DeLong notes that an alternative estimate that does not take into account the superiority of the goods that are available today compared to 1798 would imply that people today are about eight times as rich as in 1798. For discussion of conceptual and empirical issues about measuring wealth that underlie this disparity, see William Nordhaus, "Do Real-Output and Real-Wage Measures Capture Reality? The History of Lighting Suggests Not," in *The Economics of New Goods*, ed. Timothy F. Bresnahan and Robert J. Gordon (U of Chicago Press, 1997).

33. For a more detailed explanation, see Elizabeth Willott, "Recent Population Trends," in *Environmental Ethics*, 2nd ed., ed. David Schmidtz and Elizabeth Willott (Oxford University Press, 2012).

34. See Amartya Sen, *Poverty and Famines* (Oxford University Press, 1981).

35. For further discussion of contemporary research on food security, see Rosamond Naylor, ed., *The Evolving Sphere of Food Security* (Oxford University Press, 2014), and especially Naylor's introduction to that volume.

36. One might interpret the arguments in Judith Jarvis Thomson, "A Defense of Abortion," *Philosophy & Public Affairs* 1 (Fall 1971), as having the implication that there are no fundamental positive rights of the sort described here.

37. Onora O'Neill, "Rights, Obligations, and World Hunger," reprinted in *Global Ethics*, ed. Thomas Pogge and Keith Horton (Paragon, 1987), 153.

38. United Nations, CESCR General Comment No. 12: The Right to Adequate Food (Art. 11.15), footnote omitted (United Nations, 1999). See Thomas Pogge, fn 11 of "Shue on Rights and Duties", in Beitz and Goodin 2011, for further discussion of the genesis of this interpretation of rights by the UN in the work of Henry Shue.

39. For this kind of argument, see Judith Jarvis Thomson, "A Defense of Abortion," *Philosophy & Public Affairs* 1 (Fall 1971).

40. Note the connection to the "inefficacy objection," discussed at length in Chapter 4, "Consumer Ethics."

41. Thomas Pogge, *World Poverty and Human Rights*, 2nd ed. (Polity, 2008), 264. Compare Jeffrey Sachs, *The End of Poverty* (Penguin, 2005), 290, which is the basis for Pogge's claim.

PETER SINGER

Famine, Affluence, and Morality

Singer argues that you are ethically required either to give away most of your wealth to help those who are suffering in lesser-developed countries, or else to do something of comparable ethical significance instead. One way of understanding his main argument is that given the circumstances you always find yourself in, unless you do something of such significance, you are morally no different from a person who refuses to save a drowning child when it is easy, riskless, but merely financially costly to do so. If he is right, then your actions are almost always immoral, and complying with morality would require you to change the way you live your life in far-reaching ways. (Singer is an influential philosopher at Princeton University.)

As I write this, in November 1971, people are dying in East Bengal from lack of food, shelter, and medical care. The suffering and death that are occurring there now are not inevitable, not unavoidable in any fatalistic sense of the term. Constant poverty, a cyclone, and a civil war have turned at least nine million people into destitute refugees; nevertheless, it is not beyond the capacity of the richer nations to give enough assistance to reduce any further suffering to very small proportions. The decisions and actions of human beings can prevent this kind of suffering. Unfortunately, human beings have not made the necessary decisions. At the individual level, people have, with very few exceptions, not responded to the situation in any significant way. Generally speaking, people have not given large sums to relief funds; they have not written to their parliamentary representatives demanding increased government assistance; they have not demonstrated in the streets, held symbolic fasts, or done anything else directed toward providing the refugees with the means to satisfy their essential needs. At the government level, no government has given the sort of massive aid that would enable the refugees to survive for more than a few days. Britain, for instance, has given rather more than most countries. It has, to date, given £14,750,000. For comparative purposes, Britain's share of the nonrecoverable development costs of the Anglo-French Concorde project is already in excess of £275,000,000, and on present estimates will reach £440,000,000. The implication is that the British government values a supersonic transport more than thirty times as highly as it values the lives of the nine million refugees. Australia is another country which, on a per capita basis, is well up in the "aid to Bengal" table. Australia's aid, however, amounts to less than one-twelfth of the cost of Sydney's new opera house. The total amount given, from all sources, now stands at about £65,000,000. The estimated cost of keeping the refugees alive for one year is £464,000,000. Most of the refugees have now been in the camps for more than six months. The World Bank has said that India needs a minimum of £300,000,000 in assistance from other countries before the end of the year. It seems obvious that assistance on this scale will not be forthcoming. India will be forced to choose between letting the refugees starve or diverting funds from her own development program, which will mean that more of her own people will starve in the future.[1]

These are the essential facts about the present situation in Bengal. So far as it concerns us here, there is nothing unique about this situation except its magnitude. The Bengal emergency is just the latest and most acute of a series of major emergencies in various parts of the world, arising both from natural and from man-made causes. There are also many parts of the world in which people die from malnutrition and lack of food independent of any special emergency. I take Bengal as my example only because it is the present concern, and because the size of the problem has ensured that it has been given adequate publicity. Neither individuals nor governments can claim to be unaware of what is happening there.

What are the moral implications of a situation like this? In what follows, I shall argue that the way people in relatively affluent countries react to a situation like that in Bengal cannot be justified; indeed, the whole way we look at moral issues—our moral conceptual scheme—needs to be altered, and with it, the way of life that has come to be taken for granted in our society.

In arguing for this conclusion I will not, of course, claim to be morally neutral. I shall, however, try to argue for the moral position that I take, so that anyone who accepts certain assumptions, to be made explicit, will, I hope, accept my conclusion.

I begin with the assumption that suffering and death from lack of food, shelter, and medical care are bad. I think most people will agree about this, although one may reach the same view by different routes. I shall not argue for this view. People can hold all sorts of eccentric positions, and perhaps from some of them it would not follow that death by starvation is in itself bad. It is difficult, perhaps impossible, to refute such positions, and so for brevity I will henceforth take this assumption as accepted. Those who disagree need read no further.

My next point is this: if it is in our power to prevent something bad from happening, without thereby sacrificing anything of comparable moral importance, we ought, morally, to do it. By "without sacrificing anything of comparable moral importance" I mean without causing anything else comparably bad to happen, or doing something that is wrong in itself, or failing to promote some moral good, comparable in significance to the bad thing that we can prevent. This principle seems almost as uncontroversial as the last one. It requires us only to prevent what is bad, and not to promote what is good, and it requires this of us only when we can do it without sacrificing anything that is, from the moral point of view, comparably important. I could even, as far as the application of my argument to the Bengal emergency is concerned, qualify the point so as to make it: if it is in our power to prevent something very bad from happening, without thereby sacrificing anything morally significant, we ought, morally, to do it. An application of this principle would be as follows: if I am walking past a shallow pond and see a child drowning in it, I ought to wade in and pull the child out. This will mean getting my clothes muddy, but this is insignificant, while the death of the child would presumably be a very bad thing.

The uncontroversial appearance of the principle just stated is deceptive. If it were acted upon, even in its qualified form, our lives, our society, and our world would be fundamentally changed. For the principle takes, firstly, no account of proximity or distance. It makes no moral difference whether the person I can help is a neighbor's child ten yards from me or a Bengali whose name I shall never know, ten thousand miles away. Secondly, the principle makes no distinction between cases in which I am the only person who could possibly do anything and cases in which I am just one among millions in the same position.

I do not think I need to say much in defense of the refusal to take proximity and distance into account. The fact that a person is physically near to us, so that we have personal contact with him, may make it more likely that we *shall* assist him, but this does not show that we *ought* to help him rather than another who happens to be further away. If we accept any principle of impartiality, universalizability, equality, or whatever, we cannot discriminate against someone merely because he is far away from us (or we are far away from him). Admittedly, it is possible that we are in a better position to judge what needs to be done to help a person near to us than one far away, and perhaps also to provide the assistance we judge to be necessary. If this were the case, it would be a reason for helping those near to us first. This may once have been a justification for being more concerned with the poor in one's own town than with famine victims in India. Unfortunately for those who like to keep their moral responsibilities limited, instant communication and swift transportation have changed the situation. From the moral point of view, the development of the world into a "global village" has made an important, though still unrecognized, difference to our moral situation. Expert observers and supervisors, sent out by famine relief organizations or permanently stationed in famine-prone areas, can direct our aid to a refugee in Bengal almost as effectively as we could get it to someone in our own block. There would seem, therefore, to be no possible justification for discriminating on geographical grounds.

There may be a greater need to defend the second implication of my principle—that the fact that there are millions of other people in the same position, in respect to the Bengali refugees, as I am, does not make the situation significantly different from a situation in which I am the only person who can prevent something very bad from occurring. Again, of course, I admit that there is a psychological difference between the cases; one feels less guilty about doing nothing if one can point to others, similarly placed, who have also done nothing. Yet this can make no real difference to our moral obligations.[2] Should I consider that I am less obliged to pull the drowning child out of the pond if on looking around I see other people, no further away than I am, who have also noticed the child but are doing nothing? One has only to ask this question to see the absurdity of the view that numbers lessen obligation. It is a view that is an ideal excuse for inactivity; unfortunately most of the major evils—poverty, overpopulation, pollution—are problems in which everyone is almost equally involved.

The view that numbers do make a difference can be made plausible if stated in this way: if everyone in circumstances like mine gave £5 to the Bengal Relief Fund, there would be enough to provide food, shelter, and medical care for the refugees; there is no reason why I should give more than anyone else in the same circumstances as I am; therefore I have no obligation to give more than £5. Each premise in this argument is true, and the argument looks sound. It may convince us, unless we notice that it is based on a hypothetical premise, although the conclusion is not stated hypothetically. The argument would be sound if the conclusion were: if everyone in circumstances like mine were to give £5, I would have no obligation to give more than £5. If the conclusion were so stated, however, it would be obvious that the argument has no bearing on a situation in which it is not the case that everyone else gives £5. This, of course, is the actual situation. It is more or less certain that not everyone in circumstances like mine will give £5. So there will not be enough to provide the needed food, shelter, and medical care. Therefore by giving more than £5 I will prevent more suffering than I would if I gave just £5.

It might be thought that this argument has an absurd consequence. Since the situation appears to be that very few people are likely to give substantial amounts, it follows that I and everyone else in similar circumstances ought to give as much as possible, that is, at least up to the point at which by giving more one would begin to cause serious suffering for oneself and one's dependents—perhaps even beyond this point to the point of marginal utility, at which by giving more one would cause oneself and one's dependents as much suffering as one would prevent in Bengal. If everyone does this, however, there will be more than can be used for the benefit of the refugees, and some of the sacrifice will have been unnecessary. Thus, if everyone does what he ought to do, the result will not be as good as it would be if everyone did a little less than he ought to do, or if only some do all that they ought to do.

The paradox here arises only if we assume that the actions in question—sending money to the relief funds—are performed more or less simultaneously, and are also unexpected. For if it is to be expected that everyone is going to contribute something, then clearly each is not obliged to give as much as he would have been obliged to had others not been giving too. And if everyone is not acting more or less simultaneously, then those giving later will know how much more is needed, and will have no obligation to give more than is necessary to reach this amount. To say this is not to deny the principle that people in the same circumstances have the same obligations, but to point out that the fact that others have given, or may be expected to give, is a relevant circumstance: those giving after it has become known that many others are giving and those giving before are not in the same circumstances. So the seemingly absurd consequence of the principle I have put forward can occur only if people are in error about the actual circumstances—that is, if they think they are giving when others are not, but in fact they are giving when others are. The result of everyone doing what he really ought to do cannot be worse than the result of everyone doing less than he ought to do, although the result of everyone doing what he reasonably believes he ought to do could be.

If my argument so far has been sound, neither our distance from a preventable evil nor the number of other people who, in respect to that evil, are in the same situation as we are, lessens our obligation to mitigate or prevent that evil. I shall therefore take as established the principle I asserted earlier. As I have already said, I need to assert it only in its qualified form: if it is in our power to prevent something very bad from happening, without thereby sacrificing anything else morally significant, we ought, morally, to do it.

The outcome of this argument is that our traditional moral categories are upset. The traditional distinction between duty and charity cannot be drawn, or at least, not in the place we normally draw it. Giving money to the Bengal Relief Fund is regarded as an act of charity in our society. The bodies which collect money are known as "charities." These organizations see themselves in this way—if you send them a check, you will be thanked for your "generosity." Because giving money is regarded as an act of charity, it is not thought that there is anything wrong with not giving. The charitable man may be praised, but the man who is not charitable is not condemned. People do not feel in any way ashamed or guilty about spending money on new clothes or a new car

instead of giving it to famine relief. (Indeed, the alternative does not occur to them.) This way of looking at the matter cannot be justified. When we buy new clothes not to keep ourselves warm but to look "well-dressed" we are not providing for any important need. We would not be sacrificing anything significant if we were to continue to wear our old clothes, and give the money to famine relief. By doing so, we would be preventing another person from starving. It follows from what I have said earlier that we ought to give money away, rather than spend it on clothes which we do not need to keep us warm. To do so is not charitable, or generous. Nor is it the kind of act which philosophers and theologians have called "supererogatory"—an act which it would be good to do, but not wrong not to do. On the contrary, we ought to give the money away, and it is wrong not to do so.

I am not maintaining that there are no acts which are charitable, or that there are no acts which it would be good to do but not wrong not to do. It may be possible to redraw the distinction between duty and charity in some other place. All I am arguing here is that the present way of drawing the distinction, which makes it an act of charity for a man living at the level of affluence which most people in the "developed nations" enjoy to give money to save someone else from starvation, cannot be supported. It is beyond the scope of my argument to consider whether the distinction should be redrawn or abolished altogether. There would be many other possible ways of drawing the distinction—for instance, one might decide that it is good to make other people as happy as possible, but not wrong not to do so.

Despite the limited nature of the revision in our moral conceptual scheme which I am proposing, the revision would, given the extent of both affluence and famine in the world today, have radical implications. These implications may lead to further objections, distinct from those I have already considered. I shall discuss two of these.

One objection to the position I have taken might be simply that it is too drastic a revision of our moral scheme. People do not ordinarily judge in the way I have suggested they should. Most people reserve their moral condemnation for those who violate some moral norm, such as the norm against taking another person's property. They do not condemn those who indulge in luxury instead of giving to famine relief. But given that I did not set out to present a morally neutral description of the way people make moral judgments, the way people do in fact judge has nothing to do with the validity of my conclusion. My conclusion follows from the principle which I advanced earlier, and unless that principle is rejected, or the arguments shown to be unsound, I think the conclusion must stand, however strange it appears.

It might, nevertheless, be interesting to consider why our society, and most other societies, do judge differently from the way I have suggested they should. In a well-known article, J. O. Urmson suggests that the imperatives of duty, which tell us what we must do, as distinct from what it would be good to do but not wrong not to do, function so as to prohibit behavior that is intolerable if men are to live together in society.[3] This may explain the origin and continued existence of the present division between acts of duty and acts of charity. Moral attitudes are shaped by the needs of society, and no doubt society needs people who will observe the rules that make social existence tolerable. From the point of view of a particular society, it is essential to prevent violations of norms against killing, stealing, and so on. It is quite inessential, however, to help people outside one's own society.

If this is an explanation of our common distinction between duty and supererogation, however, it is not a justification of it. The moral point of view requires us to look beyond the interests of our own society. Previously, as I have already mentioned, this may hardly have been feasible, but it is quite feasible now. From the moral point of view, the prevention of the starvation of millions of people outside our society must be considered at least as pressing as the upholding of property norms within our society.

It has been argued by some writers, among them Sidgwick and Urmson, that we need to have a basic moral code which is not too far beyond the capacities of the ordinary man, for otherwise there will be a general breakdown of compliance with the moral code. Crudely stated, this argument suggests that if we tell people that they ought to refrain from murder and give everything they do not really need to famine relief, they will do neither, whereas if we tell them that they ought to refrain from murder and that it is good to give to famine relief but not wrong not to do so, they will at least refrain from murder. The issue here is: Where should we drawn the line between conduct that is required and conduct that is good although not required, so as to get the best possible result? This would seem to be an empirical question, although a very difficult one. One objection to the Sidgwick-Urmson line of argument is that it takes insufficient account of the effect that moral standards can have on the decisions we make. Given a society in which a wealthy man who gives five percent of his income to famine relief is regarded as most generous, it is not surprising that a proposal that we all ought to give away half our incomes will be thought to be absurdly unrealistic. In a society which held that no man should have more than enough while others have less than they need, such a proposal might seem narrow-minded. What it is possible for a man to do and what he is likely to do are both, I think, very greatly influenced by what people around him are doing and expecting him to do. In any case, the possibility that by spreading the idea that we ought to be doing very much more than we are to relieve famine we shall bring about a general breakdown of moral behavior seems remote. If the stakes are an end to widespread starvation, it is worth the risk. Finally, it should be emphasized that these considerations are relevant only to the issue of what we should require from others, and not to what we ourselves ought to do.

The second objection to my attack on the present distinction between duty and charity is one which has from time to time been made against utilitarianism. It follows from some forms of utilitarian theory that we all ought, morally, to be working full time to increase the balance of happiness over misery. The position I have taken here would not lead to this conclusion in all circumstances, for if there were no bad occurrences that we could prevent without sacrificing something of comparable moral importance, my argument would have no application. Given the present conditions in many parts of the world, however, it does follow from my argument that we ought, morally, to be working full time to relieve great suffering of the sort that occurs as a result of famine or other disasters. Of course, mitigating circumstances can be adduced—for instance, that if we wear ourselves out through overwork, we shall be less effective than we would otherwise have been. Nevertheless, when all considerations of this sort have been taken into account, the conclusion remains: we ought to be preventing as much suffering as we can without sacrificing something else of comparable moral importance. This conclusion is one which we may be reluctant to face. I cannot see, though, why it should be regarded as a criticism of the position for which I have argued, rather than a criticism of our ordinary standards of behavior. Since most people are self-interested to some degree, very few of us are likely to do everything that we ought to do. It would, however, hardly be honest to take this as evidence that it is not the case that we ought to do it.

It may still be thought that my conclusions are so wildly out of line with what everyone else thinks and has always thought that there must be something wrong with the argument somewhere. In order to show that my conclusions, while certainly contrary to contemporary Western moral standards, would not have seemed so extraordinary at other times and in other places, I would like to quote a passage from a writer not normally thought of as a way-out radical, Thomas Aquinas.

> Now, according to the natural order instituted by divine providence, material goods are provided for the satisfaction of human needs. Therefore the division and appropriation of property, which proceeds from human law, must not hinder the satisfaction of man's necessity from such goods. Equally, whatever a man has in superabundance is owed, of natural right, to the poor for their sustenance. So Ambrosius says, and it is also to be found in the *Decretum Gratiani*: "The bread which you withhold belongs to the hungry; the clothing you shut away, to the naked; and the money you bury in the earth is the redemption and freedom of the penniless."[4]

I now want to consider a number of points, more practical than philosophical, which are relevant to the application of the moral conclusion we have reached. These points challenge not the idea that we

ought to be doing all we can to prevent starvation, but the idea that giving away a great deal of money is the best means to this end.

It is sometimes said that overseas aid should be a government responsibility, and that therefore one ought not to give to privately run charities. Giving privately, it is said, allows the government and the noncontributing members of society to escape their responsibilities.

This argument seems to assume that the more people there are who give to privately organized famine relief funds, the less likely it is that the government will take over full responsibility for such aid. This assumption is unsupported, and does not strike me as at all plausible. The opposite view—that if no one gives voluntarily, a government will assume that its citizens are uninterested in famine relief and would not wish to be forced into giving aid—seems more plausible. In any case, unless there were a definite probability that by refusing to give one would be helping to bring about massive government assistance, people who do refuse to make voluntary contributions are refusing to prevent a certain amount of suffering without being able to point to any tangible beneficial consequence of their refusal. So the onus of showing how their refusal will bring about government action is on those who refuse to give.

I do not, of course, want to dispute the contention that governments of affluent nations should be giving many times the amount of genuine, no-strings-attached aid that they are giving now. I agree, too, that giving privately is not enough, and that we ought to be campaigning actively for entirely new standards for both public and private contributions to famine relief. Indeed, I would sympathize with someone who thought that campaigning was more important than giving oneself, although I doubt whether preaching what one does not practice would be very effective. Unfortunately, for many people the idea that "it's the government's responsibility" is a reason for not giving which does not appear to entail any political action either.

Another, more serious reason for not giving to famine relief funds is that until there is effective population control, relieving famine merely postpones starvation. If we save the Bengal refugees now, others, perhaps the children of these refugees, will face starvation in a few years' time. In support of this, one may cite the now well-known facts about the population explosion and the relatively limited scope for expanded production.

This point, like the previous one, is an argument against relieving suffering that is happening now, because of a belief about what might happen in the future; it is unlike the previous point in that very good evidence can be adduced in support of this belief about the future. I will not go into the evidence here. I accept that the earth cannot support indefinitely a population rising at the present rate. This certainly poses a problem for anyone who thinks it important to prevent famine. Again, however, one could accept the argument without drawing the conclusion that it absolves one from any obligation to do anything to prevent famine. The conclusion that should be drawn is that the best means of preventing famine, in the long run, is population control. It would then follow from the position reached earlier that one ought to be doing all one can to promote population control (unless one held that all forms of population control were wrong in themselves, or would have significantly bad consequences). Since there are organizations working specifically for population control, one would then support them rather than more orthodox methods of preventing famine.

A third point raised by the conclusion reached earlier relates to the question of just how much we all ought to be giving away. One possibility, which has already been mentioned, is that we ought to give until we reach the level of marginal utility—that is, the level at which, by giving more, I would cause as much suffering to myself or my dependents as I would relieve by my gift. This would mean, of course, that one would reduce oneself to very near the material circumstances of a Bengali refugee. It will be recalled that earlier I put forward both a strong and a moderate version of the principle of preventing bad occurrences. The strong version, which required us to prevent bad things from happening unless in doing so we would be sacrificing something of comparable moral significance, does seem to require reducing ourselves to the level of marginal utility. I should also say that the strong version seems

to me to be the correct one. I proposed the more moderate version—that we should prevent bad occurrences unless, to do so, we had to sacrifice something morally significant—only in order to show that even on this surely undeniable principle a great change in our way of life is required. On the more moderate principle, it may not follow that we ought to reduce ourselves to the level of marginal utility, for one might hold that to reduce oneself and one's family to this level is to cause something significantly bad to happen. Whether this is so I shall not discuss, since, as I have said, I can see no good reason for holding the moderate version of the principle rather than the strong version. Even if we accepted the principle only in its moderate form, however, it should be clear that we would have to give away enough to ensure that the consumer society, dependent as it is on people spending on trivia rather than giving to famine relief, would slow down and perhaps disappear entirely. There are several reasons why this would be desirable in itself. The value and necessity of economic growth are now being questioned not only by conservationists, but by economists as well.[5] There is no doubt, too, that the consumer society has had a distorting effect on the goals and purposes of its members. Yet looking at the matter purely from the point of view of overseas aid, there must be a limit to the extent to which we should deliberately slow down our economy; for it might be the case that if we gave away, say, forty percent of our Gross National Product, we would slow down the economy so much that in absolute terms we would be giving less than if we gave twenty-five percent of the much larger GNP that we would have if we limited our contribution to this smaller percentage.

I mention this only as an indication of the sort of factor that one would have to take into account in working out an ideal. Since Western societies generally consider one percent of the GNP an acceptable level for overseas aid, the matter is entirely academic. Nor does it affect the question of how much an individual should give in a society in which very few are giving substantial amounts.

It is sometimes said, though less often now than it used to be, that philosophers have no special role to play in public affairs, since most public issues depend primarily on an assessment of facts. On questions of fact, it is said, philosophers as such have no special expertise, and so it has been possible to engage in philosophy without committing oneself to any position on major public issues. No doubt there are some issues of social policy and foreign policy about which it can truly be said that a really expert assessment of the facts is required before taking sides or acting, but the issue of famine is surely not one of these. The facts about the existence of suffering are beyond dispute. Nor, I think, is it disputed that we can do something about it, either through orthodox methods of famine relief or through population control or both. This is therefore an issue on which philosophers are competent to take a position. The issue is one which faces everyone who has more money than he needs to support himself and his dependents, or who is in a position to take some sort of political action. These categories must include practically every teacher and student of philosophy in the universities of the Western world. If philosophy is to deal with matters that are relevant to both teachers and students, this is an issue that philosophers should discuss.

Discussion, though, is not enough. What is the point of relating philosophy to public (and personal) affairs if we do not take our conclusions seriously? In this instance, taking our conclusion seriously means acting upon it. The philosopher will not find it any easier than anyone else to alter his attitudes and way of life to the extent that, if I am right, is involved in doing everything that we ought to be doing. At the very least, though, one can make a start. The philosopher who does so will have to sacrifice some of the benefits of the consumer society, but he can find compensation in the satisfaction of a way of life in which theory and practice, if not yet in harmony, are at least coming together.

NOTES

1. There was also a third possibility: that India would go to war to enable the refugees to return to their lands. Since I wrote this paper, India has taken this way out. The situation is no longer that described above, but this does not affect my argument, as the next paragraph indicates.

2. In view of the special sense philosophers often give to the term, I should say that I use "obligation" simply as the abstract noun derived from "ought," so that "I have an obligation to" means no more, and no less, than "I ought to." This usage is in accordance with the definition of "ought" given by the *Shorter Oxford English Dictionary*: "the general verb to express duty or obligation." I do not think any issue of substance hangs on the way the term is used; sentences in which I use "obligation" could all be rewritten, although somewhat clumsily, as sentences in which a clause containing "ought" replaces the term "obligation."

3. J. O. Urmson, "Saints and Heroes," in *Essays in Moral Philosophy,* ed. Abraham I. Melden (Seattle and London, 1958), p. 214. For a related but significantly different view see also Henry Sidgwick, *The Methods of Ethics,* 7th ed. (London, 1907), pp. 220–221, 492–493.

4. *Summa Theologica,* II-II, Question 66, Article 7, in *Aquinas, Selected Political Writings,* ed. A. P. d'Entreves, trans. J. G. Dawson (Oxford, 1948), p. 171.

5. See, for instance, John Kenneth Galbraith, *The New Industrial State* (Boston, 1967); and E. J. Mishan, *The Costs of Economic Growth* (London, 1967).

QUESTIONS

1. What is Singer's reply to the objection that there is a morally relevant difference between POND and CHARITY because in the latter but not the former there are millions of other people who are at least equally well placed to help? Whatever you think of Singer's reply, can you think of additional good examples of situations in which many other people are at least as well placed to act as you, but yet you are morally required to assist strangers at some non-trivial cost to yourself?

2. In the paragraph that begins "I begin with the assumption . . . ," Singer presents an argument for his main conclusion that is slightly different from his argument as represented in the introduction to this chapter. A notable difference in this argument is that it explicitly invokes Singer's Principle of Preventing Bad Occurrences ("If it is in our power to prevent something bad from happening. . . ."). Put the version of Singer's argument from this part of his paper into standard form using the

stronger version of the Principle of Preventing Bad Occurrences. Then compare the argument when the weaker version of that principle is substituted into the argument. Explain clearly in your own words why the former argument has more demanding implications, and why the former but not the latter appears to imply utilitarianism.

3. How would Singer respond to the objection that helping the poor should be the responsibility of governments and not of individuals? Can you think of reasons for and against aiming at political change rather than direct donations to help with the problem of global hunger? What about other global problems? What would Deaton say about these questions?

4. Examine the charity rankings at www.GiveWell.org. What might GiveWell say about Singer's Empirical Premise?

5. If Singer's Empirical Premise were false, and instead the best way of helping the world's poor was simply to buy products made by them and to vote for good foreign policy, what would utilitarianism then imply we should do? Explain why utilitarianism implies that what it is right to do is highly sensitive to complex empirical issues that may often be difficult to know about. Is this a problem for utilitarianism? What arguments might be given that it is a problem, and what arguments might be given that it is not a problem for that general ethical theory?

6. In order to produce enough food for the global poor, might we have an obligation to degrade our own environment—to make the air that we breathe and the water that we drink unhealthy? Imagine for the sake of argument that making intensive use of our farmland in a way that had these side effects was the only way of feeding the world. What would Singer say about such a scenario?

Paul Ehrlich

Overpopulation and the Collapse of Civilization

Ehrlich outlines a number of global problems caused by humans and their interaction with the environment, and he argues that overconsumption and overpopulation are the primary causes of these problems. (Ehrlich is an influential ecologist at Stanford University.)

A major shared goal . . . is reducing the odds that the "perfect storm" of environmental problems that threaten humanity will lead to a collapse of civilization. Those threats include climate disruption, loss of biodiversity (and thus ecosystem services), land-use change and resulting degradation, global toxification, ocean acidification, decay of the epidemiological environment, increasing depletion of important

Paul Ehrlich, "Overpopulation and the Collapse of Civilization," *MAHB Blog,* November 2013, http://mahb.stanford.edu/blog/overpopulation-and-the-collapse-of-civilization/

resources, and resource wars (which could go nuclear). This is not just a list of problems, it is an interconnected complex resulting from interactions within and between what can be thought of as two gigantic complex adaptive systems: the biosphere system and the human socio-economic system. The manifestations of this interaction are often referred to as "the human predicament." That predicament is getting continually and rapidly worse, driven by overpopulation, overconsumption among the rich, and the use of environmentally malign technologies and socio-economic-political arrangements to service the consumption.

All of the interconnected problems are caused in part by overpopulation, in part by overconsumption by the already rich. One would think that most educated people now understand that the larger the size of a human population, ceteris paribus, the more destructive its impact on the environment. The degree of overpopulation is best indicated (conservatively) by ecological footprint analysis, which shows that to support today's population sustainably at current patterns of consumption would require roughly another half a planet, and to do so at the U.S. level would take four to five more Earths.

The seriousness of the situation can be seen in the prospects of Homo sapiens' most important activity: producing and procuring food. Today, at least two billion people are hungry or badly in need of better diets, and most analysts think doubling food production would be required to feed a 35% bigger and still growing human population adequately by 2050. For any chance of success, humanity will need to stop expanding land area for agriculture (to preserve ecosystem services); raise yields where possible; increase efficiency in use of fertilizers, water, and energy; become more vegetarian; reduce food wastage; stop wrecking the oceans; significantly increase investment in sustainable agricultural research; and move feeding everyone to the very top of the policy agenda. All of these tasks will require changes in human behavior long recommended but thus far elusive. Perhaps more critical, there may be insurmountable biophysical barriers to increasing yields—indeed, to avoiding reductions in yields—in the face of climate disruption.

Most people fail to realize the urgency of the food situation because they don't understand the agricultural system and its complex, non-linear connections to the drivers of environmental deterioration. The system itself, for example, is a major emitter of greenhouse gases and thus is an important driver of the climate disruption that seriously threatens food production. More than a millennium of change in temperature and precipitation patterns is now entrained, with the prospect of more crop-threatening severe storms, droughts, heat waves, and floods—all of which are already evident. Thus maintaining—let alone expanding—food production will be ever more difficult in decades ahead.

Furthermore, agriculture is a leading cause of losses of biodiversity and the critical ecosystem services supplied to agriculture itself and other human enterprises, as well as a major source of global toxification, both of which pose additional risks to food production. The threat to food production of climate disruption alone means that humanity's entire system for mobilizing energy needs to be rapidly transformed in an effort to hold atmospheric warming well below a lethal 5°C rise in global average temperature. It also means we must alter much of our water-handling infrastructure to provide the necessary flexibility to bring water to crops in an environment of constantly changing precipitation patterns.

Food is just the most obvious area where overpopulation tends to darken the human future—virtually every other human problem from air pollution and brute overcrowding to resource shortages and declining democracy is exacerbated by further population growth. And, of course, one of our most serious problems is the failure of leadership on the population issue, in both the United States and Australia. The situation is worst in the U.S. where the government never mentions population because of fear of the Catholic hierarchy specifically and the religious right in general, and the media keep publishing ignorant pro-natalist articles, and in Australia even advertise on prime-time TV to have more kids.

A prime example was a ludicrous 2010 *New York Times* screed by David Brooks, calling on Americans to cheer up because "Over the next 40 years, the U.S.

population will surge by an additional 100 million people, to 400 million." Equal total ignorance of the population-resource-environment situation was shown in 2012 by an article also in the *New York Times* by one Ross Douthat "More Babies, Please" and one by a Rick Newman in the *USNews* "Why a falling birth rate is a big problem," both additional signs of the utter failure of the US educational system.

A popular movement is needed to correct that failure and direct cultural evolution toward providing the "foresight intelligence" and the agricultural, environmental, and demographic planning that markets cannot supply. Then analysts (and society) might stop treating population growth as a "given" and consider the nutritional and health benefits of humanely ending growth well below 9 billion and starting a slow decline. In my view, the best way to accelerate the move toward such population shrinkage is to give full rights, education, and job opportunities to

women everywhere, and provide all sexually active human beings with modern contraception and backup abortion. The degree to which that would reduce fertility rates is controversial, but it would be a win-win for society. Yet the critical importance of increasing the inadequate current action on the demographic driver can be seen in the decades required to change the size of the population humanely and sensibly. In contrast we know from such things as the World War II mobilizations that consumption patterns can be altered dramatically in less than a year, given appropriate incentives.

The movement should also highlight the consequences of such crazy ideas as growing an economy at 3–5% per year over decades (or forever) as most innumerate economists and politicians believe possible. Most "educated" people do not realize that in the real world a short history of exponential growth does not imply a long future of such growth. . . .

QUESTIONS

1. What does Ehrlich cite as the main challenges in the domain of food? Why does he think these are the main challenges, and how are they related to population? Ehrlich claims that nearly every human problem is made worse by overpopulation. What arguments do you think he would give in support of this claim for each major human problem?

2. Ehrlich thinks it is "crazy" to think that economies can sustain high rates of economic growth, and he calls economists and politicians "innumerate" who believe that economies can sustain this growth. What does his argument seem to be for these claims, and how does it compare to the Malthusian argument discussed in the chapter introduction?

3. Ehrlich claims that the best way to accelerate the move toward population shrinkage is to give full rights, education, and job opportunities to women everywhere, and provide all sexually active human beings with modern contraception and backup abortion. Suppose that in addition to this, or as a consequence of this, another factor associated with zero population growth is, say, several times greater wealth than is currently enjoyed by those in high population growth areas. So, suppose that we achieved zero population growth, and that in so doing we made it the case that all of those people were three times as wealthy as their counterparts are now. How might Ehrlich argue that this would reduce consumption and reduce harmful effects on the environment? Can you think of an objection to such an argument? (Note that people tend to consume much more when they are much richer.)

4. Do an internet search to learn more about what "ecological footprint" analysis means, and therefore what Ehrlich means by claiming we would need more Earths to support our consumption. How might the following fantastic example be used to raise an objection to the basic idea that Ehrlich defends that overpopulation is best indicated by ecological footprint analysis: Imagine that by ignoring exploding population while at the same time cutting down most of the world's trees now, we could build a super-green-machine over the next 50 years that would remove the need for

us to ever have any negative impact on the environment or use natural resources ever again—and it would also allow us to prevent anyone from going hungry now or in the future at the same time. Can you think of a more realistic objection to Ehrlich's claim that overpopulation is best measured by ecological footprint analysis based on this example, together with the claim of some experts that "The coming 50 years are likely to be the final period of rapidly expanding, global human environmental impacts,"[1] partly because human population might by then naturally stabilize and start to decline if we continue to promote economic growth and proper nutrition?

NOTE

1. David Tilman et al., "Agricultural Sustainability and Intensive Production Practices," *Nature* 418 (August 8, 2002): 676.

AMARTYA SEN

Hunger and Entitlements[1]

Sen begins by arguing that in contemporary times hunger is especially ethically intolerable because, he claims, we now have the capacity to guarantee adequate food for all. At the same time, he argues that an analysis of hunger in terms of per capita food supply is inadequate, and that an alternative analysis in terms of "entitlements" (in his specific sense) is better able to explain historical cases of famine, and thus is crucial to understanding how we can best guarantee adequate food for all. (Sen is the 1998 Nobel Laureate in Economics.)

HUNGER IN THE MODERN WORLD

Hunger is not a recent phenomenon. Nor is famine. Life has been short and hard in much of the world, most of the time. Both chronic undernourishment and recurrent famines have been among the causal antecedents of the brutishness and brevity of human life in history.

Hunger in the modern world is more intolerable than past hunger not because it is typically more intense, but because it is now so unnecessary. The enormous expansion of productive power that has taken place over the last few centuries has made it possible, for the first time in history, to guarantee adequate food for all. It is in this context that the persistence of chronic hunger and the recurrence of virulent famines must be seen as being morally outrageous and politically unacceptable. If politics is "the art of the possible," then conquering world hunger has become a political issue in a way it could not have been in the past. . . .

ENTITLEMENT FAILURES

When millions of people suddenly die in a famine, it is hard to avoid the thought that there must have been a major decline in the output and availability of food in the economy. But while that is sometimes the case, there have frequently been famines in which food output and availability have remained high and undiminished. Indeed some famines have occurred in periods of peak food availability for the economy as a whole (e.g., the Bangladesh famine of 1974).

The real issue is not primarily the overall availability of food, but its acquirement by individuals and families. If a person lacks the means to acquire food, the presence of food in the market is not much consolation. To understand hunger, we have to look at people's entitlements, i.e., what commodity bundles (including food) they can make their own. The entitlement approach to hunger concentrates on the determination of command over commodities, including food. Famines are seen as the result of entitlement failures of large groups, often belonging to some specific occupations (e.g., landless rural labourers, pastoralists).[2]

The entitlement of a person stands for the set of different alternative commodity bundles that the person can acquire through the use of the various legal channels of acquirement open to someone in his position. In a private ownership market economy, the entitlement set of a person is determined by his original bundle of ownership (what is called his "endowment") and the various alternative bundles he can acquire starting from each initial endowment, through the use of trade and production (what is called his

"exchange entitlement mapping"). A person has to starve if his entitlement set does not include any commodity bundle with adequate amounts of food. A person is reduced to starvation if some change either in his endowment (e.g., alienation of land, or loss of labour power due to ill health), or in his exchange entitlement mapping (e.g., fall in wages, rise in food prices, loss of employment, drop in the price of the good he produces and sells), makes it no longer possible for him to acquire any commodity bundle with enough food.

The approach of analyzing famines in terms of declines of entitlements of particular occupation groups has been used in recent years to study many famines, e.g., the Bengal famine of 1943, the Sahel famines in the 1970s, the Bangladesh famine of 1974, the Ethiopian famines of 1973–85, the Malawi (in fact, Nyasaland) famine of 1949–50, and also various historical famines.[3]

For the bulk of humanity, about the only substantial asset that a person owns is his or her ability to work, i.e., labour power. If a person fails to secure employment, then that means of acquiring food (through getting a job, earning an income and buying food with that income) fails. If, in addition to that, the laws of the land do not provide any social security arrangements, e.g., unemployment insurance, the person will fail to secure the means of subsistence.

And that can be the end of the tale—at least for that erstwhile person.

This elementary analysis points immediately to two aspects of the action needed to combat hunger and famine. There is, on the one hand, the need for a better functioning economic system, to provide people with regular means of income and survival. There is, on the other hand, need for security in providing economic support to vulnerable individuals (or families) when they fail to get that support from the regular economic system itself. Importance has to be attached to functioning economic mechanisms that provide means and entitlements to the population. And at the same time, attention also has to be paid to public security measures that can be used to guarantee entitlements to those who happen to remain vulnerable to fluctuation and instability in earning an income and acquiring economic power (e.g., landless labourers falling victim to employment decline or a fall in real wages).

OUTPUT, AVAILABILITY, AND ENTITLEMENTS

Seeing hunger as entitlement failure points to possible remedies immediately, since we are induced to understand and address the forces that generate deprivation and help sustain it. Food problems have often been discussed in terms of the output and availability of food without going into the question of entitlement—this is a tradition that received much encouragement from Malthus's famous "Essay on Population" (1798).[4] It is particularly important to understand the relevance of seeing famines and intensification of hunger as entitlement failures which can occur even when food availability is not reduced, and even when the ratio of food to population—on which Malthus concentrated—may have gone up sharply. The relentless persistence of famines and the enormous reach of world hunger, despite a steady and substantial increase in food availability, makes it imperative for us to reorient our approach away from food availability and towards the ability to command food.

... [T]he actual command over food that different sections of the population can exercise depends on a set of legal and economic factors, including those governing ownership, transfer, production and exchange. It is, thus, quite possible for some groups, e.g., a particular occupation group such as landless rural labourers, to have a sharply reduced food entitlement, even when the overall availability of food in the economy is unaffected or enhanced. Most famines hit some particular occupation groups, and there is no paradox in the fact that a famine can occur, e.g., in Bengal in 1943, in Ethiopia in 1973, or in Bangladesh in 1974, without any significant decline in food output and availability, with members of particular occupation groups losing the

means of acquiring food and succumbing to starvation and death.[5] ...

ECONOMIC PRESSURES AND PUBLIC ACTION

While famines are related to disastrous declines of entitlements, endemic hunger and regular undernourishment are associated with inadequate entitlements on a sustained basis. Some economies of the world have not experienced famines in any real sense in recent years, but have nevertheless suffered from chronic hunger on a regular but non-acute basis. Examples can be found in South Asia. including India, Pakistan and Bangladesh, as well as in Latin America, in addition to parts of Africa. In a sense, combatting endemic hunger is a harder problem than conquering famines, since the extreme deprivation involved in famine situations can be speedily remedied, in a way that a sustained eradication of entitlement inadequacies for all sections of the population cannot be easily achieved.

The two components of the long-run elimination of famines ... viz, maintenance of economic stability and provision of social security, have corresponding counterparts in the battle against endemic hunger as well. The nature of the economy and its functioning are obviously important in making it possible to earn—without social security support—enough income and means of command over food and other necessities to avoid endemic deprivation. However, no matter how efficient the economic system might be, inadequacy of entitlements on a regular basis (with possibly a pattern of seasonality) is particularly hard to avoid in the poorer developing countries. This is where social security, in a different role, becomes relevant again. Supplementary public support as a means of providing regular nourishment (and command over other necessities), to counter endemic hunger and deprivation, is needed in most developing countries. This is no less crucial a challenge for social security planning than the task of entitlement guarantees to eliminate famines, discussed earlier. . . .

A CONCLUDING REMARK

The problem of world hunger is not a purely economic one, even though the economic issues are of major importance and call for adequately deep investigation. Even the notion of entitlement, which has obvious economic content, cannot escape having legal connotations, political implications and social relevance. This diversity need not however lead to a fragmented approach, since the connections can be explicitly explored and systematically integrated. . . . However, despite that diversity, the roles of the actions of the respective agents relate closely to each other, since they cannot be seen in isolation from other agents and their actions. It is precisely this feature of a unified focus over diverse fields of investigation that gives the research programme described here its particular character. The programme is undoubtedly ambitious. But the stakes are high. Many millions of lives are involved.

NOTES

1. For helpful comments I am most grateful to Sudhir Anand, Max Bond, Sukhamoy Chakravarty, Jean Drèze, Eric Hobsbawm, Lal Jayawardena, Martha Nussbaum, Siddiq Osmani, Robert Pringle and V. K. Ramachandran.

2. On this general approach, see Amartya Sen, *Poverty and Famines: An Essay on Entitlement and Deprivation* (Oxford: Clarendon Press, 1981).

3. Sen, ibid.

4. However, in a paper published two years later ("An Investigation of the Cause of the Present High Price of Provisions," 1800), Malthus makes implicit but extensive use of entitlement-centred reasoning to discuss the pattern of hunger in a class-divided society. Even though he evidently saw no ethical objection whatsoever to such inequalities (and viewed the prospect of everyone starving "together" as a "tragic" possibility), his analysis is deeply illuminating on the cause-effect relationships between inequalities of ownership and hunger. On Malthus' modelling of famines, see Sen, *Poverty and Famines* (1981), Appendix B. The relevance of ownership, employment, wages and prices to the acquirement of food and in the causation of hunger was also discussed with clarity by Adam Smith, David Ricardo and Karl Marx, pointing inter alia to the possibility of famines without any decline in food availability (on these see Amartya Sen, "Food, Economics and Entitlements," Elmhirst Lecture at the Triennial Meeting of the International Association of Agricultural Economists at Malaga. 1985; WIDER Working Paper No. l, 1986; published in *Lloyds Bank Review*, 160, 1986).

5. In the case of the Bangladesh famine of 1974, food output per head was in fact at a peak, on which—and on several other important aspects of that famine, and famines in general—see M. Alamgir, *Famine in South Asia—Political Economy of Mass Starvation in Bangladesh* (Boston: Oelgeschlager, 1980). See also Ravallion's penetrating analysis in *Markets and Famines* (1987).

QUESTIONS

1. Explain in your own words why a region's per capita food supply is an inadequate predictor of hunger according to Sen, and how his alternate analysis is supposed to be more adequate. Use a clear example to illustrate.
2. In light of his analysis of famines and hunger, how exactly does Sen see a form of "social security" as essential to solving the problem of hunger? What does he mean by "social security"—what specific initiatives does he seem to have in mind? How should these initiatives be guided by the concept of adequate entitlements (in Sen's sense) to food?
3. What do you make of the objection to the existence of positive rights in the sense of a right to food defined by the United Nations? Examine the UN Declaration of Human Rights, and discuss for each the extent to which each alleged right in the sense defined by the UN (as involving a duty to respect, protect, and fulfil) would likely be rejected by those who believe in only negative fundamental rights.

4. Might Sen's analysis help us understand why poor people, even in developed nations like our own, are disproportionately likely to have inadequate medical care, to drink polluted water, and to breathe polluted air? Do the same arguments tell in favor and against initiatives to ensure entitlements in these cases, as in the case of the global poor that Sen describes? How is the idea of special obligations based on reciprocity, as discussed in connection with Beitz's argument in the introduction to this chapter, relevant to answering this question?

5. In light of Deaton's arguments (which are developed in more detail in the last chapter of his book *The Great Escape*), what possible difficulties might we expect to encounter in implementing initiatives to guarantee adequate food for all? What difficulties might we expect in light of Banerjee and Duflo's arguments? How might these difficulties be relevant to deciding what we should do to help the global poor? Do they lead to any important objections to Sen's policy recommendations?

ANGUS DEATON

Response to Effective Altruism

Many arguments that we should give to charity depend essentially on the premise that, roughly, we have the ability to dramatically help the global poor by giving a relatively small fraction of our wealth to charity. Deaton argues against this empirical premise. He outlines a number of reasons why it is difficult to design successful initiatives to help the world's poor, and why foreign aid and many familiar forms of charity are not only *not* dramatic helps but are also ethically problematic. At the end of his article, Deaton offers alternative actions that he argues are better ways of doing good than familiar forms of charity—namely, particular forms of political advocacy and casting one's lot with the poor. (Deaton is the 2015 Nobel Laureate in Economics.)

Helping others is good, not least because of the happiness it brings to the giver. And it is hard not to admire . . . Peter Singer. But why do the world's poor have such a passive role in all of this happiness creation? Why are they not asked if they wish to participate, if they too feel the warm glow? Singer does nothing to persuade us that they have volunteered to be the objects of the "effective" altruism he endorses; indeed, Gallup and Afrobarometer polls show that Africans' own priorities lie

Angus Deaton, "Response to 'The Logic of Effective Altruism,'" *Boston Review,* July 1, 2015. https://bostonreview.net/forum/logic-effective-altruism/angus-deaton-response-effective-altruism elsewhere. Instead, the evidence for effectiveness, on which the recipients might have their own views, is outsourced to technical outfits, such as GiveWell, that evaluate projects and organizations. GiveWell is Consumer Reports for altruists, listing value for money and establishing the minimum cost of saving a child's life.

It is an illusion that lives can be bought like cars. For a start, the evidence is nearly always in dispute. The alleged effectiveness of the Deworm the World Initiative—which, at the time of this writing, ranked fourth in GiveWell's list of top charities—runs contrary to the latest extensive review of the evidence by the Cochrane Collaboration, an organization that compiles medical research data. Maybe Cochrane is wrong, but it is more likely that the effectiveness of deworming varies from place to place depending, among many other things, on climate and on local arrangements for disposing of human waste.

More broadly, the evidence for development effectiveness, for "what works," mostly comes from the recent wave of randomized experiments, usually done by rich people from the rich world on poor people in the poor world, from which the price lists for children's lives are constructed. How can those experiments be wrong? Because they consider only the immediate effects of the interventions, not the contexts in which they are set. Nor, most importantly, can they say anything about the wide-ranging unintended consequences.

However counterintuitive it may seem, children are not dying for the lack of a few thousand dollars to keep them alive. If it were so simple, the world would already be a much better place. Development is neither a financial nor a technical problem but a political problem, and the aid industry often makes the politics worse. The dedicated people who risked their lives to help in the recent Ebola epidemic discovered what had been long known: lack of money is not killing people. The true villains are the chronically disorganized and underfunded health care systems about which governments care little, along with well-founded distrust of those governments and foreigners, even when their advice is correct.

In today's Rwanda, President Paul Kagame has discovered how to use Singer's utilitarian calculus against his own people. By providing health care for Rwandan mothers and children, he has become one of the darlings of the industry and a favorite recipient of aid. Essentially, he is "farming" Rwandan children, allowing more of them to live in exchange for support for his undemocratic and oppressive rule. Large aid flows to Africa sometimes help the intended beneficiaries, but they also help create dictators and provide them with the means to insulate themselves from the needs and wishes of their people.

The industry does not ignore the evidence; indeed the World Bank, the U.S. Agency for International Development, and its European counterparts use the same evidence GiveWell does, and they help to create more. They are also infinitely better organized and funded than the NGOs, so if it were possible to use this sort of evidence to eliminate global poverty, they would be better placed to do so than a handful of wealthy individuals working through NGOs. Yet these official aid agencies cannot solve the political conundrum and must bear some of the burden of responsibility for the oppressive dictatorships that fester in Africa.

Like Singer, I am privileged to teach at Princeton. I too see students who want to relieve suffering in the world. Should they go to Dhaka or Dakar? Focus on bed nets or worms? I tell them to go to Washington or London and to work to stop the harm that rich countries do; to oppose the arms trade, the trade deals that benefit only the pharmaceutical companies, the protectionist tariffs that undermine the livelihoods of African farmers; and to support more funding to study tropical disease and health care. Or they could go to Africa, become citizens, and cast their lot with those they want to help. That is how they can save the lives of African kids.

QUESTIONS

1. Deaton claims that "Development is neither a financial nor a technical problem, but a political problem." Explain in your own words what he means by this. Taking your explanation as a premise,

put the argument Deaton would give against Singer's "Famine, Affluence, and Morality" into standard form.

2. How does Deaton use the track record and facts about the World Bank, USAID, and their European counterparts to argue against the reliability of the advice from www.GiveWell.org? Put Deaton's argument here into standard form.

3. If people in developing countries don't want our help, in what ways, if any, does this make it ethically problematic to create and participate in initiatives intended to help them? What if these initiatives help them on balance, but hurt some of them? What if they also put us in control of their economies and their future, rather than putting them in control? How might this be related to Deaton's suggestion that if we want to really help Africans, we should go to Africa, become citizens, and cast our lot with them? What argument do you think he would give for that suggestion? Explain.

4. Read more online about the Deworm the World Initiative and Cochrane's criticism of it. Write a paragraph explaining the most interesting ways in which this case study might be taken by Deaton to illustrate his main conclusions.

BILL GATES

The Great Escape Is an Excellent Book with One Big Flaw

Bill Gates responds to some of Deaton's arguments. (Along with his wife Melinda, Gates leads the Bill and Melinda Gates Foundation, one of the largest philanthropic organizations in the world focused on helping the poor.)

The other day I spoke at an employee event at the Gates Foundation. We do these "unplugged" sessions periodically. I open with a few remarks and then spend an hour or so taking questions from the team. I see our senior staff quite often, but these sessions are a great way to connect with the larger group.

I told the staff: If you want to learn about why human welfare overall has gone up so much over time, you should read *The Great Escape: Health,*

Wealth, and the Origins of Inequality, by Angus Deaton, a distinguished Princeton economist who has spent decades studying measures of global poverty. It's quite accessible, and the first six chapters teach you a lot about economics. But the seventh and final chapter takes a strange turn: Deaton launches a sudden attack on foreign aid. It's by far the weakest part of the book; if this is the only thing you read about aid, you will come away very confused about what aid does for people.

Deaton's parting shots came as a surprise to me, because it's clear from the rest of the book that we see the world in similar ways. His first paragraph is dead-on: "Life is better now than at almost any time in history. More people are richer and fewer people live in dire poverty. Lives are longer and parents no longer routinely watch a quarter of their children die." (I would have cut "almost" from the first sentence, but otherwise I could not agree more.) Picking up on the title of the old Steve McQueen movie, he calls this improvement in human welfare the Great Escape.

I have long believed that innovation is a key to improving human lives. Advances in biology lead to lifesaving vaccines and drugs. Discoveries in computer science lead to new software and hardware that connect people in powerful new ways. Deaton does a good job of documenting how innovations helped spark the Great Escape.

But the Great Escape, Deaton says, "is far from complete." Innovations reach only those who can afford to pay for them. And that has led to great inequality. The rest of the book examines where this inequality comes from, whether it matters, and what if anything can be done about it.

One of Deaton's most helpful passages explains how you measure human welfare in the first place. He argues that there's no single good measure, but health and GDP are the best two that we have. You probably have heard about gross domestic product, or GDP, but you might not know how it's calculated, how it's different from gross national product, or why on its own GDP is not a great measure of the quality of people's lives. Deaton provides a lucid and succinct explanation.

He is also humble about the limits of economic analysis. In this entertaining passage, he goes after economists who make unfounded assertions about economic growth:

> Economists, international organizations, and other commentators are fond of taking a few high-growth countries and looking for some common feature or policy, which is then held up as the "key to growth"— at least until it fails to open the door to growth somewhere else. The same goes for attempts to look at countries that have done badly (the "bottom billion") and divine the causes of their failure. These attempts are much like trying to figure out the common characteristics of people who bet on the zero just before it came up on a roulette wheel; they do little but disguise our fundamental ignorance.

Unfortunately, this humility goes out the window once Deaton starts criticizing foreign aid. After examining the history of GDP in countries that get aid, he concludes that aid doesn't cause growth. In fact he makes an even stronger claim—that aid keeps poor countries from growing—and says the most compassionate thing we can do is to stop giving it.

In other words, in one chapter, Deaton dismisses people who think they know why countries fail to grow. In the next, he asserts that countries fail to grow because of aid.

Deaton makes another common mistake among aid critics: He talks about foreign aid as if it's one homogeneous lump. He judges money for buying vaccines by the same standard as money for buying military hardware.

It seems obvious that programs should be measured against their original purpose. Did the program have a good goal, and did it achieve the goal? Instead, Deaton and other aid critics look at, say, aid that was designed to prop up some American industry, see that it didn't raise GDP in poor countries, and conclude that aid must be a failure.

That's a shame, because programs that are actually designed to improve human welfare—especially health and agriculture—are some of the best spending that a rich country can do on behalf of the poor. They help the poor benefit from the very innovations Deaton writes about so glowingly. And their success rate is at least as good as the track record of venture capital firms. No one looks around Silicon Valley and says, "Look at all the startups that go under!

Venture capital is such a waste. Let's shut it down." Why would you say that about aid?

Deaton spends a lot of time on the concern that foreign aid undermines the connection between governments and their people. The idea is that leaders of countries that get a lot of aid will worry more about what their donors think than what their citizens think.

This argument always strikes me as strange. For one thing, many countries—Botswana, Morocco, Brazil, Mexico, Chile, Costa Rica, Peru, Thailand, Mauritius, Singapore, and Malaysia, to name a few—have grown so much that they receive hardly any aid today. Deaton doesn't cite any evidence that aid undermined their institutions or democratic values. And his over-emphasis on institutions leads him to make sweeping statements like "drugs and vaccines save lives, but the pernicious effects are always there." I have to wonder what pernicious effects came from eradicating smallpox, and whether these effects could be worse than a disease that killed millions of people every year for centuries.

Deaton is right to point out some problems with aid. For example, too much goes to upper-middle-income countries rather than focusing on the poorest people. More aid can be directed to specific goals like vaccination. And aid shouldn't be used to replace domestic funding. But I wish he had spent more time than he does exploring better ways to give aid. Most importantly, we need to help develop a system that identifies the goals of every type of aid and makes it easier to measure which approaches work best in various situations.

If you read *The Great Escape*—and there's a lot to recommend in it—you should also read something else to balance out Deaton's negative views on aid. I've highlighted a few recommendations in the Other Reviews box at the bottom of this page. They'll give you a clearer sense of what's working, what isn't, and how we can make our efforts even more effective in the years ahead.[1]

NOTE

1. Editor's note: Gates highlights Abhijit Banerjee and Esther Duflo (2011), *Poor Economics: A Radical Rethinking of the Way to Fight Global Poverty* (PublicAffairs) and Charles Kenny (2010), *Getting Better: Why Global Development Is Succeeding* (Basic Books).

QUESTIONS

1. What is the "one big flaw" in Deaton's views, according to Gates?
2. Why does Gates think it is a mistake to think of aid as "one homogenous lump"? Explain in your own words. Can you give an example not discussed by Gates that he might use to illustrate his point (even if you disagree with his point)? What specific forms of investment does Gates say are some of the best spending that a rich country can do on behalf of the poor?
3. Suppose we grant the premise that aid always has negative unintended consequences. How does Gates use the example of smallpox to argue that Deaton's conclusions do not follow from this premise alone?
4. How does what Gates says about Silicon Valley support his claim that some aid programs are some of the best spending that a rich country can do on behalf of the poor? Suppose that the majority of the aid spending he has in mind was a failure—would this be an important objection to his argument? Why or why not? Explain and illustrate using examples.

ABHIJIT BANERJEE AND ESTHER DUFLO

More Than One Billion People Are Hungry in the World

But What If the Experts Are Wrong?

Banerjee and Duflo describe a number of approaches to helping the poor that are influential among economists, and identify complications for each based on empirical facts about the choices of the poor. One upshot is a better understanding of the right questions to ask to investigate with further empirical research, in order to identify reliable ways to combat hunger as the developing world gets slowly richer. (Banerjee and Duflo are professors of economics at MIT. In 2010, Duflo was awarded the John Bates Clark Medal, the prize for the top economist in America under age 40.)

For many in the West, poverty is almost synonymous with hunger. Indeed, the announcement by the United Nations Food and Agriculture Organization in 2009 that more than 1 billion people are suffering from hunger grabbed headlines in a way that any number of World Bank estimates of how many poor people live on less than a dollar a day never did.

But is it really true? Are there really more than a billion people going to bed hungry each night? Our research on this question has taken us to rural villages and teeming urban slums around the world, collecting data and speaking with poor people about what they eat and what else they buy, from Morocco to Kenya, Indonesia to India. We've also tapped into a wealth of insights from our academic colleagues. What we've found is that the story of hunger, and of poverty more broadly, is far more complex than any one statistic or grand theory; it is a world where those without enough to eat may save up to buy a TV instead, where more money doesn't necessarily translate into more food, and where making rice cheaper can sometimes even lead people to buy less rice.

But unfortunately, this is not always the world as the experts view it. All too many of them still promote sweeping, ideological solutions to problems that defy one-size-fits-all answers, arguing over foreign aid, for example, while the facts on the ground bear little resemblance to the fierce policy battles they wage.

Jeffrey Sachs, an advisor to the United Nations and director of Columbia University's Earth Institute, is one such expert. In books and countless speeches and television appearances, he has argued that poor countries are poor because they are hot, infertile, malaria-infested, and often landlocked; these factors, however, make it hard for them to be productive without an initial large investment to help

Abhijit Banerjee and Esther Duflo, "More Than One Billion People are Hungry in the World: But What if the Experts are Wrong?" *Foreign Policy,* April 25, 2011. http://foreignpolicy.com/2011/04/25/more-than-1-billion-people-are-hungry-in-the-world/

them deal with such endemic problems. But they cannot pay for the investments precisely because they are poor—they are in what economists call a "poverty trap." Until something is done about these problems, neither free markets nor democracy will do very much for them.

But then there are others, equally vocal, who believe that all of Sachs's answers are wrong. William Easterly, who battles Sachs from New York University at the other end of Manhattan, has become one of the most influential aid critics in his books, *The Elusive Quest for Growth* and *The White Man's Burden*. Dambisa Moyo, an economist who worked at Goldman Sachs and the World Bank, has joined her voice to Easterly's with her recent book, *Dead Aid*. Both argue that aid does more bad than good. It prevents people from searching for their own solutions, while corrupting and undermining local institutions and creating a self-perpetuating lobby of aid agencies. The best bet for poor countries, they argue, is to rely on one simple idea: When markets are free and the incentives are right, people can find ways to solve their problems. They do not need handouts from foreigners or their own governments. In this sense, the aid pessimists are actually quite optimistic about the way the world works. According to Easterly, there is no such thing as a poverty trap.

This debate cannot be solved in the abstract. To find out whether there are in fact poverty traps, and, if so, where they are and how to help the poor get out of them, we need to better understand the concrete problems they face. Some aid programs help more than others, but which ones? Finding out required us to step out of the office and look more carefully at the world. In 2003, we founded what became the Abdul Latif Jameel Poverty Action Lab, or J-PAL. A key part of our mission is to research by using randomized control trials—similar to experiments used in medicine to test the effectiveness of a drug—to understand what works and what doesn't in the real-world fight against poverty. In practical terms, that meant we'd have to start understanding how the poor really live their lives.

Take, for example, Pak Solhin, who lives in a small village in West Java, Indonesia. He once explained to us exactly how a poverty trap worked. His parents used to have a bit of land, but they also had 13 children and had to build so many houses for each of them and their families that there was no land left for cultivation. Pak Solhin had been working as a casual agricultural worker, which paid up to 10,000 rupiah per day (about $2) for work in the fields. A recent hike in fertilizer and fuel prices, however, had forced farmers to economize. The local farmers decided not to cut wages, Pak Solhin told us, but to stop hiring workers instead. As a result, in the two months before we met him in 2008, he had not found a single day of agricultural labor. He was too weak for the most physical work, too inexperienced for more skilled labor, and, at 40, too old to be an apprentice. No one would hire him.

Pak Solhin, his wife, and their three children took drastic steps to survive. His wife left for Jakarta, some 80 miles away, where she found a job as a maid. But she did not earn enough to feed the children. The oldest son, a good student, dropped out of school at 12 and started as an apprentice on a construction site. The two younger children were sent to live with their grandparents. Pak Solhin himself survived on the roughly 9 pounds of subsidized rice he got every week from the government and on fish he caught at a nearby lake. His brother fed him once in a while. In the week before we last spoke with him, he had eaten two meals a day for four days, and just one for the other three.

Pak Solhin appeared to be out of options, and he clearly attributed his problem to a lack of food. As he saw it, farmers weren't interested in hiring him because they feared they couldn't pay him enough to avoid starvation; and if he was starving, he would be useless in the field. What he described was the classic nutrition-based poverty trap, as it is known in the academic world. The idea is simple: The human body needs a certain number of calories just to survive. So when someone is very poor, all the food he or she can afford is barely enough to allow for going through the motions of living and earning the meager income used to buy that food. But as people get richer, they can buy more food and that extra food goes into building strength, allowing people to produce much more than they need to eat merely to stay alive. This creates a link between income today and income tomorrow: The very poor earn less than they need to be able to do significant work, but those who have enough to eat can work even more. There's the poverty trap: The poor get poorer, and the rich get richer and eat even better, and get stronger and even richer, and the gap keeps increasing.

But though Pak Solhin's explanation of how someone might get trapped in starvation was perfectly logical, there was something vaguely troubling about his narrative. We met him not in war-infested Sudan or in a flooded area of Bangladesh, but in a village in prosperous Java, where, even after the increase in food prices in 2007 and 2008, there was clearly plenty of food available and a basic meal did not cost much. He was still eating enough to survive; why wouldn't someone be willing to offer him the extra bit of nutrition that would make him productive in return for a full day's work? More generally, although a hunger-based poverty trap is certainly a logical possibility, is it really relevant for most poor people today? What's the best way, if any, for the world to help?

The international community has certainly bought into the idea that poverty traps exist—and that they are the reason that millions are starving. The first U.N. Millennium Development Goal, for instance, is to "eradicate extreme poverty and hunger." In many countries, the definition of poverty itself has been connected to food; the thresholds for determining that someone was poor were originally calculated as the budget necessary to buy a certain number of calories, plus some other indispensable purchases, such as housing. A "poor" person has essentially been classified as someone without enough to eat.

So it is no surprise that government efforts to help the poor are largely based on the idea that the poor desperately need food and that quantity is what matters. Food subsidies are ubiquitous in the Middle East: Egypt spent $3.8 billion on food subsidies in the 2008 fiscal year, some 2 percent of its GDP. Indonesia distributes subsidized rice. Many states in India have a similar program. In the state of Orissa, for example, the poor are entitled to 55 pounds of rice a month at about 1 rupee per pound, less than 20 percent of the market price. Currently, the Indian Parliament is debating a Right to Food Act, which would

allow people to sue the government if they are starving. Delivering such food aid is a logistical nightmare. In India it is estimated that more than half of the wheat and one-third of the rice gets "lost" along the way. To support direct food aid in this circumstance, one would have to be quite convinced that what the poor need more than anything is more grain.

But what if the poor are not, in general, eating too little food? What if, instead, they are eating the wrong kinds of food, depriving them of nutrients needed to be successful, healthy adults? What if the poor aren't starving, but choosing to spend their money on other priorities? Development experts and policymakers would have to completely reimagine the way they think about hunger. And governments and aid agencies would need to stop pouring money into failed programs and focus instead on finding new ways to truly improve the lives of the world's poorest.

Consider India, one of the great puzzles in this age of food crises. The standard media story about the country, at least when it comes to food, is about the rapid rise of obesity and diabetes as the urban upper-middle class gets richer. Yet the real story of nutrition in India over the last quarter-century, as Princeton professor Angus Deaton and Jean Drèze, a professor at Allahabad University and a special advisor to the Indian government, have shown, is not that Indians are becoming fatter: It is that they are in fact eating less and less. Despite the country's rapid economic growth, per capita calorie consumption in India has declined; moreover, the consumption of all other nutrients except fat also appears to have gone down among all groups, even the poorest. Today, more than three-quarters of the population live in households whose per capita calorie consumption is less than 2,100 calories in urban areas and 2,400 in rural areas—numbers that are often cited as "minimum requirements" in India for those engaged in manual labor. Richer people still eat more than poorer people. But at all levels of income, the share of the budget devoted to food has declined and people consume fewer calories.

What is going on? The change is not driven by declining incomes; by all accounts, Indians are making more money than ever before. Nor is it because of rising food prices—between the early 1980s and 2005, food prices declined relative to the prices of other things, both in rural and urban India. Although food prices have increased again since 2005, Indians began eating less precisely when the price of food was going down.

So the poor, even those whom the FAO would classify as hungry on the basis of what they eat, do not seem to want to eat much more even when they can. Indeed, they seem to be eating less. What could explain this? Well, to start, let's assume that the poor know what they are doing. After all, they are the ones who eat and work. If they could be tremendously more productive and earn much more by eating more, then they probably would. So could it be that eating more doesn't actually make us particularly more productive, and as a result, there is no nutrition-based poverty trap?

One reason the poverty trap might not exist is that most people have enough to eat. We live in a world today that is theoretically capable of feeding every person on the planet. In 1996, the FAO estimated that world food production was enough to provide at least 2,700 calories per person per day. Starvation still exists, but only as a result of the way food gets shared among us. There is no absolute scarcity. Using price data from the Philippines, we calculated the cost of the cheapest diet sufficient to give 2,400 calories. It would cost only about 21 cents a day, very affordable even for the very poor (the worldwide poverty line is set at roughly a dollar per day). The catch is, it would involve eating only bananas and eggs, something no one would like to do day in, day out. But so long as people are prepared to eat bananas and eggs when they need to, we should find very few people stuck in poverty because they do not get enough to eat. Indian surveys bear this out: The percentage of people who say they do not have enough food has dropped dramatically over time, from 17 percent in 1983 to 2 percent in 2004. So, perhaps people eat less because they are less hungry.

And perhaps they are really less hungry, despite eating fewer calories. It could be that because of improvements in water and sanitation, they are leaking fewer calories in bouts of diarrhea and other ailments. Or maybe they are less hungry because of the decline of heavy physical work. With the availability of drinking water in villages, women do not need to carry heavy loads for long distances; improvements in transportation have reduced the need to travel on foot; in even the poorest villages, flour is now milled using a motorized mill, instead of women grinding it by hand. Using the average calorie requirements calculated by the Indian Council of Medical Research, Deaton and Drèze note that the decline in calorie consumption over the last quarter-century could be entirely explained by a modest decrease in the number of people engaged in heavy physical work.

Beyond India, one hidden assumption in our description of the poverty trap is that the poor eat as much as they can. If there is any chance that by eating a bit more the poor could start doing meaningful work and get out of the poverty trap zone, then they should eat as much as possible. Yet most people living on less than a dollar a day do not seem to act as if they are starving. If they were, surely they would put every available penny into buying more calories. But they do not. In an 18-country data set we assembled on the lives of the poor, food represents 36 to 79 percent of consumption among the rural extremely poor, and 53 to 74 percent among their urban counterparts.

It is not because they spend all the rest on other necessities. In Udaipur, India, for example, we find that the typical poor household could spend up to 30 percent more on food, if it completely cut expenditures on alcohol, tobacco, and festivals. The poor seem to have many choices, and they don't choose to spend as much as they can on food. Equally remarkable is that even the money that people do spend on food is not spent to maximize the intake of calories or micronutrients. Studies have shown that when very poor people get a chance to spend a little bit more on food, they don't put everything into getting more calories. Instead, they buy better-tasting, more expensive calories.

In one study conducted in two regions of China, researchers offered randomly selected poor households a large subsidy on the price of the basic staple (wheat noodles in one region, rice in the other). We usually expect that when the price of something goes down, people buy more of it. The opposite happened. Households that received subsidies for rice or wheat consumed less of those two foods and ate more shrimp and meat, even though their staples now cost less. Overall, the caloric intake of those who received the subsidy did not increase (and may even have decreased), despite the fact that their purchasing power had increased. Nor did the nutritional content improve in any other sense. The likely reason is that because the rice and wheat noodles were cheap but not particularly tasty, feeling richer might actually have made them consume less of those staples. This reasoning suggests that at least among these very poor urban households, getting more calories was not a priority: Getting better-tasting ones was.

All told, many poor people might eat fewer calories than we—or the FAO—think is appropriate. But this does not seem to be because they have no other choice; rather, they are not hungry enough to seize every opportunity to eat more. So perhaps there aren't a billion "hungry" people in the world after all.

None of this is to say that the logic of the hunger-based poverty trap is flawed. The idea that better nutrition would propel someone on the path to prosperity was almost surely very important at some point in history, and it may still be today. Nobel Prize–winning economic historian Robert Fogel calculated that in Europe during the Middle Ages and the Renaissance, food production did not provide enough calories to sustain a full working population. This could explain why there were large numbers of beggars—they were literally incapable of any work. The pressure of just getting enough food to survive seems to have driven some people to take rather extreme steps. There was an epidemic of witch killing in Europe during the Little Ice Age (from the mid-1500s to 1800), when crop failures were common and fish was less abundant. Even today, Tanzania experiences a rash of such killings whenever there is a drought—a convenient way to get rid of an unproductive mouth to feed at times when resources are very tight. Families, it seems, suddenly discover that an older woman living with them (usually a grandmother) is a witch, after which she gets chased away or killed by others in the village.

But the world we live in today is for the most part too rich for the occasional lack of food to be a big part of the story of the persistence of poverty on a large scale. This is of course different during natural or man-made disasters, or in famines that kill and weaken millions. As Nobel laureate Amartya Sen has shown, most recent famines have been caused not because food wasn't available but because of bad governance—institutional failures that led to poor distribution of the available food, or even hoarding and storage in the face of starvation elsewhere. As Sen put it, "No substantial famine has ever occurred in any independent and democratic country with a relatively free press."

Should we let it rest there, then? Can we assume that the poor, though they may be eating little, do eat as much as they need to?

That also does not seem plausible. While Indians may prefer to buy things other than food as they get richer, they and their children are certainly not well nourished by any objective standard. Anemia is rampant; body-mass indices are some of the lowest in the world; almost half of children under 5 are much too short for their age, and one-fifth are so skinny that they are considered to be "wasted."

And this is not without consequences. There is a lot of evidence that children suffering from malnutrition generally grow into less successful adults. In Kenya, children who were given deworming pills in school for two years went to school longer and earned, as young adults, 20 percent more than children in comparable schools who received deworming for just one year. Worms contribute to anemia and general malnutrition, essentially because they compete with the child for nutrients. And the negative impact of undernutrition starts before birth. In Tanzania, to cite just one example, children born to mothers who received sufficient amounts of iodine during pregnancy completed between one-third and one-half of a year more schooling than their siblings who were in utero when their mothers weren't being treated. It is a substantial increase, given that most of these children will complete only four or five years of schooling in total. In fact, the study concludes that if every mother took iodine capsules, there would be a 7.5 percent increase in the total educational attainment of children in Central and Southern Africa. This, in turn, could measurably affect lifetime productivity.

Better nutrition matters for adults, too. In another study, in Indonesia, researchers tested the effects of boosting people's intake of iron, a key nutrient that prevents anemia. They found that iron supplements made men able to work harder and significantly boosted income. A year's supply of iron-fortified fish sauce cost the equivalent of $6, and for a self-employed male, the yearly gain in earnings was nearly $40—an excellent investment.

If the gains are so obvious, why don't the poor eat better? Eating well doesn't have to be prohibitively expensive. Most mothers could surely afford iodized salt, which is now standard in many parts of the world, or one dose of iodine every two years (at 51 cents per dose). Poor households could easily get a lot more calories and other nutrients by spending less on expensive grains (like rice and wheat), sugar, and processed foods, and more on leafy vegetables and coarse grains. But in Kenya, when the NGO that was running the deworming program asked parents in some schools to pay a few cents for deworming their children, almost all refused, thus depriving their children of hundreds of dollars of extra earnings over their lifetime.

Why? And why did anemic Indonesian workers not buy iron-fortified fish sauce on their own? One answer is that they don't believe it will matter—their employers may not realize that they are more productive now. (In fact, in Indonesia, earnings improved only for the self-employed workers.) But this does not explain why all pregnant women in India aren't using only iodine-fortified salt, which is now available in every village. Another possibility is that people may not realize the value of feeding themselves and their children better—not everyone has the right information, even in the United States. Moreover, people tend to be suspicious of outsiders who tell them that they should change their diet. When rice prices went up sharply in 1966 and 1967, the chief minister of West Bengal suggested that eating less rice and more vegetables would be both good for people's health and easier on their budgets. This set off a flurry of outrage, and the chief minister was greeted by protesters bearing garlands of vegetables wherever he went.

It is simply not very easy to learn about the value of many of these nutrients based on personal experience. Iodine might make your children smarter, but the difference is not huge, and in most cases you will not find out either way for many years. Iron, even if it makes people stronger, does not suddenly turn you into a superhero. The $40 extra a year the self-employed man earned may not even have been apparent to him, given the many ups and downs of his weekly income.

So it shouldn't surprise us that the poor choose their foods not mainly for their cheap prices and nutritional value, but for how good they taste. George Orwell, in his masterful description of the life of poor British workers in *The Road to Wigan Pier*, observes:

> The basis of their diet, therefore, is white bread and margarine, corned beef, sugared tea and potatoes—an appalling diet. Would it not be better if they spent more money on wholesome things like oranges and wholemeal bread or if they even, like the writer of the letter to the *New Statesman*, saved on fuel and ate their carrots raw? Yes, it would, but the point is that no ordinary human being is ever going to do such a thing. The ordinary human being would sooner starve than live on brown bread and raw carrots. And the peculiar evil is this, that the less money you have, the less inclined you feel to spend it on wholesome food. A millionaire may enjoy breakfasting off orange juice and Ryvita biscuits; an unemployed man doesn't. . . . When you are unemployed . . . you don't want to eat dull wholesome food. You want something a little bit "tasty." There is always some cheaply pleasant thing to tempt you.

The poor often resist the wonderful plans we think up for them because they do not share our faith that those plans work, or work as well as we claim. We shouldn't forget, too, that other things may be more important in their lives than food. Poor people in the developing world spend large amounts on weddings, dowries, and christenings. Part of the reason is probably that they don't want to lose face, when the social custom is to spend a lot on those occasions. In South Africa, poor families often spend so lavishly on funerals that they skimp on food for months afterward.

And don't underestimate the power of factors like boredom. Life can be quite dull in a village. There is no movie theater, no concert hall. And not a lot of work, either. In rural Morocco, Oucha Mbarbk and his two neighbors told us they had worked about 70 days in agriculture and about 30 days in construction that year. Otherwise, they took care of their cattle and waited for jobs to materialize. All three men lived in small houses without water or sanitation. They struggled to find enough money to give their children a good education. But they each had a television, a parabolic antenna, a DVD player, and a cell phone.

This is something that Orwell captured as well, when he described how poor families survived the Depression:

> Instead of raging against their destiny they have made things tolerable by reducing their standards.
>
> But they don't necessarily lower their standards by cutting out luxuries and concentrating on necessities; more often it is the other way around—the more natural way, if you come to think of it. Hence the fact that in a decade of unparalleled depression, the consumption of all cheap luxuries has increased.

These "indulgences" are not the impulsive purchases of people who are not thinking hard about what they are doing. Oucha Mbarbk did not buy his TV on credit—he saved up over many months to scrape enough money together, just as the mother in India starts saving for her young daughter's wedding by buying a small piece of jewelry here and a stainless-steel bucket there.

We often see the world of the poor as a land of missed opportunities and wonder why they don't invest in what would really make their lives better. But the poor may well be more skeptical about supposed opportunities and the possibility of any radical change in their lives. They often behave as if they think that any change that is significant enough to be worth sacrificing for will simply take too long. This could explain why they focus on the here and now, on living their lives as pleasantly as possible and celebrating when occasion demands it.

We asked Oucha Mbarbk what he would do if he had more money. He said he would buy more food. Then we asked him what he would do if he had even more money. He said he would buy better-tasting food. We were starting to feel very bad for him and his family, when we noticed the TV and other high-tech gadgets. Why had he bought all these things if he felt the family did not have enough to eat? He laughed, and said, "Oh, but television is more important than food!"

QUESTIONS

1. What is a poverty trap in the sense discussed by Banerjee and Duflo? Summarize in one or two clear sentences why Banerjee and Duflo believe that being caught in a poverty trap may not be a good explanation for why many of the global poor are malnourished. Put their main argument for this conclusion into standard form. What do Easterly and Moyo, as reported by Banerjee and Duflo, think is the best way of helping the global poor—and how does their view compare and contrast to Deaton's view? Does Banerjee and Duflo's discussion suggest that they disagree with Easterly, Moyo, or Deaton?

2. Why do Banerjee and Duflo think that when food prices go down, the poor often consume fewer calories? Give examples of two different things they often choose to consume more of, according to Banerjee and Duflo, when food prices go down. (Try to identify three—or even four—different factors discussed in the article that are each allegedly part of the explanation.)

3. If a particular poor person always has enough money to buy adequate nutrition, but chooses to buy junk food instead and is malnourished as a result, is that poor person food insecure according to the definition given in the chapter introduction (lacking reliable access—both physically and economically—to proper nutrition)? Explain. Note that food security, which is the definition used by most contemporary commentators and international organizations such as the United Nations to analyze hunger, is a concept that emerged for analyzing hunger in the wake of Sen's influential arguments, which overturned analyses of hunger in terms of food supply per capita. In light of

Banerjee and Duflo's discussion, is there a different concept for analyzing hunger that should re-place food security?

4. Banerjee and Duflo claim that "If there is any chance that by eating a bit more the poor could start doing meaningful work and get out of the poverty trap zone, then they should eat as much as pos-sible." How would you describe what the word "should" means, exactly, in this context? What does their discussion reveal about human behavior, and how is it relevant to public policy that is based on the premise that humans will always choose what is best for themselves? How might these ex-amples be used to argue that sometimes people are not blameworthy for not helping themselves, even when they have the ability to do so? What are objections and replies to such an argument?

5. Consider the following summary of actual empirical evidence from neuroscience: "*Stress Reduces Self-Control.* Everyone experiences situations in which our willpower fades, and we abandon self-control for choices that we later regret. Maier et al. assessed how stress affects self-control in young adults that have a healthy lifestyle but reported indulging in fast-food treats regularly. Com-pared to control participants, participants who were experimentally stressed preferred tastier foods more often in a two-choice taste test, regardless of whether their choice was less healthy and in disagreement with their self-imposed dietary restrictions. Brain imaging revealed more-active reward and taste circuits in stressed participants and less activity in regions associated with self-control. This suggests that stressed individuals prefer immediate reward over following a long-term goal."[1] Do you think the poor tend to be more stressed than average? What might this imply about the choices of the poor vs. average, given this evidence? Is this relevant to the question of blameworthiness in the previous set of questions? For an in-depth discussion connected to the issues discussed here, read the book by Mullainathan and Shafir in Further Reading.

6. What is India's Right to Food Act? (Do an internet search to learn more about it.) Are there wor-ries, according to Banerjee and Duflo, about it having unintended effects? What are they exactly? Some critics have claimed that the act amounts to, not food security, but "vote security." What do these critics mean by this?

NOTE

1. This report is from Laura Schuhmacher, "Stress Reduces Self-Control," *Science* 349 (2015): 1067–1068, citing research in Maier et al., "Acute Stress Impairs Self-Control in Goal-Directed Choice by Altering Multiple Functional Connections within the Brain's Decision Circuits," *Neuron* 87 (2015): 621–631.

3 } Food Justice

This chapter examines the *food justice movement* and the concept of *food justice*. The food justice movement identifies a range of problems with the food system, which are seen as *injustices*. What are these problems? Are they injustices? What kinds of injustice are at issue? This chapter also discusses the *food sovereignty* movement and its critique of the global food system as fundamentally unjust.

THE FOOD JUSTICE MOVEMENT

The *food justice movement* is a social justice movement. It aims to transform the food system in order to address a range of problems, including:

- Racism, classism, sexism, and exclusionary practices in the food system and in the alternative food movement
- Lack of equal participation in decision-making about food
- Low wages and poor working conditions for agricultural workers, fast-food workers, and other food service workers
- Indigenous peoples losing access to foods that were traditionally central to their identity, culture, and economy (what are called *first foods*)
- The environmental unsustainability of many contemporary forms of industrial agriculture
- Hunger, malnutrition, and food insecurity (not being able to reliably afford enough food)
- Inadequate access to high-quality food, including:
  - *Food deserts*—neighborhoods where a significant percentage of people have poor access to healthy food, because they live far from a grocery store or another source of healthy food and do not have access to a car
  - *Food swamps*—neighborhoods with a concentration of fast-food restaurants and other sources of unhealthy food
- The high cost of healthier foods like fruits, vegetables, and whole grains, as compared to less healthy foods such as processed and packaged food[1]

The readings in this chapter describe some of these problems. "Witnesses to Hunger" discusses the scope of food insecurity in the United States and its health and developmental effects on children, and "Angel's Story" describes one family's experience with food insecurity. The reading "Food Justice and Collective Food Relations" discusses the loss of first foods. The reading "If They Only Knew: The Unbearable Whiteness of Alternative Food" discusses racial exclusion in the alternative food movement—how the movement unwittingly excludes non-white voices and how it ignores race-based food justice issues.

Ending hunger and food insecurity is a goal of the food justice movement, but importantly, *the food justice movement is not just about giving people more food*. It addresses a range of ways in which people are not treated fairly in the food system. And the food justice movement aims not only to produce better outcomes—for example, to improve access to healthy food in food deserts, and to increase the wages of fast-food workers—but also to give individuals and communities more control over what they eat, more control over food within their communities, and more power to shape the food system as a whole. In this way, the food justice movement is, for some proponents, not only a critique of the structure of the food system and the outcomes it produces, but a critique of who has power and control to shape the food system in this way. The food justice movement critiques the power that large companies—including agribusiness companies such as Monsanto, large food manufacturers such as Kraft, restaurant chains such as Starbucks, and retailers such as Walmart—have to shape government policy, to shape food environments, and ultimately to shape what individuals eat.

In the words of some of its proponents:

> A socially just food system is one in which power and material resources are shared equitably so that people and communities can meet their needs, and live with security and dignity, now and into the future.[2]
>
> Food Justice is communities exercising their right to grow, sell, and eat healthy food. Healthy food is fresh, nutritious, affordable, culturally-appropriate, and grown locally with care for the well-being of the land, workers, and animals. People practicing food justice leads to a strong local food system, self-reliant communities, and a healthy environment.[3]
>
> Food justice is the right of communities everywhere to produce, process, distribute, access, and eat good food regardless of race, class, gender, ethnicity, citizenship, ability, religion, or community.[4]

These definitions differ slightly, reflecting the fact that different organizations understand food justice differently. But they all reflect an understanding of food justice as requiring both more equitable access to resources and more decision-making power for communities.

The food justice movement is distinct from the *alternative food movement*, which predates the food justice movement. (*Alternative food* is food that is not produced using the standard industrial methods detailed in Chapter 7, "Industrial Animal Agriculture," and Chapter 9, "Industrial Plant Agriculture." Michael Pollan discussed the alternative food movement in "The Food Movement, Rising" in Chapter 1, and alternative food, including local and organic food, is discussed more in Chapter 10, "Alternatives to Industrial Plant Agriculture.") As we discuss later in this chapter, some proponents of the food justice movement see it as a way to remedy problems with the alternative food movement, in particular its perceived elitism, racism, and classism. Though they are distinct, there is significant overlap between the food justice and alternative food movements, particularly in their opposition to mainstream industrial agriculture and the food industry.

WHAT IS JUSTICE?

As we've been describing, the food justice movement identifies a range of problems with the food system, and frames these problems as *injustices*. This raises some ethical questions:

1. Are these problems with the food system *injustices*?
2. If they are injustices, what kind of injustices are they?
3. What, if anything, should be done about these injustices?
4. Whose responsibility is it to address these injustices?

Question 1 asks whether these problems with the food system—for example, widespread food insecurity—are injustices. When a state of affairs is referred to as an injustice, this typically implies that it is wrongful and that there are duties to remedy it. A state of affairs can have bad features but nonetheless be the best possible state of affairs—because all other states of affairs would also have bad features, ones which are even worse. For example, sending your kid to the dentist even though it is painful and scary for her is a bad state of affairs, but not sending her to the dentist and running the risk of dental disease is an even worse state of affairs. In addition, a state of affairs can be bad, even though no one has done anything morally wrong in bringing about that state of affairs and no one has a moral duty to remedy it. For example, when your child is in pain while getting a shot at the doctor, this is bad, even though no one has done anything wrong and no one has a duty to remedy this bad state of affairs. But when a state of affairs is referred to as an injustice, this typically implies that it is not only bad, it *is* wrongful and that there *are* duties to remedy it.

Justice, most basically, is about fair relations between people and about people getting what they are owed by society. States of affairs that are unjust are typically wrong and wrong *because* they are unfair or, more specifically, because someone is not getting what they are owed. Justice is about fair relations between *existing people*. It is also about fair relations between *existing people* and *future people*, and future people getting what they are owed, which is known as *intergenerational justice*. Some theorists claim that animals fall under the purview of justice, and so justice is also about fair relations between people and animals, and animals getting what they are owed.

Some theories of justice concern justice within a single society. What are fair relations between people in the same society? What are individuals and groups owed by society? What system of government, what laws and institutions, what economic system, and what social practices and social norms are consistent with fairness between people living in the same society? *Global justice*, in contrast, concerns justice between nations and justice between people throughout the world, not just people in the same society. (More about global justice later in the chapter.)

Justice requires, at a minimum, that people have basic liberties and political rights. All people are owed these things. So, for example, a government that is not democratically elected, but maintains power through violence, is an oppressive and unjust government. In addition, justice requires that people have these liberties and rights equally. For example, a government that denies the vote to ethnic minorities is unjust. Justice also requires that there are fair procedures for making decisions, what's known as *procedural justice*.

Another dimension of justice is *distributive justice*, which is concerned with the fair distribution throughout society of important things. Theories disagree about what must be distributed fairly: goods and services (such as income and health care), well-being, opportunities (such as educational opportunities), capabilities (such as being healthy), or something else? Theorists also disagree about what counts as a just or fair distribution. Does fairness require that there is an equal distribution of important things, such as everyone having the same income, or everyone having equal educational opportunities? Or is a fair distribution one that reflects what people deserve based on their own choices and efforts—such that it's fair, for example, if some people make more money than others as a result of getting more education or working longer hours? Or does justice require only that everyone has an adequate level of important things, not that these things are distributed equally or according to deservingness? Or does fairness not require any particular distribution, but simply require that people acquire things in fair ways—for example, people acquire money by earning it or being given it, not by stealing it? Or should we stopping worrying about what's a fair distribution, and just try to achieve the distribution that maximizes overall utility or social welfare, as utilitarianism demands?

Along with identifying what counts as a fair or just distribution, distributive justice is also concerned with identifying the laws and institutions—for example, educational policies or tax policies or food assistance policies—that will achieve this distribution. The most influential theory of distributive justice is that proposed by John Rawls in his book *A Theory of Justice*.[5] Views about what kind of laws and institutions are just depend upon a view about the purpose of governments and social institutions. Is the primary task of governments to ensure conditions in which individuals can be self-determining and lead good lives of their own choosing (as *liberalism* would have it)? Or is the task of governments to promote the well-being of communities, in conformity with their shared values and resulting sense of group identity (as *communitarianism* would have it)? Or something else?

Some philosophers, notably some feminist philosophers, use *justice* and *injustice* to refer to a broader range of social conditions beyond laws, policies, and public institutions. It's not only the actions of governments, the distribution of goods, or the structure of public institutions that can be unjust. Social attitudes, social norms, and social practices can also constrain people's options and life chances in ways that seem unfair, and thus seem like instances of injustice. The idea is that justice requires *social equality* of multiple sorts. These philosophers use *social equality* to refer not only to distributive equality (an equal distribution of important things), but also to refer to equal social standing or equal social status. There are many ways in which people from different groups are not accorded equal social standing or status, including: they have less decision-making power when it comes to collective decisions; they are less likely to occupy formal positions of authority; they have less social power or influence over others' behavior; they are allowed less autonomy or control over themselves; and their perspectives and values are not represented in mainstream culture. For example, in the United States, women and people of color are less likely to hold elected office than men and whites. To give another example, some critics of the alternative food movement say that it reflects the experience and values of middle-class white people—a culturally dominant group—and does not reflect the perspectives of low-income people and people of color; in this way, the criticism goes, the alternative food movement reflects and perpetuates a form of social inequality.

SYSTEMIC INJUSTICE AND OPPRESSION

Consider one form of injustice, oppression. Though "oppression" calls to mind tyranny by a ruling class, oppression can also result from the everyday actions of well-intentioned people: "in unquestioned norms, habits, and symbols, in the assumptions underlying institutional rules and the collective consequences of following those rules," according to Iris Marion Young.[6] As Young argues in the reading "Five Faces of Oppression," justice requires social conditions that allow all people to develop and exercise their individual capacities. A tyrannical government or a lack of resources can prevent people from developing and exercising their individual capacities; but so, too, can other social conditions that treat people differently based upon their social groups.

Following Young, we can identify five types of oppression:

- *Exploitation*, when the labor or energy of one group benefits another group, without being equally benefited or compensated. Chapter 11, "Workers," discusses the poor treatment of some workers in the food system and considers whether this is exploitation and, if so, why.
- *Marginalization*, in which some groups are cut off from work opportunities and from social cooperation more generally. Examples of marginalized groups that are excluded from work opportunities at a high rate are old people, immigrants, and young people of color.
- *Powerlessness*, in which groups have power exercised over them but are not able to exercise power over others. The powerless are not treated as respectfully as the powerful, and they have less autonomy or control over their own work. A paradigm example of a powerless group is the working class/nonprofessionals in relation to the middle class/professionals.
- *Cultural imperialism*, in which the dominant group in a society establishes its culture as the norm. For non-dominant groups, the "dominant meanings of a society render the particular perspective of one's own group invisible at the same time as they stereotype one's group and mark it out as the Other."
- *Violence*, in which some groups are subject to systematic violence. Young gives the examples of women, blacks, gay men, and lesbian women as groups that are subject to systematic violence in the United States.

These five forms of oppression are five ways in which people are constrained based upon membership in social groups. If we apply the concept of social equality here, we can say that the five forms of oppression are multiple ways in which people are not treated as social equals and, hence, are treated unjustly. The oppression of different groups consists of different combinations of these five forms of oppression, as Young explains. For example, working-class white men experience powerlessness and exploitation, but not violence or marginalization. Gay men, as a group, experience severe cultural imperialism and violence, but not exploitation or powerlessness. In other words, groups can experience some forms of oppression and social inequality but not others.

Oppression has three important features, according to Young. First, the oppression of one social group always benefits another group, which is privileged in relation to the oppressed group. Oppressed groups in the United States would include, among other groups: racial/ethnic minorities (in relation to whites, a privileged group), women (in relation to men), people who are disabled (in relation to people who are typically abled), people who are queer (in relation to straight people), transgender people (in relation to cisgender people, i.e., those who identify as the gender they were assigned at birth), and the poor and working class (in relation to the middle class and affluent people).

Second, oppression need not involve the intention to harm or to oppress. While oppression involves some instances of intentional harm—"The raped woman, the beaten Black youth, the locked-out worker, the gay man harassed on the street"—oppression is primarily a result of everyday actions that neither intended to be nor seen as harmful or oppressive. Relatedly, Margaret Andersen and Patricia Hill Collins draw a distinction between racism or racial inequality, on the one hand, and racial prejudice, which is a "hostile attitude toward a person who is presumed to have negative characteristics associated with a group to which he or she belongs."[7] Even when people are not prejudiced—that is, even when people do not have hostile attitudes—racism or racial inequality or oppression can still exist.

Third, oppression is *structural*. When we talk about oppression and injustice—such as racial injustice or racism, or gender injustice or sexism— part of what we're talking about are attitudes and norms that work to the advantage of some groups over others. For example, Young discusses the social norm that menial labor should be done by people of color. But injustice, inequality, and oppression are not just about attitudes and norms.[8] There's a material reality corresponding to these attitudes and norms: people in some groups have fewer goods and opportunities, and less power, than people in other groups. There are laws, policies, social institutions, and social practices that help to perpetuate this material reality, in concert with the ways that our social norms and attitudes perpetuate it. For example, the denial of voting rights to women in the United States before 1920 (a lack of equal basic rights) was supported by social views about women (a form of oppression and social inequality) and by the denial of educational and employment opportunities to women. There is a complex structure of social categories, attitudes, social norms, other social practices, laws, policies, and institutions that reinforce each other. This is referred to as *structural injustice* or *systemic injustice*. It is also referred to as structural inequality or systemic inequality.

WHY JUSTICE MATTERS MORALLY

As you may recall from its definition in the previous chapter, *utilitarianism* is the moral view that one must always perform the action that maximizes well-being. For a utilitarian, if treating someone unjustly maximizes well-being—maybe the person you treat unjustly will never know they are being treated unjustly, or maybe you and others get *such* a thrill out of treating that person unjustly that it outweighs his or her loss of well-being, and so on— then utilitarianism requires treating that person unjustly. This is because, to utilitarianism, justice is only *instrumentally* important: It is morally important only insofar as it is an instrument for producing well-being.

Many moral theories deny this claim that justice is only instrumentally important. They claim that justice is *intrinsically* important—important in itself and not simply because of its consequences. Such theories claim that unjust acts are typically wrong *simply because they are unjust* and not because they have the effect of failing to maximize well-being. This is in fact what is claimed by most *deontological* theories, which provide general theories of ethics that define right and wrong not in terms of maximizing some good thing such as well-being, but rather in terms of doing what is right as defined in other terms, such as doing what is just, respecting people's basic rights, and so on. Suppose that you treat someone unjustly but you and others get *so* much pleasure out of doing so that you, in fact, maximize the total amount of well-being in the world by treating that person unjustly; deontological theories, unlike utilitarianism, claim that what you do is nevertheless wrong. When the state allows men to vote but bars women from doing so, this is unjust. So far as it is morally objectionable, deontological theories tend to claim that it is morally objectionable simply because it is unjust and not, as utilitarians say, because it fails to maximize well-being. Similarly, when some people enslave others, as some food workers are enslaved, this is wrong. Utilitarians say it is wrong because the system fails to maximize happiness. But deontological theories often deny this and claim it is wrong simply because it is unjust. (See Chapter 11, "Workers," for further discussion of food workers. See Chapter 4, "Consumer Ethics," for further discussion of general ethical theories such as utilitarianism and deontological theories.)

IS FOOD JUSTICE ABOUT JUSTICE?

Now return to the list of problems identified by the food justice movement. Notice how we can roughly map these problems onto forms of injustice identified by philosophers. Hunger and malnutrition, food insecurity, lack of access to healthy food in food deserts, and the high cost of healthier foods are all distributive justice issues, or issues of fair distribution throughout society of important things. Food deserts are also seen as a racial justice issue, because they were caused in part by racist housing policies. Low wages and poor working conditions for workers are a form of exploitation as well as a distributive justice issue. Racism in the food system—for example, discrimination against African-American farmers by the USDA—is an issue of procedural justice, an issue of fair procedures for making decisions, and marginalization. The environmental unsustainability of industrial agriculture is an issue of intergenerational justice—future generations are given less than their share of certain environmental goods. Racism, classism, and exclusionary practices in the alternative food movement are an example of cultural imperialism and other forms of social inequality, as discussed more later in the chapter.

There is an additional form of justice at play in the food justice movement, as Kyle Powys Whyte argues in "Food Justice and Collective Food Relations." Food justice requires that groups have those experiences and social relations involving food that are central to their way of life, free from interference by others. In other words, food justice requires *collective self-determination* with regards to food and the food-related aspects of a way of life. Whyte sees food as a "hub" for a variety of relations and experiences that make up a group's way of life—what he terms *collective food relations*. He gives the example of *manoomin* (wild rice), which is an important source of nutrition for the Anishinaabe people in the Great Lakes region, and is also central to their social, cultural, and economic life. Manoomin is used in ceremonies and celebrations, and camps where Anishinaabek harvest the wild rice are "places that intermingle hard work with storytelling, dances, rituals, games, courting, and education that strengthen bonds between Anishinaabek of different families and generations," as Whyte explains.

Because collective food relations are so important to groups' ways of life, the collective self-determination of groups requires that groups' collective food relations—such as the Anishinaabe collective food relations involving manoomin—are free from interference from other groups, unless that interference is justified by sufficiently weighty moral reasons. The underlying ethical idea is that justice requires collective self-determination, "that human groups have the right to decide their own destinies free from any external compulsion or interference from other human groups, unless there is a morally weighty reason for this compulsion or interference."

Whyte's account raises a number of interesting and deep questions. Do we have a special moral reason not to interfere with groups' collective relations—a moral reason *in addition* to our moral reasons not to harm individuals, or violate their autonomy, or interfere with their self-determination? That is, are there special moral reasons against interfering with groups' collective relations, in addition to the reasons we have for not interfering with individuals' actions? What counts as compulsion or interference with collective food relations? What counts as a morally weighty reason for compulsion or interference with collective food relations? What counts as a group? Whyte writes that a "morally weighty reason should be one that the affected group . . . would accept as a legitimate reason." So interference with a group's collective food relations can be justifiable, but the reason for interfering has to be mutually recognizable as a legitimate reason. What if collective food relations are unjust or otherwise morally problematic from the perspective of outsiders but are seen as legitimate by the group?[9]

JUSTICE AND ALTERNATIVE FOOD MOVEMENTS

The poor get diabetes; the rich get local and organic.

—*Mark Winne*[10]

Along with critiquing the mainstream, industrial food system, food justice activists and scholars have also critiqued the alternative food movement as paying too little attention to injustice and social inequality.

First, the alternative food movement is criticized as paying too little attention to the needs of low-income people. The organic food movement is criticized as not addressing food insecurity, nor addressing the fact that low-income people have difficulty affording healthier foods like fruits, vegetables, and whole grains, which cost more per calorie than processed foods—not to mention that they cannot afford organic food, which is typically more expensive than non-organic.

Along with being insufficiently responsive to the food insecurity of low-income consumers, the alternative food movement is also criticized as perpetuating other forms of social inequality. Food justice activists have argued that the alternative food movement is a "monoculture": it is homogeneous, having mostly white and middle-class adherents.[11] Its goals and narrative resonate with middle-class white people, but do not take into account the experience of low-income people and people of color and so do not resonate with them. In her reading in this chapter, Julie Guthman points out that the alternative food movement evokes an agrarian past—small farmers working the land—that is "far more easily romanticized by whites than others," since non-whites in the United States were systematically denied land ownership.

Similarly, food justice scholars Alkon and Agyeman critique the advice given by food writer Michael Pollan, not to "eat anything your great-grandmother wouldn't recognize as food." Alkon and Agyeman write:

> Some [of our great-grandmothers] were enslaved, transported across the ocean, and forced to subsist on the overflow from the master's table. Others were forcibly sent to state-mandated board-ing schools, in which they were taught to despise, and even forget, any foods they would previ-ously have recognized. . . . Of course it is not these histories that Pollan intends to invoke when he urges readers to choose fruits and vegetables over processed foods. But because of his privileged positionality, Pollan fails to consider the effects of race on food access and the alternative mean-ings his words may hold for people of color in the United States. In this same way, whites in the food movement often simply do not see the subtle exclusivities that are woven into its narrative.[12]

The alternative food movement, Alkon and Agyeman write, does not see the ways in which it reflects the experience merely of white people and excludes others.

In her reading in this chapter, Julie Guthman also argues that alternative food projects—such as community gardens, education programs, organic farms, and food trucks—are *white spaces*, even when these projects are located in or meant to serve communities of color. "In sum . . . even these more race-conscious projects tend to get coded as white. They are coded so not only because of the prevalence of white bodies . . . it also appears that the associations of the food, the modes of educating people to its qualities, and the ways of de-livering it lack appeal to the people such programs are designed to entice." Notice the differ-ence between the projects Guthman describes and a project such as the West Oakland farmers market—a farmers market located in a predominantly black, low-income neighbor-hood, with products, displays, music, and special events that expressed African-American identity and celebrated black culture.[13]

Guthman argues that the alternative food movement engages in a problematic form of universalism—"the assumption that values held by whites are normal and widely shared." Recall Iris Marion Young's notion of cultural imperialism, a form of oppression in which the dominant group in a society establishes its culture as the norm. For non-dominant groups, the "dominant meanings of a society render the particular perspective of one's own group invisible at the same time as they stereotype one's group and mark it out as the Other," in Young's words. What Guthman describes is perhaps a variant or form of cultural imperial-ism: The alternative food movement treats the values of middle-class white people as obvi-ously correct and widely shared.

DOES THE ALTERNATIVE FOOD MOVEMENT REINFORCE SOCIAL INEQUALITY?

Guthman describes some of her students' disappointing experiences working with alterna-tive food projects that are meant to address food insecurity or lack of access to healthy foods. As she describes these projects, they lack appeal to the low-income people of color in the communities that they are meant to serve. Part of the problem is that the projects weren't offering what people in the community wanted—for example, community members wanted a Safeway, not a food truck that offers organic food.

This lack of appeal is certainly a *practical* problem for these projects: They are unlikely to be effective if the community is not interested in taking advantage of them. But are such projects also *ethically* problematic in some way? Is it ethically problematic to go into a community, as an outsider, and start a program that isn't responsive to the desires and tastes of the people it's meant to serve? In general, it is not ethically problematic to offer someone a service that lacks appeal to her. For example, if you hate a certain sort of music and we offer you repeated opportunities to listen to it, this project will not be effective but also is not ethically problematic. But there are aspects to these alternative food projects that might seem suspect. What if a project comes across as nagging or paternalistic, less a friend trying to get a friend to listen to a certain sort of music and more a parent trying to get a child to eat broccoli? What if the program is meant to serve mostly poor people of color, but it is run by mostly middle-class white people?

One potential worry is that these projects are predicated on a form of social inequality, such as the attitude that low-income people and people of color are not experts on what they need, or the norm that low-income people or people of color don't need to be allowed to speak for themselves. A related ethical concern is that such projects will reinforce attitudes and norms privileging middle-class people and white people— for example, the attitude that middle-class people know what's best (even for other people), or the norm that white people are in charge. In the reading "Five Faces of Oppression," Iris Marion Young describes, as an example of *marginalization*, how recipients of public assistance are treated: They are not given "the right to claim to know what is good for them," because public assistance agencies decide for them what they need. Instead, they "are subject to patronizing, punitive, demeaning, and arbitrary treatment by the policies and people associated with welfare bureaucracies." Though the alternative food projects Guthman describes are not examples of public assistance, the same dynamic might be at play: The people who are running food projects decide what people need, rather than letting the people being served decide what they need.

When an alternative food project provides a service for community members that they do not want, or does not seek their input, and when this service is provided in a way that does not resonate with community members, is this an instance of failing to treat community members respectfully or as social equals? More generally, does the alternative food movement reflect and reinforce forms of social inequality and injustice? If so, what should be done?

GLOBAL JUSTICE AND THE GLOBAL FOOD SYSTEM

We have so far been considering food justice issues within the United States. Let's turn now to justice issues with the global food system. Recall that several readings in Chapter 1 discuss ethically troubling aspects of the global food system: hunger and malnutrition, the harsh treatment of farm laborers on large farms, small farmers who remain in dire poverty even as multinational corporations profit from the crops they grow, and the significant contribution of agriculture to climate change. Are these bad aspects of the global food system *injustices*? If so, are they injustices that people in developed countries such as the United States have an ethical responsibility to address?

Our preceding discussion of justice focused on justice within a single nation. *Global justice*, in contrast, concerns justice between all people in the world. Global justice covers a range of issues about the duties that individuals have toward individuals in other societies, how governments ought to treat other governments, and what's required of international institutions, non-governmental organizations, and businesses. These issues include: Can members of one society treat members of another *unjustly* rather than merely wrong? If so, who has a duty to redress those injustices? If justice requires a certain distribution within a society, does it also require the same distribution among people the world over? Or, on the contrary, do certain principles of justice only hold among people in the same society? What does justice require of entities besides nations and individual people, such as the United Nations or the World Trade Organization? What does global justice require of multinational companies? What does it require of charities and other non-governmental organizations?

Two global ethics issues that are particularly important to food ethics are as follows:

1. How does global justice demand that individuals, nations, and other entities respond to hunger and malnutrition among the world's poor?
2. What kind of global economy is just? And, in particular, are the trade and agricultural policies that structure the global food system just?

Chapter 2, "Global Hunger," introduced us to these issues, and we continue that discussion here. Many scholars and activists hold that the global food system is profoundly unjust. The food system's contribution to environmental degradation and global climate change, which are seen to threaten the well-being of future generations, is seen as an issue of inter-generational justice: Future generations are owed an environment comparable to ours and, instead, will get one in worse shape. The export of fast food and processed foods from West-ern countries is seen as unjust: When these foods enter the market in low- and middle-income countries, they drive out local foods and food practices—a form of cultural imperialism—and cause increases in diet-related illness in local populations.[14] Another perceived injustice concerns control of land, water, and other natural resources—for example, when farmland is concentrated in large landholdings controlled by multinational corporations, rather than divided more equitably among native small farmers, this is seen as unjust.[15]

Gender injustice is seen as pervading the food system. Women and girls are more likely to experience malnutrition than men. "Twice as many women suffer from malnutrition as men, and girls are twice as likely to die from malnutrition as boys," according to the Food and Agriculture Organization of the United Nations.[16] In addition:

> Having an adequate supply of food does not automatically translate into adequate levels of nutrition. In many societies women and girls eat the food remaining after the male family members have eaten. Women, girls, the sick and disabled are the main victims of this "food discrimination," which results in chronic undernutrition and ill-health.[17]

In restaurants, women are less likely to hold the highest-paying jobs and are systemati-cally paid less than men for the same work. Men average $9.77/hour as cooks; women aver-age $8.97. Men average $12.34 as supervisors; women average $10.91.[18] Women are an increasingly large portion of the agricultural workforce worldwide—what's known as the "feminization of agriculture"—but have unequal access to land, agricultural inputs, and other resources necessary to farming. As a result, women's farms are less productive on average than men's farms. As Bina Agarwal explains:

> The majority of studies, however, find lower yields on women's plots/farms. This is not attributable, however, to women's lesser capability as farmers but to one or more of the following constraints: women's lower access to inputs, especially fertilizers; insecure land rights; lower access to male labor, oxen, and extension services; and difficulties in ensuring timely ploughing, weeding, or transportation. A few studies also demonstrate that if women had access to the same inputs and extension services as men, they would have higher outputs than male farmers. . . .[19]

Because women rely on farming to feed themselves and their families, their unequal access to resources for farming impairs their food security and survival. It also has significant impacts on the overall productivity of agriculture and food availability:

> The overwhelming conclusion derived from the existing body of work is, therefore, two fold. On the one hand, if women had the same access to inputs as men, production would increase substantially on their farms. According to FAO's 2011 State of Food and Agriculture Report, reducing the constraints faced by women farmers could raise yields on their farms by 20–30% and raise total agricultural output in developing countries by 2.5–4%, thus making a significant impact on food availability (FAO 2011). On the other hand, if we fail to bridge the gender gaps in access to production inputs and services, the growing proportion of women in farming is likely to remain confined to low productivity agriculture. Infrastructure development and other measures taken to revive agriculture would fail to reach them. In turn, this would undercut world potential for increasing agricultural output and ensuring food security. The situation would be exacerbated further by the predicted effects of climate change, which will impinge negatively on the incomes and nutrition of millions of poor farmers, and specially on women and children.[20]

Agarwal brings out that gender injustices in the food system cascade into further injustices, contributing to global poverty and also to hunger, malnutrition, and food insecurity among the poor.

A particularly important consequence of food insecurity and malnutrition among the poor is its effects upon children. As Marianna Chilton describes in "Witnesses to Hunger," food insecurity during the early years of life has negative effects on children's health and development, and thus on their long-term well-being. In this way, food insecurity and malnutrition among the poor contribute to what's known as the *intergenerational transmission of inequality*.[21]

The current empirically-based thinking about the intergenerational transmission of inequality is that many desirable cognitive abilities and behavioral dispositions require proper development of our brains very early in our lives to achieve—in many cases, they require proper development in the womb before we are even born. Furthermore, this development is importantly undermined if very early in our lives we have suboptimal nutrition, exposure to toxins, or exposure to stress hormones in the womb.[22] Sadly, poor people, in virtue of being poor, are far more likely to be exposed to all of these detrimental factors that prevent proper development, and if they are exposed to these things very early in life, this handicaps them throughout their lives relative to the average, more affluent members of society. The nature of these handicaps is such that they can never really be removed later no matter how much money we pour into education and other social welfare initiatives. As a result of all of this, there is a connection between being conceived by parents at the bottom of the socioeconomic ladder and ending up there later in life, even when other factors are held fixed. And the fact that these handicaps are fixed for all time by events very early in one's life implies that this is a particularly thorny problem—it cannot be solved just by increasing spending on social welfare programs in general but requires targeted approaches that improve prenatal and early childhood nutrition.

DOES THE GLOBAL FOOD SYSTEM PERPETUATE POVERTY AND INJUSTICE?

Along with raising issues of gender justice, intergenerational justice, exploitation, cultural imperialism, and related forms of justice, the global food system is seen as fundamentally unjust because it is believed to contribute to global poverty, and to hunger, malnutrition, and food insecurity among the global poor. There is intense disagreement about the effect of specific trade and agricultural policies on the global poor, as well as disagreement about which kind of global economic system is most likely to reduce global poverty and hunger.[23] But from one perspective, the existing global food system works to the advantage of wealthier countries and to the disadvantage of lower income countries, and perpetuates poverty and food insecurity in developing countries. Countries with more power and wealth are seen as using their greater power to secure terms of trade that are favorable to them (recall the discussion of the World Trade Organization in Chapter 2). Existing international trade rules, as well as regulations within countries, allow multinational corporations to control large land holdings in low-income countries and grow crops for export using industrial methods. International institutions such as the World Bank encourage these efforts, on the view that the best way to reduce poverty and food insecurity is to incorporate developing economies into the global economy—and in particular, to transform agriculture in developing countries so that it is industrialized and more efficient, and produces more crops for export, rather than growing diversified crops for local markets.[24] Critics of these efforts claim that they have not been effective at reducing poverty and food insecurity; rather, they drive small farmers off the land and out of farming, increasing landlessness and food insecurity among the poor in those countries, as well as driving out local forms of agriculture that are more environmentally sustainable, including those practiced by indigenous people.[25]

This state of affairs in which some countries have so much more than others, and in which the better-off implement policies favoring themselves, is often seen as involving multiple forms of injustice. Countries with more wealth and power take advantage of poorer countries' vulnerability to secure trade rules that disproportionately benefit themselves—this is seen as exploitative and coercive. (See Chapter 11, "Workers," for discussion of the concepts of coercion and exploitation.) These disparities in power and wealth are seen as a legacy of *colonialism*, the establishment of colonies by Western powers in Africa, Asia, and America, which included violent coercion of colonized countries and the extraction of natural resources—a case of violent oppression. People in all countries, but especially developing countries, are seen as lacking control over agricultural and trade policies, a failure of democratic norms; as a result, these policies serve the interests of developed countries and multinational corporations rather than serving the interests of people in developing countries or representing their wishes. The existing trade rules allow exchanges that are seen as unfair, because some groups or countries benefit more than others. These unfair exchanges produce a result that is seen as unjust: there is a vast differential in wealth between low-income and high-income countries, vast differentials in wealth between high-income and low-income groups within individual countries, and significant rates of extreme poverty and food insecurity.

Whether these features of the global food system are in fact *injustices*, and not merely bad states of affairs, depends upon one's theory of global justice. Consider, for example, whether the persistence of extreme poverty and food insecurity is unjust, such that people in developed countries like the United States have justice-based obligations to address it. It might seem that if rates of extreme poverty and food insecurity could be reduced by changes to the global economy and increased aid, but these changes don't occur, then this is obviously unjust. But is it? Similarly, it might seem that if people in developed countries like the United States could reduce extreme poverty and food insecurity by supporting these changes, but they don't, then they have acted unjustly toward people in other countries. But have they? Consider a few ways in which one might argue these points. (In Chapter 2, "Global Hunger," we also discuss contrasting views about whether people in developed countries have moral obligations to help the global poor.)

One argument for the conclusion that the persistence of extreme poverty and food insecurity is not unjust is this: Justice requires maximizing the overall well-being of all the people in the world, and this is true of global justice as well as justice within societies. According to this view, if the state of affairs that has maximum overall well-being is one that includes extreme poverty, then this extreme poverty is not an injustice. But note that even if extreme poverty is not unjust and we do not have justice-based obligations to address it, we still have might have other ethical obligations to help the world's poor. For example, as explained in Chapter 2, Peter Singer argues that you are ethically required either to give away much of your wealth to help the extremely poor in lesser-developed countries or else to do something of comparable ethical significance instead.

Next consider a different sort of argument for the conclusion that people in developed countries do not act unjustly when they fail to address extreme poverty and food insecurity in developing countries: Obligations of justice hold only between people in the same society; thus, our failure to address poverty in other societies is not unjust. According to one way of spelling out this argument, obligations of justice hold only between people who are engaged in a cooperative venture for mutual benefit, and people in developed countries are not engaged in such a cooperative venture with the poor in developing countries, and thus people in developed countries do not have obligations of justice toward the poor in developing countries. In response, one might argue that the global economy does involve the relevant kind of economic cooperation between people living in different countries, and thus people in developed countries do have obligations of justice toward people in developing countries. (Recall from Chapter 2, "Global Hunger," that Charles Beitz makes just this point, arguing that relations of reciprocity do hold between people in different nations, and thus justice-based obligations to address poverty apply globally and not just within nations.)

Next consider a different sort of argument for the conclusion that the persistence of extreme poverty and food insecurity is not unjust: justice requires fair terms of cooperation between nations and between people living in different countries, but justice does not require that cooperative activity results in everyone achieving a certain standard of living. So long as the global economy is characterized by terms of cooperation that are fair, the resulting distribution of wealth is fair and is not unjust—even if some people live in extreme poverty and are food insecure. In response to this argument, one might reply that the terms of cooperation are not fair, for the reasons mentioned earlier, namely that trade and economic policies disproportionately benefit wealthier countries, and poorer countries agree to these terms of trade because they are exploited or coerced into agreeing. According to this reply, the poverty and food insecurity in poorer countries are unjust to the extent that they result from these unfair terms of cooperation between richer and poorer countries.

As this discussion has demonstrated, whether a state of affairs is unjust is a highly complicated question, which depends on the nature of the state of affairs and the events that led up to it (for example, was someone coerced? Was it the result of fair terms of cooperation?), and also depends upon one's theory of justice (do obligations of justice require that everyone have a certain level of important things, or just require fair terms of cooperation?) and also depends upon one's view about the scope of justice (do obligations of justice apply only to the members of one's own society or nation, or do they apply globally?).

DOES THE GLOBAL ECONOMY VIOLATE THE HUMAN RIGHTS OF THE GLOBAL POOR?

Another way of arguing that poverty and food insecurity are unjust appeals to our negative duties not to harm others. Thomas Pogge gives such an argument in his influential paper, "Are We Violating the Human Rights of the World's Poor?"[26] Pogge argues that the rules and institutions that govern the global economy produce high and avoidable rates of poverty in developing countries, and that when citizens of developed countries participate in these arrangements, they are violating the human rights of the world's poor.

First, Pogge makes the case that a significant percentage of the world's people do not have access to an adequate standard of living:

> Following the *Universal Declaration* [United Nations Universal Declaration of Human Rights], we might define a poor individual as one who does not have access "to a standard of living adequate for the health and well-being of himself and of his family, including food, clothing, housing and medical care." This is a vague definition, but it clearly includes a large percentage of the world's population. In 2005, the median annual income was $465, which means that half the world's people were living on less than $9 a week (the global average weekly income was $66). This surely sounds like poverty, but one must bear in mind that basic foodstuffs may cost in a poor country only half, a third, or an even smaller fraction of what they cost in the United States. So, depending on the prices of basic necessities in the various poor countries, some in the poorer half may plausibly be said to enjoy (and some in the top half to lack) an adequate standard of living. Still, such plausible adjustments do not alter the fact that a large percentage of the world's people lack the income necessary for basic survival and sustenance according to the *Universal Declaration*'s definition. This includes almost all those who, in 2005, belonged to the poorest thirty percent of humanity and thus lived on less than $4 a week. Even with substantially lower prices of basic necessities, their standard of living cannot plausibly be deemed adequate.[27]

Pogge thinks that we could reduce global poverty levels below what they are, if we modified the rules and institutions governing the global economy; but we—citizens of wealthy nations—do not advocate for that change. Pogge notes that "the shortfall of the world's poor from an adequate standard of living was about 2 percent of global household income or 1.2 percent of world income (the sum of all gross national incomes). . . . . Given these facts, it would be very hard indeed to make a good case for the claim that the massive poverty persisting today was not reasonably avoidable."[28] In other words, these high rates of poverty are easily avoidable, and it would not take much for citizens of wealthy countries to dramatically reduce global poverty.

These high and avoidable rates of poverty are not only bad for people, they are a human rights deficit, Pogge argues, because all people have a human right to a secure standard of living. When we, citizens of wealthy nations, support the institutions and rules that allow avoidable poverty to continue, this amounts to imposing institutions on other people that prevent their human rights from being fulfilled. This, Pogge argues, is a violation of our duty to respect others' rights—that is, the duty "'not to take any measures that result in prevent-ing' a human being from having secure access to the object of a human right."[29] So, in other words, our support for institutions that produce high and avoidable rates of poverty is a violation of the human rights of the world's poor.

Notice that Pogge argues that our support for institutions that produce avoidable poverty is a violation of a *negative duty*; a negative duty, recall, is a duty to refrain from acting in a certain way. Many proponents of human rights believe that we also have *positive duties* to take active steps to ensure that others' human rights get fulfilled. On an influential way of understanding human rights, part of claiming that there is a human right to something (e.g., food) is claiming that others have duties to *respect*, *protect*, and *fulfill* rights. Duties to re-spect rights are negative duties, which require only that we do *not* act in some way; but duties to protect and fulfill rights are positive duties, which require active intervention. For example, the UN Committee on Economic, Social and Cultural Rights understands the right to food as involving duties on governments and individuals not to interfere with existing access to food (*duties to respect*), as well as duties to protect people's food access from in-terference from others (*duties to protect*), duties to strengthen people's access to food (*duties to fulfill/facilitate*), and duties to provide.

Of course, this is just one way of understanding the right to food, and one way of under-standing human rights more generally. As discussed in Chapter 2, not all ethicists agree that human rights involve positive duties to facilitate rights fulfillment and provide access to the object of the right, as opposed to just involving negative duties. Similarly, not all ethicists agree that the situation of the global poor amounts to an injustice or a human rights violation, even if it is a terrible state of affairs. In addition, not everyone agrees with Pogge that the global economy perpetuates poverty that could be avoided with better rules and institutions.[30]

OPPOSITION TO NEOLIBERALISM

Assume, for the sake of argument, that the problems just described ought to be remedied, whether or not they are all injustices or human rights violations. In general terms, how should these problems be solved? By charities and non-governmental organizations providing more assistance and aid? Or do these problems demand systemic changes—that is, changes to laws, policies, and institutions? Can these problems be corrected by better policies, better trade rules, and better regulation within the existing global food system, such as minimum wage laws and stricter environmental regulations?[31] Or are these problems an inevitable result of the basic structure of the global food system, in which case justice demands a radically different global food system?

Some scholars and activists think the latter. In their view, the root problem is that the food system, like the global economy more generally, is *industrialized*, *globalized,* and based in *neoliberalism,* the political economic system emphasizing free market capitalism and a minimal state. Some scholars and activists see neoliberalism in particular as the root cause of many problems with the global food system. To understand this criticism, it's necessary to understand what scholars and activists critical of neoliberalism mean by "neoliberalism." This description, by food scholars Alison Hope Alkon and Teresa Mares, is representative:

> Neoliberalism is a political economic philosophy that asserts the primacy of the market in attending to human needs and well-being, and re-orients the state towards the facilitation of market mechanisms. . . . [N]eoliberalism's ostensible objective is increased efficiency, which its adherents believe is derived from the free flow of capital. Some of neoliberalism's most important components include deregulation (the removal of laws restricting the ways that markets can function, or that favor one industry or product over another), trade liberalization (the removal of protectionist tariffs designed to foster local consumption), and the privatization of state enterprises and public services. Each of these practices results in the market's growing influence over various aspects of social life. Indeed, scholars and critics use the term neoliberal subjectivities to denote the ways that this market logic increasingly pervades individuals' and communities' everyday thoughts and practices as we embrace such ideals as individualism, efficiency, and self-help.[32]

Neoliberal policies are seen as driving the globalization of the food system and encouraging the spread of industrial agriculture:

> Most fundamentally, the liberalization of trade for agricultural commodities was essential to the formation of a corporate food regime. . . . Often mandated by international agencies such as the World Bank and International Monetary Fund in exchange for loans, the removal of tariffs and state assistance that once protected farmers in the global south forced them to compete with subsidized exports from industrialized countries and land grabs by multinational corporations. This devastated the economic livelihoods of peasant farmers and also yielded the consolidation and corporatization of the food industry worldwide.[33]

Along with free markets and free trade, another component of neoliberalism is the scaling back or dismantling of government programs—for example, reducing levels of food assistance and other welfare programs. Thus, neoliberalism is held responsible both for agricultural and trade policies that perpetuate poverty and food insecurity in developing countries, and for inadequate levels of government food assistance in the United States that perpetuate food insecurity among low-income people.

Return to the alternative food movement mentioned previously. As we noted, it has come in for some criticism on grounds that it is culturally imperialist. A different criticism comes from some activists and scholars who argue it fails to mount a significant challenge to neoliberalism, and even shores up the ideology behind neoliberalism.[34] Alternative food projects are criticized for proposing private and market-based solutions to problems, and thereby reinforcing the neoliberal view that the government does not have responsibility for addressing these problems and that private, market-based solutions are preferable. For example, when the alternative food movement encourages individuals to choose locally grown, sustainably produced food, this implies that the solution to environmentally unsustainable agriculture is a market-based one, not government-based like changes in agricultural policy. Similarly, when non-profit organizations start community gardens in low-income communities to increase food security and food access among residents, this is an example of private citizens solving a problem that ought to be solved by government with better-funded food assistance programs.

FOOD SOVEREIGNTY

This criticism of the alternative food movement finds it not alternative enough, as simply tinkering with the status quo in a way that does not root out its fundamental injustices. A radical departure from the status quo is proposed by the *food sovereignty* movement. As described in more detail in the reading "Food Security and Food Sovereignty," by Paul B. Thompson, the food sovereignty movement is a social movement that grew out of La Via Campesina, a peasants' movement originating in Latin America. The movement comprises a "diverse amalgamation of small-scale, peasant, and landless famers, rural workers, women, youth, and indigenous peoples," as one proponent describes it.[35] It proposes smaller-scale food systems that are democratically controlled at the local and regional level, rather than globalized, industrialized food systems controlled by multinational companies and by international agreements made between national governments. As described by Alkon and Mares:

> Food sovereignty is the International Peasant Movement's demand that all people have the right "to healthy and culturally appropriate food produced through ecologically sound and sustainable methods, and their right to define their own food and agriculture systems." In many parts of the global south, and in some regions of the global north, it has become a rallying cry against the ways that the global agribusiness system devastates the livelihoods of smallholder farmers. In contrast to a corporate food regime characterized by monopolistic control of production, governance by multilateral organizations and nation-states in the global north, vast reliance on chemical inputs, and increasing disparities in food access amid growing food production, the food sovereignty approach prioritizes production for local and domestic markets, demands fair prices for food producers, and emphasizes community control over productive resources such as land, water, and seeds. Food sovereignty moves beyond a focus on food security—access to sufficient food—to advocate for communities' rights to produce for themselves rather than remain dependent on international commodities markets.[36]

The food sovereignty movement advocates for greater local and national control of agriculture and food policies, and embraces a range of goals that are perceived as compatible with—and furthered by—this control. These goals include communal control of land, water, and seeds (rather than private land-holders owning very large farms and multinational corporations owning seeds), respect for the farming practices of peasants and indigenous peoples, gender equality, and greater income equality, which is expected to follow from changing how land, other natural resources, and food are controlled.

The food sovereignty movement rejects mainstream approaches to increasing food security, and it rejects many of the assumptions seen to underlie these approaches—for example, the assumption that the best way to address poverty is to incorporate the global poor into the global economy, and the assumption that ensuring food security for all people requires increasing agricultural outputs and efficiency through industrial methods. For many proponents, food sovereignty is seen as an alternative to the "food security" paradigm. As explained by William Schanbacher:

> Many multilateral organizations such as the World Bank, IMF, WTO, and the United Nations (UN) have utilized the term *food security* to describe the global effort to eliminate hunger and malnutrition. . . . The concept of food security emerged in the 20th century as post-WWII reconstruction efforts and the decolonization of many Third World countries created a global food regime that was managed through complex local, national, and international relations. With the creation of the IMG, World Bank, and more recently, the WTO, food security is increasingly sought through economic policies including trade liberalization, privatization, deregulation of national industry, and the opening of economic markets. The guiding principle for these multilateral institutions is the idea that economic growth, via market mechanisms, provides the most suitable solution for curbing poverty and achieving food security. However, critics of these strategies point to how a purely market-based approach to food security remains entrenched in neocolonial power structures that have failed to create a just global food system. . . .
>
> Given these failures, an alternative concept and movement known as food sovereignty is garnering worldwide interest and support. . . .
>
> [A] critical analysis of the food security and food sovereignty models reveals fundamental antagonisms between the way hunger and malnutrition are conceived within these two constructs. Ultimately, the food security model is founded on, and reinforces, a model of globalization that reduces human relationships to their economic value. Alternatively, the food sovereignty model considers human relations in terms of mutual dependence, cultural diversity, and respect for the environment. Because food security has not been achieved for hundreds of millions of the world's poor, it is imperative that the food sovereignty model take center stage in the fight against global hunger and malnutrition. Furthermore, not only do we need to conceive of food as a human right, but, as food sovereignty argues, our definition of food should include the ways in which the poor deserve to have access to healthy, nutritious, and culturally important types of food. . . . Ultimately, if food sovereignty's demands are not met, the current global food system constitutes a massive violation of human rights.[37]

According to the food sovereignty movement, the right way to reduce poverty and food insecurity is not to impose industrial agricultural methods and incorporate small farmers into the global economy. The reading "Food Security and Food Sovereignty" describes in more detail the food sovereignty movement's critique of the food security paradigm, and the reading "Declaration of Nyéléni" sets out the principles of the food sovereignty movement in more detail.

Critics of anti-neoliberalist views such as food sovereignty believe that globalized markets are essential for improving the situation of the global poor, and that it would be a grave mistake to disassemble the globalized economy based on free trade, and that this would actually have the effect of making the poor far worse off. Some experts think that making global trade even freer than it actually is would reduce poverty in developing countries and reduce inequality between developing and developed countries.[38]

FURTHER ISSUES

1. *Collective Self-Determination and Oppressive Practices*
In the reading "Food Justice and Collective Food Relations," Kyle Powys Whyte emphasizes
the importance of the collective self-determination of groups. Whyte emphasizes that one
form of injustice is interfering with groups' collective relations; justice requires not interfering with groups' collective relations, unless there is a morally weighty reason for this compulsion or interference. What if groups' collective relations treat some members unjustly, as
judged from our perspective? What does justice demand in these cases? What does justice
demand when there is a conflict between the group's self-determination and sovereignty
(right to govern itself), on the one hand, and the equality and self-determination of individual group members, on the other hand?

2. *Food Deserts and Institutional Racism*
Food deserts—neighborhoods without a supermarket or other sources of healthier foods—
are a food justice issue. Lack of access to healthy food could be seen as a distributive justice
issue: There's an unfair distribution of food resources; richer neighborhoods have many
more supermarkets per capita than poorer neighborhoods, which contributes to an unfair
distribution of health outcomes. But food deserts are also seen by some theorists and activists as a racial justice issue, because they are rooted in a history of *institutional racism*.
Racist housing policies during the twentieth century allowed whites but not blacks to obtain
mortgages, purchases houses in the suburbs, and accumulate wealth. Low-income urban
communities of color are a legacy of these racist housing policies—and these communities
are now more likely to be food deserts. What is the appropriate response to historical injustice, for instance this history of institutional racism?

3. *Fair Opportunity vs. Equality of Outcomes*
Does justice demand that people have healthier diets, or just that they have *the opportunity*
to have healthier diets? Suppose that someone can afford to eat healthy food and has access
to it in her neighborhood, but she prefers eating unhealthy food. Does justice require that she
eat healthfully, or just that she has a meaningful opportunity to eat healthfully? What if she
prefers eating unhealthy food because she was raised eating it, because this was all her
family could afford? Did she have a meaningful opportunity to develop healthy preferences?
Does she now have a meaningful opportunity to have a healthy diet?

FURTHER READING

Food Justice

Alkon, Alison Hope, and Julian Agyeman. 2011. *Cultivating Food Justice: Race, Class, and Sustainability.* Cambridge, MA: MIT Press (especially "Introduction: the Food Movement as Polyculture,"
pp. 1–20).
Allen, Patricia. 2010. "Realizing Justice in Local Food Systems." *Cambridge Journal of Regions,
Economy and Society* 3: 295–308.

DuPuis, E. Melanie, Jill Lindsey Harrison, and David Goodman. 2011. "Just Food?" in Alkon and Agyeman, *Cultivating Food Justice*, 283–307.

Food and Agricultural Organisation (FAO). 2011. *The State of Food and Agriculture*. Rome: FAO.

Powers, Madison. "Emerging Issues of Justice in the Global Food System." *FEW Resources.org*. http://www.FEWResources.org/food-overview-of-issues.html (accessed January 28, 2016).

Food Sovereignty

Alkon, Alison Hope, and Teresa Marie Mares. 2012. "Food Sovereignty in US Food Movements: Radical Visions and Neoliberal Constraints." *Agriculture and Human Values* 29: 347–359.

Schanbacher, William D. 2010. *The Politics of Food: The Global Conflict between Food Security and Food Sovereignty*. Santa Barbara, CA: ABC-CLIO, LLC (especially Chapter 1, "Globalization, Development, Food Security, and the Emergence of a Global Food Regime," pp. 1–23, and Chapter 4, "Human Rights, Human Responsibilities, and the Capabilities Approach," pp. 77–95).

Justice and Human Rights

Pogge, Thomas. 2011. "Are We Violating the Rights of the World's Poor?" *Yale Human Rights and Development Law Journal* 14, no. 2: 1–33.

Powers, Madison. "Global Justice Overview." *FEW Resources.org*. http://www.fewresources.org/global-justice-overview.html (accessed January 28, 2016).

Rawls, John. 1971. *A Theory of Justice*. Cambridge, MA: Harvard University Press.

Young, Iris Marion. 1991. *Justice and the Politics of Difference*. Princeton, NJ: Princeton University Press.

The Effects of Globalized, Industrialized Agriculture on the Global Poor

Anderson, Kym. 2015. "Food Price and Trade Policy Biases," in Ronald J. Herring, ed., *Oxford Handbook of Food, Politics, and Society*, 1st ed. New York: Oxford University Press. http://www.oxfordhandbooks.com/view/10.1093/oxfordhb/9780195397772.013.009/oxfordhb-9780195397772-e-009.

Powers, Madison. "Developing Economies & Human Development." *FEW Resources.org*. http://www.FEWResources.org/global-development-issues.html (accessed January 28, 2016).

———. "Natural Resource Curse." *FEW Resources.org*. http://www.FEWResources.org/natural-resource-curse.html (accessed January 28, 2016).

Ritzer, George, and Elizabeth L. Malone. 2000. "Globalization Theory: Lessons from the Exportation of McDonaldization and the New Means of Consumption." *American Studies* 41: 97–118.

Sandler, Ronald L. 2014. "Food Systems" (ch. 1) and "Food Security and the Ethics of Assistance" (ch. 2) in *Food Ethics: The Basics*. New York: Routledge, 4–44, 45–73.

Schanbacher, William D. 2010. "Introduction" and "The Underside of Development" (ch. 2) in *The Politics of Food: The Global Conflict between Food Security and Food Sovereignty*. Santa Barbara, CA: ABC-CLIO, LLC, vii–xvii, 25–51.

Food Deserts

Handbury, Jessie, Ilya Rahkovsky, and Molly Schnell. 2015. "Is the Focus on Food Deserts Fruitless? Retail Access and Food Purchases across the Socioeconomic Spectrum." http://www.brown.edu/

academics/economics/sites/brown.edu.academics.economics/files/uploads/Jesse%20Handbury_
Is%20the%20focus%20on%20food_Paper.pdf.
Morales, Alfonso. 2011. "Growing Food and Justice: Dismantling Racism through Sustainable Food
Systems," in Alkon and Agyeman, *Cultivating Food Justice*, 149–176.

Food Insecurity in the United States

Jacobson, Kristi, and Silverbush, Lori, directors. 2013. *A Place at the Table*. Magnolia Pictures.
Winne, Mark. 2009. *Closing the Food Gap: Resetting the Table in the Land of Plenty*. Boston: Beacon
Press.
Witnesses to Hunger website. n.d. http://www.centerforhungerfreecommunities.org/our-projects/
witnesses-hunger.

Indigenous Peoples and First Foods

Nelson, Melissa K. 2014. "Protecting the Sanctity of Native Foods," in The Worldwatch Institute, ed.,
State of the World 2013: Is Sustainability Still Possible? Washington, DC: Island Press.
Norgaard, Kari Marie, Ron Reed, and Carolina Van Horn. 2011. "A Continuing Legacy: Institutional
Racism, Hunger and Nutritional Justice on the Klamath," in Alkon and Agyeman, *Cultivating
Food Justice*.

Collective Self-Determination and Oppressive Practices

Casal, Paula. 2003. "Is Multiculturalism Bad for Animals?" *Journal of Political Philosophy* 11, no. 1: 1–22.
Okin, Susan Moller. 1999. "Is Multiculturalism Bad for Women?" in *Is Multiculturalism Bad for
Women?* Princeton, NJ: Princeton University Press, 7–24.

Restaurant Workers

Jayaraman, Saru. 2013. *Behind the Kitchen Door*. Ithaca, NY: Cornell University Press.

NOTES

1. For a discussion of the price differential between categories of foods (e.g., sugary drinks, fruits and vegetables, fats, etc.), see Eric Finkelstein and Laurie Zuckerman, *The Fattening of America: How the Economy Makes Us Fat, If It Matters, and What to Do about It* (Hoboken, NJ: Wiley, 2008), 19–22.

2. Patricia Allen, "Realizing Justice in Local Food Systems." *Cambridge Journal of Regions, Economy and Society* (2010) 3: 295–308, P. 297.

3. Just Food, "What Is Food Justice?" http://justfood.org/advocacy/what-is-food-justice

4. Institute for Agriculture and Trade Policy, "Draft Principles of Food Justice." http://www.iatp .org/documents/draft-principles-of-food-justice#sthash.Q4XHqUQm.dpuf

5. John Rawls, *A Theory of Justice* (Cambridge, MA: Harvard University Press, 1971). For criticisms of Rawls's view and a discussion of how justice is conceived by food activists, see E. Melanie Dupais, Jill Lindsey Harrison, and David Goodman, "Just Food?" in *Cultivating Food Justice: Race, Class, and Sustainability* (Cambridge, MA: The MIT Press, 2011), pp. 283–307.

6. Iris Marion Young, *Justice and the Politics of Difference* (Princeton, NJ: Princeton University Press, 1991), 41.

7. Margaret L. Andersen and Patricia Hill Collins, *Race, Class and Gender: An Anthology,* 7th ed. (Independence, KY: Wadsworth, 2009), 67.

8. Ibid., 67.

9. Susan Moller Okin, "Is Multiculturalism Bad for Women?" in *Is Multiculturalism Bad for Women?* (Princeton, NJ: Princeton University Press, 1999), 7–24. Paula Casal, "Is Multiculturalism Bad for Animals?" *Journal of Political Philosophy* (2003) 11, no. 1: 1–22.

10. Mark Winne, *Closing the Food Gap: Resetting the Table in the Land of Plenty* (Boston: Beacon Press, 2009), 125.

11. Alison Hope Alkon and Julian Agyeman, "Introduction: The Food Movement as Polyculture," in Alison Hope Alkon and Julian Agyeman (eds.), *Cultivating Food Justice: Race, Class, and Sustainability* (Cambridge, MA: MIT Press, 2011), pp. 1–20.

12. Ibid., 3.
Alison Hope Alkon and Teresa Marie Mares, "Food Sovereignty in US Food Movements: Radical Visions and Neoliberal Constraints." *Agriculture and Human Values* (2012) 29: 347–359, see pp. 352–355.

13. George Ritzer and Elizabeth L. Malone. "Globalization Theory: Lessons from the Exportation of McDonaldization and the New Means of Consumption." *American Studies* (2000) 97–118; Popkin, Barry M., Linda S. Adair, and Shu Wen Ng. "Now and Then: The Global Nutrition Transition: The Pandemic of Obesity in Developing Countries." *Nutrition Reviews* 70, no. 1 (January 2012): 3–21. doi:10.1111/j.1753-4887.2011.00456.x.

14. Saturnino M. Borras and Jennifer C. Franco. "Food, Justice and Land." In *The Oxford Handbook of Food, Politics, and Society*, edited by Ronald J. Herring, 1st ed. (New York: Oxford University Press, 2015).

15. Food and Agriculture Organization, "Women Play a Decisive Role in Household Food Security, Dietary Diversity and Children's Health" (2016). http://www.fao.org/gender/gender-home/gender-programme/gender-food/en/

16. Ibid.

17. Heidi Shierholz, "Low Wages and Few Benefits Mean Many Restaurant Workers Can't Make Ends Meet," *EPI Briefing Paper* #383 (2014); Roberto Ferdman, "There's a Big Gap between What Men and Women Make in the Restaurant Industry," *Washington Post*, August 28, 2014. See, too, the Jayuraman reading in Chapter 11, "Workers."

18. Bina Agarwal. "Food Security, Productivity, and Gender Inequality." In *The Oxford Handbook of Food, Politics, and Society*, edited by Ronald J. Herring, 1st ed. (New York: Oxford University Press, 2015). http://www.oxfordhandbooks.com/view/10.1093/oxfordhb/9780195397772.013.002/oxfordhb-9780195397772-e-002, p. 286.

19. Ibid., 286–287.

20. A. Aizer and J. Currie. "The Intergenerational Transmission of Inequality: Maternal Disadvantage and Health at Birth." *Science* 344, no. 6186 (May 23, 2014): 856–861. doi:10.1126/science.1251872.

21. Ibid.

22. Ronald L. Sandler, "Food Systems" (ch.1) and "Food Security and the Ethics of Assistance" (ch.2) in *Food Ethics: The Basics* (New York: Routledge, 2014), 4–44, 45–73.
William D. Schanbacher, "Introduction" and "The Underside of Development" (ch. 2) in *The Politics of Food: The Global Conflict between Food Security and Food Sovereignty* (Santa Barbara, CA: ABC-CLIO, LLC, 2010), vii-xvii, 25–51.

23. Ibid. For discussion of the effects of effects of agricultural and development policies on the global poor, see Madison Powers, "Developing Economies & Human Development." *FEW Resources. org.* Accessed January 28, 2016. http://www.FEWResources.org/global-development-issues.html, and

Madison Powers, "Food, Fairness, and Global Markets," forthcoming in the Oxford Handbook of Food Ethics, eds. Anne Barnhill, Mark Budolfson, and Tyler Doggett (New York: Oxford University Press). For discussion of export-led agricultural policies in particular, see Madison Powers, "Natural Resource Curse." *FEW Resources.org.* Accessed January 28, 2016. http://www.FEWResources.org/natural-resource-curse.html.

24. Thomas Pogge, "Are We Violating the Rights of the World's Poor?" *Yale Human Rights and Development Law Journal* 14, no. 2 (2014): 1–33.

25. Ibid., pp. 1–2.

26. Ibid., p. 23.

27. Ibid., p. 9.

28. See Chapter 2, "Global Hunger," for further discussion of this issue. For a concise discussion of whether or not the globalization and industrialization of agriculture exacerbate food insecurity among the global poor, see Sandler 2014, chapters 1–2.

29. Sandler, 41.

30. Alkon and Agyeman 2012, 348. Citations removed from excerpted passage.

31. Ibid., 348–349. Citations removed from excerpted passage.

32. Alison Hope Alkon and Teresa Marie Mares, "Food Sovereignty in US Food Movements: Radical Visions and Neoliberal Constraints." *Agriculture and Human Values* 29 (2012): 347–359.

33. Schanbacher, viii.

34. Alkon and Mares, 347. Citations removed from excerpted passage.

35. Schanbacher, vii–ix

36. Kym Anderson, "Food Price and Trade Policy Biases." In *The Oxford Handbook of Food, Politics, and Society,* edited by Ronald J. Herring, 1st ed. (New York: Oxford University Press, 2015). http://www.oxfordhandbooks.com/view/10.1093/oxfordhb/9780195397772.013.009/oxfordhb-9780195397772-e-009.

MARIANNA CHILTON

Witnesses to Hunger

These two readings are excerpts from *A Place at the Table*, a companion book to the documentary film *A Place at the Table*. Both readings discuss malnutrition and food insecurity. The first excerpt, written by Marianna Chilton, discusses the scope of food insecurity in the United States and describes the negative effects of food insecurity on children's health and development. The second excerpt, written by the Food Research Action Council (FRAC), an anti-hunger and anti-poverty organization, describes the experience of one father whose family was food insecure. These readings help make clear why food insecurity is a particularly bad form of deprivation, and why food security is seen as a particularly important social justice goal.

. . . Some people might think that hunger is a moral problem. Some think it's political. Some consider it a mere economic problem. Although hunger is each of these, it is also a major public health problem. Not only does hunger hold us back today, but it will burden us for generations if we don't take bold action to treat and prevent it.

In the film [*A Place at the Table*] you see me interviewing a young woman with her son. I am asking her questions about depression, about her child's health, and about food insecurity. One of the questions is, "In the last twelve months, did you ever cut the size of your meals or skip meals because there wasn't enough money for food?" It's one of eighteen questions in the Household Food Security Survey Module, taken from the US Department of Agriculture's Economic Research Service (ERS).[1] I was carrying out an interview for our Children's HealthWatch study, which is a multi-site research and surveillance study that investigates how public policies affect the health and well-being of young children under the age of four. The answers to my questions tell us whether the mother is "food-insecure" or has experienced depressive symptoms. Our research shows that, compared to young children in food-secure households, infants and toddlers in food-insecure households are:

- Thirty percent more likely to have a history of hospitalization
- Ninety percent more likely to be reported in fair or poor health
- Nearly twice as likely to have iron deficiency anemia
- Two-thirds more likely to be at risk for developmental delays[2]

These are just a few of the health consequences. (For more information on the effects of hunger on very small children, please see the Children's Health-Watch website, www.childrenshealthwatch.org.) The most significant of these is the impact that food insecurity has on child development. Any kind of nutritional deprivation, however short, in the first three years of life can have lifelong consequences for children. It affects their cognitive development and ability to get along with others, their stature, their weight, and their brain at a much deeper level.

In those first one thousand days of life, the foundation and architecture of the brain is built at a rapid pace. In fact, during the first few years of life, seven hundred new neural connections (or synapses) are formed each second. (For more information, visit the Center for the Developing Child website, http://developingchild.harvard.edu/.) Because good nutrition provides the building blocks for brain development, any type of nutritional deprivation can slow down or truncate brain growth, causing lifelong consequences. In addition, research shows that a child's development is not based on nutrition alone but also on the amount of interaction between the caregiver and the child. So if a family is food-insecure and the mom is depressed, the child is deprived of both essential nutrients and the social stimulation necessary for social and cognitive development.

After age three or four, that window for cognitive, social, and emotional development begins to close. Economists show that it will be far more costly to bring a child up to speed after that window of opportunity is gone.[3] Imagine the public health problems that are unleashed because of poor child development. Not only are such children more liable to poor health, but add the other grim possibilities—poor school performance, higher dropout rates, lack of job skills, low wages, depression, maybe prison, and/or more likely high-risk teen pregnancy, which begins the cycle of hunger and poverty anew.

In America, approximately one in four (nine million) young children under the age of six lived in food-insecure households in 2010. Households experiencing even more severe forms of food insecurity are those where parents limit the size and quantity of their children's meals or their children do not eat for a whole day because there is not enough money for food. Very few families ever admit that their children "go hungry," by these USDA standards. And some research shows that families do try to protect the youngest children from experiencing food insecurity, at the expense of others in the household. Back in 2006, approximately 0.4 percent of children under age six (140,000 children) were reported to be food-insecure at this level of severity.[4] During the economic downturn, this rate of severe food insecurity increased by 250 percent. Now there are 533,000 very young children who are at severe risk.[5]

All this happens without much public outcry or substantive political discussion and with no public acknowledgment from US government agencies. The American public can't "see" the problem, and the moms who know about it are so busy struggling to pull out of their predicament that they can't take the time to figure out how to advertise their plight. This is why the story of Barbie Izquierdo—one of the young mothers we took to Congress and the first mother to join Witnesses to Hunger—is so important. Consider her son Aiden, age two when filming started, who has displayed signs of speech delay. Barbie described her hunger to us, and how the struggle manifests itself in her children's behavior and in her depression. Thankfully, our social work team encouraged her to seek early intervention services, and Aiden is doing much better. So is Barbie. But imagine the millions of women like Barbie, and the nine million children under age six, who are in food-insecure homes.

Hunger doesn't happen just by itself, when everything else is fine. It happens when a family has to make a trade-off—pay for rent when they need to pay for food, or pay for heat rather than groceries.[6] Children's HealthWatch has shown that housing insecurity and energy insecurity (not being able to pay utility bills) are harmful to children's health as well, but our latest research shows that food insecurity is also related to making what we call health care trade-offs. Too often food-insecure families are not seeing a doctor, or not buying medicine, in order to be able to have money for food, or vice versa. Parents sacrifice not only their food in order to feed their kids but their own health.

In our work with Children's HealthWatch, a Philadelphia woman described the trade-offs she had to make to prevent her children's acute asthma attacks. After one of her children was hospitalized, she had to buy a nebulizer to deliver the asthma medication through a mist, yet had no funds. She said in her interview in January 2010 that she had to make the terrible choice of paying for a nebulizer, which insurance would not cover, or paying for food. She said she had to ask herself, "Do you want to breathe? Or do you want to eat?"

* * *

We started Witnesses to Hunger out of frustration at the way people continue to ignore hunger, try to deny it exists, or worse, are indifferent. The women we met through Children's HealthWatch and other research among the emergency food cupboards of Philadelphia were trying so hard to make it and to provide the best for their children. What our science didn't capture in the interviews was the anguish and sometimes the tears that a mother showed when she was answering our questionnaire. There was a lot of pain there. There was also a lot of energy, enthusiasm, grit, entrepreneurial spirit, and street genius. Yet these positive characteristics were being ignored and shut out from the halls of Congress.

As part of Witnesses to Hunger, my team and I gave digital cameras to forty-two women in Philadelphia, several of whom we met in the emergency room through our research with Children's HealthWatch. We asked them to take the lead in describing their experiences of raising their children and to give us their ideas for improving the systems meant to help them.

Now we have a traveling exhibit of their photos, a website searchable by woman, child, topic, or policy issue, and an expert speakers bureau of women who know hunger and poverty best. We visit politicians on

Capitol Hill in Washington, DC, provide testimony, speak at press conferences, and run webinars.

Through Witnesses to Hunger, low-income mothers utilize their photos as a way to open the door to serious conversations on a topic so few people seem to want to discuss. Who best to inform the public and policymakers about how well the programs work than the participants in these programs and those who know hunger and poverty firsthand? And they do so without shame. They engage us with a strong dose of naked truth, expertise, and hope. As an organizing tool to get low-income people to solve the problems most important to their families and communities, Witnesses to Hunger can be started anywhere. It's also a way for the rest of us to pause, listen, witness, and engage.

The moms involved in Witnesses to Hunger have insisted that beyond speaking about policy change, they want to provide encouragement and support to other women and girls. We have started a woman-to-woman peer mentoring program to navigate the chaos of the social services systems in Philadelphia. In addition, the women have developed a tool kit that anyone can use to start Witnesses to Hunger in their own communities. Witnesses to Hunger currently reaches across the state of Pennsylvania—to Scranton, Harrisburg, Johnstown, and Clearfield County. Witnesses has also spread the word to Providence, Rhode Island, Martha's Vineyard Island in Massachusetts, and most recently Baltimore, Maryland, and Boston, Massachusetts.

Anti-hunger organizations can do more to ensure the participation of those who know hunger and poverty best, but it's hard work. It demands that nonprofits pay attention to those things that may not be part of their particular mission, but may be central to the larger mission of human development—the mission of experiencing a life worth living. When the women speak about nutrition assistance, they may also have other related troubles. For example, in the film you see Tianna Gaines, now the chair of the Witnesses to Hunger advisory board and a Witness herself, testifying at the Russell Senate Building about poverty and hunger in 2009. You might remember the way she looked out at Senator Casey, Senator Harkin, the other ladies of Witnesses, and the Senate staffers and said so simply and so powerfully, "This is . . . un, this is unnecessary."

Tianna was homeless at the time. So while some people may have thought she was doing amazing things, such as providing testimony to the Senate, Tianna was still returning "home" to her three young children and her husband in a musty, broken hotel room on the outskirts of Philadelphia. And if a woman so poised, so smart and savvy, could speak out in Congress, it *is* unnecessary—unacceptable—that such a person should be homeless.

At the opening of the photo exhibit of Witnesses to Hunger in December 2008, we had a full house despite torrential, freezing rains. Barbie Izquierdo was so thrilled to speak at the exhibit, but she went home afterward to an unsafe house that was imploding. Barbie lived in a house she could not afford to fix, a house located on a warring drug dealers' street, and that night rainwater from the leaks through the roof was spilling over the buckets she'd put out to catch it. In her basement was two to three feet of water. Her children's laundry was floating about in plastic bags, and the washing machine was covered in mud.

Such are the stories from Witnesses to Hunger that go way beyond hunger. They reveal the full experience of what it means to be a human being living in poverty. And they make us question our very humanity when we simply accept that so many among us, through no fault of their own, are so hungry and so poor.

Remember how Barbie's speech ends the film: Do you feel my hunger? Do you feel my pain? What she is saying is, I am no different than you. You and I are the same. We are a part of the human family. How can this not grip you? It's like looking in the mirror.

SOME URGENT PROPOSALS

Hunger knocks the breath out of you. But that doesn't mean we can't solve it. The primary solution is a comprehensive anti-hunger policy that can stimulate economic growth and protect our most vulnerable citizens.

The safety net works but needs urgent improvement. Children's HealthWatch has strong evidence that the safety net programs can help improve child health and well-being.

1. The Supplemental Nutrition Assistance Program (SNAP), the food stamp program, is an effective and efficient way to address and prevent hunger. Children's Health Watch research shows that SNAP benefits help protect child health.
   • SNAP improves the odds that a child will experience healthy development.
   • SNAP reduces the odds of severe and moderate food insecurity.
   • SNAP is associated with a reduction in the odds of having to make a health care trade-off.

For more information, see our report "The SNAP Vaccine: Boosting Children's Health" at www.childrenshealthwatch.org.

2. The Special Supplemental Nutrition Program for Women, Infants, and Children (WIC) is a program for pregnant and lactating moms and for young children up to age five. A family must be at 185 percent of the poverty level or lower to be eligible. Shockingly, child poverty in our country is so high that 53 percent of babies (up to their first birthday) born today are participating in the WIC program.
   • Children under age three who receive WIC benefits are more likely to be in excellent or good health compared to eligible children who do not receive WIC benefits.
   • Receipt of WIC benefits is linked to a decrease in the risk of developmental delays in young children.

• WIC is associated with decreased levels of stress—a composite measure of food insecurity and depressive symptoms.

For more information, visit www.childrenshealthwatch.org.

3. Just as housing insecurity and energy insecurity are related to food insecurity and fair to poor child health, our research shows that programs that help to alleviate some of those stresses have a positive public health impact. The Low-Income Home Energy Assistance Program (LIHEAP) is associated with a decreased risk of food insecurity and poor child health, and children receiving housing subsidies have better growth outcomes than children in families who do not receive this benefit.

For more information, visit www.childrenshealthwatch.org.

So these programs can work—but they should be expanded, not pinched back. For instance, housing subsidies have long waiting lists, and the Housing Choice Voucher Program (Section 8) is so strapped for funding that even the waiting lists are closed in some cities. So while the "net" is there, it's hardly within reach of many of those who need it.

As Barbie explains in the film, SNAP allotments do not adequately cover the cost of food. Our research shows that in Philadelphia a family of four receiving the maximum allotment of food stamps—assuming no other income—would find it impossible to buy the items on the USDA Thrifty Food Plan on which the allotment allowance is based. For more information, see our report "The Real Cost of a Healthy Diet, 2011" at www.centerforhungerfreecommunities.org. . . .

NOTES

1. Gary Bickel, Mark Nord, Cristofer Price, William Hamilton, and John Cook, *Measuring Food Security in the United States: Guide to Measuring Household Food Security* (Alexandria, VA: US Department of Agriculture, Food and Nutrition Service, Office of Analysis and Evaluation, 2000).

2. John T. Cook and Deborah A. Frank, "Food Security, Poverty, and Human Development in the United States," *Annals of the New York Academy of Sciences* 1136 (2008): 193–209.

3. James J. Heckman, "Skill Formation and the Economics of Investing in Disadvantaged Children," *Science* 312, no. 5782 (2006): 1900–1902.

4. Mark Nord, Margaret Andrews, and Steven Carlson, *Food Insecurity in the United States, 2006* (Washington, DC: US Department of Agriculture, Economic Research Service, 2007).

5. Alisha Coleman-Jensen, Mark Nord, Margaret Andrews, and Steven Carlson, *Statistical Supplement to Household Food Security in the United States in 2010* (Washington, DC: US Department of Agriculture, Economic Research Service, September 2011).

6. Deborah A. Frank, Patrick H. Casey, Maureen M. Black, Ruth Rose-Jacobs, Mariana Chilton, Diana Cutts, et al. "Cumulative Hardship and Wellness of Low-Income, Young Children: Multi-Site Surveillance Study," *Pediatrics* 125, no. 5 (2010): e1115–e1123.

Food Research Action Center

Angel's Story

To understand how families end up in the unhappy situation of skimping on food so as to pay rent, visit with a father like Angel. Angel, who is shy about sharing his last name, lives in Washington, DC, with his wife and two daughters. He and his wife are legal residents and their children are US citizens. Angel moved to the United States from El Salvador about twenty-five years ago, and he speaks English well enough to get by, but not well enough to land a high-skill professional job. He is a hard worker and a devoted family man, and the best job he can find is one stocking shelves and taking inventory thirty-five hours a week at a local grocery store. He wants to work more hours, but his employer keeps him at just under full-time.

Angel earns about $1,400 a month and spends $1,000 of that on his high rent. That leaves $400 a month for groceries for his family of four, clothing for his two girls, bus transportation, electricity, and other necessities.

Angel says that he knows cheaper rent would take some of the pressure off the family budget. However, rents are high in the city, and he doesn't know how to drive. That rules out a move to a more affordable home in the suburbs. More important, Angel wants to stay in the family's current neighborhood because he says it is good for his two daughters. His older daughter's elementary school, which she loves, is walking distance from home. His younger daughter will join her sister at the same school in about a year's time. Angel believes that the most important thing for his children is stability. To give his daughters that, the family continues to spend a prohibitive amount on rent and spends very little on food. For years the family has lived on a diet of eggs, rice, and beans. Angel could barely afford a few of the discounted vegetables offered at the grocery store where he works.

Things improved greatly for the family once Angel started visiting a counselor, named Carlos Merchan, at a local health clinic. Merchan works with low-income men and helps them become better fathers, providers, and family men. Merchan says that Angel, like many of the fathers he works with, was extremely anxious about the scarcity of food in the home. Most of the men Merchan works with hold low-wage jobs and don't earn enough to fully support a household. "They worry constantly about bringing in enough money to take care of their family's needs," says Merchan. "When they can't pay for it all, they feel like they've failed as men."

Angel, he observed, was so anxiety-ridden about food for his family that he couldn't move forward with any other area of his life. "You can't talk to a father about child development and the importance of reading to your child when that father is worried about having enough food in the house," says Merchan. "You have to help the family take care of the basics first." Merchan helped Angel apply for food stamps, and the family was accepted into the program. Angel talked about the difference that food stamps make in the life of his family: "I feel so good every time I open the refrigerator. There's meat, fish, and vegetables. There's fruit that the girls like— strawberries and grapes—and there's vegetables like broccoli and carrots." When asked what the family is now eating for dinner, Angel took a long, satisfied breath and described each meal with great affection and pleasure: "Ahhhh! We now have carne asada, fish fillets, and chicken breast! We have salad, too, and vegetables. All I can say is, 'Thanks be to God and to the government for food stamps!'"

Carlos Merchan says that SNAP benefits give families who live with great uncertainty in their lives some basic measure of security: "So much is uncertain in their lives. Will they still have their job tomorrow? Will they be able to afford a hospital visit if somebody gets hurt or sick? What will they do if the rent goes up? With food stamps, these families can count on one certain thing—they will have enough food for the kids." Merchan says that once families feel secure that one of their basic needs has been

met, they can move forward with other parts of their lives. For example, now that Angel isn't as worried about food, he is starting to focus on a new project— learning how to drive. If Angel learns to drive, he might be better able to take on side jobs to help bring in more income. "Food stamps help families get some of their confidence back," says Merchan. "They feel more confident that things might get better in the future."

Food assistance like SNAP is critical because, like Angel and his family, millions of households simply don't have enough money for food. A recent report by FRAC called "A Tightening Squeeze" finds that the median household's spending on food, when measured against the cost of a diet for a low-income family, fell from 2000 to 2010. The report cites some factors that may be driving this unhappy statistic: stagnant or declining wages, rising housing prices, and food inflation. The trends for the median low-income household and the median black or Hispanic household were especially of concern: all three kinds of household spent a monthly amount on food that was not adequate to support decent nutrition and health, even as defined by the government's inadequate definition of the amount of food needed for an emergency diet.

When families, senior citizens, single adults, and especially children suffer food deprivation, the health repercussions can be brutal. Young children are especially vulnerable, and women who skimp on the quality and quantity of their meals throughout their pregnancies have higher rates of low-birthweight babies, one of the most important factors linked to negative impacts on child development. Children who are hungry are more likely to act up in school, more likely to be absent or tardy, and more likely to repeat a grade.

So many Americans move in and out of joblessness or poverty that the SNAP safety net helps a surprisingly large part of the population. Professor Mark Rank of Washington University has estimated, based on a longitudinal analysis, that half of all children in the United States receive SNAP benefits at some time by age twenty, often for just a few months, and that half of all adults do so at some time between the ages of twenty and sixty-five. In short, the

Supplemental Nutrition Assistance Program, which helps buffer vulnerable Americans from the creeping, insidious damage that malnourishment and hunger can wreak on their health, has helped a remarkable number of people over the years.

QUESTIONS

1. What are some of the health and developmental consequences of living in a food-insecure household during the first three years of life? What might be the long-term impact of these health and development problems on people's lives?

2. Hunger and malnutrition have direct impacts on families, but they also have indirect impacts. What kind of trade-offs do families make in order to pay for food? How did Angel's anxiety about feeding his family impact him?

3. Marianna Chilton is the founder of Witnesses to Hunger. Go to the Witnesses to Hunger website and read about a few of the women profiled. How has poverty and food insecurity affected them and their children?

4. What, if anything, is owed to food-insecure people? If something is owed, who owes it?

5. An influential idea in political philosophy, egalitarianism, is that states of affairs are objectionable to the extent to which they contain certain kinds of inequalities. A rival idea, sufficientarianism, is that inequalities are only objectionable when and because the worse-off people do not have *enough*. The food inequalities these readings describe are objectionable on both grounds. But other inequalities might, to sufficientarians, be unobjectionable. What are some examples? Do you think such inequalities are unjust and objectionable?

KYLE POWYS WHYTE

Food Justice and Collective Food Relations

In this reading, Kyle Powys Whyte discusses the importance of food not only as a source of nutrition but as a *hub* for many collective relations required for a good life. Food brings together the cultural, social, economic, and spiritual aspects of a way of life. Food justice requires that people have food-related goods, such as adequate nutrition, and it requires that people have opportunities for equal participation in decision-making about agriculture and food, but it also requires something more: that human groups have a right to exercise and adapt their collective food relations free from external compulsion or interference. Whyte describes the role of manoomin (wild rice) in the collective food relations of the Anishinaaeb in the Great Lakes region. He describes how activities by Settler Americans have threatened these collective food relations, an instance of food injustice.

WHAT IS FOOD JUSTICE?

What is food justice? Food justice is commonly understood as the norm that everyone should have access to safe, healthy and culturally-appropriate foods no matter one's national origin, economic statuses, social identities, cultural membership, or disability. A second dimension of food justice, as commonly understood, is the norm that everyone who works within a food system, from restaurant servers to farm workers, should be paid livable and fair wages and work in safe conditions no matter one's national origin, economic statuses, social identities, cultural membership, or disability (Schanbacher 2010; Alkon and Agyeman 2011; Jayaraman 2013).

Another dimension of food justice, which is found in the words and writing of advocates but is perhaps less commonly appreciated, is that food justice should account for the value of food in relation to the *self-determination* of human groups such as urban communities of color, Indigenous peoples and migrant farmworkers, among many other groups (Alkon 2009; Schanbacher 2010; Settee 2010; Adamson 2011; Alkon and Agyeman 2011; Holt-Giménez 2011; Norgaard, Reed, and Van Horn 2011; Desmarais and Wittman 2013; Hospes 2014; Werkheiser and Noll 2014). Reflecting on the claims of food justice advocates, *my goal in this essay is to outline a norm of food justice that is based on the value of food in relation to the self-determination of human groups.*

In what follows, I begin by describing the first two dimensions of food justice; I then discuss the role of food in collective self-determination and introduce the idea of *collective food relations*, discussing in particular the role of *manoomin* (wild rice) in the collective self-determination of the Anishinaabe in the Great Lakes region; I then explain how disrupting collective food relations can be a form of food injustice; lastly, I discuss some specific further examples that illustrate these ideas.

FOOD JUSTICE, DISTRIBUTION AND DEMOCRACY

Food justice is often described in terms of moral norms that should govern some of the key social institutions that make up our food systems. Food systems are complex chains of food production, distribution, consumption and the recirculation of food refuse. Such chains are sometimes referred to as the *farm-to-fork* continuum. Here, social institutions refer specifically to laws, policies and governmental and non-governmental organizations. Key institutions in a food system include corporate food product labeling practices, labor laws and unions, agricultural subsidies, food testing and safety regulations, national food assistance and international food aid programs, and nonprofit organizations working globally to address chronic malnourishment.

The first rather common food justice norm is that everyone should have access to safe, healthy and culturally-appropriate foods no matter one's national origin, economic statuses, social identities, cultural membership, or disability. The second norm is that everyone who works within a food system, from restaurant servers to farm workers, should be paid livable and fair wages and work in safe conditions no matter one's national origin, economic statuses, social identities, cultural membership, or disability. Both norms see food has having value because it provides goods such as nutrition, the fulfillment of cultural preferences, and financial stability. It is up to social institutions to distribute these goods to everyone.

Many definitions of food and food labor reflect the understanding of food as providing nutrition, the fulfillment of cultural preferences, and financial stability. The Food and Agricultural Organization of the United Nations (UN FAO) understands food security as existing "when all people, at all times, have physical, social and economic access to sufficient, safe and nutritious food which meets their dietary needs and food preferences for an active and healthy life" (2014). The United Farm Workers union supports the vision of winning "dignity and respect for America's farm workers through better working conditions and a living wage" (United Farm Workers 2014) and the Restaurant Opportunities Center organization seeks "to improve wages and working conditions for the nation's restaurant workforce" (Restaurant Opportunities Center 2014).

Both food justice norms can be used to identify injustices in social institutions, from international aid to labor laws to agricultural subsidies. And there are many examples of food justice issues in the U.S. and abroad. A recent review article shows some evidence that members of minority and low-income populations in the U.S. suffer relatively higher rates of foodborne illness. A potential reason why is that food safety is inadequately regulated in the retail outlets and food service locations that are frequented by members of these groups (Quinlan 2013). A report by the Michigan Civil Rights Commission found farmworkers in the state "living in housing that was extremely substandard, including structural defects, lack of clean running water, exposed wires, overcrowding, close proximity to fields (and thus pesticides) and poor sanitation" (2010, 2–3). Globally, UN FAO estimates that roughly 805 million people worldwide "do not have enough food to lead a healthy active life," most of whom live in developing countries in which political and economic institutions fail to ensure people have enough resources to feed themselves (Food and Agricultural Organization of the United Nations 2014). In each of these U.S. and global cases, groups who suffer food injustice are also often the least likely to have access to opportunities to influence key social institutions in a food system. Farm workers, minority populations and poor people, and other groups tend to have too few

financial resources, and too little time and political representation, to lobby, sway the shape of laws and policies, hire attorneys and consultants, impact voting numbers and participate prominently in public participation and comment opportunities. Food justice, then, often also involves the democratic norm everyone should have the opportunity to participate equally and in culturally-appropriate ways in the social institutions that shape how the food they eat is produced, distributed and used and how food refuse is recirculated.

FOOD AND COLLECTIVE SELF-DETERMINATION

Many advocates of food justice—from scholars to organizers to community leaders—claim that food justice involves even more than the distributive and democratic norms just enumerated. They claim that norms of food justice should also account for the value of food in relation to the *self-determination* of human groups such as urban communities of color, Indigenous peoples and migrant farmworkers, among many other groups. Here, I refer to self-determination as the widely-embraced moral norm that human groups have the right to decide their own destinies free from any external compulsion or interference from other human groups.

Consider how food justice advocates use concepts associated with self-determination—such as community self-reliance and food sovereignty. The organization Just Food defines food justice as "*communities exercising their right* to grow, sell, and eat healthy food. Healthy food is fresh, nutritious, affordable, culturally-appropriate, and grown locally with care for the well-being of the land, workers, and animals. People practicing food justice leads to a strong local food system, *self-reliant communities*, and a healthy environment" (JustFood.org 2014, emphasis added). As a key element of food justice, the Detroit Food Justice Task Force cites food sovereignty, including "liberating land . . . for the production of food *for communities*," "hosting *collective* meals in our communities as a way of connecting people across generations and cultural backgrounds . . .," and "forging new models of *collective control* of land and waterways" (Detroit Food Justice Task Force 2014, emphasis added). The Indigenous Circle of the People's Food Policy Project in Canada sees "food sovereignty" as embodying the idea of "food as sacred, part of the web of relationships with the natural world that define culture and community" (People's Food Policy Project 2014, 9).

The concepts of community self-reliance, collective meals, community rights and food sovereignty express claims about the value of food as a contributor to a group's *collective* self-determination. Collective self-determination refers to a group's ability to provide the cultural, social, economic and political relations needed for its members to pursue good lives. Food contributes to collective self-determination through its integral roles in family and ceremonial life, as a source of nourishment and income, as a facilitator of trust and good will in society, as a carrier of a group's heritage and knowledge, and as a vital good that political leaders are entrusted to protect through laws and policies. Gustavo Esteva's popular essay referred to this sense of food as "*comida*," or "food-in-context," where "the context is necessarily the social context, the whole human world which comida embeds . . ." (Esteva 1994, 6). This relationship between food and self-determination differs from how food is often understood in the distributive and democratic food justice norms discussed in the first paragraph. In those norms, food is associated with goods such as nutritional intake, fulfillment of cultural preferences and financial stability.

I will refer to the special relationships between food and collective self-determination as *collective food relations*. Food justice, then, refers to a norm that human groups have a right to exercise and adapt their collective food relations free from external compulsion or interference from other human groups, unless there is a morally weighty reason for this compulsion or interference. By weighty reason, I refer to a category of reasons deemed legitimate by the group in question and offered in response to cases of severe moral depravity, such as abuses to

fundamental rights to life and freedom from unlawful detention by a group's political leaders or judicial system, or cases of dire need, such as imminent starvation. Food injustice, then, can occur when a group's collective food relations are wrongfully interfered with or coerced by the actions of another group.

How do collective food relations work in relation to food justice? Consider the example of an Indigenous peoples, the *Anishinaabek*[1] of the Great Lakes region, which refer to over a hundred Ojibwe, Odawa and Potawatomi communities and nations spanning areas known by many Settler Americans (including U.S. and Canadian citizens) primarily as Minnesota, Wisconsin, Michigan and Ontario. Due to 19th century forced relocations, Anishinaabek also live in other areas, such as what is often referred to as Oklahoma and Kansas.

Some important parts of many Anishinaabe communities and nations are the seasonal group activities of tending, cultivating, gathering, harvesting, processing, distributing, storing, and consuming diverse animal and plant foods and recirculating the refuse and unharvested materials in the ecosystem. These native foods, often called *first foods*, include walleye, blueberries, deer, hare, maple, sturgeon and wild rice, among many others. Each year, the activities associated with first foods renew the family, community, cultural, economic, social and political relationships that connect Anishinaabe persons with one another and with all the plants, animals and other entities in the environment, such as water, that are associated with these foods.

The seasonal activities and relationships make it possible for Anishinaabe persons to achieve good lives in ways that they could not achieve through their individual efforts alone. That is, it takes collective action for individuals to have consistent access to diverse sources of nutrition; to feel secure in their social and cultural identities through the food they eat; to have the family and economic support to make free decisions about maintaining or adapting their diets to suit more informed preferences; and to respond to challenges such as climate change. The seasonal group activities and community relationships can be seen as collective food relations that help to make it possible for people to attain a quality of life they could not attain by themselves.

Consider how the relationship between collective action and living well works in the case of the collective food relations of one particular Anishinaabe first food. Wild rice, or *manoomin*, grows in shallow, clear and slow-moving waterways and ripens early in the fall, when it is gathered and then processed through activities such as drying, parching, hulling, and winnowing. Manoomin helps to promote basic nutrition for Anishinaabek owing to its rich vitamin, mineral and protein contents. As a dried good, it can be stored and used for food security in winter and spring months. Consistent access to manoomin is protected by a political and economic system involving rice chiefs and committees, who have stewardship responsibilities to monitor the rice beds and related ecological conditions, look out for and punish poachers or early harvesters, determine the right times to harvest, and advise different families about where and when they can set up rice camps, in which entire families temporarily settle close to the rice beds during August and September. The natural resources and environmental agencies of many Anishinaabe Tribal governments, such as the Leech Lake Band of Ojibwe or the Little Traverse Bay Bands of Odawa Indians, devote staff time to learning about the biology and ecology of manoomin through engagement with elders and ricers and performing in-house scientific research and habitat restoration (Great Lakes Restoration Initiative 2014).

Anishinaabe treaty organizations, such as the Great Lakes Indian Fish and Wildlife Commission (GLIFWC) and Chippewa Ottawa Resource Authority (CORA), engage in research and policy advocacy to protect manoomin in ceded territories where many Anishinaabe communities exercise rights to steward and harvest the plant. Treaty organizations were established to represent different Tribes who are signatories to treaties such as the 1842 Treaty of La Pointe in Minnesota, Wisconsin and Michigan and the 1836 Treaty of Washington in Michigan. Many treaties protect Indigenous rights to harvest and gather certain species, such as manoomin.

Treaty organizations are responsible for playing a part in ensuring that sustainable populations of species harvested and gathered by Tribal members exist. For example, in the case of GLIFWC, the treaty organization "focuses on the preservation and enhancement of manoomin in ceded territory lakes. Annual surveys are performed on existing beds to determine density and overall health of the bed. Select lakes are also reseeded for the purpose of enhancement or re-establishing old beds. Recently, GLIFWC completed a comprehensive wild rice lake inventory in the ceded territories with documentation necessary to develop and launch a comprehensive wild rice management plan" (Great Lakes Indian Fish & Wildlife Commission 2013). This information is often used in policy context as evidence to show that environmental threats, such as mining, are harming rice populations, which is a violation of treaty rights (Great Lakes Indian Fish & Wildlife Commission 1995; Great Lakes Indian Fish & Wildlife Commission 2013).

Anishinaabe-led nongovernmental organizations, such as the White Earth Land Recovery Project or the Native Wild Rice Coalition, are involved in a diverse range of projects to focus and stimulate cultural life and economic viability around manoomin (Johnston 1993; LaDuke 2003; Andow et al. 2009). Individual families across the Great Lakes advocate for their right to steward and harvest in areas where Settler Americans are not accustomed to their doing so, such as Odawa/Potawatomi Lee Sprague and his family. Recently, Sprague and his son established harvesting and a rice camp on a lake in Michigan where most of the Settler American residents had little awareness of Anishinaabe ricing even though there is a substantial amount of naturally growing manoomin (Jimenez 2014).

Access to the nutritional value of manoomin requires family, economic, social and political relations; these relations are, in turn, made possible through manoomin. Other foods, such as the commodity cheese and spam distributed to some Anishinaabe through U.S. food assistance programs, or microwave meals, cannot replace manoomin as comparable contributors to the establishment and maintenance of these relationships. Yet, for many Anishinaabe, what I just described represents only the surface of Anishinaabe-manoomin collective food relations. For example, the rice camps are supposed to be places that intermingle hard work with storytelling, dances, rituals, games, courting, and education that strengthen bonds between Anishinaabek of different families and generations. At other times of the year, manoomin is used during feasts, ceremonies and other celebratory or holiday gatherings. The different manoomin cleaning processes, such as sorting, are time consuming and done throughout the fall and winter with family members. Anishinaabe harvesting of manoomin only removes about 15% of the seeds, leaving the rest for natural reseeding and other animals to eat. Manoomin not only brings Anishinaabe together, but a number of waterfowl, muskrat, deer and invertebrates eat the seeds or use the plant for cover and brooding. These activities help to recycle and to spread the seed (Vennum 1988; GLIFWC 2006; Great Lakes Indian Fish & Wildlife Commission 2013).

Manoomin is tightly woven into the fabric of collective food relations that connect Anishinaabe to their bodies, ecosystem, culture and heritage, and social, economic and political institutions (Vennum 1988; GLIFWC 2006; Great Lakes Indian Fish & Wildlife Commission 2013). Anishinaabe scholars such as Scott Lyons and Deb McGregor would likely advise that even referring to manoomin as a noun does not do justice to the fact the Anishinaabemowin language consists of mostly verbs, which differs from the predominance of nouns in English (Lyons 2010; McGregor 2008). Indeed, manoomin is usually expressed as a verb, such as the verb form *manoominike*, which conveys complex notions of the collective actions associated with the plant that I have described earlier in this essay. So by using nouns I am already capitulating to the linguistic norms and epistemologies of Settler Americans.

Anishinaabe group lives are hard to imagine without manoomin. Indeed, Anishinaabe migrated to the Great Lakes region from the East Coast hundreds of years ago because they had been instructed to settle in the land where food grows on the water. According to one Anishinaabe elder, "There is no substitute for wild rice. My whole way of being as an Indian would be destroyed. I can't imagine being without it. And there is no substitute for this lake's

rice" (Great Lakes Indian Fish & Wildlife Commission 1995). Manoomin is intrinsically valuable to the very constitution and expression of Anishinaabe group identities (Vennum 1988; Johnston 1993; Great Lakes Indian Fish & Wildlife Commission 1995; LaDuke 2003; Andow et al. 2009).

This account of manoomin is meant to express that the value of foods is not just that they provide goods such as nutrition, the fulfillment of cultural preferences and financial stability. In the case of manoomin, the food is a kind of hub whose value lies in how it can bring together many of the collective relations required for people to live good lives. The hub-like quality of certain foods, such as manoomin, allows them to convene biological, ecological, cultural, social, economic, political and spiritual aspects of a way of life. While social institutions such as rice committees, ceremonies, and treaty organizations help to distribute goods associated with manoomin, from nutrition to cultural preference fulfillment, it is *not obvious* to many Anishinaabe persons that these social institutions would be able to thrive very well if another food were *instantly* substituted for manoomin. Speaking of treaties, for example, Norman Deschampe, former Minnesota Chippewa Tribal President, said, "We are of the opinion that the wild rice rights assured by treaty accrue not only to individual grains of rice, but to the very essence of the resource. We were not promised just any wild rice; that promise could be kept by delivering sacks of grain to our members each year. We were promised the rice that grew in the waters of our people, and all the value that rice holds" (Andow et al. 2009, 3). The "very essence" of manoomin and "all the value" it holds refer to the collective food relations that I have described.

It must be noted that manoomin cannot *just* be replaced. Here, though, I must caution readers to also note that my brief account of manoomin is only a slice of Anishinaabe life. Not only are Anishinaabe communities and nations involved with many foods, but Anishinaabe persons and families live diverse lifestyles both within and outside of the jurisdictions of Indigenous governments. Manoomin can mean many different things to many different Anishinaabe persons. As with any human group, dialogue and debate exists about the ultimate meaning of significant aspects of life such as first foods. However, it is nonetheless true, as the sources I have cited bear out, that Anishinaabe governments, treaty organizations, non-governmental organizations and families invest enormous energies into the protection, harvesting and consumption of manoomin and desire future generations to continue these activities. Finally, it is certainly the case that Anishinaabe societies are not static but adaptive, and there is always the possibility of a future in which manoomin figures less prominently than it does now. Yet, as I hope to show in the next section, all forms of adaptations are not equal in a moral sense, and there is a key difference between adaptation that Anishinaabe see as morally legitimate and adaptation coerced and dictated by Settler Americans.

FOOD INJUSTICE AS INTERFERENCE WITH COLLECTIVE FOOD RELATIONS

Despite it being hard to imagine Anishinaabe identity without manoomin, Settler Americans have done quite a bit to threaten it. Neighboring Settler American groups engage in activities such as mining, damming, growing commercial paddy rice for mass distribution, and recreational boating that directly affect manoomin and its habitat—especially the relationships between manoomin and water. These activities can change water levels, water flow, and water quality in ways inhospitable to manoomin; they can also change the diversity of plants and animals in ways that alter the suitability of the habitat for manoomin. Many Anishinaabe are also concerned that Settler Americans who breed and grow varieties of commercial paddy rice for mass harvest have not taken enough precautions to ensure that these varieties do not overtake naturally growing manoomin. Moreover, in the mid-20th century, Settler Americans became interested in eating "wild rice" and some Anishinaabe people adapted by

selling their harvest to others who would finish it off reservation. The Anishinaabe rice was sold at a premium price since it was hand harvested. In the 1960s and 1970s, when Settler Americans determined how to domesticate wild rice, this reduced the price, closing Anishinaabe people out of the market (Wallwork 1997). Settler Americans further destroyed the market through laws and policies that allowed Settler companies to market wild rice as if it were harvested and processed by Anishinaabek (LaDuke 2007).

In states such as Minnesota, manoomin has declined by half in the last 100 years (Great Lakes Indian Fish & Wildlife Commission 1995; Andow et al. 2009). In Michigan, it is commonly accepted that only 12 locations of naturally growing manoomin are left and residents have largely forgotten that it is an important part of the heritage of the territory. Declines and threats to manoomin in such a short time period put immense and rapid pressures on the collective food relations of Anishinaabe groups—forcing them to adapt at an uncomfortable pace. Without manoomin, Anishinaabe lose an integral glue holding together biological, family, social, cultural, economic, ecological, political and spiritual dimensions of group life. Anishinaabe nations today face many challenges, including relatively higher rights of diabetes, food insecurity and hunger (Sarch and Spicer 2008; Cho et al. 2014). Certain ceremonies are becoming less common (Wallwork 1997). The U.S. has for some time distributed foods to Anishinaabe communities that are low in nutritional and cultural value. According to some, the U.S. has improved the quality and distribution of commodity foods relative to previous quality and distribution. Yet Anishinaabe persons in nations such as White Earth nonetheless see the protection and revitalization of manoomin as integral to fully addressing problems of nutrition, cultural decline and poverty (Siple 2011).

Importantly, Anishinaabek see Settler American threats to manoomin as breakdowns in these parties' responsibilities to respect the collective food relations of Anishinaabek (Vennum 1988; Johnston 1993; Great Lakes Indian Fish & Wildlife Commission 1995; LaDuke 2003; Andow et al. 2009). Ironically, activities such as recreational boating or eating paddy rice or mining are part of the collective food relations that Settler American groups rely on to pursue what they deem are good lives, such as being able to enjoy cheap or mass-produced foods. These settler groups have pursued the establishment and continuance of their collective food relations *at the expense of* Anishinaabe collective food relations. That is to say, Settler Americans have engaged in external compulsion of Anishinaabe collective food relations by pressuring Anishinaabek to abandon ricing and dictating the pace of Anishinaabe adaptation; they have also interfered with Anishinaabe collective food relations through pollution and commercial rice production. Settler Americans fail to grant moral consideration to the special value of first foods such as manoomin as key hubs for Anishinaabe collective self-determination that cannot be replaced easily.

These activities exemplify one form of food injustice, when one group impacts a shared food web in ways that interfere with the collective food relations of another group or compel these collective food relations to change, without having a morally weighty reason for doing so. Compulsion and interference are harmful when they target the hub-like qualities of food that are hard to replace. Moreover, there are no morally weighty reasons that Settler Americans can offer to defend their harmful compulsion of and interference with Anishinaabe collective food relations. A morally weighty reason, as I understand it, would be a reason why threatening manoomin is a tough but necessary tradeoff in order to avoid some far more terrible outcome to community members' lives (e.g. imminent starvation) or avoid the commission of heinously immoral actions (e.g. violations of fundamental rights to life and to be free from unlawful detention). The fact that others derive benefit from interfering with a group's collective food relations is not itself a morally weighty reason to do so. Furthermore, this morally weighty reason should be one that the affected group, in this case Anishinaabek, would accept as a legitimate reason. Since such considerations would have to be legitimate to Anishinaabek, they could not rest on colonial or racist portrayals of Anishinaabe collective food relations or privilege Settler ways of life over Anishinaabe ways of life.

A large literature exists where food justice is described in terms of what I am calling collective food relations (Hofrichter 1993; Pulido 1996; Pellow 2007; Alkon and Agyeman 2011; Holt-Giménez 2011; Estabrook 2012; Patel 2013; Jayaraman 2013). Indigenous peoples in particular are often targets of food injustice in other parts of the Great Lakes region where I live and work at the time of the writing of this essay. The Mohawk Indian Territory, which spans U.S. and Canadian borders, is among the most polluted Indigenous communities in North America because of historic and ongoing industrial operations of companies such as General Motors (GM). The Mohawk Council of Akwesasne, the Tribal government, discovered mercury, PCBs and other chemicals in some of the fish populations depended on by Tribal members. For example, in the 1980s, people in the region found out that the closed GM plant had two dormant sludge pits containing PCBs. New York State wildlife epidemiologists found high levels of PCBs in fish and other aquatic wildlife. A three part risk study (fish, wildlife, breast milk) focused on contamination in fish found that "PCB, dioxin, and mercury throughout the study area exceeded criteria for the protection of piscivorous wildlife" (Sloan and Jock 1990, 26).

The toxicants have affected culturally- and economically-significant fish species (such as perch and bullhead), whose harvesting and consumption formed the fabric of Mohawk communities for hundreds of years. The toxicants have entered mothers' breast milk through fish consumption. Native scholar Elizabeth Hoover writes that "In communities such as Akwesasne, the relationship between fish—whose duty it is to cleanse the water and offer themselves as food—and humans—whose role it is to respectfully harvest these fish—has been interrupted by environmental contamination" (Hoover 2013). Hoover describes how different family relationships and cultural ceremonies no longer include fish. Yet simply switching to other food sources is not so easy an alternative for Mohawks.

Groups such as the Mohawk Mother's Milk Project (LaDuke 1999), the Akwesasne Environmental Task Force (Tarbell and Arquette 2000), and the St. Lawrence River Institute of Environmental

Sciences are seeking to better understand the full impact of contamination. Arquette, of the Akwesasne Task Force, argues that "When traditional foods such as fish are no longer eaten, alternative diets are consumed that are often high in fat and calories and low in vitamins and nutrients. This type of dietary change has been linked to many health problems such as type II diabetes, heart disease, stroke, high blood pressure, cancer, and obesity" (Arquette et al. 2002, 261). The context of Arquette's words is actually an anecdote from when a Settler toxicologist congratulated members of the Akwesasne community for lessening their consumption of contaminated fish. The community members had to educate the toxicologist about how refraining from eating certain fishes is actually part of a larger interference to Mohawk collective food relations because of the health, cultural and many other tradeoffs involved.

Currently, the Task Force is developing and implementing holistic forms of risk assessment that capture how food contributes to collective self-determination, both for the sake of the Mohawks but also to educate Settler Americans. For the Mohawks, then, interference with fish erodes collective food relations that support health, family life, subsistence, and culture. There are no morally weighty reasons why groups of Settler Americans should engage in industrial activities (or fail to clean them up) that threaten Mohawk first foods.

COLLECTIVE FOOD RELATIONS BEYOND INDIGENOUS PEOPLES

Other groups experience food injustice in ways that can be described as wrongful interference in their collective food relations. In Detroit, Michigan, a city of about 700,000 residents, trends starting in the 1950s led to the decline of the street car system and population shifts to suburbs from which African-Americans were segregated and unwelcome. This resulted in today's situation where roughly 80%

of the population is African-American, 30% of Detroiters live below the poverty line, one in five lack good transportation options, and African-American Detroiters live on average 1.1 miles farther from supermarkets than residents of mostly white neighborhoods (White 2011).

Most Detroiters rely on relatively expensive and unhealthy food that they buy from some 1,000 food retailers, found mostly in impoverished neighborhoods, such as liquor stores, gas stations, party stores, dollar stores, bakeries, pharmacies, and convenience stores. 69.1% of Detroiters are obese or overweight; 21% of Detroit's youth are overweight. Detroiters die from heart disease at a rate 50% higher than the national average (White 2011). African-American organizations such the Detroit Black Community Food Security Network (DBCFSN) and D-Town Farm are actively expressing views tying food injustice to collective food relations.

Scholar and DBCFSN board member Monica White discusses how members of these organizations feel they "cannot count on others to provide them with healthy foods because availability to such food is based on race and class privilege. They note that those who live in more affluent communities have mechanisms to monitor available food. They also have easy access to safe and clean food and a wider range of healthy food options" (White 2010, 199). Malik Yakini, founder of the DBCFSN, argues regarding African-Americans, that "much of our traditional food culture has been lost over the past generation, due to the rush towards convenience in the post-World War II period, and then the fast food proliferation which occurred in Detroit and other places throughout the country. Our families today rarely sit down and eat a meal that's prepared from scratch" (Wallace 2011).

For many African-American Detroiters, the solution for achieving food justice is also closely tied to collective food relations. The *Be Black and Green* website, inspired by Yakini, seeks to network, support and promote Black farmers, gardeners and food activists. The philosophy behind the website is to advocate "African self-determination" and "to build a Black Food Sovereignty movement." Self-determination and food sovereignty are discussed in terms of Black people's heritage from "Africans enslaved to work on large and small agricultural projects . . . [and] expertise in growing rice, indigo and other plants . . ." Moreover, after the end of slavery in the U.S., "most people of African descent continued to be tied to the land either through tenant farming, sharecropping or in some cases ownership. Millions of Africans migrating from Georgia, South Carolina, Arkansas, Tennessee, Mississippi, Florida, and Louisiana to 20th century industrial cities like Detroit, Chicago, Gary and Cleveland brought their agricultural heritage with them. 'Be Black and Green' is a call to reclaim our agricultural heritage. It is a call to embrace our ancestral mandate to recognize the interconnectedness and interdependence of all things and to work always for the greatest good. It implores us to dare to use our own cultural experience as the foundation for forward movement. It situates us within our own historical continuum" (Be Black and Green 2014).

The African-American community has created important organizations that seek to achieve food justice through unique collective food relations. DBCFSN founded the D-Town Farm, which "utilizes sustainable, earth-friendly food production techniques to produce thousands of pounds of high-quality fresh produce each year" (White 2010, 196). The goal, for Yakini, is to "grasp larger control over the food system and to build self-reliance in our community" (White 2010, 196). DBCFSN has also created the U-Jamma Food Buying Club and engaged in numerous actions to influence the Detroit City Council, which led to the creation of the Detroit Food Policy Council, which seeks to bolster the conditions needed for groups such as African-American Detroiters to cultivate unique collective food relations in ways that do not limit other groups' ability to do so (White 2010). White claims that organizations associated with Be Black and Green, such as The DBCFSN and D-Town Farm, and others also are viewed as a first step in building partnerships with other community-based organizations, as well as public agencies, so that residents can work to rebuild their city (White 2011).

DBCFSN recognizes the importance of African-American collective food relations at the same time that it acknowledges the reality that other groups who share the Detroit region inevitably influence African-American Detroiters' collective self-determination. The policy-related work of DBFCSN shows that food justice not only involves establishing food sovereignty based on establishing a group's unique food relations, but also ensuring that other groups acknowledge and take responsibility for the ways in which pursuit of their own collective self-determination can commit food injustice. This effort to establish intergroup responsibilities is shared by the other groups discussed in this essay. Anishinaabe Treaty organizations, Tribal governments and families engage in widespread advocacy to educate Settler Americans about their responsibilities to consider the moral importance of manoomin. A good example is the bi-annual *Nibi* (water) and Manoomin Symposium, which one of the member nations of the Chippewa Tribe of Minnesota hosts and invites representatives of research institutions, private industry, and state government in order to build accountability toward Anishinaabe ways of life.

THE SIGNIFICANCE OF FOOD JUSTICE

In the work just discussed, food justice is understood as more than norms ensuring people's access to certain amounts of healthy, affordable and culturally appropriate food and ensuring opportunities to participate democratically in law and policy. Food justice is a matter of refraining from compelling or interfering with the collective food relations that serve as part of the undergirding of a group's collective self-determination. Because each communities' collective food relations are unique, other groups have a responsibility not to compel or interfere with the hub-like qualities of foods that are important to different groups, whether African-American Detroiters or Anishinaabek in the Great Lakes region. This sense of food justice highlights both the importance of group control over collective food relations but also the inevitable interdependence of groups within shared food webs. On my interpretation of the claims of many food justice advocates, there is a norm of food justice that requires all of us, as members of human groups, to consider how the collective food relations to which we belong interact with the collective food relations to which other human groups belong.

Satisfying this norm is a heavy responsibility, which is perhaps why some food justice advocates see this norm as a matter of human rights. La Via Campesina, along with other global organizations, has defined food sovereignty as a human right, "the right of peoples to healthy and culturally appropriate food produced through ecologically sound and sustainable methods, and their right to define their own food and agriculture systems" (Claeys 2013). But it is a human right to collective self-determination, not just a right to have access to a commodity. Monica White argues that while the work of D-Town Farm is certainly in "agreement with humanitarian agencies and human rights advocates that all citizens should have access to healthy food," there is far more to it than having enough healthy food. This is because ". . . they are not interested in relying on governmental or humanitarian bodies to deliver this food. Instead, they choose to provide food for themselves and their community. In providing an alternative behavioral option to dependence on the state, they prefer to act in ways that demonstrate agency and empowerment" (White 2010, 206). I see White's remarks about the significance of food justice as in line with the value placed on first foods by Indigenous peoples. The Mystic Lake Declaration, written by diverse Indigenous peoples and aimed at an international and human rights audience, claims that "We declare our Native Nations and our communities, waters, air, forests, oceans, sea ice, and traditional lands and territories to be 'Food Sovereignty Areas,' defined and directed by Indigenous Peoples according to our customary laws, free from extractive industries, unsustainable energy development, deforestation, and free from using food crops and agricultural lands for large scale biofuels . . ." (2009). Reflecting on these previous remarks and declarations from many groups, perhaps increasing the number and quality of dialogues connecting different groups, Indigenous, African-American and peoples and communities of many other heritages and nations, can eventually lead to the development of specific moral and human rights protocols of how to enact intergroup responsibilities in relation to diverse groups—which may promise to move us closer to really achieving global food justice.

NOTE

1. I tried to use English spellings of words in Anishinaabemowin (the language of the Anishinaabek) that can be identified by diverse Ojibwe, Potawatomi and Odawa people and people who work in relation to this language. I recognize that there are many accents and spelling systems and that the one I am using is in some ways the least similar to how members of my Tribe (Potawatomi) engage in English language spelling.

REFERENCES

Adamson, J. 2011. Medicine Food: Critical Environmental Justice Studies, Native North American Literature, and the Movement for Food Sovereignty. *Environmental Justice* 4 (4):213–219.

Alkon, AH. 2009. Breaking the Food Chains: An Investigation of Food Justice Activism. *Sociological Inquiry* 79:289–305.

Alkon, AH, and Agyeman, J. 2011. *Cultivating Food Justice: Race, Class, and Sustainability.* Cambridge, MA: MIT Press.

Arquette, M, Cole, M, Cook, K, LaFrance, B, Peters, M, Ransom, J, Sargent, E, Smoke, V and Stairs, A. 2002. Holistic Risk-Based Environmental Decision-Making: A Native Perspective. *Environmental Health Perspectives* 110 (2):259–264.

Be Black and Green. *Planting the Seeds of the Urban Tomorrow* 2014. Available from www.beblackandgreen .com.

Cho, P, Geiss, LS, Burrows, NS, Roberts, DL, Bullock, AK, Toedt, ME. 2014 "Diabetes-Related Mortality Among American Indians and Alaska Natives, 1990–2009." *American journal of public health* 104.S3: S496–S503. Read more: http://ajph.aphapublications.org/doi/abs/10.2105/AJPH.2014.301968

Claeys, P. 2013. From Food Sovereignty to Peasants' Rights: An Overview of Via Campesina's Struggle for New Human Rights.

Desmarais, A, and H. Wittman. 2013. Farmers, Foodies & First Nations: Getting to Food Sovereignty in Canada. *Presented at Yale Agrarian Studies Conference: Food Sovereignty: A Critical Dialogue.*

Detroit Food Justice Task Force. *Food Justice* 2014. Available from http://www.detroitfoodjustice.org/.

Estabrook, B. 2012. *Tomatoland: How Modern Industrial Agriculture Destroyed Our Most Alluring Fruit.* New York, NY, USA: Andrews McMeel Publishing.

Esteva, Gustavo. 1994. Re⊠Embedding Food in Agriculture. *Culture & Agriculture* 13 (48):1–12.

Food and Agricultural Organization of the United Nations. 2014. *The State of Food Insecurity in the World 2014. Strengthening the Enabling Environment for Food Security and Nutrition.* Rome, Italy: Food and Agricultural Organization of the United Nations

Food and Agriculture Organization of the United Nations. 2014. *Food Security Statistics* 2014 [cited December 28 2014]. Available from http://www.fao.org/economic/ess/ess-fs/en/.

Great Lakes Indian Fish and Wildlife Commission. 1983. *Constitution of the Great Lakes Indian Fish and Wildlife Commission.* Odanah, WI: Great Lakes Indian Fish and Wildlife Commission.

———. 1995. *Sulfide Mining: The Process and the Price, a Tribal and Ecological Perspective.* Odana, WI, USA Great Lakes Indian Fish and Wildlife Commission.

———. 2006. *The Goodberry: Growing up Ojibwe, Mazina'igan Supplement*: Great Lakes Indian Fish & Wildlife Commission.

———. 2013. *Manoomin (Wild Rice).* [Viewed October 15 2013]. Available from www.glifwc.org/WildRice/wildrice.html.

Great Lakes Restoration Initiative. 2015. *Great Lakes Restoration Initiative* 2014 [viewed January 25 2015]. Available from http://greatlakesrestoration.us/.

Hofrichter, R. 1993. *Toxic Struggles: The Theory and Practice of Environmental Justice.* Philadelphia, PA, USA: New Society Publishers.

Holt-Giménez, E. 2011. Food Security, Food Justice, or Food Sovereignty? Crises, Food Movements, and Regime Change. In *Cultivating Food Justice: Race, Class, and Sustainability*, edited by A. Alkon and J. Agyeman. Cambridge, MA: MIT Press.

Hoover, E. 2013. Cultural and Health Implications of Fish Advisories in a Native American Community. *Ecological Processes* 2 (1):1–12.

Hospes, O. 2014. Food Sovereignty: The Debate, the Deadlock, and a Suggested Detour. *Agriculture and Human Values* 31 (1):119–130.

Jayaraman, S. 2013. *Behind the Kitchen Door.* Ithaca, NY, USA: Cornell University Press.

Jimenez, J. 2014. Experts Survey, Harvest Wild Rice. *Iosco County News Herald*, September 24.

JustFood.org. 2014. *What Is Food Justice?* 2014 [cited December 27 2014]. Available from JustFood.org.

LaDuke, W. 2007. Rickeepers: A Struggle to Protect Biodiversity and a Native American Way of Life. *Orion* 26:18–23.

———. 1999. *All Our Relations: Native Struggles for Land and Life.* Cambridge, MA: South End Press

Lyons, SR. 2010. *X-Marks: Native Signatures of Assent*: U of Minnesota Press.

McGregor, D. 2008. Linking Traditional Ecological Knowledge and Western Science: Aboriginal Perspectives from the 2000 State of the Lakes Ecosystem Conference. *The Canadian Journal of Native Studies* XXVIII (1):139–158.

Mystic Lake Declaration 2009. *Native Peoples Native Homelands Climate Change Workshop II.*

Norgaard, K, Reed, R, and Van Horn, C. 2011. A Continuing Legacy: Institutional Racism, Hunger and Nutritional Justice on the Klamath. *Cultivating Food Justice: Race, Class, and Sustainability*:23–46.

Patel, R. 2013. *Stuffed and Starved: From Farm to Fork: The Hidden Battle for the World Food System.* London, UK: Portobello Books.

Pellow, DN. 2007. *Resisting Global Toxics: Transnational Movements for Environmental Justice.* Cambridge, MA: The MIT Press.

People's Food Policy Project. 2014. Resetting the Table: A People's Food Policy for Canada.

Pulido, L. 1996. *Environmentalism and Economic Justice: Two Chicano Struggles in the Southwest.* Tucson, AZ: University of Arizona Press.

Quinlan, JJ. 2013. Foodborne Illness Incidence Rates and Food Safety Risks for Populations of Low Socioeconomic Status and Minority Race/Ethnicity: A Review of the Literature. *International journal of environmental research and public health* 10 (8):3634–3652.

Restaurant Opportunities Center. 2014. *About Us* 2014 [cited December 28 2014]. Available from http://rocunited.org/about-us/#sthash.0iRkmMqO.dpuf

Sarche, M., and Spicer P., 2008: Poverty and Health Disparities for American Indian and Alaska Native Children: Current Knowledge and Future Prospects. *Annals of the New York Academy of Sciences* 1136:126–136.

Schanbacher, W.D. 2010. *The Politics of Food: The Global Conflict between Food Security and Food Sovereignty*: ABC-CLIO.

Settee, P. 2010. Indigenous Food Sovereignty. *Centre for the Study of Social Exclusion & Inclusive Policy*, University of Pondicherry, India, 8 Oct. 2010.

Siple, Julie. 2011. A Return to Traditional Foods Helps Some Fight Hunger on White Earth Reservation *Minnesota Public Radio News*, October 4.

Sloan, R., and K. Jock. 1990. Chemical Contaminants in Fish from the St. Lawrence River Drainage on Lands of the Mohawk Nation at Akwesasne and near the General Motors Corporation/Central Foundry Division, Massena, NY, Plant. New York State Department of Environmental Conservation.

Tarbell, A., and M. Arquette. 2000. Akwesasne: A Native American Community's Resistance to Cultural and Environmental Damage. In *Reclaiming the Environmental Debate: The Politics of Health in a Toxic Culture*, edited by R. Hofrichter. Cambridge, MA: MIT Press.

United Farm Workers. 2014. *The Movement at a Glance* 2014 [cited December 28, 2014]. Available from http://ufw.org/_page.php?menu=about&inc=fwmglance.html.

Vennum, T. 1988. *Wild Rice and the Ojibway People*: Minnesota Historical Society Press.

Wallace, H. 2011. Malik Yakini of Detroit's Black Community Food Security Network. *Civileats.com*, December 19th.

Werkheiser, I., and S. Noll. 2014. From Food Justice to a Tool of the Status Quo: Three Sub-Movements within Local Food. *Journal of Agricultural and Environmental Ethics* 27 (2):201–2010.

White, M. 2010. Shouldering Responsibility for the Delivery of Human Rights: A Case Study of the D-Town Farmers of Detroit. *Race/Ethnicity: Multidisciplinary Global Contexts* 3 (2):189–211.

———. 2011. D-Town Farm: African American Resistance to Food Insecurity and the Transformation of Detroit. *Environmental Practice* 13 (4):406–417.

———. 2011. Sisters of the Soil: Urban Gardening as Resistance in Detroit. *Race/Ethnicity: Multidisciplinary Global Contexts* 5 (1):13–28.

QUESTIONS

1. What are collective food relations? What are some of the Anishinaabek collective food relations involving manoomin?
2. How have the Anishinaaeb's collective food relations been interfered with by Settler Americans?
3. Why are food and food relations particularly important for a group's collective self-determination? What is Whyte's answer to this question?
4. Whyte understands *collective self-determination* as the "moral norm that human groups have the right to decide their own destinies free from any external compulsion or interference from other human groups." One component of food justice, according to Whyte, is "that human groups have a right to exercise and adapt their collective food relations free from external compulsion or interference from other human groups, unless there is a morally weighty reason for this compulsion or interference." What, in your view, is a morally weighty reason for interfering with collective food relations? When would justice allow one group to interfere with another group's collective food relations?

IRIS MARION YOUNG

Five Faces of Oppression

Iris Marion Young analyzes one form of injustice, oppression. Though oppression traditionally referred to "the exercise of tyranny by a ruling group," oppression can also result from
social conditions that treat people differently based upon their social groups. Young identifies five types of oppression: exploitation, marginalization, powerlessness, cultural imperialism, and violence.

*Someone who does not see a pane of glass does not
know that he does not see it. Someone who, being
placed differently, does see it, does not know the
other does not see it.*

*When our will finds expression outside ourselves
in actions performed by others, we do not waste
our time and our power of attention in examining
whether they have consented to this. This is true for
all of us. Our attention, given entirely to the success
of the undertaking, is not claimed by them as long
as they are docile. . . .*

*Rape is a terrible caricature of love from which
consent is absent. After rape, oppression is the
second horror of human existence. It is a terrible
caricature of obedience.*

—Simone Weil

I have proposed an enabling conception of justice.
Justice should refer not only to distribution, but also
to the institutional conditions necessary for the development and exercise of individual capacities and
collective communication and cooperation. Under
this conception of justice, injustice refers primarily
to two forms of disabling constraints, oppression and
domination. While these constraints include distributive patterns, they also involve matters which
cannot easily be assimilated to the logic of distribution: decisionmaking procedures, division of labor,
and culture.

Many people in the United States would not
choose the term "oppression" to name injustice in
our society. For contemporary emancipatory social
movements, on the other hand—socialists, radical
feminists, American Indian activists, Black activists,
gay and lesbian activists—oppression is a central
category of political discourse. . . .

OPPRESSION AS A STRUCTURAL CONCEPT

One reason that many people would not use the term
oppression to describe injustice in our society is that
they do not understand the term in the same way as
do new social movements. In its traditional usage,
oppression means the exercise of tyranny by a ruling
group. Thus many Americans would agree with
radicals in applying the term oppression to the situation of Black South Africans under apartheid.
Oppression also traditionally carries a strong con-
notation of conquest and colonial domination. The
Hebrews were oppressed in Egypt, and many uses
of the term oppression in the West invoke this
paradigm.

Iris Marion Young, "Five Faces of Oppression", in *Justice and the Politics of Difference* (Princeton, NJ: Princeton University
Press, 2011).

Dominant political discourse may use the term oppression to describe societies other than our own, usually Communist or purportedly Communist societies. Within this anti-Communist rhetoric both tyrannical and colonialist implications of the term appear. For the anti-Communist, Communism denotes precisely the exercise of brutal tyranny over a whole people by a few rulers, and the will to conquer the world, bringing hitherto independent peoples under that tyranny. In dominant political discourse it is not legitimate to use the term oppression to describe our society, because oppression is the evil perpetrated by the Others.

New left social movements of the 1960s and 1970s, however, shifted the meaning of the concept of oppression. In its new usage, oppression designates the disadvantage and injustice some people suffer not because a tyrannical power coerces them, but because of the everyday practices of a well-intentioned liberal society. In this new left usage, the tyranny of a ruling group over another, as in South Africa, must certainly be called oppressive. But oppression also refers to systemic constraints on groups that are not necessarily the result of the intentions of a tyrant. Oppression in this sense is structural, rather than the result of a few people's choices or policies. Its causes are embedded in unquestioned norms, habits, and symbols, in the assumptions underlying institutional rules and the collective consequences of following those rules. It names, as Marilyn Frye puts it, "an enclosing structure of forces and barriers which tends to the immobilization and reduction of a group or category of people" (Frye, 1983a, p. 11). In this extended structural sense oppression refers to the vast and deep injustices some groups suffer as a consequence of often unconscious assumptions and reactions of well-meaning people in ordinary interactions, media and cultural stereotypes, and structural features of bureaucratic hierarchies and market mechanisms—in short, the normal processes of everyday life. We cannot eliminate this structural oppression by getting rid of the rulers or making some new laws, because oppressions are systematically reproduced in major economic, political, and cultural institutions.

The systemic character of oppression implies that an oppressed group need not have a correlate oppressing group. While structural oppression involves relations among groups, these relations do not always fit the paradigm of conscious and intentional oppression of one group by another. Foucault (1977) suggests that to understand the meaning and operation of power in modern society we must look beyond the model of power as "sovereignty," a dyadic relation of ruler and subject, and instead analyze the exercise of power as the effect of often liberal and "humane" practices of education, bureaucratic administration, production and distribution of consumer goods, medicine, and so on. The conscious actions of many individuals daily contribute to maintaining and reproducing oppression, but those people are usually simply doing their jobs or living their lives, and do not understand themselves as agents of oppression.

I do not mean to suggest that within a system of oppression individual persons do not intentionally harm others in oppressed groups. The raped woman, the beaten Black youth, the locked-out worker, the gay man harassed on the street, are victims of intentional actions by identifiable agents. I also do not mean to deny that specific groups are beneficiaries of the oppression of other groups, and thus have an interest in their continued oppression. Indeed, for every oppressed group there is a group that is *privileged* in relation to that group.

The concept of oppression has been current among radicals since the 1960s partly in reaction to Marxist attempts to reduce the injustices of racism and sexism, for example, to the effects of class domination or bourgeois ideology. Racism, sexism, ageism, homophobia, some social movements asserted, are distinct forms of oppression with their own dynamics apart from the dynamics of class, even though they may interact with class oppression. From often heated discussions among socialists, feminists, and antiracism activists in the last ten years a consensus is emerging that many different groups must be said to be oppressed in our society, and that no single form of oppression can be assigned causal or moral primacy (see Gottlieb, 1987). The same discussion has also led to the recognition that group differences cut across individual lives in a multiplicity of ways that can entail privilege and oppression for the same person in different respects. Only a plural explication of the concept of oppression can adequately capture these insights.

Accordingly, I offer below an explication of five faces of oppression as a useful set of categories and distinctions which I believe is comprehensive, in the sense that it covers all the groups said by new left social movements to be oppressed and all the ways they are oppressed. I derive the five faces of oppression from reflection on the condition of these groups. Because different factors, or combinations of factors, constitute the oppression of different groups, making their oppression irreducible, I believe it is not possible to give one essential definition of oppression. The five categories articulated in this chapter, however, are adequate to describe the oppression of any group, as well as its similarities with and differences from the oppression of other groups. But first we must ask what a group is.

THE CONCEPT OF
A SOCIAL GROUP

Oppression refers to structural phenomena that immobilize or diminish a group. But what is a group? Our ordinary discourse differentiates people according to social groups such as women and men, age groups, racial and ethnic groups, religious groups, and so on. Social groups of this sort are not simply collections of people, for they are more fundamentally intertwined with the identities of the people described as belonging to them. They are a specific kind of collectivity, with specific consequences for how people understand one another and themselves. Yet neither social theory nor philosophy has a clear and developed concept of the social group (see Turner et al., 1987).

A social group is a collective of persons differentiated from at least one other group by cultural forms, practices, or way of life. Members of a group have a specific affinity with one another because of their similar experience or way of life, which prompts them to associate with one another more than with those not identified with the group, or in a different way. Groups are an expression of social relations; a group exists only in relation to at least one other group. Group identification arises, that is, in the encounter and interaction between social collectivities that experience some differences in their way of life and forms of association, even if they also regard themselves as belonging to the same society.

As long as they associated solely among themselves, for example, an American Indian group thought of themselves only as "the people." The encounter with other American Indians created an awareness of difference; the others were named as a group, and the first group came to see themselves as a group. But social groups do not arise only from an encounter between different societies. Social processes also differentiate groups within a single society. The sexual division of labor, for example, has created social groups of women and men in all known societies. Members of each gender have a certain affinity with others in their group because of what they do or experience, and differentiate themselves from the other gender, even when members of each gender consider that they have much in common with members of the other, and consider that they belong to the same society.

Political philosophy typically has no place for a specific concept of the social group. When philosophers and political theorists discuss groups, they tend to conceive them either on the model of aggregates or on the model of associations, both of which are methodologically individualist concepts. To arrive at a specific concept of the social group it is thus useful to contrast social groups with both aggregates and associations.

An aggregate is any classification of persons according to some attribute. Persons can be aggregated according to any number of attributes—eye color, the make of car they drive, the street they live on. Some people interpret the groups that have emotional and social salience in our society as aggregates, as arbitrary classifications of persons according to such attributes as skin color, genitals, or age. George Sher, for example, treats social groups as aggregates, and uses the arbitrariness of aggregate classification as a reason not to give special attention to groups. "There are really as many groups as there are combinations of people and if we are going to ascribe claims to equal treatment to racial, sexual, and other groups with high visibility, it will be mere favoritism not to ascribe similar claims to these other groups as well" (Sher, 1987a, p. 256).

But "highly visible" social groups such as Blacks or women are different from aggregates, or mere "combinations of people" (see French, 1975; Friedman and May, 1985; May, 1987, chap. 1). A social group is defined not primarily by a set of shared attributes, but by a sense of identity. What defines Black Americans as a social group is not primarily their skin color; some persons whose skin color is fairly light, for example, identify themselves as Black. Though sometimes objective attributes are a necessary condition for classifying oneself or others as belonging to a certain social group, it is identification with a certain social status, the common history that social status produces, and self-identification that define the group as a group.

Social groups are not entities that exist apart from individuals, but neither are they merely arbitrary classifications of individuals according to attributes which are external to or accidental to their identities. Admitting the reality of social groups does not commit one to reifying collectivities, as some might argue. Group meanings partially constitute people's identities in terms of the cultural forms, social situation, and history that group members know as theirs, because these meanings have been either forced upon them or forged by them or both (cf. Fiss, 1976). Groups are real not as substances, but as forms of social relations (cf. May, 1987, pp. 22–23).

Moral theorists and political philosophers tend to elide social groups more often with associations than with aggregates (e.g., French, 1975; May, 1987, chap. 1). By an association I mean a formally organized institution, such as a club, corporation, political party, church, college, or union. Unlike the aggregate model of groups, the association model recognizes that groups are defined by specific practices and forms of association. Nevertheless it shares a problem with the aggregate model. The aggregate model conceives the individual as prior to the collective, because it reduces the social group to a mere set of attributes attached to individuals. The association model also implicitly conceives the individual as ontologically prior to the collective, as making up, or constituting, groups.

A contract model of social relations is appropriate for conceiving associations, but not groups. Individuals constitute associations, they come together as already formed persons and set them up, establishing rules, positions, and offices. The relationship of persons to associations is usually voluntary, and even when it is not, the person has nevertheless usually entered the association. The person is prior to the association also in that the person's identity and sense of self are usually regarded as prior to and relatively independent of association membership.

Groups, on the other hand, constitute individuals. A person's particular sense of history, affinity, and separateness, even the person's mode of reasoning, evaluating, and expressing feeling, are constituted partly by her or his group affinities. This does not mean that persons have no individual styles, or are unable to transcend or reject a group identity. Nor does it preclude persons from having many aspects that are independent of these group identities.

The social ontology underlying many contemporary theories of justice, I pointed out in the last chapter, is methodologically individualist or atomist. It presumes that the individual is ontologically prior to the social. This individualist social ontology usually goes together with a normative conception of the self as independent. The authentic self is autonomous, unified, free, and self-made, standing apart from history and affiliations, choosing its life plan entirely for itself.

One of the main contributions of poststructuralist philosophy has been to expose as illusory this metaphysic of a unified self-making subjectivity, which posits the subject as an autonomous origin or an underlying substance to which attributes of gender, nationality, family role, intellectual disposition, and so on might attach. Conceiving the subject in this fashion implies conceiving consciousness as outside of and prior to language and the context of social interaction, which the subject enters. Several currents of recent philosophy challenge this deeply held

Cartesian assumption. Lacanian psychoanalysis, for example, and the social and philosophical theory influenced by it, conceive the self as an achievement of linguistic positioning that is always contextualized in concrete relations with other persons, with their mixed identities (Coward and Ellis, 1977). The self is a product of social processes, not their origin.

From a rather different perspective, Habermas indicates that a theory of communicative action also must challenge the "philosophy of consciousness" which locates intentional egos as the ontological origins of social relations. A theory of communicative action conceives individual identity not as an origin but as a product of linguistic and practical interaction (Habermas, 1987, pp. 3–40). As Stephen Epstein describes it, identity is "a socialized sense of individuality, an internal organization of self-perception concerning one's relationship to social categories, that also incorporates views of the self perceived to be held by others. Identity is constituted relationally, through involvement with—and incorporation of—significant others and integration into communities" (Epstein, 1987, p. 29). Group categorization and norms are major constituents of individual identity (see Turner et al., 1987).

A person joins an association, and even if membership in it fundamentally affects one's life, one does not take that membership to define one's very identity, in the way, for example, being Navaho might. Group affinity, on the other hand, has the character of what Martin Heidegger (1962) calls "thrownness": one *finds oneself* as a member of a group, which one experiences as always already having been. For our identities are defined in relation to how others identify us, and they do so in terms of groups which are always already associated with specific attributes, stereotypes, and norms.

From the thrownness of group affinity it does not follow that one cannot leave groups and enter new ones. Many women become lesbian after first identifying as heterosexual. Anyone who lives long enough becomes old. These cases exemplify thrownness precisely because such changes in group affinity are experienced as transformations in one's identity. Nor does it follow from the thrownness of group affinity that one cannot define the meaning of group identity

for oneself; those who identify with a group can redefine the meaning and norms of group identity. Indeed, in Chapter 6 I will show how oppressed groups have sought to confront their oppression by engaging in just such redefinition. The present point is only that one first finds a group identity as given, and then takes it up in a certain way. While groups may come into being, they are never founded.

Groups, I have said, exist only in relation to other groups. A group may be identified by outsiders without those so identified having any specific consciousness of themselves as a group. Sometimes a group comes to exist only because one group excludes and labels a category of persons, and those labeled come to understand themselves as group members only slowly, on the basis of their shared oppression. In Vichy France, for example, Jews who had been so assimilated that they had no specifically Jewish identity were marked as Jews by others and given a specific social status by them. These people "discovered" themselves as Jews, and then formed a group identity and affinity with one another (see Sartre, 1948). A person's group identities may be for the most part only a background or horizon to his or her life, becoming salient only in specific interactive contexts.

Assuming an aggregate model of groups, some people think that social groups are invidious fictions, essentializing arbitrary attributes. From this point of view problems of prejudice, stereotyping, discrimination, and exclusion exist because some people mistakenly believe that group identification makes a difference to the capacities, temperament, or virtues of group members. This individualist conception of persons and their relation to one another tends to identify oppression with group identification. Oppression, on this view, is something that happens to people when they are classified in groups. Because others identify them as a group, they are excluded and despised. Eliminating oppression thus requires eliminating groups. People should be treated as individuals, not as members of groups, and allowed to form their lives freely without stereotypes or group norms.

This book takes issue with that position. While I agree that individuals should be free to pursue life plans in their own way, it is foolish to deny the reality of groups. Despite the modern myth of a decline of parochial attachments and ascribed identities, in modern society group differentiation remains endemic. As both markets and social administration increase the web of social interdependency on a world scale, and as more people encounter one another as strangers in cities and states, people retain and renew ethnic, locale, age, sex, and occupational group identifications, and form new ones in the processes of encounter (cf. Ross, 1980, p. 19; Rothschild, 1981, p. 130). Even when they belong to oppressed groups, people's group identifications are often important to them, and they often feel a special affinity for others in their group. I believe that group differentiation is both an inevitable and a desirable aspect of modern social processes. Social justice, I shall argue in later chapters, requires not the melting away of differences, but institutions that promote reproduction of and respect for group differences without oppression.

Though some groups have come to be formed out of oppression, and relations of privilege and oppression structure the interactions between many groups, group differentiation is not in itself oppressive. Not all groups are oppressed. In the United States Roman Catholics are a specific social group, with distinct practices and affinities with one another, but they are no longer an oppressed group. Whether a group is oppressed depends on whether it is subject to one or more of the five conditions I shall discuss below.

The view that groups are fictions does carry an important antideterminist or antiessentialist intuition. Oppression has often been perpetrated by a conceptualization of group difference in terms of unalterable essential natures that determine what group members deserve or are capable of, and that exclude groups so entirely from one another that they have no similarities or overlapping attributes. To assert that it is possible to have social group difference without oppression, it is necessary to conceptualize groups in a much more relational and fluid fashion.

Although social processes of affinity and differentiation produce groups, they do not give groups a substantive essence. There is no common nature that members of a group share. As aspects of a process, moreover, groups are fluid; they come into being and

may fade away. Homosexual practices have existed in many societies and historical periods, for example. Gay men or lesbians have been identified as specific groups and so identified themselves, however, only in the twentieth century (see Ferguson, 1989, chap. 9; Altman, 1981).

Arising from social relations and processes, finally, group differences usually cut across one another. Especially in a large, complex, and highly differentiated society, social groups are not themselves homogeneous, but mirror in their own differentiations many of the other groups in the wider society. In American society today, for example, Blacks are not a simple, unified group with a common life. Like other racial and ethnic groups, they are differentiated by age, gender, class, sexuality, region, and nationality, any of which in a given context may become a salient group identity.

This view of group differentiation as multiple, cross-cutting, fluid, and shifting implies another critique of the model of the autonomous, unified self. In complex, highly differentiated societies like our own, all persons have multiple group identifications. The culture, perspective, and relations of privilege and oppression of these various groups, moreover, may not cohere. Thus individual persons, as constituted partly by their group affinities and relations, cannot be unified, themselves are heterogeneous and not necessarily coherent.

THE FACES OF OPPRESSION

Exploitation

. . . The central insight expressed in the concept of exploitation, then, is that this oppression occurs through a steady process of the transfer of the results of the labor of one social group to benefit another. The injustice of class division does not consist only in the distributive fact that some people have great wealth while most people have little (cf. Buchanan, 1982, pp. 44–49; Holmstrom, 1977). Exploitation enacts a structural relation between social groups.

Social rules about what work is, who does what for whom, how work is compensated, and the social process by which the results of work are appropriated operate to enact relations of power and inequality. These relations are produced and reproduced through a systematic process in which the energies of the have-nots are continuously expended to maintain and augment the power, status, and wealth of the haves.

Many writers have cogently argued that the Marxist concept of exploitation is too narrow to encompass all forms of domination and oppression (Giddens, 1981, p. 242; Brittan and Maynard, 1984. p. 93; Murphy, 1985; Bowles and Gintis, 1986, pp. 20–24). In particular, the Marxist concept of class leaves important phenomena of sexual and racial oppression unexplained. Does this mean that sexual and racial oppression are nonexploitative, and that we should reserve wholly distinct categories for these oppressions? Or can the concept of exploitation be broadened to include other ways in which the labor and energy expenditure of one group benefits another, and reproduces a relation of domination between them?

Feminists have had little difficulty showing that women's oppression consists partly in a systematic and unreciprocated transfer of powers from women to men. Women's oppression consists not merely in an inequality of status, power, and wealth resulting from men's excluding them from privileged activities. The freedom, power, status, and self-realization of men is possible precisely because women work for them. Gender exploitation has two aspects, transfer of the fruits of material labor to men and transfer of nurturing and sexual energies to men.

Christine Delphy (1984), for example, describes marriage as a class relation in which women's labor benefits men without comparable remuneration. She makes it clear that the exploitation consists not in the sort of work that women do in the home, for this might include various kinds of tasks, but in the fact that they perform tasks for someone on whom they are dependent. Thus, for example, in most systems of agricultural production in the world, men take to market the goods women have produced, and more often than not men receive the status and often the entire income from this labor.

With the concept of sex-affective production, Ann Ferguson (1979; 1984; 1989, chap. 4) identifies another form of the transference of women's energies to men. Women provide men and children with emotional care and provide men with sexual satisfaction, and as a group receive relatively little of either from men (cf. Brittan and Maynard, pp. 142–48). The gender socialization of women makes us tend to be more attentive to interactive dynamics than men, and makes women good at providing empathy and support for people's feelings and at smoothing over interactive tensions. Both men and women look to women as nurturers of their personal lives, and women frequently complain that when they look to men for emotional support they do not receive it (Easton, 1978). The norms of heterosexuality, moreover, are oriented around male pleasure, and consequently many women receive little satisfaction from their sexual interaction with men (Gottlieb, 1984).

Most feminist theories of gender exploitation have concentrated on the institutional structure of the patriarchal family. Recently, however, feminists have begun to explore relations of gender exploitation enacted in the contemporary workplace and through the state. Carol Brown argues that as men have removed themselves from responsibility for children, many women have become dependent on the state for subsistence as they continue to bear nearly total responsibility for childrearing (Brown, 1981; cf. Boris and Bardaglio, 1983; A. Ferguson, 1984). This creates a new system of the exploitation of women's domestic labor mediated by state institutions, which she calls public patriarchy.

In twentieth-century capitalist economies the workplaces that women have been entering in increasing numbers serve as another important site of gender exploitation. David Alexander (1987) argues that typically feminine jobs involve gender-based tasks requiring sexual labor, nurturing, caring for others' bodies, or smoothing over workplace tensions. In these ways women's energies are expended in jobs that enhance the status of, please, or comfort others, usually men; and these gender-based labors of waitresses, clerical workers, nurses, and other caretakers often go unnoticed and undercompensated.

To summarize, women are exploited in the Marxist sense to the degree that they are wage workers. Some have argued that women's domestic labor also represents a form of capitalist class exploitation insofar as it is labor covered by the wages a family receives. As a group, however, women undergo specific forms of gender exploitation in which their energies and power are expended, often unnoticed and unacknowledged, usually to benefit men by releasing them for more important and creative work, enhancing their status or the environment around them, or providing them with sexual or emotional service.

Race is a structure of oppression at least as basic as class or gender. Are there, then, racially specific forms of exploitation? There is no doubt that racialized groups in the United States, especially Blacks and Latinos, are oppressed through capitalist superexploitation resulting from a segmented labor market that tends to reserve skilled, high-paying, unionized jobs for whites. There is wide disagreement about whether such superexploitation benefits whites as a group or only benefits the capitalist class (see Reich, 1981), and I do not intend to enter into that dispute here.

However one answers the question about capitalist superexploitation of racialized groups, is it possible to conceptualize a form of exploitation that is racially specific on analogy with the gender-specific forms just discussed? I suggest that the category of *menial* labor might supply a means for such conceptualization. In its derivation "menial" designates the labor of servants. Wherever there is racism, there is the assumption, more or less enforced, that members of the oppressed racial groups are or ought to be servants of those, or some of those, in the privileged group. In most white racist societies this means that many white people have dark- or yellow-skinned domestic servants, and in the United States today there remains significant racial structuring of private household service. But in the United States today much service labor has gone public: anyone who goes to a good hotel or a good restaurant can have servants. Servants often attend the daily—and nightly—activities of business executives, government officials, and other high-status professionals. In our society there remains strong cultural pressure to fill servant jobs—bellhop, porter, chambermaid, busboy, and so on—with Black and Latino workers. These jobs entail a transfer of energies whereby the servers enhance the status of the served.

Menial labor usually refers not only to service, however, but also to any servile, unskilled, low-paying work lacking in autonomy, in which a person is subject to taking orders from many people. Menial work tends to be auxiliary work, instrumental to the work of others, where those others receive primary recognition for doing the job. Laborers on a construction site, for example, are at the beck and call of welders, electricians, carpenters, and other skilled workers, who receive recognition for the job done. In the United States explicit racial discrimination once reserved menial work for Blacks, Chicanos, American Indians, and Chinese, and menial work still tends to be linked to Black and Latino workers (Symanski, 1985). I offer this category of menial labor as a form of racially specific exploitation, as a provisional category in need of exploration.

The injustice of exploitation is most frequently understood on a distributive model. For example, though he does not offer an explicit definition of the concept, by "exploitation" Bruce Ackerman seems to mean a seriously unequal distribution of wealth, income, and other resources that is group based and structurally persistent (Ackerman, 1980. chap. 8). John Roemer's definition of exploitation is narrower and more rigorous: "An agent is exploited when the amount of labor embodied in *any* bundle of goods he could receive, in a feasible distribution of society's net product, is less than the labor he expended" (Roemer, 1982, p. 122). This definition too turns the conceptual focus from institutional relations and processes to distributive outcomes.

Jeffrey Reiman argues that such a distributive understanding of exploitation reduces the injustice of class processes to a function of the inequality of the productive assets classes own. This misses, according to Reiman, the relationship of force between capitalists and workers, the fact that the unequal exchange in question occurs within coercive structures that give workers few options (Reiman, 1987; cf. Buchanan, 1982, pp. 44–49; Holmstrom, 1977). The injustice of exploitation consists in social processes that bring about a transfer of energies from one group to another to produce unequal distributions, and in the way in which social institutions enable a few to accumulate while they constrain many more. The injustices of exploitation cannot be eliminated by redistribution of goods, for as long as institutionalized practices and structural relations remain unaltered, the process of transfer will re-create an unequal distribution of benefits. Bringing about justice where there is exploitation requires reorganization of institutions and practices of decisionmaking, alteration of the division of labor, and similar measures of institutional, structural, and cultural change.

Marginalization

Increasingly in the United States racial oppression occurs in the form of marginalization rather than exploitation. Marginals are people the system of labor cannot or will not use. Not only in Third World capitalist countries, but also in most Western capitalist societies, there is a growing underclass of people permanently confined to lives of social marginality, most of whom are racially marked—Blacks or Indians in Latin America, and Blacks, East Indians, Eastern Europeans, or North Africans in Europe.

Marginalization is by no means the fate only of racially marked groups, however. In the United States a shamefully large proportion of the population is marginal; old people, and increasingly people who are not very old but get laid off from their jobs and cannot find new work; young people, especially Black or Latino, who cannot find first or second jobs; many single mothers and their children; other people involuntarily unemployed; many mentally and physically disabled people; American Indians, especially those on reservations.

Marginalization is perhaps the most dangerous form of oppression. A whole category of people is expelled from useful participation in social life and thus potentially subjected to severe material deprivation and even extermination. The material deprivation marginalization often causes is certainly unjust, especially in a society where others have plenty. Contemporary advanced capitalist societies have in principle acknowledged the injustice of material deprivation caused by marginalization, and have taken some steps to address it by providing welfare payments and services. The continuance of this welfare state is by no means assured, and in most welfare state societies, especially the United States, welfare redistributions do not eliminate large-scale suffering and deprivation.

Material deprivation, which can be addressed by redistributive social policies, is not, however, the extent of the harm caused by marginalization. Two categories of injustice beyond distribution are associated with marginality in advanced capitalist societies. First, the provision of welfare itself produces new injustice by depriving those dependent on it of rights and freedoms that others have. Second, even when material deprivation is somewhat mitigated by the welfare state, marginalization is unjust because it blocks the opportunity to exercise capacities in socially defined and recognized ways. I shall explicate each of these in turn.

Liberalism has traditionally asserted the right of all rational autonomous agents to equal citizenship. Early bourgeois liberalism explicitly excluded from citizenship all those whose reason was questionable or not fully developed, and all those not independent (Pateman, 1988, chap. 3; cf. Bowles and Gintis, 1986, chap. 2). Thus poor people, women, the mad and the feebleminded, and children were explicitly excluded from citizenship, and many of these were housed in institutions modeled on the modern prison: poorhouses, insane asylums, schools.

Today the exclusion of dependent persons from equal citizenship rights is only barely hidden beneath the surface. Because they depend on bureaucratic institutions for support or services, the old, the poor, and the mentally or physically disabled are subject to patronizing, punitive, demeaning, and arbitrary treatment by the policies and people associated with welfare bureaucracies. Being a dependent in our society implies being legitimately subject to the often arbitrary and invasive authority of social service providers and other public and private administrators, who enforce rules with which the marginal must comply, and otherwise exercise power over the conditions of their lives. In meeting needs of the marginalized, often with the aid of social scientific disciplines, welfare agencies also construct the needs themselves. Medical and social service professionals know what is good for those they serve, and the marginals and dependents themselves do not have the right to claim to know what is good for them (Fraser, 1987a; K. Ferguson, 1984, chap. 4). Dependency in our society thus implies, as it has in all liberal societies, a sufficient warrant to suspend basic rights to privacy, respect, and individual choice.

Although dependency produces conditions of injustice in our society, dependency in itself need not be oppressive. One cannot imagine a society in which some people would not need to be dependent on others at least some of the time: children, sick people, women recovering from childbirth, old people who have become frail, depressed or otherwise emotionally needy persons, have the moral right to depend on others for subsistence and support.

An important contribution of feminist moral theory has been to question the deeply held assumption that moral agency and full citizenship require that a person be autonomous and independent. Feminists have exposed this assumption as inappropriately individualistic and derived from a specifically male experience of social relations, which values competition and solitary achievement (see Gilligan, 1982; Friedman, 1985). Female experience of social relations, arising both from women's typical domestic care responsibilities and from the kinds of paid work that many women do, tends to recognize dependence as a basic human condition (cf. Hartsock, 1983, chap. 10). Whereas on the autonomy model a just society would as much as possible give people the opportunity to be independent, the feminist model envisions justice as according respect and participation in decisionmaking to those who are dependent as well as to those who are independent (Held, 1987b). Dependency should not be a reason to be deprived of choice and respect, and much of the oppression many marginals experience would be lessened if a less individualistic model of rights prevailed.

Marginalization does not cease to be oppressive when one has shelter and food. Many old people, for example, have sufficient means to live comfortably but remain oppressed in their marginal status. Even if marginals were provided a comfortable material life within institutions that respected their freedom and dignity, injustices of marginality would remain in the form of uselessness, boredom, and lack of self-respect. Most of our society's productive and recognized activities take place in contexts of organized social cooperation, and social structures and processes that close persons out of participation in such social cooperation are unjust. Thus while marginalization definitely entails serious issues of distributive justice, it also involves the deprivation of cultural, practical, and institutionalized conditions for exercising capacities in a context of recognition and interaction.

The fact of marginalization raises basic structural issues of justice, in particular concerning the appropriateness of a connection between participation in productive activities of social cooperation, on the one hand, and access to the means of consumption, on the other. As marginalization is increasing, with no sign of abatement, some social policy analysts have introduced the idea of a "social wage" as a guaranteed socially provided income not tied to the wage system. Restructuring of productive activity to address a right of participation, however, implies organizing some socially productive activity outside of the wage system (see Offe, 1985, pp. 95–100), through public works or self-employed collectives.

Powerlessness

. . . An adequate conception of oppression cannot ignore the experience of social division reflected in the colloquial distinction between the "middle class" and the "working class," a division structured by the social division of labor between professionals and nonprofessionals. Professionals are privileged in relation to nonprofessionals, by virtue of their position in the division of labor and the status it carries. Nonprofessionals suffer a form of oppression in addition to exploitation, which I call powerlessness.

In the United States, as in other advanced capitalist countries, most workplaces are not organized democratically, direct participation in public policy decisions is rare, and policy implementation is for the most part hierarchical, imposing rules on bureaucrats and citizens. Thus most people in these societies do not regularly participate in making decisions that affect the conditions of their lives and actions, and in this sense most people lack significant power. At the same time, as I argued in Chapter 1, domination in modern society is enacted through the widely dispersed powers of many agents mediating the decisions of others. To that extent many people have some power in relation to others, even though they lack the power to decide policies or results. The powerless are those who lack authority or power even in this mediated sense, those over whom power is exercised without their exercising it; the powerless are situated so that they must take orders and rarely have the right to give them. Powerlessness also designates a position in the division of labor and the concomitant social position that allows persons little opportunity to develop and exercise skills. The powerless have little or no work autonomy, exercise little creativity or judgment in their work, have no technical expertise or authority, express themselves awkwardly, especially in public or bureaucratic settings, and do not command respect. Powerlessness names the oppressive situations Sennett and Cobb (1972) describe in their famous study of working-class men.

This powerless status is perhaps best described negatively: the powerless lack the authority, status, and sense of self that professionals tend to have. The status privilege of professionals has three aspects, the lack of which produces oppression for nonprofessionals.

First, acquiring and practicing a profession has an expansive, progressive character. Being professional usually requires a college education and the acquisition of a specialized knowledge that entails working with symbols and concepts. Professionals experience progress first in acquiring the expertise, and then in the course of professional advancement and rise in status. The life of the nonprofessional by comparison is powerless in the sense that it lacks this orientation toward the progressive development of capacities and avenues for recognition.

Second, while many professionals have supervisors and cannot directly influence many decisions or the actions of many people, most nevertheless have considerable day-to-day work autonomy. Professionals usually have some authority over others, moreover—either over workers they supervise, or over auxiliaries, or over clients. Nonprofessionals, on

the other hand, lack autonomy, and in both their working and their consumer-client lives often stand under the authority of professionals.

Though based on a division of labor between "mental" and "manual" work, the distinction between "middle class" and "working class" designates a division not only in working life, but also in nearly all aspects of social life. Professionals and nonprofessionals belong to different cultures in the United States. The two groups tend to live in segregated neighborhoods or even different towns, a process itself mediated by planners, zoning officials, and real estate people. The groups tend to have different tastes in food, decor, clothes, music, and vacations, and often different health and educational needs. Members of each group socialize for the most part with others in the same status group. While there is some inter-group mobility between generations, for the most part the children of professionals become professionals and the children of nonprofessionals do not.

Thus, third, the privileges of the professional extend beyond the workplace to a whole way of life. I call this way of life "respectability." To treat people with respect is to be prepared to listen to what they have to say or to do what they request because they have some authority, expertise, or influence. The norms of respectability in our society are associated specifically with professional culture. Professional dress, speech, tastes, demeanor, all connote respectability. Generally professionals expect and receive respect from others. In restaurants, banks, hotels, real estate offices, and many other such public places, as well as in the media, professionals typically receive more respectful treatment than nonprofessionals. For this reason nonprofessionals seeking a loan or a job, or to buy a house or a car, will often try to look "professional" and "respectable" in those settings.

The privilege of this professional respectability appears starkly in the dynamics of racism and sexism. In daily interchange women and men of color must prove their respectability. At first they are often not treated by strangers with respectful distance or deference. Once people discover that this woman or that Puerto Rican man is a college teacher or a business executive, however, they often behave more respectfully toward her or him. Working-class white men, on the other hand, are often treated with respect until their working-class status is revealed. . . .

Cultural Imperialism

Exploitation, marginalization, and powerlessness all refer to relations of power and oppression that occur by virtue of the social division of labor—who works for whom, who does not work, and how the content of work defines one institutional position relative to others. These three categories refer to structural and institutional relations that delimit people's material lives, including but not restricted to the resources they have access to and the concrete opportunities they have or do not have to develop and exercise their capacities. These kinds of oppression are a matter of concrete power in relation to others—of who benefits from whom, and who is dispensable.

Recent theorists of movements of group liberation, notably feminist and Black liberation theorists, have also given prominence to a rather different form of oppression, which following Lugones and Spelman (1983) I shall call cultural imperialism. To experience cultural imperialism means to experience how the dominant meanings of a society render the particular perspective of one's own group invisible at the same time as they stereotype one's group and mark it out as the Other.

Cultural imperialism involves the universalization of a dominant group's experience and culture, and its establishment as the norm. Some groups have exclusive or primary access to what Nancy Fraser (1987b) calls the means of interpretation and communication in a society. As a consequence, the dominant cultural products of the society, that is, those most widely disseminated, express the experience, values, goals, and achievements of these groups. Often without noticing they do so, the dominant groups project their own experience as representative of humanity as such. Cultural products also express the dominant group's perspective on and interpretation of events and elements in the society, including other groups in the society, insofar as they attain cultural status at all.

An encounter with other groups, however, can challenge the dominant group's claim to universality.

The dominant group reinforces its position by bringing the other groups under the measure of its dominant norms. Consequently, the difference of women from men, American Indians or Africans from Europeans, Jews from Christians, homosexuals from heterosexuals, workers from professionals, becomes reconstructed largely as deviance and inferiority. Since only the dominant group's cultural expressions receive wide dissemination, their cultural expressions become the normal, or the universal, and thereby the unremarkable. Given the normality of its own cultural expressions and identity, the dominant group constructs the differences which some groups exhibit as lack and negation. These groups become marked as Other.

The culturally dominated undergo a paradoxical oppression, in that they are both marked out by stereotypes and at the same time rendered invisible. As remarkable, deviant beings, the culturally imperialized are stamped with an essence. The stereotypes confine them to a nature which is often attached in some way to their bodies, and which thus cannot easily be denied. These stereotypes so permeate the society that they are not noticed as contestable. Just as everyone knows that the earth goes around the sun, so everyone knows that gay people are promiscuous, that Indians are alcoholics, and that women are good with children. White males, on the other hand, insofar as they escape group marking, can be individuals.

Those living under cultural imperialism find themselves defined from the outside, positioned, placed, by a network of dominant meanings they experience as arising from elsewhere, from those with whom they do not identify and who do not identify with them. Consequently, the dominant culture's stereotyped and inferiorized images of the group must be internalized by group members at least to the extent that they are forced to react to behavior of others influenced by those images. This creates for the culturally oppressed the experience that W.E.B. Du Bois called "double consciousness"—"this sense of always looking at one's self through the eyes of others, of measuring one's soul by the tape of a world that looks on in amused contempt and pity" (Du Bois, 1969 [1903], p. 45). Double consciousness arises when the oppressed subject refuses to coincide with these devalued, objectified, stereotyped visions of herself or himself. While the subject desires recognition as human, capable of activity, full of hope and possibility, she receives from the dominant culture only the judgment that she is different, marked, or inferior.

The group defined by the dominant culture as deviant, as a stereotyped Other, *is* culturally different from the dominant group, because the status of Otherness creates specific experiences not shared by the dominant group, and because culturally oppressed groups also are often socially segregated and occupy specific positions in the social division of labor. Members of such groups express their specific group experiences and interpretations of the world to one another, developing and perpetuating their own culture. Double consciousness, then, occurs because one finds one's being defined by two cultures: a dominant and a subordinate culture. Because they can affirm and recognize one another as sharing similar experiences and perspectives on social life, people in culturally imperialized groups can often maintain a sense of positive subjectivity.

Cultural imperialism involves the paradox of experiencing oneself as invisible at the same time that one is marked out as different. The invisibility comes about when dominant groups fail to recognize the perspective embodied in their cultural expressions as a perspective. These dominant cultural expressions often simply have little place for the experience of other groups, at most only mentioning or referring to them in stereotyped or marginalized ways. This, then, is the injustice of cultural imperialism: that the oppressed group's own experience and interpretation of social life finds little expression that touches the dominant culture, while that same culture imposes on the oppressed group its experience and interpretation of social life. . . .

Violence

Finally, many groups suffer the oppression of systematic violence. Members of some groups live with the knowledge that they must fear random, unprovoked attacks on their persons or property, which have no motive but to damage, humiliate, or destroy the person. In American society women, Blacks, Asians, Arabs, gay men, and lesbians live under such threats of violence, and in at least some regions Jews, Puerto Ricans, Chicanos, and other Spanish-speaking Americans must fear such violence as well. Physical violence against these groups is shockingly frequent. Rape Crisis Center networks estimate that more than one-third of all American women experience an attempted or successful sexual assault in their lifetimes. Manning Marable (1984, pp. 238–41) catalogues a large number of incidents of racist violence and terror against blacks in the United States between 1980 and 1982. He cites dozens of incidents of the severe beating, killing, or rape of Blacks by police officers on duty, in which the police involved were acquitted of any wrongdoing. In 1981, moreover, there were at least five hundred documented cases of random white teenage violence against Blacks. Violence against gay men and lesbians is not only common, but has been increasing in the last five years. While the frequency of physical attack on members of these and other racially or sexually marked groups is very disturbing, I also include in this category less severe incidents of harrassment, intimidation, or ridicule simply for the purpose of degrading, humiliating, or stigmatizing group members.

Given the frequency of such violence in our society, why are theories of justice usually silent about it? I think the reason is that theorists do not typically take such incidents of violence and harassment as matters of social injustice. No moral theorist would deny that such acts are very wrong. But unless all immoralities are injustices, they might wonder, why should such acts be interpreted as symptoms of social injustice? Acts of violence or petty harassment are committed by particular individuals, often extremists, deviants, or the mentally unsound. How then can they be said to involve the sorts of institutional issues I have said are properly the subject of justice?

What makes violence a face of oppression is less the particular acts themselves, though these are often utterly horrible, than the social context surrounding them, which makes them possible and even acceptable. What makes violence a phenomenon of social injustice, and not merely an individual moral wrong, is its systemic character, its existence as a social practice.

Violence is systemic because it is directed at members of a group simply because they are members of that group. Any woman, for example, has a reason to fear rape. Regardless of what a Black man has done to escape the oppressions of marginality or powerlessness, he lives knowing he is subject to attack or harassment. The oppression of violence consists not only in direct victimization, but in the daily knowledge shared by all members of oppressed groups that they are *liable* to violation, solely on account of their group identity. Just living under such a threat of attack on oneself or family or friends deprives the oppressed of freedom and dignity, and needlessly expends their energy.

Violence is a social practice. It is a social given that everyone knows happens and will happen again. It is always at the horizon of social imagination, even for those who do not perpetrate it. According to the prevailing social logic, some circumstances make such violence more "called for" than others. The idea of rape will occur to many men who pick up a hitch-hiking woman; the idea of hounding or teasing a gay man on their dorm floor will occur to many straight male college students. Often several persons inflict the violence together, especially in all-male groupings. Sometimes violators set out looking for people to beat up, rape, or taunt. This rule-bound, social, and often premeditated character makes violence against groups a social practice.

Group violence approaches legitimacy, moreover, in the sense that it is tolerated. Often third parties find it unsurprising because it happens frequently and lies as a constant possibility at the horizon of the social imagination. Even when they are caught, those who perpetrate acts of group-directed violence or harassment often receive light or no punishment. To that extent society renders their acts acceptable. . . .

APPLYING THE CRITERIA

. . . The presence of any of these five conditions is sufficient for calling a group oppressed. But different group oppressions exhibit different combinations of these forms, as do different individuals in the groups. Nearly all, if not all, groups said by contemporary social movements to be oppressed suffer cultural imperialism. The other oppressions they experience vary. Working-class people are exploited and powerless, for example, but if employed and white do not experience marginalization and violence. Gay men, on the other hand, are not qua gay exploited or powerless, but they experience severe cultural imperialism and violence. Similarly, Jews and Arabs as groups are victims of cultural imperialism and violence, though many members of these groups also suffer exploitation or powerlessness. Old people are oppressed by marginalization and cultural imperialism, and this is also true of physically and mentally disabled people. As a group women are subject to gender-based exploitation, powerlessness, cultural imperialism, and violence. Racism in the United States condemns many Blacks and Latinos to marginalization, and puts many more at risk, even though many members of these groups escape that condition; members of these groups often suffer all five forms of oppression.

Applying these five criteria to the situation of groups makes it possible to compare oppressions without reducing them to a common essence or claiming that one is more fundamental than another. . . .

REFERENCES

Ackerman, Bruce. 1980. *Social Justice and the Liberal State*. New Haven: Yale University Press.

Alexander, David. 1987. "Gendered Job Traits and Women's Occupations." Ph.D. dissertation, Economics, University of Massachusetts.

Altman, Dennis. 1982. *The Homosexualization of American Society*. Boston: Beacon.

Boris, Ellen and Peter Bardaglio. 1983. "The Transformation of Patriarchy: The Historic Role of the State." In Irene Diamond, ed., *Families, Politics and Public Policy*. New York: Longman.

Bowles, Samuel and Herbert Gintis. 1986. *Democracy and Capitalism*. New York: Basic.

Brittan, Arthur and Mary Maynard. 1984. *Sexism, Racism and Oppression*. Oxford: Blackwell.

Brown, Carol. 1981. "Mothers, Fathers and Children: From Private to Public Patriarchy." In Lydia Sargent, ed., *Women and Revolution*. Boston: South End.

Buchanan, Allen. 1982. *Marx and Justice.* Totowa, N.J.: Rowman and Allanheld.

Coward, Rosalind and John Ellis. 1977. *Language and Materialism.* London: Routledge and Kegan Paul.

Delphy, Christine. 1984. *Close to Home: A Materialist Analysis of Women's Oppression.* Amherst: University of Massachusetts Press.

Du Bois, W.E.B. 1969 [1903]. *The Souls of Black Folk.* New York: New American Library.

Easton, Barbara. 1978. "Feminism and the Contemporary Family." *Socialist Review* 39 (May/June): 11–36.

Epstein, Steven. 1987. "Gay Politics, Ethnic Identity: The Limits of Social Constructionism." *Socialist Review* 17 (May–August) 9–54.

Ferguson, Ann. 1984. "On Conceiving Motherhood and Sexuality: A Feminist Materialist Approach." In Joyce Trebilcot, ed., *Mothering: Essays in Feminist Theory.* Totowa, N.J.: Rowman and Allanheld.

———. 1989. *Blood at the Root.* London: Pandora.

Ferguson, Kathy. 1984. *The Feminist Case against Bureaucracy.* Philadelphia: Temple University Press.

Fiss, Owen. 1976. "Groups and the Equal Protection Clause." *Philosophy and Public Affairs* 5 (Winter): 107–76.

Foucault, Michel. 1977. *Discipline and Punish.* New York: Pantheon.

Fraser, Nancy. 1987a. "Women, Welfare, and the Politics of Need Interpretation." *Hypatia: A Journal of Feminist Philosophy* 2 (Winter): 103–22.

French, Peter. 1975. "Types of Collectivities and Blame." *The Personalist* 56 (Spring): 160–69.

Friedman, Marilyn. 1985. "Care and Context in Moral Reasoning." In Carol Harding, ed., *Moral Dilemmas: Philosophical and Psychological Issues in the Development of Moral Reasoning.* Chicago: Precedent.

——— and Larry May. 1985. "Harming Women as a Group." *Social Theory and Practice* 11 (Summer): 297–34.

Frye, Marilyn. 1983a. "Oppression." In *The Politics of Reality.* Trumansburg, N.Y.: Crossing.

Giddens, Anthony. 1981. *A Contemporary Critique of Historical Materialism.* Berkeley and Los Angeles: University of California Press.

Gilligan, Carol. 1982. *In a Different Voice.* Cambridge: Harvard University Press.

Gottlieb, Roger. 1987. *History and Subjectivity.* Philadelphia: Temple University Press.

Habermas, Jürgen. 1987. *The Theory of Communicative Competence.* Vol. 2: *Lifeworld and System.* Boston: Beacon.

Hartsock, Nancy. 1983. *Money, Sex and Power.* New York: Longman.

Heidegger, Martin. 1962. *Being and Time.* New York: Harper and Row.

Held, Virginia. 1987b. "A Non-Contractual Society." In Marsha Hanen and Kai Nielsen, eds., *Science, Morality and Feminist Theory.* Calgary: University of Calgary Press.

Holmstrom, Nancy. 1977. "Exploitation." *Canadian Journal of Philosophy* 7 (June): 353–69.

Lugones, Maria C. and Elizabeth V. Spelman. 1983. "Have We Got a Theory for You! Feminist Theory, Cultural Imperialism and the Demand for 'the Woman's Voice.'" *Women's Studies International Forum* 6: 573–81.

Marable, Manning. 1984. *Race, Reform and Rebellion: The Second Reconstruction in Black America, 1945–82.* Jackson: University Press of Mississippi.

May, Larry. 1987. *The Morality of Groups: Collective Responsibility, Group-Based Harm, and Corporate Rights.* Notre Dame: Notre Dame University Press.

Murphy, Raymond. 1985. "Exploitation or Exclusion?" *Sociology* 19 (May): 225–43.

Offe, Claus. 1985. *Disorganized Capitalism.* Cambridge: MIT Press.

Pateman, Carole. 1988. *The Sexual Contract.* Stanford: Stanford University Press.

Reich, Michael. 1981. *Racial Inequality.* Princeton: Princeton University Press.

Reiman, Jeffrey. 1987. "Exploitation, Force, and the Moral Assessment of Capitalism: Thoughts on Roemer and Cohen." *Philosophy and Public Affairs* 16 (Winter): 3–41.

Roemer, John. 1982. *A General Theory of Exploitation and Class.* Cambridge: Harvard University Press.

Ross, Jeffrey. 1980. Introduction to Jeffrey Ross and Ann Baker Cottrell, eds., *The Mobilization of Collective Identity.* Lanham, Md.: University Press of America.

Rothschild, Joseph. 1981. *Ethnopolitics.* New York: Columbia University Press.

Sartre, Jean-Paul. 1948. *Anti-Semite and Jew.* New York: Schocken.

Sennett, Richard and Jonathan Cobb. 1972. *The Hidden Injuries of Class.* New York: Vintage.

Sher, George. 1987a. "Groups and the Constitution." In Gertrude Ezorsky, ed., *Moral Rights in the Workplace.* Albany: State University of New York Press.

Symanski, Al. 1985. "The Structure of Race." *Review of Radical Political Economy* 17 (Winter): 106–20.

Turner, John C., Michael A. Hogg, Penelope V. Oakes, Stephen D. Rucher, and Margaret S. Wethrell. 1987. *Rediscovering the Social Group: A Self-Categorization Theory.* Oxford: Blackwell.

QUESTIONS

1. Cultural imperialism, according to Young, is a form of oppression in which a group is stereotyped and marked as Other, and the group's perspective on itself is rendered invisible to others. What does it mean for a group to be marked as Other? What are some examples?

2. Young notes that different oppressed groups experience different combinations of exploitation, marginalization, powerlessness, cultural imperialism, and violence. What are some examples of groups that experience some but not all of these forms of oppression?

3. Young notes that welfare programs are meant to reduce the material deprivation (e.g., poverty) experienced by people who don't have jobs. But, Young argues, people receiving welfare are unjustly denied the rights and freedoms that others enjoy. Some public health experts have proposed that government food assistance should not be able to be used to buy sugary soda and other sugary drinks because they are unhealthy foods. What do you think Young would say about this proposal? Do you think the proposal is unjust?

4. Young thinks that the working class/nonprofessionals are typically not treated with the same respect as the middle class/professionals, where treating someone with respect is "to be prepared to listen to what they have to say or to do what they request." This is why people wear professional dress—"white collar" business suits, for example—when they are trying to get a loan or a job. Do you agree with Young that this occurs? Do you agree that it is unjust to treat people with more respect if they comport themselves like white-collar professionals?

JULIE GUTHMAN

"If They Only Knew"
The Unbearable Whiteness of Alternative Food

In this excerpt from her paper, "If They Only Knew: The Unbearable Whiteness of Alternative Food," Julie Guthman critiques alternative food projects as "white spaces" that are characterized by two aspects of whiteness, *color-blindness* and *universalism*. She also describes some disappointing experiences that her students had while volunteering with food justice projects, such as community gardens, that did not appeal to the communities they were intended to help. Guthman provides examples of food justice projects that attempt to address one form of injustice or social inequality—food insecurity, lack of access to healthy food—while arguably overlooking and reinforcing other forms of social inequality.

Julie Guthman, "If Only They Knew: The Unbearable Whiteness of Alternative Food." In Alison Hope Alkon and Julian Agyeman, eds., *Cultivating Food Justice: Race, Class, and Sustainability*. Excerpted from Chapter 12, © 2011 Massachusetts Institute of Technology, by permission of The MIT Press .

"If people only knew where their food came from . . .." This phrase resounds in alternative food movements. My students voice it in the classroom, and it is often the first sentence of papers they write. It undergirds many of the efforts of local food system activists, who focus a good deal of effort in encouraging more personalized relationships between producers and consumers. It is the end goal for contemporary muckraking led by the likes of Eric Schlosser and Michael Pollan whose writings on industrial food production practices often evoke a "yuck" reaction. It animates the long list of ingredients on upscale restaurant menus.

The phrase warrants additional parsing. Who is the speaker? How do we identify those who do not know the source of their food? What would they do if they only knew? Do they not know now? When pushed, those who employ this rhetoric will argue that such an unveiling of the American food supply would necessarily trigger desire for local, organic food, and people would be willing to pay for it. And then, so the logic goes, the food system would be magically transformed to one that is ecologically sustainable and socially just. To be sure, many alternative food advocates in the United States see lack of knowledge as the most proximate obstacle to a transformed food system, and in their elevated esteem for farmers—and chefs—relative to others who make their living in the provision of food, these advocates think that consumers should be willing to pay the "full cost" of food (Allen et al. 2003). This assertion is made in respect to the growing sense that food in the United States is artificially cheap due to both direct and indirect subsidies to agriculture, which include not only crop payments but also water, university research and extension, and even immigration policy. It follows that food produced in more ecologically sustainable and socially just ways would necessarily cost more. As stated by Michael Pollan (2008, 184), whose paeans to the local and organic have made him a hero of sorts of the alternative food movement: "Not everyone can afford to eat high-quality food in America, and that is shameful: however, those of us who can, should."

While there is much to say about the perverse ecological, social and health-related effects of the industrialized food system (Magdoff, Foster, and Buttel 2000; Kimbrell 2002; Pollan 2006), this chapter takes on the cultural politics of "if they only knew" and "paying the full cost" as it relates to alternative food. By alternative food, I refer to the broad range of practices and programs designed to bring producers and consumers into close proximity and to educate people of the value of local, sustainably grown, and seasonal food. Alternative food institutions thus include the relatively prolific (and thus decreasingly alternative) farmers markets, subscription farms that function as community supported agriculture (CSA), farm-to-school programs, community gardens, and a variety of hands-on educational programs and demonstration sites (Allen et al. 2003). Defined as such, my critique of alternative food will partially extend to some of the more race-conscious efforts toward those ends, specifically those that come under the banner of food justice—what I will later refer to as the alternatives to the alternatives. . . . I want to argue that many of the discourses of alternative food hail a white subject and thereby code the practices and spaces of alternative food as white. Insofar as this coding has a chilling effect on people of color, it not only works as an exclusionary practice, it also colors the character of food politics more broadly and may thus work against a more transformative politics. . . .

CODING ALTERNATIVE FOOD AS WHITE

Thus far, existing research suggests that African Americans especially, do not participate in alternative food institutions such as farmers markets and CSAs proportionate to the population (e.g., Hinrichs and Kremer 2002; Payne 2002; Perez, Allen, and Brown 2003). While it may also be the case that working-class or, more likely, less formally educated whites do not participate equal to their numbers either, they have not been subject to the same sort of scrutiny regarding their food provisioning practices, including attempts to engage them in alternative food practice. . . .[1]

This point must not be construed as a claim that African Americans do not participate in these markets at all (which surely varies by region) or, worse, a blanket indictment of African American food provisioning practices. For example, a study of a farmers market in a working-class predominantly African American neighborhood in Chicago found that shoppers at that market were much happier with the food at the farmers market relative to nearby stores, although the study did not suggest much breadth in participation (Suarez-Balcazar et al. 2006). I myself have noted a loyal following of African American shoppers and activists who attend the markets in my home region, although through informal conversations I have learned that many are highly cognizant of the "whiteness" of these spaces in ways that they themselves have had to overcome. . . .

Another caveat is that whiteness is a messy and controversial concept to work with, variably referred to as the phenotype of pale bodies, an attribute of particular (privileged) people, a result of historical/ social processes of racialization, a set of structural privileges, a standpoint of normalcy, or a particular set of cultural politics and practices (Frankenberg 1993; Kobayashi and Peake 2000). My interest in using whiteness is to make the invisible visible, to decenter white as "normal" or unmarked. I do so cognizant of the critique that the prominence given to whiteness scholarship has effectively recentered whiteness, as noted by McKinney (2005) and Sullivan (2006). Nevertheless, as Rachel Slocum (2006) first noted, community food movements have been slow to address issues of white privilege, which she attributes both to the persistent invisibility of whiteness as a racial category and to resistance within the movement to embrace an antiracist practice for fear of offending allies. So there is work to be done. . . .

For some scholars of whiteness, the point is to encourage more reflexivity among whites regarding their privileged social position. Building on the work of Frankenberg, whose point was to bring into view the "social geography of race," several scholars have highlighted the presumptions and effects of those who inhabit white bodies. So, according to McKinney (2005), the purpose of an engagement with whiteness is not to determine who is racist or not, but to uncover what whites think about being white and what effects that has on a racial system. Her position is that one can be nominally nonracist

and still contribute to a racial society. Further augmenting this line of argument, Sullivan (2006) makes the point that the unconscious habits of white privilege are in some respects more pernicious than the explicit racism of white supremacy because it is not examined. She draws particular attention to how non-recognition of being the beneficiaries of privilege allows whites to retain a sense of being morally good. . . .

In this argument, I am drawing from geographers of whiteness who as a whole seem less concerned with white personhood and instead focus on the work that whiteness as an unmarked category does in shaping social relations and, hence, space (Holloway 2000; Dwyer and Jones 2003; Schein 2006; Shaw 2006). . . . So it is not only a matter of making white people, those inhabiting pale-skinned bodies, accountable as to their effects on others (Frankenberg 1993; Lipsitz 1998; McKinney 2005)—although that is an important project in its own right. Rather, it is also a matter of showing how discourses associated with whiteness are implicated practically and spatially. No space is race neutral; there is an iterative coding of race and space (Thomas 2005; Saldanha 2006; Schein 2006). . . .

With this concern in mind, two related manifestations of whiteness are particularly important for how they define alternative food practice and space. One is colorblindness. For many, *colorblindness* or the absence of racial identifiers in language, or both, are seen as nonracist (Frankenberg 1993; McKinney 2005). Refusing to see (or refusing to admit) race difference for fear of being deemed racist has its origins in liberal thought, yet as many have remarked, the doctrine of colorblindness does its own violence by erasing the violence that the social construct of race has wrought in the form of racism (Holloway 2000; Brown et al. 2003). Inversely, colorblindness erases the privilege that whiteness creates. This is the point made by various scholars who have considered how whiteness acts as property—a set of expectations and institutional benefits historically derived from white supremacy that in their contemporary invisibility work to naturalize inequalities (Roediger 1991; Harris 1993; Lipsitz 1998).

The second manifestation of whiteness is universalism: the assumption that values held primarily by whites are normal and widely shared . . . This move erases difference in another way by refusing to acknowledge the experience, aesthetics, and ideals of others, with the pernicious effect that those who do not conform to white ideals are justifiably marginalized (Moore, Pandian, and Kosek 2003). In other words, when particular, seemingly universal ideals do not resonate, it is assumed that those for whom they do not resonate must be educated about these ideals or be forever marked as different. . . .

* * *

Many of what might be called the alternatives to the alternatives have been created in the name of food justice or food security or both. Particularly in light of the dearth of healthy food venues in many low-income African American neighborhoods (the so-called food desert problem), these programs are premised on the idea that low-income African Americans lack access, or perhaps exposure, to this food. As such, they are more race conscious in their practices and rhetoric and seek, as Slocum (2007) puts it, "to bring this good food to others."

I have learned something about these too, primarily through my students who as part of the Community Studies undergraduate major at UCSC do six-month field studies with food- and agriculture-related social justice organizations. Many choose to work with food justice or food security projects. During the field study, they are expected to write field notes and updates, and upon their return they are required to analyze their notes and prepare a capstone essay or thesis. These notes and formal papers are the basis of the evidence I present in this section. Admittedly, some of these data should be taken with a grain of salt, given that they reflect student disappointments relative to their pre-field study expectations (see Guthman 2008a for an extended discussion of this). . . .

For example, many students note that organic or farm fresh food does not always resonate in the communities and projects they study. In a required faculty update letter, one student working at a gardening and environmental education project reported, "Often times the girls show up with Jack in the Box for breakfast, eating it while working. The newly

hired market manager . . . is openly opposed to eating vegetables." Another student wrote of a field trip where she accompanied African American youth to a nearby intentional community and organic demonstration farm. As she reports it in her thesis most of the youth were repulsed by the food. "Eww! This lasagna is vegetarian?" inquired one girl. "This shit is organic," stated another. Later the youth were asked to say what they thought organic means. Many used the terms "disgusting," "gross," or "dirty" (Tattenham 2006). . . .

A student cited earlier wrote of another field trip to a nearby organic farm. The director of the youth program had said that it would be a good idea for the youth to "get their hands dirty" and pick fruit. As my student described it, the African American chaperone, as well as the youth, had scowls on their faces as they left for the field trip. In talking to the youth later, she learned that they resented the expectation to work not only for free, but also for white farmers (Tattenham 2006). In a somewhat similar vein, the letter from the student at the environmental education project went on to say:

> I am also working at a community garden that is run by [the same organization]. It is approximately one acre and is located within public housing. It is far from a productive garden. It is under funded and run by a seventy year old woman with no gardening experience. She is assisted by teenagers [who] drag their feet and have little interest in being there, perhaps because their tasks mainly consist of weeding. They have little access to the growing or harvesting [of] crops and are unable to see the whole process through. They are used as laborers instead of gardeners. There is little outside expertise brought in and no community involvement.

. . . Some of my students observe that such projects lack resonance precisely because they are alternatives. In a conversation with her African American neighbor one day, my student mentioned that she worked for the organization that brought a truck load of organic fruits and vegetables to their neighborhood. Her neighbor's response to why she did not shop from the truck (which was both convenient and sold at below market prices) was "Because they don't sell no food! All they got is birdseed." She went on to exclaim, "Who are they to tell me how to eat? I don't want that stuff. It's not food. I need to be able to feed my family." When my student asked her what she would like the truck to offer, the neighbor said, "You know, what normal grocery stores have" (Tattenham 2006). Another student working at an umbrella organization for several different projects . . . noted that organizational staff had heard from community members on several occasions that what they really wanted was a Safeway supermarket in their neighborhood.

Of course the problems I describe here have not gone unnoticed by movement activists and project leaders. I have attended many public meetings of the sustainable agriculture/alternative food movements where people of color or whites working in communities of color insist that the messages of these movements are, simply put, "too white." Accordingly, many of these projects are making explicit efforts to attract African Americans, as names such as The Peoples' Grocery, Mo' Betta Foods, Food from the Hood, Mandela's Farmers' Market, Black to Our Roots, and Growing Power amply demonstrate. These organizations endeavor to rework some of the whitened idioms associated with alternative food practice, specifically as a way to enroll African Americans in their projects.

For example, as described by Alkon (2008), the West Oakland farmers market (Mandela market) frames its work in terms of black identity. It publicizes the plight of African American farmers (who are few and far between in California), and encourages community support of these farmers in the name of racial justice. She describes how vendors see their work in terms of providing alternatives to the supermarkets that have abandoned the cities and, as one put it, "sell poison." The market also emphasizes black cuisine and culture. And unlike, say, the nearby Berkeley farmers market, food is sold substantially below supermarket prices (some vendors have been subsidized at times). Mo' Better Foods similarly sees its work in terms of rectifying a history where African Americans have been consistently stripped of landholding possibilities. They also work to establish a more positive relationship to agrarian production among African American consumers.

Still, leaders and staff of these organizations constantly have to struggle to create and maintain an African American presence, sometimes at the expense of keeping out white people who want to do good, including interns. Another one of my students, who worked in a community garden in a largely African American community, wrote in her field notes (not publicly available) of the discussions she often had with her supervisor. "She often tells me and other people who come into [the name of the garden] wanting to help out, that 'we are not trying to serve the anarchist/hippy/crust sector' of [that city]. This makes sense because she wants to serve the African American/Latino families and not groups of privileged white people who come around 'wearing ripped up clothes and generally insulting everyone.'" The student went on to note that the "struggle for inclusivity in the garden was complicated by the inadvertent creation of white spaces which put off a majority of the low income people."

In sum, the evidence my students provide suggests that even these more race-conscious projects tend to get coded as white. They are coded so not only because of the prevalence of white bodies, as salient as that is. As some of their field notes illustrate, it also appears that the associations of the food, the modes of educating people to its qualities, and the ways of delivering it lack appeal to the people such programs are designed to entice. It is worth considering why this seems to be the case. Is it a lack of knowledge?

"IF THEY ONLY KNEW"?

In her dissertation entitled "Black Faces, White Spaces: African Americans and the Great Outdoors" Carolyn Finney (2006) found a tendency among whites to attribute the lack of participation of African Americans in the U.S. national parks to such things as different values, lack of interest, or the costs of getting there. When she queried African Americans on the same issue, many rejected those sorts of prompts and responded to an open-ended prompt of "exclusionary practices." Not all respondents specified these practices, but those who did pointed to issues such as cultural competency, white privilege, and varying levels of commitment by environmental groups.

I want to argue for a similar phenomenon with these spaces of alternative food provision. And the exclusionary practices I want to point to are a pervasive set of idioms in alternative food practice that are either insensitive or ignorant (or both) of the ways in which they reflect whitened cultural histories and practices (Kobayashi and Peake 2000). "Getting your hands dirty in the soil," "if they only knew," and "looking the farmer in the eye" all point to an agrarian past that is far more easily romanticized by whites than others (Guthman 2004). It is important to recall that U.S. agricultural land and labor relations are fundamentally predicated on white privilege. As elucidated by Romm (2001), land was virtually given away to whites at the same time that reconstruction failed in the South, Native American lands were appropriated, Chinese and Japanese were precluded from landownership, and the Spanish-speaking *Californios* were disenfranchised of their ranches. So, when I teach Wendell Berry, a poet of agrarianism much beloved by the sustainable agriculture movement, I do so not to depict Berry as a racist because of his skin color, but instead to show how a romanticized American agrarian imaginary erases the explicitly racist ways in which, historically, American land has been distributed and labor has been organized, erasures that ramify today in more subtle cultural coding of small-scale farming. For African Americans, especially, putting your hands in the soil is more likely to invoke images of slave labor than nostalgia. Such rhetoric thus illustrates a lack of cultural competency that might be deemed an exclusionary practice.

Yet, it is the rhetoric of paying the full cost that best demonstrates what Lipsitz (1998) has called "the possessive investment in whiteness," referring to the relationship between whiteness and wealth accumulation and other structural privileges in U.S. society. To return to this quote from Michael Pollan: "Not everyone can afford to eat high-quality food in America, and that is shameful; however, those of us who can, should." What at first appears to be a compassionate statement that acknowledges class disparities is, in effect, a punt. It assumes the persistence of inequality and, for that matter, ignores that the racialized land and labor relationships embedded in the

U.S. food system continue to contribute to structural inequality. As such, it puts people who cannot afford to eat high-quality food beyond consideration—the very definition of an exclusionary practice. As Barack Obama stated, when he was a presidential candidate running against John McCain, "it's not that he doesn't care, it's just that he doesn't get it."

IF WHO ONLY KNEW?

. . . In terms of activism, we need to think a lot more about the ethics of "bringing good food to others" in alternative food. My underlying concern is that because alternative food tends to attract whites more than others, whites continue to define the rhetoric, spaces, and broader projects of agrifood transformation. As I have argued elsewhere (Guthman 2008b), the current menu reflects a fairly delimited conception of the politics of the possible, with a tremendous emphasis on market-driven alternatives, which often take root in the most well-resourced localities. This is an enormous problem given that race intersects with agriculture and food in myriad ways, yet many substantial health and livelihood inequalities are barely addressed through existing social movement activity. Insofar as people of color die younger due to such lack of attention, the problem in its totality surely meets Gilmore's (2002) definition of racism. In other words, the implications of these perhaps minor exclusions are far reaching.

In that vein, it is worth taking note that those African Americans who do participate in alternative food have tended to become involved because they have been sickened (literally or figuratively) by industrial food provisioning practices. Still, with a persistent dearth of people of color in alternative food spaces, and perhaps in the absence of explanations that might render their indifference to alternative food practice understandable, the rhetoric of "if they only knew" appears to be vindicated. The goodness of the food continues to go without saying. This is the hallmark of whiteness and its presumption of normativity; it goes to the deeper way in which colorblindness and acts of doing good can work to separate and scold others.

My point, however, is not to disable activists and advocates who have good intentions, out them for being overtly racist, or even to claim that without whiteness food activism would take a substantially different course and be wildly successful. My immediate goal for this chapter is to encourage much deeper reflection on the cultural politics of food activism. Saldanha (2006, 11) is surely right that "the embodiment of race . . . encompasses certain ethical stances and political choices. It informs what one can do, what one should do, in certain spaces and situations." Following Sullivan (2006), whites need to think about how to use the privileges of whiteness in an antiracist practice. In the realm of food politics, this might mean turning away from proselytizing based on universal assumptions about good food. Perhaps a place to start would be for us whites to state how much we do not know to open up the space that might allow for others to define the spaces and projects that will help spurn the transformation to a more just and ecological way of providing food.

NOTE

1. In contrast, community gardens seem to have significant participation of Latino immigrants (Terwilliger 2006) and farmers markets are frequently peopled by both Asian Americans and South, Southeast, and East Asian immigrants. Such observations would seem to support the case for a cultural politics of these spaces.

REFERENCES

Alkon, Alison. 2008. Paradise or Pavement: The Social Construction of the Environment in Two Urban Farmers Markets and their Implications for Environmental Justice and Sustainability. *Local Environment: The International Journal of Justice and Sustainability* 13 (3): 271–289.

Allen, Patricia, Margaret FitzSimmons, Michael Goodman, and Keith Warner. 2003. Shifting Plates in the Agrifood Landscape: The Tectonics of Alternative Agrifood Initiatives in California. *Journal of Rural Studies* 19 (1): 61–75.

Brown, Michael K., Martin Carnoy, Elliott Currie, Troy Duster, David B. Oppenheimer, Marjorie M. Shultz, and David Wellman. 2003. Of Fish and Water: Perspectives on Racism and Privilege. In *Whitewashing Race: the Myth of a Color-Blind Society,* ed. M. K. Brown, M. Carnoy, E. Currie, T. Duster, D. B. Oppenheimer, M. M. Shultz, and D. Wellman, 34–65. Berkeley: University of California.

Dwyer, Owen J., and John Paul Jones. 2003. White Socio-spatial Epistemology. *Social & Cultural Geography* 1 (2): 209–222.

Finney, Carolyn. 2006. Black Faces, White Spaces: African Americans and the Great Outdoors. PhD diss., Department of Geography, Clark University, Worcester, MA.

Frankenberg, Ruth. 1993. *White Women, Race Matters: The Social Construction of Whiteness.* Minneapolis: University of Minnesota.

Gilmore, Ruth Wilson. 2002. Fatal Couplings of Power and Difference: Notes on Racism and Geography. *Professional Geographer* 54 (1): 15–24.

Guthman, Julie. 2004. *Agrarian Dreams? The Paradox of Organic Farming in California.* Berkeley: University of California Press.

Guthman, Julie. 2008a. Bringing Good Food to Others: Investigating the Subjects of Alternative Food Practice. *Cultural Geographies* 15 (4): 425–441.

Guthman, Julie. 2008b. Neoliberalism and the Making of Food Politics in California. *Geoforum* 39 (3): 1171–1183.

Guthman, Julie, Amy W. Morris, and Patricia Allen. 2006. Squaring Farm Security and Food Security in Two Types of Alternative Food Institutions. *Rural Sociology* 71 (4): 662–684.

Harris, Cheryl I. 1993. Whiteness as Property. *Harvard Law Review* 106 (8): 1709–1791.

Hinrichs, Claire G., and K. S. Kremer. 2002. Social Inclusion in a Midwest Local Food System. *Journal of Poverty* 6 (1): 65–90.

Holloway, S. R. 2000. Identity, Contingency and the Urban Geography of "Race." *Social & Cultural Geography* 1 (2): 197–208.

Kimbrell, Andrew, ed. 2002. *The Fatal Harvest Reader.* Washington, DC: Island Press.

Kobayashi, Audrey, and Linda Peake. 2000. Racism Out of Place: Thoughts on Whiteness and an Anti-racist Geography in the New Millennium. *Annals of the Association of American Geographers* 90 (2): 392–403.

Lipsitz, George. 1998. *The Possessive Investment in Whiteness.* Philadelphia: Temple University Press.

Magdoff, Fred, John Bellamy Foster, and Frederick H. Buttel, eds. 2000. *Hungry for Profit.* New York: Monthly Review Press.

McKinney, Karyn D. 2005. *Being White: Stories of Race and Racism.* New York: Routledge.

Moore, Donald S., Anand Pandian, and Jake Kosek. 2003. Introduction: The Cultural Politics of Race and Nature: Terrains of Power and Practice. In *Race, Nature, and the Politics of Difference,* ed. D. S. Moore, J. Kosek, and A. Pandian, 1–70. Durham, NC: Duke University Press.

Payne, Tim. 2002. U.S. Farmers' Markets 2000: A Study of Emerging Trends. *Journal of Food Distribution Research, Food Distribution Research Society* 33 (1) (March). <http://agmarketing.extension.psu.edu/Com-FarmMkt/PDFs/emerg_trend_frm_mrkt.pdf> (accessed July 19, 2007).

Pollan, Michael. 2006. *The Omnivore's Dilemma: A Natural History of Four Meals.* New York: Penguin.

Pollan, Michael. 2008. *In Defense of Food: An Eater's Manifesto.* New York: Penguin.

Roediger, David R. 1991. *The Wages of Whiteness: Race and the Making of the American Working Class.* New York: Verso.

Romm, Jeff. 2001. The Coincidental Order of Environmental Injustice. In *Justice and Natural Resources: Concepts, Strategies, and Applications,* ed. K. M. Mutz, G. C. Bryner, and D. S. Kennedy, 117–137. Covelo, CA: Island Press.

Saldanha, Arun. 2006. Reontologising Race: The Machinic Geography of Phenotype. *Environment and Planning D: Society & Space* 24 (1): 9–24.

Schein, Richard H. 2006. Race and Landscape in the United States. In *Landscape and Race in the United States,* ed. R. H. Schein, 1–21. New York: Routledge.

Shaw, Wendy S. 2006. Decolonizing Geographies of Whiteness. *Antipode* 38 (4): 851–869.

Slocum, Rachel. 2006. Anti-racist Practice and the Work of Community Food Organizations. *Antipode* 38 (2): 327–349.

Slocum, Rachel. 2007. Whiteness, Space, and Alternative Food Practice. *Geoforum* 38 (3): 520–533.

Suarez-Balcazar, Yolanda, Louise I. Martinez, Ginnefer Cox, and Anita Jayraj. 2006. African-Americans' Views on Access to Healthy Foods: What a Farmers' Market Provides. *Journal of Extension* 44 (2). <http://www.joe.org/joe/2006april/a2.php> (accessed July 19, 2007).

Sullivan, Shannon. 2006. *Revealing Whiteness: The Unconscious Habits of Racial Privilege.* Indianapolis: Indiana University.

Tattenham, Katrina. 2006. Food Politics and the Food Justice Movement. Senior thesis, Community Studies, University of California, Santa Cruz.

Terwilliger, Kaley. 2006. Sowing the Seeds of Self-Determination: Why People Are Community Gardening in Los Angeles County. Senior thesis, Community Studies, University of California, Santa Cruz.

Thomas, Mary. 2005. "I Think It's Just Natural": The Spatiality of Racial Segregation at a US High School. *Environment & Planning A* 37:1233–1248.

QUESTIONS

1. What is whiteness, according to Guthman? How, according to Guthman, are alternative food projects "white spaces"? How is this exclusionary? Guthman thinks that the fact that alternative food projects are white spaces may "work against a more transformative politics." How so?

2. Guthman writes that "colorblindness erases the privilege that whiteness creates." What does this mean? Why does Guthman believe it?

3. What is universalism? In what way is the alternative food movement characterized by a problematic form of universalism, according to Guthman? One of Iris Marion Young's five forms of oppression is *cultural imperialism,* in which the dominant group establishes its culture and perspective as the norm and makes other cultures invisible or marks them as Other. Do you think that the universalism described by Guthman is a form of cultural imperialism? If so, why? If not, how do the two differ?

4. Is there anything wrong with a community food project that's meant to serve poor people of color but is run by middle-class white people who don't live in that community? If there is a problem, what is it?

5. The food justice projects that Guthman describes are attempts to address one form of injustice, such as food insecurity or lack of access to healthy foods. Are there other forms of injustice or social inequality that these projects are not addressing? If so, is it problematic that the food insecurity projects do not address them? If so, why?

Declaration of Nyéléni

The Declaration of Nyéléni was adopted in 2007 at the first Forum for Food Sovereignty, held in the village of Nyéléni, Mali. It was signed by about 500 delegates, who were peasants, indigenous peoples, workers, activists and others from more than 80 countries. It expresses the principles and goals of the food sovereignty movement.

27 February 2007 (Nyéléni Village, Sélingué, Mali)—We, more than 500 representatives from more than 80 countries, of organizations of peasants/family farmers, artisanal fisher-folk, indigenous peoples, landless peoples, rural workers, migrants, pastoralists, forest communities, women, youth, consumers, environmental and urban movements have gathered together in the village of Nyéléni in Sélingué, Mali to strengthen a global movement for food sovereignty. We are doing this, brick by brick, have been living in huts constructed by hand in the local tradition, and eating food that is being produced and prepared by the Sélingué community. We give our collective endeavour the name "Nyéléni" as a tribute to and inspiration from a legendary Malian peasant woman who farmed and fed her peoples well.

Most of us are food producers and are ready, able and willing to feed all the world's peoples. Our heritage as food producers is critical to the future of humanity. This is specially so in the case of women and indigenous peoples who are historical creators of knowledge about food and agriculture and are devalued. But this heritage and our capacities to produce healthy, good and abundant food are being threatened and undermined by neo-liberalism and global capitalism. Food sovereignty gives us the hope and power to preserve, recover and build on our food producing knowledge and capacity.

Food sovereignty is the right of peoples to healthy and culturally appropriate food produced through ecologically sound and sustainable methods, and their right to define their own food and agriculture systems. It puts those who produce, distribute and consume food at the heart of food systems and policies rather than the demands of markets and corporations. It defends the interests and inclusion of the next generation. It offers a strategy to resist and dismantle the current corporate trade and food regime, and directions for food, farming, pastoral and fisheries systems determined by local producers. Food sovereignty prioritises local and national economies and markets and empowers peasant and family farmer-driven agriculture, artisanal fishing, pastoralist-led grazing, and food production, distribution and consumption based on environmental, social and economic sustainability. Food sovereignty promotes transparent trade that guarantees just income to all peoples and the rights of consumers to control their food and nutrition. It ensures that the rights to use and manage our lands, territories, waters, seeds, livestock and biodiversity are in the hands of those of us who produce food. Food sovereignty implies new social relations free of oppression and inequality between men and women, peoples, racial groups, social classes and generations.

In Nyéléni, through numerous debates and interactions, we are deepening our collective understanding of food sovereignty and learned about the reality of the struggles of our respective movements to retain autonomy and regain our powers. We now understand better the tools we need to build our movement and advance our collective vision.

Declaration of the Forum for Food Sovereignty, Nyéléni (2007). http://nyeleni.org/spip.php?article290

WHAT ARE WE FIGHTING FOR?

A world where . . .

. . . all peoples, nations and states are able to determine their own food producing systems and policies that provide every one of us with good quality, adequate, affordable, healthy, and culturally appropriate food;

. . . recognition and respect of women's roles and rights in food production, and representation of women in all decision making bodies;

. . . all peoples in each of our countries are able to live with dignity, earn a living wage for their labour and have the opportunity to remain in their homes;

. . . where food sovereignty is considered a basic human right, recognised and implemented by communities, peoples, states and international bodies;

. . . we are able to conserve and rehabilitate rural environments, fish stocks, landscapes and food traditions based on ecologically sustainable management of land, soils, water, seas, seeds, livestock and other biodiversity;

. . . we value, recognize and respect our diversity of traditional knowledge, food, language and culture, and the way we organise and express ourselves;

. . . there is genuine and integral agrarian reform that guarantees peasants full rights to land, defends and recovers the territories of indigenous peoples, ensures fishing communities' access and control over their fishing areas and eco-systems, honours access and control over pastoral lands and migratory routes, assures decent jobs with fair remuneration and labour rights for all, and a future for young people in the countryside;

. . . where agrarian reform revitalises interdependence between producers and consumers, ensures community survival, social and economic justice and ecological sustainability, and respect for local autonomy and governance with equal rights for women and men . . . where it guarantees the right to territory and self-determination for our peoples;

. . . where we share our lands and territories peacefully and fairly among our peoples, be we peasants, indigenous peoples, artisanal fishers, pastoralists, or others;

. . . in the case of natural and human-created disasters and conflict-recovery situations, food sovereignty acts as a kind of "insurance" that strengthens local recovery efforts and mitigates negative impacts . . . where we remember that affected communities are not helpless, and where strong local organization for self-help is the key to recovery;

. . . where peoples' power to make decisions about their material, natural and spiritual heritage are defended;

. . . where all peoples have the right to defend their territories from the actions of transnational corporations;

WHAT ARE WE FIGHTING AGAINST?

Imperialism, neo-liberalism, neo-colonialism and patriarchy, and all systems that impoverish life, resources and eco-systems, and the agents that promote the above such as international financial institutions, the World Trade Organisation, free trade agreements, transnational corporations, and governments that are antagonistic to their peoples;

The dumping of food at prices below the cost of production in the global economy;

The domination of our food and food producing systems by corporations that place profits before people, health and the environment;

Technologies and practices that undercut our future food producing capacities, damage the environment and put our health at risk. Those include transgenic crops and animals, terminator technology, industrial aquaculture and destructive fishing practices, the so-called white revolution of industrial dairy practices, the so-called "old" and "new" Green Revolutions, and the "Green Deserts" of industrial bio-fuel monocultures and other plantations;

The privatisation and commodification of food, basic and public services, knowledge, land, water, seeds, livestock and our natural heritage;

Development projects/models and extractive industry that displace people and destroy our environments and natural heritage;

Wars, conflicts, occupations, economic blockades, famines, forced displacement of people and confiscation of their land, and all forces and governments that cause and support them; post disaster and conflict reconstruction programmes that destroy our environments and capacities;

The criminalization of all those who struggle to protect and defend our rights;

Food aid that disguises dumping, introduces GMOs into local environments and food systems and creates new colonialism patterns;

The internationalisation and globalisation of paternalistic and patriarchal values that marginalise women, diverse agricultural, indigenous, pastoral and fisher communities around the world. . .

WHAT CAN AND WILL WE DO ABOUT IT?

Just as we are working with the local community in Sélingué to create a meeting space at Nyéléni, we are committed to building our collective movement for food sovereignty by forging alliances, supporting each other's struggles and extending our solidarity, strengths, and creativity to peoples all over the world who are committed to food sovereignty. Every struggle, in any part of the world for food sovereignty, is our struggle.

We have arrived at a number of collective actions to share our vision of food sovereignty with all peoples of this world, which are elaborated in our synthesis document. We will implement these actions in our respective local areas and regions, in our own movements and jointly in solidarity with other movements. We will share our vision and action agenda for food sovereignty with others who are not able to be with us here in Nyéléni so that the spirit of Nyéléni permeates across the world and becomes a powerful force to make food sovereignty a reality for peoples all over the world.

Finally, we give our unconditional and unwavering support to the peasant movements of Mali and ROPPA in their demands that food sovereignty become a reality in Mali and by extension in all of Africa.

Now is the time for food sovereignty!

PAUL B. THOMPSON

Food Security and Food Sovereignty

In this excerpt from his book *From Field to Fork: Food Ethics for Everyone* (Oxford University Press, 2015), philosopher Paul Thompson explains how the food sovereignty movement resists the idea of food security, and instead sees food sovereignty—"the ability to control the structure and organization of one's local food system"—as having central

Paul Thompson, "Food Security and Food Sovereignty," from *Field to Fork: Food Ethics for Everyone* (2015), 72–79. Excerpted by permission of Oxford University Press, USA.

importance. Thompson also discusses how different theories of economic justice—Rawlsian, Marxist, and libertarian—would assess the treatment of food system workers.

There is widespread recognition that food is, in one sense at least, *quite* different from many other social goods. Everyone must have food to survive, and when inequality in access to food reaches an extreme point, people die of starvation. Well before the point of starvation, children are especially vulnerable to the diseases of hunger and food deprivation. The Food and Agricultural Organization (FAO) of the United Nations maintains a "hunger portal" that reports global statistics on undernourishment and encourages visitors to delve more deeply into the complex causes of hunger on a global basis. As of this writing, FAO notes areas of progress on the global front but still reports approximately 842 million people in the world subsisting with less than adequate food.[1] There is thus a stark sense in which secure access to food is morally compelling in a manner that transcends philosophical argument. This fact is acknowledged in the United Nations International Declaration of Human Rights. As noted already, the policy-oriented literature that has grown up around the imperative of securing universal access to food has defined the goal as "food security."

It is not possible to do justice to the way that food security has been approached by economists, nutritionists, and food policy specialists over the last fifty years. It must suffice to say that the core notion has been a person's ability to consume a diet that is nutritionally adequate, given current age, gender, daily expenditure of calories, and general state of health. Malnutrition can surface in the form of inadequate calories or an imbalance of nutrients, the latter being the case when diets become insufficiently varied. Anyone at a significant risk of being unable to consume a nutritionally adequate diet over a specified time horizon would be considered "food insecure." But food insecurity can take many forms. Victims of natural disasters such as a typhoon, drought, volcanic eruption, or tsunami experience periods of extreme but short-lived food insecurity. Their needs can often be met by emergency shipments of food

through the World Food Program, one of FAO's more capable agencies. Ironically, such victims of disaster stimulate the most compelling moral response on the part of the food secure. To be sure, there is a genuine need. Nevertheless, although it may take a year or more for local agriculture to recover, these are the most solvable problems in food security. The more intractable ethical problems of food security concern people whose poverty prevents them from having access to adequate diets even when food is available and plentiful in local markets.[2]

However, there is also a line of thought that runs like this: a *nation* will not be secure if it is vulnerable to short-term collapses in the food supply. The tradition of political economy has tended to evaluate food security in terms of a nation's ability to produce enough to supply their military garrisons and to have secure supply lines to them. This way of thinking about the ethical/political significance of food systems goes back to the ancient world, but it was forcefully articulated by James Harrington, an English theorist of social justice in the seventeenth century. Harrington stressed the connection between military security and a nation's ability to feed its army, linking both to more traditional arguments praising the moral character of farmers.[3] Here notice that it is not so much a natural disaster as the potential for war that drives Harrington's thinking on food security. There is a longstanding policy tradition that has been skeptical of trade as a reliable source of food and thus a guarantor of food security. Whether or not this skepticism is justifiable, it has carried over into present-day debates on food security in the form [of] a dual conception. On the one hand, *people* enjoy food security when they have access to a nutritionally adequate diet; on the other hand, a *nation* is food secure when it has secure access to enough food for everyone that it wants to feed. And today as in the classical period of political economy, there is skepticism about the reliability of international trade.

Over the last decade, a new voice has entered this debate. Via Campesina began as a loose-knit Latin American group representing a variety of peasant farming interests. It has expanded and now reflects the viewpoint of poor or marginalized people across the globe. Farmers do have a special kind of vulnerability when food security is being negotiated. If policymakers in the national capital *do* decide that food security (in either sense) can be guaranteed by trading on international markets, local farmers may be facing stiff competition from imported grain—grain whose production may have been subsidized in rich countries. In the meantime, policymakers in the national capital may be hoping that local farmers will stop growing subsistence crops and switch to something like cocoa, coffee, or biofuels—crops that generate foreign exchange. Advocates for Via Campesina started to resist the idea of food security. *Their* interest is not simply one of having access to a nutritionally adequate diet. Indeed, what they fear most is being placed in a position where they must earn money to purchase a nutritionally adequate diet grown on foreign soil. So Via Campesina has argued that what matters morally is *food sovereignty*—the ability to control the structure and organization of one's local food system.[4]

Unfortunately, as compelling as this argument is for the small farmers that Via Campesina represents, it is not an idea that necessarily travels well. Some have presumed that food sovereignty is just another label for the long-lived way of defining food security at a national level, and they have then taken the view that this cannot be achieved unless a nation produces enough to feed its entire population within its national boundaries. No European nations are food secure by this standard, and none are taking steps to achieve it. Thus, there is some degree of skepticism about food sovereignty among the policy specialists that have focused on getting nutritionally adequate diets to poor people for the last fifty years. Others have seized the term as a banner for all manner of social justice activism in the food systems of the industrial world. Food sovereignty then becomes a moniker for increasing the wages of fast-food workers and for labor organizers in the fields with tomato pickers. In some quarters, food sovereignty is advanced as a reason why traditional farmers and artisanal food processors ought to be exempt from national food safety regulations. As ethically laudable as these causes may be, it is far from clear how they meld with the goals of Latin American peasant farmers who are trying to preserve both their local markets and a farming way of life.

Nevertheless, there does seem to be something philosophically important now being advanced under the flag of food sovereignty. For Via Campesina, at least, the idea points to the way entire rural communities, local cultures, and longstanding social relations are brought together through the production, preparation, and consumption of food. If you are living in a Latin American village where most people are farmers, it is easy to see how the production, preparation, and consumption of food integrates families into a community. The continuance of the community depends upon people caring for one another and looking after the ways that they have long endured through the production, preparation, and consumption of their food. The survival and maintenance of these food practices is critical to the sustainability of these communities in every sense of the word. It is the basis of their economic livelihood. It is what binds them to their natural environment, and one can be sure that they have a keen sense of what is needed to preserve it. But finally, it is in the performance of these practices that the institutions and relationships of the local community are reproduced over time. Destruction of this nexus of institutions and material practices means destruction of the community. Individuals might survive, to be sure. They might even move to the city and work in a factory where their net income will be higher than it is today. They might achieve what FAO calls food security by doing this, but would that be justice?

A TEMPORARY CONCLUSION

The facts clearly show that the industrial food system relies heavily on low-wage labor, and that food industry firms—including farms, processors, and retailers—are well represented among the bad actors of labor relations. Bad-faith negotiations, exploitation and violation of work rules, and even felony violations of basic civil and human rights are all too common in the industrial food system. No theory of justice would countenance the more extreme acts of injustice perpetrated by food industry firms, but they are able to get away with it largely because the people who are victimized by these practices often find themselves in desperate straits due to poverty, lack of education, and vulnerabilities that relate to their immigration status, work history, or family situations. From the perspective of these workers, there is no sharp distinction between being victimized by violations of the law and legally sanctioned victimization through part-time, minimum-wage employment and work rules that keep people at or near the poverty level.

While Rawlsian or Marxist conceptions of justice would find the treatment of food-system workers in many countries (and especially the United States) to be inconsistent with the philosophical dictates of social justice, there are other views. Farming and food-system employment have always been poorly compensated, in part because the skills needed for this work have historically been virtually ubiquitous. When anyone could do the manual work of farming, food processing and cooking, there was no reason for employers to pay more than the lowest wage that the market would bear. And even as economic growth and social change have produced a working class having little to no familiarity with farming and food production, there have always been plenty of immigrants with farm backgrounds who are eager to take on these jobs. If this is just the workings of the labor market, then philosophers with a certain kind of libertarian or neoliberal mindset may find the circumstances of food-system workers to be regrettable but still not a true injustice. The appropriate response will occur when enough of them attain the education that will allow them to compete for better jobs. When no one will take these food-system jobs because there are better jobs to be had, scarcity in the labor pool will force food industry firms to pay more.

There *is* work to be done in discerning how these contrasting philosophical approaches to economic justice would apply to the industrial food system, but the picture that I have just drawn suggests that the philosophical problem of justice is one that must be addressed at a level of abstraction where it is largely irrelevant that we are talking about food-system employment, as distinct from employment in building construction, manufacturing, or some other sector of the industrial economy. Indeed, the economic situation of fast-food workers or grocery employees would seem to have everything to do with the structure of retail employment and very little to do with the fact that these businesses happen to be engaged in selling food products to retail customers. So, without denying the social relevance or immediacy of these issues, we can conclude that these problems of social justice would not give rise to a form of food ethics that would be different from every other application of the theory of justice.

It is less clear that traditional theories of justice articulate what is at stake for the peasant farming villagers of Via Campesina. On the one hand, contemporary social theorists who share Marx's skepticism of capitalism have argued that the global food system should be understood as a systemic nexus that functions to extract the last shred of economic value from the production, distribution, and consumption of food and to repress any form of political action against it. Everyone needs to eat. Therefore, control of food is a powerful locus for both profit-taking and the exercise of social control. Food sovereignty is, on this view, a mode of resistance against this totalizing food regime. "Food politics" starts to look like something that is both novel and deeply significant for the way that it cuts to the heart of everything that matters. On the other hand, the driving forces that are identified by this analysis may not be very new at all: neoliberal promotion of trade and global institutions such as the World Bank are pushing toward a kind of food security that threatens small farming villages, and the big winners are corporations who first manufacture the seeds and chemicals and then control the trade in grain and manufactured food products right down to the retail level. Opponents of global capital and advocates of small farmers have a ready-made common enemy. Once again, the argument starts to circle back to a common theme. It is starting to look like the food connection is rather accidental. A Marxist is not surprised to find issues of justice in a neoliberal corporate food regime, but they are symptomatic of issues that exist *throughout* a capitalist economy. Food winds up merely as a convenient tool for raising peoples' consciousness of a more widespread type of oppression.

There is, in conclusion, a sociological question: is "the new politics of food" a *transformational* social movement, or will it exhaust itself in a few political reforms that leave the overall structure of contemporary society intact?[5] If the latter, the food movement will be like the labor movement, the civil rights movement, and the women's movement before it. In either case, there are philosophical questions that demand an answer. Those who look for transformational power in the new emphasis on food may see these issues as having a salience or universality that earlier social movements have lacked. If the food movement achieves significant but non-transformative change, it will still be important to articulate why food practices involve matters of ethical importance. The chapters that follow offer suggestions for articulating and analyzing several key topics in food ethics, but leave open the question of whether food sovereignty amounts to a comprehensive or transformational approach to problems in social justice.

In a nutshell, it may be the way that food moves *across* so many distinct and distinguishable contested terrains that provides a germ of insight. The intersectional nature of food-system issues is the key lesson to take from a review of social justice activism and the continuing injustices in farming and food industry firms. It is the way that food brings these issues together that matters for social movements, that gives them salience and some hope for effectiveness.

NOTES

1. Food and Agricultural Organization, Hunger Portal, http://www.fao.org/hunger/en/, accessed December 15, 2013.

2. Paul B. Thompson, "Food Aid and the Famine Relief Argument (Brief Return)," *The Journal of Agricultural and Environmental Ethics* 23 (2010): 209–227.

3. James A. Harrington, *The Common-Wealth of Oceana* (London: J. Streater for Livewell Chapman, 1656).

4. Miguel Altieri, "Agroecology, Small Farms and Food Sovereignty," *Monthly Review* 61, no. 3 (2009): 102–113; Raj Patel, "What Does Food Sovereignty Look Like?," *Journal of Peasant Studies* 36 (2009): 663–673; William D. Schanbacher, *The Politics of Food: The Global Conflict Between Food Security and Food Sovereignty* (Santa Barbara, CA: ABC-CLIO, 2010).

5. Eric Holt Giménez and Annie Shattuck, "Food Crises, Food Regimes and Food Movements: Rumblings of Reform or Tides of Transformation?," *Journal of Peasant Studies* 38 (2011): 109–144.

QUESTIONS

1. Who are La Via Campesina? What does "food sovereignty" mean to them? Thompson writes that "food sovereignty" has been seized "as a banner for all manner of social justice activism in the food systems of the industrial world." What are some examples?

2. Proponents of food sovereignty see food sovereignty, rather than food security, as the central goal or aim that should guide food system reform. Why? Is food security too narrow a goal, in their view? Have efforts to achieve food security had bad effects, in their view?

3. Thompson thinks that the food sovereignty movement directs our attention to something philosophically important about food, namely that "entire rural communities, local cultures, and longstanding social relations are brought together through the production, preparation, and consumption of food." How might the industrialization and globalization of agriculture threaten this?

4 Consumer Ethics

Many chapters in this textbook highlight disturbing facts about the foods that we eat—for example, that they are produced in ways that appear to do serious harm to people, non-human animals, and the environment. As one example, intensive animal agriculture ("factory farming") has negative impacts on the animals involved, as well as negative impacts on humans as a consequence of dangerous working conditions, environmental pollution, and the malnutritional consequences of a "Western diet" that relies heavily on animal products.[1] As another example, even vegan staples like tomatoes and berries are often harvested by people who have to work in conditions that harm them.

Chapters 7 through 11 focus on identifying these ethically problematic features of contemporary food production, and ask whether they are the w*rong* way of producing food and thus should be substantially changed. The focus of those chapters might be called *production ethics*, where the central question is whether it is wrong to produce goods in the way they are actually produced—and if so, how we should do things instead, and specifically what the best alternative production method is from a broadly ethical point of view that correctly accounts for everything that is important. Is it permissible to farm animals in ways that predictably degrade the environment and harm them? Is the way workers are actually treated on strawberry farms unjust? In what ways should humans and non-human animals be treated in food supply chains? And so on. Other chapters focus on issues in food ethics about justice and other values related to the distributional consequences and economic structure of the food system. Is it unjust that some have so much to eat while others have so little? Is there a moral requirement for those who are not hungry to help those who are hungry? Is the economic system underlying food distribution exploitative? And so on.

This chapter focuses on a different set of issues, which might be called *consumer ethics*, where the central question is whether it is wrong to *consume* items—to buy or ingest or otherwise make use of items, such as particular food items—if those items are produced in a way that is wrong.

THE SIMPLE PRINCIPLE ABOUT CONSUMER ETHICS

At first glance, it might seem that consumer ethics is straightforward and does not raise any difficult issues, and that the correct theory of consumer ethics is easy to identify: namely, that if something is produced in a way that is wrong, then it is always wrong to be a consumer of it. For the sake of having a name for it, we might call this the Simple Principle about consumer ethics. This Simple Principle is attractive to many people when they first consider these issues. If this principle is true, then anytime something is produced in a way that is wrong, it immediately follows that it is wrong to be a consumer of that thing. If sweatshop labor is wrong, it is wrong to wear sweatshop-produced clothes. If cosmetics were made by wrongfully hurting animals, it is wrong to buy them. If it is wrong to raise animals for food, it is wrong to eat those animals.

Now consider how the Simple Principle about consumer ethics combines with specific claims in production ethics to yield an argument that consuming a particular product is wrong:

> Specific claim from production ethics: Factory-farmed pork chops are produced in a way that is wrong.
> Simple Principle about consumer ethics: For any x: If x is produced in a way that is wrong, then it is wrong to be a consumer of x.
> Hence, Conclusion: It is wrong to be a consumer of factory-farmed pork chops.

This argument is *valid*, which means that if the premises are all true, then the conclusion must be true too as a matter of logic. In other words, if both the first premise and the second premise in this example are true, then there is no way the conclusion could fail to be true too, given that the argument is valid and has only those two premises.

Are the premises true? What do they even mean? *Factory farming* is the practice of raising animals at a high-stocking density for meat or another animal product. So the first premise is claiming that pork chops produced in that way are wrongfully produced. Whether factory farming is wrong is the topic of Chapter 7, "Industrial Animal Agriculture," and we won't say anything more about it. Let's focus instead on whether the second premise is true. It says that no matter the value of x—pork chops, sweatshirts, phones—*if* that thing was produced in a wrongful way, then it is wrong to *consume* it: to buy it, to eat it, to otherwise use it. Is that true?

EVALUATING ETHICAL PRINCIPLES

As with any purported ethical principle we encounter, there are a number of questions we should ask ourselves about the Simple Principle. The most obvious question is whether it is true. At first glance, it is tempting simply to consult our intuitions and see whether it seems true, and to take this initial reaction to settle the matter. However, our initial intuitions about ethical principles are often mistaken, so this is not the most reliable way to go. Instead, we do better to use the best tools and practices of critical thinking to evaluate the purported principles we encounter and the arguments in which they appear. These are the tools of philosophy and other critical thinking disciplines, and sharpening these tools is an important goal of this textbook.

One of the first steps when evaluating an argument is to carefully think through the *logical structure* and *implications* of that argument, so as to more clearly identify the claims and principles that it invokes, and other principles that also have to be true if the principles it invokes are true. This helps us clarify what exactly the argument is, and thereby puts us in a good position to determine whether it is valid. If so, we might then determine whether we should believe that its premises are actually true. Although this can sound easy, in practice this is difficult work, and it takes a lot of practice for all of this to become second nature—but once it does become second nature, there is a large reward.

In the case of our example here, the argument is given to us clearly, so there is no difficult task of argument identification. However, there are a number of further philosophical questions that it is useful to consider as a means to thinking more carefully and productively about whether the Simple Principle is true, or whether instead some other principle about consumer ethics is true—and if so, which.

First, whenever we consider a purported ethical principle, it is useful to consider whether there might be *counterexamples* to that principle—in other words, whether there are any examples ("cases") we can identify where the principle gives a mistaken verdict about what it is right or wrong to do in that case. This is useful because if we can be confident that we've found a counterexample to a principle, then we can be confident that principle is mistaken—and by showing us one way in which a principle is false, counterexamples usually point the way toward different or more nuanced principles that are more plausible in retrospect after we've thought carefully about the counterexamples. As a result, the method of searching for counterexamples and then reflecting on their implications provides a useful method for making progress toward identifying the ethical principles that are ultimately most plausible—and a method that is much more reliable than simply relying on our initial intuitions without any further critical thinking. For example, consider the principle that it is always wrong to tell a lie. Is that principle true? Some people think it clearly isn't and, in arguing for that, they might create examples like this: You are hiding a family wanted by the Nazis in your house. The Nazis come to your door and ask if the family is there. If you lie, you'll save the family. If you don't lie, they'll die. In this example, you might think, it is permissible to lie. If so, it is a counterexample to the principle that it is always wrong to tell a lie.

So, the method of finding counterexamples and then trying to identify more plausible principles in light of those counterexamples is a good method for making progress toward principles that give the right verdict about what it is right and wrong to do. But there is still a worry about the potential unreliability of this method, which is that our intuitions about cases—for example, our judgments about which cases are *counter*examples—are based in bias rather than insight into what's morally true. How can we guard against this more insidious kind of unreliability in our ethical reflection, which may derive from implicit biases of which we are not immediately aware?

This is a good, difficult question because it poses a deep philosophical question about the limits of critical thinking and the limits of ethics. For our purposes here, a preliminary answer is that we should take a number of further steps in critical thinking to guard against such biases. For example, we should ask what ultimate values or fundamental ethical principles, if any, could make sense of the principles and judgments we are inclined to endorse, even by our own lights, and what objections other people might raise to these values and principles from their different perspectives. And we should do this in a way that is intellectually honest, charitable to the reasoning of others, and that gives proper weight to the likelihood that they might be right and we might be wrong (or that the issue might be merely one of convention, rather than ethical fact). In order to do as good of a job as we can in guarding against bias in this way, we should celebrate the intellectual challenge and uncertainty involved when trying to answer these difficult questions, which derives from the fact that these issues are always more complicated than they appear. If we do all of that, then we can hope to avoid being overconfident in the provisional conclusions we reach, and in the process we will make further progress by learning from each other and by discovering important new objections and theoretical considerations that we otherwise would have missed. At the very least, in this way we can engage in critical thinking to the best of our abilities, and in a way that similarly benefits others.

EVALUATING THE SIMPLE PRINCIPLE ABOUT CONSUMER ETHICS

With those principles for evaluating ethical principles in mind, recall again the Simple Principle about consumer ethics: For any x: If x is produced in a way that is wrong, then it is wrong to be a consumer of x. The previous section suggests that when evaluating this principle, we should ask the following questions: Are there counterexamples to it? What ultimate values, if any, could ground it? What other objections can be raised to it from other perspectives, and how might it be defended? And in light of all of that, are there more plausible alternative principles about consumer ethics?

To get a feel for how the debates over these issues go, both in connection to the Simple Principle and other consumer ethics principles, consider first the question of whether there are counterexamples to the Simple Principle. To get the flavor of the one kind of alleged counterexample, imagine someone who proposes that there is nothing wrong with watching NCAA sports on television, even though NCAA athletes are exploited in a way that makes it the case that the product being consumed—namely, NCAA sports on television—is wrongfully produced. Similarly, such a person might claim that there is nothing wrong with using electricity to watch a movie in one's home even if it is produced by a coal power plant, even though coal-generated electricity is produced in a way that is wrong because it generates a lot of pollutants as well as greenhouse gasses that do serious harm to people when there are much better ways of producing electricity available. Finally, such a person might expect us to agree that, at the very least, a dumpster diver who eats factory-farmed meat from the garbage has done nothing wrong, even if we think that factory-farmed meat is produced in a way that is wrong.

As these examples indicate, there are some good objections to the Simple Principle: Imagine that the pork chop is still in its original packaging, and that it is not even past its freshness date—your neighbor has simply told you that he will throw it away unless you will eat it, because he is about to leave the country on a trip. If there would be nothing wrong with eating a perfectly good pork chop if it was purchased and thrown away by someone else, even if that product was produced in a way that is wrong, then that amounts to agreeing that there really is a counterexample to the Simple Principle, and thus that that principle is false. In other words, it amounts to agreeing that the following *objection* to the Simple Principle (that is, argument against the Simple Principle) is a *sound argument* (that is, an argument that is both valid and has all true premises, and thus must have a true conclusion as well):

> Factory-farmed pork chops are produced in a way that is wrong.
> If the Simple Principle is true and factory-farmed pork chops are produced in a way that is wrong, then it is always wrong to be a consumer of factory-farmed pork chops.
> It is not wrong to be a consumer of factory-farmed pork chops in the "dumpster diving" example described.
> Hence, the Simple Principle is not true.

Many people will be tempted to agree with this kind of argument against the Simple Principle based on one or more of the preceding examples (NCAA sports, coal-generated electricity, factory-farmed meat acquired through dumpster diving) or others. At the same time, even if you share the temptation to reject the Simple Principle on this basis, we noted in the previous section that it is a good idea to ask further critical questions about the sort of intuitions that generate that kind of temptation. Along those lines, one important further observation is that *if* you were to agree that one or more of the preceding examples provides a genuine counterexample to the Simple Principle, that would *not* appear to commit you to the radical view that it is *always* perfectly OK to be a consumer of anything regardless of how that thing was produced. That radical principle, too, seems overly simple. That there are counterexamples to the Simple View might instead be taken only to indicate the need for a more nuanced principle about consumer ethics that escapes both the counterexamples and the radical conclusion that it is always OK to consume anything no matter how it was produced. So far, that's good news for an intuition that the preceding examples are genuine counterexamples to the Simple Principle, because there would be special reason to be suspicious of them if following them would have radical implications that were themselves implausible.

From this starting point, the next step for understanding current debates in consumer ethics is to note that many general ethical theories initially seem to avoid the (alleged) counterexamples to the Simple Principle, and at the same time seem also to avoid the problematic implication that all consumer choices whatsoever are permissible. However, as we will see, things are more complicated than this initial appearance, because when these theories are examined more closely, it is unclear whether they can really give such an attractive account of consumer ethics that both avoids counterexamples and is consistent with a plausible theory of ultimate values and fundamental ethical principles.

In what follows, we discuss the prospects for principles of consumer ethics derived from the following general ethical theories:

- Consequentialism
- Deontology
- Virtue ethics

CONSEQUENTIALISM

Consequentialism is the view that doing something is permissible—and morally right—if and only if choosing it has better (expected) consequences than all of the other things one could have chosen to do instead—and thus that a choice is wrong if it does not have the best (expected) consequences. Consequentialist views differ depending on what they claim makes for better or worse consequences. For example, the most frequently discussed consequentialist theory is utilitarianism, which maintains that the only thing that matters for determining better or worse consequences is the total sum of well-being in the world that results. As a result, utilitarianism is the theory that doing something is permissible—and morally right—if and only if choosing it has the best expected consequences *of all the actions that one could have chosen for the total amount of well-being in the world.* The italicized part at the end brings out that the notion of *opportunity cost* is crucially important on a consequentialist view: As just explained, consequentialism ranks options based on their consequences, and requires that one choose the best option on that metric. Further, whichever option is chosen necessarily comes at the opportunity cost of not having chosen an alternative option. So, in general, the course of action that one chooses is morally permissible if and only if it does not have the opportunity cost that one did not choose an alternative course of action that had better consequences.

At first glance, utilitarianism and other consequentialist theories might appear to provide a principled vindication of the intuition that some of the preceding examples are genuine counterexamples to the Simple Principle, while at the same time providing an attractive account of why some consumer behavior is nonetheless wrong. For example, as Peter Singer and Jim Mason argue in their reading in this chapter, utilitarianism seems to provide a good explanation of why dumpster diving is not wrong even when the product consumed was produced in a way that is wrong: The explanation is that if the product is not purchased but is merely taken from a dumpster, it makes no difference to the amount of harm that is caused in the making of that product, and so dumpster diving will not make a difference to how bad the world is for anyone else, but it will make it better for the dumpster diver (assuming for the sake of argument that she enjoys the product taken from the dumpster). On the other hand, when enough people purchase products like elephant tusks or factory-farmed pork chops in the marketplace, this additional demand for those products will ultimately result in producers making more of those things, which does make the world much worse in some ways without making it much better. So while it makes things better for the consumer, it makes for unhappy elephants and pigs that suffer and die in order to make more tusks and pork chops, not to mention making for indirect negative consequences for humans that would result from the loss of a beautiful species, and from additional environmental degradation caused by additional factory farming. Importantly, these consequences for the amount of well-being in the world would be negative on *net*, even after accounting for the pleasure that those additional consumers would get from consuming those additional tusks and pork chops—because, after all, there's only so much pleasure one can get from an elephant tusk on the wall, or a short dinner that includes a pork chop, and that seems clearly outweighed by hours or months of intense suffering by a large sentient animal. As a result, utilitarianism—and consequentialism in general—implies that it would be wrong to choose to have many more consumers of tusks and of pork chops, since that would make the world worse rather than better.

So far, so good for the consequentialist story. It can explain why the Simple Principle is mistaken and why the radical alternative that everything is permitted is also mistaken. But now consider what might be called the *inefficacy objection.* The inefficacy objection is, roughly, that even if it is true that a large number of additional consumers of an objectionable product like elephant tusks would make the world worse, nonetheless it makes no difference whether there is one more or one less single individual consumer of such a product, because (the objection claims) the addition or deletion of a single consumer would not make any difference to the quantity produced in the sort of large marketplaces that are the norm in Western society. In other words, if you buy a pork chop from a store every day, this will probably make no difference to how much pork the store orders, and thus will make no difference to how much pork the wholesaler that supplies the store orders, and so on—and thus will ultimately make no difference to how many pigs are raised for meat.

The inefficacy objection is onto at least something correct—namely, that it seems very *unlikely* that the addition of one single consumer would make any difference to anything other than the well-being of that consumer. So, if, for example, it would make no difference to elephants or to pigs or to anyone else if you were one additional consumer of their tusks or pork chops, but yet being a consumer of those things would make you happy, then, bracketing other considerations, it might at first glance seem that consequentialism implies that you are actually morally *required* to be a consumer of those things, because that is the course of action that will actually have the best consequences, contrary to what consequentialism may have initially seemed to imply.[2]

THE EXPECTED CONSEQUENCES REPLY TO THE INEFFICACY OBJECTION

To make the inefficacy objection a little more vivid, note that everyone can agree that there is a dramatic ethical difference between the following two ways of consuming a pork chop: in the first case, a dumpster diver pulls a pork chop from the garbage and eats it; in the second case, a man enjoys a pork chop at Jimmy's You-Hack-It-Yourself BBQ, where customers brutally cut their meat from the bodies of live animals, which are kept alive throughout the excruciating butchering process. (Suppose that once a pig bleeds to death, customers shift their efforts to a new live pig.)[3] Everyone can agree that enjoying a pork chop at Jimmy's You-Hack-It-Yourself BBQ is objectionable, whereas enjoying a pork chop acquired through dumpster diving is far less objectionable. According to a utilitarian like Singer, the *only* relevant difference between these two ways of consuming a pork chop is that the welfare consequences of eating at Jimmy's are substantially negative on balance, whereas a dumpster diver's consumption has no negative effect on welfare. But now consider the inefficacy objection: If you purchase a factory-farmed pork chop at a normal restaurant, are the welfare effects more like those of buying a pork chop at Jimmy's, or more like those of acquiring a pork chop through dumpster diving? Isn't it very unlikely that as a single consumer you would make any difference to the number of pigs who are raised on factory farms by buying one pork chop? And if that is right, does that imply eating a pork chop at a normal restaurant is much more like eating one from a dumpster than from Jimmy's in terms of its consequences—thus undermining Singer's argument?

In response to these questions, it is important to see that even if the addition of one single consumer is very *unlikely* to make a difference, that doesn't settle the matter even on consequentialist grounds, because what matters is not only the most likely outcome of a choice, but also the low-probability risks that are imposed by that choice, and how good or bad the outcome would be if those low-probability risks were actualized. To get an intuitive feel for this point, think about why it would be wrong to accept an ice cream cone for free if that meant imposing a 1-in-100 risk on an innocent person of being killed: The explanation is that what matters is not only the most *likely* outcome of that choice (namely, that you get a free ice cream cone and no one gets hurt), but also the low-probability risk that is imposed by that choice (namely, that you get a free ice cream cone but an innocent person is killed who would have been fine if you hadn't taken that ice cream cone). As a more realistic example, consider why it would be wrong for an engineer who drives a commuter train to send text messages while driving his or her train every day: The explanation is that although each act of sending messages has a very low probability of resulting in any harm, nonetheless each choice to send messages is an impermissible "gamble" from an ethical point of view, because of the way it increases the chance of catastrophe from what it would be if he or she were not sending messages, and because the expected value of texting is so low.

Similarly, in response to the inefficacy objection, Peter Singer argues that the choice to consume a product that is produced in a way that is wrong is often the wrong thing to do even if it is likely to make no difference, because he claims that choosing to consume that product nevertheless has *some* chance of making a difference, and if it did make a difference, it would make things so dramatically worse that consuming that bad product is similarly an impermissible gamble from an ethical point of view. Here is Singer:

> . . . a large number of consumers rejecting animal flesh must make a difference. Perhaps for every 10,000 vegetarians there is one fewer [factory farm] 20,000 bird chicken unit than there would otherwise be. Perhaps not: this is merely an example and I have no idea what the true figure would be; but there must be some point at which the number of vegetarians makes a difference to the size of the poultry industry. There must be a series of thresholds, hidden by the market system of distribution, which determine how many factory farms will be in existence. In this case one more person becoming a vegetarian will make no difference at all, unless that individual, added to the others who are already vegetarians, reduces demand below the threshold level at which a new factory farm would have started up (or an existing one would have remained in production, if the industry is declining).

Singer continues:

> Looking at one's own decision to be a vegetarian, it may seem frustrating that one cannot be sure that one has saved even a single animal from a miserable life on a factory farm; but from a utilitarian perspective it really makes no difference whether each vegetarian is personally responsible for saving ten chickens a year from this fate, or one vegetarian in 10,000 makes the difference that will save 100,000 birds. Utilitarianism judges actions by their likely consequences, and so it ranks the certainty of saving ten chickens equally with the 1 in 10,000 chance of saving 100,000. As long as I have no idea whether or not my own decision to go vegetarian is the decision that takes the demand for chickens below the threshold, the strength of this reason for being a vegetarian is unaffected."[4]

In order to really understand consequentialism, it is essential to understand Singer's logic here. On a consequentialist theory the ethical reasons for action one has are a function of the *expected consequences* of one's available options—more precisely, they are a function of the *expectation* associated with each of those options, where the expectation of each option is the sum of: the goodness of the possible outcomes that could result from choosing it, each multiplied by the probability that that outcome would obtain conditional on that choice being made. On a consequentialist view, one must always choose the option that has the best *expected consequences* in this particular sense of the greatest *expectation of good*, keeping in mind that the expectation associated with some options might be driven almost entirely by very low-probability risks[5] that choosing that option would entail, as in the preceding example in which one has the option to choose to impose a 1-in-100 risk of death on an innocent person in exchange for an ice cream cone. Singer's response to the inefficacy objection relies on this rigorous understanding of consequentialism, and claims that despite the low probability of making a difference, purchasing a pork chop is wrong because of the expected consequences of doing so, in a way analogous to the ice cream cone case in the sense that low-probability risks dominate the correct way of thinking about the expected consequences of one's options.

But are the two cases truly analogous in the relevant way? On reflection, as Grace Boey suggests in her reading in Chapter 1 and Mark Budolfson suggests in his reading in this chapter, it is not obvious how the math is going to work out in everyday consumer ethics cases, such as deciding whether to eat a factory-farmed pork chop. Both authors seem to think that, unlike the ice cream cone case, it isn't obvious what the probability is of a single consumer having an effect on production quantities, and it isn't obvious whether that probability is greater than infinitesimal. Budolfson stresses that these are empirical issues, and he claims that we cannot know the answers to these questions without investigating the actual workings of the marketplace. He also argues, based on a description of some aspects of the animal products marketplace, that the probability of making a difference is *actually* lower than defenders of consequentialism such as Singer often assume, and more important that whatever that probability is, the effect you would have if you did make a difference is *actually* much lower than it would have to be for the logic of a consequentialist argument like Singer's to work.

In his first reading in this chapter on consequentialism, Eliot Michaelson notes a number of other important considerations that consequentialists might cite in response. In evaluating the disagreement between Budolfson and Singer, one issue is whether we are convinced by Budolfson's argument that consequentialism *actually* has implications that are the opposite of what advocates such as Singer claim. Budolfson's argument here depends on empirical claims, and, as Michaelson notes, there are some reasons to think that things might be more complicated than Budolfson assumes. At the same time, it is useful to note that even if we are not convinced by Budolfson's claims about what is *actually* the case, that is consistent with being convinced by a more modest version of his argument: namely, that it is at least *very unclear* whether consequentialism has the implications that Singer takes it to have for buying factory-farmed animal products and other examples in consumer ethics.

If that is so, then it is unclear that consequentialism is a viable replacement for the Simple Principle. It is unclear that consequentialism will imply that it is wrong to eat food that is wrongfully produced. If you think it is wrong to do so and if consequentialism does not imply it is wrong, then you need a different principle to link the wrongness of production with the wrongness of consumption.

RIGHTS-BASED DEONTOLOGY

Whereas consequentialist theories require us to always maximize the good or maximize expected goodness, deontological theories are theories according to which it is sometimes wrong to maximize the good and where we have duties other than the duty to maximize the good.

The most familiar deontological theory is a rights-based deontological theory, which maintains that people have some fundamental rights that it is wrong to violate even when the lives of other people can on balance be somewhat improved by doing so. (Fundamental rights are discussed at greater length in Chapter 2, "Global Hunger.") For example, if I poison everyone in a tiny village merely because doing so allows me to produce chocolate more cheaply, that is wrong, and it is wrong because doing so violates the rights of the villagers.[6] By contrast, on a consequentialist view, whether or not it is wrong depends on how much good I do by means of my chocolate production. If the chocolate is particularly delicious, and if everyone really loves chocolate, and if there aren't that many villagers . . . then what I've done is OK. In fact, if consequentialism is true, *not* producing this chocolate might be wrong.

Assuming a rights-based explanation of the wrongness of the *production* of a good such as the chocolate in the preceding story, it may then appear that no more needs to be said to explain why it would be wrong to be a *consumer* of that good: After all, fundamental rights are violated in the *production* of that good, and so it might seem to follow immediately on a deontological theory that it would then be wrong to be a *consumer* of that good.

As an example of this kind of reasoning in food ethics, Tom Regan argues that animals have rights to life that make it wrong to kill them for trivial reasons just as people have fundamental rights to life that make it wrong to kill them for trivial reasons, and on this basis he concludes that animal agriculture is wrong because it violates animals' rights to life for trivial reasons. (Accepting that animals have rights is not as radical as it may initially seem, because it need not be understood to imply that animals are in every way just as important as humans, or even that their right to life is just as inviolable as humans, or that the particular right to life that humans have should not take ethical priority over the rights of animals, etc. Also, accepting that animals have rights appears consistent with thinking that humans have many other rights that they lack, such as the right to vote, because many of these other rights are plausibly grounded in particular capacities and social relations that humans have but animals lack.)

From this conclusion about the wrongness of *producing* goods in a way that violates rights, he takes it to immediately follow with no further argument or explanation needed that *consuming* those goods is also wrong:

> Since [animal agribusiness] routinely violates the rights of these animals, for the reasons given, it is wrong to purchase its products. That is why, on the rights view, vegetarianism is morally obligatory, and why, on that view, we should not be satisfied by anything less than the total dissolution of commercial animal agriculture as we know it, whether modern factory farms or otherwise.[7]

Regan is here assuming that if farming animals routinely violates their rights, then it is wrong to consume those animals. Is that assumption true? If it were true that a good was produced in a way that violated basic rights, would it be *possible* that it was nonetheless permissible to be a consumer of that good, even on a deontological view? Why or why not?

It turns out that this question is in the ballpark of the question we considered earlier of whether the Simple Principle of consumer ethics is true. In fact, an interesting question to ask is whether Regan is simply assuming the Simple Principle here because he thinks it is so obvious that it requires no argument or even statement. Again, the Simple Principle is that: For any *x*: If *x* is produced in a way that is wrong, then it is wrong to be a consumer of *x*.

Having noted the connection between the basic structure of Regan's argument and the Simple Principle, the next question to ask is whether some of the same alleged counterexamples to the Simple Principle that we noted earlier also apply to the basic structure of Regan's argument. It turns out that they do. Here are some examples analogous to those, now in a modified form to make them apply as clearly as possible to deontological ethics:

> There is nothing wrong with using electricity to watch a movie in one's home even if it is produced by a power company that violates the basic rights of a lot of people in the vicinity by knowingly doing serious harm to them with a lot of pollutants as well as greenhouse gasses for no particularly good reason (because other alternative forms of energy that would not do those harms are available and economical).
>
> There is nothing wrong with being a consumer of medical knowledge that benefits the health of all people now, even if that knowledge was produced by unethical experiments long ago that violated people's basic rights.
>
> There is nothing wrong with dumpster diving and eating factory-farmed meat from the garbage, even though it is produced by a factory farm that knowingly violates the rights of animals for no particularly good reason.

Should a deontological theorist who agrees that one of these goods is produced in a way that violates rights immediately conclude that it is wrong to be a consumer of that good? Regan would say yes. But some other deontological theorists would say no, and would insist that in all three of these cases an individual's consumption of the good can be permissible and not even particularly objectionable, even if that good is produced in a way that violates rights. Those deontologists who believe it is permissible and not even objectionable to consume medical knowledge that was originally produced in a way that is wrong are apt to justify their view by noting first that *after all, the people who were harmed are long dead.* And although Regan is correct that the *producers'* actions were wrong because they violated rights, what matters on a rights-based deontological view for evaluating *consumers'* actions is whether *consumers* violate rights— and, because the victims at issue are long dead, those who disagree with Regan will argue that it is not possible that *consumers* now violate those victims' rights (even though it is true that *producers* violated their rights), and so it is not wrong to be a consumer of those goods now.

If you find it compelling that it is not possible for people now to violate the basic rights of people who are long dead, then you agree that the answer to the question of whether a good was produced in a way that violated rights can differ from the answer to the question of whether being a consumer of that good violates people's rights. And if that is correct, then Regan's argument for vegetarianism is in trouble, because animals are long dead by the time that we decide whether to be consumers of them at supermarkets and restaurants. To put it another way—and to return to an example from above—as consumers it is not as if we are typically at anything like Jimmy's You-Hack-it-Yourself BBQ described before; instead, supermarkets and restaurants are more like dumpster diving with respect to the deadness of the animal. So, if *killing* is assumed to violate the rights of animals, then it does not seem clear why Regan thinks that being a *consumer* of animals violates their rights, since consumers do not kill animals; producers do. Similar remarks apply to the example of consuming medical knowledge that was produced by killing people long ago, and to other analogous examples in consumer ethics where producers have violated the rights of people, but yet consumers are so removed from those evils that it is unclear why they should be thought to violate anyone's rights by being a consumer.

This kind of complication for rights-based deontology as a theory of consumer ethics is only made worse if the main premise of the inefficacy objection described earlier is correct that a single consumer's decision to consume a good cannot be expected to make a difference to the harm and rights violations that happen in the production of ethically contentious goods, and if the primary cause of those harms and violations is the wrong actions of regulators and producers *rather than consumers*, as in the power generation example given previously. If so, then it is even harder to see how a consumer could be thought to violate rights or other familiar deontological constraints merely by consuming those goods.

For all of the reasons given, there is more work for deontologists to do on consumer ethics—not only to clarify what principles of consumer ethics are most plausible on a deontological theory, but also what substantive conclusions are correct about specific consumer decisions, because there appears to be no *obvious* deontological consumer ethics that delivers the verdict that it is wrong to be a consumer of, for example, factory-farmed meat, elephant tusks, blood diamonds, and many other ethically contentious products that would be condemned by many people.

KANTIAN ETHICS

In response to all of this, it is worth considering the idea that Kantian ethics might offer a straightforward deontological reply to the set of worries just articulated, or might at least offer a theory of consumer ethics that resolves any lingering worry about the ability of deontological theories to offer a plausible consumer ethics in light of the inefficacy objection. To consider this in more detail, it is useful to begin with a summary of the *Kantian universalizability test* from Robert Johnson, which many philosophers take to represent the core of Kantian ethics:

> First, formulate a maxim that enshrines your reason for acting as you propose. Second, recast that maxim as a universal law of nature governing all rational agents, and so as holding that all must, by natural law, act as you yourself propose to act in these circumstances. Third, consider whether your maxim is even conceivable in a world governed by this law of nature. If it is, then, fourth, ask yourself whether you would, or could, rationally *will* to act on your maxim in such a world. If you could, then your action is morally permissible. If your maxim fails the third step, you have a "perfect" duty admitting "of no exception in favor of inclination" to refrain from acting on it. If your maxim fails the fourth step, you have an "imperfect" duty requiring you to pursue a policy that can admit of such exceptions. If your maxim passes all four steps, only then is acting on it morally permissible.[8]

To evaluate the prospects of a Kantian consumer ethics on the basis of this test, it is useful to begin by noting how an ideal Kantian might make ethical decisions, and then consider whether such an agent might act on consumption maxims that pass the Kantian universalizability test, but yet do not clearly counsel against consuming goods that are *produced* in a way that is wrong. If that is possible, then such a Kantian test does not provide a viable replacement for the Simple Principle and does not support the sort of conclusions that Regan draws, and may not ultimately offer as straightforward a theory of consumer ethics as it might initially appear. With that in mind, and in light of the Kantian universalizability test described previously, we might understand *ideal* Kantian ethical reasoning as deriving maxims that apply in specific situations from a general "way of life maxim" that captures the general goal of respecting others with appropriate respect for oneself, such as:

> I will to respect the agency and interests of humanity [and perhaps also the interests of other sentient creatures] and, subject to that constraint, promote my own projects and interests.

With this ideal way of life maxim in hand, an ideal Kantian might then derive specific maxims for action in specific circumstances. In the cases of consumer ethics at issue, the more specific maxim that follows from this general maxim might appear to be something like:

> In connection with consumer goods, I will: that I not interfere in the agency of others or violate familiar constraints against harming others or violating their rights, that I support just institutions, regulations, and other forms of social progress that would eliminate current forms of harm and deprivation of agency and that would promote our collective interests, and subject to those constraints, that I promote my own projects and interests.

This maxim appears to pass all four steps of the universalizability test, which if true means that actions based on this maxim are permissible on the standard interpretation of the Kantian view quoted previously.

However, it appears that a person who acts on such a maxim may permissibly consume factory-farmed meat and other products that many ethicists such as Singer and Regan condemn, as by doing so one would not obviously violate any of the constraints mentioned in the first part of the maxim, partly because (as we've noted already) doing so appears not to violate rights or familiar constraints against harming others or interfere with their agency (at least assuming that a single consumer's choices make no difference), and partly because doing so is consistent with also, at the same time, supporting proper regulation and other forms of social progress to redress the relevant harms in the background.

In light of this, there appears to be no *straightforward* Kantian consumer ethics that is a viable replacement for the Simple Principle, or that delivers the verdict that it is wrong to be a consumer of factory-farmed meat, elephant tusks, blood diamonds, and many other ethically contentious products that would be condemned by many people. In light of this, it appears that Kantian ethicists must either endorse the idea that it is permissible to be a consumer of these products, or, as they are almost certain to do, attempt to identify some further or more subtle basis for condemning those products on such a view. Michaelson discusses this in more detail in his second reading in this chapter, and begins to investigate the much larger set of issues that are relevant to properly evaluating the prospects for Kantian principles of consumer ethics. (See also Christine Korsgaard's discussion in Chapter 7 of these issues and their connection to Kantian theory.)[9]

OTHER DEONTOLOGICAL ALTERNATIVES

Recall this argument from earlier in the chapter:

> Specific claim from production ethics: Factory-farmed pork chops are produced in a way that is wrong.

Simple Principle about consumer ethics: For any x: If x is produced in a way that is wrong, then it is wrong to be a consumer of x.

Hence, Conclusion: It is wrong to be a consumer of factory-farmed pork chops.

Previously, we noted that there are some alleged counterexamples to the Simple Principle, and that these are taken to be genuine counterexamples even by many people who accept a deontological ethical theory.

In this section, we explore the possibility of replacing the Simple Principle in arguments like the one just presented with a different premise that attempts to avoid some of the counterexamples to the Simple Principle, and thus provide what many will take to be a more plausible principle of consumer ethics. Consider in particular:

Principle about Benefiting from Wrongdoing

For any x: If x is produced in a way that is wrong, then it is wrong to be a consumer of x *if by being a consumer of* x *one benefits from that wrongdoing.*

For example, if one invests in a company that uses human slaves to profit, one thereby benefits from wrongdoing; according to this principle doing so is wrong fundamentally for that reason. Similarly, if factory-farmed pigs are produced in a way that is wrong and one would benefit from consuming them, then it is wrong for one to consume them.

As you may already see, this principle will be attractive to many in light of the problems we've seen already for the Simple Principle, consequentialism, and other theories because it has some promise of avoiding some of the problems for those, while capturing an intuitive idea that many people will think is the key to explaining why it is wrong to consume some goods that are produced in a way that is wrong. However, it will also come as no surprise to you that this principle is itself subject to some objections and alleged counterexamples. Let's turn to a quick overview of those.

A first objection to this principle is that it implies that it is wrong to consume almost everything. To see why, consider the wide range of everyday consumer goods that are *not* discussed at length in this book. Basically, most of those products require a lot of fossil fuels to be produced and/or to reach you as a consumer, and fossil fuels are objectionable and have a very large "harm footprint" for a wide range of reasons—most important, because of pollution, and because oil companies themselves have, historically, engaged in serious mistreatment of people, particularly in foreign countries where a large amount of oil is extracted.[10] In addition, everyday consumer goods require inputs of materials, electricity, labor, and other things to produce, and for all of these reasons many everyday goods have surprisingly large "harm footprints" in the same way that we've seen that food from contemporary agriculture has a surprisingly large harm footprint.[11] So, if the idea is, as the principle in question says, that it is wrong to *benefit from wrongdoing* as a consumer, then it is unclear why it doesn't follow from that principle that it is wrong to be a consumer of *everything* in our society, even goods that most people would agree are obviously permissible to purchase, such as, say, a can of corn—because basically all consumer goods have a surprisingly large harm footprint.

To illustrate the idea that in our society the harm footprints of even innocuous-seeming products are surprisingly high, let's focus on the harm footprints of a variety of foods, which are obviously the goods we are most concerned with in this book. Here are some estimates based on numerical data where available, and on the informed judgment of one of the authors of this book (Budolfson) when numbers are not readily available:[12]

FOOTPRINT / UNIT OF NUTRITION						Mark Bryant Budolfson		
	GHG		Land	Water		Other Pollution	Animal Harm	Human Worker Harm
	kg CO2eq / kg protein	kg CO2eq / 10,000 kcal	sq. meters / kg protein	liters / kg protein	liters / 10,000 kcal	(judgment) / unit of nut.	(judgment) / unit of nut.	(judgment) / unit of nut.
Beef	102	93	656	75969	60645			
Lamb	160	133	120	66985	42348			
Pork	46	51	51	30231	26104			
Chicken	25	29	28	11925	10316			
Farmed Salmon	54	58	7					
Mussels	6	8	2					
Eggs	38	31	36	12468	10951			
Milk	60	31	34	25270	13049			
Cheese	54	33	34	15843	9789			
Butter	42	3		131091	8669			
Lentils	10	8	20	22767	17125			
Beans	22	14	20	23590	14562			
Rice	116	24		28960	6000			
Tomato	125	61		24318	11889			
Potato	155	33		14208	3727			
Broccoli	71	59		10106	8382			
Carrots	33	8		20968	4756			
Oranges	51	8		80000	12174			
Bananas	45	6		72477	8876			
Peaches	45	11		100000	23333			
Strawberries	75	16		51791	10844			
Grapes	63	6		96508	9075			
Apples	135	7		316154	15808			
Almonds	11	4		76099	27798			
Peanuts	5	2		15403	7009			
Cabbage	25	13		21875	11200			
Lettuce	25	23		17426	15800			

As you can see, it appears that most animal products have a high harm footprint. But at the same time, it appears that most ordinary vegan staples *also* have a surprisingly high harm footprint due to harms to workers, the environment, and indirect harm to humans via pollution and climate change described in earlier chapters. Even if many vegan staples do not have as high of a harm footprint as, say, pork, it may thus seem that the actual way they are produced is wrong. Does it then follow from the Principle about Benefiting from Wrongdoing that it is wrong to consume all foods? Or does it perhaps follow that it is wrong to consume all foods except for peanuts and mussels?

As these examples from the food domain illustrate, when one digs deeper into the facts about how goods are produced in our society and their harm footprints, especially given the dependence of almost all goods on large inputs of fossil fuels, it is easy to see how someone might think that our entire industrial society must be reformed—even if that would merely require elegant regulation that requires producers and consumers to pay the true costs of production and consumption—and that in that sense of needing to be reformed, almost all goods in our society are arguably produced in a way that is actually wrong. If that is correct, then the Principle about Benefiting from Wrongdoing seems to imply that it is wrong to consume almost everything—which might seem incorrect even if it is correct that almost everything is produced in a way that is wrong.

Thinking carefully about the harm footprint of vegan staples also suggests that even if we set aside the inefficacy objection, things might still be more complicated than they appear for arguments for a near-vegan diet such as the consequentialist argument offered by Peter Singer earlier in the chapter, and the argument Tristram McPherson offers in his reading for this chapter based on a more subtle principle. At the very least, the harm footprint of many vegan staples suggests that by the lights of arguments like Singer and McPherson's, it might not be enough merely to go vegan: One might also be required by their arguments to be *a particular kind* of vegan that also avoids berries, vegan dark chocolate,[13] and many other vegan staples that have a high harm footprint.

In addition, some specific animal products such as mussels generally have a much *better* harm footprint along every dimension than almost all vegan staples, because almost all vegan staples have substantial land and water footprints, which means that they take away land and water from wildlife, which can lead to serious harm to those animals, as well as imposing costs on humans and the environment more generally. In contrast, mussels have essentially no animal harm or other harm footprint at all—partly because mussels are not conscious and so harvesting them does not involve animal harm, and partly because the land, water, and greenhouse gas footprint of mussels is miniscule, and much lower than most vegan staples. For these reasons, both Singer and McPherson seem to allow that eating mussels and some similar creatures is likely permissible, and so their views are not really "vegan" in the familiar sense of that term.[14]

Taking things further—and much more controversially—it might even be suggested that factory-farmed chicken presents a challenge to pro-vegan arguments in light of the trade-offs that have to be made, because although chickens are clearly sentient, it may seem unclear why pro-vegan arguments seem to take their interests to always trump the interests of, say, human workers, who are harmed in the production of berries and many other vegan staples. Further, chicken delivers a lot of nutrition in a small and user-friendly package, and it is more environmentally friendly than other leading meats, especially when it is raised intensively on factory farms, where the efficiency gains in production also translate into efficiency gains from the standpoint of greenhouse gas emissions and other environmental impacts relative to organic versions of leading meats.

The upshot of all of this is that principles of consumer ethics face an important objection based on the fact that arguably nearly everything available for consumption in our society is produced in a way that is wrong. The objection is particularly pressing to the Principle about Benefiting from Wrongdoing, as that principle might then seem to overgeneralize and mistakenly imply that it is wrong to consume most ordinary products.

VIRTUE ETHICS AND AVOIDING COMPLICITY WITH WRONGDOING

A more general thought along the lines of the Principle about Benefiting from Wrongdoing is that it is wrong to be *complicit* in wrongdoing, in a sense of being connected to and/or associated with wrongdoing in a more general sense that is difficult to pin down exactly. For example, in the case of medical knowledge acquired via immoral experiments, one has the option of *dissociating* oneself from that medical knowledge and its corrupt source by refusing to accept it—perhaps as a symbolic gesture to express that the historical acts that lie behind that knowledge were wrong, and that one will have no part of that tainted medicine. As Thomas E. Hill writes, seemingly in support of the idea that this kind of dissociation is in fact required:

> To deplore the corruption inwardly seems insufficient. Even if one does not personally contribute to the wrong-doing, and so avoids the charge of complicity considered earlier, still it seems that one should break off the association. . . . The point, on this view, is not so much to keep one's own hands clean as to avoid white-washing the bloody deeds of others.[15]

In support of this view, Hill appeals to the ethical authority of Kant:

> But where the vice is a scandal, i.e. a public display of contempt for a strict law of duty that, accordingly, carries infamy with it, one's existing association must be broken off or avoided as much as possible, even though the law of the land does not punish the offense. It must be broken off, since continued association with such a person deprives virtue of all honor, and puts it up for sale to anyone rich enough to corrupt a parasite with the pleasures of luxury.[16]

As Hill's and Kant's words here show, there are some philosophers who appear happy to endorse all of the consequences of the Simple Principle and are thus happy to agree that, for example, it is wrong to make use of medical knowledge if that knowledge was produced by unethical experiments long ago on people long dead. Presumably, these philosophers would also be happy to endorse the suggestion in the last section that it is wrong to consume nearly everything in contemporary society. On such a view, true virtue requires that one refuse to connect oneself to/associate with those kinds of evils, and thus true virtue requires one to make very costly sacrifices in those cases when one could benefit from those things.

Although McPherson does not discuss these issues at length in his paper, it is important to note that the principle that he defends is an important proposal for capturing what he takes to be the kernel of truth in these ideas, while at the same time avoiding the radical sacrifices that seem to be required by Hill's view and the Principle of Benefiting from Wrongdoing. In other words, McPherson's principle is intended to provide a plausible solution to the over-generalization problem for simple principles based on complicity in or benefiting from wrongdoing articulated previously. Thus, McPherson's principle and his related discussion have more general importance than debates about vegetarianism, as it is relevant to debates about consumer ethics in general, and to very general questions about what individual people should do in regrettable circumstances.

Many philosophers who identify with *virtue ethics* are apt to agree with views such as Hill's or McPherson's. Virtue ethical theories are theories according to which actions should be judged based on what a virtuous agent would do. From the perspective of virtue ethics, consumer ethics can appear to be a straightforward matter of deciding what kind of person you want to be—do you want to be an excellent person who cultivates virtues of integrity, humility, and other virtues, or don't you? Philosophers in the virtue tradition are apt to see this as the most pressing question, rather than questions about the intricate analysis of consequentialist and deontological reasons for and against consumer choices. And they are apt to see it as a straightforward matter to connect the wrongness of production to conclusions about what a virtuous person should do—and thus are apt to see much of the discussion in the previous sections involve a vast over-analysis. As a leading statement of this kind of view, consider this passage from Hill:

> Rather than argue directly with [those] who say, "Show me why what I am doing is immoral," I want to ask, "What sort of person would want to do what they propose?" The point is not to skirt the issue with an ad hominem, but to raise a different moral question, for even if there is no convincing way to show that the destructive acts are wrong . . . we may find that the willingness to indulge in them reflects the absence of human traits that we admire and regard [as] morally important. . . . Consider, for example, the Nazi who asks, in all seriousness, "Why is it wrong for me to make lampshades out of human skin—provided, of course, I did not myself kill the victims to get the skins?" We would react more with shock and disgust than with indignation, I suspect, because it is even more evident that the question reveals a defect in the questioner than that the proposed act is itself immoral.

Hill continues:

> Sometimes we may not regard an act [as] wrong at all though we see it as reflecting something objectionable about the person who does it. Imagine, for example, one who laughs spontaneously to himself when he reads a newspaper account of a plane crash that kills hundreds. Or, again, consider an obsequious grandson who, having waited for his grandmother's inheritance with mock devotion, then secretly spits on her grave when at last she dies. Spitting on the grave may have no adverse consequences and perhaps it violates no rights. The moral uneasiness which it arouses is explained more by our view of the agent than by any conviction that what he did was immoral. Had he hesitated and asked, "Why shouldn't I spit on her grave?" it seems more fitting to ask him to reflect on the sort of person he is than to try to offer reasons why he should refrain from spitting.[17]

Commenting on Hill's view as articulated here and elsewhere, Mark Timmons writes:

> Hill rejects those attempts to explain [for example] proper environmental concern that appeal either to rights, to intrinsic value, or to religious considerations. Rather, Hill advocates an alternative to such views that focuses on ideals of human excellence as a basis for understanding proper moral concern for the natural world. In particular, Hill claims that insensitivity to the environment reflects either ignorance, exaggerated self-importance, or a lack of self-acceptance that are crucial for achieving the human excellence of proper humility.[18]

Bernard Williams seems to have at least somewhat related thoughts in mind in connection with what he takes to be the right way of thinking about one of his most famous examples:

> George, who has just taken his Ph.D. in chemistry, finds it extremely difficult to get a job. He is not very robust in health, which cuts down the number of jobs he might be able to do satisfactorily. . . . An older chemist, who knows about this situation, says that he can get George a decently paid job in a certain laboratory, which pursues research into chemical and biological warfare. George says he cannot accept this, since he is opposed to chemical and biological warfare.

Williams continues:

> The older man replies that he is not too keen on it himself, come to that, but after all George's refusal is not going to make the job or the laboratory go away; what is more, he happens to know that if George refuses the job, it will certainly go to a contemporary of George's who is not inhibited by any such scruples and is likely if appointed to push along the research with greater zeal than George would. Indeed, it is not merely concern for George and his family, but (to speak frankly and in confidence) some alarm about this other man's excess of zeal, which has led the older man to offer to use his influence to get George the job. . . . What should [George] do?[19]

This famous example from Williams challenges us to explain even outside the domain of consumer ethics what we should do even when what we do does not make a difference in a consequentialist way.

Whatever conclusions we ultimately reach about consumer ethics, all of these examples encourage us to consider whether what matters most in answering questions about what we should do is whether at the end of the day we can look *ourselves* in the mirror and be happy with ourselves, our choices, and what we stand for. We should also ask whether we can look *others* in the eye even when they are powerless, oppressed, and lack the ability to speak for themselves, and say to them: "Don't worry, I am on your side. You can count on me. I am not an oppressor. I am the kind of person who will stand up for you." One of the most important recurring points in this textbook is that non-human animals in industrial agriculture are among the most powerless and oppressed creatures in our society, along with farm workers, and many others connected to our food systems. These individuals lack the power to stand up to those who are oppressing them. Someone must stand up for them.

Perhaps the most fundamental question in consumer ethics is whether each of us must stand up for the poor and oppressed with our consumer actions (as Singer, McPherson, Hill, and others would argue), and, if so, why exactly. A bigger ethical question is whether it is a more general truth that each of us is typically required to take action that aims to *directly help* such people (for example, as Singer seems to argue in Chapter 2, "Global Hunger"). An alternative view is that we may instead stand up for them in a way that is much more indirect, but yet ethically sufficient, merely by taking action in other ways, such as by voting for policy changes, or by becoming agents of change in other ways, such as by starting ethical businesses and non-profit organizations that incrementally move things in a better direction (of the sort exemplified by many of the firms described by Michelle Paratore and Austin Kiessig in their readings in Chapter 10, "Alternatives to Industrial Plant Agriculture"). A more radical alternative view is that, perhaps because of the alleged inefficacy and costs of individual action on all of these fronts, we have no demanding obligations at all as individuals to take action on any of these fronts.

FURTHER ISSUES

1. *Individual vs. Collective Action*
If we assume for the sake of argument that the inefficacy objection is correct, is there a difference on a consequentialist view between what you have ethical reason to do *as an individual person* and what *we collectively* have ethical reason to do? How should we think about this question from the perspective of other general ethical theories? Is it coherent to think that a collective ought to stop buying *x* but yet no individual is required to stop buying *x*? (In connection with these questions, consider reading the selection from Derek Parfit in the Further Reading section.) What arguments could be given in favor of the idea that instead of worrying about our *consumer choices*, we should instead focus on helping the poor and oppressed by *political action*? Might this involve a duty to protest? Or merely a duty to vote in particular ways? Or something in between?

2. *Kantian Ethics*

After doing the readings in this chapter, especially from Michaelson, and the reading from Korsgaard in Chapter 7, "Industrial Animal Agriculture," what do you think is the best version of a Kantian view regarding factory farms? In particular, how should the view answer the question of what we collectively should do about factory farms and why exactly, and the question of what exactly you as a single individual should do about it? Are these importantly different questions even on a Kantian view? Do you think a different kind of deontological theory / virtue ethics / complicity theory ultimately fares better than a Kantian view? Why or why not?

3. *Virtue Ethics*

Thomas E. Hill raises the possibility of locating the badness of consumption not in that action or its consequences, but in the kind of character it would take to perform it. In other words, on Hill's view what should bother us about meat-eating, if we're convinced meat production is wrong, isn't the consumption itself or its consequences, but rather the sort of person we'd have to be in order to go on consuming, knowing what we do about the production. However, much of the time when we say somebody would have to have bad character to do *x*, that is because it is bad to do *x*. But it looks like we won't be able to say this if we adopt Hill's strategy. What else can we say about why the action would be indicative of bad character? It also appears that on Hill's view it does not follow that the action is wrong, or that there's moral reason not to perform it. Just that there's something wrong with the sort of person who would do it. Is that enough? For more on these questions, read Hill's papers cited in the Further Reading section.

4. *Doing Philosophy*

After reading the introduction to this chapter, are you tempted to think a particular principle of consumer ethics is true despite all of the complications raised there? What is it exactly? Can you formulate it clearly enough that it applies to every interesting example you can think of—and so that it isn't like a fortune teller's prediction, which can be interpreted in whatever way one wants in connection to a particular example? Can you think of counterexamples to the principle you identified? If so, that's good—that means you did a good job clearly formulating it, and then testing it. As you think about it more, and think about alternative principles and objections and replies that others might raise, and as you do the readings for this chapter, what are some additional objections to it, and what are some other considerations that you think are relevant, perhaps of the sort outlined herein for evaluating principles? If at the end of your work on this chapter you have answered each of these questions, and have some progress to report in response to each, then you are truly doing philosophy.

In light of the previous questions, do you now find some of the general ethical theories discussed in this chapter more or less plausible than you initially did? What general family of ethical theory do you think is most promising in connection with consumer ethics? What about as a general ethical theory? These are big questions about normative ethics. In light of what you've learned and your own thinking, how would you structure a paper to argue for or against some of these general views? Can you think of an important point that is relevant that the authors in this textbook have not explicitly discussed, but that should be taken into account? How would you structure a short paper to make the point most clearly and most crisply? Focus on making the main argument for that point as clearly and decisively as possible, considering objections and replies in the process. Examine McPherson's model paper in his reading in this chapter for some guidance.

5. *The Inefficacy Objection as an Objection to Consequentialism*

The inefficacy objection might be used to argue not only that consequentialism doesn't have the implications that Singer takes it to have, but, further, that consequentialism itself must be mistaken. As a first pass at such an argument, we might consider the following:

> In most cases, as a single individual your consumption "makes no difference" in the sense that it makes no one worse off, including those people and animals that are harmed in the production of goods; at the same time, your consumption does make you better off.
>
> If consequentialism is true, and if your consumption makes you better off and makes no one worse off, then you are required to consume.
>
> It is false that you are required to consume in most cases.
>
> Hence, Consequentialism is not true.

The first premise follows from the inefficacy objection. The second premise allegedly follows from consequentialism and the last premise, which claims that it is false that consumption is required in the consumer ethics cases at issue.

In evaluating this argument, it is important to note that even if the inefficacy objection is correct, choosing to consume still has important opportunity costs in the sense that choosing to consume comes at the cost of not doing other things instead, which are ruled out by choosing to consume. For example, even if my purchasing elephant tusks does not have an effect on the number of elephants that are killed, it still has the opportunity cost that the money I spend on the tusks is not invested in other ways—and if any of those other options I have for investing that money (or for doing other things instead) should be expected to have better consequences than spending money on conspicuous consumption of elephant tusks, then consequentialism still entails that it is wrong to buy the tusks, for reasons independent of the harms to elephants in the production of those tusks. Of particular importance, if giving the same amount of money to charity would do much more good than spending it on the tusks, then consequentialism implies that it would be wrong to spend the money on the tusks, even on the assumption that the inefficacy objection is correct that no one, including elephants, would be made worse off by purchasing the tusks. (In connection with this point, see Singer's reading in Chapter 2, "Global Hunger.")

The upshot is that consequentialism does not actually imply that if your consumption would make you better off and no one worse off, then it is required. Instead, consequentialism requires you to do whatever would do the most good, and even if the inefficacy objection is correct, it appears that there will often be options that are better ways of doing good than consumption.

With the preceding in mind, here is a second pass at an argument against consequentialism itself that is based on the inefficacy objection:

> In most cases, as a single individual your consumption "makes no difference" in the sense that it makes no one worse off, including those people and animals that are harmed in the production of goods. This is true even in connection with "ethically contentious goods" that on average do much more harm to others per unit consumed than their benefits to consumers—in other words, goods that in the aggregate have terrible consequences for the world.
>
> If consequentialism is true and the previous premise is true, then you have no reason not to consume most ethically contentious goods based on the fact that on average they do much more harm per unit consumed than their benefits to consumers. In other words, if consequentialism is true and the previous premise is true, the fact that these goods have terrible consequences for the world in the aggregate gives you no reason not to consume them.

It is false that the fact that these goods have terrible consequences for the world in the aggregate gives you no reason not to consume them.

Hence, Consequentialism is not true.

How should we evaluate this argument? Should we be convinced by it? (See also the next set of questions.)

6. *Consequentialism and Collective Harm*

Read the articles in the Further Reading section by Kagan, "Do I Make a Difference?" and by Nefsky, "Consequentialism and the Problem of Collective Harm: A Reply to Kagan." How would Kagan respond to the objection to consequentialism developed in the previous question? How does that compare to Singer's response to the inefficacy objection? What do you think of the inefficacy objection in connection with climate change? Does it make a difference to the amount of greenhouse gasses in the atmosphere every time a person, say, drives her car to work? Even if it does make a difference, what are the further complications noted by Kagan? What objections does Nefsky raise to Kagan's argument? How do the prospects of consequentialism as a general ethical theory look in light of the debate between Kagan and Nefsky? How does their debate illuminate or complicate the more general ethical issue of what you have reason to do when it doesn't seem to make a difference what you do? Note that this is a more general ethical issue, to which there are connections to many things in this chapter, such as the inefficacy objection and the ability or inability of familiar ethical theories to provide a satisfying response to that objection.

CLOSELY RELATED READINGS IN OTHER CHAPTERS

Grace Boey, "Eating Animals and Personal Guilt," Chapter 1
Peter Singer, "Famine, Affluence, and Morality," Chapter 2
Angus Deaton, "Response to Effective Altruism," Chapter 2
Peter Singer, "All Animals Are Equal," Chapter 7
Torbjörn Tännsjö, "It's Getting Better All the Time," Chapter 7
Christine Korsgaard, "Getting Animals in View," Chapter 7
Elizabeth Harman, "The Moral Significance of Animal Pain and Animal Death," Chapter 8
Roger Scruton, "Eating Our Friends," Chapter 8

FURTHER READING

Appiah, Kwame Anthony. 1992. "Racism and Moral Pollution." *Philosophical Forum.*
Barry, Christian, and David Wiens. 2014. "Benefiting from Wrongdoing and Sustaining Wrongful Harm." *Journal of Moral Philosophy.*
Barry, Christian, and Gerhard Øverland. forthcoming. *The Responsibilities of the Affluent to the Poor: Doing, Allowing, and Enabling Harm.* Cambridge University Press.
Mark Budolfson. forthcoming. "The Inefficacy Objection to Consequentialism and the Problem with the Expected Consequences Response." *Philosophical Studies.*
———. "The Inefficacy Objection to Deontology: What It Is, Why It Is Important, and the New Type of Deontological Reason Needed to Reply to It."
Chignell, Andrew, Terence Cuneo, and Matt Halteman, eds. 2015. *Philosophy Comes to Dinner.* Philadelphia: Taylor & Francis.
Driver, Julia. 2015. "Individual Consumption and Moral Complicity," in Ben Bramble and Bob Fischer, eds., *The Moral Complexities of Eating Meat.* Oxford University Press.

Hill, Thomas E. 1979. "Symbolic Protest and Calculated Silence." *Philosophy & Public Affairs.*

————. 1983. "Ideals of Human Excellence and Preserving Natural Environments." *Environmental Ethics.*

Kagan, Shelly. 2011. "Do I Make a Difference?" *Philosophy & Public Affairs.*

Lepora, Chiara, and Bob Goodin. 2013. *On Complicity and Compromise.* Oxford University Press.

Nefsky, Julia. 2011. "Consequentialism and the Problem of Collective Harm: A Reply to Kagan." *Philosophy & Public Affairs.*

————. forthcoming. "Fairness, Participation, and the Real Problem of Collective Harm." *Oxford Studies in Normative Ethics.*

————. forthcoming. "Individual Consumption and Collective Impact," in *Oxford Handbook of Food Ethics.*

Nestle, Marion. 2000. "Ethical Dilemmas in Choosing a Healthful Diet: Vote with Your Fork!" *Proceedings of the Nutrition Society.*

O'Neill, Onora. 1996. *Toward Justice and Virtue*, Chapter 4. Cambridge University Press.

Parfit, Derek. 1984. "Five Mistakes in Moral Mathematics," in *Reasons and Persons.* Oxford University Press.

Sandler, Ronald, and Philip Cafaro, eds. 2005. *Environmental Virtue Ethics.* Lanham, MD: Rowman & Littlefield.

Schwartz, David. 2010. *Consuming Choices: Ethics in a Global Consumer Age.* Lanham, MD: Rowman & Littlefield.

Singer, Peter, and Jim Mason. 2007. *The Ethics of What We Eat.* Emmaus, PA: Rodale.

Singer, Peter. 1980. "Utilitarianism and Vegetarianism." *Philosophy & Public Affairs.*

Thomson, Judith Jarvis. 1986. *Rights, Restitution, and Risk.* Cambridge, MA: Harvard University Press.

Wallace, Kathleen. forthcoming. "A Kantian Perspective on Individual Responsibility for Sustainability", in *Ethics in the Anthropocene,* Eds. Kenneth Schockley and Andrew Light, MIT Press.

Williams, Bernard. 1973. "A Critique of Utilitarianism," in Jack Smart and Bernard Williams, eds., *Utilitarianism: For and Against.* Cambridge University Press.

Young, Iris Marion. 2011. *Responsibility for Justice.* Oxford University Press.

NOTES

1. Many independent experts agree that the Western diet of, for example, an average citizen of the UnitedStates involves an unhealthy reliance on animal products, where this is largely a consequence of industrial animal agriculture, which has made animal products less expensive than ever before compared to plant-based foods, thereby resulting in the overconsumption of animal products. Similar remarks may apply to many other unhealthy aspects of the Western diet, which can also be seen largely as a consequence of analogous price incentives created by consumers by what might be called the "agribusiness-congressional-industrial" complex. (Here echoing U.S. President Dwight Eisenhower's warnings about the negative effects of the "military-industrial complex," which he originally intended to call the "military-congressional-industrial complex" before revising the term to avoid angering Congress.)

2. At least assuming there are no other things that would buy more happiness for the cost of the tusks and pork chops—which, for reasons we discuss in what follows, is generally not the case for reasons independent of harms in the production of goods.

3. If this example seems callous at first glance, it may help to note that its purpose is, by analogy, to make salient some of the horrors of animal farming of the sort discussed in Chapter 7, "Industrial Animal Agriculture."

4. Peter Singer, "Utilitarianism and Vegetarianism," *Philosophy and Public Affairs* 9 (1980): 335–336.

5. Risks in this sense are not always bad: for example, imagine that you have a choice between receiving one dollar for sure, or a 1-in-100 chance of receiving $1,000,000. The second bet with the very low

probability of winning is the better one, and the explanation is that the expectation of taking the second, risky bet is better than the first, because even when the value you'd get from an additional $1,000,000 is multiplied by 1/100, that is still much greater than the value for you of one additional dollar. So, the risky bet is much better than the sure-thing bet in this case, and the explanation is that the riskier bet has a better expectation—that is, greater *expected value*—in the sense explained in the main text.

6. Actual chocolate tends to have some different, but nonetheless highly worrisome features of its own production; see, for example, http://grist.org/food/a-guide-to-ethical-chocolate/.

7. Tom Regan, *The Case for Animal Rights*, updated ed. (Berkeley: University of California Press, 2004), 351.

8. Robert Johnson, "Kant's Moral Philosophy," *Stanford Encyclopedia of Philosophy* ([2004] 2008), http://plato.stanford.edu/entries/kant-moral.

9. For another Kantian view, see Onora O'Neill, *Toward Justice and Virtue* (Cambridge University Press, 1996), Chapter 4. For some further critical discussion of deontological ethical theories, consumer ethics, and the inefficacy objection, see Mark Budolfson, "The Inefficacy Objection to Deontology," where similar complications are noted for rule-utilitarianism and other deontological views not discussed here.

10. For examples, see Peter Maass, *Crude World* (New York: Vintage, 2010).

11. Following standard use of terminology regarding *footprints*, we can understand the *harm footprint* of a particular good as the average amount of harm that is done per good of that type in the overall production of all of those goods of that type.

12. The spreadsheet that contains the relevant calculations, data sources, and a description of the methodology behind this chart is available at www.budolfson.com/footprints. In brief, the numbers are based on the best data easily available, including in peer-reviewed sources, and the cells that do not have numbers are based on my own judgment, which aims for empirical accuracy, which the reader can judge for him-self or herself, perhaps in conjunction with my more detailed explanation of the methodology. The shading is done by the default three-color shading algorithm in Microsoft Excel 2010. Main sources of numerical data are D. Nijdman et al., "The Price of Protein: Review of Land Use and Carbon Footprints from Lifecycle Assessments of Animal Food Products and Their Substitutes," *Food Policy*, 2012; K. Hamerschlag, "What You Eat Matters," Environmental Working Group, 2011; CleanMetrics greenhouse gas footprint data, accessed at www.foodemissions.com/foodemissions/Calculator.aspx; M. Mekonnen et al., "The Green, Blue, and Grey Water Footprint of Crops and Derived Crop Products," *Hydrology and Earth System Sciences*, 2011; M. Mekonnen et al., "A Global Assessment of the Water Footprint of Farm Animal Products," *Ecosystems*, 2012; and the USDA National Nutrient Database for Standard Reference. Of particular note, the specific numbers for greenhouse gas footprints that I use from Hamerschlag and CleanMetrics are near the median estimates reported in Nijdam, which is a survey of the peer-reviewed literature on land and greenhouse gas footprints, and are also in line with the numbers reported in other peer-reviewed publications.

13. See, e.g., http://grist.org/food/a-guide-to-ethical-chocolate.

14. Peter Singer and Jim Mason seem to agree that it is permissible to eat mussels and other sustainably sourced mollusks in *The Ethics of What We Eat* (Emmaus, PA: Rodale, 2007); for McPherson, these are creatures likely to be outside the scope of the "vegan" principle he defends.

15. Thomas E. Hill, "Symbolic Protest and Calculated Silence," *Philosophy & Public Affairs* 9 (1979): 91, 98.

16. Ibid., p. 98. The passage is from Kant's *The Metaphysical Principles of Virtue*.

17. Hill, "Ideals of Human Excellence and Preserving Natural Environments," *Environmental Ethics* 5 (1983).

18. Mark Timmons, ed., *Disputed Moral Issues* (Oxford University Press, 2007), 542–543.

19. Bernard Williams, "A Critique of Utilitarianism," in J. J. C. Smart and B. Williams, *Utilitarianism: For and Against* (Cambridge University Press, 1973), 97–98.

TRISTRAM MCPHERSON

How to Argue for (and against) Ethical Veganism

McPherson begins with a short essay within an essay that presents a clear argument that it is wrong to kill animals and that it is wrong to eat meat. The clarity of this essay serves as a model for students to emulate when writing a short philosophy essay. It is also the point of departure for the remainder of McPherson's paper, where he considers a number of important objections and replies in connection with that initial argument. In light of these, McPherson ultimately defends a principle he calls "Anti-Complicity," which he argues fares better than alternative principles of consumer ethics such as the Simple View. That principle, in turn, is essential to the rigorous argument for near-veganism that his paper as a whole defends. (McPherson is a philosopher at The Ohio State University.)

This paper has two goals. The first is to offer a carefully reasoned argument for *ethical veganism*: the view that it is (at least typically) wrong to eat or otherwise use animal products. The second goal is to give you, the reader, some important tools for developing, evaluating, and replying to reasoned arguments for ethical conclusions. I begin by offering you a brief essay, arguing that it is wrong to eat meat. This essay both introduces central elements of my case for veganism, and serves as one helpful model of a short ethics essay. In the remainder of this paper, I use the model essay as a target, to illustrate important strategies for developing objections to ethical arguments. I will also illustrate a range of important ways for the vegan to reply to these objections. You can use the models and skills I illustrate here in your own essays, and in your reasoned evaluation of ethical arguments. I conclude that the arguments and replies offered in this paper add up to a powerful reasoned case for ethical veganism. You can practice the skills I illustrate here to deciding for yourself—in a reasoned way—whether my conclusion is correct.

I begin with the promised model essay:

IT IS WRONG TO EAT MEAT

Most of us think that it would be wrong to adopt a puppy from a shelter, in order to take it home and torture it until it dies. However, we do not think it is wrong to eat a steak for dinner. In this essay, I will argue that these views are hard to square with each other, and that the second view is false: it is wrong to eat meat. My argument has the following structure:

1. It is wrong to make animals suffer
2. If it is wrong to make animals suffer, then it is wrong to kill animals
3. If it is wrong to kill animals, then it is wrong to eat meat
   C. It is wrong to eat meat.

This argument is *valid*. This means that the conclusion must be true if all of the premises are true. I will defend each of these premises in turn.

First, why think that it is wrong to make animals suffer? To begin, think about why it is wrong to make another person suffer. Part of the most plausible explanation is that because suffering is awful to experience, it is wrong to inflict suffering. Because an animal's suffering is awful for it, this explanation entails that it is wrong to make an animal suffer.

This premise of my argument assumes that animals *can* suffer, which is mildly controversial. For example, René Descartes suggested that animals are just complicated machines with no inner lives (1991 [1640], 148). However, Descartes' views are scientifically indefensible (see Allen and Trestman 2014, §7.1), so I set them aside.

You might object to my case for my first premise that it is only wrong to make a creature suffer if that creature is an ethical agent: the sort of being who can be morally responsible for its actions. But this is false. It is wrong to make babies suffer, and they are not ethical agents. You might object that it is only wrong to make *human beings* suffer. This is implausible for several reasons. First, think about torturing a baby: what is wrong with this is surely the nature of the suffering inflicted, not the fact that the baby has a human genetic code. Second, imagine a non-human animal with a miraculous mutation, which has the ability to speak, reason, and feel as much as you or I do. Surely the mere fact that such an animal is not genetically human does not make it okay to torture it (compare Peter Singer's argument against such "speciesism" in his 1977). And, finally, think again about the case I began this essay with: it is wrong to torture a puppy. But surely the central explanation here is just the same as with a human victim: torture will inflict horrible suffering on the puppy, and it is wrong to inflict such suffering.

Some authors, like Carl Cohen (1986, 867), insist that all suffering is not equal: human suffering is much more ethically important than animal suffering. My argument is compatible with this thesis. I am not arguing that torturing a puppy is just as bad as torturing a human being. I think the latter is typically much worse. My claim is only that making the puppy suffer is wrong, and that the pleasure a human being might take from torturing it does not justify inflicting that suffering.

Next, I argue that if it is wrong to make animals suffer, it is wrong to kill them. Some people find the idea that it is wrong to kill animals much less intuitive than the idea that it is wrong to make them suffer. However, an example shows that this combination of views—that it is wrong to make animals suffer, but not to kill them—is difficult to defend. Suppose that there is a cow that has a disease that will be fatal unless treated by giving the cow a painful medical operation. If the cow would go on to have a long and pleasant life after the operation, performing this operation seems good, not wrong. This shows that an ordinarily wrongful act—inflicting suffering on a cow—can be permissible if it is necessary to save the cow's life. But if *saving* an animal's life can justify inflicting suffering that would otherwise be wrong, it is hard to understand how *taking* that animal's life could be a matter of ethical indifference.

We can bolster this initial argument by combining it with a plausible explanation of why it is wrong to kill animals. One important reason why killing a *person* is typically wrong is that killing typically deprives the victim of an objectively valuable future. That is, killing someone deprives them of the valuable experiences activities, projects, etc. that they would otherwise have had (compare Marquis 1989, §II; I do not claim, with Marquis, that this is the "primary" thing wrong with killing). This principle applies to animals as well: just as suffering can make an animal's life go badly, pleasant experiences can make it go well. So, just as with humans, it is plausible that it is (typically) wrong to kill animals because doing so deprives them of a valuable future.

Finally, I argue that if it is wrong to kill animals, it is wrong to eat meat. Killing and eating are, obviously, not the same thing: in our economically specialized society, many meat-eaters never even see the animals they eat alive, let alone make them suffer or kill them. However, this doesn't mean that eating meat is okay. To see why, consider an analogy.

There is a new restaurant in town: the food is sensational, and the prices are very low. How do they do it? Here's how: the owner kidnaps world-class chefs, and enslaves them at the restaurant. Suppose that the owner is connected with the mob, and going to the police would just get you killed. Your patronizing the restaurant does not enslave anyone, but it still seems wrong. The explanation for why it is wrong is roughly that by patronizing the restaurant, you would be *complicit* in wrongdoing: you would be benefiting from a wrongful act (enslavement), while economically supporting the wrongdoer (the slaver).

Making animals suffer may be less awful than enslaving another human being. But the same form of explanation applies to eating meat. The raising of animals for food causes those animals a horrifying amount of suffering, and early death (see Mason and Singer 1990 for some of the literally grisly details). If it is wrong to kill animals and to cause them to suffer, then the industry that produces our meat acts wrongly on a massive scale. It is wrong to eat meat because in doing so you are complicit with that massive and systematic wrongdoing.

In this essay I have argued that it is wrong to eat meat. One clarification of this conclusion is in order: like many ethical claims, it should be read as a claim about what is *typically* true. It is typically wrong for you to break all of my fingers, but if doing so is the only way to prevent nuclear catastrophe, break away! Similarly, there may be unusual circumstances in which it is permissible or even required to eat meat. Nonetheless, if my argument is sound, each of us does wrong almost every time we sit down to a meal that contains meat.

I have written "It is Wrong to Eat Meat" as a model short philosophy essay. Unless your professor tells you otherwise, you would do well to emulate several of the stylistic features of this essay:

- The introduction offers a brief clear motive for the question addressed, states the essay's thesis, and previews the argument to come;
- The argument of the paper is summarized in valid premise/conclusion form;
- The essay does not waste words: every sentence is dedicated to developing the central argument, explaining a concept, introducing an objection or replying to it, or doing other important work. Even the conclusion does important work, introducing a crucial clarification of the argument.
- The essay does not use lengthy quotes from its sources: instead, it cites those sources after

stating (in my own words) key claims that I take from them.

The argument of this essay is also an excellent target for reasoned objections. I now discuss how to offer such objections.

First, let's back up a bit and think about the activity that we are engaged in. We are seeking to make and to evaluate reasoned arguments about ethics. For example, the model essay did not just disagree with the claim that it is okay to eat meat; it offered reasons for thinking that claim is incorrect, and it organized those reasons into an argument. Making an argument does not simply aim to persuade your reader. I know, for example, that no reasoned argument is as likely to change eating habits as grisly video footage of life inside the animal factories that produce our meat. If philosophers aimed simply to persuade, we would write clever advertising, rather than carefully argued essays. Instead, my aim as a philosopher is to seek the truth together with my audience, in a way that respects the ability of each person involved to find the truth herself, using her own ability to reason. My aim now is to offer you some tools to enable you to skillfully engage in this sort of respectful argumentation.

For many of you, the conclusion of the model essay is a challenge to your ethical views. You may be tempted to reply to this sort of challenge by simply disagreeing with the conclusion. Resist this temptation: if an author offers you an argument, and you ignore the argument and simply reject their conclusion, it is very difficult to seek the truth together with you. So, when you are presented with an argument, your central question should be: does this argument give me good reason to accept its conclusion? The model argument appears to be *valid*: the truth of its premises would logically ensure the truth of the conclusion. When you object to a valid argument, you should focus on objecting to its premises, not the conclusion. This is because the argument purports to offer you reasons to accept its conclusion, and if you cannot explain why you should reject those reasons, you aren't providing a compelling reply to the argument.[1] On the other hand, if you can identify a good reason to reject one of the premises of an argument, you have made an important and constructive contribution, by explaining why a reasonable person should not be persuaded by the argument. This is why it is important to learn how to offer reasoned objections to the premises of an argument.

Developing reasoned objections is in part a creative task, and there is no recipe for doing it well. However, there are several useful general strategies for finding good objections. Taking the model essay as a target, I will introduce some of these strategies, and illustrate them with exemplary objections to the model essay. Another important philosophical skill is to assess the import of potential objections. Because of this, when I consider each objection I will discuss whether the objections can be answered, whether it calls for some amendment to the model essay's argument, or whether it constitutes a promising line of objection to the overall strategy of the model argument. The point of carefully exploring objections and replies is to arrive ultimately at the best arguments that can be made on each side of an ethical issue, like the issue of whether it is wrong to eat meat. Because objections should target the premises of an argument (as I have emphasized), I will organize my discussion by focusing on each premise in turn.

PREMISE ONE: INFLICTING SUFFERING

Premise One of the model argument says:

1. It is wrong to make animals suffer

In this section, I consider objections to this principle that are instances of three general strategies for identifying objections: looking to extreme cases, appealing to an obscured distinction, and appealing to a competing ethical principle.

One excellent way to find objections to ethical principles is to look to extreme cases (Hájek *forthcoming-b*, §4; this and Hájek *forthcoming-a* are excellent sources of heuristics for doing philosophy, although they are

most suited for somewhat advanced philosophy students). There are several relevant *types* of extreme cases. One type of extreme case involves *raising the stakes*. Suppose, for example, that some generic supervillain will incinerate the earth unless you torture this puppy. It is surely required (and not wrong) to torture the puppy in that case. So it is not *always* wrong to cause animals to suffer.

It is not enough to find an objection: you should also think about how someone sympathetic to the argument that you are objecting to should reply to your objection. In this case, there is a decisive reply to this objection: the conclusion of the model essay already granted that it is only *typically* wrong to eat meat. Because scenarios involving comic-book supervillains are extremely atypical, this is not an effective objection to the argument of the model essay. There is an important lesson here: make sure that you interpret the argument you are objecting to accurately and fairly. Failure to do this is so common it has its own name: the *straw man* fallacy.

A different sort of extreme case is more potent. If we arranged animals on a continuum of cognitive sophistication, we would notice that puppies (which featured in the model argument) are relatively close to us on that continuum. So: what happens to the model argument as we move to animals farther away from us on that continuum? Here is one salient example: oysters and other bivalves lack brains, and so are almost certainly incapable of suffering. Because one cannot make an oyster suffer, it cannot be wrong to eat an oyster for the reasons suggested in the model essay.[2] Because there is nothing atypical about eating oysters, this case is an important objection to the argument in the model essay.

One important way to reply to an objection is to concede that it requires one to modify one's argument. This objection to the model argument is powerful, and the best reply is thus concessive. I grant that the model argument does not explain why it is wrong to eat oysters, and so I conclude that the conclusion of the model argument should be restricted to apply only to eating animals that can suffer.

This in turn raises a further question: *which* animals, exactly, can suffer? Here there are formidable methodological barriers to investigation (Allen and

Trestman 2014, §4). The core problem is that we have no direct access to animals' experiential states, so we must reason about their inner lives on the basis of behavioral, functional, neurobiological and evolutionary considerations. Unsurprisingly, the strongest case for suffering can be made for mammals, where the evolutionary and neurobiological parallels with humans are closest. However, we should not assume that only mammals can experience pain; some have argued that there is evidence for pain experience in all vertebrates (Varner 2003), and in many cases we may simply lack adequate empirical knowledge to be able to assess the issue. Especially hard cases include cephalopods such as squid, which are behaviorally very sophisticated but evolutionarily distant from us. My approach to this issue invokes a modest sort of precautionary principle: Because we are not in a position to be confident about whether birds, fish, and cephalopods can suffer, we are not in a position to know whether we act wrongly when we eat them. Indifference to the possibility that we act wrongly is a vice, and we should avoid eating these animals on that basis.

A second powerful way to find objections to a premise is to identify an important distinction that the argument for that premise ignores. For example, one could argue that Premise One of the model essay becomes less plausible once we make the distinction between *being in pain* and *suffering*. Some philosophers grant that many animals can be in pain. However, they suggest that suffering requires something in addition to being in pain that most non-human animals lack. For example, perhaps it requires a conscious belief: that *I am having this pain* (for discussion, see Akhtar 2011, 496–499). An objector might argue that it is suffering in this sense—and not merely being in pain—that is ethically significant. If this were true, then my argument would at very least be incomplete: I would need to discuss the nature of suffering more carefully, and then explore which animals can experience it.

The best reply to this objection begins by emphasizing that the important issue here is not how we should use the word *suffering* (in philosophy you should usually avoid fighting about how to use words). It is rather whether conscious belief (or something like it) is required for pain to be ethically

significant. If we are clear on this point, another extreme case shows why this objection fails. The most intense pains tend to fully occupy us: one is unlikely to be thinking anything—let alone *this pain is happening to me*—when in utter agony. But surely it is wrong to inflict utter agony on someone, because of how awful it feels (compare Rachels 2011, 898). This shows that it can be wrong to inflict pain that does not count as suffering in the objector's stipulated sense. If this is true of agonizing pains, it should be true of less intense pains. And if it is true for our own case, it should be true for animals as well. I thus conclude that this objection fails.

A third way to object to an ethical premise is to identify and defend an independently plausible ethical principle that conflicts with it. You may have encountered such a principle in your previous study of ethics, or you might be able to develop one yourself. One example of this strategy is to argue against Premise One of the model argument by appealing to contractualism, which is one of the most influential contemporary approaches to ethics and political philosophy. The basic idea of contractualism is that moral (or political) principles are principles that reasonable persons would agree to as rules to govern their lives together. So understood, contractualism can seem to cast serious doubt on the ethical significance of animals. As Peter Carruthers notes, according to the contractualist, "Morality is viewed as constructed *by* human beings, in order to facilitate interactions *between* human beings . . ." (1992, 102, emphasis his). Because it is hard to see how a principle like Premise One would help to facilitate such interactions, contractualism may seem to give us good reasons to reject this premise.

I have two interlocking replies to this objection. First, the most plausible forms of contractualism do not have the implications that the objector claims. Exemplary here is T. M. Scanlon's extremely influential contractualist ethical theory. Scanlon is careful to argue that his theory can be extended to protect animals (1998, 177–84). Further, Scanlon is clear that we have strong reasons that are not based in the contractual principle, so his view is compatible with the idea that we might have such reasons not to harm animals. Other philosophers have been more ambitious, offering contractualist arguments on behalf of animals (Rowlands 2002, Ch. 3; Talbert 2006).

Of course, there are some contractualist theories that have the implications that Carruthers suggests. But these are controversial views among contractualists, and contractualism itself is only one of a number of controversial and competing general ethical theories. Because of this controversy, however, it is unlikely that we should be confident in the truth of these contractualist theories. Without such confidence, however, it is hard to see how these theories could give us good reasons to reject Premise One. Further, the case of animals is exactly one where these theories appear implausible. Because it is obviously wrong for me to torture puppies just for fun, it counts against a moral theory that implies otherwise. This sort of case is part of a deep and more general challenge. As Martha Nussbaum (2006) and others have argued, many of our most important moral concerns address the interests of distinctively vulnerable parties (such as children, the severely mentally handicapped, and animals), and not simply the interactions between equally capable adult humans. A contractualism that ignores these interests is indefensible. In light of these considerations, it will be very difficult to mount a compelling case against Premise One of my argument that appeals to contractualism.

In this section I have considered three kinds of objections to Premise One of my argument. An important part of my reply has been concessive, refining the premise that I want to defend: so refined, the thesis states that it is typically wrong to inflict pain on a range of animals, including at least all mammals. So refined, I have suggested that it is very difficult to reasonably reject this premise.

PREMISE TWO: KILLING ANIMALS

Premise Two of the model argument says:

2. If it is wrong to make animals suffer, then it is wrong to kill animals

This premise is *conditional.* In order to successfully object to a conditional, one would need to find a reasonable way to accept the *antecedent* (i.e. the first part) of the conditional, while rejecting the *consequent* (i.e. the second part). Here, this would mean granting that it is wrong to make animals suffer, and arguing that it is nonetheless okay to kill them. I will consider three strategies for objecting to this premise. These strategies all target my explanation of why we should accept this premise. This was the idea that the wrongness of killing is well-explained by the fact that killing deprives the victim of a valuable future. The first strategy appeals to a competing explanation, the second strategy objects that my explanation is incomplete, and the third objects that my explanation has a false presupposition.

Just as a promising objection can be based in a competing ethical principle, so we can base an objection in a competing ethical explanation. In arguing for Premise Two, I offered a general explanation of the wrongness of killing: that killing can be wrong because it deprives the victim of a valuable future. One seemingly competing explanation is that killing you would be wrong because it would violate your autonomy. *Violation* here includes two important and separable ideas. First, killing you would interfere with your exercise of your autonomy. You cannot live your life in the way you choose if you are dead. Second, killing you would be a way of failing to respect your autonomy: if I take myself to be licensed to kill you, I take myself to have the right to ride roughshod over your own view of how your life should go.

In certain cases, this explanation of the wrongness of killing may seem markedly superior to the "valuable future" explanation offered in the model essay. For example, suppose that Alice is near death and in pain, but wishes to continue living. If I inject her with a lethal dose of morphine, I wrongly kill her. (Notice that this is another instance of using an extreme case to make a point.) The best explanation here is that I have wrongly failed to respect her right to autonomously determine whether she continues to live. By contrast, it is not clear that I deprive her of a valuable future at all. Because most non-human animals are not autonomous agents (there may be borderline cases of non-human agency, such as chimpanzees), this competing explanation suggests that Premise Two is false.

To see why this objection is not promising, notice that the autonomy-violation explanation also clearly fails in some cases. Because you are an autonomous agent, I should not force you to go to bed at a certain time, even if it is good for you to do so. By contrast, I act *rightly* when I paternalistically force my three-year-old son to go to bed at an appropriate time. This is because he is not an autonomous agent. It would obviously be very wrong to kill my son, but since he is not an autonomous agent, this cannot be explained in terms of autonomy violation.

You might think that this leaves us at an impasse: we have two candidate explanations of the wrongness of killing (valuable future-deprivation and autonomy-violation) and counter-examples to each. Does this show that both must be bad explanations? No. A better diagnosis is that each of these accounts provides a *typically sufficient but not necessary* explanation of the wrongness of killing. That is: killing can be wrong *either* because it violates autonomy, *or* because it deprives the victim of a valuable future (or both). On this account, one of the reasons why it is uncontroversial that it is wrong to kill an adult human in a range of ordinary circumstances is that there are several different things wrong with such killing. Because Premise Two of the model argument requires only that the valuable future-deprivation explanation is typically sufficient, this reply vindicates that premise.

Another important way to object to an ethical principle or explanation is to argue that it is *incomplete*. Whenever someone offers a principle or explanation, it is always a good idea to ask: is that *all* that is doing the important explanatory work here? Or have I only been given a part of the best ethical principle that applies to this sort of case? For example, one might think that a future's merely *being valuable* is not sufficient to explain why we must not eliminate it. Suppose that my wife and I were debating whether to have another child. If we did, that child would almost certainly have a valuable future. But it seems clear that I do no wrong simply by preventing that future: my having had a vasectomy does not make me akin to a murderer. Michael Tooley (1972)

proposes an explanation of this fact: in order for it to be wrong to deprive an entity of a valuable future, that entity needs to have the capacity to care about its own continued existence. Because the child I do not conceive does not currently exist, it cannot care about its future existence, and hence I do not wrong it by preventing its future, on Tooley's view. One might appeal to Tooley's view to argue that it is not wrong to kill most animals because they are not cognitively sophisticated enough to care about their continued existence.

It is not obvious whether some animals can care about their futures in the relevant way. However, I set this aside, and instead focus on arguing against Tooley's explanatory claim (notice that I do so by appealing to extreme cases reasoning). Suppose that artificial intelligence research advances to the point that we are capable of creating intelligent and autonomous androids, capable of almost everything humans are: sophisticated reasoning, love, physical and emotional pain, etc. Suppose this type of android is programmed to be simply incapable of caring about its own continued existence, although it can and typically does care deeply about particular others. In light of this programming, such androids would be predictably prone to certain tragic behavior: they would sometimes lay down their lives to save others from inconsequential harms. It would be obviously wrong to kill such an android—even with its consent—to save yourself from a splinter. The android's inability to care about its future is a rational imperfection, but not one that licenses killing it.

We can square our judgments about the nonexistent child and the android if we suggest that the android is (imagined to be) an ethically significant being that now exists, while the non-existent child is a merely possible entity. We can then amend our ethical explanation as follows: it is wrong to deprive existing creatures of valuable futures, but it is not wrong to prevent non-existing entities from coming into existence. This explanation implies that it is wrong to kill existing animals, and so supports Premise Two.

A third way to object to an explanation is to argue that it has a false presupposition. That is: it works only by implicitly assuming some false claim. One crucial presupposition of my explanation of the wrongness of killing animals is that if I refrain from killing a cow today, there is a single moral patient—the cow—that will enjoy various pleasant cow experiences in the future. The objector suggests that we have reason to doubt this, if we think carefully about the conditions for the continued existence of a given moral patient.

The objection can be initially motivated by another extreme case: suppose that a mad scientist was able to map the neural structure of our brains, and then *swap* those structures: your brain is "wiped" and then rebuilt in accordance with the map of my brain, so that your body is now the home of beliefs, desires, and "memories" near identical to mine (pre-operation), and vice-versa. Suppose that the mad scientist performs this swap shortly after I injected my own heart with a slow-acting but lethal poison. Arguably, thanks to the mad scientist's intervention, I will have survived, and succeeded in killing you, rather than myself.

Some philosophers use cases like these to argue that *psychological continuity* is required for personal identity or ethically significant survival. In the case above, the idea is that I survive the operation because the surviving body houses a psychology that is continuous with my pre-operation psychology. This sort of case matters to my argument for the following reason. Suppose that the psychological connections across the life of a cow are not very rich. Then, in killing the cow now, I may be depriving *it* of only an inconsequential amount of valuable future. I will also be preventing a series of future "cows" from coming into existence and enjoying life. But as we saw from the nonexistent child case, it appears not to be wrong to refrain from bringing into existence beings with valuable futures.

This leads us to the central issue: do animals have rich enough psychological connections to underwrite the intuitive thought that a given cow (e.g.) is the same moral patient over time? I am cautiously optimistic that they do, in at least many cases. For example, many animals appear capable of various forms of memory (Allen and Trestman 2014, §7.4). However, as with questions about animal pain and suffering, answers here are likely to vary substantially across

species in ways that require careful empirical work to tease out.

It is worth making two further points. First, theories of personal identity—and related claims about the persistence of a given moral patient—are extremely difficult to assess. The view that psychological continuity is the criterion of ethically significant survival is controversial. And on many competing views—on which organism continuity, or brain continuity can underwrite ethically significant survival, for example—the objection will fail immediately. Second, the precautionary approach to practical ethics that I advocated in the preceding section is again relevant here. This objection certainly reveals deep complexities ignored by the argument of the model essay. However, we should only be content to reject that argument if these complexities lead us to be confident that it is not wrong to kill animals.

In this section I have argued that the appeal to autonomy-violation complements—rather than competes with—the valuable future-deprivation account of the wrongness of killing. I also argued that it can be wrong to kill a being that is incapable of caring about its own continued existence. In discussing this issue, I amended the ethical principle I endorse to claim that it is wrong to deprive an *existing* moral patient of the valuable future that it would otherwise have. And I argued that many animals are probably the same moral patient across time (although I granted that the issues here are quire complex).

PREMISE THREE: USING ANIMAL PRODUCTS

Premise Three of the model argument is the claim that:

3. If it is wrong to kill animals, then it is wrong to eat meat

I argued for this claim by defending another ethical principle: that it is wrong to be complicit in wrongdoing: to benefit from that wrongdoing, and to support it. Here we can ask two questions: should we accept this principle, and does it really support Premise Three? In this section I begin by considering an objection to the idea that this principle supports Premise Three, before considering whether this principle is objectionably incomplete.

It is always wise to consider whether an ethical principle really supports the conclusion it is intended to. Consider a case that illustrates this sort of objection to Premise Three. Suppose Alice is driving carefully on a country road, when a deer jumps in front of her truck without warning. The deer is killed instantly, and Alice moves its carcass to the side of the road and leaves. Zoe, who lives nearby, sees all of this. Zoe knows how to dress a deer carcass and has a taste for venison. She takes the carcass home, dresses it, cooks some, and eats it (compare Bruckner 2016 for further discussion of cases like this one). In this scenario, Zoe knowingly prepared and ate meat. But in doing so, Zoe is not complicit in any wrongdoing: Alice's killing of the deer was neither malicious nor negligent, so it is hard to see how it could be wrong. This is a case where eating meat is not complicit in wrongful killing, so it is a case where Premise Three fails to hold, even if the principle I offer is true.

I am happy to grant the objector this case. Recall that my conclusion is that eating meat is *typically* wrong. This case helpfully brings out another atypical exception. The objection lacks more general force exactly because in the overwhelming majority of cases, the meat that we eat *is* wrongfully produced (at least if the arguments for Premises One and Two are sound).

We saw in the previous section that a good strategy for finding objections to an explanation is to challenge its completeness. The same is true for ethical principles like my complicity principle. We can challenge the completeness of my principle by arguing that complicity with the wrongful treatment of animals could only be wrong if it tended to make a difference to how much wrongful treatment there was (see Appiah 1986–7 for a version of this view about complicity). I will call this the *efficacy objection*. This objection has significant force: one might wonder what the point of avoiding complicity is, if it makes no difference to how much animal suffering occurs.

Because I take this to be the single most important challenge to the argument of the model paper, I will offer three potentially complementary replies. (Please note that I offer multiple replies to help illustrate the issues here. In general you should focus on developing the single strongest reply to an objection as clearly as you can, rather than offering multiple replies.)

The first reply accepts the objection, and claims that it is wrong to eat meat because doing so *does* tend to make a difference to the amount of mistreatment of animals. This might seem absurd: by the time I buy a chicken at the store (for example) it is already dead. And the idea that every chicken bought will cause another one to be raised, made to suffer, and then killed, is plainly false. Peter Singer (1980, 335–6, and following him, Norcross 2004, Kagan 2011, and Rachels 2011) has replied to this challenge in the following way: There must be some change in demand for chicken that the market would notice. For example, Singer imagines that for every 10,000 vegetarians, there would be one fewer 20,000-bird broiler factory, harming and killing 100,000 chickens a year. He imagines further that if we were just below the threshold—if, for example, 1,009,999 people were vegetarians—the last 9,999 vegetarians would save no chickens, because demand for chicken would be just above the threshold that triggers a change in supply. Given these assumptions, and given that we do not know exactly how many other vegetarians there are, someone becoming vegetarian has only a 1/10,000 chance of making any difference to the number of chickens made to suffer and die.

That sounds depressing. But Singer argues that we should pay attention to the other numbers: if one *is* that 1/10,000, one will save 100,000 chickens a year. In light of this, the *expected* effect of becoming vegetarian is the effect you would have if you make a difference divided by your chance of making that difference; in the example, saving 100,000/10,000 = 10 chickens a year from short but awful lives. Of course, these precise numbers are merely illustrative; Singer grants that we do not know where exactly the thresholds are. But he suggests that the structure of probable effects will be similar on any reasonable hypothesis about these thresholds. So, according to

Singer, while any reduction or increase in one's meat consumption has a tiny chance of making a difference to the amount of wrongful animal suffering and death, the difference you will make if you do make a difference will be correspondingly huge. And this, it might be claimed, is what makes it wrong to eat meat. If Singer's reasoning is sound, it answers the efficacy objection: complicity is wrong in part because it has an ethically significant chance of making an ethically significant difference. While Singer's reply is promising, his argument is somewhat complex, and relies on some controversial assumptions (see Budolfson *forthcoming* for an important reply). In light of this, I will explore alternative ways of replying to the efficacy objection.

Singer's argument illustrates two important ideas worth keeping in mind in your ethical reasoning. First, sometimes the *expected* effects of your actions are ethically significant, and not just their actual effects. (In this case, the alleged expected effect of being a vegetarian is sparing ten chickens a year from short and awful lives, even if for most vegetarians, there is no actual effect on chicken well-being.) Second, in thinking about the effects of an action, it is sometimes important to step back from focusing on the particular act, and think about how that act fits into overall patterns.

A second response to the efficacy objection appeals to these patterns in another way, by focusing on the ethical significance of what groups of people do together. One advantage of this approach is that it is uncontroversial that meat-eaters as a group *do* make a difference to the amount of animal suffering: if there were no omnivores there would be no factory farms.

I will introduce the key idea with another example. Suppose that there are two small cities, Upstream and Downstream, along the same river. The river is the only available source of water for the households in each city. Each household in each city draws its water from the river as the river comes into the city, and dumps its sewage in the river as it flows out of the city. The sewage dumped in the river in Upstream flows down the river and pollutes the drinking water drawn from the river in Downstream. As a result, the people in Downstream are constantly getting seriously ill and dying. Suppose that each household in Upstream could, at small cost, bury their sewage instead of dumping it in the river. If everyone in Upstream did this, it would end the health catastrophe in Downstream. However, given the number of other households that are actually polluting, a single person in Upstream burying his sewage would not save anyone in Downstream from illness or death.

It seems plausible that the sewage-dumpers in Upstream *together* wrongfully cause massive amounts of suffering and death in Downstream. Anyone in Upstream who dumps her sewage in the river is thus part of a group that acts wrongly. It is easy to cease to be part of that group, however: one need only bury one's sewage. It seems plausible that one should bury one's sewage in this situation, rather than dump it into the river. We could explain this by appealing to the following ethical principle: if one can avoid being part of a group that together does serious wrong, then one acts wrongly by continuing to be a member of that group. This principle applies neatly to eating meat. Together, the meat-eaters make a tremendous difference: without their demand for meat, no one would cause animals to suffer and die in order to produce it. So the meat-eaters together make vast amounts of wrongful pain and death happen to animals. So, by the ethical principle just proposed, one acts wrongly by continuing to be a member of that group.

This reply answers the efficacy objection by appealing to group efficacy. However, the issue of when exactly it is wrong to remain a part of an ethically objectionable group is very complicated. (Sometimes, for example, it is only by being part of such a group that one can mitigate the bad things the group does.) So I will explore another alternative response to the efficacy objection, which is the one I find most promising.

This response directly rejects the efficacy objection, and defends the claim that complicity with wrongdoing can be a sufficient explanation for wrongdoing, even if it has no expected bad effects. I will defend this response in three ways: by appealing to a plausibly analogous ethical principle, by clarifying the anti-complicity principle, and by appealing to a variant on an earlier case that helps to distinctively motivate it.

The first thing to notice is that there are other plausible ethical principles that require us to act even when our doing so will not make a difference. For example, the duty of *fair play* requires that one not benefit from successful cooperative institutions without making a fair contribution to them; i.e., that one not *freeride* (see e.g. Klosko 2004). Consider, as an example, sneaking onto a public bus without paying the fare.

Second, it may be useful to more precisely state the principle that I endorse (see McPherson *2016-b* for more detailed discussion):

Anti-Complicity It is typically wrong to aim to benefit by cooperating with the wrongful elements of others' plans

When introducing a principle, it is often useful to briefly explain each of the elements of that principle. I now do this for Anti-Complicity. My talk of "plans" here should not be taken to apply only to patterns of explicit reasoning; rather it should include the pattern of goals that explain an individual's or institution's behavior. If my unconscious desire to humiliate my rival explains all of my behavior, humiliating my rival counts as my plan, even if I would never consciously admit this is what I am up to. My talk of "benefit" should similarly be read in an expansive way: smoking does more harm than good, but if one seeks the enjoyment of a cigarette, one is aiming at benefit in the sense I am interested in. We should understand "cooperating" in the following way: our plans often call for others to act in certain ways. For example, if I make widgets for sale, my plan includes others' buying those widgets. Of course, it is not crucial that any particular person buys my widgets. So anyone who buys a widget counts as cooperating with my plan. Finally plans can be disjunctive: someone can plan to read the newspaper, buy some tools at the store, and then use the tools to torture a puppy. The clearly wrongful part here is the puppy torturing. Buying the tools is instrumental to the wrongful behavior, and is arguably wrongful for that reason, and reading the newspaper is not a wrongful part of the plan. It is most clear that we should not cooperate with the wrongful part of the plan.

Anti-Complicity is plausible in part because it can explain the wrongness of certain acts that cannot be explained by either the group or individual efficacy explanations. Return to the example in the model essay: the restaurant that kidnaps and enslaves chefs to make its food. Suppose the restaurant is *demand-insensitive*: it's partly a money-laundering operation, and so it will remain in business even if no one ever patronizes it. This means that neither an individual, nor the whole group of patrons, have any chance of reducing the amount of slavery in the restaurant by refusing to patronize it. Still, it seems wrong to go to the restaurant and enjoy the fruits of the slave chefs' unwilling labors. Anti-Complicity can explain why, while principles that demand that the individual or group make a difference cannot.

If the arguments earlier in the paper are correct, the meat industry has a wrongful plan: to produce meat in a way that involves egregious amounts of pain and early death, and then to sell that meat. They do not, of course, typically sell it directly to consumers. But consumers buying meat is clearly part of their plan: for if consumers do not buy, then wholesalers will not either, and the meat industry's plan would not be economically viable. (This is why meat-industry groups sometimes advertise directly to consumers: to increase consumer-level demand for their goods.) So, in buying meat, one is cooperating with their wrongful plan. And Anti-Complicity suggests that doing so is typically wrong.

Of the three explanations that I have discussed here (individual efficacy, group efficacy, and Anti-Complicity), I prefer the last. However, it is worth emphasizing that, as with explanation of the wrongness of killing, it is not clear that these explanations compete. Rather, if each is sound, they could be complementary explanations of the wrongness of eating meat. This means that the objector has her work cut out for her. For each of the three explanations that I have discussed, she must either debunk the relevant explanatory principle, or argue that the principle does not entail that it is wrong to eat meat. For example, one might insist that individual efficacy is required for wrongdoing in these cases, and then argue against the Singer-style reasoning. I take this to be the most promising way to reject the argument, but to nonetheless be a very difficult task.

THE IMPLICATIONS OF THE ARGUMENT: VEGANISM

In the previous three sections, I have considered several objections to each of the three premises of the model argument, and refined that argument in light of those objections. I now want to consider the broader implications of the argument, as refined. I will begin by considering two objections to the argument that target gaps between the premises and my overall thesis: ethical veganism.

An obvious but important objection at this stage notes that my aim in this paper is to argue for ethical veganism: the view that it is (at least typically) wrong to eat or otherwise use animal products. However, the model argument concludes only that it is wrong to eat *meat*. The model argument itself thus fails to establish ethical veganism. I grant this objection. However, the argument I have developed in this paper naturally extends to support ethical veganism.

The first point to notice is that it is possible to imagine farming with animals in a way that does not involve shortening their lives or making them suffer. My argument does not suggest any objection to using animal products made on such farms. However, when we turn from possible to actual animal farming, we find that my case against killing animals and making them suffer applies to almost all of the institutions that produce animal products (with the exceptions of some shellfish farms). The reasons lie in the interaction between biology and economics. Consider a single example: even the most humane dairy farm will typically produce as many male calves as female, and almost all of the males will be killed early, so as not to be an economic burden. That means that the central plan of almost any economically viable dairy farming operation involves raising cows to be killed (or to be sold to another operation, knowing the latter operation will kill them), a practice that I have argued above is typically wrong. And this in turn means that the overall argument I have proposed applies here: the core plan of economically viable dairy farms involves systematic wrongdoing, and I have argued that it is wrong to be

complicit with such wrongdoing. But one would be complicit with such wrongdoing if one were to buy and consume the milk (e.g.) produced on such farms, and hence buying and consuming such milk would be wrong. This example generalizes to the institutions that produce almost all of our animal products: eggs, cheese, leather, etc. And for this reason I think that my argument supports ethical veganism as opposed to a requirement to be a vegetarian who merely refrains from eating meat.

A second worry about my overall argument is that the initial simple statement of the argument in premise and conclusion form in the model essay is misleading. In the preceding sections, I have emphasized various ways that this argument should be refined, but there is a general worry that should be explored. The conclusion of the model argument emphasized that it is only *typically* wrong to eat meat. And as I explained in my initial discussion of Premise One, this qualifier should be read back into the premises. So the argument should look like this:

1. It is typically wrong to make animals suffer
2. If it is typically wrong to make animals suffer, then it is typically wrong to kill animals
3. If it is typically wrong to kill animals, then it is typically wrong to eat meat
   C. It is typically wrong to eat meat.

The first thing to do is to verify that this statement of the argument, like the statement in the model essay, is valid. It is: the addition of the word "typically" does not alter the logical form of the argument, which is: *P, if P then Q, if Q then R, so R*, which is a slightly more complex variant of the classic *modus ponens* argument form. However, there are two connected worries about the argument as given. First, the reference to typicality points us at a range of ordinary cases, but every sort of exception that we have identified for each premise is an exception that must hold for the argument as a whole. The discussion has identified a raft of "atypical" exception cases: cases of making animals suffer to avoid ethically awful alternatives, cases of eating oysters and other animals incapable of experiencing pain, and cases of eating meat (like some roadkill) that was not wrongfully produced.

These cases do not exhaust the set of potential exceptions that the argument permits. And one might worry that as a result, the argument might be far too weak to support anything resembling veganism. To begin to see the force of this worry, notice that I have granted that human suffering and death may tend to be substantially more ethically significant than the suffering and death of non-human animals. This is because, as we saw above, killing you or making you suffer would be wrong for multiple reasons: some have to do with the awfulness of suffering, and the deprivation of your future, and others have to do with the ethical significance of your autonomy.

In light of this, my argument at least suggests that the most central and pressing human interests should typically take priority over the welfare of non-human animals. For example, my conclusion is compatible with the idea that we should typically harm or kill a non-human animal if doing so is needed to prevent suffering or death to a human being. This is practically relevant: in various times and places, animal products have been an essential element of the only feasible nutritionally adequate human diets. For example, in many parts of the world, owning a cow—or even a handful of chickens—can offer crucial protection against certain forms of malnutrition. I take it to be a virtue of my argument that it is compatible with cases like these counting as legitimate exceptions to the vegan principle.

At this point, however, one may wonder whether the case for veganism has any practical bite at all. After all, becoming a vegan involves a non-trivial sacrifice of real goods. Consider three sorts of examples. First, there is a sea of delicious animal-involving food, so as a vegan one sacrifices access to a range of interesting aesthetic goods. Second, food is deeply meaningful to many people, and animal products are centrally involved in many important cultural traditions and occasions. To be a vegan is thus to complicate one's relationship to those traditions and meanings. Finally, because shared values are central to many personal and professional relationships, veganism could be an impediment to such relationships, especially in cultural contexts where veganism is seen as threatening.

If the fact that veganism required one to sacrifice goods like these typically rendered omnivorism

permissible, then veganism would not typically be ethically required, as I claim. Instead, it would be an admirable but non-obligatory ideal. However, I do not think that the sorts of sacrifices just mentioned suffice to make omnivorism permissible. The core issue here is how weighty the considerations in favor of veganism that I have developed in this paper are. The issue is complex, but I think that a reasonable heuristic can be derived from the initial example in the model paper: *some circumstances* would warrant torturing the stray puppy imagined in that example. But those circumstances would be comparatively dire. I contend that only similarly dire circumstances would warrant ordering the sirloin steak for dinner. And the sacrifices typically involved in becoming vegan, while significant, fall well below this threshold.

Challenging this heuristic would be yet another natural way to object to the argument of this paper. However, I think the heuristic is basically sound. And if it is, the argument of the paper suggests that we ought to eschew almost all animal products in almost all ordinary circumstances. We ought, in other words, to be vegan.

PEDAGOGICAL CODA

I conclude this paper by returning to my pedagogical aims: to aid you in thinking about how to make (and critically examine) philosophical arguments in ethics. In order to do so, I will review the basic elements of philosophical argument that I have sought to explain and illustrate in this paper.

The argument of the model essay began with a vivid *example*: the claim that it would be wrong to torture a puppy in a specific scenario. This case supported a *general principle*: that it is wrong to make animals suffer. The case supported the principle in part because the case seems *representative* of the principle. It does not seem that there is some unique feature of puppies that explains why it is wrong to torture them, for example. This principle was also supported by an underlying *ethical explanation*: it is wrong to cause animals to suffer, *because of how awful it is to experience suffering.* Although general principles themselves appear explanatorily illuminating, explanations and general principles can be different. One way to see this is to notice that there can be multiple good explanations of a single ethical principle, as in the case of the future-deprivation and autonomy-violation explanations of the wrongness of killing. In making arguments, cases, general principles, and explanations are likely to be the most important elements to develop. These elements should fit together in a rationally compelling way, and one good way to do that is to put these elements together into a valid argument, as I again did in the model essay.

In critically examining an argument, you might in principle target the structure of the argument itself: for example, showing that the argument contains some fallacious reasoning. Or you might challenge the ethical claims the argument makes about specific cases: for example, you could try to argue that there is nothing wrong with torturing puppies. (But I dearly hope you don't do that!) It is far more common for it to be useful to challenge the general principles and explanations offered in an argument. I have discussed several important ways of executing these challenges. First, it can be useful to look to extreme cases, to see if principles are really generally applicable. For example, the model argument appeals to suffering to explain why it is wrong to eat meat. But some animals (such as oysters) cannot suffer. So the model argument cannot explain why it is wrong to eat them. Second, it can be useful to see if an argument only works because it obscures an ethically important distinction. I discussed this issue using the example of the contrast between being in pain and suffering. Third, it is always a good idea to ask if there is a superior competitor to the general principle or ethical explanation offered in an argument. Examples of this strategy discussed above were the objection from contractualism, and the objection that autonomy violation is the best explanation of why killing is typically wrong. Fourth, a very natural objection to an explanation or principle is that it is *incomplete.* For example, I considered the idea that it is only wrong to deprive a creature of its valuable future *if* that creature is capable of caring about that future. And I discussed the idea that complicity with

wrongdoing is only morally objectionable if such complicity can make a difference to the extent of the underlying wrongdoing. Fifth, another important type of objection to some explanations is that those explanations rest on false presuppositions. For example, I considered the possibility that most animals do not have valuable futures in the ethically relevant sense, because most animals lack rich enough psychological connections to remain the same moral patient from one day to the next. Finally, another important way to challenge an argument is to show that there is a gap between an explanation offered in support of an ethical principle, and the principle itself. For example, the case of eating blamelessly produced roadkill suggests that there is a gap between its being wrong to kill animals, and its being wrong to eat meat, because some meat does not come from animals that were wrongfully killed.

I take these to be some of the most important tools for critically analyzing philosophical arguments. However, there are many more to be discovered. One very good habit to get into when reading philosophical papers is to ask: what kind of argument is this? How is this author objecting to that argument? If you do that consistently, you will soon have a very rich repertoire of tools for evaluating others' arguments, and making your own. One final note about how to use these tools. Probably the most important place to use the tools I have discussed in this paper is in revising your own paper. Once you have a draft of your paper in hand, you should be merciless in carefully reading through it, asking: how compelling is this argument? How could someone reasonably object to it? Are their objections sound? In my view, it is most important to use these tools to examine arguments for the conclusions that you most care about. Only by doing so can you determine whether these conclusions are reasonable, or whether you are guilty of wishful thinking, only accepting them *because* you care about them.[3]

NOTES

1. This paragraph simplifies in several ways. First, in some arguments the premises (even if true) simply fail to support the conclusion, even given a charitable interpretation. Clearly demonstrating that fact can be a powerful way of objecting to such an argument. Second, some

philosophers have argued that it can be legitimate to object to certain arguments as a whole, without criticizing either specific premises or the logical structure of the argument. For discussion relevant to our topic, see McPherson 2014 and *2016-a*.

2. There might, however, be other arguments that count against eating animals that cannot suffer: for example, one could offer environmental objections to how some such animals are raised or harvested, or appeal to the idea that simply being a fellow animal is morally significant.

3. One final bit of guidance: you should always recognize help you have received in writing a paper! I am indebted to many people for helpful comments and discussion of ideas related to this paper. These include Mark Budolfson, David Plunkett, Tyler Doggett, Andrew Chignell, Sean Walsh, Derek Baker, Tom Dougherty, Gideon Rosen, and Katie Batterman, to audiences at Rhodes College, Bowling Green State University, Charles Sturt University, and Virginia Commonwealth University, and to many of my students for discussion. I am also indebted to Liz Harman, whose talk about ethical vegetarianism first started me thinking systematically about it. Parts of this paper draw significantly on my 2014, and especially my *2016-b*.

WORKS CITED

Akhtar, Sahar. "Animal Pain and Welfare: Can Pain Sometimes Be Worse for Them Than for Us?" *Oxford Handbook of Animal Ethics*. Eds. Tom Beauchamp and R. G. Frey. Oxford University Press, 2011. 495–518.

Allen, Colin, and Michael Trestman. "Animal Consciousness." *The Stanford Encyclopedia of Philosophy* (Summer 2014 Edition). Ed. Edward N. Zalta. <http://plato.stanford.edu/archives/sum2014/entries/consciousness-animal/>.

Appiah, Kwame Anthony. "Racism and Moral Pollution." *Philosophical Forum* 18.2–3 (1986). 185–202.

Bruckner, Donald W. "Strict Vegetarianism is Immoral" in *The Moral Complexities of Eating Meat*, Eds. Robert Fischer and Ben Bramble. Oxford University Press: 2016. 30–47.

Budolfson, Mark. "The Inefficacy Objection and the Problem with the Expected Consequences Response", *Philosophical Studies, forthcoming*.

Carruthers, Peter. *The Animals Issue*. Cambridge: Cambridge University Press, 1992.

Cohen, Carl. "The Case for the Use of Animals in Biomedical Research." *The New England Journal of Medicine* 315, 1986. 865–869.

Descartes, Rene. *The Philosophical Writings of Descartes Vol. III*. Ed. and Tr. John Cottingham, Robert Stoothoff, Dugald Murdoch, and Anthony Kenny. Cambridge, Cambridge University Press, 1991.

Hájek, Alan. "Heuristics for Philosophical Creativity." *forthcoming* in *The Philosophy of Creativity*. Eds. Elliot Samuel Paul and Scott Barry Kaufman. Oxford: Oxford University Press. *Cited as forthcoming-a*.

———. "Philosophical Heuristics and Philosophical Methodology." *forthcoming* in *The Oxford Handbook of Philosophical Methodology*. Eds. Herman Cappelen, Tamar Gendler, and John Hawthorne. Oxford: Oxford University Press. *Cited as forthcoming-b*.

Kagan, Shelly. "Do I Make a Difference?" *Philosophy and Public Affairs* 39.2 (2011). 105–141.

Klosko, George. The Principle of Fairness and Political Obligation (New Edition). Rowman and Littlefield, 2004.

McPherson, Tristram. "A Case for Ethical Veganism." *Journal of Moral Philosophy* 11(6), 2014. 677–703.

———. "A Moorean Defense of the Omnivore?" in *The Moral Complexities of Eating Meat*, Eds. Robert Fischer and Ben Bramble. Oxford University Press: 2016. 118–134. *Cited as 2016-a*.

———. "Why I am a Vegan (and You Should be One Too)." in *Philosophy Comes to Dinner*, Eds. Andrew Chignell, Terence Cuneo, and Matthew Halterman. Routledge: 2016. 73–91. Cited as *2016-b*.

Marquis, Don. "Why Abortion is Immoral." *Journal of Philosophy* 86.4, April 1989. 183–202.

Mason, Jim and Peter Singer. *Animal Factories* Revised and Updated Edition. Harmony: 1990.

Norcross, Alasdair. "Puppies, Pigs, and People: Eating Meat and Marginal Cases." *Philosophical Perspectives* 18 (Ethics), 2004. 229–245.

Nussbaum, Martha. *Frontiers of Justice*. Harvard: Belknap, 2006.

Rachels, Stuart. "Vegetarianism." *Oxford Handbook of Animal Ethics*. Eds. Tom Beauchamp and R. G. Frey. Oxford: Oxford University Press, 2011. 877–905.

Rowlands, Mark. *Animals Like Us*. Verso: 2002.

Scanlon, T. M. *What We Owe to Each Other*. Cambridge, MA: Belknap: 1998.

Singer, Peter. *Animal Liberation*. New York: Avon, 1977.

———. "Utilitarianism and Vegetarianism." *Philosophy and Public Affairs*. 9.4 (Summer 1980), 325–337.

Talbert, Matthew. "Contractualism and Our Duties to Nonhuman Animals." *Environmental Ethics* 28 (Summer 2006). 202–215.

Tooley, Michael. "Abortion and Infanticide." *Philosophy and Public Affairs* 2.1 (August 1972). 37–65.

Varner, Gary. *In Nature's Interests*. Oxford: Oxford University Press, 1998.

QUESTIONS

1. What are the main objections that McPherson considers to each premise of the argument in the model essay? Explain the main point of each objection in your own words in one or two clear sentences.
2. What exactly does McPherson's Anti-Complicity Principle say? How does it differ from the principles outlined in the introduction to this chapter? Explain using clear examples that illustrate the differences. Can you think of reasons why someone might think that McPherson's principle does a better or a worse job than the principles discussed in the chapter introduction of capturing what we often think is intuitively wrong in cases where a person might be described as "complicit in wrongdoing"?
3. Why does McPherson favor adding the Anti-Complicity Principle to the argument? What are the alternatives he considers? Why do you think he favors Anti-Complicity over alternative principles? How do you expect he would argue against alternatives?
4. Can you think of clear cases that could be taken to be counterexamples to the Anti-Complicity Principle? How do you think McPherson would respond? How would you respond?

MARK BUDOLFSON

The Inefficacy Objection to Utilitarian Theories of the Ethics of the Marketplace

Budolfson argues that the inefficacy objection raises an important problem for utilitarian arguments in consumer ethics, including for Peter Singer's arguments for vegetarianism. He examines an "expected consequences" response to the inefficacy objection on behalf of such utilitarians, which claims that the expected effect of one individual's consumption on production is roughly equal to the average effect on production of everyone's actions of that type. Budolfson argues that we should not expect this response to work given readily available knowledge about the workings of markets. He argues that in light of those facts about the actual workings of markets, we should expect conclusions opposite to those of Singer's to be true. (Budolfson is a philosopher at the University of Vermont.)

Mark Budolfson, "The Inefficacy Objection to Utilitarian Theories of the Ethics of the Marketplace." Printed with the author's permission.

The signature ethical problem of the global consumer society is our responsibility for the unethical practices that lie behind the products we buy.

—Peter Singer

Americans would be healthier if they reduced their consumption of animal products, and any desirable level of animal consumption could be sustained without factory farming. Furthermore, eliminating factory farms would save billions of animals from intense suffering each year, improve public health, reduce food prices in lesser developed countries, reduce energy costs by reducing the price of biofuels, reduce air and water pollution, reduce the irrational consumption of scarce groundwater resources, reduce greenhouse gas emissions, reduce health-care costs and thereby reduce the national deficit, and allow family farmers to compete more effectively against agribusiness conglomerates.

In light of the preceding, and the fact that the U.S. government could adopt efficient regulations that would largely eliminate factory farming without causing any weighty negative side effects, the U.S. government should adopt such regulations. However, in the meantime factory farming continues. Does this mean that each American *as an individual person* is required to stop consuming animal products from factory farms, at least when s/he can do so without dramatic inconvenience?

At first glance, it might seem that the answer to this individual-level question is "yes," just as the answer to the collective-level question of whether we should eliminate factory farms is "yes." However, even if it is clear what solution is best at the level of public policy, this does not mean that it is clear what *individuals* have ethical reason to do in the absence of such policy—especially if factory farming is a problem to be solved only by policy and cannot realistically be solved by individual ethics or by individual people "voting with their dollars."

In what follows I argue that the question of what individuals are required to do about factory farms is indeed more complicated than it initially appears—and, for similar reasons, most questions about what individuals are required to do when products are produced in morally objectionable ways are more complicated than they initially appear. As I argue at greater length elsewhere, I think these complications have general importance, because they ultimately call into question whether familiar ethical theories can explain many of the most important facts about modern moral life.

To see how things get complicated, in this paper I'll focus on utilitarian arguments that it is wrong to consume animal products from factory farms, such as those offered by Peter Singer. The intuitive idea behind Singer's arguments is that purchasing and eating meat from factory farms is wrong because it has unacceptable consequences on balance for welfare. For example, if I purchase and eat a factory-farmed chicken, the idea is that my gustatory pleasure is greatly outweighed by the suffering that the chicken experiences in order to bring me that pleasure; as a result, Singer would claim that the (expected) effect on overall wellbeing of my eating that chicken is unacceptably negative on balance, even if I really enjoy eating it—and similar reasoning explains why it is in general impermissible for individual people to consume animal products from factory farms and other products that are produced in a way that is wrong.[1]

Furthermore, note that Singer's reasoning can seem decisive even if one endorses an ethical view other than act utilitarianism. That is because on any plausible view, the welfare effects of one's actions are ethically important. In particular, even on deontological and virtue theories, it is generally wrong to bring about significant harm or suffering for no significant reason, even if doing so would not violate any rights or agreements. For example, if I know that bad weather has destroyed the food supply for animals in my area except for some berries that grow deep in the woods on my property, it would be wrong for me to burn all of those berries in my outdoor fireplace simply to provide a very fleeting pleasant aroma, if I know that this would cause all of the animals in my area to starve to death painfully—and one doesn't have to be a traditional consequentialist to endorse this thought. As a result, if Singer's argument about eating meat are sound on the assumption that act utilitarianism is true, then it seems like they are also sound on the assumption that any other plausible ethical theory is true, because if Singer is right about the welfare effects of eating meat, those considerations would trump any other considerations that a plausible ethical theory could say are relevant to determining what we are required to do.

However, even if we agree with Singer's premises about the magnitude of animal suffering in the world, and the comparative unimportance of gustatory and other human pleasures, there is an important objection to his argument—the inefficacy objection—that claims that his conclusion about the welfare effects of consumption by an individual does not follow, and, upon careful reflection, turns out to be false. That is because, according to the inefficacy objection, an individual's decision to consume animal products cannot really be expected to have any effect on the number of animals that suffer or the extent of that suffering, given the actual nature of the long and complex supply chain that stands in between individual consumption decisions and production decisions; at the same time, an individual's decision to consume animal products does have a positive effect for that individual. As a result, according to the inefficacy objection utilitarian premises about the value of suffering vs. pleasure, together with the actual empirical facts about the workings of the marketplace, entail that the (expected) welfare effect of an individual's decision to consume many ethically objectionable products is *positive* on balance, in contrast to what utilitarians like Singer assume. So, if the inefficacy objection is sound, it undermines the idea that it is generally wrong for individuals to consume products that are, on utilitarian grounds, produced in a way that is extremely wrong.

In light of this challenge from the inefficacy objection, it is perhaps no surprise that utilitarians have unified behind a particular response, which claims that the inefficacy objection invariably overlooks the significance of low-probability threshold effects. Here is Alastair Norcross's presentation of such a response:

> Suppose that there are 250 million chicken eaters in the US, and that each one consumes, on average, 25 chickens per year . . . Clearly, if only one of those chicken eaters gave up eating chicken, the industry would not respond. Equally clearly, if they all gave up eating chicken, billions of chickens (approximately 6.25 billion per year) would not be bred, tortured, and killed. But there must also be some number of consumers, far short of 250 million, whose renunciation of chicken would cause the industry to reduce the number of chickens bred in factory farms. The industry may not be able to respond to each individual's behavior, but it must respond to the behavior of fairly large numbers. Suppose that the industry is sensitive to a reduction in demand for chicken equivalent to 10,000 people becoming vegetarians. (This seems like a reasonable guess, but I have no idea what the actual numbers are, nor is it important.) For each group of 10,000 who give up chicken, a quarter of a million fewer chickens are bred per year. It appears, then, that if you give up eating chicken, you have only a one in ten thousand chance of making any difference to the lives of chickens, unless it is certain that fewer than 10,000 people will ever give up eating chicken, in which case you have no chance. Isn't a one in ten thousand chance small enough to render your continued consumption of chicken blameless? Not at all. While the chance that your behavior is harmful may be small, the harm that is risked is enormous.[2]

The goal of this response from Norcross is to argue that in the cases at issue, for any single individual, the *expected effect* of that individual's action—in the particular example discussed here, the action of purchasing one chicken—is equal to the *average effect* of all actual acts of that type across society, in the sense of "expected effect" familiar from the notion of "expectation" in expected utility theory[3]—and similarly for other collective action situations in which the inefficacy objection might initially seem to show that utilitarianism has absurd implications by the lights of its own defenders such as Singer and Norcross. If this response were correct, then utilitarians would be able to respond to the inefficacy objection in a way that appears fully satisfactory by their own lights.

In what follows, I will argue that this response to the inefficacy objection presented by Norcross does not ultimately work, and that the inefficacy objection is ultimately sound.

To begin to see the problem with the response outlined by Norcross, consider the following case:

> Richard makes paper T-shirts in his basement that say "HOORAY FOR CONSEQUENTIALISM!," which he then sells online. The T-shirts are incredibly cheap to produce and very profitable to sell and Richard doesn't care about waste per se, and so he produces

more T-shirts than he is likely to need, and then sells whatever the excess turns out to be at the end of the month at a nearly break-even amount to his hippie neighbor, who burns them in his wood-burning stove. For many years Richard has always sold between 13,000 and 16,000 T-shirts each month, and he's always printed 20,000 T-shirts at the beginning of each month. Nonetheless, there is a *conceivable* increase in sales that would cause him to produce more T-shirts—in particular, if he sells over 19,000 this month, he'll produce 25,000 T-shirts at the beginning of next month; otherwise he'll produce 20,000 like he always does. So, the system is genuinely sensitive to a precise tipping point—in particular, the difference between 19,000 purchases and the "magic number" of 19,001.

Suppose that a consumer knows all of these facts about Richard's business, and is considering buying a T-shirt for himself. What is the expected effect on the number of T-shirts produced of that consumer purchasing a T-shirt? The correct answer is essentially zero, because given what is known about the history of demand for Richard's T-shirts and how production quantities are determined, there is virtually no chance that exactly 19,001 people are going to buy Richard's T-shirts this month and trigger a dramatic threshold effect—which, of course, is not to claim that there is *zero* chance of that happening, but rather that the odds of that happening—of exactly 19,001 of Richard's T-shirts being sold and no more—is certainly dramatically lower than 1/5,000 or any other number that would drive the expected effect of an individual buying one T-shirt anywhere near the consequence that 1 additional T-shirt is produced.

This shows that the reasoning behind Norcross's response is flawed, because insofar as his response is taken to show that consuming meat should be expected to have significant bad effects for animal welfare (i.e., equal to the average effect of each such purchase across all of society), similar reasoning would show that buying one T-shirt in the story above should be expected to result in approximately 1 additional T-shirt being produced, which is the wrong result.[4] The problem with the reasoning is that it overlooks the fact that we can know enough about the supply chains in both cases to know that threshold effects are not sufficiently likely and are not of sufficient magnitude to drive the expected effect of

consumption anywhere close to the average effect. For the sake of giving a name to the more general mistake illustrated by Norcross's reasoning of illegitimately assuming that the expected effect of a single individual's action must equal the average effect of all actual actions of that type, we might call that mistake the "Average Effects Fallacy."

In response, it might be insisted that there is a crucial disanalogy between the T-shirt case just described and e.g. our actual situation with respect to factory farmed animal products. One obvious difference might seem to be the amount of waste: in particular, in the T-shirt case, a significant amount of the product is "wasted." However, although the T-shirt case is indeed a dramatization aimed primarily at making vivid why the reasoning behind the response is invalid as presented, upon further reflection there is less of a difference to a typical case involving the consumption of animal products than it might initially appear, and more importantly there is no crucial disanalogy with respect to the expected effect of an individual's consumption decisions. For example, consider the meat that goes out of date in a wholesaler's meat locker or on a supermarket shelf, and is then sold to a dog food plant or "rendered" into feed for other animals. Is that meat "wasted"? What is the difference between that meat and the "wasted" T-shirts in the story above that Richard sells to his neighbor?

For current purposes it doesn't really matter whether such things are labeled as "wasted" or not—what matters is that there is reliably at least a small amount of "wasted"-like meat at each stage of the supply chain that serves as sufficient "slack" to create buffers that prevent an individual's decision to purchase meat from making any difference to the number of animals that are produced at the far other end of the supply chain. Most importantly, the crucial issue is not about the *magnitude* of these buffers, but rather about their *reliability*: as long as we can know—as we can—that there are sure to be buffers of non-trivial size throughout the supply chain (even if they are not nearly as large as the buffers in the T-shirt example), that reduces the probability of a single individual making a difference to a level that appears to become nearly infinitesimal.

So, the key empirical argument here relevant to consumer ethics is that (1) Many products we consume are delivered by a massive and complex supply chain in which there is some *reliable* amount of *slack*—in the form of waste, inefficiency, and so on—at many links in that chain. (2) That slack serves as a buffer to absorb any would-be effects from the links before. Furthermore, (3) Production decisions are insensitive to the informational signal generated by a single consumer because the sort of slack just described together with other kinds of noise in the extended transmission chain from consumers to producers, and are also insensitive to a single individual's action because production decisions themselves are generally not made in the way assumed by utilitarians in their responses to the inefficacy objection. (Conclusion 1) This ensures that significant-enough threshold effects are not likely-enough to arise from an individual's consumption decisions to justify equating the expected effect on wellbeing of an individual's decision with anything approaching the average effect of such decisions. As a result, (Conclusion 2) For many products in modern society, it is empirically implausible that even a lifetime of consumption decisions by a single individual would make any difference to quantity produced and thus the harm that lies behind those products. So, (Main Conclusion) Utilitarianism cannot explain why it is wrong to consume those products.

For an illustration, consider the supply chain for American beef. When ranchers who own their own grazing land decide how many cattle to raise, their decisions are sensitive to their own financial situation, the number of cattle their land can support, the expected price of any additional feed that will be needed, bull semen and other "raw materials" that go into cattle production, and the expected price that the cattle will fetch when they are ultimately sold to feedlots. Of these, small changes in the last item—the price that cattle will fetch at the feedlot—are of the least importance, because insofar as ranchers judge that capital should be invested in raising cattle rather than other investments, they will tend to raise as many cattle as they can afford to breed and feed within that budget, letting the ultimate extent of their profits fall where it may at the feedlot. Many ranchers also use the nutritional well-being of their herd as a buffer to absorb adverse changes in market conditions, feeding their cattle less and less to whatever

point maximizes the new expectation of profits as adverse conditions develop, or even sending the entire herd to premature slaughter if, say, feed prices rise to levels that are unacceptably high. This serves to shift the ranchers' emphasis in decision-making relevant to herd size even further away from the price of beef. As a result, even if an individual's consumption decisions managed to have a $0.01 effect on the price of cattle at feedlots, the effect on the number of cattle produced would be much smaller than it would have to be in order for the (vanishingly small) probability of such a threshold effect to justify equating the expected marginal effect of an individual's consumption of beef with the average effect of such consumption decisions. More importantly, because animal production is so many links in the supply chain away from grocery stores and restaurants, and because the intervening links typically involve some small but non-negligible amount of waste, inefficiency, and other forms of slack serve as a buffer to absorb any effect that your personal consumption might otherwise have. These facts suggest that there is good empirical reason to think that the expectation of a single individual's consumption decisions on production is nearly zero and is not to be equated with the average effect of similar consumption decisions across society, contrary to what the response to the inefficacy objection by Norcross suggests. A similar upshot emerges even in a more vertically integrated industry such as the poultry industry, where demand is relatively inelastic; nonetheless, because profits are dependent mostly on the cost of inputs such as feed and fuel, a similar story about the expected effect of a single consumer's purchases remains true.[5]

To more completely evaluate the prospects for utilitarian arguments regarding consumer ethics, another important consideration is that even if you would convince many others to be a vegetarian by becoming one yourself, that does not does not translate into strong welfare-based reasons to become a vegetarian. That is because even if your vegetarian lifestyle ultimately caused, implausibly, one hundred others to become vegetarians who would not otherwise have done so, their collective consumption decisions might still not have any appreciable effect on the number of animals that are raised and mistreated, because the actual mechanisms in the marketplace may be insensitive to the distributed effects of even one hundred consumers. Of course, this reasoning does not hold true when applied to an influential person like Peter Singer who really does influence enough people to make a difference, but it does hold true when applied to almost everyone else, which means that utilitarianism does not require most individuals to become vegetarians, even if it requires a few influential people like Peter Singer to be vegetarians. For example, just as morality does not require each of us to act as if we had the talents, influence, and resources that Warren Buffett has, so too morality does not require us to act as if we had the talents, influence, and resources that Peter Singer has.

A related complication is that individual vegetarian acts often have negative unintended consequences that must also be properly accounted for. Like the positive "indirect effects" discussed in the preceding paragraph, this is also a genuine complication that must be taken into proper account in a consequentialist analysis. For example, if I am a vegetarian, I might easily alienate others with my vegetarian acts insofar as they tend to be interpreted as self-righteous, and thus cause others to adopt a policy of never reducing their consumption of meat and never taking vegetarian arguments seriously. And if vegetarians are generally interpreted as self-righteous, that might lead to a consensus among most members of society that vegetarians are radical, self-righteous jerks who should not be taken seriously and who should be scoffed at by others—which then raises the cost of making vegetarian choices for everyone, and is counterproductive in other ways.[6] (Here it may be useful to note that many undergraduate students respond to vegetarian eaters by pledging to eat more meat to "cancel out" the effects of the vegetarians.)

In sum, the key issues here relevant to consumer ethics are that many products we consume are delivered by a massive and complex supply chain in which there is waste, inefficiency, and other forms of slack at each link. Arguably, that slack serves as a buffer to absorb any would-be effects from the links before. Furthermore, production decisions are insensitive to the informational signal generated by a single consumer because the sort of slack just described

together with other kinds of noise in the extended transmission chain from consumers to producers ensures that significant-enough threshold effects are not likely enough to arise from an individual's consumption decisions to justify equating the effect of an individual's decision with anything approaching the average effect of such decisions. As a result, for many products in modern society, it is implausible that even a lifetime of consumption decisions by a single individual can be expected to make any difference to the harm that lies behind those products, and so it is implausible that we have strong utilitarian reasons not to consume those products.

A more general philosophical upshot is that when evaluating utilitarian reasons for individual action, the knowledge available to agents about the mechanisms at play in their specific situations matters greatly, especially when outcomes depend on collective action—and it is a mistake to think that there is any simple argument that shows that individuals always have decisive utilitarian reasons to "cooperate" and perform "pro-social" actions whenever the stakes for society are high of our collective action.

NOTES

1. See Peter Singer (1980). "Utilitarianism and Vegetarianism," *Philosophy & Public Affairs*.

2. Alastair Norcross (2004). "Puppies, Pigs, and People," *Philosophical Perspectives*, pp. 232–3. See also Peter Singer, ibid, and Shelly Kagan (2011). "Do I Make a Difference?" *Philosophy & Public Affairs*.

3. In particular, the "expected effect" of an action in this sense is the *expectation* associated with that action, based on the sum of all of the values of all of the possible outcomes of that action weighted by their probability conditional on that action. See Michael Resnik (1987), *Choices: An Introduction to Decision Theory*, U of Minnesota Press for further discussion of expected utility theory.

4. Note that this result is not undermined by the observation (often enthusiastically made by consequentialists) that in collective action situations, as the probability of making a difference goes down, the magnitude of the difference that would be made goes up. As the discussion above illustrates, what matters is whether the difference that would be made increases in a way that is relevantly proportional to the decrease in the probability of making a difference—and as the discussion here illustrates, in real

world collective action problems it is often empirically un-realistic to think that it does.

5. See for example the comments of poultry industry expert Ed Fryar in Ryssdal, K. (2015). "Why chicken wings cost more this time of year," *Marketplace*, 5 January 2015: http://www.marketplace.org/topics/business/why-chicken-wings-cost-more-time-year

6. For some other suggestive empirical results that vindicate this as a serious general worry, see Julia Minson and Benoit Monin (2011), "Do-Gooder Derogation," *Social Psychological and Personality Science*, and Benoit Monin et al. (2008), "The Rejection of Moral Rebels: Resenting Those Who Do the Right Thing," *Journal of Personality and Social Psychology*.

QUESTIONS

1. Does Budolfson consider the possibility that by deciding to be a vegetarian one might influence many other people, leading them to become vegetarians, who might then influence other people, and so on? (What does Peter Singer say about this in "Utilitarianism and Vegetarianism"?) Does Budolfson miss something important here, or are his arguments convincing?

2. If Budolfson's arguments are correct, does it follow that it is permissible to consume everything? Why or why not?

3. Do Budolfson's arguments assume that utilitarianism or some form of consequentialism is true? Explain.

4. How might someone argue that the inefficacy objection also raises problems for deontological ethical theories? Give the best example possible of how someone might argue that they do not raise problems, and of how someone might argue that they do raise problems.

5. How would Budolfson's argument apply to other cases? What would be the implications for what individual people have reason to do in the cases discussed by Williams and Hill, cases of voting in elections, cases (discussed by papers in the Further Reading section) of divesting from investments in institutions doing wrong discussed by Appiah, and cases discussed by Kagan and Nefsky, such as climate change? Does utilitarianism or Budolfson's arguments gain or lose plausibility from careful consideration of these cases and related arguments? Explain.

ELIOT MICHAELSON

Act Consequentialism and Inefficacy

Michaelson argues that even if Budolfson's argument is convincing against an "expected consequences" response to the inefficacy objection, this may not undermine the force of consequentialist considerations in our actual world, and so Budolfson might be incorrect about what consequentialism *actually* implies in the consumer ethics cases we care about.

In addition, Michaelson emphasizes that further progress from a consequentialist point of view requires being more clear about what values are relevant to the goodness of outcomes, and how exactly we should value trade-offs and risky gambles with those values. Michaelson emphasizes that these are difficult but important questions that are often glossed over in consumer ethics discussions. (Michaelson is a philosopher at King's College London.)

A variety of purchasing and eating practices—vegetarianism, veganism, pescatarianism, locavorism, etc.—are often motivated along broadly act consequentialist lines. That is, these sorts of practices are often motivated by the thought that individual decisions not to purchase meat (I'll focus on just this example here) *matter* for the world. Or, at the very least, that this sort of decision has a decent chance of mattering. Fewer animals will lead short and unhappy lives, fewer animals will die badly, and the world will generally be a better, happier place. The reasoning here seems hard to dispute: you should do what maximizes expected goodness. Purchases *signal* the market to produce more or less of a certain good, or to deliver it in one way as opposed to another. These signals can be expected to result in better or worse outcomes. You should therefore signal the market to produce fewer goods that, overall, reduce the goodness of the world. So unless one wants to cast doubt on the entire apparatus of market signaling, it will be hard to dispute that—assuming that treating animals how we do on contemporary factory farms is generally a bad thing—we will have strong consequentialist reasons to refrain from purchasing meat. Or so it would seem.

There is, however, a serious concern with this line of reasoning, and one that has been lurking in the background of such arguments for some time. Suppose that one derives some non-trivial enjoyment from eating meat. How should the value of this enjoyment be weighed against the value of this market signaling effect? The enjoyment, recall, is basically guaranteed (leaving aside cases of food-poisoning, or just bad cooking). The signal may or may not lead to a change in production and distribution practices. And, at the end of the day, consequentialists care about *consequences* (or at least expected consequences). It looks, therefore, like empirical facts about *how likely* it is that one's purchasing habits will have an effect on subsequent production and distribution practices may matter quite a bit for whether act consequentialism will recommend adopting a vegetarian set of eating and purchasing practices.

To illustrate the point, consider the following example: suppose that all of the world's chickens are produced by a global monopoly called "Chicken Demon."[1] Chicken Demon is run by an eccentric billionaire, "The Colonel," who loves nothing more than torturing and killing chickens. Chicken Demon raises as many chickens in as many countries the world over as the available resources will permit; the operation is not sensitive to profits and The Colonel effectively has an endless supply of money to support Chicken Demon if it slides into unprofitability. The Colonel is a good free-market capitalist, however, so if people are willing to pay for the byproduct of his chicken-torturing and -killing enterprise, i.e. chicken carcasses, he is more than willing to sell these carcasses for a tidy profit. The important thing is that The Colonel, and hence Chicken Demon, isn't motivated by the amount of money coming in. What The Colonel cares about is torturing and killing chickens, and he has the resources to pursue that goal to his heart's content. So while *there is* a market signal generated by global chicken-demand, Chicken Demon's behavior is *insensitive* to that signal. In this scenario, act consequentialism can offer no reason to refrain from eating chicken. One's choosing to eat chicken or not to do so will send a market signal, but that signal is *guaranteed* to have no effect on the morally relevant behavior, i.e. torturing and killing chickens. So the act consequentialist's argument for vegetarianism turns out to be *contingent* on certain empirical facts—and, in particular, on producers exhibiting a certain degree of sensitivity to market signaling. For act consequentialism to recommend being vegetarian, there needs to be at least some chance that one is going to make a difference.

This much has long been acknowledged by consequentialists like Peter Singer, Alastair Norcross, and Shelly Kagan. What these authors have claimed is that our world is relevantly different from the world of my Chicken Demon example. In our world, the individuals and corporations that produce chickens and other foodstuffs are sensitive to the decisions of consumers. The question is just how sensitive they are, and how we are to conceive of this sensitivity as mattering for the subsequent state of the world. To help us get this question in view, let us consider a contrasting scenario, one of perfect market sensitivity.

Suppose once more that there is a global chicken monopoly, "Chicken Angel." Chicken Angel, run by the eccentric billionaire "The Corporal," is concerned to eliminate all waste and unnecessary harm in the chicken-production industry. As a result, when one wants to purchase a chicken, one enters an order at a Chicken Angel franchise. Chicken Angel then undertakes to raise one more chicken in their facilities. One to two months later, a chicken carcass is delivered to one's door (in the unlikely event that one's chicken dies of natural causes before maturity, delays may ensue). In contrast to Chicken Demon, Chicken Angel is *perfectly sensitive* to market signals; for every purchase of a chicken, one more chicken is raised and killed. Thus, supposing that the pleasure one derives from eating that chicken is less weighty, morally speaking, than the harm done to the chicken, act consequentialism will tell straightforwardly against ever ordering a chicken from Chicken Angel.[2]

Of course, we live in neither the world of Chicken Demon nor the world of Chicken Angel. And we might well wonder: what does act consequentialism recommend in our world? Singer, Norcross, and Kagan have all claimed that, in the morally relevant sense, our world is more like the world of Chicken Angel. We can expect to make a difference. Thus, we should refrain from purchasing meat. Recently, however, Mark Budolfson has argued that the reasoning behind Singer, Norcross, and Kagan's confidence here is in fact misguided; it is based on what

he calls the "Average Effects Fallacy." I will argue, briefly, that although Budolfson's reasoning is persuasive, this may not undermine the force of act consequentialist considerations in our world.

Singer, Norcross, and Kagan all reason more or less as follows. Suppose that chickens are in fact purchased in batches of 25. And suppose that your local butcher will order a new batch whenever 23 chickens have been sold. At the end of the day, he throws out any remaining chickens. This means that you will be a *difference maker* only if you purchase the 23rd chicken. Otherwise, nothing will change in the world as the result of your purchase (the butcher will never go out of business as the result of selling one less chicken). Your chance of being a difference maker would seem, naturally enough, to be 1 in 25. So it looks like you have a 1 in 25 chance of being a difference maker with respect to 25 chickens. The expected badness of your act is thus equivalent to killing one chicken yourself.[3] In other words, the badness of the purchase is equivalent to the average badness of twenty-five people choosing to kill twenty-five chickens together. This is what Budolfson means when he says that Singer, Norcross, and Kagan equate the moral value of an individual's meat purchase with the average effect of everybody's purchases. Hence the title "Average Effects Fallacy," since Budolfson thinks that this reasoning has gone substantially off-course.

The problem, as Budolfson points out, is that purchases often aren't distributed in a random series. In fact, we are generally well aware that they are not so distributed. Suppose that, aside from your own purchases, the number of chickens purchased per day at the local butcher can be accurately modeled by rolling two twelve-sided dice. There are days when just 2 chickens are sold, and days when 24 are. But there will be many more days when 12 chickens are sold. Likewise, there are many, many days when fewer than 12 chickens will have been sold by the time you find yourself considering whether to buy a chicken than there will be days when 22 have already been sold. Given this sort of purchasing series, the expected badness of your chicken purchase will be far less than the badness of killing one chicken. Days when you would make the difference—tipping the shop from 22 to 23 chickens—will be exceedingly rare. Supposing that you are aware of all this, then you should expect to have far less of a bad effect on the world by purchasing a chicken at the butcher shop than you should expect to have if you were to kill a chicken yourself. That, in turn, makes it substantially easier for the badness of this act to be swamped by its potential upside, e.g. your gustatory pleasure. That is, to justify buying a chicken, the pleasure one will obtain from eating that chicken needn't outweigh the badness of killing a chicken, but rather the badness of killing a chicken multiplied by the slight chance that one's action will actually lead to a chicken getting killed.

But is the badness of purchasing a chicken *in fact* swamped in our world? Here, things are far from clear. On the one hand, reflection on how the meat-production industry operates indicates that, in the actual world, meat producers may be relatively insensitive to market signals. For one thing, supply chains involve a number of layers (retailers, distributors, wholesalers, slaughterhouses, producers, etc.), offering multiple opportunities for an individual market signal to get lost along the way. For one's signal to make a difference, it must get transmitted from the point of purchase (at the butcher's shop, say) all the way up to the farmers who are actually raising the relevant sort of animal. Every step along the way, however, is at least somewhat waste-tolerant. That is, meat processors, packers, and farmers are all used to some of their product going unsold. That, in turn, means that a whole lot of individual signals are going to have to get lost before one actually gets through. Each layer is a bit like the butcher we considered above, who only cared whether 23 chickens had been sold and was perfectly willing to throw out a few chickens at the end of the day. Another relevant consideration is that demand for meat products tends not to fluctuate randomly in the real world, aside from chance events like disease outbreaks and negative media reports. Rather, demand for meat grows roughly in accord with population and wealth. What's more, meat distributors may also be willing to supplement standing orders (for, say, 25 chickens) with much smaller batches (of, say, 5 chickens) when demand unexpectedly spikes in a region. Finally,

there is plausibly excess demand for meat products in the real world—particularly in the developing world—meaning that the question is not so much whether so much meat can be sold, but where and at what price. Given how cheap it is to produce meat in many places around the world, what stands in the way of more meat production is plausibly the lack of available land and water rather than a lack of potential profit. We thus appear to be far closer to the world of Chicken Demon than one might initially have anticipated.

On the other hand, the negative effects of raising and killing chickens are also far worse in our world than we have been supposing so far. Labor exploitation is rampant in the meat-production industry, and is not easily avoided by purchasing free-range or other "ethically-treated" meat products. Consumers have shown relatively little interest in treating workers, as opposed to animals themselves, more humanely. Likewise, the negative environmental effects of raising chickens in the way we do must also be factored in.

Where does this leave us? Do we make a difference via our consumption habits? The answer would seem to be: possibly, but very little if we do. Still, that small chance may still be enough to offer a consequentialist justification for being vegetarian. One might, for instance, think that it is unacceptable to give one's child some medicine that will make her recover faster from a minor cold if that medicine has even a one in a million chance to killing her. On the other hand, we might find this trade-off acceptable if what we're dealing with isn't a minor cold, but something causing her significant discomfort. Much hinges on the costs that are to be tallied on the other side of the ledger. For many people, giving up meat is likely to strike them as a serious cost in terms of gustatory pleasure. But we are often rather terrible as weighing potential costs and benefits. For one thing, once one learns to cook vegetarian and navigate the vegetarian culinary world, there is scant evidence that one ends up enjoying food any less. So whatever gustatory pleasure-based costs are incurred by vegetarians may well be only short-duration costs. What's more, the potential health benefits of vegetarianism are well-documented, and living a longer life is presumably of some non-trivial value.[4] These considerations make it unclear just how the ledger will lean; much depends on some actual, and rather complicated, empirical facts that we cannot simply discern from the armchair.

What Budolfson's response to the Singer/Norcross/Kagan line should make clear, however, is the following. Whereas act consequentialism might have initially seemed appealing in that it explained why, if we ought collectively to refrain from purchasing meat, then we ought individually to do so, this transition from the collective to individual ought relies on some highly questionable empirical assumptions. The act consequentialist can only justifiably endorse this sort of argument if certain contingent features of the world turn out to be a particular sort of way. What's more, it is highly questionable whether the world turns out to be this way. For dedicated vegetarians, this is likely to seem like an odd result. What was hoped for was an argument for vegetarianism *per se*, not an argument for vegetarianism that is held hostage by certain recondite details about the market for meat products— let alone an argument that depends on certain recondite details that look unlikely to obtain in the real world! If one is looking for an argument for vegetarianism *per se*, or even in a range of situations that look rather similar to our own, then Budolfson is surely correct in pointing out that act consequentialism looks poorly situated to provide such an argument.

NOTES

1. This is an exaggerated version of Mark Budolfson's "waste" example from his "The Inefficacy Objection to Consequentialism, and the Problem with the Expected Consequences Response," forthcoming in *Philosophical Studies*.

2. Two brief notes here: first, it may well be that there are restaurants in the real world that are relevantly similar to Chicken Angel, though on a smaller scale. Second, something akin to the Non-Identity Problem rears its head here (see chapter 9 introduction for discussion). Basically, we might ask whether it is better for one more chicken to live a bad life than to lead no life at all. I will tentatively assume here that the answer is "No," as reasoning along these lines leads to absurd consequences. [Editor's note: on this issue, see also Torbjörn Tännsjö's essay in chapter 7.]

3. See Singer, P. "Utilitarianism and Vegetarianism," *Philosophy and Public Affairs* 1980; 9: 325–37, Norcross, A. "Puppies, Pigs, and People," *Philosophical Perspectives* 2004; 18: 229–45, and Kagan, S. "Do I Make a Difference?" *Philosophy and Public Affairs* 2011; 39: 105–41.

4. See Key, T.J., P.N. Appleby and M.S. Rosell, "Health Effects of Vegetarian and Vegan Diets," *Proceedings of the Nutrition Society* 2006; 65(1): 35–41 and McEvoy, C.T., N. Temple and J.V. Woodside, "Vegetarian Diets, Low-Meat Diets, and Health: A Review," *Public Health Nutrition* 2012; 15(12): 2287–2294.

QUESTIONS

1. Both Michaelson and Budolfson emphasize that consequentialist reasons for action depend on empirical facts. What are five examples outside of consumer ethics, each from a different area of life, where what it is morally required to do about an important issue depends on empirical facts that reasonable people might disagree about on a consequentialist view? In light of this, what disciplines of empirical study seem to be most frequently relevant on a consequentialist view? Is it plausible that what we are required to do is so sensitive to these particular kinds of empirical facts?

2. Michaelson claims that neither the Chicken Demon nor the Chicken Angel case is a good analogy to the workings of actual markets. Which does he think is closer to a correct description of those markets? What would Budolfson say? After carefully considering both of these authors' arguments, what do you think? What further empirical questions do you think are most important to answer in order to have a confident view about how to think about these issues?

3. In the second to the last paragraph, Michaelson identifies some questions about the values that are relevant to the goodness of outcomes, and how exactly we should value trade-offs and risky gambles with those values. Do you think there are other important values he might emphasize here as well? What are they exactly? In light of all that, how do you think we should make trade-offs between these values, and how should we take risks when those values are involved in the possible outcomes of those gambles?

4. Someone might argue that even if you can't generally expect to make a difference when you purchase goods that are delivered by a long and complex supply chain, nonetheless you can expect to make a difference by buying directly from a very small-scale producer, such as a local meat CSA (community-shared agriculture collective; for something analogous, see the reading from Joel Salatin in Chapter 8, "Alternatives to Industrial Animal Agriculture"). Further, it could be claimed that these meat CSAs are worth promoting because they are the primary driver of making things better in our society with respect to meat production among the things that you have the power to influence as a single individual. In light of this, if you care about the well-being of animals, it could be argued that you have some reason to buy meat from these CSAs, in addition to other complementary reasons you have for doing so, such as sustaining the culture and craftsmanship of such traditional producers, and so on. What should we make of this argument? Could it be a good argument for buying meat from a consequentialist point of view? How do these consequentialist reasons compare to the consequentialist reasons that Michaelson thinks it is plausible that we have? Do these reasons pull in a different direction than the reasons Michaelson discusses?

ELIOT MICHAELSON

A Kantian Response to Futility Worries?

This paper discusses one distinctive deontological position, Kantianism. Michaelson explains why he believes that Kantian ethics can offer a reasonable explanation for why it is that we, *collectively*, shouldn't purchase and eat animals, largely following Christine Korsgaard's arguments (see her reading in Chapter 7, "Industrial Animal Agriculture"). However, Michaelson asks whether, even granting such an explanation, Kantians can explain why each of us *as an individual* shouldn't eat animals. He argues that this question is more difficult to answer than it initially appears, and he articulates some of these challenges.

In this chapter we've seen that there is a serious question whether act utilitarians can justifiably move from the claim that we, collectively, shouldn't purchase or consume meat to the claim that we, individually, shouldn't purchase or consume meat. Having observed this, it is natural to wonder whether similar kinds of problems are going to arise for other sorts of ethical theories. For instance, ethicists in the Kantian tradition might seem well-situated to respond to this sort of worry and to justify this transition from the way that we ought, collectively, to act to the way we ought, individually, to act. The

Eliot Michaelson, "A Kantian Response to the Futility Worries?" Printed with the author's permission.

purpose of this essay will be to explore whether this is really the case.

One way of putting the basic Kantian suggestion is as follows: one should act only in such a way that one could coherently will that everyone else act in this same manner in relevantly similar situations.[1] Suppose, therefore, that we want to know whether we should purchase or consume meat. If we were all to purchase or consume meat, the Kantian will reason, then many, many animals will have to be killed in order to feed us. Supposing that we can provide some further reason for thinking that we, together, would be acting badly or irrationally if we were to kill many, many animals merely in order to feed ourselves, then we will have reason to think that we, collectively, should refrain from purchasing and eating meat. Since it would prove impossible to coherently will that everyone purchase or consume meat, the idea goes, we should refrain from purchasing or consuming meat ourselves. Prima facie then, it looks like the Kantian is in a significantly better position than the act utilitarian to offer a full-throated defense of vegetarianism.

We need, therefore, first to ask whether there are good Kantian reasons for thinking that it is bad or somehow incoherent for us, collectively, to kill numerous non-human animals in order to feed ourselves. Kant himself is often taken to think that the only sort of value that non-human animals can obtain is as *mere means*. That is, non-human animals are valuable only in relation to rational creatures like human beings, who are valuable in and of themselves. Here is how Kant puts the point:

> Beings the existence of which rests not on our will but on nature, if they are beings without reason, still have only a relative worth, as means, and are therefore called things, whereas rational beings are called persons because their nature already marks them out as an end in itself, that is, as something that may not be used merely as a means.[2]

It is largely due to reasoning like this that the Kantian strain of ethical theory was long thought to be hostile to vegetarianism.

Recently, however, Christine Korsgaard has claimed both that Kant himself has been misunderstood to some degree and that there is absolutely nothing at odds between Kantian ethical theory and vegetarianism. In particular, Korsgaard has argued that respecting each other ineliminably requires respecting not just each other's rational selves, but also our animal selves. Korsgaard's basic idea seems to be that part of what it is for us to respect each other is for us to respect each other in ways that have little or nothing to do with each other's rationality. So, for instance, we should not cause each other to suffer; to do so would be to evince a fundamental lack of respect for each other. But, while causing each other to suffer might well impair the other's rationality, the harm done seems to be fundamentally against the other's animal self, which incurs some basic natural harm when it is caused to suffer. Putting the point slightly differently, we can coherently imagine some sub-group of human beings who have been trained to exhibit equal rationality whether or not they are suffering physical pain. Still, causing these beings to physically suffer would be to do them harm, and thus to exhibit extreme disrespect for them. If that's right, then part of what it is to respect each other as human beings is to respect each other in ways that are not essentially tied to our rationality, in ways that we can respect or disrespect animals as well as human beings.[3]

Korsgaard's argument can then be completed as follows: in failing to respect each other's animal selves, we are failing to respect each other. We are disrespecting part of what makes us valuable. In failing to respect the animal selves of non-human animals, then, we likewise evince a lack of respect for each other, since we treat the non-rational part of us—which still helps to make human beings valuable—as though it were of little or no value. Since we cannot rationally will that we all disrespect each other, we likewise cannot rationally will that we all disrespect non-human animals. To treat non-human animals as though they lacked value via their animal selves *just is* to treat the animal self as lacking in value—which is thus, in turn, to treat human beings as though they lacked a certain sort of value which they in fact possess.[4]

It seems at least plausible, therefore, that Kantian ethicists can offer a reasonable explanation for why it is that we, collectively, shouldn't purchase and eat animals. To purchase and eat animals is to disrespect their animal selves—and thus to disrespect our own animal selves. What though of what we should do not collectively, but individually, on the Kantian picture?

The worry here is basically this: supposing that one knows a sufficient amount about the way that animals are treated in one's society—enough to know that one's purchasing some meat is overwhelmingly unlikely to make any difference—is it still reasonable to think that one might be able to consume and eat meat *without* evincing disrespect for animals? After all, one knows, among other things, that: if I don't eat this meat, then it is overwhelmingly likely to go to waste. What could be more disrespectful towards an animal than not only to cause it to suffer and die prematurely, but then to let its meat go to waste?

Sometimes, it seems to be ethically important not just what we physically do, but also how we think about what we're doing. Many philosophers in fact think of actions as being partly individuated by the mental states standing behind them. One might, for instance, perform the very same set of bodily actions when *accidentally* tripping as opposed to *intentionally* tripping. Nonetheless, these look like very different sorts of actions. Or consider an example with more ethical weight: suppose that you are an air force general deciding what to bomb. You might (i) choose to bomb a factory located right next to a school because you think that factory is of great strategic value, or (ii) choose to bomb the factory *because* it is located right next to a school, and you expect that the loss of their children's lives will help to demoralize the enemy. In both cases, one gives the same order and expects the same relevant results: a destroyed factory and a number of dead children. Many people, however, think that, even if (i) is objectionable, it is a decidedly better thing to do than (ii).

Now back to our main topic. Suppose that one knows a good amount about how overwhelmingly unlikely it is that one is going to affect any animals' lives by refraining from purchasing or eating meat. Can one now intend: to purchase or consume meat *so as to minimize meat waste*? And, supposing that one can form such an intention, would

acting on that intention exhibit disrespect for animals' selves in the same way that purchasing or consuming meat *because one finds it tasty* more plausibly does?

Kantians like Korsgaard have hardly addressed this question, so we can only speculate as to how they might be tempted to respond. One possibility would be for the Kantian to claim that, in a modern capitalist society like ours, it is simply understood that, in purchasing a good, one is implicitly endorsing the way in which that very good is produced. Certainly, many will, on reflection, deny that they endorse the horrid labor conditions that went into producing their clothing or sneakers. Perhaps they will claim that they weren't even aware of these conditions. But such protestations are in bad faith, the Kantian might claim; even if they weren't aware of the conditions under which their clothing was made, these individuals *ought to have known*. Sometimes it is appropriate to hold individuals accountable for what they ought to have known, not just what they happened to know.[5] When it comes to purchasing and consuming meat, ignorance will be no excuse and nor will a surfeit of knowledge. Knowing that one will not make a difference is simply not enough to exculpate oneself from endorsing the way treat animals when one chooses to either purchase or consume meat.

Still, a worry remains. Suppose that one were living in a society where, unlike our own, one's purchasing choices were viewed as no reflection at all of what one implicitly endorses. Chicken purchases in the Chicken Demon scenario considered in the previous reading might constitute one example of this. Or consider a society in which no one would even think of accusing someone else of hypocrisy were that other to wear a fur coat to a rally against the continued production of fur. A society like this is likely to seem strange to us, I grant, but it is hardly inconceivable. The worry, however is this: in this sort of society, it is not at all clear that one would be exhibiting any disrespect for the animal selves of non-human animals if one were to purchase or consume meat *so as to minimize meat waste*. If that is correct, then the Kantian ethicist, like the act consequentialist, proves to be in no position to offer us an argument for vegetarianism *per se*. Rather, it turns out that the Kantian ethicist can only offer us a contingent argument for vegetarianism, one that depends for its validity on certain things in the world turning out to be the case. Like the act utilitarian then, it looks like it is going to be either difficult or impossible for the Kantian to endorse a maxim like the following: do not, under any normal circumstances, purchase or eat animals. Rather, the best she will be able to do is: do not, under normal circumstances in a society relevantly similar to our own, purchase or eat animals. For many of us, this apparent failure of generality is more than a tad disappointing.[6]

NOTES

1. See the introduction to this chapter for more on the Kantian categorical imperative.

2. Immanuel Kant, *Groundwork of the Metaphysics of Morals*, trans. and ed. Mary Gregor, Cambridge: Cambridge University Press, 1996; 4: 428, p. 36.

3. Korsgaard, C. 1996. *The Sources of Normativity*, Cambridge University Press; Korsgaard, C. 2011. "Interacting with Animals: A Kantian Approach", in *The Oxford Handbook of Animal Ethics*, ed. T. Beauchamp and R. G. Frey, Oxford: Oxford University Press, 2011; pp. 108–9. See also Korsgaard's essay "Getting Animals in View" in chapter 7.

4. Korsgaard, C. 2011; p. 109.

5. Child negligence laws are a good example of this. If one were to starve one's child to death, it is no excuse to claim—even truthfully—that one was somehow unaware that children need food to survive. Rather, the fact that one *ought to have known* this will turn out to be enough.

6. Similar issues are explored with respect to deontological theories in general, not just Kantian ones, in M. Budolfson, "The Inefficacy Objection to Deontology"

QUESTIONS

1. According to Michaelson, how should Kantian ethics answer the question of what exactly we *collectively* should do about factory farms and why? Do you think the answer he outlines is the best answer to this question that a Kantian can give? Are there more attractive alternative deontological theories that provide more plausible answers to this question? Why or why not? How do these compare in plausibility to consequentialism and virtue ethics alternatives?

2. According to Michaelson and the introduction to this chapter, how might a Kantian try to answer the question of what exactly each of us *individually* should do about factory farms and why? Why is this a different and arguably more difficult question than what we collectively should do? Do you think there are better answers to this question that a Kantian can give beyond those considered in this textbook? Are there more attractive alternative deontological theories that provide more plausible answers to this question? Why or why not? How do these compare in plausibility to consequentialism and virtue ethics alternatives?

3. What do you think Thomas E. Hill and Bernard Williams would say about the discussions of Kantian ethics in this textbook by Korsgaard, Michaelson, and others? How would their view agree or differ? To begin to work toward a more detailed answer to this question, read the papers by Hill and Williams in the Further Reading section.

4. Pope Francis claims that "It is contrary to human dignity to cause animals to suffer or die needlessly."[7] When Pope Francis appeals to the notion of "contrary to human dignity" here as the grounding for the claim that it is wrong to cause animals to suffer, to what extent do you think he intends to offer the very same grounding as Michaelson and Korsgaard? How do you think values of human dignity are related to values of what God commands and desires on the Pope's view?

PETER SINGER AND JIM MASON

Freeganism and Food Waste

Singer and Mason describe a community of *freegans* who eat only the discarded food of others that would otherwise go to waste, and who try similarly in the rest of their lives to avoid any impact themselves by merely making use of the unused excess created by others. Because it produces the best results, Singer and Mason describe this way of life as "impeccably consequentialist," even when it involves eating some meat that is sure to go to waste. They also note its appeal to non-consequentialists since it empowers one to reject oppressive and counterproductive social norms, allowing one to reject the priorities set by consumer society, to withdraw entirely from the industrial food system, to reduce the net amount of food waste in our society—the magnitude of which is itself staggering—and ultimately to reject consumer society altogether. In an appendix, Singer and Mason also discuss the promise of in vitro meat, whereby real meat is produced in a petri dish, with therefore no need for animals to be raised and slaughtered to produce that meat. (Peter Singer is a philosopher at Princeton University, and Jim Mason is an author and attorney.)

It's about 7.30 p.m. on a mild Tuesday evening in Melbourne, Australia. We're in a small Toyota station wagon with Tim, Shane, G (Gareth), and Danya. They're all in their 20s, wearing old denim or waterproof jackets, except for G, who is wearing a jacket that might once have been more stylish and formal, but is now so worn that it would have suited Charlie Chaplin in *The Tramp*. The comical appearance is reinforced by the fact that G is tall and lanky, and this jacket was made for someone much smaller. We park in the Safeway parking lot, but avoid the customer entrance, heading instead to the delivery ramp. A dumpster bin stands at the side. The lid is chained and locked, but the chains have enough slack to allow you to raise the lids and insert an arm. G and Danya get their arms in and start bringing out loose potatoes, plastic wrapped packages of broccoli, a bunch of asparagus, plastic packs of flat Lebanese

bread, and a small can of tuna. The tuna can is dented, the broccoli is looking a little tired, and some of the potatoes have a slight greenish tinge. We collect what we want, throw the rest back, replace the plastic bags and other trash that has come out accidentally, and leave the area at least as tidy as we found it.

We move around the corner to where there is another bin, this time unlocked. We throw the lid open to reveal boxes of strawberries. Tim says strawberries are not worth taking since they usually taste bad. Instead he picks out some tomatoes and capsicums, two large bottles of orange juice, loaves of whole meal bread, white rolls, packs of croissants, and maybe thirty packets of flat bread. Shane comes up with a long piece of fish. "Ah, Blue Grenadier!" he says, but he's laughing, because it smells really bad, and he throws it back. "There's some really skank

Peter Singer and Jim Mason, "Freeganism and Food Waste," from *The Ethics of What We Eat: Why Our Food Choices Matter* (Emmaus, PA: Rodale, 2006).

stuff down here," Danya warns. "Watch out for the orange plastic bags; they're full of bad meat." We pick up the pile of food we have collected but put back most of the bread, keeping just a few of the flat breads and one pack of croissants. "We don't need that much, and there might be others coming after us," Tim explains.

Shane and G have gone somewhere else and return with cartons full of small bottles of orange juice. But they sample one, and it's fizzy. They try another, same thing. It goes back in the dumpster. We head off to another group of supermarkets. Danya, who is sitting next to Shane, complains about the bad fish smell that still lingers on Shane's hands.

The next bin we visit is standing by the loading dock and isn't locked, so this time we climb up onto the dock and investigate the contents from above. Danya is delighted to find several cakes, still in clear plastic display boxes. It's her 21st birthday today, and she claims one as a birthday cake. She also finds a tray of chicken breasts and one of chicken drumsticks. "Are they cold?" Tim asks. Yes, they still feel cold. That means they haven't been out of refrigeration long, and that makes them acceptable. Two dozen eggs, still in their cartons, are another find worth taking. So too are a bag of sugar, some tins of tomatoes, a large pack of Chinese noodles, and a torn bag of pasta shells. "Does anyone drink Coke?" G asks. He's found a pack of 24 cans. Shane says yes, he'll have them. The carton is ripped, but the cans are intact, so he starts loading them into another cardboard box. G pulls out a chocolate cake covered in cream, removes the plastic packaging, takes a large bite, and pronounces it good. There are large packs of toilet paper. "That's good, we always need them," says Shane. There is even an electric toothbrush, still in its package.

While we are going through the bin, the roller door behind us starts moving, and an employee who looks about 16 comes out with a wheelie bin to empty into the dumpster. He doesn't look particularly surprised to see us there, but he says, "If security comes around you'll be in trouble." Tim nods assent and offers assistance in unloading the contents of the wheelie bin into the dumpster. The exchange is polite and friendly. We never see any security people, and

this turns out to be the only encounter with anyone from one of the stores this evening. That's fairly typical. If they are asked to leave, they say, they just go.

We move on to another supermarket up the road. The bins here are chained down again, but the gap is wide enough for G to spot some coffee he wants. It's too far down for even his long arm to reach, so for the first and only time tonight we see some real "dumpster diving" as G gets his upper body right into the bin, only his legs sticking out the top. The booty is eight 250-gram vacuum-sealed packets of an imported Italian Arabica coffee, just a couple of days past the expiration date.

By now the back of the car is getting full and we are hungry, so we head home to cook. Home is an office-warehouse building that the group has been squatting in for about six months—apparently there is a legal dispute about who owns it, and the property had been vacant for years before they moved in. They've furnished it almost entirely with discarded items and had electricity and gas put back on, so it's comfortable and very spacious. Tonight Tim does most of the cooking, with some advice and assistance from others. He chops up the asparagus, zucchini, broccoli, and fresh tomatoes and opens two tins of tomatoes as well. That all goes into a pot and gets cooked up. Meanwhile the pasta is boiling away, and when everything is ready we serve ourselves some pasta and add the sauce. If this were a restaurant they'd probably call it "Pasta Primavera." We wash it down with sparkling organic apple juice from New Zealand, in individual bottles. We've had better meals in restaurants, but we've had worse too.

Although some of the items we got were past their use-by date or had damaged packaging, with others there was no obvious reason why they had been thrown out. The expiration date on the eggs was still two weeks in the future and none were broken. The cans of Coke and the Chinese noodles weren't damaged or about to go bad. The toilet paper and electric toothbrush would have lasted indefinitely. "You find stuff and can't figure out why it has been thrown away," Tim says. "We got cartons of organic breakfast cereal and the use-by date was two months ahead." "And what about this organic apple juice?" we ask, holding up the bottle we've just enjoyed drinking. "That had a use-by date about a year ago," Tim says, and everyone laughs at our evident discomfort. "But don't worry, it's perfectly fine." And indeed it was. We experienced no after-effects, from that or any of the other ingredients in the meal. Nor have any of the others ever had any stomach problems from a dumpster meal.

After we've eaten, Danya goes out with a friend to celebrate her birthday, and the rest of us start talking about lifestyles and "dumpstering." G says he got started about two years ago when he was reading George Bataille, the French writer and thinker who died in 1962. In contrast to conventional economists, who start from the problem of scarcity and how best to overcome it, Bataille analyzed the prevailing social and economic order by seeing what it does with its excess. So the next time G passed a supermarket's dumpster, he looked in. "There were about a hundred bananas in there," he said. That got him really excited, and he has been dumpstering ever since. Now he gets all his meals from dumpstering, living from the excess of corporate capitalism. Some days are better than others, he says, but you can always find a meal. G is studying at university. In Australia, students without enough money to live on are eligible for government financial support, but G feels no need for it and hasn't applied. "I can live without money."

Tim takes a slightly different view. He earns some money, but goes dumpstering in order to save for things he can't get free. "It's a question of priorities. Beyond wanting to save money, it's about how you want to spend it. Whether you want to be just a mindless consumer, or whether you want to put your money into useful stuff, and save money for things that are tools, like keeping a car on the road that I need, buying laptops, and digital-video players. It means that you are able to have access to resources that we couldn't otherwise afford."

Shane has been dumpstering for about five years. Dumpstering, he says, is empowering. "Think of the single mother who has to scrape together enough money to be able to buy a tin of baked beans and some white bread for herself and her kid. If she had the confidence to go around the back and walk up to the bin, she could get much better food for nothing.

But she can't transcend the cultural shame. For us, it's culturally acceptable to do it, and we have the skills and the confidence as well. So although none of us has a high-paying job, we live a very comfortable lifestyle, much better than we could afford on what we earn if we had to pay for everything we use."

Tim says it's important to think about dumpstering in its political and economic context. "We have to get away from the simplistic idea that 'you're eating out of a bin, therefore you're a dero,'" he says, using Australian slang for a derelict, a homeless vagrant. "That's going to prevent the single mother from getting food out of the bin. We have the political analysis that enables us to rise above that way of thinking." Shane agrees: "What's better about dumpstering is that you're not buying into that whole process of consumption. Even buying organic food involves being part of the consumer economy. Dumpstering really does break the consumer chain."

"But the people who buy organic could say that they're changing the system," we interject. "By giving money to organic farmers, they're encouraging farmers to grow more organics. What you're doing isn't changing the system, you're just living off a glitch in the system." That provokes Shane and Tim to a critique of the extent to which organic farming has become part of the system of agriculture and marketing, rather than a real alternative to it. Shane acknowledges that some forms of community-supported farming and organic cooperatives could be a real alternative, but in his view, the "local yuppie organic store" certainly isn't. Dumpstering is much more radical. "It's an act of withdrawal—a withdrawal from the whole process of industrial food production and marketing."

G comes back into the discussion, saying that dumpstering has "an ethical dimension . . . We're saving food that would otherwise totally go to waste—perfectly good food. We're recycling it." Tim adds: "It's got to be the lowest-impact form of food consumption." Then he goes on to say that because you don't need much money, you can spend your time doing something socially useful, rather than getting a meaningless job to earn money to buy food. To judge by the leaflets and notices stuck on boards in the house, people living there are spending time on campaigns for indigenous Australians, against duck shooting, for environmental protection, and against the war in Iraq.

Apart from all that, this way of getting food just seems to be a lot of fun. "It's a daily victory against the system," Tim says. "Every day you come home and think 'I've won.' It may be only a small victory, but I've won." Shane talks about the "rush" of finding great stuff, and G mentions the communal aspect of dumpstered meals: "There's a really good alternative economy in terms of the way you can share and distribute your food as well. Every meal you can share with a couple of people, and there's never any hassle or concern about where the food is coming from. You know it is from this resource that is kind of . . . unending. It's a permanent gift." G also relishes the challenge of getting a few things and working out what you're going to cook with them. That sparks a lot of reminiscing about the good things they've found, and, amidst laughter, they discuss the great and the not-so-good meals they've made entirely from dumpstered food.

Our evening of dumpstering in Melbourne could have been replicated in any large city in the U.S., Canada, or much of Europe. Nobody knows how many people do it, but at the time of writing, www. Meetup.com listed 1,888 people interested in dumpstering, and the New York City group alone had 199 members.[1] We had imagined that dumpstering would retrieve only old or blemished food and were astonished by the non-perishable items in perfect condition we found in dumpster bins; later we discovered that our gleanings were typical of what is thrown out in many countries. A New York dumpster diver recounts finding dumpsters full of expensive packages of gourmet nuts and dried fruit, luxury chocolates, three or four 50-pound bags of bagels regularly thrown out by a single deli, and large quantities of non-perishable food like rice pilaf mixes and instant soups.

Some of this waste is easily explained. Bakeries, donut stores, delis, and salad bars often advertise that they bake fresh, or get freshly made food every day, and they also like to keep their racks and salad bowls full, so that customers don't get the impression that they are buying the dregs after other customers

have picked them over. This combination ensures that at the end of the day a lot of perfectly good food gets thrown out. A small fraction of it may be donated to food banks or shelters for homeless people, but most of it is simply put in the bin, probably because the stores are worried about undermining their own sales—if the word gets around that you can get something for free at 10 p.m., fewer people will buy it at 8 p.m. But the reasons for trashing non-perishable goods are more mysterious. On some products, stores get lower prices for ordering large quantities, so it can be cheaper for them to order more and put what they don't sell in the trash than to buy only what they can sell. Perhaps more importantly, shelf space is a limited resource, and stores regularly clear out shelves for new deliveries. The store may have a long-term contract with a supplier to provide a specified quantity of a product each week. If an item has not sold as well as expected, the old stock will be dumped, even if it is not out of date, to make way for the new stock.

Many dumpster divers began as vegans but became convinced that boycotting animal products is not radical enough. Even products that contain no animal ingredients can hurt animals, when land is cleared to grow crops or when oil companies go into wilderness areas to provide the fuel needed to truck the goods around the country. Some of them began calling themselves "freegans," a term that is a deliberate play on "vegans." An anonymous vegan has said that being a freegan means that "you are boycotting EVERYTHING! . . . That should help you get to sleep at night."[2] While freegans are more radical than vegans in refusing to purchase any kind of food at all, they are also more flexible, in that they see no ethical objection to eating animal products that have been thrown out. They want to avoid giving their money to those who exploit animals. Once a product has been dumped, whether it gets eaten or turned into landfill can make no difference to the producer. Some freegans still don't like the idea of dining on a corpse, and—although they are prepared to eat food from dumpsters—they know about fecal contamination on meat and see health risks in eating anything that has passed through a slaughterhouse. But their reasoning is impeccably consequentialist: If you oppose the abuse of animals, but enjoy eating meat, cheese, or eggs—get it from a dumpster.

Freeganism is not only about free food. Behind it lies a view about how to live one's life, one that rejects the priorities set by the consumer society and the lifestyle that results from accepting those priorities. Because most people see their status as linked to wealth and what they can buy, they are locked into working, often in unsatisfying jobs, to earn the money they need to enhance their status. Freegans reject that idea of status and do not even need to earn money to satisfy their basic needs. They point out that we all have far more consumer goods than people did in the 1950s—when most people had smaller homes, and no one had DVDs, microwave ovens, cell phones, or personal computers—and yet surveys show that we are no happier now than we were then. Freegans see happiness as something that comes from doing things, rather than having things. If they work at all, it will be because they see the work they are doing as worthwhile in itself. To a far greater extent than people who pay for everything they consume, freegans' time is, as Tim said, their own, to enjoy or to use for working for what they believe in. They are thus doubly free—free from subordination to the consumer ethos and free from the need to work to satisfy their needs. They think that an alternative, less exploitative economic system is possible, but they are under no illusion that taking food from dumpsters will in itself bring that system about. Instead they see dumpster diving both as a way of detaching themselves from the present system and, at the same time, as part of a broader life of resistance to that system.[3]

Dumpster diving may not be an option many consumers are likely to explore, but there's still a lesson to draw. Many of agriculture's ill effects on laborers, animals, and the environment could be reduced if we ate what would otherwise be wasted. According to Dr. Timothy Jones, an archaeologist at the University of Arizona who led a U.S. government-funded study of food waste, more than 40 percent of the food grown in the United States is lost or thrown away—that's about $100 billion of wasted food a year. At least half of this food, Jones says, could have been safely consumed. Waste could also be reduced by having better storage facilities. Some of the waste is completely pointless and reflects nothing more than a casual disregard for what went into producing the food, from the suffering of the animals, to the labor of the workers, to the natural resources consumed and the pollution generated. Jones examined what stores, restaurants, and individuals throw out and found that 14 percent of household garbage was perfectly good food that was in its original packaging and not out of date. About a third of this edible food was dry-packaged goods, and canned goods that keep for a long time made up another 19 percent. Jones speculated that discounts for bulk purchases lead people to buy more food than they want to keep, but he admits to some bafflement, remarking: "I just don't understand this."[4] As consumers, we have direct control over our own waste. We'd do well to follow the advice our mothers gave us: Eat your leftovers.

APPENDIX: ANIMAL-FREE MEAT?

Skum-skimming wasn't hard to learn. You got up at dawn. You gulped a breakfast sliced not long ago from Chicken Little and washed it down with Coffiest. You put on your coveralls and took the cargo net up to your tier. In blazing noon from sunrise to sunset you walked your acres of shallow tanks crusted with algae. If you walked slowly, every thirty seconds or so you spotted a patch at maturity, bursting with yummy carbohydrates. You skimmed the patch with your skimmer and slung it down the well, where it would be baled, or processed into glucose to feed Chicken Little, who would be sliced and packed to feed people from Baffinland to Little America. Every hour you could drink from your canteen and take a salt tablet. Every two hours you could take five minutes. At sunset you turned in your coveralls and went to dinner—more slices from Chicken Little—and then you were on your own.[5]

That is Frederick Pohl and C. M. Kornbluth's fantasy, in *The Space Merchants,* of how we might one day produce our food. "Chicken Little" is a vast lump of meat, hundreds of feet across, growing in a culture that is fed on algae. The idea has attracted more eminent and realistic figures than science fiction writers. In 1932, Winston Churchill wrote: "Fifty years hence, we shall escape the absurdity of growing a whole chicken in order to eat the breast or wing, by growing these parts separately under a suitable medium."[6] Churchill was better at predicting Hitler's aggressive intentions than the future of food production, but it may be only his timing that was astray. Within the animal movement, there are some who hope that, just as the development of the internal combustion engine has eliminated the suffering of millions of horses and oxen previously used to transport people and heavy goods, so eventually the development of *in vitro* meat will eliminate the suffering of billions of animals now used for meat.

We already have vegetarian burgers, sausages, bacon bits, and many other meat-like products. In China, when the spread of Buddhism led to abstention from meat during religious festivals, the Emperor's chefs devised ways of making gluten and tofu resemble various forms of meat and seafood, so that the Emperor could continue to dine on the classic dishes of Chinese cuisine. Today, this tradition is still practiced in Chinese vegetarian restaurants. Some vegetarians object to "fake meat" because it may leave the impression that meat dishes set the culinary benchmark, and some meat eaters don't like it because the taste and texture are not the same as that of meat. In vitro meat would not be fake meat, it would really be meat, with an identical taste and texture. In theory, growing meat in culture should be more efficient than producing entire animals, since as Churchill suggested, we should be able to grow pure boneless steak or chicken breast, without producing inedible bone, unhealthy fat, and undesirable internal organs. Cultured meat should also have less impact on the environment than factory farms because it would not produce any manure.

Scientists can already produce small amounts of muscle tissue in a laboratory. In 2001, a scientist from the University of Amsterdam, together with two Dutch businessmen, took out a patent on a process for producing meat by bathing muscle cells in a nutrient solution and inducing them to divide. Several scientists in the United States as well as the Netherlands are working on producing edible meat, but so far without success. It may eventually prove possible; the real question is, whether it will be possible for such meat to compete economically with meat from living animals.

One scientist has estimated that the current cost of producing muscle tissue in a laboratory equates to $5 million per kilogram! But only 50 years ago, the exorbitant cost of building a computer meant that few people imagined that they would ever become affordable to ordinary families. If, one day, cultured meat becomes an efficient way of producing food, we see no ethical objection to it. Granted, the original cells will have come from an animal, but since the cells can continue to divide indefinitely, that one animal could, in theory, produce enough cells to supply the entire world with meat. No animal will suffer in order to provide you with your meal.[7]

NOTES

1. www.meetup.com, visited January 30, 2006.
2. Anonymous, "Why Freegan?" Food Not Bombs Houston, December 30, 2002, http://fnbhouston.org/20021230-2815.html.
3. Our account of freeganism draws on Web sites like http://freegan.info/ and the writings of Adam Weissman.
4. Lance Gay, "Food Waste Costing Economy $100 billion, Study Finds," Scripps Howard News Service, August 10, 2005, www.knoxstudio.com/shns/story.cfm?pk=GARBAGE-08-10-05&cat=AN
5. Frederick Pohl and C. M. Kornbluth, *The Space Merchants,* Ballantine, New York, 1952.
6. Winston Churchill, *Thoughts and Adventures,* Thornton Butterworth, London, 1932, pp. 24–27.
7. For more information on progress in making cultured meat, see www.new-harvest.org.

QUESTIONS

1. What do you think are the most interesting ethical questions regarding freeganism? Is freeganism a "mind-blowing" ethical way of living, in that it is far superior to the most virtuous ways of living that are more familiar to us (even if it does not appeal to you personally)? For example, in what ways do you imagine that freegans would argue that their way of life is preferable from an ethical point of view to veganism as it is normally practiced? How might it be argued to better realize the reasons we have to dissociate ourselves from wrongdoing in the sense articulated herein by Thomas E. Hill?

2. Do you agree that eating factory-farmed meat from a dumpster is "impeccably consequentialist"? What does that mean? What should we say about such behavior on a deontological view that argues that the *production* of factory-farmed meat is wrong? What would the freegans discussed by Singer and Mason say?

3. Setting aside freeganism, what is the right way for the rest of us to think about food waste? Once we see the enormous amount of food wasted by an average American, does it seem that each of us has an obligation to reduce food waste? What should governments and other institutions do about the problem? What is your university doing about it, and what do you think they should be doing? In what ways does what Singer and Mason seem to suggest we should do about it differ from what Michelle Paratore seems to suggest we should do about it (in her reading in Chapter 10)?

4. Is food waste irrational? In answering this question, it may help to imagine a case such as this: Imagine a well paid but very busy mother of two children, who is also juggling a job and other responsibilities. She wants her family to eat healthy, even though she and they are so busy. So, she always keeps fresh fruit and vegetables on hand, knowing that sometimes they won't end up using them, but it is valuable to her to have the *option* to use them: Having them around all the time means that her family ends up eating healthier, and if she didn't have them around she wouldn't have time to go get them every time they actually wanted to consume them, and so they all wouldn't eat as healthy. Is this irrational? Couldn't this be what is best for this family? (Compare: A wealthy family should also buy insurance, even though it is likely to go to "waste.") What percentage of food waste in wealthy nations do you think is ultimately explained by something like these incentives? In this story, do you think there is a good ethical objection to the mother's behavior? Why or why not? What objections could be raised to arguments for or against different positions on this issue? How does this kind of consideration complicate what outcomes government and other actors should desire in society regarding food waste, given our competing values of maximizing nutrition in households, minimizing the impact of agriculture, feeding the world, and so on?

5 Food and Identity

Food practices are one way in which we form our personal identities and group identities. In other words, we are what we eat, as individuals and as groups, in some sense. This chapter discusses some ways in which food practices are central to personal and group identities, and identifies some of the resulting ethical issues.

FOOD PRACTICES AND GROUP IDENTITY

The popular saying "You are what you eat" is not just a nutritional adage. If you eat Vegemite every day, you are probably Australian; if you nosh on grits and collard greens, chances are high that you are from the southern US; if you eat steak and lobster regularly, you are most likely middle or upper class; and, if you normally consume salad and other "lighter fare," you are probably a woman.
— *Amy E. Guptill, Denise A. Copelton, and Betsy Lucal,* Food & Society: Principles and Paradoxes[1]

Food practices and customs are one way in which we construct personal identities and group identities, and they are a powerful way to communicate our identities to others. Simply put, what you eat and how you eat it make you a certain kind of person, and this serves as a signal to others. As Guptill, Copelton, and Lucal explain: "What foods we eat, how and when we prepare, serve, and consume them, are all types of identity work—activity through which we define for ourselves and others who we are socially and culturally."[2] For example, part of identifying as Italian or Korean or Peruvian for many people is appreciating traditional or distinctive Italian or Korean or Peruvian foods. Religions prescribe certain food practices, including eating special foods as part of rituals, eating special foods on holidays, not eating certain foods, and periodically fasting, as is further discussed in Chapter 6, "Food and Religion." Having a religious identity can include observing these food practices. Families have food traditions or food practices that help to create a shared identity as a family—for example, eating specific or traditional foods on holidays, or sharing a special meal each week (such as Sunday dinner or pizza night).

The readings in this chapter discuss several examples of food practices central to personal and group identities. For example, the Australian food product Vegemite, a paste made from brewer's yeast, is inextricable from Australian national identity, as explained in the reading "Food and Identity: Fitting In and Standing Out." Vegemite is associated with Australia, eating Vegemite is associated with being Australian, and rejecting Vegemite is seen as "a rejection of everything 'Aussie.'" Coca-Cola is another example of a food linked with a national identity, in this case American identity, as Mark Weiner describes in his reading in this chapter. Another example is kimchi and Korean identity.

The food experiences we have, and the food practices that develop significance for social groups, are largely determined by the society we live in and our position in that society. A complex example, frybread, is discussed in the reading "Commod Bods and Frybread Power: Government Food Aid in American Indian Culture" by Dana Vantrease. Frybread is a kind of fried dough that was first created by indigenous peoples in the United States in the nineteenth century, using food aid provided by the U.S. government. Frybread is now an iconic cultural food and cultural symbol, as Vantrease describes it, but one that represents both indigenous culture *and* the loss of traditional foodways. Another complex example is soul food, described in the reading "Food and Identity: Fitting In and Standing Out." Soul food originated among enslaved Africans in the United States, and it now has a variety of positive and negative meanings for African-Americans. Soul food is embraced as part of a positive black cultural identity and a source of ethnic pride by some African-Americans but rejected by others as unhealthy and as not distinctively African-American.

FOOD PRACTICES, GROUP BOUNDARIES, AND SOCIAL INEQUALITY

Because they are so strongly linked with group identity, food practices are an effective way to monitor group boundaries, identifying some people as insiders, identifying others as outsiders, and shoring up the distinction. This has both positive and negative implications. Participating in shared, unique food practices—food practices that are "ours" and not "theirs"—can bring groups of people closer together, giving them feelings of commonality and solidarity, making them feel connected to a shared history. But, as Mark Weiner notes, group-based food practices can also serve as a locus of the hostility that exists between groups: "Because Coca-Cola has served as an icon of American consumer society, it also possesses another quality unique among foods: the emotional hostility it arouses."

Group-based food practices can also reinforce social inequalities between groups, including inequalities between groups based on race/ethnicity, class, gender, or other social categories. As Guptill et al. write, "differences in eating patterns help distinguish social groups from each other, becoming a form of cultural capital . . ., the relatively rare and highly valued knowledge, skills, attitudes, and tastes that help define an elite status."[3] Some food practices confer social status, by signaling that someone has resources or insider knowledge. For example, "knowing and using upperclass table manners—knowing which fork to use for what foods, for example—marks a person as having a particular class status in society."[4] Consuming certain foods—typically more expensive foods—is also a marker of class status. For example, serving caviar and expensive champagne at a party rather than chips and beer, or in Chinese culture, serving shark's fin soup. Or, in the United States, shopping at Whole Foods rather than Sam's Club. Which practices confer social status vary by community and by culture, and change over time. Lobster is now a high-status food in the United States, because it's expensive, but it used to be an abundant, low-status food eaten by fishermen and fed to animals.[5]

Stereotypes about how people eat, and how they relate to food, can reinforce social inequalities. For example, in the reading "'Now Then—Who Said Biscuits?' The Black Woman Cook as Fetish in American Advertising," Alice Deck discusses the "Mammy" stereotype existing in American culture since slavery: a stereotyped African-American cook and domestic worker who enjoys cooking and who "exists to do nothing but prepare and serve food, along with a hearty helping of her homespun wisdom about life." This stereotyped portrayal of African-American women as servants of white people, and more-over as happily embracing this status as part of their identities, is analyzed by Deck as reinforcing the subordinate status of African-Americans.

As you read in "Five Faces of Oppression" in Chapter 3, Iris Marion Young observes that one dimension of racial oppression is the assumption that oppressed racial groups ought to be servants of privileged groups: "In most white racist societies this means that many white people have dark or yellow-skinned domestic servants, and in the United States today there remains significant racial structuring of private household service." The history of racial oppression undergirding the Mammy stereotype, along with the persisting assumption that menial labor should be done by people of color, is a clear instance of racial injustice. (The concepts of oppression and justice are discussed in more detail in Chapter 3, "Food Justice.")

The reading "The Sexual Politics of Meat" by Carol Adams is a famous articulation of the idea that certain foods and eating habits are gendered—that is, associated with masculine or feminine identity. Adams argues that "a mythology that meat is a masculine food and meat eating, a male activity, permeates all classes." This association of meat with masculinity has many facets. Meat is a food that symbolizes power and is perceived to provide strength and virility. Men are presumed to enjoy meat, to need it, and to have the prerogative to eat it. Women are associated with non-meat foods, and in particular vegetables, which are perceived as a feminine food and a "second-class" food.

Work by psychologists has confirmed, in some ways, the phenomenon theorized by Adams.[6] For example, one study of American undergraduates found that men and women whose favorite foods are described as "steak and other kinds of beef" are rated as more masculine and less feminine than men and women whose favorite foods are described as "sushi and other kinds of fish" or "vegetable stir fry and other vegetable dishes."[7]

Gender and gender identities shape food practices in other ways, too. As discussed in the next section, some kinds of food work are seen as feminine and are more likely to be performed by women (such as home cooking), whereas other food-related work is seen as masculine and is more likely to be performed by men (such as being a professional chef).

GENDER, IDENTITY, AND FOOD WORK

There are many gender-based differences in food work. In the United States, the majority of farm operators are men (30% of farm operators are women, and only 14% of principal operators are women).[8] In the restaurant industry, women are 52% of restaurant workers, but are much more likely to be food servers and greeters than men, whereas men are more likely to be cooks.[9]

These gender differences in food work correspond to the perception that certain kinds of food work are feminine, and others are masculine. For example, a scholar studying Australian farm women who do tractor work—an agricultural practice traditionally considered "men's work"—found that these women made efforts to reassert their femininity while performing this traditionally masculine job.[10] The women emphasized that they were doing this work to help their families, or emphasized that they did the housework and cooking for their families. These findings are consistent with prior research showing that women with jobs traditionally considered masculine (for example, women military officers) emphasized the "feminine" aspects of their jobs, and men with jobs traditionally considered feminine (for example, men who are nurses) emphasized the "masculine" aspects of their job.[11] Though the women farmers who drive tractors challenge notions of masculinity and femininity in one respect, by doing tractor work, their accompanying efforts to reassert their femininity implicitly validate the idea that driving a tractor is "a man's job" and cooking dinner for the family is "women's work."

Another example of food work coded masculine or feminine is that few women are recognized as great chefs. Part of the reason, according to one author, is that the attributes we associate with being a great chef—being a leader, a businessman, a risk-taker, an expert, a competitor, a renegade—are attributes that we associate only with men. *Chefs* are men. Women are merely *cooks*.[12]

A significant gender-based difference in food work is that women do the majority of feeding work within their families. Surveys in a wide range of countries show that women do 85%–90% of household food preparation (as measured in hours of work).[13] *Feeding work* includes cooking, but also much more: shopping, planning, cleaning up, understanding family members' preferences, keeping track of what's in the refrigerator, learning about food, and so forth.

For some women, feeding work is a source of joy and satisfaction, and an expression of a feminine identity that they embrace. For example, in her article "Female Identity, Food, and Power in Contemporary Florence," written in 1988, Carole Counihan described the important role of cooking for their families in Italian women's identity. Their identity had traditionally been other-directed and centered around meeting their families' needs. Cooking for their families was an expression of this identity. Cooking was also a source of power for Italian women, because it put them at the center of the family and gave them influence over their children—"In giving them food, she has given them her mores, values, and worldview."[14] But the younger Italian women studied by Counihan experienced a conflict between this identity—which pulls them toward time-consuming homemaking and cooking—and their desire to work outside the home for wages. While homemaking expressed one aspect of these women's identities, and gave them one kind of power and fulfillment, working for wages gave them another kind of power and fulfillment that they also wanted. As Counihan writes:

> Urban Italian women, like many others in the urban industrial West, are undergoing a transition in their status and power relative to men. They are challenging the dominance of men over women inherent in the traditional division of labor where men control the public, political, wage-labor sphere and women the domestic sphere of reproduction and nurturance. Today women are increasingly participating in wage work and gaining access to exchange values so important to status and self-definition in modem consumerist Italy. . . . Women at the same time

suffer a strong and debilitating identity conflict because of the unresolved contradiction between their public and domestic roles. They consider both roles essential to their self-esteem and self-fulfillment today, and yet cannot materially perform both roles effectively. Hence they suffer frustration and self-doubt.[15]

Fast forward to 2013. The writer Emily Matchar finds that domestic food work remains an important expression of some women's personal identities, but with an interesting twist.[16] Matchar reports that an increasing number of college-educated women in the United States are embracing intensive homemaking—including food-related work like raising backyard chickens, beekeeping, canning vegetables, and making jam—as a form of resistance to the industrial food system and a form of virtuous living:

> My baby boomer mother does not can jam. Or bake bread. Or knit. Or sew. Nor did my grandmother, a 1960s housewife of the cigarette-in-one-hand-cocktail-in-the-other variety, who saw convenience food as a liberation from her immigrant mother's domestic burdens. Her idea of a fancy holiday treat was imported lobster strudel from the gourmet market. . . . Around the country, women my age (I'm 29), the daughters and granddaughters of the post–Betty Friedan feminists, are embracing the very homemaking activities our mothers and grandmothers so eagerly shucked off. We're heading back to jam-canning and knitting needles, both for fun and for a greater sense of control over what we eat and wear. . . . [M]any women (and a few men) are diving into domesticity with a sense of moral purpose. The homemade jar of jam becomes a symbol of resistance to industrial food and its environment-defiling ways. This view has been brewing for a while, a thick stew of Slow Food and locavorism and DIY brought to a boil by recession and anxiety. Suddenly, learning the old-fashioned skills of our great-grandmothers seems not just fun, but necessary and even virtuous.[17]

For other women, feeding work is not fun and empowering, but is stressful and unsatisfying. A study of 150 black, white, and Latina mothers in the United States found that cooking home-cooked meals is, for many of them, time-consuming, frustrating, and stressful.[18] Cooking takes time away from other valuable experiences and requires navigating family members' different preferences. "We rarely observed a meal in which at least one family member didn't complain about the food they were served," the study reports. The lower-income mothers studied often had cramped kitchens and lacked "basic kitchen tools like sharp knives, cutting boards, pots and pans," making it virtually impossible to cook a meal from scratch.[19]

CONFLICTS BETWEEN IDENTITIES AND MORAL BELIEFS

Emily Matchar describes women who embrace feeding work and homemaking with a sense of moral purpose. A different kind of experience is detailed by the novelist Jonathan Safran Foer in his book *Eating Animals*. He describes two food practices that express multiple aspects of his identity, and are meaningful for that reason, but conflict with his emerging conviction that it is morally wrong to eat meat. The first is eating turkey on Thanksgiving, a food practice that's woven into Foer's and many Americans' national identity, cultural identity, and family identity. The second food practice is eating his grandmother's special dish, chicken and carrots, that she made for him when he was young. This "singular dish" symbolizes, to Foer, his grandmother's love of her family and her personal history as a Holocaust survivor, a history that is central to his family's self-understanding:

> Growing up, my brothers and I thought our grandmother was the greatest chef who ever lived. We would literally recite those words when the food came to the table, and again after the first bite, and once more at the end of the meal: "You are the greatest chef who ever lived." And yet we were worldly enough kids to know that Greatest Chef Who Ever Lived would probably have more than one recipe (chicken with carrots) and that most Great Recipes involved more than two ingredients. . . .
>
> In fact, her chicken and carrots probably was the most delicious thing I've ever eaten. But that had little to do with how it was prepared, or even how it tasted. Her food was delicious because we believed it was delicious. We believed in our grandmother's cooking more fervently than we believed in God. Her culinary prowess was one of our family's primal stories, like the cunning of the grandfather I never met, or the single fight of my parents' marriage. We clung to those stories and depended on them to define us. We were the family that chose its battles wisely, and used wit to get out of binds, and loved the food of our matriarch. . . . More stories could be told about my grandmother than about anyone else I've ever met—her otherworldly childhood, the hairline margin of her survival, the totality of her loss, her immigration and further loss, the triumph and tragedy of her assimilation. . . .
>
> We are made of stories. I'm thinking of those Saturday afternoons at my grandmother's kitchen table, just the two of us—black bread in the glowing toaster, a humming refrigerator that couldn't be seen through its veil of family photographs. Over pumpernickel ends and Coke, she would tell me about her escape from Europe, the foods she had to eat and those she wouldn't. It was the story of her life—"Listen to me," she would plead—and I knew a vital lesson was being transmitted, even if I didn't know, as a child, what that lesson was. . . .
>
> If my wife and I raise our son as a vegetarian, he will not eat his great-grandmother's singular dish, will never receive that unique and most direct expression of her love, will perhaps never think of her as the Greatest Chef Who Ever Lived. Her primal story, our family's primal story, will have to change.[20]

These practices put Foer in a quandary: They are deeply meaningful shared practices, yet participating in them conflicts with Foer's personal morality, according to which eating meat is morally wrong. This personal morality is part of his personal identity, and when he acts contrary to it, he is not *being himself*: "To accept the factory farm . . . would make me less myself, less my grandmother's grandson, less my son's father." In other words, these food practices that are part of his personal and group identities also conflict with his identity. Foer's solution to this conflict is to reinvent the practices, for example by having a Thanksgiving dinner that does not include turkey. This reinvention allows him to express his group identity by participating in the shared experience (albeit a modified, vegetarian version of it), while remaining true to his moral beliefs.

PERSONAL IDENTITY AND SOCIAL GROUPS

We've been using the terms *personal identity*, *group identity*, and *social group* while relying on an intuitive understanding of them. But it's worth examining them in closer detail. Someone's *personal identity* is, roughly, her understanding of who she is or what kind of person she is. Personal identity is "a socialized sense of individuality, an internal organization of self-perception concerning one's relationship to social categories, that also incorporates views of the self perceived to be held by others," as one theorist puts it.[21] Our identities include seeing ourselves as certain kinds of people, or people with certain personal characteristics—for example, seeing oneself as an intellectual or an activist. Someone can have a personal characteristic, but not identify or not strongly identify as having that characteristic—for example, someone who's become an outgoing person but still sees himself as a shy person. Our identities also include seeing ourselves as members of groups, such as families, and communities, and social groups based on race, ethnicity, gender, class, sexuality, nationality, religion, or other categories. For example, someone could simultaneously identify as a woman, gay, white, an American, an intellectual, working class, and a person of Italian descent.

In the reading "Five Faces of Oppression" (in Chapter 3 of this book), Iris Marion Young argues that personal identity is largely determined by our membership in social groups. Social groups determine individual identities in part because our group membership determines how others see us, which in turn influences how we see ourselves. Also, individuals typically share group practices and norms; so group membership largely determines which practices and norms we adopt, according to Young. In some cases, social groups have extensively different practices and norms than other groups. For example, according to Young, there is a division between the working class and the middle class "in nearly all aspects of social life," including living in different neighborhoods and having "different tastes in food, décor, clothes, music, and vacations, and often different health and educational needs."

Though group membership largely forms individual identity, it does not wholly form it. Individuals have their own styles, Young notes, and can transcend or reject group identities. In addition, individuals can reject specific practices or norms accepted by a social group that they belong to. As we just noted, Jonathan Safran Foer came to reject the practice of serving turkey at Thanksgiving, despite the significance of this practice as an expression of family and cultural identity.

Individuals are members of multiple social groups, which are inter-related and form identities in complex ways. What it's like to be a member of one group (for example, men) depends upon one's membership in other groups (for example, African-Americans or Latinos or whites). The experience of being a man is different for African-American men than for Latino men or white men; for example, African-American men are stereotyped as aggressive and are more likely to be subjected to violence. An individual's position in the *system of social relations*—the complex structure of norms, attitudes, institutions, laws, and other social practices that comprise group differences—is the intersection of multiple, inter-related forms of social relations. This is known as intersectionality. (See Chapter 3, "Food Justice," for further discussion of social inequality.)

GROUP IDENTITY

"Group identity" is used to refer to a group's own understanding of the group—the group's shared understanding of "who we are." "Group identity" is also used to refer to a more broadly shared understanding of the group that may be at odds with the group's understanding of itself. For example, how Muslim Americans understand and experience the identity "Muslim American" may be quite different from how other Americans understand this identity. The phrase "group identity" is also used to refer to that part of an individual's personal identity that derives from her membership in and identification with a group. As noted previously, each individual's personal identity typically includes multiple group identities: Italian American, working class, intellectual, and so on.

Though we've defined a group identity as a "shared understanding" of a group, this understanding is sometimes implicit and not well recognized, even as it shapes our attitudes and social experience. In particular, dominant groups may fail to recognize that their group has a specific identity, instead experiencing their group, and its norms and practices, as universal or the normal way to be. This is an aspect of what Iris Marion Young refers to as *cultural imperialism*, which is one form of oppression. The dominant group's cultural expression and understanding gets widely disseminated and becomes the norm, while other groups' cultural expression is marked as Other, as a deviation from the norm. An example is *whiteness*, the cultural and ethnic/racial identity of white Americans. In "Vegans of Color" (not included here), Breeze Harper discusses how people who are white can fail to notice how spaces are white spaces, instead experiencing them as race-"neutral."[22] For example, Harper argues, vegan events are white spaces that are experienced by white participants as race-"neutral." This failure to recognize whiteness because it is perceived as "neutral" functions to exclude people of color. As we discuss in other chapters (Chapter 3, "Food Justice" and Chapter 10, "Alternatives to Industrial Plant Agriculture"), one persistent criticism of the organic and local food movements in the United States is that their adherents are mostly white and middle-class people, and that the movements' concerns and language express these identities in exclusionary ways.

CONSUMERISM AND IDENTITY

It's pretty easy to see how traditional dishes or special home-cooked meals, shared with family and friends, could have a place in shaping our personal and group identities. But much of our food consumption does not have this character. Eating is not always a social experience; sometimes we eat alone. We often eat packaged foods and beverages, or fast food, not home-cooked meals. How does *this* kind of food consumption shape our personal and group identities?

One worry is that eating has shifted from an organized ritual that affirmed family identity to a consumerist activity in which our individual consumption choices construct our personal identity.[23] Whereas eating was traditionally a social activity, it is now increasingly an individual activity. Whereas being part of a family and a community used to be a central part of our personal identity, now our individual consumption choices predominate. Explaining this view, Jeremy Iggers writes, "[E]very choice we make about what we consume makes a statement about who we are, and no one hears that statement louder than we do ourselves."[24] These food choices speak so loudly in part because they come with meanings attached— literally, foods come in packages covered in words. As Iggers notes: "Virtually everything we consume nowadays comes in a package, and every package carries a message, even if only by omission, as in the case of the yellow-and-black generic packaging. A world of irregular natural forms is replaced by a preinterpreted world of packages."[25]

This raises a cluster of interesting questions: Have societies in developed countries become increasingly consumerist—that is, preoccupied with the acquisition of consumer goods? Has individual consumption of "pre-interpreted" packaged food products replaced meaningful social experiences involving eating? If so, are these bad results? How so? Is individual consumption of food typically less meaningful than social experiences involving food? What about consumption of packaged and prepared food products? Is this consumption typically less meaningful than consumption of home-cooked foods?

In the reading "Consumer Culture and Participatory Democracy: The Story of Coca-Cola," Mark Weiner discusses another concern with consumerism, namely that consumerism undermines democracy. One worry here is that consumerism is an ethos that encourages paying more attention to oneself and one's stuff than to others, and thus inhibits focusing on the common good. A related worry is that consumerism encourages us to think that buying things is the best way to participate in public life—instead of, for instance, becoming active in the community or engaging in political activism. Some criticisms of consumerism are based in criticism of neoliberalism, the political economic system emphasizing free-market capitalism and a minimal state. For example, Julie Guthman and Melanie DuPuis argue that under neoliberalism, consumption of purchased goods is seen as a primary source of well-being and as the main way for individuals to participate in public life. Under neoliberalism, buying things is even seen as a mark of good citizenship: the way we help our country thrive is to buy more things.[26]

Weiner has a more positive spin on the consumption of consumer goods, at least in the case of Coca-Cola. He argues that this consumption can be a meaningful experience that makes us feel connected to a wider group of people than we otherwise would. By providing a shared experience, consumer goods can create an imagined community that serves as the basis of joint political action.

ACCOMMODATING AND RESPECTING OTHERS' FOOD PRACTICES

What is the ethical significance of the fact that people's food practices are important to their group identities? Does this create moral duties on the part of others, for example, duties to accommodate or tolerate these practices, or duties not to interfere with or change these practices?

One question is whether food practices that would otherwise be prohibited should be tolerated because of their centrality to group identities or their cultural significance. A series of cases in the United States around the Santerian religious practice of animal sacrifice are relevant here. Santeros argue that they should be allowed to sacrifice animals, even though the method of sacrifice would otherwise fall foul of animal cruelty laws, since the practice is central to their religious and cultural identities. Similar justifications for otherwise prohibited behavior are enshrined in law in the European Union. (Think about bullfighting. Whereas it would typically be wrong and illegal in the European Union to repeatedly stab a bull for sport, it is not illegal to do so in Madrid in a bullfight, since bullfighting is a protected cultural tradition in Spain.) Recently, the president of the British Veterinary Association argued that traditional Jewish and Muslim methods of slaughter are inhumane and should be banned. One line of response is empirical—deny that the method is inhumane—but another response is ethical—argue that even if the slaughter is inhumane it ought to be permitted nonetheless because it is central to group identities.[27]

Relatedly, another question is whether provision should be made for food practices that are central to personal and group identities. "For example," Ronald Sandler writes, "if there are not religiously appropriate foods in school lunch programs, then students may have to choose between eating and being faithful to their values/traditions. Similarly, social events, both public and private, at which culturally appropriate foods are not available may unintentionally exclude or marginalize people."[28] Should school lunches include kosher options, Halal options, and vegan options? Another set of issues concerns interference with group food practices. Recall that in "Food Justice and Collective Food Relations" (in Chapter 3 of this book), Kyle Powys Whyte argues that one of the demands of food justice is that groups have a right to exercise their collective food relations without interference from other groups, unless there is a morally weighty reason for the interference.

The reading "Cultural Food Colonialism" by Lisa Heldke takes up a related topic: the ethics of members of one culture trying out and experimenting with the food practices of another culture. Heldke notes that we typically find it unproblematic to casually try out new cuisines—to try new "ethnic" restaurants, or to try cooking recipes from other cuisines. But, Heldke argues, we should have a critical attitude toward this casualness. Cuisines and food practices are central to cultures, so casually engaging with and experimenting with other cultures' food practices can be disrespectful toward those cultures, in the same way that casually trying out another culture's spiritual practices would be disrespectful.

Heldke introduces the concept of *cultural food colonialism*, the appropriation of another culture's food practices. Cultural food colonialism involves casual or glib engagement with another culture's food practices, and it involves the attitude that other cultures' cuisines are "available to us." This "available to us" attitude is at the root of colonialism—the establishment of colonies by Western powers in Africa, Asia, and America, which involved the appropriation of natural materials, such as land and minerals, but also the appropriation of cultural practices, such as "art, music, stories, systems of government, medicine, cooking." The "available to us" attitude, Heldke writes, "often operated under the view that everything they found in the new setting was a resource available for them to take up and use." Heldke wants us to see present-day food adventuring in the United States—trying out bits and pieces of cuisines without appreciating the culture they come from—as a related form of cultural colonialism. Because food practices are central to culture, treating food practices glibly or casually amounts to treating *the culture* disrespectfully. Casually engaging with others' cuisines and food practices is ethically problematic in two additional ways, according to Heldke. Treating a culture disrespectfully may harm members of the culture. And because it is based in the attitude that cultures are "available to us," it can reinforce this attitude and make us more likely to condone other forms of mistreatment.

FURTHER ISSUES

1. *Cultural Imperialism*

Cultural imperialism, as Lisa Heldke defines it, is the imposition of cultural practices by an economic or political power. Heldke gives the example of United States businesses such as McDonald's and Coca-Cola selling their products in developing countries and thereby displacing local foods. If people in these countries choose to buy these products, in what sense is it an *imposition* to sell them? Is this one example of how the voluntary and mutually beneficial actions of individuals can be part of a larger pattern in which one group maintains advantage over another group? Similarly, if immigrants to the United States open a restaurant serving their cuisine, in what sense could it be an *appropriation* of their culture to eat at their restaurant? You are buying a product that they are voluntarily offering for sale. In what sense, then, is a problematic appropriation taking place?

2. *Social Groups*

What are social groups? According to Iris Marion Young, "A social group is a collective of persons differentiated from at least one other group by cultural forms, practices, or way of life" ("Five Faces of Oppression"). Is this an adequate definition of social groups? What is the connection between *social groups* and *social categories*? Some theorists refer to gender and racial categories as *social categories*, and to gender and race as *social constructs*. What are *social* categories, and what is the contrasting kind of category?

3. *Food Products, Advertising, and Group Identity*

Matt Weiner describes how the Coca-Cola Company used advertising and marketing to turn Coca-Cola into a national icon and a symbol of America. If a food is central to group identity as the result of commercial marketing or advertising, does this make the food a less authentic component of identity? Less important? Less deserving of respect? More generally, why are foods such a big part of group identities? Heldke assumes that food is a crucial, central part of a culture and so disrespecting food is disrespecting a culture. Why does food play such a role? Are there cultures in which it does not?

FURTHER READING

Anderson, E. N. 2005. *Everyone Eats: Understanding Food and Culture.* New York: New York University Press.

Casal, Paula. 2003. "Is Multiculturalism Bad for Animals?" *The Journal of Political Philosophy* 11, no. 1: 1–22.

Counihan, Carole, and Penny Van Esterik. 2013. *Food and Culture: A Reader.* New York: Routledge.

Curtin, Deane W., and Lisa M. Heldke. 1992. *Cooking, Eating, Thinking: Transformative Philosophies of Food.* Bloomington: Indiana University Press.

Guptill, Amy E., Denise A. Copelton, and Betsy Lucal. 2013. *Food & Society: Principles and Paradoxes.* Cambridge, UK; Malden, MA: Polity.

Harper, Breeze. 2011. "Vegans of Color, Racialized Embodiment, and Problematics of the 'Exotic,'" in Alison Hope Alkon and Julian Agyeman, eds., *Cultivating Food Justice: Race, Class, and Sustainability.* Cambridge, MA: MIT Press, 221–238.

Heldke, Lisa M. 2003. *Exotic Appetites: Ruminations of a Food Adventurer.* New York: Psychology Press.

Matchar, Emily. 2013. *Homeward Bound: Why Women Are Embracing the New Domesticity* New York: Simon & Schuster.

McIntosh, Peggy. 2015. "White Privilege: Unpacking the Invisible Knapsack." http://www.feministezine .com/feminist/modern/WhitePrivilege-MalePrivilege.html (accessed August 12, 2015).

Sandler, Ronald L. 2015. "Food and Culture," in *Food Ethics: The Basics.* New York: Routledge.

Williams-Forson, Psyche A. 2006. *Building Houses Out of Chicken Legs: Black Women, Food, and Power.* Chapel Hill: University of North Carolina Press.

Williams-Forson, Psyche A. 2007. "Chickens and Chains: Using African American Foodways to Understand Black Identities," in Anne Bower, ed., *African American Foodways: Explorations of History and Culture.* Urbana: University of Illinois Press.

NOTES

1. Amy E. Guptill, Denise A. Copelton, and Betsy Lucal, *Food & Society: Principles and Paradoxes* (Cambridge, UK; Malden, MA: Polity, 2013), 18–19.

2. Ibid., 18.

3. Ibid., 4.

4. Ibid., 4.

5. Ibid., 8.

6. Matthew B. Ruby and Steven J. Heine, "Meat, Morals, and Masculinity," *Appetite* 56, no. 2 (2011): 447–450; Rozin, Paul, Julia Hormes, Myles Faith, and Brian Wansink, "Is Meat Male? A Quantitative Multimethod Framework to Establish Metaphoric Relationships," *Journal of Consumer Research* 39, no. 3 (2012): 629–643.

7. Rozin et al., "Is Meat Male?," 634–635.

8. United States Department of Agriculture. "Women Farmers Control 7 percent of U.S. farmland, Account for 3 Percent of Sales." *2012 Census of Agriculture Highlights*, September 2014. http://www.agcensus.usda.gov/Publications/2012/Online_Resources/Highlights/Women_Farmers/Highlights_Women_Farmers.pdf.

9. Restaurant Opportunities Centers United, "Ending Jim Crow in America's Restaurants: Racial and Gender Occupational Segregation in the Restaurant Industry" (New York: ROC United, 2015), 3–4.

10. Barbara Pini. "Farm Women: Driving Tractors and Negotiating Gender," *International Journal of Sociology of Agriculture and Food* 13, no. 1 (2005): 1–18.

11. Ibid., 1.

12. Charlotte Druckman, "Why Are There No Great Women Chefs?" *Gastronomica: The Journal of Food and Culture* 10, no. 1 (Winter 2010): 24–31.

13. "Women and Hunger: 10 Facts," *World Food Programme.* http://www.wfp.org/our-work/preventing-hunger/focus-women/women-hunger-facts.

14. Carole M. Counihan, "Female Identity, Food, and Power in Contemporary Florence," *Anthropological Quarterly* 61, no. 2 (April 1988): 51. doi: 10.2307/3317156, p. 56.

15. Ibid., 51.

16. Emily Matchar, *Homeward Bound: Why Women Are Embracing the New Domesticity* (New York: Simon & Schuster, 2013).

17. Emily Matchar, "The New Domesticity: Fun, Empowering or a Step Back for American Women?" *The Washington Post*, November 18, 2011. https://www.washingtonpost.com/opinions/the-new-domesticity-fun-empowering-or-a-step-back-for-american-women/2011/11/18/gIQAqkg1vN_story.html.

18. S. Bowen, S. Elliott, and J. Brenton, "The Joy of Cooking?" *Contexts* 13, no. 3 (August 1, 2014): 20–25. doi:10.1177/1536504214545755.

19. Ibid., 23.

20. Jonathan Safran Foer, *Eating Animals* (New York: Little, Brown and Company, 2009), 4–5, 14–15.

21. Steven Epstein, "Gay Politics, Ethnic Identity: The Limits of Social Constructionism," *Socialist Review* 17 (May-August 1987): 9–54; as cited in Young, "Five Faces of Oppression" (see ch. 3 of this volume).

22. Breeze Harper, "Vegans of Color, Racialized Embodiment, and Problematics of the 'Exotic,'" in *Cultivating Food Justice: Race, Class, and Sustainability*, ed. Alison Hope Alkon and Julian Agyeman (Cambridge, MA: The MIT Press, 2011), 221–238.

23. This view is defended in Jeremy Iggers, *Garden of Eating: Food, Sex, and the Hunger for Meaning* (New York: Basic Books, 1996), 60–63, 99–106.

24. Ibid., 98.

25. Ibid., 63.

26. Julie Guthman and Melanie DuPuis, "Embodying Neoliberalism: Economy, Culture, and the Politics of Fat," *Environment and Planning D: Society and Space* 24, no. 3 (2006): 427–48. doi:10.1068/d3904, pp.442–444.

27. For an overview of the issues in this paragraph (and some focused ethical argument about the Santeria case), see Paula Casal, "Is Multiculturalism Bad for Animals?" *Journal of Political Philosophy* 11, no. 1 (2003): 1–22. Note that while the Santeria case is relevant to food ethics, it is not a food case. Sacrificed animals are not eaten. For discussion of the British Veterinary case, see Kevin Rawlinson, "Top Vet Calls for Reform of Kosher and Halal Slaughter Practices," *The Guardian*, March 5, 2014. http://www.theguardian.com/world/2014/mar/06/reform-of-kosher-and-halal-slaughter-practices.

28. Ronald L. Sandler, "Food and Culture," in *Food Ethics: The Basics* (New York: Routledge, 2015), 168–186 (see especially 169–170).

AMY E. GUPTILL, DENISE A. COPELTON, AND BETSY LUCAL

Food and Identity: Fitting In and Standing Out

In this reading, the authors describe two examples of foods tightly linked to group identities. The first example is Vegemite, a paste made from brewer's yeast that is part of Australian national identity (but is disgusting to many non-Australians). The second example is soul

Amy E. Guptill, Denise A. Copelton, and Betsy Lucal, "Food and Identity: Fitting In and Standing Out," reprinted from *Food and Society: Principles and Paradoxes* (Cambridge, UK: Polity Press, 2012).

food, a style of cuisine first developed by African-Americans under slavery and now embraced by many, but not all, African-Americans as an important part of African-American identity.

In October 2006, newspaper headlines announcing "US Bans Vegemite" enraged Australians at home and abroad (Healey 2006). One Australian in New York exclaimed, "in Australia the slogan is that Vegemite puts a rose in every cheek; but today America has slapped the cheek of every Australian" (Nichols 2006: para 6). Just the thought of the US banning this quintessential Australian food seemed a rejection of everything "Aussie."

Vegemite is a brown vitamin-rich paste made from brewer's yeast popular in Australia where it is spread on toast like peanut butter or jam. It was created by the Fred Walker Cheese Company in 1922 as the Australian counterpart to the popular British spread Marmite. As a former British colony, Australia initially "held on tightly to all things British," but by the 1920s, Australian entrepreneurs were introducing Aussie-made products as competitors to popular British items like Marmite (Richardson 2003: 60). Vegemite's popularity grew slowly until World War II when Vegemite was indelibly linked with nationalist sentiment. It was included in Australian soldiers' rations, a fact the company advertised heavily, in part to explain why Vegemite was in short civilian supply. This created a solid link between Australian national identity and Vegemite ("The Vegemite Story").

The 2006 Vegemite controversy stemmed from false media reports that customs officials were not permitting travelers to enter the US with Vegemite, paired with the US Food and Drug Administration's (FDA) restrictions on folic acid supplementation. Folic acid is the synthetic form of folate, a water-soluble B vitamin hailed for its role in preventing birth defects. Because excessive amounts of folic acid may mask vitamin B12 deficiencies, the FDA restricts folic acid supplementation to enriched breads, cereals, flours, and other grain products. Brewer's yeast is rich in naturally occurring folate, so these FDA restrictions do not apply. Although the FDA denied an import ban, and media reports later

clarified that imports for personal use were legal, the anger it provoked indicates how closely Vegemite is linked with Australian national identity (Bosch 2006; "US Government Denies" 2006).

Two years later, Australians were again outraged when, in an effort to promote local food vendors, the Beijing Organizing Committee for the 2008 Olympics prohibited teams from shipping imported food into Olympic Park for athletes' consumption. While the ban applied to all national teams, the Australian team was particularly incensed because it severely limited athletes' access to Vegemite. Louise Burke, the Australian Olympic team nutritionist, explained that the foods they planned to ship, including Vegemite, were "not readily available in China" and that such foods were "crucial" because they provide "familiar foods in the heat of competition," making "athletes feel at home" (English 2008: para 9–10). The Australian team considered Vegemite necessary for ensuring optimal performance and winning medals. Happily, disaster was averted when, upon their arrival in Beijing, Australian athletes found Vegemite in their official welcome bags ("Australian Athletes" 2008).

Rozin and Siegal (2003: 63) call Vegemite "the best predictor of national identity of any food in the world." Their survey of undergraduates at a large Australian university found that students who were at least third-generation Australians were more likely than non-Australian students to report liking Vegemite. Students closely associated Vegemite with "Australia," second only to its strong association with "toast." The link between Vegemite and Australian national identity persists, despite the fact that the Vegemite brand is now wholly owned by the US company, Kraft Foods.

The popular website YouTube.com is filled with video clips of non-Australians trying Vegemite for the first time. Typically, these depict the novice preparing toast and spreading it with butter and a thin layer of Vegemite in the Australian tradition. However, unlike Australians, the novice usually grimaces, spitting out the first bite. On one hand, these videos demonstrate the novice's adventurous spirit and willingness to cross cultural thresholds by sampling food associated with a cultural "other." However, the predictable negative reaction signifies that incorporation of foodways often occurs on the culinary terms set by the novice. In short, eating Vegemite marks Australians *as Australians,* while not eating it or reacting negatively to it marks one *as not Australian.* . . .

FOOD AND RACIAL-ETHNIC IDENTITY

The US is often depicted as a cultural melting pot. Given the unique combinations of native peoples and immigrant groups and their distinctive food traditions, the culinary landscape is diverse (Gabaccia 1998). Many cultural groups maintain and reinvigorate distinctive foodways to retain and express their unique heritage, while simultaneously adapting new culinary elements to create a hybrid cuisine. The Gullah, for example, descendants of slaves from the coastal islands of South Carolina and Georgia, have been especially successful in preserving foodways centered on rice, rice cultivation, and food self-reliance through gardening and foraging over generations of changing social contexts (Beoku-Betts 1995). In other cases, ethnic foods have become largely untethered from their cultural origins. The prevalence and variation of hybrid cuisines illustrate the heterogeneous origins of foodways.

"Soul food" is a rich example of a dynamic, hybrid cuisine (Opie 2008). It is "distinctively African American but was influenced by Europeans, who introduced corn to African foodways and then provided cornmeal, meat, fish, and other ingredients as rations to the first enslaved Africans in southern North America" (Opie 2008: 134). Enslaved and poor African Americans fashioned a culinary repertoire reliant on less valuable cuts and types of meat, such as pig ears and feet, chitterlings, ham bones, and chicken, and used strong flavorings to spice up and extend meals to feed large families over several days. Based on diverse African ancestries and the deprivations imposed by slavery and Reconstruction, these culinary skills served poor African Americans well in times of scarcity.

In the early decades of the twentieth century, African Americans from the southern US began moving to northern cities in large numbers in what is called the Great Migration. Seeking industrial work and escape from poverty, tenant farming, sharecropping, and blatant discrimination in the South, poor African-American southerners brought to the North the culinary repertoire on which prior generations had relied (Poe 2002). During and after the Great Migration, southern African-American foodways offered psychological comfort to migrants in northern cities, functioning as a comfort food that reminded them of home (Poe 2002). African-American foodways also offered new arrivals business opportunities in the form of neighborhood groceries and restaurants, appealing prospects to new migrants because of their low start-up costs, the relatively few skills required for entry, and migrants' established familiarity with cooking techniques (Poe 2002). However, upper-class African Americans in northern cities often rejected the foodways of poorer migrants, preferring instead to eat like their white upper-class counterparts in an attempt to assimilate to the dominant white culture (Poe 2002).

Working-class African-American foodways were more difficult to maintain during the economic hardship and food scarcity caused by the Great Depression in the 1930s. Food assistance programs, including the distribution of surplus commodities, soup kitchens, and breadlines offered an array of non-ethnic products to many poor African-American families. Wealthy white families also sometimes shared extra food with their African-American cooks and domestic servants, who brought leftovers home to their hungry families (Opie 2008). The once-thriving black-owned restaurants and grocers faced difficulty during these lean times and, because of the refusal of many white-owned banks to extend credit to black business owners, many small grocers and restaurants closed (Poe 2002).

Beginning in the 1950s and continuing into the 1970s, African-American social movements valorized

African-American culinary traditions, renaming the cuisine "soul food" (Opie 2008; Poe 2002). The Black Power and Black Nationalist movements, for example, called for the creation of a distinctive Afrocentric consciousness and culture to contest the devaluation of African-American culture in white America. These movements sought to develop and promote a new, positive black cultural identity that would unite African Americans. Along with music and literature, African-American foodways were a key part of this Afrocentric culture (Opie 2008). According to Opie (2008), African-American authors began publishing cookbooks and defining soul food as an important part of a unique African-American heritage. The Black Power movement, in particular, championed soul food as a distinctively African-American creation and urged blacks to take pride in this unique culinary legacy. African-American celebrities, including James Brown and Muhammad Ali, invested in African-inspired chain restaurants as the popularity of soul food soared (Opie 2008).

Nevertheless, like upper-class black northerners during the Great Migration, some African Americans continued to criticize soul food. Soul food held "complex meanings in the 1960s, serving as a source of ethnic and family pride to some and as a reminder of slavery and nutritional miseducation to others" (Opie 2008: 181). Despite endorsing Black Nationalism and welcoming the creation of a unique Afrocentric culture, the black separatist movement known as the Nation of Islam (NOI), popularized by figures such as Elijah Muhammad and Malcolm X, rejected soul food on both religious and cultural grounds. As a religious movement preaching a unique brand of Islam, the NOI rejected pork, a soul food staple, believing pigs to be unclean and prohibited under Islam. Additionally, the NOI rejected soul food on the grounds that its strong reliance on animal products and frying made it unhealthy and, as such, part of a white conspiracy to undermine the physical and political vitality of African Americans. Elijah Muhammad, the head of the NOI throughout the 1950s and 1960s, preached that white elites "promoted the consumption of unhealthy processed food and spicy and greasy food in order to weaken and eventually wear out black(s)" (Opie 2008: 159).

Additionally, some question the distinctiveness of soul food as an African-American culinary tradition, claiming that soul food represents regional southern foodways more generally. White southerners regularly publish cookbooks on "southern" cuisine that prominently feature many of the same dishes commonly associated with soul food, like sweet potato pie, chitterlings, greens, fried fish, and pulled pork. Nevertheless, soul food has maintained its pivotal position as an emblem of black cultural identity. Soul restaurants remain popular, and soul-themed canned goods and convenience foods, including Sylvia's brand, now appear in conventional supermarkets.

REFERENCES

"Australian Athletes Get Vegemite in Welcome Pack." 2008. The Daily Telegraph, July 31. Retrieved February 21, 2012 (www.dailytelegraph.com.au/news/australian-athletes-get-vegemite-in-welcome-pack/story-e6freyp0-1111117071758).

Beoku-Betts, Josephine. 1995. "'We Got Our Way of Cooking Things': Women, Food and the Preservation of Ethnic Identity Among the Gullah." Gender & Society 9(5): 535–56.

Bosch, Torie. 2006. "Is Vegemite Banned in the United States?" Slate, October 25. Retrieved January 15, 2012 (www.slate.com/id/2152218/).

English, Ben. 2008. "Beijing Bans our Athletes' Vegemite." Adelaide Now, April 29. Retrieved January 15, 2012 (www.adelaidenow.com.au/news/beijing-bans-our-athletes-vegemite/story-e6freo8c-1111116202433).

Gabaccia, Donna R. 1998. We Are What We Eat: Ethnic Food and the Making of Americans. Cambridge, MA: Harvard University Press.

Healey, Kelvin. 2006. "Ultimate Insult as US Bans Vegemite." The Sunday Mail, October 22, p.35.

Nichols, Michelle. 2006. "Vegemite Outrage Spreads." Herald Sun, October 24. Retrieved December 2, 2009 (www.heraldsun.com.au/news/world/vegmite-outrage-spreads/story-e6frf7lf-1111112408593).

Opie, Frederick Douglass. 2008. Hog and Hominy: Soul Food from Africa to America. New York: Columbia University Press.

Poe, Tracey N. 2002. "The Origins of Soul Food in Black Urban Identity: Chicago, 1915–1947," in C. Counihan (ed.), Food in the USA. New York: Routledge, pp. 91–108.

Richardson, Kay. 2003. "Vegemite, Soldiers, and Rosy Cheeks." Gastronomica 3(4): 60–2.

Rozin, Paul, and Siegal, Michael. 2003. "Vegemite as a Marker of National Identity." *Gastronomica* 3(4): 63–7.

"US Government Denies It's Banned Vegemite." 2006. NineMSN. Retrieved April 1, 2012. (http://news.ninemsn .com.au/article.aspx?id=155019).

QUESTIONS

1. The authors describe how vegemite is a part of Australian national identity and loved by most Australians, whereas many non-Australians can't stand it. What are other examples of foods associated with specific countries? Are there specific foods associated with your geographic region (e.g., Texas barbecue)? With your religion? With the other groups that you are part of?
2. According to the authors, what are the positive meanings and negative meanings that African Americans attach to soul food?

DANA VANTREASE

Commod Bods and Frybread Power: Government Food Aid in American Indian Culture

Commodity foods—distributed to over 250 tribes by the United States government as food aid—are a complex symbol of American Indian identity. They symbolize both American Indian culture and the U.S. government's subjugation and displacement of indigenous peoples—in particular, the loss of traditional foodways. Vantrease describes the complex role of commodity foods and debate about them.

INTRODUCTION

The US government's Food Distribution Program on Indian Reservations (FDPIR) provides food items free of charge to over 250 American Indian tribes. Government food aid has become a significant aspect of modern American Indian foodways. Perhaps the best example, frybread, is an iconic cultural food enjoyed at powwows, feasts, and other American

Dana Vantrease, "Commod Bods and Frybread Power: Government Food Aid in American Indian Culture", from *Journal of American Folklore*, 126, no. 499 (Winter 2013), 55–69. © 2013 by the Board of Trustees of the University of Illinois. Reprinted with permission of the University of Illinois Press.

Indian celebrations. The flat discs of fried dough were created roughly 150 years ago, with ingredients and implements—wheat flour, lard, and steel pots—introduced by Europeans and provided by the US government. Thus, although frybread is a cultural symbol, it also reflects governmental dietary assimilation efforts. After generations of consuming and in large part subsisting on government food aid, American Indians have developed complex ethnic food symbols related to food aid that evoke both ethnic pride and deep sorrow.

The FDPIR foods are commonly called "commodity foods" or "commods" because the foods come from government purchases of surplus agricultural commodities. Among American Indians, one often hears the commodity food program referenced with humorous expressions about commodity recipes like frybread and supplied foodstuffs like cheese bricks and canned meat. . . .

This essay begins by describing the history of the commodity food program. I then show how today, commodity foods are used as super-tribal identity symbols. Because of the non-Native origins of these foods, a sense of irony is recognized and reflected in Indian humor. In some instances, Indians use very dark humor to talk about their history of hardship, and commodity foods are also an emblem of that continuing struggle. Finally, there is a movement to abandon commodity and commodity-derived foods based on values of pride and authenticity.

COMMODITY FOODS AS AMERICAN INDIAN FOODS

Before Europeans arrived, American Indian foodways were based on a tribe's collective ethno-ecological awareness of its environment (Hufford 1986). For example, bison used to be the main source of food for Plains Indians. Tribes in the East typically cultivated maize, beans, and squash, while tribes in the Northwest often fished and gathered berries. These cultural food traditions were largely destroyed when, over the course of the nineteenth century, many Indian tribes were displaced to unfamiliar land in the Western United States. Others were restricted to a fraction of their former territory. Bound to fixed parcels of land, they were not able to continue their foodways.

The government implemented a "policy designed to make farmers out of the American Indians and thereby to help assimilate them into white society" (Hurt 1987:96). As part of this effort, the government provided food rations intended as temporary assistance while tribes made the transition to self-sufficient commercial farming centers (US Department of State 1868). By the late nineteenth century, however, the campaign was floundering due to inadequate governmental aid and education, cultural resistance from nomadic tribes, and placement of Indians on barren lands (Hurt 1987:134).

Lacking a successful sustenance system and in some cases being accused of preferring "to survive on governmental annuities rather than to labor in the fields for their food," many American Indians became wholly dependent on these food subsidies (US Congress 1891:6). As a result, the government, in its role as the chief foodstuff provider, came to all but dictate the dietary intake of these indigenous groups.

The rations the US government supplied were, without exception, foreign to the American Indians and foreign to North America. Beef and salt pork replaced bison, deer, and fish; wheat flour replaced cornmeal; refined sugar replaced honey, maple syrup, and dried fruits. The deliberate omission of Native foodstuffs intended to aid the government's goals of "civilizing" American Indians into general society. An 1832 treaty outlines typical low-cost and shelf-stable provisions as received by the Sauk and Fox Indians: "articles of subsistence as follows: thirty-five beef cattle; twelve bushels of salt; thirty barrels of pork; and fifty barrels of flour" (US Department of State [1832] 1904). In the case of Navajos, "in the autumn of 1865, the Army issued the Navahos meal, flour, and bacon" (Brown 2001:33). Shipments of food were meant to slow down endemic starvation and did not have an emphasis on nutrition. Most foods were heavily processed and preserved to endure the journey. Still, sometimes the provisions were so poor in quality that they were officially condemned as being "unfit for soldiers" (Brown 2001:33).

Today, the US Department of Agriculture (USDA), a government agency, still supplies food commodities free of charge to nearly 100,000 people in over 250 tribes through the FDPIR (USDA 2012b:1). Available foods today include canned meats, canned beans, canned vegetables, canned soups, canned fruits, bottled juices, cereals, rice, dried pasta, flours, processed cheese food, powdered egg mix, shelf stable milk, buttery spread, and vegetable oil (USDA 2012a).

In many ways, today's FDPIR resembles the early distribution of rations to Indians. It is still run by the government. Most commodity foods are shelf-stable and preservative-heavy to endure storage and delivery. Many have questionable nutrition value. Most are not native to North America. Finally, although the aid is still meant to provide *"supplemental* foods" (USDA 1990:1), it is often used as the *"primary* source of food" (US Senate 1993) (emphasis added).

COMMODITY FOODS AS SYMBOLS OF AMERICAN INDIAN IDENTITY

Commodity foods have now been part of life on Indian reservations for generations, and for many American Indians today, they symbolize that experience. Many commodity foods are not widely available outside reservations, or come in distinct packaging emphasizing their separateness from non-Indian foodways. The host of an American Indian-produced radio program announced that American Indians "take pride in saying if you weren't raised on commodities you're not a real Indian" (Native America Calling 2005). As a shared badge of group membership, commods are the basis of jokes, songs, and other cultural expressions.

The first commod-themed expression that caught my attention was "commod bod." I was attending a "frybread workshop" put on by Wunk Sheek as part

of the month-long "Native November" celebration. An American Indian staff member demonstrated her method of making frybread, and students were invited to join in the cooking. The frybread became part of a "traditional feast" that included deer stew, acorn squash, and wild rice. As one student reached for an extra helping of frybread, another teased, "Hey, you workin' on that commod bod or what?" Literally, "commod bod" is esoteric terminology for "commodity [food] body." The expression is humorous because in the common American idiom, to "work on" one's body means exercise. The activity referenced—eating fried starchy bread—has the opposite effect of exercise. Thus, the playful rhyming term "commod bod" indicates a reversal of typical ideals. As a student of folklore, I was intrigued. . .

Frybread

While not distributed by FDPIR, frybread is synonymous with the commodity food experience. According to lore, frybread "came about as a necessity to keep Indian people alive in times of starvation. They got creative with the rations that were given to them when everybody was starving" (Rexford 2005:1). Although frybread is still commonly made from FDPIR ingredients, it has grown from last resort to an esteemed food. According to Ray Red Corn, his American Indian company sells over 200,000 pounds of frybread mix each year through outlets including Wal-Mart (personal e-mail correspondence).

Frybread recipes vary from tribe to tribe and family to family. There are "as many different recipes for this modern pan-Indian flatbread as there are Native cooks to make it" (Kavasch 1995:11). A typical recipe calls for making plain white flour into dough with water and baking powder, forming it into discs, and then deep frying to a golden color. One of my classmates, a member of the Bad River Band of Lake Superior Chippewa Indians, told me that the FDPIR flour was the only kind of flour her aunt, an expert frybread maker, used (anonymous personal communication). Recipes are passed down through generations, and are a point of familial and tribal pride. The recipe for Red Corn

Fry Bread Mix, for example, Red Corn recalls "came from Aunt Mary McFall, a full-blood Osage woman that took my non-Indian mother under her wing in 1933 and taught her Osage Feast traditions" (personal e-mail correspondence). A mockumentary film called *More Than Frybread* takes frybread pride to an exaggerated extreme, portraying over-the-top personalities of the competitors in a "frybread championship" representing all twenty-two of Arizona's federally-recognized tribes (*More Than Frybread* 2011).

Frybread is symbolic of Indian identity. Frybread is a defining element of powwows, the tribal and pan-tribal ceremonial gatherings that feature Native regalia, dancing, and singing.

> At powwows and other Indian celebrations there are as many booths for selling fried bread as there are hotdog stands at a country fair. Some families earn their traveling money to go from one powwow to the next by buying a big sack of flour, making it up into fried bread, hanging up a cardboard sign, and selling it as fast as it can be cooked. (Hungry Wolf 1980:209)

At powwows, where different tribes and non-Indians intermingle, it is common to see Indians wearing T-shirts printed with "Frybread Power," "Fry Bread Investigator," or "Got Frybread?" The shirts help identify Indians from non-Indians in the absence of traditional regalia.

There are many other signs of frybread's status as cultural symbol. The legislature of South Dakota, home of the Great Sioux Nation, declared it the state bread (South Dakota Legislature 2005). One newspaper columnist jokingly proposed the "frybreadth" as a unit of measure "based on the standard size of a piece of auntie's frybread" (Long Feather 2001). In 2006, I received an e-mail forward titled "You Might Be from the Rez if" (anonymous personal communication), listing various experiences that indicate an upbringing on a reservation. I later found portions of it duplicated online in an Internet message forum (pigheaded 2011). One in particular caught my attention: "You eat mutton stew and frybread for breakfast," in reference to pairing a traditional Navajo dish. To most American Indians, frybread is the traditional culture-specific food. . . .

Commodity foods occupy a place in Indian culture that is similar to the crawfish in Cajun culture (Gutierrez 1985). Both are historically "poor people's food." The Cajuns turned this free "insect" into a delicacy through skillful cooking, much as American Indians turn commodity food into frybread. Furthermore, in the same way commodities are viewed by outsiders—and joked about by insiders—as being disgusting, many non-Cajuns see crawfish as insects and thus "repulsive" (Gutierrez 1985:180). Both groups use their foods as a symbol of uniqueness and unity.

AMBIVALENCE AND RESISTANCE

Although commods are a shared Indian experience that spans generational, geographical, and tribal divisions, they also embody government subjugation and displacement of Indian culture. . . .

Indian Ambivalence toward Commods

As they were displaced from their territories, Indians lost the ability to support themselves using the cultural methods they had developed. The reservations' landscapes and climates were in most cases unfamiliar and infertile. Even Indians who stayed on a portion of their former land often lost access to the wildlife they had formerly hunted. The US government undertook efforts to re-educate Indians, including forcibly removing children from their families to attend boarding schools. The stated goal was to replace the Indian ways, which depended on particular land and resources, and make the Indian reservations into European-style farming communities. These programs were largely failures. This troubled history is very much alive in Indian attitudes toward commodity foods.

Many Indians resent their position of dependency on the government for food. In the same Native call-in show where the host identified commods as part of being a "real Indian," callers referred to the foods as "government handouts" and "America's leftovers" (Native America Calling 2005). These terms reflect the perception that commodities are foods bought up by the US government because they are unwanted or exceed the needs of other Americans. On the Pine Ridge Reservation in South Dakota, where over 50 percent of the population is below the federal poverty line (US Department of Commerce 2000), Vic Glover stated, "Why would anyone want them [commodity foods], you might wonder. They're free, is why" (Glover 2004:66). Suffice it to say that reliance on government food aid is not a point of pride.

The loss of traditional Indian foodways is another sorrowful occurrence that Indians today associate with government food aid. Traditional foods have long played a role in the spiritual life of American Indians. For example, the Navajo creation myth tells of humans emerging from corn ears. Many tribes have myths that show reverence for sources of food, or incorporate food into traditional ceremonies. All tribes had particular methods and sources for food that had developed for generations before European colonization. Many of these food traditions have been diminished or extinguished. A survey conducted shortly after bison was added to the FDPIR program indicated that respondents favored commodity cheese by a 2 to 1 margin and were "not accustomed to the taste [of bison]" (USDA 2004:5). Frybread and other commods have taken part of the blame. Although it is often said that "no 'traditional' Indian meal is complete without a big pile of fried bread" (Hungry Wolf 1980:209), some Indians reject frybread because the flour, leavening, cooking oil, and even cooking implements used to make it were introduced by Europeans. There is a movement, sometimes using the slogan "Decolonize Your Diet," to cut back or eliminate foods that are not native to the Americas from the Indian diet (bumper stickers and other items are offered for sale at http://www .cafepress.com/decolonizenow). This slogan analogizes commodity and other non-native foods to colonists who have invaded the Indian diet. This is an argument from tradition alone. Others cite the need for biodiversity, stewardship of natural resources,

or health concerns (discussed below) as reasons to revive Indian food traditions. Some people take the challenge to eat only "native" sources of food for a week or a month as a way to learn more about traditional foodways (Dooglas 2011).

Finally, many people blame commods, and by extension the US government, for diabetes, obesity, and associated health problems, including coronary artery disease and hypertension. "Diabetes was uncommon among Native Americans before World War II but recently has grown at a rate 234% higher than for all other U.S. ethnic groups and has attained epidemic status among Indian peoples" (Dillinger et. al 1999: 174). Commodity foods have "been roundly blamed as a factor in the diet-related diseases like diabetes and obesity" (Fogarty 2005). In a 2004 survey conducted by the USDA, respondents complained the foods were not diabetic friendly and flagged 60 percent of the foods as having "too much fat, grease, salt/sodium, and/or sugar" (USDA 2004:4).

Cultural Resistance to Commods through Humor

Indians use humor to present perceived truths about commodity foods. Many jokes address the perceived quality of the foods, or lack thereof:

> Did you hear about the tribal office mouse that came upon a piece of commodity cheese on the floor?
> He passed it up because it didn't meet the minimum daily nutritional requirements suggested by the USDA! (anonymous personal communication)

The irony of this joke revolves around the surprise that the mouse, usually lured by cheese, voluntarily turns it down. The humor lies in the perception that while the USDA oversees the FDPIR, it distributes food that does not meet its own dietary standards. A second irony is that the animal has the good sense to avoid low-quality commods, while humans line up to get them. Thus it implies that the commodity program has turned people into animals, or worse. . . .

Another theme in Indian commodity humor is government malfeasance or ineptitude. . . .

Barre Toelken recounts the following joke, passed around Navajo country during the harsh winters of the mid-1950s, about the misguided government aid efforts:

> Did you hear about the [Navajo] woman who heard a plane circling her place and ran out to see what it was?
> She got out there and was killed by a case of condensed milk. (Toelken 2003:153)

Here, as in other American Indian humor, a heartbreaking subject is inserted into an innocuous framework. The form of the joke ("Did you hear . . . ?") is commonplace, and generally sets up a silly or trivial punch line. In this case, it leaves the audience the senseless tragedy of a woman killed by the presumably well-intentioned government action of delivering food aid. Doubly ironic, the "aid" is all of one type—condensed milk—and its value to the woman, had she lived, was questionable. The condensed milk is not a meal, and Navajo, like other Indians, are mostly lactose intolerant. The joke-teller and audience would have known this all too well.

This dark and at times bleak commodity food humor draws from a larger body of dark Indian humor. For example, Custer and Columbus jokes have long been told by American Indians. "What did one Indian say to the other when Columbus landed? 'Well, there goes the neighborhood!'" (Taylor 1971:421). On the surface, this joke is a straightforward role reversal, putting a phrase stereotypical of bigoted white American suburbanites in the mouth of a fifteenth-century Indian, talking about a white man. On another level, the punch line is funny because it is grossly disproportionate to the wars, plagues, conquest, and starvation that followed from Columbus. . . .

"[S]hared Columbus and Custer jokes alone have bound together Indian groups who agree on little else except resistance to Euro-American colonization" (Gibbon 2003:202). Commodities are one more thread to strengthen this intertribal bond of social catharsis. "The bottom line," according to Northern Cheyenne artist Bentley Spang, "is we are pretty darn funny people. Humor has helped us deal with incredible adversity and hardship over the years and is still an integral part of life today" (quoted in Bates 2004:242).

The Great Frybread Debate

In January 2005, Cheyenne and Muscogee activist Suzan Shown Harjo leveled a pointed attack on unfit or inauthentic foods: "My New Year's Resolution: No More Fat 'Indian' Food" (Harjo 2005). While many Indians associate frybread with survival in difficult conditions, to Harjo it symbolizes past and current hardships:

> Frybread is emblematic of the long trails from home and freedom to confinement and rations. It's the connecting dot between healthy children and obesity, hypertension, diabetes, dialysis, blindness, amputations and slow death. (Harjo 2005)

Moreover, while most Indians embrace commodity foods to some extent as a cultural emblem, Harjo points out that non-Indians have adopted the emblem as well. Frybread is the new "firewater" in stereotypical portrayals of American Indians, the default icebreaker at Indian social events, and the way that well-meaning non-Indians try to relate to Indians. Charged responses from other Indians included message board debates on sites like www.indianz.com, a Native America call-in show devoted to the article, and an Tucson newspaper article claiming that Harjo had sparked the yet-to-be-resolved "great fry bread debate" (Native America Calling 2005; swrussel 2005; Wagner 2005).

In the same year as Harjo's article, the South Dakota legislature debated making frybread the official bread of South Dakota. Before the vote, Mary Anne Bear Heels McCowan of the Rosebud Sioux Tribe told legislators, "This will show that South Dakota is proud of all the contributions of its citizens," including Indians. Kibbe Conti, a dietitian and member of the Oglala Sioux Tribe, disagreed: "It's a food that has contributed to our downfall. In our history we have replaced a lot of our food with fry bread and it is not a superior food compared to what we had before" (quoted by *Native American Times* 2005). The measure passed, but with less than unanimous support.

This debate bears many similarities to the ongoing debate in the African American community over soul food. American Indians and African

Americans experienced similar histories of food displacement and colonization. Just as commodities are an artifact of the reservation system, African American soul food is an artifact of enslavement (Iré 1997:255). Like commodities, "soul foods" are used as ethnic signifiers and considered traditional. And like commodities, items like chitterlings, fried chicken, and cobblers are linked to numerous health problems. The documentary film *Soul Food Junkies* presents many viewpoints on the issue, from those that call soul food "the authentic American cuisine" to others that call it "the death food . . . because it will kill you" (*Soul Food Junkies* 2012). Writer and journalist Lolis Eric Ellie presents an idea that could just as easily apply to the frybread debate:

> Food is about culture. There can be at times a sense that culture is static, and so soul food is black culture, because we need to hold on to it, because that's our ancestors. Well, our ancestors change! (quoted in *Soul Food Junkies* 2012)

By this view, the existence of a tradition is not the end of the story. It is just as important to acknowledge that traditions like frybread and commodities can change, that culture is dynamic.

CONCLUSION

This paper presents the commodity food system and its influence on American Indian foodways. Over the generations since Indians were restricted to reservations, government food aid has become part of American Indian culture and traditions. Expressions of commodity food humor, constructed by and targeted for the pan-Indian community, have emerged in conversation, radio, newspapers, Internet exchanges, clothing, music, and films. Commodity humor's role is twofold: it contributes to a sense of unified modern Indian identity and provides an opening to discuss serious topics of health, self-determination, and authentic Indian identity.

REFERENCES

Bates, Sara, ed. 1995. *Indian Humor*. San Francisco: American Indian Contemporary Arts. Quoted in *Native Universe: Voices of Indian America*, ed. Gerald McMaster and Clifford E. Trafzer. 2004. Washington, DC: National Museum of the American Indian and *National Geographic*.

Brown, Dee Alexander. 2001. *Bury My Heart at Wounded Knee: An Indian History of the American West*. New York: Holt.

Dillinger, Teresa L., Stephen C. Jett, Martha J. Macri, and Louis E. Grivetti. 1999. Feast or Famine? Supplemental Food Programs and Their Impacts on Two American Indian Communities in California. *International Journal of Food Sciences and Nutrition* 50(3):173–87.

Dooglas, Carl. 2011. Decolonizing Diets: The Traditional Foods Challenge. http://recycledminds.blogspot.com/2011/10/decolonizing-diets-traditional-foods.html.

Fogarty, Mark. 2005. Commodities Program Serves Lowest Number of People in 20 Years. *Indian Country Today*, January 20. http://web.archive.org/web/20060506083031/ http://www.indiancountry.com/content.cfm?id=1096410206.

Gibbon, Guy. 2003. *The Sioux: The Dakota and Lakota Nations*. Malden, MA: Blackwell.

Glover, Vic. 2004. *Keeping Heart on Pine Ridge: Family Ties, Warrior Culture, Commodity Foods, Rez Dogs and the Sacred*. Summertown, TN: Native Voices.

Gutierrez, Paige C. 1985. The Social and Symbolic Uses of Ethnic/Regional Foodways: Cajuns and Crawfish in South Louisiana. In *Ethnic and Regional Foodways in the United States*, ed. Linda Keller Brown and Kay Mussell, pp. 169–82. Knoxville: University of Tennessee Press.

Harjo, Suzan. 2005. My New Year's Resolution: No More Fat "Indian" Food. *Indian Country Today*, January 20. http://indiancountrytodaymedianetwork.com/ictarchives/2005/01/26/my-new-years-resolution-no-more-fat-indian-food-94439.

Hufford, Mary. 1986. The Organization of Environmental Difference. In *One Space, Many Places: Folklife and Land Use in New Jersey's Pinelands National Reserve*, pp. 34–49. Washington, DC: American Folklife Center.

Hungry Wolf, Beverly. 1980. *The Ways of My Grandmothers*. New York: HarperCollins.

Hurt, Douglas R. 1987. *Indian Agriculture in America*. Lawrence: University Press of Kansas.

Iré, Jennifer. 1997. The Power of the Pepper: From Slave Food to Spirit Food. In *Through the Kitchen*

Window, ed. Arlene Voski Avakian, pp. 255–63. Boston: Beacon.

Kavasch, E. Barrie. 1995. *Enduring Harvests: Native American Foods and Festivals for Every Season*. Old Saybrook, CT: Glove Pequot Press.

Long Feather, Cheryl. 2001. Four Directions. *Bismarck Tribune*, June 13:1B.

More than Frybread. 2011. Dir. Travis Holt Hamilton. Phoenix, AZ: Holt Hamilton Production. DVD, 96 min.

Native America Calling. 2005. *Greasy Debate*, Prod. Tara Gatewood for Koahnic Broadcast Corporation [KBC], on KNBA, 90.3 FM, Anchorage, AK. February 15. Radio broadcast.

Native American Times. 2005. Frybread an Official Food? Health Expert Not Thrilled with South Dakota Idea. February 11. http://nativetimes.com/index.asp?action=displayarticle&article_id=5982.

pigheaded. 2011. You Might Be from the Rez If. . . . *powwows.com*, September 20. http://www.powwows.com/gathering/archive/index.php?t-61090.html.

Rexford, Cathy. 2005. Invasion of the Frybread Snatchers: Something Is Wrong in Native America. *Institute of American Indian Arts Chronicle*. http://www.iaiachronicle.org/archives/FRYBREADSNATCHERS.htm.

Soul Food Junkies. 2012. Dir. Byron Hurt. Plainfield, NJ [independent production]. DVD, 64 min.

South Dakota Legislature. House. 2005. *An Act to Designate Fry Bread as the Official Bread of South Dakota*. 80th Legislature. H.R. 1205.

swrussel. 2005. Harjo on Frybread. http://64.38.12.138/boardx/topic.asp?TOPIC_ID=12452.

Taylor, J. Golden, ed. 1971. *The Literature of the American West*. Boston: Houghton Mifflin.

Toelken, Barre. 2003. *The Anguish of Snails: Native American Folklore in the West*. Logan: Utah State University Press.

US Congress. Board of Indian Commissioners. 1891. *Annual Report*. 52nd Cong., 1st sess.

US Department of Agriculture [USDA]. 1990. *Evaluation of the Food Distribution Program on Indian Reservations*. Washington, DC: Department of Agriculture. http://www.fns.usda.gov/ora/menu/Published/FoodDistribution/FDStudies.htm (accessed February 20, 2007).

———. 2004. *2004 Commodity Acceptability Progress (CAP) Report*. Washington, DC: Department of Agriculture. http://origin.www.fns.usda.gov/fdd/caps/2004/cap04-fdpir04.pdf (accessed April 21, 2012).

———. 2012a. *FDPIR Foods Available for 2012*. Washington, DC: Department of Agriculture. http://www.fns.usda.gov/fdd/foods/fy12-fdpirfoods.pdf (accessed April 21, 2012).

———. 2012b. *Food and Nutrition Service Food Distribution Nutrition Program Fact Sheet*. March. Washington, DC: Department of Agriculture. http://www.fns.usda.gov/fdd/programs/fdpir/pfs-fdpir.pdf.

US Department of Commerce. Bureau of the Census. 2000. *Summary File 3—Sample Data Geographic Area: Pine Ridge Reservation and Off-Reservation Trust Land*. Washington, DC: Department of Commerce.

US Department of State. [1832] 1904. Treaty with the Sauk and Foxes. *Indian Affairs: Laws and Treaties*, Vol. 2, compiled and Ed. Charles J. Kappler, pp. 635ff. Washington, DC: Government Printing Office. http://memory.loc.gov/cgi-bin/ampage?collId=llsl&fileName=015/llsl015.db&recNum=2.

US Department of State. 1868. Fort Laramie Treaty. *U.S. Statutes at Large*. Vol. 15, pp. 635–48.

US Senate. 1993. Committee on Indian Affairs and Senate Committee on Nutrition and Forestry. *Barriers to Participation in the Food Stamp Program and Other Programs of the Department of Agriculture by People Residing on Indian Lands*. 103rd Cong. 1st sess.

Wagner, Angie. 2005. Indian Fighting the Curse of Fry Bread: Fat Diabetes. *Tucson Citizen Newspaper*, August 22. http://tucsoncitizen.com/morgue2/2005/08/22/188241-indians-fighting-curse-of-fry-bread-fat-diabetes/.

QUESTIONS

1. Does the experience of cooking and eating commodity foods help to create a shared cultural identity among present-day American Indians, according to Vantrease? Does this experience connect them to their history and traditions? How or how not?

2. Some object to the role commodity foods play in the life and cultural expression of indigenous peoples in the United States. What are their objections?

3. According to Vantrease, both soul food and commodity foods are artifacts of displacement and confinement. What does this mean? How does this history give soul foods and commodity foods an ambivalent place in African-Americans' and indigenous peoples' minds?

4. Recall Kyle Powys Whyte's notion of "collective food relations": the variety of relations and experiences involving food that help make up a group's way of life ("Food Justice and Collective Food Relations," in Chapter 3). Are there collective food relations that include commodity foods? Recall Whyte's discussion of the role of manoomin (wild rice) in the collective food relations of the Anishinaaeb in the Great Lakes region. Is manoomin a hub for collective food relations in a different way than commodity foods? Did commodity foods displace other collective food relations?

5. Commodity foods are a form of government food assistance. Do commodity foods help to achieve food justice, by helping to address hunger, food insecurity, and poverty? Do they work against food justice in some other way, or have they worked against food justice in the past?

MARK WEINER

Consumer Culture and Participatory Democracy: The Story of Coca-Cola

Coca-Cola is a symbol of American national identity and the "American Way of Life." Mark Weiner describes how a deliberate advertising and marketing campaign during World War II helped to create this association. While some theorists think that consumerism undermines democracy by focusing our attention on our own interests rather than the common good, Weiner suggests that consumer goods can provide a shared experience that links people together in an "imagined community."

As any foreign traveler can attest, the relation between food and national identity is close and strong, as deeply intertwined, perhaps, as the twin yearnings of hunger and love. Not only do citizens of most nations come to perceive some aspect of their cuisine as distinctive, nations themselves are typically associated with particular foods. Consider the people of Japan, whose collective identity is firmly based on their shared consumption of rice, or those of Scotland, who take pride in their distinguished tradition of distilling fine whiskey. These national symbols, of course, are far from arbitrary: the food that represents a nation is frequently said to reveal the special values of the people who live there. A carafe of wine, for example, often serves as the national symbol of France, in part because the complex fragrance of the

Mark Weiner, "Consumer Culture and Participatory Democracy: The Story of Coca-Cola during World War II." From *Food and Foodways* (Philadelphia: Taylor & Francis, 1996), Vol. 6(2), 109–129.

beverage is a powerful reminder of French concern for aesthetic subtlety. Similarly, a steaming cup of hot tea recalls the nation of England, partly because the leisurely manner in which it must be consumed brings to mind British ideals of civil discourse. Countries are what they eat, or at the very least, people tend to think of nations in culinary terms.

The United States is hardly unique then in possessing a national icon drawn from the world of comestibles. Symbolically unifying its diverse multi-ethnic society, Coca-Cola is what Roland Barthes has called a "totem-drink," and more than any other food (except, perhaps, hamburgers, with which it is often served), this beverage has come to symbolize the American nation.[1] Speak with people in India, China, Austria, or Egypt, just about anywhere, and many will tell you that Coke and the United States are closely associated, if not synonymous. But while a Bordeaux recalls the celebrated complexity of the French palate, and tea the special esteem in which the British hold polite conversation, Coca-Cola *is* special among patriotic symbols in at least one important respect: the national characteristic it represents is a political one, a democratic vision of consumer abundance known as the "American Way of Life." Inexpensive, simple for the palate, and providing a sweet, caffeinated release, Coca-Cola indeed not only embodies the egalitarian, self-directed spirit of consumer society in the United States, but also explicitly served as an international symbol of that society during the Cold War. This cultural status is reflected in documents as diverse as Billy Wilder's comedy film classic *One, Two, Three,* the renowned "World and Friend" cover of Henry Luce's *Time* magazine, and Stanley Kubrick's *Dr. Strangelove.*[2]

Because Coca-Cola has served as an icon of American consumer society, it also possesses another quality unique among foods: the emotional hostility it arouses. Other culinary symbols have certainly caused great anger when they were removed from stores (one thinks of the recent shortage of domestic rice in Japan, or of Gorbachev's ill-fated attempt to curtail vodka consumption in the Soviet Union). But no other foods, except Coca-Cola, have aroused such strong negative feelings when they were merely introduced to the open marketplace, for in serving as a primary symbol of the "American Way of Life," Coke often is viewed not simply as a food but also as a social danger. Coca-Cola may be inexpensive, critics announce, but it also is the same everywhere, and so intimates the approach of cultural uniformity. The drink may be simple for the palate, easily enjoyed by all, but it also is sold from machines, and so exists outside of sanctioned locations of community ritual. Coca-Cola may provide an innocent, sweet release, but that sweetness seems to conceal the fact that Coke is manufactured by a single multinational corporation, a major locus of economic power. Such criticisms animated what Mark Pendergrast has characterized as the series of "threats and rumors [Coke faced] at midcentury around the world," including French protests of the late 1940s and early 1950s, and such criticisms continue to undergird the cynicism many direct toward Coke today.[3]

How was Coca-Cola forged into this hotly contested symbol? That story began in the 1920s, when company president Robert Woodruff initiated a series of reforms important for the growth of his organization, including an increased emphasis on the sale of Coca-Cola in bottles, especially from gasoline stations, as well as a campaign to standardize the beverage, to make certain that "every bottle and fountain drink [would] taste exactly the same across the United States."[4] In the 1930s Coke deftly employed film and radio to market cheap distraction to people enduring difficult times, utilized new methods of electric refrigeration in its sales (Coca-Cola tastes best over ice), and used Madison Avenue to emphasize the critical role the beverage played in the culture of the drugstore soda fountain—which at the time lay "at the heart of America's social activity."[5] But while the 1920s saw Coke become portable, accessible and uniform, and the 1930s witnessed how Coke become more widely consumed and "increasingly . . . performed a social function," in order to understand how Coca-Cola became deeply linked with *American* identity, one must look to World War II.[6] For it was only during the war, when savvy business executives placed Coke within the smithy of global conflict, within its peculiar cultural and psychological circumstances, that this already popular beverage was transformed into an icon of *national* values.

This essay examines that transformation and the tactics The Coca-Cola Company used to create it, in order to explore a widely held political judgment of the consumer society Coke represents.[7] Scholars generally believe that consumer society is hostile to the republican ideal of participatory democracy, which valorizes the active involvement of citizens in public decision-making. Many assert not only that the self-focused ethic of consumerism diminishes commitment to the common good, the foundation of a democratic republic, but that the fluid meaning of commodities masks the concentrated, anti-democratic power of capital. Recently, scholars have developed and periodized this judgment by focusing their attention on the 1930s and 1940s, especially on World War II, when a "far-reaching ideological redefinition of polity and society [allegedly] began to take hold." This redefinition, which ushered in "the social contract of cold war liberalism," reconceived consumer items as one of the primary rights of citizenship and so refigured citizenship, in the words of Jean-Christophe Agnew, "in the seemingly innocuous language of soft drinks, arms, and household appliances."[8] This transition formed an anti-democratic turning-point in American history because civic self-perceptions were altered in a way that privatized political consciousness, and the fluid language of commodities in which those self-perceptions were articulated served to conceal corporate power.

Although I agree that historical evidence supports this perspective, I believe that the story of Coca-Cola during World War II can also support a somewhat different conclusion. During the war, certainly, Coca-Cola did come to play a role in how Americans understood their identity as citizens, and The Coca-Cola Company did become tightly intertwined with the American state, setting the stage for its enormous postwar expansion. But the wartime tale of Coke may not be simply one of declining democratic politics, for the history of Coca-Cola also reveals how a consumer item, a product of concentrated economic power that appealed to individual desires, could be used by the people who drank it for ends that were not private but communal. Coca-Cola was unique among most consumer products in being a *food*, an item whose meaning is rarely fluid but is instead created through social-practice; but it is partly for this reason that I believe the story of Coca-Cola suggests a different evaluation of consumer society as a whole from that held by many critics. This evaluation, which I discuss in my conclusion, is sensitive to the ways in which consumer goods can be used in morally profound interactions between individuals and within communities . . .

[During World War II, Coca-Cola] undertook a series of sophisticated advertising campaigns which surrounded Coke with the language of American identity. . . . In discussing this campaign, which was based on the semiotic use of the = symbol, I hope to offer a rough architectural sketch of Coke's cultural meaning, especially its status as a consumer good with associations at once private and public. . . .

* * *

[T]he promotionals seem odd today for the manner in which they so clearly reveal the intent of the advertiser: to associate Coke with interactions that are not private but have *communal* significance. In one typical ad, a soldier on leave relaxes at a drug-store lunch counter, telling stories of battle to an admiring boy, who is flanked by the smiling figures of his mother and sister. All are sipping Coke, and they seem to be joined in their talk by a prominent red Coke dispenser and a series of unfilled Coca-Cola drinking glasses. As the man stares intently into the boy's eyes, his hands form two parallel lines that suggest the movement of a plane or vehicle in combat, lines that also appear to place a subliminal = sign between the soda dispenser and the boy and his family. The headline above this warm, patriotic image states plainly, "Have a Coca-Cola = Howdy, Neighbor," while the subhead explains, ". . . or greeting friends at home and abroad."[9] Another advertisement from the campaign depicts two sailors greeting a civilian family containing a mother, father, and two admiring blonde daughters. While one of the sailors looks on and smiles, the other reaches his hand left, across the center of the image, to shake that of the father, who bows slightly. Almost directly below the point where the civilian and military hands meet is a table bedecked with sweets and Coca-Cola. The headline of the image states, "Have a 'Coke' = You're invited to our house"; the subhead notes ". . . or how to make sailors feel at home."

The number and variety of Coke advertisements that employed the juxtapositional force of the = is overwhelming, and a search through any popular middle-class magazine of the time will uncover scores of them. Even here, through mere written description, one can easily imagine their emotional force. GI letters in Coca-Cola archives, in fact, testify to that intensity, expressing in indignant tones the frustration that followed when The Coca-Cola Company seemed to promise the public more than it could deliver. "As staunch but frustrated Coca-Cola fans," wrote one group of bitter seamen from North Africa, for instance,

> we are a little puzzled by your new advertising policy. In your ad of the July 24 issue of the POST, is that Marine in the desert seeing a mirage? Must be, for we have the palm trees, the sand, but no cokes. . . . Here's to the fulfillment of your mirage. Don't just "tell it to the marines."[10]

Viewed together as a steady stream of images, Coca-Cola promotionals reveal the power and clarity with which Coke associated its very private product with communal life—how within the larger context of U.S. propaganda, the company provided its beverage with meanings that were not restricted to the "private 'why'" but instead were more broadly national. For when Coke used the techniques of advertising to associate its product with a variety of intimate rituals constituting American social life (as well as with the notion of American cultural ambassadorship), it also asserted by implication that American social life depended upon Coca-Cola for its very existence. And the implication of *that* assertion was clear enough: that the United States, as it was known and loved, was almost inconceivable without Coke. During World War II, the masters of persuasion were fast attempting to become the masters of American identity.

COCA-COLA AND THE MEMORY OF HOME

But did soldiers actually come to perceive Coke as a symbol of the United States or of their own identity? The evidence in the third part of my discussion suggests that they did. The headquarters of The Coca-Cola Company in Atlanta, Georgia, contain extensive archival holdings concerning the history of company products, materials intended largely for in-house marketing use. Among these astonishingly rich documents are scores of letters from American soldiers pleading with company executives to send packages of Coke to specific regiments in the field, correspondence that testifies to the special place the beverage held in the minds of servicemen abroad. . . .

While other comestible items seem to have played a similar role in servicemen's lives, especially milk and ice cream, apparently none were so powerful as Coca-Cola.[11] Reading G.I. correspondence about the beverage, in fact, can be a deeply moving experience, for it paints a highly charged portrait of Coke as the only stable object in a world of total chaos, as the one familiar point-of-reference in acutely disorienting situations. "No ice cream, no milk, no eggs, no white bread, no butter, punk coffee, tea, tea, tea, no chicken, no steaks, no vegetables, no fruit, warm beer," wrote one soldier from England, where shortages were especially severe. "[But even here] I can buy ICE COLD COCA-COLA!!! Ain't it a wonderful world?"[12] "I always thought it was a wonderful drink," wrote another soldier from the South Pacific, "but on an island where few white men set foot, it is a God-send. . . . I can truthfully say that I haven't seen smiles spread over a bunch of boys' faces as it did when they saw the Coca-Cola in this God-forsaken place."[13] For men in the field, Coca-Cola was a firm rock in a sea of cultural confusion, a morale-boosting token of a place that seemed exceedingly remote.

Indeed, servicemen's writings indicate that Coke was such a powerful talisman of the United States that it reminded them of *actual moments* of their experience as civilians, Coca-Cola triggered memories of the *specific* events in their prewar lives. Most importantly, G.I. letters attest that Coke was a potent, even Proustian conjurer of the social life of the drugstore soda fountain, in which the beverage had played an increasingly important role since the 1930s. Again and again, soldiers noted the connection between Coca-Cola and their local gathering place. "The ole 'Coke' sign," wrote one serviceman from Sicily, "brings every soldier back to his moments in his favorite drug store, where he sat and conversed with his friends."[14] "The Officers' Club, we call it 'Tony's Tavern,' was merely a tent pitched on the sand," wrote another, "but in there, with a blue ribbon tied around it, the 'Coke' would always draw such comments as, 'Boy I'd give a month's pay for an ice-cold Coke.' The shape of the bottle, the memory of the refreshing taste, brought to mind many happy memories."[15] Even Gen. Eisenhower, a noted Coca-Cola aficionado, told reporters, "Being a general is a lonely life. I wish I could be home and go down to the cafe this morning and have a coke with the gang."[16] Countless newspaper articles about G.I. life tell a similar story. "The first thing Colonel Moore did after leaving the station," observed a reporter for *Life*, "was go uptown in Villisca to his old drugstore and buy a Coke and a hamburger, the first in 16 months."[17] In other words, soldiers seem to have perceived Coke as a part of the peaceful rituals of domestic fellowship, and it recalled for them the friends they had cultivated within those folk conventions. . . .

Moreover, while G.I. letters reveal that Coke was important to servicemen on a personal level, that it reminded them of their own private stories, they also exhibit that soldiers perceived the beverage as an equally evocative symbol of the American polis, of the United States as an abstract political entity. Letters housed in Coca-Cola archives, in fact, suggest that soldiers understood Coke as a symbol of civic significance precisely because it was so closely connected with their individual experience. In servicemen's writings, for example, we find numerous seemingly paradoxical statements that link conceptions of communal, national sacrifice with the noncommunal, antipolitical desire to drink a sweet, fizzy beverage. "Since I've come across," wrote one enthusiastic soldier to his parents, "I've met and

talked with some of the greatest men in the world, *real men who have gone through Hell and come out again, but would go back for a cold Coca-Cola.*"[18] "'An American airman may be able to carry plenty of thunder to the Japs,'" one officer told a local reporter, "'provided he can have . . . a Coca-Cola to drink occasionally, to help him keep in touch with the American way of life.'"[19] These sentiments indicate precisely what Agnew's historical portrait would predict: that Coca-Cola did play a role in American civic consciousness, that soldiers did come to describe their own identity as citizens using "the language of soft drinks." Soldiers' letters seem to tell us, in other words, that under the special psychological conditions of war—at a moment when men craved the comfort of the familiar—Woodruff's patriotic promise refigured not only Americans' conceptions of government, but also their inner lives.

COCA-COLA AND PARTICIPATORY POLITICS?

The transformation of Coke into a national icon, we have seen, contained a number of separate but related components: first, the cooperation between the American state and Coca-Cola, embodied in the story of T.O.'s; second, as revealed in advertising, the attempt of Coca-Cola to associate its product with the mundane but meaningful aspects of daily life, a project facilitated by its rhetorical use of the = sign; and third, the emotional response of American servicemen to Coke, a beverage that for many was strongly linked to peaceful, civilian life. If Coca-Cola became a national icon under these circumstances, did that icon advance a democratic, participatory vision of society or did it serve to hinder the republican political ideal many of us find so compelling? If we live in the "World of Coca-Cola," if we are, as The Coca-Cola Company implicitly claims, a "community" brought together around a mass-market good, then how might we characterize that community in regards to the civic responsibilities felt by its members? These issues concern the more general debate over consumer society I raised at the start of this discussion and invite the question: When American soldiers claimed to be fighting for the right to purchase Coke, were they in fact fighting for an impoverished notion of political life?

I would like to suggest that they were and that they were not. That the politics implicit in Coca-Cola is an impoverished vision of politics, inimical to the type of participatory political vision on which the United States was founded strikes me as a reasonable position to take. A strong body of scholarly literature certainly exists that reveals how a privatized, consumerist understanding of national life can have a disastrously corrosive effect upon civic fellowship. This literature, which bears much in common with the literature of philosophical antiliberalism, asserts that the "commodification of politics," embodied in the story of Coca-Cola, offers little hope of a future communitarian social order. Instead, consumer society conceals the antidemocratic relations of economic power on which it is based, and encourages an ethic of individual self-focus incompatible with republican ideals of virtue and community. In regard to Coke, such criticisms seem not only immanently valid but also functionally linked. For if Woodruff's promise induced servicemen to consider one of the most important functions of the state to be to supply brand-name consumer products to its citizens, then that allegedly "patriotic" commitment to fulfill *individual* desires seems simultaneously to have concealed the *institutional* machinations it presupposed. As Agnew has noted, of those servicemen who asserted that they were fighting to preserve their ability to drink Coca-Cola, how many also saw themselves as fighting for The Coca-Cola *Company*? During the war, the business of America remained business.[20]

But there are other ways of understanding the role of consumer goods in society and the story of Coca-Cola as well. For instance, Timothy Breen, in his challenging analysis of eighteenth-century commercial culture, suggests that everyday consumer items provided Americans with a shared "language of consumption" that ultimately served as a "language for revolution," that consumer goods became "good to think" in political ways.[21] More

specifically, Breen focuses his attention, as we have here, on a particular beverage—tea—explaining how it served as a medium through which nationalist consciousness grew and ultimately exploded into revolutionary action. The reason why Americans displayed such marked political solidarity beginning in 1773, writes Breen, a solidarity not evident during the Townshend protest, was that the Tea Act "affected an item of popular consumption found in almost every colonial household," an item very much like Coca-Cola which "appear[ed] on the tables of the wealthiest merchants and the poorest labourers." In creating a *material* commonalty among Americans, tea became an ideal medium through which "to transmit perceptions of liberty and rights," and a way in which *"ideological* abstractions acquired concrete meaning."[22] Breen's analysis suggests that commodities generally can provide "a shared framework of consumer experience" that allows individuals to "reach out to distant strangers, to perceive, however dimly, the existence of an 'imagined community'" and then to take political action when the liberties and rights of that community are infringed.

Similarly, Lizabeth Cohen's powerful analysis of Chicago working-class culture from 1919 to 1939 richly illustrates how commodities have not always served as forces of privatization, but, at times, have reinforced group identities. In particular, Cohen's discussion of how Americans of varied ethnic backgrounds "encountered" mass culture "at the grassroots"—a discussion that centers, in part, on a study of grocery stores—suggests that mass-market goods are not consumed by isolated individuals, but by groups of people in acts of shared experience. In doing so, Cohen suggests that goods can create situations in which morally profound loyalties are formed and sustained. "A commodity," she writes, "could just as easily help a person reinforce ethnic or working-class culture as lose it. What mattered were the experiences . . . that the consumer brought to the object."[23] Speaking of shopping at local groceries, for instance, Cohen notes that in acts of consumption, buyers brought "their own values to every exchange" and thus, while "ethnic workers [during the 1920s] came to share more in the new consumer goods" they did so "in their own stores, in their own neighborhoods, and in their own ways."[24] Cohen's analysis implies, in other words, that consumer goods can have potentially democratic political significance because their meanings are not based solely on the associations ascribed to them by Madison Avenue, but instead are rooted in a history of sentimental interaction between the people who buy them. Consumers form *real* communities around what they purchase, communities that hold affective and even political meanings for their members. . . .

NOTES

This essay is adapted from "Democracy, Consumer Culture, and Political Community: The Story of Coca-Cola During World War II," which was presented at "Eating for Victory: American Foodways and World War II," held at the University of Colorado-Boulder; 8–9 October 1993. I wish to thank Philip Mooney and Brookie Keener of The Coca-Cola Company, who offered invaluable access to historical materials and provided a model of corporate openness to scholarly inquiry; my anonymous reviewers for their criticism and advice; Amy Bentley, Meg Jeffrey, and Mark Pendergrast for their assistance; and, though he was not party to writing this essay, Jean-Christophe Agnew for his indispensable teaching.

1. Roland Barthes, "Wine and Milk," *Mythologies,* trans. Annette Lavers (New York: Hill and Wang, 1972), 58.

2. Billy Wilder. *One, Two, Three* (1961): "World and Friend," *Time* (15 May 1950), front cover: Stanley Kubrick, *Dr. Strangelove, or How I Learned to Stop Worrying and Love the Bomb* (1964). See also Dusan, Makavejev, *The Coca-Cola Kid* (1985), Jamie Uys, *The Gods Must Be Crazy* (1982), and the variety of works of American literature in which Coca-Cola plays an iconic role, for example, Arthur Miller, *Death of a Salesman* (1949), and Saul Bellow, *Seize the Day* (1956). On Coca-Cola as icon and as folklore, see Christia Murken-Altrogge, *Coca-Cola Art: Konswn, Kult, Kurst* (Munich: Klinhards and Biernmann, 1991), and Paul Smith, "Contemporary Legends and Popular Culture: "It's the Real Thing." *Contemporary Legend: The Journal of the International Society for Contemporary Legend Research* 1 (1991): 123–52. See also E. J. Kahn, Jr., *The Big Drink: The Story of Coca-Cola* (New York Random House, 1960), 3–12.

3. Mark Pendergrast, *For God, Country and Coca-Cola: The Unauthorized History of the Great American*

Soft Drink and the Company That Makes It (New York: Charles Scribner's Sons, 1993), 244. On French protest, see Richard Kuisel, *Seducing the French: The Dilemma of Americanization* (Berkeley: The University of California Press, 1993). See also Kahn. *The Big Drink,* 20–44.

4. Mark Pendergrast, *For God, Country, and Coca-Cola.* 169. General information about the history of Coca-Cola can be obtained from Pendergrast's extensive work. See also Frederick Allen, *Secret Formula: How Brilliant Marketing and Relentless Salesmanship Made Coca-Cola the Best Known Product in the World* (New York: Harper Business, 1994).

5. Ibid., 178. For evocative though non-scholarly comments on soda, fountain culture, see Paul Dickson. *The Great American Ice Cream Book* (New York: Atheneum, 1972). See also John J. Riley, *A History of the American Soft Drink Industry: Bottled Carbonated Beverages 1807–1957* (Washington: American Bottlers of Carbonated Beverages, 1958).

6. Pendergrast, *For God, Country, and Coca-Cola,* 178.

7. For an early examination of the place of Coca-Cola in World War II, see John Morton Blum, *V Was for Victory: Politics and American Culture During World War II* (San Diego: Harcourt Brace Jovanovich, 1976), 38, 107–8, See also Kahn, *The Big Drink,* 12–19. My analysis differs from the work of Blum, Pendergrast, Allen and Kahn in being driven primarily by the theoretical concerns raised in Jean-Christophe Agnew. "Coming Up for Air: Consumer Culture in Historical Perspective." *Intellectual History Newsletter* 12 (1990): 3–21; Robert Westbrook, "'I Want a Girl, Just Like the Girl That Married Harry James': American Women and the Problem of Political Obligation in World War Two," *American Quarterly* 42 (December 1990); and Robert Westbrook, "Fighting for the American Family: Private Interests and Political Obligations of World-War II," in *The Power of Culture: Critical Essays in American History,* ed. Richard Wrightman Fox and T. J. Jackson Lears (Chicago: The University of Chicago Press, 1993), 195–221.

8. Agnew, "Coming Up for Air," 14.

9. "Have a Coca-Cola = Howdy, Neighbor," *Life* (5 June 1944), back cover.

10. [Seven seamen stationed in North African waters] to The Coca-Cola Company (8 September 1943).

11. On milk, ice cream, and Coca-Cola, see for instance Hedda Hopper, "The Lusty Laughton." *The Washington Post* (21 October 1943): "Little Hard Liquor Available in Africa," *Herald-Courier* [Bristol, Virginia] (28 November 1943): and "U.S. Flyers Crave Ice Cream, Soft Drinks," *The Baltimore Sun* (17 November 1943). On

the significance of ice cream in American cultural history, see Dickson, *The Great American Ice Cream Book,* and Patricia M. Tice, *Ice Cream for All* (Rochester: Strong Museum, 1990).

12. Whitey [soldier stationed in England] to Ronnie (1 August 1943).

13. Corp. Richard E. Storekman, "Coca-Cola in South Pacific: Letter Tells of Joy it Brings to Soldier There," *Republican Register* [Mt. Carmel, Illinois] (16 July 1943).

14. Louis [soldier stationed in Sicily] to The Coca-Cola Company (10 September 1943).

15. John [Captain, Army Air Force] to Advertising Manager. The Coca-Cola Company (3 August 1943).

16. "Mother of 'Ike' Tells Hope," *New York Journal American* (10 November 1942). Eisenhower's comments were widely printed in publications of the time.

17. "Col. Moore's Homecoming," *Life* (16 August 1943).

18. Tommy [somewhere in Australia] to Mom and Dad (7 February 1943), transcribed copy.

19. "Lieut. Thomas R. Waddell Jr. Smuggles Pup as Jungle 'Pal': Former Local Youth Describes Activities of Air Combat Units," *The Florida Times-Union* (16 July 1943).

20. Agnew, "Coming Up for Air." 16. For a discussion of some of these issues in the context of corporate historical presentations, see also Mark Weiner, "We Are What We Eat or, Democracy, Community, and the Politics of Corporate Food Displays." *American Quarterly* (June 1994), 227–50.

21. Breen, "'Baubles of Britain,'" 76.

22. Ibid., 98, 104. Emphasis added.

23. Cohen, *Making a New Deal,* 106.

24. Ibid., 116.

QUESTIONS

1. Weiner writes that "the food that represents a nation is frequently said to reveal the special values of the people who live there." How, according to Weiner, does Coca-Cola represent American values and the "American Way of Life"?

2. Weiner discusses, but doesn't fully accept, the view that consumerism undermines democracy because the "self-focused ethic of consumerism diminishes commitment to the common good." What does this mean? Do you think it's true?

3. How, according to Weiner, can consumer goods provide a shared experience that links people together? Do you think the shared experience of drinking Coca-Cola is the kind of experience that motivates political action? What about the shared experience of eating organic food or locally grown food?

4. In *The Garden of Eating* the writer Jeremy Iggers argues that being part of a family and a community used to be a central part of our personal identity, but now our personal identity is mainly determined by which consumer products we choose: "[E]very choice we make about what we consume makes a statement about who we are, and no one hears that statement louder than we do ourselves." Does this seem true to you? In your opinion, what is the "statement" about oneself made by choosing to drink a Coca-Cola? What would Weiner say?

CAROL ADAMS

The Sexual Politics of Meat

This article by writer and activist Carol Adams is a modern classic. Adams argues that meat is associated with masculinity—"a mythology" that "permeates all classes." Men are presumed to enjoy meat, to need it, and to have the prerogative to eat it. Women are associated with non-meat foods, and in particular vegetables, which are perceived as a feminine food and a "second-class" food.

I left the British Library, where I was doing research on some women of the 1890s whose feminist working-class newspaper advocated meatless diets, and went through the cafeteria line in a restaurant nearby. Vegetarian food in hand, I descended to the basement. A painting of Henry VIII eating a steak and kidney pie greeted my gaze. On either side of the consuming Henry were portraits of his six wives and other women. However, they were not eating steak and kidney pie, nor anything made of meat. Catherine of Aragon held an apple in her hands. The Countess of Mar had a turnip, Anne Boleyn—red grapes, Anne of Cleaves—a pear, Jane Seymour—blue grapes, Catherine Howard—a carrot, Catherine Pair—a cabbage.

People with power have always eaten meat. The aristocracy of Europe consumed large courses filled with every kind of meat, while the laborers consumed the complex carbohydrates. Dietary habits proclaim class distinctions, but they proclaim patriarchal distinctions as well. Women, second-class citizens, are more likely to eat what are considered to be second-class foods in a patriarchal culture: vegetables and fruits and grains, rather than meat. The sexism in meat eating recapitulates the class distinctions with an added twist: a mythology that meat is a masculine food and meat eating, a male activity, permeates all classes.

Meat-eating societies gain male identification by their choice of food, and meat textbooks heartily endorse this association. We learn from *The Meat We Eat* that "a liberal meat supply has always been associated with a happy and virile people." *Meat Technology* informs us that the "virile Australian race is a typical example of heavy meat-eaters." Leading gourmands refer "to the virile ordeal of spooning the brains directly out of a barbecued calf's head."[1] *Virile: of or having the characteristics of an adult male,* from *vir* meaning *man.* Meat eating measures individual and societal virility.

Meat is a constant for men, intermittent for women, a pattern painfully observed in famine situations today. Women are starving at a rate disproportionate to men. Lisa Leghorn and Mary Roodkowsky surveyed this phenomenon in their book *Who Really Starves: Women and World Hunger.* Women, they conclude, engage in deliberate self-deprivation, offering men the "best" foods at the expense of their own nutritional needs. For instance, they tell us that "Ethiopian women and girls of all classes are obliged

Carol Adams, "The Sexual Politics of Meat," reprinted from *Heresies 21: Food Is a Feminist Issue* (Heresies Collective, 1987), 51–55.

to prepare two meals, one for the males and a second, often containing no meat or other substantial protein, for the females."[2]

In fact, men's protein needs are less than those of pregnant and nursing women, and the disproportionate distribution of the main protein source occurs when women's need for protein is the greatest. Curiously, we are now being told that one should eat meat (or fish, vegetables, chocolate, and salt) at least six weeks before becoming pregnant if one wants a boy. But if a girl is desired, no meat please, rather milk, cheese, nuts, beans, and cereals.[3]

Fairy tales initiate us at an early age into the dynamics of eating and sex roles. The King in his counting house ate four-and-twenty blackbirds in a pie (originally four-and-twenty naughty boys), while the Queen ate bread and honey. Cannibalism in fairy tales is generally a male activity, as Jack, after climbing his beanstalk, quickly learned. Folktales of all nations depict giants as male and "fond of eating human flesh."[4] Witches—warped or monstrous females in the eyes of a patriarchal world—become the token female cannibals.

A Biblical example of the male prerogative for meat rankled Elizabeth Cady Stanton, a leading nineteenth-century feminist, as can be seen by her terse commentary on Leviticus 6 in *The Woman's Bible*: "The meat so delicately cooked by the priests, with wood and coals in the altar, in clean linen, no woman was permitted to taste, only the males among the children of Aaron."[5]

Most food taboos address meat consumption, and they place more restrictions on women than on men. The common foods forbidden to women are chicken, duck, and pork. Forbidding meat to women in non-technological cultures increases its prestige. Even if the women raise the pigs, as they do in the Solomon Islands, they are rarely allowed to eat the pork. When they do receive some, it is at the dispensation of their husbands.[6] In Indonesia, "flesh food is viewed as the property of men. At feasts, the principal time when meat is available, it is distributed to households according to the men in them. . . . The system of distribution thus reinforces the prestige of men in society."[7]

Worldwide this patriarchal custom is found. In Asia, some cultures forbid women to consume fish,

seafood, chicken, duck, and eggs. In equatorial Africa, the "prohibition of chicken to women is common."[8] For example, the Mbum Kpau women do not eat chicken, goat, partridge, or other game birds. The Kufa of Ethiopia punished women who ate chicken by making them slaves, while the Walamo "put to death anyone who violated the restriction of eating fowl."[9]

Correspondingly, vegetables and other non-meat foods are viewed as women's food. This makes them undesirable to men. The Nuer men think that eating eggs is effeminate. In other groups, men require sauces to disguise the fact that they are eating women's foods. "Men expect to have meat sauces to go with their porridge and will sometimes refuse to eat sauces made of greens or other vegetables, which are said to be women's food."[10]

In technological societies, cookbooks reflect the presumption that men eat meat. A random survey of cookbooks reveals that the barbecue sections of most cookbooks are addressed to men and feature meat. The foods recommended for a "Mother's Day Tea" do not include meat, but readers are advised that on Father's Day, dinner should include London Broil because "a steak dinner has unfailing popularity with fathers."[11] In a chapter on "Feminine Hospitality," we are directed to serve vegetables, salads, and soups. The new *McCall's* cookbook suggests that a man's favorite dinner is London broil. A "Ladies Luncheon" would consist of cheese dishes and vegetables, but no meat. A section of one cookbook entitled "For Men Only" reinforces the omnipresence of meat in men's lives. What is for men only? London broil, cubed steak, and beef dinner.[12]

Twentieth-century cookbooks only serve to confirm the historical pattern found in the nineteenth century, when British working-class families could not afford sufficient meat to feed the entire family. "For the man only" appears continually in the menus of these families when referring to meat. In adhering to the mythologies of a culture (men need meat; meat gives bull-like strength), the male "breadwinner" received the meat. Social historians continually report that the "lion's share" of meat went to the husband.

What, then, was for women during the nineteenth century? On Sundays, they might have a modest but good dinner. On the other days, their food was bread with butter or drippings, weak tea, pudding, and vegetables. One observer noted, "The wife, in very poor families, is probably the worst fed of the household." His comment was recorded in 1863 by Dr. Edward Smith in the first national food survey of British dietary habits, which revealed that the major difference in the diet of men and women in the same family was the amount of meat consumed. In one rural county of England, the investigators were told that the women and children "eat the potatoes and look at the meat."[13]

Where poverty forced a conscious distribution of meat, men received it. Many women emphasized that they had saved the meat for their husbands. They were articulating the prevailing connections between meat eating and the male role: "I keep it for him; he *has* to have it." Sample menus for South London laborers "showed extra meat, extra fish, extra cakes, or a different quality of meat for the man." Women ate meat once a week with their children, while the husband consumed meat and bacon "almost daily," according to Smith.

Early in the present century, the Fabian Women's group in London launched a four-year study in which they recorded the daily budget of thirty families in a working-class community. These budgets were collected and explained in a compassionate book, *Round About a Pound a Week*. Here is perceived clearly the sexual politics of meat: "In the household that spends 10s [shillings] or even less on food, only one kind of diet is possible, and that is the man's diet. The children have what is left over. There must be a Sunday joint, or, if that is not possible, at least a Sunday dish of meat, in order to satisfy the father's desire for the kind of food he relishes, and most naturally, therefore, intends to have." More succinctly, we are told: "Meat is bought for the men. The leftover meat from the Sunday dinner is eaten cold by him the next day."[14] Poverty also determines who carves the meat. As Cicely Hamilton discovered during this same period, women carve when they know there is not enough meat to go around.[15]

In situations of abundance, sex-role assumptions about meat are not so blatantly expressed. For this reason, the diets of English upper-class women and men are much more similar than the diets of upper-class women and working-class women. Moreover, with the abundance of meat available in the United States, as opposed to the restricted amount available in England, there has been enough for all, except when meat supplies were controlled. For instance, at a time when enslaved black men received half a pound of meat per day, enslaved black women often found that they received little more than a quarter pound a day at times.[16]

During wartime, government rationing policies reserve the right to meat for the epitome of the masculine man, the soldier. With meat rationing in effect for civilians during World War II, the per capita consumption of meat in the Army and Navy was about two-and-a-half times that of the average civilian. Russell Baker observed that World War II began a "beef madness . . . when richly fatted beef was force-fed into every putative American warrior."[17] In contrast to the recipe books for civilians, which praised complex carbohydrates, cookbooks for soldiers contained variation upon variation of meat dishes. One survey conducted of four military training camps reported that the soldier consumed 131 grams of protein, 201 grams of fat, and 484 grams of carbohydrates daily.[18] Hidden costs of warring masculinity are to be found in the provision of male defined foods to the warriors.

Women are the food preparers; meat has to be cooked to be palatable for people. Thus, in a particular culture, women accede to the dietary demands of their husbands, especially when it comes to meat. The feminist surveyors of women's budgets in the early twentieth century observed:

> It is quite likely that someone who had strength, wisdom, a vitality, who did not live that life in those tiny, crowded rooms, in that lack of light and air, who was not bowed with worry, but was herself economically independent of the man who earned the money, could lay out his few shillings with a better eye to a scientific food value. It is quite as likely, however, that the man who earned the money would entirely refuse the scientific food, and demand his old tasty kippers and meat.[19]

A discussion of nutrition during wartime contained this aside: it was one thing, they acknowledged, to demonstrate that there were many viable alternatives to meat, "but it is another to convince a man who enjoys his beefsteak."[20] The male prerogative to eat meat is an external, observable activity implicitly reflecting a recurring fact: meat is a symbol of male dominance.

It has traditionally been felt that the working man needs meat for strength. A superstition analogous to homeopathic principles operates in this belief: in eating the muscle of strong animals, we will become strong. According to the mythology of patriarchal culture, meat promotes strength; the attributes of masculinity are achieved through eating these masculine foods. Visions of meat-eating football players, wrestlers, and boxers lumber through our brains in this equation. Though vegetarian weightlifters and athletes in other fields have demonstrated the equation to be fallacious, the mythology and the myth remain: men are strong, men need to be strong, thus men need meat. The literal evocation of male power is found in the concept of meat.

Meat is king: this noun describing meat is a noun denoting male power. Vegetables—a generic term meat-eaters use for all foods that aren't meat—have become as associated with women as meat is with men, recalling on a subconscious level the days of Woman the Gatherer. Since women have been made subsidiary in a male-dominated, meat-eating world, so has our food: the foods associated with second-class citizens are considered to be second-class protein. Just as it is thought a woman can't make it on her own, so we think that vegetables can't make a meal on their own, despite the fact that meat is only second-hand vegetables, and vegetables provide, on the average, more than twice the vitamins and minerals of meat. Meat is upheld as a powerful, irreplaceable item of food. The message is clear: the vassal vegetable should content itself with its assigned place and not attempt to dethrone king meat. After all, how can one enthrone women's foods, when women cannot be kings?

Men who decide to eschew meat eating are deemed effeminate; the failure of men to eat meat announces that they are not masculine. Nutritionist Jean Mayer suggested that "the more men sit at their desks all day, the more they want to be reassured about their maleness in eating those large slabs of bleeding meat, which are the last symbol of machismo."[21] The late Marty Feldman observed. "It has to do with the function of the male within our society. Football players drink beer because it's a man's drink, and eat steak because it's a man's meal. The emphasis is on 'man-sized portions,' 'hero' sandwiches; the whole terminology of meat-eating reflects this masculine bias."[22] Meat-and-potatoes men are our stereotypical strong and hearty, rough and ready, able males. Hearty beef stews are named "Manhandlers." One's maleness is reassured by the food one eats. During the 1973 meat boycott, men were reported to observe the boycott when dining out with their wives or eating at home, but when they dined without their wives, they ate London broil and other meats.[23]

What is it about meat that makes it a symbol and celebration of male dominance? Superficially, we might observe that the male role of hunter of meat has been transposed to the male role of eater of meat. But there is much more to meat's role as symbol than this.

Both the words "men" and "meat" have undergone lexicographical narrowing. Originally generic terms, they are now closely associated with their specific referent. Meat no longer means all foods; the word man, we realize, no longer includes women. Meat represents *the essence or principal part of something* according to the *American Heritage Dictionary*. Vegetable, on the other hand, represents the least desirable characteristics: *suggesting or like a vegetable, as in passivity or dullness of existence, monotonous, inactive.* Meat is *something one enjoys or excels in,* vegetable becomes representative of someone who doesn't enjoy anything: a *person who leads a monotonous, passive or merely physical existence.*

A complete reversal has occurred in the definition of the word vegetable. Whereas its original sense was to *be lively, active,* it is now viewed as dull, monotonous, passive. To vegetate is to lead a passive existence, just as to be feminine is to lead a passive existence. Once vegetables are viewed as women's food, by association they become viewed as "feminine," passive.

Men's need to disassociate themselves from women's food (as in the myth in which the last Bushman flees in the direction opposite from women and their vegetable food) has been institutionalized in sexist attitudes toward vegetables, and the word vegetable is used to express criticism or disdain. Colloquially, it is a synonym for a person severely brain-damaged or in a coma. In addition, vegetables are thought to have a tranquilizing, dulling, numbing effect on people who consume them, and so, we can't possibly get strength from them. According to this perverse incarnation of Brillat-Savarin's theory that you are what you eat, to eat a vegetable is to become a vegetable.

In her essay, "Deciphering a Meal," the noted anthropologist Mary Douglas suggests that the order in which we serve foods, and the food we insist on being present at a meal, reflect a taxonomy of classification which mirrors and reinforces our larger culture. A meal is an amalgam of food dishes, each a constituent part of the whole, each with an assigned value. In addition, each dish is introduced in a precise order. A meal does not begin with dessert, nor end with soup. All is seen as leading up to and then coming down from the entree, which is meat. The pattern is evidence of stability. As Douglas explains, "The ordered system which is a meal represents all the ordered systems associated with it. Hence the strong arousal power of a threat to weaken or confuse that category."[24] To remove meat is to threaten the structure of the large patriarchal culture.

Marabel Morgan, one expert on how women should accede to every male desire, reported in her *Total Woman Cookbook* that one must be careful about introducing foods which are seen as a threat: "I discovered that Charlie seemed threatened by certain foods. He was suspicious of my casseroles, thinking I had sneaked in some wheat germ or 'good-for-you' vegetables that he wouldn't like."[25]

Mary McCarthy's *Birds of America* provides a fictional illustration of the intimidating aspect to a male of woman's refusal of meat. Miss Scott, a vegetarian, is invited to a NATO General's house for Thanksgiving. Her refusal of turkey angers the General. Not able to take this rejection seriously, as male dominance requires a continual recollection of itself on everyone's plate, the General loads her plate up with turkey and then ladles gravy over the potatoes as well as the meat, contaminating her subsidiary foods as well. McCarthy's description of his actions with the food mirrors the war-like customs associated with military battles. "He had seized the gravy boat like a weapon in hand-to-hand combat. No wonder they had made him a Brigadier General—at least that mystery was solved." The General continues to behave in a bellicose fashion and, after dinner, proposes a toast in honor of an eighteen-year-old who has enlisted to fight in Vietnam with the rhetorical question. "What's so sacred about a civilian?" This upsets the hero, necessitating that the General's wife apologize for her husband's behavior: "Between you and me," she confides in him, "it kind of got under his skin to see that girl refusing to touch her food. I saw that right away."[26]

Male belligerence in this area is not limited to fictional military men. Husbands who batter their wives—who, according to social scientists, are insecure men who feel powerless and not sufficiently masculine—have often been triggered to do violence against women by the absence of meat.

This is not to say that women's failure to serve meat is the cause of the violence against them. This is patently not true. The true cause of a gun going off is not the trigger. The causes of domestic violence reside within the batterer and male-dominated society.[27] Yet, as a trigger to this accepted violence meat is hardly a trivial item. "Real" men eat meat. Failing to honor the importance of this symbol catalyzes male rage. As one battered woman reported. "It would start off with him being angry over trivial little things, a trivial little thing like cheese instead of meat on a sandwich."[28] Another battered wife stated, "A month ago he threw scalding water over me, leaving a scar on my right arm, all because I gave him a pie with potatoes and vegetables for his dinner, instead of fresh meat."[29]

Men who become vegetarians challenge an essential part of the masculine role. They are opting for women's food. How dare they? Refusing meat means a man is effeminate, a "sissy," a "fruit." Indeed, in 1836, one response to the vegetarian regimen of that day, known as Grahamism, charges that "Emasculation is the first fruit of Grahamism."[30]

Choosing not to eat meat means that men repudiate their masculine privileges. *The New York Times* explored this idea in an editorial on the masculine nature of meat-eating. Instead of "the John Wayne type," epitome of the masculine meat-eater, the new male hero is "vulnerable" like Alan Alda, Mikhail Baryshnikov, and Phil Donahue. According to the *Times,* they might eat fish and chicken, but not red meat. Alda and Donahue, among other men, have not only repudiated macho food but also the macho role. Writes the editor, "Believe me, the end of macho marks the end of the meat and potatoes man."[31] Believe me, we won't miss either.

NOTES

1. Waverly Root and Richard de Rochemont, *Eating in America: A History* (New York: William Morrow, 1976), p. 279.

2. Lisa Leghorn and Mary Roodkowsky, *Who Really Starves: Women and World Hunger* (New York: Friendship Press, 1977), p. 21.

3. Lloyd Shearer, "Intelligence Report: Does Diet Determine Sex?", summarizing the conclusions of Dr. Joseph Stolkowski. *Parade Magazine,* June 27, 1982, p. 7.

4. William and Ceil Baring-Gould. *The Annotated Mother Goose* (New York: Bramhall House, 1962), p. 103.

5. Elizabeth Cady Stanton, *The Woman's Bible* (Seattle: Coalition Task Force on Women and Religion, 1974, reprint of the 1898 edition published in New York by European Publishing Co.), p. 91.

6. Frederick J. Simoons, *Eat Not This Flesh: Food Avoidances in the Old World* (Madison: University of Wisconsin, 1967), pp. 108

7. Leghorn and Roodkowsky, *Who Really Starves: Women and World Hunger,* p. 20.

8. Simoons, p. 73.

9. *Ibid.*

10. Bridget O'Laughlin. "Mediation of Contradiction: Why Mbum Women do not eat Chicken" in Michelle Rosaldo and Louise Lamphere, *Woman, Culture and Society* (Stanford: Stanford University Press, 1974), p. 303.

11. Sunset Books and Sunset Magazines, *Sunset Menu Cook Book* (Menlo Park, Ca.: Lane Magazine and Book Co., 1969), pp. 139, 140.

12. *Oriental Cookery* from ChunKing and Mazola Corn Oil. This cookbook was called to my attention by Karen Lindsey.

13. Dr. Edward Smith, *Practical Dietary for Families, Schools, and the Labouring Classes* (London: Walton and Materly, 1864).

14. Maud Pember Reeves, *Round About a Pound a Week* (London: Virago Press, 1979, reprint of 1913 edition published by G. Bell and Sons), pp. 144, 97, 113, et seq.

15. Cicely Hamilton, *Marriage as a Trade* (London: The Women's Press, 1981, reprint of 1909 edition), p. 75.

16. Todd L. Savitt, *Medicine and Slavery: The Diseases and Health Care of Blacks in Antebellum Virginia* (Urbana and Chicago: University of Illinois Press, 1978), p. 91.

17. Russell Baker, *The New York Times,* April 3, 1973, p. 43.

18. Aaron M. Altschul, *Proteins: Their Chemistry and Politics* (New York: Basic Books, Inc., 1965), p. 101, footnote.

19. Reeves, p. 131.

20. Helen Hunscher and Margerita Huyck, *Nutrition,* p. 414.

21. *The Boston Globe,* n.d. (circa 1975).

22. Marty Feldman, quoted in Ryan Berry, *The Vegetarians* (Brookline, Mass: Autumn Press, 1979), pp. 31–32.

23. *The New York Times,* April 15, 1973, p. 38.

24. Mary Douglas, "Deciphering a Meal," in *Implicit Meanings; Essays in Anthropology* (London: Routledge and Kegan Paul, 1975), pp. 273, 258.

25. Marabel Morgan, *The Total Woman Cookbook* (New Jersey: Fleming H. Revell Co., 1980), p. 13.

26. Mary McCarthy, *Birds of America* (New York: New American Library, 1965), pp. 166–173.

27. Though I use the term 'battered wives,' I am referring to a phenomenon not bounded by a marriage license.

28. R. Emerson Dobash and Russell Dobash, *Violence Against Wives: A Case Against the Patriarchy* (New York: The Free Press, 1979), p. 100.

29. Erin Pizey, *Scream Quietly or the Neighbors Will Hear* (Hammondsworth, England: Penguin Books, 1974), pp. 34–35.

30. James C. Whorton, "'Tempest in a Flesh-Pot': The Formulation of a Physiological Rationale for Vegetarianism," *Journal of the History of Medicine,* 32 (1977), p. 122.

31. *The New York Times,* editorial, August 17, 1981.

QUESTIONS

1. Explain what Adams means by "'Real' men eat meat."
2. Adams discusses what she calls the "male prerogative to eat meat." She gives historical examples of women eating no meat, or eating very little of it, so that men in their families would have larger servings of meat. She then notes: "In situations of abundance, sex-role assumptions about meat are not so blatantly expressed . . . with the abundance of meat available in the United States . . . there has been enough for all, except when meat supplies were controlled." The "male prerogative to eat meat" does not require women to forgo eating meat, when there's enough meat for everyone. In these circumstances, how else might the "male prerogative to eat meat" manifest itself?
3. Adams writes that "Men who become vegetarians challenge an essential part of the masculine role. They are opting for women's food. How dare they? Refusing meat means a man is effeminate, a 'sissy,' a 'fruit.'" Is this an accurate description of how vegetarianism is now understood in your community?
4. According to Adams, meat is associated with men, masculinity, and "masculine" traits such as strength, and vegetables are associated with women, femininity, and "feminine" traits such as passivity. Do you agree? Can you find a food commercial or other advertisement that associates meat-eating with masculinity, men, or "masculine" traits? Can you find an advertisement that associates meat-eating with femininity, women, or "feminine" traits? Can you find an advertisement that associates eating vegetables with masculinity, men, or "masculine" traits? Can you find an advertisement that associates eating vegetables with femininity, women, or "feminine traits"?

ALICE A. DECK

"Now Then—Who Said Biscuits?"

The Black Woman Cook as Fetish in American Advertising

Alice Deck analyzes several early twentieth-century advertisements that depict African-American women as "Mammy" figures—a stereotyped African-American cook and domestic worker who enjoys cooking and serving white people. Deck discusses the historical origins of Aunt Jemima ads, one example of Mammy figures in advertising.

Alice A. Deck, "'Now Then—Who Said Biscuits?' The Black Woman Cook as Fetish in American Advertising, 1905–1953." From *Kitchen Culture in America: Popular Representations of Food, Gender, and Race* (University of Pennsylvania Press, 2001), 69–77; 79–80.

One of the prevailing images of black women in American culture that has persisted since the early days of slavery is that of the quintessential cook and housekeeper. In novels,[1] films,[2] television sitcoms, and print ads for cooking products, the black domestic is portrayed as a very large, dark earth mother who represents fecundity, self-sufficiency, and endless succor. This black cook/domestic, often referred to as Mammy,[3] exists to do nothing but prepare and serve food, along with a hearty helping of her homespun wisdom about life, to her own black family and to the white families for whom she works. Mammy's legendary creativity with preparing food is attributed to her "magical" powers with blending just the right foods and spices to delight those whom she feeds. The black cook, according to both popular imagery and culinary historians, works best not from printed recipes but from a memory that links her to previous generations of slave women and black earth mothers.[4] Given her propensity for improvisation, to "add a little of this and a little of that" as the spirit may move her on a given day, the same dish never tastes exactly the same no matter how many times she may prepare it.[5] Though she is sometimes portrayed in the popular media with a black male companion, Mammy's large breasts, muscular arms, and wide hips signify a unifying of male and female sexualities. She usually needs no other to complete her, yet many others in her orbit can be completed by her. All of this renders the black Mammy, as we see her depicted in American popular culture, as a fetish—an idealized representation of an autonomous black woman. . .

During the first decade of the twentieth century, the Washburn-Crosby milling company ran a series of black-and-white ads for its Gold Medal flour that featured a black woman dressed as a Mammy, standing next to either a large sack of flour or a table laden with breads, cakes, and pies that she presumably baked. In all of its primary and secondary details, a 1910 publication of the ad exemplifies the idealized representation of the black woman cook as a cross-cultural fetish. Primarily, the ad attempts to convey the idea that no matter which of the particular American regional recipes used, one can make superior biscuits with Gold Medal flour. It appeals to the

potential buyer's sense of belonging to a nation unified by a particular type of baked bread. Yet the secondary discourse emerging from the specific details of this particular picture relies on the viewer's familiarity with the nineteenth-century idealization of the southern black Mammy—wearing a white bandanna and a checkered apron—as the sole authority on baking biscuits. The black woman stands alone in this ad with only the large sack of flour and a tabletop. The isolation from other people signifies her autonomy, yet she is tied to the white sack of flour by the visual similarities between its tied ends and the tips of her white bandanna. Hence she is as much defined as a cook by her relationship to the flour sack as she exemplifies the image of reflexivity—her Mammy costume is the signifier of itself as autonomous agency.

An integral part of the Mammy's attire is the broad smile displaying clean, even, white teeth because it suggests not only a cheerful personality but also pleasure in what she does. This cheerful aspect actually works to counterbalance the potentially aggressive signals contained in the pointed ends of her bandanna and the sharp angles of her elbows and hands. Her right index finger points toward the viewer but, like her gaze, is at an angle as though to soften the implied command/reprimand. Her left hand is balled into a fist placed on her left hip, which, in other contexts, could suggest anger, defiance, or a sassy retort. In the context of the caption at the top of the frame ("Now then—Who said Biscuits?"), the woman's body language suggests a friendly command to use the product or even a friendly challenge to a biscuit bake-off using Gold Medal flour. Not only is the black woman the only person pictured in the ad, she dominates the right side of the ad's frame such that her left elbow can barely be contained within the black border. All of this says that the black woman is a powerful, uncontested authority on baking biscuits and we had better trust her endorsement of the product.

In a 1905 ad for Gold Medal flour that appeared in the July issue of *McClure's Magazine*, the same woman is photographed in the same costume on the left side of the frame and cropped at an angle that draws our attention to Mammy's broad shoulders and the width of her hips. In contrast to the taller, more angular image of the 1910 ad, in this one the Mammy's spherical shape emphasizes her womanly fecundity and nurturing skills. Her large arms are posed to suggest that she could cradle the potential consumer and viewer of the ad next to her ample bosom. In contrast to the sharp points on the bandanna in the 1910 ad, the ends of Mammy's bandanna in the 1905 ad are short, small, and suggestive of a soft bow on the top of her head. It is the mark of a female being who, in the context of the message written below the picture, personifies the natural forces of the physical body. . .

The overall appearance of the black woman in the two ads for Gold Medal flour draws on another one first used to sell pancake flour at the World's Columbian Exposition of May–November 1893 in Chicago. There, a woman named Nancy Green was hired by the Davis Milling Company to mix a processed pancake flour and cook pancakes on an open griddle. Nancy Green was padded to fill out her physique and then attired in a full-skirted dress and a white apron, with a bandanna tied around her head. She answered to the name of Aunt Jemima, and while cooking pancakes, she greeted guests, sang songs, and told stories of life ("her past life") on a Louisiana plantation. The Aunt Jemima exhibit attracted large crowds, and many merchants who attended placed orders for the pancake flour. After the exposition, Nancy Green, as Aunt Jemima, began participating in sales promotions across the country.[6] An image of her face was placed on the outside of the box containing the pancake flour that to this day bears the name of Aunt Jemima.

Of particular relevance to this chapter is the contextualizing "life story" of Aunt Jemima that was created as early as 1895 and printed in the thousands of ads and pamphlets that were distributed nationally. Aunt Jemima, according to her "biographers," was a slave before the Civil War on a Louisiana plantation owned by Colonel Higbee. After the war, she chose to remain on the plantation as Colonel Higbee's cook, and she took pleasure in serving her famous pancakes to the many guests who came to visit. Missing from this "biography" of Aunt Jemima is any mention of a wife for Colonel Higbee. One study suggests that the creators of the Aunt Jemima legend wanted the white woman consumer to insert herself into the story as Colonel Higbee's wife and the mistress of his plantation, to imagine herself being waited on by contented black servants and a doting husband.[7] My own reading of this omission is based on the historical accounts of the relationship between the southern white master and black women slaves who were assigned to work in his house. It was sometimes a relationship based on sexual coercion due in part to a tacit agreement among white southern men that a gentleman, no matter his wife's protests against it, was entitled to have a paramour.[8] Other reasons include the death or infertility of the white mistress or, if she had given birth to children, her subsequent disinterest in sex.[9] The absence of any references to Colonel Higbee's wife in the legend merely foregrounds a historical reality that some southern white women relinquished many of their conjugal and domestic duties to a female slave, including feeding their infants, children, and husbands. This white-wife gap in the legend allows Aunt Jemima to serve alone as Colonel Higbee's mistress. She, as his uncontested female subordinate, satisfied his desire to be fed on her limitless supply of warm food, personal devotion, and loyalty. The effect all of this may have had on white women who read the legend of Aunt Jemima in the turn-of-the-century ads for the processed pancake flour was a desire not just to hire a black cook but to replace Aunt Jemima altogether as the primary source of Colonel Higbee's nourishment.

Aunt Jemima's loyalty to Colonel Higbee was without bounds. According to the version of the legend printed on a 1926 ad appearing in the *Pictorial Review,* she never revealed her secret recipe for her famous pancakes until after Colonel Higbee died. She then sold it to the representative of a northern milling company, which developed it into a product that people all over the United States could use to make pancakes as good as those made originally by Aunt Jemima. Aunt Jemima agreed to attend the Columbian Exposition in 1893, and to travel the country selling the pancake flour for the milling company afterwards, out of the goodness of her heart and an earnest desire to help Americans enjoy their breakfasts.

In his *Slave in a Box: The Strange Career of Aunt Jemima,* M. M. Manring explains that this legend encompassed an idea about the Old South and its usefulness to the new post–Civil War United States. The Old South, as imagined by postbellum white southerners in their diaries and letters, was a place of white leisure, an abundance of well-prepared food, and a host of contented black people who did all of the work.[10] The imaginary Old South did not disappear after the Civil War, primarily because of ad campaigns that featured people like Aunt Jemima and Rastus, the black man on the Cream of Wheat cereal box, who were so dedicated to domesticity in the service of white people; hence the Old South was a New South only in its desire to share its culture with northern white entrepreneurs and to forget any cultural and political differences that may have led to the Civil War. Unlike the millions of blacks who migrated north beginning in the late nineteenth century through the first three decades of the twentieth century, Aunt Jemima never tried to forget her southern culture and assimilate into the northern urban lifestyle. She sold her pancake flour out of a belief that southern "down home" cooking could be adapted to a northern, faster-paced lifestyle and retain its high standards of nourishment. . .

The ads discussed in this chapter show how the product manufacturers and the advertising agencies—all white males—gave form to white middle-class America's deep-laying desires for black domestic servants and being catered to by contented black women concerned only with satisfying their sensorial cravings. It is an ostensibly venerable depiction, but beneath its surface lies the political determination to keep the black woman forever in that class as a happy servant. Even when she is not physically present in the ad, representations of her image on boxes of pancake flour, small dolls, and kitchen utensils render the idea of her subordination palpable.

NOTES

I wish to thank Kal Alston, Cathy Johnson Adams, Juliana Chang, Maurice Manring, and Rychetta Watkins for a series of stimulating conversations about this topic while I was developing this chapter.

1. In novels such as Harriet Beecher Stowe's *Uncle Tom's Cabin* (1852), William Faulkner's *The Sound and the Fury* (1929), Fannie Hurst's *Imitation of Life* (1933), Margaret Mitchell's *Gone with the Wind* (1934), Margaret Walker's *Jubilee* (1966), and Toni Morrison's *Song of Solomon* (1977) and *Tar Baby* (1982), a black woman known for her associations with food preparation, with feeding other characters, and with emotional nurturing plays a central role.

2. See *Hallelujah,* 1929; *Imitation of Life,* 1934; *Gone with the Wind,* 1939; *Clara's Heart,* 1988; *Ghost,* 1990; and *Soul Food,* 1997.

3. Mammy was a name given to black women who worked in any number of capacities in white homes on antebellum southern plantations. There is considerable scholarly debate as to the accuracy of popular representations of Mammy. See Deborah Gray White's *Aren't I a Woman? Female Slaves in the Plantation South,* Trudier Harris's *From Mammies to Militants: Domestics in Black American Literature,* and Patricia Turner's *Ceramic Uncles and Celluloid Mammies: Black Images and Their Influence on Culture.* In this chapter, I will be referring to Mammy as a cook and examining how she is portrayed in ads for American cooking products.

4. By black earth mothers I am referring specifically to Mary McLeod Bethune (1875–1955), founder of Bethune Cookman College and in 1935 the National Council of Negro Women, and Dorothy Height (b. 1912), president since 1957 of the National Council of Negro Women. Their recipes for traditional African American dishes are routinely included in cookbooks such as *Celebrating Our Mothers' Kitchens* published by the National Council of Negro Women (1994).

5. In her novel *Sula,* Toni Morrison's description of a once thriving, culturally rich black community includes a reference to Reba's Grill, a black-owned eatery whose owner "cooked in her hat because she couldn't remember the ingredients without it" (3). Wearing a hat while preparing food in this instance meets more than a sanitation requirement. The hat is endowed with magical properties. In *The Welcome Table: African American Heritage Cooking,* Jessica B. Harris discusses the fact that many black cooks, women and men, did not and do not cook from a printed recipe, nor do they use measuring cups and spoons. The best recipes are passed down orally from one generation to the next. See Harris, 83.

Two excellent cultural and historical studies of the Aunt Jemima figure and its impact on American advertising are M. M. Manring's *Slave in a Box: The Strange*

Career of Aunt Jemima (see esp. chap. 3, "From Minstrel Show to the World's Fair: The Birth of Aunt Jemima," 60–78); and Doris Witt's *Black Hunger* (see esp. chap. 1. "Look Ma, the Real Aunt Jemima . . .," 21–53).

6. Maurice Manring makes this argument in his *Slave in a Box*, "The Absent Mistress," 139–42.

7. I refer specifically to the sexual harassment of slave women by white men as described in *The History of Mary Prince, A West Indian Slave, Related by Herself* (1830) and in Harriet Brent Jacobs's *Incidents in the Life of a Slave Girl* (1861). As a domestic servant living in close proximity to the white family, the slave woman/concubine was also the victim of the slave mistress's jealousy. See Minrose Gwin. "Green-Eyed Monsters of the Slaveocracy: Jealous Mistresses in Two Slave Narratives." See the following historical studies for discussions of the sexual plight of female slaves in the plantation South: Eugene Genovese, *Roll, Jordan, Roll: The World the Slaves Made,* 413–31; Herbert Gutman, *The Black Family in Slavery and Freedom, 1750–1925,* part 1; and Deborah Gray White, *Aren't I a Woman? Female Slaves in the Plantation South,* 27–118.

8. Two American novels, Margaret Mitchell's *Gone with the Wind* (1936) and Margaret Walker's *Jubilee* (1966), include a portrayal of a white wife who refused to have a sexual relationship with her husband after giving birth to his child or children. Walker includes it as an explanation for the birth of her central character, the mulatto slave Vyry, whose black slave mother, Hetty, died from having too many babies too soon by her white master. See *Jubilee*, 3–14.

9. See Manring, *Slave in a Box*, 95–109.

WORKS CITED

Aunt Jemima products. "Poor Aunt Jemima Had to Mix Everything Herself!" Advertisement. *Pictorial Review* March 1920: 63.

Faulkner, William. *The Sound and the Fury.* New York: Vintage Books, 1954.

Genovese, Eugene. *Roll, Jordan. Roll: The World the Slaves Made.* New York: Pantheon Books, 1976.

Gutman, Herbert. *The Black Family in Slavery and Freedom, 1750–1925.* New York: Pantheon Books, 1974.

Gwin, Minrose. "Green-Eyed Monsters of the Slaveocracy: Jealous Mistresses in Two Slave Narratives." *Conjuring: Black Women, Fiction, and Literary Tradition.* Ed. Marjorie Pryse and Hortense Spillers. Bloomington: Indiana University Press, 1985, 39–52.

Harris, Jessica B. *The Welcome Table: African American Heritage Cooking.* New York: Simon and Schuster, 1995.

Harris, Trudier. *From Mammies to Militants: Domestics in Black American Literature.* Philadelphia; Temple University Press, 1982.

Manring, M. M. *Slave in a Box: The Strange Career of Aunt Jemima.* Charlottesville: University Press of Virginia, 1998.

Mitchell, Margaret. *Gone with the Wind.* New York: Avon Books, 1964.

Morrison. Toni. *Suta.* New York: Plume, 1982.

———. *Song of Solomon.* New York: Plume, 1982.

———. *Tar Baby.* New York: Plume, 1982.

National Council of Negro Women. *Celebrating Our Mothers' Kitchens.* Memphis: Wimmer, 1994.

Stowe, Harriet B. *Uncle Tom's Cabin.* New York: Macmillan, 1994.

Walker, Margaret. *Jubilee.* New York: Bantam Books, 1966.

Washburn-Crosby products. "Now Then—Who Said Biscuits?" Advertisement for Gold Medal flour, 1906.

———. "Good Bread—Good Nature." Advertisement for Gold Medal flour. *McClure's Magazine,* July 1905: 1.

Witt, Doris. *Black Hunger: Food and the Politics of U.S. Identity.* New York: Oxford University Press, 1999.

QUESTIONS

1. The author analyzes some early twentieth-century advertisements depicting African-American women as "Mammy" figures. What is the Mammy stereotype?

2. According to the Mammy stereotype, a Mammy is a respected and trusted authority on cooking. How is this portrayal—which might seem like a superficially positive portrayal—problematic?

3. Part of the Mammy stereotype is that Mammies are contented and enjoy cooking. How does the "happy servant" stereotype function to reinforce racial discrimination?

LISA M. HELDKE

Cultural Food Colonialism

Lisa Heldke is a "food adventurer"—someone who likes to try out new foods, especially new and different "ethnic" cuisines. In this reading, an excerpt from her book *Exotic Appetites: Ruminations of a Food Adventurer*, Heldke introduces the concept of *cultural food colonialism* and argues that food adventuring can be a form of it. *Cultural colonialism* is the appropriation of cultural practices, and *cultural food colonialism* is the appropriation of cuisines or food practices. We tend to think it's unproblematic to casually try out new cuisines. But food practices are central to cultures, and therefore co-opting food practices can be injurious to a culture. Casually engaging with and experimenting with other cultures' food practices can be disrespectful, just as casually engaging with their spiritual practices would be disrespectful.

I was becoming a food adventurer, and I (mostly) didn't look back. After eating my way through the inexpensive ethnic restaurants of Chicago and Evanston during graduate school (the weekend I defended my dissertation I celebrated with meals at both an Indian and a Peruvian restaurant), I moved to a small town in Minnesota, and then to another small town in Minnesota. . .

Despite the dearth of opportunities for food adventuring in my own town, I managed to scrape by. On weekend visits to Minneapolis/St. Paul, trips to professional conventions, sabbaticals in other towns, and summer vacations, I collected eating adventures in restaurants serving all sorts of ethnic cuisines, ranging from the relatively routine (Vietnamese food in Minneapolis/St. Paul) to the more unusual (Tibetan food at "America's Second Only Tibetan Restaurant" in Bloomington, Indiana). . .

"Experiment" was my middle name; I'd try (nearly) anything once, and I actively sought any and all opportunities to increase the number and range of eating adventures I had. Experimentation had its risks and dangers—the dangers of ordering a dish that was too spicy, too full of "weird" foods—but that risk was just part of the experiment, part of the adventure. I was not alone on my quests; wherever I adventured, I could always be sure of company. No matter what crowd I was in, there was always someone else like me, eager to eat things they'd never heard of before.

Over time, though, I started to have some suspicions about my food adventuring. For one thing, various experiences made me feel uncomfortable about the easy acquisitiveness with which I approached a new kind of food, the tenacity with which I collected adventures—as one might collect ritual artifacts from another culture without thinking about the appropriateness of removing them from their cultural setting. Other experiences made me reflect on the circumstances that conspired to bring these cuisines into my world in the first place. On my first visit to an Eritrean restaurant, for

Lisa Heldke, "Cultural Food Colonialism," from *Exotic Appetites: Ruminations of a Food Adventurer* (New York: Routledge, 2013). Reproduced with permission of Routledge Publishing Inc.

example, I found myself thinking about how disturbing and how complicated it was to be eating the food of people who were in the middle of yet another politically and militarily induced famine. An offhand remark in a murder mystery I was reading started me thinking about the *reasons* there were so many Vietnamese restaurants in Minneapolis/St. Paul, reasons directly connected to the Vietnam War and the resultant dislocation of Vietnamese and Hmong people.[1]

CULTURAL COLONIALISM: WHAT IS IT?

Eventually, I put a name to my activity, to my penchant for cooking and eating ethnic foods—most frequently and most notably the foods of economically dominated or "third world" cultures.[2] The name I chose was "cultural food colonialism" because, as I had come to see, my adventure eating was (and continues to be) strongly motivated by an attitude with deep connections to Western colonialism. When I began to examine my tendency to go culture hopping in the kitchen and in restaurants, I found that the attitude with which I approached such activities often bore an uncomfortable resemblance to the attitude of, say, nineteenth- and early twentieth-century European painters, anthropologists, and explorers who set out in search of ever "newer," ever more "remote" cultures that they could co-opt, borrow from freely and out of context, and use as the raw materials for their own efforts at creation and discovery. . .

Of course, my eating was not simply colonizing; it was also an effort to play, and to learn about other cultures in ways I intended to be respectful. But underneath, or alongside, or over and above all these other reasons, I could not deny that I was motivated by a deep desire to have contact with, and to somehow own an experience of, an Exotic Other, as a way of making myself more interesting. Food adventuring, I was coming to decide, made me a participant

in cultural colonialism, just as surely as eating Mexican strawberries in January made me a participant in economic colonialism. . .

CULTURAL FOOD COLONIALISM?

Food colonialism is a familiar notion—but in ordinary usage, it refers to things such as the disruption of local, self-sufficient food systems and their replacement with export economies, or the practice of multinational food firms moving their growing and production facilities "offshore" in order to exploit cheap labor and land.[3] Such material or economic food colonialism produces real poverty, malnutrition, and starvation in dominated economies, even as it produces artificially cheap foodstuffs for inhabitants of dominant economies. As such, it merits—and has received—considerable attention from both academic and nonacademic writers.

In contrast to such a familiar form of colonialism, identifying a form of colonialism as *cultural* might seem odd, even positively wrong to some readers; isn't colonialism *by definition* an economic or political relationship? A woman once responded to my discussion of various cultural forms of food colonialism quite angrily by saying, "Exploitation happens in our culture because our economy rewards multinational corporations such as Dole, not because I sometimes eat in a Chinese restaurant." She went on to say "'Cultural food colonialism' as distinct from economic food colonialism is a speculative construct which depends on someone else's reading of my motives. . . ."[4] In other words, cultural colonialism has no objective, external manifestations; it goes on—if at all—only in my head. As such, its existence can never be strictly verified, and its effects surely cannot be very damaging (to colonizer or colonized) if or when it does occur.

I disagree. As one way to make the notion of cultural colonialism comprehensible, if not compelling, consider a concept that is its close relative—the familiar notion of cultural imperialism. Cultural imperialism refers to the practice through which an economic or political power imposes its social or cultural practices and belief systems on another culture. Cultural imperialism both supports and is supported by economic and political forms of imperialism; it helps to make those other forms effective and powerful.[5]

In the most extreme forms of cultural imperialism, the imperial power may, as a matter of explicit policy, root out indigenous practices and replace them with its own in order to subdue and control a people. A notorious example of this in the United States was the system of boarding schools (often missionary schools run by the Catholic Church) for Native American children. Euroamerican governmental and religious officials forcibly removed Native children from their homes, and sent them to faraway schools from which they often were not allowed to return for years at a time. At school the boys' long hair was cut (a direct assault on the sacred traditions of many Native nations), and boys and girls were forbidden to speak their languages, eat their own foods, or engage in their own spiritual practices. They were forbidden to observe all the most central, daily, routine, and significant ways in which their cultural selves were defined and encouraged; in short, they were not allowed to be Lakotah, Ojibwe, Navajo, Hopi.

In other cases the imposition of the imperial culture may appear (even to inhabitants of the indigenous culture) less a systematic attempt to destroy the indigenous culture and more of a supposedly "benign," or even "welcome" side effect achieved in the process of pursuing other goals. Consider the "creation of a demand"—notice the absence of an agent in that phrase!—for U.S. fast foods, U.S. movies, and U.S. clothing in many contemporary third world nations. While first world businesses like McDonald's and Coca-Cola do not explicitly state as their goal the obliteration of indigenous foodways in places where they set up outlets, the erosion of those foodways and their replacement by desires for french fries and hamburgers constitutes an effect that is by no means simply accidental.

Cultural imperialism refers to the *imposition* of cultural practices by an economic or political power; cultural colonialism, as I shall be using the term, refers to the *appropriation* of such practices by such a power. In both cases, the cultural forms exist alongside, and work in the support of, economic and political forms. . .

I once talked with a woman who had grown up in a Scandinavian household in Minnesota, and who had welcomed the appearance of any new cuisine to the region as a way to alleviate what she saw as the unremitting boredom of the predominant food. She saw variety as an unproblematically positive thing to seek. I could sympathize; having grown up in a nearby region, I know that "white food" doesn't refer to a racial classification. But at the same time, I felt disappointed that she regarded her own heritage only as a limit, as something to be outgrown or cast aside. While I spent a number of years assiduously ignoring all the foods I grew up eating, in recent years I've found myself returning to some of these foods—a move that coincides with my philosophical turn toward theorizing about my own white identity. I see this exploration of my food heritage as in part an attempt to understand and connect myself to my particular ethnic location within the white racial system. As such, it is not an unthinking, romantic return to my roots, but rather a critical, reflective attempt to come to terms with those roots, to understand how they continue to shape my current ways of being in the world.

It would be grossly simplistic to say that rejecting one's culinary heritage is akin to refusing to acknowledge one's racial or ethnic identity. However, I do think there is something suspicious and troubling about a white person who valorizes all "ethnic" cuisines while simultaneously denigrating her own. Like the Euroamerican who idolizes the noble savage of North America and bemoans the loss of innocence in one's own culture, the food colonizer who has no time for her own food heritage creates a false image of both her own culture and the other's. . .

THE OTHER AS RESOURCE

As food adventurers, we have only accomplished part of our task when we have identified a cuisine as exotic and authentic. We must also see that cuisine as available to us—as something we are entitled to consume at will. This step is vital; without it, we would leave ourselves with tantalizing but utterly inaccessible ways to increase our cultural capital. So we must somehow define these exotic cuisines—and the people who create them—as available to us *in principle*. We must make our access to them utterly legitimate, as *we* define "legitimate."

That this is a step in the cultural colonization process—and a necessary step at that—tends to be invisible to adventurers, for a couple of reasons. One is that we tend to see food as the sort of thing one would *always* have access to, as a matter of course. Who would ever wonder if they have the right to eat another culture's cuisine, for heaven's sake? While we might think twice before trying on someone else's religious beliefs, or buying their archaeological treasures, or perhaps even playing their musical instruments, we tend to see food as just food—not the sort of thing that needs protecting, or that can be harmed in any way by someone else eating it or cooking it. We don't need to overcome any compunctions about eating the food of the Other, because, where food is concerned, no compunctions exist.

By now it's clear that I believe that thinking about a cuisine in this way—as either so tough or so superficial that it can't possibly be harmed—is wrong. In a sense, this entire book is my attempt to show why a cuisine is the sort of thing that can be harmed, in ways that bring harm to a culture. I can't, in a paragraph, dissolve this erroneous view. But I can contribute to its dissolution by suggesting that we look at food here slightly differently. Think not simply of eating someone else's food, but of walking into the middle of someone else's dining room or kitchen while their family is eating. Or into their meal of celebration or mourning. Deep and significant strands often connect a culture's foods and their customs and practices; practices central to the identity of a culture. (Think of wafer and wine in Christian communion, of matzoh at the Jewish Passover seder.) Given these connections, it is possible for the glib borrowing of foods engaged in by food colonizers to constitute a form of injury to another culture. Consider: it is generally recognized that to treat another culture's social and cultural practices casually or disrespectfully can actually harm members of that culture. In

the contemporary American context it may seem hard to believe that food practices could ever be as sensitive or significant as religious practices or moral imperatives, but it is still the case that they play important roles in cultures. (Indeed, they play an important role in mainstream American culture also; the largest demonstration I witnessed during my years in graduate school was a protest over the university's decision to change from Coke to Pepsi—or maybe Pepsi to Coke.) Recognizing that food is never just food, we may begin to realize that co-opting someone else's cuisine has the potential to affect another culture, just as does co-opting a spiritual practice.[6]

The other reason that this step—defining the Other as available in principle—tends to be invisible to adventurers is that availability is such a familiar element of so much of Western colonialist ideology that it has come to seem like a given, a fact of life. . .

Westerners invading indigenous African, Asian, and American cultures have often operated under the view that everything they found in the new setting was a resource available for them to take up and use. This view has extended not only to natural materials—minerals, timber, land—but also to people's very cultural products—art, music, stories, systems of governance, medicine, cooking. Explorers, artists, and entrepreneurs alike have treated the artistic and intellectual products of indigenous cultures—like their mineral deposits—as diamonds in the rough, raw materials awaiting refinement at the more capable hands and minds of colonizers. . .

It can be wonderful to explore the wealth of foods the world has produced, to hop from cuisine to cuisine. But when all I know of a culture is what I learn from the inside of a restaurant, I have a very limited picture indeed. Out of this experience, I create a superficial image of a culture, an image that treats that culture as if it were designed for my use and pleasure. This way of eating is harmful both to colonizer and colonized, for it reifies and reduces colonized people, substitutes for authentic relations to food the exotic quick fix and normalizes colonialism, encouraging us to condone it in its other, more destructive economic and political forms.

Furthermore, in the midst of my colonizing eating and cooking, I miss my own tradition. And I think my missing it is something more than mere nostalgia for something that never was, that my desire to be tied to a food tradition is not simply a consequence of romanticizing the notions of tradition and authenticity. Knowing who I am means knowing where I come from—and that means, in part, knowing what people in my past cooked and ate. I cannot replace my own food traditions by stuffing others' into the place where my own could be. All this succeeds in doing is violating their integrity, and leaving me feeling like a wannabe, someone who sees other traditions as rich, vibrant, interesting, and sees her own as at best boring, at worst, nonexistent.

In critically discussing this issue, I do not advocate some kind of hands-off policy for white people. Nor do I mean to suggest that ethnic groups are always utterly justified when they install roadblocks to their cultures. I mean only to question the *absoluteness* with which Euroamerican adventurers presume our right to explore whatever we want, and our concomitant belief that others have no legitimate right to deny our access.

NOTES

1. Sara Paretsky, in her 1985 book *Killing Orders* (New York: Ballantine, 1985), writes, "I stopped for a breakfast falafel sandwich at a storefront Lebanese restaurant . . . The decimation of Lebanon was showing up in Chicago as a series of restaurants and little shops, just as the destruction of Vietnam had been visible here a decade earlier. If you never read the news but ate out a lot you should be able to tell who was getting beaten up around the world" (36).

2. On the term "third world," cultural theorist Trinh T. Minh-ha writes in *Woman Native Other: Writing Postcoloniality and Feminism* (Bloomington: Indiana University Press, 1989), "To survive, [it] must necessarily have negative and positive connotations: negative when viewed in a vertical ranking system—'underdeveloped' compared to overindustrialized, 'underprivileged' within the already Second sex—and positive when understood sociopolitically as a subversive, 'non-aligned' force. Whether 'Third World' sounds negative or positive also depends on who uses it. Coming from you Westerners, the word can hardly mean the same as when it comes from Us members of the Third World. Quite predictably, you/we who condemn it most are both we who buy in and they who deny any participation in the bourgeois mentality of the West" (97–98). I am uncomfortable with this term, but I have chosen to use it anyway—primarily because none of the alternatives is any better. I do not encase the term in quotation marks, but that doesn't mean that I take it to be unproblematic.

3. For a detailed account of the modern Western food system, with attention to the colonialist relations it establishes between north and south, see David Goodman and Michael Redclift, *Refashioning Nature: Food, Ecology and Culture* (London: Routledge, 1991).

4. Marjorie Ireland, personal correspondence, June 28, 1991.

5. This is obviously a very truncated and simplified definition of cultural imperialism. For an interesting discussion of the complexity of this concept, see John Tomlinson, *Cultural Imperialism: A Critical Introduction* (Baltimore: Johns Hopkins University Press, 1991).

6. For most Euroamerican eaters to imagine what it would mean for our food to be injured by the practices of some other culture, we must turn to the arena of the health and safety of our food supply. There, we have very vivid ideas about the susceptibility of our food to the influences of others. Recall when U.S. inspectors found traces of cyanide in some grapes in a shipment from Chile. The response to Chilean fruit imports was immediate, and nearly hysterical.

The fact that we have trouble thinking of harms to our food practices that are not health-related is no virtue, on my view, but represents the degraded relationship to food that many of us in the United States now experience. For more on this general relationship, see Jeremy Iggers, *The Garden of Eating: Food, Sex, and the Hunger for Meaning* (New York: Basic Books, 1996).

QUESTIONS

1. In your opinion, is there something wrong with the Americanization of food—with cuisines being modified, in restaurants in the United States, to suit the tastes of American consumers? More generally, is there something wrong with cuisines being adapted to suit the tastes of members of a dominant culture?

2. *Cultural colonialism* is the appropriation of cultural practices, whereas *cultural imperialism* is the imposition of cultural practices by an economic or political power. An example of cultural imperialism mentioned by Heldke is American businesses such as McDonald's and Coca-Cola selling their products in developing countries, and thus displacing local foods. If people in these countries choose to buy these products, in what sense is it an *imposition* to sell them? Similarly, if immigrants to the United States open a restaurant serving their cuisine, in what sense could it be an *appropriation* of their culture to eat at their restaurant? What do you think Heldke would say?

3. Part of cultural food colonialism, according to Heldke, is seeing other cuisines as "available to us" to enjoy and use as we wish. This is analogous to the attitude of Western colonial powers invading Africa, Asia, and America, who saw raw materials and cultural products as "available for them to take up and use." In what ways is it problematic to see cultural products as "available to us"? Is it problematic just because it encourages mistreatment, or is it problematic in and of itself?

4. Heldke thinks that cuisines should be treated respectfully, similar to how a culture's religious beliefs and spiritual practices should be treated respectfully. "Recognizing that food is never just food, we may begin to realize that co-opting someone else's cuisine has the potential to affect another culture, just as does co-opting a spiritual practice." Do you agree? What does it take to treat a cuisine respectfully, in your opinion?

6 } Food and Religion*

In this introduction, we survey some of the many food ethical issues that arise within various religious traditions and also consider some ethical positions that such traditions take on food. To say the least, we do *not* attempt to address all the ethical issues concerning food that arise in religious contexts, nor do we attempt to cover every tradition's take on food. We look at just a few traditions and a few interesting writings on food ethics and religion: What do they say about the ethics of eating? Why do they say these things? If your own tradition is not represented, we hope the selected texts can serve nonetheless as a starting point for reflecting on what your tradition has to say about these issues and why it says those things.

* * *

Food has a prominent place in numerous religions. In the Christian and Jewish traditions, Adam and Eve originally sinned by eating. For Muslims and the ancient Norse, feasting is an important part of the heavenly afterlife. To Buddhists, Hindus, and Rastafaris, some foods are pollutants. Some religions offer food to their gods. Others bless food to make it an object of proper concern or of connection to the divine. Still others require us to eat this or that. In these traditions, food serves as a symbol, a community-builder, an identity-shaper, a source of joy and reverence. Our focus in this chapter is on religion and food ethics.

Here we use the terms "food ethics" and "religion" ecumenically as big tents under which many importantly different sorts of things may be grouped. Among the wide range of food ethical issues we consider in this chapter, for example, are religious views about the ethics of keeping, hurting, and killing animals, killing plants, dominion over creation, wastefulness, purity, blessing, atonement, and the connection between food and character. We realize, moreover, that it might be a stretch to label some of the views engaged by selected readings in this chapter as "religious" on a stringent understanding of that term; Lisa Kemmerer's "Indigenous Traditions," for instance, addresses some views that are recognizably spiritual but perhaps not religious in a strict sense. We hope that our ecumenical usage of the term can bring these important traditions to bear on the discussion without reducing them to something they are not.

How, then, does an engagement with religious traditions (broadly construed) illuminate and complicate the task of thinking through the ethics of eating?

---

*Matthew C. Halteman is a co-author of this chapter.

THE SURFACE COMMANDS OF VARIOUS RELIGIONS

When you think about food and religion, some things that might come to mind straight away are *bans* on certain foods: Rastafaris should abstain from pork. Muslims should, too. Yet *The Quran* is otherwise quite liberal about animals used for farming. It simply prohibits eating

> carrion, blood, the flesh of swine, and that which has been dedicated to other than Allah, and those animals killed by strangling or by a violent blow or by a head-long fall or by the goring of horns, and those from which a wild animal has eaten, except what you slaughter, and those which are sacrificed on stone altars. (5:3)

Leviticus is more restrictive, forbidding Jews from eating pigs and also quite a bit more, telling the Israelites that they may eat any animal with a divided hoof who *also* chews the cud but may not eat cud-chewers who lack divided hoofs (Leviticus 11:3). It tells them they may eat water-dwellers with fins and scales but forbids eating water-dwellers without fins and scales (or even the eggs of such animals). It forbids eating *most* insects with wings who walk on all fours (11:20) and forbids eating

> the eagle and the vulture and the buzzard, and the kite and the falcon in its kind, every raven in its kind, and the ostrich and the owl and the sea gull and the hawk in its kind, and the little owl and the cormorant and the great owl, and the white owl and the pelican and the carrion vulture, and the stork, the heron in its kind, and the hoopoe, and the bat. (11:13–19)

Chapter 8 of the Buddhist *Lankavatara-sutra* is still more wide-ranging in its prohibitions on eating meat and even proscribes some drinks and vegetables:

> The Bodhisattvas, mighty beings,
> Consume no alcohol; they eat
> No meat, no garlic, and no onion.
> This the Conquerors, the leaders of the flock, have taught. . . .[1]

Other prohibitions concern *how* you eat rather than with *what* you eat. For example, the Hindu *Bhagavadgita* states:

> With [food] shall you sustain the gods so that the gods may sustain you. By sustaining one another, you shall achieve the highest good.
>   For so sustained by sacrifice, the gods will give you the food of your desire. Who so enjoys their gifts yet gives them nothing is a thief, no more nor less.
>   Good men who eat the leavings of the sacrifice are freed from every taint, but evil are they and evil do they eat who cook only for their own sakes.
>   From food do all contingent beings derive and food derives from rain; rain derives from sacrifice and sacrifice from works. (III, 11–14)[2]

The passage encourages its readers to make food for the gods and not just for themselves. They should eat while also leaving some for the gods to eat, too. Note that whereas the *Bhagavadgita* enjoins readers to eat what's left of sacrifice, to leave the best bits for the gods, some ancient religions took the opposite approach:

> Many of the [ancient] Greeks' neighbors found [Greek] eating habits showed irreverence before heaven: the gods had to be content with the discards of sacrifice—"the tail-end and the gall-bladder, the bits you can't eat."[3]

Some religions restrict how one may eat in a different way: The religious views of some Buddhists require them to beg for food and then mix whatever they get: popcorn, hot dogs, carrot cake, grits. Likewise, St. Francis of Assisi reportedly felt that his Christian commitment compelled him to mix his food with ashes.[4] Doing so kept him attuned to his view that food is just a source of fuel for his real, spiritual life.

Yet in some religious traditions, food is not simply a source of fuel and eating not simply a necessary, mundane activity. In, for example, the Eastern Orthodox tradition, eating brings the eater closer to God. In that tradition, there is a rhythm of fasts and then feasts designed to ensure this closeness. So, too, in Islam, *iftar* follows the fast of Ramadan. Like Easter feasts in the Eastern Orthodox tradition, *iftar* is a communal affair. These feasts are not simply venues for filling up after a time of deprivation, like splurging at a lonely Las Vegas buffet after a day hiking Red Rock Canyon solo. Rather, these feasts are occasions for communities to gather, to celebrate, to share stories, to bond.

It's striking that in all three major monotheistic religions, eating together plays an identity-shaping role in important communal rituals like the Jewish Passover Seder, the Christian Eucharistic meal, and the Islamic feast of Eid al-Fitr. (You might compare the motivations here with the community-building motivation behind local agriculture that we describe in Chapter 10, "Alternatives to Industrial Plant Agriculture.")

It's also striking that the feasts often go with fasts. The feast of Eid Al-Fit follows the month of Ramadan, a month with tight restrictions on when one may eat. Jews observe Yom Kippur by fasting for 25 hours, but they feast before then.

Fasts are independently interesting. Some Buddhists eat a single meal a day and never in the evening or at night. Part of the Buddhist justification for restricting *when* one may eat is to restrict *how much* the devout eat. This raises a general issue about how much to eat that crops up in many other traditions as well. For example, St. Thomas Aquinas writes,

> The vice of gluttony becomes a mortal sin by turning man away from his last end: and accordingly, by a kind of reduction, it is opposed to the precept of hallowing the Sabbath, which commands us to rest in our last end. . . . (Q[122], A[1])

Aquinas's advice coheres with some from Gandhi:

> [There is] a great deal of truth in the saying that man becomes what he eats. The grosser the food, the grosser the body. Plain living is said to go hand in hand with high thinking. . . . Plain living may itself be said to be a mode of fasting. . . .
>
> The *Bhagavadgita* enjoins not temperance in food but "meagerness": meagerness is perpetual fast. Meagerness means just enough to sustain the body for the service for which it is made. . . . (Gandhi, 1965: 50, 52)

Aquinas's advice resonates, too, with this Indic proverb: The one who eats once a day is a yogi [divine]; the one who eats twice a day is a bhogi [pleasure-seeker]; the one who eats three times a day is a rogi [a sick man].

Aquinas and Gandhi, Catholicism and Hinduism, might agree on these points. They might agree that one should eat very little or only as much as one needs. But why, according to these traditions, are these commands correct? Catholicism and Hinduism might here diverge. This raises a new issue.

THE DEEPER COMMANDS OF VARIOUS RELIGIONS AND WHAT THEY TELL US ABOUT ETHICS

The preceding food rules can be thought of as "surface" moral rules. They do nothing to *explain* why you should or shouldn't do this or that. Standing alone, they can look somewhat odd or archaic or superstitious. What could the ethical objection to *onions* be? Why *should* one mix foods, ruining their taste? Felipe Fernandez-Armesto claims,

> It is pointless to seek rational and material explanations for dietary restrictions, because they are essentially suprarational and metaphysical. Meanings ascribed to food are, like all meanings, agreed conventions about usage: ultimately, they are arbitrary.[5]

Trying to justify this claim, Fernandez-Armesto points out that the Jewish philosopher Maimonides defended the prohibition on eating pork with a patently false theory according to which pork is too moist and full of "superfluous matter" to be a proper subject of eating (ibid.). Yet to conclude from poor Maimonides' error that dietary restrictions are always—or even typically—beyond reason is a mistake. That some attempted justifications for surface commands are spurious, after all, hardly demonstrates that attempted justifications are always or even typically spurious.

In this chapter, we take a more sanguine view according to which some surface commands have reasonable, compelling bases. For example, the Doniger reading in this chapter articulates some surface principles of Indic religions. But it also starts to articulate deeper, plausible justifications that make sense of those surface commands.

The character of this relationship between what we're calling deep and surface religious commands may come into sharper relief in view of some parallel observations about the moral theory utilitarianism, according to which one is required to maximize well-being. If utilitarianism is true, it is typically—but not always—wrong to steal. That is because stealing typically—but not always—fails to maximize well-being. It might make the thief happy but at the cost of making others much more unhappy. The surface moral requirement, if utilitarianism is true, is that (typically) you shouldn't steal. The deeper requirement that explains *why* you typically shouldn't steal is that you are required to maximize well-being. Maximizing well-being is the only deep requirement, if utilitarianism is true. It explains a multitude of surface requirements: don't lie, don't cheat, don't steal, and so on.

In its surface requirements, utilitarianism might agree with other moral theories. So, for example, a virtue ethical theory will imply that it is typically—but not always—wrong to steal. That is because stealing typically—but not always—is not what a perfectly virtuous agent would do: A perfectly virtuous agent might find herself in a tight spot some time, a spot in which stealing is the only way to avert catastrophe. But such a case is atypical. Typically, not stealing is a sign of good character. The surface requirement, if virtue ethics is true, is that you typically shouldn't steal. On that virtue ethics agrees with utilitarianism. But they differ on the deeper explanation of that surface requirement. (For more on virtue ethics and utilitarianism, see Chapter 4, "Consumer Ethics.")

One of the signal things that religion offers to food ethics is a stock of ethical principles that serve as deep explanations for various surface commands and permissions. So, for example, the Quaran's injunction not to eat carrion or swine is explained by a prohibition on eating the harmful, the impure, and the unclean. Allah is the arbiter of what is harmful, impure, and unclean, but the Quaran is straightforward about which things are.

Ahimsa, the command not to injure, not to injure *any* living thing, is an important component of Buddhism, Hinduism, and Jainism. It offers a straightforward explanation of why it is wrong to make agricultural workers suffer as is described in the Estabrook reading in Chapter 1, "The Ethically Troubling Food System," and in the Holmes reading in Chapter 11, "Workers"—doing so injures living things.

What does the command imply or explain about what to eat? How is this command to be carried out in a world in which it is nearly impossible to get food without injuring living things? What sort of food production practices does it support? What sort of *diet*? These are hard questions in Indic food ethics.

Shalom—peace and flourishing of all creatures—is one of the key ideas of Judaism and, in particular, of the Torah. Again, it offers a straightforward explanation of why it is wrong to make agricultural workers suffer, though one different from the Indic explanation: Doing so is neither peaceful nor conducive to flourishing.

Yet it raises big, difficult questions: How to promote the peace and flourishing of all creatures? What does such a commandment imply about food? About food production? Food consumption? About the treatment of animals and food workers?

Finally, to Christians the command to love your neighbor—the claim that you should love your neighbor—is very important. (To Jews, too. It's in *Leviticus* and, in fact, comes very shortly after an agricultural commandment: "When you reap the harvest of your land, you shall not reap your field right up to its edge, neither shall you gather the gleanings after your harvest. And you shall not strip your vineyard bare, neither shall you gather the fallen grapes of your vineyard. You shall leave them for the poor and for the sojourner" [*Leviticus* 19: 9–10]). This command, too, offers a third straightforward explanation of why it is wrong to make agricultural workers suffer: They are your neighbors and making them suffer is not loving.

What else does the requirement to love your neighbor imply about food? What does it imply about killing animals? What does it imply about less obvious topics like subsidies for American farmers that have the effect of producing huge quantities of food that then flood foreign markets, leading to farmers in those countries going out of business? Is that consistent with loving your neighbor? Is it expressive of such love? Are those foreign farmers your neighbors? Are far-off farmers within your country your neighbors? Are animals your neighbors? Are food workers? Is the environment? Are future generations? What is it to show love to these things?

Hard questions! As we said, one of the signal things that religion provides is certain moral principles, but the spelling out of those principles' implications with respect to food ethics is fraught. As Matthew C. Halteman writes,

> Those who go to the Bible looking for an open highway to the one true Christian diet usually end up perplexed. The bookends of Eden and the peaceable kingdom (cf. Isa 11:6–9) might seem to show that God's ideal for human beings is a plant-based diet, but the giving of animals to Noah for food and Jesus eating fish (among other things) complicate the picture, suggesting that eating animals is permissible, at least in some circumstances. The strict dietary laws of the Hebrew Bible seem to show that reservations about unrestrained omnivorism have a divine precedent, but Paul enjoins us not to let dietary differences inhibit fellowship. A diet of vegetables emboldens Daniel in the lion's den, yet Paul curiously appears to associate vegetarianism

with weak faith. Evidence of God's love and care for animals abounds throughout the scriptural record, but that record also includes animal sacrifice, at least until the Passover lamb gives way to the Last Supper—an event memorialized in the sacrament of a simple vegetarian meal. The debate that ensues from these tensions has ancient roots in both Judaism and Christianity, and the biblical interpretation involved in discerning their contemporary significance traverses controversial theological and philosophical terrain.[6]

Halteman believes that discerning what the deep commands of what one's religion are is itself tricky, and then discerning what those commands imply about food is trickier still. But this is not to say these deep commands have no such implications. The Halteman reading in this chapter argues that Christian principles militate against industrial animal agriculture.

The implications of the deep commands of one's religion might be acceptable across a wide spectrum of outlooks on the world, whether religious or not. Some atheists, agnostics, Buddhists, Christians, Jains, and Jews might come to agree about various parts of surface food morality. For example, they might agree—indeed, some do agree—that veganism is the ideal diet.

As the Kemmerer reading demonstrates, some indigenous traditions—like some Buddhist traditions—endorse that all animals—human and otherwise—have life forces or souls or spirits and, moreover, these migrate after death to other animals. So an animal might be a relative. But, also, because it is, say, ensouled, the animal is subject to suffering, and, because it is ensouled, it has moral status and, like persons, should not be made to suffer without good reason.

The moral command underlying some people's veganism is something like: Minimize harm to sentient beings. When you put together this moral command with the empirical claim that veganism is better than other dietary regimes at minimizing such harm, you get a commitment to veganism as the moral ideal. These are points on which atheist vegans might agree with the Buddhist.[7]

The deeper command to minimize harm is endorsed on Christian grounds by Joel Salatin in Chapter 8, "Alternatives to Industrial Animal Agriculture." But there are important points of difference: Salatin understands his commitment to the specific type of animal farming he practices as an explicitly Christian one and also explicitly denies that animals have souls.[8] It is because of this lack of souls, Salatin thinks, that killing animals is not harming them. Whereas the Buddhist view is not only that animals—like all sentient things—have souls but that those might be the souls of re-incarnated humans. This is a deeper-still explanation of why one should minimize harm, one that Salatin will reject.[9]

Relatedly, consider the surface command not to eat pig. Rastafari, Islamic, Hindu, Buddhist, and Jewish views agree on this and agree on a deeper justification for this: Don't sully yourself. Put that together with the claim that eating pig sullies oneself and the prohibition on eating pig follows. That's a prohibition that atheist vegans will abide, too, but typically not because of agreement on the deeper commandment.

And note that even agreement on the deeper commandment can lead to disagreement about surface commandments. Consider a longer version of the Buddhist *Lankavatara-sutra* quotation from earlier:

> The Bodhisattvas, mighty beings,
> Consume no alcohol; they eat
> No meat, no garlic, and no onion.
> This the Conquerors, the leaders of the flock, have taught. . .

For flesh is food for wild and ravening beasts.
It is unfitting food, the Buddha taught. . .

All flesh, of animals as well as one's friends,
Derives from unclean substances, both blood and sperm;
And those who feed on flesh become a source of fear.
Therefore yogis shall refrain from eating meat.
Every kind of flesh, all onions and garlic,
Alcoholic drinks in various forms,
Leeks, wild garlic also—these indeed
Are foods that yogis shall reject. . . .[10]

This passage articulates not only a view on *what* not to eat—flesh, onion, garlic—but also views on *why* not to eat it—because doing so is dirty or inferior or makes one fearsome. The implication is that eating pig is not the only dietary practice that will sully you, but so, too, will the practice of eating onion. That's a point Jews, Rastafaris, and Muslims will demur on. So, too, will atheists and Christians. Christianity differs strikingly from the other major monotheistic religions in both its permissiveness about what to eat and in its lack of concern with cordoning off some foods as unclean. Islam only cordons off a few, but it cordons off some. But Christianity seems to cordon none off. So far as there are restrictions on what to eat, the restrictions have to do with gluttony or with the expiation of sin. Peter, in Acts 10, has a vision in which he is told all food is now clean, even pigs, garlic, and onions.[11] The claim that garlic is unclean is, then, not one that Christians endorse. And the argument for that claim—that it is unclean—is one that a Christian will eschew, but it will be appealing to members of other religious communities, even if the particular claim about *garlic* being unclean will not.

Even the ostensibly baffling surface command to mix the flavor out of your food is defensible against the background of deeper moral principles. It makes sense against the background of a deeper command to turn yourself away from bodily pleasures and the point that food provides a source of great bodily pleasure. As H. L. Seneviratne writes,

> In the ideal Buddhist life, that of the monk, food is to be ingested merely as necessity. The practice of begging for food eradicates both the social origin and the uniqueness of food items and flavors and thereby expresses indifference to those qualities such as texture and flavor which are so important in the food ingestion of the laity. The inevitable mixing of food which takes place in this method of food gathering, considered to lower flavor, is repeated in the monk's conscious act of mixing immediately before ingestion.[12]

Relatedly, in the Christian tradition, Augustine writes,

> Although the purpose of eating and drinking is to preserve health, in its train there follows an ominous kind of enjoyment, which often tries to outstrip it, so that it is really for the sake of pleasure that I do what I claim to do and mean to do for the sake of my health.[13]

Augustine not only sets out what food's purpose is but counsels against going in for too much enjoyment of food—that would tempt one to sin. This, then, makes sense of St. Francis's practice, mentioned earlier, mixing of food and ash. He should do so lest, as Augustine warned, he be distracted by the pleasure of eating.

There is a related justification underpinning the prohibition on overconsumption. (Compare with the purely secular ideas mentioned in the introduction to Chapter 12,

"Overconsumption and Obesity.") The Judeo-Christian tradition provides religious, ethical grounds for not overconsuming: Overconsumption leads to weakness in the face of temptation. (Augustine claims, "[T]he snare of concupiscence awaits me in the very process of passing from the discomfort of hunger to the contentment that comes when it is satisfied" [235].) It leads to (disordered) desire for wordly things rather than (rightly ordered) desire for otherworldly ones. (Augustine again: "The Israelites in the desert deserved rebuke, not because they wanted meat, but because in their greed for food they sulked and grumbled against the Lord" [237].) And, generally, overconsumption leads to bad behavior. In C. S. Lewis's book *The Screwtape Letters*, the character Screwtape—a devil—claims, "[Mere excess in food's] chief use is as a kind of artillery preparation for attacks on chastity."[14] And the rich man in the Christian parable of Lazarus, the man who refuses to feed Lazarus and goes to hell as a result is led by the pleasure he gets in eating to commit a crime of negligence toward Lazarus. (If the food were foul, he'd have been more likely to give some to Lazarus.)

Discussing the parable of Lazarus, William Ian Miller writes, "For that earlier economic order [eating too much] was, in a sense, murder or a kind of criminal negligence, like drunk driving is for us."[15] And impoverished human beings aren't the only earthlings going hungry when some of us eat too much, as Lisa Kemmerer reminds us in her reading in this chapter in describing the agricultural practices of the Bhima Saoras of central and southeast India:

> Their broad-minded attitude [that they are just one species among many all of which depend on the land for survival] restricts the amount of land that they are willing to take for crops, even though many of their own children die of starvation each year. The Bhima Saoras' spiritual understanding of their rightful place in the natural world prevents them from contributing to the massive human overpopulation problem that has devastated landscapes and destroyed animal communities throughout most of the world, too often driving animals to extinction. (316)

Considerations like these raise a final justification for not overconsuming, recognizable in both secular and religious contexts: When you overconsume, you take more than your share of food. In a world in which millions of people do not have enough to eat, and billions of animals are both displaced by our agricultural expansion and killed for the excessively rich diets of affluent people, overconsumption might be especially objectionable.

WHAT ELSE RELIGION MAKES AVAILABLE TO ADHERENTS

One thing, then, that religion provides to its adherents is a set of moral guidelines to steer their consumption. There are the surface guidelines like that you shouldn't eat onions and the deeper ones like that you shouldn't pollute yourself.

There are other things religion provides that matter to food ethics. In addition to providing substantive *moral theses*—for example, you should love your neighbor—that yield substantive moral conclusions, it might provide substantive metaphysical theses—for example, all animals have souls or all living things have souls. It might even provide something still grander, what you might think of as a cosmic vision. Let's think of such a vision as an intersubjective, communal, evolving way of both understanding and being in the world. The vision often encompasses origin myths, folklore, oral history, sacred texts, and other sources of wisdom such as philosophy, literature, and lived experience. It can provide an earnest, savvy, and ultimately pragmatic identity politics (i.e., a set of rules for deciding who is a member of the community and who is not, who is a good or successful member of the community and who is not, etc.). These, in turn, can provide practitioners with an identity and social glue.

Neither the metaphysical theses nor the cosmic vision is a moral thesis. But, combined with moral theses, they might yield insights about whether to kill a yak or some number of fish. They might have implications about whether it is permissible to kill plants.

As Kemmerer notes in her reading in this chapter, some religious groups have a certain metaphysical vision of the world—one according to which animals, plants, even rocks are spiritual beings who, moreover, are all related—and then a certain moral view—you should minimize harm to spiritual beings and, when you do harm them, you should atone. The implication for food ethics is that you should minimize harm and offer thanks for the food you get.

It's a conclusion lots of people have arrived at independently. Religion might, then, provide substantive justifications for conclusions you could arrive at otherwise—for example, atheist vegans and Buddhists agree that one shouldn't eat pork but differ about why. And Rastafaris agree that one shouldn't eat pork, but their justifications differ still further. The Rastafari justification is overdetermined: Like all forms of meat, pork derives from death and, because of this, is to be avoided. Also, independently, pork is to be avoided because pigs are tainted animals.

These justifications provide different adherents with different reasons to avoid eating pork. For some moral theories, the reasons for which you do things are *very* important. From the deontological perspective of Immanuel Kant, for instance, to act well, it is not enough to, for example, save a baby from drowning. You have to save the baby from drowning for the right reasons. Whatever the right reason—and ethicists differ on what the right reason is—one wrong reason is that saving the baby would make you famous. If you save the baby for that reason, Kant would deem your act less morally impressive than saving the baby for the right reason.

So while the atheist vegan, the Buddhist, and the Rastafari agree that eating pork is wrong, they disagree on the reason(s) that it is wrong. And this disagreement is morally significant and is attributable—not to be too grand about it—to the cosmic visions that Buddhism and Rastafarianism endorse. Indeed, these groups might disagree among themselves, and these disagreements can be traced to differences in their cosmic visions.

We finish this chapter by discussing three other religious ideas that are important for food ethics, each interestingly pertinent to an adherent's efforts to conform her life to her religion's cosmic vision.

SYMBOLISM

According to utilitarianism, an action is permissible if and only if no other option produces more well-being. An act is required if and only if all other options produce less well-being. So, for example, if you have a choice between doing something that makes your little brother happy but affects no one else and doing something that makes him sad but affects no one else, utilitarianism implies you are required to do the former. If you have a choice between doing something that makes him really happy but affects no one else, doing something else that makes him equally happy but affects no one else, and doing something that makes him sad, utilitarianism implies you are required to do one of the first two actions but permitted to do either one.

Now think about, say, abstaining from eating pork. It might be that doing so makes you unhappy and affects no one else—not even a pig—and that eating pork would make you happy and affect no one else. If so, then utilitarianism implies you should eat the pork. What if you're a Muslim? Well, if it really won't make a difference to happiness, you should eat the pork, according to utilitarianism. Even though doing so is forbidden by your religion. For some religious people, though, acting morally is not simply a matter of producing the most well-being but, rather, of being a certain sort of person or standing for certain things or siding with God. Such a person abstains from pork not because of its effects on well-being but, rather, because doing so is a way of showing her devotion to God or a way of indicating the alignment of her being with a certain vision of the world. Refusing to eat animals is like wearing a flag lapel pin or voting for a candidate who is sure to win anyway: It's a way of showing support for something. But, in the food case, because our eating practices are often central parts of our identities, showing support for this dietary regime over that one is also, typically, a way of showing who you are. Moreover, its value is not reducible to the effects it produces.

In the *Laws of Manu* reading in this chapter, as in the introduction to Chapter 5, "Food and Identity," eating is made out to be a way to display one's character. This display might have a value in itself, apart from its effects on anyone else.

Actions might be good for what they symbolize as well as what they produce. The *refusal* to eat can be a way to bring oneself closer to God—this is a good reason for a religious person to do it, a reason based on effects. Refusal to eat might also improve one's character. Again, this is a good reason to do it, a reason based on its effects. And it has further good effects: For some believers, it increases their awareness of their dependence on God, makes them contrite and humble, or more attuned to spiritual concerns. Yet it is also valuable because it symbolizes something—in this case, abstinence from sin, a strengthening of the will, and a general alignment of one's life with one's cosmic vision.

For some vegetarians, the refusal to eat meat is something they think they *should* do, that is, that they are morally required to do. When you ask them why they abstain, however, they often say things that, on reflection, seem off-topic: "It is wrong to kill animals for food" or "Do you know how animals are hurt on factory farms"? In situations like these, the philosophical (if somewhat flat-footed) response might be something like: "I'm not asking about killing and hurting animals. I'm asking why you don't *eat* them."

But it could be that what the vegetarian has in mind is something like: "I believe meat is wrongly produced. If I eat it, I symbolize that I am indifferent to that wrongdoing. I shouldn't symbolize that. So I shouldn't eat meat."

And while, as Chapter 12, "Overconsumption and Obesity," demonstrates, overconsumption is a fraught, complex topic; there is a kind of overconsumption that this idea about symbolism is well-positioned to criticize. As we write these paragraphs, several thousand children are dying from hunger-related causes. And, as we write these paragraphs, some well-off college student, having already eaten plenty, is having an extra burrito just because he wants to see if he can pack it in. It's not the case that if he *stopped eating so much* he would thereby be able to save the people dying from hunger-related causes. It's not like the college student who eats one too many burritos could've shipped the offending burrito to a starving child and thereby saved a life. But, all the same, by eating too much the student might be doing wrong because he is symbolizing that he is willing to take more than his share. As Robert Adams writes, it is an important part of Christian and Hindu thought that

> A central part of living well is being for the good and against evils. We face the question, how we can be for and against goods and evils that we are relatively powerless to accomplish or prevent. One of the most obvious answers is that we can give more reality to our being for the goods and against the evils by expressing our loyalties symbolically in action. For this reason acts of martyrdom represent a particularly important possibility for living well for people who find themselves in situations of comparative helplessness. . . .[16]

VIRTUE

As we said before, food is often tied up with personal identity. Both as individuals and as members of particular communities and social groups, people tend to think of themselves as defined, at least in part, by their food choices: Ana is a feminist vegan, Pat is a freerangetarian who keeps chickens, Keith loves a good steak with his teammates on game day.

When it comes to the communities and social groups that shape culinary identity, religious communities often play a particularly influential and often morally inflected role in the lives of their adherents. If Darryl eats no pork because he's Muslim, for instance, his abstinence from pork is likely to be an important part of how he thinks of himself. If he eats no pork just because he's never liked the taste of it, less so. A religiously motivated refusal to eat pork might, for Darryl, be part of what makes his life meaningful to him, a life with the qualities and narrative he wants it to have, as the author of his own life. A vivid example, described in the introduction to Chapter 5, "Food and Identity," comes from Jonathan Safran Foer's book *Eating Animals*. Foer recounts his grandmother's flight from the Nazis and how, even when starving, she kept kosher. She stayed true to her convictions even when that meant going hungry rather than eating pork. Keeping kosher gave meaning to her life, as she confirms when she says, "If nothing matters, there's nothing to save."

For a different example of the way that religious commitment can shape food choices and the underlying traits of character they aim to mold and express, consider Confucianism. In Confucianism, manners—not only food-related manners but certainly including those—are highly important. Manners build character and also display respect for others. The Confucian text *Mencius* claims, "[T]hose who have propriety (li) respect others" (Mencius 4B:28).

Glossing the passage, Tae Wan Kim and Alan Strudler write,

> Li, it seems, is a pattern of behavior, whereas respect is an attitude that one may take when engaging in ritual with a person worthy of respect. One may show respect for a person by engaging in appropriate ritual behavior, and one may deserve respect by engaging in appropriate ritual together; both the respector and respectee must collaborate in ritual for meaningful respect to occur, on our reading of Confucius.[17]

Manners are important in part because they express moral virtue (rather than because they produce the best consequences). But they are also important because they build moral character.

There is an idea—not only in Confucianism but also in, say, Eastern Orthodox Christianity and the Jewish tradition of Jonathan Safran Foer's grandmother—that what you eat, how you eat, and with whom you eat are expressive, indeed even constructive, of who you are. Lots of things we regularly, frequently do are not nearly so expressive or constructive of character—how you breathe, when you go to bed—but in some religious traditions what you eat (and refuse to eat) shows off and even creates who you are.

AUTHENTICITY

Finally, return to the cosmic vision that some religions offer. As we said, that vision itself offers various non-ethical theses: Garlic makes you fearsome. Each living thing is ensouled. And so on. These can be poured into your ethical grinder, churning out substantive conclusions: Don't eat garlic. Give thanks for any food you get since that food was once a living, ensouled thing. And so on. As we said, the vision can itself offer substantive ethical theses: Stand with God against factory farming. Be kind to all living creatures. And so on. It can also offer substantive justifications for theses you might be antecedently committed to: Mind your manners *in order to* build character. Don't be a cannibal *because* doing so offends God. And so on.

There is something else that one might think the cosmic vision offers, something that manifests clearly at the table and in the kitchen: The principles with food ethical implications, whether surface or deep, can serve the purpose of guiding people toward a flourishing or a God-pleasing life, or both. Food and the regulation of food plays such a huge role in the spiritual disciplinary regimes of these religions because food connects us to every level of being in the cosmic vision—what we eat affects the health of our bodies, the sustainability of ecosystems and human communities, the well-being of other creatures, and on and on and on. As such, any effort to envision holistic flourishing within a harmonious order of things—a cosmic vision that motivates a sustainable identity that is compatible with human beings doing well with one another and by the rest of the world—will obviously have to say quite a bit about how, what, and when human beings should eat.

Religious food ethics, from a certain perspective, can be seen to have practical advantages over ethics like Harman's or Singer's in Chapters 7, "Industrial Animal Agriculture," and 8, "Alternatives to Industrial Animal Agriculture," insofar as the latter usually tries to begin from a neutral standpoint that has very little power to compel a person viscerally or habitually into action, whereas religious food ethics shapes and cultivates a person's deepest ways of apprehending the world and its significance. Relatedly, this line of thought goes, part of the reason that food ethics is so central in religions is that eating is such a holistic endeavor that connects us to everything else that chances are good that if we eat badly, we might well end up being-in-the-world badly as well.

As the Halteman reading discusses, the cosmic vision thus holds out a model for living a purposeful life. If one aligns one's daily attitudes and actions with that purpose, one will live an authentic life—that is, a life that exemplifies genuine adherence to the commitments that arise from one's professed cosmic vision. The goal is to live into this cosmic vision and concretize it in one's daily affairs to whatever finite extent is possible given the inevitable limitations of being human. In doing so, one will live a life that is mindfully in sync with the flourishing of the whole, at least as this order of things is framed within that specific religious vision.

Mindfulness of the humble place of humankind in the grand scheme of things, however, doesn't come naturally to most human beings. As such, religious efforts to live in accordance with a cosmic vision typically require the adoption of spiritual disciplines—repetitive daily practices that remind adherents of their unchecked tendency to live without regard for the whole, and that entrench, through the doing, more mindful habits of thought and practice. Thus, a Jewish person might take up the daily discipline of kosher vegetarianism in hopes of being in more genuine accord with the shalomic vision,[18] or a Buddhist might adopt veganism as a means of more deeply instantiating the karmic vision.[19]

But if such cosmic visions have the power to inspire people to live more mindfully in certain regards, they also have the power to entrench hierarchies, promote and exploit systemic injustices, and foment legalism and exclusion. Indeed, some people[20] think that some religious visions of the world have done especially egregious harm where "food animals" are concerned. The Halteman reading in this chapter provides a different perspective on this issue, asking whether paying closer attention to food ethics can help to reinvigorate religious visions and make them more authentic. Halteman considers this question from a Christian perspective, but others in the chapter speak to it, too.

FURTHER ISSUES

1. *Moral Taint*

An important idea for some religious groups is that members should remain pure. (You hear discourse about this having to do with food, with social groups, with sex.) What does this—being pure—mean? Does being pure have moral importance? Consider an example derived from one by Kwame Anthony Appiah: You work in a hardware store. Someone comes in, looking for a knife to use in a fight. If you don't sell it to him, he'll just go to a nearby store and get exactly the same knife. You are about to put the knife on the shelf where the customer will buy it. Is that permissible? Will you be "tainted," in Appiah's evocative word, by the crime? In what ways might eating certain foods be considered to "taint" one morally?

2. *Moral Motivation*

Part of what is powerful about religious food ethics is its provision of a cosmic vision. And part of what is powerful about a cosmic vision is its ability to compel adherents to live a life that lines up with their values. This is well and good if the values are good values, but it is easy to imagine a cosmic vision that leads to very bad things. (Various visions have led to very bad things. ISIS does not lack for a cosmic vision.)

This raises interesting issues about moral motivation. Some think that you must be motivated—*to some extent*—to do whatever you judge you morally should do. They think there is a necessary connection between judging you ought to do something and being motivated to do that action. Others think that the connection is contingent: It's possible to judge you ought to do something and be motivated to do it but also possible to judge you ought to do it while not being motivated to do it.

Can you think of examples that support the second position? And what do you make of a version of the first position according to which the moral motivation is *very powerful*, that if you judge you ought to do something, you are very powerfully motivated to do it? In a short stand-up routine that is easy to find online—"Louis C.K.'s Justification for Eating Meat"— the comedian Louis C.K. provides a counterexample. What is the justification for eating meat that he offers in that video? Is it part of a cosmic vision?

3. *Food as Fuel*
A Buddhist/Franciscan view is that food is simply fuel. Against this, consider this passage from Dan Barber's *The Third Plate*:

> Without cuisine, Glenn [Roberts] said, farming systems can't last. "They don't," he said. "Maybe for our lifetime, or for our children's lifetime, but eventually, forget it. Food and cuisine have to be an important part of our culture, and not just something that fuels the culture in one way. Food as fuel is a dangerous concept. That's where we are right now—food as fuel. It's why nothing tastes good, and why our farming systems are collapsing. . . . [T]he culture of food is as important, if not more important, than the production of food."[21]

Roberts makes a couple of *causal* claims. First, he claims that the view that food is simply fuel, if sufficiently widespread, *produces* food that is not particularly flavorful—if it's just fuel, it might as well be a nutrition pill, so why need it be flavorful? Second, he claims that the view that food is fuel, if sufficiently widespread, *produces* "collapse" in farming systems. What do you think he has in mind? One idea might be that the view, if spread wide enough, produces environmental damage that undermines farms—how might that happen? Why would it happen?

4. *Farms as Organisms*
The Austrian mystic Rudolf Steiner—"mystic" is not meant to be pejorative, but it is hard to classify Steiner's spiritual views—claimed that farms are themselves organisms. He claimed that life on those farms is, like the lives of cells within your body, something to be preserved and supported. There are cases in which things on a farm need to be rooted out but, as with your body, this is a sign that something is not right within the body. The problem on the farm—late blight on your tomatoes, for example—is like a bacterial infection you pick up.

Compare this view to the Buddhist metaphysical view according to which all living things are ensouled or the traditional Melanesian metaphysical view in which animate and inanimate objects alike are viewed holistically as members of a single community.

The Steiner view supports "biodynamic farming" and is popular among some organic farmers. After reading about organic farming in Chapter 10, "Alternatives to Industrial Plant Agriculture," consider whether these views—Steiner's, the Buddhist, the traditional Melanesian's—have implications for, say, organic farming. If so, what are they?

5. *Profiting from Wrongdoing and Having Others Do Wrong*
Counter to stereotype, not all Buddhists are vegetarian. As mentioned previously, some Buddhists are *required* to eat what is given to them, flesh or otherwise. About this, Charles Goodman writes,

Though all Buddhist traditions attach moral significance to animal life and animal suffering, not all Buddhists practice vegetarianism. For example, Theravāda monks, who live by begging, are expected to eat whatever food is placed in their bowl, including meat, without preference or discrimination. However, they are forbidden to eat meat from an animal if they have seen, heard, or suspected that the animal in question was killed specifically for them.[22]

This is importantly connected to issues about consumption we discuss in Chapter 4, "Consumer Ethics." It is also connected to this interesting passage about Buddhism from H. L. Seneviratne:

> The carnivorousness of the Sinhalese has baffled many who reason that since Buddhism proposes nonviolence toward all beings, the Sinhalese, who are Buddhist, should not eat meat. This is certainly a logical expectation, but the ordinary Sinhalese people think differently. They hold that what is non-Buddhist is killing, and not eating—a position which is perfectly in keeping with the doctrinal Buddhist idea that *karma* is volition and not action. The large majority of the Buddhist Sinhalese do abhor killing, often hesitating to kill even pests, and certainly avoid killing for purposes of food. Who then does the killing? Muslims and Christians. . . .
>
> A more difficult logical problem faces those Buddhist Sinhalese who actually do kill, such as the seafaring communities of the southern and southwestern seaboard. The dilemma is solved by the resort to the well-known distinction, made by many [Buddhist] peasants. . ., between merit and demerit. These fisherman admit that when killing fish, they actually commit unwholesome karma, which produces demerit. But they believe that merit gained by good works cancels the demerit. How do these fisherman gain merit? By avoiding fishing on the sacred full-moon days and by feeding Buddhist monks with a portion of the catch.[23]

What is it for merit to cancel demerit? How plausible it is *in general* that merit cancels demerit? How plausible is it in this case?

What do you think of the ethics of Buddhists profiting from actions by Muslims and Christians that the Buddhists are themselves unwilling to do and that they think would be wrong for them to do? After examining their readings about consumption in Chapters 1 and 4, what do you think Grace Boey and Tristram McPherson would think?

FURTHER READING

Dominion

Adams, Carol J. 2012. "What about Dominion in *Genesis*?" in York and Baker, *A Faith Embracing All Creatures*. Eugene, OR: Cascade.

Greenway, William. 2015. *For the Love of All Creatures: The Story of Grace in Genesis*. Grand Rapids, MI: Eerdmans.

Scully, Matthew. 2002. *Dominion*. New York: St. Martin's Press.

Singer, Peter. 2002. "Man's Dominion. . . A Short History of Speciesism," in *Animal Liberation*. New York: Harper Collins.

World Religions and Food

Augustine. 1961. *Confessions*. New York: Penguin.

Camosy, Charles. 2013. *For Love of Animals: Christian Ethics, Consistent Action*. Cincinnati, OH: Franciscan Media.

Chaudry, M. M. 1992. "Islamic Food Laws: Philosophical Basis and Practical Implications," *Food Technology* 46: 92.

Doniger, Wendy. 2009. *The Hindus: An Alternative History*. New York: Penguin.

Gandhi, M. K. 1965. *Fasting in Satyagraha*. Ahmedabad: Navjivan.

Goodman, Charles. 2009. *Consequences of Compassion*. New York: Oxford University Press.

———. 2014. "Ethics in Indian and Tibetan Buddhism," *The Stanford Encyclopedia of Philosophy* (Fall 2014 ed.), ed. Edward N. Zalta. http://plato.stanford.edu/archives/fall2014/entries/ethics-indian-buddhism/.

Gross, Aaron S. 2015. *The Question of the Animal and Religion*. New York: Columbia University Press.

Grumett, David, and Rachel Muers. 2010. *Theology on the Menu: Asceticism, Meat and Christian Diet*. New York: Routledge.

Halteman, Matthew C. 2008. *Compassionate Eating as Care of Creation*. Washington, DC: Humane Society of the United States Faith Outreach.

———. 2013. "Knowing the Standard American Diet by Its Fruits: Is Unrestrained Omnivorism Spiritually Beneficial?" *Interpretation* 67 (4): 383–395.

Kalechofsky, Roberta. 1992. *Judaism and Animal Rights*. Boston: Micah Books.

Kemmerer, Lisa. 2012a. *Animals and World Religions*. New York: Oxford.

———2012b. "Islamic Traditions," in *Animals and World Religions*. New York: Oxford.

———, and Anthony Nocella. 2011. *A Call to Compassion: Religious Perspectives on Animal Advocacy*. New York: Lantern.

Komjathy, Louis. 2011. "Daoism: From Meat Avoidance to Compassion-Based Vegetarianism," in Kemmerer and Nocella, *A Call to Compassion*. New York: Lantern.

Linzey, Andrew. 1994a. *Animal Theology*. Chicago: University of Illinois Press.

———. 1994b. "Vegetarianism as a Biblical Ideal," in *Animal Theology*. Chicago: University of Illinois Press.

Phelps, Norm. 2011. "Buddhism and Animal Liberation: The Family of Sentient Beings," in Kemmerer and Nocella, *A Call to Compassion*. New York: Lantern.

Regenstein, J. M., M. M. Chaudry, and C. E. Regenstein. 2003. "The Kosher and Halal Food Laws," *Comprehensive Reviews in Food Science and Food Safety* 2: 111–127.

Rosen, Steven J. 2011. "Vaishnava Hinduism: Ahimsa and Vegetarianism," in Kemmerer and Nocella, *A Call to Compassion*. New York: Lantern.

Schwartz, Richard. 2001. *Judaism and Vegetarianism*. New York: Lantern.

Waldau, Paul, and Kimberley Patton, eds. 2006. *A Communion of Subjects: Animals in Religion, Science, & Ethics*. New York: Columbia University Press.

Webb, Stephen. 2001a. *Good Eating*. Grand Rapids, MI: Brazos.

———. 2001b. "The Once and Future Peace" in *Good Eating*. Grand Rapids, MI: Brazos.

———. 2001c. "The Diet of Christian Vegetarianism" in *Good Eating*. Grand Rapids, MI: Brazos.

Wirzba, Norman. 2011. *Food and Faith*. New York: Cambridge University Press.

York, T., and A. Alexis-Baker. 2009. *A Faith Embracing All Creatures: Addressing Commonly Asked Questions about Christian Care for Animals*. Eugene, OR: Cascade.

NOTES

1. We use the translation from Shabkar, *Food of Bodhisattvas* (London: Shambala, 2004), 56–57.

2. We take the translation from Robert Charles Zaehner, ed. *The Bhagavad-gita* (New York: Oxford University Press).

3. Felipe Fernandez-Armesto, *Near a Thousand Tables* (New York: Free Press), 135; quotation within it is from Menander.

4. See Francine Prose, *Gluttony* (New York: Oxford University Press, 2003).

5. Fernandez-Armesto, *Near a Thousand Tables*, 32.

6. Matthew Halteman, "Knowing the Standard American Diet by Its Fruits: Is Unrestrained Omnivorism Spiritually Beneficial?" *Interpretation* 67 (2013): 391.

7. Though some atheist vegans may bristle at the thought that their commitments are in any way consonant with the views of the devout, Bruce Friedrich has argued that "a belief in animal liberation qualifies as religion under the Free Exercise Clause jurisprudence of the United States Constitution." See Bruce Friedrich, "The Church of Animal Liberation: Animal Rights as 'Religion' under the Free Exercise Clause," *Animal Law Review* 21 (Fall 2014): 65–119. http://works.bepress.com/cgi/viewcontent.cgi?article=1038&context=bruce_friedrich (accessed May 28, 2015).

8. Note that there is a parallel between Salatin and the Buddhist even here, though. The Buddhist insists that animals have souls but also insists that only human souls are capable of "awakening." So there is something metaphysically special about us, Buddhists and Salatin agree, though they disagree on what the specialness is.

9. Wendy Doniger writes, "In Tibet. . . I met a Buddhist who said he would eat yak, but not fish, on moral grounds. That is, if you kill a yak, you destroy one soul but feed many people, but you have to kill many fish, and destroy many souls, to feed the same number of people. It occurred to me that it is a good thing that Tibet does not border on whaling waters" (*The Hindus: An Alternative History*. New York: Penguin, 2009, p. 10). The shallow command here is something like: "You should eat big animals rather than small." The deeper command is something like: "You should minimize harm." When that deeper command is combined with the Buddhist view that each animal has a soul, it yields the conclusion that killing one ensouled big thing—a yak—and getting a lot of food is preferable to killing many ensouled little things—fish—to get the same amount of food. That's the justification for the shallow command.

10. Shabkar. *Food of Bodhisattvas* (London: Shambala, 2001), 56–57.

11. Note that traditional Christian permissiveness about what to eat at the level of surface commands is compatible with a conviction of Christian conscience that one ought not to eat various foods for spiritual or moral reasons that arise from deeper commands. If a Christian were to believe, for instance, that she could not genuinely abide in the two deepest commands of the Christian vision—love God with all your heart, soul, and mind and love your neighbor as yourself—while purchasing and consuming animal products, then she would have good reason to believe herself obligated to eschew certain foods even though there are no operative shallow commands that prohibit their consumption.

12. H. L. Seneviratne, "Essence of Food and the Essence of Experience," in *The Eternal Food*, ed. R. S. Khare (Albany: State University of New York Press, 1992), 188–189.

13. Augustine, *Confessions* (New York: Penguin, 1961), 235.

14. C. S. Lewis, *Mere Christianity* and *The Screwtape Letters* (San Francisco: HarperCollins, 2003), 330.

15. William Ian Miller, *The Anatomy of Disgust* (Cambridge, MA: Harvard University Press, 1997), 97.

16. Robert M. Adams, *Finite and Infinite Goods* (New York: Oxford University Press, 1999), 225.

17. Tae Wan Kim and Alan Strudler, "Workplace Civility," *Business Ethics Quarterly* 22 (2012): 563. For more on manners, see Eske Møllgaard, "Confucian Ritual and Modern Civility," *Journal of Global Ethics* 8 (2012): 227–237, and Karen Stohr, *On Manners* (New York: Routledge, 2011).

18. See Roberta Kalechofsky, *Judaism and Animal Rights* (Boston: Micah Books, 1992).

19. See Norm Phelps, "Buddhism and Animal Liberation: The Family of Sentient Beings," in *A Call to Compassion: Religious Perspectives on Animal Advocacy*, ed. Lisa Kemmerer and Anthony Nocella (New York: Lantern, 2011).

20. See the Singer (2002) and Camosy (2013) readings in the Further Reading section of this chapter for some relevant literature.

21. Dan Barber, *The Third Plate* (New York: Penguin, 2014): 380.

22. Charles Goodman, "Ethics in Indian and Tibetan Buddhism," *The Stanford Encyclopedia of Philosophy* (Fall 2014ed.), ed. Edward N. Zalta. http://plato.stanford.edu/archives/fall2014/entries/ethics-indian-buddhism/.

23. H. L. Seneviratne, "Essence of Food and the Essence of Experience," in *The Eternal Food*, ed. R. S. Khare (Albany: State University of New York Press, 1992), 186–187.

MATTHEW C. HALTEMAN

Compassionate Eating as Care of Creation[1]

Through careful interpretive analysis, the piece argues that the Christian cosmic vision reveals the wrongness of industrial animal agriculture and that taking up more intentional eating practices is a morally significant spiritual discipline for Christians. It also testifies to our claim in the introduction that religious food ethics have practical advantages over purely secular ethics insofar as the latter usually tries to begin from a neutral perspective that has very little power to compel a person, whereas religious food ethics hooks into one's deepest commitments.

INTRODUCTION: DISCOVERING THE MORAL AND SPIRITUAL SIGNIFICANCE OF EATING

Compassionate stewardship of the animal kingdom is one of the primary responsibilities accorded to human beings in many religious creation narratives. But the question of how best to respect and to honor the creatures under human care is one that religious people too often neglect to ask. This omission is especially unfortunate given the compelling evidence of fallenness in the social and commercial practices that presently govern human relationships to animals. The most troubling of these practices is industrial farm animal production—an industry whose methods Pope

Matthew C. Halteman, "Compassionate Eating as Care of Creation," from the eponymous *Compassionate Eating as Care of Creation* (Humane Society of the United States, 2008, 2010).

Benedict XVI has described as the "degrading of living creatures to a commodity."[2]

Within the growing circle of religious people who are aware of the methods and implications of industrial agriculture, there is increasing consensus that the plight of farmed animals is a serious moral concern. But for the great majority, the question of what goes on in concentrated animal feeding operations (or CAFOs) and slaughterhouses may seem too distant from everyday religious concerns to merit significant attention. Given the gravity of the human problems and environmental crises currently looming large, an honest person of faith can hardly be faulted for asking: "Don't we have more important things to worry about than what's for dinner?"

But if daily food choices may at first seem far removed from the most pressing concerns of religious people, a closer look at these dietary decisions reveals that they have troubling consequences not just for billions of animals, but for the food, commerce, and education systems of developing countries, the dignity of those employed in industrial farms and slaughterhouses, the integrity of our rural communities, the health of an increasingly obese and diseased human population, the accessibility of the healthcare systems that treat these ills, the sustainability of the earth's natural resources, and even the hastening of global climate change. As this evidence of the unintended consequences of industrial animal farming continues to mount, it is becoming increasingly clear that, far from being a trivial matter of personal preference, eating is an activity that people of faith have good reason to regard as deeply morally and spiritually significant.

If the goal, after all, is to become increasingly mindful of the role humanity is called to serve in the flourishing of the world as a whole—a goal widely shared among the cosmic visions of many world religions—then it makes perfect sense for religious people to seek to become much more intentional about the daily activity that connects them perhaps more directly than any other to the whole of creation: eating! The simple question of what to eat can prompt us daily to live out our religious vocations of service to the world—to bear witness to the marginalization of the poor, the exploitation of the oppressed, the

suffering of the innocent, and the degradation of the natural world, and to participate in the reconciliation of these ills through intentional acts of love, justice, mercy, and good stewardship. Indeed, if it is the renewal rather than the degradation of creation that we profess to serve, we must address ourselves with more imagination, conviction, and honesty to the moral and spiritual significance of eating.

My aim here is to clarify this general idea that eating more intentionally can be a compelling discipline for living out one's faith by developing a case study of how this strategy might apply within my own spiritual tradition, Christianity. But if I speak from within a specific tradition, many of the guiding insights I explore—for instance, that religious visions of reality can provide strong inspiration for ethical living, that human beings and animals share an ontological bond as fellow creatures, that authentic dominion is displayed in compassion rather than tyranny, and that courageous moral imagination can excavate new epiphanies from ancient texts—are insights that resonate deeply with the thought and practice of many other religions.[3] I submit these reflections, then, without any pretense that Christianity has a corner on food ethical wisdom, in the spirit of promoting interfaith dialogue on matters of shared religious interest and in hope that any reader concerned with ethical eating, religious or otherwise, might find value in a case study that positions Christ-followers as potential fellow travelers on this path.

IMAGINATION: ENVISIONING THE PEACEABLE KINGDOM

One of the perennial temptations that Christians have faced throughout the history of the church is that of living as if the good news of the Gospel of Jesus—God's promise to redeem and transform all of creation—is relevant only to human beings. This oversight is particularly troubling, given the clarity of the scriptural record both on God's original intentions for the created order and on God's promise to regenerate it from its currently fallen state. Whether we interpret the relevant passages literally or figuratively, our creation and redemption narratives make it abundantly clear that God's highest aspiration for creation is the institution of a cosmic harmony in which human beings created in God's image promote the flourishing of the whole of God's world to God's glory.

As the narrative goes, in fact, the first dignity God bestows upon human beings—our very first opportunity to exercise the love, power, and creativity of the divine image within us—is the charge to care for the natural world and the animal creatures with whom we share it. As the drama unfolds, however, human disobedience disrupts this harmony, leading to a downward spiral of selfishness and alienation that estranges us from God, from ourselves, and from the creatures entrusted to our care. Nevertheless, God resolves to redeem the created order by becoming incarnate in Jesus Christ, the "new Adam" who not only defeats human sin through his death and resurrection, but will one day return to usher in and reign over a "peaceable kingdom" in which the harmony of creation is so fully restored that the scriptures describe it with images of children playing amidst venomous snakes, leopards and lambs lying down together, and lions eating straw. An exhilarating vision, to be sure!

For some help discerning the implications of this vision for Christian attitudes and actions toward our fellow creatures, I'll draw on an insightful prayer by the Baptist theologian Walter Rauschenbusch on the kinship of humans and animals as fellow creatures of God. Prays Rauschenbusch in "For the World,"

O God, we thank thee for this universe, our great home; for its vastness and its riches and for the manifoldness of the life which teems upon it and of which we are a part. [. . .] Enlarge within us the sense of fellowship with all the living things, our little brothers, to whom thou hast given the earth as their home in common with us. We remember with shame that in the past we have exercised the high dominion of man with ruthless cruelty so that the voice of the earth, which should have gone up to thee in song, has been a groan of travail. May we realize that they live not for us alone but for themselves and for thee, and that they love the

sweetness of life even as we, and serve thee in their place better than we in ours.[4]

There are four insights here that can aid us in understanding the ideal of "living toward the peaceable kingdom." The first insight is that the entirety of creation belongs to God. While few Christians would contest this statement in principle, the ways in which we treat creation in practice suggest that either we don't really mean what we say, or perhaps more likely, our sense of what God's ownership of creation should mean for our daily lives has been dulled by our immersion in consumer culture—a culture which promotes the idea that anything we desire can be rightfully ours for a price. By keeping our attention focused completely on the short-term benefits that *we* enjoy through the use of creation as a "resource," consumer culture blinds us to the costs of our consumption for other human beings, animals, and the earth, seducing us into living as if creation were ours to dispense with as we please. But the world belongs to God. And the upshot of this insight for our purposes is that living toward the peaceable kingdom must begin with a renewed awareness of whose will it is the ultimate fulfillment of creation to serve—God's, not our own.

Rauschenbusch is well aware, of course, that coming to terms with this insight will not be an easy task for fallen human beings. Presumably this is why he petitions God for help in the very next line, praying for a more expansive "sense of fellowship with all living things" through which we may reawaken to our humble station as creatures, indeed as kin to the animals with whom we share the earth as our God-given home. This second insight that we too are creatures and that our fellow creatures enjoy a mandate to call the earth their home and to flourish here among us fits hand in glove with the first insight. For the more we come to accept our standing as creatures among other creatures, the better we are able to see our well-being as linked to the well-being of the whole—one creation whose ultimate purpose is to serve the glory of God. The upshot of this second insight, then, is that living toward the peaceable kingdom transforms our conceptions of human flourishing in view of God's call to seek what is best for creation as a whole—a whole of which human beings are but one integral part.

Before anyone starts to worry that this second insight blurs the line between humans and animals or otherwise diminishes human beings in some way, let us turn our attention to the third insight, which is that God intended this all-species kinship to be facilitated through the "high dominion" of human beings created specially in God's image. Far from a demotion in rank, this call to seek what is best for the whole of creation elevates us to a station much higher than most of us have dared to imagine, much less sought to fulfill: it is a call to bring our own highest aspirations for the cosmos into line with God's, a call to exercise the love, power, and creativity of God's image within us toward the end of enabling the total flourishing of God's world. The upshot of this third insight, in summary, is that living toward the peaceable kingdom elevates humankind by realizing our unique potential to exemplify God's image through the loving and merciful treatment of all God's creatures.

Lest we forget, this once-and-future peaceable kingdom is for now just an ardent hope. Sadly, the fault of creation's languishing in the meanwhile falls squarely on us, its "groans of travail" a testimony to our selfishness and disobedience. And so Rauschenbusch's prayer is, perhaps above all else, a prayer of repentance, a reminder—and here is the fourth insight—that God's call to high dominion is fundamentally incompatible with cruelty to animals, indifference to their suffering, and the conceit that they are here for us to do with as we please. These, we confess, are not acts befitting our dominion, but acts of tyranny, betrayals of God and our fellow creatures for which shame is our just yield. Rauschenbusch well knows, nonetheless, that the end of genuine repentance is not shame but rebirth, and thus he closes the prayer with the hope that our approach to dominion may be transformed through a realization of the inherent dignity of animals, creatures whose lives are not ultimately measured by their usefulness to us, but by their value to God and to themselves. The upshot of this fourth insight, finally, is that living toward the peaceable kingdom challenges us to repent of our self-serving treatment of animals as

mere objects so that we may become more mindful of their inherent dignity as creatures of God deemed worthy in God's sight.

In view of these four insights, it should be clear that the ideal of living toward the peaceable kingdom is nothing less than an inkling of a new world order. It is an invitation to reconsider, in a dazzling new light, our relationships to God, other human beings, fellow creatures, the Earth, and ourselves. It is a call to imagine what creation might be like if we were to live today as though the kingdom of God has already arrived, grounding our present attitudes and actions toward all of God's creatures in the hope of honoring the dignity that will be theirs when God's redemptive work is complete.

CONVICTION: PRACTICING COMPASSIONATE EATING AS A SPIRITUAL DISCIPLINE

My guiding suggestion is that compassionate eating is a compelling way to turn the lofty aspirations of this vision of the peaceable kingdom into concrete convictions practiced on a daily basis. In developing this suggestion, I should clarify, first, why the activity of eating is a particularly fruitful starting point for taking up the call to creation care. The main insight here is disarmingly simple: thinking through the ethics of eating forces us to be mindful of the impact of our consumer habits on every link in the great chain of being.

Virtually every meal offers ample food for thought about the world and our place within it. A traditional breakfast of eggs and bacon raises the question of what life is like for the chickens and pigs who are used to produce the food. The drive-thru "value meal" at lunchtime prompts our suspicion that some people somewhere are getting less than they deserve so that we can save a buck or two. The tomato salad at dinner gives us pause to consider the environmental costs of trucking produce thousands of miles so that we can eat "fresh" vegetables anytime of the year. In short, raising questions about the way we eat leads us directly to deeper questions about our relation to the whole—questions that aspiring stewards of creation should be asking.

But if eating is an *enlightening* starting point as an activity that can illuminate our daily connectedness to the rest of creation, it is also an *empowering* starting point as an activity over which many of us have a significant degree of personal control. Relatively few of us can decide overnight to become full-time activists, ecologists, creation-friendly farmers, or even hybrid car owners. By contrast, a great many of us *are* able to change our eating habits in ways that can have transformative effects in our own lives and the world at large. Moreover, because eating is often a communal activity, the convictions of a few can inspire a great many, as friends and family, teachers and students, pastors and congregations begin to see that eating more intentionally is something they too can find morally and spiritually invigorating—as well as delicious, nutritious, and cost-effective.

In suggesting that compassionate eating can be a Christian spiritual discipline, my contention is that the repetitive daily practice of remembering and taking care to reduce the hidden costs of our food choices may serve to supplant thoughtless, damaging patterns of consumption with more intentional, compassionate habits. Practicing this discipline is an act of repentance because it reminds us, each time we eat, that all of us make decisions every day that contribute to the unnecessary suffering of other creatures and the degradation of creation. But compassionate eating is also an act of redemption because the daily activity of seeking out less cruel, more socially and ecologically responsible choices—even though it can never fully extricate us from the web of fallen institutions and practices in which we are always already entangled—nevertheless serves to propel us in the right direction. Limited though our power is, the seemingly insignificant practices of eating less meat, supporting less intensive farming methods, or adopting a greener diet have a way—like mustard seeds—of giving rise to greater things.

HONESTY: FACING THE TRUE COST OF FOOD

Having envisioned the ideal of the peaceable kingdom and developed a concrete strategy for living out the convictions inspired by it, we are now in a better position to get honest about the true cost of food. My focus here will be on the cost of our dietary choices for other animals, but I could just as easily canvas the many human and environmental costs of industrial animal agriculture.[5] It is crucial to remember, too, that in reality these divisions are artificial, and that all of these problems ultimately spring from the same root: human fallenness. As creatures made in the image of God and dignified with the high calling to care for creation, we are the ones to whom God has entrusted the wellbeing of the animal kingdom and the natural world, and so the degradation of these on our watch because of our poor choices is ultimately evidence of our own decadence. While it is natural for each of us to find different aspects of this same basic problem more and less compelling (some of us are moved most deeply by the plight of the global poor, others by the suffering of animals or the degradation of the natural world), we would do best to cultivate a holistic sensitivity to all of the above, acknowledging that the flourishing of the whole is our ultimate aspiration.

As we strive to cultivate this holistic outlook, the need is paramount for an open spirit that does not retreat into denial or defensiveness in the face of these problems. For though our sacred texts provide general guidelines as to what a life of authentic Christian discipleship should look like, they do not directly address the question of how we should respond to the specific forms of alienation, suffering, and decline that have arisen in the wake of industrial agriculture over the past sixty years. Indeed, those who look to the Bible for an unobstructed path to the one true Christian diet usually end up perplexed. The bookends of Eden and the peaceable kingdom might seem to show that God's ideal for human beings is a plant-based diet. But the giving of animals to Noah for food and Jesus eating fish complicate the picture, suggesting that eating animals is permissible, at least in some circumstances. The strict dietary laws of the Hebrew Bible seem to show that reservations about unrestrained omnivorism have a divine precedent, but Paul enjoins us not to let dietary differences inhibit fellowship. A diet of vegetables emboldens Daniel in the lion's den, yet Paul curiously appears to associate vegetarianism with weak faith. Evidence of God's love and care for animals abounds throughout the scriptural record, but the record also includes animal sacrifice, at least until the Passover lamb gives way to the last supper—an event memorialized in the sacrament of a simple vegetarian meal.

The debate that ensues from these tensions has ancient roots in both Judaism and Christianity, and the biblical interpretation involved in discerning their contemporary significance traverses controversial theological and philosophical terrain.[6] When we combine the complexity of the biblical record with the knowledge that taking a stand on these issues requires sacrificing some of the conveniences to which we've grown accustomed (say, having access to unlimited quantities of inexpensive animal products), we may find ourselves tempted to exploit the Bible's lack of specific directives on these matters for our own selfish purposes. In such moments of weakness, we must remember St. Paul's injunction, in the absence of obvious, uncontroversial scriptural directives, to follow the Spirit where it leads and to know it by its fruits: love, joy, peace, patience, kindness, generosity, faithfulness, gentleness, and self-control. As we contemplate the consequences of the way we eat, we must consider whether these are the fruits of our daily choices. If, after honest discernment, the answer to this question is "no," then we must ready ourselves to take steps toward doing better.

As we consider the consequences of our daily choices, finally, we must take great care to remember that we are dealing here with the fallenness of the agricultural system at large—a system in which we are all involved at some level. As such, when the temptation arises to assign blame, we must strenuously resist the urge to scapegoat people who work in the industry—be they agribusiness people or workers on industrial farms—as "the real culprits" who bear the brunt of the responsibility. Farmers, after all, are just one link in a long supply chain and they are generally at the mercy of competitive markets that must answer to shareholders who demand high returns and consumers who demand low prices. If anything, the buck stops with those of us who have the power to demand positive changes or to patronize new and better markets. In short, we should humbly discern the planks in our own eyes before attending to specks in the eyes of others.

What, then, are some of the hidden costs to animals of our dependence on industrial agriculture? Other readings in this volume provide more comprehensive coverage of the gory details, but the short story is that the vast majority of animals used for food are raised in confinement systems that cause them acute and chronic suffering, that systematically frustrate their species-appropriate interests, and that nearly always result in their deaths. Roughly nine billion animals are slaughtered annually for food in the U.S. alone (not including billions of fish) so that Americans can consume over 200 pounds of meat per person per year—almost twice the global average. At the same time as we exploit, kill, and eat this historically unprecedented number of animals, we know more than ever before about their complex cognitive, emotional, and social lives, not just from the work of scientists and animal ethicists, but from our daily experience with the companion animals who live in almost 70% of our households.

Although Christians haven't been particularly well attuned to these hidden moral costs in the past, the time has come to be wary as serpents. By any defensible moral standard of welfare, a great many of the billions of animals raised and slaughtered for food every year by the industrial agricultural complex are enduring lives unbefitting creatures of God. If we ignore these animals' suffering, we do so at the peril of turning our backs on the scriptural record of God's original intentions for creation and God's plan for redeeming it. As Anglican theologian Andrew Linzey has observed, the redemptive power of Christ's gospel is for every creature. "To stand for Jesus," Linzey argues, "is to stand for a ministry of reconciliation to the whole of creation [. . .], to stand for active compassion for the weak [against exploitation by the powerful], to stand for animals as God's creatures, against all purely humanistic accounts of animals as things, commodities, resources, here for us."[7]

In failing to be moved by the suffering of animals in the industrial system, moreover, we must also deny the validity of both our own experience and contemporary scientific accounts of the kinds of beings these animals are. Just like the cats and dogs we cherish as our companions, the chickens, turkeys, pigs, cattle, sheep, laying hens, and dairy cows we use for food are unique individuals—sentient beings who are fully capable of feeling pain and experiencing psychological trauma. The structure of their bodies is significantly similar to our own, their nervous systems transmit pain in the same ways, and they manifest similar types of behavior when in pain or under stress. They form lasting bonds with members of their own species, and they experience significant trauma when these bonds are broken. Like us, they seek out pleasure and fulfillment, avoid pain and discomfort, and fight for their lives when faced with the threat of imminent death.

Note that none of this is to say that their suffering is on a moral or psychological par with human suffering. But please notice, too, that it doesn't need to be on a par with human suffering in order to count as something bad, even as something terribly evil—something that God-appointed stewards of creation should take great care to avoid inflicting or supporting without strong reasons for doing so. Though we could argue indefinitely over what constitutes a good reason to inflict this kind of suffering on animals, I hope that many of us can agree that the overproduction of inexpensive comfort food for comparatively affluent people at the expense of poorer people and our collective health is not a particularly attractive candidate.

ONWARD TOWARD THE PEACEABLE KINGDOM: WISDOM FOR THE JOURNEY

My final task is to highlight some of the unique advantages of this approach and offer some concluding advice on how to put these advantages to work as we take up the discipline of compassionate eating.

The first advantage of our approach is that it provides an *accessible, distinctively Christian framework* for coming to appreciate the moral and spiritual significance of some urgent contemporary issues that many Christians may otherwise find alienating or off-putting. Many Christians, for instance, are suspicious that "animal compassion" demotes human interests, or that "environmentalism" worships nature. Within this framework, however, such Christians can see the merits of deep concern for animals and the environment as perfectly consistent with our fundamental commitment to a theocentric universe in which human beings have been dignified with a special calling. Once attuned to this consistency, we can engage the causes of animal compassion and environmentalism not as "outside threats," but as productive challenges that can provoke our discovery of invigorating new possibilities for discipleship within our own tradition.

A second advantage of our approach is that it is *ecumenical*—it is inclusive of the interests of a wide variety of people, including different types of Christians, people of other faith traditions, and even some non-religious people. Christians of a conservative stripe can appreciate our strategy's emphasis on the sovereignty of God, the authority of scripture, and the importance of personal responsibility to the moral and spiritual life. Christians of a more progressive stripe may resonate with its emphasis on social justice, its sensitivity to the importance of engaging culture and questioning the status quo, and its call to make the imitation of Jesus a more salient feature of Christianity's contemporary witness. People of other faith traditions may find something useful in our strategy's emphases on revisiting the metaphysical vision of their tradition with fresh eyes for the purpose of inspiring more compassionate habits, and on the usefulness of spiritual disciplines for entrenching those habits (an approach to seeking authenticity that has been employed for millennia by pilgrims from virtually every spiritual heritage). Finally, non-religious people with a passion for the human, animal, and environmental concerns addressed here can perhaps see in our strategy an opportunity to make allies of people they once viewed as adversaries.

A third advantage of our approach is its *holism*. Rather than emphasizing the interests of just one aspect of the created order at the expense of others, the focus of our strategy is squarely on the flourishing of the whole. By highlighting the intimate connections among the different interests represented in creation and by recognizing that the degradation of any one of them has repercussions for the well-being of the others, we end up in a better position both to discern what moral and spiritual flourishing means for us and to negotiate conflicts of interest with the principles of compassion, justice, and sustainability in mind.

The fourth and most significant advantage of our approach is that the discipline of compassionate eating has its moral and spiritual sights set on *liberation and transformation rather than legalism and conformation*. Compassionate eating, as we have described it, begins not with a code of laws to which we are obliged to conform, but with the vision of an ideal toward which we are called to strive. Instead of saying "This activity is bad; don't do it!", our approach says "Practicing this discipline is liberating; take up the call and experience transformation!". The transformation we have in mind here, recall, is not a "once-and-for-all" arrival at a perfected state, but rather a disciplined process of ongoing striving that proceeds in full view of our fallen limitations, challenging us, nonetheless, to shoot ever higher as progress is achieved.

The goal of compassionate eating, in summary, is not some this-worldly utopia, nor is our disposition toward those who disagree with us one of separatist judgment. The two-fold aim, rather, is this: (1) to live as faithfully as we can toward the peaceable kingdom in which the harmony among human beings, animals and the natural world will be restored; and (2) to commit ourselves in the meanwhile to bringing pressure to bear on the institutions of the fallen world (of which we remain a part) in the hopes of raising the world's consciousness and advancing whatever improvements are possible under the specific fallen conditions in which we find ourselves. Promoting a "one-size-fits-all" legalism is a sure-fire way to achieve irrelevance. If this witness really matters to us, if we really believe in its transformative power, we must adapt it to the particular communities we serve, grounding our words and deeds in intimate knowledge of and respect for the cultural and socio-economic circumstances of the people with whom we live and work.

At the end of the day, it is the faithfulness of our discipleship rather than its impact on the world that matters most. Being a witness, after all, sometimes means being a martyr, and there will surely be times when the different choices we feel called to make will be met with indifference, cynicism or even contempt by the world at large, indeed perhaps even by our own friends or family. We must persevere, holding out hope that the many individual and social goods of compassionate eating—dare I say fruits of the spirit—will flourish.

NOTES

1. This reading is an abridged, revised version of Matthew C. Halteman, *Compassionate Eating as Care of Creation*, Washington, D.C.: Humane Society of the United States Faith Outreach, 2008. I am grateful to HSUS Faith Outreach for their encouragement to republish the piece here, and to *Interpretation* for permission to repurpose a passage from my "Knowing the Standard American Diet by Its Fruits: Is Unrestrained Omnivorism Spiritually Beneficial?", Interpretation, 67 (4), 383–395.

2. Since the original publication of this piece, Pope Francis has upped the ante in bringing Catholic concern for animals to public attention with his 2015 encyclical *Laudato Si': On Care for Our Common Home*. This encyclical is available in its entirety at http://w2.vatican .va/content/francesco/en/encyclicals/documents/papa-francesco_20150524_enciclica-laudato-si.html, as accessed on August 21, 2015.

3. Those interested in more direct engagements with the traditions of Buddhism, Daoism, Hinduism, indigenous religions, Islam, Judaism, Wicca, and others can find a wealth of resources in two recent anthologies: *A Communion of Subjects: Animals in Religion, Science, & Ethics*, Paul Waldau and Kimberly Patton, eds., New York: Columbia University Press, 2006; and *Call to Compassion: Religious Perspectives on Animal Advocacy*, Lisa Kemmerer and Anthony J. Nocella II, eds., New York: Lantern Books, 2011. Lisa Kemmerer's *Animals*

and World Religions (Oxford: Oxford University Press, 2012) is another excellent resource.

4. Walter Rauschenbusch, "For This World," in *For God and the People: Prayers of the Social Awakening*, New York: The Pilgrim Press, 1910, 47–48.

5. The original version of this piece addresses the human and environmental fallout as well. See Halteman 2008.

6. On Judaism, see Roberta Kalechofky, *Judaism and Animal Rights: Classical and Contemporary Responses* (Boston: Micah Books, 1992). On Christianity, see Andrew Linzey, *Animal Theology* (Chicago: University of Illinois Press, 1994); and *A Faith Embracing All Creatures* (Alexis-Baker and York, eds.; Eugene: Wipf and Stock, 2012).

7. Andrew Linzey, *Animal Gospel*, 11–18.

QUESTIONS

1. Halteman suggests that facing the fallout of our collective eating habits requires honesty, conviction, and imagination. But he intentionally frontloads the discussion of imagination, claiming that doing so is strategically important. Why does he believe that the discussion of imagination should come first? Can you think of any instances in your own experience where an expansion of your imagination has resulted in an increased sense of moral curiosity or responsibility?

2. The Christian cosmic vision of the "peaceable kingdom" that Halteman describes is clearly an ideal that is difficult or impossible to actualize in the real world. As such, it may seem hopelessly "pie in the sky" to some people. Is that a problem for Halteman's view? In your opinion, are spiritual or moral ideals better or worse to the degree that they are realizable in the here and now? If so, why? If not, why not? How might an unrealizable ideal be morally edifying and even practically useful?

3. What do you think of the idea of intentional eating practices functioning as a spiritual discipline? Could this idea work outside of a religious context, or does it require a robust cosmic vision in order to work?

4. On Halteman's account, an honest look at the consequences of our collective eating habits confronts us with serious moral and practical problems for human beings, animals, and the environment. Up against problems this huge, one might worry that a single individual's eating practices don't make any difference. Still, Halteman seems to think that a commitment to compassionate eating is important, even if its impact on the world is negligible. Drawing on the chapter introduction's accounts of symbolism, virtue, and authenticity, help Halteman defend his view against this worry. Now criticize Halteman's view on utilitarian grounds. Consider the Singer and Korsgaard readings in Chapter 7, "Industrial Animal Agriculture." What, if anything, would their objections be?

WENDY DONIGER

Compassion toward Animals, and Vegetarianism

This selection comes from Doniger's response to J. M. Coetzee's *The Lives of Animals*, a novella that's in part about industrial animal agriculture and partly about dealing with people whose moral views differ—sometimes quite dramatically—from one's own. Doniger provides a *very* brief history of Buddhist, Hindu, and Jain thought on killing animals (and other living things) for food and also on using those animals for food by, for example, milking them.

It's full of fascinating, short arguments on consumption and oblation. Unlike the purely secular arguments in the book *The Lives of Animals*, Doniger puts forward arguments according to which certain foods are pollutants and also a startling argument according to which living things, being divine, are *ipso facto* edible. She shows a way toward vegetarianism rather than the "two natural extremes of raw flesh [omnivorism] and grass [veganism]."

... After about the sixth century B.C.E., most Hindus, Buddhists, and Jains did indeed feel that people should not eat animals, in part, as is generally argued, because they themselves might be reborn as animals, but more because they feared that animals might retaliate in the afterworld. A Vedic text from 900 B.C.E. tells of a boy who went to "the world beyond" (that is, the world to which one goes after death—the theory of rebirth is not yet reflected in this text) and saw a man cut another man to pieces and eat him, and another man "eating a man who was screaming," and another man "eating a man who was *soundlessly* screaming." When he returned to earth, his father explained that the first man represented people who, when they had been in *this* world, had cut down trees and burnt them, the second people who had cooked for themselves animals that cry out, and the third people who had cooked for themselves rice and barley, which scream soundlessly.[1]

Now, we might regard this as an extreme ecological program—to ban not only the eating of animals, but the burning of fuel and the consumption of vegetables (there was one Hindu, in the twentieth century, who claimed to have recorded the screams of carrots that were strapped down to a table and chopped up). But in fact this is not what this text argues for. When the terrified boy asked his father, "How can one avoid that fate?" his father told him that he could easily avoid it simply by offering oblations to the gods before consuming fuel, animals, and vegetables. This is an example of . . . rationalization . . .: invent the gods and blame *them*.

Other parts of this same text do express a kind of submerged guilt at the slaughter of animals, perhaps even compassion, though the ostensible point of the myth is to justify the slaughter: in the beginning, cattle had the skin that humans have now, and humans had the skin that cattle have now. Cattle could not bear the heat, rain, flies, and mosquitoes,

Wendy Doniger, "Reflections," in J. M. Coetzee, *The Lives of Animals*. Edited by Amy Gutmann. © 1999 Princeton University Press. Reprinted by permission of Princeton University Press.

and asked humans to change skins with them; in return, they said, "You can eat us and use our skin for your clothing." And so it was. And the sacrificer puts on the red hide of a cow so that, when he goes to the other world, cattle do not eat him; otherwise, they would eat him.[2] Another common ploy to assuage guilt—which is to say, to silence compassion—was to assert that the animal willingly sacrificed itself.[3] On yet other occasions an attempt was made to convince the animal that it was not in fact killed. Thus in the hymn of the horse sacrifice in the *Rig Veda,* ca. 1000 B.C.E., the priest says to the horse, "You do not really die through this, nor are you harmed. You go on paths pleasant to go on."[4]

Hindu legal texts generated a great deal of what we now call "language" to sidestep this deep ambivalence. The most famous of these texts, *The Laws of Manu,* composed in the early centuries of the Common Era, ricochets back and forth between the vegetarian and sacrificial stances:

> As many hairs as there are on the body of the sacrificial animal that he kills for no (religious) purpose here on earth, so many times will he, after his death, suffer a violent death in birth after birth. The Self-existent one himself created sacrificial animals for sacrifice; sacrifice is for the good of this whole (universe); and therefore killing in a sacrifice is not killing. Herbs, sacrificial animals, trees, animals (other than sacrificial animals), and birds who have been killed for sacrifice win higher births again. On the occasion of offering the honey-mixture (to a guest), at a sacrifice, and in rituals in which the ancestors are the deities, and only in these circumstances, should sacrificial animals suffer violence, but not on any other occasion; this is what Manu has said.[5]

Outside the sacrificial arena, the cow that generously gives her milk replaces the steer that must be slaughtered to provide food;[6] Hindu myths imagine the transition from hunting to farming, from killing to milking, from blood sacrifice to vegetable sacrifice.[7]

We may see a variant of this argument in a part of *Gulliver's Travels.* . . . When Gulliver finds himself unable to live on either the vegetarian fare of the Houyhnhnms or the flesh that is the food of the horrid Yahoos, he devises a solution: "I observed a cow passing by; whereupon I pointed to her, and expressed a desire to let me go and milk her." Henceforth

Gulliver survives, in perfect health, on a diet of milk and a bread made of oats—two civilized alternatives to the two natural extremes of raw flesh and grass.

In Hindu myths of this genre, the humans among the animals eat "fruits and roots"; in the Buddhist variants, they eat nothing at all (not being true humans yet) or they eat the earth itself, which is delicious and nourishing, and is sometimes called the earth-cow.[8] (Shame, too, . . . enters in here: when people begin to hoard the food given by the earth-cow, they build houses to hide both the food and their newly discovered sexuality; for people who watch others copulating say, "How could anyone treat someone else like that?" and throw clods of earth at them.)[9] These two strategies, one realistic and one fantastic, provide natural alternatives to the food that men do in fact share with *unmythical* animals: meat.

But it is not quite so simple. Vegetarianism and compassion for animals are not the same thing at all. . . . It is usual for most *individuals* to eat meat without killing animals (most nonvegetarians, few of whom hunt or butcher, do it every day) and equally normal for an individual to kill without eating the kill—or, indeed, any other meat (what percentage of hit men or soldiers devour their fallen enemies?). Indeed, one historian of ancient India has suggested that vegetarianism and killing were originally mutually exclusive: that in the earliest period of Indian civilization, meat-eating householders would, in time of war, consecrate themselves as warriors by giving up the eating of meat.[10] They either ate meat *or* killed. In later Hinduism, the strictures against eating and killing continued to work at odds, so that it was regarded as better (for most people, in general: the rules would vary according to the caste status of the person in each case) to kill an Untouchable than to kill a Brahmin, but better to eat a Brahmin (presuming that one came across a dead one) than to eat an Untouchable (under the same circumstances). It is within this world of revisionist scripture and unresolved ambivalence that we must come to terms with Gandhi's twisted vegetarianism—rightly problematized by "the blond man" who argues with Norma.

Nevertheless, the logical assumption that any animal that one ate had to have been killed by *someone* led to a natural association between the ideal of vegetarianism and the ideal of nonviolence toward living creatures. And this ideal came to prevail in India, reinforced by the idea of reincarnation and its implication that humans and animals were part of a single system of the recycling of souls: do not kill an animal, for it might be your grandmother, or your grandchild, or you.

COMPASSION TOWARD ANIMALS, AND INDIVIDUAL HUMAN SALVATION

But compassion for animals is seldom the dominant factor in South Asian arguments for vegetarianism. Buddhists and Jains cared . . . for individual human salvation, more, really, than they cared for animals; they refrained from killing and eating animals to protect their own souls from pollution (and even, as Norma nastily but correctly points out, to protect their bodies from social pollution). Yet it seems to me that this argument for individual salvation could be adopted in a secular form in the Western conversation more often than it is. It is an argument often made against capital punishment, that it should be abolished not because of its evil effects upon criminals but because it is bad for *us,* bad for us to be a people who kill people like that. So, too, whether or not we can argue that killing animals for food or experimentation is bad for the universe, for the food supply, for medical advances, or even whether or not we can prove that animals suffer as we do, or know that they are going to die, we might take from the South Asian context the very wise argument that *we* know that they are going to die, and that *that* makes it bad for us to kill them.

COMPASSION FOR ANIMALS AS NONOTHER

Let me turn now to the argument, implicit in the rebirth scenario, that we must not kill and eat animals because they are like us. In India, this argument begins the other way around: the Vedic myths of sacrifice (before the theory of rebirth) close the gap between humans and animals in the other direction, by including humans with animals as sacrificial beasts. The Sanskrit term *Pashu* (cognate with Latin *pecus,* cattle [as in Pecos Bill or impecunious—meaning having no cattle, no bread, no money]) designates sacrificial and domestic animals, animals that we keep until we slaughter them, either in ritual or for food, or both. These are the animals that we own and measure ourselves by; they are the animals that are us. *Mriga,* related to the verb "to hunt" (*margayati,* from which is also derived the noun *marga,* "a trail or path"), designates any animal that we hunt, in particular a deer. But just as "deer" in English comes from the German *Tier,* meaning any wild animal, a meaning that persisted in English for some time (Shakespeare used the phrase "small deer" in this sense), so too in Sanskrit the paradigmatic *mriga,* the wild animal par excellence, is the deer, just as the paradigmatic *pashu* is the cow (or, more precisely, the bull). But *mriga* is also the general term for any wild animal in contrast with any tame beast or *pashu. Pashus* are the animals that get sacrificed, whatever their origins; *mrigas* are the animals that get hunted. In both cases, the ancient Indians defined animals according to the manner in which they killed them.

The Vedas and Brahmanas often list five basic kinds of sacrificial animal or *pashu*: bull (*go,* which can also mean "cow"), horse, billygoat, ram, and human being (person, particularly male person or man).[11] The later Vedic tradition then opens the gap by distinguishing humans from animals in sacrificing only animals; *The Laws of Manu* lists *pashus, mrigas,* and humans as three separate groups—though one Hindu commentator glosses this by saying that, even though humans are in fact *pashus,* they are mentioned separately because of their special preeminence.[12] And still later Hinduism once again narrows the gap between humans and animals by joining humans and animals together as creatures *not* to be sacrificed, in contrast with vegetables (which remain stubbornly other).[13]

To imply that humans are sacrificial victims just like other animals, and to imply that neither humans nor animals should be sacrificial victims, are two very different ways of expressing the belief that we are like animals. So, too, the decision not to kill and/ or eat animals follows from the belief that, since animals are nonother, to eat them is a kind of cannibalism. On the other hand, the belief that animals are *so* other as to be gods gives yet another swing to the pendulum and produces a reason to eat such animals after all—to eat them ritually, which lands us back at square one. The argument that humans (but not animals) are created in the image of god is often used in the West to justify cruelty to animals, but most mythologies assume that animals, *rather than humans,* are the image of god—which may be a reason *to eat them.*

The belief that animals are like us in some essential way is the source of the enduring and widespread myth of a magic time or place or person that erases the boundary between humans and animals. The place is like the Looking-Glass forest where things have no names, where Alice could walk with her arms around the neck of a fawn. The list of people who live at peace among animals would include Enkidu in the epic of *Gilgamesh* and the many mythical children who are raised as cubs by a pack of animals, like Romulus and Remus, Mowgli, and Tarzan, like Pecos Bill (suckled by a puma) and Davy Crockett (raised among mountain lions). T. H. White, translator of a medieval bestiary, imagined the young King Arthur's education by Merlin the magician as taking place among ants and geese and owls and badgers.[14] This myth is very different from the mythologies of bestiality, which imagine a very different sort of intimacy (though the two intersect uncomfortably in the image of "lying down with" animals, literally sleeping with animals).[15] Our myths generally do *not* define animals as those with whom we do not have sex (though the president's elegant wife, Olivia Garrard, favors this distinction).

The ideal state of humans among animals is not one in which wild animals become tame (like Elsa the Lioness in *Born Free,* or the Lone Ranger's horse Silver). It is a state in which a human becomes one of the animals. Or rather, more precisely, a human becomes part of the society of the animals but remains a human, like Barbara Smuts among the nonhuman primates; the adopted child in the myth must eventually return to the human world. In contrast with the rituals of cultural transformation, in which we cease to eat flesh by becoming quintessentially cultural and eating bread or milk instead, these are myths of natural transformation, in which we become quintessentially natural and eat what animals eat (food that may in fact include other animals).

NOTES

1. *Jaiminiya Brahmana* 1.42–44; Wendy Doniger O'Flaherty, *Tales of Sex and Violence: Folklore, Sacrifice, and Danger in the Jaiminiya Brahmana* (Chicago: University of Chicago Press, 1985), 32–35.

2. See the story of "How Men Changed Skins with Animals," *Jaiminiya Brahmana* 2.182–83; also in O'Flaherty, *Tales of Sex and Violence.* For a discussion of this genre of prevarication in other religions, see Jonathan Z. Smith, "The Bare Facts of Ritual," in *Imagining Religion* (Chicago: University of Chicago Press, 1982), 53–65.

3. See the discussion of the willingness of the sacrificed animal in Wendy Doniger O'Flaherty, "The Good and Evil Shepherd," in *Gilgul: Essays on Transformation, Revolution, and Permanence in the History of Religions, Dedicated to Zwi Werblowsky,* ed. S. Shaked, D. Shulman, and G. G. Stromsa (Leiden: E. J. Brill, 1987), 169–91.

4. *Rig Veda* 1.162.21; Wendy Doniger O'Flaherty, *The Rig Veda: An Anthology, 108 Hymns Translated from the Sanskrit* (Harmondsworth: Penguin Classics, 1981), 91.

5. *The Laws of Manu* 5.38–41; *The Laws of Manu,* a new translation of the *Manavadharmasastra,* by Wendy Doniger, with Brian K. Smith (Harmondsworth: Penguin Classics, 1991), 103.

6. Wendy Doniger O'Flaherty, *Women, Androgynes, and Other Mythical Beasts* (Chicago: University of Chicago Press, 1980), 239–54.

7. Wendy Doniger O'Flaherty, *Other Peoples' Myths: The Cave of Echoes* (New York: Macmillan, 1988; reprint, University of Chicago Press, 1995), 82–96.

8. Wendy Doniger O'Flaherty, *The Origins of Evil in Hindu Mythology* (Berkeley and Los Angeles: University of California Press, 1976), 29, 321–46.

9. *Digha Nikaya,* Aggañña Suttanta 27.10; *Visuddhimagga* 13.49; cited by O'Flaherty, *Origins of Evil,* 33.

10. Jan Heesterman, *The Inner Conflict of Tradition* (Chicago: University of Chicago Press, 1985).

11. *Atharva Veda* 11.2.9, with Sayana's commentary.

12. Govindaraja on *Manu* 1.39. In *Manu-Smrti, with Nine Commentaries,* ed. Jayantakrishna Harikrishna Dave (Bombay: Bharatiya Vidya Series, no. 29, 1975).

13. O'Flaherty, *Other Peoples' Myths,* 82–83.

14. T. H. White, *The Once and Future King* (London: Fontana Books, 1962); pt. 1, "The Sword in the Stone." The culmination of the animal education comes in chap. 23.

15. Wendy Doniger O'Flaherty, "The Mythology of Masquerading Animals, or, Bestiality" (in *In the Company of Animals,* ed. Arien Mack, *Social Research: An International Quarterly of the Social Sciences* 62, no. 3 [Fall 1995]: 751–72).

QUESTIONS

1. Doniger puts forward various Indic explanations of why one at least sometimes should not eat meat. What are they? Which are *moral*? Which are *prudential*? Which are motivated by concern for animals? Which are motivated by concern for oneself or other people? Which are motivated by disgust? What does reincarnation have to do with various prohibitions?

2. Consider Doniger's arguments from premises about the effects on us of meat eating or animal killing. What do those premises imply, if anything, about slaughterhouse work?

3. Explain the difference between the prudential case against killing animals and the "compassion"-based case.

4. Explain the distinction between the types of ideals Doniger describes at the end—our becoming wild and wild animals becoming tame. What do these ideals teach us about food ethics?

5. In the Jewish Torah, eating sea creatures lacking fins and scales is forbidden: "anything that does not have fins and scales you may not eat; *for you it is unclean*" (Deuteronomy 14:10; cf. Leviticus 11:9–10). The idea is not just that you will be tainted if you eat a fish without scales but that you will be tainted *because* uncleanliness will move contagiously from the fish to you. How does this idea compare to the Indic ideas Doniger mentions about pollutants? How does it compare to the idea in Chapter 4, "Consumer Ethics," that it is wrong to eat food that is wrongly produced because in doing so you are *complicit* in wrongdoing?

Selections from *Laws of Manu*

This is an ancient Indic religious text. The editor nicely describes it as a text that "ricochets" between prohibiting eating meat and allowing it on the condition that it is properly blessed. It thus captures a common position in the food ethics world: Meat eating—like meat raising—is morally permissible but only under certain quite strict conditions. Whereas a secular take on this—expressed in the Salatin reading in Chapter 8, "Alternatives to Industrial Animal Agriculture"—is that those conditions have to do with the lives of animals, the stress in *The Laws of Manu* is on blessing the food you eat.

Wendy Doniger and Brian Smith, trans., *Laws of Manu* (New York: Penguin, 1992), 102–104.

[*1*] When the sages had heard these duties of a Vedic graduate thus declared, they said this to the great-souled Bhṛgu, who was born of fire: [*2*] "My lord, how can Death have power over priests who know the teaching of the Veda and who fulfil their own particular duty as it has just been described?" [*3*] Bhṛgu, the son of Manu, who was the soul of religion, replied to the great sages:

Listen to the fault through which Death tries to kill priests. [*4*] Through failure to study the Vedas, the neglect of proper conduct, inattentiveness to duties, and eating the wrong food, Death tries to kill priests.

[*5*] Garlic, scallions, onions, and mushrooms, and the things that grow from what is impure, are not to be eaten by twice-born men. [*6*] The red sap of trees, and any exudations from a cut (in a tree), the "phlegmatic" fruit, and the first milk of a newly-calved cow—you should try not to eat these. [*7*] (And do not eat) a dish of rice with sesame seeds, or a spice cake made of flour, butter, and sugar, or a cake made of rice, milk and sugar, if these are prepared for no (religious) purpose; or meat that has not been consecrated; or food for the gods, or offerings; [*8*] or the milk of a cow within ten days of calving, or the milk of a camel or of any animal with a whole, solid hoof, or of a ewe, or of a cow in heat or a cow whose calf has been taken from her; [*9*] and avoid the milk of women, the milk of all wild animals in the wilderness except the buffalo, and all foods that have gone sour or fermented. [*10*] But among foods that have gone sour or fermented, yogurt can be eaten, and all foods made with yogurt, as well as whatever is extracted from auspicious flowers, roots, and fruits.

[*11*] Do not eat carnivorous birds or any birds that live in villages, or any whole-hoofed animals that have not been specially permitted; or little finches, [*12*] the sparrow, the aquatic bird, the goose, the waterbird, the village cock, the crane, the wildfowl, the moorhen, the parrot, and the starling; [*13*] birds that strike with their beaks, web-footed birds, the paddy-bird, birds that scratch with their toes, and birds that dive and eat fish; or meat from a butcher or dried meat; [*14*] or the heron or the crane, the raven or the wagtail; or (animals) that eat fish, or dung-heap pigs, or any fish. [*15*] Someone who eats the meat of

an animal is called an eater of that animal's meat; someone who eats fish is an eater of every animal's meat; therefore you should avoid eating fish. [*16*] But sheat-fish and red fish may be eaten if they are used as offerings to the gods or the ancestors, and "striped," "lion-faced," and "scaly" fish can always be eaten.

[*17*] You should not eat solitary or unknown wild animals or birds, nor any animals with five claws, not even those listed among the animals that may be eaten. [*18*] They say that, among the animals with five claws, the porcupine, hedgehog, iguana, rhinoceros, tortoise, and hare may be eaten, as well as animals with one row of teeth, except for the camel.

[*19*] Any twice-born person who knowingly eats mushrooms, a dung-heap pig, garlic, a village cock, onions, or scallions, will fall. [*20*] If he unknowingly eats (any of) these six, he should perform the "Heating" vow or the "Ascetic's Moon-course" vow; and for (eating any of) the others, he should fast for a day. [*21*] A priest should perform the "Painful" vow once a year in any case, in order to clean himself from anything (forbidden) that he has unknowingly eaten; but (he should do it) specially for (anything that he has eaten) knowingly.

[*22*] Wild animals and birds that are permitted (to be eaten) may be killed by priests for sacrifices and for the livelihood of dependents; for Agastya did this long ago. [*23*] Indeed, in the ancient sacrifices of the sages that were offered by priests and rulers, the sacrificial cakes were made of edible wild animals and birds. [*24*] Any food that is permitted (to be eaten) and is not despised may be eaten if oil is added to it, even if it has been kept overnight; and so can what is left over from an oblation. [*25*] But the twice-born may eat anything that is made of barley and wheat, or dishes cooked with milk, without adding oil, even when they have been standing for a long time.

[*26*] The list of what can be eaten and cannot be eaten by the twice-born has thus been declared, leaving nothing out. Now I will tell the rule for eating and not eating meat.

[*27*] You may eat meat that has been consecrated by the sprinkling of water, or when priests want to have it, or when you are properly engaged in a ritual, or when your breath of life is in danger. [*28*] The Lord

of Creatures fashioned all this (universe) to feed the breath of life, and everything moving and stationary is the food of the breath of life. [29] Those that do not move are food for those that move, and those that have no fangs are food for those with fangs; those that have no hands are food for those with hands; and cowards are the food of the brave. [30] The eater who eats creatures with the breath of life who are to be eaten does nothing bad, even if he does it day after day; for the Ordainer himself created creatures with the breath of life, some to be eaten and some to be eaters. [31] "Eating meat is (right) for the sacrifice": this is traditionally known as a rule of the gods. But doing it on occasions other than this is said to be the rule of ogres. [32] Someone who eats meat, after honouring the gods and ancestors, when he has bought it, or killed it himself, or has been given it by someone else, does nothing bad.

[33] A twice-born person who knows the rules should not eat meat against the rules, even in extremity; for if he eats meat against the rules, after his death he will be helplessly eaten by them (that he ate). [34] The guilt of someone who kills wild animals to sell them for money is not so great, after his death, as that of someone who eats meat for no (religious) purpose. [35] But when a man who is properly engaged in a ritual does not eat meat, after his death he will become a sacrificial animal during twenty-one rebirths. [36] A priest should never eat sacrificial animals that have not been transformed by Vedic verses; but with the support of the obligatory rule, he may eat them when they have been transformed by Vedic verses. [37] If he has an addiction (to meat), let him make a sacrificial animal out of clarified butter or let him make a sacrificial animal out of flour; but he should never wish to kill a sacrificial animal for no (religious) purpose.

[38] As many hairs as there are on the body of the sacrificial animal that he kills for no (religious) purpose here on earth, so many times will he, after his death, suffer a violent death in birth after birth. [39] The Self-existent one himself created sacrificial animals for sacrifice; sacrifice is for the good of this whole (universe); and therefore killing in a sacrifice is not killing. [40] Herbs, sacrificial animals, trees, animals (other than sacrificial animals), and birds

who have been killed for sacrifice win higher births again. [41] On the occasion of offering the honey-mixture (to a guest), at a sacrifice, and in rituals in which the ancestors are the deities, and only in these circumstances, should sacrificial animals suffer violence, but not on any other occasion; this is what Manu has said.

[42] A twice-born person who knows the true meaning of the Vedas and injures sacrificial animals for these (correct) purposes causes both himself and the animal to go to the highest level of existence. [43] A twice-born person who is self-possessed should never commit violence that is not sanctioned by the Veda, whether he is living in (his own) home, or with a guru, or in the wilderness, not even in extremity. [44] The violence to those that move and those that do not move which is sanctioned by the Veda and regulated by the official restraints—that is known as non-violence, for the law comes from the Veda.

[45] Whoever does violence to harmless creatures out of a wish for his own happiness does not increase his happiness anywhere, neither when he is alive nor when he is dead. [46] But if someone does not desire to inflict on creatures with the breath of life the sufferings of being tied up and slaughtered, but wishes to do what is best for everyone, he experiences pleasure without end. [47] A man who does no violence to anything obtains, effortlessly, what he thinks about, what he does, and what he takes delight in. [48] You can never get meat without violence to creatures with the breath of life, and the killing of creatures with the breath of life does not get you to heaven; therefore you should not eat meat.

[49] Anyone who looks carefully at the source of meat, and at the tying up and slaughter of embodied creatures, should turn back from eating any meat.

[50] A man who does not behave like the flesh-eating ghouls and does not eat meat becomes dear to people and is not tortured by diseases. [51] The one who gives permission, the one who butchers, the one who slaughters, and the one who buys and sells, the one who prepares it, the one who serves it, and the eater—they are killers. [52] No one is a greater wrong-doer than the person who, without reverence to the gods and the ancestors, wishes to make his flesh grow by the flesh of others.

[*53*] The man who offers a horse-sacrifice every year for a hundred years, and the man who does not eat meat, the two of them reap the same fruit of good deeds. [*54*] A man who eats pure fruits and roots, or who eats what hermits eat, does not reap fruit (as great as that) of refraining from eating meat. [*55*] "He whose *meat* in this world do I eat will in the other world *me eat.*" Wise men say that this is why meat is called meat. [*56*] There is nothing wrong in eating meat, nor in drinking wine, nor in sexual union, for this is how living beings engage in life, but disengagement yields great fruit.

NOTES

[7] Meat is consecrated by sprinkling water on it and saying Vedic verses over it at the public (*śrauta*) sacrifices. The sacrificial foods should be offered first to the gods (and the priests), and only then may the remnants be eaten by other people.

[8] Animals with a whole, solid hoof (*ekaśapha*) are the class of equines.

[9] Buffalo were evidently still found in the wild at this period in India, though they were also already widely domesticated.

[11] The general prohibition against eating whole-hooved animals, which has already been stated in 5.8,

admits at least one important exception: the horse that is slaughtered and eaten in the horse-sacrifice.

[19] Here, as elsewhere, the "fall" might be from caste, in this world, or into hell, in the next.

[22] One commentator on this verse says Agastya did this to feed his children. Agastya is also said to have easily digested several demons and the entire ocean in order to help the gods, who were in a sense his dependents at that time (*Mahābhārata* 3.97, 100–103).

[54] The commentators explain that a person should merely refrain from eating the meat specifically prohibited by the teachings. The verse implies that it is better to eat all sorts of foods except meat (or except certain meats) than to subsist on hermit-food alone.

[55] This translation of this much-quoted verse is based on that of Charles Lanman, who attempted to capture the Sanskrit pun: meat is called *māṃsa* because he (*sa*) eats me (*mām*) in the other world if I eat him now. A similar pun is made in Vedantic texts on the metaphor for the soul, the swan (*haṃsa*), said to express the identity of the individual soul (*ātman*) and the world-soul (*brahman*): 'I am he' (*ahaṃsa*).

[56] The implication is that these activities are permitted under the specified circumstances, but that, even then, it is better to refrain from them and, perhaps, to refrain from engagement in life in general (*pravṛtti*), which is here, as often, explicitly contrasted with a word that means disengagement (*nivṛtti*) from life in general.

QUESTIONS

1. The prohibition on eating mushrooms, garlic, and so on in the reading is based on their *impurity*. A consumer will himself become impure by eating them. This is a very different sort of explanation against why you shouldn't eat mushrooms than, say, Tristram McPherson's explanation in Chapter 4, "Consumer Ethics," of why you shouldn't eat meat. What are some other moral requirements that might be explained in terms of avoiding impurity? If you are a member of a religious group, are there prohibitions in your religious tradition that are purity based? What are they?

2. The teachings stress the importance of *blessing* food in order to make what would otherwise be impermissibly consumed permissibly consumed. Is blessing important to you? Is blessing *food*? (In the Talmud, God Himself is blessed before eating.) Why is blessing important? Does it *recognize* significance that was already there? *Bestow* significance on something that had none before? How does this fit in with various indigenous traditions that the Kemmerer reading in this chapter discusses?

3. The stunning diversity of things that might be eaten—that the teachings mention as edible—reminds us of how few things we eat. This is connected with questions about hunger and food waste that are explored in Chapter 4, "Consumer Ethics." They are also connected with questions about the virtues of thrift and the vice of wastefulness. Are such things virtues in your religious tradition? Why are they virtues?

4. The reading articulates the view that the eater of an animal, its buyer, its butcher, and its seller are all *killers* of the animal. The view is not simply that the eater is somehow responsible for the killing but is herself a killer. Why might you think that? What might you think about the view that even if the eater does not kill the animal, the eater is as much or as little to blame as the killer?

LISA KEMMERER

Indigenous Traditions

This piece widely surveys the views of a host of indigenous religions and cosmic visions nominally on the subject of animals, but, really, on much more, including the environment, consumption, even food workers. Common to most is a view according to which compassion toward animals is required and that animals are to be treated with respect. But how to interpret these notions is difficult and, as Kemmerer spells out, those varying interpretations lead to substantively different ethical views.

We are as one: earth, sky, all living things, the two-legged, the four-legged, the winged ones, the trees, the grasses.
  —*Sioux myth of White Buffalo Woman*

Quetzalcoatl became famous for his moral principles. He had great respect for all forms of life. He did not believe in killing flowers by picking them, or killing any of the animals of the forest.
  —*Aztec myth of Quetzalcoatl*

. . . Indigenous religious traditions do not share a founder (as do Buddhists, and Muslims, for example); nor do they share a particular body of sacred texts (as do Hindus and Jews, for example). Indigenous religious traditions tend to be similar in critical ways, but

each tradition is distinct and separate. I use the term "indigenous traditions" throughout this chapter, but I use the term only as a generalization. While most indigenous religious traditions will fit within the patterns mentioned herein—the vast majority, in fact—it is always likely that there is an exception to the rule.

"INDIGENOUS"

. . . . Though all humans are indigenous only to Africa—or perhaps certain regions of Africa—most of us use this term to mean something quite different. For the purposes of this chapter, *indigenous religious traditions* refer to spiritual beliefs and practices that existed before the advent of Jewish, Confucian, Daoist, or Hindu traditions (which means that they also existed before Buddhist, Christian, and Islamic beliefs and practices). These ancient belief systems and their associated lifeways have, of course, changed across centuries, but there has been much more continuity than change, particularly in their mythology, which I will turn to shortly. The beliefs and lifeways of indigenous peoples persisted as identifiable religious traditions for centuries—most often until they were damaged or destroyed by Western influence—and each indigenous religious tradition is unique. . . . .

This chapter explores beliefs, myths, and practices from a plethora of indigenous peoples around the world. This kaleidoscope of indigenous religious beliefs and practices demonstrates that despite a lack of shared origins and texts, indigenous religious traditions tend to share important similarities concerning rightful relations between humans and nonhumans.

MYTH

Myth, perhaps most appropriately described as sacred wisdom, is critical to understanding religions. Myths contain a people's worldview; they "encapsulate and condense . . . views of the world, of ultimate reality, and of the relationships between the Creator, the universe, and humanity" (Henare, 201–2). For example, sub-Saharan African mythology answers "questions of meaning and value" about a people's place, and relations with the larger world (Opoku, 351). Maori (New Zealand) myths contain a people's worldview and spiritual vision (Henare, 202). Myths of the Koyukon (interior Alaska), called Distant Time stories, contain the sacred word of the Koyukon and are best understood in relation to the historic position of the Bible in Western societies (Jette, "On Ten'a"). Similarly, Koyukon myths provide people "with a foundation for understanding the natural world" (R. Nelson, *Make,* 18, 227).

Myths are a living reality intended to guide daily life. Stories told through myths are "believed to have occurred in remote times" but are also believed to affect "daily life and human destiny" (Silva, 307). Myth is not about the past, ultimately, but about the present. For instance, the Nahua (Mesoamericans dwelling in the mountains of Mexico, near Mexico City), describe myth as an ever-present truth (Silva, 307). In the Arctic, myth is believed to tie traditional Koyukon people to their past while governing daily life (C. Thompson). Mayans (northern Central American region, including present-day nations of Guatemala, Belize, western Honduras, El Salvador, and southern Mexico) continue to use myth to teach children (Montejo, 177). Myths tell people who they are and how to live.

SACRED NATURE, SACRED ANYMALS

Indigenous peoples do not generally hold an idea of "nature" separate and apart from humanity or from the spirit world. Instead, they most often view the supernatural world as here, among us, and they tend to view humans as just one part of a perpetual sacred life that encompasses the entire cosmos (Prabhu, 58): "For indigenous people, the environment and the supernatural realm are interconnected" (Montejo, 176–77). Indigenous peoples in India, for example, generally accept that "there is no distinction between the sacred and the profane or even between nature and humans" (Prabhu, 58). The Arapaho (South/Central America) view creation as an ongoing process in which the sacred is ever-present in the natural world. Melanesian indigenous people believe that humans, plants, and animals are all infused with spirit, and "the environment is a place of worship" that sustains all forms of life (Namunu, 251). Melanesian indigenous people teach their young that we are all "surrounded with creative energies flowing through trees, grasses, streams, and rivers, mountains, sea, sky and all the galaxies, animals, birds, and humans. . . . The ecosystem [is] viewed with awe" (Namunu, 251).

Myths teach humanity to find the sacred in and through all aspects of the natural world (J. Brown, 26), and expose humanity as just one part of an ongoing sacred life that includes the entire cosmos. For example, indigenous peoples in India feel that humans, "nature, and the supernatural are all bound in a mutual relationship" (Prabhu, 57).

Supernatural and natural become one in the indigenous worldview, and mythology invariably provides a spiritual outlook of admiration and respect for the natural world *in and of itself* (Clark, 124). For indigenous peoples, nature is often viewed as a "temple, and within this sanctuary [people ought to show] great respect to every form, function, and power. . . .[R]everence for nature and for life is *central* to their religion" (J. Brown, 37). Humans must show respect to iguanas and eels (as well as rivers and trees), and respect is built into many indigenous religious beliefs and practices (Kwiatkowska-Szatzscheider, 268, 271). Koyukon Distant Time stories, for example, teach people to *serve* nature—all of nature—the dominant force (Jette, "On Superstitions," 88). The West African term *Nyam* refers to "an enduring power and energy" that is within all life forms, such that "all forms of life are deemed to possess certain rights, which cannot be violated" (Riley, 479).

The Western dualistic division of nature and humanity, or nature and civilization, stands in stark contrast to the indigenous view, in which humans are part of the world around them, and in which the entirety of the natural world shares in the powers of the spiritual world. Whether birch tree or lilac, Mexican long-tongued bat or Chinese paddlefish, cliff or beach—everything that indigenous people find in the world around them is considered sacred.

INDIGENOUS PHILOSOPHY AND MORALITY

Oneness and Interdependence

Just as indigenous peoples tend to view the earthly and the sacred as one, so they tend to recognize their own villages as part of a larger community that includes *all* of the natural world—poplar trees, minke whales (further endangered by plastics in our oceans), red-billed tropicbirds, geraniums, Tasmanian devils (the world's largest marsupial carnivore, currently endangered), sword ferns, and rugged mountains. Traditional Melanesians, for example, view the entire world, animate and inanimate, as part of their community (Namunu, 251). Haida people (western Canada) feel that their identity is "based on the land, the trees, and the whole of life within" (Suzuki, xxxiv); the land and all creatures "represent their history, their culture, their meaning, their very identity" (Suzuki and Knudtson, xxxi).

Indigenous peoples also tend to understand their expansive community is interdependent. Indigenous myths generally "illustrate the fact that all living things and natural entities, have a role to play in maintaining the web of life," whether grass snake or raccoon dog, human or grape vine (Cajete, 629). All beings are equal, and balance is essential. Myths of the Koyukon (interior Alaska) explain how Raven created a harmonious universe in which all beings both control and are controlled in equal measure. A Warao hunter (Orinoco Delta, Venezuela) "expects to be hunted" by others, such as boa constrictors and jaguars, even as he hunts (Wilbert, 396–97).

Indigenous peoples often feel a sense of responsibility to maintain the "continuity and balance of the cosmos" (Kwiatkowska-Szatzscheider, 271). The Cree (North Dakota, Montana, and north into Canada) note that "when humans live in balanced reciprocity with animals, each creates the continued conditions for the survival of the other as members of a society" (Feit, 423). When people do not live in a respectful and reasonable way, the web of life is shaken, endangering the existence of all who live in the extended community. The Nahua (near Mexico City) understand that their surroundings (*cemanahuac,* "that which surrounds us") are not only essential for their survival, but for the survival of all that dwell therein (Silva, 303, 319): All of nature is "important for the existence of any one being" (Silva, 303, 319).

Mayan *Popol Vuh* creation stories, for instance, highlight interconnections between humans, anymals, plants, and the land. Mayan myths remind that "the lives of humans, plants, animals, and the supernatural world" are interconnected in a deep kinship (Montejo, 180). Their creation stories tell humans that they have been placed into, and are dependent on, a larger, preexistent world. In the *Popol Vuh* there is a

> collective survival that must exist between humans, plants, and animals. Humans are not separate . . . [because] according to Mayan creation myths, corn . . . entered into the body and became the flesh of human beings. This, in turn, explains the profound respect, appreciation, and compassion that Mayans feel for trees and animals for whom they pray during the cyclical ceremonies of the Mayan new year. (Montejo, 177–78)

Human bodies are formed with corn, symbolic of the reality that humans cannot live without plant life. In the *Popol Vuh,* anymals of the earth—and the plants and land itself—do not belong to people; "rather, people belong to the earth" (Henare, 202).

Similarly, one of the "cardinal beliefs in the traditional religious heritage of Africa is the interconnectedness [and interdependence] of all that exists" (Opoku, 353). Indigenous sub-Saharan Africans understand humans to be "an inextricable part of the environment" and find "themselves to be in a neighborly relationship with . . . earth, trees, animals and spirits" (Opoku, 351). They do not see themselves as separate and distinct from nuguni cattle or Africana sheep, "but rather as beings in relation with the world around them" (Opoku, 353).

The Warao people (Orinoco Delta, Venezuela) also have no sense of separation between humanity and the rest of the living world. They "identify all animals (including themselves) by the root form 'arao,' meaning 'life'" (Wilbert, 393). Their own name entails the word for all life: *W-arao.* Their species classification system categorizes humans *with* other species, neither distinct nor separate.

The Warao classify species according to eco-niches (water, land, trees, or air), according to where they *sleep* (Wilbert, 393). They categorize species according to those who sleep *in* the ground, *on* the ground (terrestrial), in flood-forest pools and channels or swamp streams (aquatic), in tree trunks, or in tree overstories (arboreal) (Wilbert, 394). Life forms are thus viewed as aquatic, terrestrial, or aerial (including arboreal); humans belong in the category of *terrestrial animals* along with two-toed ungulates like the Chacoan peccary and the southern pudu.

Interestingly, according to Warao species categorization, one species can fit into more than one category, and individuals from one species can also be put in two different categories. For example, human communities that dwell and sleep in trees would fall into a different category from human communities that live and sleep on the ground. Given the interconnected nature of indigenous understandings, this makes perfect sense.

Warao cosmology is based on a vertical slice of the earth's surface, but their understanding of community is horizontal: "Hierarchical station and inborn advantage" are irrelevant (Wilbert, 394). While Warao categories differentiate according to ecological zones, those who rest in trees are not better than water sleepers or land nappers. For the Warao, "merit for all is vested in balanced complementary diversity," through a dynamic of reciprocity (Wilbert, 394).

Ayllu is an Andean, Quechua word that refers to one's extended family, their larger community, including the feathered Peruvian booby, the wooly Bolivian ram, and the slick new Peru blue tetra—all protected by Quechua morality. For the Quechua, "it is not only that everything is alive, but that everything is a person with whom one converses and shares, equally" (Valladolid, 655).

> In this worldview humans are the equals of the maise, the llama, the mountains, the stars, rocks, lakes, the departed who are also alive, and so on. All are nature;

humans do not feel alienated from her, nor superior to her. Humans are not distant from nature, they are part of nature. Humans feel that all are their *ayllu,* a Quechua word that in its broadest sense refers to the family that extends beyond just the human relatives. The rocks, the rivers, the sun, the moon, the plants, the animals are all members of the *ayllu.* All those that are found in the territory where they live in community are their *ayllu.* (Valladolid, 656)

Anymals, and the lands on which they depend, have their respected place in the *ayllu.* From the smallest beetle to the majestic mountain protector, *Apu Huanshan*—"all are important," and all are one community (Valladolid, 657–58).

Respect, Responsibility, and Compassion

Because indigenous peoples consider anymals (and often plants and earth as well) to be part of their community, indigenous peoples tend to respect the totality of the natural world (VanStone, 122). Kinship entails certain proper and required behaviors (McLuhan, 56, 99), whether one is dealing with a transparent sea cucumber (recently "discovered" deep in the ocean) or the United Kingdom's great crested newt (which stands dangerously close to extinction because of human population expansion and agricultural development).

Waswanipi people (Canadian subarctic) recognize that all creatures are "bound together," not only through "common mythic origins," but also by their "kindred 'human' qualities, their capacity for consciousness, [and] their inherent and unquestioned 'social' worth" (Suzuki, 68). This recognition of anymals as inherently valuable entails human responsibilities. Consequently, indigenous ethics do not generally focus only on (or apply only to) human beings. Instead, they teach interspecies moral codes that help humans to live harmoniously and peacefully among other animal communities. Because anymals and humans are kin, because anymals are recognized as *people,* indigenous myths frequently teach human responsibilities with regard to the extended family of beings (Noske, 185; Kinsley, *Ecology,* 33).

The Yup'ik people of northwestern Alaska consider anymals—from polar bears to ring seals (once endangered by hunting, now endangered by global climate change)—to be part of their moral community (Feinup-Riordan, 543). In the Yup'ik understanding, part of maturity as members of an interdependent, interrelated, interspecies community is to learn how to behave in the context of *shared cultures,* that is, to learn how to behave compatibly and respectfully within the diverse cultures of a myriad beings and communities. Similarly, the Koyukon (interior Alaska) uphold "a code of moral and social etiquette" that extends to all creatures (R. Nelson, *Make,* 228; Kwiatkowska-Szatzscheider, 268, 271). Indigenous peoples in western Canada speak of anymals "with the same respect [they] have for humans," insisting that the forests be protected because anymals "have a right" to the forests on which they depend for survival (Suzuki, xxxv). As individuals of one community among many, Australian Aborigines (Northern Territory), have a "moral obligation to learn to understand, to pay attention, and to respond" to other individuals and communities, whether wallaby or wombats (Suzuki, 47, italics removed). The peoples of the great plains of North America also felt it necessary to uphold a host of moral obligations across species, including polite communication and "truthful speech, generosity, kindness, and bravery" (Harrod, 91). The moral obligations of peoples of the Great Plains extend to all "beings whom humans meet in their everyday life—the animals, plants," and nature more generally (Harrod, 91).

Myths that convey a moral message often remind indigenous peoples to respect every aspect of the natural world, and to show compassion for other members of their extended community, including anymals and plants. Mayan myths, contained in the *Popol Vuh,* "ensure respect and compassion for other living beings" (Montejo, 177) and obligate people to show "understanding, respect, and compassion" for all of creation (Montejo, 183). While some myths offer rewards, others use threats to encourage humans to follow the moral path laid out by ancestors. Mayan myths, for example, warn against abuse and destruction of any aspect of the natural world, and reinforce these teachings with stories of a horrible fate that awaits those who fail to show compassion and respect for the surrounding landscape and other living beings (Montejo, 183).

Indigenous ethics generally require human beings to treat anymals with great respect. For example, before clearing a new patch of ground, the Bhima Saoras of central and southeast India show respect and compassion by offering a prayer to acknowledge that they are "robbing" wild creatures of their homes, and thereby endangering the lives of these members of their extended community. In that same prayer, they ask "creatures big and small" to "go away with their children," so that people might cultivate the land without causing harm to Indian game chickens or gaur (ox family) (Prabhu, 57). The Bhima Saoras recognize clearing

> a patch of forest for cultivation as an encroachment on the right to life of the other creatures of the forest. Not wanting to clash with them, they ask the animals to move away with their children. The terms they use, such as 'children,' reveal their belief that the animals of the forest have the same status [as human beings]. (Prabhu, 57)

For the Bhima Saoras, Bengal tigers, dawn bats, jambu fruit doves, and the slender loris are part of their moral community. They deserve respect, and human relations with anymals entail moral and spiritual obligations. The Bhima Saoras view themselves as but one species among many living in the same interspecies community, all of which depend on the land for survival. Their broad-minded attitude restricts the amount of land that they are willing to take for crops, even though many of their own children die of starvation each year. The Bhima Saoras' spiritual understanding of their rightful place in the natural world prevents them from contributing to the massive human overpopulation problem that has devastated landscapes and destroyed anymal communities throughout most of the world, too often driving anymals to extinction (Prabhu, 57).

The Nicobarese (Nicobar Islands, east of mainland India) also view the entirety of the natural world as part of their sacred moral community. They talk to plants while they gather leaves, begging forgiveness for taking the plant's leaves and explaining why they have done so. "For the Nicobarese, there is animate life even in plants and trees," and they must maintain polite and respectful relations with these green and growing beings (Prabhu, 57–58). Their conversations with plants reveal humility—a recognition that they do not own other living entities—and that they cause harm by taking plants' leaves. Their words are directed to the leaves and the plants, but their conversation is an ongoing dialogue with the cosmos, a conversation that is fundamentally spiritual in nature. The indigenous people of the Nicobar Islands, through this ongoing communication, are reminded that they cannot take perpetually. The plants need their leaves, and there is a limit to that which humans may take and legitimately ask forgiveness.

The Nahua (near Mexico City) consider all that dwell in the *cemanahuac* ("that which surrounds") to be included in their moral sphere (Silva, 319). They see power in the world around them, and believe that the forest can bring harm to those who overexploit, or who lack reverence. Like the Nicobarese, the Nahua ask permission before taking anything from the trees. "Everything that exists in nature has its limits, can be exhausted, and is invaluable" (Silva, 319). The Nahua know that they cannot live without their ecosystem, and they view everything within the natural world as worthy of respect.

As part of a larger, mutually dependent community with a shared morality, the Nahua expect that other creatures will also take from human beings. For example, the Nahua do not seek to eliminate "competitive" species, but expect other anymals to eat part of their crops and food stores (Silva, 319–20). When they see a Mexican jay enjoying a few of their freshly planted seeds, or a field mouse seeking sustenance in their food stores, they are neither surprised nor moved to deadly violence. For the Nahua, sharing is common sense: How could any reasonable human being thrive while forcing others to starve?

Sharing is a compassionate act, and interspecies indigenous ethics require compassion: Humans are to be compassionate toward anymals, and anymals, in their turn, will then show compassion for needy and dependent human beings. (The topic of anymals' compassion is covered in the section on hunting.) Given that anymals and humans are considered to be part of one and the same community, an ethic of compassion is consistent with community moral expectations around the world. Compassion is praised and encouraged, and selfish or cruel behaviors are discouraged. For instance, an Iroquois myth records how a man, in his time of need and desperation, was saved by anymals because they "remembered his kindness to them in former days, how he had never slain an animal unless he really needed it for food or clothing, how he had loved and protected the trees and the flowers" (Spence, 259).

The Aztec myth of Quetzalcoatl explains how a great hero, the son of a union between a goddess and the sun, taught humanity the art of being human. In this myth, compassion and respect for life—all life—are central to what it means to be human. Quetzalcoatl taught the Aztec people

> how to raise corn and cotton, weave cloth, work with gold, jade, feathers, wood, and stone, and write, paint, and dance. Quetzalcoatl became famous for his moral principles. He had a great respect for all forms of life. He did not believe in killing flowers by picking them, or killing any of the animals of the forest. (Rosenberg, 494)

Andean cultivation is a ritual infused with love "not only for their plants and animals, but also for the whole landscape that accompanies them in the nurturance of their fields, or *'chacras,'* which they consider to be members of their family, or *ayllu*" (Valladolid, 651–52). Andean peasants willingly share with their *ayllu*, their extended family—nature. They expect natural elements and wild creatures to share what they cultivate, so these experienced agriculturalists plant

> a furrow for the hail, another one for the frost, another for insects, because they recognize all of these realities of nature as members of their *ayllu*. They do not worry when the frost lightly burns the leaves of their crops; they say, "The frost has come to take its portion." (Valladolid, 657)

When the snow comes late in spring and destroys leafy vegetables, when a busy mole uproots growing greens, Andean peasants recognize that the whole family, the larger community, has come to the table. With such an outlook there is little room for anger or disappointment when a deer mouse or silvery-throated jay shares in the bounty; there is no incentive to eradicate other species or prevent anymals from taking what they need to live—even if they take that which humans have cultivated.

Autonomy

Australian Aborigine (Northern Territory) codes of behavior require that humans respect the autonomy of individual creatures, whether sea eagle, numbat, yabby, brolga, goanna, Australian fur seal, koala, or little lesser bilby (who has not been sighted since the 1960s, and is likely extinct). Australian Aborigines do not consider it their rightful role to control or manipulate other species; each anymal community is autonomous: "No species, no group or country is 'boss' for another; each adheres to its own Law. Authority and dependence are necessary within parts, but not between parts" (Suzuki, 47, italics removed).

Chewong (Malaysia) morality also requires humans to respect the autonomy of other creatures. A Chewong story tells of two young people who suffered for failing to respect a squirrel's autonomy. The young couple did not intend to be cruel: They captured a squirrel and kept her as a much-loved pet, robbing her of individual freedom, as well as her proper place in the wilds. As a result, the "guardian of all animals . . . went into a fury at the plight of a single, tiny squirrel" (Suzuki, 43–44). The anymal guardian brought a raging storm down on the couple, snuffing out not only their lives, but their souls, for such a "grave offense" against the squirrel (Suzuki, 43–44). In the Chewong worldview, each creature has a role to play, "and proper behavior on the part of humans vis-à-vis [anymals] must be observed" (Suzuki, 44, italics removed). For example, as this story demonstrates, wild anymals must not be trapped and detained, or domesticated.

The Desana (northwestern Amazon, in Colombia) also respect the autonomy of anymals by giving a wide berth to critical wild habitat—places frequented by anymals. They hold particular water holes and wallows as sacred sanctuaries for wildlife alone, protected from human meddling by Vaimahse, the great protector of anymals. Humans are expected to scrupulously avoid such places, and if they pass close by, they must pass in silence. Humans are not to disturb the ocelot or anaconda who come for a drink or a bath (Suzuki, 117).

Humans must respect anymals, and to respect anymals, they must respect their autonomy. Indigenous myths teach people to leave anymals free and in the wild, and to avoid interfering with the lives of these myriad independent individuals.

Great Peace

In the process of living among and pursuing blue grouse and herring, indigenous peoples often come to know anymals—their kin—intimately. Consequently, there is considerable dissonance between the closeness they often come to feel for anymals and any necessity they might have to kill anymals for food or clothing. The Makah (western Washington State), once dependent on whales, often commented on the terribly sad cry of a dying whale. Indigenous hunters in India, anticipating the horrors of death, ask forgiveness before an arrow leaves their bow, and simultaneously reiterate that "the arrow is supposed to be a messenger of remorse" (Prabhu, 58). Myths indicate that the tension of killing one's kin is as old as human-anymal relations.

Many indigenous creation stories tell of a time when there was no bloodshed (Harrod, 44), a time when animals lived peacefully in community with one another, sharing one language and one culture. A Hopi myth recalls a time when "many Hopis lived at Oraibi, with birds and animals living as equals among them" (D. Brown, 14). The Cherokee remember a time of universal peace, when "humans and animals freely communicated," including hoary marmot and human and great blue heron (Bierlein, 115). The Cheyenne of the Great Plains remember the original creation, a world where "people and animals lived in peace. None, neither people nor animals, ate flesh" (Erdoes, 390).

A Navajo (North America) myth recalls a time when there was plenty of food for everyone and all creatures "spoke the same language, and they all had the teeth, claws, feet, and wings of insects" (Rosenberg, 499). Navajo people remember that these early humans could remove their wings, they lived in caves, and humans "ate only what food they could gather and eat raw, such as nuts, seeds, roots, and berries"—they were vegan, holding to a completely plant-based diet (Rosenberg, 499).

Indigenous myths also record how "the interrelatedness of the creation is disturbed"—why and how killing and predation broke the original great peace (Harrod, 44). Cherokee myths recall that humans greedily began to kill anymals for fur and food: "It was easy to do at this time, as the animals were completely unprepared to be hunted and they walked up to human beings, trusting them. Then the animals became angry" (Bierlein, 115). The bears met in council, and committed to open warfare (Spence, 249). Then the deer met in council, then fish and reptiles, and finally birds and insects. They were all angry with humans, and decided to inflict humans with various punishments, such as nightmares and disease (Bierlein, 115).

Maori mythology (New Zealand) holds Tane as the father and protector of forests, birds, and insects, and Tangaroa as the father and protector of fish and reptiles (Rosenberg, 388). When the gods squabbled, Tu (the god of humans) attacked Tane's children by hanging nooses to trap birds. "Once caught, he defiled them" by cooking and eating them (Rosenberg, 390). He then attacked Tangaroa's children by weaving nets, and pulling fishes from the sea. "These too he defiled by cooking them, and [eating] them" (Rosenberg, 390).

This Maori myth explains why people eat other creatures, why "the warrior god and his human children have dominated and eaten the children of [the] gods of earth and sea" (Rosenberg, 390). The explanation portrays flesh eating as a cruel aberration. In this myth human predation began when the gods squabbled, when the god Tu conquered the anymals' protector deities and proceeded to destroy and defile anymals, taunting those who had been conquered. Humans are cast as warlike and deadly in Maori mythology, consuming fish and birds as their vicious god taught them. And their deadly diet assures that there will be no peace on Earth: Angry seas and wild storms pound and threaten human villages (Rosenberg, 390). Maori myths explain how the original peace was broken, and how this has made life more difficult, and more tragic, for all.

Cheyenne myths (North America, Great Plains region) speak of a long-ago world that was created as an interrelated whole, where all beings shared kinship: Minnows, black-capped chickadees, and people "lived together as friends" (Harrod, 49). In a fascinating turn of events (that looks much like projection), Buffalo People begin to feel superior (being large and powerful), and come to believe that they are entitled to kill and eat Human People. In response, Humans remind Buffalo that all creatures have been created equally—one should not eat the other. Yet they also assert that, if one creature *is* to reign supreme, it ought to be Humans. At an impasse, Human People and Buffalo People decide to have a contest—a race—to determine who will be the dominant species. Interestingly, humans admit that they are slower—that they would lose the contest they have chosen (an admittance of inferiority even before the contest begins!)—so birds are pitted against buffalo *on behalf of humans*.

On the day of the great race, Slim Buffalo Woman lines up next to hummingbird, meadowlark, hawk, and magpie—four against one, and not one human at the starting line, not one human fast enough to join the contest. At the end of the race, only magpie remains, defeating Slim Buffalo Woman by a mere hair—or perhaps a feather. As a result, "people became more powerful than the buffalo and all the other animals"—even the birds, who raced for physically challenged humans (Erdoes, 390–92).

While the race itself is a marvel of revealing details, human domination is somehow thought to be justified by this myth—perhaps because the story reveals the arbitrary nature of human power and the injustice that lies at the core of our reign of terror. In any event, the myth describes how the community of beings was broken, at which point Humans eat flesh, and Buffalo must live in fear and terror (Harrod, 50).

Indigenous myths that remember a Great Peace, a vegan world where all species consumed only plants and plant products, and shared space peacefully, invariably remember this vegan world as superior. Indigenous myths portray the present state of perpetual violence, of predation and consumption, as inferior to the original great peace. Interspecies violence—eating one another—is identified as a great loss for all involved. . . .

Hunting

Indigenous hunters who do not use mechanized transport or modern weapons must live and work close to anymals whom they kill for food. Indigenous hunters, to be successful, must discover the sleeping places of the hooded skunk, know what the mountain beaver prefers to eat, learn the quirks and habits of the river otter, yet ultimately kill these familiar members of their extended family. For indigenous peoples, who view all creatures as kin, who recognize anymals as "creatures who possess consciousness and life," the necessity of hunting, fishing, and trapping creates a "moral dilemma" (Harrod, 45). The Inuit hunter, for example, can experience "considerable psychological pain in the process of slaying [anymals] that he believes are endowed with the vitality, sentience, and sacredness inherent in his own human kin" (Suzuki, 104).

Not surprisingly, many indigenous myths reveal the troubled conscience of indigenous hunters (Serpell, 29).

> Native American tribal cultures experienced feelings of ambivalence and guilt about the killing of animals. One of the ways some native cultures seem to have dealt with their uneasy feelings is by developing a mythology or worldview according to which it was believed that the animals "gave" her or his life as a "gift." (Kheel, 101)

Indeed, indigenous peoples sometimes hold a cyclical view of life in which anymals willingly give their temporary bodies to become human food, and then return to be born again. The Cree and Koyukon hold this point of view, believing that caribou and spruce grouse have the power to decide whether or not to be captured or killed.

Indigenous peoples who believe that brush rabbits and ruffed grouse *choose* to die to feed and clothe humans also believe that they will make this compassionate and generous choice only if people maintain proper, respectful behavior and attitudes toward those they hunt. Those who do not wish to die for humans will not do so. Those who do not wish to return to woodlands or prairies near a particular village will not do so. Humans must show extreme respect for anymals on which they depend for survival if they are to be successful in their hunt or when fishing.

Respect requires balance, not taking more than is needed, and treating the lives of sentient individuals with respect. Many indigenous myths explain human moral obligations with regard to anymals—what they must do to respect and preserve natural ecosystems (Opoku, 357). Koyukon Distant Time stories, for example, include many myths that explain how people ought to relate to nature in order to maintain balance and harmony (VanStone, 61). Indigenous myths are filled with stories that offer "a complex of metaphors that teach . . . proper relationship[s] and respect for the natural world" (Cajete, 628). Not surprisingly, indigenous religious beliefs and practices limit what hunters might legitimately do to gorillas and pythons, wildebeests and black-bellied whistling-ducks. "When humans live in balanced reciprocity with animals, each creates the continued conditions for the survival of the other as members of a society" (Feit, 423).

Victoria Tauli-Corpuz, who grew up among the Igorot, in a small community in the northern Philippines, remembers an important indigenous concept that means something like "'exercise caution,' 'don't do it,' or 'have limits,'" which guides human relations with "other human beings, other creations (animal, plant, microorganism), the spirit world, and nature in general" (Tauli-Corpuz, 281). She also remembers a closely related concept that specifically restricts what humans may do to anymals; this understanding is best translated as "taboo, forbidden, holy, or sacred" (Tauli-Corpuz, 281). These restricting forces are central to Igorot life. For the Igorot people, these two concepts are "fundamental principles which underpin

the traditional religion of the Igorots and by which every Igorot should live" (Tauli-Corpuz, 281). In their understanding, humans must use restraint if they are to stay within the bounds of that which is morally acceptable and they must always maintain respectful relations with the natural world.

Indigenous hunting is rooted in necessity, and limiting what humans may do to yellow-rumped warblers, long-eared jerboa, snubfin dolphin, and Caribbean monk seals (pronounced extinct in 2008) is central to indigenous morality. Hunting without necessity is *contrary* to indigenous spiritual beliefs and practices; such killing is dangerous, taboo, and contrary to ancient lifeways. A Waswanipi Cree hunter (Canadian subarctic), while noting that technology and modern techniques allow humans to take life beyond what is necessary, cautions against doing so. He notes that killing anymals "for fun or self-aggrandizement" demonstrates "the ultimate disdain" for other creatures (Suzuki, 106, italics removed). The Cree believe that anymals decide whether or not to be hunted, and such disdain would surely lead to starvation; no anymal would return to give his or her life to such a hunter.

Kinship and Community

Indigenous peoples generally recognize humanity as just one form of life amid many forms of life—one community of animals amid many communities of animals. Each community, and each being, is unique but fundamentally similar; each community and each being is important in its own right and to the larger whole. Additionally, there is no conception of the autonomous individual, free to do as he or she chooses. Nor is there any single community more important than all others. Indigenous people tend to be keenly aware of their debt and dependence in relation to the larger whole. For most indigenous peoples, there is no such thing as a "species barrier"; in the indigenous understanding, species are interdependent, fluid, and interconnected, and this understanding is reflected in their language and their morality.

The central feature of proper interspecies relations in nearly every indigenous culture is to view every other individual, whether Nicaraguan seed-finch or tiger salamander, as part of self and community. In keeping with other indigenous peoples, for example, the Chewong do not have a word for humans as separate from anymals. Similarly, the Haida include anymals in the language they use to refer to their personal family members, referring "to whales and ravens as 'brothers' and 'sisters'" (Suzuki, xxxii). The Haida also recognize other communities as composed of individuals of a particular type, just like human communities: They refer to "fish and trees as the finned and tree people" (Suzuki, xxxii). These various peoples are not understood to be separate and distinct, but are viewed as part of a larger family and community of beings. Like human races, the various living beings look different but are fundamentally similar. Jenny Leading Cloud of the White River Sioux (Dakotas, Minnesota, Nebraska, and north into Canada) comments:

> Man is just another animal. The buffalo and the coyote are our brothers; the birds, our cousins. Even the tiniest ant, even a louse, even the smallest flower you can find—they are all relatives. We end our prayers with the words *mitakuye oyasin*—"all my relations"—and that includes everything that grows, crawls, runs, creeps, hops, and flies on this continent. (Erdoes, 5)

Similarly, Cree (North American Plains) recognize coyotes, magpies—all creatures—as members of communities in a world rich with communities of every stripe and speckle (Feit, 428). In the traditional Cree worldview, anymals are understood to be part of the same larger community to which humans belong:

> The animal world is a part of the same kind of social world that humans inhabit, and in much conversation a social metaphor serves to talk about the whole world. . . . [M]any of the actions of animals are intelligible and predictable. The whole world is therefore a socially informed world, in which habit and learning rather than natural law explain the actions of animals and other nonhuman persons. As a result, communication between all beings is possible, and animals can in their turn interpret and understand the actions and needs of humans. (Feit, 421)

The Cree therefore believe that anymals decide whether or not to allow a hunter to eat; muskrats and snow geese willingly give themselves to a morally worthy hunter, as a generous gift (Kinsley, *Ecology,* 13). When asked why animals permit themselves to be killed, the Cree response is similar to how we might explain sharing food with the poor in our own communities: Deer and geese are aware of the needs of hungry fellow creatures, and share accordingly. The implication is that offering your body to those who have nothing else to eat "is a responsible thing to do as a moral social being"—as a member of a larger, interdependent community of beings (Feit, 421). The gift of food and life, given to those who are dependent and at their mercy, further demonstrates to the Cree, and many other indigenous communities, that rainbow trout, Gunnison sage-grouse, and antelope are compassionate, generous, upstanding members of the larger community, and are therefore greatly deserving of respect.

REFERENCES

Bierlein, J. F. *Parallel Myths.* New York: Ballantine, 1994.

Brown, Dee. *Folktales of the Native American: Retold for Our Times.* New York: Henry Holt, 1979.

Brown, Joseph Epes. *The Spiritual Legacy of the American Indian.* New York: Crossroad, 1991.

Cajete, Gregory. "Indigenous Education and Ecology: Perspectives of an American Indian Educator." In *Indigenous Traditions and Ecology: The Interbeing of Cosmology and Community,* edited by John A. Grim, 619–38. Cambridge, MA: Harvard University Press, 2001.

Erdoes, Richard, and Alfonso Ortiz, eds. *American Indian Myths and Legends.* New York: Pantheon, 1984.

Feinup-Riordan, Ann. "A Guest on the Table: Ecology from the Yup'ik Eskimo Point of View." In *Indigenous Traditions and Ecology: The Interbeing of Cosmology and Community,* edited by John A. Grim, 541–58. Cambridge, MA: Harvard University Press, 2001.

Feit, Harvey A. "Hunting, Nature, and Metaphor: Political and Discursive Strategies in James Bay Cree Resistance and Autonomy." In *Indigenous Traditions and Ecology: The Interbeing of Cosmology and Community,* edited by John A. Grim, 411–52. Cambridge, MA: Harvard University Press, 2001.

Harrod, Howard L. *Renewing the World: Plains Indian Religion and Morality.* Tucson: University of Arizona Press, 1987.

Henare, Manuka. *"Tapu, Mana, Mauri, Hau, Wairua*: A Maori Philosophy of Vitalism and Cosmos." In *Indigenous Traditions and Ecology: The Interbeing of Cosmology and Community,* edited by John A. Grim, 197–221. Cambridge, MA: Harvard University Press, 2001.

Jette, Jules. "On Superstitions of the Ten'a Indians (Middle Part of the Yukon Valley, Alaska)." *Journal of the Royal Anthropological Institute of Great Britain* (1895).

————. "On Ten'a Folk-Lore." *Journal of the Royal Anthropological Institute of Great Britain.* 38 (1908): 298–367.

Kheel, Marti. "License to Kill: An Ecofeminist Critique of a Hunters' Discourse." In *Women and Animals: Feminist Theoretical Explorations,* edited by Carol Adams and Josephine Donovan, 85–125. Durham, NC: Duke, 1995.

Kinsley, David. *Ecology and Religion: Ecological Spirituality in Cross-Cultural Perspective.* Englewood Cliffs, NJ: Prentice-Hall, 1995.

Kwiatkowska-Szatzscheider, Teresa. "From the Mexican Chiapas Crisis: A Different Perspective for Environmental Ethics." *Environmental Ethics* 19 (1997): 267–78.

McLuhan, T. C. *Touch the Earth.* New York: Promontory, 1971.

Montejo, Victor D. "The Road to Heaven: Jakaltek Maya Beliefs, Religion, and the Ecology." In *Indigenous Traditions and Ecology: The Interbeing of Cosmology and Community,* edited by John A. Grim, 175–96. Cambridge, MA: Harvard University Press, 2001.

Namunu, Simeon B. "Melanesian Religion, Ecology, and Modernization in Papua New Guinea." In *Indigenous Traditions and Ecology: The Interbeing of Cosmology and Community,* edited by John A. Grim, 249–80. Cambridge, MA: Harvard University Press, 2001.

Nelson, Richard K. *Make Prayers to Raven: A Koyukon View of the Northern Forest.* Chicago: University of Chicago Press, 1983.

Noske, Barbara. "Speciesism, Anthropocentrism, and Non-Western Cultures." *Anthrozoos* 10: 4 (1997): 183–90.

Opoku, Kofi. "Animals in African Mythology." In *A Communion of Subjects: Animals in Religion, Science, and Ethics,* edited by Paul Waldau and Kimberley Patton, 351–59. New York: Columbia University Press, 2006.

Prabhu, Pradip. "In the Eye of the Storm: Tribal Peoples of India." In *Indigenous Traditions and Ecology: The Interbeing of Cosmology and Community,* edited by John A. Grim, 47–70. Cambridge, MA: Harvard University Press, 2001.

Riley, Shamara Shantu. "Ecology Is a Sistah's Issue Too: The Politics of Emergent Afrocentric Ecowomanism." In *Worldviews, Religion, and the Environment: A Global Anthology,* edited by Richard C. Foltz, 472–81. Belmont, CA: Thompson, 2003.

Rosenberg, Donna. *World Mythology: An Anthology of the Great Myths and Epics.* Lincolnwood, IL: NTC, 1994.

Serpell, James. "Animal Protection and Environmentalism: The Background." In *Animal Welfare and the Environment,* edited by Richard D. Ryder, 27–39. Melksham, UK: Duckworth, 1992.

Silva, Javier Galicia. "Religion, Ritual, and Agriculture among the Present-Day Nahua of Mesoamerica." In *Indigenous Traditions and Ecology: The Interbeing of Cosmology and Community,* edited by John A. Grim, 303–24. Cambridge, MA: Harvard University Press, 2001.

Spence, Lewis. *North American Indians: Myths and Legends.* London: Studio, 1985.

Suzuki, David, and Peter Knudtson. *Wisdom of the Elders: Sacred Native Stories of Nature.* New York: Bantam, 1993.

Taulli-Corpuz, Victoria. "Interface between Traditional Religion and Ecology among the Igorots." In *Indigenous Traditions and Ecology: The Interbeing of Cosmology and Community,* edited by John A. Grim, 281–302. Cambridge, MA: Harvard University Press, 2001.

Thompson, Chad, and Helen Thompson. *A Teacher's Guide to Bakkaatugh Ts'uhuniy: Stories We Live By.* Fairbanks: Yukon Koyukuk School District and Alaska Native Language Center, University of Alaska Press, 1989.

Valladolid, Julio, and Frederique Apffel-Marglin. "Andean Cosmovision and the Nurturing of Biodiversity." In *Indigenous Traditions and Ecology: The Interbeing of Cosmology and Community,* edited by John A. Grim, 639–70. Cambridge, MA: Harvard University Press, 2001.

VanStone, James W. *Athapaskan Adaptations: Hunters and Fishermen of the Subarctic Forests.* Chicago: Aldine, 1974.

Wilbert, Werner. "Warao Spiritual Ecology." In *Indigenous Traditions and Ecology: The Interbeing of Cosmology and Community,* edited by John A. Grim, 377–407. Cambridge, MA: Harvard University Press, 2001.

QUESTIONS

1. Some traditions view non-violence as the ideal. Others don't and, indeed, think it's an impossibility. Do the latter views imply that anything goes when it comes to getting food?

2. Several traditions support the importance of making amends and "mitigating" violence one commits in getting food (for example, the violence in shooting a deer). Why are making amends and mitigating important? Are they important (just) for one's own well-being, as in some of the Indic views discussed in this chapter?

3. Strikingly, some of the traditions discussed lament violence against non-sentient things and even against non-living things—which? Why? What is the upshot for a vegan diet? What are some connections between this lamentation and the point Carol Kaesuk Yoon makes in her reading in Chapter 10, "Alternatives to Industrial Plant Agriculture?"

4. In Chapter 9, "Industrial Plant Agriculture," we mention the view that it is wrong to, say, pollute a river because of its effects on the river rather than, say, because of its effects on fish in the river or on people who drink from it. One justification for this—alluded to in the hunting section of Kemmerer's reading—is that pollution makes for an *imbalance* in nature. How so? What, if anything, is wrong with such an imbalance?

7 Industrial Animal Agriculture

This chapter is about what we call "industrial animal agriculture" and what is commonly called "factory farming." It is a system described in Jonathan Safran Foer's reading in Chapter 1, "The Ethically Troubling Food System," involving the high-density stocking of animals for the purpose of producing food.

Instead of using the term "factory farm" (which may have negative connotations), the Environmental Protection Agency (EPA) uses the term "AFO" which stands for *Animal Feeding Operation*. When an AFO reaches a certain size, it is then called a "CAFO," for *Concentrated Animal Feeding Operation*. The EPA describes the meaning of these terms as follows:

> [AFOs] are agricultural enterprises where animals are kept and raised in confined situations. AFOs congregate animals, feed, manure and urine, dead animals, and production operations on a small land area. Feed is brought to the animals rather than the animals grazing or otherwise seeking feed in pastures, fields, or on rangeland. There are approximately 450,000 AFOs in the United States. Concentrated animal feeding operations (CAFOs) are a relatively small number of AFOs that are regulated by the EPA.[1]

The term "factory farm" is used by ordinary people to refer to both AFOs and CAFOs and, for our purposes, the distinction does not matter. This chapter is about the general practice of industrial animal agriculture in our society, which includes everything under the wider category of AFOs. Some might prefer to use the term "factory farming" to refer to this, some not—some academic discussions focus only on CAFOs. But our focus here is on the general nature and consequences of contemporary industrial animal agriculture—that is, the practice of confined, high-density production of animals for the purpose of eating them or their products—their milk, their eggs. It's about the effects of such farms on people, the environment, and animals. And it's about the ethics of this sort of farming.

WHAT INDUSTRIAL ANIMAL AGRICULTURE IS

While something like industrial agriculture has been used with fish since the fifth century B.C.E. in China, and while snails have been farmed in this way since Roman times (and probably quite a bit earlier), the history of doing so with larger animals starts much more recently.

The Humane Society reading in this chapter estimates that, circa 2010, over 10 billion land animals were farmed on industrial animal farms in the United States alone. These animals include various sorts of birds—chickens for meat, chickens for eggs, geese, ducks—cows for milk, cattle for beef, and pigs. If we add fish that are raised both on-shore in tanks but also in floating farms in the sea, the number is significantly higher.[2]

Raising animals in this way makes for high efficiency in, roughly, the sense of maximizing profits and minimizing the price of food at the supermarket. Here's a simplified example to see how it works. (This chapter's Humane Society reading, "The Welfare of Animals in the Meat, Egg, and Dairy Industry," makes it more realistic.)

> You keep the chickens as close together as you can, for example in a large shed. This requires food being grown elsewhere and shipped in. But the one, compact location enables you to save on space for your farm. It enables you to feed the chickens in a central location rather than either having them forage for their own or feeding them at various far-flung spots. It enables you to care for them in a single spot. But the crowding is stressful for the chickens and they peck at each other. As a result, you debeak them. Doing it with anesthetic would cost money. Doing it without does not. So you do it without. Also, the crowding makes engaging in natural chicken behaviors like dustbathing and wingspreading impossible. This adds to stress. Also, the crowding makes chickens susceptible to disease. Rather than risk a disease wiping everyone out, you can use preventative antibiotics. This costs more than not doing so but guards against catastrophic risk. (Yet the use of antibiotics also helps to produce drug-resistant super-bugs.)
>
> Antibiotics, too, help to promote growth. If you are raising chickens for meat, you want to produce the most meat for the least amount of money. The ideal is a chicken that's going to produce a lot of meat without costing you much in terms of, say, feed. So you breed for the fastest-growing chicken who'll eat the least amount of feed.
>
> Finally, if you are raising chickens for eggs, you don't want any males—they produce no eggs. Financially, it makes sense to kill them quickly before they cost you anything—in fact, it makes best financial sense not to spend money euthanizing them, but merely to throw them in masse into the dumpster, where those that are not suffocated by the weight of others gradually starve to death or die in some other unpleasant way. (Similarly, if you are raising cows for milk, you don't want male cattle, and what it makes best financial sense to do is raise those males for veal, which has even worse consequences for animal welfare.) The animals that are killed for food are typically killed in slaughterhouses, venues detailed in the Jonathan Safran Foer reading in Chapter 1, "The Ethically Troubling Food System," and the Timothy Pachirat reading in Chapter 11, "Workers."

The industrial farming of different animals will, of course, proceed differently. And these differences affect animals differently. So whereas tight-packing is stressful to chickens because it inhibits wingspreading, it will, obviously, not be stressful for that reason for cattle or pigs. Whereas chickens are debeaked, pigs have their tails docked. And whereas there is no need to put a hen into a small crate to keep her from crushing her young while nursing them, that is a common practice on industrial pig farms where pigs are given little enough room that crushing is a real danger. This is detailed, too, in the Humane Society reading on animal welfare in this chapter.

EFFECTS OF INDUSTRIAL ANIMAL AGRICULTURE ON PEOPLE

In brief, that is what industrial animal agriculture is. We can turn now to what it does: what it does to people, to the environment, and to farmed animals. The Pew Commission, Nestle, Humane Society, and Singer readings in this chapter detail these effects.

The effects of industrial animal agriculture on people can be somewhat hard to determine since some of the effects are not immediately perceptible. Others are. For example, people who live near AFOs report stench and sickness from contaminated water and from gases and parasites. Workers on industrial farms deal with debilitating injuries and death: death from falling into manure lagoons, death from various threats in meat-packing plants.

People who live farther away might deal with contamination from seepage due to farm waste. People might deal with contamination due to excess waste being spread on fields and then draining off into the water supply. They might deal with contaminated meat.

People who live farther away might deal, too, with farm-bred viruses and antibiotic-resistant bacteria. Industrial animal farms are, in various ways, good breeding grounds for viruses and bacteria. The stress on the animals weakens their immune systems. Their proximity to each other makes passage of viruses easy. The antibiotics they take wipe out some bacteria but, in doing so, clear the field for the "fittest" bacteria.[3]

And to say that many of the other harms lack immediacy and perceptibility is not to say that they are not serious. If I release poison into the ground that slowly poisons the water you drink, the effects might not be immediate, and you might not perceive that you are slowly being poisoned, but the health effects could be very serious indeed. More generally, many serious harms from environmental pollution have this structure: People are seriously harmed relative to how healthy they would have been without the pollution, yet they are unaware of this fact because it is a state of affairs that unfolds very slowly and in a way that is imperceptible to them—or that is not perceptible until it is too late. One of the implications of the Pew Foundation and HSUS reports in this chapter is that these kinds of serious harms are happening to some people in society as a result of industrial farms.

MARKET FAILURE, EXTERNALITIES, AND HARMS TO SOCIETY

The time inconsistency and imperceptibility of the harms just discussed is part of the explanation of why serious harms might continue even if they are much larger than the benefits that come from allowing them. The basic explanation is that if people do not know that they are suffering harms, then they will not tend to pay more to avoid them—so, the market will not tend to take care of the problem. And at the same time, those who profit from imposing those harms are well aware of the costs to them of having to clean up their act, and so they are often willing to pay any amount less than that to prevent better regulations—and, as a result, government also often does not take care of the problem, as a result of the familiar dynamics of lobbying, campaign contributions, and so on.

Earlier we noted that industrial farming is highly efficient in, roughly, the sense of producing food at maximum profit and lowest cost at the supermarket. But in light of the harms identified previously and throughout this chapter, one big-picture worry we should have is whether this way of producing food might *not* be the way of producing food that has the least cost *to all of us in society*. That is because the way of minimizing costs for farmers might involve a system whereby, for example, law and regulations do not require them to properly dispose of animal feces and other pollutants. This might allow farmers to save a little money and thus minimize *their* costs and the costs of their products on supermarket shelves, but this might end up costing everyone else even more in the form of worse health than the amount saved by the farmers and by us at the supermarket—for example, when that pollution harms everyone else physically, decreases the value of their property, artificially drives up the price of other things, and makes the environment they live in unpleasant. Because these costs are not paid by producers or consumers, they are not reflected in the prices of the goods in the marketplace, which means that inefficient outcomes are then irrationally incentivized by the distorted market prices that result.

For example, if it costs producers only $20 to make each unit of a good because government subsidies ensure that the price of the materials and energy is only $10 per unit even though those things really cost society $1,000 per unit to provide, and if producers don't have to pay any of the costs of the pollution from their factories, which amount to an additional $1,000 per unit produced in harm to the people in the city where her factory is located, and if people are only willing to pay $50 for each unit of the good that is produced and no more, then it is easy to see how this situation could lead to production and consumption that makes society increasingly worse off over time. (The market price for the good that emerges might be $40, which makes both producers and consumers better off with each unit that is sold, while at the same time society gets poorer and poorer with each unit produced.) Many critics of industrial agriculture believe that this sort of irrational incentive structure is actually in place in our society's food system.

The logic of this incentive structure is important because it is a recurring example of how markets can be distorted, and how market-based societies sometimes fail to thrive in the way they ideally could as a result of these incentives. It also illustrates how a particular food product that has a very low market price might not actually be *cheap* from the point of view of society—its true cost to society might be much higher, and perhaps so high that it should not even be produced, as in the example in the previous paragraph. To illustrate some common terminology that is used by economists and other experts to describe this important kind of *perverse incentive structure*, we might say that in the example in the previous paragraph the producers *externalize* the costs of the pollution they produce, and that those costs are a *negative externality*, because they negatively affect people in a way that is *external* to the prices paid in the production and consumption of those goods. In such situations, free market exchanges can fail to make society better off, even though normally they do make society better off when this kind of *market failure* does not happen.

The harms we've discussed so far in connection with industrial animal farms are largely side effects of the huge amount of food that they produce. But this system also provides jobs—these are discussed in some detail in Chapter 11, "Workers"—and it also makes food that is easy to get and cheap at the store or in the restaurant. For reasons we've just noted, there is a serious conversation to be had about whether the total cost of "cheap" beef is less than the total cost of free-range beef—see Chapter 8, "Alternatives to Industrial Animal

Agriculture"—or cheaper than no animal products at all.[4] The total cost will include not just what the consumer pays at the store or in the restaurant but what the animal "pays" in getting there, what the environment "pays" as a result of the animal being raised, what workers "pay" to produce it, and what society pays to deal with the effects of raising and eating this food.

EFFECTS OF INDUSTRIAL ANIMAL AGRICULTURE ON THE ENVIRONMENT

Consider one environmental cost of industrial animal agriculture. The billions of penned animals on industrial farms need to be fed. Since they need to be fed, farmers need to get food for them. And once they get fed, they make waste. These simple points about industrial animal agriculture underlie most of their environmental effects.

Animals on industrial farms cannot feed themselves. Food needs to be bought for them and then given to them. And they need a lot of food: many times more than would be required if humans ate that food directly rather than using it to first grow animals to then eat. So, as the number of animals on these farms rises, so too does the amount of food that needs growing. This leads to forest and other lands being turned into farmland. That, in turn, leads to loss of habitat for wildlife, loss of biodiversity, and, in the case of forests that are clear-cut, loss of carbon sinks that remove greenhouse gasses from the atmosphere, and the replacement of them with sources of greenhouse gasses, as agricultural fields are net emitters.

The food that is grown for animals—often called *feed* when it is fed to them rather than to humans—is typically derived from industrial plant agriculture, and it is often derived from corn or soy[5] that is grown using the synthetic fertilizers, pesticides, and so on that are crucial to contemporary industrial plant agriculture. Their manufacture and distribution requires fossil fuels. The crops are grown in ways that disturb soils, releasing trapped greenhouse gas. Some of these issues are detailed in the Humane Society reading, and the negative effects of the feed production that lies behind industrial animal products are discussed in much more detail in Chapter 9, "Industrial Plant Agriculture."

That's what goes into animals on industrial farms. Another environmental problem is what comes out. Animal feces are a valuable resource in the right quantity, because they can be used as fertilizer. (This is part of an argument for some form of animal agriculture. See Chapter 8, "Alternatives to Industrial Animal Agriculture.") Yet too much waste is produced to be useful fertilizer. It collects in "lagoons," where it threatens to overrun or to leech into water. It gets sprayed on fields where it runs off and becomes a pollutant that renders water undrinkable, unswimmable, and, for aquatic animals, uninhabitable. In too concentrated a form, it renders soil unusable. And animal excrement produces greenhouse gases (GHGs), just like animals' burps and farts do. It produces stench and respiratory illness for those nearby.

People who live in the future will deal with environmental problems that are indirect results of industrial farming but traceable in part to the quantities of GHGs produced by industrially farmed animals and to the clear-cutting that is done to grow food for factory-farmed animals. When GHGs from crops that are grown to feed animals are taken into account, and the associated deforestation in some areas associated with grazing and cultivating this feed, most experts estimate that around 10% to 15% of all global GHG emissions are the result of animal agriculture.[6] By comparison, all of the world's commercial airline emissions account for only about 2% of global GHG emissions, and all of the world's road transport emissions (including, but not limited to, automobile emissions) account for about 10%.[7] So, globally, consuming animal products is an even larger contributor to climate change than driving automobiles.

This may be quite surprising. To understand why these numbers are so high, it is useful to note that in these estimates only about 10% of animal GHG emissions are from manure that is not reused in agriculture, and only about 5% are from energy use in animal and other industrial activity such as packaging. The bigger factors are that about 40% of animal agriculture emissions are due to the growing of feed crops (with a little over half of that from nitrous oxide emissions from either fertilizer use or manure use connected with growing those feed crops, and a little under half from carbon dioxide emissions from the growing of the crops), about 10% are from land use changes as a result of the clearing of additional land for grazing and feed crops, and about 40% are from enteric fermentation releases of methane, which are almost all from ruminant animals such as cows.[8]

Enteric fermentation might be unfamiliar, so let's take a minute to explain what that means, and why that is such a large fraction of the total. Methane is a familiar gas, and it is basically the gas that is burned by a natural gas stovetop. We also release that gas when we fart, and cows do too. But cows also release it when they belch, and that turns out to be a much larger source of methane from them, because of the particular way that cows digest what they eat, which is called enteric fermentation. Cows have a multi-chambered stomach, as do the other animals classified as "ruminants," which in animal agriculture include, most importantly, goats and sheep as well as cows. This allows them to mix some saliva and other fluids with the stuff they eat in one chamber, separate out the nutritious stuff from liquids, and then regurgitate it, mix some other saliva and bacteria with it, and send that stuff off to one of those chambers to ferment for a while before they ultimately digest it all. This is useful to them, because it allows them to digest some rough stuff that we wouldn't be able to digest, which also allows them to graze in areas that are otherwise unsuitable for agriculture. But in the process of all of this fermentation and regurgitation, methane is produced and most of it is belched out, with a little bit also exiting through the other end. And when you multiply that methane by over 3.5 billion ruminants in animal agriculture on the planet, that's a lot of methane, which scientists have good methods for measuring. When it is added up, that is a huge amount of methane, which also happens to be a much more potent greenhouse gas than carbon dioxide.

The combination of all of these factors explains why animal agriculture is such a large contributor to the global GHG problem. These problems only stand to get worse given, for example, a UN Food and Agriculture Organization (FAO) projection that production of meat will go from 229 tons at the turn of the century to 465 tons by the middle of it and that milk production will go from 580 tons to 1,043 tons.[9] This rise in demand is due to a rise in population but also a rise in demand for animal products among increasingly wealthy populations, especially in Asia. (For further discussion of these important projections about rising consumption of meat, and their implications for the challenge of feeding the world without destroying the environment, see Chapter 9, "Industrial Plant Agriculture.")

EFFECTS OF INDUSTRIAL ANIMAL AGRICULTURE ON ANIMALS

Some effects on animals are easy to determine. Farmed salmon have organ and skeletal deformities at a rate that outstrips the rate in wild salmon. Because they are stocked in high-density pens, they fail to exercise as much as their wild peers. Because of this stocking, they are more susceptible to the rapid spread of disease and parasites than their wild peers.[10]

Other effects on animals can be somewhat hard to determine since determining some of these effects requires knowledge of animal minds that can be tricky to acquire. On the one hand, just imagining how we would feel, if we were in animals' place, is not a good way to get knowledge of animal minds. To determine whether force-feeding a goose hurts it, or is otherwise bad for it, it is no good imagining what force-feeding would be like for you. Physiologically, you are just too different from a goose. On the other hand, refusing to trust any sort of imaginative insight into the lives of animals is also clearly a mistake. To determine whether an animal thrashing around and yelping is uncomfortable is not hard. To insist that, well, we don't know whether those effects mean something different in animals than in us is a bridge too far. Even ardently supportive pieces on industrial animal agriculture accept that industrial animal agriculture's effects on animals include physical pain, psychological pain, and death.

The physical pain comes from two different sources: One is the conditions the animals are kept in: where they are kept and with whom, what and how much they are fed, and so forth. Another is the type of animal they are. So while hens suffer from being kept in battery cages, unable to spread their wings and suffer from being jostled and attacked by larger birds they have nowhere to run from, hens also suffer from being products of extensive selective breeding that is designed for maximum efficiency: the most meat for the least money. The faster a bird grows and the less it eats, the better. As the reading "The Welfare of Animals in the Meat, Egg, and Dairy Industry" notes,

> The poultry industry has used selective breeding to produce birds whose bodies "are on the verge of structural collapse." Studies consistently show that approximately 26–30% of broiler chickens suffer from gait defects severe enough to impair walking ability, and additional research strongly suggests that birds at this level of lameness are in pain. [According to] professor John Webster of the University of Bristol School of Veterinary Science . . . , "Broilers are the only livestock that are in chronic pain for the last 20 per cent of their lives. They don't move around, not because they are overstocked, but because it hurts their joints so much."[11] (1)

In addition to the physical pain of being industrially farmed, animals suffer psychological pain owing to their dense confinement and the attendant inability to engage in natural behaviors. We can't be 100% sure what this is like, and there is a danger of anthropomorphizing our feelings about this, but, as the reading "The Welfare of Animals in the Meat, Egg, and Dairy Industry" and its numerous citations note, it is clear that crowding is distressing to animals.

These are the effects on the living, but, as many of the readings in this chapter note, industrial animal farms kill billions of creatures each year. Death comes, of course, from animals being killed in slaughterhouses but also from animals simply not being needed and being quickly disposed of as when male chicks, useless for egg farms, are killed right away.

As Torbjörn Tännsjö stresses in his reading in this chapter, the flipside of these billions of deaths is the billions of lives that precede them. Industrial farming makes life possible for billions of animals each year. The billions of chickens on industrial American farms would simply not exist if it were not for industrial farms. And while these lives are painful in various ways and are shorter than a natural lifespan, industrial farms provide medical care and protection from predation and the elements. These are features of industrial animal agriculture that deserve consideration in an ethical reckoning.

THE ETHICS OF INDUSTRIAL ANIMAL AGRICULTURE

So, is the treatment of animals in industrial animal agriculture permissible? If not, what would make it permissible? These are hard questions partly because they depend on what the alternatives to industrial animal agriculture are. We will build up to answering them.

It is clear that industrial animal agriculture produces various goods: a great deal of food and a great deal of jobs. The food is highly in demand and, as we noted, will only become in more demand.

Also, although this is more controversial, the Tännsjö view just articulated is that minimally decent lives are themselves goods, and so simply adding more minimally decent animal lives to the world is a good thing.

But, of course, these aren't the only relevant issues. Consider whether the effects enumerated in the previous section are bad for animals. Do they diminish animals' welfare? Do animals have an interest in not experiencing these effects? Yes. Expanding on a point Peter Singer makes in his essay in this chapter, rocks don't have interests, so when you kick a pile of pebbles, this is not bad for the pebbles; it does not go against the pebbles' interests. But animals have interests in virtue of being sentient. When you kick your dog, this is bad for the dog. This, as Singer argues, is because they have an interest in not suffering. We'll talk about animal welfare and animal interests more in the next chapter. But on any plausible notion of welfare, it's a diminishment of welfare to experience significant physical pain and psychological distress. Depending on how welfare is construed, it may or may not be a diminishment of animals' welfare to be killed. Insofar as not engaging in natural behaviors or being confined causes animals distress or pain, it is a diminishment of their welfare not to engage in natural behaviors or to be confined. But it's controversial whether engaging in natural behaviors or having liberty is itself a component of animal welfare.

Whether death is bad is controversial and is an issue that Korsgaard's, Singer's, and Tännsjö's readings deal with. (The issue is also discussed in Chapter 8, "Alternatives to Industrial Animal Agriculture.") Some maintain that death is only bad for beings of a certain psychological complexity and that animals on farms lack this psychological complexity (as do various mentally handicapped and very young and very old humans). Others maintain that animals have the requisite psychological complexity. This raises hard ethical issues about the badness of death and hard psychological issues about the nature of animals' mental lives.

Yet, putting death aside, some treatment on industrial farms is clearly bad for animals, for example the physical and psychological pain from crowding, debeaking, and excessive growth.

To say that these aspects of farm life are *bad* for animals is consistent with saying that the farm environment is not the worst possible environment. It is also clear that it is better in various ways than a natural environment. As the Pew Commission reading notes, the farms protect against certain diseases that life in the wild would expose animals to. The farms protect against predators. Animals are protected from the elements. Animals get medical care. Perhaps animals on farms die more quickly and less painfully than animals in the wild, because they are usually killed in slaughterhouses rather than dying of disease and injury or being eaten by other animals.

However, it is important to distinguish *good* conditions from conditions that *could be worse*. It is important to distinguish conditions that are *good overall* from conditions that are *good in some ways*. Compare: If you have an overprotective parent who never lets you leave the house even when you're in your twenties, that is not good overall. Yet being kept in your house does protect you from various dangers outside your house. Similarly, the conditions on industrial farms can be good in some ways but still be bad for animals overall.

Also, to say that this suffering is bad is not to say that producing it is wrong. Of course, it is sometimes permissible to hurt animals or to stress them. The question is just *when* it is permissible and *why*. If a great white shark attacks you, it is permissible to hurt it or even to kill it to save your life. If a mosquito is biting you, it is permissible to crush it. But the situation on industrial farms is quite different. The animals are doing us no harm. Is it permissible to hurt them simply in order to get food from them? In order to get food for cheap? In order to get food for cheap while, at the same time, providing employment and money to farmers and other workers?

The reading "All Animals Are Equal" by Peter Singer provides one argumentative strategy for answering these questions. Singer asks us to consider whether it would be permissible to hurt *people* in such a situation, a situation in which doing so provides us food for cheap, provides money to others. He compares the claim that it is permissible to hurt animals for food with the claim that it is permissible to hurt people with the mental lives of animals for food. When we're comparing our treatment of people who have mental lives like animals, and our treatment of animals, the only difference between them that might be a morally relevant difference is that the people are human beings, whereas the animals are members of another species. But, Singer argues, species membership is not actually a morally relevant difference, a difference that can explain why it is permissible to treat people and animals differently. Species membership does not morally justify treating one group of sentient creatures differently from another. Singer argues that species membership is no more morally relevant than being *white* or being *male*. To think that being a person has the requisite moral relevance is to be a *speciesist*.

In response to Singer's argument, it might be argued that Singer assumes that being industrially farmed is painful but is not entitled to assume this. One way of developing this is to claim we have no idea what it is like for animals to undergo the treatment they undergo on farms. On the one hand, this seems overly pessimistic. While there is debate about the exact nature of the mental lives of farm animals, and, especially, about whether our theories of those mental lives anthropomorphize those animals,[12] that they are sentient creatures is not controversial. On the other hand, if it's true, that might motivate a *precautionary* approach. If you don't know whether what you're doing is hurting a baby, you wouldn't—and shouldn't—go ahead with it just because, hey, maybe it is not hurting the baby after all. (For further discussion of these issues see Chapter 9, "Industrial Plant Agriculture," and Chapter 10, "Alternatives to Industrial Plant Agriculture.")

This uncertainty shows up in response to a different worry one might have about industrial animal farms. When a cat mercilessly beats a toy, there is no problem. (In fact, because it is a toy, "merciless" might strike you as odd.) But when people see cats mercilessly toying with mice or birds, they sometimes feel a shock of revulsion or horror or discomfort. It's one thing for a cat to kill an animal to eat it—that's what cats do to survive—but it's another thing to treat an animal like a toy. Which isn't to say the cat does anything *wrong*. It's a cat—it does neither right nor wrong. But our discomfort about the toying cat might stem from the fact that the cat is treating a sentient creature as a toy. And this sentient creature, as Korsgaard notes, has a life with its own rhythm, social structures, relationships,

> even a narrative structure to the course of an individual life that we can recognize and describe—even if they cannot. Among social animals, for instance, certain male individuals rise to positions of power and leadership in middle age, only to be deposed by younger members when they are older. Females move through a distinct set of roles in family life as daughters, then mothers, then grandmothers in much the same way that, in many cultures, human females do.[13]

Treating a creature like that as a toy is no way to treat such a thing. Similarly, the worry goes, industrial farming treats animals like machines for making food. And, the objection goes, that is no way to treat a sentient creature.

Why not? And *which* creatures is this no way to treat? When a bus driver treats a bus like a machine, there is no issue. But consider this quotation from Charles Gerard:

> The goose is nothing, but man has made of it an instrument for the output of a marvelous product, a kind of living hothouse in which there grows the supreme fruit of gastronomy (i.e., its liver).[14]

But a goose is not a living hothouse. It is a sentient creature that enjoys doing certain things, none of which are being a hothouse. Treating it like a hothouse is failing to treat it appropriately and is *ipso facto* wrong. As many of the books and articles cited in Chapter 11, "Workers," note, treating an animal as a hothouse might lead, as a matter of psychological fact, to a sort of psychological brutalization of workers: They start to treat various sentient things, not just non-human animals, as machines.

Along with ethical worries about the treatment of animals, a different sort of worry stems from the externalizing of the costs of industrial agriculture in the sense of *externalities* described further previously. The stench of industrial farms, for example, afflicts people in the surrounding areas. That cost is concentrated there rather than distributed among all the people who benefit from the farm and the food it produces. (The people who live nearby mightn't benefit at all from the farm.) Climate change driven by greenhouse gas emissions afflicts people far off in both time and space from industrial farms. They, too, might reap no benefits while bearing this cost of industrial farming. The issue is that there seems to be something morally objectionable about having people bear costs when those people are not properly compensated. (And then what would proper compensation be?)

So, is it morally impermissible to treat animals and people in these ways in order to produce animal-source food? We have enumerated some reasons for and against. The force of those reasons depends in part on what the alternatives are. If the only choices were actual industrial animal agriculture or a type that was worse for people and animals, then our actual industrial animal agriculture would be permissible. But, as a matter of fact, there are other alternatives.

For example, we could opt for the abolition of industrial animal agriculture and all other forms of animal agriculture. Many fewer of these animals will exist. Humans will have much less animal-source food, so some humans' welfare will be diminished in various ways from eating less animal-source food. But overall long-term human welfare might be improved.

We could, instead, opt to abolish industrial animal agriculture while adopting a very different form of animal agriculture, such as free-range animal agriculture. As we discuss in Chapter 8, "Alternatives to Industrial Animal Agriculture," animal welfare is plausibly higher in free-range animal agriculture, though not necessarily higher along every dimension, for example because animals may be more exposed to the elements or predation. Probably way fewer animals can feasibly be raised for food, in non-industrial animal agriculture. So fewer animals will exist on this alternative, too. Humans will have less animal-source food. Also animal-source food will be more expensive, typically. So some humans' welfare will be diminished in various ways from eating less animal-source food. But overall long-term human welfare might be improved. On the other hand, widespread adoption of free-range animal agriculture runs the risk of using a great deal of land, which would reduce the amount of land available for plant agriculture and would have dire environmental consequences.

A more radical alternative is developing genetically engineered animals that do not suffer or suffer much less, or developing "synthetic meat" that is real muscle fiber grown in a petri dish that is never part of a living animal.[15] As an intermediate alternative, we could retain industrial animal agriculture but improve animals' welfare, by, for example, banning cages and crates of all sorts as in some European countries. On this alternative, maybe humans will have somewhat less animal-source food, and maybe it'll be a bit more expensive. This sort of system is discussed in the Tännsjö reading that follows. Tännsjö argues that such a system produces the most happiness overall and *ipso facto* should be adopted. He argues:

> A well-designed industrial animal agricultural system is the agricultural system that maximizes happiness.
> We are morally required to adopt the agricultural system that maximizes happiness.
> Hence, We are morally required to adopt a well-designed industrial animal agricultural system.

R. M. Hare (1999) accepts the second premise of this argument but denies the first, instead endorsing that a free-range system maximizes happiness. The Singer reading in this chapter, by contrast, hints that a system with no animal agriculture maximizes happiness. If utilitarianism is true, and one of these alternatives produces the most happiness, then it should be adopted.

But there are non-utilitarian reasons to think that industrial animal agriculture is impermissible. These are the reasons that come from harming animals without good reason *and* where the good reason is not our own happiness. To a utilitarian, whether or not industrial animal agriculture is permissible depends entirely on how much happiness it produces. So if eaters were happy *enough* about eating industrially produced food, industrial farms might well be permissible. To some non-utilitarians, the happiness of consumers is beside the point. What matters might be just that animals are being made to suffer just so we can eat them. Or what matters might be that animals are being treated merely as tools or machines when, instead, they are owed better treatment. Or what matters might be that humans are being forced to bear costs that they need not bear.

These are hard issues. Even if we were to resolve them, we might still be left with a question about what to make of our resolution. For example, if industrial animal agriculture is morally impermissible, what should be done? Well, the farming is wrong, so it should be stopped. But you don't farm. What should you do?

One question we might ask is: What should I as an individual do? What should I consume? We discuss this in Chapter 4, "Consumer Ethics."

Another question we might ask is: What alternatives to industrial animal agriculture, in its current form, should be supported? What should we throw our weight behind? Improved industrial agriculture? Non-industrial animal agriculture? The abolition of animal agriculture?

And then a related question is: *How* should one support these alternatives? By purchasing certain products? By eating them? By lobbying policymakers?

A FURTHER COMPLICATION: WHAT FOOD SYSTEM WOULD BE IDEALLY BEST VS. WHAT FOOD SYSTEM IS BEST IN OUR ACTUAL NON-IDEAL CIRCUMSTANCES

To illustrate a further complication that must be taken into account in answering these questions, consider this important argument in favor of contemporary industrial agriculture, including industrial animal agriculture:

1. If (a) the world grows richer and more populous as many experts predict and (b) people continue to consume far more animal products as they get richer as many experts predict, then only intensive animal agriculture that incorporates many of the practices of contemporary industrial animal and plant agriculture will allow us to meet that demand without leading to a catastrophe of failing to feed very many people and destroying the environment.
2. We should expect these experts to be correct about both (a) and (b).

Hence, Even if the ideal solution to food systems challenges, including animal welfare concerns, would involve wealthier people eating far less animals than experts predict and a less intensive form of agriculture for both animals and plants, nonetheless we should actually promote more intensive agriculture in our actual non-ideal circumstances, because the form of agriculture that would be best in ideal circumstances would actually lead to catastrophe in our non-ideal circumstances, given that wealthy people will predictably not eat far less animal products.

In other words, this argument claims that regardless of what we think would be ethically ideal, nonetheless people are going to consume far more animals than is ideal, and if we don't produce them using industrial means, we are going to starve people and destroy the planet. So, we should produce animals in a more intensive way, because the animal welfare cost of doing so is a trade-off we ethically must make in order to avoid the even bigger catastrophe of failing to feed people and destroying the planet.

This argument illustrates that there is arguably an important distinction between two different things that are of fundamental ethical importance: namely, what would be best in what we might call, following philosophical usage, *ideal theory*—that is, what would be ethically right if everyone was disposed to perfectly comply with morality—and what would be best in *non-ideal theory*—that is, what is ethically right given the predictable behavior of actual human beings, which is often far from ethically perfect. To illustrate the difference using an example from outside the domain of food, note that even if in ideal circumstances (where all human behaved perfectly ethically) we would leave all of our doors unlocked and everyone would let anyone use whatever property they wanted at all times, nonetheless in our actual non-ideal circumstances (where we know that many people are disposed to behave unethically) it would often be ethically wrong to behave in that way, because doing so would likely lead to catastrophe (for oneself, for one's family, etc.), and instead the best outcome from an ethical point of view would result from behaving very differently.

This highlights why there are arguably two different but fundamentally important ethical questions about food systems and other problems regarding ethics and society: namely, what would be ethically right in ideal theory versus what is actually right in non-ideal actuality. Many philosophers take the latter issue to be the most relevant to questions of both *practical ethics*—what we should actually do in practice—and *public policy*—roughly, what package of government policy, civil society initiatives, and market-based initiatives we should actually implement. As one more example to illustrate the allegedly greater relevance of non-ideal theory to practical ethics and public policy, David Schmidtz notes that we would find a traffic control system that was designed for ideal people to be ethically unacceptable if it predictably led to far greater fatalities in practice, even if it would truly be the optimal system for drivers very different from us and more ethically ideal.[16] Similarly, one might think that a food system that would be best for ideal humans would be ethically unacceptable if it predictably would actually lead to catastrophe for actual non-ideal humans—just as the argument in this section claims.

BIG-PICTURE QUESTIONS ABOUT FOOD SYSTEMS, AND HOW BEST TO LEVERAGE INDIVIDUAL ACTION, GOVERNMENT, INDUSTRY, AND ADVOCACY FOR POSITIVE CHANGE

In light of all this, some important "big-picture" questions to consider after reading this chapter and the following three chapters are as follows:

1. Is there a better way to produce food than the actual way it is produced, and is there a better overall *food system*, which includes the food distribution and socio-economic systems in which agricultural systems are embedded?
2. If so, what would be the ideally best food system, assuming everyone was disposed to act in a way that was perfectly ethical—that is, willing to stop eating animal products if necessary, and so on?
3. What food system is it actually best to aim for, given the actual dispositions of people, including their dispositions to sometimes respond less than ethically?

4. Given a particular conception of what food system we should actually aim for, what is the best way of getting there from here? That is, given the complex workings of the food system, what actions would best move us in the right direction, distinguishing actions by individual people like you, by our government, by industry leaders, by community organizations, by charities, and so on, and taking into account the complex feedbacks and interactions between those actions?

To illustrate the importance of the last question, which has not been discussed so far, note that one thing that many of the readings in this chapter leave out is the motivation for treating animals in the ways detailed herein: It's not sadism. It's more like an interest in maximizing profit, which in an extremely competitive industry is arguably necessary for remaining in business rather than going bankrupt. This is important. It shows that the industry is sensitive to things like consumer boycotts. If people refuse to pay money for pork that comes from a certain sort of industrial farm, one that keeps pregnant pigs in small crates, the industry will change. However, that change might come slowly. Marion Nestle details a stark example of how slow that change can be in her reading in this chapter.

But change has come, to some extent, and perhaps more change is on the way. In recent years, California's Proposition 2 banned confinement of animals in crates that prevent them from standing and turning around on California farms. It passed by nearly a two-thirds majority. Similar measures have been adopted in several other states. Regarding these and other, more general changes, Tim Carman writes,

> It would appear that corporate America is catching up to public opinion. Since December [2012], a string of fast-food chains, pork producers and other major companies have committed to raising sows without gestation crates or buying meat from suppliers that have dumped the confinement system. It started late last year when Smithfield Foods, the nation's largest pork producer, announced that 30 percent of its own sows would be moved from gestation crates to group housing by the end of 2011, a sign the company was at last fulfilling a pledge it had made in 2007.
>
> In January, Hormel Foods decided to jump on board, announcing it would convert all of its company-owned farms to group sow housing before 2018. A month later, McDonald's promised to work with its suppliers to eliminate gestation crates, and two of the fast-food giant's competitors, Burger King and Wendy's, soon followed suit. Others have joined the movement . . . as well: Denny's, Safeway and two food-service companies, the Compass Group and Bon Appetit Management.[17]

Explaining why this is happening, Carman writes,

> Participants inside (and outside) the pork and restaurant industries say this seemingly sudden movement against gestation crates actually has been in the works for years, the result of a number of factors. Prime among them . . . is public opinion. To date, eight states have passed laws prohibiting the crates, including Florida, Arizona, Colorado and Michigan. Some of those laws were approved in public referendums, like California's, which garnered more than 60 percent of the vote.[18]

And the technology available to pig farmers is improving,[19] with redesigned pens and feeding chutes that allow some of the benefits of crating—pigs get protected from more aggressive pigs, and the aggressive pigs don't eat all the food—without confining pigs to crates. And similar remarks apply along some analogous dimensions to dairy cows, veal calves, beef cattle, and chickens. For example, here is Temple Grandin describing welfare improvements in the cattle industry in the last decades:

> In 1999 McDonald's Corporation started auditing handling and stunning practices in the plants that supply them with beef. They used a scoring system that I developed for the American Meat Institute . . . and I trained the HACCP food safety auditors from their grinder suppliers to do handling and stunning audits. The results of the McDonald's audits clearly showed huge improvements. . . . The industry became serious about improving handling and stunning after McDonald's removed one large plant from the approved supplier list and suspended several others for varying lengths of time. Both McDonald's and Wendy's are conducting audits of handling stunning. During my travels in the U.S. I have observed that the cleanliness of meat plants is better in plants that are audited by McDonald's or Wendy's compared to plants that are not audited. Audits by restaurant companies have raised both food safety and animal welfare standards. Being a practical person I base standards of animal treatment on what would the general public accept. I have taken many non-meat industry people to a well run slaughter plant and most people found it was acceptable.[20]

Despite these improvements for cattle, Grandin claims that much of the egg industry did not meet the same standard of acceptability:

> My background in working with animals is in cattle and pigs. When I visited a large egg layer operation and saw old hens that had reached the end of their productive life, I was horrified. . . . Some egg producers got rid of old hens by suffocating them in plastic bags or dumpsters. The more I learned about the egg industry the more disgusted I got. Some of the practices that had become "normal" for this industry were overt cruelty. Bad had become normal. Egg producers had become desensitized to suffering. There is a point there: economics alone must not be the sole justification for an animal production practice. When the egg producers asked me if I wanted cheap eggs I replied, "Would you want to buy a shirt if it was $5 cheaper and made by child slaves?"[21]

But once again, Grandin believes that McDonald's and other corporations are crucial to improving welfare by setting standards of "minimal decency" that will be adhered to in practice because of the market power of McDonald's and other large customers of producers:

> I predict that animal welfare standards will evolve into two categories. A minimum decent standard for large scale commercial use and higher welfare standards for niche markets with higher income consumers. Throwing live hens in the trash violates most people's idea of minimum decent standards. It is my opinion that the new McDonald's standards for egg laying hens are a minimum decent standard that the egg industry really needed. . . . An example of a higher welfare standard for hens would be free range hens. . . . Minimum decent standards need to be implemented worldwide. [22]

Here Grandin explains some of the workings of and feedbacks within the food system that may not be obvious at first glance, and she highlights what she takes to be some of the less obvious "leverage points" that may be excellent opportunities to move things in a different direction.[23] She also takes a stand on the two big-picture questions highlighted at the beginning of this section: She thinks that we should have "minimum decent standards" for animal welfare as a goal, and she gives some indication of how she thinks we can best move things in that direction.

In the following three chapters we consider other arguments relevant to these big-picture questions about what food system we should want and how best to achieve it. Then, at the end of Chapter 10, we revisit the big-picture questions at the start of this section and outline one general framework for thinking about them (sustainable intensification) that has recently become influential among many experts.

FURTHER ISSUES

1. *The Real Cost of Cheap Food*
Industrial animal agriculture makes cheap food available in at least the following way: It makes, say, Sausage McMuffins, Double Cheeseburgers, and McChicken sandwiches available at McDonald's for $1. Yet there are costs in addition to the dollar that are associated with the burger: costs to workers and people who live nearby, costs—obviously—to animals, costs to the environment. There's a whole genre of articles about this: "The Hidden Cost of Cheap Food." One issue: Is this food really cheap? How so? How not? Another issue: What enables McDonald's to make money off these $1 products is that McDonald's does not bear many of the costs associated with producing them. Is that fair or just? If not, is it permissible?

2. *Who Profits from Contemporary Industrial Agriculture?*
Early in this chapter, we said that industrial agriculture is, roughly, producing the most food at maximum profit. One might think that what industrial agriculture is really about is not exactly producing the most food at maximum profit for the *farmer* but, rather, producing the most food at maximum profit for *the large agribusiness companies that farmers are dependent on (or in some cases work for) in contemporary industrial agriculture*. This suggests a criticism of the industrial agricultural model—both industrial animal agriculture and industrial plant agriculture—namely, that it is unjust because it favors the rich over the poor. Spell out that criticism more rigorously. Is it compelling? Does it point to something of genuine ethical concern—perhaps not only about inequalities in who profits from work but also in the distribution of power in society?

3. *The Benefits of Adding Lives*
Tännsjö's argument relies on the thesis that it is better to add happy lives than to not add any lives. And then it relies on the thesis that you should bring about the best outcome. You might reject either of these theses. Instead of thinking you make a world better simply by *adding* good lives, you might think that betterness is calculated by, say, averaging the quality of lives. No one thinks we can know the *precise* amount of goodness any life has in it, but some people think we can know the rough amount. They think that the total amount of goodness is the average amount of goodness. What do you think of the additive view? The averaging view? What are the implications of the averaging view for Tännsjö's argument?

4. *What's So Good about Liberty? What's So Good about Naturalness?*
Part of what produces psychological distress in industrially farmed animals is that those animals lack liberty and live profoundly unnatural lives. The Singer and Tännsjö readings suggest that what is wrong with the lack of liberty and the unnaturalness is just that those things produce psychological distress, that there is nothing *in itself* objectionable about a lack of liberty and a lack of naturalness. Is that right? What would Korsgaard say?

5. *Genetic Modification*

The Adam Shriver articles cited herein point out that, in the future, we might be able to genetically engineer animals in order to eliminate or greatly reduce the suffering they experience on some farms. Would it be permissible to do so? Why or why not? Now consider this reply to Shriver from a letter to the editor by the philosopher N. Ann Davis:

> To the Editor:
>
> Adam Shriver applauds the possibility that we may soon be able to reduce the discomfort of the animals we choose to raise in the horrific warehouses of factory farms through neuroscience. I'd like to propose an alternative: that we consider using neuroscience and genetic engineering to modify humans so that they derive less pleasure from consuming large amounts of animal flesh and more pleasure from consuming things like tofu.
>
> Another option, of course, is that we leave both humans and animals unmodified and instead encourage the humans to use their superior intelligence, freer wills and more developed moral sense to see how deeply repellent it is for humans to continue to devote so much energy to find new ways of exploiting animals so that they can have tasty morsels on their plates.

Explain Davis's objection to Shriver. Is it persuasive? Why or why not?

6. *In Vitro Meat*

As briefly noted earlier, researchers have recently demonstrated the ability to grow meat in a petri dish that is genuine meat in the sense that it is genetically animal flesh, but yet it is synthetic meat in the sense that it has never been part of a living animal, apart from some initial "starter" materials. Advocates of this in vitro meat promote it as "cruelty-free meat." Assuming that this kind of meat can be grown economically and made commercially attractive in other ways (i.e., can be made to taste good), what are some arguments for and against its widespread adoption? Is it a good objection to this kind of meat that it is unnatural? How natural are other food products?

FURTHER READING

Industrial Fishing and Aquaculture

Greenberg, Paul. 2010. "Salmon," in *Four Fish*. New York: Penguin.

Grescoe, Taras. 2008. "An Economy of Scales," in *Bottomfeeder*. New York: Bloomsbury.

Hilborn, Ray, and Ulrike Hilborn. 2012. *Overfishing: What Everyone Needs to Know*. New York: Oxford University Press.

Humane Society of the United States. n.d. "The Welfare of Animals in the Aquaculture Industry," http://www.humanesociety.org/assets/pdfs/farm/hsus-the-welfare-of-animals-in-the-aquaculture-industry-1.pdf.

Naylor, Rosamond, et al. 2000. "Effect of Aquaculture on World Fish Supplies," *Nature* 405: 1017–1024.

The Environmental Effects of Industrial Animal Agriculture

Gerber, P. J., H. Steinfeld, B. Henderson, A. Mottet, C. Opio, J. Dijkman, A. Falcucci, and G. Tempio. 2013. "Tackling Climate Change through Livestock—A Global Assessment of Emissions and Mitigation Opportunities." Food and Agriculture Organization of the United Nations.

Humane Society of the United States. n.d. "The Impact of Industrialized Animal Agriculture on the Environment." http://www.humanesociety.org/assets/pdfs/farm/hsus-the-impact-of-industrialized-animal-agriculture-on-the-environment.pdf.

Pew Commission on Industrial Farm Animal Production. 2008. *Putting Meat on the Table: Industrial Farm Animal Production in America*, 22–29.

Singer, Peter, and Jim Mason. 2007. *The Ethics of What We Eat*. Emmaus, PA: Rodale.

The Ethics of Industrial Animal Agriculture

Anomaly, Jonathan. 2014. "What's Wrong with Factory Farming?" *Public Health Ethics* 8: 1–9.

Carruthers, Peter. 1990. *The Animals Issue*. New York: Cambridge University Press.

Coetzee, J. M. 1999. *The Lives of Animals*. Princeton, NJ: Princeton University Press.

———. 2003. *Elizabeth Costello*. New York: Viking.

Cohen, Carl. 1997. "Do Animals Have Rights?" *Ethics and Behavior* 7: 91–102.

Frey, R. G. 1980. *Interests and Rights: The Case against Animals*. New York: Oxford University Press.

———. 1983. *Rights, Killing, and Suffering: Moral Vegetarianism and Applied Ethics*. Oxford: Blackwell.

Gruen, Lori. 2011. "Eating Animals," in *Ethics and Animals*. New York: Cambridge University Press.

Hare, R. M. 1999. "Why I Am Only a Demi-Vegetarian," in Jamieson, *Singer and His Critics*.

Jamieson, Dale, ed. 1999. *Singer and His Critics*. Cambridge, MA: Wiley-Blackwell.

Korsgaard, Christine M. 2011. "Interacting with Animals: A Kantian Account," in *The Oxford Handbook of Animal Ethics*, ed. Tom Beauchamp and R. G. Frey. New York: Oxford University Press.

———. 2005. "Fellow Creatures: Kantian Ethics and Our Duties to Animals," in *The Tanner Lectures on Human Values*, Vol. 25, ed. Grethe B. Peterson. Salt Lake City: University of Utah Press.

Mason, Jim, and Singer, Peter. 1990. *Animal Factories,* updated ed. New York: Harmony Books.

McGinn, Colin. 1997. "Frey: Beyond the Moral Pale," in *Minds and Bodies*. New York: Oxford University Press.

Pollan, Michael. 2006. *The Omnivore's Dilemma*. New York: Penguin.

Scott, James. 2012. *Two Cheers for Anarchism*. Princeton, NJ: Princeton University Press.

Singer, Peter. 1980. "Utilitarianism and Vegetarianism," *Philosophy and Public Affairs* 9: 325–337.

Singer, Peter, and Jim Mason. 2007. "The Ethics of Eating Meat," in *The Ethics of What We Eat*. Emmaus, PA: Rodale.

Ethology

Balcombe, Jonathan. 2006. *The Pleasurable Kingdom*. New York: MacMillan.

Dawkins, Marian Stamp. 2007. "Feelings Do Not a Science Make," *Bioscience* 57: 83–84.

Palmer, Clare. 2010. *Animal Ethics in Context*. New York: Columbia University Press.

Improvements

Bittman, Mark. 2015. "Hens, Unbound," *New York Times,* January 1, 2015.

Carman, Tim. 2012. "Pork Industry Gives Sows Room to Move," *Washington Post,* May 29, 2012.

Gates, Bill. 2013. "Future of Food." https://www.gatesnotes.com/About-Bill-Gates/Future-of-Food.

Sebo, Jeff, and Dale Jamieson, "The Future of Meat," forthcoming.

Sebo, Jeff, and Peter Singer, "Animal Activism," forthcoming.
Shriver, Adam. 2009. "Knocking Out Pain in Livestock," *Neuroethics* 2: 115–124.
Shriver, Adam. 2010. "Not Grass-Fed, But At Least Pain-Free," *New York Times,* February 19, 2010.

Racism, Sexism, Speciesim

Adams, Carol. 1990. *The Sexual Politics of Meat.* New York: Continuum.
Spiegel, Marjorie. 1988. *The Dreaded Comparison.* London: Heretic.

NOTES

1. EPA, "Animal Feeding Operations," 2016. https://www.epa.gov/npdes/animal-feeding-opera-tions-afos. In their reading in this chapter, the Pew Commission call industrial animal agriculture the "IFAP system," the Industrial Farm Animal Production system.

2. www.fishcount.org.uk estimates that *at least* 37 billion farmed fish are killed worldwide and *at most* 120 billion are. Not all of these are killed in the United States, but even a small fraction would greatly increase the number of creatures farmed in the U.S. each year. The Humane Society estimates that more than 1 billion fish were farmed in the United States in 2005. See "An HSUS Report: The Welfare of Animals in the Aquaculture Industry," http://www.humanesociety.org/assets/pdfs/farm/hsus-the-welfare-of-animals-in-the-aquaculture-industry-1.pdf.

3. Anomaly (2014) clearly and persuasively expands on the points in this paragraph.

4. There is a related serious conversation to be had about whether relatively few "big box" stores are cheaper overall than the model of smaller, more numerous stores they replaced.

5. The prevalence of corn in the diet of animals that are not designed to eat it is (surprisingly rivetingly) discussed in Pollan (2006).

6. For the high end of this range, see "FAO 2013": P. J. Gerber, H. Steinfeld, B. Henderson, A. Mottet, C. Opio, J. Dijkman, A. Falcucci, and G. Tempio, "Tackling Climate Change through Livestock—A Global Assessment of Emissions and Mitigation Opportunities" (Rome: Food and Agriculture Organization of the United Nations [FAO], 2013); note that this study is by many of the same authors as and supersedes the slightly higher earlier estimates of H. Steinfeld, P. Gerber, T. Wassenaar, V. Castel, M. Rosales, and C. de Haan, "Livestock's Long Shadow"(Rome: UN FAO, 2006); for the low end, see "EPA 2012" (USA Environmental Protection Agency, 2012), "Non-CO2 Global Inventory: Appendix." By adding the same proportion of indirect to direct emissions from FAO 2013 to the estimates of direct emissions from animal agriculture that are the focus of EPA 2012, one arrives at approximately 10% of the global GHG emissions. Compare also Intergovernmental Panel on Climate Change WG3 AR5, Chapter 11, where the relevant discussion is based on the same sort of estimates as EPA 2012, and compare the claim that "the livestock sector may be responsible for 8–18% of GHGs, a significant share considering their projected growth" in Mario Herrero and Philip Thornton, "Livestock and Global Change: Emerging Issues for Sustainable Food Systems," *Proceedings of the National Academy of Sciences* 110 (2013): 20878–20881; see also Mario Herrero et al., "Biomass Use, Production, Feed Efficiencies, and Greenhouse Gas Emissions from Global Livestock Systems," *Proceedings of the National Academy of Sciences* 110 (2013): 20888–20893.

7. Intergovernmental Panel on Climate Change (IPCC) WG3 AR5 (2014), ch. 8, p. 606, where domestic and international aviation are reported to be a little less than 1 GT CO2eq and road transport emissions 5 GT CO2eq, out of total global emissions of 49 GT CO2eq. The bulk of the rest of global GHG emissions are from power plants and industrial sources. (For global totals, see IPCC WG3 AR5 Technical Summary, p. 42.)

8. The numbers in this paragraph are from P. J. Gerber, H. Steinfeld, B. Henderson, A. Mottet, C. Opio, J. Dijkman, A. Falcucci, and G. Tempio, "Tackling Climate Change through Livestock—A

Global Assessment of Emissions and Mitigation Opportunities" (Rome: UNFAO, 2013). Many commentators believe that GHGs from land use changes due to animal agriculture are poorly quantified, and they are likely to be higher than these estimates.

9. From the executive summary of H. Steinfeld, P. Gerber, T. Wassenaar, V. Castel, M. Rosales, and C. de Haan, "Livestock's Long Shadow," UN FAO. ftp://ftp.fao.org/docrep/fao/010/a0701e/a0701e00.pdf.

10. See Greenberg (2010), Grescoe (2008), and HSUS (n.d.).

11. http://www.humanesociety.org/assets/pdfs/farm/welfare_overview.pdf

12. See Balcombe (2006) and then Dawkins (2007), a review of Balcombe.

13. http://thepointmag.com/2012/examined-life/getting-animals-view

14. Quoted at http://www.foodreference.com/html/qgoose.html and at numerous other spots on the Web. We have not been able to find the original source.

15. Shriver (2009, 2010) details the former option. Alok Jha reports on the latter in "Synthetic Meat: How the World's Costliest Burger Made It on to the Plate," *The Guardian*, August 5, 2013.

16. David Schmidtz, "Nonideal Theory: What It Is and What It Needs to Be," *Ethics* 121 (4): 772–796.

17. Tim Carman, "Pork Industry Gives Sows Room to Move," *Washington Post*, May 29, 2012. https://www.washingtonpost.com/lifestyle/food/pork-industry-gives-sows-room-to-move/2012/05/25/gJQAISlxyU_story.html.

18. Ibid. On hens, see, too, Mark Bittman, "Hens, Unbound" (op-ed), *New York Times*, December 31, 2014. http://ift.tt/1Bj1cQ3. Proposition 2 requires increased space for farmed animals. It went into effect on January 1, 2015. As of this writing, gestation crates are banned in nine states; veal crates were banned in three; "battery" cages for hens are banned in two.

19. These two sources report on some developments. The latter also has a short, readable history of the industrial farming of pigs: Theresa Everline, "The Quest to Build a Better Pig," fastcoexist.com, February 17, 2015. http://www.fastcoexist.com/3041802/the-quest-to-build-a-better-pig-thats-easier-to-raise-humanely; and Sujata Gupta, "Porklife: Building a Better Pig," mosaicscience.com, June 17, 2014. http://mosaicscience.com/story/porklife-building-better-pig.

20. Temple Grandin, "Corporations Can Be Agents of Great Improvements in Animal Welfare and Food Safety and the Need for Minimum Decent Standards," paper presented at National Institute of Animal Agriculture, April 4, 2001. http://www.grandin.com/welfare/corporation.agents.html.

21. Ibid.

22. Ibid. For some recent developments in connection with Grandin's predictions, see Stephanie Strom, "McDonald's Plans a Shift to Eggs from Only Cage-Free Hens," *New York Times*, September 9, 2015. www.nytimes.com/2015/09/10/business/mcdonalds-to-use-eggs-from-only-cage-free-hens.html.

23. For further relevant discussion of the importance of this kind of "systems thinking," that is, understanding the nature of complex systems in order to move things in the right direction—including the importance of understanding aspects such as feedbacks and leverage points—see Donella Meadows, *Thinking in Systems* (White River Jonction, VT: Chelsea Green, 2008).

Pew Commission Says Industrial Scale Farm Animal Production Poses "Unacceptable" Risks to Public Health, Environment

This is a summary of a lengthy report on industrial animal agriculture. The summary focuses mostly on effects on people: health effects, effects on people deriving from the environment, effects on rural America. It includes a short discussion of animal welfare. The report argues that there are serious, pressing problems with our system of industrial animal agriculture. To rectify them, the report makes a series of recommendations, including banning non-thereapeutic uses of certain drugs, improving handling on animal waste, banning gestation crates and small cages, and increasing funding for animal science.

April 29, 2008—The current industrial farm animal production (IFAP) system often poses unacceptable risks to public health, the environment and the welfare of the animals themselves, according to an extensive 2½-year examination conducted by the Pew Commission on Industrial Farm Animal Production (PCIFAP), in a study released today.

Commissioners have determined that the negative effects of the IFAP system are too great and the scientific evidence is too strong to ignore. Significant changes must be implemented and must start now. And while some areas of animal agriculture have recognized these threats and have taken action, it is clear that the industry has a long way to go.

PUBLIC HEALTH

Over the past five decades, the number of farms producing animals for food has fallen dramatically, yet the number of food animals produced has remained roughly constant. It is the concentration of farm animals in larger and larger numbers in close proximity to one another, along with the potential of IFAP facilities to affect people, that give rise to many of the public health concerns that are attributed to IFAP. Animals in such close confinement, along with some of the feed and animal management methods employed in the system, increase pathogen risks and magnify opportunities for transmission from animals to humans. This increased risk is due to at least three factors: prolonged worker contact with animals, increased pathogen transmission within a herd or flock, and the increased opportunities for the generation of antimicrobial resistant bacteria (due to imprudent antimicrobial use) or new strains of viruses. Stresses induced by confinement may also increase the likelihood of infection and illness in animal populations.

Communities near IFAP facilities are subject to air emissions that can significantly affect certain segments of the population. Those most vulnerable—children, the elderly, and individuals with chronic or acute pulmonary or heart disorders—are at particular risk. The impacts on the health of those living near IFAP facilities have increasingly been the subject of epidemiological research. Adverse community health effects from exposure to IFAP air emissions fall into two categories: (1) respiratory symptoms, disease and impaired function, and (2) neurobehavioral symptoms and impaired function.

ENVIRONMENT

As with public health impacts, much of IFAP's environmental impact stems from the tremendous quantities of animal waste that are concentrated on IFAP premises. Animal waste in such volumes may exceed the capacity of the landscape to absorb the nutrients and neutralize pathogens. Thus, what should be a valuable byproduct (e.g., fertilizer) becomes a waste that must be disposed of.

According to the EPA, the annual production of manure produced by animal confinement facilities exceeds that produced by humans by at least three times. Unlike most human sewage, the majority of IFAP is spread on the ground untreated. Manure in such large quantities carries excess nutrients and farm chemicals that find their way into waterways, lakes, groundwater, soils and airways. Excess and inappropriate land application of untreated animal waste on cropland contributes to excessive nutrient loading and, ultimately, eutrophication of surface waters. Eutrophication is an excess of nutrients in a

body of water, mostly nitrates and phosphates from erosion and runoff of surrounding lands, that causes a dense growth of plant life and the death of aquatic animal life due to lack of oxygen.

IFAP runoff also carries antibiotics and hormones, pesticides, and heavy metals. Antibiotics are used to prevent and treat bacterial infections and as growth promoters. Pesticides are used to control insect infestations and fungal growth. Heavy metals, especially zinc and copper, are added as micronutrients to the animal diet.

According to a 2006 UN report, globally, greenhouse gas emissions from all livestock operations account for 18% of all anthropogenic greenhouse gas emissions, exceeding those from the transportation sector. IFAP can produce greenhouse gases such as methane and carbon dioxide. Other greenhouse gases, primarily nitrous oxide, arise mainly from the microbial degradation of manure.

Air quality degradation is also a problem in and around IFAP facilities because of the localized release of significant quantities of toxic gases, odorous substances, and particulates and bioaerosols that contain a variety of microorganisms including human pathogens. Some of the most objectionable compounds are the organic acids, which include acetic acid, butyric acids, valeric acids, caproic acids, and propanoic acid; sulfur containing compounds such as hydrogen sulfide and dimethyl sulfide; and nitrogen-containing compounds including ammonia, methyl amines, methyl pyrazines, skatoles and indoles.

It is also recognized that ammonia emissions from livestock contribute significantly to the eutrophication and acidification of soil and water. Some level of nutrient overload occurs naturally, but this process can be accelerated by human activities. Acidification can put stress on species diversity in the natural environment.

ANIMAL WELFARE

IFAP methods for raising food animals have generated concern and debate over just what constitutes a reasonable life for animals and what kind of quality of life we owe the animals in our care. It is an ethical dilemma that transcends objective scientific measures, and incorporates value-based concerns. Physical health as measured by absence of some diseases or predation, for example, may be enhanced through confinement since the animals may not be exposed to certain infectious agents or sources of injury that would be encountered if the animals were raised outside of confinement. It is clear, however, that good animal welfare can no longer be assumed based only on the absence of disease or productivity outcomes. Intensive confinement (e.g. gestation crates for swine, battery cages for laying hens) often so severely restricts movement and natural behaviors, such as the ability to walk or lie on natural materials, having enough floor space to move with some freedom, and rooting for pigs, that it increases the likelihood that the animals suffer severe distress.

Good animal welfare can also help to protect the safety of our nation's food supply. Scientists have long recognized that food safety is linked to the health of the animals that produce the meat, dairy and egg products that we eat. In fact, scientists have found modern intensive confinement production systems can be stressful for food animals, and that stress can increase pathogen shedding in animals.

RURAL AMERICA

Life in rural America has long been challenged by persistent poverty. The causes are many, but among them is the lack of economic diversity in rural economies. Workers have few options in the event of a plant closure or other dislocation, and unemployment rates are high. Consequently, IFAP is frequently considered an attractive new source of economic opportunity by local economic development officials, but with this transition comes significant change including public health threats.

The industrialization of American agriculture has transformed the character of agriculture itself and, in so doing, the face of rural America. The family-owned farm producing a diverse mix of crops and food animals is largely gone as an economic entity, replaced by ever-larger operations producing just one animal species, or growing just one crop, and many rural communities have fared poorly.

As the food animal industry shifted to a system of captive supply transactions controlled by production contracts, economic power shifted from farmers to livestock processors or so-called integrators. Farmers relinquished their once autonomous, animal husbandry decision-making authority in exchange for contracts that provide assured payment, but require substantial capital investment. Once the commitment is made to such capital investment, many farmers have no choice but to continue to produce until the loan is paid off. Such contracts make it nearly impossible for there to be open and competitive markets for most hog and poultry producers, who must enter into contracts with the integrators (meat packing companies) if they are to sell their production.

Although the proponents of the industrialization of animal agriculture point to the increased economic efficiency of IFAP operations, the Commission is concerned that the benefits may not accrue in the same way to affected rural communities. In fact, industrialization leading to corporate ownership actually draws investment and wealth from the communities in which specific IFAP facilities are located.

The Commission's recommendations focus on appropriate siting of IFAP facilities in order to prevent further degradation of air, water, and soils and to minimize the impact on adjacent communities.

Below are the Commission's key recommendations.

1. Ban the non-therapeutic use of antimicrobials in food animal production to reduce the risk of antimicrobial resistance to medically important antibiotics and other microbials.
2. Implement a disease monitoring program for food animals to allow 48-hour trace-back of those animals through aspects of their production, in a fully integrated and robust national database.
3. Treat IFAP as an industrial operation and implement a new system to deal with farm waste

to replace the inflexible and broken system that exists today, to protect Americans from the adverse environmental and human health hazards of improperly handled IFAP waste.

4. Phase out the most intensive and inhumane production practices within a decade to reduce the risk of IFAP to public health and improve animal wellbeing (i.e., gestation crates and battery cages).

5. Federal and state laws need to be amended and enforced to provide a level playing field for producers when entering contracts with integrators.

6. Increase funding for, expand and reform, animal agriculture research.

"The goal of this Commission is to sound the alarms that significant change is urgently needed in industrial farm animal production," says John Carlin, PCIFAP Chairman and former Kansas governor. "I believe that the IFAP system was first developed simply to help increase farmer productivity and that the negative effects were never intended. Regardless, the consequences are real and serious and must be addressed."

Our energy, water and climate resources are undergoing dramatic changes that, in the judgment of the Commissioners, will require agriculture to transition to much more biologically diverse systems, organized into biological interactions that exchange energy, improve soil quality, and conserve water and other resources. "Long-term success will depend on the nation's ability to transform from an industrial economy that depends on quickly diminishing resources to one that is more sustainable, employing renewable resources and understanding of how all food production affects public health and the environment," says Michael Blackwell, PCIFAP Vice Chair and former dean of the University of Tennessee College of Veterinary Medicine and former Assistant Surgeon General, (Ret.) USPHS.

The PCIFAP consists of 15 Commissioners who bring individual knowledge and expertise in diverse fields, including public policy, veterinary medicine, public health, agriculture, animal welfare, the food industry and rural society. The Commission assessed the current state of industrial animal agriculture based on site visits to production facilities across the country; consultation with industry stakeholders, public health, medical and agriculture experts; public meetings; peer-reviewed technical reports; staff research; and Commissioners' own expertise. PCIFAP is a project of The Pew Charitable Trusts and the Johns Hopkins Bloomberg School of Public Health.

QUESTIONS

1. There's an interesting bit in the report about welfare *not* being the absence of bad things. Why isn't it the absence of bad things? How does this understanding of welfare square with the views developed in the introduction to Chapter 8 "Alternatives to Industrial Animal Agriculture"?

2. With the exception of part of the fourth recommendation, the report's recommendations all aim to benefit humans. (Some aim to benefit animals, too. But all aim to benefit humans.) Is that "speciesist," to use the term from Peter Singer's reading later in the chapter? Why or why not?

MARION NESTLE

Pew Commission on Industrial Farm Animal Production: Update

This is a short summary of a follow-up to the Pew Commission report. Nestle was a member of the Pew Commission. The gist of the follow-up is that the recommendations of the Commission have largely been ignored.

I was a member of this Pew Commission, which produced a landmark report in 2008: *Putting Meat on the Table: Industrial Farm Animal Production in America.*

Our report's conclusion: The current system of raising farm animals poses unacceptable risks to public health, to communities near Confined Animal Feeding Operations (CAFOs), and to the environment.

Our key recommendations:

1. Ban the nontherapeutic use of antimicrobials in food animal production.
2. Define nontherapeutic use of antimicrobials as any use in food animals in the absence of microbial disease or documented microbial disease exposure.
3. Implement new systems to deal with farm waste.
4. Phase out gestation crates, restrictive veal crates, and battery cages.
5. Enforce the existing environmental and antitrust laws applicable to food animal production.
6. Expand animal agriculture research.

Recently, the Johns Hopkins Center for a Livable Future (CLF) did an in-depth analysis of what has

happened with these recommendations. Its dismal conclusion: The problems have only gotten worse.

Many hoped the release of the report, which occurred within a year of a change in the administration, would help trigger a sea change in the federal government's approach to regulating the food animal production industry . . . Early administrative appointments to top regulatory posts held promise for meaningful changes.

CLF's review of the policy-landscape changes in the five years since the release of the report paints a very different picture. Contrary to expectations, the Obama administration has not engaged on the recommendations outlined in the report in a meaningful way; in fact, regulatory agencies in the administration have acted regressively in their decision-making and policy-setting procedures.

In addition, the House of Representatives has stepped up the intensity of its attacks on avenues for reform and stricter enforcement of existing regulations, paving the way for industry avoidance of scrutiny and even deregulation, masked as protection of the inappropriately termed "family farmer."

The assaults on reform have not been limited to blocking policies . . . Instead, the policy debate . . . has shifted to the implementation of policies such as "ag-gag," agricultural certainty, and right-to-farm laws, all of which are designed to further shield unsavory

Marion Nestle, "Pew Commission on Industrial Animal Production: Update" (October 2013). http://www.foodpolitics.com/2013/10/pew-commission-on-industrial-farm-animal-production-update/

industry practices from the eye of the public and the intervention of regulators.

This week, some of the Commission members answered questions from ProPolitico reporter Helena Bottemiller Evich. Ralph Loglisci reports in Civil Eats on that meeting and his conversation with former Pew Commission director Robert Martin, who is now the Center for a Livable Future's Director of Food System Policy:

I think issues are going to drive change at some point. You've got this big group of people who want to see change. The problems of antibiotic resistance are worsening—the problems of 500 million tons of (animal) waste we produce each year are worsening and the ground in many areas of the country is really saturated with phosphorous. You can't transport the material, so you've got to disperse the animals. So, the problems are reaching really a crisis point. So that could really force action too.

Is there any hope? It sounds like things will have to get worse before they get better. But how much worse?

I wish there were better news. Food safety, animal welfare, and environmental advocates: get together and get busy!

QUESTIONS

1. The gulf between what the Commission recommended and what actually happened is striking. What would it take to make the recommendations more effective?
2. Is there any cause for optimism in Nestle's blogpost? If so, what is it?

HUMANE SOCIETY OF THE USA

The Welfare of Animals in the Meat, Egg, and Dairy Industries

This heavily researched essay briefly summarizes conditions on industrial farms for chickens, turkeys, geese, pigs, cattle, and fish. It explains conditions on industrial farms, explains some of the logic that produces those conditions, and then spells out those conditions' effects on animal welfare. It is part of a series on farms that you can find at http://www.humanesociety.org/news/publications/whitepapers/farm_animal_welfare.html.

Humane Society of the United States, "An HSUS Report: The Welfare of Animals in the Meat, Egg, and Dairy Industries." http://www.humanesociety.org/assets/pdfs/farm/welfare_overview.pdf

Each year in the United States, approximately 11 billion animals are raised and killed for meat, eggs, and milk. These farm animals—sentient, complex, and capable of feeling pain and frustration, joy and excitement—are viewed by industrialized agriculture as commodities and suffer myriad assaults to their physical, mental, and emotional well-being, typically denied the ability to engage in their species-specific behavioral needs. Despite the routine abuses they endure, no federal law protects animals from cruelty on the farm, and the majority of states exempt customary agricultural practices—no matter how abusive—from the scope of their animal cruelty statutes. The treatment of farm animals and the conditions in which they are raised, transported, and slaughter within industrialized agriculture are incompatible with providing adequate levels of welfare.

BIRDS

Of the approximately 11 billion animals killed annually in the United States, 86% are birds—98% of land animals in agriculture—and the overwhelming majority are "broiler" chickens raised for meat, approximately 1 million killed each hour. Additionally, approximately 340 million laying hens are raised in the egg industry (280 million birds who produce table eggs and 60 million kept for breeding), and more than 270 million turkeys are slaughtered for meat.

On factory farms, birds raised for meat are confined by the tens of thousands in grower houses, which are commonly artificially lit, force-ventilated, and completely barren except for litter material on the floor and long rows of feeders and drinkers. The most significant assault on their welfare is fast growth. The poultry industry has used selective breeding to produce birds whose bodies "are on the verge of structural collapse." Studies consistently show that approximately 26-30% of broiler chickens suffer from gait defects severe enough to impair walking ability, and additional research strongly

suggests that birds at this level of lameness are in pain. On October 14, 1991, *The Guardian* quoted professor John Webster of the University of Bristol School of Veterinary Science who stated, "Broilers are the only livestock that are in chronic pain for the last 20 per cent of their lives. They don't move around, not because they are overstocked, but because it hurts their joints so much."

Market weight is reached after 6–7 weeks for broiler chickens, approximately 99 days for turkey hens, and 136 days for tom turkeys. The birds are hastily caught and can suffer dislocated and broken hips, legs, and wings, as well as internal hemorrhages during the process. The birds are put into crates stacked one atop another on trucks. During their journey to slaughter, they are not given any food or water and are afforded little if any protection from extreme temperatures.

Like birds raised for meat, chickens in the egg industry suffer immensely—beginning right after hatching. Male chicks are considered byproducts, as they are unable to lay eggs and are not bred for meat production. Millions each year are gassed, macerated, sucked through a vacuum system, or thrown into garbage bins where they are left to die from dehydration or asphyxiation. Most female chicks are mutilated without any pain relief. To help prevent potential outbreaks of feather-pecking and other injurious behavior that can result from intensive confinement in barren conditions, tips of their sensitive beaks are seared off with a hot blade.

More than 95% of egg-laying hens in U.S. animal agriculture are intensively confined in small, wire "battery cages" stacked several tiers high and extending down long warehouses. Hens are given less space than the area of a letter-sized sheet of paper in which to eat, sleep, lay eggs, and defecate. The intensive confinement makes it impossible for them to engage in nearly all of their natural behavior, including dustbathing, foraging, or nesting, the most significant source of frustration for battery caged hens. While many countries are phasing out the abusive battery cage system, U.S. egg producers still overcrowd hens in barren cages so small the birds can't even spread their wings.

When their productivity wanes, hens may be "force molted" through low-nutrient feed, until they lose 30–35% of their body weight—to induce another laying cycle. After two years when hens may no longer be profitable, the majority are "depopulated," removed from their cages, a process that can cause broken limbs in nearly one in four hens, and then sent to slaughter or gassed on farm. As with broiler chickens and other animals, egg-laying hens are given little protection from extreme temperatures during their journey to slaughter.

At the slaughter plant, the birds are uncrated, dumped onto conveyors, and hung upside-down in shackles by their legs. In the United States, birds are typically not rendered unconscious before they are slaughtered, as the U.S. Department of Agriculture (USDA) does not interpret the federal Humane Methods of Slaughter Act to extend to farmed birds.

Shackled and inverted, their heads pass through an electrified water bath before their throats are cut, usually by machine. As slaughter lines run at rapid speeds (up to 8,400 chickens per hour), mistakes can occur and up to 3% of birds may still be conscious as they enter tanks of scalding water intended to loosen their feathers.

Although chickens, turkeys, and eggs are the more common products from fanned birds, *pâté de foie gras* is another food item produced from birds. French for "fatty liver," foie gras is made from the livers of overfed ducks and geese. Ducks and geese are force-fed via a long tube inserted down their esophagi with an unnatural quantity of food pumped directly into their stomachs.

Force-feeding birds to produce foie gras is detrimental to their welfare, causing the birds' livers to become diseased. Birds force-fed for foie gras may suffer from a number of significant welfare problems, including frustration of natural behavior, injury, liver disease, lameness, diseases of the respiratory and digestive tracts, and higher rates of mortality compared to non–force-fed ducks.

The majority of the world's foie gras is made from duck livers, and approximately 80% is produced in France. In the United States, three facilities produce livers for foie gras, slaughtering in total more than 500,000 ducks annually.

PIGS

More than 116 million pigs, intelligent and highly social animals, are slaughtered annually in the United States.

In industrial pig production, sows (adult female pigs) are customarily put through consecutive cycles of impregnation, giving birth, and nursing, all while intensively confined. During their four-month pregnancies, approximately 80% of sows are kept in stalls—individual metal "gestation crates" that are 0.6 m (2 ft) wide and 2.1 m (7 ft) long—so small, the animals are unable to turn around. The USDA's Agricultural Research Service reported in its March 2005 issue of *Agricultural Research,* "Confining pregnant sows in stalls is a major well-being issue. It curtails movement and social interaction and fails to provide dirt or hay to satisfy their instincts to use their snouts to root for food." Despite this understanding about the welfare issues arising from confinement in gestation crates, their use is still prevalent throughout much of the U.S. pork industry, although they have been banned in other countries. However, there is a growing concern in the U.S. with confining sows in gestation stalls and many states and companies are phasing out the practice.

Right before giving birth, the sows are moved into equally restrictive "farrowing crates," stalls designed to separate the mother pig from her nursing piglets, to protect them from crushing, but are so small she can only stand up and lie down. After the piglets are weaned prematurely, the cycle begins again for the mother pig, who averages 2.1–2.5 litters each year. Once they can no longer reproduce efficiently, the sows are sent to slaughter.

Pigs raised for meat undergo mutilations—including castration and tail docking—without any pain relief. For six months, they are confined in pens until they reach the average market weight around 122 kg (270 lb). As with birds, the pigs are given little protection from extreme heat or cold while on the trucks transporting them to slaughter.

According to the federal Humane Methods of Slaughter Act, pigs and other animals considered "livestock" are to be "rendered insensible to pain" before they are shackled and killed. However, a January 2004 report by the U.S. General Accounting Office on the USDA's enforcement of the Act found that some animals are still conscious as they are hung upside down and their throats are being cut.

CATTLE

Every year in the United States, approximately 35 million cattle are raised for beef, 9 million cows for milk, and 450,000 calves for veal.

Most cattle raised for beef are castrated, dehorned, and branded, painful procedures often performed without any anesthesia. For seven months, calves graze on the range before they are transported to feedlots, where they are fattened on unnatural diets. Within six months, they reach market weight of 544 kg (1,200 lb) and are trucked to slaughter. As with other animals to be killed for food, cattle are not given any food, water, or protection from the elements during the journey.

Cows in the dairy industry endure annual cycles of artificial insemination, mechanized milking for 10 out of 12 months (including 7 months of their 9-month pregnancies), and giving birth. Many are routinely given hormones to increase milk yield. According to John Webster, "[t]he amount of work done by the [dairy] cow in peak lactation is immense. To achieve a comparable high work rate a human would have to jog for about six hours a day, every day." In the U.S. industry, cows, overwhelmingly Holsteins, produce an average of 729 days of milk, which corresponds to 2.4 lactations, before they are considered "spent" and are sent for slaughter at an average of less than 5 years of age. Cows can naturally live more than 20 years.

A byproduct of the dairy industry is a calf per year per cow. According to a U.S. Department of Agriculture fact sheet, "[m]ale dairy calves are used in the veal industry. Dairy cows must give birth to continue producing milk, but male dairy calves are of little or no value to the dairy farmer." As a result,

within their first few days of life, the calves are taken from their mothers. Females will likely join the dairy line, while some males are sold to veal farmers. Indeed, the veal industry would likely not exist without the dairy industry. Calves raised for veal are intensively confined and tethered in individual stalls so small they can't turn around during their entire 16- to 18-week lives before slaughter. Veal crates are widely known for their inherent cruelty. As with conventional battery cages and gestation crates, veal crates are being phased out in Europe, yet are still in use in the United States, though some states and companies are beginning to phase them out.

Cattle suffer the same mistreatment as pigs during both their transport and slaughter. Additionally, typically during or after transport, some cattle can have difficulty getting up from a recumbent position. Nonambulatory cattle—referred to as "downers" by the industry—are animals who collapse for a variety of metabolic, infectious, toxic, and/or musculoskeletal reasons and are too sick or injured to stand or walk on their own. Data from federally inspected slaughter facilities estimate 1.1–1.5% of U.S. dairy cows go down in a year, but this does not include those who collapse on-farm. A 2007 review of nonambulatory cattle suggests that the number of downed cattle on U.S. farms or feedlots or who are sent to slaughter in any given year may approach 500,000. It has been reported that dairy cows account for approximately 75% of downed cattle.

AQUATIC ANIMALS

A significant animal welfare problem in the U.S. is aquaculture—the factory farming of fish. According to the USDA's Census of Aquaculture completed in 2005, nearly 1.3 billion fish were raised for human consumption annually, with the industry dominated by catfish, trout, tilapia, bass, and salmon. Aquaculture production systems can cause great suffering for farmed fish.

Since the mid-1980s, the aquaculture industry has expanded approximately 8% per year, and the numbers of farmed fish are expected to continue to increase, perhaps surpassing the numbers of wild-caught animals from the world's fisheries. Tore Håstein of Norway's National Veterinary Institute addressed the World Organisation for Animal Health (OIE) Global Conference on Animal Welfare in 2004 and reported that aquaculture has "developed to become the fastest growing food production sector in the world . . . and it will continue to grow in the years to come."

With the expansion of the fish farming industry comes growing concern for the well-being of increasing numbers of aquatic animals raised and killed for human consumption. A review of recent scientific literature on fish welfare and stress, as well as debates on pain and consciousness in fish, reflect the escalating interest in the well-being of farm-raised fish.

The welfare of farmed fish may be most easily observed through their response to stressors. Their environment can affect welfare if water quality is degraded or if stocking densities are inappropriate for the species in question. Additionally, farmed fish are vulnerable to a variety of diseases and parasites which can degrade their health, and susceptibility to these problems increases with stress. Handling fish throughout the many stages of production may introduce more challenges to their well-being. And, as with other species, both transport and slaughter pose potential problems for farmed fish.

PRODUCTIVITY AND WELFARE

Domesticated animals have been selectively bred, over many generations, with an aim toward improving productivity and feed efficiency. Breeders have been highly successful in creating genetic lines of animals who rapidly gain weight, grow to unprecedented sizes, lay greater numbers of eggs, produce higher milk yields, and give birth to larger litters.

The breeding goal of pushing animals toward their biological limit and seeking maximum output with minimum input has been pursued without due regard to animal welfare. According to Donald Broom, Colleen Macleod Professor of Animal Welfare in the Department of Clinical Veterinary Medicine at Cambridge University, "efforts to achieve earlier and faster growth, greater production per individual, efficient feed conversion and partitioning, and increased prolificacy are the causes of some of the worst animal welfare problems." Indeed, problems and diseases can result as genetic side-effects of selective breeding programs that attempt to improve production efficiency. One of the worst production diseases, in scope and severity, is debilitating leg problems and lameness (the inability to walk normally) for broiler chickens, turkeys, pigs, and dairy cows. Intense selection for high milk yield has also led to an increase in the incidence of clinical mastitis. For egg-laying hens, the increase in production has caused osteoporosis-induced loss of structural bone mass so severe that these birds commonly experience bone fractures. Such selective breeding for economically important traits at the expense of overall health is a blight on the animal production industries.

Productivity is often touted as a sign of good welfare. The logic rests on the proposition that animals who are healthy and unstressed are able to channel more of their metabolic resources toward reproduction and growth. While it is true that individuals who are sick or stressed may suffer setbacks in growth or become less likely to reproduce, the tie between productivity and welfare is severed when economic returns on whole herds or flocks are used as the evidence that productivity is high. This is because crowding more animals into smaller spaces can result in more meat or eggs per unit of space (and thus, high productivity), but individual animals' welfare may be severely compromised by increasing stocking density, and may actually result in a slight decline in individual productivity.

Asserted agricultural ethicist Bernard Rollin, University Distinguished Professor, Professor of Philosophy, Professor of Animal Sciences, and Professor of Biomedical Sciences at Colorado State University, "in industrial agriculture, this link between productivity and well-being is severed. When productivity as an economic metric is applied to the whole operation, the welfare of the individual animal is ignored."

CONCLUSION

There are no federal laws regulating the treatment of the billions of animals raised for meat, eggs, and milk while they are on the farm, and the federal Humane Methods of Slaughter Act has been interpreted by the USDA as not affording minimal protections to farmed birds or fish, animals who make up the overwhelming majority of those raised for consumption. Many of the conditions and customary industrial agricultural practices endured by farm animals must fundamentally change to enable higher standards of welfare.

For more detailed information on animal agriculture and its impacts, please see www.FarmAnimal-Welfare.org.

The original version of this article, which includes almost 200 footnotes to support the claims above, is available online at: http://www.humanesociety.org/assets/pdfs/farm/welfare_overview.pdf

QUESTIONS

1. On p. 353, the article states and rejects a theory about the relation between productivity of farm animals and their welfare. What is the theory? Why does the article reject it?
2. Does the article offer a theory of what animal welfare consists in? If so, what is it? If not, is that problematic?
3. As we noted in the introduction, some states have eliminated the battery cages discussed on p. 350. Which of the effects on chickens' welfare will that eliminate? Which won't it?
4. If animals are not doing well, how do farms achieve high productivity?

PETER SINGER

All Animals Are Equal

In this paper, Peter Singer argues against "speciesism" and against the moral permissibility of hurting and killing animals on industrial animal farms. He argues that animals deserve "equal consideration" to humans and that it would be wrong to hurt and kill, say, severely mentally handicapped humans on industrial farms so it must be wrong to hurt and kill relevantly similar animals, animals with mental lives like those humans.

One of the key moves in the article is the comparison of the mental capacities of certain non-human animals and certain humans. The idea is that there are *some* people whose mental lives are like the mental lives of animals that we farm. Because Singer thinks it would be wrong to farm the former, he thinks it is wrong to farm the latter.

In recent years a number of oppressed groups have campaigned vigorously for equality. The classic instance is the Black Liberation movement, which demands an end to the prejudice and discrimination that has made blacks second-class citizens. The immediate appeal of the black liberation movement and its initial, if limited, success made it a model for other oppressed groups to follow. We became familiar with liberation movements for Spanish-Americans, gay people, and a variety of other minorities. When a majority group—women—began their campaign, some thought we had come to the end of the road. Discrimination on the basis of sex, it has been said, is the last universally accepted form of discrimination, practiced without secrecy or pretense even in those liberal circles that have long prided themselves on their freedom from prejudice against racial minorities.

One should always be wary of talking of "the last remaining form of discrimination." If we have learnt anything from the liberation movements, we should have learnt how difficult it is to be aware of latent prejudice in our attitudes to particular groups until this prejudice is forcefully pointed out.

A liberation movement demands an expansion of our moral horizons and an extension or reinterpretation of the basic moral principle of equality. Practices that were previously regarded as natural and inevitable come to be seen as the result of an unjustifiable prejudice. Who can say with confidence that all his or her attitudes and practices are beyond criticism? If we wish to avoid being numbered amongst the oppressors, we must be prepared to re-think even our most fundamental attitudes. We need to consider them from the point of view of those most disadvantaged by our attitudes, and the practices that follow from these attitudes. If we can make this unaccustomed mental switch we may discover a pattern in our attitudes and practices that consistently operates so as to benefit one group—usually the one to which we ourselves belong—at the expense of another. In this way we may come to see that there is a case for a new liberation movement. My aim is to advocate that we make this mental switch in respect of our attitudes and practices towards a very large group of beings: members of species other than our own—or, as we popularly though misleadingly call them, animals. In other words, I am urging that we extend to other species the basic principle of equality that most of us recognize should be extended to all members of our own species.

All this may sound a little far-fetched, more like a parody of other liberation movements than a serious objective. In fact, in the past the idea of "The Rights of Animals" really has been used to parody the case for women's rights. When Mary Wollstonecraft, a forerunner of later feminists, published her *Vindication of the Rights of Women* in 1792, her ideas were widely regarded as absurd, and they were satirized in an anonymous publication entitled *A Vindication of the Rights of Brutes*. The author of this satire (actually Thomas Taylor, a distinguished Cambridge philosopher) tried to refute Wollstonecraft's reasonings by showing that they could be carried one stage further. If sound when applied to women, why should the arguments not be applied to dogs, cats, and horses? They seemed to hold equally well for these "brutes"; yet to hold that brutes had rights was manifestly absurd; therefore the reasoning by which this conclusion had been reached must be unsound, and if unsound when applied to brutes, it must also be unsound when applied to women, since the very same arguments had been used in each case.

One way in which we might reply to this argument is by saying that the case for equality between men and women cannot validly be extended to nonhuman animals. Women have a right to vote, for instance, because they are just as capable of making rational decisions as men are; dogs, on the other hand, are incapable of understanding the significance of voting, so they cannot have the right to vote. There are many other obvious ways in which men and women resemble each other closely, while humans and other animals differ greatly. So, it might be said, men and women are similar beings and should have equal rights, while humans and nonhumans are different and should not have equal rights.

The thought behind this reply to Taylor's analogy is correct up to a point, but it does not go far enough. There are important differences between humans and other animals, and these differences must give rise to some differences in the rights that each have. Recognizing this obvious fact, however, is no barrier to the case for extending the basic principle of equality to nonhuman animals. The differences that exist between men and women are equally undeniable, and the supporters of Women's Liberation are aware that these differences may give rise to different rights. Many feminists hold that women have the right to an abortion on request. It does not follow that since these same people are campaigning for equality between men and women they must support the right of men to have abortions too. Since a man cannot have an abortion, it is meaningless to talk of his right to have one. Since a pig can't vote, it is meaningless to talk of its right to vote. There is no reason why either Women's Liberation or Animal Liberation should get involved in such nonsense. The extension of the basic principle of equality from one group to another does not imply that we must treat both groups in exactly the same way, or grant exactly the same rights to both groups. Whether we should do so will depend on the nature of the members of the two groups. The basic principle of equality, I shall argue, is equality of consideration; and equal consideration for different beings may lead to different treatment and different rights.

So there is a different way of replying to Taylor's attempt to parody Wollstonecraft's arguments, a way which does not deny the differences between humans and nonhumans, but goes more deeply into the question of equality and concludes by finding nothing absurd in the idea that the basic principle of equality applies to so-called "brutes." I believe that we reach this conclusion if we examine the basis on which our opposition to discrimination on grounds of race or sex ultimately rests. We will then see that we would be on shaky ground if we were to demand equality for blacks, women, and other groups of oppressed humans while denying equal consideration to nonhumans.

When we say that all human beings, whatever their race, creed, or sex, are equal, what is it that we are asserting? Those who wish to defend a hierarchical, inegalitarian society have often pointed out that by whatever test we choose, it simply is not true that all humans are equal. Like it or not, we must face the fact that humans come in different shapes and sizes; they come with differing moral capacities, differing intellectual abilities, differing amounts of benevolent feeling and sensitivity to the needs of others, differing abilities to communicate effectively, and differing capacities to experience pleasure and pain. In short, if the demand for equality were based on the actual equality of all human beings, we would have to stop demanding equality. It would be an unjustifiable demand.

Still, one might cling to the view that the demand for equality among human beings is based on the actual equality of the different races and sexes. Although humans differ as individuals in various ways, there are no differences between the races and sexes as such. From the mere fact that a person is black, or a woman, we cannot infer anything else about that person. This, it may be said, is what is wrong with racism and sexism. The white racist claims that whites are superior to blacks, but this is false—although there are differences between individuals, some blacks are superior to some whites in all of the capacities and abilities that could conceivably be relevant. The opponent of sexism would say the same: a person's sex is no guide to his or her abilities, and this is why it is unjustifiable to discriminate on the basis of sex.

This is a possible line of objection to racial and sexual discrimination. It is not, however, the way that someone really concerned about equality would choose, because taking this line could, in some circumstances, force one to accept a most inegalitarian society. The fact that humans differ as individuals, rather than as races or sexes, is a valid reply to someone who defends a hierarchical society like, say, South Africa, in which all whites are superior in status to all blacks. The existence of individual variations that cut across the lines of race or sex, however, provides us with no defense at all against a more sophisticated opponent of equality, one who proposes that, say, the interests of those with I.Q. ratings above 100 be preferred to the interests of those with I.Q.s below 100. Would a hierarchical society of this sort really be so much better than one based on race or sex? I think not. But if we tie the moral principle of equality to the factual equality of the different races or sexes, taken as a whole, our opposition to racism and sexism does not provide us with any basis for objecting to this kind of inegalitarianism.

There is a second important reason why we ought not to base our opposition to racism and sexism on any kind of factual equality, even the limited kind which asserts that variations in capacities and abilities are spread evenly between the different races and sexes: we can have no absolute guarantee that these abilities and capacities really are distributed evenly, without regard to race or sex, among human beings. So far as actual abilities are concerned, there do seem to be certain measurable differences between both races and sexes. These differences do not, of course, appear in each case, but only when averages are taken. More important still, we do not yet know how much of these differences is really due to the different genetic endowments of the various races and sexes, and how much is due to environmental differences that are the result of past and continuing discrimination. Perhaps all of the important differences will eventually prove to be environmental rather than genetic. Anyone opposed to racism and sexism will certainly hope that this will be so, for it will make the task of ending discrimination a lot easier; nevertheless it would be dangerous to rest the case against racism and sexism on the belief that all significant differences are environmental in origin. The opponent of, say, racism who takes this line will be unable to avoid conceding that if differences in ability did after all prove to have some genetic connection with race, racism would in some way be defensible.

It would be folly for the opponent of racism to stake his whole case on a dogmatic commitment to one particular outcome of a difficult scientific issue which is still a long way from being settled. While attempts to prove that differences in certain selected abilities between races and sexes are primarily genetic in origin have certainly not been conclusive, the same must be said of attempts to prove that these differences are largely the result of environment. At this stage of the investigation we cannot be certain which view is correct, however much we may hope it is the latter.

Fortunately, there is no need to pin the case for equality to one particular outcome of this scientific investigation. The appropriate response to those who claim to have found evidence of genetically-based differences in ability between the races or sexes is not to stick to the belief that the genetic explanation must be wrong, whatever evidence to the contrary may turn up: instead we should make it quite clear that the claim to equality does not depend on intelligence, moral capacity, physical strength, or similar matters of fact. Equality is a moral ideal, not a simple assertion of fact. There is no logically compelling reason for assuming that a factual difference in ability between two people justifies any difference in the amount of consideration we give to satisfying their needs and interests. The principle of the equality of human beings is not a description of an alleged actual equality among humans: it is a prescription of how we should treat humans.

Jeremy Bentham incorporated the essential basis of moral equality into his utilitarian system of ethics in the formula: "Each to count for one and none for more than one." In other words, the interests of every being affected by an action are to be taken into account and given the same weight as the like interests of any other being. A later utilitarian, Henry Sidgwick, put the point in this way: 'The good of any one individual is of no more importance, from the point of view (if I may say so) of the Universe, than the good of any other.'[1] More recently, the leading figures in contemporary moral philosophy have shown a great deal of agreement in specifying as a fundamental presupposition of their moral theories some similar requirement which operates so as to give everyone's interests equal consideration—although they cannot agree on how this requirement is best formulated.[2]

It is an implication of this principle of equality that our concern for others ought not to depend on what they are like, or what abilities they possess—although precisely what this concern requires us to do may vary according to the characteristics of those affected by what we do. It is on this basis that the case against racism and the case against sexism must both ultimately rest; and it is in accordance with this principle that speciesism is also to be condemned. If possessing a higher degree of intelligence does not entitle one human to use another for his own ends, how can it entitle humans to exploit nonhumans?

Many philosophers have proposed the principle of equal consideration of interests, in some form or other, as a basic moral principle; but, as we shall see in more detail shortly, not many of them have recognized that this principle applies to members of other species as well as to our own. Bentham was one of the few who did realize this. In a forward-looking passage, written at a time when black slaves in the British dominions were still being treated much as we now treat nonhuman animals, Bentham wrote:

> The day may come when the rest of the animal creation may acquire those rights which never could have been witholden from them but by the hand of tyranny. The French have already discovered that the blackness of the skin is no reason why a human being should be abandoned without redress to the caprice of a tormentor. It may one day come to be recognized that the number of the legs, the villosity of the skin, or the termination of the os sacrum, are reasons equally insufficient for abandoning a sensitive being to the same fate. What else is it that should trace the insuperable line? Is it the faculty of reason, or perhaps the faculty of discourse? But a full-grown horse or dog is beyond comparison a more rational, as well as a more conversable animal, than an infant of a day, or a week, or even a month, old. But suppose they were otherwise, what would it avail? The question is not, Can they *reason*? nor, Can they *talk*? but, Can they *suffer*?[3]

In this passage Bentham points to the capacity for suffering as the vital characteristic that gives a being the right to equal consideration. The capacity for suffering—or more strictly, for suffering and/or enjoyment or happiness—is not just another characteristic like the capacity for language, or for higher mathematics. Bentham is not saying that those who try to mark "the insuperable line" that determines whether the interests of a being should be considered happen to have selected the wrong characteristic. The capacity for suffering and enjoying things is a prerequisite for having interests at all, a condition that must be satisfied before we can speak of interests in any meaningful way. It would be nonsense to say that it was not in the interests of a stone to be kicked along the road by a schoolboy. A stone does not have interests because it cannot suffer. Nothing that we can do to it could possibly make any difference to its welfare. A mouse, on the other hand, does have an interest in not being tormented, because it will suffer if it is.

If a being suffers, there can be no moral justification for refusing to take that suffering into consideration. No matter what the nature of the being, the principle of equality requires that its suffering be counted equally with the like suffering—in so far as rough comparisons can be made—of any other being. If a being is not capable of suffering, or of experiencing enjoyment or happiness, there is nothing to be taken into account. This is why the limit of sentience (using the term as a convenient, if not strictly accurate, shorthand for the capacity to suffer or experience enjoyment or happiness) is the only defensible boundary of concern for the interests of others. To mark this boundary by some characteristic like intelligence or rationality would be to mark it in an arbitrary way. Why not choose some other characteristic, like skin color?

The racist violates the principle of equality by giving greater weight to the interests of members of his own race, when there is a clash between their interests and the interests of those of another race. Similarly the speciesist allows the interests of his own species to override the greater interests of members of other species.[4] The pattern is the same in each case. Most human beings are speciesists.

I shall now very briefly describe some of the practices that show this.

For the great majority of human beings, especially in urban, industrialized societies, the most direct form of contact with members of other species is at mealtimes: we eat them. In doing so we treat them purely as means to our ends. We regard their life and well-being as subordinate to our taste for a particular kind of dish. I say "taste" deliberately—this is purely a matter of pleasing our palate. There can be no defense of eating flesh in terms of satisfying nutritional needs, since it has been established beyond doubt that we could satisfy our need for protein and other essential nutrients far more efficiently with a diet that replaced animal flesh by soy beans, or products derived from soy beans, and other high-protein vegetable products.[5]

It is not merely the act of killing that indicates what we are ready to do to other species in order to gratify our tastes. The suffering we inflict on the animals while they are alive is perhaps an even clearer indication of our speciesism than the fact that we are prepared to kill them.[6] In order to have meat on the table at a price that people can afford, our society tolerates methods of meat production that confine sentient animals in cramped, unsuitable conditions for the entire durations of their lives. Animals are treated like machines that convert fodder into flesh, and any innovation that results in a higher "conversion ratio" is liable to be adopted. As one authority on the subject has said, "cruelty is acknowledged only when profitability ceases."[7] . . .

Since, as I have said, none of these practices cater for anything more than our pleasures of taste, our practice of rearing and killing other animals in order to eat them is a clear instance of the sacrifice of the most important interests of other beings in order to satisfy trivial interests of our own. To avoid speciesism we must stop this practice, and each of us has a moral obligation to cease supporting the practice. Our custom is all the support that the meat-industry needs. The decision to cease giving it that support may be difficult, but it is no more difficult than it would have been for a white Southerner to go against the traditions of his society and free his slaves: if we do not change our dietary habits, how can we censure those slaveholders who would not change their own way of living?

The same form of discrimination may be observed in the widespread practice of experimenting on other species in order to see if certain substances are safe for human beings, or to test some psychological theory about the effect of severe punishment on learning, or to try out various new compounds just in case something turns up. . . .

In the past, argument about vivisection has often missed the point, because it has been put in absolutist terms: Would the abolitionist be prepared to let thousands die if they could be saved by experimenting on a single animal? The way to reply to this purely hypothetical question is to pose another: Would the experimenter be prepared to perform his experiment on an orphaned human infant, if that were the only way to save many lives? (I say "orphan" to avoid the complication of parental feelings, although in doing so l am being overfair to the experimenter, since the nonhuman subjects of experiments are not orphans.) If the experimenter is not prepared to use an orphaned human infant, then his readiness to use nonhumans is simple discrimination, since adult apes, cats, mice, and other mammals are more aware of what is happening to them, more self-directing and, so far as we can tell, at least as sensitive to pain, as any human infant. There seems to be no relevant characteristic that human infants possess that adult mammals do not have to the same or a higher degree. (Someone might try to argue that what makes it wrong to experiment on a human infant is that the infant will, in time and if left alone, develop into more than the nonhuman, but one would then, to be consistent, have to oppose abortion, since the fetus has the same potential as the infant—indeed, even contraception and abstinence might be wrong on this ground, since the egg and sperm, considered jointly, also have the same potential. In any case, this argument still gives us no reason for selecting a nonhuman, rather than a human with severe and irreversible brain damage, as the subject for our experiments.)

The experimenter, then, shows a bias in favor of his own species whenever he carries out an experiment on a nonhuman for a purpose that he would not think justified him in using a human being at an equal or lower level of sentience, awareness, ability to be self-directing, etc. No one familiar with the kind of results yielded by most experiments on animals can have the slightest doubt that if this bias were eliminated the number of experiments performed would be a minute fraction of the number performed today.

Experimenting on animals, and eating their flesh, are perhaps the two major forms of speciesism in our society. By comparison, the third and last form of speciesism is so minor as to be insignificant, but it is perhaps of some special interest to those for whom this article was written. I am referring to speciesism in contemporary philosophy.

Philosophy ought to question the basic assumptions of the age. Thinking through, critically and carefully, what most people take for granted is, I believe, the chief task of philosophy, and it is this task that makes philosophy a worthwhile activity. Regrettably, philosophy does not always live up to its historic role. Philosophers are human beings, and they are subject to all the preconceptions of the society to which they belong. Sometimes they succeed in breaking free of the prevailing ideology: more often they become its most sophisticated defenders. So, in this case, philosophy as practiced in the universities today does not challenge anyone's preconceptions about our relations with other species. By their writings, those philosophers who tackle problems that touch upon the issue reveal that they make the same unquestioned assumptions as most other humans, and what they say tends to confirm the reader in his or her comfortable speciesist habits.

I could illustrate this claim by referring to the writings of philosophers in various fields—for instance, the attempts that have been made by those interested in rights to draw the boundary of the sphere of rights so that it runs parallel to the biological boundaries of the species homo sapiens, including infants and even mental defectives, but excluding those other beings of equal or greater capacity who are so useful to us at mealtimes and in our laboratories. I think it would be a more appropriate conclusion to this article, however, if I concentrated on the problem with which we have been centrally concerned, the problem of equality.

It is significant that the problem of equality, in moral and political philosophy, is invariably formulated in terms of human equality. The effect of this is that the question of the equality of other animals does not confront the philosopher, or student, as an issue itself—and this is already an indication of the failure of philosophy to challenge accepted beliefs. Still, philosophers have found it difficult to discuss the issue of human equality without raising, in a paragraph or two, the question of the status of other animals. The reason for this, which should be apparent from what I have said already, is that if humans are to be regarded as equal to one another, we need some sense of "equal" that does not require any actual, descriptive equality of capacities, talents or other qualities. If equality is to be related to any actual characteristics of humans, these characteristics must be some lowest common denominator, pitched so low that no human lacks them—but then the philosopher comes up against the catch that any such set of characteristics which covers all humans will not be possessed only by humans. In other words, it turns out that in the only sense in which we can truly say, as an assertion of fact, that all humans are equal, at least some members of other species are also equal—equal, that is, to each other and to humans. If, on the other hand, we regard the statement "All humans are equal" in some non-factual way, perhaps as a prescription, then, as I have already argued, it is even more difficult to exclude non-humans from the sphere of equality.

This result is not what the egalitarian philosopher originally intended to assert. Instead of accepting the radical outcome to which their own reasonings naturally point, however, most philosophers try to reconcile their beliefs in human equality and animal inequality by arguments that can only be described as devious.

As a first example, I take William Frankena's well-known article "The Concept of Social Justice." Frankena opposes the idea of basing justice on merit, because he sees that this could lead to highly inegalitarian results. Instead he proposes the principle that

all men are to be treated as equals, not because they are equal, in any respect, but simply because they are human. They are human because they have emotions and desires, and are able to think, and hence are capable of enjoying a good life in a sense in which other animals are not.[8]

But what is this capacity to enjoy the good life which all humans have, but no other animals? Other animals have emotions and desires and appear to be capable of enjoying a good life. We may doubt that they can think—although the behavior of some apes, dolphins, and even dogs suggests that some of them can—but what is the relevance of thinking? Frankena goes on to admit that by "the good life" he means "not so much the morally good life as the happy or satisfactory life," so thought would appear to be unnecessary for enjoying the good life; in fact to emphasize the need for thought would make difficulties for the egalitarian since only some people are capable of leading intellectually satisfying lives, or morally good lives. This makes it difficult to see what Frankena's principle of equality has to do with simply being human. Surely every sentient being is capable of leading a life that is happier or less miserable than some alternative life, and hence has a claim to be taken into account. In this respect the distinction between humans and nonhumans is not a sharp division, but rather a continuum along which we move gradually, and with overlaps between the species, from simple capacities for enjoyment and satisfaction, or pain and suffering, to more complex ones.

Faced with a situation in which they see a need for some basis for the moral gulf that is commonly thought to separate humans and animals, but can find no concrete difference that will do the job without undermining the equality of humans, philosophers tend to waffle. They resort to highs sounding phrases like "the intrinsic dignity of the human individual";[9] they talk of the "intrinsic worth of all men" as if men (humans?) had some worth that other beings did not,[10] or they say that humans, and only humans, are "ends in themselves," while "everything other than a person can only have value for a person."[11]

This idea of a distinctive human dignity and worth has a long history; it can be traced back directly to the Renaissance humanists, for instance to Pico della Mirandola's *Oration on the Dignity of Man.* Pico and other humanists based their estimate of human dignity on the idea that man possessed the central, pivotal position in the "Great Chain of Being" that led from the lowliest forms of matter to God himself; this view of the universe, in turn, goes back to both classical and Judeo-Christian doctrines. Contemporary philosophers have cast off these metaphysical and religious shackles and freely invoke the dignity of mankind without needing to justify the idea at all. Why should we not attribute "intrinsic dignity" or "intrinsic worth" to ourselves? Fellow-humans are unlikely to reject the accolades we so generously bestow on them, and those to whom we deny the honor are unable to object. Indeed, when one thinks only of humans, it can be very liberal, very progressive, to talk of the dignity of all human beings. In so doing, we implicitly condemn slavery, racism, and other violations of human rights. We admit that we ourselves are in some fundamental sense on a par with the poorest, most ignorant members of our own species. It is only when we think of humans as no more than a small sub-group of all the beings that inhabit our planet that we may realize that in elevating our own species we are at the same time lowering the relative status of all other species.

The truth is that the appeal to the intrinsic dignity of human beings appears to solve the egalitarian's problems only as long as it goes unchallenged. Once we ask why it should be that all humans—including infants, mental defectives, psychopaths, Hitler, Stalin, and the rest—have some kind of dignity or worth that no elephant, pig, or chimpanzee can ever achieve, we see that this question is as difficult to answer as our original request for some relevant fact that justifies the inequality of humans and other animals. In fact, these two questions are really one: talk of intrinsic dignity or moral worth only takes the problem back one step, because any satisfactory defence of the claim that all and only humans have intrinsic dignity would need to refer to some relevant capacities or characteristics that all and only humans possess. Philosophers frequently introduce ideas of dignity, respect, and worth at the point at which other reasons appear to be lacking, but this is hardly good enough. Fine phrases are the last resource of those who have run out of arguments.

In case there are those who still think it may be possible to find some relevant characteristic that distinguishes all humans from all members of other species,

I shall refer again, before I conclude, to the existence of some humans who quite clearly are below the level of awareness, self-consciousness, intelligence, and sentience, of many non-humans. I am thinking of humans with severe and irreparable brain damage, and also of infant humans. To avoid the complication of the relevance of a being's potential, however, I shall henceforth concentrate on permanently retarded humans.

Philosophers who set out to find a characteristic that will distinguish humans from other animals rarely take the course of abandoning these groups of humans by lumping them in with the other animals. It is easy to see why they do not. To take this line without re-thinking our attitudes to other animals would entail that we have the right to perform painful experiments on retarded humans for trivial reasons; similarly it would follow that we had the right to rear and kill these humans for food. To most philosophers these consequences are as unacceptable as the view that we should stop treating nonhumans in this way.

Of course, when discussing the problem of equality it is possible to ignore the problem of mental defectives, or brush it aside as if somehow insignificant.[12] This is the easiest way out.

What else remains? My final example of speciesism in contemporary philosophy has been selected to show what happens when a writer is prepared to face the question of human equality and animal inequality without ignoring the existence of mental defectives, and without resorting to obscurantist mumbo jumbo. Stanley Benn's clear and honest article "Egalitarianism and Equal Consideration of Interests"[13] fits this description.

Benn, after noting the usual "evident human inequalities" argues, correctly I think, for equality of consideration as the only possible basis for egalitarianism. Yet Benn, like other writers, is thinking only of "equal consideration of human interests." Benn is quite open in his defence of this restriction of equal consideration:

> . . . not to possess human shape is a disqualifying condition. However faithful or intelligent a dog may be, it would be a monstrous sentimentality to attribute to him interests that could be weighed in an equal balance with those of human beings . . . if, for instance, one had to decide between feeding a hungry baby or a hungry dog, anyone who chose the dog would generally be reckoned morally defective, unable to recognize a fundamental inequality of claims. This is what distinguishes our attitude to animals from our attitude to imbeciles. It would be odd to say that we ought to respect equally the dignity or personality of the imbecile and of the rational man . . . but there is nothing odd about saying that we should respect their interests equally, that is, that we should give to the interests of each the same serious consideration as claims to considerations necessary for some standard of well-being that we can recognize and endorse.

Benn's statement of the basis of the consideration we should have for imbeciles seems to me correct, but why should there be any fundamental inequality of claims between a dog and a human imbecile? Benn sees that if equal consideration depended on rationality, no reason could be given against using imbeciles for research purposes, as we now use dogs and guinea pigs. This will not do: "But of course we do distinguish imbeciles from animals in this regard," he says. That the common distinction is justifiable is something Benn does not question; his problem is how it is to be justified. The answer he gives is this:

> . . . we respect the interests of men and give them priority over dogs not *insofar* as they are rational, but because rationality is the human norm. We say it is *unfair* to exploit the deficiencies of the imbecile who falls short of the norm, just as it would be unfair, and not just ordinarily dishonest, to steal from a blind man. If we do not think in this way about dogs, it is because we do not see the irrationality of the dog as a deficiency or a handicap, but as normal for the species, The characteristics, therefore, that distinguish the normal man from the normal dog make it intelligible for us to talk of other men having interests and capacities, and therefore claims, of precisely the same kind as we make on our own behalf. But although these characteristics may provide the point of the distinction between men and other species, they are not in fact the qualifying conditions for membership, to the distinguishing criteria of the class of morally considerable persons; and this is precisely because a man does not become a member of a different species, with its own standards of normality, by reason of not possessing these characteristics.

The final sentence of this passage gives the argument away. An imbecile, Benn concedes, may have no characteristics superior to those of a dog; nevertheless this does not make the imbecile a member of "a different species" as the dog is. Therefore it would be "unfair" to use the imbecile for medical research as we use the dog. But why? That the imbecile is not rational is just the way things have worked out, and the same is true of the dog—neither is any more responsible for their mental level. If it is unfair to take advantage of an isolated defect, why is it fair to take advantage of a more general limitation? I find it hard to see anything in this argument except a defense of preferring the interests of members of our own species because they are members of our own species. To those who think there might be more to it, I suggest the following mental exercise. Assume that it has been proven that there is a difference in the average, or normal, intelligence quotient for two different races, say whites and blacks. Then substitute the term "white" for every occurrence of "men" and "black" for every occurrence of "dog" in the passage quoted; and substitute "high I.Q." for "rationality" and when Benn talks of "imbeciles" replace this term by "dumb whites"—that is, whites who fall well below the normal white I.Q. score. Finally, change "species" to "race." Now retread the passage. It has become a defense of a rigid, no-exceptions division between whites and blacks, based on I.Q. scores, notwithstanding an admitted overlap between whites and blacks in this respect. The revised passage is, of course, outrageous, and this is not only because we have made fictitious assumptions in our substitutions. The point is that in the original passage Benn was defending a rigid division in the amount of consideration due to members of different species, despite admitted cases of overlap. If the original did not, at first reading strike us as being as outrageous as the revised version does, this is largely because although we are not racists ourselves, most of us are speciesists. Like the other articles, Benn's stands as a warning of the ease with which the best minds can fall victim to a prevailing ideology.

NOTES

1. *The Methods of Ethics* (7th Ed.), p. 382.

2. For example, R. M. Hare, *Freedom and Reason* (Oxford, 1963) and J. Rawls, *A Theory of Justice* (Harvard, 1972); for a brief account of the essential agreement on this issue between these and other positions, see R. M. Hare, "Rules of War and Moral Reasoning," *Philosophy and Public Affairs,* vol. 1, no. 2 (1972).

3. *Introduction to the Principles of Morals and Legislation,* ch. XVII.

4. I owe the term speciesism to Richard Ryder.

5. In order to produce 1 lb. of protein in the form of beef or veal, we must feed 21 lbs. of protein to the animal. Other forms of livestock are slightly less inefficient, but the average ratio in the United States is still 1:8. It has been estimated that the amount of protein lost to humans in this way is equivalent to 90 percent of the annual world protein deficit. For a brief account, see Frances Moore Lappé, *Diet for a Small Planet* (Friends of The Earth/Ballantine, New York, 1971), pp. 4–11.

6. Although one might think that killing a being is obviously the ultimate wrong one can do to it, I think that the infliction of suffering is a clearer indication of speciesism because it might be argued that at least part of what is wrong with killing a human is that most humans are conscious of their existence over time and have desires and purposes that extend into the future; see, for instance, M. Tooley, "Abortion and Infanticide," *Philosophy and Public Affairs,* vol. 2, no. I (1972). Of course, if one took this view one would have to hold—as Tooley does—that killing a human infant or mental defective is not in itself wrong and is less serious than killing certain higher mammals that probably do have a sense of their own existence over time.

7. Ruth Harrison, *Animal Machines* (Stuart, London, 1964). For an account of farming conditions, see my *Animal Liberation* (New York Review Company, 1975) from which "Down on the Factory Farm" is reprinted in this volume [*Animal Rights and Human Obligations*].

8. In R. Brandt (ed.), *Social Justice* (Prentice Hall, Englewood Cliffs, 1962), p. 19.

9. Frankena, op. cit. p. 23.

10. H. A. Bedau, "Egalitarianism and the Idea of Equality," in *Nomos IX: Equality,* ed. J. R. Pennock and J. W. Chapman, New York, 1967.

11. C. Vlastos, "Justice and Equality," in Brandt, *Social Justice,* p. 48.

12. For example, Bernard Williams, "The Idea of Equality," in *Philosophy, Politics, and Society* (second series), ed. P. Laslett and W. Rundman (Blackwell, Oxford, 1962), p. 118; J. Rawls, *A Theory of Justice,* pp. 509–10.

13. *Nomos IX: Equality;* the passages quoted are on p. 62ff.

QUESTIONS

1. What does Singer mean by "speciesism"? Why does Singer think that speciesists are importantly like racists and sexists?

2. What does Singer mean by "equal consideration"? If an abortion clinic refuses to see a male patient who cannot get pregnant, is that consistent with giving him equal consideration? If you read to your son but not to your cat, is that consistent with giving the cat equal consideration? If you read to your son but not to your daughter, is that consistent with giving the daughter equal consideration?

3. What is Thomas Taylor's argument against giving women the right to vote? What, if anything, is wrong with that argument? Read the Carol Kaesuk Yoon article in Chapter 8, "Alternatives to Industrial Animal Agriculture." Her reasoning is in some ways like Taylor's. Explain how.

4. Singer is a utilitarian but claims that the reasoning in "All Animals Are Equal" does not assume that utilitarianism is true. Is he right? What does utilitarianism imply about the permissibility of industrial animal agriculture?

5. Singer is *not* opposed to hurting animals in general. He thinks this is sometimes permissible. When? Why? How can he both hold that position while also holding that hurting them on industrial farms is wrong?

TORBJÖRN TÄNNSJÖ

It's Getting Better All the Time

A plausible utilitarian view is that industrial animal agriculture is wrong because it fails to maximize well-being. Another plausible utilitarian view is that free-range animal agriculture is permissible—required even—because it maximizes well-being. In this reading, Tännsjö claims that both views are false. He argues that industrial animal agriculture is required because it is the agricultural system that maximizes well-being. His view is not that *any* industrial system does so but, rather, that an industrial system that (a) raises enormous numbers of animals and (b) gives them tolerably good lives produces more happiness than any alternative.

Has the world become better or worse since the 1970s, when Peter Singer's arguments regarding famine relief and animal welfare first appeared? The present chapter is based on an unpublished talk, presented in a discussion with Singer in 2003,[1] and at several other occasions when we have met since

Torbjörn Tännsjö, "It's Getting Better All the Time." Printed with permission of the author.

then, where I answer this question by comparing the situation in 1975 to the situation in 2000. I haven't updated the statistics since 2000, but the trends I discuss seem to have continued. The upshot is that the world became better, much better, between 1975 and 2000 for both people and animals. And since then it has improved even more.

In my discussion I take (classical) hedonistic utilitarianism for granted, which is the view that the *happiness* of individual people and animals is the only thing that matters when judging how good or bad the world is, and that happiness enjoyed by one individual matters just as much as the same happiness enjoyed by any other.[2] Judging from Singer's most recent book, I have the impression that he too now accepts this view.[3]

Further, I assume *total* hedonistic utilitarianism, which is the view that what matters is the *total* amount of happiness in the world. According to this view, we ought to maximise the *total* amount of happiness in the world. This contrasts with other possible hedonistic utilitarian theories, such as the view that what matters is the *average* amount of happiness in the world and thus that we ought to maximize the *average* amount of happiness in the world.

COMPARISON I: PEOPLE

Let us assume, then, that total hedonistic utilitarianism is correct. This means that there are two ways of making the world a better place, either by making existing individuals happier, or by making (additional) happy individuals. That these two ways of making the world a better place are on equal terms is a bold claim of course. This is not the place to defend it; I have done so elsewhere. Two observations are in place, however, one about population ethics, and the other one about what has been called the deprivation theory of the (instrumental) badness for an individual of being killed.

Concerning population ethics it is of note that, according to total hedonistic utilitarianism we make the world a better place by adding happy individuals

to it. The claim is even stronger, however. According to total hedonistic utilitarianism, if we are presented with the choice, we ought to create a world with billions and billions of creatures leading lives just worth living (each with a net balance of happiness over pain), rather than a world where a billion creatures lead extremely happy lives. This is what Derek Parfit has nicknamed the repugnant conclusion.[4] The total hedonistic utilitarian maintains that this conclusion is acceptable, although the reasons why are too complex to go into in the present context.[5] It should just be noted that it is a premise of my argument here that both ways of making the world a better place, either by improving the situation of existing individuals, or by the mere addition of happy individuals, are indeed on equal terms.

Now to the deprivation theory about the instrumental badness of being killed. Some have argued against the kind of argument I here put forward that even on utilitarian grounds it must be problematic to raise an animal and then kill it for food. When we kill it, rather than keep it alive, we harm it. We deprive it of the future happiness it would have had, had we not killed it but instead kept it alive. This is true and relevant according to hedonistic utilitarianism. We do indeed deprive this animal of future happiness and this is as such problematic. Utilitarianism is an impartial view, however. If there is compensation in other lives for the happiness that is not realised in the life of this animal, then no harm has been done. When it comes to animals we raise for food it is clear that, unless we kill them, and replace them, there will be no resources available for us to keep many of them alive for long time. So the fact that we kill and eat the animals we raise for this purpose is what makes possible for us to sustain over time a big population of them.

Given these assumptions, what about the situation of the world today, as compared with 1975? Well, simple population statistics informs us that, while some 4 billion people lived 1975, the world now sustains a population of 7 billion people. Let us make the rather pessimistic assumption that people living in poverty (with an income of less than one US dollar a day) lead lives worth not experiencing. We then find that the number of people living such lives is roughly the same today as in 1975 (about 1 billion people). At least, since the measurement was invented (in 1987), the number of people living in poverty has been the same (1.2 billion). This, as such, is a scandal, of course, but in our assessment it means: no difference!

We also see that the people who live privileged lives, materially like the ones most of us lead, is also about the same, 1 billion. Again this means, given the assumptions in this paper, no difference!

It is reasonable to assume that the number of people living lives worth living means compensation for the misery experience by those who don't. This was true already in 1975, I am prepared to argue, and it is even more true today, when some 2 billion have entered the picture, living lives better than those lived by the poor people.

COMPARISON II: OTHER SENTIENT ANIMALS

What has happened to the population of other sentient animals? If we consider animals kept by people for food and other products, the following picture emerges. I will focus on a few important species:

1975	2000
Cattle 1.2 billion	1.3 billion
Chickens 5.9 billion	14.7 billion
Goats 0.4 billion	0.7 billion
Horses 0.06 billion	0.06 billion
Pigs 0.7 billion	0.9 billion
Sheep 1.0 billion	1.1 billion

There has been an increase in the population of these animals kept in captivity from 8 billion to 17 billion. The probable explanation of this fact is that there is a causal connection: We hold more animals because we eat them, and because we who eat them

become more numerous. The number of dogs, cats, and rabbits, and so forth, held as pets, moreover, is constantly growing.

What about the number and fate of wild mammals and birds? Here it is impossible to find relevant statistics. How many of these animals were there in 1975, and how many are there now? I have questioned many experts on this, and most are reluctant to make even a rough estimate. One has been willing to do so, however. His conjecture, built on speculations about the average number of members of various different species, is that there are 100 billion birds (most of them small or middle-sized), and 50 billion mammals (where rodents, bats, and insectivores dominate the picture completely). According to the same assessment, there is really no reason to believe that the population of these animals has decreased during the relevant period (1975–2000).[6]

If the rough picture here drawn is correct, if the number of wildlife has at least not decreased, and if the number of sentient animals kept in captivity (for food, other products, or as pets) has increased, does this mean improvement or decline?

My strong intuition is that it means improvement.

Here two non-moral, factual assumptions are essential to my argument.

First of all, animals living in captivity are for most of the time (on the whole) living lives worth experiencing.

Secondly, wildlife are living lives that are, most of the time, worth experiencing, even if they may well lead worse lives than animals held in captivity. This is not to deny that, certainly, animals held in captivity often experience a terrible time awaiting their being butchered (being transported, kept in narrow slaughterhouses, being actually killed in a less than painful manner). And this is even truer of wildlife (often suffering from famines, actually starving to death, or being hunted down and eaten alive slowly by predators). However, my conjecture is that both animals held in captivity and wildlife experience *on average* enough happiness to compensate for these terrors.

THE FUTURE

Even if the negative aspects of happiness should not be neglected, the positive ones are, in the long run, more important. So if we want to continue with a kind of moral progress, beyond the point where we have solved the problems of world poverty and animal misery, we should see to it that the number of sentient beings is constantly increasing. How should this be accomplished?

In the future, an important task for humanity will be to colonise space. This will ensure that an almost indefinite increase of the sum-total of happiness, for an indefinite period of time, can take place. By putting our eggs in more than one basket in this way, we also have some reassurance against natural or self-inflicted disasters that threaten to put an end to sentient life in our region of universe. Many Noah's arks, containing both human beings and other sentient animals, carefully selected with respect to their chances of leading good and secure lives together, should be sent out in the near space.

Ought we to become vegetarians? If my argument is correct, we should do nothing of the sort.

It is sometimes claimed that, if we become vegetarians, then the world can sustain an even larger human population. This is probably true, but from the point of view of total hedonistic utilitarianism, irrelevant. Other species, capable of experiencing happiness, are no less important than human beings. And by keeping animals in captivity, providing them with good living and dying conditions, exchanging one generation for another, we can see to it that much happy life is constantly kept going.

Here one of the most urgent tasks emerges, with respect to the situation in the world. The living and dying conditions of animals held in captivity are in many respects terrible, and they could rather easily be improved. If the animals raised for food experience good living and dying conditions, then they do indeed lead lives worth experiencing, and they have our interest in raising and eating them to thank for their lives.

Finally, when we consider wildlife, we must be prepared to think in terms of extinction of entire species. Those animals, living poor wild lives, having to predate on others, or being constantly subjected to attacks from predators, famines, and the like, should probably not exist at all. They certainly will not be among the species allowed to occupy a place on Noah's space-ark.[7]

NOTES

1. The 7th international conference of the international society for utilitarian studies, Lisbon, 11-13 April, 2003.

2. I defend this stance in *Hedonistic Utilitarianism. A Defence* (Edinburgh: Edinburgh University Press, 1998).

3. Katarzyna de Lazari-Radik and Peter Singer, *The Point of View of the Universe* (Oxford: Oxford University Press, 2014).

4. See his *Reasons and Persons* (Oxford: Oxford University Press, 1984), sections 148–149.

5. In my book *Taking Life: Three Theories of the Ethics of Killing* (New York: Oxford University Press, 2015) I defend the repugnant conclusion, as well as the deprivation theory about the instrumental badness of death for an individual.

6. Recent statistics indicate a loss among animals in wildlife. http://www.scientificamerican.com/podcast/episode/wildlife-population-plummeted-since-1970/ However, this is compatible with the possibility that there is compensation in the number of mammals (rodents and birds) living in symbiosis with human beings in the cities. I have no means to assess this. However, in the present context, even if it should turn out that the net effect is loss, rather than increase, my point remains that the world is not getting worse because of poverty and factory farming, rather it is getting worse (along this important dimension), if it does, because of other human activities that are harming wildlife (which are not obviously tied up with global poverty or animal agriculture).

7. I have a chapter on animal ethics in my book *Taking Life: Three Theories of the Ethics of Killing* (New York: Oxford University Press, 2015); in the book I argue that utilitarianism can best cater for our considered intuitions, not only about the killing of animals, but about killing in general. I also defend both the repugnant conclusion and the deprivation theory about the instrumental badness of death for an individual, alluded to in the opening of this chapter.

QUESTIONS

1. In your own words, explain Tännsjö's argument. How would Singer respond to that argument? (Hint: Utilitarianism is a premise in Tännsjö's argument. Singer would accept it.)
2. Consider a world that is just like our world except that it has one extra, *barely* happy person. Does that world contain more well-being than our world? Is that world better than our world?
3. Relatedly, what does Tännsjö's view imply about human procreation? Are we required to have more and more happy children? Why or why not?
4. Why does Tännsjö believe industrial animal agriculture produces more well-being than free-range agriculture? Is he right about that? Why or why not?

CHRISTINE KORSGAARD

Getting Animals in View

Korsgaard outlines some radically non-utilitarian ethical considerations about animals.

As she notes, the anti-utilitarian philosopher Immanuel Kant argued that it is wrong to hurt animals, as industrial animal farms routinely do, but that this is wrong *only* because of its effects on humans. Basically, Kant thought that hurting animals would harden one's heart and that that would lead to mistreatment of humans. Kant thought that animals, lacking certain rational capacities, do not matter morally except insofar as they affect people.

Korsgaard defends a view that is inspired by Kant but according to which it is wrong to hurt animals—not in any situation, but in the situations we find ourselves in on industrial animal farms—and not because of the effects of doing so on people. It is wrong to hurt animals on industrial farms because of its effects on animals. And also because doing so embodies an objectionable attitude toward animals, the attitude that they are "mere means" to the end of human consumption.

What sorts of philosophical problems do we face because of the existence of non-human animals? Most humane people would agree that their existence presents us with some moral and legal quandaries. And recently, but only recently, philosophers have taken a serious interest in the character of animal

Christine Korsgaard, "Getting Animals in View." The essay originally appeared in issue 6 of *The Point Magazine*, and it is reprinted here with their permission.

minds. But I have come to think that animals present us with a philosophical problem deeper than either of those—that the existence of non-human animals is the source of a profound disturbance in the way that human beings conceptualize the world. It is almost as if we—I'm using "we" to mean "us human beings" here—are unable to get them firmly into view, to see them for what they really are.

Many people, to take one small example, find nothing odd about the sentence, "I live alone with a cat." Okay, granted, someone might also say, "I live alone with a child," at least so long as the child was a very small one.[1] But "I live alone with four children" would be starting to put the language under stress, even if they were all toddlers, while "I live alone with four cats" would not. Here's another example: People wondering about whether there might be life on other planets sometimes ask, "Are we alone in the universe?" Just look around!

Well, you may reply, they mean to ask whether there is any other *intelligent* life in the universe. Right. Just look around! Animals also seem to pop in and out of our moral view. Most people would agree that it is wrong to hurt or kill a non-human animal without a good reason, but then it turns out that any reason, short of malicious pleasure, is reason enough. We want to eat the animal, and to raise her cheaply for that purpose; we can learn from doing experiments on her; we can make useful or attractive products out of her; she is interfering with our agriculture or gardening; or maybe we just don't feel comfortable having her come so near. Her interests have weight, we insist—but never weight enough to outweigh our own.

Then there is the disturbing use of the phrase "treated like an animal." People whose rights are violated, people whose interests are ignored or overridden, people who are used, harmed, neglected, starved or unjustly imprisoned standardly complain that they are being treated like animals, or protest that after all they are not just animals. Of course, rhetorically, complaining that you are being treated like an animal is more effective than complaining that you are being treated like a thing or an object or a stone, for a thing or an object or a stone has no interests that can be ignored or overridden. In the sense

intended, an object *can't* be treated badly, while an animal can. But then the curious implication seems to be that animals are the beings that it's all right to treat badly, and the complainant is saying that he is not one of *those*.

Do we need that contrast, between the beings it is *all right* to treat badly and the ones it is not? My otherwise favorite philosopher, Immanuel Kant, seemed to think so. In his essay "Conjectures on the Beginning of Human History," Kant traces the development of reason through a series of steps, the last of which is this:

> The fourth and last step which reason took, thereby raising man completely above animal society, was his . . . realization that he is the true *end of nature* . . . When he first said to the sheep "the pelt which you wear was given to you by nature not for your own use, but for mine" and took it from the sheep to wear it himself, he became aware of a prerogative which . . . he enjoyed over all the animals; and he now no longer regarded them as fellow creatures, but as means and instruments to be used at will for the attainment of whatever ends he pleased. This notion implies . . . an awareness of the following distinction: man should not address other *human beings* in the same way as animals, but should regard them as having an equal share in the gifts of nature. . . . Thus man had attained a position of *equality with all rational beings,* because he could claim *to be an end in himself* . . . and not to be used by anyone else as a mere means to other ends.

Non-human animals, on this showing, are the ultimate and final Other. They are the beings we can still use as mere means once we have given up the idea that other human beings are there for our purposes—once we've rejected the ideas that women are *for* housework and childcare, that girls are *for* sex, that boys are *for* fighting wars that serve older men's interests, and that people of color are *for* harvesting the fields and doing the menial jobs that all of us hate. Is that, to revert to this symposium's theme, what animals are for? Are they there so that there will be someone we can still use as mere means to our ends?

Not being what Kant called a "mere means" is not a privative condition—a way of being useless, say. It's a positive condition, which Kant calls being an "end in yourself." For a human being, it means that your choices should be respected and your ends promoted, that you have rights that the community should be prepared to uphold, that your happiness is valuable and your suffering should be cured or mitigated or met with tenderness when it is beyond cure. "Morality" is our name for demanding this kind of treatment from one another, and for meeting that demand. When we do use others to serve our own purposes—for of course we do—it must be done in a way that is consistent with all this, and then we are not treating them as "mere means," but at the same time as ends in themselves. But why shouldn't the other animals also be treated as ends in themselves?

I'll come back to that question. But first, let me respond to those readers who are now tempted to protest that there are plenty of people who *do* treat the other animals as ends in themselves. After all, it is notorious these days that more people than ever not only live with companion animals, but treat them like human children, keeping them in the house, providing them with toys and furniture, buying them medical insurance, bribing their affection with treats and burying them in graveyards when they die. Of course it's also true that in tough economic times when there is no longer money for such indulgences, these companion animals are turned loose onto the streets and into shelters in a way that human children ordinarily are not. But even those of us who are convinced that *we* would never treat our beloved pets in this way should remember that keeping an animal for affection and companionship is also a way of *using* the animal. Is it using the animal as a "mere means"?

It could be. Even among people, of course, it is possible to use someone for affection and companionship without keeping her existence and value as an independent being firmly in view. In *Middlemarch,* George Eliot tells the story of Dorothea, an idealistic young woman hungry to do some good in the world, who marries an older man whom she conceives to be a scholar engaged in a great work. Eliot writes:

We are all of us born in moral stupidity, taking the world as an udder to feed our supreme selves: Dorothea

had early begun to emerge from that stupidity, but yet it had been easier to her to imagine how she would devote herself to Mr. Casaubon, and become wise and strong in his strength and wisdom, than to conceive with that distinctness which is no longer reflection but feeling—an idea wrought back to the directness of sense, like the solidity of objects—that he had an equivalent center of self, whence the lights and shadows must always fall with a certain difference.

Eliot's purpose, at the particular moment at which this passage occurs, is to emphasize that Dorothea has failed to understand Casaubon's feelings. She has not quite managed to get his "center of self" into her view. But the moment is also one of moral revelation, a moment in which Dorothea grasps that "there is as great a need on his side as on her own" and so acquires "a new motive." Eliot is accusing her heroine, just a little, of having used Casaubon as a mere means to give significance and purpose to her own life. How much easier, then, to do something like that to a creature whose "center of self" you may not—rightly or wrongly—grant to be the "equivalent" of your own.

Is it because the other animals have lesser "centers of self" that so many people suppose they are not entitled to be treated as ends in themselves? In his Tanner Lectures, written as a work of fiction called *The Lives of Animals,* J. M. Coetzee imagines a professional philosopher who says: "It is licit to kill animals because their lives are not as important to them as ours are to us." George Eliot reminds us how hard it is to keep in view—not just to tell yourself, but to feel with "the directness of sense"—that other *people's* lives are as just important to them as yours is to you. But we are at least theoretically committed to the importance, and the equal importance, of every human life. Many of our religious and philosophical traditions try to explain this equal importance. We, these traditions assert—we human beings, that is—are all God's children, or have some special sort of intrinsic value that the other animals lack. But what makes it possible to believe such things at all is probably the thing that Coetzee puts in his philosopher's mouth: the passionate sense of importance that each of us attaches to himself or herself. After all, every human being pursues the things that are important to himself and to those whom he loves as if they were important *absolutely,* important in deadly earnest—for what else can we do? And just by doing that, we claim our own standing as ends in ourselves. For when we claim that the things that are important to us should be treated as important absolutely, just because they are important to us, we also claim that we are important ourselves.[2] But the other animals also pursue the things that are important to them and their loved ones as if they were important in deadly earnest. Why then should we think they must be less important to themselves than we are to ourselves?

Some of the philosophical views about the nature of animal minds are, among other things, attempts to answer that question. The other animals are not conscious at all, some people argue, or their consciousness is so fleeting and ephemeral that it just does not add up to the consciousness of a self, so nothing really could matter to them in quite the same that way it does to us. A less extreme version of that last view—one that even many defenders of the moral claims of animals, such as Peter Singer, endorse—is that animals live so thoroughly in the moment that their deaths are not regrettable, although their suffering is.

That might seem puzzling. After all, when we consider our fellow human beings, we often regard a capacity for living in the moment as a good thing. The human mind can be so cluttered and overshadowed with worries about the future and regrets about the past that we fail to enjoy the present—the only thing, after all, that is real. So why would the fact that the other animals live in the moment, supposing it is a fact, make their deaths less regrettable? Jeff MacMahan offers this explanation:

> . . . the lives of persons typically have a narrative structure that may demand completion in a certain way. People autonomously establish purposes for their lives, form patterns of structured relations with others, and thereby create expectations and dependencies that require fulfillment. The importance of later events in a typical human life may thus be greatly magnified by their relation to ambitions formed and activities engaged in earlier . . . In the lives of animals, however, this potential for complex narrative unity is entirely absent. There are no projects that require completion,

mistakes that demand rectification, or personal relations that promise to ripen or mature. Rather, as Aldous Huxley once put it, "the dumb creation lives a life made up of discreet and mutually irrelevant episodes." And each day is merely more of the same.

According to this argument, to deprive a human being of life is worse than to deprive another animal of life, because you are depriving the non-human animal only of "more of the same," while you may be disrupting the narrative unity of the human being's life.

I have mixed reactions to this kind of argument. On the one hand, animal lives are not the same every day—rather, at least for many of them, they have a rhythm that is set by the seasons of the year, and by the age of breeding, and may involve the raising of families, migrations, the building of homes, preparation for the winter and so on. Many mother animals raise new young every year or so, and most of those die and presumably are forgotten, but in some social animals, the bonds that result from family ties are permanent and important. Relationships, families and larger social groups persist over time. For some animals there is even a narrative structure to the course of an individual life that *we* can recognize and describe—even if they cannot. Among social animals, for instance, certain male individuals rise to positions of power and leadership in middle age, only to be deposed by younger members when they are older. Females move through a distinct set of roles in family life as daughters, then mothers, then grandmothers in much the same way that, in many cultures, human females do.

Which brings me to the other side of what bothers me about this—that human lives also have established rhythms set by the seasons of the year and the age of breeding, and that many human lives, especially when you look at the species historically, or at less developed nations, have been pretty much the same every day. You get up, do some work, eat breakfast, then do some more work. You tend the children and prepare the food, or you feed the animals, or you hoe the fields, or you go to the factory, depending on when and where your life takes place, but you go to work, and then you have supper, and then go to bed and start over. Each day is merely more of the same. Perhaps it is exactly those lives that most challenge the ability of the more privileged members of developed nations to feel with "the directness of sense" that every person's life is just as important to her as ours are to us.

Yet there is clearly something right about Mac-Mahan's picture. I think it is this: we human beings, unlike the other animals, think of ourselves and our lives in normative terms. We are governed not merely by instinctive likes and dislikes, attractions and aversions, enjoyment and suffering, but by values. Being reflective animals, we endorse or reject our likes and dislikes, attractions and aversions, pleasures or pains, declaring them to be good or bad. Each of us identifies himself in terms of certain roles, relationships, occupations and causes, all of them governed by normative standards, which it is then the business of our lives to live up to. And so we come to think of ourselves as worthy or unworthy, lovable or unlovely, good or bad.

Philosophers disagree about what exactly it is about our nature that makes us like this— whether it is rationality, or a special kind of sentiment, or something else. However that may be, this kind of evaluative self-conception is a condition that gives a strange extra dimension to human life, both a special source of pride and interest, and a profound cause of suffering. It is not that nothing is important to the other animals, for instinctive desire and aversion have an imperative character all their own. But that does not seem to suffuse whatever sense of their own being the other animals have. Some of the other animals seem to have moments of pride, but they don't seem in general to think of themselves as worthy or unworthy beings. Some of them certainly want to be loved, but they don't seem to worry about being lovable. Thinking of yourself as having a kind of identity that is at once up to you and subject to normative assessment is a distinctive feature of being human. It gives a human being's life, in his own eyes, the character of a *project,* of something at which he can succeed or fail. That possibility of success or failure is what gives human life the kind of narrative structure that MacMahan describes.

If this is right, it shows that human lives are important to human beings in *a way* that the lives of the other animals are not important to them. But it does not show that our lives are *more* important than theirs. It is not that our lives have a kind of importance that the lives of the other animals lack. It is rather that our lives have a kind of importance *for us* that the other animals' lives do not have *for them.* And I am prepared to make a further claim here: that there is nothing that is therefore *missing* from the lives of the other animals.

This is where things start to get a little bit dizzying, conceptually speaking. The difficulty is that everything that is important must be important because it is important *to* someone: to some person or animal. What makes it important to that person or animal is that it satisfies some desire or conforms to some standard that applies to that person or animal. But the standard of normative success and failure, which goes with the project of making yourself into a worthy or an unworthy being, does not apply to the other animals. There is nothing missing from the lives of the other animals because they fail to see themselves as good or bad, successes or failures. The standards that we use when we measure ourselves in these ways apply to us in virtue of something about our nature, and do not apply to them.

Perhaps a comparison will help. John Stuart Mill famously claimed that it is better to be Socrates dissatisfied than a pig satisfied.[3] Mill believed this because he held that human beings have access to what he called "higher pleasures"—for instance, the pleasures of poetry. But for whom is it better? Would it be better *for the pig* if he were Socrates? Temple Grandin, in her book *Animals Make Us Human,* reports that there is nothing pigs love more than rooting around in straw. Poetry is not good for a pig, so it is not something valuable that is missing from the pig's life, something he would get access to if he were changed into Socrates, any more than rooting around in straw is something valuable that is missing from your life, something you would get access to if you were changed into a pig. But isn't poetry a higher pleasure than rooting around in straw? If what makes a pleasure "higher" is, as Kant and others have suggested, that it cultivates our capacity for even deeper and greater pleasures of the very same kind, then we must have that capacity before the pleasure can be judged a higher one for us. Since the pig lacks that capacity, poetry is not a higher pleasure for a pig. Of course, we might try the argument that, so far as we can tell, none of the pig's pleasures are "higher" in this sense. But then perhaps it is only for us jaded human beings that the lower pleasures seem to grow stale. So long as the straw itself is fresh, pigs apparently *never* lose their enthusiasm for rooting around in straw.

There's a notorious philosophical problem about thoughts that begin, "if I were you . . ." When I tell you what I would do if I were you, I must bring something of myself with me, usually some standard for the assessment of actions that also applies to you, or a superior ability to apply some standard that we already share. Otherwise it's a foregone conclusion that whatever *you* would do if I weren't offering you advice is exactly what I would do if I were you. But the standard I bring with me may be one that does not apply to you or that you do not share. David Hume reminds us of the famous story of the advice Parmenio gave to Alexander the Great. *"Were I Alexander,* said Parmenio, *I would accept of these offers made by Darius. So would I too,* replied Alexander, *were I Parmenio."* This problem pervades our efforts to think about the other animals, for when we try to think about what it is like to be another animal, we bring our human standards with us, and then the other animals seem to us like lesser beings. A human being who lives a life governed only by desires and instincts, not by values, would certainly be a lesser being. But that doesn't mean that the other animals are lesser beings. They are simply beings of a different kind. When we look at the other animals through the lens of our own standards, just as when we look at them through the lens of our own interests, we cannot get them properly in view.

We are all born, as Eliot says, in moral stupidity, unable to see others except through the lens of our own interests and standards. Kant suggested that it took four steps for us to emerge from this moral stupidity, but perhaps there is a fifth step we have yet to take. That is to try to look at the other animals and their lives unhindered by our own interests and specifically human standards, and to see them for what they really are. What is important about the other animals is what we have in common: that they, like us, are the kinds of beings to whom things *can* be important. Like us, they pursue the things that are important *to* them as if they were important *absolutely,* important in deadly earnest—for, like us, what else can they do? When we do this, we claim our own standing as ends in ourselves. But our only reason for doing that is that it is essential to the kinds of beings we are, beings who take their own concerns to be important. The claim of the other animals to the standing of ends in themselves has same ultimate foundation as our own—the essentially self-affirming nature of life itself.

NOTES

1. There's interference here from another use of "I live alone with" in which it means, "I have sole charge of": "I can't go out whenever I please; I live alone with an autistic child." That's obviously not what is meant by "I live alone with a cat," but it might be what's meant by "I live alone with a child." But notice that very small babies, like animals, get called "it." It's tempting to speculate that this practice dates from the days when human infant mortality rates were higher and babies, like nonhuman animals, were regarded as fungible.

2. These remarks are a loose reading of Kant's claim that "representing" ourselves as ends in ourselves is a subjective principle of human action. See *Groundwork of the Metaphysics of Morals,* 4:429.

3. Actually Mill claims, on p. 10 of *Utilitarianism,* that it is better to be a human being dissatisfied than a pig satisfied, and better to be Socrates dissatisfied than a fool satisfied, so I am merging his claims by taking Socrates as the exemplar of humanity here.

QUESTIONS

1. How would Korsgaard respond to Singer's argument against industrial animal agriculture?
2. How would she reply to Tännsjö's argument?

3. What is wrong with Kant's view, according to Korsgaard? Why is Korsgaard's view nevertheless *Kantian*?
4. What is the point Korsgaard makes in the "treating like an animal" paragraph? Is she making an argument? What is its conclusion?
5. Korsgaard is, in this essay, guarded about the implications of her view for industrial animal agriculture. What, if anything, does her view imply about the permissibility of engaging in it? Of reasons for or against engaging in it?
6. What is the point Korsgaard makes in the paragraphs about pets, the ones starting with "I'll come back to this question. . . ."?
7. Consider Korsgaard's view about the badness of animal death. How does it compare with the view Elizabeth Harman articulates in Chapter 8, "Alternatives to Industrial Animal Agriculture"? What does it imply about the death for purely mindful people who live entirely in the moment? Are their deaths bad? Why or why not?
8. There are things that are important to Korsgaard. These things might be lacking in your life. Is your life thereby worse, period? Worse for you? Why or why not?

8) Alternatives to Industrial Animal Agriculture

This chapter discusses some alternatives to industrial animal agriculture. One alternative is simply not to raise animals at all and only raise plants. In Chapter 9, "Industrial Plant Agriculture," and Chapter 10, "Alternatives to Industrial Plant Agriculture," we turn to a discussion of plant agriculture. In this chapter we mostly focus on alternatives to industrial animal agriculture that do involve raising animals. We explain these alternatives and then sketch some ethical considerations for and against them.

WHAT FREE-RANGE FARMING IS

Free-range farming is a system of raising animals for food. In the ideal, it involves raising domestic animals outdoors in ways that take advantage of their natural tendencies and make them well off. So for pigs it might involve giving the animals plenty of room outdoors to roam, places to build nests, areas in which to forage, and so on. It might involve giving them toys to play with and man-made piles of things in which to forage, neither of which is at all natural but both of which take advantage of pigs' natural proclivities.

In three very important ways, being free-range farmed differs from living in the wild. First, the animals are better protected from predators and the weather. A chicken in the wild is raccoon bait. Of course, some chickens on farms are, too. Ideally, though, the farmer protects the animals throughout their lives from raccoons and also from snowstorms, hailstorms, and so forth.

Second, animals on farms are, unlike animals in the wild, under the control of humans. This leads to restrictions on what the animals can do but also to things like the animals receiving medical treatment and regular supplies of food and drink, if necessary.

Third, the lives of animals on free-range farms are shorter—often much shorter—than the natural lives of animals. Because animals are being raised for food and because many animals taste best when they are younger, animals on free-range farms are killed well before the end of their natural lifespans. However, ideally, on a free-range farm, this death is as painless and stress-free as possible. That is an improvement on, say, death by lupine disembowelment, beheading by raccoon, or assembly-line slaughter at a meatpacking plant.

As the repeated use of "ideally" thus far suggests, what we just described is an endpoint on a farming spectrum. There are various sorts of farming that come close to the ideal in some ways—by giving animals access to the outdoors, for example—but not in others—by giving them nasty deaths or castration without anesthetic or only limited opportunities to indulge their natural proclivities. . . . Also, some farms will come quite close to the ideal with some animals—the pigs, say—but far from it in others—perhaps the rabbits. There is a vegetarian agricultural ideal, too, in which animals are raised for their products but no animals get killed. As we will discuss, few, if any, farms live up to the vegetarian ideal since most kill animals or have those animals shipped off for killing. It could be that few, if any, farms meet the free-range ideal. Few, if any, might actually give animals happy lives and painless, stress-free deaths. In the state of Vermont, for example, state regulations make approximating the ideal difficult. State regulations about slaughtering lead to many animals being shipped quite long distances to large slaughterhouses, where the animals are slaughtered factory-style. For at least some, this is a stressful, painful way to die. If so, few, if any, Vermont farms achieve the free-range ideal.

We can only guess about how many farms get close to the free-range ideal. There are no statistics about this. Neither are there any statistics about how many animals are free-range-farmed. This is at least partly because "free-range" is a barely legally regulated term in the United States. The USDA applies it only to meat birds and, in that case, it means that the producers have demonstrated to the USDA that the bird was been *allowed access* to the *outside*. This chapter's notion of free-range farming is significantly more involved than that, and there is little information about how many animals in the United States are raised in this more involved way.

Be careful not to confuse this notion with other notions, some of which are legally regulated by the USDA. For example:

Free-range. This label indicates that the flock was provided shelter in a building, room, or area with unlimited access to food, fresh water, and continuous access to the outdoors during their production cycle. The outdoor area may or may not be fenced and/or covered with netting-like material. This label is regulated by the USDA.

Cage-free. This label indicates that the flock was *able* to freely roam a building, room, or enclosed area with unlimited access to food and fresh water during their production cycle. It does not indicate that the flock *did* roam freely. Neither does it specify what constitutes roaming.

Natural. As required by USDA, meat, poultry, and egg products labeled as "natural" must be minimally processed and contain no artificial ingredients. However, *the natural label does not include any standards regarding farm practices* and only applies to processing of meat and egg products. . . .

Humane. Multiple labeling programs make claims that animals were treated humanely during the production cycle, but the verification of these claims varies widely. *These labeling programs are not regulated under a single USDA definition.*

It is also important not to confuse *free-range* agriculture with *traditional* agriculture. Free-range agriculture can be highly technologically sophisticated and radically different from old methods. It can involve raising animals that have not been traditionally raised for food.

It can involve farmers from groups that have traditionally been excluded from farming. On the connection between free-range agriculture, organic agriculture, and traditional attitudes about farms and farmworkers, see Chapter 10, "Alternatives to Industrial Plant Agriculture," and its suggestions for further reading.

ANIMAL WELFARE

We should pause for a minute to discuss animal well-being, something that came up in the previous chapter. The free-range ideal involves well-off animals. What makes an animal well off?

One component of a well-off life might be freedom from pain. As we discussed in the last chapter, animals on industrial farms suffer in various ways and thereby lack this sort of well-being. Yet freedom from pain can't be the whole of well-being, otherwise an animal that is put into a coma, and thereby inured from pain, would be well off—but such an animal obviously is not well off. Such an animal is not suffering—that's good!—but also isn't enjoying anything—that's less good. So another component of animal welfare might be the presence of various pleasant mental states.

On one theory of well-being, *hedonism*, all there is to being well off is being free of bad states *and* having good ones. If hedonism is true, a person who is happy all the time and never in any pain is a person who is doing well. A person who relentlessly suffers is not.

It sounds plausible, but as an objection to this view, consider a variation on a famous philosophical thought experiment from Robert Nozick: You have a choice between, on the one hand, going on with your own life or, on the other hand, going into a virtual reality machine that will simulate that life exactly, giving you the same experiences, pleasurable and painful.[1] If hedonism is true, these lives are equally good since you experience the same pleasures and pains in each. Are they equally good? If hedonism is true and we get the machine to up the pleasant experiences and diminish the unpleasant ones, then the life in the machine is *better* than your actual life. Is it better? If not, then pleasure and the absence of pain can't be the only components of a good life since the life in a machine has more of both.

As a way of seeing that there might be more to a good life than pleasant and painful mental states, consider this: In the machine, you have experiences as of, say, eating ice cream. These feel good. But you don't actually eat ice cream. So far as you want to eat ice cream, you aren't getting what you want. Getting what you want might be an important part of well-being. On some theories—*desire-satisfaction theories of well-being*—getting what you want is the *only* component of a good life. So far as pigs want to root around, then, a free-range farm gives them what they want, and a confinement operation does not.

Of course, we could modify hedonism and desire-satisfaction theories so that a good life is a function of getting what you want and also having pleasant mental states and freedom from unhappy ones.

But just being happy and getting what you want might not be all it takes to make a good *human* life. Imagine a situation where you took a pill that greatly simplified your desires: all you want to do is take care of your bodily needs and, say, doodle. And along with getting the pill, assume that you get an endless supply of paper and pencils and have no problem satisfying your bodily needs.

Would you take the pill? Would a life on that pill be better than your real life? You'd get everything your heart desires. You might be happier and free from suffering. Yet the life would be missing various things that we value in our own lives: friendship, family, problem-solving, playing, love, freedom, health (depending on how the pill works), and so on.

Are these things—friendship et cetera—good *in themselves* and not just good because they contribute to happiness? Are they good not just because people want them? According to *objective list theories of well-being*, some things might be good for you, might increase your well-being, even if they neither make you happy nor get you what you want.

Which goods, if any, should go on the list for the animals we farm? Health? Play? Family? Freedom? When you read about industrial and free-range farms, consider which of these goods animals get on those farms.

COMPARING FREE-RANGE FARMING AND INDUSTRIAL ANIMAL AGRICULTURE

Here is a way to start thinking about the comparison between industrial animal agriculture and free-range farming: The vast majority of animals we eat are produced on the industrial farms discussed in the previous chapter. The number of animals produced by free-range farms is significantly lower than the number of animals produced by industrial farms. And this makes good economic sense and so will likely continue. Because free-range-farmed animals are living something like their natural lives and since, for many animals we eat, their natural lives involve a fair bit of roaming around, free-range-farmed animals need much more space than industrially farmed animals. Because free-range-farmed animals are provided a comparatively stress-free and painless death, fewer of them can be slaughtered in a day than can factory-farmed animals. So free-range farming produces fewer animals, given the same time and same space, as industrial farming.

To boot, the type of life and type of death experienced by a factory-farmed and free-range-farmed pig will typically be quite different. When he summarizes research on animal well-being, David Fraser writes,

> [A]s people formulated and debated various proposals about what constitutes a satisfactory life for animals in human care, three main concerns emerged: (1) that animals should feel well by being spared negative affect (pain, fear, hunger etc.) as much as possible, and by experiencing positive affect in the form of contentment and normal pleasures; (2) that animals should be able to lead reasonably natural lives by being able to perform important types of normal behavior and by having some natural elements in their environment such as fresh air and the ability to socialize with other animals in normal ways; and (3) that animals should function well in the sense of good health, normal growth and development, and normal functioning of the body.[2]

Similarly, the influential "Five Freedoms" framework has it that:

> The welfare of an animal includes its physical and mental state and we consider that good animal welfare implies both fitness and a sense of well-being. Any animal kept by man must, at least, be protected from unnecessary suffering.

An animal's welfare, whether on farm, in transit, at market or at a place of slaughter, should be considered in terms of the "five freedoms." These freedoms define ideal states rather than standards for acceptable welfare.

1. Freedom from Hunger and Thirst—by ready access to fresh water and a diet to maintain full health and vigor.
2. Freedom from Discomfort—by providing an appropriate environment including shelter and a comfortable resting area.
3. Freedom from Pain, Injury or Disease—by prevention or rapid diagnosis and treatment.
4. Freedom to Express Normal Behavior—by providing sufficient space, proper facilities, and company of the animals' own kind.
5. Freedom from Fear and Distress—by ensuring conditions and treatment that avoid mental suffering.[3] (http://www.fawc.org.uk/freedoms.htm)

In this light, it is clear why industrial farming offends and why the free-range alternative appeals: The latter keeps animals healthy. It enables happy states ("positive affect") and puts up some safeguards against the infliction of suffering. There is no need, for example, to dock free-range pigs' tails or to debeak free-range chickens, if they have enough space to stay out of each other's way. It enables animals to socialize and to otherwise lead reasonably natural lives. A free-range's pig's life is in those ways more pleasant than a factory-farmed pig's.

But because free-range farming does not involve confinement and does involve being outdoors, it involves various risks: predator- and weather-related risks, for example. These go into the well-being calculus, too.

Sometimes very different lives are hard to compare in terms of well-being. It is hard, for example, to figure out whether a happy, successful athlete is better off than a happy, successful entrepreneur. (What's easy is comparing things like how much money each has or how many hours each works.) To adapt an example from Jean-Paul Sartre, it is hard to figure out whether you will be better off if you join a band of freedom fighters or stay home to take care of your sick mother.

Yet simply because two lives are quite different, it doesn't follow that it is impossible to rank them in terms of well-being. Also, just from the fact that it is impossible to give a precise value to how much well-being a life has, it doesn't follow that it is impossible to roughly quantify how much well-being a life has. No one doubts that life as a successful basketball player is better than life as an enslaved subject for painful human research, even though those lives are so different (and even though the latter life will be better in various ways than the former—the subject might well be participating in valuable experiments or form bonds with other subjects that are deeper and more meaningful than sporting relationships).

Similarly, when he argued in favor of industrial animal farming in the last chapter, Torbjörn Tännsjö was not arguing that each animal on an industrial farm was better off than each animal on a free-range farm. On the contrary, Tännsjö's view is that the average well-being is quite a bit lower on an industrial farm. He just believes that that *sum* of well-being on industrial farms is so much higher because there are so many animals industrially farmed and they all have lives that are at least minimally worth living, and so make the world at least slightly better by their existence.

THE ETHICS OF FREE-RANGE FARMING

Free-range farming raises some ethical issues that we have already dealt with in our discussion of industrial animal agriculture: Is it wrong to hurt animals just to produce cheaper meat? Is it permissible to do the environmental damage that animal agriculture does just to raise animals for meat? Free-range farming, in the ideal, tries to minimize these bad effects.

Though much discussion of animal agriculture focuses on whether it is morally permissible to cause animals to suffer, or to kill them, it is also worth thinking about whether it is morally permissible to raise animals for food at all, even in cases where the animals have free-range, happy lives.

Notice that when we raise them, we also *use* them. On a dairy farm, a cow is not only raised but is also used, as if she were a tool for producing milk. Is that morally significant?

Also, what's the difference between raising and using? Consider a worm farm. You feed the worms, watch them build their tunnels, feed them, watch them. That's it. You aren't getting anything from them. (Are you getting the enjoyment of watching them? You might not. You might feed them and then not watch them, the way kids do with goldfish after several days.) With the worm farm, you are raising the worms: giving them a home, food, protecting them. But you aren't using them. A farmer's relationship to her chickens is typically different. She raises them—gives them a home, provides for food and protection—but she also takes their eggs. A farmer's relationship to her cows is typically even more different. She not only raises them and takes their milk, but she impregnates them routinely so as to make sure they have milk. Whereas you don't have to do much to a chicken to induce her to lay eggs, you have to keep a cow lactating to get the milk. The chickens—and even more clearly the cows—are tools we use to produce foods.

So we have two sets of questions: Is it permissible to keep animals for food? If so, why? Is it permissible to use animals for food? If so, why? To answer the first question, it helps to answer another question: *How* is it permissible to keep animals?

THE ETHICS OF KILLING ANIMALS

Let's assume, for the sake of argument, that it is permissible to raise animals and give those animals good lives. Free-range farming involves killing these happy animals. What can be said for and against the permissibility of doing both of those?

Here's a common enough thought, voiced and defended in the Salatin and Scruton readings that follow: Killing animals to eat them is not wrong. This is because death is no great harm to animals. By contrast, *hurting* animals to eat them is a great harm to those animals and is wrong; so industrial farming is not morally permissible. Moreover, since raising them in captivity is better for them than letting them run free—and be disemboweled, beheaded by predators, and so on—there is nothing wrong with raising animals in captivity. So, the argument concludes, free-range agriculture is at least permissible.

Another case for free-range farming allows that killing domestic animals might well be a great harm to them. The case then insists that this great harm is compensated for by benefits elsewhere: The death of one pig leads to the farmers raising a new, happy pig. And the death of one pig leads to ham and bacon, both of which people greatly enjoy. Generally, this argument goes, free-range farming is the agricultural option that produces the most overall happiness. In the previous chapter, Tännsjö disputed this and argued that industrial farming produces the most happiness (and Singer, implicitly, argued that a vegan agriculture system does). There is a hard question here about who is correct. Let's assume, for the sake of argument, that the proponent of free-range agriculture is. *Utilitarianism* claims that the option available to us that maximizes happiness is what we are *morally required* to do. So there's a utilitarian case for free-range farming. It is defended in the Hare (1999) reading in Further Reading. Such an argument would lead not only to free-range farming being *morally permissible* but, to boot, *morally required*.

As we noted, the utilitarian argument for free-range farming can concede that death is a very bad thing. It just insists that it's a very bad thing that is, nevertheless, morally permissible to do like, for example, amputating someone's arm so they can survive or stealing Juan's boat to save Clare's life. Against this line of utilitarian argument, one might note that it seems to imply all sorts of awful things about how we should treat people. We might be morally required, for example, to free-range farm other people if only enough happiness were produced by it. That is, if free-range farming *humans* somehow produced more options than any other, utilitarianism implies we are morally required to free-range farm humans. But, the objection concludes, there would be no such moral requirement, so utilitarianism is false.

Tännsjö, by contrast, accepts the utilitarianism but rejects the claim the free-range farming is the agricultural system that maximizes well-being. How should we sort out how much well-being an agricultural option produces? We'd have to tot up how much well-being industrial farming produces, how much free-range farming produces, how much vegetarian agriculture produces, how much vegan agriculture produces. And that's just the start. Now imagine a slightly tweaked industrial farming system, one that improves animal welfare slightly at minimal increase in the cost of food. How much well-being would that produce in the short run? In the long run? Extremely difficult questions! This shows not that Hare is wrong when he claims that free-range agriculture maximizes well-being. It just shows we have little reason to believe he is right and so have little reason to believe he is right to claim that free-range farming is morally permissible because it maximizes well-being.

Most of these objections show up in the Harman selection to follow. Harman argues that *if* industrial farming is wrong, then so is free-range farming; part of what explains why industrial farming is wrong explains, too, why free-range farming is wrong. If she is right and industrial farming is wrong, then free-range farming isn't a morally viable alternative. If so, we might turn to vegetarian or vegan agriculture. "Vegetarian" and "vegan" usually refer to dietary policy. We focus instead on forms of agriculture that either involve raising no animals—vegan agriculture—or that involve raising animals for their products but not their flesh—vegetarian agriculture.

It is important to keep whether vegetarian *agriculture* is the way to go from the question of whether meat-*eating* is permissible. Imagine that you accidentally run over a couple of rabbits on your drive home from work. What should you do with them? Is it wrong to eat them? Even if it's wrong to raise animals for food and wrong to kill animals for food, here you have some dead bodies that look quite yummy. What can you permissibly do with them?

Even if you learn that it would be wrong to raise the rabbits for food, that doesn't tell you what you should do in *this* case.

Or imagine that you run a farm for egg-laying hens. One old, old hen dies. Is it wrong to eat her? That is not a question addressed in this chapter but, rather, it is addressed in Chapter 4, "Consumer Ethics." The question in this chapter is whether it is permissible to *raise* animals for their products without *killing* the animals. Here the focus is on farming practices—such as vegetarian agriculture—not on individual consumption practices—such as vegetarianism.

The case for and against these farming practices is outlined below and in the readings that follow.

THE ETHICS OF VEGETARIAN ANIMAL AGRICULTURE

The objections to free-range agricultural systems just canvassed focused largely on the fact that in free-range agricultural systems, we kill animals for food. What if we raise animals for food without killing them for their flesh? Is such a system morally permissible?

Let's use the term "vegetarian animal agricultural system" to refer to an agricultural system that *might* involve raising animals for their products but not for their flesh. The vegetarian ideal involves no killing of animals. For example, it might involve raising chickens for eggs rather than chicken wings and even when the hens are too old to produce eggs, they are, in the vegetarian ideal, not killed. It might involve raising cows for milk rather than burgers and even when the cows are too old to produce milk they are, in the vegetarian ideal, not killed. Note that some vegetarian animal agriculture is industrial: there are industrial farms that produce animal-source foods for vegetarians—milk, eggs—but without killing the animals. These farms would raise most of the animal welfare, environmental and human health concerns that non-vegetarian animal agriculture raises. Since we have discussed these issues in the previous two chapters, we will ignore them here.

What about free-range vegetarian animal agriculture—a form of animal agriculture that, in the ideal, gives animals happy lives and does not kill them? A first comment is that the ideal that animals are not killed for food is hardly ever met. In practice, almost no one adheres to this ideal—doing so makes no economic sense. Male chickens on an egg farm are close to useless. Older female chickens on an egg farm are close to useless. Male cows on a dairy are close to useless. But these animals cost money to keep around, so it makes economic sense just to be rid of them. As Suzanne Podhaizer writes,

> [I]f you're a dairy-eating vegetarian, animals are dying to provide you with slices of tangy cheese to augment your hummus and sprout sandwiches.
>
> Needless to say, only female animals produce milk and cream, and pregnancy is a prerequisite of lactation. The male offspring of heifers, however, don't figure into the dairy farm equation. A farm only needs a couple of stud animals, if they're not using artificial insemination, and dairy cattle, while they can be tasty, are typically smaller and leaner than breeds raised for meat. The doddering little steers—with their expressive eyes, skinny legs and prodigious appetites—are considered expendable.

Most of the "bob calves," as they are called, get slaughtered when they are just a few days old. . . .

These animals . . . are the lucky ones. The most robust, healthy-looking babes . . . are shipped off to conventional veal producers in Pennsylvania, Canada or the Midwest. There they live in confinement, often in the dark, until they're big enough to be converted into scaloppini and schnitzel. Anemia accounts for the pale color of the meat.

For many dairymen, these creatures are just another waste product—like manure—to be disposed of.[4]

So our current practices of raising cows for milk and chickens for eggs do not conform to the vegetarian ideal. Male cattle and female cattle past the milk-producing age are just an economic drag on farms. So they are killed and turned to food for us or our pets. (Something similar happens with male chicks and female chickens past the egg-laying point.) This is normal operating procedure on farms you might not think of as farms in the meat business.

This is not an objection to vegetarian animal agriculture. It's just pointing out that existing egg and dairy farms don't meet the ideal standards of vegetarian animal agriculture. They might not do the killing themselves, but the killing gets done. And in the non-ideal system we are currently in, it has been speculated that animal *use*, as on vegetarian farms, leads as a matter of fact to animal *abuse*.[5] The point isn't that the abuse can't be helped. It's more like: Given the sorts of fallible, non-ideal creatures we are, if we start off with a system of using animals, we'll start edging into a system where we use and abuse them.

But consider the ideal vegetarian system: No animals—male or female—are ever killed. No animals are abused. Nevertheless, animals are still held in captivity and used for their milk, say, or eggs. Is there something morally wrong with that? This brings us back to the questions about control and use discussed previously.

Let's approach them indirectly via a modification of a *Twilight Zone* episode:[6] Aliens come to Earth. They give us good lives. They let us do as we please, more or less. There's no leaving our own states or countries, much less any space exploration. Would this somewhat minimal sort of control be permissible? Is the case analogous to vegetarian animal agriculture's treatment of birds and mammals? When he mentions this topic, Singer speculates that "the life of freedom is preferred." By people, sure. By other animals? Cats? Cows? Chickens? What about very young people, toddlers and babies?

Let's add that the aliens regularly take our blood. They regularly impregnate women since the blood of pregnant women is especially useful. Moreover, the whole system of person-confinement is designed to produce the most, best blood. It is the reason for being of our confinement. Would this be morally permissible? Is the case analogous to vegetarian agriculture's treatment of cows? (It's importantly different from the treatment of chickens since eggs, unlike milk, are a naturally occurring byproduct of daily hen life. This fact, and its moral importance, is discussed in the McPherson reading in Chapter 4, "Consumer Ethics").[7]

If this alien scenario strikes you as morally wrong, does the free-range vegetarian scenario strike you the same way? If not, is that just because people are people, cows and chickens aren't? That view is discussed and roundly criticized in the Singer reading in Chapter 7, "Industrial Animal Agriculture." Singer would conclude that both vegetarian animal agriculture and human "agriculture" are wrong.[8]

THE VEGAN UTOPIA?

If the case against vegetarian animal agriculture is successful and the case against killing animals for food is successful, the last candidate for a permissible agricultural system is a *vegan* agricultural system, one in which plants are raised, but animals are not raised for their flesh nor their products.

A few points can be raised about it. First, a vegan agricultural system would not be utopian for us. We would lose out on food that some of us find delicious. Second, as Salatin details in his reading in this chapter, animals have a valuable role to play in agriculture as sources of fertilizer and as grazers of land. Third, they have a valuable role to play as a source of food that can graze on land that would otherwise not be fit to grow food.

Fourth, a vegan agricultural system is not some utopia for cows and chickens and other animals. So far as these animals exist in a vegan agricultural system, they exist without the protection that farmers provide them shelter and healthcare.

Moreover, fifth, animals will be killed in the course of farmwork and will be killed in the process of turning habitat into farmland. And, obviously, finally, the vegan agricultural system will involve billions of plant deaths daily.

Is there something wrong with killing plants? Yoon argues that killing an animal is no worse than killing a plant. (And also that if one is *wrong*, so is the other.) But this, as Yoon notes, is extremely surprising since plants appear not to suffer from being killed and appear not to be deprived of anything particularly good by being killed. (Compare: A person who is in a terminal coma and taken off life-support is deprived of life, but the life he is deprived of is not a good life. It's a life of nothingness. That's what most of us think a plant is deprived of.) Yoon's response is that plants show signs of being attached to their lives—they work to protect them—and that our understanding of the mental lives of other beings is not so great that we should rule out the possibility that they do have a life worth having and do, in a way, suffer. (She might have also noted that some early proponents of a vegetarian diet, Pythagoras and the Buddha, were also skittish about killing plants.[9])

The Singer reading from Chapter 7, "Industrial Animal Agriculture," notes that critics of giving women various rights mocked that if you gave them to women, you'd soon be giving them to *beasts*. Yoon's article suggests that if you give rights to beasts, you'll soon be giving them to *plants* and wonders then what you are going to kill for food.

FURTHER ISSUES

1. *The Ethics of Free-Range Agriculture*
Here are four different positions on free-range agriculture. Critically evaluate each.

- It's morally worse than industrial farming and, in fact, morally wrong.
- It's morally better than industrial farming, but still wrong.
- It's morally permissible (in some forms).
- It's morally required.

Scruton and Salatin argue for the permissibility of free-range agriculture, but their arguments are very different. Explain the differences. Explain how their arguments differ from a utilitarian argument for free-range agriculture. How would Harman object to each?

2. *Natural Human Lives*

When we think about what makes a human well-off, we might not (explicitly) talk about living a "natural" life, but that's a common thing that comes up when talking about animal welfare, as the animal scientist David Fraser notes. Why is there this difference between humans and animals? Or is there no such difference and living a natural life is an important part of human well-being? (Note that when food ethicists like Wendell Berry praise farming, they often praise how it immerses the farmer in a natural way of life.)

What does natural mean here? What are "natural lives" for domestic animals that have evolved side by side with humans? Is it intrinsically important that animals have "natural lives"? Or is this important only insofar as it increases the likelihood that animals experience enjoyment rather than suffering, or that their desires are satisfied rather than frustrated?

3. *Animal Welfare*

What are the views of animal welfare used by scientists, farmers, and other experts? How do these views of animal welfare compare to the theories that ethicists have created? Is, for example, the theory David Fraser gives in this chapter a hedonistic theory? A desire-satisfaction theory? An objective list theory? Something else?

4. *Pets*

As we said, the ideal vegetarian system isn't—and probably never will be—instantiated. But it would go some ways towards addressing concerns like Salatin's about how animals are needed to keep ecosystems healthy. Female animals could provide eggs or milk as well as manure and grazing and then, once past their egg-laying, child-bearing age, just provide the manure and grazing. The male animals would do so from the start. But these male animals and older females would be something like pets. As the Harman reading brings out, it would seem to most pet-owners to be horrific to kill their pets rather than give them a short, painful surgery that extends their life. Would this be wrong? Why?

Generally, are there differences between pets and animals we keep for food that explain why we *do* treat them differently? Does that explain why we *may*—are morally permitted to—treat them differently? How so?

FURTHER READING

Free-Range Farming, Vegan and Vegetarian Agriculture, and the Ethics of Them

Adams, Carol. 2010. *The Sexual Politics of Meat,* 20th anniversary ed. New York: Bloomsbury Academic Press.

Bramble, Ben, and Bob Fischer, eds. 2015. *The Moral Complexities of Eating Meat.* New York: Oxford University Press.

Diamond, Cora. 1978. "Eating Meat and Eating People," *Philosophy* 53: 465–479.

Engel, Mylan. 2000. "The Immorality of Eating Meat," in Louis Pojman, ed., *The Moral Life.* New York: Oxford University Press.

Fearnley-Whittngstall, Hugh. 2007. *The River Cottage Meat Book*. Berkeley, CA: Ten Speed Press.
———. 2008. *The River Cottage Cookbook*. Berkeley, CA: Ten Speed Press.
Foer, Jonathan Safran. 2009. *Eating Animals*. New York: Little, Brown.
Francione, Gary. 2012. "Animal Welfare, Happy Meat, and Veganism as the Moral Baseline," in David Kaplan, ed., *The Philosophy of Food*. Berkeley: University of California Press.
Hare, R. M. 1999. "Why I Am Only a Demi-Vegetarian," in Jamieson, *Singer and His Critics*.
Halteman, Matthew C. 2010. *Compassionate Eating as Care of Creation*. Washington, DC: Humane Society of the United States.
Haynes, Richard P. 2012. "The Myth of Happy Meat," in David Kaplan, ed., *The Philosophy of Food*. Berkeley: University of California Press.
Jamieson, Dale, ed. 1999. *Singer and His Critics*. Cambridge, MA: Wiley-Blackwell.
Kingsolver, Barbara. 2007. *Animal, Vegetable, Miracle*. New York: Harper.
McMahan, Jeff. 2008. "Eating Animals the Nice Way," *Daedalus* 137: 66–76.
McWilliams, James. 2015. "Inside Big Ag," *VQR*. http://www.vqronline.org/nonfiction-criticism/2015/04/inside-big-ag-dilemma-meat-industry.
Niman, Nicole Hahn. 2009. *Righteous Porkchop*. New York: William Morrow.
———. 2014. *Defending Beef*. White River Junction, VT: Chelsea Green.
Nobis, Nathan. 2008. "Reasonable Humans and Animals: A Case for Vegetarianism," *Between the Species* 13: 8.
Norcross, Alastair. 2004. "Puppies, Pigs, and People," *Philosophical Perspectives* 18: 239–245.
Podhaizer, Suzanne. 2008. "The Veal Deal," *Seven Days*, August 27. http://www.sevendaysvt.com/vermont/the-veal-deal/Content?oid=2135007.
Pollan, Michael. 2006. *The Omnivore's Dilemma*. New York: Penguin.
Regan, Tom. 1983. *The Case against Animal Rights*. Berkeley: University of California Press.
Scruton, Roger. 2006. *Animal Rights and Wrongs*. New York: Continuum.
———. 2008. "A Carnivore's Credo," *Harper's* May 2006, pp. 21–26.
Scully, Matthew. 2002. *Dominion*. New York: St Martin's.
Singer, Peter. 1980. "Utilitarianism and Vegetarianism," *Philosophy and Public Affairs* 9: 325–337.

Some History of the Ethics of Free-Range Farming

Stuart, Tristram. 2008. *The Bloodless Revolution*. New York: Norton
Williams, Howard, ed. 2003. *The Ethics of Diet*. Champaign, IL: University of Illinois Press.

The Harm of Death (and, More Particularly, the Harm of Death to Domestic Animals)

Bradley, Ben. 2009. *Well-Being and Death*. New York: Oxford University Press.
Kamm, Frances Myrna. 1998. *Death and Whom to Save from It*. New York: Oxford University Press.
Midgeley, Mary. 1998. *Animals and Why They Matter*. Athens, GA: University of Georgia Press.
Nagel, Thomas. 1983. "Death," in *Mortal Questions*. Cambridge: Cambridge University Press.
Norcross, Alastair. 2012. "The Significance of Death for Animals," in Ben Bradley et al., eds., *The Oxford Handbook of the Philosophy of Death*. New York: Oxford University Press.
Velleman, J. David. 2000. "Well-Being and Time," in *The Possibility of Practical Reason*. New York: Oxford University Press.

Utilitarianism: What It Is and Why You Should (or Shouldn't) Endorse It

Driver, Julia. 2011. *Consequentialism*. New York: Routledge.
———. 2009. "The History of Utilitarianism," *Stanford Encyclopedia of Philosophy*.
Kagan, Shelly. 1997. *Normative Ethics*. Boulder, CO: Westview Press.

(Human and Animal) Welfare

Balcombe, Jonathan. 2006. *Pleasurable Kingdom*. London: St Martin's.
Crisp, Roger. 2014. "Well-Being," in Edward N. Zalta, ed., *Stanford Encyclopedia of Philosophy* (Winter 2014 ed.), http://plato.stanford.edu/archives/win2014/entries/well-being/.
Fraser, David. 2008. *Understanding Animal Welfare: The Science in Its Cultural Context*. Cambridge, MA: Wiley-Blackwell.
Grandin, Temple, ed. 2010. *Improving Animal Welfare*. Cambridge, MA: CAB International.
———, and Catherine Johnson. 2005. *Animals in Translation*. New York: Scribner.
Hearne, Vicki. 1994. *Animal Happiness*. New York: HarperCollins.
Streiffer, Robert, and John Basl. 2011. "Ethical Issues in the Application of Biotechnology to Animals in Agriculture," in Tom L. Beauchamp and R. G. Frey, eds., *The Oxford Handbook of Animal Ethics*. New York: Oxford University Press.

On the Use of Animals in Agriculture

Balfour, Eve. 2006. *The Living Soil*. Bristol: The Soil Association.
Berry, Wendell. 1977. *The Unsettling of America: Culture and Agriculture*. San Francisco: Sierra Club.
Donaldson, Sue, and Will Kymlicka. 2011. *Zoopolis*. New York: Oxford University Press.
Kirschenmann, Fred. 2011. *Cultivating an Ecological Conscience*. Berkeley: Counterpoint.
Korsgaard, Christine. 2011. "Interacting with Animals," in Thomas Beauchamp and R. G. Frey, eds., *The Oxford Handbook of Animal Ethics*. New York: Oxford University
Salatin, Joel. 2007. *Everything I Want to Do Is Illegal*. Swoope, VA: Polyface Press.

NOTES

1. Robert Nozick, *Anarchy, State, Utopia* (New York: Basic Books, 1971).
2. David Fraser, *Understanding Animal Welfare: The Science in Its Cultural Context* (Cambridge, MA: Wiley-Blackwell), 70–71.
3. Farm Animal Welfare Committee, "Report on Farm Animal Welfare in Great Britain," 2009. https://www.gov.uk/government/uploads/system/uploads/attachment_data/file/319292/Farm_Animal_Welfare_in_Great_Britain_-_Past__Present_and_Future.pdf.
4. Suzanne Podhaizer, "The Veal Deal," Seven Days, August 27, 2008. http://www.sevendaysvt.com/vermont/the-veal-deal/Content?oid=2135007.
5. Donaldson and Kymlicka (2011), cited in the Further Reading section, makes this argument.
6. The episode we are modifying is "To Serve Man" (http://www.imdb.com/title/tt0734684/).
7. These questions about our treatment of animals recall similar questions about the treatment of slaves in the nineteenth century. See Marjorie Spiegel, *The Dreaded Comparison* (London: Heretic, 1988).

8. A further consideration is the environmental impact of raising animals. On the one hand, it is uncontroversial that a free-range vegetarian system will take up room and uncontroversial that, if it involves cows, will involve creatures that produce plenty of greenhouse gases. On the other hand, it is controversial what the net impact of such systems is. Proponents argue not just that they aren't too bad, are worth the cost, but, rather, are a *net positive*. Niman (2014), cited in the "Further Reading" section, makes this case and surveys recent research. McWilliams (2015) responds.

9. And we might note that this characterization of Pythagoras is controversial. To what extent he was even opposed to the eating and killing of animals is controversial.

JOEL SALATIN

Animal Welfare

In this selection, Joel Salatin valuably makes a battery of arguments that free-range farming is permissible: one starts from a premise about its environmental effects, another from its effects on animals, a third from its effects on humans. (There's a religious case in the background, too.)

The paper is also valuable for its remarks about the dangers of empathizing with animals, as when one thinks, "It must be wrong to stop an animal's life short. Just think about what it would be like for *me* to have my life cut short." This is a common pattern of reasoning but can be mistakenly used. For example, when some think about gavage—the process of force-feeding waterfowl to produce *foie gras*—they are repulsed. But, for some the repulsion comes from imagining what force-feeding would be like for us. And since our physiology and psychology are so different from fowls', it's a mistake to infer that since it'd be terrible for us to be force-fed, it is terrible for them.

. . . Unlike a cat, which relishes the chance to play with a mouse for a long time before finally killing and eating it, I do not scratch, beat, and paw animals before killing them. We honor and respect them both in life and in death. And just for the record, humans are not animals. Animals don't sin. Animals don't have souls.

This notion that modern humankind has evolved beyond killing animals is simply the result of too

Joel Salatin, "Animal Welfare," from *Everything I Want To Do Is Illegal: War Stories from the Local Food Front* (Swoope, VA: Polyface, 2011).

many people being totally disconnected from life. Anyone connected to life understands the cycles of life, which include death, decay, and regeneration. We've raised a generation on Bambi and Thumper rather than Thanksgiving hog killin' and the Christmas goose. Those who say they've achieved a spiritual Nirvana by being at one with the animals are only showing just how disconnected they are from real life cycles.

To be sure, I have no problem with vegans or vegetarians. I have no problem with animal worshippers—the ones who say a person is a cat is a fly is a grasshopper. The problem comes when they try to use the political process to outlaw meat consumption. Interestingly, these folks vilify the religious right for trying to impose their ideas on others, but have no problem when the shoe is on the other foot.

This became quite apparent to me in the early 1990s when I was asked by the Humane Society of the U.S. to help write the humane standards for a wonderful book they put together called *The Humane Consumer and Producer Guide*. In my mind, this is still one of the best national directories ever compiled to connect humane farmers with people who want to buy their food from these kinds of farmers. Anyway, in the standards, it was considered inhumane to abort a fetus from a heifer in the third trimester of the pregnancy.

If a heifer is not going to be used for breeding, farmers will sometimes abort the calves in order for the heifer to gain faster as a beef animal. Early in the pregnancy, drugs can be used. Often heifers are spayed. But if a heifer enters a feedlot already heavy with calf, farmers will induce abortions in order to simplify their operation and put the calories on backfat rather than into milk and a baby calf. Amazingly, the people who are so concerned about abortions in the third trimester of a bovine pregnancy tend to support that action in humans. Isn't that incredible?

It's as inconsistent as the pro-lifers eating disrespected, factory-farmed meat out of Costco. I agree with Matthew Scully, author of *Dominion*: The people who should be most concerned about respecting and honoring animals are the members of the religious right. Instead these folks defend the right to abuse animals, to disrespect their chickenness and pigness.

And they even applaud their own ability to find the cheapest food. I wonder if they think the best church comes from hiring the cheapest pastor.

Invariably, when animal rights advocates come to the farm and we begin talking about things like castration or embryo abortion, they always assume that I'm a fellow rabid human baby abortionist. As a farmer who has helped many cows deliver calves, the moment of ecstasy is when you reach in and the calf pulls away. That's when you know the calf is alive. And no farmer ever looks at his assistant and says, "Oh, good, this fetal mass is moving."

Rather, we exclaim, "Oh boy! It's alive! Let's get this little guy out of here." And if it's alive then, was it alive yesterday? How about the day before that? And the day before that? If any animal welfare groups want my respect, they will have to come out passionately in favor of a human pro-life position. In my soul, I cannot see how a person wanting desperately to save a tree or save a baby whale has no remorse at snuffing out a wiggling, very much alive human baby in what should be its safest environment, a mother's womb. The rise of the abortion movement coincided perfectly with our culture's disconnection to the land.

The wonder of life, the mystery and majesty of chicks hatching and pigs farrowing creates a deep appreciation for new life. Even the satisfaction of seeing cows get bred—knowing the value of that developing calf—makes farmers want to protect these developing babies. We farmers know they are the future. They are our survival. We do everything possible to bring those babies to term. People who don't see that routinely, who don't experience that, can easily lose that sense of awe. And when babies no longer instill awe, we've not become a higher developed society, we've become crass and harsh.

I don't know how many people have said to me, "How can you butcher those animals? I just don't think I could do it. They're so cute." I could just as easily turn the question around: "How could you live in a townhouse divorced from fields and woods and vibrant life? I just don't think I could do it. It's so sterile and dead."

A lot of this is just in the way we've been brought up, what we've experienced. I've grown up on the farm, battling possums and raccoons. And rats. Oh, I hate rats. When you find a hundred half-dead chicks stuffed down a hole under the brooder house, you develop a keen distaste for rats.

We had a guy come to one of our seminars sporting a PETA bumper sticker. That stands for People for the Ethical Treatment of Animals. Out here in farmland, we call it People Eating Tasty Animals. My favorite is this rendition: PETA—Indian word for poor hunter. Anyway, this fellow decided that if he couldn't kill it, he shouldn't eat it. Because every time we eat meat, we are vicariously taking an animal's life. He had been a vegetarian for several years.

The first morning of the seminar, we gave him a knife and let him kill some chickens. He appreciated our honoring them in life, and our honoring them in death. It was quite an epiphany for him, and he ate chicken the next night. Can you imagine a Tyson slaughter plant allowing this guy to come in and kill chickens? They have all sorts of no trespassing and security signs posted. This is part of the problem with the food system. We have made it unfriendly to people, to the extent that people can't be connected to it even if they wanted to. This inherently breeds disconnect, misunderstanding, and mistrust.

On our farm, we've changed the name of our pastured shelters from pens to shelters, partly as a response to this animal welfare movement. Pens sound like a shortened version of penitentiary. It has all sorts of negative connotations. In farm country, pens do not carry that kind of negativity. When we put animals in a pen, it's usually because they are receiving special care. If they aren't in a pen, they are just out there on the range so to speak, fighting the elements and surviving with minimal care. But in a pen, that's where they get special attention.

For urbanites, however, pen holds an entirely different meaning. They think it smacks of confinement, being enslaved, penned up and not free to move. In fact, some animal welfare folks visited us and castigated me for having the broilers out in these pens. They thought it was awful. I assured them that if the birds were not in a pen, they would be destroyed by predators and weather. And if one happens to get out, all it does is run around and around trying to get back in. They instinctively know that

the pen means safety. And they don't want to be away from their buddies.

As we began realizing our language liability, we changed the word to shelter. Shelter sounds more like nurturing and care. Of course, it's a lot harder to say and we had to work hard at going to all this extra speech effort, but it has paid big dividends. We haven't had any complaints for some time now. . . .

Another blind spot in the animal welfare community is horse slaughter. I have been deeply chagrined with the effort to prohibit horse slaughter for human consumption in the U.S. I expect that by the time this book comes out, the final abattoir will be out of business. What legislation couldn't do, the judiciary has done. And it's a shame. I couldn't disagree more with my friends in the animal welfare movement over this issue. Although horse meat is not a staple of the American diet, it is consumed, with relish, in other cultures.

To deny farmers the extra value created by a vibrant horse meat sales option just because I don't like the idea of eating the Black Stallion is myopic to the extreme. Talk about the religious right. Give me a break. Since when did horses become sacred over llamas or cows or pigs? I guess since Flicka. A slaughtered horse is a slaughtered horse. Just because the meat goes to dog and cat food, does that make the killing act more noble?

Horses get old and stiff and crotchety. Allowing a useful market when they no longer can stay healthy is only reasonable. To what animal will we ascribe this non-human food status next? Squid? Lobster? And this is what concerns me. When I read the arguments these folks are putting out, it is clear to me that their real agenda is to make all animal slaughter illegal. All of it.

To do that, philosophically, a person must equate animals with humans. And that is an untenable position. Let me explain why from an ecologist's point of view. Tillage is generally destructive to soil. Historically, all sustainable tillage schemes are on a 5–7 year rotation, in which the land is tilled only about 2 years out of 7. The in between years of grass rebuild the soil.

Grass is nature's most efficient soil builder. It's also the most efficient carbon sequestration mechanism.

Much better even than forest. Planting annual crops year after year requires large off-field inputs in both organic and conventional chemical systems. In all sustainable systems, tillage only 2 out of 7 years is all the soil can stand without hefty imported amendments. From a land healing and atmosphere cleaning perspective, nothing is as efficacious as grass. Grass value only increases on marginal lands. Millions of acres on the planet are not suitable for crop production, but they grow wonderful forages.

In fact, now we know that today's dense eastern forests did not exist before Europeans came to the continent. The Indians maintained savannahs by lighting routine fires to beat back encroaching trees. This manipulation encouraged more grass to grow stimulating herbivore populations. Manure is magic. Always has been; always will be. Even with all we know about soil fertility, we still don't know what the X factor is in manure that makes it better than the artificially reconstituted elements found in manure.

Without perennial meadows and grasses, we would have a more eroding landscape and a dirtier atmosphere. How do grasslands stay healthy? They regenerate and proliferate through routine mowing. That mowing is most efficiently performed by animals. Certainly some folks would say that animals on the landscape do not necessitate carnivorous humans. And while that may be true, part of the human responsibility is to steward the landscape to make it capture more solar energy, to sequester more atmospheric carbon, and to make it more productive than it would be if left to its natural devices.

Grass-based meat is a whole different nutritional item than grain-based meat. The recent discoveries regarding the B vitamins, conjugated linoleic acid, and the polyunsaturated fats, including the omega 3:omega 6 ratio, are proving that all of the alleged human health problems associated with meat consumption are a result of artificially producing that meat. We've had numerous customers who return to meat after a decade of vegetarianism destroys their health. I suggest skeptics contact the Weston A. Price Foundation for corroboration, or log onto <eatwild .com> for cutting-edge nutritional findings.

Whatever is wrong with eating meat and poultry is a result of producing it in factory farms and feedlots.

Whatever environmental degradation, human health problems, or animal welfare issues impugn meat and poultry consumption can be rectified and turned into positives with a fundamentally different production style.

Beautifully, this fundamentally different production style would result in the 70 percent of North America's tilled farmland being converted to perennial grasslands. Only 30 percent of the grain acreage is for people, pigs, and poultry. If we really want to heal the land, atmosphere, and our bodies on a massive scale—not to mention getting the petroleum out of agriculture—the fastest way to accomplish that is to increase demand for 100 percent grass finished beef and milk in this country. That is far more healing than anything else.

Finally, I actually have more respect for true vegans than I do vegetarians if the issue is animals equal humans. Vegetarians who eat eggs and dairy but refuse to eat meat because killing animals is wrong have no understanding of animal life cycles. Where do they think eggs and cheese come from? They certainly don't come from geriatric livestock. They come from productive, virile, breeding-age animals. And as those animals age, they must be culled from the herd before they become unproductive.

The symbiotic relationship between grasslands, ecology, and herds of herbivores is a natural principle. It has been functioning for millennia. For anyone to suggest that eliminating these relationships could be normal is to not recognize historical principles. When we begin looking at nutrient density, nothing beats meat, dairy, and poultry. Extricating animals from the landscape is not healthy for anyone or anything.

Certainly some people thrive on a vegetarian diet. I don't know anyone who thrives on a vegan diet. I've met many folks who are on a vegan diet, but I've never met a healthy one. Many times the diet works great as a cleansing or detoxifying regimen, but just because something works great as a temporary curative doesn't mean that continuing it is better. Antibiotics that knock out infection are great, but continuing to take them beyond the point of cure isn't healthy. Virtually all of the supposed animal-protein-induced toxicities are the result of factory farming. Grass-based changes everything.

Anyone wanting to invoke religious reasons for not eating animals should realize that Jesus certainly ate meat. So did Mohammed. So did Indians. I realize that in the Garden of Eden the lion didn't eat the lamb, but we haven't been in Eden for a long time. And it won't return because of our imposition; it will return only because outside spiritual forces intervene in our world.

I am all about caring for animals. On our farm, we do chores before we eat breakfast. Always. I would much rather deny myself rather than my animals. But that doesn't mean I worship them, or that they are human.

A chef was out one time to see the pigs and we walked up to the pig pasture. He had never seen live pigs before. His only acquaintance with pigs was pork. These pigs were scratching on trees, rooting in the dirt, lounging under bushes, nibbling at weeds and grass. He stood quietly for a while, mesmerized by the theater before him and the actors enjoying their parts. Finally he said, "I don't know anything about pigs. But I think if I were a pig, this is the way I'd like to live."

To me, that said it all. And that is the attitude we take toward the animals. I don't pay much attention to the folks who think children are dogs are rats are crickets. And I wish politicians wouldn't either. If our culture continues to destroy direct farmer-consumer local food commerce, people will continue to become more and more unreasonable in their thinking. Supposing themselves to become wise, they've become fools. And fools often pass laws.

That is one reason why we invite and encourage people to come out to our farm to visit, to touch, to see, to smell. Real husbandry on a real place in a real time helps to punch through the academic and theoretical disconnects pontificated by the radical animal welfare elite. I am native. That should not be illegal.

QUESTIONS

1. What is Salatin's case against vegetarianism?
2. What is Salatin saying about the connection between the thesis that abortion is permissible and the thesis that killing animals for food is not?
3. What is Salatin's environment-based case for the permissibility of free-range agriculture?
4. What is Salatin's animal-based case for the permissibility of free-range agriculture?
5. What is Salatin's human-health-based case for the permissibility of free-range agriculture?
6. What point is Salatin making with his claims that "humans are not animals" and that "animals don't sin"?
7. What is Salatin's case that hurting animals while raising them for food is not always permissible but killing them while raising them for food is always permissible?

ROGER SCRUTON

Eating Our Friends

In this selection, Roger Scruton makes several important contributions. Many of these stem from claims about the role of animals in our daily lives and duties that arise from that role. Our cows, like our dogs, and unlike the squirrels that live behind our houses, are members of our community. How does that affect our duties to them?

Scruton argues in resolutely non-utilitarian terms for the permissibility of free-range farming. His argument, though subtle, hinges on the unsubtle premise that death is not bad for animals.

After endorsing that killing free-range animals is permissible, Scruton gives an independent argument for the permissibility of eating animals, an argument that distinguishes animals coming from, say, Joel Salatin's Polyface Farm, on the one hand, and, on the other, chicken McNuggets.

. . . What are our obligations and do they permit us to eat animals?

If animals had rights then there would be absolute limits to the things that we could do to them. We could not, for example, kill them, breed them for our purposes, train them without their consent or take them into captivity. We certainly could not raise them for food, still less raise them in the kind of conditions that have become normal in the industrialized world. But the moral problem arises either because animals do not have rights, so that the principles that impede our invasions of other people do not serve to protect them, or because they have rights, but rights so differently ordered from those of humans, as to leave whole areas of human conduct towards them undetermined. I happen to think that the attribution of rights to animals is unhelpful, since it involves uprooting the concept of a right from the moral and legal practices that give it sense. . . . But, whether or not I am justified in that approach hardly matters. For the question concerns not *their rights* but *our duties*. And if I am right even the proponent of virtue ethics must recognize the concept of duty or obligation as an indispensable part of ethical thinking, with a logic that is not straightforwardly derivable from the concept of the good life.

Obligations make distinctions. They bind me to some things, and leave me free from others. For example, I have an obligation to my daughter, to see that she is properly fed and educated, which I do not have to your daughter. Kindness is not shown by ignoring that obligation in order to satisfy the need of some stranger. On the contrary, that would be a sign of callousness, an inability to respond to real and legitimate claims.

Some obligations are undertaken: as when we promise something. Others arise independently of our choice, like the obligations to parents, to country and to neighbours. Others still arise by an invisible hand, to use Adam Smith's expression, from behaviour that has no such intention. Obligations to animals are often like this. The person who enjoys eating meat

Roger Scruton, "Eating Our Friends," from *A Political Philosophy* (New York: Bloomsbury, 2007), 56–63.

is putting himself into relation with the creatures on his plate. He is doing something which creates an obligation that he must fulfil. It would be a mark of callousness to ignore this obligation, to behave with complete indifference towards the life and sufferings of the creatures that he eats. But what exactly *is* the obligation?

Animals bred or kept for our uses are not honorary members of the moral community, as pets or "companion animals" are. Nevertheless, the use that we make of them imposes a reciprocal duty to look after them, which spreads forward from the farmer to the slaughterer and from the slaughterer to the consumer, all of whom benefit from these animals, and all of whom must therefore assume some part of the duty of care. If these animals were moral beings then we could not, morally speaking, make use of them as we do—just as we cannot enslave human beings or breed them for food. And if the life of an animal bred for food were simply one long torment, the only relief from which is the final slaughter, we should certainly conclude the practice to be immoral. Utilitarians might disagree, since a utilitarian can justify any amount of suffering, provided the greater happiness is achieved by it. But that is one of the things that is wrong with utilitarianism. Moreover, until we have specified duties, moral judgement cannot begin, and duties cannot be assigned by the Greatest Happiness principle. Their ground lies in the past, not the future, and they cannot be overridden merely because some good can be achieved by disobeying them.

To criticize battery pig farming as violating a duty of care is surely right and proper. But the argument does nothing to condemn other livestock practices. There is surely scope, here, for some comparative judgements. Consider the traditional beef farmer, who fattens his calves for 30 months, keeping them on open pasture in the summer and in warm roomy barns in the winter, feeding them on grass, silage, beans and maize, attending to them in all their ailments, and sending them for slaughter, when the time comes, to the nearby slaughterhouse, where they are instantly despatched by a humane killer. Surely, such a farmer treats his cattle as well as cattle can be treated. Of course, he never asked them whether they wanted to live in his fields, or gave them the choice of lifestyle

during their time there. But that is because he knows—from instinct rather than from any philosophical theory—that cattle cannot make such choices, and do not exist at the level of consciousness for which freedom and the lack of it are genuine realities.

Animals raised for meat are, for the most part, gregarious, gentle and dependent. They are unhappy in isolation and emotionally dependent on the proximity of their kind. In the winter they must be sheltered; in the summer, if they are lucky, they are out to grass, or (in the case of the pig and the chicken) free to roam in a place where they can hunt for scraps of food. Human standards of hygiene are alien to their nature and their affections, unlike ours, are general and transferable, without tragic overtones. Such animals, tended in the traditional way, by a farmer who houses them together in the winter and allows them to roam in the summer, are as happy as their nature allows. Assuming that their needs are satisfied, only two questions arise in the farmer's mind, which is when and how they should be killed—for that they must be killed is evident, this being the reason why they live. Death is not merely a moral question. There is an economic aspect which no farmer—and no consumer—can afford to ignore. And I suspect that those who believe that it is immoral to raise animals for meat have in mind the moment of death and the economic calculation that prompts us to cut short a life in its prime.

Here the metaphysical distinction between humans and other animals once again comes to the fore. Human beings are conscious of their lives as their own; they have ambitions, hopes and aspirations; they are fatally attached to others, who cannot be replaced in their affections but whose presence they feel as a need. Hence there is a real distinction, for a human being, between timely and untimely death. To be 'cut short' before one's time is a waste—even a tragedy. We lament the death of children and young people not merely because we lament the death of anyone, but because we believe that human beings are fulfilled by their achievements and not merely by their comforts.

No such thoughts apply to domestic cattle. To be killed at 30 months is not intrinsically more tragic than to be killed at 40, 50 or 60. And if the meat is at its best after 30 months, and if every month thereafter represents an economic loss, who will blame the farmer for choosing so early a death? In so doing he merely reflects the choice of the consumer, upon whose desires the whole trade in meat, and therefore the very existence of his animals, depends.

But what about the manner of death? That it should be quick is not in dispute. Nevertheless, there is a distinction between sudden death and death preceded by terror, and to the conscientious farmer, who has looked after his animals from day to day, living with them and providing for their needs, this terror is not merely unwelcome but a betrayal of trust and a dagger of accusation. Livestock farmers, therefore, prefer to see their animals despatched suddenly and humanely in the place where they have lived, by skilled slaughterers who know how to kill an animal without awakening it from its soporific routine.

Livestock farming is not merely an industry—it is a relation, in which man and animal are bound together to their mutual profit, and in which a human duty of care is nourished by an animal's mute recognition of dependency. There is something consoling and heart-warming in the proximity of contented herbivores, in the rituals of feeding them, catching them, and coaxing them from field to field. This partly explains why people will continue in this time-consuming, exhausting and ill-paid occupation, resisting the attempts by bureaucrats and agribusinesses to drive them to extinction. Anybody who cares for animals ought to see this kind of husbandry as a complex moral good, to be defended on the one hand against those who would forbid the eating of meat altogether, and on the other hand against those carnivores who prefer the unseen suffering of the battery farm and the factory abattoir to the merest suggestion of a personal risk.

The life of the cattle farmer is not an easy life, nor is the relation between man and animal always as harmonious as it appears in the numerous children's books devoted to life on the farm. Nevertheless, as with all forms of husbandry, cattle farming should be seen in its full context—and that means, as a feature of the total ecology of the countryside. Traditional livestock farming involves the maintenance of pastureland, properly enclosed with walls or hedges. Wildlife habitats spring up as the near-automatic by-products of the boundaries and shady places required by cattle.

This kind of farming has shaped the English landscape, ensuring that it retains its dual character as producer of human food and complex wildlife habitat, with a beauty that is inextricably connected to its multifarious life. In this way, what is, from the point of view of agribusiness, an extremely wasteful use of land, becomes, from the point of view of the rest of us—both human and animal—one of the kindest uses of land yet devised.

I have abbreviated the story. But it could be expanded into a full vindication of livestock farming, as conferring benefits on all those, the animals included, who are part of it. When animals raised for their meat are properly looked after, when all duties of care are fulfilled, and when the demands of sympathy and piety are respected, the practice cannot be criticized except from a premise—the premise of animal rights—which I believe to be incoherent. Of course, the result of raising animals in this way will change the character of meat-eating, which will become not only more expensive, but more ceremonial—as it was before the battery farm. The animal brought to the table will have enjoyed the friendship and protection of the one who nurtured him, and his death will be like the ritual sacrifices described in the Bible and Homeric literature—a *singling out* of a victim, for an important office to which a kind of honour is attached.

Such it seems to me would be the life of the virtuous carnivore, the one who is prepared to eat only his friends. The real force of the vegetarian argument stems, I believe, from a revulsion at the vicious carnivore: the meat-eating character as this has evolved in these days of gluttony and indulgence. And it is entirely true that the indifference of modern carnivores to the methods used to reduce the cost of their habit is a morally repulsive characteristic against which it is wholly natural to rebel. The repulsiveness is enhanced by the solipsistic fast-food culture, and by the removal of food from its central place in domestic life and in the winning of friends. From Homer to Zola meat has been described as the focus of hospitality, the primordial gift to the stranger, the eruption into the world of human conflict of the divine spirit of peace. Take all that away, reduce meat to an object of solitary greed like chocolate, and the question naturally arises: why should *life* be sacrificed, just for this?

As I indicated, this question has a religious dimension. From the point of view of morality it has a clear and rational answer: namely, that the life that is sacrificed would not exist, but for the sacrifice. A great number of animals owe their lives to our intention to eat them. And their lives are (or can easily be made to be) comfortable and satisfying in the way that few lives led in the wild could possibly be. If we value animal life and animal comfort, therefore, we should endorse our carnivorous habits, provided it really is *life,* and not living death, on which those habits feed. From the point of view of religion, however, the question presents a challenge. It is asking the burger-stuffer to *come clean*; to show just why it is that his greed should be indulged in this way, and just where he fits into the scheme of things, that he can presume to kill again and again for the sake of a solitary pleasure that creates and sustains no moral ties. To such a question it is always possible to respond with a shrug of the shoulders. But it is a real question, one of many that people now ask, as the old forms of piety dwindle. Piety is the remedy for religious guilt, and to this emotion we are all witting or unwitting heirs. And I suspect that people become vegetarians for precisely that reason: that by doing so they overcome the residue of guilt that attaches to every form of hubris, and in particular to the hubris of human freedom.

I believe, however, that there is another remedy, and one more in keeping with the Judaeo-Christian tradition. We should not abandon our meat-eating habits, but *remoralize* them, by incorporating them into affectionate human relations, and using them in the true Homeric manner, as instruments of hospitality, conviviality and peace. That was the remedy practised by our parents, with their traditional "Sunday roast" coming always at midday, after they had given thanks. The lifestyle associated with the Sunday roast involves sacrifices that those brought up on fast food are unused to making—mealtimes, manners, dinner-table conversation and the art of cookery itself. But all those things form part of a complex human good, and I cannot help thinking that, when added to the ecological benefits of small-scale livestock farming, they secure for us an honourable place in the scheme of things, and neutralize more effectively than the vegetarian alternative, our inherited burden of guilt.

Furthermore, I would suggest not only that it is permissible for those who care about animals to eat meat; they have a duty to do so. If meat-eating should ever become confined to those who do not care about animal suffering then compassionate farming would cease. All animals would be kept in battery conditions and the righteous vegetarians would exert no economic pressure on farmers to change their ways. Where there are conscientious carnivores, however, there is a motive to raise animals kindly. And conscientious carnivores can show their depraved contemporaries that it is possible to ease one's conscience by spending more on one's meat. Bit by bit the news would get around, that there is a right and a wrong way to eat; and—failing some *coup d'état* by censorious vegetarians—the process would be set in motion, that would bring battery farming to an end. Duty requires us, therefore, to eat our friends.

QUESTIONS

1. What's the argument of the last paragraph? Previously, Scruton's argument had seemed to be for the conclusion that free-range agriculture is *permissible*. Then, in the last paragraph, Scruton reveals that he holds that free-range agriculture is the morally *required* agricultural system (and that eating free-range animals is, for some of us, required)—why?

2. What is Scruton's argument that battery farming—industrial farming—is wrong?

3. Unlike most authors on animals and food, Scruton includes an argument about the permissibility of *killing* animals and another, separate one about the permissibility of *eating* them. What are they? How do they differ from each other?

4. Does Scruton's argument about how the "reason why [animals] live is to be food" support the permissibility of killing animals by, say, hunting them?

5. Scruton makes a "metaphysical distinction" between humans and other animals. What is it? Why does it matter, according to Scruton, to whether it is permissible to kill humans? Are severely mentally handicapped people on the human side of the distinction? What might Scruton's view about free-range farming the severely mentally handicapped be?

ELIZABETH HARMAN

The Moral Significance of Animal Pain and Animal Death

In this selection, Harman argues against a common defense of free-range farming, one voiced in the readings from Scruton and Salatin readings. The defense holds that though there is something seriously wrong with hurting animals—that is why industrial animal farming is wrong—there is nothing seriously wrong with killing animals. Since, the defense goes, free-range farming involves killing but no hurting, it is not seriously wrong. In fact, it is permissible.

Harman argues that *if* hurting animals is seriously wrong, then killing them is seriously wrong, too. So, she argues, if Scruton and Salatin are right that industrial animal farming is wrong because it hurts animals, they should hold that free-range farming is wrong, too.

ABSTRACT

This article addresses the question: "What follows from the claim that we have a certain kind of strong reason against animal cruelty?" It deals with the ethics of killing animals. It finds the following common assumption highly puzzling and problematic: despite our obligations not to commit animal cruelty, there is no comparably strong reason against painlessly killing

Elizabeth Harman, "The Moral Significance of Animal Pain and Animal Death," from *The Oxford Handbook of Animal Ethics,* eds. Beauchamp and Frey (2011). Reprinted by permission of Oxford University Press.

animals in the prime of life. It argues that anyone who accepts this view is committed to the moral position that either we have no reasons against such killings or we have only weak reasons.

ANIMAL CRUELTY
AND ANIMAL KILLING

In this paper, I will be concerned with this question: what follows from the claim that we have a certain kind of *strong* reason against animal cruelty? In particular, what follows for the ethics of killing animals? My discussion will be focused on examination of a view that I take some people to hold, though I find it deeply puzzling. The view is that although we have strong reasons against animal cruelty, we lack strong reasons against painlessly killing animals in the prime of life; on this view, either we have no reasons against such killings, or we have only weak reasons. My attention will be focused on animals of intermediate mental sophistication, including dogs, cats, cows, and pigs, while excluding more mentally sophisticated animals such as humans and apes, and excluding less mentally sophisticated creatures such as fish and insects. Whether any of what I say also applies to the animals I am excluding is a topic for further work.

I am interested in the claim that we have a certain kind of *strong* reason against animal cruelty. As will emerge, I take our reasons against animal cruelty to be strong in several ways. One way they are strong is the following: if an action would cause significant suffering to an animal, then that action is *pro tanto* wrong; that is, the action is wrong unless justified by other considerations. Such a view of animal cruelty is part of a more general non-consequentialist view on which there is a moral asymmetry between causing *harm* and causing *positive benefit*: our reasons against harming are stronger and of a different type than our reasons in favor of benefiting (and our reasons against preventing benefits).

Here is the claim that I take to be believed by some people, and which I plan to examine:
The Surprising Claim:

> (a) we have strong reasons not to cause intense pain to animals: the fact that an action would cause intense pain to an animal makes the action wrong unless it is justified by other considerations; and

> (b) we do not have strong reasons not to kill animals: it is not the case that killing an animal is wrong unless it is justified by other considerations.

The Surprising Claim seems to lie behind the following common belief:

> While there is something deeply morally wrong with factory farming, there is nothing morally wrong with "humane" farms on which the animals are happy until they are killed.

Some people think that factory farming is morally wrong, and that it is morally wrong to financially support factory farming, because factory farming involves subjecting animals to intense suffering. By contrast, "humane" farms do not subject animals to suffering, but they do kill animals in the prime of life. Some people who believe factory farming is morally wrong also believe that this "humane" farming is morally permissible. They appear to believe that while we have strong moral reasons not to cause animals pain, we lack strong moral reasons against killing animals in the prime of life.[1]

I find the Surprising Claim puzzling. My goal in this paper is to examine the Surprising Claim. I will ask: how could the Surprising Claim be true? In section 2, I will argue that the Surprising Claim is not true. I will then consider four views on which the Surprising Claim is true; each view rejects one of the claims made in my argument of section 2. I will ask what can be said in favor of each view, and whether any of these views is true. I will argue that each view is false. The fourth view I will consider is Jeff McMahan's time-relative interests view; one of my conclusions will thus be that this well-known view is false. Finally, I will draw some lessons about the relationship between the significance of animal pain and the significance of animal death.

AN ARGUMENT AGAINST THE SURPRISING CLAIM

In this section, I will argue that the Surprising Claim is false.

The Surprising Claim:

(a) we have strong reasons not to cause intense pain to animals: the fact that an action would cause intense pain to an animal makes the action wrong unless it is justified by other considerations; and (b) we do not have strong reasons not to kill animals: it is not the case that killing an animal is wrong unless it is justified by other considerations.

Consider part (a) of the Surprising Claim. If (a) is true, what explains its truth? It seems that it must be true because animals have moral status, and because any action that significantly harms something with moral status is impermissible unless justified by other considerations.

Here is an argument that the Surprising Claim is false:

1. If it is true that we have strong moral reasons against causing intense pain to animals, such that doing so is impermissible unless justified by other considerations, then part of the explanation of this truth is that animals have moral status.
2. If it is true that we have strong moral reasons against causing intense pain to animals, such that doing so is impermissible unless justified by other considerations, then part of the explanation of this truth is that significantly harming something with moral status is impermissible unless justified by other considerations.
3. If an action painlessly kills a healthy animal in the prime of life, then that action significantly harms the animal.
4. If it is true that we have strong moral reasons against causing intense pain to animals, such that doing so is impermissible unless justified by other considerations, then painlessly killing a healthy animal in the prime of life is

impermissible unless justified by other considerations (1, 2, 3).
5. Therefore, the Surprising Claim is false (4).

I endorse this argument. I think it gives the right account of why the Surprising Claim is false. In the next three sections, I will discuss four views on which the Surprising Claim is true; those views reject this argument.

FIRST VIEW: KILLING AN ANIMAL DOES NOT HARM IT

Consider this view:

First View: An action that painlessly kills an animal in the prime of life deprives the animal of future life, which would be a positive benefit to the animal, but does not harm the animal.

According to the First View, death is *bad for* animals, but a proponent of the First View would point out that there are two ways that events can be bad for a being: an event can be or lead to something that is in itself bad for the being, such as suffering, or an event can be a deprivation of something that would have been in itself good for the being. A being is *harmed* when it undergoes something that is in itself bad, but a being is not typically harmed when it is merely prevented from something good.

According to the First View, claim 3 is false: while death is bad for animals in that it deprives them of futures that would be good for them, it does not harm them because it does not involve anything that is in itself bad for them, such as pain. A proponent of the First View would grant that claim 1 is true: animals have moral status. A proponent of the First View would also grant that claim 2 is true, but only if we have a suitably narrow understanding of what *harming* involves. In particular, a proponent of the First View would deny that claim 2 is true if "harming" is understood so broadly as to encompass all cases of failing to positively benefit, and all cases of preventing positive benefits.

A proponent of the First View would be *correct* in asserting that claim 2 is true only on a suitably narrow understanding of "harming"; indeed, that is the reading I intend in stating the claim and the understanding of "harming" I will use throughout the paper. There are many cases of failing to positively benefit people, or of preventing positive benefits to people, that do not generate strong reasons—there are many such cases in which it is false that the behavior is wrong unless justified by other considerations. For example, if I decide, on a lark, to give a particular acquaintance $200 and write her a check, but then I rip up the check, then my action prevents positive benefit to her but it is not the case that my action is wrong unless justified by other considerations; my action requires no justification.

Painless animal death involves no *bad experiences*. Rather, it involves failing to have future life. When death is bad for some being, typically that is because it is deprived of a future that would be good; so the badness of death consists in the failure to have some *good experiences* (and, for persons, the failure to have other things that make life meaningful and valuable). But suffering death then looks like it constitutes experiencing a failure to get a benefit *rather than* a harm. A proponent of the First View would say that this shows that in killing something, one is not *harming* it, but merely depriving it of a positive benefit.

The First View is false because, while it is typically the case that when a being fails to get a benefit, the being is not harmed, nevertheless some actions that deprive a being of a benefit do thereby harm the being. If someone deafens you (causes you to become permanently deaf), she simply deprives you of the benefit of hearing, but she thereby harms you. If someone steals your money, she simply deprives you of the benefit the money would have provided, but she thereby harms you.[2]

In particular, actively and physically interfering with a person in such a way that she is deprived of a benefit does typically harm that person. And if this is true of persons, it should also be true of animals. But killing an animal does actively, physically interfere with the animal in such a way that the animal is deprived of a benefit. So killing an animal is harming that animal.[3]

SECOND AND THIRD VIEWS: DEATH IS NOT BAD FOR ANIMALS BECAUSE ANIMALS LACK SUFFICIENT PSYCHOLOGICAL CONNECTION WITH THEIR FUTURES

In this section, I will consider two more views on which the Surprising Claim is true. Both views are more specific elaborations of the following basic idea:

> When a person dies, she *loses out* on the future she would have had. She had expectations, hopes, plans, and dreams that are thwarted. Animals, however, do not *lose out* on their futures. They do not have the right kind of psychological connection to their future lives to be losing out on them.

Here is one way of making this basic idea more precise. It is an argument that would be offered by someone who endorses the Second View:

(i) The death of a person is bad for her only because it frustrates her desires and plans for the future.
(ii) Therefore, death is bad in general only because it frustrates desires and plans.
(iii) Animals do not have desires and plans for the future.
(iv) Therefore, animals' deaths are not bad for them.

The Second View is more radical than the First View. The First View granted that death is bad for animals but denied that animals are harmed by being killed. The Second View denies that death is bad for animals at all. It follows that animals are not harmed by death, and that claim 3 is false.

The Second View is false because its claim (i) is false. It is true that *one way* death is bad for most persons is that it frustrates their desires and plans for the future. But a person might not have any desires and plans for the future, yet her death could still be bad for her. Consider someone who is depressed and wants to die; she is so depressed that she lacks any desires about the future and has no plans for the future. Suppose she in fact would recover from her depression and have a good future if she continued to live (because her family is about to intervene and get her treatment). If she dies now, then death deprives her of a good future and is bad for her. But death does not frustrate her desires and plans. In a more far-fetched example, consider someone who *truly* lives in the moment. She enjoys life but has absolutely no expectations or desires about the future, and no plans for the future. If she dies now, her death is bad for her, although it frustrates no desires or plans.

Just as a person's death may be bad for her because she is losing out on a future life that would be good for her (even if she lacks desires and plans for the future), similarly an animal's death may be bad for it because the animal loses out on a future life that would be good for it, even if the animal lacks desires and plans for the future. This is why the Second View is false.

While the Second View is committed to claim (i), which is too strong, there is another way to make out the basic idea I outlined at the beginning of this section:

> Third View: It is true that animal pain matters morally. But it is a mistake to conclude that this is because *animals* have moral status. Rather, animals lack moral status. But *stages* of animals have moral status. Animal pain matters morally because an animal stage is in pain. What is better or worse for the *animal* does not matter morally, though what is better or worse for stages of it does.

The Third View assumes a certain metaphysical picture. It assumes that there are entities called "animal stages" that are temporal stages of animals; these animal stages exist briefly. An animal's life is made up of the existence of many animal stages in a series. An animal is a mereological sum of many animal stages.[4]

According to the Third View, claim 1 is false. While animal pain matters morally, it does not matter because *animals* have moral status. Rather, only *animal stages* have moral status. The Third View grants that claim 2 is true: if an action would harm something with moral status, then that action is wrong unless other considerations justify it. In this view, while animals are harmed by being killed, there is not thereby any reason against killing animals, because animals lack moral status.

Animal stages have moral status, which is why we have reasons against causing animals to suffer; but animal stages are not harmed when animals are killed.

The Third View makes a number of seemingly counterintuitive claims. Some of these claims may seem false, though they are in fact true. For example, the Third View implies these two claims:

(v) There are some things that can be harmed but that lack moral status.

(vi) There are some things that lack moral status although they are entirely made up of stages that have moral status.

The Third View implies claim (v) because it holds that animals can be harmed but that animals lack moral status. The Third View implies claim (vi) because it holds that animals are entirely made up of animal stages, yet animals lack moral status.

It might seem that anything that can be harmed has moral status. Indeed, some philosophers write as though this is the case.[5] However, plants can be harmed, but plants lack moral status: the mere fact that an action would harm a plant does not provide a reason against the action. For example, suppose that I place a picnic table in my backyard, depriving a dandelion growing there of light. I harm the dandelion, but there is not thereby any reason against my action. (Our reasons to take care of the environment stem from our reasons to treat persons and animals well, but not from the moral status of plants.)[6]

It might seem that if something is entirely made up of stages that *have* moral status, then it too must have moral status. To see that this is false, let us consider some unusual entities that are made up of persons. One such entity is Longy: Longy is the mereological sum of several non-temporally-overlapping persons, including me. Suppose that Frank punches me. Frank harms me, and I have moral status; this is what makes it wrong of Frank to punch me (absent justification). When he punches me, Frank also harms Longy. It might seem fine to grant that Longy too has moral status. But this would be a mistake: entities like Longy do not have moral status.

Another example will enable us to see that entities like Longy do not have moral status. Suppose Bill is considering whether to do something that would cause major injury to you but would prevent worse injury to someone one hundred years from now; call her Gertrude. Bill justifies his action by saying, "Consider Thingy, which consists of the mereological sum of you and Gertrude. The action I am considering would hurt Thingy, but only in order to prevent worse injury to Thingy." This justification fails, and it fails because while Thingy lacks moral status, *you* have moral status.[7]

So, while the Third View is committed to claims (v) and (vi), which may appear to be false, those claims are true, so they are no problem for the Third View.

I will raise a different objection to the Third View, which comes out of what we have just been considering.

Consider a young cat that could lead a long, happy life if it is given serious surgery that would cause it quite a bit of pain (even with painkillers) for a few days, followed by a month of serious discomfort. Otherwise the cat will die within a few days, without experiencing much discomfort. In this case, it is permissible to do the surgery. My objection to the Third View is that the Third View cannot explain *why* it is permissible to do the surgery. It is not in general permissible to cause serious pain and injury to one morally significant entity in order to benefit others, but according to the Third View, that is what one would be doing. One would be causing pain and suffering to one animal stage, a morally significant entity, in order to benefit several different animal stages, other morally significant entities. (Note that I am denying that it is permissible to cause serious pain and injury to one in order to provide *positive benefits* to other morally significant entities; we sometimes use the word "benefit" to refer to the *prevention of pain or harm,* but that is not what is at issue in this case, because according to the Third View, no animal stage is harmed when an animal dies.)

Even more seriously, according to the Third View, what one would be doing in this case is causing serious pain and injury to one morally significant entity in order to cause there to be created some further morally significant entities who are happy but who otherwise would not exist at all. Doing that kind of thing is even more morally problematic than causing suffering to one being in order to benefit another who independently exists. (When the benefit is to an independently existing being, then one consideration in

favor of causing the suffering is that otherwise there will be some beings who lose out on some benefits; but when the benefit would be to some beings who would not otherwise exist, then if one does not cause the suffering, it is not the case that there are some entities that lose out on some benefits they could have had.[8])[9]

The surgery on the cat is permissible. To account for the permissibility of the surgery, we need both these claims:

• While the action harms an entity that has moral status, it also benefits that entity.
• It is not the case that the action harms an entity that has moral status but the action does not also benefit that entity.

Thus, we need both of these claims:

• Animals have moral status.
• Animal stages lack moral status.

The fact that animals have moral status provides a justification for the surgery: while it harms the cat, a morally significant being, it also provides benefits to *that very being.* If animal stages had moral status, the surgery would be impermissible, because it would involve harming one morally significant entity—the stage of the cat during the recovery—in order to provide benefits that are not to that same entity, but to a different entity.

Because the surgery on the cat is permissible, the Third View must be false.

FOURTH VIEW: MCMAHAN'S TIME-RELATIVE INTERESTS VIEW

In this section, I will discuss a fourth view on which the Surprising Claim is true. Like the First View, the Fourth View grants that we have *some reasons* against killing animals; the Fourth View denies that these reasons are *strong.*

My discussion of the more extreme Third View will enable us to see why the less extreme Fourth View is also false.

The Fourth View is a view of Jeff McMahan's. He calls it the "time-relative interests view."[10] On this view, the badness of death for a morally significant being is not a direct function of what the being loses out on in dying; the badness of death is not simply a matter of how good the lost life would have been. Rather, it also matters what the being's *psychological relationship* is with that potential future life. If a being is such that, were it to continue to live, there would be only weak psychological connections between its current stage and its future life, then the goodness of that future is *less of a loss* for it than if the being would have stronger psychological connections with its future life: the being currently has less of an interest in continuing to live than if the psychological connection he would have to a future life would be stronger. This view has the virtue that it can explain why, as is plausible, the death of a ten year old is worse for the ten year old than the death of a one month old is bad for the one month old: while the infant loses out on more life, so loses more, the ten year old would have much greater psychological connections with its future if it continued to live. According to the time-relative interests view, the one month old has a weaker interest in continuing to live than the ten year old has.

The implications of the time-relative interests view for animal death are that animal death is not very bad for animals because animals do not have very strong psychological connections to their future selves: they do not have *strong interests* in continuing to live. But the view does not hold (nor is it plausible) that animals lack *any* psychological connections to their future selves; so the view does not hold that animal death is not bad for animals, nor that we have no reasons against killing animals. The view grants that animals have *some interest* in continuing to live.[11] The view supports the following claim:

> We have strong reasons against causing animal pain, and we have some reasons against painlessly killing animals in the prime of life, but these reasons are weakened by animals' lack of deep psychological continuity over time.

(Note that I stipulated at the beginning of the paper that I am only concerned with animals of intermediate mental sophistication, including dogs, cats, cows, and pigs, and excluding humans, apes, fish, and insects. My claims about the time-relative

interests view's implications regarding animals are restricted to these animals of intermediate mental sophistication.)

The Fourth View can grant claims 1 and 2 of the argument of section 2. But the Fourth View denies claim 3: it holds that, while death is a harm to animals, it is a minor harm. On this view, killing an animal does not *significantly* harm the animal, and it is not the case that killing an animal is wrong unless justified by other considerations.

I will now argue that the time-relative interests view is false, for reasons similar to the reasons the Third View is false. My argument relies on some substantive claims about the nature of the psychological connections that animals have over time, and the way the time-relative interests view would handle these connections.[12] In particular, I assume that on the time-relative interests view, an animal now has greater psychological connection to its nearer future life than to its farther future life, and that an animal now has negligible psychological connection to its future life a sufficient amount of time into the future, such as five years into the future. It follows from this that, on the time-relative interests view, while it is currently in an animal's interest to continue to live for the next several months (at least), an animal currently lacks any interest in being alive five years from now, currently lacks any interest in having particular good experiences five years from now, and currently lacks any interest in avoiding particular bad experiences five years from now—any experiences it would have five years from now are so psychologically remote that the animal currently has no interests regarding those experiences.

My objection relies on two cases.

> Billy is a cow with a serious illness. If the illness is not treated now and is allowed to run its course, then Billy will begin to suffer mildly very soon, the suffering will get steadily worse, Billy will be in agony for a few months, and then Billy will die. If the illness is treated now, Billy will undergo surgery under anesthetic tomorrow. Billy will suffer more severely over the next two weeks (from his recovery) than he would have from the illness during that time, but then he will be discomfort-free and he will never suffer agony; he will be healthy and able to live a normal life.

It is permissible to do the surgery on Billy. This is permissible because, while the surgery will cause

Billy to suffer, which he now has an interest in avoiding, it will prevent worse suffering to Billy, which he also now has an interest in avoiding.

> Tommy is a horse with a serious illness. If the illness is not treated now and is allowed to run its course, Tommy will live an ordinary discomfort-free life for five years, but then Tommy will suffer horribly for several months and then die. If the illness is treated now, then Tommy will undergo surgery under anesthetic tomorrow. Tommy will suffer over the following two weeks, but not nearly as severely as he would five years from now. Tommy will be completely cured and will be able to live a healthy normal life for another fifteen years.

It is permissible to do the surgery on Tommy. This is in fact permissible because Tommy has an interest in getting to live a full life, and though he has an interest in avoiding the pain of recovery from surgery, it is overall in his interests to have the surgery.

But the time-relative interests view cannot explain why it is permissible to do the operation on Tommy. On that view, Tommy has a reasonably strong interest in avoiding pain in the immediate future; he has no interest in avoiding suffering five years from now or in avoiding death five years from now. While the time-relative interests view can easily account for the permissibility of the surgery on Billy, it cannot account for the permissibility of the surgery on Tommy.

Because the time-relative interests view cannot accommodate the truth that it is permissible to do the surgery on Tommy, and the truth that the two surgeries on Tommy and Billy are permissible for the same basic reasons, the time-relative interests view must be false.

CONCLUSION

What lessons have emerged from our examination of the Surprising Claim and the four views? The basic lesson is that if we have strong moral reasons not to cause animal pain, we must also have strong moral reasons not to kill animals, even painlessly. In section 2, I argued that this is true. I have considered four ways one might reject this argument and argued that each one fails.

The background picture I have been assuming is one on which our reasons against causing harm to animals are strong in two ways: these reasons are strong in that an action that would significantly harm is *wrong* unless other considerations justify it; furthermore, I have assumed that, just as the harming of persons cannot typically be justified by benefits to *other* persons, similarly the harming of animals cannot typically be justified by benefits to other beings. I have also assumed that harm to an animal can be justified by the prevention of greater harm and/or of death for that very animal, just as is true for persons.

One might try to develop a view on which the kinds of agent-relative constraints that apply to persons do not apply to animals or animal stages. On such a view, it would be permissible to harm one animal or animal stage in order to provide positive benefits to a distinct entity. If this view is correct, then my objections to the Third View are wrong-headed: the Third View can hold that the cat surgery is permissible. However, a view like this sees our reasons against causing suffering to animals as *much weaker* than I have been taking them to be, and as very different in kind from our reasons against harming persons. The lesson appears to be that it is possible to hold that we have reasons against causing animal pain, while lacking reasons against killing animals, but at the cost of holding that our reasons against causing animal pain are weak reasons.

NOTES

1. Someone might believe we should *support* "humane" farming because it is so much morally *better* than factory farming, without believing "humane" farming is morally unproblematic; this person need not believe the Surprising Claim.

2. One might object that by stealing your money, the thief violates a right of yours but does not harm you. The more general point I want to make about this case is that sometimes an action has a *strong* reason against it, such that the action is impermissible unless it is justified by other considerations, although the action is simply the deprivation of positive benefit. Stealing is one example. Killing is, I claim, another.

3. I discuss the asymmetry between harming and benefiting, and what harm is, in my "Can We Harm and Benefit in Creating?" *Philosophical Perspectives* 18 (2004): 89–113, and my "Harming as Causing Harm," in *Harming Future Persons: Ethics, Genetics and the Nonidentity Problem,* ed. Melinda Roberts and David Wasserman (Dordrecht and London: Springer, 2009), pp. 137–54. In those papers, I claim that killing and deafening are harming, and also that if a being dies or is deaf, then the being suffers a harm. Here I make only the former claim. Here I claim that killing or deafening a being is harming that being; I don't take a stand on whether if a being dies or is deaf, then the being suffers a harm.

4. I am using the term "temporal stages" for what are also often called "temporal parts." See "Temporal Parts" by Katherine Hawley in *The Stanford Encyclopedia of Philosophy,* ed. Edward N. Zalta (Spring 2009), available at http://plato.stanford.edu/entries/temporal-parts/ (accessed 7/31/10).

5. See Bonnie Steinbock, *Life Before Birth: The Moral and Legal Status of Embryos and Fetuses* (New York: Oxford University Press, 1992), and Joel Feinberg, "The Rights of Animals and Unborn Generations," in *Philosophy and Environmental Crisis,* ed. William T. Blackstone (Athens: University of Georgia Press, 1974), pp. 43–63.

6. I argue that some things can be harmed although they lack moral status in my "The Potentiality Problem," *Philosophical Studies* 114 (2003): 173–98.

7. One might think that entities like Longy and Thingy must not have moral status for a different reason: that they would generate *double-counting* of moral reasons. For example, if Frank punches me, if Longy and I both have moral status, then it seems there are thereby *two* moral reasons against his action: that he harms me, and that he harms Longy. But it is not the case that these are distinct moral reasons. I do not think that this is a successful objection to the claim that entities like Longy and Things have moral status. If one claims that they have moral status, one can also claim that mereologically overlapping entities do not generate distinct moral reasons. See footnote 21 of my "The Potentiality Problem."

8. I discuss differences in our reasons regarding beings whose existence is affected by our actions, and our reasons regarding independently existing beings, in my "Harming as Causing Harm," in *Harming Future Persons: Ethics, Genetics and the Nonidentity Problem,* ed. Melinda Roberts and David Wasserman (Dordrecht and London: Springer, 2009), pp. 137–54.

9. As I have articulated it, the Third View denies that any animal stage with moral status loses out when an animal dies. One might ask how long animal stages exist for, and what makes two distinct animal stages distinct. These are details that would have to be worked out by anyone who endorsed the Third View.

10. McMahan, *The Ethics of Killing: Problems at the Margins of Life* (New York: Oxford University Press, 2002).

11. Note that what a being "has an interest in" is a matter of what is *in the being's interests,* not a matter of what the being desires or wants.

12. I am also assuming that the time-relative interests view sees the badness of the death of animals as sufficiently diminished that it does not count as the kind of significant harm that is pro tanto wrong to cause.

REFERENCES

Feinberg, Joel. "The Rights of Animals and Unborn Generations." In *Philosophy and Environmental Crisis,* edited by William T. Blackstone, 43–63. Athens: University of Georgia Press, 1974.

Harman, Elizabeth. "Can We Harm and Benefit in Creating?" *Philosophical Perspectives* 18 (2004): 89–113.

———. "Harming as Causing Harm." In *Harming Future Persons: Ethics, Genetics and the Nonidentity Problem,* edited by Melinda Roberts and David Wasserman, 137–54. Dordrecht and London: Springer, 2009.

———. "The Potentiality Problem." *Philosophical Studies* 114 (2003): 173–98.

Hawley, Katherine. "Temporal Parts." In *The Stanford Encyclopedia of Philosophy,* edited by Edward N. Zalta (Spring 2009), available at http://plato.stanford.edu/entries/temporal-parts/.

McMahan, Jeff. *The Ethics of Killing: Problems at the Margins of Life.* New York: Oxford University Press, 2002.

Steinbock, Bonnie. *Life Before Birth: The Moral and Legal Status of Embryos and Fetuses.* New York: Oxford University Press, 1992.

QUESTIONS

1. In your own words, explain what the Surprising Claim is and what Harman's argument against it is.
2. What point is Harman making with the example of giving your pet a painful medical procedure?

3. What is the view Harman attributes to McMahan? How does that view compare with the view Scruton endorses? What is Harman's objection to McMahan's view?

4. On which moral points do Harman and Salatin agree? Disagree? On which points does she agree or disagree with Scruton?

CAROL KAESUK YOON

No Face, but Plants Like Life Too

Yoon raises a common objection to vegan agriculture and defense of killing animals for food: If it is wrong to kill animals, it is also wrong to kill plants. It isn't wrong to kill plants. Hence, it isn't wrong to kill animals.

Yoon's view seems to be something like: If it is wrong to kill pigs for food, it is wrong to kill pig*weed* for food. People who aren't ethical vegetarians often take this position and find it *very* compelling. People who are ethical vegetarians are often confronted with this position and find it *very* far from compelling. What, if anything, is each side missing?

At any rate, Yoon describes her journey from omnivore to vegetarian and back, but the real interest of the article is the paragraphs about whether plants feel pain and, if so, how we would assess this. When thinking about this, it is worth noting that the sphere of creatures we think experience pain has steadily *in*creased. We thought cats were insensate and were wrong about that. We thought all fish were insensate and were wrong about that. Are plants next on the list of living things we are wrong about?

Several years ago, after having to drive for too long behind a truck full of stinking, squealing pigs being delivered for slaughter, I gave up eating meat. I'd been harboring a growing distaste for the ugliness that can be industrial agriculture, but the real issue was a long-suppressed sympathy for its—or really, my—victims. Even screaming, reeking pigs, or maybe especially screaming, reeking pigs, can evoke stark pity as they tumble along in a truck to their deaths.

If you think about it, and it's much simpler not to, it can be hard to justify other beings suffering pain, fear and death so that we can enjoy their flesh. In particular, given our many connections to animals, not least of all the fact that we are ourselves animals,

Carol Kaesuk Yoon, "No Face, but Plants Like Life Too," in *The New York Times* (March 14, 2011). http://www.nytimes.com/2011/03/15/science/15food.html

it can give a person pause to realize that our most frequent contact with these kin might just be the devouring of them.

My entry into what seemed the moral high ground, though, was surprisingly unpleasant. I felt embattled not only by a bizarrely intense lust for chicken but nightmares in which I would be eating a gorgeous, rare steak—I could distinctly taste the savory drippings—from which I awoke in a panic, until I realized that I had been carnivorous only in my imagination.

Temptations and trials were everywhere. The most surprising turned out to be the realization that I couldn't actually explain to myself or anyone else why killing an animal was any worse than killing the many plants I was now eating.

Surely, I'd thought, science can defend the obvious, that slaughterhouse carnage is wrong in a way that harvesting a field of lettuces or, say, mowing the lawn is not. But instead, it began to seem that formulating a truly rational rationale for not eating animals, at least while consuming all sorts of other organisms, was difficult, maybe even impossible.

Before you hit "send" on your hate mail, let me say this. Different people have different reasons for the choices they make about what to kill or have killed for them to eat. Perhaps there isn't any choice more personal or less subject to rationality or the judgment of others. It's just that as far as I was concerned, if eating a tofu dog was as much a crime against life as eating bratwurst, then pass the bratwurst, please.

So what really are the differences between animals and plants? There are plenty. The cells of plants, and not animals, for example, harbor chloroplasts, tiny green organelles that can turn the energy of light into sugar. Almost none of these differences, however, seem to matter to any of us trying to figure out what to eat.

The differences that do seem to matter are things like the fact that plants don't have nerves or brains. They cannot, we therefore conclude, feel pain. In other words, the differences that matter are those that prove that plants do not suffer as we do. Here the lack of a face on plants becomes important, too, faces being requisite to humans as proof not only that one is dealing with an actual individual being, but that it is an individual capable of suffering.

Animals, on the other hand—and not just close evolutionary relations like chimps and gorillas, but species further afield, mammals like cows and pigs—can experience what pretty much anyone would agree is pain and suffering. If attacked, these animals will look agonized, scream, struggle and run as fast as they can. Obviously, if we don't kill any of these animals to eat them, all that suffering is avoided.

Meanwhile, whether you pluck a leaf or slice a trunk, a plant neither grimaces nor cries out. Plants don't seem to mind being killed, at least as far as we can see. But that may be exactly the difficulty.

Unlike a lowing, running cow, a plant's reactions to attack are much harder for us to detect. But just like a chicken running around without its head, the body of a corn plant torn from the soil or sliced into pieces struggles to save itself, just as vigorously and just as uselessly, if much less obviously to the human ear and eye.

When a plant is wounded, its body immediately kicks into protection mode. It releases a bouquet of volatile chemicals, which in some cases have been shown to induce neighboring plants to pre-emptively step up their own chemical defenses and in other cases to lure in predators of the beasts that may be causing the damage to the plants. Inside the plant, repair systems are engaged and defenses are mounted, the molecular details of which scientists are still working out, but which involve signaling molecules coursing through the body to rally the cellular troops, even the enlisting of the genome itself, which begins churning out defense-related proteins.

Plants don't just react to attacks, though. They stand forever at the ready. Witness the endless thorns, stinging hairs and deadly poisons with which they are armed. If all this effort doesn't look like an organism trying to survive, then I'm not sure what would. Plants are not the inert pantries of sustenance we might wish them to be.

If a plant's myriad efforts to keep from being eaten aren't enough to stop you from heedlessly laying into that quinoa salad, then maybe knowing that plants can do any number of things that we typically think of as animal-like would. They move, for one thing, carrying out activities that could only be called behaving, if at a pace visible only via time-lapse photography.

Not too long ago, scientists even reported evidence that plants could detect and grow differently depending on whether they were in the presence of close relatives, a level of behavioral sophistication most animals have not yet been found to show.

To make matters more confusing, animals are not always the deep wells of sensitivity that we might imagine. Sponges are animals, but like plants they lack nerves or a brain. Jellyfish, meanwhile, which can be really tasty when cut into julienne and pickled, have no brains, only a simple net of nerves, arguably a less sophisticated setup than the signaling systems coordinating the lives of many plants. How do we decide how much sensitivity and what sort matters?

For those hoping to escape these quandaries with an all-mushroom diet, forget it. In nearly every way that you might choose to compare, fungi are likely to be more similar to us than are plants, as fungi are our closer evolutionary relations.

If you think about it, though, why would we expect any organism to lie down and die for our dinner? Organisms have evolved to do everything in their power to avoid being extinguished. How long would any lineage be likely to last if its members effectively didn't care if you killed them?

Maybe the real problem with the argument that it's O.K. to kill plants because they don't feel exactly as we do, though, is that it's the same argument used to justify what we now view as unforgivable wrongs.

Slavery and genocide have been justified by the assertion that some kinds of people do not feel pain, do not feel love—are not truly human—in the same way as others. The same thinking has led to other practices less drastic but still appalling. For example, physicians once withheld anesthetics from infants during surgery because it was believed that these not-quite-yet-humans did not feel pain (smiles were gas, remember).

Yet even as we shake our heads over the past, we continue to fight about where to draw the line around our tribe of those deemed truly human. We argue over whether those who love others of the same gender deserve full human rights. We ask the same about fetal humans.

The dinner menu pushes us further still. Do other species of animal deserve our consideration? Do plants? Fungi? Microbes?

Maybe this seems all nonsense to you. Perhaps you're having trouble equating a radish to a lamb to a person whose politics you hate to your beloved firstborn. It's not surprising. It is reliably difficult for us to accept new members into our tribe, the more so the less like us they seem. It can be infinitely inconvenient to take the part of every individual we come across, to share with it that most precious of commodities: compassion.

What should we have for dinner tonight? Who knows?

Human beings survive by eating other living things. I really want not only to eat, but to survive. Yet a nakedly logical way to judge the value of one kind of organism over another—the rightness of a plant's death versus an animal's—seems, to me, out of reach.

My efforts to forgo meat didn't last more than a couple of years. Still, I wonder what our great-grandchildren will think of us. Will we have trouble explaining to them why we killed animals or perhaps even plants for food? And if so, what on Earth will we be eating?

QUESTIONS

1. Yoon writes, "I couldn't actually explain to myself . . . why killing an animal was any worse than killing . . . plants. . . ." Why not?
2. Does Yoon believe plants feel pain? Or does she just believe they try to avoid death?
3. You will die if you don't kill and then eat the pig in front of you. The pig will die if it doesn't eat you. Do McPherson and Singer think that killing the pig is permissible in this case?
4. One of Yoon's arguments seems to be: It is bad for the plant if it dies. Therefore, it is wrong to kill the plant. Is this good reasoning? Does Yoon's conclusion follow from her premise? Why or why not?

9 〉Industrial Plant Agriculture

In this chapter, we explain what industrial *plant* agriculture is, present some considerations for it and against it, and bring out some moral concerns it raises. It is in some ways a companion piece to Chapter 7, "Industrial Animal Agriculture," since in developed countries, and increasingly in other countries, the dominant form of agriculture combines industrial animal agriculture with industrial plant agriculture.

WHAT INDUSTRIAL PLANT AGRICULTURE IS

Industrial plant agriculture is the source of the vast majority of food in developed nations. To a first approximation, industrial agriculture involves producing as much as possible per unit of land area given basic constraints of economic profitability and technological possibility. In practice, this generally means that industrial farms have larger "capital inputs" of fertilizer, irrigated water, fossil fuels (to run machinery), and so on per unit of land area than alternative forms of agriculture, and are in this way much more "intensive" than alternatives such as organic agriculture.

In somewhat more detail, when it comes to plants, industrial agriculture typically involves more than one of the following:

- Large-scale farms that feature a preponderance of monocultures—concentrations of single crops rather than a multitude in a given area over a given period of time where
- Those farms are concentrated in comparatively advantageous locations (e.g., soy and corn monoculture fields in the Midwestern United States, banana monoculture plantations in equatorial regions, rice paddy monoculture in Southeast Asia and other relevantly similar locations, and oil palm monoculture plantations in Indonesia and other similar locations), where
- Crops are raised with liberal application of (synthetic) fertilizer, pesticides, herbicides, insecticides, and irrigated water, where
- Crops may be genetically modified organisms (GMOs), organisms whose genetic code has been modified using biotechnology, and
- Crops and agricultural inputs are traded in a global marketplace that is increasingly dominated by multinational companies. This globalization of trade is part of the

growing neoliberal global economic order, which emphasizes a minimally regulated global marketplace that is constrained only by international agreements, such as those associated with the World Trade Organization (WTO).

This definition of industrial agriculture is deliberately vague, but it gives you the idea: Your uncle's vegetable patch in Ypsilanti, Michigan—non-industrial. Your cousin-in-law's enormous canola farm, growing genetically modified canola outside of Regina, Saskatchewan—industrial.

The readings in this chapter are about what the industrial farming of plants is, what can be said for and against it, and what the moral upshot of all this is: Are we ethically required to have an agricultural system that is (largely) industrial? Are we, instead, morally required to have an agricultural system that is (largely) non-industrial? Are we, instead, permitted to have a mixed system, with large industrial and large non-industrial parts? What is best from an ethical point of view?

The readings in this chapter focus only on a particular set of questions about industrial agriculture. Other chapters and readings in this book are also relevant to the ethics of industrial agriculture. When it comes to animals, industrial agriculture involves factory farming, a topic we discussed at length in Chapter 7, "Industrial Animal Agriculture," and won't discuss much here. For additional concerns about workers, see Chapter 11, "Workers." And, of course, the cases for and against industrial agriculture are, near enough, the flip sides of the cases for and against organic and local alternatives to industrial agriculture that are discussed in the next chapter.

FOOD JUSTICE AND FOOD SOVEREIGNTY CRITIQUES OF INDUSTRIAL AGRICULTURE

Recall from Chapter 3, "Food Justice," that some scholars see the global food system as unjust in myriad ways: Workers are mistreated; large companies have too much power over policies, standards, and consumers; the export of fast food and processed foods from Western countries displaces local food practices; and the global food system is seen as contributing to global poverty, and to hunger, malnutrition, and food insecurity among the global poor. In the view of some critics, the root cause of these injustices is that the global food system, like the global economy more generally, is *industrialized, globalized,* and based in *neoliberalism,* the political economic system emphasizing free-market capitalism and a minimal state. The food sovereignty movement proposes a wholesale alternative to the status quo: smaller-scale food systems that are democratically controlled at the local and regional level, rather than globalized, industrialized food systems controlled by multinational companies and by international agreements made between national governments.

Critics of anti-neoliberalist views such as food sovereignty believe that globalized markets are essential for improving the situation of the global poor, and that it would be a grave mistake to completely disassemble the globalized economy based on free trade, and that this would actually have the effect of making the poor far worse off. Some experts think that the goal should be to make global trade even freer than it actually is, and to change agricultural policies that distort markets. For example, many farmers in developing countries have to compete with imported crops from developed countries, the production of which was heavily subsidized by the developed countries' governments. These farmers are unable to sell their own, less subsidized crops at much of a profit because of the competition from the cheaper, subsidized imports. To help these farmers compete, the argument goes, we should reduce or eliminate developed countries' subsidies—an instance of making trade less regulated and freer.

In this chapter, we discuss a central debate about industrial agriculture: whether industrial methods are necessary to feed the world in coming decades, or whether alternative agricultural systems can do just as well or better at feeding the world. Recall from Chapter 3, "Food Justice," that some proponents of food sovereignty might resist how we frame these issues and would argue that ensuring that the world has a large enough food supply should not be the central aim guiding food system reform. Rather, they would see food sovereignty—"the ability to control the structure and organization of one's local food system," as Paul Thompson puts it—as centrally important. In fact, some proponents of food sovereignty argue that concern with having an adequate global food supply, along with the assumption that global food security requires the industrialization and globalization of agriculture, has been used to justify agricultural and economic reforms that harm the poor, harm the environment, and exacerbate inequalities. (For more detail about the food sovereignty movement's critique of the "food security" paradigm, see the reading "Food Security and Food Sovereignty" in Chapter 3, "Food Justice.")

In this chapter, we put many of these issues of economic justice and global justice to the side. We do not focus on the global food system as an *economic* system that is industrialized and globalized, but focus instead on the *agricultural methods* of industrial agriculture. We consider the alleged benefits and harms of these methods—harms and benefits to the environment, to human health, and to workers.

THE HISTORY OF INDUSTRIAL AGRICULTURE

Industrial agriculture is a relatively recent phenomenon. Until quite recently, all agriculture was non-industrial agriculture. Farming vast quantities of land by hand using organic methods was too work-intensive to be viable for one family of farmers, so farms tended to be small or in some cases owned by rich landholders who could pay others to do the manual labor. Sufficient quantities of organic fertilizer had to be produced and distributed. Fields had to be weeded and kept free of pests.

But a dramatic shift to industrial agriculture has happened. In 1900, the average size of a farm in the United States was roughly 150 acres. In 2000, the number was roughly 450. Regarding these changes, the United States Department of Agriculture (USDA) writes:

> American agriculture and rural life underwent a tremendous transformation in the 20th century. Early 20th century agriculture was labor intensive, and it took place on a large number of small, diversified farms in rural areas where more than half of the U.S. population lived. These farms employed close to half of the U.S. workforce, along with 22 million work animals, and produced an average of five different commodities. The agricultural sector of the 21st century,

on the other hand, is concentrated on a small number of large, specialized farms in rural areas where less than a fourth of the U.S. population lives. These highly productive and mechanized farms employ a tiny share of U.S. workers and use 5 million tractors in place of the horses and mules of earlier days.[1]

Industrial agriculture aims for the production of the greatest quantity of food in the smallest amount of space with the least labor, all for the ultimate goal of maximum profits. But these aims were also more or less pursued pre-industrially, and have been the aims of many farmers since the dawn of agriculture. So what has changed?

The difference is that in order to achieve these goals now, farmers must invest large amounts of capital in recent technological advances, which have in turn made possible huge increases in crop yields both overall and per unit of land area, and reductions in the amount of land and labor necessary to achieve those yields. These technological changes and economic forces explain the transformation away from an agriculturally focused society, which has occurred in almost every developed nation.

As a result of this transformation, there has been a large increase in the amount of food produced on agricultural land. This was made possible by nineteenth-century plant and soil science that suggested that what plants need from the soil is just a few nutrients, nutrients that could be given directly to plants in the form of fertilizer, and by selective breeding that led to much higher yielding seeds. It was made possible, too, by important subsequent technological advances and investments in machinery, synthetic fertilizers, weed, fungus, and pest killers ("herbicides," "fungicides," and "pesticides," respectively), irrigation (sometimes in the form of large public works projects paid for by taxpayers, such as large dam and water transportation infrastructure, but also including technology such as improved drilling, center pivot irrigation, and so on), and by GMOs that produced more food and promised a reduced need for herbicides and pesticides.

Previously, farmers had, of course, worked to fertilize, kill weed, fungi, and pests, and plant high-yielding, hardy plants. But recent technological advances have massively improved that situation and enabled farmers to work much larger farms without much more work. A U.S. government official described this new form of agriculture as containing "the makings of a new revolution. It is not a violent red revolution like that of the Soviets, nor is it a White Revolution like that of the Shah of Iran. I call it the Green Revolution."[2] His term "Green Revolution" caught on, and it is now widely used to refer to the large increases in crop yields in the 1950s, 1960s, and 1970s that were associated with the development and deployment of important instances of the technologies described previously, especially as implemented in developing world nations in Asia and Latin America.

Larger farms located in the most advantageous places also enabled farmers to benefit from economies of scale: as farmers produced more, the costs they needed to pay for that production went down proportionately. This was aided by ever larger and more capable machinery. Larger farms reduced the number of farms, freeing up people to do other jobs. And the productivity of those large farms in certain especially agriculturally apt places enabled those farms to produce enough for places near and far. For example, whereas small states on the East Coast used to grow their own wheat, huge wheat producers in the Midwest and Great Plains—possessed of better natural resources than New England for growing wheat—eliminated that need. Whereas some places are unsuitable for growing much given their soil and climate, megafarms in suitable spots made it possible to grow and then ship widely. But, at the same time, to make the most efficient use of many of these technologies and thus maximize the profitability of their farms, many farmers need to shift almost exclusively to monoculture—that is, planting all the same crop over a large area, and suppressing the growth of absolutely everything else. This is necessary because, for example, the combine harvester can very efficiently harvest many rows of corn, but it can't harvest— or can't harvest well—a row of corn, strawberries, and potatoes.

However, shifting to monocultures has some downsides. One downside is that small farms find it increasingly difficult to survive. Another downside is the increased risk of devastating pest and disease outbreaks. (If a pest likes one row of corn, it is going to like all the rows. The Irish potato famine came about because one disease—late blight—found nothing but a certain sort of vulnerable potato to infect. To guard against this, monocultures then need to be treated with even heavier doses of pesticides, herbicides, and fungicides. Which leads to pesticide-resistant pests and weeds and fungi. Which leads to better pesticides, and so on. Which leads to better pests, and so on. You see how this goes. (For more, see the Altieri reading in the "Further Reading" section.)

Also, planting monocultures repeatedly over time denudes the soil. A diversity of plants takes a diversity of nutrients out of the soil, whereas a monocrop takes the same nutrients year after year—where plants, like people, vary in which nutrients they need to thrive. If the same resources are taken out year after year, this depletes that resource. This necessitates using more fertilizer to provide those nutrients. Which then get sucked out year after year. Which necessitates using more fertilizer. Which weakens the soil's ability to hold nutrients. Which leads to leeching into waterways. You see how that goes, too.

REASONS TO ENGAGE IN INDUSTRIAL AGRICULTURE

Supporters of industrial agriculture see it as having many benefits:

- It is a high-yielding form of agriculture, meaning that it allows farmers to produce more crops per acre than alternatives such as organic agriculture.
- It is more environmentally friendly than alternative systems along some dimensions— because it takes less land under industrial agriculture to produce any given amount of crops, many environmental harms are lower *per unit of crops produced* than they would be under alternatives.
- It is less work-intensive than its non-industrial predecessors and alternatives.
- Its larger yields and environmental benefits are arguably necessary to feed the world without destroying it, in the sense that a growing world population requires more and more food, which would lead to catastrophe for humans and the environment if we did not rely on industrial agriculture to meet that basic need. The basic thought is that if we don't use industrial agriculture, we will either have to greatly increase the amount of land under cultivation which brings various environmental bads *or* we can hold fixed the amount of land used which will bring about starvation since not enough food will be produced.
- GMOs offer further nutritional, yield, and environmental benefits even beyond these general benefits of industrial agriculture.

In light of these alleged benefits of industrial agriculture, many advocates conclude that we should promote industrial agriculture whenever possible, and that we should use GMOs whenever possible to achieve further benefits.

As a prelude to turning a critical eye to such arguments in favor of industrial agriculture, let's first expand on each of its alleged benefits.

First, proponents of industrial agriculture claim that, per acre, more food is produced by the industrial system than by any alternative. Consider this from the U.S. Environmental Protection Agency about industrial corn production:

> Corn farming has become exponentially more efficient. If U.S. farmers in 1931 wanted to equivalently yield the same amount of corn as farmers in 2008, the 1931 farmers would need an additional 490 million acres![3]

Generalizing this point, James McWilliams writes:

> What [small-scale, organic, i.e. non-industrial] agriculture is unable to do with enough reliability is something that a viable system of global food production *must* always do: produce increasing quantities of food on the same, or even smaller, amount of land than is currently under conservation.[4]

McWilliams confidently asserts that industrial agriculture can, does, and will produce "increasing quantities of food" and that non-industrial does not because it cannot. However, when we turn a critical eye to this assertion, it is not immediately clear whether it is correct. It is not even clear precisely what McWilliams is saying: When he makes the comparison, which industrial techniques do the industrial farms use, which do the non-industrial farms use? What are they growing? When? (Is that food being fed directly to people or to animals which people then eat?[5]) How much food is being produced per person? Over how many years? (These issues are discussed in the Kirschenmann reading in Chapter 10, "Alternatives to Industrial Plant Agriculture.")

Yet despite the importance of these critical questions, and although there is not complete consensus on the empirical question of the yield benefits of industrial agriculture, there is something to what McWilliams is saying. The weight of the evidence does indicate that in developed nations industrially grown crops have higher yields than organic crops, at least with respect to many staple crops (i.e., many of the most widely consumed crops).[6] At any rate, the evidence makes clear that some forms of industrial agriculture can reliably produce a lot of food. This is good for people—more food! It is also good for the environment—less land is used for agriculture, and so, as Norman Borlaug stresses in his reading in this chapter, land we don't need for farming can be used for people and animals to enjoy. As the world's population rises while the amount of arable and habitable land does not increase, it is ever more important to use agricultural land as judiciously and efficiently as we can. That industrial agriculture can do so is a mark in its favor.

This is by no means an insignificant consideration, especially in light of the threats posed by climate change, where greenhouse gas emissions from agriculture are responsible for a large percentage of the climate change problem. There is significant disagreement about the magnitude of agriculture's contribution to the problem, but one important factor is that land use changes caused by increasing demand for agriculture lead to rainforest and other lands being converted into agricultural fields. This means that those areas of land that have up until now been "carbon sinks" (areas that, on balance, subtract greenhouse gasses from the atmosphere via photosynthesis and other well-understood processes) are transformed into "carbon sources" in the form of agricultural fields that are net emitters of greenhouse gasses. This provides just one more crucial example of why there are reasons to prefer a global system of agriculture that effectively minimizes the amount of land devoted to agriculture.

Another important part of the equation is that experts predict a steadily increasing demand for biofuels—fuels that are derived from plants, such as ethanol. Biofuels require agricultural land to grow, which subtracts from the land available for meeting the more basic need for food. Biofuels are alternatives to fossil fuel energy, and demand for biofuels is expected to increase as incentives increase for alternatives to fossil fuel energy, where those incentives will be largely driven by increasing concern over pollution and climate change. (This is somewhat ironic in connection with biofuels and climate change, given the land use changes that are implied by increased use of biofuels.) This is a significant part of the equation going forward, and further supports the idea that industrial agriculture is more environmentally friendly than alternative forms of agriculture that have lower yields, because it minimizes the amount of land needed to meet our overall (food- and energy-based) agricultural needs.

A second alleged benefit of industrial agriculture is that the synthetics that go into industrial farming make it less work-intensive than at least one form of non-industrial farming, namely, small-scale organic farming. Farming industrially, one can kill weeds by spraying herbicide rather than uprooting. One can kill insects by spraying insecticides rather than using more work-intensive organic methods like simply crushing bugs or attracting good pests to manage bad pests or planting crops to draw pests away. (Also, one can plant GMOs that are weed- and bug-resistant. Not so on organic farms.) This lessening of work is good in one way for farmworkers who have to do less of the back-breaking work that is detailed by Seth Holmes in Chapter 11, "Workers." (However, if the technology obviates the need for some farmworkers to work at all, or increases the exposure to herbicides and pesticides of those who do work, then it is bad in quite another way for the farmworkers.)

It is also good for those people who can do something other than farming. As Descrochers and Shimizu stress, there were and are places that grow all their food organically on a small scale for people nearby. Some of these—like Joel Salatin's farm as described in Chapter 8, "Alternatives to Industrial Animal Agriculture," and the farms Bill McKibben describes in Chapter 10, "Alternatives to Industrial Plant Agriculture"—are places we have in mind when we idealize unconventional agriculture. But others—like subsistence farms in low-income countries or American farms in the late 1800s—are not. The labor that goes into such farms is difficult and time-consuming and, Desrochers and Shimizu claim, not as rewarding as it is sometimes made out to be. They welcome the drop in the U.S. farmworker force from 41% of our population in 1900 to 2% of our population in 2000.[7] So they see industrialization's decreasing reliance on human labor as a second mark in favor of industrial agriculture. Even if—and it's a big if—the farming life is one to be cherished and idealized, it is a mark in industrial agriculture's favor that it doesn't *require* so many farmers, that people in industrialized farming countries are free to choose other work.

Finally, there is also some evidence to support the claim that industrially grown crops are on average no worse than non-industrial organic crops on general nutritional grounds.[8] However, there is also some evidence that organics are on average better than industrial crops with respect to antioxidants and other micronutrients,[9] and the relevant pro-industrial studies also tend to ignore the potential effects of prolonged exposure to low levels of pesticides and other chemical residues, which are often higher for industrial crops.[10] However, the levels of these chemicals in both industrial and organic crops are generally lower than the limits that regulators in the United States deem safe for human consumption, so advocates of industrial agriculture argue that there is no good reason to prefer organics even when this factor is taken into proper account.[11]

GENETICALLY MODIFIED FOOD

The use of genetically modified (GM) crops is seen to offer additional benefits along all of the dimensions just noted. As Pamela Ronald argues in her entry in this chapter, GM crops have higher yields and thus require less land, thrive on less water, require less pesticides per unit of yield, and can withstand particular pesticides that enable farms to use forms of agriculture that better forestall erosion. Some GM crops are also more nutritious, as some are created with nutritional improvements in mind, such as the GM-variety of rice, golden rice, which gives consumers extra vitamin A and thus helps to ward off a vitamin A deficiency that leads to blindness.

Arguments for and against these alleged additional benefits of GM crops get more of a hearing in the readings in this chapter, but it is worth stressing here that the idea behind genetic modification is an ancient idea: Modify plants in order to improve them in various ways. What has changed is the technological means by which these improvements are carried out. Whereas it used to be done by cross-breeding of plants (or, in the mid-twentieth century, radiation), it can now be done by the direct insertion of genes into a genome. Another change is that the new genes aren't simply limited to the genes of plants.

The central ethical question to ask about GM crops is whether these most recent technological changes have any ethical significance, or whether instead GM crops are no more ethically worrisome than non-GM crops, which despite being non-GM are nonetheless almost always the product of genetic manipulation using the older technologies of cross-breeding and radiation.

The most persistent worry about GMs is that they involve greater risks than their non-GM alternatives, risks that are difficult to quantify and perhaps even difficult to identify. If GMs did involve a much greater threat than their alternatives, then this would be an excellent reason for thinking that GM technology is especially worrisome from an ethical point of view.

As a first step toward discussing the alleged risks of GM foods, it is useful to make a number of distinctions. First, it is useful to distinguish between risks associated with *growing* GM crops and risks associated with *eating* GM crops. Second, it is useful to distinguish between ethical principles that claim that it is wrong to impose risks when doing so is a bad bet because of the *expected consequences* of doing so,[12] and *strong precautionary principles* that maintain that it is wrong to impose risks when extremely bad outcomes are possible and there is significant-enough uncertainty about their probability, even when experts tend to agree that imposing those risks is not a bad bet in terms of expected consequences.[13]

The risks that are most frequently discussed with *growing* GM food are that a food system that is highly dependent on GM crops risks a widespread catastrophic collapse that could lead to mass starvation, or could at least cause large economic damage. Such a collapse could arise from a blight that might arise for GM crops, or from those crops becoming sterile for unanticipated reasons. Further, even if GM crops promise environmental benefits in the short run, over the long run dependence on GM crops could be argued to increase our need to use herbicides and pesticides in the long run. (This controversial view is argued for by Philpott in his reading for this chapter.) The most frequent risks associated with *eating* GM crops are that we might develop allergies to those crops, or more generally that we might not be able to digest and extract nutrients from them, or that they might turn out to be carcinogenic.

A further common objection to GMOs is that they empower large multinational corporations such as Monsanto to control the world's food supply in a way that is dangerous or unjust. One primary mechanism for that control is agricultural trade and intellectual property rules within the WTO, especially those that prevent farmers from using part of their harvest to grow the next year's crop, and instead force farmers to become more and more dependent on corporations for seeds and herbicides.

In response to these objections to GMOs, one important thing to note is that these worries might appear to apply to *all* monoculture, and not only to GM crops. This leads to the critical question of whether, once we appreciate this point, there is then any special objection to GM crops per se, rather than more general objections to monoculture and thus to industrial agriculture as it is generally practiced, whether or not it uses GM crops. If there is not any ethically relevant difference between GM crops and non-GM crops in connection with these worries, then the leading arguments against GM crops should be understood not as arguments against GMs per se, but against monoculture and industrial agriculture more generally.

However, at the same time, even though these common objections to GMs also apply to non-GM industrial monoculture, they may have more force when directed at GMs. For example, GM crops might have a higher probability of negative side effects or collapse than their non-GM alternatives in otherwise identical contexts. This is because the use of targeted genetic manipulation might make GMs inherently more problematic or fragile, especially specific subsets of GMs, such as those with "terminator technology" that means that only one generation of that crop can be grown, with subsequent generations of seeds of that crop sterile and thus not able to grow. More scientifically controversial arguments are also sometimes made, especially by non-scientists, such as that since we have evolved to process the types of plants that we have traditionally eaten, we should expect to get optimal nutrition from (and minimize allergies to) "natural" permutations of those plants, where these "natural" permutations include the results of traditional selective breeding, but do not include the results of more high-tech genetic engineering.

REASONS NOT TO ENGAGE IN LARGE-SCALE INDUSTRIAL AGRICULTURE

Whereas various synthetics and GMOs are potentially boons for industrial agriculture, they are also at the heart of the case against industrial agriculture. That case comprises multiple parts, one about the environment, one about health, and one about workers.

The Union of Concerned Scientists summarizes the environmental case against industrial agriculture thus:

> Intensive monoculture depletes soil and leaves it vulnerable to erosion. Chemical fertilizer runoff . . . add[s] to global warming emissions and create[s] oxygen-deprived "dead zones" at the mouths of major waterways. Herbicides and insecticides harm wildlife. . . . Biodiversity in and near monoculture fields takes a hit, as populations of birds and beneficial insects decline.[14]

Adding some irony to this, environmental degradation and global warming isn't just a general problem for humankind, but also counts against the main selling point of industrial agriculture, its ability to feed future generations. This point is emphasized by many researchers, including the Intergovernmental Panel on Climate Change (IPCC), which issues authoritative summaries of scientific consensus on climate change under the auspices of the United Nations. The worry is that climate change has already reduced crop yields relative to what they would have been without human interference in the climate, and that in the future as the effects of climate change become worse the effects on some staple crops could be catastrophic.[15] This suggests that the current industrial model may be not only environmentally harmful in the short run but, because of the effects of climate change, ultimately self-defeating.

The second consideration against industrial agriculture is that it may be bad for human health. One worry follows on from the environmental concern mentioned previously: When pesticides get into water supplies, they can sicken people and animals. Another worry has to do with consumption of food grown with synthetic inputs. It is a precautionary worry, a worry that we have no idea what consuming synthetic pesticides and other synthetics is doing to our bodies. As Samuel Fromartz cracks, "Although the potential risks incurred by pesticide exposures over a lifetime are unknown, people who choose to eat organic . . . have, in effect, decided to opt out of an ongoing social experiment into whether pesticides are safe. Given the number of pesticides that were once freely used but have since been removed from the market for health reasons, this is not a wild or unreasonable choice."[16] This is all tied in to skepticism about the safety of conventional pesticides and fertilizers. This is a common concern among the general public but, it should be said, not among scientists.

Worries about the health effects of synthetic pesticides and fertilizers ramify into concerns about the health of workers who apply them. Whereas the case for conventional agriculture that stems from workers has to do with how it has freed up workers, the case against stems from effects of conventional agriculture on those workers who are still engaged in it and, in some cases, on those workers' unborn children. This case is not discussed in this chapter but is taken up in Chapter 11, "Workers."

THE ETHICS OF INDUSTRIAL AGRICULTURE

So much for considerations for and against industrial agriculture. How do these considerations work together to issue a verdict on whether industrial agriculture is morally permissible? Or morally required? On whether industrial agriculture is best all things considered, or whether an alternative would be better?

The main argument in the literature that industrial agriculture is *morally required* starts from the fact that, currently, many studies indicate that something on the order of 842 million people worldwide do not have enough to eat. Yearly, 3.1 million children die from causes related to this lack of nourishment.[17] As Borlaug notes, this isn't simply an issue about producing enough food but, rather, about producing enough and then properly distributing it. Is there a moral requirement to alleviate hunger by producing enough food and then distributing it properly? Whose hunger are we required to alleviate? Who are "we"? Why are we so required? These are important questions to think about when thinking about claims like Borlaug and Dowswell's and Desrochers and Shimizu's about industrial agriculture's ability to produce more food than alternative forms of agriculture.

Implicitly, Borlaug and Dowswell and Desrochers and Shimizu seem to be arguing:

> Industrial agriculture is the only way to feed the world.
> If only one form of agriculture can feed the world, we should adopt it.
> Hence, we should adopt industrial agriculture.

The idea behind this argument is totally straightforward and reminiscent of an argument from the end of the introduction to Chapter 7: We should go for industrial agriculture since that is the only way to feed the world. It's consistent with this argument that people are currently going hungry, despite the widespread use of industrial agriculture; though industrial agriculture produces enough food to feed the world, this food is not distributed in ways that prevent hunger. It's also consistent with this argument that industrial agriculture by itself will not feed the world, but must be paired with different ways of distributing food. It's also consistent with this argument that industrial agriculture is environmentally bad and even that it is bad for human health. The second premise of the arguments displayed at the opening of this paragraph encodes that *even if* a form of agriculture is bad for the environment and human health, we should go for that form of agriculture if it's the only one that feeds the world. Even if an option has significant downsides, sometimes we should adopt it. Certain medications have significant downsides, but you should take them all the same.

Evaluating the argument is tricky. The first premise is empirical and not ethical at all: Without saying anything about what is good or bad, right or wrong, it just makes a testable claim about food production. Well, it seems to. But what is the premise saying exactly? That in the short term industrial agriculture is the only way to feed the world? That in the long term it is the only way to feed the world? At any rate, this premise implies that *no* form of non-industrial agriculture *can* feed the world.

What is the evidence that this premise is true? What is it about industrial agriculture that makes it so it can feed the world? What is it about *all* the varieties of non-industrial agriculture that make them unable? And note that the argument is claiming that non-industrial is un*able* to produce sufficient food. It is not simply claiming that industrial agriculture produces *more* food than non-industrial. It is not simply claiming that non-industrial *does not* produce sufficient food. It is claiming that *no matter the mode of non-industrial farming,* no matter how the food is distributed, no matter which foods we grow, non-industrial agriculture *cannot* produce enough food to feed the world.

In response to these questions, proponents of the argument for industrial agriculture have a further substantive argument to offer for the first premise that industrial agriculture is the only way to feed the world. This supporting argument relies on a claim about how much food we need to produce in the future, as well as a claim about the amount of food that can be produced by industrial versus organic agriculture in the future. Basically, the argument relies on two premises: that we must produce 60%–120% more food in 40 to 50 years, and that organic agriculture is unable to produce that much more food—and, in the course of this argument, it is usually emphasized that even if we use all of the higher yielding tools of industrial farming, it will still be a challenge even then to meet that future demand for food.[18] (See the text box following this section for a more detailed explanation of the argument for the claim that we must produce 60%–120% more food in 40 to 50 years.)

The argument we have been considering is committed to the strong claim that *only* industrial agriculture can feed the world. Proponents of industrial agriculture can weaken that premise, though, and still make a powerful argument in industrial agriculture's favor. They could concede instead that non-industrial agriculture can feed the world but only at a great environmental cost since non-industrial agriculture, the argument goes, will need to use significantly more land as farmland than industrial agriculture will.

More precisely:

Industrial agriculture is among the ways to feed the world.
It is the form of agriculture that is best, on balance, taking into account effects on humans and the environment.
If multiple forms of agriculture can feed the world, but industrial agriculture is best, then we should adopt the latter.
Hence, we should adopt industrial agriculture: preserve it where it is; spread it where it isn't.

Since we have adopted it in the United States and elsewhere, the argument implies we should keep it here and spread it elsewhere. (The Borlaug reading insists it should be adopted in, for example, sub-Saharan Africa.) The ideas behind the second premise are that industrial agriculture conserves the most land and enables the fewest people to farm and because of these two facts has the best effects.

Again, this argument has an empirical, non-ethical component and an ethical component. About both, you might ask, "Are they true? What is our evidence for them?" More specifically, you might ask, "Why is industrial best?" or "If it is best, why should we adopt it? Why do we do wrong if we adopt a second-best policy?"

A criticism of the argument is that the second premise is false and that industrial agriculture is not best for the environment, that its well-documented environmental drawbacks and impacts on human health outweigh the benefits in terms of land saved or labor hours saved.

From these concerns about industrial agriculture and its effects springs this argument against the permissibility of industrial agriculture.

Industrial agriculture is environmentally awful.
It is wrong to farm in environmentally awful ways when there are viable alternatives.
There are viable alternatives.
Hence, industrial agriculture is wrong.

Or

Industrial agriculture is worse for humans and animals than other options.
In this case, using a form of agriculture that is worse for humans and animals than other options is wrong.
Hence, industrial agriculture is wrong.

And here the first premise might include economic concerns or environmental concerns or concerns about food, concerns echoing the environmental concerns about industrial animal agriculture in Chapter 7, "Industrial Animal Agriculture."

This conclusion doesn't say much about which form of agriculture is right: If industrial agriculture is wrong and some form of agriculture is permissible, then it follows that the permissible form of agriculture must be non-industrial. But which form of non-industrial agriculture? Two possibilities are the subject of the next chapter.

The arguments for and against industrial agriculture raise a cluster of tricky, interesting empirical issues, as we highlighted earlier. They also raise tricky, interesting issues about, among other things, duties to feed the hungry and duties to future generations, the ethics of imposing risks, and environmental ethics. We'll briefly discuss those later, and they are also discussed in a number of other chapters, as indicated later as well.

HOW MUCH FOOD WILL WE NEED IN THE FUTURE?

Mark Budolfson

Experts often answer the question of how much food we will need in the future by using mathematical models of how the world's demand for food will evolve given the expected growth of both human population and per capita wealth. The main assumptions of many leading models are that as a person's wealth increases, his or her food consumption increases, both of overall calories and, especially important, of meat. Then, when the details of this relationship between wealth and meat consumption are combined with population growth projections, and projections about the increasing wealth of people in developing nations where most of that population growth will also occur, and assumptions about the grain needed to feed all of the additional animals demanded, those assumptions entail that we will likely need 60%–120% more overall food production in 40 to 50 years compared to our production now.[19]

For example, consider that Africa has more than one billion people now, and is expected to have over a billion *more* people in 40 years and will be much wealthier as well; China and India have billions of people who will also be much wealthier in 40 years (and those places will also have more people),[20] and each of those billions will therefore (according to the assumptions of the model under discussion) consume far more meat than their counterparts in those locations do now. And, crucially, feeding people meat requires much more crop production than feeding people plants. Producing meat requires grazing area or grain and other types of inputs from plant agriculture to feed the animals involved, often takes *many times* more acres to produce than it would to feed those people the same amount of nutrition by feeding them plants rather than meat. In short, when people's diets shift toward meat, this disproportionately increases the amount of land that is needed to provide them with the same amount of nutrition—which in the future will also be multiplied by increasing numbers of people.

On the basis of these models of future food demand, together with the claim that organic agriculture would not be able to produce that much more food, some leading proponents of industrial agriculture argue that industrial agriculture is the only system capable of feeding the world into the future.

Note that the connection claimed between wealth and meat consumption by these models is an *empirical claim*: it says that as a matter of fact, the world is one particular way rather than another, even though we can imagine the world being a different way without imagining anything impossible or contrary to the laws of nature. For an example of how the world could be different, imagine that once people become wealthy enough, they tend to have lots of education and the leisure to read a book like this one, and partly as a result they tend to be more worried about the environment and their health, and they tend to have good vegetarian alternatives available to them, and as a result of all of those factors and more they tend to eat *less* meat. Doesn't that seem like a *possible* way the world could work, even if it does not actually work that way? It seems possible in this sense (even if not actual), which illustrates why the premise we are considering is an empirical claim, because it claims that the world is not that way, and that instead meat consumption tends to always increase as people get wealthier.

Given that this is an empirical claim, a good critical question to ask is whether there is any *empirical evidence* that supports that claim: in other words, evidence that does not amount merely to an *intuition* or *feeling* that the world is that way, but involves actual observations of the world that, once we learn them, increase the probability that the world actually is that way rather than some other way. In fact, there is some impressive empirical evidence offered in support of the further premise and the details of the relationship it assumes between wealth and meat consumption. The evidence is based on facts about the actual meat consumption per capita in nations around the world, which of course differ substantially in the levels of wealth per capita of their citizens. Based on that *data* (that is, actual observations about the world), agricultural economists then estimate the "best fit" relationship between per capita income and meat consumption (and the consumption of other agricultural products). The result is the detailed numerical relationship that is used in the argument that the world will need to produce much more food in the future.[21] So, there is some impressive empirical evidence in support of the claim we have been considering about the relationship between wealth and meat consumption, and there is similarly impressive evidence for the other empirical assumptions of the model.

However, it is worth noting that such data, even when it is *powerful evidence* that strongly supports a particular empirical conclusion, seldom conclusively rules all alternative possibilities. So, even when we have good evidence for an empirical claim, there are often further critical questions that we should ask, and other alternative explanations of the data that we should seek to identify and then consider. For example, in connection with the claim under consideration here that increases in wealth always lead to increases in meat consumption, we might note that the assumed relationship extrapolates from facts about meat consumption *across* nations, but it does not focus on facts about how meat consumption has evolved over time *within* individual nations as they have become increasingly wealthy in per capita terms. In light of this, it is possible (in the absence of further empirical evidence) that, for example, some of the difference between nations in meat consumption is driven by cultural factors, and that when we look *within* wealthy nations at how their meat consumption has evolved over time, we will find that meat consumption per capita is actually declining in each of the most wealthy nations, and thus that within each nation there seems to be a level of per capita wealth above which meat consumption begins to decline—just as we noted was an interesting possibility earlier in this discussion.

In fact, this alternate possibility is supported by some further empirical evidence we get when we actually look at how meat consumption has evolved over time within many of the wealthiest nations, such as the United States. In the United States., per capita meat consumption has declined since 2003, while per capita wealth has increased substantially.[22] And apart from chicken, the per capita consumption of which rose steadily in the United States between World War II until 2003 before stopping its growth recently, U.S. per capita consumption of other meat has remained flat or declined since the early 1990s, when Americans were half as wealthy per capita as they are now.[23] Similar remarks apply to many other wealthy countries, such as the United Kingdom.[24]

So, does this show that there is an important objection to the main argument for industrial agriculture in the literature? It is important to see that even if the model of future meat and agricultural needs that we have discussed is based on assumptions that are not perfectly true in every way, that does not immediately show that it is a bad model, and does not immediately show that we should doubt that the predictions of that model are true. That is because good models often have assumptions that are known to be false in some ways, and what matters most is often not whether their assumptions are perfectly true, but rather whether we should expect their predictions to be correct, or whether we should expect them to be much more accurate predictions than those of alternative models that we could feasibly construct— or perhaps more precisely still, whether we should expect the assumptions and predictions of the model to be roughly correct within the empirical range that we care about.[25] To illustrate this, consider an analogy: suppose we want to know what would happen if the United States printed enough extra money to send a newly created $1,000 in an envelope to every citizen. A good model for predicting what effect this would have might assume, among other things, that all people would spend versus save a particular fraction of this money (perhaps as a function of their wealth). Notice that this assumption implies that all people (with the same level of wealth) will spend versus save the exact same amounts—but that is obviously false! Of course all of those people would not act exactly the same way! But even though this is sufficient to show that that assumption is not exactly true, that does not mean that it is a bad assumption to make for the purposes of constructing a model, or that the model itself could not be a good predictive model.

With this in mind, it is important to note that in the particular model of future food needs that we have been discussing, the vast majority of the predicted increase in future needs is due to changes in developing nations, where people are mostly still much poorer than the levels at which per capita meat consumption slows to near zero or falls. As a result, even if we assume that the assumed relationship between wealth and meat consumption is not entirely correct because above some high threshold of wealth individuals eat less meat, that does not give us any reason to doubt the general prediction of the model that we will need much greater quantities of agricultural output to feed the world in the future.

At the same time, this highlights some empirical reason for optimism that the world is not condemned forever to inevitably increasing meat consumption. As a further objection to the main argument we have been considering, it might even be hoped that by quickly bringing the world out of poverty and increasing global education, especially education about the dangers of climate change and deforestation, and about meat consumption as a primary driver of those harms, we might be able to "bend the curve downward" that represents the relationship between wealth and meat consumption, and thus not only feed the world without destroying it, but also feed the world without even damaging it too badly. (More specific ways in which we might hope to reduce demand for meat are discussed in Chapter 10, "Alternatives to Industrial Plant Agriculture.")

POPULATION CONTROL

Returning to the main argument from the last section, that industrial agriculture is morally required, consider the simplest version of that argument:

> Industrial agriculture is the only way to feed the world.
> If only one form of agriculture can feed the world, we should adopt it.
> Hence, we should adopt industrial agriculture.

In objection to the first premise, we might say something we alluded to in Chapter 2, "Global Hunger": Even if we grant that industrial agriculture is the only *agricultural* way to feed the world, there are some non-agricultural alternative ways to feed the world into the future, such as to adopt population control policies that would stop population growth. In support of this alternative, someone could argue that even though industrial agriculture is the best way to feed the world *given expected population growth*, the reasons against adopting industrial agriculture are so powerful that the right response is instead to stop population growth, which would also allow us to feed the world, since we already produce enough food to feed the current world population. (In connection with this, see the reading by Paul Ehrlich in Chapter 2.)

One objection to this alternative is that when population control policies have been implemented in the past, arguably the "cure has been worse than the disease" in the sense that they have involved ethical horrors worse than those they were intended to prevent. For example, dramatic population control policies like forced sterilization involve extreme coercion that prevents the exercise of what many people take to be fundamental personal freedoms. Further, population growth has already essentially stopped in the developed world, and so this extreme coercion would have to be imposed entirely on the developing world, which seems unjust. Along with seeming to discriminate against those in the developing world, it seems to violate the rights of people to procreate. In reply, one might question whether people do have a right to procreate and whether they have a right to procreate as often as they would like. These are topics of ongoing concern and controversy.

Consider instead non-coercive measures of population control. Some favor attempting to stop population growth with policies that promote economic development, female empowerment, and education, all of which are widely thought to be the primary drivers of uncoerced population growth reductions.[26] These non-coercive population policies would have the further welcome effect of allowing us simultaneously to aid the poorest and most oppressed people in the developing world, rather than heaping even more oppression upon them. Of course, we should not assume that non-coercive population policies could reduce population growth fast enough to solve the challenge of feeding the world, meaning that arguments like the preceding one remain important. Neither should we assume that we must choose between either adopting a purely agricultural policy, or else a purely population control policy. We might well need to adopt both, or elements of both.

FEEDING THE HUNGRY

The idea that it's wrong to allow widespread hunger and we are required to prevent it even though it has serious costs for the environment and human health can seem obvious. But, like a lot of ethical claims that seem obvious, it is less certain than you might think. These points are discussed in detail elsewhere in the book, so we will just mention them here: Duties to alleviate hunger nationally and internationally are discussed in Chapter 2, "Global Hunger," and Chapter 3, "Food Justice."

That we in the present have a duty to feed *future* people is even less certain than that we have a duty to feed present people. Both one case for industrial agriculture and one case against it depend on claims about the need to feed future people. Proponents of industrial agriculture claim that only it can feed the coming 9 billion people. Opponents of industrial agriculture claim that present-day usage of conventional techniques will hinder our ability to feed the many in the future—we are burning out our resources now and so we won't be able to avail ourselves of them in the future. Both cases raise a series of moral issues: What sacrifices must we make *now* so that people in the future will be fed? Does the fact that someone does not currently exist make it so that it is morally permissible to deprive them of food in the future? These are examples of important philosophical questions in the general area of *intergenerational justice*.

THE NON-IDENTITY PROBLEM

Answering these questions is complicated by *the non-identity problem*.

A case that made the problem famous in the philosophical literature is closely related to some of the agricultural practices discussed in this chapter and in Chapter 8, "Non-Industrial Animal Agriculture." It goes like this: Imagine that we are considering whether to adopt Depletion Policy, a policy that makes our lives better in the present but at the cost of making the lives of future people significantly worse. Now add a wrinkle: The way in which we make our lives better not only lowers the quality of life for future people but also *changes which people exist* in the future, that is, changes the identities of which people exist. So if we adopt Depletion, we make our lives better than it would be if we don't do so, we make the lives of future people worse than if we don't do so, but also, importantly, we make it so that certain people—let's call them Anna, Billy, and Cleo—exist in the future. If we don't adopt Depletion, our own lives are worse, the lives of future people are better than they are if we had adopted Depletion, but, importantly, the people that exist are not Anna, Billy, and Cleo but, instead, Derrick, Evan, and Fahrid. Is it permissible to adopt Depletion? If the lives of future people are bad enough, many people say, "No! It's wrong to adopt Depletion." And many people think that the wide-scale adoption of industrial agriculture just is the adoption of Depletion—that is, widespread adoption of industrial agriculture makes our lives better in the present but makes the lives of future people significantly worse.

However, consider an objection to that line of thought: By adopting Depletion, we make our own lives better. And, also, we do not make the lives of anyone worse *than they would have been*. In particular, we do not make the lives of Derrick, Evan, and Fahrid worse than they would have been if we hadn't adopted Depletion. For, if we hadn't adopted Depletion, they wouldn't even exist. If Derrick, Evan, and Fahrid complain that Depletion has made them worse off, this objection claims that they are mistaken. If it hadn't been for Depletion, they wouldn't exist at all. If anything, they should be *grateful* we adopted Depletion, for it made their existence possible.

In this way, Depletion is very different from a case like this: Lucy gets pregnant. She has always taken a certain prescription drug to deal with joint pain. Her physician tells her that that prescription drug will significantly worsen her child's life, but there's a different drug she can take for her joint pain that won't: It's the same price, as easy to take, and just as effective. But Lucy can't be bothered to make the switch. As a result, her baby, Leo, is born with some severe physical problems that require multiple risky surgeries and cause him significant chronic pain. In this case, it is much easier to explain why Lucy did something wrong: Her decision not to change prescription drugs makes Leo's life much worse than his life would have been if Lucy had merely switched prescription drugs at trivial cost to herself.

The important difference between Lucy's wrong decision, on the one hand, and adopting Depletion on the other, is that Lucy's decision does not change whether or not Leo exists—he exists either way—and so her decision ensures that *Leo* lives a much worse life, rather than that *Leo* lives a much better life. For this reason, it is much easier to explain why Lucy's decision is wrong, because there is a person, Leo, who is made much worse off by her decision. In contrast, there is no person who would exist whether or not Depletion is adopted, and so there is no person of whom we can say that adopting Depletion ensures that *that person* leads a worse life rather than a better life. The important philosophical upshot is that even if we are inclined to think that adopting Depletion would be wrong even in light of the preceding objection, there is still an important ethical puzzle that needs to be solved: namely, how to explain why adopting Depletion is wrong despite the fact that it does not make anyone much worse off in the straightforward way that Lucy's wrong action makes Leo much worse off. And if we cannot ultimately identify any good way of explaining that, the more disturbing implication is that perhaps we should be less confident that adopting Depletion is wrong.

All of this is important when you are thinking about food for the following reasons. Some of the case against the most intensive contemporary forms of industrial agriculture is that they are *in the long term* less productive than more sustainable alternatives, such as those that are less dependent on maximal synthetic inputs and that prioritize long-term soil health over maximal short-term yields. The case is that it's significantly worse *for future generations* to degrade the environment in the way that current forms of industrial agriculture do. But what does that mean? It does *not* mean that the same people will exist regardless of whether or not we continue to pursue those forms of industrial agriculture, and that *those* people will have a worse life if we do. Rather, *if* we continue with these forms of industrial agriculture, what will happen is that certain children will be born and those kids will be born into a depleted environment. If, instead, we use a more environmentally beneficial agricultural system, kids will be born into a better environment, but *which* kids are born will be different. If we go on with industrial agriculture, Mike, Miguel, and Miranda will be born. If we go with a non-industrial alternative, Noa, Nigel, and Nora will be. So it's not as if *Mike* can complain that *his* life is worse than it would have been thanks to our industrial agriculture policies. On the contrary, if we hadn't pursued that policy, Mike never would've been born. So the agriculture case is quite different from the case of Lucy and Leo because, again, in that case, the same child will be born regardless of the decision that is made.

In sum, the non-identity problem is the problem of explaining why it is wrong to do certain things, things that have bad consequences for future generations even though doing those things changes which people exist. The people who exist if we pursue Depletion are *non-identical* to the people who exist if we don't. Should thinking through this problem change our thinking about what it is wrong to do with respect to future generations?

IMPOSING RISKS

Imagine a slight tweak to the Lucy case. She starts taking pills that merely *might* cause Leo to be cognitively impaired. But let's say Lucy is lucky and no harm comes to Leo. All the same, was it permissible for her to have taken the pills?

We ask because part of the case against industrial *growing* is that it subjects workers to various risks and doing so is wrong. (These are detailed in the Estabrook reading in Chapter 1, "The Ethically Troubling Food System.") Part of the case against *eating* industrially produced food is that it subjects consumers to various risks and doing so is wrong. Of course, the case can't *simply* be that, say, conventional growing is risky and *simply because of that* wrong. For there is no duty to always and everywhere avoid risks of harm. Going to class usually subjects you to some chance of catching a cold or the flu. All the same, that's permissible.

Yet consider this example, inspired by Fran Krause: You are driving home from class. There's a person-shaped lump in the road. You can safely drive around it or drive over it. What should you do? To some, it is obvious you should drive around it. You are doing something wrong if you drive over it. Even if it turns out to just be a mannequin.[27]

What if driving around it were itself risky? For example, what if driving around it would be very dangerous—you'd drive up on a crowded sidewalk or dangerously close to the edge of a cliff? In that case, it might well be wrong to drive around the lump. You are permitted to risk it.

The worries about industrial growing and eating raise a related suite of risk-questions: When feeding yourself, is it permissible to risk your health? When feeding children or peers, is it permissible to risk their health? Do you have to have their consent to risk their health?

What's at the heart of some of the worries about GMOs and also at the heart of some worries about synthetic pesticides and fertilizers—that the residue that's left on food is actually harmful despite our *currently* thinking it's not—is that we simply do not know what these risks are. It is as if you are driving home from class and you can't even tell if the lump in the road is person shaped. Or as if a government spokesman with a questionable track record on these things tells you the lump is trash-shaped rather than person-shaped. (It is worth noting that there is a big discrepancy between scientists and [American] non-scientists about the riskiness of consuming GMOs. A recent Pew survey found that 88% of scientists in the American Association for the Advancement of Science hold that it is safe to eat genetically modified food. By contrast, 37% of the general public hold that same view; see Lynas, 2015, in the "Further Reading" section.)

What's at the heart of other worries is that we know perfectly well what the risks are, and we cannot justify imposing them on workers. It is wrong to risk the health of workers and their unborn children just to grow conventional produce that is cheaper by a few pennies. That's the idea.

This bears on one of the arguments we made in favor of industrial agriculture:

Industrial agriculture is among the ways to feed the world.
It is the form of agriculture that is best for the environment—human and natural.
If multiple forms of agriculture can feed the world, but industrial agriculture is best for the human and natural environment, we should adopt the latter.
Hence, we should adopt it.

It might be that this argument is unsound because the third premise is false. It might be that even though industrial agriculture is *actually* best for the human and natural environment, we shouldn't adopt it because it's risky. Or, alternatively, it might be that this argument is false because industrial agriculture is *not* best for the human environment because it *actually* has terrible health consequences for people, worse consequences than some alternatives.

DUTIES TO CARE FOR THE ENVIRONMENT

Finally, consider this more direct challenge to that argument in favor of industrial agriculture: It's not best for the environment. Indeed, critics allege, it is terrible for the environment and significantly worse than some anti-industrial alternatives. There's nothing about risk here. The idea is that industrial agriculture in fact has certain environmental effects and those effects are bad enough that it is wrong to go in for industrial agriculture.

But what is wrong with spoiling the environment? Consider the possibility that we have duties not to spoil the environment. Whence come these duties? Are they duties to the animals that use the environment, including ourselves? So, for example, Leon has a duty not to pollute a certain river because doing so harms the fish in it or because it pollutes Maria's water supply? The idea here is not that it is never permissible to harm fish or to harm Maria. There might well be cases where that is permissible. The idea would just be that there are clearly *other* cases where harming them is wrong, cases where you don't have sufficiently good reason to harm them, and this case is one of them. This sort of reasoning is familiar from Chapter 7, "Industrial Animal Agriculture."

Duties to the environment might, instead, derive from something else. For example, they might derive from duties simply to other people to, for example, treat the environment as some common good. So, for example, does Leon have a duty not to pollute a certain river but not because of its effects on fish but, rather, because he is entitled to a certain share of the river and, by polluting it, he eats into Maria's share and, in fact, ruins it? To take an agricultural example, farmers near the Mississippi River have used so much phosphorous that the phosphorous runs off into the Mississippi, traveling into the Gulf of Mexico, where it makes an enormous dead zone. This dead zone shrinks the area in which fishermen can catch fish.

Are the duties not to harm, duties to the environment itself, so that even if no sentient creature were harmed by our doing so, it might still be wrong to pollute a river? On this view, just as it makes sense to think we can harm sentient creatures, it makes sense to think we can harm non-sentient things—we hesitate to call them "beings," much less "creatures." And just as it can be wrong to harm sentient things, it can be wrong to harm non-sentient ones. So, on this view, pollution might be wrong *simply* because it harms the environment. Even if you could pollute a river without harming *any* sentient creature or without taking more than your share, it might still be wrong to do so. This view is expanded upon in Lisa Kemmerer's essay in Chapter 6, "Food and Religion."

CONCLUSION

As we have defined it, industrial agriculture is a scalar notion: A system can be more or less industrial and where it falls on the scale depends on weighing up various features that are themselves open to interpretation: How big is a big farm? How close to the monocultural ideal—same crop, same place, planting after planting—does it come? How much is a preponderance of GMOs? And so on.

When thinking about the cases for and against industrial agriculture, it is helpful to fasten on to *which* features are responsible for *which* goods (and which bads). Certain synthetic fertilizers are bad for the environment. Could they be taken from industrial agriculture without loss? If you took those fertilizers, would you have to take other things? If, instead, you have GMOs, do you *have* to have certain synthetics? *Must* those synthetics be bad for the environment? To what extent do objections to GMOs ultimately apply just as much to *all* industrial agriculture—and insofar as those objections do apply to all industrial agriculture, do they lose plausibility because they would prove too much if taken to be sound?

So far as the considerations presented against industrial agriculture are forceful, are they forceful against *any* industrial system? Or just the present one? If the former, then it would be good to have an alternative to industrial agriculture. The next chapter looks at two.

FURTHER ISSUES

1. *Prioritarianism*
Industrial agriculture raises an issue about *priority* for the worst off. When Earl Butz notoriously said, "Before we go back to organic agriculture, somebody is going to have to decide what 50 million people we are going to let starve," he was conveying that non-industrial

agriculture—not only organic agriculture—was going to fail to produce enough food and that it is owed to the people who will otherwise starve that the U.S. farms industrially.[28]

Some people would go beyond that and insist that we have a duty to help the worst off *because they are the worst off*. Is there a duty to help the worst off that goes beyond a duty to help those in need? Are there extra reasons to help the worst off because they are worst off? Why would there be? Some hold it is especially morally important to help the worst off. In some cases, this is quite plausible: You have an exclusive choice between giving some food to someone starving and someone who's not hungry. To whom should you give it? Not a hard question—give it to the starving person. Or you have an exclusive choice between making the very rich and the very poor both $100 richer or making the very rich $50 richer and the very poor $150 richer. What should you do? This case is fairly straightforward, because you can improve well-being more by giving to the poor than to the rich in these cases, dollar for dollar.

Prioritarianism goes further, and it insists that the interests of the worst off have *priority* over the interests of the rest even when equivalent amounts of well-being are at stake. On such a view, being worst-off itself provides reason to benefit that worst-off person. So, on a prioritarian view, the second option, giving the very poor more money, has some extra thing to recommend it: It makes the worst off better off. On some prioritarian views, consideration of priority always trumps other considerations, while on other prioritarian views, it might be permissible to prefer the first option if that is the *more fair* option, but, all the same, the second option would have something to recommend it, namely, that it's best for the worst off.

2. *Taking More Than Your Share*

Industrial agriculture raises an issue about taking more than one's share. Think of the environment as a good for the public to use. (This is already an ethically loaded way to think about this. Is the environment a good for the public to use?) Assume it is and that each should get a share of that good. When you use more than your share of farmland—as with industrial farms in South America and Africa that feed China—or when you render land unusable—as with dead zones—and thus deprive others of their share, you act unfairly because you take more than your share.

When you act unfairly here, do you act wrongly? Are all instances of unfair acting instances of wrongful acting? Sometimes unfair action at least seems to be permissible. Imagine if you and your brother share a medicine. Half is his; half is yours. You almost never use the medicine and, anyway, your condition isn't so serious. But your brother uses that same medicine regularly to treat a quite serious condition. One day, he runs out of his share. If he doesn't tap into yours, he'll suffer terribly. If he just takes some of your share, that's taking more than his share and acting unfairly. But it might be permissible here.

3. *Externalizing Costs*

Many people who suffer from environmental damage due to industrial farming are not the same people who benefit from it. The people whose water supply is depleted or polluted, the future individuals whose soil is degraded, the people whose air quality is worsened are people who suffer, but most of the people who benefit might be quite far away. The people whose homes are threatened by climate change might be people who benefit not at all from industrial agriculture. Or consider industrial agricultural workers: They take all the risks to make conventional food. Non-workers get the bulk of the rewards, as the readings in Chapter 11, "Workers," make clear. (The workers themselves are hardly reaping great benefits from the system.)[29]

In plenty of cases, there is nothing objectionable about one person or group bearing the costs while another person or group benefits. If you bake cookies and then *give* them to your brother—you love him, and it's his birthday—there's nothing objectionable about that. In plenty of other cases, however, there is something objectionable, as in a case in which your brother acquires cookies by charging them to your credit card without your permission. Industrial agriculture externalizes costs. In doing so, is it more like the former cookie case or the latter?

4. *Worries about GMOs*
Which worries strike you as the most powerful about GMOs? Worries about safety of consuming? There is a wide gap between scientific consensus about whether eating GM food is safe and American public opinion about that. Something at the heart of some of the worries about GMOs and also at the heart of some worries about synthetic pesticides and fertilizers— that the residue that's left on food is actually harmful despite our *currently* thinking it's not—is that we simply do not know what the risks are and that we have been wrong about such risks in the past. It is as if you are driving home from class and you can't even tell if the lump in the road is person shaped. Or as if a government spokesman with a good but not perfect track record of these things tells you the lump is trash-shaped rather than person-shaped. Under what conditions is it permissible—or required—for a non-expert majority to veto a course of action widely endorsed by experts?

Instead, are worries about the naturalness of GMOs most troubling? What is so great about "natural" products? (What is so suspicious about non-natural products? What does "natural" even mean here?)

5. *Industrial Agriculture and Population Control*
Without extremely coercive policies to quickly reduce global population growth to zero, one might question whether non-coercive population policies could reduce population growth fast enough to solve the challenge of feeding the world. If so, and if coercive population control policies would be ethically atrocious violations of fundamental human rights, the main argument that industrial agriculture is morally required might be revised as follows:

> Industrial agriculture is the only form of agriculture that allows us to feed the world in a way that does not violate fundamental human rights.
> If only one form of agriculture allows us to feed the world in a way that does not violate fundamental human rights, we should adopt it.
> Hence, we should adopt it.

Nonetheless, even if one ultimately endorses this argument, one might *also* endorse an argument that noncoercive population growth policies that benefit the poor and oppressed are *also* essential to feeding the world in a way that is ethically acceptable. The argument might be that:

> Meeting people's most fundamental needs of basic nutrition is much more ethically important than—and takes ethical priority over—almost everything else, except respecting people's most fundamental human rights.
> Hence, we must do whatever is necessary to feed the world, even if that means harming the environment, human health, and other valuable things.
> Yet, if it is necessary to harm other valuable things to feed the world, we have an obligation to minimize those harms, because those are still very significant harms.
> The way of feeding the world that minimizes harms to other valuable things is to adopt industrial agriculture in combination with noncoercive population policies.
> Hence, we are required to adopt both industrial agriculture and noncoercive population policies.

Note that whereas earlier arguments simply claimed that it would be wrong not to feed the world, the first premise attempts to add a more fundamental explanation of that claim, and argues that it follows from (allegedly) fundamental facts about what is ethically important, and how those values are to be prioritized, and how further trade-offs are to be made between those values.

This argument and the assumptions behind it raise a series of important questions that recur throughout the book. The claims that meeting fundamental needs of nutrition is important and not harming the environment is important raise claims about what is valuable. This raises a general question: Which things, if any, are ethically valuable? Being fed? Being free to have as many children as one wants? Conserving the environment? And these questions raise general questions of their own: If something is valuable, why is it valuable?

Also, the first premise makes a claim about *relative* value: It claims that meeting nutritional needs is *more* important than many other things. This raises a general question: If things are valuable, which things have *more* value than others? How do values *combine*? If a certain agricultural policy makes it so that present people can be well fed and have as many children as they would like while *also* making it so that future people have less food and a degraded environment, is that better than a system in which the freedoms of present-day people are limited somewhat but the quality of life for future people is much improved?

And then the first inference makes a further claim: *If* it's more important to do one thing than another, then you *should*—you *must*—do the former. This raises another question: *Should* we do what is best? If consequentialism is true, then, yes, of course. If not, no.

FURTHER READING

The History of Industrial Agriculture

Fernandez-Armesto, Felipe. 2002. *Near One Thousand Tables*. New York: Free Press.

Gaud, William. 1968. "The Green Revolution: Accomplishments and Apprehensions," speech to the Society for International Development. http://www.agbioworld.org/biotech-info/topics/borlaug/borlaug-green.html.

Pollan, Michael. 2001. "The Organic-Industrial Complex," *New York Times,* May 13.

———. 2006. *The Omnivore's Dilemma*. New York: Penguin.

———. 2008. *In Defense of Food*. New York: Penguin.

Stoll, Steven. 1998. *The Fruits of Natural Advantage*. Berkeley, CA: University of California Press.

———. 2003. *Larding the Lean Earth*. New York: Macmillan.

The Ethics of Risk-Taking

Gardiner, Stephen. 2006. "A Core Precautionary Principle," *The Journal of Political Philosophy* 14: 33–60.

Guerrero, Alexander. 2007. "Don't Know, Don't Kill," *Philosophical Studies* 136: 59–97.

Harsanyi, John. 1975. "Can the Maximin Principle Serve as a Basis for Morality?" *The American Political Science Review* 69: 594–606.

Lockhart, Ted. 2000. *Moral Uncertainty and Its Consequences*. New York: Oxford University Press.

Quiggin, John. 2013. "Complexity, Climate Change and the Precautionary Principle (Climate Change Working Paper: C07#3), Australian Research Council Federation Fellow, University of Queensland. http://www.uq.edu.au/rsmg/WP/Climate_Change/WPC07_3.pdf.

Sunstein, Cass. 2001. *Laws of Fear*. New York: Cambridge University Press.

GM Crops and Other Genetically Modified Organisms (GMOs)

Fedoroff, Nina. 2004. *Mendel in the Kitchen*. Washington, DC: Joseph Henry Press.

Lynas, Mark. 2015. "How I Got Converted to G.M.O. Food," *New York Times,* April 24.

Ronald, Pamela. 2008. *Tomorrow's Table: Organic Farming, Genetics, and the Future of Food*. New York: Oxford University Press.

Sandler, Ronald. (2015). "Bioengineering," in *Food Ethics: The Basics*. New York: Routledge.

Productivity

Rodale Institute. 2011. *Farming Systems Trial 30-Year Report*. Kutztown, PA: Rodale Institute.

Seufert, Verena, Navin Ramankutty, and Jonathan Foley. 2012. "Comparing the Yields of Organic and Conventional," *Nature* 485: 229–232.

The Environmental Impact of Industrial Agriculture

Altieri, Miguel. n.d. "Modern Agriculture: Ecological Impacts and the Possibilities for Truly Sustainable Farming." http://nature.berkeley.edu/~miguel-alt/modern_agriculture.html. Accessed May 2, 2016.

Desrochers, Pierre, and Hiroko Shimizu. 2012. *The Locavore's Dilemma*. Washington, DC: Public Affairs.

Fromartz, Samuel. 2006. *Organic Inc*. New York: Mariner Books.

Hurst, Blake. 2009. "The Omnivore's Delusion," *The American*, July 30, 2009. http://www.aei.org/publication/the-omnivores-delusion-against-the-agri-intellectuals/.

McWilliams, James. 2010. *Just Food*. Boston: Back Bay Books.

Union of Concerned Scientists. 2016. "Industrial Agriculture." http://www.ucsusa.org/our-work/food-agriculture/our-failing-food-system/industrial-agriculture#.VYR9-1Wqqkp. Accessed May 2, 2016.

The Non-Identity Problem

Barnes, Elizabeth. 2015. *The Minority Body*. New York: Oxford University Press.

Boonin, David. 2014. *The Non-Identity Problem and the Ethics of Future People*. New York: Oxford University Press.

Gardner, Molly. 2015. "The Non-Identity Problem," *wi-phi*. http://www.wi-phi.com/video/nonidentity-problem.

Parfit, Derek. 1984. *Reasons and Persons*. New York: Oxford University Press.

Roberts, Melinda. 2015. "The Nonidentity Problem," *Stanford Encyclopedia of Philosophy* (Winter 2015 edition). http://plato.stanford.edu/archives/win2015/entries/nonidentity-problem/.

Roberts, Melinda, and Wasserman, David. 2009. *Harming Future Persons*. Dordrecht: Springer.

Duties to the Environment

Goodpaster, Kenneth. 1978. "On Being Morally Considerable," *Journal of Philosophy* 75: 308–325.

Jamieson, Dale. 2008. "The Value of Nature" in *Ethics and the Environment*. New York: Cambridge University Press.

Rolston, Holmes, III. 1988. *Environmental Ethics: Duties to and Values in the Natural World*. Philadelphia: Temple University Press.

Schmidtz, David, and Elizabeth Willott, eds. 2012. *Environmental Ethics*, 2nd ed. New York: Oxford University Press.

Procreation Ethics

Benatar, David. 2006. *Better Never to Have Been*. New York: Oxford University Press.

Conly, Sarah. 2015. *One Child*. New York: Oxford University Press.

Connelly, Matthew. 2009. *Fatal Misconception*. Cambridge, MA: Harvard University Press.

Hannan, Sarah, Samantha Brennan, and Richard Vernon, eds. 2015. *Permissible Progeny*. New York: Oxford University Press.

Roberts, Melinda. 1998. *Child Versus Childmaker*. Lanham, MD: Rowman and Littlefield.

————. 2010. *Abortion and the Moral Significance of Merely Possible Persons*. Dordrecht, Netherlands: Springer.

Shiffrin, Seana Valentine. 1999. "Wrongful Life, Procreative Responsibility, and the Significance of Harm." *Legal Theory* 5: 117–148.

NOTES

1. Carolyn Dimitri, Anne Effland, and Neilson Conklin, "The 20th Century Transformation of U.S. Agriculture and Farm Policy" (Economic information bulletin; no. 3) (USDA, June 2005). http://www.ers.usda.gov/media/259572/eib3_1_.pdf (see figure 3).

2. Gaud, William. "The Green Revolution: Accomplishments and Apprehensions," speech to the Society for International Development, 1968. http://www.agbioworld.org/biotech-info/topics/borlaug/borlaug-green.html.

3. Gayland Ward Seed, "Major Crops Grown in the U.S.," 2013. http://www.gaylandwardseed.com/research/archives/11-2013. The numbers are based on USDA data. For updated numbers, see "Corn: Background," 2016. http://www.ers.usda.gov/topics/crops/corn/background.aspx.

4. McWilliams, James. *Just Food* (Boston: Back Bay Books, 2010), 5.

5. On this question, see "U.S. Could Feed 800 Million People with Grain That Livestock Eat," *Cornell Chronicle*, August 7, 1997. http://www.news.cornell.edu/stories/1997/08/us-could-feed-800-million-people-grain-livestock-eat.

6. See Seufert et. al., "Comparing the Yields of Organic and Conventional Agriculture," *Nature* 485 (2012): 229232.

7. Dimitri et al., "20th Century Transformation," cited in note 1 of this chapter. On the rewards—and lack thereof—of farming, see Bren Smith, "Don't Let Your Children Grow Up to Be Farmers" (op-ed), *New York Times*, August 9, 2014, http://www.nytimes.com/2014/08/10/opinion/sunday/dont-let-your-children-grow-up-to-be-farmers.html?_r=0, and the responses it precipitated. See, too, Blake Hurst, "The Omnivore's Delusion," *The American*, July 30, 2009, http://www.aei.org/publication/the-omnivores-delusion-against-the-agri-intellectuals/, and see the much-debated claims that farmer suicide rates are increasing—e.g., Madeleine Thomas, "How Can We Stop Farmer Suicides?" *Grist*, April 16, 2015, http://grist.org/food/how-can-we-stop-farmer-suicides/.

8. See Smith-Spangler et al., "Are Organic Foods Safer or Healthier Than Conventional Alternatives?" *Annals of Internal Medicine* 157 (2012): 348–366.

9. See Baranski et al., "Higher Antioxidant and Lower Cadmium Concentrations and Lower Incidence of Pesticide Residues in Organically Grown Crops," *British Journal of Nutrition* 112 (2014): 794–811.

10. See Environmental Working Group, "Shopper's Guide to Pesticides in Produce" (2015), http://www.ewg.org/foodnews/summary.php, and *Consumer Reports,* "Pesticide Use in Produce" (2015), www.consumerreports.org/content/dam/cro/magazine-articles/2015/May/Consumer Reports_From Crop to Table Report_March 2015.pdf.

11. See Smith-Spangler et al. (2012), referenced in note 8. The U.S. Environmental Protection Agency (EPA) claims that the "EPA sets limits on how much of a pesticide residue can remain on food and feed products, or commodities. These pesticide residue limits are known as tolerances. Tolerances are set to protect you from harmful levels of pesticides on your food. Inspectors from the Food and Drug Administration and the United States Department of Agriculture monitor food in interstate commerce to ensure that these limits are not exceeded" (from http://www.epa.gov/pesticides/food/viewtols.htm). In setting the tolerance, the EPA must make a safety finding that the pesticide can be used with "reasonable certainty of no harm" (from http://www.epa.gov/safepestcontrol/food-and-pesticides).

12. See Chapter 4, "Consumer Ethics," for more discussion of this notion of expected consequences.

13. For philosophical discussion of precautionary principles, see Sunstein (2001) and Gardiner (2006), listed in the "Further Reading" section of this chapter.

14. Union of Concerned Scientists, "Industrial Agriculture," 2016. http://www.ucsusa.org/our-work/food-agriculture/our-failing-food-system/industrial-agriculture#.VyewKaMrJE4.

15. J. R. Porter et al., "Food Security and Food Production Systems," in *Climate Change 2014* (Contribution of Working Group II to the Fifth Assessment Report of the IPCC), ed. C. B. Field et al. (Cambridge: Cambridge University Press, 2015), 485–533; D. Lobell et al., "Climate Trends and Global Crop Production Since 1980," *Science* 333 (2011): 616–620.

16. Samuel Fromartz,. *Organic Inc.* (Boston: Mariner Books, 2006), 3.

17. World Food Programme, "Hunger Statistics." 2016. http://www.wfp.org/hunger/stats.

18. For representative sources cited in support of these premises, see David Tilman et al., "Global Food Demand and the Sustainable Intensification of Agriculture," *Proceedings of the National Academy of Sciences* 108 (2011): 20260–20264, and Verena Seufert et al., "Comparing the Yields of Organic and Conventional Agriculture," *Nature* 485 (2012): 229–232. See also further discussion and citations in the text box.

19. As a leading example of this kind of model, see Tilman et al., as cited in note 17. For an accessible summary, see the graphic "A World Demanding More" in Jonathan Foley, "A Five Step Plan to Feed the World," *National Geographic,* http://www.nationalgeographic.com/foodfeatures/feeding-9-billion. See also the detailed explanation of the assumptions about the relationship between wealth and meat consumption that drive the calculations on pp. 7–10 of UN FAO (2006), *Livestock's Long Shadow* (full report). For the range reported here of 60%–120%, see Tara Garnett and Charles Godfray, *Sustainable Intensification in Agriculture* (Food Climate Research Network and Oxford Martin Programme on the Future of Food, University of Oxford, 2012), 12.

20. See p. 1, table 1, of United Nations, *World Population Prospects* (2015 revision), http://esa.un.org/unpd/wpp/Publications/Files/Key_Findings_WPP_2015.pdf.

21. See especially Tilman (cited in note 17), p. 20261, UN FAO (cited in note 18), p. 9, and Gordon Conway, *One Billion Hungry* (Cornell University Press, 2012), p. 11.

22. See USDA numbers for disappearance (which is a *proxy* for consumption—that is, a measurable quantity that appears to be so closely correlated with the quantity that we are interested in that it might be taken as a guide to it in the absence of more direct data) accessible online at: http://www.ers.usda.gov/data-products/livestock-meat-domestic-data.aspx. For another proxy based on livestock slaughter numbers, see: http:// www.ers.usda.gov/datafiles/Livestock_Meat_Domestic_Data/Meat_statistics/Livestock_and_poultry_slaughter/SlaughterCountsFull.xls. In addition to the fall of

per capita meat consumption, these numbers indicate that *total aggregate* U.S. meat consumption has also declined slightly since 2006.

23. For a nice depiction of this, see Jonathan Corum, "A Century of Meat," *New York Times*, March 15, 2011, http://www.nytimes.com/imagepages/2011/03/15/science/15food_graphic.html.

24. See http://faostat3.fao.org/home/E. See also the graph in Conway (cited in note 20), p. 11, which is one of the few major sources that explicitly notes the possibility of a downward trend in per capita demand beyond some threshold.

25. What exactly the conditions are under which a predictive model is a good model is a controversial issue in the philosophy of science. For a classic, controversial, and highly *pragmatist* view (i.e., one that does *not* see the *truth* of the assumptions of models as particularly important), see Milton Friedman, "The Methodology of Positive Economics," in *Essays in Positive Economics* (Chicago: University of Chicago Press, 1953).

26. See Amartya Sen, *Development as Freedom* (New York: Knopf, 1999), Chapter 9, which argues that female empowerment is the most important factor of these. For historical discussion of population control policies, see Matthew Connelly, *Fatal Misconception* (Cambridge, MA: Harvard University Press, 2010).

27. The example comes from Fran Krause's cartoon strip "Deep Dark Fears."

28. Butz makes a related argument, one involving the work-intensivity of organic agriculture, too, when he says, "If the family farm I grew up on had not adjusted, we would be shucking corn by hand, and we would be knocking potato bugs off potatoes with a wooden handle. . . . The family farm has to adjust. It has to produce more in the days ahead to survive" (quoted at http://downfalldictionary. blogspot.com.es/2014/01/earl-l-butz-just-plane-stupid-joke_5639.html).

29. Something like this will happen with any sort of agricultural system that has a class of farmers and a class of eaters: Some of the costs will be borne exclusively by the farmers. What makes industrial agriculture different is the severity of the costs and the concentration of short-term environmental costs on relatively few people in the present—people who work on farms and people who live near farms—and then the severity and concentration of long-term environmental costs on relatively few people who don't much benefit from industrial agriculture—low-income countries that will suffer most severely from climate change.

Norman Borlaug

Feeding a World of 10 Billion People

Borlaug is widely cited as the father of the Green Revolution. In this piece, he gives an (admittedly partial) overview of the Green Revolution, and he makes a case for industrial agriculture.

Norman Borlaug. 2003, "Feeding a World of Ten Billion People". IFDC, 4–8; 20–21.

AGRICULTURE AND POPULATION

In geologic terms, the domestication of plant and animal species is a recent event. Archaeological evidence indicates that all the primary cereals, economically important legumes, root crops, and animal species that are our principal sources of food were domesticated some 10,000 to 12,000 years ago. The process may well have begun when Neolithic women, faced with food shortages when their menfolk failed to bring home enough food from hunting forays, decided that something had to be done and began searching for a means to ensure a more permanent and reliable supply. This was achieved by sowing seed of the same wild grain species they had been collecting for untold millennia to supplement their meat diet. Thus, agriculture was born, and with it, permanent human settlements and the beginning of civilization. With the development of agriculture, the condition of humankind began to improve markedly, and human numbers, estimated to have been 15 million at that time, began to increase at an accelerated rate. A more stable food supply resulted in better nutrition and the development of a settled way of life, leading to higher survival rates and yet more rapid population growth.

World population presumably doubled four times—to about 250 million—from the beginning of agriculture to the start of the Christian era. It doubled again, to 500 million, by about 1650. The next doubling of the population required only 200 years, producing a population of one billion by 1850. At about that time the discovery of the nature and cause of infectious diseases—the dawn of modern medicine—began to lower death rates. It took only 80 years for the next doubling—to two billion people—which occurred about 1930. Shortly thereafter, the development of sulfa drugs, antibiotics, and improved vaccines led to a further substantial reduction in death rates, especially among infants and children. The next doubling of population took only 45 years—to about 1975, when global population reached four billion. The next doubling is projected by 2020, again only 45 years, representing a 533-fold increase since the discovery of agriculture.

While growth of world population overall is now slowing, the current rate in much of the developing world is still frighteningly high. Over the next 50 years, world population is likely to swell to 9-10 billion people, with 90% being born in low-income developing countries, and very likely into conditions of poverty. Hopefully, the UN predicts that by the end of the 21st century, world population will stabilize at 10-11 billion people, and much of the poverty that still haunts the world will have been abated. I must confess that I am less optimistic than many about how fast world population will slow, given the persistence of poverty and illiteracy.

There are two aspects to the problem of feeding the world's people. The first is the complex task of producing sufficient quantities of the desired foods to satisfy people's needs. The second task, equally or even more complex, is to distribute the food equitably. The chief impediment to equitable food distribution is poverty—lack of purchasing power. About 42% (2.6 billion) of the world's people are farmers and rely largely on their own agricultural efforts to feed themselves. Millions of these rural poor remain food insecure. Thus, only by increasing agricultural productivity in food-deficit areas can both aspects of the world food problem be ameliorated. . . .

FOOD PRODUCTION AND THE ROLE OF SCIENCE

By the early-1800s, German scientist Justus von Liebig and French scientist Jean-Baptiste Boussingault had established important theoretical foundations in soil chemistry and crop agronomy. Sir John Bennett Lawes produced superphosphate in England 1n 1842, and shipments of Chilean nitrates (nitrogen) began arriving in quantities to European and North American ports in the 1840s. However, the use of organic fertilizers (animal manure, crop residues, green manure crops) remained dominant into the early 1900s. Of course, the most skillful and dedicated users of organic fertilizers (which also included human waste) were the Chinese, Japanese, and Koreans.

The groundwork for more sophisticated genetic improvement of crop plant species was laid by Charles Darwin, in his writings on the variation of life species (published in 1859), and by Gregor Mendel through his discovery of the laws of genetic inheritance (reported in 1865). Darwin's book immediately generated a great deal of interest, discussion and controversy. Mendel's work was largely ignored for 35 years. The rediscovery of Mendel's work in 1900 provoked tremendous scientific interest and research in plant genetics.

The first decade of the 20th century brought a fundamental scientific breakthrough that was followed by the rapid commercialization of the breakthrough. In 1909, Fritz Haber, Nobel Laureate in Chemistry (1918), demonstrated the synthesis of ammonia from its elements. Four years later—in 1913—the company BASF, thanks to the innovative solutions of Karl Bosch, began operation of the world's first ammonia plant. The expansion of the fertilizer industry was soon arrested by WWI (ammonia used to produce nitrate for explosives), then by the great economic depression of the 1930s, and then again by the demand for explosives during WWII. However, after the war, rapidly increasing amounts of nitrogen became available and contributed greatly to boosting crop yields and production.

By the 1930s, much of the scientific knowledge needed for high-yielding agricultural production was available in the United States. However, widespread adoption was delayed by the great economic depression of the 1930s, which paralyzed the world's agricultural economy. It was not until WWII brought a much greater demand for food supplies that the new research findings began to be applied widely (excluding nitrogen fertilizer), first in the United States and later in many other countries.It is only since WWII that inorganic fertilizer use, and especially the application of low-cost nitrogen derived from synthetic ammonia, has become an indispensable component of modern agricultural production (nearly 80 million nutrient tons of nitrogen are now consumed annually). . . .

Professor Vaclav Smil of the University of Manitoba, who has studied nitrogen cycles for most of his professional life, estimates that 40% of the world's

6 billion people are alive today thanks to the Haber-Bosch process, which produces 80 million tons per year of chemical nitrogen (Smil, 1999). It would be impossible for organic sources to replace this amount of nitrogen. In fact, Smil calculates that organic sources of nitrogen could only feed 4 billion of the world's people, not the 6.2 billion we currently have. This message on the importance of chemical nitrogen was not lost on China, the world's greatest organic recycler, which beginning in the late 1970s relied increasingly on chemical fertilizer to raise yields and rapidly expand its food production.

THE GREEN REVOLUTION

Over the past four decades, sweeping changes have occurred in the factors of production used by farmers in many parts of the developing world but nowhere more dramatic than in India, Pakistan, China and other developing countries of Asia (Table 9.1).

High-yielding semi-dwarf varieties are now used on 84% and 74% of the wheat and rice area, respectively; irrigation has more than doubled—to 175 million ha; fertilizer consumption has increased more than 30-fold and now stands at about 70 million tons of total nutrients; tractor use has increased from 200,000 to 4.8 million units; and cereal production has tripled—from 309 to 962 million tons.

In describing the rapid spread of the new wheat and rice technology across Asia, William Gaud, the USAID Administrator, in a talk given on March 8, 1968, to the Society for International Development in Washington D.C., said:

> These and other developments in the field of agriculture contain the makings of a new revolution. It is not a violent Red Revolution like that of the Soviets or the White Revolution in Iran. But rather, I call it a Green Revolution.

Thus, the term "Green Revolution" was coined. To me, it symbolizes the process of applying agricultural science to develop modern techniques for Third World food production conditions. I believe that there has tended to be too much focus on the wheat and

TABLE 9.1   Changes in Factors of Production in Developing Asia.

	Adoption of Modern Varieties		Irrigation	Fertilizer Nutrient Consumption	Tractors	Cereal Production
	Wheat	**Rice**				
	(M ha/% area)		(million ha)	(million tons)	(million)	(million tons)
1961	0 / 0%	0 / 0%	87	2	0.2	309
1970	14 / 20%	15 / 20%	106	10	0.5	463
1980	39 / 49%	55 / 43%	129	29	2.0	618
1990	60 / 70%	85 / 65%	158	54	3.4	858
2000	70 / 84%	100 / 74%	175	70	4.8	962

Source: FAOSTAT, July 2002; author's estimates of modern variety adoption based on CIMMYT and IRRI data.

rice varieties themselves, as if they alone can produce miraculous results. Certainly, modern varieties can shift yield curves higher due to more efficient plant architecture and the incorporation of genetic sources of disease and insect resistance. However, modern, disease-resistant varieties can only achieve their genetic yield potential if systematic changes are also made in crop management, such as in dates and rates of planting, fertilization, water management, and weed and pest control. Moreover, many of these crop management changes must be applied simultaneously if the genetic yield potential of modern varieties is to be fully realized. For example, higher soil fertility and greater moisture availability for growing food crops also improve the ecology for weed, pest, and disease development. Thus, complementary improvements in weed, disease, and insect control are also required to achieve maximum benefits.

The Green Revolution has been a much-debated subject. During the late 1960s, the initial euphoria over the high-yielding wheat and rice varieties—and more intensive crop production practices—was followed by a wave of criticism. Some criticism reflected a sincere concern about social and economic problems in rural areas that were not—and cannot—be solved by technology alone. Some criticism was based on premature analyses of what was actually happening in areas where the Green Revolution technologies were being adopted. Some criticism focuses on issues of environmental damage and sustainability. Many of these criticisms have some element of truth to them. Obviously, wealth has

increased in irrigated areas, relative to less-favored rainfed regions, thus increasing income disparities. Cereals, with their higher yield potential, have displaced pulses and other lower yielding crops, but with a net gain in total calories produced. Farm mechanization has displaced low-paid laborers, although many have found better-paying jobs off the farm in towns and cities. High-yielding cereal varieties have replaced lower yielding land races, generally with significant improvements in disease resistance, especially in the case of wheat (Borlaug, 2000).

For those whose main concern is protecting the "environment," what would the world have been like without the technological advances that have occurred? Had the global cereal yields of 1950 still prevailed in 1999 we would have needed nearly 1.2 billion ha of additional land of the same quality instead of the 660 million that was used. Obviously, such a surplus of land was not available, and certainly not in Asia, where the population has increased from 1.2 to 3.8 billion over this time period. Moreover, if more environmentally fragile land had been brought into agricultural production, the impact on soil erosion, loss of forests and grasslands, biodiversity and extinction of wildlife species would have been much more severe.

The debate on benefits and shortcomings of the Green Revolution must be framed within the larger context of population growth. The continuing decline in the real price of cereals also needs to be considered. Lower food costs benefit everybody in society but especially the poor consumer. Finally, the very strong growth linkages between Green Revolution technology and industrial development are also apparent. Indeed, much of Asia's spectacular economic development in industry and services over the past 20 years has followed in the wake of the agricultural revolutions that preceded them.

Despite the successes of smallholder Asian farmers in applying Green Revolution technologies to triple cereal production since 1961, millions of miserably poor people remain, especially in South Asia. Huge stocks of grain have accumulated in India over the past several years, while tens of millions need more food but do not have the purchasing power to obtain it. China has been more successful in achieving broad-based economic growth and poverty reduction than India. Nobel Economics Laureate, Professor Amartya Sen, attributes the difference to the greater priority that the Chinese government has given to investments in rural education and health care services (Sen, 2000). Nearly 80% of the Chinese population is literate, whereas only 50% of the Indian population can read and write. Only 9% of Chinese children are malnourished compared with 45% in India. With a healthier and better educated rural population, China's economy has been able to grow about twice as fast as the Indian economy over the past two decades and today China has a per capita income nearly twice that of India. . . .

AGRICULTURE AND THE ENVIRONMENT

The current backlash against agricultural science and technology evident in some industrialized countries is hard for me to comprehend. Thanks to science and technology that has permitted increasing yields on the lands best suited to agriculture, world farmers have been able to leave untouched vast areas of land for other purposes.

Had the U.S. agricultural technology of 1940—when relatively little chemical fertilizer and agricultural chemicals were used—still persisted today we

would have needed an additional 233 million ha (575 million acres) of agricultural lands of the same quality to match 1997–98 average production of 700 million tons for the 17 main food and fiber crops produced in the United States. The area spared for other land uses is slightly greater than all the land in 25 states east of the Mississippi River.

If the 1950 average global cereal grain yield had still prevailed in 1998, instead of the 600 million ha that were used for production, we would have needed nearly 1.8 billion ha of land of the same quality to produce the current global harvest (Figure 9.1).

This amount of land generally was not available, especially in highly populated Asia. Moreover, had more environmentally fragile land been brought into agricultural production, the impact on soil erosion, loss of forests, grasslands, and biodiversity, and extinction of wildlife species would have been enormous.

The attacks against chemical fertilizers are also difficult to understand. Biochemically, it makes no difference to the plant whether the nitrate ion it "eats" comes from a bag of fertilizer or decomposing organic matter. Yet, to hear many uninformed people, chemical fertilizer is seen more as a poison than the plant food that it really is. Equally misinformed is the notion that "organically" produced food has higher nutritive value. This is not so.

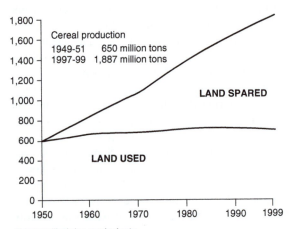

*Uses milled rice equivalents.
Source: FAO Production Yearbooks and AGROSTAT.

FIGURE 9.1   World Cereal* Production—Areas Saved Through Improved Technology, 1950–99.

Although the affluent nations can certainly afford to pay more for food produced by the so-called "organic" methods, the one billion chronically undernourished people of the low-income, food-deficit nations cannot. Indeed, it would be impossible for organic sources to replace the 80 million tons of nitrogen contained in chemical fertilizer. If we tried to do it with cattle manure, the world beef population would have to increase from about 1.5 billion to 6-7 billion head, with all of the resulting overgrazing, erosion and destruction of wildlife habitat this would cause. It would produce quite a heap of animal dung, too, and quite an aroma!

One might have thought that GMOs would have been warmly received by the green movement. So far, in cotton, maize and soybeans alone in the United States, pesticide use has been reduced by 21,000 tons due the use of varieties with insect resistance and herbicide tolerance. These reductions in pesticide use have increased farmer income by US $1.5 billion (Gianessi, 2002).

In the not too distant future—when science rather than emotions and ideology becomes more dominant—I predict that many environmentalists will embrace GMOs as a powerful "natural" tool to achieve greater environmental protection.

AGRICULTURE AND PEACE

Almost certainly, the first essential component of social justice is adequate food. And yet there are almost 1 billion people who go to bed every night hungry. Particularly disheartening are the 150 million young children who go hungry each day, with this undernourishment often leading to irreversible damage to their bodies and minds. . . .

Since agriculture provides employment for most people in low-income developing countries, it is not surprising that when this sector is allowed to falter, armed conflict often ensues. It is troubling to see the persistence of large military budgets around the world, including in the United States. In total something on the order of US $800 billion is spent annually on the military. The United States accounts for half of this total (about US $400 billion) and spends 40 times more on the military than it does on overseas development assistance. Indeed, trends in foreign assistance for agricultural and rural development have been declining, not only in the United States but also in many other donor countries and institutions as well. In 2000, the World Bank reported its lowest level of support to agriculture in its history.

REFERENCES

Borlaug, Norman E. 2000. The Green Revolution Revisited and the Road Ahead. Norwegian Nobel Institute, Oslo.

Gianessi, Leonard. 2002. Plant Biotechnology: Current and Potential impact for improving Pest Management in Us. Agriculture, National Center for Food and Agricultural Policy, Washington, D.C.

Sen, Amartya. 2000. Development as Freedom. Anchor Books, New York.

Smil, Vaclav. 1999. Long-range Perspectives on Inorganic Fertilizers in Global Agriculture, Travis P. Hignett Memorial Lecture, IFDC, Muscle Shoals, Alabama.

QUESTIONS

1. What are the considerations Borlaug enumerates in favor of conventional farming?
2. What are the worries he has about it? Do these worries show that conventional farming is seriously problematic? If so, how? If so, what remedies suggest themselves? (What remedies suggest themselves to Borlaug?)
3. One sort of worry Borlaug does not do much to address is that the Green Revolution is a form of objectionable cultural imperialism, that it imposes culture on unwilling subjects. Explain what the problem is. How do you think Borlaug should respond to it?

PIERRE DESROCHERS AND HIROKO SHIMIZU

Selections from *The Locavore's Dilemma*

This selection is from Desrochers and Shimizu's book that might equally have been called *The Non-Industrial Agriculturist's Dilemma*. From a marketing perspective, it is obvious why it is not titled that, but it would be more accurate since the book isn't really about local agriculture in particular. Rather, the book is a robust defense of industrial agriculture. The selection here defends conventional, industrially produced food on several grounds: the prosperity it's brought for workers and consumers, its environmental impact (compared to organic agriculture), and its high yield.

WHAT IS OUR BEEF WITH?

Food production and distribution is a complex business, so let us begin by making the obvious point that not all "local" food is created equal and that some of it is perfectly fine with us. For instance, New Hampshire maple syrup, California strawberries, Alaskan salmon and crabs, Washington apples, Florida oranges, Michigan cherries, and Iowa corn are among the best and most affordable in the world and, as a result, have long been enjoyed by nearby and distant consumers alike. Competitively priced, high-quality seasonal local fruits and vegetables have also long been sought after by nearby grocers and restaurateurs alike. "Hobby" gardening is its own psychic reward and should not be judged by economic criteria. In isolated rural areas where land is cheap, game animals abundant, and economic opportunities limited, it often makes perfect sense to cultivate large vegetable gardens along with fruit and nut trees; to keep animal coops while having a few grass-fed ruminants roam over the surrounding pastureland; and

to supply one's pantry, root cellar, and freezer with the results of hunting, fishing, and harvesting wild food of various kinds. Local food items that might not be the most delicious or economical might also have other redeeming qualities, such as an orchard that survives on "pick-your-own" family outings or an otherwise average vineyard to which a gourmet restaurant has been added. Some overpriced local food might also be sold for charitable purposes.

"Local when sensible" is obviously not our concern, nor do we believe that most committed locavores sincerely promote the cultivation of pineapples or bananas in the American snowbelt; in our experience, they would rather have local residents get by without them. We don't even disagree with their belief that "eating locally means eating seasonally," which, in turn, results in "deprivation lead[ing] to greater appreciation." In our view, food masochism should be left to the realm of personal preferences. Rather, we draw the line where local food is deemed desirable simply *because of its geographical origin* and is not more affordable, nutritious, safer, or better tasting than alternatives produced further away.

PHYSICAL GEOGRAPHY AND AGRICULTURAL SPECIALIZATION

As with all economic activities, a range of factors affects the profitability of agricultural endeavors, from the costs of various inputs (from diesel to insurance) and tax policies to consumers' shifting demands and producers' marketing abilities. More than any other sector, however, the success or failure of agricultural productions depends on where they take place. True, innovative behavior can sometimes overcome the shortcomings inherent to poorer, rockier, or less leveled soils; unsuitable climate for certain crops; less abundant water; or the poor quality of pastureland. Yet, as Adam Smith observed over two centuries ago, in many cases the "natural advantages which one country has over another in producing particular commodities are sometimes so great, that it is acknowledged by all the world to be in vain to struggle with them." For instance, with the help of the greenhouse technologies of his day, Smith observed, decent grapes could be grown in Scotland from which a very good wine could be made—but "at about 30 times the expense for which at least equally good can be brought from foreign countries." He then asked rhetorically if it would be reasonable to adopt a law "to prohibit the importation of all foreign wines, merely to encourage the making of claret and burgundy in Scotland?" Doing so, he points out, "would be a manifest absurdity" inasmuch as Scottish people would have to use thirty times as many resources than if they were to import wine from Southern Europe, resources which would then be no longer available to create wealth in other activities more suited to local conditions.

Smith's example was deliberately extreme in order to make his point, but many significant productivity differences between locations are often not obvious to nonspecialists. For example, fruit and vegetable producers located in more humid regions typically face more serious fungus problems than those located in drier ones. Some apple varieties are less resistant to cold weather than others. Dairy farmers whose pastureland is chock full of clover and high quality grass have less need to buy additional feed for their cows than competitors whose animals graze on poorer vegetation. Producers who benefit from a substantially longer growing season can justify massive investments in the development of new plant varieties that yield more berries over longer periods of time.

Whether obvious or more subtle, however, the most glaring shortcoming of the locavores' economic rhetoric is that it ignores productivity differentials—and therefore production costs—between agricultural locations. As all of agricultural history illustrates, trade between regions that specialize in products for which they have significant advantages (say, wine or wheat) delivers more food for less money than if producers in both regions tried to grow a range of crops unsuitable to their soil and climate. Though this is a basic fact of agricultural life, a growing number of local food activists argue that present-day regional specialization is largely the result of agricultural subsidies that benefit a few select crops such as corn. Get rid of these "comparative advantage mirages," they argue, and the economic profitability of monocultures will quickly be overtaken by those of polycultures—plots of land on which multiple and complementary plants and animals are produced. These arguments, however, do not stand up in light of the available historical evidence.

First, large-scale monocultures long predate modern subsidies and are as ancient as urbanization and maritime transportation—as is attested by, among other evidence, the large grain and olive-oil trade of Mediterranean antiquity. For instance, during Ancient Athens' peak period, its soft bread wheat supply was imported by ships from production zones located in what is now southern Russia, the Aegean islands, and the Greek mainland. Because of their poorer soil and drier climate, producers in Athens' hinterland could not compete with these foreigners and instead focused their efforts on growing barley (mostly for local consumption) and replanted lands formerly devoted to grain production with vineyards and olive and fig orchards, the output of which was both consumed domestically and exported over long distances.

The case made by food activists on behalf of poly-cultures is similarly weak. In short, polycultures—thanks to the supposed positive effects of the interactions of their attendant species—are said to deliver large amounts of food from little more than "soil, water, and sunlight." To bolster their case, pro-ponents of alternative agricultural systems often point to the Japanese farmer Takao Furuno who, on his seven-acre Kyushu farm, produces enough rice, vegetables, duck meat and eggs, fish, and vegetables to feed 100 local families. How this approach funda-mentally differs from old-fashioned subsistence agri-culture—now often labeled "globally-important ingenious agricultural heritage systems" (GIAHS) by activists and sustainable development theorists—isn't clear to us. After all, subsistence agriculture (GIAHS) is built on "natural ecological processes" rather than "against them; . . . endowed with nutrient-enriching plants, insect predators, pollinators, nitro-gen-fixing and nitrogen-decomposing bacteria, and a variety of other organisms that perform various ben-eficial ecological functions;" and characterized by "small farm size" and "diversified production based on mixtures of crops, trees, and animals with high genetic variability, maximum use of local resources, and low dependence on off-farm inputs" (such as synthetic chemicals manufactured in distant loca-tions). Or, as the historian Peter Garnsey observed in 1988, the ancient Greek and Roman small farmer "traditionally practiced mixed farming, the poly-cropping of arable and trees on the same land with the addition of a little livestock." Nice indeed, unless one remembers that subsistence farming everywhere always delivered very little return and low standards of living for all the hard labor required.

Of course, what really sets Furuno and other modern polyculture "pioneers" apart from their pre-decessors is that they benefit from much more ad-vanced technologies and knowledge—agricultural machinery, electricity, carbon fuels, refrigeration, transportation, electric fences, the help of agricultural extension scientists, etc.—and much wealthier cus-tomers, thanks to the fact that they ply their trade in societies in which long-distance trade, urbanization, and commercial agriculture have long displaced subsistence agriculture. Like all subsistence farmers before them, however, practitioners of "modern" polycultures exhibit comparatively low productivity and thus entail many more man-hours per unit of output. According to one sympathetic report, Furu-no's approach "requires far more intensive and con-tinuous management than does its industrial counterpart" and he "must carefully monitor the per-formance of each crop and apply any new insights the following season—requirements that add consider-ably to a farmer's labor hours." According to Matt Liebman, Iowa State University's cropping system diversification and polyculture expert, this method can require almost twice the labor hours as that of a conventional agribusiness approach. Lower produc-tivity and longer hours are then translated into higher price tags for consumers. There are good practical reasons why subsistence agriculture systems were supplanted by large-scale monocultures in all devel-oping economies a long time ago and they are still very relevant today. The importance of differences in soil and climate, along with the overall resources (in-cluding manpower) required to produce food, cannot be overlooked.

In the end, the fact that many otherwise prosper-ous locations are not amenable to a locavore life-style is too obvious to be ignored by proponents of locavorism, although they sometimes find a simple way around it. Perhaps the most telling example in this respect is that of writer Barbara Kingsolver who left her home outside of Tucson, Arizona, and relocated full-time with her family to a farm in Washington County in rural Virginia, "a place that could feed us: where rain falls, crops grow, and drinking water bubbles right up out of the grounds." She chronicled their experiences in a book that became a bestseller, *Animal, Vegetable, Miracle: A Year of Food Life.* We have no doubt that life in Washington County is pleasant if you can make a go of it. To most people, however, a location like Tucson—despite the fact that it was in its third year of drought when the Kingsolvers left and resi-dents wouldn't last long without massive food imports—offers more opportunities for personal development.

TIME AND TRADE-OFFS

Finally, another point lost on many locavores is that the one thing that money cannot buy is more time, thus making it the scarcest commodity of all. Once this is factored into many proposals to increase the production of "cheap and healthy" food, the end result doesn't look affordable anymore. For instance, the National Sustainable Agriculture Information Service recommends that food miles be reduced by having people eat minimally processed, packaged, and marketed food in season; can, dry, and preserve fruits and vegetables by themselves; and plant a garden and grow as much of their own food as possible. Add in the inconveniences of shopping at farmers' markets compared to conventional supermarkets and the time devoted to preparing meals increases drastically.

No doubt, people can accomplish many things cheaply—such as, say, growing organic tropical products in Maine—if their time and extra trouble are not factored in. In real life, however, most of us are happy to buy a house built by other people who specialize in various trades. The same is true where our food is concerned. Sure, many people are currently (re)discovering the joys of gardening or supporting local farmers out of a sense of duty. Michael Pollan might wax poetic over the fact that, by the end of the Second World War "more than 20 million [Victory] home gardens were supplying 40% of the produce consumed in America," but this relative success (after all, 40% was still not even a majority of the supply) owed much to a drastic reduction in the number of male farm workers and didn't last once more abundant and cheaper produce again became available through normal commercial channels. As a writer in the *Ladies' Home Journal* observed in 1929, "Primitive men spent nearly all his time getting, caring for, and preparing food. In a real sense, the aim of human progress has been to make these processes ever easier and easier. The less time we are forced to spend thinking about food, the more we have for higher things, so called." Many people might be yearning to connect with nature, community, and local food, but

much historical evidence suggests that most won't find it as rewarding as they first believed it to be.

As a result of urbanization and long distance trade in agricultural and other products, consumers in advanced economies now enjoy a much larger, diversified, and affordable year-round food supply than would have otherwise been the case. Because of the dramatically increased productivity that resulted from geographical specialization and economies of scale, numerous remunerative jobs were created in both the agricultural and nonagricultural sectors. For instance, according to 2000–2002 numbers, the average value of agricultural production per worker was about $50,000 in the United States and $40,000 for the United Kingdom compared to the much more "local" and labor intensive agricultural sectors of Nigeria and India, where these figures are respectively about $700 and $400. The United States and the United Kingdom could easily create the kind of jobs that Nigeria and India have in abundance, but much wealth would be destroyed in the process and a lower standard of living ensured for all. Besides, as the celebrity chef Anthony Bourdain observes, the "labor-intensive pastoral vision" of local food activists implies that "either lots of the citizens of wealthy countries like America and Italy are going to have to take up farming again," something which he rightly thinks unlikely, or else, "importing huge numbers of poor brown people from elsewhere—to grow those tasty, crunchy vegetables for more comfortable white masters. So, while animals of the future might be cruelty-free . . . what about life for those who have to shovel the shit from their stalls?"

Why is it that American and British agricultural workers are so much more productive than their Nigerian and Indian counterparts and, as a result, enjoy a much higher standard of living? Hard work is not the issue, for if anything Indian and Nigerian subsistence farmers work even harder than food producers in the U.S. and U.K. Rather, the difference between the two groups is that those in more advanced economies—where people specialize in what they do best in the most favorable locations and trade extensively with each other—belong to a much more sophisticated and geographically extended division of labor than subsistence farmers enjoy. Greater self-sufficiency has always been a one-way road to poverty, even at the national level. As was obvious to the geographer Jacques Redway more than a century ago:

> If a country or an inhabited area produces all the foodstuffs and commodities required by its people, the conditions are very fortunate. A very few nations, notably China and the United States, have such diverse conditions of climate, topography, and mineral resources, that they can, if necessary, produce within their national borders everything needed by their peoples. The prosecution of such a policy, however, is rarely economical; in the history of the past it has always resulted in weakness and disintegration. China is to-day helpless because of a policy of self-seclusion; and the marvelous growth of Japan began when her trade was thrown open to the world.

Of course, China's economic growth in the last few decades was entirely contingent on its becoming part of the international division of labor and on relying ever more on foreign goods and markets. Suffice it to say here that it is now the world's largest importer of soybeans (over 50 million tons a year as of this writing) to feed its hogs and chickens, even though soybeans are native to China and the country is the world's fourth largest producer of this commodity (although it lags significantly behind the top three, the U.S., Brazil, and Argentina).

True, increasing agricultural productivity and letting in cheaper imports will always hurt inefficient agricultural producers and their workers. On the other hand, cheaper prices mean that consumers have more income available to spend on other things—and all of us are consumers. In the end, if the economic case made by locavores was sensible, it would not stop at the "foodshed next door" but would revert all the way back to subsistence agriculture. And why stop there? Why not adopt a stance similar to that of the Horse Association of America a century ago? When faced with the advent of gasoline and diesel-powered engines, it "emphasized that reliance on horses kept money within the community whereas the use of tractors required an outflow of the cash required to purchase and operate the equipment."

The real key to economic development and improved standards of living, as Adam Smith identified

so long ago, is to make "a smaller quantity of labour produce a greater quantity of work." Creating miserable "local" jobs is easy, but creating prosperity and a higher standard of living requires long distance trade.

LOCAVORISM AND THE (MIS) MANAGEMENT OF NATURAL RESOURCES

An article of faith among locavores is that because their impacts are so concentrated in a few locations, modern industrial agriculture does more damage to the environment than smaller-scale and less technology-intensive operations. Ironically, the low productivity practices now advocated by locavores are the ones that previous generations of environmental activists believed were the cause of problems such as deforestation, massive soil erosion, depletion and compaction, and outright ecological collapse.

In an often quoted passage, Plato complained more than 2000 years ago that if Athens' hinterland hills had once been "covered with soil," the plains "full of rich earth," and the mountains displaying an "abundance of wood," by his time many mountains could "only afford sustenance to bees" while, as in small islands, all the "richer and softer parts of the soil [had] fallen away, and the mere skeleton of the land [was] being left." Even though some scholars now suggest that the Greek philosopher was exaggerating to make a point, fears of widespread land mismanagement and irremediable top soil losses recurred from then on. To give but one more recent illustration, in their 1939 classic *The Rape of the Earth: A World Survey of Soil Erosion* (a book which reviewed the vast literature of the time on the topic), British writers Graham Vernon Jacks and Robert Orr Whyte argued that "as the result solely of human mismanagement, the soils upon which men have attempted to found new civilizations are disappearing, washed away by water and blown away by wind"; that the "destruction of the earth's thin living cover is proceeding at a rate and on a scale unparalleled in history, and when that thin cover—the soil—is gone, the fertile regions where it formerly lay will be uninhabitable deserts," just as had happened to "former civilizations and empires whose ruined cities now lie amid barren wastes that once were the world's most fertile lands." Erosion, they proclaimed, was the "modern symptom of maladjustment between human society and its environment. It is a warning that nature is in full revolt against the sudden incursion of an exotic civilization into her ordered domains."

As is now obvious, although much damage was done in some areas, the global catastrophe predicted by past activists never materialized because of the adoption of a number of tools and strategies, from contour plowing, windbreaks, legume fallow crops, mulching and alley cropping to deferred and rotational grazing, drip irrigation, re-vegetation and no-till agriculture. Unfortunately, one of the greatest advances in combating erosion in the last decades— "no-till" agriculture, which leaves the root systems of previous crops undisturbed, thereby retaining organic matter and greatly discouraging erosion—is decried by many activists because of its reliance on rDNA-modified plants and synthetic herbicides.

Be that as it may, the key point is that by concentrating the growing of crops in ever more suitable locations, long distance trade not only maximized output and drastically lowered prices, but also significantly reduced the environmental impact of agriculture. For instance, the agricultural economist Dennis Avery observes that with the rise of the American corn and wheat belts in the 19th century, grain growers in Virginia's Shenandoah Valley could no longer compete with producers whose yields were three times higher than theirs and whose farm machinery didn't get damaged by buried rocks. In short order they had no choice but to switch to cattle grazing and wood production for which their land was better suited. As a result, in today's Shenandoah Valley wildlife is more common than in colonial and precolonial times, the area has gained beauty and the "huge soil erosion losses that cropping inflicted on its steep, rocky slopes" has long ended. True, the ecosystems of grain producing states from Indiana to

Montana have been profoundly altered, but because their land is more productive and less prone to erosion, more grain is now being produced on fewer acres and, overall, more habitat is available for wildlife. Avery further argues that, because of similar land use changes in many other locations, severe erosion problems are now largely confined "to poor countries extending low-yield farming onto fragile soils."

Of course, Avery was far from being the first agricultural analyst to observe this phenomenon. To quote but one other writer, the Marxist theorist Karl Kautsky observed in 1899 that "as long as any rural economy is self-sufficient it has to produce everything which it needs, irrespective of whether the soil is suitable or not. Grain has to be cultivated on infertile, stony and steeply sloping ground as well as on rich soils." In time, however, the emergence of commodity production and overseas competition meant that "it was no longer necessary to carry on producing grain on unsuitable soils, and where circumstances were favorable it was taken off the land and replaced by other types of agricultural production," such as orchards, cattle, and dairy farming.

International trade is also beneficial in terms of overall water usage, as exporting food from locations where it is abundant to regions where it isn't reduces the need to drain surface waters and aquifers in these less-productive areas. For instance, a country that imports one ton of wheat instead of producing it domestically is said to save about 1,300 cubic meters of local (or "indigenous") water. As food production represents approximately 70% of human water use, the issue is not insignificant. Trading agricultural products grown in water-rich regions to drier ones is now often subsumed under the labels of "virtual," "embedded," "embodied," or "hidden" water to describe the environmental benefits of the practice, but it has long been a reality because of simple economic incentives.

Perhaps the least heralded triumph of high-yield agriculture and international trade is that, along with urbanization, they have played a crucial role in the expansion of forested areas in significant parts of the Earth in the last two centuries. Contrary to the common belief that massive deforestation is a recent occurrence (with the bulk of it taking place in the tropical regions of the world during the last five decades), it is now acknowledged by specialists that perhaps as much as nine-tenths of all deforestation caused by human beings since the emergence of civilization occurred before 1950 as people needed to clear vast tracts of forested land in order to provide themselves with shelter, food, warmth, and a multitude of implements. A reversal of these trends (not attributable to wars, epidemics, or collapse of civilizations) began in the early decades of the 19th century in certain European countries through a process since labeled "forest transitions." In France, the forest area expanded by one-third between 1830 and 1960, and by a further quarter since 1960. Similar processes, although of varying intensity and scope, have been occurring in all major temperate and boreal forests and in every country with a per capita Gross Domestic Product (GDP) now exceeding U.S. $4,600 (roughly equal to the GDP of Chile) and in some developing economies, most notably China and India.

While in some cases this outcome can be traced back to aggressive governmental policies, these efforts would have been unthinkable without drastically improved agricultural and forestry productivity (including the development of tree or "fiber farms") that reduced harvesting pressures in other locations. Of course, this transition also owed much to the more efficient transformation of wood into various products and to carbon-fuels that were the basis of substitutes for organic fibers, dyes, and animal feed (when automobiles, tractors, and trucks became substitutes for horses).

Turning our back on the global food supply chain, and, in the process, reducing the quantity of food produced in the most suitable locations will inevitably result in larger amounts of inferior land being put under cultivation, the outcome of which can only be less output and greater environmental damage. Such problems would obviously be made worse by the locavores' rejection of technology-based approaches such as no-till farming. Unfortunately, these considerations are never addressed by locavores, whose primary focus is on reducing the distance that foodstuff travels between producers and final consumers.

QUESTIONS

1. In "What Is Our Beef With?" Desrochers and Shimizu explain in a roundabout way the thesis they are arguing against—what is it?

2. In "Physical Geography and Agricultural Specialization," Desrochers and Shimizu make an economic argument stemming from a claim about productivity differentials. What is a productivity differential? What work do productivity differentials do in Desrochers and Shimizu's argument? What is the conclusion of that argument? What point are they making in the paragraph about ancient Athenian monocultures? What does it have to do with contemporary local food production?

3. What is the point "proponents of alternative agricultural systems" are making with the example of Takao Furuno? Desrochers and Shimizu point out two significant costs of Furuno's system—what are they?

4. Desrochers and Shimizu write that "many otherwise prosperous locations are not amenable to a locavore lifestyle." So what? What does it have to do with the point they make about Barbara Kingsolver? What is that point? It is connected to what they say in the first paragraph of "Time and Trade-Offs?" That paragraph and the one that follows also offer an important rejoinder to the end of the Bill McKibben selection in the next chapter—what is McKibben's point there? How would Desrochers and Shimizu respond?

5. Explain the "article of faith" in the first paragraph of "Locavorism and the (Mis)management of Natural Resources" and Desrochers and Shimizu's rejoinder to it in that paragraph.

6. How did long-distance trade "significantly [reduce] the environmental impact of agriculture"? Which environmental impacts do they have in mind? Desrochers and Shimizu use this claim about environmental impacts to make an implicit argument. What's the argument? Against whom is it directed?

PAMELA RONALD

The Truth about GMOs

Ronald begins by summarizing what she takes to be some clear advantages of GM crops, concluding that they "appear to be precisely the kind of triumph of biology over chemicals envisioned by Rachel Carson, food security experts, and organic farmers who have long dreamed of reducing the use of synthetic chemicals and enhancing biological diversity on farms." At the same time, she notes ethically problematic facts about the current GM food system, such as the threat of domination by one multinational corporation, which focuses on benefiting farmers in the developed rather than developing world. She also notes the worry about weeds and pests developing resistance to engineered herbicide and pesticide properties of many GM crops and notes that there are ways of mitigating these threats, but emphasizes that these threats are not always mitigated in practice. She discusses worries about health risks and finds them to be without empirical merit. In the second half of her article, she considers explanations for why many people are skeptical of GM crops despite what she takes to be the scientific evidence, and she concludes by arguing that much is at stake in the GM debate, because much is to be gained by their widespread adoption.

Mama Moses has been growing bananas on her farm in southwestern Uganda for twenty years. She farms only bananas, which is typical of subsistence farmers in Sanga, the impoverished village where she lives. Last year, when she saw the flowers on her banana plants begin to shrivel and yellow bacteria ooze from the cut stems, she knew her crop was doomed. Within months the bacterial infection turned her healthy crop into a black, wilted mess.

Banana *Xanthomonas* wilt disease (BXW) is one of the greatest threats to banana production in Eastern Africa. Cultural practices provide some control, but they are ineffective during epidemics. More than a thousand kinds of banana can be found worldwide, but none has robust resistance to BXW. Even if resistance were identified, most scientists believe that breeding a new variety using conventional methods would take decades, assuming it is even possible.

BXW creates precisely the sort of food insecurity that affects the world's poorest people. Bananas and plantains are the fourth most valuable food crop after rice, wheat, and maize. Approximately one-third of the bananas produced globally are grown in sub-Saharan Africa, where bananas provide more than 25 percent of the food energy requirements for more than 100 million people.

For anyone worried about the future of global agriculture, Mama Moses's story is instructive. The world faces an enormous challenge: with changing diets and population growth of 2–3 billion over the next 40 years, UNESCO predicts that food production will need to rise by 70 percent by 2050. Many pests and diseases cannot, however, be controlled

Pamela Ronald, "The Truth about GMOs," in *The Boston Review* (September 6, 2013). http://www.bostonreview.net/forum/pamela-ronald-gmo-food

using conventional breeding methods. Moreover, subsistence farmers cannot afford most pesticides, which are often ineffective or harmful to the environment.

Yet many emerging agricultural catastrophes can almost certainly be avoided thanks to a modern form of plant breeding that uses genetic engineering (GE), a process that has led to reduced insecticide use and enhanced productivity of farms large and small.

In spite of these benefits, genetic engineering is anathema to many people. In the United States, we've seen attempts to force labeling of genetically modified organisms (GMOs). In much of Europe, farmers are prohibited from growing genetically engineered crops and so must import grain from the United States. And "GMO-free" zones are expanding in Japan.

The strong distrust of GE foods is curious. Opponents typically profess a high degree of concern for human welfare and the environment. They want the same things that scientists, farmers, food security experts, and environmentalists want: ecologically sound food production accessible to a growing global population. But their opposition threatens the great strides that have been made toward these goals through deployment of new technologies.

For 10,000 years, we have altered the genetic makeup of our crops. Conventional approaches are often crude, resulting in new varieties through a combination of trial and error, without knowledge of the precise function of the genes being moved around. Such methods include grafting or mixing genes of distantly related species through forced pollinations, as well as radiation treatments to induce random mutations in seeds. Today virtually everything we eat is produced from seeds that we have genetically altered in one way or another.

Over the last twenty years, scientists and breeders have used GE to create crop varieties that thrive in extreme environments or can withstand attacks by pests and disease. Like the older conventional varieties, GE crops are genetically altered, but in a manner that introduces fewer genetic changes. Genetic engineering can also be used to insert genes from distantly related species, such as bacteria, directly into a plant.

Given that modern genetic engineering is similar to techniques that have served humanity well for thousands of years and that the risks of unintended consequences are similar whether the variety is derived from the processes of GE or conventional gene alteration, it should come as no surprise that the GE crops currently on the market are as safe to eat and safe for the environment as organic or conventional foods. That is the conclusion reached by diverse agricultural and food experts. There is broad consensus on this point among highly regarded science-based organizations in the United States and abroad, including the American Medical Association, the National Academy of Sciences, the World Health Organization, and European Commission Joint Research Centre. In the seventeen years since GE crops were first grown commercially, not a single instance of adverse health or environmental effects has been documented.

To understand why farmers have embraced GE crops and how they benefit the environment, consider genetically engineered cotton. These varieties contain a bacterial protein called Bt that kills pests such as the cotton bollworm without harming beneficial insects and spiders. Bt is benign to humans, which is why organic farmers have used Bt as their primary method of pest control for 50 years. Today 70–90 percent of American, Indian, and Chinese farmers grow Bt cotton.

Recently, a team of Chinese and French scientists reported in the journal *Nature* that widespread planting of Bt cotton in China drastically reduced the spraying of synthetic chemicals, increased the abundance of beneficial organisms on farms, and decreased populations of crop-damaging insects. Planting of Bt cotton also reduced pesticide poisonings of farmers and their families. In Arizona farmers who plant Bt cotton spray half as much insecticide as do neighbors growing conventional cotton. The Bt farms also have greater biodiversity. In India, farmers growing Bt cotton increased their yields by 24 percent, their profits by 50 percent, and raised their living standards by 18 percent, according to one common standard that measures household expenditures.

GE papaya, engineered to withstand a devastating viral infection, has been similarly successful. First developed in 1998, it is now grown by 99 percent of Chinese and about 70 percent of Hawaiian papaya farmers. The GE papaya carries a snippet of the viral genome that immunizes it against infection. Conventional and organic papayas, which lack resistance, are infected with thousands-fold higher levels of the virus. There is currently no other method—organic or conventional—that can adequately control the disease.

Genetic engineering can be used not only to combat pests and diseases, but also to enable farmers to use less harmful chemicals to control crop-choking weeds. That is why 80–90 percent of the cotton, corn, soybeans, and sugar beets grown by U.S. farmers is genetically engineered for resistance to an herbicide called glyphosate. Farmers and home gardeners prefer glyphosate because it is much less toxic than earlier herbicides; indeed, the Environmental Protection Agency's "worst case risk assessment of glyphosate's many registered food uses concludes that human dietary exposure and risk are minimal." Glyphosate kills the weeds but not the herbicide-tolerant crop. This approach greatly reduces the need for ploughing or digging, the conventional and organic method for controlling weeds. In Argentina and the United States, the use of herbicide-tolerant soybeans is associated with a 25–58 percent decrease in the number of tillage operations. Such reduced tillage practices correlate with reduced soil erosion and a significant drop in greenhouse gas emissions. In 2005 the decreased tillage that accompanied planting of herbicide-tolerant soybeans was equivalent to removing 4 million cars from the roads.

There are dozens of other useful traits in the GE pipeline: nitrogen-efficient crops that reduce fertilizer run off; golden rice, a provitamin A–enriched rice; cassava that is resistant to viral infection; and drought-tolerant corn. My laboratory at the University of California, Davis has genetically engineered rice for tolerance to flooding and resistance to disease.

Some of these crops, such as cassava and golden rice, are important to poor farmers and their families in developing countries who lack nutrients and cannot pay the price of improved seed. Consumption of golden rice, within the normal diet of rice-dependent poor populations, could provide sufficient vitamin A to reduce substantially the estimated 2,200–6,850 deaths caused every day by vitamin A deficiency and save the sight of several hundred thousand people per year. This "biofortification" approach complements conventional supplementation, such as the World Health Organization's distribution of Vitamin A pills, which costs many times more and often does not reach the rural poor who have little access to roads.

These well-documented benefits of GE crops, which have been repeated around the world, appear to be precisely the kind of triumph of biology over chemicals envisioned by Rachel Carson, food security experts, and organic farmers who have long dreamed of reducing the use of synthetic chemicals and enhancing biological diversity on farms.

Considering our long history of plant genetic manipulation and the success of modern GE seeds in enhancing the sustainability of our farms and food supplies, why do some consumers still express grave unease over the planting of GE crops?

Much of the concern relates to a general distrust of large corporations, in particular, Monsanto, which produces a large proportion of the world's seeds. GE opponents fear that such corporations are taking advantage of farmers. Yet one need only observe the overwhelming farmer adoption of GE crops in the United States and elsewhere to conclude that the GE crop varieties on the market are useful to farmers. It is unlikely that experienced and skilled farmers would buy GE seeds if their farm operations did not benefit economically. Many U.S. farmers prefer Bt seed because it reduces reliance on sprayed insecticides that can harm farm workers and the environment. A recent Supreme Court case, *Bowman v. Monsanto,* highlighted the lengths farmers will go to obtain the seed, even when non-GE conventional alternatives are available.

The practice of buying seeds from seed companies has been criticized by opponents of GE seed. But seed purchasing is the norm in any non-subsistence farming system, whether or not the seed is genetically engineered, a fact that points to the abundant misinformation that plagues the debate over genetic engineering of crops.

Farmers often prefer to buy hybrid seed, a type of seed that inherits its useful traits, such as high yield, from two genetically distinct parents. These beneficial traits are lost in the second generation, so it makes no sense to save the seed from a crop and replant. The production of hybrid seed benefits the farmers, who are able to reap the advantages of the high-yielding seed, and the seed companies, which are able to reap a tidy profit each year the farmer buys the seed. Seed companies do produce seeds that can be replanted, but they are often lower yielding or susceptible to disease, which is why many crops grown by conventional and organic farmers are hybrids. Hybrid seed is not generated through genetic engineering and has been available since the 1920s. Genetic engineering does not, in and of itself, affect the ability of farmers to save their seed.

The priority for Monsanto and other for-profit seed companies is to produce high-quality seed for farmers in the developed world who can pay for them. But most farmers live in less developed countries and grow crops such as cassava or rice, which are not a priority for crop improvement in the developed world. For this reason, we need strong investment in public-sector research to develop improved seed for farmers who otherwise cannot afford it. We also need regulation of the seed industry to ensure fair dealing and to avoid the rise of a single company monopolizing the world's seed supply.

Today, more and more countries are exploring the use of genetic engineering for a greater variety of crops. Currently there are 30 commercialized GE crops cultivated worldwide. By 2015 there will be more than 120. Half will come from national technology providers in Asia and Latin America and are designed for domestic markets. The reduced dominance of U.S. seed companies may alleviate concerns of consumers who oppose genetic engineering because they see it only as a tool of large U.S. corporations.

Another common fear of anti-GE activists is the emergence of "super weeds" in the fields of herbicide-tolerant crops. Indeed, one drawback to using a single herbicide is that overuse can lead to the evolution of weeds that are resistant to that herbicide. For example, the liberal use of glyphosate has spurred the evolution of herbicide-resistant weeds. Twenty-four glyphosate-resistant weed species have been identified since herbicide-tolerant crops were introduced in 1996. But herbicide resistance is a problem for farmers who rely on a single herbicide regardless of whether they plant GE crops. For example, 64 weed species are resistant to the much more toxic herbicide atrazine, and no crops have been genetically engineered to withstand it. So even if herbicide-tolerant plants were nowhere to be found, conventional farmers would still have to develop strategies to manage weeds that are resistant to herbicides.

Farmers face similarly complex issues when controlling pests. One limitation of using any insecticide, whether it is organic, synthetic, or genetically engineered, is that insects can evolve resistance to it. For example, one crop pest, the diamondback moth (*Plutella xylostella*), has evolved resistance to Bt toxins under open-field conditions. This resistance occurred in response to repeated sprays of Bt toxins to control this pest on conventional (non-GE) vegetable crops.

Partly on the basis of the experience with the diamondback moth, scientists predicted that pests would evolve resistance to Bt crops if they were deployed widely in monocultures. For this reason, U.S. farmers who plant Bt crops are required to deploy a "refuge strategy": creating refuges of crop plants that do not make Bt toxins. This promotes survival of susceptible insects and has helped to delay evolution of pest resistance to Bt crops.

Global pest-monitoring data suggest that Bt crops have remained effective against most pests for more than a decade. Failure to provide adequate refuges appears to have hastened resistance of pink bollworm in India. In contrast, Arizona cotton growers who planted adequate refuges saw no increase in pink bollworm resistance. This example emphasizes the need to deploy a crop diversity strategy and crop rotation to reduce the evolution of insect resistance. This is the case for organic and conventional farmers too. Farmers cannot rely on seed alone to eliminate pests.

Perhaps the greatest concern surrounding GE foods is their effect on human health. Opponents regularly point out that GMOs have never been proven safe, which creates a great deal of anxiety. This is a difficult claim to rebut because GMOs don't define a testable class—in the same way that the Federal Aviation Administration can't test "planes" but can test individual aircraft—and because there is no evidence of harm for scientists to explore.

Yet individual GE crops have been studied extensively. A vast scientific literature considers the potential risk associated with GE crops. To help bridge the gap between consumers and scientists, one of my former students, Karl Haro von Mogel, and his colleague Anastasia Bodnar have created the GENetic Engineering Risk Atlas, a database that currently lists 600 studies examining safety, environmental impact, food composition, and other aspects of GE crops. One-third of these studies are not funded by companies that stand to profit from the results, and these studies support the scientific consensus that genetic engineering of crops is not inherently riskier than conventional methods of crop improvement.

There are a few intensely promoted and controversial studies that claim to refute the broad scientific consensus. For example, a study published last year purported to show that corn engineered for tolerance to glyphosate caused tumors and early death in rats. However, this finding was widely dismissed by scientists not involved with the study, including the European Food Safety Authority and six French science academies. They reported, "The authors' conclusions cannot be regarded as scientifically sound because of inadequacies in the design, reporting and analysis of the study as outlined in the paper."

Although the GE crops currently on the market are safe, every new variety must be assessed on a case-by-case basis. Each new plant variety, whether it is developed through genetic engineering or conventional approaches of genetic modification, carries a risk of unintended consequences. Whereas each new genetically engineered crop variety is assessed by three governmental agencies, conventional crops are not regulated. To date, compounds with harmful effects on humans or animals have been documented only in foods developed through conventional breeding approaches. For example, conventional breeders selected a celery variety with relatively high amounts of psoralens in order to deter insects that damage the plant. Some farm workers who harvested such celery developed a severe skin rash—an unintended consequence of this non-GE breeding strategy.

With all of the scientific evidence arrayed in support of the safety and environmental benefits of the GE crops currently on the market, we must look to other sources to understand opposition.

To some extent, it is a product of our political culture. There is often little critical scrutiny of the issues within a particular "tribe." For example, just as many on the political right discount the broad scientific consensus that human activities contribute to global warming, many on the left disregard the decades of scientific studies demonstrating the safety and wide-reaching benefits of GE crops.

Both the left and the right (and the center) discard reason when it doesn't suit their politics. Some activist groups manufacture uncertainty to stoke fear in consumers. They demand more testing despite the fact that GE crops are the most highly regulated crops on the market. As Daniel Engber aptly remarks in *Slate,* the success of the manufactured-uncertainty strategy "shows how the public's understanding of science has devolved into a perverse worship of uncertainty, a fanatical devotion to the god of the gaps."

Anti-science campaigns can have devastating consequences. Consider the anti-vaccination movement led by actress Jenny McCarthy and discredited physician Andrew Wakefield, which claims a link between the administration of the measles, mumps, and rubella vaccine and the appearance of autism and bowel disease. Many newspapers have promoted their views and many parents have chosen not to vaccinate their children, invoking a personal-belief exemption to skirt public school requirements.

The result has been a worldwide outbreak of measles and whooping cough. Marin County, California, home to a wealthy, educated populace, recently experienced the largest outbreak of whooping cough in the nation. Health care workers descended on Marin as if it were a third-world country to reeducate parents about the importance of vaccinating their children. Even today, despite the revocation of Wakefield's medical license because of his fraudulent claims and undisclosed conflicts of interest, the notion that vaccines can cause autism or other problems remains prevalent in some places, especially certain liberal, affluent ones.

In the case of the vaccine fraud, skepticism isn't a product of political culture so much as scientific illiteracy. The respected science journalist Michael Specter points out that consumers have a tendency to trust anecdotes over peer-reviewed results, which may explain why today "the United States is one of the only countries in the world where the vaccine rate for measles is going down."

A similar lack of comprehension likely afflicts opponents of modern crop varieties. Consumers have a tendency to group all "GMOs" together without regard to the purpose of the engineering, the needs of the farmer, or the social, environmental, economic, or nutritional benefits. They may be unaware that research organizations and scientists they otherwise trust agree that all GE crops currently on the market are safe to eat and safe for the environment, that each new crop variety is evaluated on a case-by-case basis, and that because each GE crop is different, testing them as a group is simply not possible and contesting their safety, in general, makes no sense.

This misunderstanding of the nature of GE crops underlies the labeling campaigns we have seen in recent years. These are not only public campaigns. Grocery giant Whole Foods has declared that within five years it will require labeling of all GMO foods sold in its stores. The implication of this labeling is that there is something worrisome about GMOs that consumers need to be warned about.

But to those of us who farm, carry out scientific research, or regulate food safety, it is clear that a GMO label provides scant information to the consumer and hinders the advancement of sustainable agriculture. The Food and Drug Administration does not support a GMO label because there are no known health effects. Almost all food would require such a label because virtually every crop grown for human consumption has been genetically modified in some way: bananas are sterile plants with artificially induced triple chromosomes, some varieties of California-certified organic rice were developed through radiation mutagenesis, and most cheeses use genetically engineered rennet as a key ingredient.

In other words, unless you forage for wild berries, hunt game, or catch wild salmon, you are consuming a food that has been genetically altered. For this reason, the FDA has concluded there is no universal or logical definition of GMO food. The FDA already requires stringent testing of food products and labeling of those that carry an ingredient found to be potentially harmful (such as peanuts), so there is no nutritional need for more labeling. The claim that consumers have a right to know what is in their food, prevalent during a 2012 referendum campaign to require GMO labeling in California, is also specious. Consumers have a right to know about potentially harmful ingredients, but a right to know about the presence of harmless GE ingredients is tantamount to a right to know that fruits contain sugars.

Whole Foods either believes that it can safeguard the food supply better than the FDA can, or it simply wants to sell more of its high-priced products. A. C. Gallo, president of Whole Foods, recently told the *New York Times,* "Some of our manufacturers say they've seen a 15 percent increase in sales of products they have labeled."

To reap greater profits is a perfectly legitimate goal for a corporation such as Whole Foods. But what about the health of families, farmers, and the environment? For those of us who want to advance sustainable agriculture, the fears promoted by Whole Foods and popular media figures such as Dr. Oz do a major disservice. These anti-GE forces have much to gain financially, but at great cost to farmers and their families in less developed countries, who benefit from what plant genetics can offer.

Once upon a time, if we needed more food, we could simply plough more land or cut down more rainforests for cultivation. No longer. This approach causes environmental damage and ignores the need of poor farmers in developing nations to enhance the productivity of their farms to ensure local food security.

It is time to change the debate about food production. Let's frame discussions about agriculture in the context of environmental, economic, and social impacts—the three pillars of sustainability. Rather than focusing on how a seed variety was developed, we must ask what most enhances local food security and can provide safe, abundant, and nutritious food to consumers. We must ask if rural communities can thrive and if farmers can make a profit. We must be sure that consumers can afford food. And finally we must minimize environmental degradation. This includes conserving land and water, enhancing farm biodiversity and soil fertility, reducing erosion, and minimizing harmful inputs. We must work together to identify the most appropriate technology to address a particular agricultural problem.

In the last twenty years we have seen dramatic advancements in plant genetics. In 2000 the first plant genome was sequenced after seven years at a cost of $70 million. This year the same project is expected to take two or three minutes and cost $99. Through genomic sequencing of diverse plant species and varieties, we have already learned an astonishing amount about the genetic diversity of our food crops. Seed is just one of many components needed for sustainable food production, but it is an important one. We would be foolish not to take advantage of the advances in plant genetics.

In the case of bananas and BXW, we may be able to control the disease by introducing genes from other plant species, such as rice, that confer resistance. Such resistance genes are widespread in plants and animals and are highly effective at controlling bacterial infection. These genes have already been incorporated in virtually all crops that we eat today, through conventional genetic approaches.

If millions of small-scale farmers see their banana crops wiped out for want of new disease-resistant varieties, it will be due both to the failure of world's agricultural scientists to make their voices heard and to the resistance of ideological opponents of modern genetic techniques. This is suffering that we can prevent.

QUESTIONS

1. What does Ronald take to be important connections between the anti-GM movement and the anti-vaccine movement? What might some take to be important disanalogies? What is the strongest single argument (whether you agree with it or not) that you can construct on the basis of Ronald's discussion and using other resources against the conclusions of those who are anti-GM and anti-vaccine (i.e., a single argument that applies to both views)? Put this argument into standard form. What objections might be raised to the argument?
2. What reasons does Ronald give to think that new conventional crop varieties are often more risky than GM varieties, given current regulatory standards?
3. Is Ronald in favor of labeling GM foods? What is her argument on that issue?
4. What might someone who objects to GM crops and much of industrial agriculture on the grounds of a strong precautionary principle say in response to Ronald's arguments? What do you think she might say in response?

Editor's note [from Boston Review]: The author is an employee of the University of California, Davis, a public institution. Her research is funded by the NSF, NIH, USDA, DOE, and the Bill and Melinda Gates Foundation. She is not funded by Monsanto.

ROSAMOND NAYLOR

GMOs and Preventing Hunger

Naylor highlights food security reasons for including GM crops in a range of tools we should often deploy to meet the challenges of feeding people in a way that is sustainable, especially given increasing threats from climate change and other factors in the coming decades. She argues that deploying GM crops in developing nations is often likely to be especially wise, and she discusses some of the resistance to GMs in those nations. Like Ronald, she also highlights a number of ethically problematic facts about the current GM food system.

Zambia became a poster child for the anti-GMO lobby in 2002 when then-President Levy Mwana-wasa refused to accept food aid that contained any genetically modified grain. Several other African countries followed suit, claiming that if the European Union worried about the health and safety of GE crops, then Africa should also be concerned. With more than thirteen million people in Southern Africa at risk of starvation due to crop failure from drought, the United Nations issued a statement endorsing the food-safety protocols of donor countries and encouraging the acceptance of GE food aid.

More than a decade later, the debate continues, with only four African countries—Egypt, Sudan, Burkina Faso, and South Africa—permitting the production of GE crops for sale. Uganda is now on the verge of becoming the fifth, in light of its ailing banana sector. Despite the importance of bananas for home consumption and rural incomes, however, the acceptance of GE crops for production and sale is mixed. Most banana growers in Uganda would like an immediate solution to the BXW epidemic and are willing to accept GMOs. But consumers remain wary.

Why the scare, especially when food security throughout the country is in jeopardy? For most countries, the issue revolves around two ideas about the ethics of food—first, that everyone has the right to know what is in their food, and second, that food carries strong cultural symbolism worth preserving. But this ethical stance, when focused specifically on health, ignores an important counterfactual: in the absence of GMOs, the same crops would be grown with pesticides or herbicides that are proven to be damaging to human health. In some of the world's poorest countries, lead-based pesticides are still widely used, causing lead poisoning and long-term cognitive impairment within the farming population. Moreover, anti-GMO advocates are silent about beer made from GE yeast, soft drinks made from GE high fructose corn syrup, and pharmaceuticals (including insulin) produced with genetic modification.

While there is little evidence of health risk from GMO consumption, the possibility that GE material might spread from one farm to another unintentionally, or to the wild where it can alter natural ecosystems irreversibly, is a serious problem. Sound biosafety

Rosamond Naylor, "The Truth about GMOs: Response," in *The Boston Review* (September 6, 2013). http://www.bostonreview.net/forum/truth-about-gmos/preventing-hunger

protocols for GE crops are extremely important, and Uganda should not adopt GE bananas until such measures are firmly in place.

Beyond biosafety, there are reasons to be concerned about who will actually benefit from the introduction of GE crops. Africa accounted for only 2 percent of the 170 million hectares of GE crops harvested worldwide in 2012. The United States, not surprisingly, occupied the leading role, with almost 70 million hectares under cultivation, followed by Brazil, Argentina, Canada, and India. South Africa was the largest producer on the African continent, with 2.9 million hectares sown to GE maize, soybeans, and cotton. Africa's small market for GE crops, along with limited competition in the industry (GE seeds are mostly controlled by a handful of international companies), could well preclude widespread participation by smallholders. Large seed companies typically have their eye on scale and profit margins. Unless special licensing arrangements are made with governments—which have not been skillful at operating seed companies in the past—or with nonprofit groups or local firms, GMO-planting prospects for small farmers throughout most of sub-Saharan Africa appear quite limited.

Despite such reasonable concerns, is there a wider role for GE crops in fighting persistent hunger and improving rural incomes in sub-Saharan Africa and South Asia, where most of the world's chronic malnutrition is found? Yes, especially when considering the potential impacts of climate change. Most climate scientists agree that the world is likely to experience higher temperatures, decreased soil moisture, and more extreme flooding events in the decades to come. Subtropical regions are likely to face an increase in the frequency and severity of droughts. By 2050, growing-season temperatures in many tropical and subtropical countries will surpass even the warmest seasons of the past century. Staple crops in both sub-Saharan Africa and South Asia are already grown at well above their optimum temperatures, placing them at high risk from climate change. Sub-Saharan Africa, with only five percent of its agricultural land irrigated, is particularly vulnerable to the combined effects of extreme heat and dry soil conditions. These concerns about climate change are important because multiple genes control heat and drought tolerance in plants, making it difficult to breed for these traits using conventional techniques.

It would be unwise to limit the world's agricultural toolkit at a time when pests, diseases, and climate change threaten the food security of many low-income countries. The ethics of GMOs and the range of possibilities in solving world hunger need to be discussed openly. To say no to GE crops without debate would be an imprudent form of triage most countries would regret.

QUESTIONS

1. What are two widely held ethical values that Naylor notes that are relevant to GM crops? What does she argue is a complicating factor for arguments from these values to anti-GM conclusions? Explain.
2. Should people who are anti-GM crops also be opposed to drinking beer, drinking soda, and to using many contemporary pharmaceuticals? What is the argument that they should be, suggested by Naylor's discussion? How are these considerations relevant to the question of whether we should be against GM crops?
3. Was it ethically wrong for the United Nations to encourage developing nations to accept GM food as aid, assuming the majority of citizens of those developing nations do not want GM food? Would it be wrong for the United Nations to incentivize acceptance of GM foods in such situations if a minority of the population of those nations was otherwise in danger of severe malnutrition? What about incentivizing acceptance of GM crops when there is no emergency?
4. What are the negative effects of climate change on agriculture, especially in developing nations, that Naylor highlights?

TOM PHILPOTT

Why I'm Still Skeptical of GMOs

Philpott suggests that GM crops might have short-term benefits, but that these might hide even larger long-term costs, on the grounds that their deployment might predictably make us need to use massively more pesticides and herbicides in the future.

Over the weekend [of January 4, 2014], listservs, blogs, and Twitter feeds lit up with reactions to Amy Harmon's *New York Times* deep dive into the politics behind a partial ban on growing genetically modified crops on Hawaii's main island.[1] The fuss obscured a much more significant development that occurred with little fanfare (and no *Times* attention) [on January 3, 2014], when the US Department of Agriculture took a giant step toward approving a controversial new crop promoted by Dow Agrosciences that could significantly ramp up the chemical war on weeds being waged in the Midwest's corn and soybean fields.[2] Since the '90s, the widespread use of corn and soy crops genetically engineered to withstand the herbicide Roundup has led more weeds to resist that chemical. Farmers have responded by using even more chemicals.[3] Dow's new product promises to fix that problem. The company is peddling corn and soy seeds engineered to withstand not just Roundup, but also an older and much more toxic herbicide called 2,4-D. In a January 3 [2014] press release, the company noted that "an astonishing 86 percent of corn, soybean and cotton growers in the South have herbicide-resistant or hard-to-control weeds on their farms," as do more than 61 percent of farms in the Midwest.[4] "Growers need new tools now to address this challenge," Dow insisted.

Use of 2,4-D—the less toxic half of the infamous Vietnam-era defoliant Agent Orange—had been dwindling for years, but the rise of Roundup-resistant superweeds has revived it. Farmers have been using it to "burn down" superweed-ridden fields before the spring planting of corn and soybeans.[5] But if Dow gets its way, they'll be able to resort to it even after the crops emerge. Dow has downplayed the concern that the new products will lead weeds to develop resistance to 2,4-D. But in a 2011 paper,[6] weed experts from Penn State University—hardly a hotbed of anti-GMO activism—concluded that chances are "actually quite high" that Dow's new product will unleash a new plague of super-duper-weeds that resist both Roundup and 2,4-D. (I laid out the details of their argument in [another article].[7]) In their model for how the new product would affect herbicide application rates on soybeans, they project that glyphosate (Roundup) use will hold steady, but that "other herbicides," mostly 2,4-D, will spike—meaning a windfall for Dow but nothing good for the environment.

The USDA, which oversees the introduction of new GMO crops, appeared set to green-light Dow's new wonderseeds at the end of 2012. But in May of [2013], after a firestorm of criticism from environmental groups, the department slowed down the process,[8] announcing in a press release it had decided that release of the novel products "may significantly

Tom Philpott, "Why I'm Still Skeptical of GMOs," in *Mother Jones* (January 7, 2014). http://www.motherjones.com/tom-philpott/2014/01/usda-prepares-greenlight-chemical-war-weeds affect the quality of the human environment," and that a thorough environmental impact statement (EIS) was necessary before such a decision could be made.[9]

Then on [January 3, 2014], the USDA reversed itself—it released the draft of the promised EIS, and in it, the department recommended that Dow's 2,4-D-ready crops be unleashed upon the land. Once the draft is published in the Federal Register on January 10, [2014] there will be a 45-day public comment period, after which the USDA will make its final decision. At this point, approval seems imminent—probably in time for the 2015 growing season, as Dow suggested in its press release reacting to the news.[10]

Why did the USDA switch from "may significantly affect the quality of the human environment" to a meek call for deregulation? As the USDA itself admits in its [January 3, 2014] press release, the department ultimately assesses new GMO crops through an extremely narrow lens: whether or not they act as a "pest" to other plants—that is, they'll withhold approval only if the crops themselves, and not the herbicide tsunami and upsurge in resistant weeds they seem set to bring forth, pose a threat to other plants.[11] And Dow's new corn and soy crops don't cross that line, the USDA claims. I explained the tortured history and logic behind the USDA's "plant pest" test in [another article].[12] Long story short: It's an antiquated, fictional standard that doesn't allow for much actual regulation.

US farmers planted about 170 million acres of corn and soy in 2013—a combined land mass roughly equal to the footprint of Texas.[13] Every year, upwards of 80 percent of it is now engineered to resist Monsanto's Roundup.[14] It's chilling to imagine that Dow's 2,4-D-ready products might soon enjoy a similar range.

Given the USDA's regulatory impotence in the face of such a specter, perhaps the Hawaiian activists who pushed for that ban aren't quite as daft as the *New York Times* portrayed them in its recent piece. The big biotech companies don't operate on the island that imposed the partial ban on GMOs. But as another *New York Times* piece, this one from 2011, shows, they do operate on other islands within the state—using them as a testing ground for novel crops and a place to grow out GMO seeds, taking advantage of the warm climate that allows several crops per year.[15] According to the *Times,* GMO seeds are now bigger business in Hawaii than tropical staples like coffee, sugarcane, and pineapples—and the GMO/agrichemical giants have "have stepped into the leading, and sometimes domineering role, once played by the islands' sugar barons." As for Dow, it cops to having field-tested its 2,4-D-ready corn there.[16]

NOTES

1. http://www.nytimes.com/2014/01/05/us/on-hawaii-a-lonely-quest-for-facts-about-gmos.html

2. http://www.aphis.usda.gov/newsroom/2014/01/eis_ge_products.shtml

3. See Figure 5 at http://www.scribd.com/doc/158931501/Superweeds-How-Biotech-Crops-Bolster-the-Pesticide-Industry

4. http://newsroom.dowagro.com/press-release/dow-agrosciences-statement-about-usda-announcement-regarding-draft-environmental-impac

5. https://ag.purdue.edu/btny/weedscience/Documents/BurndownMadness.pdf

6. http://www.jstor.org/pss/10.1525/bio.2012.62.1.12

7. http://www.motherjones.com/tom-philpott/2012/01/dows-new-gmo-seed-puts-us-agriculture-crossroads

8. http://www.motherjones.com/tom-philpott/2013/05/shocking-everyone-usda-sticks-it-monsanto-and-dow%E2%80%94-least-temporarily

9. http://www.aphis.usda.gov/newsroom/2013/05/brs_24d_and_dicamba.shtml

10. http://newsroom.dowagro.com/press-release/dow-agrosciences-statement-about-usda-announcement-regarding-draft-environmental-impac

11. http://www.aphis.usda.gov/newsroom/2014/01/eis_ge_products.shtml

12. http://www.motherjones.com/environment/2011/07/usda-deregulate-roundup-gmo-tom-philpott

13. http://www.nass.usda.gov/Newsroom/2013/03_28_2013.asp

14. http://www.nass.usda.gov/Newsroom/2013/03_28_2013.asp

15. http://www.nytimes.com/gwire/2011/08/22/22greenwire-king-corn-takes-root-in-hawaii-28466.html

16. http://www.aphis.usda.gov/brs/aphisdocs/09_23301p.pdf

QUESTIONS

1. What are superweeds? What are super-duper-weeds? Why are they potentially a problem for GM crops? Why is this problem for GM crops a problem for people?
2. How should utilitarians think about a situation where we can certainly make ourselves much better off over the next decade, but at the cost of greater harms in the further future?
3. What would happen if all pesticides and herbicides were banned, along with all GMOs? Do you think Philpott thinks we should do this? If not, what, exactly, does he think we should do?
4. Do Philpott's objections apply equally to non-GM industrial monoculture? Explain.
5. If you were in charge of protecting our drinking water and ensuring that we had healthy air to breathe, would you ban all pollutants? What would be the costs of banning all pollutants? Why might someone argue that there are different "optimal" levels of pollution from different sources that we should endorse given our actual circumstances? How might such a person think that such "optimal" levels should be calculated? What would a utilitarian say about "optimal" levels? What would someone say who thought that everyone had a fundamental human right to clean water and clean air? Would those who endorse these different ethical frameworks differ on what levels they thought were "optimal"? In what ways? Would these levels be much higher in developing nations than in developed nations? Would it be an injustice to have much higher levels as the targets of policy in developing nations than in developed nations? How are these questions relevant to these issues about genetically modified foods, and to food systems policy in general?

10) Alternatives to Industrial Plant Agriculture

The selections in this chapter discuss small- and medium-scale organic farms and networks of small-scale local farms. These forms of agriculture are embraced by some as alternatives to the industrial model discussed in Chapter 9, "Industrial Plant Agriculture." They are also embraced by some as alternative ways of structuring the food system. This chapter introduces and evaluates these two alternatives.

* * *

Remember that industrial agriculture, when it comes to plants, typically involves more than one of the following:

- Large-scale farms that feature a preponderance of monocultures—concentrations of single crops rather than a multitude in a given area over a given period of time—where
- Those farms are concentrated in comparatively advantageous locations (e.g., soy and corn monoculture fields in the Midwestern United States, banana monoculture plantations in equatorial regions, rice paddy monoculture in Southeast Asia and other relevantly similar locations, and oil palm monoculture plantations in Indonesia and other similar locations), where
- Crops are raised with liberal application of (synthetic) fertilizer, pesticides, herbicides, insecticides, and irrigated water, where
- Crops may be genetically modified organisms (GMOs), organisms whose genetic code has been modified using biotechnology, and
- There is global trade in crops and agricultural inputs, dominated by multinational companies. This global trade is part of the neoliberal economic order.

Industrial agriculture doesn't require all of these. A country might have a bunch of large-scale, monocultural farms that use lots of synthetics pesticides and GMOs but also may *not* be involved in the global trade and also have its farms distributed all over the country. Such a system would be industrial, just not as industrial as could be. So the way we are thinking of it, industrial agriculture is a scalar notion: an agricultural system can be more or less industrial. A system that involved large-scale farming but nothing else on the list would be *less* industrial than one that involved a similar quantity of monocultural, large-scale farms that use synthetic inputs. And a system that involved all five items on the list would be more industrial than both.

The readings in this chapter focus on alternatives to industrial agriculture. In particular, they focus on two alternatives prominent in the United States. These alternatives are important because *if* the status quo is bad in various ways that we have moral reasons to prevent, then we have moral reasons to find alternatives to the industrial status quo. Yet merely knowing that the status quo is bad or objectionable in various ways does not tell us which alternatives are preferable. (Compare: If you need to give a sick patient some medicine and don't know which of three medicines to give her, finding out that she is badly allergic to one of the medicines is useful—you shouldn't give her that one. But you still don't know which alternative to give her.)

Some of the selections that follow cover *organic agriculture*: what it is, whether it is a good idea, and, if so, why. As we discussed in previous chapters, organic farms can be industrial, but they also can be clear alternatives to industrial farms, and such farms are the ones we focus on. These farms rate low on the industrial scale by not being large-scale, and by avoiding monocultures, synthetic chemicals, and GMOs.

Some of the selections that follow cover *local agriculture*. Local farms can be industrial—your next-door neighbor might have an industrial beet farm—but they also can be clear alternatives to industrial agriculture, and such farms are the ones we focus on. On the industrial agricultural model, most of our food is grown in relatively few places: tomatoes in Florida, corn in some Midwestern states, all sorts of things in the Central Valley of California. That food is then shipped to Pennsylvania, Minnesota, New Mexico, and so forth. The local alternative would involve people in Pennsylvania, Minnesota, New Mexico, and so on producing more of their own food and doing so in a non-industrial sort of way. These farms can be but needn't be organic. This alternative scores low on the industrial scale by avoiding large farms and avoiding a concentrations of farms—the local ideal is that farms will be everywhere, providing food for their communities.

There is also a way to develop the local alternative so that it scores lower on the industrial scale by withdrawing from the global, neoliberal economy. Recall from Chapter 3, "Food Justice," that some people call for a radically reformed global food system. They see the current system as pervasively unjust—mistreating workers, perpetuating poverty, degrading the environment, exploiting poorer countries, and giving power to multinational companies and international organizations rather than empowering citizens and communities. From their perspective, the problems with the global food system cannot be fixed by modest changes to policies but are the inevitable result of the basic structure of the global food system: That food system is *industrialized*, *globalized*, and based in *neoliberalism*, the political economic system emphasizing free market capitalism and a minimal state. One vision for an alternative food system is offered by the food sovereignty movement, which proposes smaller-scale food systems that are democratically controlled at the local and regional level, rather than globalized, industrialized food systems controlled by multinational companies and by international agreements made between national governments. Some critics of food sovereignty believe that globalized markets are essential for ensuring food security and improving the situation of the global poor, and that rolling back globalization would be a mistake.

In this introduction, we discuss the organic alternative first and then the local one.

WHAT ORGANIC FOOD IS AND ISN'T

When you think about organic food, what do you think of? Something nutritious? Something expensive? Something produced in an environmentally friendly way? By a family? By a family of hippies? By a local family of hippies? By a family using old-fashioned methods?

"Organic" is a legally regulated term in the United States. Food with the United States Department of Agriculture (USDA) organic seal or a variety of regional seals is certified organic by the government. (Certifying *bodies* vary from place to place in the United States, but the rules are the same.) Food that earns the certification is organic. Food that does not is conventional. To earn certification, food has to be produced according to lengthy USDA guidelines. To simplify, these guidelines state:

> Organic *crops* must not be genetically modified organisms. They cannot be irradiated. They cannot be treated with sewage sludge, synthetic fertilizers, synthetic herbicides, and most synthetic pesticides. They must come from fields making use of crop rotation and green manures.
>
> Organic *livestock* must not be treated with antibiotics or given growth hormones and must be given entirely organic food and must be provided with access to the outdoors.
>
> Organic *multi-ingredient food* must have at least 95% organic content and the remaining 5% must come from ingredients on a government-approved list.[1]

That's it. There's nothing in the guidelines about organic food being nutritious. There is nothing in the regulations about the food being grown in an environmentally friendly way. There is nothing in them about the food being grown in a low-tech way. Or by hippies. There is nothing in the guidelines about animals being well treated or even better treated than on conventional farms. There is nothing in the guidelines about workers at all, much less something mandating they be well treated. Also, importantly, there is nothing in the guidelines about the food being produced on a small scale or on a farm near its consumers. Because of this, it is *possible* for organic food to be produced in the industrial way outlined in previous chapters. It is possible for organic farms to be massive monocultures that are grown in a fashion that is harmful to the environment, to workers, to people who live nearby. What this brings out, what Joan Gussow's article that follows brings out, too, is that there is a gap between organic ideals and organic laws.

Other countries have different guidelines. The European Union guidelines are similar to the United States' guidelines.[2] So too are Canada's. Japan's and the United States' guidelines are very similar for produce and plant-based processed foods.

In the United States, food that meets these guidelines and is certified as such is organic. Food that either doesn't meet the guidelines or isn't certified as doing so is conventional.

COMPARISON OF ORGANIC AND LOCAL

As we said, it is possible for organic food to be non-local: If you are in California and buy organic peaches from Georgia, you have some organic, non-local food. It is also possible for local food to be non-organic: If you grow genetically modified tomatoes in your garden and sell them in your neighborhood, you have produced some local, non-organic food.

Furthermore, it is possible to have organic food that is grown on huge, far-off farms that grow monocultures in ways that are, on balance, damaging to the environment. This would be an industrial organic farm. The history of the organic movement and organic regulation in the United States help explain how these possibilities came to be. Before we get to that history, let us discuss some terminology.

First, the distinction between industrial agriculture and non-industrial agriculture is *not* the same as the distinction between conventional agriculture and organic agriculture.

- The organic/conventional distinction is largely about inputs. Organic farming requires limited putting of synthetics into and onto the soil. No putting GMOs into the ground. No putting conventional food into animals' diet. No putting antibiotics into them. The industrial/non-industrial distinction is not just about inputs.
- Because of this difference, the industrial/non-industrial distinction cross-cuts the organic/conventional distinction. It's possible to have organic farms that are large-scale monocultures. So it is possible to have an organic industrial farm. Similarly, it is possible to have a conventional, non-industrial farm, such as a small-scale, diversified farm that occasionally uses GMOs or synthetic herbicides. That farm would not be organic, but it would also be non-industrial.

Second, the distinction between industrial animal agriculture and free-range animal agriculture is *not* the same as the distinction between conventional and organic. There are two ways of seeing that the distinctions are different. For one thing, the free-range/industrial animal agriculture distinction applies only to livestock, not plants or processed food. There are free-range chickens and industrially farmed chickens but, obviously, no free-range apples or pretzels. Yet the organic/conventional distinction covers chickens, apples, and pretzels. It covers livestock, produce, and processed food. For another thing, even when it comes to livestock, the two distinctions are different. To meet the organic regulations, an animal needs to eat strictly organic feed. So it's easy to see how a free-range chicken could be conventional: Let it range as freely as it wants but give it some conventional feed on top of what it forages. Conversely, there are organic, industrially farmed chickens: laying hens that are fed organic feed, kept free from hormones, given access to the outdoors, otherwise treated in ways that meet the organic guidelines. Nevertheless, those guidelines do not forbid the dense-packing which is the hallmark of industrial animal farming. So it is possible to organically factory-farm laying hens.

ORGANIC HISTORY

Until quite recently, all farming would have conformed to the USDA's organic regulations. As we discussed in the previous chapter, until quite recently, there were no synthetic pesticides, fertilizers, or herbicides. There were no GMOs. There were neither irradiators nor sewage plants.

The nineteenth and twentieth centuries brought some genuine scientific breakthroughs with respect to our ability to create fertilizers, pesticides, and herbicides in laboratories and with respect to our ability to genetically modify plants in labs. The organic ban on most "synthetics" is a ban, roughly, on things made in laboratories. So whereas compost is a fertilizer, it isn't a synthetic one: It's made by piling organic matter and letting it break down. Scott's Miracle-Gro, by contrast, is produced in a factory somewhere. The ban on synthetic pesticides is not a ban on killing bugs. It's a ban on one particular method for doing so. Likewise, the organic ban on genetic modification is *not* a ban on cross-breeding plants, something that farmers have done for a very long time. The ban on GMOs is a ban on engineering genes.

These scientific advances made new agricultural techniques possible, allowing us to grow huge quantities of crops resistant to various ailments that afflicted traditional varieties. In the early twentieth century, as the techniques became more popular, ethical and political resistance to them sprouted. That resistance was not directed merely at the use of synthetics, and later at the use of genetic modification, but, rather, was directed at a whole culture around farming and eating. As Joan Gussow details in her selection in this chapter, when proponents of organic said they wanted organic regulation, the laws they got are not what they meant: "When we said organic, we meant local. We meant healthful. We meant being true to the ecologies of our regions. We meant mutually respectful growers and eaters. We meant social justice and community" (2002).

Yet the regulations about organic food do not require organic food to be produced near where it is sold or consumed. They do not require organic food to be healthful. They do not require organic food to be grown in a way that suits the ecology of the place in which they are grown. They do not require organic food to be grown in a way that is mutually respectful to growers or eaters or in a way that is just or that builds community. Those regulations were the process of protracted negotiations, engagingly detailed in Fromartz (2006), between various stakeholders. The negotiations resulted in the USDA regulations we have, regulations that do not match up perfectly—or even all that well—with one's preconceptions about organic as healthy, nutritious food grown in environmentally sustainable ways on happy family farms by well-paid workers.

THE CASE FOR NON-INDUSTRIAL ORGANIC AGRICULTURE

Regardless of how well they conform to our preconceptions, we have the regulations we have. What can be said in favor of agriculture that conforms to them?

First, as discussed in the last chapter, there are concerns about the environmental impact of industrial agriculture. Synthetic pesticides, herbicides, and fertilizer pollute the environment.[3] Certain GMOs are claimed to be partly responsible for recent collapses in honeybee and butterfly populations (though the evidence to support this is not strong). Another part of the environmental case, discussed in the industrial agriculture chapters, is the high energy costs and required fossil-fuel inputs of conventional agriculture. For example, conventional plant agriculture currently has a much higher water footprint than organic plant agriculture.[4]

This raises some issues dealt with at more length in Chapter 7, "Industrial Animal Agriculture," and Chapter 9, "Industrial Plant Agriculture."

Second, there is a consumer health case. One concern is with the health impacts of consuming the synthetic pesticides that are sprayed onto conventional produce. Organic foods are largely free of these synthetic pesticides. Concern with consuming these pesticides is common among the general public but, it should be said, not among scientists. The consumer health case is also based on the view that organic food is more nutritious than conventional, that it is not only lower in pesticides but higher in various nutrients.[5] This is a highly controversial view. (Though this is not directly related to plants, it is worth noting that the consumer health case is also a reaction to the rampant use of antibiotics on conventional animal farms. Such use makes those farms a breeding ground for antibiotic-resistant bacteria, bacteria that can then prey on animals and, the worry goes, people.)

Third, the health effects on workers also motivate anti-industrial organic agriculture. While workers get their own chapter in this book, a critical part of the case for organic agriculture is the effects on farmworkers of repeated, durable contact with synthetic chemicals.[6]

Fourth, finally, there is a case based on the health of those near agricultural land: people in schools nearby, churches, homes, and so on Drift of synthetic chemicals can have serious illeffects on people and animals who are no part of the farming set-up.

Some of these worries are worries motivated by well-known effects of synthetics. Others are motivated by *precaution*—it's unclear what the long-term effects of synthetics in one's diet are. Gussow voices this when she says, "I prefer butter to margarine because I trust cows more than chemists."[7] Samuel Fromartz voices it when he says that our repeated consumption of conventional food is something like an experiment on ourselves, testing the health effects of doing so.[8]

If this is a strong case, it is a strong case not only *against* industrial agriculture but also for one particular alternative to it, one that forgoes various synthetic chemicals and GMOs. So a response to the case might take two forms: Either it might take the form of endorsing industrial agriculture or it might take the form of accepting some form of non-industrial agriculture while rejecting the organic alternative.

THE CASE AGAINST THE ORGANIC ALTERNATIVE

One complaint about organic agriculture is that the organic laws in the United States do a bad job of codifying the ideology they are meant to codify. Organic agriculture was intended by its original proponents to be an alternative to conventional agriculture, especially conventional, industrial agriculture. Yet much of what people find distressing about conventional agriculture can be replicated by producers who follow the letter of the organic law. Organic producers can farm in a somewhat industrial fashion and can be multinational companies participating in the neoliberal, globalized food system and therefore open to the objections to neoliberalism discussed by Julie Guthman and others in Chapter 3, "Food Justice."[9] So, the objection goes, the organic would-be alternative is no real alternative to industrial agriculture.

Elsewhere in the same book, Guthman raises a different worry. Consider the organic farmer, quoted in Singer and Mason (2006), who refers to his product as "yuppy chow." Now, on the one hand, yuppies have to eat, too, and it isn't a serious objection to organic food that it feeds yuppies. Is the objection that it *only* feeds yuppies because it is financially difficult for the non-rich to subsist on organic food? That can't be quite right either: It is financially difficult for the non-rich to buy Picassos, but it isn't wrong for Picasso to produce them or for museums to buy them. On the other hand, since food, unlike Picassos, is a necessity, and *if* organic food really is superior to conventional food in the way its proponents allege, it might be unfair for it to be prohibitively priced. There is something to this objection, but precisely articulating it is hard.

Finally, as we detailed at length in the previous chapter, maybe the most pressing worry about organic agriculture is that such an agricultural system will be unable to produce enough food to feed the world. As we detailed, a version of this objection supports *industrial* agriculture and targets all forms of anti-industrial agriculture. With regard to organic agriculture—small-scale organic agriculture, remember—the objection goes:

> Wide-scale adoption of small-scale organic agriculture will not produce sufficient food to feed the world.
> If so, it is wrong to go in for wide-scale adoption of small-scale organic agriculture.
> Hence, it's wrong to go in for wide-scale adoption of small-scale organic agriculture.

The point here is not that it is wrong for you to grow organic tomatoes in your backyard. The argument says nothing about that. It says nothing about organic farms here and there. What it opposes is organic as the dominant mode of production. And it opposes that on the grounds that such a system would not produce enough food, and that any system that doesn't produce enough food is morally wrong.

When she responds to this argument, Gussow, in her reading in this chapter, notes that industrial agriculture isn't currently feeding the world. People go hungry; they starve. (See Chapters 2, "Global Hunger," and 3, "Food Justice.") There is a way of hearing Gussow's complaint so that it's irrelevant. Proponents of industrial agriculture who make the preceding argument hold that only industrial agriculture *can* feed the world though they admit that under the current system this food is not being distributed in ways that feed everyone. Gussow's response that people currently go hungry might seem, then, to be beside the point since the preceding argument and people who make it do not dispute that people currently go hungry.

But Gussow isn't making this irrelevant point. Her position is that organic agriculture can grow enough food so that, properly distributed, it can feed the world. She denies the first premise of the preceding argument. Stepping back, we should ask whether the question "Can organic farming feed the world?" is even a well-formed question. That is the topic of Fred Kirschenmann's essay. It recalls a line from James McWilliams's *Just Food* about whether organic farming can produce as much food as conventional. To McWilliams, a California organic grower responded: "It depends on the crop, the place, the farmer, the variety, the type of crop rotation used, and whether cover crops take the place of crops."[10] McWilliams describes this answer as a "hedge," but a more charitable reading is that it's simply a rejection of the question "Can organic farming feed the world?" on the grounds that the question is hopelessly vague.

THE CASE FOR LOCAL AGRICULTURE

This sort of objection to organic agriculture—that it is not productive enough—will, of course, also apply to local, non-industrial production, too, since the idea behind the objection is that *only* industrial forms of agriculture are productive enough. Kirschenmann's skepticism in the question "Can organic farming feed the world?" can be translated to "Can local farming feed the world?".

As we said, though, the local alternative should be separated from the organic alternative. As McKibben and de Bres note in their readings in this chapter, as with organic agriculture, environmental concerns are part of the motivation for a local alternative. Yet adherents also embrace local production because *local* food systems are seen as socially, economically, and aesthetically preferable to a *globalized* food system—local production builds community and builds relationships, supports the local economy, increases transparency in the food system, and allows people to have aesthetic experiences of agriculture and food that they find valuable. For some adherents, too, the local food movement is "against global, big, conventional, environmentally degrading food systems."[11] That is, local food systems are seen as the alternative to a global, industrial, neoliberal food system and, in the view of some, the organic alternative is not alternative enough.[12]

As with organic food, local production of food is seen to offer various environmental benefits: Food has to travel less far from farm to plate. As long as the transportation method is the same as it would be from a far-off farm, the reduction in miles will reduce the amount of energy used on transport and reduce the amount of emissions emitted in transport. This provides *some* reason to go in for local farms, though clearly not a decisive reason. If a local and non-local option were otherwise equally good but the local one were better for the environment, then maybe that would be a decisive reason to go for the local one. But, so far, we don't have an argument that local and non-local options are equally good.

Consider, then, the perceived advantages of a local food system over a global one. First, when you *buy* local, food money stays in the community, strengthening the local economy. And this is a benefit for the local economy. But what about the non-local farmers who do not benefit from your business?

Second, buying local putatively builds and sustains relationships between farmer and consumer/purchaser. Or at least, buying locally makes this (somewhat?) easy to do. Eas*ier* to do? And this is a benefit, a benefit local production makes possible. Again, it is clearly not decisive, but the case for local is beginning to add up. Also, local agriculture supports a way of life—a rural, agrarian life—that, as DeBres discusses, is thought to be intrinsically valuable.

Third, local production increases (the possibility of) transparency around food. Buying locally is seen to make it easy to learn about where one's food comes from, and how it was produced. At least, it makes it eas*ier* to do so. And this knowledge or facilitation of knowledge is plausibly a benefit.

Fourth, local production allows people to have aesthetic experiences that they find valuable. Based on interviews with community supported agriculture (CSA) members, Steven Schnell also concludes that eating locally grown food is embraced as a way to have a fuller experience of *place*.

Food has become a key part of many individuals' place narratives, and it has provided a key way for many to weave themselves into the broader narratives of the places they inhabit, in establishing a stronger sense of place. No longer is a tomato just a tomato; it is a tomato that came from this field, was grown in this particular way by this particular farmer. Such narratives contrast with mistrust of the abstractness and the anonymity of the globalized food system expressed by large numbers of my interviewees, and embed the individual in a web of meaning and place . . . local food has become a vital part of the "thickening" of place experience.[13]

As this discussion shows, local production is perceived as having a range of virtues. When people endorse "local" production, they are not just endorsing geographically smaller food systems; they are endorsing food systems that have these virtues. In other words, "local" is shorthand for a range of perceived virtues.[14] Of course, not all local food—that is, food grown geographically near—has these virtues. And food that is not locally grown can have these virtues.

The Bay Area group that coined the word "locavore" even has a ranking of such virtues on its website. (The ranking is advice for consumers, but it could just as well be advice for producers.)

> If not LOCALLY PRODUCED, then **Organic**. This is one of the most readily available alternatives in the market and making this choice protects the environment and your body from harsh chemicals and hormones.
>
> If not ORGANIC, then **Family farm**. When faced with Kraft or Cabot cheeses, Cabot, a dairy co-op in Vermont, is the better choice. Supporting family farms helps to keep food processing decisions out of the hands of corporate conglomeration.
>
> If not FAMILY FARM, then **Local business**. Basics like coffee and bread make buying local difficult. Try a local coffee shop or bakery to keep your food dollar close to home.
>
> If not a LOCAL BUSINESS, then **Terroir**, which means "taste of the Earth." Purchase foods famous for the region they are grown in and support the agriculture that produces your favorite non-local foods such as Brie cheese from Brie, France, or Parmesan cheese from Parma, Italy (http://www.locavores.com/how/).

THE CASE AGAINST LOCAL, NON-INDUSTRIAL AGRICULTURE

Some of this case is predictable from readings in Chapter 9, "Industrial Plant Agriculture." Any non-industrial form of agriculture is subject to the objections to non-industrial agriculture put forward there, for example the objection that non-industrial systems cannot produce enough food to feed the world. But there are local agriculture-specific arguments, arguments that would show that local, non-industrial agriculture is a mistake even if some other forms of non-industrial agriculture are not.

A common criticism of local production is that the environmental benefits are small (the food miles benefit is oversold and, anyway, the transportation of food accounts for only a fraction of the total greenhouse gas emissions and fossil fuel used in agriculture) and outweighed by environmental costs. When they discuss this, as de Bres notes, critics of local agriculture have in mind *certain* forms of local agriculture, such as one that grows tomatoes year-round, regardless of climate. A greenhouse that grows tomatoes in Quebec year-round would, indeed, be an environmental problem.

Yet such attacks only go so far. It is not part of the push for local agriculture that everyone has access to local tomatoes year-round. The criticism might just show that *if* the environmental argument for local production works, it does not support local, year-round production of tomatoes in cold places.

Also, note that the attacks here are *not* on the conclusion that local production is a good idea or morally required. Rather, they are attacks on arguments for those conclusions. Just because some arguments for a conclusion are no good, that doesn't show you that the conclusion itself is false. For any conclusion, there are countless arguments you can make for it. Some of them will be terrible, and pointing out that there are terrible arguments for the conclusion does nothing to undermine the conclusion. You argue that there's drought in California in 2015—true!—by arguing that Nostradamus predicted it—false!—and every prediction Nostradamus makes comes to pass—false! So we should ask whether local production really is a bad idea or whether the problem is just that bad arguments have been made for it.

As de Bres discusses, there are powerful considerations against a *requirement* to farm and vend locally. One is that it is difficult for people who aren't well-off to buy and eat anything like a locavore diet, at least in the United States and given current conditions. It's feasible to buy locally—McKibben touches on the economics of it—but only with much effort and, even so, only in those parts of the United States with sufficient and sufficiently diverse farms. If the local food movement is advocating practices that only the well-off can afford, this might be elitist. The movement is also unlikely to succeed in transforming the food system, if only well-off people can afford to participate in the transformation.

As discussed in Chapter 3, "Food Justice," a common criticism of the local food movement, and the alternative food movement more generally, is that is has paid insufficient attention to the needs of low-income people. Local and organic food is often unaffordable for low-income people, and the alternative food movement is perceived as doing little to address this. Nor has it addressed the broader problem of food insecurity, the inability to reliably afford food (much less healthy food, much less local and organic food).

A related criticism of the alternative food movement—of which the local food movement is a part—is that it comprises mostly white and middle-class or upper middle-class people— it is a "monoculture." *If* movement members are disproportionately white, well-off, and female, is this a problem? It might be if that movement excludes others. As discussed in Chapter 3, the alternative food movement's narrative and language are critiqued as reflecting the experience of white Americans. As we noted previously, discussing the organic alternative to industrial agriculture, Guthman argues that the movement evokes an agrarian past— small farmers working the land—that is "far more easily romanticized by whites than others" since non-whites in the United States were systematically denied land ownership. Another example is that emphasizing the value of "putting your hands in the soil" also reflects white experience: "For African-Americans, especially, putting your hands in the soil is more likely to invoke images of slave labor than nostalgia. Such rhetoric thus illustrates a lack of cultural competency that might be deemed an exclusionary practice."[15]

Another criticism which applies to both the local and organic alternatives is that they do not go far enough in opposing the status quo. One concern here is that organic and local agriculture can have some of the objectionable features of industrial agriculture—this is the problem of "industrial organic" as discussed earlier. Whereas organic farms necessarily avoid liberal application of synthetics and GMOs, they might well be large, monoculture farms concentrated in few places. And whereas a network of small-scale local farms, producing a variety of crops necessarily avoids being large-scale and avoids concentrations of, say, almond farms or garlic farms in one place, they might liberally use GMOs or synthetics.

Another concern is that the organic and local food movements, in their current form, are not an effective "counter-strategy" to globalization and neoliberalism as discussed in Chapter 3, "Food Justice," some activists and scholars argue that the alternative food movement fails to mount a significant challenge to neoliberalism, and even shores up the ideology behind neoliberalism.[16] The idea is the alternative food movement in practice serves to advocate for market-based solutions to problems—it advocates for farmers to choose alternative production methods, and for consumers to choose to purchase local and organic food. But by advocating for market-based solutions, rather than pushing for changes to agricultural and trade policies, the alternative food movement is reinforcing the neoliberal view that the government does not have responsibility for addressing these problems and that private, market-based solutions are preferable. Furthermore, as the Gussow reading brings out, industrial agriculture and popular, extant alternatives to it might *all* be missing out on various goods about workers, about food justice, and about autonomy.

SUMMING UP: BIG-PICTURE QUESTIONS ABOUT FOOD SYSTEMS AGAIN, AND SUSTAINABLE INTENSIFICATION AS ONE FRAMEWORK FOR ANSWERING THEM

We are now nearing the end of this, the fourth of four chapters on industrialization and its alternatives in plant and animal agriculture. As a result, some discussion of how we might weigh up the overall pros and cons of these alternative systems is appropriate. Recall the following big-picture questions about food systems from Chapter 7:

1. Is there a better way to produce food than the actual way it is produced, and is there a better overall *food system*, which includes the food distribution and socio-economic systems in which agricultural systems are embedded?
2. If so, what would be the ideally best food system, assuming everyone was disposed to act in a way that was perfectly ethical—that is, willing to stop eating animal products if necessary, and so on?
3. What food system is it actually best to aim for, given the actual dispositions of people, including their dispositions to sometimes respond less than ethically?
4. Given a particular conception of what food system we should actually aim for, what is the best way of getting there from here? That is, given the complex workings of the food system, what actions would best move us in the right direction, distinguishing actions by individual people like you, by our government, by industry leaders, by community organizations, by charities, and so on, and taking into account the complex feedbacks and interactions between those actions?

This chapter and the preceding chapters have highlighted many ethical values that may be relevant to answering these questions. Arguably, these ethical values sometimes pull in opposing directions. If our ethical values really do pull in opposing directions, then this means that the food system that we should aim for will involve *trade-offs* between those values, in the sense that sacrifices should be made with respect to some of them so that we can avoid making even more ethically costly sacrifices of others. As an example of one alleged trade-off we should make, we've seen some arguments for the conclusion that feeding the world requires us to make sacrifices of animal welfare or other ethically important values, especially in connection to the environment.

In thinking about how to answer the question of what agricultural system we should actually aim for given the values at stake, it is useful to introduce an influential framework for answering that question that is endorsed by many experts, called *sustainable intensification* of agriculture. Sustainable intensification is based on the premises that the best way of promoting our values requires (1) increasing the average yield per acre of agriculture worldwide, and (2) reducing the negative environmental impacts of agriculture per acre. The view is often taken to imply that, to a first approximation, we must feed the world without increasing the amount of the Earth devoted to agriculture, and (subject to that constraint) minimize the environmental impacts of so doing. Etymologically, the term is derived from the idea that we should invest substantial resources in increasing yields per acre (that's the *intensification* part), but that we should also do so in a way that doesn't undermine the long-term capacity of the land to yield similarly bountiful yields, and that doesn't make the environment worse for future generations, or compromise their ability to meet their needs in other ways (that's the *sustainability* part). (For an influential definition of sustainability along these lines, see United Nations [1987], *Our Common Future*, also known as the Brundtland Report, where sustainable development is defined as "development that meets the needs of the present without compromising the ability of future generations to meet their own needs.")

Sustainable intensification is more of a *framework* for how to answer the big-picture question of what agricultural system we should aim for, rather than a detailed *substantive theory* of what the answer is, because sustainable intensification is consistent with many different substantive answers to that question that are inconsistent with each other. For example, many proponents of the framework believe we must put more emphasis on the selective use and further development of the tools of industrial agriculture (such as GMOs, more precise application technologies for irrigation, pesticides, and fertilizer, and other tools discussed in Chapter 9, "Industrial Plant Agriculture"). In contrast, many other experts believe that we must instead put more emphasis on *agroecological intensification* to meet these goals, which includes more tools from organic agriculture such as intercropping (growing two or more crops simultaneously, in a way that allows the crops to complement each other in numerous ways, such as providing nutrients for each other, and providing pest resistance), rotation (growing multiple crops in sequence for similar reasons), agroforestry (growing perennials and annuals together for similar reasons), green manuring (using legumes and other plants as nitrogen fertilizers for soil rather than animal manure), conservation tillage (planting seed directly into the soil rather than tilling it first), and pest control that utilizes natural process whenever possible and at least does not degrade the soil.[17] As a result, the former group sees much more of a role for the tools of industrial agriculture in feeding the world, while the latter group sees much more of a role for the tools of organic agriculture, both under the banner of sustainable intensification. But it is crucial to note that most advocates of sustainable intensification see some important role for the tools of *both* approaches.

A further complexity is that proponents of the framework generally agree that given what is known about the relevant empirical issues, sustainable intensification will require a highly diverse array of initiatives that will display substantial variation from region to region and from specific location to location, depending on facts about the people, cultures, and technology involved as well as facts about the physical landscape and the local economy. This is partly because different crops grow better in some places than others, and some places can't grow a lot of nutritious plants and are too poor to import much food, but do have minimal vegetation for some livestock to graze. Locations also differ in their vulnerability to the side effects of industrial agriculture—for example, fertile fields best adapted for monoculture in the American Midwest may be less vulnerable to many environmental harms than areas close to highly fragile ecosystems. More generally, what sustainable intensification requires will be highly variable depending on people's precise location in space and time in complex *agroecosystems*, which are themselves composed of the complex ecosystems in which agriculture occurs, together with the complex social and economic systems within which they and people interact. So, although some proponents of the framework believe it may be best *in some locations and with respect to some crops* to use all of the methods of contemporary intensive agriculture, even they typically do not believe it will be best always to use all of those methods at every location. And in some locations—often when subsistence farming is the norm—many proponents believe that highly organic methods are best.[18]

Again, beyond these general statements, there is vigorous debate among proponents about the exact implications of sustainable intensification as the allegedly best "middle way" between the status quo of allegedly unsustainable forms of industrial agriculture and, at the other extreme, a highly organic food system. This disagreement exists because the empirical and normative questions that must be answered are very difficult—as they often are in connection with highly complex questions about what we should do about the world's thorniest problems. For example, regarding sustainable intensification, one group of distinguished commentators writes:

> In one sense the answer is simple: crop and livestock production must increase without an increase in the negative environmental impacts associated with agriculture, which means large increases in the efficiency of nitrogen, phosphorus and water use, and integrated pest management that minimizes the need for toxic pesticides. In reality, achieving such a scenario represents one of the greatest scientific challenges facing humankind because of the trade-offs among competing economic and environmental goals, and inadequate knowledge of the key biological, biogeochemical and ecological processes.[19]

One worry about sustainable intensification is that for all of its attractive features, the framework may predictably lead to the neglect of some ethically important values if it is used to guide policy. Perhaps most worrisome, arguably it may lead to neglect of the need to reduce food waste and/or animal consumption, and to neglect of animal welfare. That is because a focus only on increasing yields while reducing environmental impacts does not clearly highlight the vast amounts of food waste in the food system (the reduction of which may be part of the best way forward), nor does it address the consumption of animal products, which is arguably largely unnecessary in developed nations and the primary cause of many agricultural challenges. It may also appear to tell in favor of industrial animal agriculture, since intensive methods of animal agriculture are arguably the best way of meeting global demand for animal products while minimizing environmental impacts per unit of animal product produced.[20]

A focus on sustainable intensification arguably may also lead to neglect of fairness considerations, and insufficient attention to whether there are fair opportunities and benefits for the world's poorest farmers. This is because a focus only on increasing yields while reducing environmental impacts appears to tell in favor of whatever agricultural system best meets those objectives, which may be one that makes things even worse for the world's poorest farmers. As some historical evidence that a worry along these lines is important to consider, Gordon Conway argues that the last concerted effort leading to large-scale global increase in yields—the *Green Revolution* of the 1950s, 1960s, and 1970s often associated with the work of agronomists and development researchers such as Norman Borlaug—had the result that "larger landowners have reaped most of the benefits, while the poor and landless have missed out."[21] More generally, some activists and scholars would argue that sustainable intensification fails to acknowledge the problems with the current neoliberal global order, and even shores up the ideology behind neoliberalism. (Neoliberalism is discussed in more detail in Chapter 3, "Food Justice.")

In response, some proponents of sustainable intensification explicitly endorse a concern for values such as animal welfare and distributive justice in their articulation of the framework. However, it is a topic of ongoing debate whether giving voice to these worries in academic papers is sufficient to avoid the predictable result that these values would be neglected by policymaking based on the mantra of sustainable intensification. And a different objection is that if these values are included, then sustainable intensification arguably becomes such an all-encompassing framework that it has no distinctive content.[22]

Another arguably problematic feature of sustainable intensification is that it focuses on increasing the *supply* of food to meet "business as usual" projections of future demand. However, it is important to note that focusing on increasing supply is not our only option: Some people argue that we should focus instead on reducing *demand* for food in one or more ways, such as by reducing food waste (as Michelle Paratore discusses in her reading for this chapter), or by changing the preference of so many people for animal products (as discussed in Chapter 7, "Industrial Animal Agriculture"), or by reducing population growth (as discussed in Chapter 2, "Global Hunger"). As another, complementary approach, many people also argue that even without changing overall consumption quantities or people's preferences, we can still reduce the amount of agricultural inputs that are needed by changing the composition of the foods we consume, or by creating innovative new products that are made from ingredients that are less burdensome on the environment. As Bill Gates reports:

> Some exciting new companies are taking on this challenge. They are creating plant-based alternatives to chicken, ground beef, even eggs, that are produced more sustainably, and taste great. . . . Companies like Beyond Meat and Hampton Creek Foods are experimenting with new ways to use heat and pressure to turn plants into foods that look and taste just like meat and eggs. [A] chicken taco I ate was made using Beyond Meat's chicken alternative. I wasn't the only one fooled by how real it tasted. *New York Times* food writer Mark Bittman couldn't tell the difference between Beyond Meat and real chicken either. . . . Try them for yourself. I think you'll discover that you can create a nutritious, protein-rich meal that's good for you and the environment.[23]

About a year after Gates wrote this, food journalist and cookbook author Mark Bittman quit his "dream job" at the *New York Times* to join The Purple Carrot, a new company devoted to making it easy for people to eat vegan meals that are superior by their own lights to meals they are currently eating.[24] In his reading for this chapter, Austin Kiessig discusses a number of other "startups" (that is, new companies formed with the intention of growing into very large or high-impact companies) in the food domain focused on increasing yields, decreasing environmental impacts, and improving the composition of food that we consume in similar ways.

A more fundamental worry about any response to the challenges we face that focuses primarily on increasing food supply (as sustainable intensification does) is that previous success with substantial increases in supply arguably had large negative effects on the environment, and arguably were unsustainable. For example, some experts argue that the greatest success story in our past in connection with increasing food supply, the Green Revolution, had these downsides for the environment—as Gordon Conway argues:

> Green Revolution agroecosystems have shown poor resilience in the face of environmental degradation. Now, there is also evidence of increasing production problems in those places where yield growth in the Green Revolution was most marked. Of particular concern is the growing scarcity of water; in some of the most intensively cultivated districts of India, the groundwater table is falling by up to 2 meters a year. A further factor is the cumulative effect of environmental degradation, partly caused by agriculture itself. In India, fertilizers such as urea were heavily subsidized for over three decades leading to overuse and degradation of soil, declining yields, and rising levels of imports. Virtually all long-term cereal experiments in the developing countries exhibit marked downward trends in yields.[25]

Part of Conway's argument here is that because many of the yield increases associated with the Green Revolution had negative effects on the environment on balance, we should worry about the feasibility of achieving our current goals, which include reducing overall environmental impacts, by focusing primarily on achieving increases in food supply (as is the focus of sustainable intensification).

Whatever one makes of sustainable intensification itself as a framework for deciding what agricultural system is best, the preceding discussion highlights some of the challenges for *any* food systems framework that aims to answer the question of how we might best feed the world without destroying the environment during the coming decades. Together with the preceding chapters, this illustrates the general difficulties—both empirical and normative—relevant to big-picture questions about what food systems we should aim for, and how best to get there from here.

FURTHER ISSUES

1. *Relationships*

A putative good of local agriculture, discussed in the DeBres and McKibben readings, is that it facilitates establishing relationships between farmer and consumer. Yet what's so good about establishing such relationships? For whom is it good? Does it matter what sort of person you're establishing a relationship with? (What if the farmer is a jerk? What if the consumer is? Is there a good in fostering a relationship with a jerk?) What sort of pressure does relationship-forming put on a farmer? (They have to grow your food *and* befriend you? Why think the people good at growing your food will be good at or even interested in talking about it?)

2. *Vegan Locavores?*

Consider the idea that there is a requirement to eat as much local food as you can, finances permitting. This isn't a central idea of this chapter—the focus is mostly on production rather than consumption—but it is an idea prominent in some food movements. A requirement to *eat* local food restricts what one can eat or where one can live. Take someone committed to veganism. Such a person could not eat strictly local food in Vermont year-round without putting in quite intensive food-preparation work. As McKibben notes, during the winter, the vast majority of local food that is available in Vermont is animal-based: meat, eggs, dairy. To get through the winter, the Vermont vegan has to spend a fair bit of time in the summer prepping food for the winter: canning, freezing, preserving. We can even imagine cases in which being a locavore would make being a vegan impossible. What would the moral upshot of that conflict be? Are the reasons to be vegan more powerful than the reasons to be locavore? Why?

3. *Supererogation and Locaorganic Diet*

One might think, weighing all the considerations, that eating a diet of largely local organic food is *wrong*—that's a view de Bres considers. One might, instead, think it is *required*—that's another view de Bres considers. One might think, instead, that such a diet is permissible but not required. And if so, one might think it is both permissible and *supererogatory*, going above and beyond the call of duty but somehow laudable—this seems to be the view of McKibben. Supererogatory actions are actions that are permissible but not required but also actions that are especially good and beneficial for others. Giving a lot of your money to the desperately poor, so much so that you become desperately poor yourself, might be an example of a supererogatory action. Giving all your Halloween candy to your younger brother might be another. Waking up extremely early to help your roommate with her bio exam might be a third. It could be that devoting one's money to a locaorganic diet is like that: permissible, laudable, helpful to others, but not morally required. Instead, it could be that devoting one's money to a locaorganic diet is like devoting one's money to a diet of nuts and berries: permissible but idiosyncratic, just an expression of taste and not deserving any special credit. What do you think?

4. *The Alternative Food Movement*

Here's a complaint about the alternative food movement voiced in this chapter and in Chapter 3, "Food Justice": The movement assumes that its values are universally shared, but they aren't. The movement illicitly endorses *universalism*. As a result, the movement is imposing its values on some who do not share them. Some non-ethical questions: Is the complaint right that the movement makes this illicit assumption? Is it right that the movement imposes those values on people who do not share them? Some ethical questions: If so, is what the movement does wrong? Is it unjust? Why or why not?

One way in which the complaint is developed is that there is something especially offensive about the non-industrial food movement since it comprises rich, white people self-righteously imposing their views on others. Some non-ethical questions: Is the complaint right about who the movement comprises? Is it right about what those people do and to whom they do it? Some ethical questions: If so, is there something especially offensive about it? Why or why not?

Another complaint is that the alternative food movement advocates for a means of changing the food system—consumers purchase food that is organically grown and locally produced—that requires consumers to be able to afford these products, but many consumers cannot afford them. As a result, the movement ends up excluding people who support its aims but cannot afford to participate on those terms. This is exclusionary and makes the movement smaller and less effective than it could be. Is this complaint correct? Does the alternative food movement only offer its participants one means of changing the food system—that is, purchasing alternative food? Or does the movement include other forms of participation, such as political advocacy?

5. *The Allure of Old Fashion*

There's a stereotype about organic agriculture—and non-industrial agriculture in general—that it is old-fashioned and, because of this, low-tech. (When we ask our students what they think about organic food, being grown in an old-fashioned way is one of the first things they mention.)

This stereotype has *something* to it: There are some new technologies—GMOs, synthetics—that organic farms can't use. But organic farms can and do display great agricultural ingenuity.

One thing the stereotype raises is exactly how much we should dial back on advanced technology and why we should do so. Consider the bracing Menonite form of agriculture that Dan Barber describes and the anti-industrial rationale behind it:

> [Klaas Martens] explained that Mennonites forbid the use of rubber tires on their farm tractors. . . . Klaas smiled, acknowledging the severity of the decree—steel-tired tractors inch along, as slow as oxen. He said one day he got up the nerve to ask a Mennonite bishop why rubber tires were forbidden. The bishop answered Klaas's question with a question: "When do you start raising a child?" According to the bishop . . . child rearing begins not at birth, or even conception, but one hundred years before a child is born, "because that's when you start building the environment they're going to live in." Mennonites, he went on, believe that if you look at the history of tractors with rubber tires, you see failure within a generation. Rubber tires enable easy movement, and easy movement means that, inevitably, the farm will grow, which means more profit. More profit, in turn, leads to acquisition of even more land, which usually means less crop diversity, more large machinery, and so on. Pretty soon the farmer becomes less intimate with his farm. It's that lack of intimacy that leads to ignorance, and eventually to loss. . . . Klaas had just described the problem with American agriculture.[26]

On the one hand, most (non-Mennonite) proponents of organic agriculture are not opposed to rubber tires on tractors. On the other hand, all—most? many?—are opposed to certain advanced technologies. What is the difference between the technologies that makes some seem like good ideas, the other bad ideas? It can't simply be that organic, non-industrial agriculture must be good for the environment. As Barber writes a bit later in the book,

> If you have a hankering, as I do, for the old days of our young republic, when farming was what farming should be—small, family-owned, well-managed and -manicured, a platonic paradigm of sustainable agriculture—think again. Today's industrial food chain might denude landscapes

and impoverish soils, but our forefathers did much of the same. They just had a lot less horse-power. . . . Steven Stoll identifies the detrimental precedent that came to define American farm-ing: "In a common pattern, farmers who had occupied land for only 20 or 30 years reduced the fertile nutrients in their soils until they could no more than subsist. Either that, or they saw yields fall below what they expected from good settlers' country and decided to seek fresh acres elsewhere."[27]

Another thing about the old-fashioned stereotype: Julie Guthman raises concerns with the connections between the traditional farming mindset of some organic farmers and more objectionable, traditional attitudes they have (see Guthman, 2014, in the "Further Reading" section). The "beyond organic" farmer Joel Salatin, author of a reading in Chapter 8, "Alter-natives to Industrial Animal Agriculture," is revered for his largely organic techniques, but less revered for his attitudes about a woman's place on the farm. For example, his farm interns must be male (cf. Stanescu, 2010, in "Further Reading").

6. *Weighing Up Risks*

One of the more chilling passages in Barry Estabrook's chilling *Tomatoland* is the part in which he writes, "Ag-Mart . . . voluntarily stopped using five of six chemicals that had been connected to birth defects in animal experiments. But it continued to use one of those muta-gens because there was no cost-effective replacement."[28] This shows that Ag-Mart was will-ing to avoid putting people at risk. But only if it could do so without significant cost to itself. This might strike you as morally awful. But there are cases in which it is permissible: Imag-ine you can save a baby from drowning but only at the risk of paralyzing yourself—don't ask how. Are you permitted to avoid doing so? Is this case significantly different from the Ag-Mart case? If so, how? What if Ag-Mart knows that if they stop using the chemical, they will go out of business, because they will lose all of their market share to others who will continue to use the chemical and produce produce at a much lower cost? If that were true, would Ag-Mart do any good if they stopped using the chemical? If Ag-Mart wouldn't do any good by stopping using the chemical, does that mean it is permissible for them to use it?

7. *The Organic/Conventional Distinction*

In his book *Just Food* (Back Bay Books, 2010), James McWilliams complains that there is no "clear line" that separates organic from conventional. But this is not true. In the United States, "organic" is a legally defined term and it's clear which products satisfy the require-ments for being organic and which don't. The ones that do are organic; everything else is conventional. But the point McWilliams is trying to make by complaining that there is no clear line is a different point. What is it? Is it a good point?

FURTHER READING

Organic Ideology and the History of the Organic Movement

Balfour, Eve. 2006. *The Living Soil*. Bristol: The Soil Association.
Conford, Philip. 2002. *The Origins of the Organic Movement*. Edinburgh: Floris Books.
Fromartz, Samuel. 2006. *Organic, Inc.* New York: Mariner Press.
Gussow, Joan. 2002. "The Real Story of 'O,'" *Organic Gardening* Sep/Oct 2002.
Rodale, J. I. 2000. *The Encyclopedia of Organic Gardening*. Emmaus, PA: Rodale Press.

Pollan, Michael. 2001. "Behind the Organic-Industrial Complex," *New York Times Magazine*, May 13.

———. 2004. *The Omnivore's Dilemma*. New York: Penguin.

Singer, Peter, and Jim Mason. 2006. *The Ethics of What We Eat*. Emmaus, PA: Rodale Press.

Organic Regulations and Organic Ideology

Fromartz, Samuel. 2006. *Organic, Inc*. New York: Mariner Press.

Gussow, Joan Dye. 1997. "Can an Organic Twinkie Be Certified?" in Patrick Madden and Scott Chaplowe, eds., *For All Generations: Making World Agriculture More Sustainable*. West Hollywood, CA: World Sustainable Agriculture Association (WSAA).

Gussow, Joan Dye. 2001. *This Organic Life*. White River Junction, VT: Chelsea Green.

Guthman, Julie. 2014. *Agrarian Dreams,* updated ed. Berkeley: University of California Press.

Workers and Organics

Estabrook, Barry. 2009. "Politics of the Plate: The Price of Tomatoes," *Gourmet,* March 1.

Reeves, Margaret, et al. 2002. "Fields of Poison 2002." Oakland, CA: Californians for Pesticide Reform.

The Environment and Organics

Beyond Pesticides (website). http://www.beyondpesticides.org.

Estabrook, Barry. 2011. *Tomatoland*. Kansas City: Andrews McMillan.

Fromartz, Samuel. 2007. *Organic, Inc*. New York: Mariner Press.

Greenberg, Paul. 2013. "A River Runs Through It," *The American Prospect,* May.

Marshall, Jessica. 2012. "In Summer, Toxic Blue-Green Algae Blooms Plague Freshwater," *The Atlantic*, September 18.

Organic and Nutrition

Benbrook, Chuck. 2012. "The Devil in the Details," CSANR, Washington State University. http://csanr.wsu.edu/devil-in-the-details/.

Brandt, Kirsten, et al. 2011. "Agroecosystem Management and Nutritional Quality of Plant Foods: The Case of Organic Fruits and Vegetables," *Critical Reviews in Plant Sciences* 30: 177–197.

Can Organic Feed the World? (Should It?)

Anonymous. 2011. "Special Report on Feeding the World," *The Economist,* February 24.

Bittman, Mark. 2014. "Don't Ask How to Feed the 9 Billion," *New York Times,* November 12.

Schmidtz, David. 2000. "Islands in a Sea of Obligation," *Law and Philosophy* 19: 683–705.

Singer, Peter. 2010. *The Life You Can Save*. New York: Random House.

Stuart, Tristram. 2009. *Waste*. New York: Norton.

Local, Organic, and Status

Biltekoff, Charlotte. 2013. *Eating Right in America*. Durham, NC: Duke University Press.

Guthman, Julie. 2007. "Can't Stomach It: How Michael Pollan et al. Made Me Want to Eat Cheetos," *Gastronomica* 7: 75–79.

Mallory, Chaone. 2013. "Locating Ecofeminism in Encounters with Food and Place," *Journal of Agricultural and Environmental Ethics* 26: 171–189.

Paarlberg, Robert. 2010. "Attention Whole Foods Shoppers," *Foreign Policy,* April 26. http://foreign policy.com/2010/04/26/attention-whole-foods-shoppers/.

Stanescu, Vasile. 2010. "'Green' Eggs and Ham?" United Poultry Concerns. http://www.upc-online .org/thinking/green_eggs.html.

Locavorism

Barnhill, Anne. 2015. "Does Locavorism Keep It Too Simple?" in Chignell et al., *Philosophy Comes to Dinner*. New York: Routledge.

Chignell, Andrew, Terence Cuneo, and Matthew Halteman, eds. 2015. *Philosophy Comes to Dinner*. New York: Routledge.

Dieterle, J. M. 2015. *Just Food*. Lanham, MD: Rowman & Littlefield.

Goodnick, Liz. 2015. "Limits on Locavorism," in Dieterle, *Just Food*. Lanham, MD: Rowman & Littlefield.

McKibben, Bill. 2007. *Deep Economy*. New York: Henry Holt.

Navin, Mark. 2014. "Local Food and International Ethics," *Journal of Agricultural and Environmental Ethics* 27: 349–368.

Werkheiser, Ian, and Noll, Samantha. 2013. "From Food Justice to a Tool of the Status Quo," *Journal of Agricultural and Environmental Ethics* 27: 201–210.

Sustainable Intensification and Big-Picture Questions about Food Systems

Conway, Gordon. 2012. *One Billion Hungry: Can We Feed the World?* Ithaca, NY: Cornell University Press.

Garnett, Tara, et al. 2013. "Sustainable Intensification in Agriculture: Premises and Policies," *Science* 341: 33–34.

Thompson, Paul, ed. 2010. *The Ethics of Intensification*. Dordrecht, Netherlands: Springer.

Tilman, David et al. 2002. "Agricultural Sustainability and Intensive Production Practices," *Nature* 418: 671–677.

Tilman, David et al. 2011. "Global Food Demand and the Sustainable Intensification of Agriculture." *Proceedings of the National Academy of Sciences* 108: 20260–20264.

NOTES

1. We here paraphrase the guidelines found at http://www.ams.usda.gov.

2. "European Union and United States Agree to Historic New Partnership on Organic Trade" (news release), USDA, February 15, 2012, http://www.usda.gov/wps/portal/usda/usdahome?contentid =2012/02/0051.xml. The most salient differences have to do with Europe's more stringent requirements with regard to animal welfare. See "Animal Welfare," European Commission, http://ec.europa .eu/agriculture/organic/consumer-trust/animal-welfare/index_en.htm.

3. This case is thoroughly documented by the group Beyond Pesticides. Their website, http:// www.beyond.pesticides.org, has a wealth of information on the topic.

4. See Nicolas Franke and Ruth Mathews, "Gray Water Footprint Indicator of Water Pollution in the Production of Organic vs. Conventional Cotton in India" (Water Footprint Network, 2013). http://waterfootprint.org/media/downloads/Grey_WF_Phase_II_Final_Report_Formatted_06.08.2013.pdf

5. This is controverted in a Stanford study, a study that generated immediate, fierce controversy. The study is here: http://annals.org/article.aspx?articleid=1355685. An op-ed response, with lots of links to other entries in the controversy, is here: http://opinionator.blogs.nytimes.com/2012/10/02/that-flawed-stanford-study/?_php=true&_type=blogs&_r=0.

6. See Estabrook (2011) and Fromartz (2006), listed in the "Further Reading" section, for vivid descriptions of these effects.

7. Gussow, Joan Dye, 2001. *This Organic Life* (White River Junction, VT: Chelsea Green).

8. Fromartz, Samuel, 2006. *Organic, Inc.* (New York: Mariner Press: p. 3).

9. See Guthman (2014), listed in "Further Readings," especially chap. 9, for more on this.

10. James McWilliams, *Just Food* (Boston: Back Bay Books, 2010), 4.

11. David Goodman, E. Melanie DuPuis, and Michael K. Goodman, *Alternative Food Networks: Knowledge, Practice, and Politics*, 1st ed. (New York: Routledge, 2013), 12.

12. Ibid. See also Werkheiser and Noll (2013), listed in "Further Reading," 206–207; Alison Hope Alkon and Teresa Marie Mares, "Food Sovereignty in US Food Movements: Radical Visions and Neoliberal Constraints." *Agriculture and Human Values* 29 (2012): 347–359.

13. Schnell, "Food Miles, Local Eating, and Community Supported Agriculture," 625.

14. Ibid., 623.

15. Guthman, "If They Only Knew: The Unbearable Whiteness of Alternative Food," 276.

16. Alkon and Mares, "Food Sovereignty" (cited in note 12), 347–359.

17. Gordon Conway and Edward Barbier, *After the Green Revolution* (New York: Routledge, 1990); J. Pretty et al., "Resource-Conserving Agriculture Increases Yields in Developing Countries," *Environmental Science & Technology* 40 (2006): 1114–1119; Rebecca Nelson and Richard Coe, "Agroecological Intensification of Smallholder Farms," in *Oxford Handbook of Food, Politics, and Society*, ed. Ronald J. Herring (Oxford University Press, 2015).

18. In support of the claims thus far, see T. Garnett et al., "Sustainable Intensification in Agriculture: Premises and Policies," *Science* 341: 33–34 (2013); G. Conway, *One Billion Hungry: Can We Feed the World*? (Ithaca, NY: Cornell University Press, 2012); H. C. J. Godfray et al., "Food Security: The Challenge of Feeding 9 Billion People," *Science* 327: 812–818 (2010); J. Burney et al., "The Case for Distributed Irrigation as a Development Priority in Sub-Saharan Africa," *Proceedings of the National Academy of Sciences* (2013); M. Herrero et al., "Smart Investments in Sustainable Food Production: Revisiting Mixed Crop-Livestock Systems," *Science* 327: 822–825 (2010); M. Herrero et al., "Biomass Use, Feed Efficiencies, and Greenhouse Gas Emissions from Global Livestock Systems," *Proceedings of the National Academy of Sciences* (2013); H. Buffett, *Forty Chances* (Simon & Schuster, 2013); N. V. Fedoroff et al., "Radically Rethinking Agriculture for the 21st Century," *Science* 327 (2010): 833–834.

19. D. Tilman et al., "Agricultural Sustainability and Intensive Production Practices," *Nature* (2002): 672.

20. Tara Garnett and Charles Godfray, *Sustainable Intensification in Agriculture* (Food Climate Research Network and Oxford Martin Programme on the Future of Food, University of Oxford, 2012), 34.

21. Gordon Conway, *One Billion Hungry* (cited in note 21), 109.

22. Tara Garnett and Charles Godfray, *Sustainable Intensification in Agriculture* (cited in note 20).

23. Bill Gates, "Future of Food," gatesnotes (blog), March 18, 2015, https://www.gatesnotes.com/About-Bill-Gates/Future-of-Food.

24. Mark Bittman, "Why I Quit My Dream Job at the New York Times," *Time*, November 2, 2015, http://time.com/4096834/mark-bittman-why-i-quit-my-dream-job-at-the-new-york-times.

25. Gordon Conway, *One Billion Hungry* (cited in note 21), 109. Conway's footnotes to supporting sources are here omitted.

26. Barber, Dan, *The Third Plate* (New York: Penguin, 2014), 31–32.

27. Ibid., 48–49. The Stoll book is Steven Stoll, *Larding the Lean Earth* (New York: Hill and Wang, 2002).

28. Barry Estabrook, *Tomatoland* (Kansas City: Andrews McMillan), 52.

JOAN DYE GUSSOW

The Real Story of "O"

This short, passionate, oft-quoted editorial in *Organic Gardening* is about the mismatch between the legal guidelines regulating organic farming and the beliefs that motivated and sustained the organic farming movement. Gussow articulates her view about what the guidelines *should* be and notes the ways in which the actual guidelines fail to do what she holds they should do. Gussow claims the actual guidelines are not as wide as they should be: Rather than largely focusing on soil inputs, the guidelines should include coverage for workers, for sustainability, and others. She claims, too, that the actual guidelines are not as deep as they should be: Even on the points they rule on, they don't rule out enough.

There was a time when suggesting that the term organic meant more than carbon-containing was to risk labeling yourself a food faddist. There was a time when newspaper gardening columns patronizingly informed new gardeners that compost was nice for texture but otherwise useless and that manure was a much less efficient source of nutrients than a bag of 5-10-5. From the beginning, *Organic Gardening* reassured us that those folks were wrong.

Sixty years have changed everything. Now organic is a glamour word. Now the outputs of organic production can be found in supermarkets around the world. Now there are national guidelines for what it means to be organic with every i dotted and t crossed, so industrial-scale farms can follow the letter of the law and be certified.

So have we won? Not really. The "O" word is now academically respectable, but state and federal funding for organic research remains minimal. More alarmingly, given the entry into the industry of some of the largest multinational food companies, organics seems to be becoming what some of us hoped it would be an alternative to—another industrial food system that ships raw materials from wherever on the

Joan Dye Gussow, "The Real Story of 'O'," in *Rodale's Organic Life* (December 20, 2011). http://www.rodalesorganiclife.com/wellbeing/real-story-o

planet they can be most cheaply grown to factories producing everything from "organic" TV dinners to "organic" soft drinks.

This isn't what we meant. When we said organic, we meant local. We meant healthful. We meant being true to the ecologies of our regions. We meant mutually respectful growers and eaters. We meant social justice and community. Some insist that the modern world has no place for such niceties. Small-scale organic operations, they declare, will inevitably lose out to what has been called the organic-industrial complex. Its output will be delivered to high-volume superstores, where locally grown carrots will be undersold by mass-produced "organic" carrots.

Some of us don't agree that the future of organics lies in economies of scale or long-distance transport of food. We believe it lies in local markets that help sustain vibrant local economies. "Oh, sure," sneer the critics, "but local organic can't feed the world."

Industrial agriculture is not now feeding the world, of course, and shows no promise of doing so.

Instead, this high-input model keeps plunging into destitution the very farmers whose production might really help end hunger. Local organic agriculture, moreover, doesn't have to feed the world; it needs only to offer local communities techniques for feeding themselves, an offer it has widely delivered on from Mexico to Kenya. It has delivered, most notably, in Cuba, 90 miles off our southern coast, where small-scale local organic agriculture is feeding a nation.

Cut off from the inputs for "modern" agriculture by the 1989 disintegration of the Soviet Union, Cuba went organic of necessity. Now private and community urban gardens supply more than half of Cuba's vegetables. Could a similar revolution come to pass here, in a nation that "has everything"? Why not? By demonstrating the power of organic methods in our own backyards, by supporting local farmers, and by working steadily to shorten our food chains, we veterans of Organic Gardening's earlier battles can help save the kind of organic we always meant to have.

QUESTIONS

1. Gussow gives voice to the ideology behind the organic movement. This ideology was then codified into law. Which bits of the ideology made it into law? Which didn't?
2. Which are the values that "organic" goes proxy for in Gussow's mind?
3. Explain how organic agriculture, as codified in the actual organic laws, could be turned into a form of industrial agriculture. Explain Gussow's objection to industrialization. Is it compelling? Why or why not?

FRED KIRSCHENMANN

Can Organic Agriculture Feed the World?
And Is That the Right Question?

This reading by Fred Kirschenmann, a farmer and food activist, shares some of Gussow's worries that organic agriculture as currently practiced just replicates the faults of large-scale, industrial, conventional agriculture that it is meant to remedy. However, its main contribution is to note what a difficult question "Can organic feed the world?" is. Feed the world what? Under which weather conditions? For how long? Given which governmental policies? To confidently claim, as some do, that small-scale organic cannot feed the world, these questions need answering. But to answer them, they first need to be made visible.

Thomas Malthus, an English clergyman and political economist, published a treatise in 1798 that riveted the world's attention on the "problem" of human population growth.[1] Malthus argued that population growth was bound to outstrip food production, because human population would increase geometrically while the food supply could only grow arithmetically. Malthus's powerful thesis has been used to justify many social doctrines ever since, everything from "survival of the fittest" to the "green revolution" (GR).

The question "Can organic agriculture feed the world?" is posed against that backdrop. What the question is asking is this: can organic farming methods produce enough food to feed an ever-expanding human population, or will its methods of production reduce yields and therefore hasten the time of the massive famines envisioned by Malthus? The question usually raises a moral issue as well as a technical one. In his essay in praise of Norman Borlaug, Gregg Easterbrook blames all those who oppose GR agriculture for the starvation of people in Africa.[2]

Borlaug is, of course, the agronomist who helped develop the high-yielding grain varieties (and the input-intensive technologies required to produce those yields), ushering in the new era of industrial agriculture. The moral implication of Easterbrook's essay is clear: those who oppose high-input agriculture will have starving millions on their conscience.

DESCRIPTION OF THE PROBLEM

Posed this way, the food/population issue appears to be a simple matter of producing enough food and inventing the technologies capable of producing it. However, the imbalance of humans relative to the millions of other species with whom we coevolved now disrupts the biotic community and the delicate ecological relationships that have evolved over billions of years. This disruption and deterioration now

Frederick L. Kirschenmann, "Can Organic Farming Feed the World? And Is That the Right Question?" From *Cultivating an Ecological Conscience: Essays from a Farmer Philosopher* (Berkeley, CA: Counterpoint, 2011).

threaten the food supply of the human species. The reason we need to consider an alternative is that our current model of industrial agriculture is contributing, dramatically, to this ecological disruption. So while the green revolution may have enjoyed success in increasing the yields of a few crop varieties for the short term, it now threatens the ability of future generations to feed themselves.

In other words, the question "Can organic agriculture feed the world?" is a much more complex question than is often implied. This is not simply a question of whether or not the technologies to farm organically can outperform the technologies to farm industrially. The question is, how do we regain and maintain the evolutionary stability of the various ecological neighborhoods in which we humans live? Apart from such stabilization, we will lose the "ecosystem services" that provide not only food, but all of the life-sustaining elements that make human life possible on this planet.[3] So, the "agriculture" question (inside that larger question) is: What kind of agriculture can best mirror and maintain that evolutionary stability?

Niles Eldredge gives us some examples of our utter dependence on these complex biological relationships. Insects, which humans generally hold in low regard (we'd love to expunge many of them from the face of the Earth altogether), are so important, says Eldredge, that "humanity probably could not last for more than a few months" without them.[4] Most of us would probably support a proposal to eradicate termites from the face of the Earth. But Eldredge reminds us that termites, because of their symbiotic relationship with spirochete bacteria, are one of the few creatures on the planet that can digest cellulose. Consequently, we humans are absolutely dependent on termites for a huge portion of the recycling of the world's biotic material. "No recycling, no ongoing life," he says.[5] Put another way, without termites you can forget about the problem of producing enough food. There wouldn't be any humans—or much of any other kind of life as we know it—to feed!

What is often posed as the food/population problem can more accurately be described as a population/ecology problem. In other words, the real problem

with the unprecedented increase in human population is that it has led to the disruption and deterioration of the natural functioning of Earth's biotic community, and that is what threatens our future, not lack of production.

THE ECOLOGY/FOOD/ POPULATION CONNECTION

When the technologies we use to increase the production of a few species of crops and livestock accelerate ecosystem disruption and deterioration, we only hasten the time when food shortages become inevitable. In short, we are now on a downward spiral of an ever-increasing population and an ever-decreasing capacity to produce food, our powerful technologies notwithstanding. If we are to survive, we must both reduce the growth of the human species and transform agriculture so that it enhances, rather than further deteriorates, the ecological neighborhoods in which we farm.

Reducing the population of the human species is, of course, a formidable task, given its current rate of growth. Before agriculture was invented, about 10,000 years ago, the total human population on the planet had reached an estimated 10 million people over its entire evolutionary history. After agriculture was invented, the human population jumped from 10 million to about 50 million in just 3,000 years. Thereafter, the human population doubled at an ever-increasing rate. In the pre-Christian era, it took 1,600 years for the human population to double; the population went from 50 million in 3000 B.C. to 100 million in 1400 B.C. The most recent doubling took just thirty-six years, from 1969 to 1996.

Not surprisingly, the disruption of the natural functioning of biotic communities has increased along with population. But population growth, up to now, is not the major cause. The disruptions are caused by the way an increasing number of us relate to the rest of nature and how we feed ourselves from it.

For the past five years, the United States has seen the worst declines in honeybees in its history. Many states have seen bee kills as high as 85 and 90 percent. The immediate cause of the bee kills is, of course, the varroa mite, but the mite's impact might have been minor had the industrial system of agriculture not provided an environment in which it could do its damage. Derrick Jensen describes the real problem:

> The collapse was inevitable anyway. In February, the hills surrounding Modesto, California, roll with white-blossomed almond trees. Although monocropped miles of almond flowers may be beautiful, they're as unnatural as Frankenstein's monster; the staggering number of blooms to be pollinated grossly overmatches the capacity of wild pollinators like bumblebees, moths, wasps, and beetles to set fruit, causing almond ranchers to pay distant beekeepers up to $35 per hive to bring in bees for the four-week bloom.
>
> Almonds aren't the only crop needing pollination. Apples, cherries, pears, raspberries, cranberries, blueberries, cucumbers, watermelons—each of these densely packed crops requires similarly densely packed beehives to set fruit. The strengths that have made modern beekeeping the foundation upon which the agricultural infrastructure rests are precisely the weaknesses that have made beekeeping, and modern agribusiness, vulnerable to something as tiny as the mite.[6]

Thus, industrial agriculture, with its successful productivity in a few crops, has caused the ecological imbalance that now threatens the productivity of those same crops. Jensen's analysis of the honeybee destruction helps us to see that if we are truly interested in feeding the world, then we have to face up to a host of complicated questions often missing from the "feeding the world" debate.

Even the debate between Lester Brown, the World Bank, and the UN Food and Agriculture Organization (FAO) is oversimplifying the issue. Their debate hinges primarily on whether future technologies will be able to continue to increase production. The World Bank and the FAO argue that such technologies are on the horizon. Brown argues that they probably aren't.[7] Posing the question this way implies, again, that the issue can be reduced to our capacity to produce more grain through technology. However, the problem is much more complicated.

THE MANIFOLD DIMENSIONS OF THE PROBLEM

The Weather Factor

In *The Genesis Strategy,* climatologist Stephen Schneider demonstrated that both crop yields and low variability are due at least as much to weather as to technology.[8] I suppose most any farmer could have told him that: "Don't worry and fret about the crops. After you have done all you can for them, let them stand in the weather on their own."[9] Because weather is such a significant factor in our capacity to produce high yields, Schneider argues that if we want to keep the world fed, we need to implement the strategy of Joseph in the Bible, who urged Egypt's pharaoh to store part of the abundance of the seven good years, to assure themselves food for the seven bad years. Because small changes in atmospheric conditions can cause major changes in weather patterns, we should not use farming practices that help destabilize delicately balanced atmospheric conditions. Global warming may radically disrupt global weather patterns and cause dramatic increases in severe weather changes and violent storms. Those changes can dramatically alter our ability to produce food.

Insurance companies worldwide have taken note of the increased insurance losses due to weather-related natural disasters since 1980. In the entire decade of the 1980s, insurers paid only $17 billion for all weather-related natural disasters. By the end of the first half of the 1990s, insurers had already paid out $57 billion for such damages. No wonder insurance companies often stand shoulder to shoulder with environmentalists lobbying for legislation that has the potential to reduce climate change.[10] Farmers and food-related industries might do well to follow their example. After all, "If the crop of any one year was all, a man would have to cut his throat every time it hailed."[11]

Ecological farming practices, which seek to mirror and maintain the ecological neighborhoods in which they exist, are much less likely to contribute to climate change than industrial agriculture, which alters natural ecological neighborhoods for the sake of short-term yield increases of a few specialized crops. Industrial agriculture accelerates global warming through forest destruction and use of ozone-depleting chemicals, such as methyl bromide, as a soil fumigant. To the extent that organic agriculture remains true to its ecological roots, it may do a better job of feeding the world.

It's Not Just about Grain

Sixty percent of the world's population today depends on fish and seafood for 40 percent of its annual protein.[12] Insects provide "the major source of protein to roughly 60 percent of the world's population."[13] These and other vital food sources are often ignored in the feeding-the-world debate. In fact, there is a tendency to equate grain yields with food production. Easterbrook, for example, credited Norman Borlaug with saving "more lives than any other person who ever lived" because Borlaug increased grain yields of a few crops two- and three-fold.[14] But it is well known that the very technologies that accomplished the increased grain yields have seriously damaged seafood ecologies. So an important question has to be asked: did we really increase food production when we increased wheat and rice yields at the expense of seafood?

According to the International Rice Research Institute (IRRI), increased rice yields may not have improved the quality of life in the developing world that much.[15] The institute concluded that pesticides induced resistance to pests, created new pests by destroying natural predators, and increased health problems from farming with pesticides. Farm families have lost "more money from getting sick than the chemicals save by killing bugs in the field."[16]

Furthermore, the IRRI scientists expressed doubts that the GR methods had actually produced more food. While using the GR technologies, rice yields doubled and even tripled, but those same technologies killed fish previously raised in the rice paddies and fruit trees previously producing fruit on the periphery of the rice paddies. Despite increased rice yields, more food was probably not produced. As a result, the UN FAO has established farm schools to teach ecological methods to the same farmers that had previously learned GR practices from IRRI.

Vandana Shiva points out similar problems with the GR in India.[17] While the GR "miracle seeds" were more responsive to chemical fertilizer and irrigation inputs, their overall performance was inferior to the indigenous seeds selected and bred by India's farmers for centuries. She argues that considering all factors, the GR has diminished rather than enhanced India's food security.

In the industrial paradigm of agriculture, the way to feed the world is by reinventing nature to increase grain production. One has to question this paradigm because much of the increased grain production goes into alcohol and animal feed, and is not used to directly feed humans at all.

The Role of Animals

Much of our capacity to feed the world is wasted because we feed grain protein to animals instead of feeding it directly to humans. However, that is not a good reason to eliminate animals from the food system altogether, as Rifkin has argued.[18] Animals play a key role in keeping the world fed and help maintain the ecological health of the neighborhoods in which we live. Ruminant animals are the only creatures capable of transforming grass into protein that can be digested by humans. Consequently, if it weren't for animals, more than a billion acres in the United States alone could not be used for human food, because that acreage is unsuitable for annual cereal grain production, with which industrial agriculture would feed the world.

Furthermore, without animals many other foodstuffs not suitable for human consumption, such as crop residues and weather-damaged grain, could not be turned into protein for humans. Nevertheless, industrial agriculture unnecessarily feeds animals huge quantities of grain. The principal reason for feeding large quantities of grain is that industrial agriculture has concentrated animals in large feedlots and in hog and poultry barns, and concentration makes it inefficient to feed animals either forages or crop residues. Transportation costs dictate that protein fed to animals must be in concentrated form, primarily corn and soybeans.

Concentrating animals also means that animal manure becomes a huge, environmentally damaging waste-disposal problem rather than a rich source of fertilizer and organic matter to improve soil quality. Large concentrations of animals also deplete water resources in the ecological neighborhoods where they are confined and make grazing difficult, if not impossible. Disease problems and pathogen resistance are increased, which lead to increased use of antibiotics to control the increased disease. Thus, antibiotic-resistant pathogens are more likely to end up in the food system.

Organic farms that remain true to their ecological roots integrate animals into the farming system to help close nutrient cycles on the farm. The wastes from the cropping system are used as food for animals, and the wastes of animals are used to feed the crops. Integration and dispersion of animals throughout ecosystems is a much better way of maintaining ecological health and feeding the world over the long term.

The Ecological Disruption/ Food Supply Connection

Since the era of industrial agriculture began, we have lost approximately half of our topsoil, and the quality of the remaining soil has seriously deteriorated. High-yielding crops require large quantities of water. Irrigation is depleting our groundwater sources faster than nature can replenish them. Inadequate water supplies may be more of a problem than inadequate food supplies for an expanding human population. Water quality has been seriously damaged through fertilizer and pesticide runoff. Biodiversity has been reduced as a result of industrial agriculture practices. These effects of industrial agriculture are well known and documented. Their potential to seriously jeopardize our capacity to produce food in the future is obvious.

Many other adverse consequences are not as well known. In a recent *Science* magazine article on nitrogen use in Minnesota, nitrogen loading was found to be causing environmental disruptions. The study showed that "after 12 years of N addition, species richness declined by more than 50 percent."[19] Such deterioration of the biotic community, plus the atmospheric changes caused by concentrations of nitrous oxide (which is a long-lived greenhouse gas and a destroyer of the ozone layer), can seriously disrupt our ability to produce food.

Arsenic poisoning in India has been traced to irrigation.[20] Prior to the GR, arsenic, naturally present in the soil, posed no problem to humans or other animals. But irrigation concentrated the arsenic so that it caused major health problems. Although industrial agriculture increased grain production in India, it did so in some locations at the expense of human health.

Dramatic increases in world trade augment the likelihood that new pests, "invader species," will hitchhike to new ecosystems in which they did not evolve.[21] Without the natural enemies with which they coevolved, these exotic insects, nematodes, mites, and weeds can quickly become disastrous pests. In addition, industrial agriculture now depends on only about fifteen varieties of plant species worldwide for 90 percent of the calories used to feed the world.[22] The specialization of industrial agriculture (resulting in very brittle ecosystems) and increased potential for invader species disrupting brittle ecologies is a prescription for food-supply disaster. The nineteenth-century Irish potato blight and the corn leaf blight of the 1960s in the United States remind us how vulnerable genetically uniform cropping systems can be. Increased risk of invader species moving into genetically uniform ecologies may make the bee kills resulting from the hitchhiking of the varroa mite into the United States seem like a minor incident by comparison.

Contrary to Easterbrook's vision for saving Africa from starvation, the National Research Council has concluded that Africa may need to return to its more than 2,000 indigenous species of grains, fruits, vegetables, and roots to reduce the continent's vulnerability to food shortages.[23] That advice may become more critical if local ecosystems, dominated by monoculture agriculture, are disrupted by invasive species. Destabilization by invasive species could be further exacerbated by the introduction of novel, transgenic organisms, which some scientists have referred to as "aliens with a capital 'A.' "[24] The ecological risks of introducing genetically engineered organisms are similar to the problems created by introducing non-native organisms into new environments.[25,26] A diverse, ecologically integrated agriculture practiced by organic farmers may do a better job of feeding the world.

Production vs. Power

In a report to the Bruntland Commission, the issue of food and population was put into proper perspective. The report said, "The problem is not one of global food production being outstripped by population. The problem has three aspects: where the food is being produced, by whom, and who can command it."[27] Reducing the problem of hunger to adequate production simply misconstrues the problem, either inadvertently (due to a lack of understanding) or purposefully (to protect vested interests). The fact that 800 million people are starving on the planet when we have the capacity to feed everyone makes it clear that hunger is not a production problem. The global food market responds to money, but most of the 800 million who are starving have no economic power. One does not have to go to Africa to see this problem at work; in the United States, 12 million children go to bed hungry every night.

Daniel Quinn suggests that agriculture has always been totalitarian.[28] If so, then agriculture has always been more about power than about feeding people. While it is difficult to substantiate Quinn's claim historically, modern agriculture is clearly about power. Power is perhaps also the reason we talk about this subject in terms of "feeding the world" rather than "keeping the world fed." "Feeding the world" suggests someone is responsible for feeding someone else, which increases dependency. Under such terms, there can be no food security. "Keeping the world fed," however, implies that people are empowered to feed themselves, which is essential to long-term food security. Organic farms integrated into local ecologies and rooted in communities have more potential to keep the world fed than large, corporate farms owned by distant investors.

Energy to Feed the World

The industrial food system is, of course, made possible only by the availability of cheap, abundant energy, which is used at all levels: production, processing, and distribution. From the perspective of calories of energy consumed to put a calorie of food on the table, it is one of the least efficient systems known to humankind. As sources of cheap, nonrenewable, stored energy continue to be depleted, it will become increasingly necessary to rely on much more current, efficient energy sources. In a study comparing the energy efficiency of actual operating organic, no-till, and conventional farms in North Dakota, organic farms were 70 percent more energy-efficient when all energy use was calculated.[29] Ultimately, an ecological agriculture that incorporated perennial polycultures, in a manner similar to that being explored by the Land Institute in Salina, Kansas, would have an even better chance of keeping the world fed without destroying the resources upon which agriculture depends.

CAN ORGANIC AGRICULTURE FEED THE WORLD?

So what is the answer to the question, "Can organic agriculture feed the world?" First, we should not delude ourselves into believing that the human species can continue to reproduce itself at anything like its present rate without dire consequences. The human species is part of an intricate biotic community; thus, we have to maintain some kind of equilibrium within that community if we are to survive with any kind of quality of life. Feeding itself from that community is only one of a very complex set of problems which an overburdening human population poses. Maintaining the ecological relationships between diffusely coevolved species is essential to survival.

Therefore, if our population increases, we have to use fewer of our ecosystem resources and services to restore and retain the health of our ecological neighborhoods. The only kind of agriculture that can hope to keep the world fed is an ecologically oriented agriculture that mirrors and maintains the natural ecology in which it is located.

FROM FARM TO FORK: REORGANIZING THE FOOD SYSTEM

However, organic agriculture, inserted into the current industrial food system infrastructure, will fare no better at feeding the world than industrial agriculture. Apart from a radical restructuring of the food system, we will have little success in keeping the world fed. Meeting maximum production goals of a few crops and livestock in a few regions of the world, to be marketed into the global economy, cannot keep the world fed. In keeping with the sentiment of the Bruntland report, the best way to achieve food security is evolution of a people/food/land equilibrium based on local culture.

Helena Norberg-Hodge provides an intriguing example of a food system rooted in local culture.[30] Despite scarce resources and extreme climates, the Ladakh people who live in the desert highlands of the western Himalayas are well-nourished, usually healthy, and free of social and environmental stresses. The Ladakh experience corroborates one of the principles for ending hunger outlined by Francis Moore Lappé: "While slowing population growth in itself cannot end hunger, the very changes necessary to end hunger—the democratization of economic life, especially the empowerment of women—are key to reducing birth rates so that the human population can come into balance with the rest of the natural world."[31]

We still don't know the capacity of people in a local ecological neighborhood to feed themselves, once they are empowered to properly use local resources and sound ecological farming systems. Different ecological neighborhoods have different capacities, depending on such factors as local climate and land- and sea-based food resources. Exporting surpluses from one foodshed to another

could, of course, always continue to be part of the new food system. But the first priority in the new food system is food self-sufficiency in every ecological neighborhood.

Furthermore, local food systems, tied to local ecological neighborhoods, would tend to create people/food/land equilibriums through local culture as it has among the Ladakh. This vision of the restructuring of the global food system may seem bizarre in our world of global markets and global competitiveness. Regional foodshed concepts, until recently, were largely endorsed only by grassroots groups and a few prophets in the wilderness. More recently the idea is being endorsed by the U.S. Congress in programs like the Community Food Security Act and by a few faculty in land-grant universities.

Jack Kloppenburg and his colleagues at the University of Wisconsin claim that regional foodsheds are not only desirable but feasible. Bill Heffernan at the University of Missouri has suggested for some time that farms need to understand the global food market and then unhook from it. Cornelia Flora at Iowa State University suggests that food systems should integrate into the new economy, rather than follow the model of "Fordism," or mass production of uniform commodities at low prices.

The new economy relies on the production of differentiated products produced on a much smaller scale but designed to be innovative and flexible to meet the fast-changing demands of a discriminating consumer.[32] The post-Fordist economy shortens supply lines and responds to local markets. It doesn't attempt to compete in the global mass market. This localized, site-specific concept of the economy can be adapted to empower local people to feed themselves.

Furthermore, the idea of local foodsheds is catching on in many communities, especially among poor neighborhoods. Hundreds of communities are creating new food and farming markets. Organic farmers are collaborating with community organizations to exchange food for labor, community gardens are linked with local school systems to provide food for poor families and teach kids organic gardening, and businesses work with nonprofits to make food available in communities without grocery stores.

These fledgling enterprises, along with the growing farmers' markets and community-supported agriculture, are indications that the global industrial food system is not working for a growing number of people. New food systems, grounded in local culture, sound local ecological management, and local control, are likely to make up an increasing portion of the food system of tomorrow. Making such fundamental shifts in the food system is, however, bound to run into opposition. Because agriculture today is about power, corporate interests will oppose these new initiatives and continue to claim that only their way can prevent world starvation.

A FINAL OBSERVATION

Awareness that sound ecological farming and local empowerment are essential to feeding ourselves leads to a conclusion that industrial farming is fundamentally about something other than "feeding the world." Perhaps Wendell Berry said it best:

> But the *real* products of any year's work are the farmer's mind and the cropland itself.
>
> If he raises a good crop at the cost of belittling himself and diminishing the ground, he has gained nothing. He will have to begin over again the next spring, worse off than before.
>
> Let him receive the season's increment into his mind. Let him work it into the soil.
>
> The finest growth that farmland can produce is a careful farmer.
>
> Make the human race a better head. Make the world a better piece of ground.[33]

NOTES

1. T. R. Malthus, *An Essay on the Principle of Population: Text, Sources and Background, Criticism,* ed. Philip Appleman (New York: W. W. Norton & CO., 1976).

2. G. Easterbrook, "Forgotten Benefactor of Humanity," *Atlantic Monthly,* January 1997, 75–82.

3. Niles Eldredge, *Dominion: Can Nature and Culture Co-Exist?* (New York: Henry Holt & Co., 1995).

4. Ibid., 162.

5. Ibid., 163.

6. Derrick Jensen, "Hush of the Hives," *New York Times Magazine,* October 13, 1996.

7. Lester R. Brown, *Tough Choices: Facing the Challenge of Food Scarcity* (New York: W. W. Norton & Co., 1996).

8. Stephen H. Schneider, *The Genesis Strategy: Climate and Global Survival* (New York: Plenum Press, 1976).

9. Wendell Berry, "Prayers and Sayings of the Mad Farmer," in *Collected Poems,* 1357–1982 (San Francisco: North Point Press, 1984), 131.

10. Christopher Flavin, "Climate Change and Storm Damage: The Insurance Costs Keep Rising," *World Watch,* January-February 1997, 10–11.

11. Berry, *Collected Poems,* 131.

12. Tracy I. Hewitt and Katie R. Smith, *Intensive Agriculture and Environmental Quality: Examining the Agricultural Myth* (Greenbelt, Md.: Henry A. Wallace Institute for Alternative Agriculture, 1995).

13. A. A. Spindler and J. D. Schultz, "Comparison of Dietary Variety and EthnicFood Consumption among Chinese, Chinese-American and White American Women," *Agriculture and Human Values* 13 (1996): 65.

14. Easterbrook, "Forgotten Benefactor."

15. All Things Considered, National Public Radio, July 31 and August 7, 1994.

16. Ibid.

17. Vandana Shiva, *The Violence of the Green Revolution: Third World Agriculture, Ecology, and Politics* (London: Zed Books Ltd., 1991).

18. Jeremy Rifkin, *Beyond Beef The Rise and Fall of the Cattle Culture* (New York: Dutton, 1992).

19. D. A. Wedin and D. Tilman, "Influence of Nitrogen Loading and Species Composition on Carbon Balance of Grasslands," *Science* 274 (1996): 1721.

20. P. Bagla and J. Kaiser, "India's Spreading Health Crisis Draws Global ArsenicExperts," *Science* 274 (1996): 174–75.

21. Yvonne Baskin, "Curbing Undesirable Invaders," *BioScience* 46 (1996): 732–36.

22. Judy Soule, Danielle Card, and Wes Jackson, "Ecological Impact of ModernAgriculture," in *Agroecology,* ed. C. Ronald Carroll, John H. Vandermeer, and Peter Rosset, 165–88 (New York: McGraw-Hill, 1990).

23. National Research Council, *Lost Crops of Africa,* vol. 1, Grains (Washington D.C.: National Academies Press, 1996).

24. Baskin, "Curbing Undesirable Invaders."

25. Jane Rissler and Margaret G. Mellon, *The Ecological Risks of Engineered Crops* (Cambridge, Mass.: MIT Press, 1996).

26. A. A. Snow and P. M. Palma, "Commercialization of Transgenic Plants: Potential Ecological Risks," *BioScience* 47 (1997): 86–96.

27. Advisory Panel on Food Security, Agriculture, Forestry, and Environment to the World Commission on Environment and Development, *Food 2000: Global Policies for Sustainable Agriculture* (London: Zed Books, 1987).

28. Daniel Quinn, *The Story of B* (New York: Bantam Books, 1996).

29. S. A. Clancy. *Farming Practices for a Sustainable Agriculture in North Dakota* (Carrington, N.D.: North Dakota State University, Carrington Research Extension Office, 1993).

30. Helena Norberg-Hodge, *Ancient Futures: Learning from Ladakh* (San Francisco: Sierra Club Books, 1991).

31. Frances Moore Lappe and Joseph Collins, *World Hunger: Twelve Myths* (New York: Grove Press, 1986).

32. Cornelia Butler Flora, *The Sustainable Agriculturist and the New Economy* (St. Paul Minn.: Minnesota Department of Agriculture, Energy, and Sustainable Agriculture Program, 1996).

33. Berry, *Collected Poems*, 131.

QUESTIONS

1. What, exactly, is Malthus's thesis mentioned in the first paragraph? What work does Malthus's thesis do in Chapter 2, "Hunger"?
2. Kirschenmann claims that "the food/population issue" is *not* "a simple matter of producing enough food and inventing the technologies capable of producing it." First, what is the food/population issue? Second, what is Kirschenmann's argument that the issue is not a matter of producing enough food and coming up with the technologies to do so?
3. Kirschenmann blames "industrial" agriculture for various problems producing food. What is his account of industrial agriculture? (How does it differ from the account we offer in our introduction to this and the previous chapter?) Can organic agriculture be industrial, according to Kirschenmann?
4. What are the seven ways in which the problem of feeding the world has been oversimplified, according to Kirschenmann?
5. What are Kirschenmann's answers to the questions in his essay's title?

BILL McKIBBEN

A Grand Experiment

The hook here is that McKibben spends the winter in frigid central Vermont eating nothing but very local food. On this hook, McKibben hangs a series of ideas about local, small-scale, organic alternatives to industrial agriculture and hangs a series of ideas about the benefits of these alternatives. These are environmental and social benefits but also benefits to the welfare of animals and humans.

Bill McKibben, "A Grand Experiment," in *Gourmet* (July 2005). © Condé Nast. http://www.gourmet.com/magazine/2000s/2005/07/livingoffland.html

From before the first frost until after the salad greens had finally poked their heads above the warming soil, most of my food for seven months came from within a couple dozen miles of my house. For a few things, I traveled to the corners of this watershed, which covers the northwest third of Vermont and a narrower fringe along the New York shore of Lake Champlain. (I did make what might be called the Marco Polo exception—I considered fair game anything your average thirteenth-century explorer might have brought back from distant lands. So pepper and turmeric, and even the odd knob of ginger, stayed in the larder.) Eating like this is precisely how almost every human being ate until very recently, and how most people in the world still do eat today. But in contemporary America, where the average bite of food travels 1,500 miles before it reaches your lips, it was an odd exercise. Local and seasonal may have become watchwords of much new cooking, but I wanted to see what was really possible, especially in these northern climes. I know that eating close to home represents the history of American farming—but I sense it may have a future, too. The number of farms around Burlington, Vermont's chief city, has grown 19 percent in the past decade. Most of them are small, growing food for local consumers instead of commodities for export; the same trend is starting to show up nationwide. Something's happening, and I wanted to see exactly what.

I'm writing this, so you know I survived. But, in fact, I survived in style-it was the best eating winter of my life. Here's my report.

* * *

September—The farmers' market in Middlebury, Vermont, is in absolute fever bloom: sweet, sweet corn; big, ripe tomatoes; bunches of basil; melons. This is the bounty of our short but intense summer, when the heat of the long days combines with the moisture of these eastern uplands to produce almost anything you could want. It's the great eating moment of the year.

But I'm wandering the market trying to keep the image of midwinter in mind—the short, bitter days of January, when the snow is drifted high against the

house and the woodstove is cranking. I'm used to getting the winter's wood in, but not to putting the winter's food by. In our world, it's always summer somewhere, and so we count on the same produce year-round. But that takes its toll: on the environment, from endless trucking and flying and shipping; on local farmers, who can't compete with the equatorial bounty and hence sell their fields for condos; and most of all, perhaps, on taste. There's nothing that tastes like a June strawberry; whereas a January supermarket strawberry tastes like . . . nothing.

All of which explains why I'm bargaining for canning tomatoes, the Romas with perhaps a few blemishes. Though mostly I want to spend the winter buying what's available, I'll put up a certain amount. My friend Amy Trubek volunteers to help—a food anthropologist, she's the head of the Vermont Fresh Network, which partners farmers with chefs; she and her husband, Brad Koehler, one of the chefs at (and general manager of) Middlebury College's renowned dining halls, also own a small orchard and a big vegetable garden, not to mention a capacious freezer. "A lot of people associate canning with their grandmother, hostage in the kitchen for six weeks," she said. "But, hey, this is the twenty-first century. We can freeze, we can cure, we can Cryovac—we can do all this a hundred different ways." An afternoon's work, with the Red Sox beginning their stretch drive on the radio, and I've got enough tomato sauce frozen in Ziplocs to last me through the winter.

* * *

October—Fall lingers on (and the Red Sox, too). I'm already regarding the leaf lettuce in our local food co-op with a kind of nostalgia, knowing it's about to disappear from my life. And I'm regarding two small bins in the co-op's bulk section as my lifeline. They're filled with local flour, fifty-nine cents a pound. Once upon a time, the Champlain Valley was the nation's granary—but that was back before the Erie Canal opened the way west and vast rivers of grain began rolling back from the deep topsoil of the Plains. Grain farming all but disappeared from the region; the most basic component of the American diet had to be imported from Nebraska.

But there's always an oddball, and, in this case, his name is Ben Gleason, who came to Vermont, as did many others, as a part of the back-to-the-land movement of the 1970s. He found an old farm in the Addison County town of Bridport and began to plant it in a rotation of organic hard red winter wheat. Last year, for instance, he grew thirty tons on twenty-eight acres, perfectly respectable even by Midwest standards, and he ground all of it with the small, noisy machine in the shed next to his house. He only does whole-wheat flour-white would require another machine, and anyway, as he points out, it's not nearly as good for you. In any event, his is delicious—making pancakes flavorful enough to stand up to the Grade B maple syrup that's the only kind we buy. (Grade A, Fancy—it's for tourists. The closer to tar, the better.)

"There's maybe four or five hundred acres altogether that's planted in wheat around the area," said Samuel Sherman, who owns Champlain Valley Milling, in Westport, New York. Mostly he grinds wheat that arrives by train car from the west, but he'd love to see more local product. "We can sell it in a minute," he said. The proof is just down the lakeshore, in the town of Crown Point, where a young baker named Yannig Tanguy makes artisanal bread—fougasse, baguette, Swabian rye—entirely with local wheat that he grinds himself, sometimes three hundred pounds in a day. Crown Point is a poor town next to an aging paper mill—and yet the door to the little bakery keeps popping open constantly. Here's someone who wants to reserve ten loaves for an elementary school dinner the next week; here's a woman to buy a cookie and say thanks for letting her park in the tiny lot during church that morning. "It's not like I'm trying to invent anything with local food," said Tanguy. "It all obviously worked for a long time. That we're here today is proof that it worked. And it can work again."

November—The traditional Thanksgiving dinner is also the traditional local foods dinner in this part of the world. Which makes sense, since the Pilgrims weren't in any position to import much food—they just hunkered down with the beige cuisine that begins to predominate as the summer becomes mere memory. (On Cape Cod, cranberries provide a flash of deep color; here, we have beets, which make a ruby slaw.) The kind of self-sufficient all-around farm with which the colonists covered the continent has essentially

disappeared, at least outside of Amish country. Even the tiny growers in this valley specialize in order to stay afloat—I can show you a potato farmer in the hills above Rutland with fifty varieties on his three acres, or a bison wrangler on the lakeshore, or an emu rancher. Some of America's original community-supported agriculture farms (CSAs) are in this area, and none produce vegetables more glorious than those from Golden Russet Farm, in Shoreham, where Will and Judy Stevens are busy threshing dried beans when I stop by one afternoon to pick up some squash. If you pay them a few hundred dollars in the winter, they'll keep you supplied with a weekly bin of vegetables throughout the growing season and deep into the fall. But even Will and Judy go to the store for their milk.

Not so for Mark and Kristin Kimball, the young proprietors of Essex Farm, on the New York side of the lake. If you want to join their CSA, you pay more like a few thousand dollars. But when you stop by on Friday afternoons for your pickup, it's not just vegetables: they have a few milking cows, so there's milk and cheese and butter; they have a small herd of grass-fed cattle, so there are steaks and burgers; the snorting tribe of pigs behind the barn provides bacon and lard; there are chickens and turkeys. Except for paper towels and dental floss, you'd never have to set foot in a store again—think Laura Ingalls Wilder, complete with a team of big Belgians. "There's nothing inherent about modern ways that I don't support," Mark insisted. "It just so happens that working with horses is—not better than working with tractors, but more fun. It's a more dynamic relationship. You can understand an engine. You'll never understand a horse."

You can't leave the farm without Mark loading your trunk full of food—"Do you have room for another chicken in there?"—and all of it tastes of the place. As you bump down the driveway, a look in the rearview mirror reveals Mark juggling carrots and grinning. "Occasionally I feel like I'm doing some work," he said. "But usually it feels more like entertainment for myself."

Is this realistic? Could you feed Manhattan in this fashion? You could not—every place is different. (And Manhattan is lucky to have New Jersey right next door, with some of the best truck-farming soil and weather anywhere on earth.) But you could feed Essex, New York, this way—Mark figures the fifty acres they're farming can support ten families, a reminder of just how fertile the earth is in the right hands.

December—Here's what I'm missing: not grapefruit, not chocolate. Oats. And their absence helps illustrate what's happened to American agriculture, and what would be required to change it a little bit.

Once upon a time, oats were everywhere—people grew them for their horses, and for themselves. But oats aren't easy to deal with. They have a hull that needs removing, and they need to be steamed, and dried, and rolled. You can do that more efficiently on an enormous scale in places like Saskatoon, Saskatchewan, where a single mill can turn out more than half a million pounds of oat products a day. For the moment, this centralization works. But that may change if the price of oil (the lifeblood of industrial agriculture) continues to climb, or as the climate continues to shift, or if global politics deteriorates. Even now, stubborn people keep trying to rebuild smaller-scale food networks, but it's hard going against the tide of cheap goods flowing in. A few years ago, for instance, a Vermonter named Andrew Leinoff decided to go into oats—he and his friend Eric Allen found some old equipment and started experimenting. But after a few years of struggling they gave up, and a little bitterly. The state's Agency of Agriculture talks a good game—a public service ad on the radio urges Vermonters to buy 10 percent of their food from within the state—but in the opinion of many small farmers, it spends most of its time and money propping up the state's slowly withering dairy industry, not supporting the pioneers trying to build what comes next.

They sold their equipment across the border in Quebec, to an organic miller named Michel Gaudreau, who does everything from hulling spelt to pearling barley. And Gaudreau found a farmer in the province's Eastern Townships, Alex Brand, whose family had been growing oats for many years. I tracked him down, delighted to find that Brand's Fellgarth Farm was right on the edge of my Champlain watershed. But shipping a bag of oats across the border was going to be hard work—it might, they warned, require a trip to Customs. Happily, Brand had an American distributor—Joe Angello, in New York's Columbia County. By the time

all was said and done, my "local" oats had traveled on a truck from Canada to the lower Hudson Valley, and then back to Vermont in a UPS sack. Not precisely an ecological triumph. On the other hand, they were delicious—plump, if oats can be plump. So now it's pancakes only every other morning.

January—Truth be told, my eleven-year-old daughter has used the words icky and disgusting on several occasions, always in connection with root vegetables. Not potatoes, not carrots—but turnips, and parsnips, and rutabagas. It is a little hard to imagine how people got through winter on the contents of their root cellars alone.

Which is why I'm glad for the Ziplocs full of raspberries and blueberries my wife froze in the summer. And why I'm glad for the high-tech apple warehouse just down the road in Shoreham. Here's the thing about apples: the best ones rot pretty fast. Sure, those brick-hard Red Delicious and Granny Smiths can be picked in New Zealand or South Africa or China or Washington and flown and trucked halfway around the world and sit on a shelf at the supermarket for a week and still look like an apple. (Taste is another story—they've been bred for immortality, and immortality alone.) But the great apples of the Northeast—your Cortland, your Empire, your Northern Spy, and, above all, your McIntosh—are softer, more ephemeral. For generations, people solved that problem by converting them to cider—hard cider, fermented for freezerless storage. That's what most of those apple trees around New England were planted for. But there's another solution if, like Barney Hodges, you have a storage shed where you can pump in nitrogen. "We push the oxygen level down from its normal twenty percent to just under three percent. The apple's respiration is slowed to the point where the ripening process is nearly halted," he explained. Every few weeks he cracks open another room in the warehouse, and it's as if you're back in September—the apples in his Sunrise Orchard bags head out to nearby supermarkets, where he frets that they won't be kept cool.

Apples help illustrate another point, too: in the years ahead, *local* may be a more important word than *organic* in figuring out how to eat. In fact, a British study published this winter found that buying food from close to home prevented twice as much environmental damage as buying organic food from a distance.

Now, the best solution might be local and organic; most of the food I've been eating this winter falls into that category. But apples aren't easy—an orchard is a monoculture, prey to a bewildering variety of insects and blights. And very few consumers, even at the natural foods co-op, will pick up a Macoun or a Paula Red if it's clear that some other creature has taken the first nibble, so almost all the area growers do a little spraying. "How little spray can I get away with, and still produce fruit that people will buy?" asked Bill Suhr, who runs Champlain Orchards, down the road just above the Ticonderoga ferry dock. His saving grace is the cider press that's clanking away as we talk: he can take the risk of using fewer chemicals because if the apples aren't perfect, he can always turn them into cider. Absolutely delicious cider, too—I've been drinking well north of two gallons a week, and I'm not sure I'll ever go back to orange juice. And each batch, because it draws on a slightly different mix of varieties, tastes a little different: tartest in early fall, sweetest and most complex at the height of the harvest, but always tangy and deep. It may not be organic, but it's neighborly, which is good enough for me.

February—By now an agreeable routine has set in: pancakes or oatmeal or eggs in the morning, soup and a cheese sandwich for lunch (I could eat a different Vermont cheese every day of the winter, but I usually opt for a hunk off the Orb Weaver farmstead round). And for dinner, some creature that until quite recently was clucking mooing, baaing, or otherwise signaling its pleasure at the local grass and hay it was turning into protein. Also potatoes. And something from the freezer—it's a chest-type, and in a dark corner, so you basically just stick a hand in and see what vegetable comes out.

And, oh, did I mention beer? Otter Creek Brewing, a quarter mile down the road from my daughter's school, makes a stellar wit bier, a Belgian style that is naturally cloudy with raw organic wheat from Ben Gleason's farm. It's normally sold in the summer, but I hoarded some for my winter drinking. "We'd love to use local barley for the rest of our beers," said Morgan Wolaver, the brewery's owner. But that would mean someone building a malting plant to serve not just

Otter Creek but the state's seven other microbreweries. Perhaps right next to the oat mill . . .

March—I can see spring in the distance—there are still feet of snow in the woods, but the sun is September strong, and it won't be long before down in the valley someone is planting lettuce.

But there's one last place I must describe, both because it's provided many of my calories and because it embodies the idea of a small-scale farmer making a decent living growing great food. Jack and Anne Lazor bought Butterworks Farm, in the state's Northeast Kingdom, in the mid-'70s, after a stint of working at Old Sturbridge Village, in Massachusetts: dressed in nineteenth-century costumes, they milked cows by hand and talked to the tourists. As it turns out, they weren't actors—they were real farmers. Slowly they've grown their business into one of the state's premier organic dairies: their yogurt is nearly a million-dollar business. I've been living off their dried beans, too, and their cornmeal. It's great fun, then, to sit in their kitchen eating bacon and eggs and watch Anne mix up some salve for the teats of her cows, and listen to them describe their life. The talk's a mix of technical detail (they milk Jerseys, not the more common Holsteins, which means less milk but higher protein, so their yogurt needs no pectin to stay firm) and rural philosophy. "We have such a 'take' mentality," Jack said. "It's part of our psyche, because we came to this verdant land as Europeans and were able to exploit it for so long."

But here the exploitation feels more like collaboration. We stroll over to his solar barn, where the hundred cows in the herd loiter patiently, mulling over the events of the day. "That's Morel, that's Phooey, that's Vetch, that's Clover, that's Jewel . . ." It's very calm in here, no sound but cud being chewed, and it's warm out of the late winter wind. Jack, who's a talker, explained how Vermont could market itself as the Sustainable State, and how he's hoping to sell *masa harina* for making tortillas next year, and so forth. I sort of listen, but mostly I just absorb the sheer pleasure of the scene—that this place works, that I've been connected to it all winter long, that it will be here, with any luck, for the rest of my life.

Look—eating this way has come at a cost. Not in health or in money (if anything, I've spent less than I usually would, since I haven't bought a speck of processed food), but in time. I've had to think about every meal, instead of cruising through the world on autopilot, ingesting random calories. I've had to pay attention. But the payoff for that cost has been immense, a web of connections I'd never have known about otherwise. Sure, I'm looking forward to the occasional banana, the odd pint of Guinness stout. But I think this winter has permanently altered the way I eat. In more ways than one, it's left a good taste in my mouth.

QUESTIONS

1. What is McKibben's dietary policy exactly during his year of eating locally? What counts as local for him? When he encourages people to eat locally, what standard of "local" does he have in mind? (Note that various states have legal regulations about the use of "local" on packaging in their state. Does your state have such regulations? What are they?)
2. Is McKibben's view that eating locally is morally required, finances permitting? Is it that it is morally permissible and praiseworthy? That it is simply morally permissible but not particularly praiseworthy?
3. What are McKibben's arguments in favor of local eating? In favor of local *production*? In favor of local *buying*?
4. One key point McKibben makes is that buying local food enables a transparency between consumption and production. This is seen by him as a good. Why is it good? At any rate, the transparency here contrasts dramatically with the opacity between consumption in the United States and production on industrial farms. This opacity is seen by him as troubling. Why is it troubling?
5. McKibben wrote a significantly longer version of this essay as "My Year of Eating Locally" for his book *Deep Economy*. One striking idea at the end of that essay, less pronounced in this one, is that putative costs of locavorism—for example, how time-intensive it is for locavores in cold states like Vermont—bring great benefits. Read the longer essay. What benefits does McKibben have in mind? Do they eliminate the putative costs? Merely outweigh them? Would they in your case if you were a Vermont locavore?

HELENA DE BRES

Local Food: The Moral Case

The paper is on what the title says it's on. It thoroughly evaluates various ideas in the McKibben reading (without explicitly discussing the McKibben reading). It lays out various ethical arguments—economic, environmental, and social—for and against local production and consumption and critically evaluates each.

You're standing in a North American grocery store eyeing a locally grown tomato and one from Mexico. The price difference is insignificant to you. Which should you buy? Many today would say that, at least in the absence of further relevant information, the answer is obvious: buy the local tomato. We are all supposed to be "locavores" now. "Locavorism" refers to the practice of purchasing and consuming food grown within a relatively short distance from one's current location in preference to food grown further away. Exactly how short a distance varies: sometimes the term "local" refers to one's neighborhood or district, at other times to one's state, multi-state region or even nation-state. The now standard convention is to term food "local" if it is produced within a radius of one hundred miles from where one currently finds oneself; I will use that convention here.

Although many of the ideas motivating the locavore movement have a long history, the current enthusiasm in the United States for "eating local" can be traced to a highly successful consumer campaign ("Be a Local Hero / Buy Locally Grown") launched in 1999 by the Western Massachusetts organization Community Involved in Sustaining Agriculture (Hinrichs and Allen 334). Since then, campaigns have multiplied across the country, farmers markets have sprung up in many cities, supermarkets have introduced "local" labeling, consumers have signed up for regular home delivery of locally grown produce, and urban residents have begun planting vegetables or raising poultry in their own backyards or community gardens. Similar developments have occurred elsewhere, including the European Union, United Kingdom, Australasia and Japan.[1] Although locavorism began as a campaign targeted at individual consumers, many locavores are now successfully urging its adoption by public institutions, which could significantly extend its reach.[2]

The movement can be understood as a reaction to two striking changes in the food systems of industrialized countries over the past century. First, the agricultural sector has been radically transformed. Farmers as a percentage of the overall labor force have decreased, the average size of farms (whether measured in area, number of livestock or value of produce) has increased, and most farms

now specialize in one or two products. Small-scale, productively diverse, "family farms" are a dying breed. Second, food travels much further, on average, than before. International trade in food has increased four-fold since 1961 and even domestically produced food goes lengthier distances (Singer and Mason 135). Many people find these trends alarming and locavores urge us to eat locally as a way to stem the tide. Should we?

Over the past several years, a literature has emerged critiquing the local food movement on environmental and economic grounds.[3] Much of this criticism draws on arguments raised repeatedly against similar movements or practices in the past and some of it is very persuasive. However, other parts of the anti-locavore critique are not as strongly supported as their proponents (chiefly social scientists and journalists) believe them to be. Some of the opposition is glib and based on undefended normative assumptions that merit questioning. If skeptics want to make a fair and comprehensive assessment, they need to take the legitimate concerns of locavores more seriously.

In that spirit, this paper aims for a philosophically more nuanced discussion of the case for and against eating locally. I assess, in turn, locavore arguments based on environmental preservation, human health, community support, agrarian values and political concerns, along with the criticisms that have been made of those arguments. I finish by returning to that hypothetical grocery store and presenting you with a set of key considerations to weigh prior to choosing your tomato.

PRUNING THE QUESTION

Let me begin by clarifying what I will and won't be discussing here. First, I am interested exclusively in the case for and against *local* food. Many people associate locally grown food with organically fertilized, genetically unmodified produce cultivated on small-scale, independently owned, poly-culture farms in accordance with fair labor practices. But food can be all of these things without being locally grown and none of them despite being produced nearby. It's important to treat the arguments for each of these features separately, so that our assessment of one doesn't distort our assessment of the others.

Second, there are different roles to be played within the local food movement. I will mainly consider the case for *purchasing* local food (through farmers markets, supermarkets or Community-Supported Agriculture programs [CSAs]), but some of the arguments that I discuss will also apply to the case for growing local produce oneself.

Third, I will limit myself to the question of whether *relatively affluent* consumers in *industrialized* (or, to use more contentious terminology, "developed") countries should buy locally. In many parts of the world at many times of the year, local food will be pricier than non-local food. Many locavores accept that, at least under current conditions, poorer people should not have to increase their hardship by forgoing cheaper distant food. I focus, then, on the standard locavore case, which is directed at wealthier consumers who can afford to "go local" without assuming significant economic burdens. The restriction to industrialized countries is based partly on the same reason, since many people outside OECD nations are desperately poor, and partly on the fact that imported food is often unavailable in poorer countries. But there are also other reasons, addressed below, why the case for locavorism may be less contentious in "developing" countries.

Fourth, we should distinguish between two possible variants of locavorism. *Radical* locavorism is the practice of buying only local food at all times. *Moderate* locavorism is the practice of buying some local and some non-local food. I will set aside the radical version here for three reasons. First, there is very good reason to think that the widespread adoption of radical locavorism would be economically destructive, due both to the general benefits of international trade over protectionism (on which more below) and to the land use implications. If industrialized countries were to feed their large and growing populations with exclusively local produce, they would need to both dramatically increase their agricultural sectors and situate large numbers of farms right by (or within)

existing cities. This prospect may not sound too bad to the average locavore. But note that land used to farm is land not being used for urban development and that farmers who are farming are not engaging in any number of other economic activities in cities. If this happened on a large scale, the economy would suffer dramatically, given that urbanization is a huge generator of economic prosperity.[4] The effects of full-scale locavorism would be especially economically harmful for one's poorer neighbors. Not only does a higher grocery bill represent a real hardship for the cash-strapped, but restricting urban development to leave room for agriculture drives up housing prices, disproportionately affecting the worse-off. Second, even setting aside the general toll on the economy, radical locavorism would be extremely burdensome for individual consumers. While those lucky enough to live in California might eat a varied and delicious diet year-round, residents of colder or less fertile parts of the world would face a massively constrained menu, even if pickling and preserving are taken into account. Finally, for these reasons and others, radical locavorism is highly unlikely to ever be adopted on a large scale. These three considerations could be overcome if there were urgent moral reasons in favor of radical locavorism: sometimes we ought to pursue morally valuable goals even when doing so is very difficult and costly and success is unlikely. But, as I will argue below, the moral reasons in favor of buying local food are in fact often weak or absent (and there will sometimes be urgent moral reasons pointing in the exact opposite direction). Moderate locavorism, on the other hand, seems both achievable on a broad scale and not overly burdensome and is therefore much more likely to be justified.

Finally, I will be discussing the question of whether or not we are *morally required* to buy local food. The way that most locavores speak and write suggests that they do think of locavorism as a moral obligation of some sort (albeit perhaps one that can be "trumped" by other considerations). But it is possible to instead present eating locally as something that it is morally *good* (although not required) to do or—even less ambitiously—as something that it is morally *permissible* (although not especially good) to do. I will start by considering the version of locavorism that posits a moral requirement, since I believe that it is the most widely endorsed version, and turn to the other, less ambitious, positions as we go along.

IT'S NOT EASY BEING GREEN (OR HEALTHY)

Our question, then, is this: are affluent consumers in industrialized countries morally required to purchase local food in preference to non-local food (for short, "buy local") at least some of the time? One of the more popular arguments in favor of this claim rests on the idea that eating locally is better for the environment. According to the most common version of this argument, the fewer the miles that food travels, the fewer the greenhouse gas emissions produced, and the lower the contribution to environmentally harmful climate change.[5] The moral argument then takes this form:

1. Buying local food is better for the environment than buying non-local food.
2. We are morally required to do what is best for the environment.

Conclusion. We are morally required to buy local food in preference to non-local food.

The first premise of this argument has been widely criticized for focusing on too small a part of the overall picture. The reasoning goes like this. To accurately assess the respective carbon footprints of, say, a local and a "distant" tomato, we need to consider the amount of fuel used across the entire life cycle of each. Especially if you live in the Northern hemisphere, a "life cycle assessment" of this kind will often reveal that the distant tomato has burnt up less fuel by the time it gets to your kitchen than the local one has. There are two main reasons for this. First, the vast majority of the fuel used to get food into people's mouths is spent in the production phase, before "food miles" enter the picture, and food production is much more energy-intensive in some countries than others.[6] In particular, countries with

warmer climates or higher rainfall (generally located nearer the equator or in the Southern hemisphere) don't need heated greenhouses or extensive irrigation to produce crops, thus burning much less fuel.[7] Second, locavores overstate the fossil fuel advantage of local food even in the transportation phase. The number of miles that food travels is less important in this respect than the mode of transportation and the load size (Desrochers and Shimizu 99). Because boats use much less fuel than trucks and have greater storage capacity, the carbon costs, per tomato, involved in moving local tomatoes around many neighborhoods in multiple trucks may be higher than delivering them by a single large ship from a foreign country and then larger trucks across state. Locavores also tend to disregard the miles that the locavore consumer travels when going from farm to farm to pick up local vegetables, as opposed to doing one-stop shopping of distant produce at a nearby supermarket.

An additional problem with the "food miles" version of this argument is that, by virtue of focusing exclusively on the problem of climate change, it neglects the non-fuel environmental costs of agriculture. Food grown in natural conditions unsuited for its production requires massive amounts of water, fertilizers and pesticides, resulting in water depletion, soil erosion and toxicity.[8] From this broader perspective, and in light of the points made above, international trade in agricultural products, from geographical areas suited to their production, starts to look like the environmentally more responsible choice.[9]

This suggestion is likely to invite a return charge of myopia from locavores. Doesn't international trade involve distinct environmental costs in other domains that outweigh these benefits? It's true that the current system of international trade is environmentally problematic. Critics rightly worry about an environmental "race to the bottom"—incentives for states to lower standards in order to attract foreign trade—and World Trade Organization rules that hamper legitimate attempts at responsible environmental safeguards (Singer 57–70). But, due to the force of the considerations discussed above, the critics of locavorism argue, the best solution is to push for better international regulation and compliance measures (alongside improvements in the energy efficiency of transportation[10]), not to replace trade with environmentally destructive local production.

The environmental critique just rehearsed clearly presents a serious problem for what I above termed "radical locavorism." Assuming that most people will continue to want to eat a reasonably varied diet, and that most people won't be living in, say, California, widespread adoption of radical locavorism would be environmentally destructive.[11] As a result, while radical locavorism might conceivably be supported by other moral reasons, the environmental argument under consideration won't get us to a moral requirement to be a radical locavore and will arguably get us a significant way toward a moral prohibition. However, the environmental critique doesn't work against moderate locavorism, the variety that most locavores endorse. We can imagine a version of moderate locavorism that tells us to buy local when it's the environmentally friendly choice (for instance, when the food is in season locally). That said, the environmental critique does suggest, importantly, that it will be harder than it might at first have seemed to work out how to apply that principle. We certainly can't simply assume that buying the local product will always be better for the environment. In some geographical areas, that will only rarely be the case.

A similar conclusion holds concerning a second locavore argument, which appeals to the alleged contribution of local food to human health. The argument runs as follows:

1. Local food is healthier than non-local food.
2. We are morally required to do what is best for our health.

Conclusion. We are morally required to buy local food in preference to non-local food.

In support of the first premise, locavores argue that local food is more nutritious because it is likely to be fresher than food from afar. They also argue that local food is safer, both because industrialized countries have higher health and safety standards and because local produce (unlike imported food) doesn't spend time in giant centralized processing facilities where contamination is difficult to prevent and trace.

Both of these claims, critics argue, are problematic. The only way to eat locally throughout the year in most parts of the Northern hemisphere is to engage in extensive preservation and storage for the winter months. As a result, local food will not in fact be fresher than distant food for much of the year. Moreover, even if local *food* were more nutritious (by virtue of being fresher), for most people a local *diet* would not be. A healthy diet depends on adequate access to a variety of foods. A local food diet works against this goal by being less varied and more expensive than an imported food diet (Desrochers and Shimizu 151). Is local food at least less likely than distant food to carry disease, even if its nutritional benefits are exaggerated? Those who focus on the risks of contamination along the international agricultural supply chain tend to disregard the similar risks that arise in local supply chains. Some critics argue that there is in fact good reason to think that food that is processed in large-scale distant facilities is *less* likely to carry disease than food processed in small-scale local operations. Large firms can afford the kind of high-quality equipment and food safety training that is out of the reach of many small farmers.[12] They are also more likely to undergo extensive inspections. While locavores often tout the transparency advantage of buying locally, few have the time or expertise to actually undertake comprehensive safety assessments of their local farms.

As in the case of the environmental argument, these criticisms undermine the case for the radical version of locavorism, but not the moderate kind. Moderate locavores can recommend eating local food only when it is fresh and reliably safe. That said, again, the critique does suggest that the second of these recommendations, at least, is not as easy to put into practice as many locavores claim. It is also doubtful that the freshness of food tapers off dramatically at the 100-mile limit that most locavores have in mind. A more serious problem with the health argument—one that applies to radical and moderate locavorism alike—is the implausibility of its second premise. We are surely morally permitted to make less-than-optimal health choices. We may even be morally *required* to make them, for instance when the health cost is low and other significant values are at stake. (Notice that, while the second premise of the environmental argument is more plausible on its face, it too suffers from this problem.)[13]

This section has discussed two popular arguments for locavorism, along with some popular critiques of those arguments. I have argued that, while the critiques don't seriously undermine the case for moderate (as opposed to radical) locavorism, they do significantly limit the scope of any moral requirement attached to that position. Both because the connection between local production and environmental or personal health is contingent and because other values are plausibly at stake in our food purchases, the most that these two arguments can show is that buying local food will sometimes be the morally superior choice and will sometimes not be. That seems like a weaker case than the average locavore is hoping for. Can we find stronger reasons elsewhere in favor of buying locally?

CULTIVATING COMMUNITY

From the point of view of the ethically motivated consumer, the problem with the arguments discussed so far is that we will often lack the information needed to apply them to our purchasing decisions. It's hard to know in many cases whether the local or distant tomato is environmentally friendlier or healthier. In contrast, one thing we *do* know is that when we give a dollar to a local farmer, that dollar will go into our community as opposed to somewhere outside it. The appeal of this thought forms part of the motivation for a third popular locavore argument, which runs as follows:

1. Buying local food supports one's local community better than buying non-local food does.
2. We are morally required to support our local community.

Conclusion. We are morally required to buy local food in preference to non-local food.

Let's start by considering the first premise of the argument, which asserts a connection between locavorism and support for one's community. The strength of this connection depends partly on what one means by "support" and partly on whom one means when speaking of one's "community." A key fact here is that local food will often be pricier than imported food in industrialized countries, both because it is usually more energy-intensive to produce and because its inputs—land and labor—cost more. In developing countries the natural conditions are often well suited to agriculture and other more lucrative uses for land and labor are not readily available, keeping food prices down.[14] This means that when locavores select the more expensive local tomato, they have less to spend on other goods and services, including those that their fellow locals wish to sell. If we interpret "support" in narrowly economic terms, then, locavorism may support some members of one's community (farmers), but at the cost of reducing support for others (including, but not only, employees at the local supermarket). The net economic benefit for one's community as a whole may be minor at best.

The above line of criticism successfully weakens the force of the first premise of the community support argument if we interpret community support in a narrowly economic sense, which is what most critics of the argument have in mind. But there are other ways to support your local community than by increasing the monetary wealth of the people who live in it. Some locavores are clearly concerned with that narrow goal. But many who speak of "supporting your local community" are instead referring to the act of maintaining and strengthening the *relationships* that bind people who live and work close to each other.[15] For many people, strolling through farmers markets, buying from CSAs or digging in community gardens are ways to connect in a concrete way with others in their community and express commitment to sustaining that community in other domains. (One study showed that people have ten times as many conversations at farmers' markets as they do in supermarkets [Halweil 138].) If this is so, locavorism has a relational value that the economic critique doesn't address.

Let's follow this more subtle line of thought and assume that the first, empirical, premise of the argument under consideration points to a genuine and considerable benefit, if we understand "community support" to include the "relational" sense. The crucial question now is whether the second, normative, premise of the argument is defensible. Are we each under a moral requirement to support our local community (in this way)? If this second premise is to be plausible, we immediately need to introduce an amendment. Most people will agree that there are often good moral reasons to support one's local community. However, whatever the force of these reasons, they are clearly conditional. If your community is unjustly aggressing against outsiders, for instance, supporting it may be morally wrong. So premise 2 is more plausible if reformulated as follows:

2*. We are morally required to support our local community, unless doing so violates duties we have to people beyond it.

This is where a problem arises for locavorism, according to some recent critics. Their claim is that eating locally does violate duties that we have to people beyond our local community: in particular, to people *far* beyond it.[16] Consider this revised version of the community support argument, coming from the opposing camp now:

1. Buying local food supports one's local community better than buying non-local food does.
2*. We are morally required to support our local community, unless doing so violates duties we have to people beyond it.
3. We have a duty to alleviate global poverty.
4. Buying local food in preference to non-local food contributes to global poverty.
5. Buying local food in preference to non-local food violates duties we have to people beyond our local community (i.e. the global poor).

Conclusion. We are not morally required to buy local food in preference to non-local food.

In fact, the conclusion to this argument (call it "the global poverty argument") can be stated more strongly. If locavorism violates our duties to the global poor, and if those duties take priority over duties to our fellow locals, we will not only not be morally required to purchase local produce, but may actually be morally prohibited from doing so.

For many people, the most startling step in this argument will be the fourth premise. How exactly is buying local food supposed to adversely affect the global poor? Most economists agree that the developing world needs international trade to achieve the growth, income and employment necessary to escape poverty.[17] And the best products for the developing world to trade currently lie in agriculture (where, as indicated earlier, poor countries have "comparative advantage"). If producers in industrialized countries grow those crops instead—via public farm subsidies or in response to the patronage of individual locavores—they obstruct the best route out of poverty that developing countries have. In short, the line goes, when you purchase that local tomato from a relatively affluent local farmer, what you are *not* doing is purchasing a tomato from a much poorer farmer in a developing country. You are thereby unintentionally harming—or at least, not helping—some of the world's most vulnerable people.

There are two ways for locavores to press back against this critique, one empirical in nature, one normative. The empirical response denies that agricultural trade is as beneficial for the world's poor as the critics of locavorism claim that it is. The rules of the contemporary international trading system are significantly skewed in favor of OECD countries and corporate interests.[18] As a result, there is no guarantee that the gains from trade will reach the poorest citizens of developing countries, rather than being captured by large-scale commercial growers or transnational corporations.[19] Moreover, even if the world's poorest do benefit from trade, some argue that development strategies that don't rely on agricultural exports would better serve the needs of many poor countries.[20]

Although this empirical critique is important, it doesn't do much to undermine the global poverty argument. This is because, while buying distant food may not be the *optimal* means of alleviating global poverty, it is still likely to *better* promote that goal than buying food from an affluent local farmer. Moreover, supporters of international trade can address some of the problems with the current system by advocating the purchase of "Fair Trade" produce (such as coffee, chocolate and bananas produced in accordance with high labor standards), along with pushing for a reformed multilateral system that aims for fairness and genuinely embraces the "pro-poor" goals asserted in the World Trade Organization's Doha Declaration. Although we may have a long way to go, defenders of trade can argue, the best course of action for those concerned about the global poor is to continue to work for a fairer trading system from within the current regime, rather than to undercut it by reverting to food isolationism.[21]

For these reasons, locavores would do better to focus their response to the global poverty argument on its normative component. Most locavores will agree that we have strong moral reasons to alleviate global poverty and will therefore endorse the third premise of the argument. But it is open to them to draw attention to a troubling implication of premise 2*. That premise implies that if a conflict arises between supporting one's local community and fulfilling one's global duties, the global duties should take priority. But why, locavores might ask, should we assume *that*? Why don't our duties to our local community sometimes prevail?

The critics' argument for the assumption at issue is utilitarian in nature. We ought always to direct our resources to where they produce the most welfare, the line goes, and because poor people in developing countries are on average so much poorer than the residents (poor or otherwise) of industrialized countries, our dollars will produce much more welfare in their pockets than in those of our fellow locals. As the utilitarian Peter Singer puts it: "When we think ethically, we should put ourselves in the positions of all those affected by our actions, no matter where they live . . . we will, other things being equal, do better to support the farmers in developing countries" (Singer and Mason 141).

This utilitarian line is much more contentious than the critics of locavorism admit. Utilitarianism depends upon a strong principle of impartiality, according to which any concern for the local can appear to be "a kind of community-based selfishness" (Singer and Mason 141). But nobody lives in this austerely egalitarian way. Each of us daily violates utilitarian impartiality, privileging the interests of family, friends, fellow citizens and ourselves over the interests of the global poor. Moreover, most of us

consider at least some of this behavior to be morally justified. Morality seems to leave room for some significant degree of partiality.

Locavores can argue, appealing to this broad consensus, that we have morally defensible reasons to support our local community that are not based on utilitarian reasoning and that generate legitimate limits on what we can be required to do to promote global wellbeing. Some of these reasons involve concerns with fairness or reciprocity: it's often claimed that we have a duty to "give back" to our immediate community members that doesn't apply to foreigners whom we have never met. Other reasons are more personal. A flourishing local community improves the lives of you, your family and your friends. And most people agree that each of us is morally permitted to engage in activities and relationships that we personally value (within certain constraints), even if the cost is some distraction from pursuit of the impersonal good.[22] Both types of argument—the one based on fairness and the one based on personal prerogatives—suggest that, at least sometimes, supporting one's local community properly takes priority over maximally promoting the interests of the global poor.[23]

Perhaps this is the correct line to take. It does, however, face the following problem. There are many ways to give back to your community or to foster its flourishing in ways that benefit you, some of which may be more effective than purchasing local food and less likely to have the negative effect on the life prospects of the global poor that economists point to. Granting that we have legitimate moral reasons to support our local community, then, why do it in *this* way? What's so special about food?

MEANWHILE, BACK AT THE RANCH . . .

The conclusion of the previous section was that, to defend their community support argument, locavores must explain what it is about food that makes it a particularly powerful generator of community. One answer, or set of answers, can be found in the school of thought known as "agrarianism." Agrarians argue for the distinctive value—for individuals, communities and the world—of traditional agricultural ways of life. What kind of value? Different threads are present in the agrarian literature; I will present each of them in turn, before discussing their merits. One thread is broadly Aristotelian. Humans are a part of the natural world, the line goes, a world that proceeds according to a set of in-built laws and purposes. We can only flourish if we accord with these laws and purposes: if our lives "fit" appropriately with our inner nature and environment.[24] By engaging us in intimate contact with the land and climate, farming focuses our attention on the natural forces that shape our lives, encouraging us to work patiently with those forces rather than against them. The implied contrast is with a fast-paced modern industrial lifestyle that is out of sync with the rhythms of the natural world. A related thread might be labeled "Kierkegaardian," due to its emphasis on the importance for human flourishing of being connected to a particular context. Agriculture, as traditionally practiced, involved a long-term commitment, extending across many generations, to living and working on a specific piece of land. This fostered a sense of genuinely belonging to a place—of being grounded in both a concrete location and a particular lineage—that gave people a secure sense of identity and purpose. Here the contrast is with us moderns who shift from place to place, according to economic necessity or whim, and end up feeling restless, anxious and lost.[25] A further thread owes something to Marx. The pre-industrial farmer, the agrarian claims, possessed complete control over his (usually his) crops from the initial planting of the seed to the selling of the fruits at harvest. His work involved an independence of judgment and creativity that are lacking in many modern occupations. Moreover, as Marx also emphasized, the sense of alienation that many of us now feel from our work, and from the products of our and others' work, is connected to a sense of alienation from other people. The challenges of soil and weather fostered a sense of solidarity on the family farm; the direct transactions between farmer and customer did the same in the local market.

Agrarians clearly view connection to one's nature, one's context, one's work and one's fellows as essential for human flourishing and advocate traditional forms of agriculture for that reason. But the agrarian literature is also pervaded by references to the "purity," "authenticity," "integrity" and "basic dignity" of agricultural work, in ways that suggest a tight relationship between pastoral ways of life and moral virtue. Farming and ranching, we are told, promote *humility,* reminding us of our ultimate dependence on natural forces, our animal nature and our mortality.[26] Agrarian life also cultivates *temperance* and *thrift*: "agrarian farmers see, accept, and live within their limits" (Berry 2003 59), in contrast to industrial farmers and urbanites, who strive to surpass those limits by artificial means. Rural life allegedly produces a set of more social virtues, too—such as *honesty, cooperativeness* and *compassion*—growing out of a sense of interdependence, shared fate and purpose out on the farm. Finally, it is suggested that, beyond agriculture's direct connection to these particular virtues, the slow, steady and repetitive rhythms of the farming year are especially conducive to the emergence and entrenchment of moral character in general. This strikes another Aristotelian note: virtue is only attainable by the persistent practice of patterns of thought and conduct – essentially, by habit.

How does all of this connect with the community support argument discussed in the previous section? The idea is that buying local food might be a particularly effective means of fostering community, because of the essential goods built into agricultural lifestyles. By connecting us to the land, farming connects us to each other and forms the kinds of moral dispositions that are needed to sustain community over the long term.[27] Furthermore, agriculture is highly conducive to individual flourishing independently of its strengthening of social ties. To the extent that healthy groups consist of healthy individuals, this too strengthens community. For all of these reasons, agrarians argue, agriculture produces a moral harvest greater than the value of its material one. We can't all be farmers, but we might all do a bit of farming (say, in a backyard or community garden), and we might support the backbone of our community by buying local produce.

Agrarians don't tend to discuss the impact of this recommendation on the global poor. Were they to do so, they might argue that agriculture is so significant for human welfare that the value of widespread engagement in or with it outweighs the welfare cost to the global poor. Or, more likely, they might claim that, while the net impact of locavorism on global welfare may be negative, that's merely unfortunate, not immoral. We are morally obliged to make some effort to assist those suffering in foreign countries. But there are limits to that obligation. Ethics is not about improving as many people's lives as possible, in order to maximize overall value. Rather it's a matter (here quite literally) of "tending your own garden": of both fostering a set of self-directed virtues and of ensuring that the relationships that you are directly engaged in are healthy and just.

What should we make of this argument? Critics are right to dismiss some agrarian claims as implausible. Much agrarian writing is imbued with a mystical anthropomorphization of nature that is difficult to stomach.[28] And when Wirzba worries, characteristically, about "postmoderns . . . engag[ing] reality on our own terms rather than the terms set by physiology, biology, ecology, meteorology, and communal tradition" (84) he seems to have a much narrower understanding of those terms than the breadth of human experience justifies. The suggestion that farming is the natural occupation of mankind is undermined by the fact that "anatomically modern humans" did without it for "for approximately 90% of their existence" (Desrochers and Shimizu 19). Like the Aristotelian theme, the Kierkegaardian note is also overplayed. While traditional agriculture may be one way to achieve a sense of attachment and identity, it is hard to see why it is the unique or best way to do so. When Heldke claims that "we have very good reasons to dig into the *soil closest to us* much more intentionally—to *contextualize* our lives with dirt and its denizens" (45, italics in original), one wonders: why dirt, of all parts of the natural world? And, even if dirt, why farm it? Furthermore, there is the undeniable fact that for most farmers of the past and present, rural life has been anything but stable and satisfying. That life—to contest the Marxist strain, now—has also traditionally involved a

significant amount of alienation. A standard agrarian explanation for these obvious facts is that historically many agrarian farmers have been "systematically robbed" (Donahue 39; see also Orr 172), a feature that would presumably be absent in a more just system. But surely features intrinsic to agriculture—for instance, its dependence on unpredictable environmental factors and the commodity nature of its products—are a large and ineradicable part of the problem.[29] Finally, the allegedly essential connection of farming to morality is tenuous at best. Not only have many urbanites been paradigms of virtue, but small rural communities can be parochial, intolerant and sexist. This is one of several places where agrarian arguments draw on a false dichotomy between an idealized pastoral community and a demonized urban one.

In short, there are many ways, other than engagement with farming, for communities to flourish and be virtuous, some of which have worked, do work and will work better for some people than farming ever did, does or will. For this reason, the empirical connection that agrarians attempt to draw between traditional agriculture, wellbeing and morality is too weak to shore up the community support argument, our initial motivation for turning to agrarian ideas. We haven't found a compelling reason in agrarianism to think that eating locally is an especially effective generator of community, compared to other activities. This is not to deny that, in some circumstances, buying local food will in fact promote community, perhaps for broadly agrarian reasons, and that it would therefore be morally good to do it. Our duty to support our community is arguably "imperfect" in nature, allowing us discretion over which specific means of support, including locavorism, to adopt. But the foregoing does suggest that an attempt to base a general moral *requirement* to eat locally on locavorism's contribution to community is unlikely to succeed.

That said, the agrarian tradition might provide compelling reasons to buy local food that are independent of the community support argument. Many people are strongly moved by agrarian ideas, philosophically well grounded or not. For them, supporting local farms can be a powerful source of wellbeing or identification. The fact that these sentiments are linked to dubious empirical and normative beliefs (consider the Aristotelian theme) or are not universally felt (consider the Kierkegaardian theme) need not undermine their force. The agrarian vision has a symbolic quality, and symbols can be important and beneficial independently of their factual basis.[30] We might argue that, for people thus moved, living in accordance with agrarian ideals, at least to some extent, is a legitimate exercise of the general prerogative that we all have to pursue activities and relationships that we find meaningful.

This line of thought provides defensible reasons for purchasing local food, but the force of those reasons is limited in two ways. For one, agrarian reasons are by their nature restricted to the products of certain kinds of farms: those small-scale, independently owned, low-tech operations that most closely approximate the better forms of traditional agriculture. Second, the subjective reasons discussed above, taken alone, could only ground a constrained permission to eat locally: only for those who have the relevant sentiments and only to a certain extent. Acting on personal preferences is permissible only so far as it doesn't significantly harm others. So, assuming that the critics are correct that radical locavorism would be environmentally and economically destructive (harming both one's community members and foreigners), agrarians will have a subjectively grounded permission to eat locally only if not too many others join them. Beyond a certain threshold of participation, locavorism would move from the realm of permissible prerogative into the realm of moral prohibition.

GRASSROOTS POLITICS

The strongest part of the agrarian argument for local food is not so much its positive vision of a widespread return to pre-industrial diversified family farms, but its critique of modern industrial society. Some agrarians admittedly overdo this critique, ignoring the many benefits that industrial agriculture,

a globalized economy, and modernity generally have delivered to the citizens of developed countries. But we can celebrate the advances in the quality, affordability, convenience and reliability of our food supply that the modern food system has secured while at the same time regretting the losses involved and the costs imposed. Many citizens of developed countries experience a sense of disconnection from the natural environment, their fellow citizens, and non-economic values that is easily traceable to the social and economic structures of modern life. For many of these people, participation in the local food movement has provided a way to get together with others who are similarly dissatisfied and think constructively about alternative ways of structuring society. Usually these discussions begin with a focus on the many problems of large-scale industrial agriculture as it is currently practiced (including the treatment of animals, working conditions, health risks and ecological damage). But discussions within local food networks can also progress to industrial/economic ills more generally and to other moral concerns (for instance, racial or class injustice) within the local or broader community. In this way, locavorism can serve as a petri dish for political education and activism, promoting environmental sustainability, corporate social responsibility and social and global justice in arenas that include but extend beyond food.

A final argument for locavorism, then, is that local food networks can serve as "sites of resistance" (Portman 1), becoming "both the symbol and substance for structural change" (Delind 123). Why might food work well as a basis for political organizing? One explanation is that food constitutes a genuinely universal need and source of pleasure. Another is that the intimate nature of eating food and the hands-on nature of growing it affect people in a particularly direct way. A final explanation is that food activism provides opportunities for easy and immediate action. Although battling agri-business giants directly is beyond the powers of the average consumer, buying a local tomato is not. In each of these ways, buying local food can contribute to a sense of empowerment and personal investment in improving social conditions that may not be as readily obtainable by other means.[31]

These considerations provide the foundation for the following argument:

1. Buying local food in preference to non-local food promotes socially beneficial political activism.
2. We are morally required to engage in socially beneficial political activism.

Conclusion. We are morally required to buy local food in preference to non-local food.

While there is some force to this argument, that force is contingent on the efficacy of one's local food network at achieving valuable social change, something that is likely to vary dramatically across networks. In some places, depending on the priorities of one's fellow locals, political organizing based around, say, wilderness preservation or fostering the arts might work better at motivating people to care about the environment and each other than food activism would. Moreover, in some contexts a focus on the local, in whatever domain, can backfire. Many locavores are skeptical about the efficacy of centralized, top-down political action and mistrustful of government. But public regulation is often necessary for large-scale, sustainable change. To the extent that locavorism distracts individuals from higher-impact political reform, the concerns underlying the political argument could point away from rather than toward buying local food.[32]

FOOD FOR THOUGHT WHEN THINKING ABOUT FOOD

You're back in that North American grocery store trying to decide between the local tomato and one shipped in from Mexico. What is the morally correct choice? I argued in the earlier part of this paper that health concerns don't point strongly in either direction: there is no general reason to think that any particular item of local produce is any safer than a similar imported one. I also claimed that the miles that the tomatoes have travelled should not be the overriding concern when thinking about the environmental impact of your choice. If the local tomato is in season where you are, you have a fairly good environmental reason to buy it; otherwise the Mexican tomato may be the better option for the planet. When we turn to the impact of your choice on your local community, things get more complicated. Though purchasing the local tomato is unlikely to economically benefit your community much more than purchasing the Mexican one, it might do its small part to strengthen the relationships between you and your neighbors. Still, there's no very good reason to think that buying the local tomato will be *especially* effective in that regard, compared to other things you might do. And there is good reason to think that buying the foreign tomato instead will help farmers who are much worse off than your neighbors. If you self-identify as a traditional utilitarian, you can stop right there and take the Mexican tomato to the checkout. But if you're a more sophisticated utilitarian, or not a utilitarian at all, you have some more thinking to do. For one, you need to ask yourself some questions about your own values, attachments and priorities. Does buying local food help you to feel more at home in your community and more connected to the natural world? Do you already donate a significant amount of your time, energy and other resources to the global poor, such that your duty in that respect is largely already discharged? If yes, the local tomato gains ground; if no, the Mexican one does. You also need to consider what other people are doing. How many of your fellow citizens are locavores already? Would buying this local tomato contribute to a promising collective project of softening the edges of modern capitalism, reforming industrial agriculture or promoting social justice more generally? Or would it contribute instead to a worrying trend toward radical locavorism, which could only result in ecological and economic disaster? Of course, this single tomato isn't going to make a great difference either way. But your consumption choices over time, when combined with those of your fellow citizens, will. One goal of this paper has been to show that the question of how to go about making those choices is much more complex than many parties to the debate currently assume.[33]

The conclusion of our discussion could be interpreted as presenting both good news and bad news for locavores. The good news is that in many cases there will be nothing morally *wrong* with being a locavore, *contra* the harsher anti-locavore critiques. It is true that, when "local food" is used as shorthand for "ethically responsible food," locavorism can get in the way of sound moral reflection and result in harm. But, when practiced sensitively, locavorism is likely to be, at a minimum, morally *permissible*, by virtue of falling under the scope of a defensible personal prerogative and not causing significant damage. More positively, locavorism will sometimes be a morally *good* practice, by virtue of promoting valuable goals or satisfying compelling moral principles. The bad news is that locavorism is not plausibly a moral *requirement*. There are too many other ways to achieve the valuable goals and satisfy the compelling principles that are contingently connected to local food to single out buying local as a categorical obligation. The most that we can plausibly say, then, is that, depending on how the facts pan out, moderate locavorism is one morally good practice among others. That may be less than what many locavores were hoping for, but it's enough to part the clouds above many farmers' markets for a significant portion of the year.[34]

NOTES

1. The movement has been furthered by a number of popular texts, including Bittman (2008), Kingsolver et al. (2007), Pollan (2006), Smith and Mackinnon (2007) and McKibben (2007).

2. The U.S. Department of Agriculture's "Know Your Farmer, Know Your Food" program is "a USDA-wide effort to carry out President Obama's commitment to strengthening local and regional food systems." A federal Commodity Facilities Program to support construction of farmers markets, and a federal voucher program to encourage low-income seniors to shop at them, are also in operation.

3. Desrochers and Shimizu synthesizes this literature.

4. See Glaeser.

5. Non-"food miles" environmental arguments for locavorism include the claims that it promotes biodiversity, encourages land conservation and reduces packaging. See Desrochers and Shimizu (91, 104–6) for some replies.

6. Weber and Matthews estimate that transportation accounts for only 4% of the total energy used to get food to consumers in the U.S.

7. In some cases, distant farms will also be more energy efficient than your neighboring farm because they use clover pastureland instead of animal feed or are larger and can employ economies of scale in production.

8. Desrochers and Shimizu (49) claim that a country that imports one ton of wheat instead of producing it domestically can save around 1,300 cubic meters of local water.

9. This point can be strengthened by appeal to the alleged connections between international trade and economic growth and between economic growth and environmentalism.

10. McWilliams (49–50) recommends a "hub-and-spoke" system: environmentally responsible production centers, in environmentally efficient locations, combined with energy-efficient transportation lines (e.g. greater-capacity vehicles, out of hours delivery times, better route-planning, engine specifications and industrial carpooling).

11. Producing food in season and then storing it for later consumption is no solution: cold storage uses a large amount of energy.

12. Notably, local food sellers who make direct sales successfully petitioned for exemptions from the higher standards of the new food safety act passed by the U.S. Congress in 2010.

13. As does the "taste argument" for locavorism. Local food is also often claimed to be tastier than distant food. Whether or not this claim is true, it's difficult to derive a moral requirement to eat locally from it. Even if tasty food does have moral value (by virtue of contributing to a flourishing life), that value is relatively trivial and easily outweighed by competing values.

14. Food produced by the small-scale, polyculture local farms that most locavores have in mind is especially expensive. Large-scale monoculture requires less labor per unit of output, resulting in lower prices.

15. See Kingsolver, McKibben, Pollan.

16. See McWilliams 205–210; Singer and Mason 141.

17. Krugman et al. provides an accessible standard introduction to the economics of international trade.

18. Stiglitz and Charlton provides a helpful overview of the empirical research. Singer 2002 and James discuss the philosophical implications.

19. Pauw and Thurlow raise this concern in relation to Tanzania.

20. See, for example, Dercon, Dethier and Effenberger and Torrez.

21. See Navin for a more extensive discussion of these issues.

22. See Miller 2004.

23. The space opened up here will be even larger if, as non-utilitarians often insist, our duty to assist the poor is "imperfect" in nature: we have a stringent duty to assist, but the amount, form and timing of the assistance is up to us.

24. Berry (2000 14) refers to this notion as "propriety."

25. Schnell (623–625) and Delind (127–133) emphasize the importance of the idea of place within the local food movement. See also Wendell Berry (2003 24): "Industrialism prescribes an economy that is placeless and displacing. It does not distinguish one place from another. It applies its methods and technologies indiscriminately . . ." Compare the narrator of Percy's *The Moviegoer,* which invokes Kierkegaard throughout: "If I did not talk to the theater owner or the ticket seller, I should be lost, cut loose metaphysically speaking. I should be seeing one copy of a film which might be shown anywhere and at any time. There is a danger of slipping clean out of space and time" (75).

26. Barbara Kingsolver writes: "recall that whatever lofty things you might accomplish today, you will do them only because you first ate something that grew out of dirt" (xii). See also Orr: "the closeness to birth, growth, decay and death in the nurturing context of a farm has the effect of demystifying mortality and laying the psychological foundation for the healthy acceptance of our own death" (180).

27. See Delind: "[T]he relationship to a common landscape . . . is critical for holding people together . . . It is just such a connection to a commons, to land and landscape, to people and place, that [those who advocate for local food and farming] wish to strengthen and that they believe will emerge through the production and consumption of local food" (128–9).

28. See Jacquetta Hawkes' characterization of eighteenth century English rural life as a "creative, patient and increasingly skillful love-making that persuaded the land to flourish" (202).

29. See Smith, "Don't Let Your Children Grow Up To Be Farmers."

30. Miller makes a similar point about national identities, which "typically contain a considerable amount of myth" (35).

31. Andrew Light argues, similarly, that community efforts at environmental restoration can have an educational and motivational value, even if we doubt the possibility or desirability of genuine restoration of nature.

32. Guthman argues, in this vein, that the "changing the food system one meal at a time" rhetoric "all too often reproduces a neoliberal climate where broad and substantive public regulation is shunned for the 'culture of audit,' corporate social responsibility and individual consumption choice" (263).

33. In fact, more complex than I have been able to do justice to here. For instance, I haven't discussed aesthetics (other than in footnote 13), but it surely provides one important motivation for locavorism. Many people find pastoral landscapes highly attractive. The vegetable and flower gardens that have recently spread through hundreds of vacant post-industrial lots in Detroit and Chicago are beautiful in a different way.

34. I am grateful for helpful insights and comments from Howard Axelrod, Tyler Doggett, Alex Rajczi, several anonymous reviewers, and audiences at Michigan State University, Wellesley College and Mt Holyoke College.

WORKS CITED

Berry, Wendell. "The Agrarian Standard." *The Essential Agrarian Reader.* Ed. Norman Wirzba. Berkeley: Counterpoint, 2003. 23–33.

Berry, Wendell. *Life is a Miracle: An Essay Against Modern Superstition.* Washington, D.C.: Counterpoint, 2000.

Bittman, Mark. *Food Matters: A Guide to Conscious Eating with More Than 75 Recipes.* New York: Simon & Schuster, 2008.

Delind, Laura B. *Journal of Agricultural and Environmental Ethics.* 19 (2006): 212–146.

Dercon, S. "Rural Poverty: Old Challenges in New Contexts". *The World Bank Research Observer* 24.1 (2009): 1–28.

Desrochers, Pierre, and Shimizu, Hiroko. *The Locavore's Dilemma.* New York: Public Affairs, 2012.

Dethier, J.J. and Effenberger, A. "Agriculture and Development: A Brief Review of the Literature." *Economic Systems* 36.2 (2012): 175–205.

Donahue, Brian. "The Resettling of America." *The Essential Agrarian Reader.* Ed. Norman Wirzba. Berkeley: Counterpoint, 2003. 34–51.

Glaeser, Edward. *Triumph of the City: How Our Greatest Invention Makes US Richer, Smarter, Greener and Happier.* New York: Penguin, 2011.

Goodin, Robert. "What Is So Special about Our Fellow Countrymen?" *Ethics* 98.4 (1988): 663–86.

Guthman, Julie. "Commentary on Teaching Food: Why I Am Fed Up with Michael Pollan et al." *Agriculture and Human Values* 24 (2007): 261–264.

Halweil, Brian. *Eat Here.* New York: Norton, 2004.

Hawkes, Jacquetta. *A Land.* Boston: Houghton-Mifflin, 1950.

Heldke, Lisa. "Down-Home Global Cooking: A Third Option between Cosmopolitanism and Localism." *The Philosophy of Food.* Ed. David Kaplan. Berkeley: University of California, 2012. 33–51.

Hinrichs, C. Clare, and Allen, Patricia. "Selective Patronage and Social Justice: Local Food Consumer Campaigns in Historical Context." *Journal of Agricultural and Environmental Ethics* 21 (2008): 329–352.

James, Aaron. *Fairness in Practice: A Social Contract for a Global Economy.* New York: Oxford University Press, 2012.

Kingsolver, B., Hopp, S.L., and Kingsolver, C. *Animal, Vegetable, Miracle: A Year of Food Life.* New York: Harper Collins, 2007.

Kingsolver, Barbara. "Foreword." *The Essential Agrarian Reader.* Ed. Norman Wirzba. Berkeley: Counterpoint, 2003. ix–xvii.

Krugman, P.R., Obstfeld, M. and Melitz, M.J. *International Economics: Theory and Policy.* Boston: Pearson Addison-Wesley, 2012.

Light, Andrew. "Ecological Restoration and the Culture of Nature: A Pragmatic Perspective." *Environmental Ethics: An Anthology.* Ed. Andrew Light and Holmes Rolston III. Malden: Blackwell, 2003. 398–409.

McKibben, Bill. *Deep Economy: The Wealth of Communities and the Durable Future.* New York: Henry Holt and Company, 2007.

McWilliams, James. *Just Food: Where Locavores Get It Wrong and How We Can Truly Eat Responsibly.* New York: Little, Brown and Company, 2009.

Miller, David. *On Nationality.* Oxford: Oxford, 1995.

Miller, Richard. "Beneficence, Duty and Distance". *Philosophy and Public Affairs* 32.4 (2004): 357–383.

Navin, Mark C. "Local Food and International Ethics". *Journal of Agricultural and Environmental Ethics.* 27.3 (2014): 349–368.

Orr, David W. "The Uses of Prophecy." *The Essential Agrarian Reader.* Ed. Norman Wirzba. Berkeley: Counterpoint, 2003. 171–187.

Paarlberg, Robert. *Food Politics: What Everyone Needs to Know.* Oxford: Oxford, 2010.

Pauw, K. and Thurlow, J. "Agricultural Growth, Poverty and Nutrition in Tanzania." *Food Policy* 36.6 (2011): 795–804.

Percy, Walker. *The Moviegoer.* New York: Vintage International, 1998.

Pollan, Michael. *The Ominvore's Dilemma: A Natural History of Four Meals.* New York: Penguin, 2006.

Portman, Anne. "Mother Nature Has It Right: Local Food Advocacy and the Appeal to the 'Natural.'" *Ethics and the Environment* 19:1 (2014): 1–30.

Schnell, Steven M. "Food Miles, Local Eating and Community-Supported Agriculture: Putting Local Food in Its Place." *Agriculture and Human Values* 30 (2013): 615–628.

Singer, Peter. *One World: The Ethics of Globalization.* New Haven: Yale, 2002.

Singer, Peter, and Mason, Jim. *The Ethics of What We Eat.* Emmaus: Rodale, 2006.

Smith, Alisa and Mackinnon, J.B. *The 100-Mile Diet: A Year of Local Eating.* Toronto: Random House, 2007.

Smith, Bren. "Don't Let Your Children Grow Up To Be Farmers." *The New York Times.* August 9, 2014.

Stiglitz, Joseph and Charlton, Andrew. *Fair Trade for All.* New York: Oxford University Press, 2005.

Torrez, F. "La Via Campesina: Peasant-Led Agrarian Reform and Food Sovereignty." *Development* 54.1 (2011): 49–54.

Weber, Christopher L., and Matthews, H. Scott. "Food Miles and the Relative Climate Impacts of Food Choices in the United States." *Environmental Science and Technology* 42.10 (2008): 3508–3513.

Wirzba, Norman. "Placing the Soul: An Agrarian Philosophical Principle." *The Essential Agrarian Reader.* Ed. Norman Wirzba. Berkeley: Counterpoint, 2003.80–97.

QUESTIONS

1. In the previous reading, McKibben makes a series of implicit arguments in favor of local eating or buying or producing. Does de Bres cover all of them? What would she say in response to the arguments of his that she does cover?

2. Locavores often stress the value of building community. Why is it valuable? Does it matter whether your community is itself made of good people? What if your community comprises nothing but jerks? Even so, is there something to be said for building community?

3. Relatedly, locavores often stress the value of keeping money in one's community. There is clearly sometimes a *prudential* justification for this in some cases—doing so will in some cases be better *for you.* Explain the moral justification for it. Is it compelling? Why or why not?

4. De Bres seems skeptical of the simple idea that there is a moral requirement to support one's community. She seems less skeptical of the idea that there is a moral requirement to support one's community *so long as in doing so one violates no duties to creatures outside one's community.* Why does she think the second idea is more plausible? Does she actually *believe* it? Or just think it is more plausible than the simple idea?

MICHELLE PARATORE

Rising to the Food Waste Challenge

Paratore provides a summary of food waste in our society, including its sources. She then describes a panel discussion among a diverse group from business and civil society who are trying to combat food waste. She reports insightful comments from many of the panelists that illuminate important dimensions of food waste, and opportunities for combating it, that are not often discussed.

CONTEXT

According to an August 2012 report by the National Resources Defense Council, in the US we waste a whopping 40% of our food each year.[1] An estimated 64 billion pounds of surplus food is dumped into landfills each year, valued at $165 billion, and disposed of at a cost of $750 million per year. A typical American family of four throws away $1,600 in food every year—a number that's especially interesting when compared to the incremental cost to a family of four of eating healthy every year: $2,016 a year.[2]

In December 2013, Local Food Lab and Edible Startups hosted a panel highlighting innovative approaches to food waste entitled, "Rising to the Food Waste Challenge." It was a fascinating conversation and, given it felt like we barely scratched the surface, is a topic we'll address again in future events.

The purpose of this panel was to bring together and highlight organizations which are tackling this astonishing amount of waste via a range of strategies. Our panel featured:

1. Roger Gordon, Co-Founder, Food Cowboy: *DC-based startup which works with truckers,* *caterers, and supply chain companies to divert food from landfills to food banks*

2. Kelly Ernst Friedman, Program Director, Food Shift: *Oakland-based nonprofit which works collaboratively with communities to develop long-term sustainable solutions to reduce food waste, most known for their fall 2013 education campaign via ads on BART*

3. Stu Rudick, Social Impact Investor, Mindfull Investors and Co-Founder, FoodStar Partners: *Bay Area startup which works with retailers to sell soon-to-be-discarded food or produce which don't meet aesthetic standards via flash sales*

4. Patricia Kelly, Business Development, Lean Path: *Portland-based supplier of automated food waste tracking systems for hospitals, colleges, and restaurants*

5. Anea Botton, Founder, Valley Girls Foodstuffs: *Seller of value-added food products made with gleaned produce and employing at-risk teens in Sonoma County*

6. Ashley Beleny, PR, Zero Waste Energy: *Bay Area organization operating the world's largest dry fermentation anaerobic digestion facility in San Jose to convert compost into energy*

THE BARRIERS TO REDUCING FOOD WASTE

Clearly the amount of food wasted is huge. Waste spans the food value chain, with the highest share attributable to consumer losses (55% of total waste—food thrown out at home, unfinished dishes at restaurants i.e., "plate waste") though a material amount of waste also occurs at the production, processing, and retail steps. Why does this waste occur? There are a few key barriers to more efficient usage of food that are important to understand when thinking about solutions:

1) Logistics and information: The ability to match supply and demand of food is a significant challenge. Across the value chain, organizations and individuals faced with excess food often do not have an outlet for selling or donating that food. Roger highlighted that "the supply chain is 24/7 while most food banks operate Monday through Friday from 9–5. They don't have adequate resources to staff volunteers beyond that." He also cited that total food bank donations in a year are equal to the amount our supply chain wastes in 19 days (!). Stu agreed, "What's missing is information—what can you do with food that's going to be thrown out?" Both Food Cowboy and FoodStar are trying to provide that information, to truckers and retailers respectively.

Another interesting information challenge is the fact that many organizations aren't aware of the scale of food they're wasting. LeanPath is helping food service organizations like hospitals, colleges, hotels, and casinos gain transparency into their own waste. As Patricia noted, "you can't manage what you can't measure."

2) Economics: Food waste seems to be a straight-forward enemy—something most people would agree is a bad thing. However, like any systemic issue, there are incentives in place which support the status quo. The profitability of the grocery industry depends upon food waste. If consumers were to suddenly rationalize their grocery purchases to achieve near-zero waste, the grocery industry would take a massive hit. Roger cited that "adjusting the supply of produce to meet demand [in terms of what is actually consumed] would take the grocery industry from a 1.5% average profit margin to a 0.7% loss—waste is essential to our economy." How essential? $165B is about 1% of the US's ~$17T nominal GDP; we're not talking about the lifeblood of our economy, but the hit wouldn't be immaterial either.

Across the food value chain, economics work in both directions—producers, distributors, and retailers profit from their customers continuing to over-purchase and waste, but all these groups would benefit if they were able to reduce the waste that hits their own bottom line (i.e., if retailers were able to reduce the amount of unsold food they throw out, or if

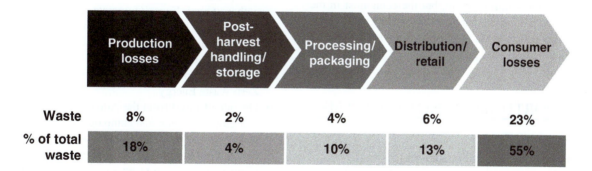

Food Waste Ecosystem

	Production losses	Post-harvest handling/ storage	Processing/ packaging	Distribution/ retail	Consumer losses
Waste	8%	2%	4%	6%	23%
% of total waste	18%	4%	10%	13%	55%

consumers could save the money they spend on food they don't eat). The fact that economics aren't working entirely against change makes solutions to this problem more feasible than in other food areas.

3) Culture/norms: Our norms promote a degree of food waste in the retail and consumer stages of the value chain. Ideas about the aesthetics of foods as well as confusion around "sell by" dates cause both retailers and consumers to discard good food.[3] We are quick to dismiss bruised apples, brown bananas, wilted greens, etc. when taste and nutritional value may be perfectly good. Anea deals with this issue on-the-ground in Sonoma where she regularly procures produce that can't be sold due to aesthetic reasons to use in her jams, pickled goods, and dried fruits. She explains, "Reeducation around produce aesthetics is hard." Her secret weapon: empowered teenagers. "Get teenagers on board and behind a cause and they'll tell everyone. They'll change the attitudes of those around them because they're influential." I love Anea's approach to making change in her community.

An obvious strategy to overcome the cultural barrier is discounting. If we go back to economics, at some point the price can be low enough that the demand for bruised, past-date, or otherwise suboptimal food would meet supply. This is what Doug Rauch, the former President of Trader Joe's, is doing with his new concept Daily Table, set to launch this May in Boston. Daily Table will take blemished food, use it to prepare meals, and sell those hot meals along with grocery staples (eggs, milk, bread, produce) at "junk food prices." However this approach raises controversy: Roger protests that, "it's not the duty of the poor to consume discarded food. This would institutionalize the problem of food waste and excuse it." I understand his point, but the economist in me can't help thinking that matching willing buyers with willing sellers at the right price is a good alternative to letting resources go to waste.

OPPORTUNITIES, NOT PROBLEMS

In a sector packed with trade-offs (big food vs. local producers, organics vs. GMOs, carbs vs. fats), few issues are win-win-win. Reducing food wastes offers the holy grail—environmental benefits, economic benefits (to an extent), and health benefits (improved nutrition by getting good food to those who need it). Beyond that, there's something visceral about food waste. As Anea pointed out, "yes there are environmental and economic reasons to not waste food but beyond that there's an innate feeling of sadness we all experience when we see food wasted." So we can add emotional benefits to that list.

As the panel pointed out, the food waste conversation should be about opportunities, not about problems. So what are the opportunities? Food Shift is working to add employment to the list of benefits from reduced waste. They're working to create jobs in food recovery, similar to what San Francisco's Food Runners do: they pick up excess food from businesses (restaurants, caterers, bakeries, hospitals, event planners, corporate cafeterias, and hotels) and deliver it (15+ tons per week) to neighborhood food programs. The challenge is to create paid jobs and not volunteer positions. I'll be curious to see how Food Shift manages to sustainably fund paid positions, beyond using grant dollars.

There are also abundant opportunities in new sectors and technologies. To name a few:

- Technologies which postpone spoilage by reducing oxygen: BluApple and FreshPaper both sell products which prolong fruit and vegetable shelf-life within the fridge; Organic Girl salad greens, along with many pre-rinsed salad producers, use technology to remove oxygen from their packaging
- Innovation which reduces time from field to fridge
- Companies which dis-intermediate retail altogether (Good Eggs, Quinciple, other online food delivery startups) to remove a step (and the corresponding waste) from the value chain
- Anaerobic digestion technology for turning food waste into energy, like that created by Zero Waste Energy
- One idea I loved from the panel is a branding/conscious consumerism campaign around food waste similar to "Eat Local"—some way to denote brands which perform above average in terms of waste so consumers can reward them with their dollars[4]

NOTES

1. Dana Gunders (2012), "Wasted: How America is Losing Up to 40 Percent of Its Food from Farm to Fork to Landfill," NRDC Issue Paper, online at: http://www.nrdc.org/food/files/wasted-food-ip.pdf

2. http://greatist.com/health/eating-healthy-cost-less-121013

3. http://www.nrdc.org/media/2013/130918.asp

4. Note: The panel was recorded and broadcast by C-SPAN, and an online video of the event is available here: http://www.c-spanvideo.org/program/FoodW.

QUESTIONS

1. According to the sources that Paratore cites, what percentage of food does the average American throw out every year? How does that compare to the amount that is lost at other points in the supply chain before reaching consumers? Suppose you learned that the large numbers for waste at the consumer stage were partly accounted for by the fact that when you cook food, it often loses weight because it loses water content—and that the report was counting that as food waste. What would you think? (Are such cooking losses something that the actual report classifies as food waste?)

2. Paratore writes that "The fact that economics aren't working entirely against change makes solutions to this problem more feasible than in other food areas." Explain in your own words what she means by this, and in doing so, provide a pair of examples that illustrates the contrast with problems in other food areas where economics might be described as working against change.

3. If you had to rank your top three ideas that Paratore discusses, based on what you expect the reduction in food waste from the idea to be, how would you rank them? As you read more online about what is working and not working with respect to food waste—and as you read other authors' takes on the problem—does that change your ranking? Are there things that Paratore does not discuss that are also promising? For each of these initiatives, what is the single best objection to it? Is there some modified version of the initiative that you think is more promising in light of that objection?

4. How would you try to make a positive difference regarding food waste, if you were an influential person who could get other people to listen to you and give you some funding to do things? Come up with ideas for:
   a. Government initiatives
   b. Initiatives you'd pursue as an individual person
   c. "Civil society" initiatives (e.g., by non-profit organizations)
   d. More "grass roots" community organizing

   How would you invest your time if you could only pursue the idea you find most promising in two of these four areas?

AUSTIN KIESSIG

What "Big Ideas" in Food Get Funded in Silicon Valley?

Kiessig highlights a wide variety of new food-related businesses that are receiving venture capital funding, and that are likely to play an important role in the evolution of the food and agriculture sectors. He provides a framework for understanding why these food startups and not others are receiving this funding.

Much has been written about the ascent of Silicon Valley (SV) as the go-to global incubator for transformational change. SV has become the Jerusalem of the techno-optimist religion. In venture capital doctrine, the absolution of humanity's sins begins with seed financing for the next spate of Big Ideas. And in an America where the federal government no longer functions (quite literally), Silicon Valley has taken on new gravity. It is ground zero for ingenuity as cathartic salvation.

The unsustainability of the modern food system is one of humanity's biggest problems. So, it's worth taking a look at which Big Ideas in food the leading SV venture capital firms (VCs) are voting for. [Editors' note: Venture capital firms provide funding for new businesses (often referred to as "startups") that aim to grow quickly into large profitable firms. VCs provide this funding in exchange for an ownership stake in those startups.]

Where are VCs placing their bets for the salvation of food? (Note: this piece will focus on venture capital financing, but not crowd-funding, angel financing, or later-stage private equity financing, all of which also play an important role in advancing Big Ideas in food.) SV's rising focus on food has already received attention from the mainstream press.[1]

Before diving in, it's important to bear in mind a few truths about the VC business model. To have a chance of being funded by a VC, a company must "walk and talk" like a high-growth technology firm. VCs look for: a) billion-dollar marketplaces; b) game-changing innovations; c) short innovation cycles that can quickly lead to high-margin revenue; and d) a promising path to "liquidity" (meaning the sale of the VC firm's equity shares in the company). One problem cited by food entrepreneurs is that food businesses often *don't* fit this profile. So as you peruse the ideas below, it's also important to consider what's *not* being financed. But, more on that later.

AGRICULTURE INPUTS: INFORMATION, RESOURCE MANAGEMENT, SEEDS

VCs love agriculture input innovations. Why? Inputs undergird all of food production, and thus represent massive marketplaces. Plus, VCs understand the imminent scarcity of inputs such as water and petroleum-derived fertilizer. If technology can reduce or supplant the need for threatened resources, it can probably be monetized. (However, because such technologies often hinge on bets about unforeseeable commodity price trends and/or government

Austin Kiessig, "What 'Big Ideas' in Food Get Funded in Silicon Valley?" Originally published at www.ediblestartups.com

distortion of markets, they bear resemblance to some of the "cleantech" investments that burned VC firms in recent years.[2])

A good place to start is with the recent sale of The Climate Corporation (CC) to Monsanto for over $1 billion. Having liquidated for about ten times the $109 million in venture funding the company has received since 2007, CC is rightly hailed as a successful venture investment, and was backed by big-name firms such as Founders Fund, Khosla Ventures, Google Ventures, NEA, Index Ventures and Atomico. CC is a "Big Data" company that processes historical and real-time weather data with predictive algorithms, and then intelligently prices crop insurance and weather informatics for farmers. CC produces something that tech-oriented VCs can understand, and they've cracked into the multi-billion dollar insurance and business intelligence marketplaces. While we may not think about risk management and production intelligence as agriculture inputs, farmers certainly do! CC is an important case study because it shows VCs that they can make money playing in agriculture.

Another interesting information-seller is Solum, which produces soil sensors and an accompanying analytical platform aimed at reducing fertilizer inputs. The company provides farmers with detailed knowledge on the health of their soil to enable precise decisions on how much additional application is needed to maximize crop yields.

VCs have also focused on companies trying to reduce water use. The Roda Group financed mOasis, a company developing a polymer gel that retains soil moisture and reduces watering intensity in arid climates. Both Banyan Water and PureSense offer technology platforms to economize water application on irrigated landscapes. And Khosla Ventures backed NanoH2O, a membrane technology company that lowers the cost of desalination (and brings farmers one step closer to using abundant salty water for their fields).

Seeds are an additional big focus of VC firms. Kleiner Perkins has two non-GMO seed companies in its portfolio: Kaiima and VoloAgri. Both are trying to coax better productivity out of crop lines without directly altering genetics, a la Monsanto.

Note that what all these companies are really selling are data-derived intelligence or intellectual property that could shift entire marketplaces. They are high-risk, but potentially high-return, with global applicability.

AG PRODUCTION & FOOD PROCESSING: MORE EFFICIENT PROTEIN, PROCESS AUTOMATION

Another concept that VCs love is substitutes for conventionally produced animal protein. If you know anything about how resource-intensive it is to raise a cow, you realize it's probably possible to produce protein far more efficiently. Furthermore, the market for proteins is large and growing as more middle-class consumers come online worldwide.

The animal protein alternatives market is currently dominated by next-generation plant-protein synthetics that closely mimic real meat. The most "buzzy" among them is Beyond Meat, which leads a class of startups investing heavily in food science and processing technique to bring the flavor, texture, and visceral eating experience of their substitutes as near as possible to "the real thing." The promise for VCs is that these companies will make delicious products with a *much* lower production cost, thereby carving out a large fraction of the global market by virtue of a favorable price point. Also in this vein is Hampton Creek, an egg substitute with exceptionally promising early market traction,[3] and Lyrical Foods, which is going after cheese.

Further down the pike are companies attempting to grow real animal cell cultures (and ultimately complex animal tissue compounds) in a lab. Rather than originating from a cow in a field, your hamburger would come from "in vitro cultivation" in an industrial incubator. Again, the investment promise of companies such as Modern Meadow is that they will someday streamline production and drop costs—although today, a single "cultured" burger costs $325,000.[4]

(Keep an eye on one more animal protein substitute: farmed insects. While I am not aware of any insect companies currently being financed by institutional VCs, they are thriving on crowd-funding sites such as Kickstarter.com.[5])

Another well-attended class of ventures is those that are automating processes in the semi-structured environment of food production. For example, Blue River Technology is using computer vision technology to automate in-field weeding and plant selection processes, which have historically relied on manual labor or excessive application of chemicals. Primary backer Khosla Ventures envisions a future where autonomous robotic vehicles diligently roam every agriculture plot around the world. A similar company is Rowbot, which is focused on fertilizer application.

And not far off will be a series of investments in flying drone vehicles used in food production. I don't know what these will look like, but some have ventured a guess.[6]

STORAGE, DISTRIBUTION, AND CONSUMPTION: SUPPLY CHAIN TRACEABILITY, NUMEROUS CONSUMER APPLICATIONS

Information is of paramount importance in distribution. Since supply chain traceability is of interest for food safety, cost control, and consumer education purposes, VCs have bolstered technology company HarvestMark, which can help track fresh food items down to the package level.

Further along the supply chain is the intersection of food and consumer purchases. Because "consumer Internet" (the intersection of internet technology and the traditional consumption of goods and services, the latter of which composes over 70% of U.S. GDP[7]) has been such a massive area of investment for VCs, the ecosystem of ventures that allow people to seek out, buy, and consume food is extremely robust.

Instead of trying to catalogue notable investments in this space, I will refer readers to Brita Rosenheim's exhaustive map of "Food Tech and Media" companies.[8] For ongoing coverage, Food and Tech Connect monitors this space very well. Expect several billion dollars to be invested in this space in coming years.

WHAT'S BEING LEFT OUT?

Anything that is regionally oriented, serves a small market, or fails to provide an "exit opportunity" for VC investors is unlikely to be funded. The reason such investments are left out is because *the business of venture capital is to make money,* and do so relatively quickly. VCs raise investment funds from limited partners (smaller investors), and promise to "close" a pool of funds and deliver returns within five to seven years. What that means is that even a company that receives investment early in the five-to-seven year life of a fund doesn't have a tremendously long time to grow and go public, be bought by a competitor, sell to a private equity firm, or otherwise recapitalize to "liquidate" equity shares. If the "exit opportunity" never manifests, the VCs can't make money, and they won't make the investment in the first place.

Contrast the five-to-seven year exit timeline with the life cycle of most agriculture and food businesses. Pistachio trees take seven years to mature after planting. Converting land from conventional to certified organic takes at least three years (and probably closer to four in practice). Building sales and distribution in a physical sales network takes much longer than in an e-commerce network. VCs simply aren't willing to wait for many food businesses to generate a competitive return on their investments.

And, even if VCs waited, a *competitive* return may never appear. Most parts of the food value chain generate modest profit margins. Contrast the 15% operating margin of Kraft Foods (a mature and profitable food company) to the 34% operating margin of

Microsoft (a mature and profitable software company). For a VC chasing "superior" returns, the profit profile of a business matters a lot.

So what "progressive food" business models are unlikely to be courted by VCs? Big Ideas that are a bit ahead of their time (such as vertical farming); "low-tech" agriculture production technologies; local foodshed farming operations; regional food processors or distributors; artisanal "mom and pop" food manufacturers; most restaurant chains; retailers targeting "food deserts"; niche cooking or nutrition education platforms; and most publications or blogs. VC is not interested in Slow Food or Slow Money. And it's important to recognize that many of the changes needed in the food system simply don't fit in the "techno-optimist" paradigm. For those changes, alternative investment channels are springing up, but may never develop at all. Future Edible Startups posts will address complementary avenues of investment in other parts of the food system.[9]

In the meantime, cutting-edge food start-up incubators such as Local Food Lab and Accel Foods, and investment enablers such as CircleUp, are trying to close the broad gap between new food businesses and institutional VC financing. As more Big Ideas (and laudable Small and Medium Ideas) in food continue to emerge, stay tuned to the evolving infrastructure of support for food companies.

NOTES

1. Jenna Wortham and Claire Cain Miller (2013), "Venture Capitalists Are Making Bigger Bets on Food Start-Ups," *New York Times*, 28 April 2013, online at: www.nytimes.com/2013/04/29/business/venture-capitalists-are-making-bigger-bets-on-food-start-ups.html

2. Randall Smith (2012), "Despite Setbacks, Investor is Bullish on Clean Technology," *New York Times*, 29 November 2012, online at: http://dealbook.nytimes.com/2012/11/29/despite-setbacks-investor-is-bullish-on-clean-technology

3. Michelle Paratore (2013), "The Future of Protein: Event Recap," ediblestartups.com, online at: http://edible-startups.com/2013/08/12/the-future-of-protein-event-recap

4. Henry Fountain (2013), "A Lab-Grown Burger Gets a Taste Test," *New York Times*, 5 August 2013, online at: www.nytimes.com/2013/08/06/science/a-lab-grown-burger-gets-a-taste-test.html

5. Michelle Paratore (2013), "Exo: Is that a cricket in my protein bar? I hope so!", ediblestartups.com, online at: http://ediblestartups.com/2013/07/31/exo-is-that-a-cricket-in-my-protein-bar-i-hope-so

6. Thomas Frey (2013), "Agriculture the New Game of Drones," online at: http://www.futuristspeaker.com/2013/08/agriculture-the-new-game-of-drones

7. See World Bank data for household final consumption expenditure % of GDP, online at: http://data.worldbank.org/indicator/NE.CON.PETC.ZS

8. See latest version online, e.g.: http://www.foodtechconnect.com/2015/09/30/food-tech-media-startup-funding-ma-and-partnerships-august-2015

9. See more online at: www.ediblestartups.com

QUESTIONS

1. What are venture capitalists? What role do they play in the economy, as partly illuminated by Kiessig's discussion? What role do they play in addressing social problems? (Feel encouraged to read some articles online in thinking about these questions.) According to Kiessig, how do venture capitalists decide whether they are interested in investing in a new food company? What effect does this have on their likelihood of their investing in companies that are unlikely to be profitable quickly, or that are focused only on making the world a better place in a way that is not profitable?

2. If society needs investment in a new kind of knowledge or technology or infrastructure, does Kiessig's discussion suggest that venture capitalists will always provide it? Who else could provide it? Is government the only other source of funding or innovation? Read some articles online about "civil society." What are two different arguments that could be given for the conclusions that, when

there is a particular technology that society needs, government should finance it? What are objections to that idea? If neither government nor venture capitalists finance something we need, how else might it be provided for society?

3. Imagine a strawberry farm that met all of the criteria for being certified organic, but it was entirely tended and harvested by a large fleet of robots and drones that were constantly flying around and were optimized to increase the yield-per-acre output of the farm by carefully applying water, organic fertilizer, and the like. What are some arguments against the desirability of such a farm? What are some possible arguments in favor of it? Would it be an "industrial" farm?

4. What is an egg substitute? What is in vitro meat? (See also the appendix to Singer and Mason's reading in Chapter 4.) Can you think of reasons why the former might have a much easier time taking market share from existing competitors than the latter? If everyone believed that the former would have a much easier time in this way than the latter, what would you expect the result to be in terms of the quantity of investments made in the former technology versus the latter? What would you expect the result to be in terms of the source of investments in the former technology versus the latter—that is venture capital, versus government, versus wealthy individuals interested in maximizing the return on their investment for society, versus wealthy individuals with a personal interest in animal welfare? Read some articles online about the sources of funding in these technologies.

5. Under what conditions could a single individual person, all by him- or herself, cause something important to be provided for society that didn't previously exist? Under what conditions could this be done regardless of what other people thought, regardless of what the government thought, and regardless of whether anyone else was willing to provide financing? Do such innovators have to be rich? (Note that not all contributions to society are large-scale transformative technologies—some are small contributions.) Consider the following quote: "We may learn something about the renewal of societies if we look at the kind of people who contribute the most to that outcome—the innovators." What are two controversial ideas in this quote? What arguments could be given in favor of those ideas, and against them? How do different societies treat innovators? Do some societies make it more difficult for innovators than others?

11 } Workers

In this chapter, we describe the conditions of some agricultural workers, meatpackers, and restaurant workers. We then explain and discuss some ethical issues that those conditions raise.

WORKERS, EMPLOYERS, AND CONSUMERS

In his essay in Chapter 1, "The Ethically Troubling Food System," Barry Estabrook writes,

> I suggest that if you're looking to experience culture shock in one of its starkest forms, drive from Naples [Florida] to Immokalee. It takes about 45 minutes on a straight road, but it's a journey from one of the most privileged enclaves of the First World (houses in Naples are fetching as much as $28 million) to the gritty squalor of the Third World. In Immokalee, a community of 20,000 dependent upon the surrounding tomato fields and citrus groves, 70 percent of the population is Latino; four in ten of its residents (and nearly half its children) live below the poverty line.
>
> To alleviate some of that poverty, a group called the Coalition of Immokalee Workers came up with a seemingly modest suggestion a few years ago: Ask giant fast food companies to pay Florida farmworkers one penny more per pound for their tomatoes. That less-than-princely sum would be small potatoes to the billion-dollar-plus corporations, but it would add $20 to a picker's daily wage of about $50.[1]

The campaign succeeded and then became a campaign to get grocery stores and food service providers—catering companies, dining hall vendors—to only buy from farms that pay these higher wages.[2] The initial CIW campaign was directed at the people charged with paying tomato pickers in the first place. Those people do wrong by not paying pickers enough, the CIW alleged, and they get away with not paying enough by wrongfully exploiting their workers.

We can distinguish two clusters of question that the CIW campaign raises. The first is about employers: Do the overseers in tomato fields treat pickers wrongly? Do the companies the tomatoes were being picked for treat those workers wrongly? If so, which of their actions are wrong? Why are they wrong? Is their treatment of the workers coercive? Exploitative? Unjust?

The second cluster is about consumers: *If* employers treat workers wrongly, do *consumers* act impermissibly by buying the employers' products? Relatedly, do consumers treat tomato pickers impermissibly by buying tomatoes that are produced in this wrongful way? This cluster of issues about consumers is closely related to questions about consumption discussed in Chapter 4, "Consumer Ethics," and is dealt with in that chapter. In this chapter, we just focus on the first cluster of questions: Do food employers do wrong with regard to workers? If so, what are the wrong actions? Why are they wrong?

In particular, we focus on employers and employees on farms, in meatpacking plants, and in restaurants.

FARMWORKERS

Farm work is discussed in the Holmes reading that follows. It was discussed in the Estabrook reading in Chapter 1, "The Ethically Troubling Food System." These selections are, of course, not synoptic. Estabrook focuses on tomato pickers on industrial farms in southern Florida, Holmes on berry pickers on industrial farms on the west coast of the United States. The pieces are not comprehensive accounts of working conditions on farms across the United States, much less the world. There are farms with happy workers with well-paying, safe jobs, jobs they willingly return to until they willingly, happily leave. Those jobs do not raise the ethical questions that we discuss in this chapter.

There are also farms with workers that are enslaved. In some ways, slavery is a complicated issue. The Coalition of Immokalee Workers' work to end slavery on tomato farms, including the Campaign for Fair Food mentioned earlier, was recognized in the United States with the Presidential Medal. Secretary of State John Kerry's remarks touch on many themes in this book:

> [I]f you dig deeper, you begin to see that modern slavery does not exist in a vacuum. It's connected to many of our other foreign policy concerns, from environmental sustainability, to advancing the lives of women and girls. . . . Wherever we find poverty and lack of opportunity, wherever rule of law is weak, wherever corruption is most ingrained, and where minorities are abused, . . . we find not just vulnerability to trafficking but zones of impunity where traffickers can prey on victims.
>
> One of the greatest zones of impunity is in the supply chains. The sources of the problem include individuals desperate for work; unscrupulous labor brokers who lie to recruit those workers; companies greedy for profits . . . ; and customers looking to just save that extra dollar or two without regard to what the implications of those savings might be.[3]

But, ethically speaking, slavery is not complicated. If there are any truths in ethics, that it is wrong to enslave people is one.

Yet the workers Holmes discusses do not seem too far removed from slavery: They work very long, hard hours for very little compensation. They have very few opportunities for advancement in their jobs and few means to improve their work conditions. They work at the mercy of their employer with few opportunities to work elsewhere. They work under the threat of being deported. Because of this threat, these workers are easily prevailed upon to work ever longer and harder and to do so for a pittance. Their employers' control seeps into more and more of the workers' lives: when and what they eat, where they sleep and bathe, how they raise their children.

It might seem like *because* slavery is wrong, it is also wrong to treat workers in the ways that they are treated on the farms Holmes discusses; treating workers that way is wrong for the same reasons enslaving workers is wrong. Is that correct? If slavery is wrong, is employing people in the conditions Holmes details wrong?

WHAT IS WRONG WITH SLAVERY?

We said if there are any truths in ethics, that it is wrong to enslave people is one. There is much agreement—these days, in most parts of the world—about this. But about *why* slavery is wrong, there is less agreement. One theory, supported by *utilitarians*, is that slavery is wrong because it doesn't produce enough well-being, that an economic system stripped of slavery produces more. The only right labor arrangement, according to utilitarians, is the one that maximizes well-being. So this explanation implies that *if* slavery were to produce sufficient well-being, slavery might be permissible or even morally required since, if utilitarianism is true, one is always and everywhere required to maximize well-being.

Rejecting that implication, some say that what is wrong with slavery is not its failure to maximize well-being, but, rather, its treating people as tools. Slavery *uses* people, where *using* someone is distinguished from a case where you need someone to get what you want while *also* treating them as an equal. For example, when you ask a McDonald's cashier for a burger or pay a plumber to get your sink fixed, you are not using them in this sense of "use." (We come back to this later in the chapter.)

A third view is that what is wrong with slavery is not its failure to maximize well-being or its using people but, rather, its systematic restriction of the freedom of autonomous creatures.

If one of these explanations of the wrongness of slavery is right, what, if anything, does that imply about the ethics of raising animals for food? Are animals autonomous creatures? Is there something wrong with restricting their freedom? Is there something wrong with using them? Do we do so on farms?

And what is it, exactly, to restrict freedom? What, if anything, is wrong with doing so? We discuss related questions in Chapter 13, "Paternalism and Public Health."

As you read through the discussions of the treatment of farmworkers, meatpackers, and restaurant workers, you should think about what is wrong with slavery and ask yourself whether what is wrong with slavery shows that the treatment of these non-enslaved workers is wrong, too.

INDUSTRIAL AGRICULTURAL WORKERS

Back to the main thread. The Holmes reading details conditions for pickers on industrial farms. These conditions include brutally hard, monotonous work. (After one day's work, Holmes wrote, "It honestly felt like pure torture.") As detailed in Chapter 9,

"Industrial Plant Agriculture," industrial plant agriculture involves the use of synthetic pesticides, fungicides, and so forth, and these have deleterious health effects on workers and, if a worker is pregnant, on the worker's fetus. In the United States, workers often live in impoverished communities with little hope of upward mobility. A large number of these workers—very conservatively 1.2 million[4]—are illegal immigrants and, hence, especially vulnerable to threats such as the threat of deportation. They often are unaware of their legal rights with regard to the racism, sexism, and wage theft they experience. That said, they are less robustly protected than other workers, lacking, for example, a right to overtime or the strict prohibition on child labor that is found in other industries.

NON-INDUSTRIAL AGRICULTURAL WORKERS

As with work on industrial farms, work on non-industrial farms is brutally hard. In some cases it involves the same synthetics as industrial agriculture. Remember from Chapter 10, "Alternatives to Industrial Plant Agriculture," that non-industrial does not mean organic. And, even on organic, non-industrial farms, the work might involve toxic organic pesticides. Like work on industrial farms, it involves low pay and few benefits.

Unlike work on industrial farms, though, it will typically involve closer relationships between employer and employee. As Margaret Gray discusses in her book *Labor and the Locavore*, however, this closeness is a double-edged sword. She describes some bosses feeling, because of their relationship with their employees, like they are entitled to exert control over the workers' lives, acting in what they perceive to be their employees' best interests. And in a recent article on the high rate of farmer suicide, Madeline Thomas writes,

> On family farms in particular, where personal issues are often intertwined with financial ones, the tension is that much higher. "Over half [the calls to a farmer suicide helpline], between 50 and 60 percent, have some type of interpersonal issue that has to be dealt with before progress can be made in the farm business," [Edward Staehr of a New York farmer crisis hotline] says. "Could be intergenerational conflict or family conflict, sibling rivalry, relationship issues, and so on."
>
> Family farms are a "hidden stress issue in agriculture," adds Val Farmer, a clinical psychologist based in Missouri who specializes in rural mental health and family relationships.[5]

What this quotation brings out, something Gray brings out, too, is that while the closeness of family farms and small-scale agriculture operations brings with it benefits, it also makes possible costs that are not present on larger-scale farms or farms with no close relation between employers and employees. (This is understandable. Falling in love makes possible various otherwise inaccessible benefits. But it also makes possible terrible, heart-wrenching costs. It's important to stress this: Gray's book makes clear that work on non-industrial farms is better in all sorts of ways than work on industrial farms. Yet it also makes clear that the differences make possible not just benefits in the lives of workers but also costs.)

MEATPACKERS

The conditions in slaughterhouses like the one that Pachirat describes are in some ways quite similar to those described by Holmes: Workers, meatpackers, work very long, hard hours for very little compensation. The work can be brutally monotonous. Steve Striffler writes, "The first complaint that virtually all [meatpackers] point to—before wages, working conditions, and supervisors—is the intolerable monotony" and then quotes a worker: "For ten years of my life I have been torturing myself, spending the best years of my life in this ugly building, without windows, watching the chickens pass by, doing the exact same thing."[6] This work comes at hours that make a normal life outside the plant hard. Meatpackers have few opportunities for advancement in their jobs and few means to improve their work conditions. They work at the mercy of their employer with few opportunities to get a job with another employer. Like agricultural workers, many work under the threat of being deported and, because of this, these workers are easily prevailed upon to work longer and harder and for little pay. To boot, the work in slaughterhouses can be disgusting, there is pervasive violence against animals, and there is the risk of great, immediate physical harm. (As Holmes notes, tomato pickers risk serious physical harm to their backs caused by repetitive, debilitating work. What they don't risk is losing fingers from sloppy knifework.)

RESTAURANT WORKERS

The conditions for restaurant workers that Jayaraman describes are in some ways better than the conditions for tomato pickers and meatpackers: The work is less debilitating, less disgusting, and less dangerous. Yet in other ways, the jobs are quite similar and the pay is even worse.

Jayaraman's reading draws attention to something that occurs in tomato fields and meatpacking plants but that is largely skipped over in the Holmes and Pachirat sections we include here: racism and sexism in the workplace.[7] This racism and sexism not only issue in insults and an unpleasant work environment but also systematically limit workers' options so that, for example, Latino men have no chance at working more visible and lucrative jobs as servers but instead are, at best, kitchen help or table-bussers.

ETHICAL ISSUES ABOUT EMPLOYERS' TREATMENT OF WORKERS

In a nutshell, that's what working conditions are like in the venues our readings look at. Is it permissible that people are given jobs with such conditions? It is easy to imagine situations in which it would be permissible: Imagine a world where those jobs are the *only* jobs, where there really is nothing but jobs with long hours, low pay, and bad working conditions but where a life without such a job is even worse. In such a world, giving people jobs like that would seem okay. In fact, depriving people of such jobs might be wrong.

But we don't live in such a world. After all, the employer could make the job less awful. Consider again the conditions detailed in the Holmes, Jayaraman, and Pachirat readings. Some of these jobs include:

- Long hours
- Physically and mentally exhausting work
- Physically debilitating work
- Dangerous, sometimes traumatic work
- Sometimes disgusting work
- Ruthless bosses
- Low pay

It is hard to believe that these awful working conditions are permissible in the actual world where it would be easy to improve them. Part of what appalls us about these conditions is that it seems like it would be easy enough to improve those conditions, that another way is possible.

And yet consider that some people work jobs that permit them to repeatedly risk being knocked unconscious—boxers and mixed martial artists. Or that require them to work long, grueling days in the heat, pouring rain, or freezing cold, repeatedly smashing into other people, greatly increasing their risks of chronic traumatic encephalopathy—NFL players. Or that require them to risk their lives daily—soldiers. (Soldiers might be especially apt points of comparison here since their working conditions can easily be truly described as long, exhausting, dangerous, and sometimes disgusting and traumatic.)

Is it permissible to furnish employees with such awful conditions? Some conditions are surprisingly hard to improve since they are driven by systemic concerns rather than purely local ones. Others could more easily be improved.

One striking thing about, say, the soldier case is that soldiers know what they are signing up for. They consent to do the job, knowing it is hard, dangerous, and sometimes disgusting. Do the food workers consent to their work conditions? Does it matter to whether it is permissible that the workers consent? Does it matter whether the employers get this consent by *exploiting* or *coercing* workers?

Consider a case where consent seems to matter: You take Julian's wallet without permission—that's wrong. Later, lesson learned, you ask Julian if you can have his wallet. He thinks it over and in a calm moment says "sure," and you take it—that's permissible, and it's permissible because Julian agreed to it.

Onora O'Neill once argued that consent matters in the workplace because, without it, the employer is using the employee, and using is wrong. This highlights a connection between the readings in this chapter and Chapter 7, "Industrial Animal Agriculture": Some claim that food workers, like factory-farmed animals, are being used. Others claim, relatedly, that workers are being treated like animals and that animals are being treated like tools. Vividly making this complaint in his novel about meatpacking in the early twentieth century, Upton Sinclair describes the job of a woman, Elzbieta, in a packing plant as "stupefying, *brutaliz-ing* work; it left her no time to think, no strength for anything. She *was part of the machine she tended.*"[8] Her bosses use her just as they might use a machine.

To bring out what seems wrong about using someone, consider a famous pair of examples from the philosophical literature: You are standing by some train tracks. A train is about to crush five people to death who are on one track. You can divert it onto a spur of track, but, if you do so, it will crush one person to death. What should you do? Most people say that it is at least permissible to switch the train onto the track with one person, even though, when you do so, you kill that person. Now consider the other member of this pair of examples: You are a doctor. Five of your patients are dying. A sixth patient shows up for his yearly physical. You can kill him and use his organs to save the five. What should you do? Fewer people say it is permissible to kill the one here. Why? How could it be wrong to kill the one to save the five here given that it was permissible to kill one to save five in the train case? Some say, "It is wrong because when the doctor kills the one he *uses* that person. By contrast, when you kill the one, you don't use her, you only use the spur—if the person gets off the track, so much the better." Some of the readings that follow support that food workers are like your sixth patient, someone used as a resource—an unwilling resource—to benefit others.

The idea is that when you get consent from workers, then, you at least do not use them. More exactly, when you get a certain sort of consent from workers, you do not use them. You might do wrong for other reasons, but you do not use them if you get a certain sort of consent. But the "certain sort" is important. We can imagine ways of telling the story of Julian and the wallet whereby Julian's saying "sure" doesn't give you permission. For example, if Julian said "sure" in his sleep, you wouldn't thereby have permission to take his wallet. Or if he said so after you'd drugged him. Or because he didn't understand your question—the only word he knows in English is "sure." Or because you held a gun to his head while "asking." This last case would be a case of consent due to *coercion*. It's an especially clear case. As you read the writings about agricultural workers and slaughterhouse workers, it is worth considering whether coercion can be achieved through threats of deportation as well as through threats of bodily harm. It's worth considering whether coercion can be achieved by economic systems like capitalism as well as by individual agents like people with guns. (Echoing language in the McMillan [2013] reading in the "Further Reading" section, the National Farm Worker Ministry writes, "In many ways, undocumented farm workers today are *forced* to leave their countries, just as agricultural workers have been *forced* to do throughout history, coming to the United States looking for a livelihood that they cannot attain in their own country." The emphasis is ours; the word choice is telling.[9])

Through a series of vivid examples, the Wertheimer reading in this chapter explores the issues raised in the preceding paragraph. One way in which these issues matter is this: If workers are consenting to their working conditions—and giving informed, clear-eyed consent—and they are in no way coerced, then it might be that there is no requirement by their employers to make their jobs better. It might be *sad* that that's the worker's job or *disgusting*. It might be that the employer is a *jerk* with terrible character. But, all the same, for the employer to provide a worker with that saddening, disgusting job rather than a better one might be permissible.

In providing a worker with a difficult and disgusting but poorly paid job, does an employer exploit the worker? To answer this, consider a pair of examples based on examples by Mikhail Valdman: Julian falls deathly sick. You have medicine to cure him but the medicine is valuable to you and so you charge Julian its market value: $100. There seems to be nothing objectionable here. What if you, knowing Julian is a millionaire, charge Julian $1,000,000?

(You reason: It's my medicine. I can do what I want with it.) In her reading in this chapter, Liberto argues that that would be not only exploitative but wrongfully so.

Why? What is the difference between these two cases such that the first involves no exploitation but the second does? Is the second transaction *coercive*? To answer these, it might help to answer more general questions: What is coercion? What is exploitation? When and why are they wrong? In her reading in this chapter, Liberto gives a series of illuminating examples of exploitation in an attempt to draw out what is distinctive and distinctively wrong about it. Her view is that wrongful exploitation involves an "Advantage Clause" that has it that "there must be something morally problematic about the gain that the exploiter achieves (e.g., the gain is unfair or is motivated by opportunism)" and also involves a "Vulnerability Clause" that has it that the exploited was in a, well, vulnerable position such as "a condition of desperation or a state of being without options" (p. 569). Recall that Iris Marion Young, in her reading from Chapter 3, "Food Justice," analyzes exploitation—not *wrongful* exploitation in particular—as a form of oppression in which the labor and energy of one group benefits another group, without reciprocal benefits. One might think that workers in agriculture and in restaurants provide labor and energy to benefit eaters while also thinking these people are not adequately compensated. If so, Young's account would imply that those workers are exploited. Would Liberto's? One interesting question is whether Young gives an account of exploitation to rival Liberto's or whether she is providing a substantive account of Liberto's Advantage and Vulnerability Clauses.

At any rate, a discussion of exploitation has clear implications for food workers since at least some of those workers are, like Julian, in bad shape—they need money. They are also vulnerable—they are not only in bad shape but also have limited options for improving their situation. (Their situation, then, is quite different from a very rich guy with a bad illness but with excellent healthcare options.) Because of their being in bad shape and being vulnerable, they are willing to do things for money that they would not otherwise do. So Liberto's analysis implies they are wrongfully exploited. And at least some of this work benefits others without appropriate compensation. So Young's analysis implies that those workers are exploited.

When you read about food workers, you can ask, Are their bosses more like you in the first example, where you charge Julian market price, or the second, where you charge him a million dollars? Perhaps it is not the bosses that are doing the exploiting. Might an economic system be exploiting food workers? A familiar Marxist idea is that not only can individual agents exploit but so, too, can economic systems like capitalism.

Compare the workers' situation to this mundane one. You need a babysitter. You are choosing between an adult, a high school student, and a middle schooler. They will do equally good work, but the middle schooler has the fewest other options for work, the greatest need for money, and the lowest expectations for pay. You offer her much less money than you would offer the adult or the high schooler. Have you exploited her? Is that objectionable?

If it is objectionable, is it made more objectionable by being exploitation of the worst off? In Valdman's antidote examples, a rich guy is being exploited. In food work cases, it's people who are already very badly off being exploited.

If it is objectionable, would it be made more objectionable if the exploitation were not just of any old middle schooler but, as with food work, exploitation of darker-skinned, foreign employees on the part of lighter-skinned Americans? Or if the exploitation were, as in some food work, of a woman—a girl—by a man?

FOOD SYSTEM WORKERS AND SOCIAL JUSTICE

The previous section considered the treatment of workers by employers: When is an employer's treatment of an employee morally impermissible? When is it coercive? When is it exploitative? Whether an individual employer treats her own workers permissibly is one kind of ethical question. Another kind of question is whether workers are treated justly as a group—whether these workers are getting what they are owed by society. Consider a series of questions about justice and food workers:

Recall from Chapter 3, "Food Justice," that one dimension of justice is distributive justice, which is concerned with the fair distribution throughout society of important things. Theories disagree about what must be distributed fairly: goods and services (such as income and health care), well-being, opportunities (such as educational opportunities), capabilities, or something else? Theorists also disagree about what counts as a just or fair distribution. Does fairness require that there is an *equal* distribution of important things, such as everyone having the same income, or everyone having equal educational opportunities? Or is a fair distribution one that reflects what people deserve based on their own choices and efforts? Or does fairness require only that everyone has an adequate level of important things, enough food or money or opportunities? Or does fairness not require any particular distribution, but simply requires that people acquire things in fair ways—for example, people acquire money by earning it or being given it, not by stealing it? Or should we just try to achieve the distribution that maximizes overall utility or social welfare, as utilitarianism demands?

Even if individual employers do not exploit or coerce their workers, can the resulting distribution of income and other important goods be unjust? If the distribution that results from food system workers getting these low wages is an unjust distribution, what is the right remedy? Should there be a higher minimum wage for workers—for example, a higher minimum wage for fast-food workers, as many in the food justice movement have argued? Should there be more redistribution of income, for example through more generous public assistance programs or subsidized social services, such as healthcare?

In the reading "Food Security and Food Sovereignty" from Chapter 3, Paul Thompson notes that the treatment and low pay of many farmworkers is unjust according to both Rawlsian and Marxist theories of justice. But, as Thompson points out, there are other views:

> Farming and food-system employment have always been poorly compensated, in part because the skills needed for this work have historically been virtually ubiquitous. When anyone could do the manual work of farming, food processing and cooking, there was no reason for employers to pay more than the lowest wage that the market could bear. And even as economic growth and social change have produced a working class having little to no familiarly with farming and food production, there have always been plenty of immigrants with farm backgrounds who are eager to take on these jobs. If this is just the workings of the labor market, then philosophers with a certain kind of libertarian or neoliberal mindset may find the circumstances of food-system workers to be regrettable but still not a true injustice. The appropriate response will occur when enough of them attain the education that will allow them to compete for better jobs. When no one will take these food-system jobs because there are better jobs to be had, scarcity in the labor pool will force food industry firms to pay more (p. 163).

So on the libertarian and neoliberal views, farmworkers' low wages are not unfair or unjust. Are those views right? When workers are paid low wages even though they perform a difficult job and work long hours, are they not getting fair wages? Or are these low wages fair, because they are the wages that the labor market supports?

This long series of questions brings out that there are several important things to keep in mind as you read the selections in this chapter: First, which aspects of food work are morally objectionable? Second, why are they objectionable? Third, who—or what—is acting objectionably? And what, if anything, ought be done to fix things?

FURTHER ISSUES

1. *Which Things Coerce and Exploit?*
It is clear that individual persons can and do exploit other persons. It is clear that individual persons can and do coerce other persons. Can things other than individuals exploit or coerce? Can companies? Can a social group? Can nations? Can economic systems? (People sometimes say that capitalism is coercive—is that just a figure of speech?)

2. *Use*
What is morally objectionable about using people? Is it something about the *attitude* of the user toward the used? Why is it objectionable—if it is—to use a person but not a toaster? Is it objectionable to use animals?

The talk of use might be metaphorical. Talk of turning animals and people into machines clearly is. What does it mean to say someone is being treated like a machine? What is wrong with doing so?

3. *Responsibility for Mistreatment*
Consider the treatment of workers in a slaughterhouse. Take some instance of mistreatment by a supervisor. Who is responsible for that? The supervisor? What if the supervisor is following his supervisor's orders? The boss of the slaughterhouse? The company's board of directors? The consumer of the product the slaughterhouse helps make? The economic and legal system, which makes the mistreatment profitable and doesn't effectively punish the supervisor?

At the end of his reading in this chapter, Pachirat wonders whether people who eat meat or slaughterhouse workers are "more morally responsible for the killing of animals." He wonders whether all the workers bear equal responsibility or only the "knocker" himself. Adrienne Martin argues that consumers who buy the fruits of wrongful labor bear *more* responsibility for what they do than employers.[10] She argues that employers are just following orders, whereas consumers aren't and, moreover, that it is easier for consumers to avoid buying wrongfully produced food than it is for employers to quit and find new employment or to lobby for better conditions. What do you think about this?

4. *Generalizing from Food Work*
Much of what is saddening about food workers has nothing peculiar to do with their being food workers. People doing all sorts of jobs work long, hard hours for low pay with little

hope of advancement. There are two quite different responses you might have to this: First, you think, "This just shows that there is nothing wrong with food work. Lots of people have jobs with such conditions and there is no ethical objection to those jobs, so there is no ethical objection to food work." Second, alternatively, you could think, "This shows that there is something wrong with a lot of jobs. Lots of people have jobs with conditions like those of food workers and, since there is an ethical objection to food work, it follows that there is an ethical objection to these other, similar jobs." Which do you prefer?

5. Inequality
Part of what chafes about food workers is the huge gap between the worst-off workers and the best-off workers: not only people with supervisory jobs in the slaughterhouse or in the fields but also the owners of the slaughterhouse or fields. (This is replicated in the NFL, where even the best-paid football players are typically much less rich than team owners. The coaches are, in some ways, worse off: They have no hope of making anything like the money the players do but also work long, brutal hours albeit without the physical violence the players' jobs include.) When are such gaps objectionable? Why are they objectionable?

6. Paternalism
What do you think of a paternalistic justification for forbidding workers to work in particularly awful agricultural jobs? Imagine someone stopping a worker from doing a job he would willingly, knowingly, freely do on the grounds that doing so is in his best interest. That's a paradigmatically paternalistic justification. Is it a *good* justification? It seems like a good justification with a young child—why? And why, if at all, is the child case relevantly different from the adult worker's case? (See also Chapter 13, "Paternalism and Public Health.")

FURTHER READING

Agricultural Labor

Bowe, John. 2003. "Nobodies," *The New Yorker*, April 21.
———. 2007. *Nobodies*. New York: Random House.
Estabrook, Barry. 2012. *Tomatoland*. Kansas City, MO: Andrews McMeel.
Gray, Margaret. 2013. *Labor and the Locavore*. Berkeley, CA: University of California Press.
Holmes, Seth. 2013. *Fresh Fruit, Broken Bodies*. Berkeley, CA: University of California Press.
McMillan, Tracie. 2012. *The American Way of Eating*. New York: Scribner.
———. 2012. "As Common as Dirt," *The American Prospect* 7:23.
———. 2013. "Interview with Seth Holmes," *Civil Eats*, October 7. http://traciemcmillan.com/articles/fresh-fruit-broken-bodies-the-human-cost-of-american-agriculture/
Marosi, Richard. 2014. "Product of Mexico," *Los Angeles Times*, December 7–14.

Class, Gender, Race, Workers

Holmes, Seth. 2013. *Fresh Fruit, Broken Bodies*. Berkeley, CA: University of California Press.
Pachirat, Timothy. 2011. *Every Twelve Seconds*. New Haven, CT: Yale University Press.
Schlosser, Eric. 2001. *Fast Food Nation*. New York: Houghton Mifflin.

Striffler, Steve. 2005. *Chicken: The Dangerous Transformation of America's Favorite Food.* New Haven, CT: Yale University Press.

Trice, Dawn Turner. 2006. "Immigration Issues Real in Delta," *Chicago Tribune*, June 11.

Coercion

Anderson, Scott. 2011. "Coercion," in *Stanford Encyclopedia of Philosophy,* ed. Edward N. Zalta. http://plato.stanford.edu/entries/coercion/

Wertheimer, Alan. 1988. *Coercion.* Princeton, NJ: Princeton University Press.

Consent

Eyal, Nir. 2011. "Informed Consent," in *Stanford Encyclopedia of Philosophy,* ed. Edward N. Zalta. http://plato.stanford.edu/entries/informed-consent/.

O'Neill, Onora. 2007. "Onora O'Neill on Medical Consent" (podcast), *Philosophy Bites.* http://philosophybites.com/2007/10/onora-oneill-on.html.

Equality

Anderson, Elizabeth. 1999. "What Is the Point of Equality?" *Ethics* 109: 287–337.

Parfit, Derek. 2002. "Equality and Priority," *Ratio* 10: 202–221.

Exploitation

Liberto, Hallie. 2014. "Exploitation and the Vulnerability Clause," *Ethical Theory and Moral Practice* 17, no. 4: 619–629.

Sample, Ruth. 2003. *Exploitation.* Lanham, MD: Rowman and Littlefield.

Valdman, Mikhail. 2009. "A Theory of Wrongful Exploitation," *Philosophers' Imprint* 9: 1–14.

Wertheimer, Alan, and Matt Zwolinski. 2012. "Exploitation," in *Stanford Encyclopedia of Philosophy* (Summer 2015 ed.), ed. Edward N. Zalta. http://plato.stanford.edu/archives/sum2015/entries/exploitation/.

Paternalism

Conly, Sarah. 2012. *Against Autonomy.* Cambridge: Cambridge University Press.

Dworkin, Gerald. 1972. "Paternalism," *The Monist* 56: 64–84.

Hands, Barbara. 2015. "Paternalism and the Law," *Philosophy Now* (June/July 2015). https://philosophynow.org/issues/71/Paternalism_and_the_Law.

Mill, J. S. 1978. *On Liberty.* Indianapolis: Hackett.

Shiffrin, Seana. 2000. "Paternalism, Unconscionability Doctrine, and Accommodation," *Philosophy and Public Affairs* 29: 205–250.

Restaurant Labor

Ehrenreich, Barbara. 2011. *Nickel and Dimed* (10th anniv. ed.). New York: Picador.

Jayaraman, Saru. 2013. *Behind the Kitchen Door*. Ithaca, NY: Cornell University Press.

McMillan, Tracie. 2012. *The American Way of Eating*. New York: Scribner.

———. 2012. "I Got Hired to Do the Hardest Job at Applebee's," *Slate,* February 15. http://www.slate.com/articles/life/food/2012/02/tracie_mcmillan_s_the_american_way_of_eating_doing_the_hardest_job_at_applebee_s.html.

Slaughterhouse Labor

Pachirat, Timothy. 2011. *Every Twelve Seconds*. New Haven, CT: Yale University Press.

Schlosser, Eric. 2001. *Fast Food Nation*. New York: Houghton Mifflin.

Sinclair, Upton. 2005. *The Jungle*. Clayton, DE: Prestwick House.

Striffler, Steve. 2005. *Chicken: The Dangerous Transformation of America's Favorite Food*. New Haven, CT: Yale University Press.

Slavery

Bowe, John. 2003. "Nobodies," *The New Yorker,* April 21.

———. 2007. *Nobodies*. New York: Random House.

Coalition of Immokalee Workers, "Anti-Slavery Campaign." http://ciw-online.org/slavery/.

Coleman, Nathaniel. "What Is Wrong with 'What Is Wrong with Slavery?'?" Unpublished manuscript. DOI: 10.1007/s11572-014-9346-x.

Estabrook, Barry. 2012. *Tomatoland*. Kansas City, MO: Andrews McMeel.

Hare, R. M. 1979. "What Is Wrong with Slavery?" *Philosophy and Public Affairs* 8: 103–121.

U.S. Department of State. 2010. "Trafficking in Persons Report," http://www.state.gov/j/tip/rls/tiprpt/2010/.

The Trolley Problem

Foot, Philippa. 1967. "The Problem of Abortion and the Doctrine of Double Effect," *Oxford Review* 5: 5–15.

Thomson, Judith Jarvis. 1985. "The Trolley Problem," *Yale Law Journal* 94: 1395–1415.

———. 2008. "Turning the Trolley," *Philosophy and Public Affairs* 36: 359–374.

Use

Guerrero, Alexander A. 2014. "Appropriately Using People as a Means," forthcoming in *Criminal Law and Philosophy*.

Kant, Immanuel. 1996. *Groundwork of the Metaphysics of Morals*. New York: Cambridge University Press.

Korsgaard, Christine. 2015. "Treated Like Animals," *Practical Ethics* (blog). http://blog.practicalethics.ox.ac.uk/2015/01/treated-like-animals-guest-post-by-christine-korsgaard/

NOTES

1. Barry Estabrook, "Politics of the Plate," *Gourmet*, May 6, 2008. http://www.gourmet.com/foodpolitics/2008/05/politicsoftheplate_05_06_08.html.

2. For more on the transformed campaign, the Fair Food Program, a campaign that now includes a commitment to improved worker treatment as well as improved worker wages, see http://ciw-online.org/campaign-for-fair-food/.

3. Online at Ciw-online.org/blog/2015/01/presidential-medal-combatting-slavery/

4. We arrived at this number using data here: http://www.splcenter.org/get-informed/publications/injustice-on-our-plates; and here: http://www.ncfh.org/uploads/3/8/6/8/38685499/fs-facts_about_farm-workers.pdf.

5. On-line at http://grist.org/food/how-can-we-stop-farmer-suicides/

6. Steve Striffler, *Chicken* (New Haven, CT: Yale University Press, 2005), 127–128.

7. The topics are discussed in various readings listed in the "Further Readings" section: Extensively in Holmes (2013) and Pachirat (2011) and also to some extent in Bowe (2007), Estabrook (2012), Schlosser (2001), and Striffler (2005).

8. Upton Sinclair, *The Jungle* (Clayton, DE: Prestwick House, 2005), 133; emphasis ours.

9. National Farm Worker Ministry, "Farm Workers and Immigration." http://nfwm.org/education-center/farm-worker-issues/farm-workers-immigration/.

10. Adrienne Martin, "Consumer Complicity in Factory Farming," in *Philosophy Comes to Dinner,* ed. Chignell et al. (New York: Routledge, 2015).

SETH HOLMES

Farm Workers

This reading comes from Seth Holmes's book *Fresh Fruit, Broken Bodies*, documenting conditions for Mexican workers on large farms in California and Washington, drawing on years of research Holmes conducted as a medical anthropologist working and living alongside farmworkers.

The reading substantiates the idea that farmworkers on industrial farms are in some ways analogous to animals on industrial farms: In order to produce benefits for others, they suffer physically and mentally and lead lives that are shortened by their positions. And, just as Peter Singer urges that animals are mistreated due to speciesism, Holmes argues that workers are mistreated due to classism, nationalism, racism, and sexism. These selections offer detailed, academic looks at portions of the big picture drawn by the Barry Estabrook reading in Chapter 1, "The Ethically Troubling Food System."

SOCIAL SUFFERING AND THE VIOLENCE CONTINUUM

During both of my summers of fieldwork on the Tanaka Brothers Farm, I picked berries once or twice a week and experienced several forms of pain for days afterward. I often felt sick to my stomach the night before picking, due to stress about picking the minimum weight. As I picked, my knees continually hurt; I tried different positions, sometimes squatting, sometimes kneeling, sometimes propped up on just one knee. Each time I stood up to take my berries to be weighed, it felt as if a warm liquid like my own blood was running down my pants and into my shoes. All day, I leaned forward to see the strawberries below the leaves, and my neck and back began to hurt by late morning. For two or three days after picking, I took ibuprofen and sometimes used the hot tub in a local private gym to ease the aches, all too aware of the inequality of having access to such amenities.

After the first week of picking on the farm, I asked two young female pickers how their knees and backs felt. One replied that she could no longer feel anything ("*Mi cuerpo ya no puede sentir nada*"), though her knees still hurt sometimes. The other said that her knees, back, and hips are always hurting ("*Siempre me duelen*"). Later that same afternoon, one of the young Triqui men I saw playing basketball every day the week before the harvest told me that he and his friends could no longer run because their bodies hurt so much ("*Ya no corremos; no aguantamos*"). In fact, even the vistas that were so sublime and beautiful to me had come to mean ugliness, pain, and work to the pickers. On multiple occasions, my Triqui companions responded with confusion to my exclamations about the area's beauty and explained that the fields were "pure work" (*puro trabajo*).

Knee, back, and hip pain are only a few of the ways in which the social context of migrant farmwork—especially living and working conditions—affects the bodies of my Triqui companions. These pains are examples of the structural violence of social hierarchies becoming embodied in the form of suffering and sickness. The shacks in which the Triqui pickers live, the grueling conditions in which they work, and the danger they face in the border desert function as mechanisms through which structural violence produces suffering. I use the word *suffering* to indicate not only physical sickness but also mental, existential, and interpersonal anguish.

Scheper-Hughes and Bourgois propose understanding violence as a continuum, including not only direct political violence but also structural, symbolic, and everyday violence.[1] They suggest that these wartime and peacetime expressions of violence potentiate, produce, conceal, and legitimate one another. Bourgois defines direct political violence as "targeted physical violence and terror administered by official authorities and those opposing [them]."[2] Structural violence is manifested as social inequalities and hierarchies, often along social categories of class, race, gender, and sexuality.[3] Symbolic violence, as defined by Bourdieu, is the internalization and legitimation of hierarchy, "exercised through cognition and misrecognition, knowledge and sentiment, with the unwitting consent of the dominated."[4] Scheper-Hughes uses the phrase "everyday violence" to describe the normalized micro-interactional expressions of violence on domestic, delinquent, and institutional levels that produce a common sense of violence and humiliation.[5] Bourgois poses this challenge to ethnographers: "to check the impulse to sanitize and instead to clarify the chains of causality that link structural, political, and symbolic violence in the production of an everyday violence that buttresses unequal power relations and distorts efforts at resistance."[6]

This chapter focuses ethnographic attention on "how the poor suffer" in this case the poorest of the poor on the farm, the Triqui strawberry pickers. Much of the suffering of Triqui migrant laborers can be understood as a direct embodiment of the violence continuum. During my fieldwork, many Triqui people experienced notable health problems affecting their ability to function in their work and families. I discuss in particular the experiences of [two] Triqui migrants whom I came to know well, Abelino [and] Crescencio. . . While the suffering of Triqui berry pickers in general is determined by their position at the bottom of various hierarchies, each of these vignettes serves to underscore the embodiment of a different expression of the violence continuum. Abelino's knee injury highlights the physical and mental suffering caused by the structural violence of segregated labor. Crescencio's headache brings to light the embodied effects of the verbal and symbolic violence of racist insult and stereotype. At the same time, each case draws linkages between the embodiment of the primary form of violence and its interactions with the rest of the violence continuum.

ABELINO AND THE PAIN OF PICKING

The first Triqui picker whom I met when I visited the Skagit Valley was Abelino, a thirty-five-year-old father of four. He, his wife, Abelina, and their children lived together in a small shack near me in the labor camp farthest from the main road. During one conversation over homemade tacos in his shack, Abelino explained in Spanish why Triqui people have to leave their hometowns in Mexico.

> In Oaxaca, there's no work for us. There's no work. There's nothing. When there's no money, you don't know what to do. And shoes, you can't get any. A shoe like this [*pointing to his tennis shoes*] costs about 300 Mexican pesos. You have to work two weeks to buy a pair of shoes. A pair of pants costs 300. It's difficult. We come here and it is a little better, but you still suffer

> in the work. Moving to another place is also difficult. Coming here with the family and moving around to different places, we suffer. The children miss their classes and don't learn well. Because of this, we want to stay here only for a season with [legal immigration] permission and let the children study in Mexico. Do we have to migrate to survive? Yes, we do.

The economic situation in the Triqui Zone of Oaxaca is both depressed and depressing. To keep their homes and support their families in Oaxaca, they must leave to work. Oaxaca's economic depression is linked to discriminatory international policies—such as NAFTA—originating in the United States as well as unequal economic practices with colonialist roots in Mexico. Abelino describes some of the ways in which the transitory nature of migration leads to suffering on many levels. Moving from place to place allows for the most earnings to be saved toward whichever goal each worker may have as well as to be sent back to family members in Oaxaca. At the same time, this ongoing movement leads to periods of homelessness, fear of apprehension and deportation, uprooting of connections and relationships outside of the migration circuit, and loss of productive studies and continuity for children. Moving from state to state also functionally disqualifies workers, including pregnant women and recent mothers, from social and health services for which they would otherwise be eligible.

Later that same night, Abelino explained the difficulty of entering the United States without official documents: "We have to migrate to survive. And we have to cross the border, suffering and walking two days and two nights, sometimes five days, to get here to work and support the American people. Because they don't work like we do. They just get rich working a light job like the shops, the offices, but they don't work in the field. We Mexicans from many Mexican states come here to maintain our families. We want to get permission to enter just for a harvest season and then return to our country."

Crossing the border from Mexico to the United States involves incredible financial, physical, and emotional suffering for Triqui migrants. Each migrant pays approximately $1,500 to $2,500 to various people along the way for rides and guidance.

They walk hurriedly in physically impossible conditions, getting speared by cactus spines, attempting to avoid rattlesnakes, climbing and jumping over numerous barbed-wire fences—all the while using no flashlights in order to avoid being seen by the Border Patrol and vigilante groups. As a rule, they do not bring enough food or water because of the weight. Every step of the way carries a fearful awareness that at any moment one might be apprehended and deported by the Border Patrol, which would entail beginning the nightmarish trek all over again after figuring out a way to scrape together enough money for another attempt.

The suffering Abelino talked about most, however, related to picking berries on the farm. After arriving in the Skagit Valley, many Triqui people attempt to obtain various types of jobs, including in construction or in the farm's processing plant, but the only job they are offered is the harvest of berries. Early in my time on the farm, Abelino explained to me the experience of picking: "You pick with your hands, bent over, kneeling like this [*demonstrating with both knees fully bent and his head bowed forward*]. Your back hurts; you get knee pains and pain here [*touching his hip*]. When it rains, you get pretty mad and you have to keep picking. They don't give lunch breaks. You have to work every day like that to make anything. You suffer a lot in work." He explained that although picking blueberries in the autumn is not as physically strenuous as harvesting strawberries in the summer, one makes significantly less money.

One day in the middle of my first summer on the farm, like the other mornings I picked, I followed Abelino, his wife, and their oldest daughter as they led the way to the field we were to pick that morning. It was pitch black before the sun rose, and we wore heavy clothes in layers to take off as the sun came up. We walked through a line, and our picking cards for the day were marked with our beginning time, though, as we came to expect, the cards were marked as though we had arrived thirty minutes later. We were assigned rows next to each other and began picking into our individual buckets without saying a word. As usual, I was quickly left behind in the row, though I had learned to pick relatively quickly using both hands at once. We picked as fast as we could while squatting, alternating back and forth from right to left to pick both rows of berries next to us.

In the middle of one of the rows, while picking, Abelino experienced acute, intense pain in his right knee during one of the countless times he pivoted from the right to the left. At the end of the day, he told me about the incident. He said it felt like his foot would not move, and then the pain suddenly began. The pain was most intense on the inside of the knee just behind the kneecap. He also felt like there was something loose moving around within his knee. He attempted to keep working for the rest of the day in the vain hope that the pain would go away. He tried picking with his knees straightened while he bent at the hips, but this hurt almost as intensely and slowed him down significantly, and he almost missed the minimum weight. At the end of the day, as we approached our cars to drive back to the camp, Abelino told our supervisor about the incident. The supervisor said simply, "OK," and drove away in his white farm pickup without any follow-up. Unsure of what to do, Abelino tried to pick again the next day in great pain and once again barely picked the minimum. Abelino ended up seeing four doctors, a physical therapist, and a Triqui healer, as well as attempting to go through the bureaucracy of worker's compensation. In the end, his pain was diagnosed by a rehabilitation medicine physician as patellar tendonitis, or inflammation of the tendons behind the kneecap.

The social and political genesis of Abelino's knee pain could not have been clearer. His pain was caused unequivocally by the fact that he, as an undocumented Triqui man, had been excluded by both international market inequalities and local discriminatory practices from all but one narrow and particularly traumatic labor position. This occupation required him to bend over seven days a week, turning back and forth, in all kinds of weather, picking strawberries as fast as he possibly could. Tendonitis is understood biomedically to be inflammation caused by repetitive strain and stress on a particular tendon. The inflammation can be brought on over years of overwork and worsened by individual straining events. Abelino's position at the bottom of the farm's ethnicity-citizenship-labor hierarchy meant that he, like hundreds of other Triqui pickers with knee, back, and hip pain, was forced into the precise conditions ripe for the harvesting of chronic joint inflammation and deterioration. Furthermore, his suffering was compounded by the fact that he, like other Triqui people from Oaxaca, had been driven by the results of international economic policies and the expansion of multinational corporations to cross a mortally dangerous border and then live in fear and remain transient wherever he worked, despondently reproducing the same situation for his children, who could not stay in school to seek a better future. In this way, his body was victim to multiple layers of structural violence.

At the beginning of the following summer, Abelino told me he was still suffering from knee pain. Nonetheless, to improve the likelihood of survival of his family and to continue working toward the goal of putting a roof on his house in San Miguel, he again attempted to pick.

CRESCENCIO'S HEADACHE: STRUCTURE AND GAZE IN MIGRANT HEALTH CARE

Crescencio . . . developed excruciating headaches after being called racist names and treated unfairly on the job and explained that he wanted treatment before he might become agitated or violent with his family. He explained that he had seen several physicians in the United States and Mexico as well as a traditional Triqui healer, but none of their therapies had been effective over the long term. He asked me if I had any medicines I could give him. Not knowing what else to do, I suggested Crescencio go to the local migrant clinic to see if they could try something new for his problem. I remembered the algorithm for headache diagnosis and treatment that I had learned in medical school and wondered if the doctors in the migrant clinic might use something similar, moving through trials of medications for tension, cluster, and migraine headaches. A week

later, Crescencio told me that he had seen one of the doctors in the clinic but that she didn't give him any medicines. He said that she had referred him for therapy and asked me what that meant. I described paying someone to sit with you, ask you questions, and listen to your answers in order to help you work through your feelings and thoughts and help you decrease your unhealthy use of substances. At the same time, I knew he barely had money to go to the clinic the first time, and it was unlikely he would spend $15 a session for psychotherapy or substance abuse therapy (though that would seem a bargain to others).

After several weeks of trying to make an appointment with the doctor who saw him at the migrant clinic, I was able to ask her about Crescencio's headache. She thought for a minute and then looked at Crescencio's chart to refresh her memory. She told me that she met with him once briefly over a month ago. She had asked him to cut back on his drinking and then return to see her for further evaluation. However, he ended up returning at a different time and seeing a different doctor, the locums physician who spoke only English. After looking at her chart note and the notes from the locums physician, she told me about Crescencio's situation from her perspective.

Well, yes, he thinks that he is the victim and thinks that the alcohol or the headache makes him beat his wife . . . but really he is the perpetrator and everyone else is the victim. And until he owns his problem, he can't really change.

I'm on the CPS [Child Protective Services] subcommittee, and so I've learned a lot about domestic violence. What we've seen is that nothing really works, none of these migraine medicines or anything, but to put people in jail because then they see a show of force. That's the only thing that works because then they have to own the problem as theirs and they start to change. It's a complex psychosocial problem, a patterned behavior. Probably his dad treated him this way, beat him, and was alcoholic, and now that's what he does. It's a classic case of domestic abuse.

He came to see me once, and I told him to come back two weeks later after not drinking. But he didn't come back two weeks later. Instead, he came back a month later and saw one of our locums. Apparently, he told the doc something about when people at work tell him what to do, it makes him mad, and that's what gives him a headache.

Obviously he has issues. He needs to learn how to deal with authority. We referred him to therapy. Do you know if he's going to therapy?

As in Abelino's health care experiences, this doctor was pressed for time and made assumptions without fully exploring the patient's psychosocial realities. In Crescencio's case, the physician made the assumption that his description of feeling agitated and angry indicated that he had already beaten his wife and continued to beat her. Without enough time to pay full attention to the patient's concerns and focus on the headache and its source, she focused primarily on assumed intimate partner violence. While paying attention to the possibility of such violence is of utmost importance, this focus may have led to a short-circuiting of the treatment possibilities for Crescencio. Without being able to explore all the possible therapies for severe headaches, the physician retrospectively advocated incarcerating people like Crescencio.

After reading in the chart that Crescencio's headaches were due to mistreatment from supervisors on the farm, the physicians recommended therapy to help him overcome his "issues" with authority and treat his substance use. Without the lenses to see that Crescencio's suffering was determined by multiple levels of social inequality and disrespect, they inadvertently blamed the headache on the patient's psychological makeup. In the end, their primary interventions were twofold. First, they told him to stop drinking cold turkey, even though drinking was the only effective intervention he had found after years of active searching. Unfortunately, though perhaps expectedly, he was not able to stop drinking. Second, the physicians referred him to therapy, without the patient understanding what this meant. Therapy performed in order to help a patient accept poor treatment from supervisors may be helpful to the patient in developing coping mechanisms in the midst of a difficult situation. Substance abuse therapy may help a patient reduce the harm of substance use and develop healthier behaviors. At the same time, therapy may also promote the patient's acceptance of his place in a labor hierarchy that may

include the disrespect and racist insults that Crescencio experienced. In this way, the migrant clinic's interventions were not only ineffective but also inadvertently complicit with the social determinants of suffering, serving to reinforce the social structures producing Crescencio's labor position and headache in the first place.

Crescencio's headache is a result most distally of the international economic inequalities forcing him to migrate and become a farmworker in the first place and more proximally of the racialized mistreatment he endures in the farm's ethnicity and citizenship hierarchy. These socially produced headaches lead Crescencio to become agitated and angry with his family and to drink, thus embodying the stereotype of Mexican migrants as alcoholic and potentially violent. The racialized mistreatment that produces his headaches is then justified through the embodied stereotypes that were produced in part by that mistreatment in the first place. Finally, due to powerful economic structures affecting the migrant clinic as well as limited lenses of perception in biomedicine, this justifying symbolic violence is subtly reinforced throughout Crescencio's health care experiences. . . .

SUFFERING THE HIERARCHY

On the Tanaka farm, the hierarchies of perceived ethnicity and citizenship correlate closely with the labor and housing pecking order. On further inspection, it becomes clear that this whole complex maps onto a hierarchy of suffering. Attending to the body in an analysis of the violence continuum in U.S.-Mexico migration allows deeper understanding of the links among class, ethnicity, citizenship, health, and sickness. In many ways, employees of the berry farm in the Skagit Valley come to embody power differentials and prejudice. The working and living conditions, degree of respect received, and access to political power of each of the groups within the labor hierarchy lead to different forms of suffering from top to bottom. A focus on the embodiment of different expressions of violence lends clarity to the reciprocal importance of social forces to bodily suffering.

In general in U.S. agriculture, the more Mexican and the more "indigenous" one is perceived to be, the more psychologically stressful, physically strenuous, and dangerous one's job. Thus where a migrant body falls on the dual ethnic-labor hierarchy shapes how much and what kind of suffering must be endured. The farther down the ladder from Anglo-American U.S. citizen to undocumented indigenous Mexican one is positioned, the more degrading the treatment by supervisors, the more physically taxing the work, the more exposure to weather and pesticides, the more fear of the government, the less comfortable one's housing, and the less control over one's own time.

Of course, the people on every level of the hierarchy suffer. Yet suffering is also roughly cumulative from top to bottom. Some of the social and mental forms of suffering are described as anxieties over profitability and increasing competition by the farm executives, over farm profitability and disrespect from supervisors by the administrative assistants, and over racist insult from supervisors and familial economic survival by the berry pickers. On the more strictly physical level of suffering, this rough accumulation continues to hold. For example, the farm executives worry most about what are sometimes called the diseases of the upper middle class, like heart disease and breast cancer. The administrative assistants worry about these sicknesses, as well as repetitive stress injury like carpal tunnel syndrome. The strawberry pickers are at risk for heart disease and many cancers but worry most about pesticide poisoning, musculoskeletal injury, and chronic pain.

The Triqui people inhabit the bottom rung of the pecking order in the Skagit. They live in the coldest and wettest shacks in the most hidden labor camp with no insulation, no heat, and no wooden ceiling under the tin roof. They hold the most stressful, humiliating, and physically strenuous jobs working seven days a week without breaks while exposed to pesticides and weather. Accordingly, the Triqui pickers bear an unequal share of sickness and pain. . . .

Mexican pickers are not paid by the hour. Instead they are called "contract workers" and are paid a certain amount per unit of fruit harvested. Most live in the camp farthest from farm head-quarters, which has no heat or insulation and no wood under the tin roof. Each day, they are told a minimum amount of fruit they must pick. The crop manager calculates the minimum to make sure that each picker brings in more than enough to be worth paying them at least the legal state minimum wage. If they pick less on two occasions, they are fired and kicked out of the camp. The first contract picker I met, Abelino, explained, "The hourly jobs, the salaried jobs are better because you can count on how much you will make. But they don't give those jobs to us."

Approximately twenty-five people, mostly mestizos with a few Mixtec and Triqui men, pick apples. The field boss, Abby, explained to me that picking apples is the hardest job on the farm. Apple pickers work five to ten hours a day, seven days a week, carrying a heavy bag of apples over their shoulders. They repeatedly climb up and down ladders to reach the apples. This job is sought after because it is known to be the highest-paid picking position.

However, the majority of pickers—350 to 400—work in the strawberry fields for one month, followed by three months in the blueberry fields. Other than a few Mixtecs, they are almost all Triqui men, women, and teenagers (agricultural workers can legally be fourteen or older). Most Triqui pickers come with other family members, and most hail from the same village, San Miguel, in the mountains of Oaxaca. The official contract pay for strawberry pickers is 14 cents per pound of strawberries. This means that pickers must bring in fifty-one pounds of deleafed strawberries every hour because the farm is required to pay Washington State minimum wage—$7.16 at the time. In order to meet this minimum, pickers take few or no breaks from 5:00 A.M. until the afternoon when that field is completed. Nonetheless, they are reprimanded by some crew bosses and called *perros* (dogs), *burros, Oaxacos* (a derogatory mispronunciation of "Oaxacans"). Many do not eat or drink anything before work so they do not have to take time to use the bathroom. They work as hard and fast as they can, arms flying in the air as they kneel in the dirt, picking and running with their buckets of berries to the checkers. Although they are referred to as contract workers, this is misleading. On a few instances, the pay per unit was changed by the crop managers without warning or opportunity for negotiation.

Strawberry pickers work simultaneously with both hands in order to make the minimum. They pop the green stem and leaves off of each strawberry and do their best to avoid the green and the rotten berries. During my fieldwork, I picked once or twice a week and experienced gastritis, headaches, and knee, back, and hip pain for days afterward. I wrote in a field note after picking, "It honestly felt like pure torture." Triqui pickers work seven days a week, rain or shine, without a day off until the last strawberry is processed. Occupying the bottom of the ethnic-labor hierarchy, Triqui pickers bear an unequal share of health problems, from idiopathic back and knee pains to slipped vertebral disks, from type 2 diabetes to premature births and developmental malformations.[7] The brief profiles below highlight the economic and physical hardships of the pickers on the farm and on the U.S.-Mexico border, touching on the importance of language, ethnicity, and education in the organization of the farm labor hierarchy.

Marcelina is a twenty-eight-year-old Triqui mother of two. She is a cousin of Samuel (introduced in chapter 1), grew up in San Miguel, and is one of the other people with whom I would share a slum apartment in Central California in the winter. Every summer, a local Skagit Valley non-profit organizes a seminar on migrant farm labor. The seminar involves a visit to a farm and labor camp as well as several brief presentations and live interviews with people from all aspects of migrant labor, from pickers to growers, Border Patrol agents to social workers. Most of the attendees are white, middle-class adults who live in the area, along with a handful of mestizo and indigenous Mexican farmworkers. Late in my first summer of fieldwork, Marcelina was invited to speak at the seminar about her experiences migrating and picking. Shyly, she approached the translator, holding her one-year-old daughter, and spoke in Spanish, her second language.

Good afternoon. I am Marcelina. I come here to the United States to work. A man left me with two children. I wanted to come here to make money, but no. I don't even make enough to send to Oaxaca to my mom who is taking care of my son. Sometimes the strawberry goes poorly, your back hurts, and you don't make anything.

I am sorry; I don't speak Spanish well. Pure Triqui. [*Chuckles*] Pure Triqui.

It's very difficult here. The farm camp manager doesn't want to give a room to a single woman. So I am living with this family over here [*pointing to a Triqui family of five in the audience*]. One gains nothing here, nothing to survive. Besides that, I have a daughter here with me, and I don't make anything to give her. Working and working. Nothing. I've been here four years and nothing.

It's very difficult for a person here. I came to make money, like I thought, "Here on the other side [of the border] there is money and good money," but no. We're not able to make enough to survive.

And then sometimes [the checkers] steal pounds. Sometimes rotten berries make it into the bucket— "Eat that one!" they say, throwing it into your face. They don't work well. And there are hardly any good berries this time of year, pure rotten ones.

This is not good. You don't make enough even to eat. I have two children, and it is very ugly here, very ugly to work in the field. That's how it is. Sometimes you want to speak up, but no. You can't speak to them.

After speaking about the difficulties of farmwork in Washington State, Marcelina was asked to talk about the migration process in general. She continued:

There in Oaxaca, we don't have work. There are no jobs there. Only the men work sometimes, but since there are many children in my family, the men didn't make money for me and my son. That's why I wanted to come here, to make money, but no—no—no. You don't make anything here; you don't have anything to survive. I wanted to work, to move ahead [*salir adelante*] with my children, to take them ahead [*salir adelante*].

I have been here four years without seeing my son.

In California, there is no work, just pruning, and you don't make any money because of the same thing, we don't know Spanish, and that is because we don't have enough money to study. Parents have to suffer in order to send their children to school, buy food and school uniforms. I have lots of sisters back there, studying, but I couldn't study. There are many children who don't go to school because they lack money. I had to leave Oaxaca so I wouldn't suffer from hunger. I hoped I would make enough to send back to support my sisters in school. I had to give up school myself.

One of the Triqui families who welcomed me most into their lives was that of Samuel, his wife, Leticia, and their four-year-old son. As described earlier, after moving from the farm in Washington to Madera, California, I shared a three-bedroom, one-bath slum apartment with Samuel, Leticia, and their son; Marcelina and her daughter; Samuel's sister and her son; Samuel's brother, his wife, and his daughter; and two other families of four. One night in the farm labor camp, while we watched a Jet Li action movie with the sound turned down and drank blue Kool Aid, Samuel described in Spanish their lives as migrant farmworkers.

Samuel: Here with Tanaka, we don't have to pay rent, but they don't pay us much. They pay 14 cents a pound. And they take out taxes, federal taxes, social security. They pay $20 a day.

. . . They don't pay fairly. If a person has 34 pounds of strawberries, 4 pounds are stolen because the checker marks only 30. It is not just. That is what bothers people most. People work a lot. They suffer. Humans suffer.

It is easy for them, but for us it is not.

In the blueberries, they steal an ounce from the little boxes and that is why the people can't move ahead [*salir adelante*]. We pick a lot of fruit, and we don't make money.

The people don't say anything. They are afraid of speaking, because the farm will fire them. We want to say things to them, but we can't because we don't have papers. Sometimes the bosses are really mean, and they'll deport you. Sometimes, when one of us says something, they point to the police, and the police can do something to us. That's why people are silent.

Seth: How much do you make each year?

Samuel: One person makes $3,000 to $5,000 a year. We are not asking to be rich. We don't come here to be rich. Yes, it's very little. They say the boss doesn't want us to earn money, and I ask myself, "Why?"

Some supervisors explain how we are going to pick or what we're supposed to do, but other supervisors are bad people or have bad tempers and don't explain well what we do or what we pick. They even scream at us,

using words you should not say. If you treat people badly, they're not going to work calmly or happily. And if we tell the boss, he might not believe us. They scream at us and call us "dumb donkeys" or "dogs." It's very ugly how they treat us.

One of Marcelina and Samuel's cousins, Joaquin, nicknamed "Gordo" or "Lobo," also lived in the slum apartment in Central California. Late in the first summer of my fieldwork, Joaquin's 1990 Aerostar minivan broke down. Most of my Triqui companions had bought old American minivans because they often cost less than $500 and could carry several people to and from the fields, the grocery store, and the local church, which gave away free food on Tuesday evenings. I stood with several of Joaquin's Triqui friends as we took turns watching and helping work on his car. At one point, the conversation turned to work, and Joaquin elaborated on the stresses and contradictions of picking.

The supervisors say they'll take away our IDs and fire us if we don't pick the minimum. They tell us we're dropping too many berries, we have to go slow so we don't drop so much. When we go slowly, we don't reach [the minimum] and "Go faster!" They tell us, "You don't know how to work," "Indian, you don't know!" We already know how to work and why the berries drop. If we go slowly, we can't make any money and we get in trouble. If we hurry up, we drop berries and they come and castigate us. "Dumb donkey!" "Dog!" We are afraid.

The first day I picked, the only people who were as slow as I was were two Latinas from Southern California and one Latino who commuted from a suburb of Seattle. After the first week, the two Latinas began picking into the same bucket in order make the minimum and keep one pay-check. The second week, I no longer saw the man from Seattle. I asked a supervisor where he had gone, assuming he had decided the work was too difficult and given up. She told me that the farm made a deal with him that if he could make it through a week picking, they would give him a job paid hourly in the processing plant. He has been "one of the hardest workers" in the plant since then. I then inquired about why the indigenous Mexicans could not get processing plant jobs. The supervisor replied, "People who live in the migrant camps cannot have those jobs; they can only pick." She considered it a farm policy without any need for explanation.

Thus marginalization begets marginalization. The indigenous Mexicans live in the migrant camps because they do not have the resources to rent apartments in town. Because they live in the camps, they are given only the worst jobs on the farm. Unofficial farm policies and practices subtly reinforce labor and ethnic hierarchies. The position of the Triqui workers, at the bottom of the hierarchy, is multiply determined by poverty, education level, language, citizenship status, and ethnicity. In addition, these factors produce each other. For example, a family's poverty cuts short an individual's education, which limits one's ability to learn Spanish (much less English), which limits one's ability to leave the bottom rung of labor and housing. Poverty, at the same time, is determined in part by the institutional racism at work against Triqui people in the first place. Segregation on the farm is the result of a complex system of feedback and feed-forward loops organized around these multiple nodes of inequality.

Beyond the Latino meta-ethnic group assigned them, Triqui strawberry pickers belong to the disadvantaged category of immigrants in the United States. Several studies show that the health status of immigrants declines with increasing time in the United States. Such health indicators as obesity, serum cholesterol, tobacco smoking, alcohol use, illicit drug use, mental illness, suicide, and death by homicide increase between first-and second-generation Mexican immigrants in this country.[8] Nutritional value of the diet of immigrants also decreases significantly during the first year in the United States.[9] Those immigrants who are undocumented have the additional negative health determinant of having to cross what one scholar has called the "most violent border in the world between two countries not at war with one another."[10] Undocumented status further increases "allostatic load"—understood biomedically as the accumulation of health risk associated with chronic stress—due to traumatic experiences crossing the border and fear of deportation.[11]

In addition, Mexican migrant farmworkers suffer poor health due to their class position. Agricultural

workers have a fatality rate five times that of all workers.[12] Moreover, agricultural workers have increased rates of nonfatal injuries, musculoskeletal pain, heart disease, and many types of cancer.[13] There is also an increased risk of stillbirth and congenital birth defects in children born near farms.[14] Furthermore, research indicates that approximately one-third to one-half of agricultural workers report chronic symptoms associated with pesticide exposure such as headache, skin and eye irritation, and flu-like syndromes.[15]

To further specify class position, migrant and seasonal farmworkers suffer the poorest health status in the agriculture industry. The vast majority of these individuals and families live below the poverty line.[16] They have increased rates of many chronic conditions, such as malnutrition, anemia, hypertension, diabetes, dermatitis, fatigue, headaches, sleep disturbances, anxiety, memory problems, sterility, blood disorders, dental problems, and abnormalities in liver and kidney function.[17] Migrant farmworkers have increased pulmonary problems to such a degree that farmwork has an effect on lung health comparable to smoking.[18] They have increased incidence of acute sicknesses such as urinary tract and kidney infections, heat stroke, anthrax, ascariasis, encephalitis, leptospirosis, rabies, salmonellosis, tetanus, and coccidioidomycosis, most of which are believed to be caused in large part by poor living and working conditions and lack of sanitary bathrooms.[19] Tuberculosis prevalence, also related to poor living conditions, is six times higher among migrant workers than in the general U.S. population.[20] and HIV infection is three times more common than in the overall U.S. and Mexican populations.[21] Finally, children of migrant farmworkers show high rates of malnutrition, vision problems, dental problems, anemia, and blood lead poisoning.[22]

Despite worse health status and a resulting need for increased health and social services, migrant farmworkers have many obstacles to accessing these services. Farmworkers are entirely or partially excluded from worker's compensation benefits in all but fifteen states.[23] The Fair Labor Standards Act of 1938 guaranteed minimum wage, time and a half wage for overtime, and restricted child labor, but it did not apply to agricultural workers. Amendments in 1966 ostensibly extended eligibility to farmworkers but disqualified the majority by excluding those on small farms and those paid piece wages. These amendments restricted child farm labor such that any age child could work nonhazardous agricultural jobs but only children at least sixteen years old could work hazardous agricultural jobs. The 1974 amendments retained the previous exclusions. Most farmworkers were excluded also by the Social Security Act and its later amendments from benefits related to unemployment, which in any case are not available to undocumented immigrants. In addition, even though migrant housing conditions are addressed in the Housing Act of 1949 and the Occupational Safety and Health Act of 1970, living conditions in labor camps continue to fall below the requirements. Finally, agricultural workers were denied the right to collective bargaining under the Wagner Act of 1935. They have gained the right to bargain only in the state of California under the Agricultural Labor Relations Act of 1975 after strong organizing by and a heavy toll of violence against the United Farm Workers (UFW). While this win led to labor improvements, the agriculture system in California for workers on farms without UFW contracts remains extremely exploitative. Furthermore, we must remember that even existing provisions for farmworkers are violated regularly because of vast power differentials and threats by employers to have undocumented migrants deported if they report violations.

Although there is a federal Migrant Health Program, it is estimated that it serves only 13 percent of the intended population of migrant workers.[24] Despite living well below the poverty line, fewer than one-third of migrant women qualify for Medicaid, primarily due to their nomadic interstate existence and their undocumented status.[25] Researchers estimate that less than 30 percent of migrant laborers have health insurance, in contrast to an estimated 84 percent of U.S. residents overall.[26] This disparity is likely to grow with the otherwise laudable health care reform of 2009 that promises—if fully implemented—to increase the rate of health insurance for U.S. citizens with no provisions for one of our most vulnerable populations, immigrant workers. Furthermore, it is estimated in California that less than 10 percent of indigenous Mexican farmworkers have health insurance, in contrast to 30 percent of their mestizo counterparts.[27] In part due to these obstacles, migrant laborers are less likely than other people to obtain preventive care, with 27 percent never receiving a routine physical exam, 25 percent never having a dental checkup, and 43 percent never receiving an eye exam.[28] In fact, many migrant workers in the United States go through significant hardships to return to Mexico for health care and cite economic, cultural, and linguistic reasons for this choice.[29] Importantly, these statistics directly contradict the popular American complaint that undocumented immigrants are the cause of the demise of the American health care system through overuse. . . .

INTERNALIZATION

During my second day picking strawberries, a tractor with long metal extensions spraying something in the air drove through the field while we picked. I asked Mateo what it was. "Do you really want to know? You sure you want the truth?" he asked. I nodded. "Dangerous insecticides," he said, shaking his head. Later in the summer, I noticed danger signs (in English only) posted on several large canisters surrounding one of the hand washing and outhouse stations at the edge of the field. Strawberry pickers worked every day without gloves as the visible pesticide residue dissolved in the mixture of strawberry juice that stained their hands dark maroon. If they ate anything, they ate it in the fields while picking, without washing their hands so as not to take time away from work and fail to pick the minimum weight. Our only education about pesticides came from a short warning cassette tape in monotone Spanish played inaudibly in one corner of a huge warehouse full of over one hundred workers and their children during one of the picker orientations. After the tape, the farm administrator in charge of the orientation asked if we had any questions. After a brief silence, he was satisfied and moved on to explain where we should sign the forms we were given, all of which were printed in English. One of the forms stated in English that we agreed not to organize.

The same week the spraying described above occurred, I received a video I had ordered from the United Farm Workers about the health dangers of pesticides. Several Triqui pickers watched it with me in the shack where Samuel's family lived. Afterward, I asked them what they thought. One told me matter-of-factly, "Pesticides affect only white Americans [*gabachos*] because your bodies are delicate and weak." Another said, "We Triquis are strong and *aguantamos* [hold out, bear, endure]." The others nodded. These ideas were reflected several times over the course of my fieldwork. One of the Triqui people with whom I traveled to Oaxaca bragged to me that there were many Triqui people in the military in Mexico because "we endure [*aguantamos*]." Here Triqui people internalized their class position through ethnic pride in perceived bodily differences that ironically aids in the naturalization and therefore reproduction of the very structures of their oppression. . . .

THE VIOLENCE OF MIGRANT FARMWORK

[The preceding] ethnography endeavors to uncover the linkages among suffering, social inequalities related to structural violence, and the normalizing symbolic violence of stereotypes and prejudices. It attempts to do this while telling the stories of indigenous Mexican migrant laborers who are largely hidden from public view. By structural violence, I mean the violence committed by configurations of social inequalities that, in the end, has injurious effects on bodies similar to the violence of a stabbing or shooting. This is what the English working men described by Friedrich Engels called "social murder."[30] Much of the structural violence

in the United States today is organized along the fault lines of class, race, citizenship, gender, and sexuality.[31]

Symbolic violence is a concept from the French sociologist Pierre Bourdieu, indicating the interrelations of social structures of inequalities and perceptions.[32] For Bourdieu, the lenses through which we perceive the social world are issued forth from that very world. Because of this, our lenses of perception match the social world from which they are produced. Thus, we come to (mis)recognize the social structures and inequalities inherent to the world as natural. Symbolic violence works through the perceptions of the "dominating" and the "dominated" (in Bourdieu's words), while it tends to benefit those with more power.[33] Each group understands not only itself but also the other to belong naturally in their positions in the social hierarchy. For example, the powerful tend to believe they deserve the successes they have had and that the powerless have brought their problems on themselves.

Structural violence—with its pernicious effects on health—and symbolic violence—with its subtle naturalization of inequalities on the farm, in the clinic, and in the media—form the nexus of violence and suffering through which the phenomenon of migrant labor in North America is produced. This [study] attempts to make sense of the lives, labor, and suffering of Triqui migrant laborers in Mexico and the United States through these concepts. More broadly, it engages a critically embodied anthropology to confront the ways in which certain classes of people become written off or deemed less human.

NOTES

1. Scheper-Hughes and Bourgois 2004; Bourgois 2001.
2. Bourgois 2001: 8.
3. Galtung 1969; Farmer 1997.
4. Bourdieu 2001.
5. Scheper-Hughes 1992, 1997.
6. Bourgois 2001: 30.
7. Holmes 2006; Kandula, Kersey, and Lurie 2004; McGuire and Georges 2003; *Migration News* 2004; Mobed, Gold, and Schenker 1992; *Rural Migration News*

2005; Rust 1990; Sakala 1987; Slesinger 1992; Villarejo 2003.

   8. Ibid.; Villarejo 2003.

   9. Villarejo 2003.

  10. McGuire and Georges 2003.

  11. Ibid.

  12. Frank et al. 2004.

  13. Ibid.

  14. Ibid.; Mobed, Gold, and Schenker 1992.

  15. Frank et al. 2004.

  16. Rust 1990; Slesinger 1992; Villarejo 2003.

  17. Slesinger 1992; Mobed, Gold, and Schenker 1992.

  18. Mobed, Gold, and Schenker 1992.

  19. Ibid.; Sakala 1987.

  20. Villarejo 2003.

  21. *Rural Migration News* 2005.

  22. Mobed, Gold, and Schenker 1992.

  23. Sakala 1987.

  24. Villarejo 2003.

  25. Kauffold et al. 2004.

  26. Health Outreach Partners 2010; Villarejo 2003; *Migration News* 2004.

  27. Mines, Nichols and Runsten 2010. See also Bade 1999.

  28. Slesinger 1992.

  29. Kauffold et al. 2004.

  30. Engels 1958.

  31. See Bourgois 1988; Eber 1995; Farmer 1992, 1997, 1999; Kleinman and Kleinman 1994; Scheper-Hughes 1992, 2002, 2003; Singer and Baer 1995. Wacquant (2004) points out potential analytical pitfalls in the overly generalized, nonspecific use of the term "structural violence." In order to avoid conflating different forms of violence, I use the phrase narrowly, staying close to Johan Galtung's (1969) as well as Scheper-Hughes and Bourgois's (2003) focus on political economic domination. The effects of structural domination are thus analyzed separately from, among other phenomena, everyday physical violence, armed political violence, and symbolic violence enacted with the complicity of the dominated (see Bourgois 2001). The phrase is helpful in indicating that social structures can do "peacetime" violence that has the same effects as other forms of violence, though on a different time scale (Engels 1958). In addition, I illustrate ethnographically the ways in which structural violence is enacted on every level of the farm's social hierarchy, not solely on the poorest or most marginalized.

  32. See Bourdieu 1997, 2001.

  33. See Bourgois 1995, 2001; Scheper-Hughes and Bourgois 2003; Klinenberg 1999.

REFERENCES

Bade, Bonnie. 1999. *"Is There a Doctor in the Field?" Underlying Conditions Affecting Access to Health Care for California Farmworkers and Their Families.* CPRC Report. [Berkeley]: California Policy Research Center, University of California.

Bourdieu, Pierre. 2000 [1997]. *Pascalian Meditations.* Stanford, CA: Stanford University Press.

———. 2001. *Masculine Domination.* Stanford, CA: Stanford University Press.

Bourgois, Philippe. 1988. "Conjugated Oppression: Class and Ethnicity among Guaymi and Kuna Banana Plantation Workers." *American Ethnologist* 15(2): 328–48.

———. 1995. *In Search of Respect: Selling Crack in El Barrio.* New York: Cambridge University Press.

———. 2001. "The Power of Violence in War and Peace: Post–Cold War Lessons from El Salvador." *Ethnography* 2 (1): 5–34.

Eber, Christine. 1995. *Women and Alcohol in a Highland Maya Town: Water of Hope, Water of Sorrow.* Austin: University of Texas Press.

Engels, Friedrich. 1958. *The Condition of the Working Class in England.* Trans. W. O. Henderson and W.H. Chaloner. Stanford, CA: Stanford University Press.

Farmer, Paul. 1992. *AIDS and Accusation: Haiti and the Geography of Blame.* Berkeley: University of California Press.

———. 1997. "On Suffering and Structural Violence: A View from Below." In *Social Suffering,* ed. Arthur Kleinman, Veena Das, and Margaret Lock, 261–83. Berkeley: University of California Press.

———. 1999. *Infections and Inequalities: The Modern Plagues.* Berkeley: University of California Press.

Frank, Arthur, Robert McKnight, Steven Kirkhorn, and Paul Gunderson. 2004. "Issues of Agricultural Safety and Health." *Annual Review of Public Health* 25: 225–45.

Galtung, Johan. 1969. "Violence, Peace, and Peace Research." *Journal of Peace Research* 6: 167–91.

Health Outreach Partners. 2010. *Breaking Down the Barriers: A National Needs Assessment on Farmworker Health Outreach.* 4th ed. Oakland, CA: Health Outreach Partners.

Holmes, Seth M. 2006a. "An Ethnographic Study of the Context of Migrant Health." *PLoS* 3 (10): e448; 1776–93. Doi: 10.1371/journal.pmed.0030448.

Kandula, Namratha, Margaret Kersey, and Nicole Lurie. 2004. "Assuring the Health of Immigrants: What the Leading Health Indicators Tell Us." *Annual Review of Public Health* 25: 357–76.

Kauffold, Andrea, Edward Zuroweste, Deliana Garcia, Carmel T. Drewes. 2004. *Breast, Cervical and Colon Cancer in Mobile Underserved Populations.* Migrant Clinicians Monograph Series. Austin, TX: Migrant Clinicians Network.

Kleinman, Arthur, and Joan Kleinman. 1991. "Suffering and Its Professional Transformation: Towards an Ethnography of Interpersonal Experience." *Culture Medicine and Psychiatry* 15 (3): 275–301.

———. 1994. "How Bodies Remember: Social Memory and Bodily Experience of Criticism, Resistance, and Delegitimation Following China's Cultural Revolution." *New Literary History* 25: 707–23.

Klinenberg, Eric. 1999. "Denaturalizing Disaster: A Social Autopsy of the 1995 Chicago Heat Wave." *Theory and Society* 28: 239–95.

Mines, Richard, Sandra Nichols, and David Runsten. 2010. "California's Indigenous Farmworkers." www.indigenousfarmworkers.org.

McGuire, Sharon, Sr., and Jane Georges. 2003. "Undocumentedness and Liminality as Health Variables." *Advances in Nursing Science* 26 (3): 185–96.

Migration News. 2004. "Labor, H-1B, Census, Health." *Migration News* 11:4.

Miyazki, Hirokazu. 2009. *The Method of Hope: Anthropology, Philosophy, and Fijian Knowledge.* Stanford: Stanford University Press.

Mobed, Ketty, Ellen Gold, and Marc Schenker. 1992. "Occupational Health Problems among Migrant and Seasonal Farm Workers." *Western Journal of Medicine* 157 (3): 367–85.

Rural Migration News. 2003. "Mexico: Migrants, Nafta." 9 (1). www.migration.ucdavis.edu/rmn.

———. 2005. "Health and Insurance." 11 (1). www.migration.ucdavis.edu/rmn.

Rust, George. 1990. "Health Status of Migrant Farmworkers: A Literature Review and Commentary." *American Journal of Public Health* 80 (10): 1213–17.

Sachs, Wolfgang, ed. 1991. *The Development Dictionary.* London: Zed Books.

Sakala, Carol. 1987. "Migrant and Seasonal Farmworkers in the United States: A Review of Health Hazards, Status, and Policy." *International Migration Review* 21 (3): 659–87.

Sassen, Saskia. 1998. *Globalization and Its Discontents.* New York: New Press.

Scheper-Hughes, Nancy. 1990. "Three Propositions for a Critically Applied Medical Anthropology." *Social Science & Medicine* 30 (2): 189–97.

———. 1992. *Death without Weeping: The Violence of Everyday Live in Brazil.* Berkeley: University of California Press.

———. 1994. "The Rebel Body: The Subversive Meanings of Illness." *Traditional Acupuncture Society Journal* 10: 3–10.

———. 1997. "People Who Get Rubbished." *New Internationalist,* no. 295: 20–22.

———. 2002. "Peace Time Crimes and the Violence of Everyday Life." *IDEAS: Journal of the National Humanities Center* 9 (1): 56–58.

———. 2003. "Why Violence: An Interdisciplinary Dialogue." Lecture, University of Massachusetts, Boston, Apr. 5.

Scheper-Hughes, Nancy, and Philippe Bourgois. 2003. "Making Sense of Violence." In *Violence in War and Peace: An Anthology,* ed. Nancy Scheper-Hughes and Philippe Bourgois, 1–31. Malden, MA: Blackwell.

———, eds. 2003. *Violence in War and Peace: An Anthology.* Malden, MA: Blackwell.

Singer, Merrill, and Hans Baer. 1995. *Critical Medical Anthropology,* Amityville, NY: Baywood Publishing.

Slesinger, Doris. 1992. "Health Status and Needs of Migrant Farm Workers in the United States: A Literature Review." *Journal of Rural Health* 8 (3): 227–34.

Villarejo, Don. 2003. "The Health of U.S. Hired Farm Workers." *Annual Review of Public Health* 24: 175–93.

Wacquant, Loïc. 2004. "On the Strategic Appeal and Analytic Perils of 'Structural Violence.'" *Current Anthropology* 45(3): 322–23.

QUESTIONS

1. Explain structural violence and symbolic violence and the difference between them. What are some examples from the reading of structural violence that workers are subjected to? Of symbolic violence? What is "the violence continuum"? Why are the things on the continuum all usefully thought of as forms of violence?

2. What are the morally significant differences between the Mexican crews and the white, teenage crews of pickers? Why is hierarchy important here? Is Holmes objecting to any hierarchy? Or just certain ones?

3. What does Holmes mean when he claims that "marginalization begets marginalization"? What is problematic about marginalization begetting marginalization?

4. Holmes claims that the Mexican workers he discusses "suffer poor health due to their class position." What is the argument for that? It is bad when people suffer poor health, but why might it be especially bad if they suffer poor health due to their class position?

5. Consider the pesticides material at the end of the reading. Workers clearly do not know what they are in for: The signs are in languages they can't read or the warnings are played too softly to hear. In the terms of the Wertheimer reading later in this chapter, do workers who are given such "warnings" consent to the risks of applying pesticides? Do they give valid consent?

6. Which of the five types of oppression identified by Iris Marion Young in Chapter 3, "Food Justice," are on display in the Holmes reading (and other readings in this chapter)?

7. At the end of his reading in Chapter 1, "The Ethically Troubling Food System," Estabrook warns against buying produce year-round from large, far-off farms—farms like he and Holmes describe—and instead advises you to "buy seasonal, local, and small-scale." Is that good advice? Why would such farms be better for workers than the farms Estabrook and Holmes describe? Might the conditions Holmes objects to be replicated on a small farm down the street from you?

TIMOTHY PACHIRAT

Slaughterhouse Workers

This reading comes from Timothy Pachirat's book about the workings of meatpacking plants. In researching the book, he spent months undercover, working various jobs in a plant and reporting in depth about the conditions of that work. What stands out here, as in the Seth Holmes reading, are the physical and mental difficulty of the work but also the status of the workers and their organization within a hierarchy—including supervisors and government officials—in the plant.

Job Number 8, Presticker: *uses hand knife to make incision along length of the cow's neck, giving the sticker access to jugular veins and carotid arteries. Must take care not to be kicked in face,* *arms, chest, neck, or abdominal area by cows that are reflexively kicking, or kicking because they have not been knocked completely unconscious.*

Timothy Pachirat, "Slaughterhouse Workers," from *Every Twelve Seconds: Industrialized Slaughter and the Politics of Sight* (New Haven, CT: Yale University Press, 2013), 140–161.

"Guys, no more livers next week."

It is James, the red-hat supervisor in charge of the cooler, and he mumbles the words as he hands Ramón and me our Friday paychecks in the warming room while we take off our gear and get ready to head home. "But don't worry," he quickly adds, "we'll try to find some work for you guys. Just come back on Monday and we'll try to find something else."

We learn later that Russia or Korea—nobody really seems to know which—has temporarily stopped importing livers, and the management has decided to stop packing them until demand picks up again. And just like that, with two days' warning, Ramón and I find ourselves out of our jobs. Driving home, Ramón is anxious, asking me repeatedly what we are going to do, whether we are going to be fired, telling me he doesn't know how to use a knife and is not sure what other kind of work he can do. I commiserate, but internally I find the possibility of a break from the endless monotony of the cooler exciting and am hopeful that this will provide an opportunity to see a different part of the slaughterhouse. On the way home we stop at a Mexican grocery store, where Ramón picks up two tamales and a forty-ounce Miller Genuine Draft. I buy cheese, chips, and salsa. As we carry our bags to the car, Ramón asks me again whether we will have to look for another job. I tell him that I just don't know.

On Monday morning, Ramón and I stand nervously in the hallway opposite the kill floor office, hands in our pockets. Javier walks by whistling. We stop him, and he says he doesn't know what we'll be doing, but we should change into our work clothes and wait near the cafeteria. After about fifteen minutes of standing around in the hallway outside the cafeteria while kill floor workers rush past us to get to their stations, Ramón decides to check in the cafeteria to see whether someone is waiting for us in there.

Equally nervous at the thought of being out of work, and, like Ramón, knowing that each second that passes after the kill floor starts operating bodes ill for our chances of being given another job, I head onto the kill floor, where I see Bill Sloan, the son of the manager, talking with Ricardo, the red-hat supervisor.

"Do you guys know where I can work?" I ask.

"Do you have any knife experience?" Bill asks.

"No, but I can learn."

Ricardo shakes his head ominously.

"Guys, do you have anything outside in the chutes? I used to work on a ranch, and I'm good with live cattle," I plead.

Ricardo and Bill glance at each other, and Bill nods his head slightly. They both talk into their radios, then Ricardo motions for me to follow him through the clean side of the kill floor, where a line of white hats is standing ready for the first carcass of the day to make its way down the chain, and duck under a half-open garage door onto the gray-hat, hide-on, dirty side. There the line has already started, and the cattle swinging from the chain appear increasingly lifelike as we move down the line against the flow of production. Finally we arrive at a raised platform behind a gated area. A man in a black T-shirt leans over a waist-high barrier, a cylindrical silver gun in his hands, and every six seconds or so there is a *pffft, pffft* as the killing bolt strikes the cow, then retracts back into the gun in the man's hands, after which the cow falls forward onto the green conveyor belt below.

We climb the steps to the platform, and as we edge our way past the shooter, I can see the glistening sweat on his neck, even though it is only half past seven in the morning. Passing through an aluminum swinging door, we are suddenly beyond the walls of the slaughterhouse in a half-open enclosure. The odor is sharp and immediate, an acidic mixture of manure, urine, and vomit that stings my eyes and throat. Cattle, hooves clapping against the floor, push their way nose to rump in a continuous stream of hide up a chute with concrete walls about four and a half feet high and a foot thick. Two men stand on either side of the chute using metal-tipped prongs connected by wires to a live electrical line, plastic paddles, and a leather whip to push, nudge, and shove the cattle one by one through a dark hole at the end of the chute. There a conveyor catches them under the belly and lifts them off their feet, propelling them forward through a metal box to the knocking box, where the man in the black T-shirt stands ready to shoot them.

Covering the whole area is a low tin roof, only three or four feet from the top of my hard hat, dully lit by long fluorescent bulbs encased in plastic covers that are speckled with bits of feces. On either side of the chutes, three foot–wide concrete walkways are bordered by chest-high walls with plastic sheeting that stretches from the top of the walls to the frame holding up the roof.

From the hole in the wall that leads into the slaughterhouse, the chute descends at a steady slope for about fifteen feet before splitting into two parallel chutes. Known collectively as the serpentine, these chutes lead down into a circular area about forty feet in diameter called the squeeze pen. The cattle's movement from the squeeze pen up the serpentine is controlled by a series of gates and trapdoors. Beyond the squeeze pen, the cramped chute leads into a huge room with a peaked ceiling fifty feet high that is open to the air near the rafters. The enormous floor space is divided into pens with metal gates; some are empty, while others hold groups of cattle. This area is followed by the scale room, where cattle are weighed, and a raised concrete ledge where transport trucks unload their cattle.

Ricardo leaves me at the top of the chute in the charge of a short stocky man with a thin mustache named Camilo. In addition to the two of us, three other men work the area between the squeeze pen and the top of the chute. Directly across from Camilo and me a short thin man named Gilberto whistles and prods the cattle through the opening in the slaughterhouse wall. The squeeze pen and lower serpentines are worked by Fernando, a tall nineteen-year-old who immediately asks me if I belong to a gang, and Raul, a quiet man in his thirties who wears a blue bandanna in place of a hard hat and listens to a Walkman.

Gilberto and Camilo explain that our job is to "keep the line tight": to keep the cattle moving up the chutes and into the knocking box. Most of the cattle are moved into the primary serpentine chute, but five or six are also kept in the secondary chute in case there is a lull in the first chute. The cattle are organized in lots by seller, and when Fernando or Raul calls "Lot!" one of the upper chute workers uses an orange hide marker to write "LOT" on the back of the last animal from that group.

The size of a lot is determined solely by the number of cattle sold to the slaughterhouse from a single source: it can be as small as one or as large as several hundred. To be able to track the overall quality and age distribution of cattle from a source, lots are kept together when they are killed, and when the knocker sees the orange "LOT" on the back of an animal, he blows a loud air horn that signals to the supervisors and the workers responsible for keeping track of the lots that one lot is ending and another is beginning.

Camilo hands me an electric shocker and emphasizes that I should not use it when a USDA inspector is present. Because there are only two approaches to the chute area, one from the back through the cattle pens and the other from the front through the kill floor, the chute workers have developed a signal: a short whistle followed by a finger pointing at the eyes means that an inspector is coming over.

After a few hours in the chutes, it becomes clear to me that both Gilberto and Camilo use the electric cattle prods extensively, sometimes sticking them under the animals' tails and into their anuses. The cattle jump and kick when shocked in this way, and many also bellow sharply. Gilberto uses the prod in almost rote fashion, shocking practically every animal, especially as they near the hole in the slaughterhouse wall that leads into the knocking box. Even when the cattle are tightly packed, with the nose of one animal pushed up against the rear of the animal in front of it—sometimes even with its head squished between the hind legs of the animal in front of it—Gilberto still delivers the electrical shock, often causing the cow to mount the animal in front of it.

Already caked in feces from their time in the feedlot, the transport truck, and the slaughterhouse holding pens, the cattle are packed so closely together as they push their way up the chutes that the defecation of one animal often smears the head of the animal immediately behind it. The impact of hooves against concrete splatters feces and vomit up over the chute walls, covering our arms and shirts, and sometimes hitting us in the face.

Running up the serpentine with swinging heads, the cattle are no more than a few inches away from us, separated only by the torso-high sides of the chute. Some poke their noses up over the chute wall to sniff at our arms and stomachs. I can run a bare hand over their smooth, wet noses, a millisecond of charged, unmediated physical contact. At close range, even caked in feces and vomit, the creatures are magnificent, awe-inspiring. Some are muscular and powerful, their horns sharp and strong. Others are soft and velvety, their coats sleek and sensuous. Thick eyelashes are raised to reveal bulging eyeballs with whites visible beneath darkly colored irises. I see my distorted reflection outlined in the convex mirror of their glossy eyes: a man wearing a hard hat, wielding a bright orange paddle. I look crazed, a carnival-mirror grotesque, upholder of a system that authorizes physical, linguistic, and social conceal-ment to allow those who consume the products of this violence to remain blind to it. And what of the cattle, what of each of the twenty-five hundred crea-tures that are run through this chute each day? What do they see as they race by? What do they experience in the final moments before their deaths?

After months of the sterile, interminable monot-ony of hanging livers in the cooler, I am shocked by this confrontation with live cattle. Almost immedi-ately, I resent Gilberto and Camilo for using electric prods (hotshots) on the animals, and after Camilo leaves the upper-chute area to take Raul's place in the lower chutes so that he can go to a doctor's ap-pointment, I lean his prod against the back wall and pick up one of the orange plastic paddles instead. The rest of the day turns into an emotionally and physically draining blur of the "Hey, hey, yah, yah" call of the chute men, the slapping of the plastic paddle against hides, the bellowing and rearing of rolling-eyed cattle, and the incessant *pffft, pffft* of the knocking gun as it punctures one skull after an-other for hours on end.

Now that I am working on the dirty side as a gray hat, I am supposed to use the dirty men's bathroom and dirty men's lunchroom. We are the dirty men, no longer meant to interact with the clean men, the white hats. The chutes and pens, though, provide an informal gathering place of their own. Maintenance workers, supervisors, and USDA inspectors all use the semi-open area of the chutes as a place to take a cigarette break, to escape the confinement of the kill floor, to stand and talk while the stream of cattle runs by.

That afternoon, finished before the rest of the kill floor because the work of the chute men is done when the last animal is run through the chutes (it will be another forty-five minutes before that same animal is hanging in the cooler as two perfectly split half-sides), I wait for Ramón in the hallway. When he emerges from the clean men's bathroom almost an hour later, his hair and shirt are damp with sweat, and his clothes and arms are covered with small white specks of intestine. Driving home, he tells me he started out the day on the dirty side, unshackling the chain from the hind leg of the animals after they were attached to the overhead rail with a sturdier hook. He could not keep up with the work, and after the morning break they moved him to the gut room, where he threaded small intestines onto a coil that releases jets of water into them to clean them. Ramón complains that the gut room smells terrible, and that the work is hard, but he can probably get used to it. Then, after a few minutes of silence as he pulls bits of intestine out of his hair and tosses them through the open window, he says that he is going to look for another job since there is no future in this plant. As I drop him off, we agree that it will be better to drive to work separately from now on since work in the chutes begins at 6:30 and ends around 4:00, while work in the gut room begins after 7:00 and does not end until close to 5:00.

Next day in the chute the disagreement between me and the other chute workers over the use of the electric prods grows more heated. Camilo has re-placed the knocker, and I am in Camilo's place in the upper chutes, standing across from Gilberto, using the plastic paddles to move the cattle. Both Gilberto and Fernando soon start yelling at me to use the elec-tric prod. It is not just a matter of keeping the line tight, of making sure that there is little or no space between the animals, but also of keeping the line moving as quickly as possible so that the knocker and shackler can build up a surplus of stunned and shackled animals before the indexer spaces them evenly on the rails. Without the electric prods, the momentum of the line of animals is sufficient to move the cattle through the opening in the slaughterhouse wall into the knocking box, but not at the pace that the chute workers want. When shocked, the animals jump into the box, moving the line more quickly and reducing the probability of an animal's balking and holding up the line behind it.

Once, when the line moves too slowly for Fernando's liking, he sprints up the walkway from the squeeze pen, grabs the plastic paddle out of my hand, and shoves the electric prod into it. "You motherfucking pussy!" he yells. "Do your job and use the fucking hotshot!"

"Why?" I yell back. "What's the point of shocking them? They're all moving through the line anyway."

"The point is pain and torture," Fernando retorts, laughing. "Now do your motherfucking job and keep this line tight!" he screams, sauntering back down the walkway to the squeeze pen.

Across the chutes, Gilberto looks at me and shrugs before shoving his electric prod into the anus of one of the animals, causing it to kick back and then lunge forward into the animal in front of it.

"Why do you have to do that?" I yell at him.

He shrugs again, smiles, and keeps working. Furious, I repeat the question.

"Okay," he finally shouts back; "you wanna know why I use this?" He shoves the tip of the electric prod across the chute in my direction. "I use this because I like to have my work. And if we don't keep these cows moving through, they're gonna call us up to the office and we're going to get fired. That's why." Later that day we talk some more, and I learn that Gilberto has three children, aged twelve, nine, and six, and today is their first day of school.

By my third day in the chutes, after several warnings from Steve, the red-hat supervisor in charge of the area on the dirty side that includes the chutes and the pens, to "keep it tight," I too increasingly rely on the electric prod. The point of using the prod is not "pain and torture," in Fernando's mocking words, but rather avoiding conflict with co-workers

and supervisors; in addition, once the abstract goal of keeping the line tight takes precedence over the individuality of the animals, it really does make sense to apply the electric shock regularly. Rather than electrocuting an individual animal, the prod keeps a steady stream of raw material entering the plant, satisfies co-workers and supervisors, and saves me from having to expend the energy it takes to move the animals with plastic paddles.

I try to take advantage of my proximity to the knocking box to learn something about the work of shooting the animals. One of the red-hat supervisors is temporarily manning the knocking gun for Camilo, and I ask him whether I could be trained to do that work. He says, "Yeah, I'll train you later. Now get back there and keep the line tight."

Later in the day, when Camilo is back at the knocking box, I ask him to teach me how to do the job. He tells me there are different controls in the knocking box area: one button powers the entire system; a lever controls the conveyor that runs under the animals after they enter the knocking box and lifts them off their feet; a second lever controls the side walls that move in and constrict the animal to keep it as still as possible before it is shot. Finally, there is a control for the overhead chains, which lift the cattle off the lower platform once they are shot and shackled.

The cylindrical gun is suspended in the air over the knocking box's conveyor, balanced with a counterweight and powered by compressed air supplied via a yellow tube. Camilo tells me that using it is not easy: the knocker has only one shot, and although the animals' bodies are restrained, their heads thrash wildly. It takes a combination of patience and good timing to hit an animal squarely in the skull about three inches above the eyes.

After shooting a couple of cattle, Camilo motions for me to take the gun. I do so while he controls the conveyor and the side restrainers. I am so focused on the gun that I do not even notice the animal that comes through on the conveyor. Its head swings back and forth wildly, eyes bulging. Then it stops moving for a moment, and I hold the gun against its skull and pull the trigger. Nothing happens. The gun has to be pressed harder against the animal's skull for the safety to be deactivated. I press again, harder, and pull the trigger. The gun recoils in my hands, and I see a hole in the animal's skull. Blood sputters, squirts, and then begins flowing steadily from the hole and the animal's eyes roll up into its shaking head. Its neck is extended and convulsing, and its tongue hangs out the side of its mouth. I look at Camilo, who motions for me to fire again. I shoot, and the animal's head falls heavily onto the conveyor below. Camilo advances the conveyor and the animal drops onto the lower conveyor, where it is shackled. There is already another animal in the knocking box, head swinging and eyes large in terror. I shoot two more animals, then Camilo takes the gun from my hands, warning, "They're looking at us." Two red-hat supervisors are standing farther down the kill floor, gesturing for me to return to the chutes.

Back in the chutes, Fernando asks, "Why you out there doing that? You want to be the knocker?" When I say maybe, he responds, "No, you don't want to do that. I don't want to do that. Nobody wants to do that. You'll have bad dreams." This is the same man who told me that the point of using electric prods was "pain and torture."

Fernando's reaction turns out to be common. In the lunchroom, heating up my food, I talk to Jill, one of the two quality-control workers. We know each other from earlier conversations about dealing with the USDA inspectors when they watch the liver-hanging work.

"So, are you working in the pens?" she asks.

"Yeah."

"How do you like it? Do you like it more than the livers?"

I shrug noncommittally.

Jill holds her nose.

"Yeah, it smells pretty bad out there," I agree, then ask, "Do you know when the livers are going to start up again?"

"No, I don't know."

"I want them to train me to do the knocking," I offer.

She looks up, surprised. "You want to be a knocker?" Her voice is incredulous.

I shrug again.

"I already feel guilty enough as it is," she says.

"Do you really feel guilty?"

"Yeah. Especially when I go out there and see their cute little faces."

"Well, basically if you work here you're killing cattle," I say defensively. "I mean, aren't we all killing these cattle in one way or another?"

There is an uncomfortable silence.

"How long have you been working here?" I ask, shifting the conversation, and I learn that she has been at the slaughterhouse for three years. She has taken classes to qualify for a USDA inspector's job, but does not want to apply for one because the work involves traveling and she has three small children at home.

The next morning, I am at work early for the free annual employee checkup provided by a company called Healthy and Well and paid for by the slaughterhouse. As an incentive to come to work an hour early, have your blood drawn to check for cholesterol levels, do a flexibility test (you sit with legs extended and see how far forward you can reach), have your blood pressure taken, and fill out a short questionnaire about your eating, sleeping, drinking, and smoking habits, the company provides a free breakfast of scrambled eggs, milk, juice, cereal, bananas, grapes, bagels, and cream cheese.

Rick, the safety coordinator, is responsible for enrolling employees for the checkup, and I sit across from him with a plate of scrambled eggs. When I tell him I want to be trained as a knocker he coughs on his eggs, then after a few minutes says, "You seem like the kind of person who would be really good for a desk job." It fits with a running conversation we have been having in which Rick has been encouraging me to start taking classes at the community college nearby and start looking for some other kind of work.

Later, I see Christian, Umberto, and Tyler, the railers from the cooler, and I join them. Christian and Umberto need to start working and eat and leave quickly. When I tell Tyler I shot three animals with the knocking gun the day before, he urges me to stop. "Man, that will mess you up. Knockers have to see a psychologist or a psychiatrist or whatever they're called every three months."

"Really? Why?"

"Because, man, that's killing," he says; "that shit will fuck you up for real."

I have no opportunity to become a knocker because my next day in the chutes, the fourth, is also my last. The day begins poorly. I am late to work, leaving me five minutes to get my gear on and get out to the chutes. Within minutes, an animal kicks up a big chunk of excrement that hits me squarely in the right eye. It stings, and I rinse it out with water from the sink at the knocker's stand, but I am worried about infection. Despite my increased use of the electric prod, Gilberto and, especially, Fernando continue to yell at me to "use the fucking hot-shot," "watch your fucking side [of the chutes]," and "turn off the fucking fan." This last concerns an ongoing fight between Fernando and me over whether to turn on a large circular fan meant to provide some air circulation in the suffocating confines of the upper-chute area.

An hour into our work, a large brown heifer collapses in the knocking box just before it reaches the conveyor belt, blocking the passageway and shutting down the production line. Four USDA inspectors arrive, along with Roger Sloan, the kill floor manager, and his son Bill. They shoot the animal with the portable handheld knocking gun and attach a cable to its front legs. A winch drags the cow through the knocking box by its legs, clearing the way for the killing to resume.

Moments later, another animal collapses just inside the passageway leading from the squeeze pen into the primary chute. Steve, the red-hat supervisor, comes out, looks at the downed animal, and tells Raul and Fernando to route the remaining cattle up the secondary chute. A few minutes later Miguel, another red-hat supervisor, comes over and after talking into his radio orders everyone to take an early morning break. After the last animals are moved through the chute into the knocking box, the line is shut down, and the downed animal is shot with the portable knocking gun and dragged by the winch through the chute into the slaughterhouse.

Unbelievably, forty minutes after we return from morning break a third cow collapses in the chute. Lower down the chute, Gilberto has been shocking the cattle with the electric prod; I am using a plastic paddle to coax the animals through the hole into the knocking box. Shocked from the rear by Gilberto's electric prod, a cow mounts the steer in front of it. When the plastic paddle I am using to push the front-most animal into the knocking box spooks the animal behind it, the line of cattle in front of the cow that has mounted the steer pushes back, flipping the cow over onto its back and pinning it between the two sides of the chute. The cow struggles to right itself, but with the narrow passageway and downward slope slick with feces and vomit, it cannot get up. It soon lies still, breathing heavily and jerking its head back and forth, while the animals behind it come to a halt. Gilberto is furious, pointing at me with the electric prod and yelling, "You did this!"

Alerted by the stopped line of cattle, Fernando sprints up from the squeeze pen. "Good fucking job, Tim," he says when he sees the downed cow. Gilberto grabs a pair of metal rings off the wall behind him and tosses them to Fernando while I stand back against the wall. Fernando inserts the rings through the cow's nostrils, clamps them shut, and attaches them to a yellow rope, which he jerks heavily, trying to make the cow, now lying flat on its back, sit up and flip over onto its legs. Steve and several line workers from inside who have been alerted to the problem by the knocker join in the pulling. The pressure on the rope stretches the cow's nostrils until they are almost translucent. Finally, the men pull so hard that they rip the cow's nostrils and the nose rings fly out, hitting Juan in the hand. "Fuck!" he screams. The animal is thrashing back and forth in the chute now, its hide completely covered with the feces and vomit that layer the chute floor.

Richard, one of the maintenance workers who has been out in the chutes designing a compressed air–powered vibrator to use instead of the hotshots, is standing next to me against the wall. He looks appalled by what is happening. Steve motions to Gilberto to begin driving the cattle over the downed cow and raises two fingers to his eyes, signaling that all of us should be on the lookout for USDA inspectors. With electric prods Gilberto and Fernando push the remaining cattle over the downed cow, and they stomp on its neck and underbelly trying to escape the electric shock. Leaning against the wall, I look at

Richard, who says shakily, "Man, this isn't right, running them other cattle over this cow like that. I'm not going to take part in this. I'm not going to stand and watch this." I nod my head in agreement, but both of us continue to stand against the wall.

After three cattle trample over the downed cow, I approach Steve and ask, "Do you really want to run the cattle over this one? If the other cattle break something in this cow, then it will never be able to get up." Steve ignores me but a moment later motions for Gilberto to stop driving the cattle over the downed cow, turns to Richard, and screams, his face only a foot from Richard's, "I'm going to get a cable and pull this beef through, and I want you to keep your fucking mouth shut about it. I don't want you to say nothing about it like the last time. Do you understand?"

Looking a bit stunned, Richard replies, "Um, yeah, I guess so."

"You keep your mouth shut," Steve says again, for emphasis.

Steve yells for some of the workers to get the cable and hook it up to the winch. But then his radio crackles with an alert from one of the red-hat supervisors inside the kill floor that the USDA is on its way. Yelling "Forget it!" he shouts at Fernando to get the water hose, which Gilberto hands to me and I hand to him, and begins hosing the hoofprints off the downed cow so that the inspectors will not be able to see that it has been trampled.

Within minutes, two USDA inspectors walk over. "What do you want me to do with this beef?" Steve asks them. The USDA veterinarian who usually inspects the live cattle says, "I want you to knock it and take it out the door."

"Which way, this way?" pointing down the chute back toward the pens.

"I don't care which way you pull it out, I just want you to take it outside. I don't want you to hang it"— meaning he does not want it processed.

Suddenly, Steve turns to me and orders, "You go see Ricardo in the lunchroom."

I assume that I will be fired because of the downed cow, as Fernando and Gilberto are in agreement that it is my fault. It is also possible that Steve does not want me present when the inspectors ask employees

how the animal went down. I go look for Ricardo; not finding him in the cafeteria, I return to the chutes. The USDA inspectors and the downed cow are gone, and the cattle are moving through the chutes again. Roger and Bill Sloan are now in the chutes with Ricardo, and Gilberto is talking to them, his hands gesturing furiously. When they are finished talking with Gilberto, Bill Sloan turns to me: "What happened?" I tell him that the animal went down when it was pushed backward by the line of cattle in front of it, omitting any reference to the nose rings and the cattle being run over the downed animal. Roger, Bill, and Ricardo confer in a small huddle. As they leave, Roger turns to Gilberto and me and says clearly, "If this happens again, you two can both go home."

Roger and Bill return to the clean side of the kill floor, but Ricardo hangs back, talking with the knocker as he works. I approach him and ask whether the livers are going to start again on Monday. When he says he thinks so, I ask if I can be moved back to work on the liver line. "I really don't like being here," I say; "we have to use the electric prods too much." Ricardo tells me he will see what he can do.

Less than an hour later, a utility worker I have never met before enters the chute area and announces, "Someone is going home." Sullen and silent since our admonishment by Roger, Gilberto and I glare at each other. "I don't know who it is," the utility worker says, "but they told me to come back here because someone here is going home." Fernando, who has moved up the chutes with the last lot of cattle to be killed before the lunch break, points at me, laughs, and says, "Yeah, tell this motherfucker to go home."

After pushing the last few cattle through the knocking box, we go to the dirty side lunchroom, where Ricardo pulls me aside and tells me that Ramón and I are both being moved back to the cooler to get ready for the livers that will be starting again next week. "We have some extra guys, so since you don't want to be out there in the chutes anymore we're gonna switch you with the other guy so you can work with the liver guys again," he says.

I walk over to the clean-side lunchroom to tell Ramon, who is happy to learn that we will be working together on the liver line again. Just before the lunch break ends, James, the supervisor in charge of the cooler, tells Ramón and me to head down and spend the afternoon cleaning off the carts and hooks in preparation for the livers on Monday. "When you guys are done with that," he says, "just go to the box room and fold some boxes. But don't work too fast so you'll still have some work to do tomorrow [Friday]. You can leave at three, but don't let anyone see you, and I'll put you down for working the whole day. Then on Monday, everything is the same as before. You guys will start at seven hanging livers downstairs in the cooler."

In my four days working as a gray hat in the chutes, I drove no fewer than six thousand individual cattle into the knocking box, watched many of them get shot through the skull at close range, and shot three with my own hands. And although I spent most of this time in the chutes driving the cattle rather than as the knocker, Tyler's words—"Man, that's killing. . . that shit will fuck you up for real"—resonate deeply. "Fucked up" is exactly how I feel; it is how I would describe many of the chute workers, and it captures the rawness and violence of the perpetual confrontation between the living animals and the men driving them, myself included. What the experiences of Fernando, Raul, Gilberto, and Camilo suggest, though, is that three and a half days in the chutes, three and a half days in close proximity to the knocking box, is insufficient to understand what it means to do the work of killing at close range. Indeed, the experiences of the other chute workers indicate that there is some undetermined length of time, different for each individual, after which "fucked up" becomes routine, normal, and it is any sign of resistance to using the electric prods, to running live animals over a collapsed one, to piling the animals up like dominoes to be killed that becomes characterized as abnormal. Like Rick, Jill, Tyler, and many of the other kill floor workers, though, I do not want to traverse the terrain of routinization and normalization. The mythologizing of the work of the knocker—the almost supernaturally evil powers invested in the act of shooting the animals by the other kill floor workers, including, notably, the chute workers themselves—makes possible the construction of a killing "other" even on the kill floor of the

industrialized slaughterhouse. It legitimizes and authorizes statements like the one made by Richard the maintenance worker, statements underscored rather than undercut by the fact that those making them are themselves contributing daily to the work of the kill floor: "I'm not going to take part in this. I'm not going to stand and watch this."

It is true. I would rather be cleaning hooks and hanging freshly eviscerated livers by the tens of thousands in the segregated confines of the cooler. The divisions of labor and space on the kill floor work to fragment sight, to fracture experience, and to neutralize the work of violence. But what I realize as I settle back into the hypnotic rhythms of wiping hooks and hanging livers by their posterior venae cavae is that this fragmentation, fracturing, and neutralization also create pockets of refuge, places of safety and sanity even here in the heart of the slaughterhouse.

The cooler and its monotonous rhythms are not only physically segregated from the correlates of killing by walls and partitions and the sterilizing effects of cold. More important, the cooler is also psychologically and morally segregated. Like Tom, Jill, and the other kill floor workers, I prefer to isolate and concentrate the work of killing in the person of the knocker, to participate in an implicit moral exchange in which the knocker alone performs the work of killing, while the work I do is morally unrelated to that killing. It is a fiction, but a convincing one, particularly for those already seeking to be convinced: of all workers in the plant, only the knocker delivers the blow that begins the irreversible process of transforming the live creatures into dead ones. Although the sticker technically kills the cow, it is unconscious by the time it reaches him. Only the knocker places the hot steel gun against the shaking, furry foreheads of creature after creature, sees his reflection in their rolling eyes, and pulls the trigger that will eventually rob them of life: only the knocker. If you listen carefully enough to the hundreds of workers performing the 120 other jobs on the kill floor, this might be the refrain you hear: "Only the knocker." It is simple moral math: the kill floor operates with 120 + 1 jobs. And as long as the 1 exists, as long as there is some plausible narrative that concentrates the heaviest weight of the dirtiest work on this 1, then the other 120 *kill floor workers* can say, and believe it, "I'm not going to take part in this. I'm not going to stand and watch this."

Months after I stopped working on the kill floor, I argued with a friend over who was more morally responsible for the killing of the animals: those who ate the meat or the 121 workers who did the killing. She maintained, passionately and with conviction, that the people who did the killing were more responsible because they were the ones performing the physical actions that took the animals' lives. Those who ate the meat, she claimed, were only indirectly responsible. I took the opposite position, holding that those who benefited at a distance, delegating this terrible work to others while disclaiming responsibility for it, bore more moral responsibility, particularly in contexts like the slaughterhouse, where those with the fewest opportunities in society performed the dirty work. My friend's position was the "120 + 1" argument, an argument replicated across myriad realms where morally dirty work is performed by a select few, out of the sight of the many who implicitly or explicitly authorize it but manage to evade responsibility for it by virtue of their citizenship, the taxes they pay, their race, their sex, or the actions of their ancestors.

But perhaps it is the preoccupation with moral responsibility itself that serves as a deflection. Perhaps there are at least some who would be willing to disavow the "120 + 1" argument and accept moral responsibility for the killing as a condition of benefiting from it, as long as they could continue to be shielded from any direct contact with or experience of it. In the words of the philosopher John Lachs, "The responsibility for an act can be passed on, but its experience cannot."[1] What might it mean, then, for all who benefit from dirty work not only to assume some share of *responsibility* for it but also to *experience* it: seeing, smelling, hearing, tasting, touching what it means to be the 1 in the 120 + 1?

NOTE

1. John Lachs, *Intermediate Man* (Indianapolis: Hackett, 1985), 13.

QUESTIONS

1. Some of the conditions that Pachirat discusses are clearly *disgusting*. Yet not all disgusting work environments are such that it is wrong to have people work in them. What are some examples of disgusting work environments where it would be permissible to have people work in them? Why is having people work such jobs permissible?

2. Similarly, some of the conditions that Pachirat discusses are clearly *saddening*. Yet not all saddening work environments are such that it is wrong to have people work in them. What are some examples of saddening work environments where it would be permissible to have people work in them? Why is having people work such jobs permissible?

3. Similarly, reading about some of the conditions that Pachirat discusses might be *enraging*. Yet not all enraging work environments are such that it is wrong to have people work in them. First, what is it that is enraging about the conditions Pachirat details? Second, what are some examples of enraging work environments where it would be permissible to have people work in them? Why is having people work such jobs permissible?

4. Finally, some of the conditions that Pachirat discusses are clearly *morally bad*. For example, workers are very harshly treated in ways that clearly make them unhappy. Whether or not this is wrong, making people unhappy is clearly bad. But in some cases, such treatment might be bad but not wrong. Coaches often treat their players in extremely harsh ways—that's bad—but it's not always wrong. When you break up with your long-term partner—sensitively, gently—you might cause much heartbreak. That's bad without being wrong. What are examples of treatment in slaughterhouses that is bad? Are there examples of treatment that is bad but not morally wrong?

5. Having distinguished disgusting work from saddening work from enraging work from bad work, we can distinguish all of these from *wrongful* work. What are the aspects of slaughterhouse work that are *morally wrong*? Why is this wrong?

6. What are some morally significant differences between the work Holmes details in the previous reading and the work Pachirat details in this one?

SARU JAYARAMAN

Restaurant Workers

The previous readings detail the conditions of workers who grow, harvest, or produce food. In the book from which this reading comes, Saru Jayaraman details the conditions of workers who serve that food in restaurants. She discusses their wages, their working conditions, and their quality of life outside the restaurant. She pays special attention to some issues about race, gender, and class that are only implicitly present in the previous readings.

Right now, earning $2.13 per hour, I don't have enough for my kids, I can't put them through college. I barely have enough to put food on the table.

—SERVER, MAN, NEW ORLEANS

I'm not even worth one cheeseburger an hour.

—BUSSER, MAN, SIX YEARS IN THE INDUSTRY, CHICAGO

We don't usually think of food service workers as poor, if we think of them at all.

I used to be a bad tipper. Even though I ate out frequently, I didn't understand what tipping really meant. Part of me resented the whole idea. Weren't servers being paid for their jobs? Why did I need to pay more than the price of my meal? Wasn't service part of the menu price? I worked hard for my money, and eating out was a guilty pleasure, so feeling compelled to leave something extra just didn't seem right. If I left $5 for a $40 meal, I felt good about myself.

It took me years to understand how tipping really works. First, I learned that my $5 is shared by many different people: the waiter who takes my order, the runner who brings out my food, and the bussers who clean my table and refill my bread basket and water. In some restaurants, the waiter has to ask a bartender to prepare the drinks, and a barback may assist. In the finest fine-dining restaurants, a captain greets customers and oversees the service they receive. All those workers get a piece of my $5.

Here's the worst part: the federal minimum wage for tipped workers is *$2.13 an hour.* That means the federal government permits restaurants nationwide to pay tipped workers an hourly wage of only $2.13, as long as the workers' tips make up the difference between $2.13 and the federal minimum hourly wage of $7.25. If the tips do not cover the difference, the employer is supposed to pay it. In 32 states, the tipped minimum wage is actually higher than the federal tipped minimum wage (e.g., $2.65 or $4.25 an hour), and in 7 states the minimum wage is the same for tipped and nontipped workers.[1] However, 13 states operate under the federal tipped minimum wage of $2.13, and another 8 states have a tipped minimum wage of less than $3.00 an hour. Thus, 21 states—almost half of the United States—allow restaurants to pay their employees less than $3.00 an hour. In several of those states, there is no state minimum wage at all. That means some restaurants in these states can get away with not paying their workers anything! As long as these restaurants bring in less than $500,000 in revenue annually (and therefore don't fall under the purview of federal law), they can force their workers to live entirely off their tips.[2]

The system is further complicated by the rules governing who gets a share of the tips. In a restaurant that complies with the law, the only workers taking a share of the tips are the nonmanagerial employees, who interact directly with customers. Ideally, a waiter collects tips from his or her tables and distributes them among the employees described above. In a "pooled house," the waiter puts all of his or her tips into a pool, and at the end of the night, all of the tips in the house are distributed among service employees using a point system—five points for captains, four points for waiters, and three points for runners, for example. In a "nonpooled house," the waiter collects his or her tips and then, using a percentage system, "tips out" the runner, bussers, bartender, and others at the end of the night.

However, many restaurants break the rules, allowing managers to take a share of the tips. Thirteen percent of workers nationwide report that managers regularly steal tips.[3] Some workers report that they've been forced to turn over all of their tips to management, and they've received a flat rate, or

"shift pay" (also illegal!). Workers who work banquets or special functions in restaurants frequently complain that "service charges"—the "gratuity" charged to customers—disappear at the end of events; these workers end up receiving a flat rate for their work, without any knowledge of how much gratuity management collected.

When I began organizing restaurant workers, I knew that restaurant workers were poor, often living below the poverty line. I understood the basics: some workers don't receive the minimum wage, some don't get proper overtime payments, some don't receive pay for all the hours they've worked, and some get paid late or not at all. Some are even charged for things that aren't their fault, like a guest walking out of the restaurant without paying the check. Most of us have heard about the plight of fast-food workers in the United States, and it's not surprising when cheap chain restaurants pay their workers poverty-level wages.

I also knew, however, that the restaurant industry laid claim to some "shining examples," restaurant owners who wanted to abolish poverty-level wages and offer workers a decent standard of living. Jason Murphy and Ben Hall, an unlikely pair of longtime friends and former dishwashers, are shining examples of employers who not only pay their workers a living wage but also offer raises, IRAs, and health insurance and have a commitment to diversity. They own the Russell Street Deli, a bustling, profitable sandwich and soup restaurant in Detroit. Later in this chapter I'll tell the story of how Jason and Ben have shattered expectations, going from dishwashers to restaurant owners, and built a business using social justice principles.

Still, fair and equitable labor practices are extraordinarily rare in the restaurant industry. Restaurant workers hold 7 of the 10 lowest-paying occupations in the United States, earning less, on average, than farmworkers and all other domestic workers.[4] Although the industry has grown steadily over the last 20 years, restaurant workers continue to earn significantly less than workers in almost every other industry. In 2010, the median wage for restaurant workers nationwide was $9.02 an hour, including tips—a wage that leaves a family of four below the federal poverty line.[5] In 2009, restaurant workers made, on average, $15,092. Workers throughout the rest of the private sector made, on average, $45,155.[6]

All of this probably sounds confusing because it *is* confusing. The minimum wage system for tipped workers is totally dysfunctional. It's a system that permits and even encourages employers to underpay their employees, and forces us, the consumers, to try to make up the difference.

THE AMERICAN DREAM AT $2.13

Claudia, a former low-wage worker in a national pancake restaurant, is a slender, young Mexican immigrant with big brown eyes and long black hair. She laughs often and loves kids. She's also one of the smartest people I know. She reads voraciously and is an articulate, outspoken advocate for the needs of workers. Thus, I was really surprised when I learned that at one point she had not been able to speak up for herself or her coworkers. In fact, it worried me. If someone as brilliant and articulate as Claudia had not been able to speak up against exploitation, how could we expect anyone else to do so?

Claudia became the only Latina server at the Houston pancake house. There were four white and two black servers working with her, and business was slower in this restaurant than in the Austin establishment. White servers were almost always chosen over Claudia and the black servers to work banquet events—the rare parties that pulled in higher-than-average tips.

Once again managers also forced Claudia to report more tips than she actually earned. They didn't want to have to pay her the difference between $2.13 and the minimum wage of $7.25. In addition, they never paid her overtime. "I would have to work off the clock," says Claudia. "They told me to clock out before doing side work. I was always scheduled to work 5:00 p.m. to 12:00 a.m., and exactly at midnight, even if I hadn't finished clearing tables, I had to clock out. Sometimes I'd stay two more hours. Late at night they'd only keep one or two people, and

we had to do all the side work: make silverware packets; clean coffee pots, orange juice pots, and the soda machine; refill the butter, syrup, and ketchup; make sure the syrups were in alphabetical order, all filled up. The tables had to be left spotless. I had to refill the sugar, salt, and pepper. I had to make sure the supply room was clean, organized, and everything labeled. I had to make sure the stockroom was refreshed, and cut lemons myself."

Worst of all, the managers forced Claudia to translate their nasty comments to the Latino bussers and dishwashers. "When the managers were mad, they'd take it out on bussers and dishwashers, and they'd make me translate all the horrible things they were saying," says Claudia. "The workers would cry when I told them they were being sent home. I would apologize and feel horrible. They would say, 'Please don't send me home. I need to make this salary.' I would say, 'I'm sorry, that's what they're making me tell you.' They saw me as a sellout. I knew that this was the only job I could get, and the only one they could get. The managers would take the most vulnerable people and take stuff out on them when things were going bad. It was inhumane, horrible, how they treated them." Although Claudia was a firebrand at school, she somehow could not bring herself to advocate for these workers on the job. She told herself she really needed the money, and tried hard to ignore the pleas of her Latino coworkers.

Claudia made about $30 to $40 a day in tips, working five to six days a week. The $2.13 she earned in wages amounted to a weekly paycheck of about $10.00 after taxes. So, in total, she earned about $150 to $200 per week. She used that money to pay for books, car payments, gas to drive the 20 miles to Prairie View, and other living expenses. She would have been homeless had it not been for the university administrator who gave her a place to stay. Sometimes Claudia had to choose between going to school or to work. "I remember having to make the choice, 'If I go to work today, I can afford to go to school tomorrow,'" she says. "Half of my income every week would go to gas. I definitely couldn't afford to get sick."

She was also hungry all the time. She couldn't afford food and tried to survive on pancakes she ate at the restaurant. "I had to eat less than $6.50 for the employee meal," says Claudia. "If I wanted an omelette, I went over $6.50. I could only afford pancakes. If you were on the schedule for only five hours, you couldn't get a meal. There were days when I wouldn't eat all day."

She was a food service worker who couldn't afford to eat.

At times Claudia and other waitresses would try to get food from the cooks. "When we were really hungry, we would flirt with the cooks to get food," she says. "Sometimes we wanted shrimp, but they wouldn't let us eat it even when it came out bad. The cooks were all Mexican, so I would put on makeup and make jokes that only Mexicans would know. I was really hungry! They would ask me for my number, and I'd say, 'Can I have three pieces of butterfly shrimp?' I'd give them a fake number, so later they'd ask me why I lied. I'd just tell them, 'I have to eat!'"

To make matters worse, the restaurant required servers to bring $20 each night as their "bank" so they could make change as necessary for guests. Claudia had to scrimp and save to bring the $20 every night; sometimes she asked her family to lend her the money. If she didn't have the $20 when she got to work, she had to ask the manager to change larger bills given to her by customers requesting change, and she'd get in serious trouble.

On the weekends the restaurant stayed open 24 hours. One extremely slow weekend night a manager asked Claudia to roll silverware in napkins for two hours. This meant that she got only one table to serve. She knew she wouldn't make any tips this way—she'd make little more than $2.13 an hour—and she'd still be asked to report that she made the minimum wage of $7.25 in tips. Meaning, with taxes, she'd have worked for free. After two hours, Claudia approached the manager and said, "I'm done with the silverware, and other servers are getting tables. Can I serve another table now?" The manager got upset with Claudia for asking this question and berated her on the dining floor. Customers watched. The manager then told her to punch out and go home, and to tell the customers at her one table that someone else would serve them. When Claudia relayed

the message to the customers, they asked to speak to the manager. They were upset by the manager's treatment of Claudia. This only enraged the manager further. She then accused Claudia of telling the customers about their exchange.

The manager realized that having three servers on a weekend night didn't work, and so the next weekend she asked only Claudia to work—but it happened to be the night of a football party. "I was alone on the floor for four hours," says Claudia, "and some people walked out without paying their bill. That night I had to stay until 7:00 a.m., and then come in the next morning at 10:00 a.m. I told the manager someone had walked out, and she said, 'We'll take care of it at the end of your shift.' But at the end of my shift, new people started coming in. The manager told me to clock out and then do my side work. Then she talked to me about the people who walked out. They owed a bill of $98. 'Why did they walk out?' she asked me. I told her, 'Because we were busy. I was the only person on the floor.' She told me that it was my fault, and that I'd have to pay the bill. I had made $80 in tips that night. So after tipping out the busser and the dishwasher, the manager took all my tips and told me I still owed the restaurant $18. I had worked from 10:00 p.m. until 9:00 a.m.—though I had clocked out at 7:00 a.m.—and instead of paying me anything, they were telling me I had to pay them."

At that point, Claudia quit. "I felt like I was being robbed," she says. She walked out to her car in the parking lot and cried.

NOTES

1. Rajesh D. Nayak and Paul K. Sonn, *Restoring the Minimum Wage for America's Tipped Workers,* technical report (New York: National Employment Law Project, 2009), 6.

2. Ibid., 7.

3. Restaurant Opportunities Centers United, *National Survey Data, 2011.*

4. U.S. Bureau of Labor Statistics, *2010 National Cross-Industry Estimates Sorted by Median Hourly Wage for All Standard Occupational Classifications,* Occupational Employment Statistics, http://bls.gov/pub/special.requests/oes/oesm10nat.zip.

5. http://aspe.hhs.gov/poverty/12fedreg.shtml; *Federal Register,* vol. 76, no. 13, January 20, 2011, pp. 36737–38. Hereafter, unless otherwise stated, "poverty line" or "poverty wage" refers to the income below which a family of four falls into poverty as defined by 2011 HHS Poverty Guidelines. A poverty wage of $10.75 assumes full-time, year-round work.

6. U.S. Bureau of Labor Statistics, *Quarterly Census of Employment and Wages,* www.bls.gov/cew (accessed January 20, 2011).

QUESTIONS

1. In a briefly famous case, a St. Louis pastor refused to tip her Applebee's server the 18% that Applebee's recommended. On her credit card receipt, the pastor wrote, "I give God 10%, why do you get 18%?" Was the pastor making a good point? What was that point, exactly?
2. What are the ethics of tipping? Is it something that is morally required in restaurants like American ones where servers are paid lower wages than most other jobs? Is it supererogatory?
3. Compare Jayaraman's account of job opportunities for non-white kitchen workers with Holmes's account of job opportunities for Mexican farmworkers. What is morally objectionable about racialized, gendered, and class-based job opportunities that they discuss? Would there be something similarly objectionable if it turned out that redheads were denied opportunities in just the way Latinas are? Would there be something similarly objectionable if non-native English speakers were? Why or why not?
4. What are the various morally objectionable ways in which Claudia is treated by the management of her pancake house? What is objectionable about them?
5. Jayaraman's description of Claudia's time at the pancake house raises concerns about gender, race, and class. What are some of them? Who is acting wrongly? What should they be doing instead?

ALAN WERTHEIMER

The Value of Consent

Full of lots of examples of cases involving consent, the Wertheimer reading explains the difference between consent—basically, agreeing—and *valid* consent—basically, the sort of agreement that makes permissible whatever the parties are agreeing to. There must be a difference: When Berti gives Alma a drug that makes her say "yes" to anything and then asks Alma if he can have her purse, Alma will say "yes"—that is, she will, in Wertheimer's terms, consent—but this is not valid consent. It is *not* permissible for Berti to take the purse even though Alma did agree to it. The reading also traces the outlines of *when* consent is valid. Although the reading is not obviously about food ethics at all, it is important to food worker ethics since it bears on the question of whether workers consent to their treatment and, if so, whether that renders that treatment permissible.

We have a rough and serviceable idea of what it is to consent to sexual relations that is adequate for ordinary purposes. But we want a deeper analysis of consent, one that will enable us to understand the moral importance of consent, one that will help us to think about what counts as giving consent, and one that will distinguish valid from invalid consent; so it seems that we should turn to an analysis of the concept of consent.

A standard picture about the role of conceptual analysis goes something like this. We start with the principle that it is morally and legally impermissible to engage in sexual relations without the other party's consent. To determine which specific behaviors should be regarded as impermissible, we analyze the concept of consent (and related concepts). We ask, in effect, "when is it proper to say that someone consents to do X"? Given an answer to that question and given the premise, we can then say when sexual relations are morally and legally permissible.

This picture greatly exaggerates what a certain kind of conceptual analysis can do. The concept of consent provides a template that organizes and focuses our attention on a set of relevant moral issues, but it cannot do much more. The question as to when we should regard it as morally or legally impermissible to engage in sexual relations will be settled by moral argument informed by empirical investigation, not metaphysical inquiries into the meaning of consent. The important question is not what consent "is," but the conditions under which consent is *morally transformative* in the relevant way.

CONSENT AS MORALLY TRANSFORMATIVE

I begin with a reminder that we are not interested in consent as a freestanding concept or word. We are interested in consent to sexual relations because consent "is an act in which one person alters the normative relations in which others stand with respect to what they may do," that is, their rights, duties, obligations, privileges, and the like.[1] B's consent may provide moral or legal *legitimation* for an action by A that would not be legitimate without B's consent, as when B's consent to surgery transforms A's act from battery to a permissible medical procedure, or when B's consent to A's use of her land absolves A of trespass. Put somewhat differently, B's consent can render A's action morally or legally *permissible*. B's consent to A's doing X may also transform the obligations and rights of third parties. In some cases, B's consent to A's doing X may curtail C's right or duty to interfere with A's conduct. If B consents to allow A to tattoo her, C may continue to think tattooing a disgusting activity. But C should not think that A is committing battery or intervene on those grounds.[2]

George Fletcher claims that consent can transform (what would otherwise be) a harmful action to a non-harmful action. In other, cases, it does not remove the actual harm, but it negates B's right to complain about the harm. If B consents to a taking of property or gives a gift, then, says Fletcher, there is no harm at all. But if B consents to box with A and is knocked out, B's consent blocks the complaint but not the harm, as captured by the expression "volenti non fit injuria" (to one who consents no harm (or wrong) is done).[3] I am not sure that Fletcher is correct. If one consents to a taking of property, one still *loses* the property, just as one who consents to be boxed in exchange for a fee still suffers the pain and bruises of the beating. So the property and boxing cases may be closer than Fletcher seems to think.[4] In any case, the moral and legal force of any economic or physical injuries that B might suffer is negated or weakened by B's consent and that is what is crucial.

Consent can also work as a promise or a way of acquiring an obligation to do something, as when B consents or promises at Time-1 to do X at Time-2. In general, it is desirable that people be able to make binding commitments on grounds of both autonomy and utility, but it is not clear whether this applies to sex. Alan Soble argues that the Antioch College policy, which requires contemporaneous explicit consent to any initial form of sexual contact, effectively trivializes consent because it does not allow people to promise to perform and because it implies that withdrawing consent is not prima facie wrong.[5] Soble has misdiagnosed the issue. With the possible exception of paying for a prostitute, people do not ordinarily rely to their detriment on another's promise to engage in sexual activity. To the extent that breaking promises is wrong precisely because others have relied on one's promise to their detriment, reneging on a promise to engage in sex is not particularly wrong. Soble is (or should be) more concerned that the Antioch policy does not allow people to consent at Time-1 to not having to explicitly consent at Time-2.

> **Default**. A asks B if he can kiss B. B says, "For God's sake, I'll tell you if I want you to stop." After some kissing and petting, A removes his clothing. B removes her own clothing, but says nothing. They have sexual intercourse.

It's hard to believe that there is anything problematic here.

Before going further, I must enter an important cautionary remark about the notion of "moral transformation." To say that B's (valid) consent is morally transformative is to say that it alters A's (or C's) reasons for actions. It is not to say that B's consent is either necessary or sufficient to an "all things considered" moral assessment of A's actions. The moral alchemy may change an act from lead to silver but not necessarily to gold—it makes "morally allowable what would not be allowable without consent, or at any rate . . . *so far* allowable, since there may be additional moral impediments to the doing of it."[6] For example, it may be wrong for A to perform surgery on B with B's consent if the procedure is not medically indicated.[7] And even if B's consent renders A's action permissible, consent does not always work "to make an action right when it would otherwise be wrong."[8] Exchanging money for sexual relations may be morally problematic even if the prostitute consents. Still, the prostitute's consent is morally transformative because it removes one important reason for regarding A's behavior as wrong.

THE LOGIC OF CONSENT ARGUMENTS

To put the point schematically, we are interested in the following sort of argument.

> *Major premise*: If B consents to sexual relations with A, it is (*ceteris paribus*) permissible for A to have sexual relations with B.[9]
> *Minor premise*: B consents (does not consent) to sexual relations with A.
> *Conclusion*: It is (not) permissible for A to have sexual relations with B.

Given the major premise, it seems that we must determine when the *minor premise* is true if we are going to determine if the conclusion is warranted. We may be tempted to think that an analysis of the concept of consent will identify the *criteria* or necessary and sufficient conditions of valid consent, and that empirical investigation can, in principle, determine if those criteria are met. If the criteria are met, then the minor premise is true and the conclusion follows. If not, then the minor premise is false and the conclusion does not follow.

If things were only so simple. Consider the following cases (in these and subsequent cases, assume that A and B have sexual relations):

Abandonment. A and B drive to a secluded spot in A's car. B resists A's advances. A says, "Have sexual relations with me or I will leave you here."

Vasectomy. A makes advances. B tells A that she will accept only if A wears a condom. A falsely tells B that he has had a vasectomy.

Fraternity Party. B is a college freshman. She has never had much to drink. She attends her first fraternity party and is offered some punch. She asks, "Does this have alcohol?" A responds, "Absolutely." She has several glasses, and becomes quite "high" for the first time in her life. When A proposes that they go to his room, she agrees.

No analysis of the meaning of consent will enable us to say whether A's conduct should be illegal in these cases. And modifiers will not help. We can say that it should be a criminal offense if A "fails to obtain *meaningful* consent, and continues to engage in sexual activity," but then we seem to need to know when consent is sufficiently "meaningful" to bar criminalization.[10]

THE PRINCIPLES OF VALID CONSENT (PVC)

To return to phraseology that I have previously introduced, the primary theoretical task is to specify the *principles of valid consent* (PVC) for legal or criminal contexts (PVC_L) and for moral but not legal contexts (PVC_M). In my view, PVC is the primary site of the philosophical action about consent. B clearly gives a token of consent in Fraternity Party. It is less clear whether her consent is valid. Tokens of consent are obviously important. If B does not token consent, then A's act is impermissible. But B's consent token renders A's act morally permissible (insofar as things turn on consent) only if B's consent meets the criteria specified by PVC.

The content of PVC_L and PVC_M may or may not vary from context to context. Consider the following cases.

Mastectomy. A physician tells his patient that she has breast cancer and that she should immediately undergo a mastectomy. He does not explain the risks of the procedure or other options. Because the patient trusts her physician, she signs a consent form.

Gangrene. A patient's leg is gangrenous and she must choose between amputation and death. She understands the alternatives, and because she does not want to die, she signs the consent form.

Dance Studio. A dance studio gets an elderly woman to contract to pay $20,000 for dance lessons by "a constant and continuous barrage of flattery, false praise, excessive compliments, and panegyric encomiums."[11]

Psychotherapist. B is undergoing psychotherapy with A. Under the grip of "transference" and strongly attracted to A, she proposes that they have sexual relations. A accepts.

Has there been valid or morally transformative consent in any or all of these cases? A full resolution would require both more information and moral argument. But setting aside, for now, the distinction between moral and legal contexts, I think that the best account of PVC might generate the following judgments: the consent in **Mastectomy** is not valid because valid consent to a medical procedure must be *informed* consent; the consent given in Gangrene is valid even though the patient reasonably believes that she had no choice but to agree; the consent given in **Dance Studio** does not give rise to a legally binding agreement because the dance studio acted illegitimately in procuring the subject's consent; the consent given in **Psychotherapist** does not render it legitimate for the psychotherapist to have sexual relations with his patient, because the therapist has a fiduciary obligation to refrain from sexual relations with his patient that cannot be waived. Period.[12]

These are just intuitions. How do we determine what is the best account of PVC for one context or another? At one level, this will turn on what is the best account of morality or on that part of morality that concerns "what we owe to each other."[13] On a consequentialist outlook, we will examine the costs and benefits of different versions of PVC and adopt those principles that generate the best consequences when all things are considered. I do not mean that the best version of PVC will be settled "case by case." We will want to know in advance whether we can regard consent as valid in one type of situation or another. But it is possible, for example, that the best version of PVC will be different for medical contexts than for sexual contexts. From a contractarian perspective, we can think of PVC_L and PVC_M as the outcome of a choice made under conditions of impartiality, perhaps as modelled by a Rawlsian veil of ignorance or along Scanlonian lines, as the principles that no one could reasonably reject as a basis for informed, unforced general agreement. Here, too, the principles will vary.

For present purposes it is not necessary to opt for one moral theory or another. The crucial and present point is that we should think of the principles of valid consent as themselves the subject or target of moral theorizing. We are used to thinking of consent principally as an "input" to moral thinking, as a factor that generates a moral result. So we might say, "B consents to sexual relations with A" (input) and thus "It is permissible for A to have sexual relations with B" (output). I am arguing that we should shift the focus of our thinking, that we should regard the principles of valid consent as an *output* of moral theorizing, as what we are trying to justify.

THE VALUE OF CONSENT

Needless to say, we are not likely to resolve the question of what is the best moral theory. Moreover, we are also not able to say with precision what account of PVC would be adopted within the framework of a given theory. We can make some progress, however,

because we can identify some moral considerations that will be relevant to what constitutes the best version of PVC on several different theoretical approaches.

We can begin by asking why consent is important or valuable. In a book published just before his death, Robert Nozick argues that the norm of "voluntary cooperation" might be regarded as the "core principle of ethics."[14] He suggests that the point of these norms is to facilitate mutually beneficial interactions. By adopting the principle that consent is (ordinarily) *sufficient* to legitimize interaction, we encourage mutually beneficial interactions. By adopting the principle that consent is (ordinarily) *necessary* to legitimize interaction, we prohibit interactions that are not to mutual benefit. Nozick's approach does not mandate mutual benefit. A person could choose to interact with others in a way that "benefits them yet is to his own detriment," so long as the choice is clearly voluntary. But the principal aim is to encourage interactions that are mutually beneficial and to discourage those that are not. Of course not every consensual transaction enhances the parties' utility *ex post*. People make mistakes. But if people typically consent only to those interactions that will improve their expected welfare, and if people typically make fairly good judgments about such matters, then consensual interactions will leave both parties better off than they otherwise would be.

We can put the norm of voluntary cooperation in terms of an ethics of *autonomy*, which also has two dimensions. To say that sexual relations are legitimate only if B consents is to protect the *negative* dimension of B's autonomy or control of her life. But that is not sufficient. B is not an autonomous agent if she is not capable of entering into relationships with others when she and they are so willing. So to say that sexual relations are (prima facie) legitimate if (and not "only if") B consents is to endorse the *positive* dimension of autonomy, the notion that people should be permitted "to seek emotional intimacy and sexual fulfillment with willing partners."[15] The distinctiveness of the two dimensions of autonomy is well illustrated by a moral or legal regime that rigorously protects everyone's right to refuse sexual contact, but places extensive restrictions on one's right to engage in sexual contact, such as restrictions on non-marital sex or homosexual relations. Under this regime, there is extensive negative autonomy, but little positive autonomy. To acknowledge the positive dimension of autonomy is to see that a common critique of liberal morality is thoroughly mistaken. It is sometimes said that a liberal morality or a concern with autonomy assumes a world of "isolated" or "atomistic" or "asocial" individuals. But to respect an *individual's* sexual autonomy is precisely to respect and facilitate her decisions to interact *with others*. It does not assume that she prefers autoerotic activity.

I need to say something more about autonomy. A common view is that autonomy refers to *control* of one's life, to the ability to shape one's life in accordance with one's desires. Some philosophers adopt a more rigorous or Kantian view, one that emphasizes its moral dimension. The Kantian conception of autonomy tracks its etymology (*auto* = self, *nomos* = law). The autonomous person is one who submits to moral laws or principles that one has made for oneself.[16] Living in accordance with one's nonmoral or non-reflective desires is not to live an autonomous life. George Sher advances a somewhat relaxed version of the Kantian line. On his "responsiveness to reasons" view, an agent is autonomous or self-directing only when she is motivated by her appreciation of the *reasons* provided by her situation, but not exclusively moral reasons.[17]

As Sher points out, the "responsiveness to reasons" view can explain what appears to be a disparate set of requirements for autonomy as well as an apparent anomaly. A's coercive threats imperil B's autonomy because A's threats make B responsive to *A*'s reasons or will, not her own. Information is important to autonomy because one's choices cannot reflect one's judgments or values without the relevant information. Psychological compulsions, phobias, and manipulation interfere with autonomy because they weaken the agent's ability to make choices that reflect her reasons, values, or conception of the good. In addition, the responsiveness-to-reasons view can explain why the capacity for a critical attitude toward one's own beliefs, desires, and choices is also a requirement of autonomy. An autonomous person must have the intellectual resources to reason about her

reasons. Interestingly, this account also explains the anomalous but important *sense* in which one may act autonomously when making decisions in response to a threat, as when a bank teller hands over money in response to the gunman's threat—"the money or your life." Although there is clearly one sense in which the gunman's threat interferes with her autonomy, the teller is also responding to the relevant reasons for action. She need not deny that she is morally responsible for her decision to turn over the money. Rather, the robber's threat renders her action *justifiable*.

It is not clear how best to understand the value of autonomy. To put the issue arithmetically, we can contrast an additive view with a multiplicative view. On the additive view, the "good" of autonomous choice is added to the value of the choice, so that it enhances the positive value of a good choice and reduces the negative value of a bad choice. On the multiplicative view, the moral value of autonomous choices depends on the value of the choices. The degree of autonomy amplifies the positive or negative value of a choice. A good autonomous choice is more valuable than a good non-autonomous choice, but a bad autonomous choice is worse than a bad non-autonomous choice. Intuitively, the multiplicative view seems closer to the truth. It seems implausible to suppose that an autonomous choice of evil is somehow better than a non-autonomous choice of evil. Even if we accept the multiplicative view, it is still morally desirable that people have the space to make autonomous unworthy choices since an autonomous worthy choice is possible only when people have the space for autonomous unworthy choices.

NOTES

1. John Kleinig, "Consent" in Lawrence Becker and Charlotte Becker (eds.), *Encyclopedia of Ethics,* second edition (New York: Routledge, 2001), 300.

2. Carl Wellman, *Real Rights* (New York: Oxford University Press, 1995), 67.

3. George Fletcher, *Basic Concepts of Legal Thought* (New York: Oxford University Press, 1996), 112.

4. B's consent (or, more accurately, B's belief that B consents) can also transform the character of her *experience.* If B consents to box with A, she will not experience the blow to her head as a hostile attack on her person,

although B may still experience the non-belief-mediated distress caused by such a blow.

5. Alan Soble, *Sexual Investigations* (New York: New York University Press, 1996), 57. The policy requires explicit consent to each new level of intimacy, for example, kissing, fondling, etc.

6. Edmund Pincoffs, "On Consenting" in Lyman T. Sargent (ed.), *Consent: Concept, Capacity, Conditions, and Constraints, Archives for Philosophy of Law and Social Philosophy,* volume 12 (1979), 108.

7. It is another question whether performing such surgery would be a wrong *to B* if B asks A to perform the procedure. For example, it may be wrong for a physician to accede to a beggar's request to have his leg amputated so that he can enhance his success as a beggar, but I am not at all sure that it would be a wrong to B.

8. Larry Alexander, "The Moral Magic of Consent II," 2 *Legal Theory* 165 (1996), 165.

9. A *ceteris paribus* clause is necessary because I do not want to beg the question whether consent is a sufficient condition for legitimacy.

10. Joan McGregor, "Why When She Says No She Doesn't Mean Maybe and Doesn't Mean Yes: A Critical Reconstruction of Consent, Sex, and the Law," 2 *Legal Theory* 175 (1995), 190.

11. *Vokes v. Arthur Murray. Inc.,* 212 So. 2d 906 (1968), 907.

12. See chapter 6 in my *Exploitation* (Princeton: Princeton University Press, 1996).

13. T.M. Scanlon, *What We Owe to Each Other* (Cambridge, MA: Harvard University Press, 1998).

14. Robert Nozick, *Invariances* (Cambridge, MA: Harvard University Press, 2001), 263.

15. Stephen J. Schulhofer, *Unwanted Sex* (Cambridge, MA: Harvard University Press, 1998), xi.

16. See Joel Feinberg, *Harm to Self* (New York: Oxford University Press, 1986), 27.

17. George Sher, *Beyond Neutrality* (New York: Cambridge University Press, 1997), 48.

QUESTIONS

1. What is the difference between consent and valid consent, according to Wertheimer?
2. What are conditions that have to be met for consent to be valid, according to Wertheimer?
3. In Wertheimer's gangrene case, is there valid consent? If so, there can be valid consent to something even when the subject knows her only other option is horrendous. What does that show about food workers who claim their consent is invalid because if they failed to give it, they would be deported?

HALLIE LIBERTO

Exploitation and the Vulnerability Clause

One worry about the treatment of workers is that they are being *coerced* into their work, and this is objectionable. The Wertheimer reading speaks to that. Another worry is that their employers *exploit* workers, and this is objectionable. But what is exploitation? Why is it objectionable? Liberto outlines some answers to both questions and provides some compelling examples of exploitation, examples that make clear how it differs from mere, unobjectionable hard-bargaining. She also argues that it is harder than it first appears to characterize *vulnerability*, an important component of wrongful exploitation.

Exploitation theorists usually stipulate two necessary and jointly sufficient conditions for an act being one of wrongful exploitation. There must be something morally problematic about the gain that the exploiter achieves (e.g. the gain is unfair or is motivated by opportunism). One might call this the "Advantage Clause." In addition, there is some predicament that must characterize the circumstances of the exploited persons (e.g. a condition of desperation or a state of being without options). I will call this the "Vulnerability Clause." The scope of this paper is limited to the second of these clauses; I am concerned with the conditions of vulnerability an individual must confront in order that we might ever correctly say that she or he has been wrongfully exploited. Such a condition will only be a necessary and not a sufficient condition of wrongful exploitation. I will say nothing about the particular "Advantage Clause" with which my account need be paired to result in a complete theory of wrongful exploitation. Mikhail Valdman has recently argued that wrongful exploitation is the extraction of excessive benefits from someone who cannot reasonably refuse one's offer. So, "being without the ability to reasonably refuse an offer" is Valdman's Vulnerability Clause. I will argue that this clause is too narrow, but that other competing theories, like Alan Wertheimer's, are too broad.

EXPLOITATION AND THE ANTIDOTE CASE

Mikhail Valdman presents a case that he believes to be unarguably an instance of wrongful exploitation: Hiker A carries with him an antidote for a deadly poison contained in the venom of a snake living in the woods. Hiker A encounters Hiker B who has just been bitten by such a snake and who has no antidote with him. The market value of the antidote is $10. However, A knows that B is worth a million dollars

and, so, charges him a million dollars for the antidote. B unhappily accepts the terms of the transaction, uses the antidote, and lives.

Perhaps Hiker A wrongly exploits Hiker B because he treats him as a mere means to his own end. Ruth Sample suggests that we treat another as a mere means if we do not take his interests into account (Sample 2003, 70–81). However, Valdman points out that we can easily imagine a slightly different version of the antidote case in which Hiker A thinks to leave Hiker B with a little money so that Hiker B can continue living a decent life, rather than extracting the whole million in the exchange. Certainly, thinks Valdman, we would still call this modified Antidote case an instance of wrongful exploitation, even though Hiker A takes Hiker B's interests into account. So, "having one's ends ignored" is too strict of a Vulnerability Clause. There will be some cases of wrongful exploitation that it leaves out.

On Allen Wood's account of exploitation, wrongful exploitation occurs when one person takes opportunistic advantage of another person's vulnerabilities (1995, pp. 150–1; see also Valdman 2009, p. 5). On this account, the Vulnerability Clause is very broad; any vulnerability meets the criterion. Valdman suggests that, on Wood's account, Hiker A would be wrongfully exploiting Hiker B even if Hiker A did not demand any money for the antidote, but rescued Hiker B *only* for the sake of the pleasure that Hiker A takes in rescuing others. Valdman does not deny that there might be something problematic about Hiker A's character in such a case, but points out that we cannot say that Hiker A *wrongs* Hiker B, no matter his motivation in this rescue scenario.

Valdman offers the following theory of wrongful exploitation: one wrongly exploits another if and only if one extracts excessive benefits from someone who cannot, or cannot reasonably, refuse one's offer (2009, p. 9). Valdman believes that only his own account of wrongful exploitation picks out what is wrong in the Antidote Case. Hiker B cannot reasonably refuse Hiker A's offer, as the poisonous venom is deadly. Hiker A extracts benefits from Hiker B in excess. If he had only asked for $10, his extraction would not have been wrong. At one million dollars, the extraction is wrong.

Valdman recognizes that his account of the wrongness of exploitation is much like Alan Wertheimer's account. Unlike Valdman, Wertheimer makes exploitation a thick term, describing exploitation as, among other things, a kind of unfairness, which is always morally problematic.[1] However, what is wrongful exploitation for Valdman, and what is exploitation at all for Wertheimer, look much the same. After all, Valdman thinks that wrongful exploitation involves the extraction of "excessive benefits," and "excessive benefits" sound an awful lot like "unfair benefits." In what remains of this Section I will highlight what Valdman lakes to be the important difference between his and Wertheimer's accounts.

According to Wertheimer, A exploits B when A transacts with B to A's advantage in a way that is unfair to B (1996, p. 16). Like with Valdman's theory, exploitation may be harmful, neutral, *or* beneficial to B. Mutually beneficial exploitation occurs when both A and B benefit from the transaction, compared to what they would have been left with if they did not transact, but A benefits *unfairly*. How is this unfairness measured?

Wertheimer thinks that there is a point or a range of points of agreement at which a transaction is fair. Exploitation, for Wertheimer, is measured by the distance between the point of fairness, otherwise called the "normative baseline," and the actual point of agreement. How is the normative baseline determined? Wertheimer considers and rejects a variety of possibilities.[2] He ultimately suggests that the best method for determining a normative baseline is to consider what two good friends would do if one was selling an item or service to the other, and neither was rushed or desperate for the sale.

The difference between Wertheimer and Valdman's accounts of exploitation is that Valdman thinks that in order for an agreement that diverges from the normative baseline of a fair transaction to be wrongful, it must be the case that the exploited party had no reasonable way of refusing the offer. Valdman thinks that for this condition to be met, one must have an urgent need that can only be satisfied by a monopolist. That is, the

exploited person must have no other or better option for transacting, and it must be the case that she truly needs to transact at all. Valdman allows one other way in which someone might lack the ability to reasonably refuse an offer, and that is if one has some compulsion or addiction that internally controls his behavior: like that had by a compulsive gambler (2009, p. 10).

Valdman thinks that his proposed condition on wrongful exploitation sets his theory apart from Wertheimer's in an important way. On Wertheimer's account, an individual might *let* himself be exploited even though he has no urgent need to enter into the transaction. Valdman thinks that we cannot call such exploitation wrongful when the exploited party "lets himself be used."

> To wrongly exploit someone is to *extract* excessive benefits from him—it is to use the fact that his back is to the wall, so to speak, to get him to accept lopsided and outrageous terms of exchange. The special wrongness of doing so is not captured by a view that considers all instances of excessive gain to involve wrongful exploitation. (2009, p. 10)

For instance, imagine a car seller who knows that he could get a better deal for his car than what the buyer is offering, but is lazy and doesn't want to hunt around. Robert Goodin agrees; he says, "We would not, I think, want to say that absolutely everyone who has ever driven a bad bargain is thereby necessarily [wrongfully] exploited. Some people just cannot be bothered to shop around for the best price available, and therefore end up paying more than is strictly necessary for their goods and services."[3] Valdman thinks that it is a disadvantage of Wertheimer's account of exploitation that such a case would be considered *wrongful* exploitation. So, in summary, Valdman proposes a Vulnerability Clause, and Wertheimer does not.

EXPLOITATION AND REASONABLE ALTERNATIVES

Both Goodin and Valdman's complaint against calling the lazy person, unwilling to investigate his options, a victim of wrongful exploitation is very reasonable. Yet, sometimes agreements are made between individuals such that a person is exploited even though he can reasonably refuse an offer, and that exploitation may still be wrongful exploitation. Before I launch into a short series of counterexamples to Valdman's Vulnerability Clause, it is important that I make the best case for Valdman possible, ensuring that I am not leveraging an attack against a straw man.

What does it mean to have "reasonable" alternatives? Obviously, Hiker B in the Antidote Case has no reasonable alternatives; his only alternative to paying Hiker A is to face death. We could interpret "reasonably" very narrowly and assume Valdman means alternatives that *no* reasonable person would accept over the terms of an offer (e.g. death, bodily injury, or large-scale material loss). However, it would be more fair to Valdman to assume that an alternative might be rendered unreasonable in virtue of a strongly held conviction on the part of the exploited person that his or her options were unreasonable. Consider the following case that I have presented elsewhere in which an exploited person holds the belief that his exploiter must be giving him a fair price.

> Perhaps the stranger is a religious minister, and the individual is a lay person of that religion, though not in the minister's own congregation (hence, the status of a stranger). If the minister is selling a piece of property and offers a price to the lay person, the lay person will assume that the minister is attempting to be good and fair, and is not just attempting to maximize his own gains. . . Any advantage that the minister attempts to secure in the transaction over the lay person is exploitative. (Liberto 2013, p. 282)

Imagine that the minister in this scenario sells a house to the lay-person for an exorbitant price. The lay-person certainly has alternatives. Namely, he could buy a different house of a similar size in a similar neighborhood at a fair price. Let us even say that he knows of available houses and knows that they cost less. However, he holds the conviction that the price proposed by the minister is the fair price. Hence, he believes that buying an alternative house for less money would be unfair to the seller of that house. He does not think that it is reasonable to treat someone unfairly.

Either Valdman must say that the minister/lay-person case is not one of wrongful exploitation, or he must say that what counts as a reasonable option depends, to some degree, on the convictions of the exploited person. Since the minister/lay-person case seems so clearly to be a case of wrongful exploitation, I will assume the latter. "Reasonable" alternatives can be constrained by the convictions held by the exploited. Even on this charitable reading of the clause, there are still cases in which wrongful exploitation occurs wherein the exploited person has reasonable alternatives.

The following case I will call *Poor Student Renter*: Imagine that a poor college student moves to his college town and seeks an apartment to rent for the academic year. The college student comes from a bad neighborhood—perhaps he is paying for school with a scholarship. His landlord, who has learned to recruit scholarship student renters for these reasons, guesses that the student is used to living in rather rough conditions, and so does not put the sort of money and upkeep into the apartment that he normally would. The poor student has many reasonable options available to him, he could do his due diligence and compare apartments, but he does not have the background to know that he is getting a bad deal. Once lodged in the apartment, he could demand better treatment. However, he doesn't have experience calling a landlord to demand better treatment, because his mother was always so far behind on paying rent that neither she nor he would have ever dreamed of calling and making demands of their landlord. He knows this is one way of solving the problem, but due to this lack of experience, he is shy about making such a phone call. Despite being terribly bright in school, he is terribly uninformed as to what options are available to him. He could, with a little embarrassment, ask his friends how they have come by their superior housing, and so become informed. But he already feels a little insecure about his social status among his friends, does not want to betray his more modest budget, and so wants to avoid this embarrassment. The landlord continues to charge him too much for a bad apartment with bad upkeep, and the student continues to pay at this rate.

Now, in this case, the obstacles preventing the student from "shopping around" are not so great that we would want to call them *unreasonable* options. He could even be described as being somewhat negligent about doing his homework on housing. The student certainly holds no conviction that his alternatives are unreasonable. However, something about his circumstances, that he is accustomed to bad apartments, that he is shy about negotiating with a landlord, that it would involve a little bit of embarrassment to ask for advice from his better informed friends, that the landlord seeks out student renters with just such backgrounds, these are aspects of vulnerability that make his landlord's exploitation of him seem wrongful.

Next, consider the following case which I will call *Lewd Promotion*: Employer, A, must make a decision about which of his equally qualified employees he will promote to a job with more pay and more responsibility. He does not have any reason relevant to the job at hand to prefer one candidate to any other. However, he does find Employee, B, very attractive, and tells her that she may have the promotion if she engages in sexual activity with him, but may keep her current position otherwise. Let us imagine that life will be very awkward for B in her current position after such an offer is refused. However, if she accepts the promotion, she will work from a different office, and will not have to see her employer except on the occasions of their sexual encounters. B could also find another job. However, the discomfort of her work environment should she refuse the offer, combined with the hassle of looking for new work, in addition to the extra money involved in the promotion, together motivates employee B to accept the conditions of this promotion.

This case certainly meets the conditions of Valdman's Advantage Clause. The benefits A extracts are excessive because A is securing sexual favors from B on top of the benefits that promoting an employee would ordinarily provide to him and the company. Also, B is vulnerable because she stands on the lower end of a power relationship with her employer. He has this sexual access to her because of their relative roles in the power structure. But it is also clear that B is, to a certain degree, letting herself be used. After all, she *does* have reasonable alternatives to the agreement; for one, she could stick with her current position and deal with the resulting awkwardness. Dealing with this sort of awkwardness is no *unreasonable* alternative. Most of us deal with some awkwardness at our work places from day to day. Also, she could look for another job. Assuming that the economy is not completely crumby, looking for a new job is not an unreasonable alternative. Despite these the other reasonable options available to B, A uses his power advantage to wrongfully exploit B by creating this condition for B's promotion.

Valdman might argue that this action wrongs Employee B, but not *in virtue of* the exploitative component of the agreement. Maybe the arrangement between the employer, A, and employee, B, is wrongful because it is coercive of B. Certainly, the case that I have described is very like other cases that would, doubtless, be coercive. For instance, if A had told B that she would be fired and black-listed from similar agencies if she did not have sex with him, then the proposal would be coercive. Even if A had made B's promotion conditional on sex, but knew that B was in desperate need of the higher pay, we might be tempted to call the scenario coercive. However, neither A's proposal nor the desperation of B's circumstances restricts B's choices in the case that I have described. A is not himself manipulating B's alternatives to his preferred scenario to make them worse.

The case of the *Poor Student Renter* and the case of *Lewd Promotion* both involve excessive benefits being reaped from individuals who do have other reasonable options available to them. They are otherwise paradigm cases of wrongful exploitation, in that they cannot be explained in terms of any other wrong. However, wrongful exploitation can also arise in actions that can also be described as other kinds of wrongs. For instance, Wertheimer, Goodin, Sample, Wood, and Valdman's theories all allow that theft and rape are wrongfully exploitative, even if those actions are also rights violations and harms. Both incidents of theft and rape are ones in which a perpetrator benefits unfairly, opportunistically, and (when the benefit can be measured quantitatively) excessively. Typically, the victims of thieves and rapists are left with no other option but to be subject to these crimes.

Yet, consider a case of rape, I will call it *Date Rape* in which a male college student, A, lures a female college student, B, away from a living-room house party and into an adjacent room to have sex with her. A forces himself on B, who plainly refuses her consent, both verbally and through some physical resistance, but A does not prevent B from screaming for help. They are close enough to other party-goers that both A and B know that a scream would be heard. Imagine that A knows that B has only recently been admitted into the social group, is still quite unknown to his friends and housemates, and worries that she still might face rejection from the group. For these reasons, A feels confident that B will not scream for help or make any other sort of fuss after the fact. Additionally, B knows the following: that there is a college culture such that it is presumed that women who drink at house parties and wear outfits such as the one B is wearing are interested in engaging in sexual activity; also, that many popular college athletes, friends or esteemed acquaintances of A and his housemates, have been accused of sexual misconduct, so A and his housemates think particularly ill of women who make accusations of this sort. B does not scream for help, though there is ample time throughout the course of the rape.

In this case, A harms B, A violates B's rights against bodily integrity violations, and A wrongfully exploits B. A gains sexual and power-related advantages from raping B without suffering any social or legal costs. He counts on features of B's psychology and environment to keep B from accessing her other options both during and after the rape. However, these other options are not unreasonable alternatives. After all, exclusion from a (bad) social group is not an unreasonable option, and B knows this. It is a striking feature of Valdman's Vulnerability Clause for wrongful exploitation that it is *more* narrow than any plausible Vulnerability Clause for rape. (I am assuming that *Date Rape* counts as an instance of rape on any plausible account of rape.)

Wertheimer's account of exploitation allows that all of these scenarios are ones of wrongful exploitation. Valdman's account of exploitation allows that

these scenarios are ones of exploitation, but not of wrongful exploitation. I have argued that these cases are, indeed, wrongfully exploitative, which means that Wertheimer's theory has at least three advantages over Valdman's: it can accommodate the wrongful exploitation that occurs when an advantage is extracted from someone with reasonable alternatives, when the extraction is only possible because the victim has: an upbringing that has habitualized him to the receipt of bad treatment; a subordinate position in a work-related power relationship; or a vulnerable physique in a culture that tolerates rape. Of course, Wertheimer's theory has the disadvantage of calling every case in which one person extracts an unfair advantage from another an act of wrongful exploitation, rendering Wertheimer's theory too broad, as Valdman suggests. I have merely shown that Valdman's "no reasonable alternatives" Vulnerability Clause is too narrow.

NOTES

1. Goodin (1987) does the same as Wertheimer in this regard.

2. For instance, some might be tempted to say that the normative baseline for a fair agreement is at some half-way point between people's reservation prices. The idea here is that people should benefit equally in a fair transaction. However, this cannot be right, since there are all sorts of clearly exploitative cases in which the exploited party actually benefits more than his or her exploiter. Consider the Antidote Case itself. Hiker A takes unfair advantage of Hiker B, even though Hiker B benefits more from the transaction than Hiker A, that is, A merely gets money, B gets his life.

Perhaps the normative baseline for a fair transaction is some function of the background conditions, or starting points of the agents in the trade? Wertheimer points out that this account is also implausible. An exploited person might be much wealthier and more privileged than the person who exploits him. Imagine a case in which a poor shop owner raises his price exorbitantly for snow shovels on the day of a storm on which customers' cars are stuck in the snow bank on the shop owner's block. The customers might be wealthy, and paying ten times the normal amount for a snow shovel might not hurt their budgets in any significant way. However, these customers are, nonetheless, exploited by the poor shop owner.

3. Goodin (1987, p. 175). See note 1.

REFERENCES

Goodin R (1987) Exploiting a situation and exploiting a person. In: Reeve A (ed) Modern theories of exploitation. Sage Publications, London

Liberto H (2013) Noxious markets vs. noxious gift relationships. Soc Theory Pract 39(2):265–287

Sample R (2003) Exploitation: what it is and why it's wrong. Rowman & Littlefield, Landham

Valdman M (2009) A theory of wrongful exploitation. Philosophers Impr 9(6):1–14

Wertheimer A (1996) Exploitation. Princeton University Press, Princeton

Wood A (1995) Exploitation. Soc Philos Policy 12:136–158

QUESTIONS

1. What are the two conditions that characterize wrongful exploitation, according to Liberto? What are some examples of exploitation other than the ones she mentions? How does Liberto's view of wrongful exploitation differ from the view of exploitation Iris Marion Young defends in Chapter 3, "Food Justice"? Which food workers discussed in this chapter are wrongfully exploited, on Liberto's account? Which food workers are exploited on Young's account?

2. At the end of the excerpt, Liberto poses a question about how to have a theory of vulnerability that is neither too narrow, like Valdman's, nor too broad, like Wertheimer's. Explain what these accounts are and why she thinks these accounts are, respectively, too narrow and too broad. What is your view of what it is for someone to be vulnerable? What are some examples of vulnerable people other than the ones she mentions? When are food workers vulnerable?

3. Say you hire a babysitter. You know that younger sitters typically charge less than older ones. So you find the youngest sitter you're comfortable with and hire that sitter. Have you exploited the sitter? If so, have you done wrong?

4. Liberto discusses the Antidote, Date Rape, Lewd Promotion, and Poor Student Renter cases. In which ways are these cases like the cases of the treatment of tomato pickers in Immokalee? Like the cases of slaughterhouse workers in the Midwest?

12) Overconsumption and Obesity

This chapter discusses obesity and the overconsumption of food. A first topic of this chapter is the causes and consequences of overconsumption and obesity. A second topic is whether there's something ethically problematic with the ways that overconsumption and obesity are discussed by experts and the public. The readings in this chapter offer different explanations of why people consume too much food and critically discuss the "obesity epidemic."

CONSEQUENCES OF OVERCONSUMPTION

To stay alive and to be healthy, people must eat enough food, eat safe food, and eat food that is relatively healthy. They also must *not eat too much food* and in particular *not eat too much unhealthy food*. What has caused the increase in rates of overweight and obesity during the past few decades? Should we be concerned about this increase, and if so, why? Why do many people purchase and eat more food than they need to meet their bodies' energy needs? Why do many people eat more food high in sugar, fat, and salt than is likely consistent with good health? Do people make a choice to overconsume unhealthy food, or is this behavior not truly chosen? If it is a choice, is it an informed choice? Is it a rational choice? These questions about the causes of overconsumption and the psychology of unhealthy eating are relevant to the ethics of efforts to change what people eat. As Chapter 13, "Paternalism and Public Health," discusses, it may be more justifiable to limit people's access to unhealthy food if their consumption of unhealthy food is not an informed, rational, or fully voluntary choice.

What is the *overconsumption of food*? For the purposes of this chapter, let's define the *overconsumption of food* as, roughly, consuming more food than is necessary to meet your body's energy needs given your level of physical activity. But note that defining overconsumption this way makes assumptions about what's important, when it comes to assessing levels of food consumption. Why should overconsumption be defined relative to the body's energy needs? Why not define overconsumption in some other way, such as consumption in excess of what's needed to maximize the individual's happiness? Or define overconsumption as consumption in excess of what's necessary to maintain one's preferred body shape?

There are multiple reasons why we might care about the overconsumption of food, so defined. We might believe that eating more than we need to meet our bodies' energy needs is wasteful. We might believe that the overconsumption of food shows disregard for one's body—it pollutes the temple of one's body, so to speak. We might think that eating more food than we need is gluttonous, and that gluttony is a vice. Ethicists could surely find many more ethical reasons to care about overconsumption.

But the primary reason why experts and policymakers seem to care about overconsumption, at this moment in history, is that overconsumption can cause people to become overweight and obese, and obesity is associated with a higher risk of developing heart disease, diabetes, high blood pressure, and other diseases. In recent decades, there's been a sharp increase in the number of people who are overweight and obese, a phenomenon often labeled the *obesity epidemic*. According to the World Health Organization, 39% of adults worldwide were overweight and 13% were obese in 2014, with obesity doubling since 1980.[1] Within the United States, rates of overweight and obesity are higher than the global average. According to the United States Centers for Disease Control and Prevention (CDC), 34.9% of Americans are obese, and an additional third of the population are overweight but not obese.[2]

The prevailing definition of overweight and obesity is based on body mass index (BMI). BMI is a function of a person's weight and height: weight (in kilograms) divided by the square of height (in meters). *Overweight* is defined as a BMI of 25 or above. *Obesity* is defined as a BMI of 30 or above. *Normal weight* is defined as a BMI between 18.5 and 25. *Underweight* is defined as a BMI below 18.5. Given the current BMI-based definitions of overweight and obesity, one third of American adults are overweight and an additional third are obese. But these definitions are controversial. Some argue that the "normal weight" range should be higher than a BMI range of 18.5–25. Others argue that BMI should not be used at all to define normal weight, because it is not a good measure of body fat. Someone with a lot of muscle but very little fat, such as a body builder, will have a high BMI just because she weighs a lot. Others argue that total amount of body fat is not a good proxy for the risk of diet-related illness, because someone's risk of disease depends upon where fat is located on his body and what other risk factors he has.[3]

These high rates of overweight and obesity have significant consequences for public health, according to mainstream public health organizations and experts. According to the CDC, people who are obese, compared to people with a normal or healthy weight, have an increased risk of high blood pressure, high cholesterol, type 2 diabetes, heart disease, stroke, arthritis, sleep apnea, some cancers, as well as other health problems. High rates of diet-related illness are a concern because these illnesses cause people to suffer, become disabled, and die prematurely. They are also a concern because they are expensive to treat. According to the CDC, the "estimated annual medical cost of obesity in the U.S. was $147 billion in 2008 U.S. dollars" and obesity-related health problems cause people to miss work, causing a loss of productivity valued at $3.38 to $6.38 billion.[4]

Notwithstanding the intense concern with obesity expressed by the CDC, and the public health community more generally, there is disagreement about the health consequences of being overweight and being obese. Some research shows that being moderately overweight is correlated with a *lower* chance of dying, as compared with being normal weight, though the significance of this finding is disputed.[5] Some scholars question whether the health effects of obesity are as severe as claimed, and they conclude that the "obesity epidemic" is overblown. In the selection "Can't Stomach It: How Michael Pollan et al. Made Me Want to Eat Cheetos," Julie Guthman discusses criticisms of the science of obesity.

Despite this controversy about the health effects of overweight and obesity, most people could agree that there is *some* level of repeated overconsumption that poses health risks and agree that this is well known. Thus, whether or not we agree that overweight and obesity are a public health crisis, we can agree that it is an interesting question why so many of us regularly overconsume when we know it is risky. Similarly, there is some level of underconsumption of healthy foods, such as fruits and vegetables, that poses health risks and is well known to pose health risks, so it is also an interesting question why so many of us eat too little healthy food.

EXPLANATIONS OF EATING PATTERNS AND OBESITY

In this chapter, we consider explanations of the overconsumption of "unhealthy foods" (such as sugary drinks and processed foods high in sugar, fat, and sodium) and the underconsumption of "healthy foods" (such as fruits, vegetables, and whole grains). We consider two types of explanation. First, explanations of why people within contemporary food environments eat as they do. Second, explanations of why contemporary food environments are structured as they are. (We focus in this chapter on eating behavior, but a more complete discussion would include other potential contributors to body weight besides eating behavior, including physical activity, genetic factors, and environmental exposure to chemicals that cause weight gain.)

Examples of the first type of explanation—why people within contemporary food environments overconsume some foods and underconsume other foods—include the following:

- Healthy foods such as fruits and vegetables are more expensive than less healthy foods, such as processed foods high in sugar and fat, and some people cannot afford to buy these healthier foods rather than the less healthy ones and so eat unhealthily (see the reading "How the Economy Makes Us Fat" by Finkelstein and Zuckerman).
- Some people live in "food deserts"—neighborhoods with poor access to grocery stores or other sources of healthier foods—and so eat unhealthily.
- Some people live in "food swamps"—neighborhoods with a high concentration of fast-food restaurants, corner stores, and other sources of unhealthy food—and so eat unhealthily.
- Many unhealthy foods are a cheap source of pleasure, and for some people, overconsuming these foods maximizes utility, so they eat unhealthily (see "How the Economy Makes Us Fat").
- We are "hard-wired" to be motivated to consume the sugary and high-fat foods and beverages that pervade the food environment, and to have trouble regulating our consumption of them, and so eat unhealthily (see "The End of Overeating" by David Kessler).
- Eating is an automatic behavior, one that we have trouble exerting psychological control over. Given the preponderance of unhealthy food around us, we eat unhealthily.

- People who eat unhealthily are not sufficiently motivated to eat healthfully, or have inadequate willpower and self-control, and so eat unhealthily (see the readings "Can't Stomach It" and "Obesity: Chasing an Elusive Epidemic").

There is controversy about many of these explanations. Some researchers question whether living in a food desert contributes to overweight and obesity, and whether opening more grocery stores in food deserts will significantly change people's purchases and health.[6] Is the higher cost of healthier foods such as fruits and vegetables the main driver of underconsumption of them, or is taste the main factor? Are overconsumption and obesity a result of insufficient motivation, or is this just a false stereotype rooted in prejudice against people who are overweight?

Many experts who study obesity support the *environmental account of obesity*.[7] According to the environmental account of obesity, each individual is situated within an environment, and individual behaviors and individual outcomes are caused by environmental factors and by the interplay between the individual and the environment. Individual behaviors and outcomes are not caused just by features of the individual. Proponents of the environmental account of obesity typically endorse an environmental approach to obesity prevention: Focus on changing features of the food environment that influence behavior and outcomes, and don't focus just on the individual and individual factors that influence behavior.

For example, obesity researchers Marlene Schwarz and Kelly Brownell explain obesity as a result of the interaction of human biology and psychology with an environment pervaded with highly palatable, convenient, aggressively marketed food. They refer to the contemporary food environment as a "toxic," or poisonous environment:

> When we use the term "toxic environment," we are referring to several layers of the world around us that interact with key elements of our biology. . . . Humans are innately predisposed to prefer sweet foods, and infants quickly learn to prefer the flavor of high fat and high salt foods. . . . Children and adults will eat more when larger portions are served. . . . These factors interact with the current environment in several ways. Driving down the highway, we see dozens of drive through windows at fast food restaurants, billboards with advertisements for inexpensive snacks, and soft drinks at drugstores, and when we stop for gas, shelf after shelf of high-fat and high-sugar snacks at gas station mini marts. It is no wonder American spending on fast food has increased eighteen-fold since 1970. A variety of good tasting snacks and meals are now highly visible and accessible for most Americans, and there is also evidence that since the 1970's, portion sizes have gotten larger, and far exceed federal guidelines. These foods are also extremely convenient[;] compared with home made meals, fast food and packaged foods are easier to obtain and ready to eat immediately, as they require little preparation. . . . In addition to the omnipresence of unhealthful foods in our current environment, these foods are also less expensive than healthful choices. . . . Another layer of the toxic environment that promotes the consumption of unhealthful foods is their heavy promotion by the food industry. The food industry is massive; in 2000 it generated nearly $900 billion in sales. . . .[8]

Along with "toxic" environment, the food environment is also referred to as an "obesogenic" environment—that is, an environment that tends to cause obesity.[9] As Egger and Swinburn put it, obesity is "a normal response to an abnormal environment, rather than vice versa."[10] The "toxic environment" and "obesogenic environment" views are examples of the first kind of explanation—explaining why people within the contemporary food environment overconsume food. Further examples are found in this chapter in the selections by Eric Finkelstein and Laurie Zuckerman, Brian Wansink, and David Kessler.

In the selection "How the Economy Makes Us Fat," Finkelstein and Zuckerman explain overconsumption as a result of the relatively cheap price of food, particularly unhealthy food. They suggest, furthermore, that people who are overweight typically make an informed, rational choice to overconsume and thereby to be overweight, and this choice maximizes their utility. (A utility-maximizing choice is a choice that, among the available choices, leads to the maximum amount of utility. *Utility* may be understood here as *happiness*, or as *satisfaction of preferences*.) According to Finkelstein and Zuckerman, people typically understand the costs and benefits of healthy eating, unhealthy eating, and poor health; for example, they understand the health risks of unhealthy eating, the financial cost of healthy eating, and the benefits of unhealthy eating, such as enjoyment. Given these costs and benefits, many people experience more utility from overconsuming, becoming overweight, and increasing their health risks than they would from not overconsuming. Finkelstein and Zuckerman argue not just that these choices maximize utility in the short run, when we're eating the delicious food and relaxing rather than exercising, but that these decisions maximize people's long-term utility *even though* they increase the risk of diet-related illness. (But note that even if the choice to eat unhealthily maximizes someone's utility, given the existing costs of healthy eating and benefits of unhealthy eating, she might still prefer to live in a food environment in which the costs of healthy eating are lower. For example, a food environment in which healthy eating is more convenient, cheaper, more delicious, and takes less psychological effort.)

An opposing view is that people who overconsume, become overweight and obese, and thereby increase their risk of illness are not making informed, rational choices to overconsume. Instead, they are making choices that are *uninformed* or *irrational* or both; or maybe their overconsumption is not truly a choice at all. For example, someone who overconsumes may not understand that he is overconsuming or the long-term health consequences of overconsumption. Or he understands these consequences but irrationally chooses to experience the positive effects of overconsumption in the short run, even though this will likely cause him much more pain and inconvenience later. For example, every day Max decides to have a soda with his lunch, even though he believes that drinking soda will eventually exacerbate his diabetes and cause painful health complications, because he irrationally judges the pleasure he gets from drinking soda to be worth the long-term costs. Or he rationally decides not to consume it but is psychologically unable to follow through on this decision. For example, Max finally decides that drinking soda with lunch is the wrong choice and decides that he'll stop doing it, but he can't manage to stop doing it.

Perhaps the "choice" to overconsume is not typically a *choice*, properly speaking. In the selection "The Mindless Margin," Brian Wansink discusses how features of the environment—such as large serving sizes—cause people to eat more, unbeknownst to them. Even if they choose to begin eating, people may not be choosing how much to eat. A complementary view is that eating is an *automatic behavior*, one of those behaviors that "occur without awareness, are initiated without intention, tend to continue without control, and operate efficiently or with little effort."[11] If eating is an automatic behavior, this suggests an explanation of why we continue to eat even when our energy needs have been met: We don't exert psychological control over our eating, once it's begun. In other words, we overconsume because when it comes to eating, we are on auto-pilot. If eating is initiated without intention and tends to continue without control, is overconsuming truly a choice? This depends, of course, on exactly how we understand *intention*, *control*, and *choice*.

An additional explanation of why we overconsume, given in the reading "The End of Overeating," is that certain foods—foods high in sugar, fat, and salt, which are called palatable foods—stimulate the *reward system* of the brain. "Eating foods high in sugar, fat, and salt makes us eat more foods high in sugar, fat, and salt," Kessler writes. "Rewarding foods tend to be reinforcing, meaning that they keep us coming back for more. I put an M&M in my mouth, it tastes good, and I return for another. The sugar and fat in the candy reinforce my desire to keep eating it." Eating foods high in sugar, fat, and salt motivates us to eat more of these foods, even if we're not hungry and would rather not eat them.

EXPLAINING THE FOOD ENVIRONMENT

We've been discussing explanations of why people eat as they do within contemporary food environments. A second kind of explanation endeavors to explain why contemporary food environments are structured as they are where that structure might be "toxic" or "obesogenic." Example explanations include the following:

- Agricultural subsidies for corn and soy have led to an excess of cheap corn and soy, which is turned into corn syrup and soybean oil and then used in sugary and high-fat processed food.
- Technological advances in food processing and distribution have increased the availability of convenient, high-calorie processed foods.
- The food industry has created a large array of processed foods that are high in fat, sugar, and salt, and which are carefully engineered to be hard to resist (see the reading "Lunchtime Is All Yours").
- The food industry spends billions of dollars on marketing and advertising in order to influence consumer preferences and behavior (see the reading "The Politics of Food Choice"), and these efforts have changed social norms about how much and what to eat.

Some obesity researchers encourage us to look for this second kind of explanation and to take a "food system perspective on obesity," as Julie Guthman puts it.[12] Rather than examining individual behavior and critiquing people's lifestyles, we instead "should incorporate the entire array of ideas, institutions, and policies that affect how food is produced, distributed, and consumed."[13] In other words, to understand obesity adequately, we need to keep the big picture in view, and not just narrowly focus on individuals' eating behaviors.

One big-picture explanation, found in the reading "The Politics of Food Choice" by Marion Nestle, is that the food industry exerts extraordinary influence over both individuals and the government, shaping individual preferences and government policy in ways that perpetuate unhealthy eating. As Nestle describes it, the food industry shapes consumers' food preferences through marketing, and it shapes government policy behind the scenes through lobbying and relationships with government officials. The food industry also shapes public opinion about healthy eating and public opinion about government regulation—for example, by describing government efforts to promote healthier diets as "totalitarian" and as unwarranted limitations on individual liberty.

As an example of another "big-picture" explanation of obesity, some scholars argue that neoliberalism—the political economic system emphasizing free market capitalism and a minimal state—contributes to increasing rates of obesity. Neoliberalism engenders the agricultural policies, cheap foods, and other conditions that encourage obesity, some scholars argue.[14] And the ideology of neoliberalism encourages obesity, they argue, because it encourages seeing consumer choice as a right—and thus seeing government regulation of the food marketplace as illegitimate. The ideology of neoliberalism also sees consumption as a feature of good citizenship, as argued here by Julie Guthman and Melanie Dupuis:

> One of the ways that neoliberal governmentality produces a certain sort of subject is through the fetish of consumer choice (along with the fetish of the market) and through the idea that choice represents a sort of right. . . . This "rights discourse," as Dean puts it, is certainly found in the politics of obesity; it undergirds, for instance, the presentations of the Center for Consumer Freedom, the key group countering the group they call the "food Nazis." In their advertisements we are told not to be swayed by those who would regulate what we eat. By exercising our choice to eat we are exercising our freedoms. . . . Consequently, as the many descriptions of modern America as the consumer society suggest, we have all but abandoned notions of citizenship as participation in the public sphere for a more individualist notion of self as the citizen consumer whose contribution to society is mainly to purchase the products of global capitalism. Whereas the role of the US consumer in the Fordist period was to work hard *and* to consume hard, in the neoliberal period of locating production off-shore only the consumption side is left to maintain US identity. . . . eating becomes the embodiment of that which today's society holds sacred: consumption. We buy and eat to be good subjects.[15]

According to the ideology of neoliberalism, Guthman and Dupuis argue, consumption is a mark of good citizenship. The ideology of neoliberalism also pins responsibility for obesity on the individual who is expected to control her own consumption, they argue:

> At the same time, neoliberalism produces a hypervigilance about control and deservingness. . . . The neoliberal critique of too much intervention returns improvement to the individual, who is expected to exercise choice and to become responsible for his or her risks. . . . In short, neoliberal governmentality produces contradictory impulses such that the neoliberal subject is emotionally compelled to participate in society as both out-of-control consumer and self-controlled subject. The perfect subject-citizen is able to achieve both eating and thinness, even if having it both ways entails eating nonfoods of questionable impact (Splenda) or throwing up the food one does eat (the literal bulimic). Those who can achieve thinness amidst this plenty are imbued with the rationality and self-discipline that those who are fat must logically lack; they then become the deserving in a political economy all too geared toward legitimizing such distinctions.[16]

Guthman and Dupuis argue that people who are able to remain thin are seen as "imbued with the rationality and self-discipline" that others lack. This judgment feeds into the stigmatization of people who are overweight—a topic discussed in the next section.

WEIGHT STIGMA

Critics of the "obesity epidemic" discourse raise concerns about the science of obesity, as mentioned previously. They also raise ethical concerns about the way that overweight and obesity are discussed. For example, in the reading "Can't Stomach It: How Michael Pollan et al. Made Me Want to Eat Cheetos," Julie Guthman critiques the "obesity epidemic" conversation as stigmatizing and belittling toward fat people. An example of a stigmatizing approach to obesity, according to its critics, is found in the reading "Obesity: Chasing an Elusive Epidemic" by Dan Callahan. He proposes applying social pressure to people who are overweight and obese, to motivate them to adopt better dietary and exercise habits. Callahan acknowledges the difficulty of applying this social pressure without leading to outright discrimination, but he advocates that we should try to achieve this "stigmatization lite." Callahan's article was intensely controversial, and it provoked a firestorm of criticism. The reading "Obesity Stigma: A Failed and Ethically Dubious Strategy" is a reply to Callahan; the authors Goldberg and Puhl argue that there is no evidence that stigmatization is effective at addressing obesity and plenty of evidence that it is harmful and counter-productive.

Ethicists disagree about whether it is ever ethically justifiable to stigmatize behaviors (such as smoking) or health states (such as being overweight), in an effort to produce healthier behavior. Whether stigma is ever ethically justifiable depends in part upon what stigma is. "Stigma" and "stigmatization" are used by some authors to refer to a specific kind of social sanction that is severe and all-encompassing, involving a loss of status, shame, and self-punishment.[17] Goldberg and Puhl cite a common definition of stigma: "an out-group is marked or branded as different on the basis of a common demographic characteristic, and then the out-group is judged deviant or inferior on the basis of that characteristic." But other authors and researchers use "stigma" and "stigmatization" more loosely so that they refer to public disapproval, social marginalization, self-directed shame, and other related phenomena.[18] Andrew Courtwright, in a discussion of the ethics of health-related stigma, defines it thus: "for an institution to stigmatize a health related characteristic or behavior involves changing norms about the desirability of the activity, marking the bearers of the trait, and excluding them from the broader community, a process that can, but does not necessarily, create a spoiled social identity."[19]

Along with questioning whether obesity discourse and antiobesity efforts are stigmatizing, critics also question the motives and attitudes that underlie concern with obesity. Julie Guthman, in her reading in this chapter, and other scholars have argued that concern with the "obesity epidemic" may not derive primarily from concern for public health, but instead reflects moral judgments about people who are overweight or obese, reflects bias against people who are overweight or obese, reflects an aesthetic preference for thinness, and is motivated by the self-interest of public health professionals (who build careers around combating obesity) and the self-interest of pharmaceutical companies and the weight-loss industry (who sell more weight-loss drugs and products if the public is intensely concerned with overweight and obesity).[20] Implicit in these criticisms is that it is ethically problematic to urge people to lose weight, or even shame them, because of, say, an aesthetic preference or a desire to sell more weight-loss drugs.

HEALTHY EATING POLICY

A variety of policies have been proposed or implemented to change what consumers purchase and eat.[21] Often these policies are implemented by the government—including legislative bodies (such as the San Francisco board of supervisors, which required McDonalds Happy Meals to have higher nutritional standards), health departments (such as the New York City Department of Health and Mental Hygiene), and regulatory bodies (such as the United States Food and Drug Administration, which banned various "raw" foods). Many schools, community organizations, and businesses also have healthy eating initiatives.

Some policies focus on providing general information about nutrition and health, or information about specific foods. Examples include nutrition education programs, efforts to revamp food labels so that they clearly communicate the nutritional content of food, and calorie posting laws requiring fast-food restaurants and other chain restaurants to indicate, on their menu boards, how many calories each item has. Other policies aim to change people's attitudes toward specific foods, or toward body weight and health. For example, a media campaign in New York City aimed to raise awareness of the sugar content and health impact of sugary drinks.[22] Media campaigns in Minnesota and Georgia aimed to increase parents' awareness of childhood obesity and motivate them to take action.[23] These media campaigns were criticized as stigmatizing and criticized for shaming children who are overweight (see the reading "Obesity Stigma: A Failed and Ethically Dubious Strategy" for an argument that stigma is both counter-productive and unethical).

Other policies focus on increasing access to healthy food. Some policies aim to increase *geographic* access to healthy food, for example: subsidies for grocery stores that locate in food deserts, subsidies and support for farmers markets that open in underserved areas, and programs encouraging corner stores in cities to offer healthy foods such as fresh fruits and vegetables. Other policies aim to increase *financial* access to healthy food. For example, programs in many states and localities provide financial incentives to participants in the Supplemental Nutrition Assistance Program (a.k.a. the food stamp program) who shop at farmers markets, in order to make fruits and vegetables more affordable for them.

Other policies focus on limiting access to unhealthy food, either by making it less available or making it more expensive. Examples of such policies include taxing sodas and other sugary drinks; banning the use of trans fat, a particularly unhealthy form of fat, in restaurants and packaged foods; requiring fast-food restaurants to make kids' meals healthier; and the (failed) New York City ban on the sale of large sugary drinks, which is discussed in Chapter 13, "Paternalism and Public Health."

These healthy eating policies have been criticized by scholars, politicians, advocates for low-income people, advocates for overweight and obese people, the food industry, and the general public. Policies that make unhealthy food more expensive, such as taxes on sugary drinks, have been criticized as unfair to low-income people, who have less money to spend on food. Many policies, but particularly media campaigns that attempt to change people's attitudes toward body weight and health, have been criticized as stigmatizing people who are overweight and obese. Some policies have been criticized as "nanny state" or "infantilizing" policies that treat consumers like children who cannot make decisions for themselves. As we discuss in Chapter 13, "Paternalism and Public Health," many policies, but particularly those limiting access to unhealthy food, have been criticized as *paternalistic*—as inappropriately limiting consumers' personal freedom for the sake of improving their health.

We started this chapter by pointing out that people overconsume, in the sense that they eat more food than they need to meet their bodies' energy needs. We noted that there is controversy about whether this overconsumption is problematic, and why. We have now come to the point that *even if* there's a problem here, it is unclear what an ethically sound response to it would be.

FURTHER ISSUES

1. *Definition of Healthy and Unhealthy Foods*

What are "healthy foods" and "unhealthy foods"? Who decides? People have different conceptions of health and healthy eating. Is it uncontroversial that processed foods and foods high in sugar, fat, and salt should count as "unhealthy foods"? Is there one conception of "unhealthy foods" that should be privileged, when making public health policy?

2. *Control over Eating and Body Weight*

Do people have control over whether they consume healthier foods rather than less healthy foods? If healthier food is not readily available in someone's neighborhood, and is unaffordable for her, does she have control over whether she eats healthier food? Do people have control over whether they overconsume unhealthy food? Dan Wikler writes: "To some commentators, then, the question of free choice of lifestyles is the key to determining responsibility for health. But which choices are free, and which are not? . . . Once addicted, the heroin addict seems to lack the capacity to choose not to seek heroin; the compulsive hand washer is visited with overwhelming anxiety if denied access to a sink. Such behavior stands in contrast to a person who slowly, deliberately, and autonomously decides to join a mountain climbing expedition simply for the adventure. The kinds of behavior which are most commonly singled out in the debate over personal responsibility for health, such as smoking, sloth, and overweight, are, however, in a gray zone. These habits seem to be matters of personal choice, but they are notoriously difficult to give up."[24] Do you agree with Wikler's characterization of overweight as both a matter of personal choice and something that involves behaviors difficult to give up?

3. *Control and Responsibility*

If people cannot control what they eat, should they be held responsible for the negative consequences of their eating? Do they deserve moral blame, if they did not have control over acting that way? Should they be held liable for the costs incurred by acting that way? Is it fair to hold people responsible for behavior that they did not control?

4. *Responsibility for Obesity*

Some ethical disagreement about obesity prevention is disagreement about whose responsibility obesity is. Who is responsible for current rates of obesity? Whose responsibility is it to reduce the prevalence of obesity going forward—individuals themselves, the government, the food industry, or society in general? Whose responsibility is it to bear the costs associated with obesity (such as higher health care costs)—for example, should individuals pay more for health insurance if they are overweight or obese? There are distinct kinds of responsibility at play in these ethical disagreements: causal responsibility, concerned with who caused something to happen; role responsibility, concerned with whose role it is to control what happens; and moral responsibility, concerned with who deserves moral blame for what happened and who should be held liable for what happened.

5. *Unhealthy Eating and Adaptive Preferences*

People the world over collectively buy a lot of processed foods that are high in sugar, salt, and fat. Many people like these foods (though we can argue about the sense in which they "like" them). For some people, these are their favorite foods. But if the food industry had never figured out how to create processed foods, some other foods would be their favorite foods (maybe apples, or homemade bread). Should we see preferences for these processed food products as adaptive preferences—that is, preferences that were formed in response to a limited range of options? Is the way that the food industry has shaped consumers' preferences morally problematic? Is it morally problematic in a way that makes consumers' preferences morally suspect?

6. *Preferences for Behavior Versus Preferences for Environments*

Finkelstein and Zuckerman argue that people who are overweight typically prefer to overconsume and are making consumption choices that maximize their long-term utility. But note that even if the choice to eat unhealthily maximizes someone's utility, given the existing costs of healthy eating and benefits of unhealthy eating, she might still prefer to live in a food environment in which the costs of healthy eating are lower. For example, a food environment in which healthy eating is more convenient, cheaper, more delicious, and takes less psychological effort.

FURTHER READING

Stigma and Weight Discrimination

Bacon, Linda. 2009. "Reflections on Fat Acceptance: Lessons Learned from Privilege." http://www.lindabacon.org/Bacon_ThinPrivilege080109.pdf.

Bayer, R. 2008. "Stigma and the Ethics of Public Health: Not Can We but Should We," *Social Science and Medicine* 67, no. 3: 463–472.

Campos, Paul. 2006. "Fat and the Politics of Fear," *Health At Every Size* 20, no. 3: 133.

Courtwright, Andrew. 2013. "Stigmatization and Public Health Ethics," *Bioethics* 27, no. 2: 74–80. doi:10.1111/j.1467-8519.2011.01904.x.

Saguy, Abigail C., and Kevin W. Riley. 2005. "Weighing Both Sides: Morality, Mortality, and Framing Contests over Obesity," *Journal of Health Politics, Policy and Law* 30, no. 5: 869–921.

Williams, Regina D. 1998. "Conquering the Fear of a Fat Body: The Journey Toward Myself," in Ophira Edut, ed., *Adios Barbie: Young Women Write about Body Image and Identity*. Seattle, WA: Seal Press.

Skepticism about the Health Risks of Overweight and Obesity

Bacon, Linda, and Lucy Aphramor. 2011. "Weight Science: Evaluating the Evidence for a Paradigm Shift," *Nutrition Journal* 10: 9.

Belluck, Pam. 2013. "Study Suggests Lower Mortality Risk for People Deemed to Be Overweight," *New York Times*, January 1. http://www.nytimes.com/2013/01/02/health/study-suggests-lower-death-risk-for-the-overweight.html?_r=0.

Campos, Paul F. 2004. *The Obesity Myth: Why America's Obsession with Weight Is Hazardous to Your Health.* New York: Gotham Books.

———. 2013. "Our Imaginary Weight Problem," *New York Times*, January 2. http://www.nytimes.com/2013/01/03/opinion/our-imaginary-weight-problem.html?_r=0.

Causes of Overconsumption and Obesity

Chaykin, Dan, director. 2012. *The Weight of the Nation*. HBO Documentary Films. http://www.imdb.com/title/tt2220150/?ref_=fn_al_tt_1.

Cohen, Deborah, and Thomas A. Farley. 2008. "Eating as an Automatic Behavior," *Preventing Chronic Disease* 5, no. 1: A23. http://www.ncbi.nlm.nih.gov/pmc/articles/PMC2248777/.

Egger, Garry, and Boyd Swinburn. 1997. "An 'Ecological' Approach to the Obesity Pandemic," *BMJ: British Medical Journal* 315 (7106): 477.

Lang, Tim, and Geoff Rayner. 2007. "Overcoming Policy Cacophony on Obesity: An Ecological Public Health Framework for Policymakers." *Obesity Reviews* 8 (s1): 165–181.

Morales, Alfonso. 2011. "Growing Food and Justice: Dismantling Racism through Sustainable Food Systems," in Alison Hope Alkon and Julian Agyeman, eds., *Cultivating Food Justice: Race, Class, and Sustainability*, 149–176. Cambridge, MA: MIT Press.

Moss, Michael. 2013. *Salt, Sugar, Fat: How the Food Giants Hooked Us*. New York: Random House.

Schwartz, Marlene B., and Kelly D. Brownell. 2007. "Actions Necessary to Prevent Childhood Obesity: Creating the Climate for Change," *The Journal of Law, Medicine & Ethics* 35, no. 1: 78–89.

Story, Mary, Karen M. Kaphingst, Ramona Robinson-O'Brien, and Karen Glanz. 2008. "Creating Healthy Food and Eating Environments: Policy and Environmental Approaches," *Annual Review of Public Health* 29, no. 1: 253–272. doi:10.1146/annurev.publhealth.29.020907.090926.

Responsibility and Obesity

Brownell, K. D., R. Kersh, D. S. Ludwig, R. C. Post, R. M. Puhl, M. B. Schwartz, and W. C. Willett. 2010. "Personal Responsibility and Obesity: A Constructive Approach to a Controversial Issue." *Health Affairs* 29, no. 3: 379–387. doi:10.1377/hlthaff.2009.0739.

Guthman, Julie. 2011. *Weighing In: Obesity, Food Justice, and the Limits of Capitalism*, 1st ed. Berkeley: University of California Press (see especially chap. 3, "Whose Problem Is Obesity?," pp. 46–65).

Kirkland, Anna. 2011. "The Environmental Account of Obesity: A Case for Feminist Skepticism." *Signs* 36, no. 2: 463–485.

Wikler, Daniel. 1987. "Who Should Be Blamed for Being Sick?" *Health Education & Behavior* 14, no. 1: 11–25.

NOTES

1. World Health Organization, "Obesity and Overweight." http://www.who.int/mediacentre/factsheets/fs311/en/ (accessed September 1, 2015).

2. Centers for Disease Control and Prevention. "Adult Obesity Facts," June 16, 2015. https://www.cdc.gov/obesity/data/adult.html.

3. Pam Belluck, "Study Suggests Lower Mortality Risk for People Deemed to Be Overweight," *New York Times,* January 1, 2013. http://www.nytimes.com/2013/01/02/health/study-suggests-lower-death-risk-for-the-overweight.html?_r=0.

4. Centers for Disease Control and Prevention, 2015.

5. Belluck,"Study Suggests Lower Mortality Risk."

6. Jessie Handbury, Ilya Rahkovsky, and Molly Schnell, "Is the Focus on Food Deserts Fruitless? Retail Access and Food Purchases across the Socioeconomic Spectrum," 2015. http://www.brown.edu/academics/economics/sites/brown.edu.academics.economics/files/uploads/Jesse%20Handbury_Is%20the%20focus%20on%20food_Paper.pdf.

7. Garry Egger and Boyd Swinburn, "An 'Ecological' Approach to the Obesity Pandemic," *BMJ: British Medical Journal* 315, no. 7106 (1997): 477–480; Marlene B. Schwartz and Kelly D. Brownell, "Actions Necessary to Prevent Childhood Obesity: Creating the Climate for Change," *Journal of Law, Medicine & Ethics* 35, no. 1 (2007): 78–89; Mary Story, Karen M. Kaphingst, Ramona Robinson-O'Brien, and Karen Glanz, "Creating Healthy Food and Eating Environments: Policy and Environmental Approaches," *Annual Review of Public Health* 29, no. 1 (2008): 253–272. doi:10.1146/annurev.publhealth.29.020907.090926.

8. Schwartz and Brownell, "Actions Necessary to Prevent Childhood Obesity."

9. Egger and Swinburn, "An 'Ecological' Approach to the Obesity Pandemic."

10. Ibid., 477.

11. Deborah Cohen and Thomas A. Farley, "Eating as an Automatic Behavior," *Preventing Chronic Disease* 5, no. 1 (2008). http://www.ncbi.nlm.nih.gov/pmc/articles/PMC2248777/.

12. Guthman, Julie. *Weighing In: Obesity, Food Justice, and the Limits of Capitalism*, 1st ed. (Berkeley: University of California Press, 2011), 19.

13. Ibid., 19.

14. Ibid., 17–20.

15. Julie Guthman and Melanie DuPuis, "Embodying Neoliberalism: Economy, Culture, and the Politics of Fat," *Environment and Planning D: Society and Space* 24, no. 3 (2006): 427–448. doi:10.1068/d3904, pp.442–443.

16. Ibid., 443–444.

17. Scott Burris, "Stigma, Ethics and Policy: A Commentary on Bayer's 'Stigma and the Ethics of Public Health: Not Can We But Should We'," *Social Science and Medicine* 67, no. 3 (2008): 473–475.

18. Ronald Bayer, "Stigma and the Ethics of Public Health: Not Can We But Should We." *Social Science and Medicine* 67, no. 3 (2008): 463–472; Ronald Bayer, "What Means This Thing Called Stigma? A Response to Burris," *Social Science and Medicine* 67, no. 3 (2008): 476–477.

19. Andrew Courtwright, "Stigmatization and Public Health Ethics," *Bioethics* 27, no. 2 (February 2013): 74–80. doi:10.1111/j.1467-8519.2011.01904.x., 78.

20. Paul Campos, "Fat and the Politics of Fear," *Health at Every Size* 20, no. 3 (Fall 2006).

21. Mary Story, Karen M. Kaphingst, Ramona Robinson-O'Brien, and Karen Glanz, "Creating Healthy Food and Eating Environments: Policy and Environmental Approaches," *Annual Review of Public Health* 29, no. 1 (2008): 253–272. doi:10.1146/annurev.publhealth.29.020907.090926; Institute of Medicine, *Accelerating Progress in Obesity Prevention: Solving the Weight of the Nation* (Washington, DC: National Academies Press, 2012), 33–54, see chaps. 5–9 (pp.127–378) for discussion of policy approaches.

22. New York City Department of Health & Mental Hygiene, "Are You Pouring on the Pounds?" http://www.nyc.gov/html/doh/downloads/pdf/pan/PouringOnPounds.pdf.

23. Kathy Lohr, "Controversy Swirls Around Harsh Anti-Obesity Ads," *The Salt*, January 9, 2012. http://www.npr.org/2012/01/09/144799538/controversy-swirls-around-harsh-anti-obesity-ads; Selena Simmons-Duffin, "New Anti-Obesity Ads Blaming Overweight Parents Spark Criticism," National Public Radio, September 27, 2012. http://www.npr.org/sections/thesalt/2012/09/27/161831449/new-anti-obesity-ads-blaming-overweight-parents-spark-criticism.

24. Daniel Wikler, "Who Should Be Blamed for Being Sick?" *Health Education & Behavior* 14, no. 1 (1987): 11–25.

BRIAN WANSINK

The Mindless Margin

In this excerpt from his book *Mindless Eating*, Brian Wansink describes one of the many studies he's conducted showing that how much we eat is influenced by the surrounding environment. Wansink's other studies have found, among other things, that people eat more candy if the candy bowl is clear rather than opaque, they eat more jelly beans if there are more colors of them, they cook more spaghetti if the spaghetti comes in a larger box, and they pour a larger drink into a squat glass than a tall and skinny glass. Wansink's work provides a *psychological* explanation for why people within the contemporary food environment overconsume.

Did you ever eat the last piece of crusty, dried-out chocolate cake even though it tasted like chocolate-scented cardboard? Ever finish eating a bag of french fries even though they were cold, limp, and soggy? It hurts to answer questions like these.

Why do we overeat food that doesn't even taste good?

We overeat because there are signals and cues around us that tell us to eat. It's simply not in our nature to pause after every bite and contemplate whether we're full. As we eat, we unknowingly—mindlessly—look for signals or cues that we've had enough. For instance, if there's nothing remaining on the table, that's a cue that it's time to stop. If everyone else has left the table, turned off the lights, and we're sitting alone in the dark, that's another cue. For many of us, as long as there are still a few milk-soaked Froot Loops left in the bottom of the cereal bowl, there is still work to be done. It doesn't matter if we're full, and it doesn't matter if we don't even really like Froot Loops. We eat as if it is our mission to finish them.[1]

STALE POPCORN AND FRAIL WILLPOWER

Take movie popcorn, for instance. There is no "right" amount of popcorn to eat during a movie. There are no rules of thumb or FDA guidelines. People eat however much they want depending on how hungry they are and how good it tastes. At least that's what they say.

My graduate students and I think different. We think that the cues around us—like the size of a popcorn bucket—can provide subtle but powerful suggestions about how much one should eat. These cues can short-circuit a person's hunger and taste signals, leading them to eat even if they're not hungry and even if the food doesn't taste very good.

If you were living in Chicago a few years back, you might have been our guest at a suburban theater matinee. If you lined up to see the 1:05 P.M. Saturday showing of Mel Gibson's new action movie,

Payback, you would have had a surprise waiting for you: a free bucket of popcorn.

Every person who bought a ticket—even though many of them had just eaten lunch—was given a soft drink and either a medium-size bucket of popcorn or a large-size, bigger-than-your-head bucket. They were told that the popcorn and soft drinks were free and that we hoped they would be willing to answer a few concession stand–related questions after the movie.

There was only one catch. This wasn't fresh popcorn. Unknown to the moviegoers and even to my graduate students, this popcorn had been popped five days earlier and stored in sterile conditions until it was stale enough to squeak when it was eaten.

To make sure it was kept separate from the rest of the theater popcorn, it was transported to the theater in bright yellow garbage bags—the color yellow that screams "Biohazard." The popcorn was safe to eat, but it was stale enough one moviegoer said it was like eating Styrofoam packing peanuts. Two others, forgetting they had been given it for free, asked for their money back. During the movie, people would eat a couple bites, put the bucket down, pick it up again a few minutes later and have a couple more bites, put it back down, and continue. It might not have been good enough to eat all at once, but they couldn't leave it alone.

Both popcorn containers—medium and large—had been selected to be big enough that nobody could finish all the popcorn. And each person was given his or her own individual bucket so there would be no sharing.

As soon as the movie ended and the credits began to roll, we asked everyone to take their popcorn with them. We gave them a half-page survey (on bright biohazard-yellow paper) that asked whether they agreed to statements like "I ate too much popcorn," by circling a number from 1 (strongly disagree) to 9 (strongly agree). As they did this, we weighed their remaining popcorn.

When the people who had been given the large buckets handed their leftover popcorn to us, we said, "Some people tonight were given medium-size buckets of popcorn, and others, like yourself, were given these large-size buckets. We have found that the average person who is given a large-size container eats more than if they are given a medium-size container. Do you think you ate more because you had the large size?" Most disagreed. Many smugly said, "That wouldn't happen to me," "Things like that don't trick me," or "I'm pretty good at knowing when I'm full."

That may be what they believed, but it is not what happened.

Weighing the buckets told us that the big-bucket group ate an average of 173 more calories of popcorn. That is roughly the equivalent of 21 more dips into the bucket. Clearly the quality of food is not what led them to eat. Once these moviegoers started in on their bucket, the taste of the popcorn didn't matter.[2] Even though some of them had just had lunch, people who were given the big buckets ate an average of 53 percent more than those given medium-size buckets. Give them a lot, and they eat a lot.

And this was five-day-old, stale popcorn!

We've run other popcorn studies, and the results were always the same, however we tweaked the details. It didn't matter if our moviegoers were in Pennsylvania, Illinois, or Iowa, and it didn't matter what kind of movie was showing; all of our popcorn studies led to the same conclusion. People eat more when you give them a bigger container. Period. It doesn't matter whether the popcorn is fresh or fourteen days old, or whether they were hungry or full when they sat down for the movie.

Did people eat because they liked the popcorn? No. Did they eat because they were hungry? No. They ate because of all the cues around them—not only the size of the popcorn bucket, but also . . . the distracting movie, the sound of people eating popcorn around them, and the eating scripts we take to movie theaters with us. All of these were cues that signaled it was okay to keep on eating and eating.

Does this mean we can avoid mindless eating simply by replacing large bowls with smaller bowls? That's one piece of the puzzle, but there are a lot more cues that can be engineered out of our lives. As you will see, these hidden persuaders can even take the form of a tasty description on a menu or a classy name on a wine bottle. Simply *thinking* that a meal will taste good can lead you to eat more. You won't even know it happened.

NOTES

1. See Brian Wansink, "Environmental Factors That Increase the Food Intake and Consumption Volume of Unknowing Consumers," *Annual Review of Nutrition* 24 (2004):455–79.

2. On average, those given the medium-sized bucket ate 6.1 grams, while those given the large bucket ate 93.5 grams. Nobody finished all of their popcorn, which had been popped in partially hydrogenated (meaning "bad" trans fat) canola oil. This study was filmed for the ABC News' Morning Edition. It can be viewed at www.MindlessEating.org. See Brian Wansink and SeaBum Park, "At the Movies: How External Cues and Perceived Taste Impact Consumption Volume," *Food Quality and Preference*, 12:1(January 2001):69–74.

QUESTIONS

1. Wansink writes, "Did they eat because they were hungry? No. They ate because of all the cues around them . . . that signaled it was okay to keep on eating and eating." Does Wansink's work show that hunger is not relevant to how much people eat? Or just that serving size *is* relevant to how much they eat?

2. In Wansink's experiment, when people with a large bucket of stale popcorn eat 500 calories worth of popcorn, do they want to eat this much? When people with a medium bucket of stale popcorn eat 326 calories worth of popcorn, do they want to eat this much? Does the size of the popcorn bucket change how much people want to consume, or does it just change how much they do consume?

DAVID KESSLER

The End of Overeating

David Kessler gives a neurophysiological explanation of why we overconsume certain foods. Foods high in sugar, fat, and salt stimulate the *reward system* of the brain. Eating these foods is reinforcing: Eating them causes us to eat more of them.

David Kessler, "The End of Overeating," from *The End of Overeating: Taking Control of the Insatiable American Appetite* (Emmaus, PA: Rodale, 2010).

For nearly a century scientists believed humans had biological mechanisms to balance the calories we consume (our energy intake) with the calories we burn (our energy expenditure). This dynamic process was supposed to allow us to maintain a relatively stable amount of fat on our bodies and limit fluctuations in weight.

We have presumed that the wisdom of the body is maintained through a feedback system known as homeostasis.[1] Like temperature or blood pressure, which the body also tries to keep within relatively narrow ranges, energy is supposed to be regulated by a homeostatic process that keeps the body's energy stores stable. By closely matching food intake and energy expenditure, this biological strategy has allowed us to consume hundreds of thousands of calories every year without losing or gaining much weight.

It's a highly sophisticated system that can be explained simply: Many parts of the body talk to one another.

The brain is the command center of an elaborate communications network essential to energy regulation.[2] This network involves the brain, the central and peripheral nervous systems, the gastrointestinal tract, the hormonal system, fat tissue, and more. The brain's hypothalamus receives signals from all these sources, integrates that information, and decides what needs to be done to maintain the body at a steady weight.

But this homeostatic system, while relevant, turns out to be less powerful than many scientists have assumed: If we could maintain energy balance effectively, we wouldn't be gaining so much weight.[3] Our bodies would compensate, either by burning more calories or by shutting down our appetites. Obviously, that is not happening.

Over the past decade, scientists have tried to explain this failure by searching for defects in the homeostatic system. Their results have been disappointing. While some genetic and chemical defects have been identified, they seem to be rare and don't adequately account for the most common forms of obesity. . .

Despite all the research focused on homeostasis, it is not the only influence on food intake. Researchers have shown that what we eat doesn't depend solely on signals sent by the brain to maintain a stable weight. Another region of the brain, with different circuitry, is also involved, and often it's in charge. This is known as the reward system.

And in America, in the fight between energy balance and reward, the reward system is winning.

Like the homeostatic system, the body's reward system is essential to survival, encouraging us to seek out pleasurable things like sex and food. Powerful biological forces are at play that make us *want* something enough to pursue it and then make us feel momentarily better once we obtain it. The anticipation of reward provides motivation to act.

Motivational pathways in our brains have developed over the millennia to keep us alive.[4] Activated by stimuli in the environment, they generate an emotional response, which then drives our behavior. In other words, we receive information and we act on it. If the message is "This is good," we move closer to gain the benefit; if the message is "This is dangerous," we're likely to withdraw.

It is possible to activate the brain's reward centers by artificially stimulating them with an electrode, which is sometimes done during animal experiments.[5] One study showed that when the far-lateral hypothalamus region was stimulated, animals ate well beyond the point where they would otherwise have stopped.

Another study demonstrated the power of the reward system even more dramatically. Food was placed at the far end of a room with an electrified floor that delivered an unpleasant shock. Animals had to walk across that floor to reach their food. The strength of that shock stopped an animal that hadn't eaten for a while from walking across the floor to obtain food. Under normal circumstances, hunger did not provide enough motive to act, given the consequences. Stimulate the reward centers, though, and the result was just the opposite: Even an animal that wasn't hungry was willing to cross the electrical floor in order to secure a reward.

Outside the laboratory, there are other stimulants, of course. And that raises provocative scientific questions. Can they also stir the reward centers of the brain? Is it possible that eating certain foods can stimulate us to keep eating—and eating and eating?

To understand how eating promotes more eating—and why homeostasis is under sustained assault—we must first understand the concept of "palatability" as the term is used scientifically. In everyday language, we call food palatable if it has an agreeable taste. But when scientists say a food is palatable, they are referring primarily to its capacity to stimulate the appetite and prompt us to eat more. Palatability does involve taste, of course, but, crucially, it also involves the motivation to *pursue* that taste. It is the reason we want more.

Palatability is largely based on how food engages the full range of our senses. Usually, the most palatable foods contain some combination of sugar, fat, and salt. The sensory properties of palatable foods—the cold, creamy pleasure of a milkshake, the aroma of chocolate cake, the texture of crispy chicken wings sweetened with a honey-mustard dipping sauce—all stimulate the appetite. And it's that stimulation, or the anticipation of that stimulation, rather than genuine hunger, that makes us put food into our mouths long after our caloric needs are satisfied . . .

Eating foods high in sugar, fat, and salt makes us eat *more* foods high in sugar, fat, and salt. We see this clearly in both animal and human research. . .

Anthony Sclafani was a graduate student at the University of Chicago in the late 1960s when he started trying to understand what promoted excess consumption. When he fed animals high-fat foods, they gained more weight than those fed chow pellets (the bland food that's typically given to laboratory rats), but his results weren't particularly dramatic.

Then, by chance, he put a rat on a lab bench near some fallen Froot Loops, the high-calorie, high-sugar cereal. He was struck by how fast the animal picked up the cereal and started to eat it.

Sclafani turned that casual observation into a more formal experiment. After familiarizing test animals with the taste of Froot Loops, he let them loose in an open field. Rats prefer to stay in corners and won't readily venture across a field to eat chow pellets, but when Froot Loops were available, they scurried over to them.

Next, Sclafani studied the effect of a "supermarket diet." The mix of foods he fed his animals could be purchased at any grocery store: sweetened condensed milk, chocolate-chip cookies, salami, cheese, bananas, marshmallows, milk chocolate, and peanut butter. After ten days, animals that were fed the supermarket diet weighed significantly more than rats that were fed bland chow. And the rats on the supermarket diet continued to gain weight, eventually becoming twice as heavy as their control counterparts. Sclafani concluded that feeding adult rats "a variety of highly palatable supermarket foods was a particularly effective way of producing dietary obesity."

Why did they keep on eating? What happened to the homeostatic ability to balance energy consumption and expenditure? Why did the rats fail to defend themselves from weight gain?

Sclafani answered those questions in a single sentence: "In the normal rat, free access to palatable foods is a sufficient condition to promote excessive weight."[6]

Coupled with evidence collected by other scientists, Sclafani's results support the idea that the biological system that's designed to maintain energy balance can go awry when animals have easy access to a variety of foods that are high in sugar and fat.

Experiments with humans show much the same thing, especially when they're offered foods they prefer.[7] In one study, participants were asked to keep track of the foods they ate for seven days and to rate their preference for each meal on a scale of 1 to 7. Most people gave higher ratings to foods with higher levels of fat and sugar. Unsurprisingly, they also ate more of them, consuming almost 44 percent more food at meals they rated a 7 than at those rated a 3 or below.

In another study, researchers at the National Institutes of Health confined male subjects to a ward in which their food intake could be monitored.[8] For the first few days the men were fed a diet designed to keep them at their current body weight; since many of them were significantly overweight, that meant an average of just under 3,000 calories a day. (Approximately 50 percent of those calories came from carbohydrates, 30 percent from fat, and 20 percent from protein.)

The participants were then allowed to eat whatever they wished from two free vending machines that contained a variety of entrées and snacks. This gave them twenty-four-hour-a-day access to meats, cheese, and bread; tortillas and pinto beans; cereal, pastry, and desserts; french fries, popcorn, and chips; fruits, vegetables, nuts, and beverages. The men were asked to follow their typical eating patterns as closely as possible.

You've probably guessed the result. Given the opportunity to eat without restriction, participants consumed an average of 4,500 calories daily—150 percent of what they actually needed to maintain a stable weight. One person consumed almost 7,000 calories, the equivalent of about seventeen quarter-pound hamburgers. In general, the study subjects also ate substantially more fat and less protein during the period of unrestricted eating; the typical diet contained 48 percent carbohydrates, 40 percent fat, and 12 percent protein.

All of this demonstrates scientifically what most of us know from experience: When offered a varied selection and large portions of high-sugar, high-fat, high-salt foods, many of us will eat them in excessive amounts.

NOTES

1. A. E. Macias, "Experimental Demonstration of Human Weight Homeostasis: Implications for Understanding Obesity," British Journal of Nutrition 91, no. 3 (2004): 479–84; L. M. Kaplan, "Body Weight Regulation and Obesity," Journal of Gastrointestinal Surgery 7, no. 4 (2003): 443–51.

2. M. W. Schwartz and D. Porte Jr., "Diabetes, Obesity, and the Brain," Science 307, no. 5708 (2005): 375–79; M. K. Badman and J. S. Flier, "The Gut and Energy Balance: Visceral Allies in the Obesity Wars," Science 307, no. 5717 (2005): 1909–14; J. G. Mercer and J. R. Speakman, "Hypothalamic Neuropeptide Mechanisms for Regulating Energy Balance: From Rodent Models to Human Obesity," Neuroscience and Biobehavioral Reviews 25, no. 2 (2001): 101–16.

Lee Kaplan, MD, PhD, director of the Weight Center, Massachusetts General Hospital (presentation at "Practical Approaches to the Treatment of Obesity," an annual Harvard Medical School Department of Continuing Education conference). "There is a central regulatory system . . . ," said Kaplan. "The body is very good at matching energy intake and energy expenditure to a very close tolerance. The tolerance is about 0.15 percent,

averaged on a daily basis. . . . The mechanism by which this process of balancing food intake and energy expenditure occurs is a simple biological feedback controlled by parts of the brain. . . . If you decrease your energy intake so that you lose weight arbitrarily, you will become hungrier so that you return the energy intake to a higher level. If you arbitrarily try to gain weight, the opposite will occur. . . . The epidemic of obesity is not divorced from the system; the epidemic of obesity is a disruption of this system. It's not McDonald's only; it's McDonald's as it disrupts this system. It's not your genes only; it's your genes as they affect the balance of this system."

In a conversation with me on November 19, 2003, James O. Hill, PhD, Professor of Pediatrics, director, Center for Human Nutrition, University of Colorado–Denver, one of the nation's leading experts on weight, emphasized the changed environment: "For most of mankind's history our challenge was getting enough food to meet our energy needs. . . . If you look at how our physiology really developed, it developed in a situation where we had to be very physically active in daily living. We had to go out and kill the wild beast. Weight was controlled simply because we had to be very physically active and our challenge was to get enough food to meet our needs."

See also M. W. Schwartz and K. D. Niswender, "Adiposity Signaling and Biological Defense against Weight Gain: Absence of Protection or Central Hormone Resistance?" Journal of Clinical Endocrinology and Metabolism 89, no. 12 (2004): 5889–97.

Those who maintain eating and exercise behaviors that led to weight loss for a year are significantly more likely not to gain that weight back. M. T. McGuire, R. R. Wing, M. L. Klem, W. Lang, and J. O. Hill, "What Predicts Weight Regain in a Group of Successful Weight Losers?" Journal of Consulting and Clinical Psychology 67, no. 2 (1999): 177–85.

3. Jutta Heckhausen and Heinz Heckhausen, Motivation and Action (New York: Cambridge University Press, 2008); Johnmarshall Reeve, Understanding Motivation and Emotion, 4th ed. (Hoboken, NJ: Wiley, 2005); Rick A. Bevins and Michael T. Bardo, Motivational Factors in the Etiology of Drug Abuse (Lincoln: University of Nebraska Press, 2004); Eva Dreikurs Ferguson and Beth Eva Ferguson Wee, Motivation: A Biosocial and Cognitive Integration of Motivation and Emotion (New York: Oxford University Press, 2000).

4. Almost a half century ago, P. J. Morgane, a faculty member in the Department of Physiology at the University of Tennessee Medical School, implanted electrodes in various regions of rats' brains, and then sent a stimulating

pulse through those electrodes for four, three-hour periods spread out over 20 days. When the far-lateral hypothalamus was stimulated, rats already fed to satiation showed a dramatic tendency to keep on eating. P. J. Morgane, "Distinct 'Feeding' and 'Hunger Motivating' Systems in the Lateral Hypothalamus of the Rat," Science 133 (1961): 887–8; P. J. Morgane, "Electro-physiological Studies of Feeding and Satiety Centers in the Rat," American Journal of Physiology 201 (1961): 838–44; P. J. Morgane, "Evidence of a 'Hunger Motivational' System in the Lateral Hypothalamus of the Rat," Nature 191 (1961): 672–4; P. J. Morgane, "Medial Forebrain Bundle and 'Feeding Centers' of the Hypothalamus," Journal of Comparative Neurology 117 (1961): 1–25.

5. Author interviews with Anthony Sclafani, PhD, Distinguished Professor, Department of Psychology, Brooklyn College, City University of New York, June 11, 2004, and August 29, 2005; A. Sclafani and D. Springer, "Dietary Obesity in Adult Rats: Similarities to Hypothalamic and Human Obesity Syndromes," Physiology and Behavior 17, no. 3 (1976): 461–71.

6. J. M. de Castro, F. Bellisle, A. M. Dalix, and S. M. Pearcey, "Palatability and Intake Relationships in Free-Living Humans: Characterization and Independence of Influence in North Americans," Physiology and Behavior 70, no. 3–4 (2000): 343–50.

7. D. E. Larson, R. Rising, R. T. Ferraro, and E. Ravussin, "Spontaneous Overfeeding with a 'Cafeteria Diet' in Men: Effects on 24-Hour Energy Expenditure and Substrate Oxidation," International Journal of Obesity and Related Metabolic Disorders 19, no. 5 (1995): 331–7.

QUESTIONS

1. How does eating highly palatable foods (those high in sugar, fat, and salt) make us want to eat more highly palatable food?
2. When we eat highly palatable food, is this because we want to eat it? Or perhaps a better question is: Do we sometimes eat highly palatable foods (think: Cheetos or milkshakes) even though we don't want to eat them?

MICHAEL MOSS

Lunchtime Is All Yours

Michael Moss describes how the Oscar Mayer company developed and marketed Lunchables, a packaged lunch for children composed mostly of processed food that's high in salt, fat, and sugar.

The public and the food companies have known for decades now . . . that sugary, salty, fatty foods are not good for us in the quantities that we consume them. So why are the diabetes and obesity and hypertension numbers still spiraling out of control? It's not just a matter of poor willpower on the part of the consumer and a give-the-people-what-they-want attitude on the part of the food manufacturers. What I found, over four years of research and reporting, was a conscious effort—taking place in labs and marketing meetings and grocery-store aisles—to get people hooked on foods that are convenient and inexpensive. I talked to more than 300 people in or formerly employed by the processed-food industry, from scientists to marketers to C.E.O.'s. Some were willing whistle-blowers, while others spoke reluctantly when presented with some of the thousands of pages of secret memos that I obtained from inside the food industry's operations. . .

Sometimes innovations within the food industry happen in the lab, with scientists dialing in specific ingredients to achieve the greatest allure. And sometimes, as in the case of Oscar Mayer's bologna crisis, the innovation involves putting old products in new packages.

The 1980s were tough times for Oscar Mayer. Red-meat consumption fell more than 10 percent as fat became synonymous with cholesterol, clogged arteries, heart attacks and strokes. Anxiety set in at the company's headquarters in Madison, Wis., where executives worried about their future and the pressure they faced from their new bosses at Philip Morris.

Bob Drane was the company's vice president for new business strategy and development when Oscar Mayer tapped him to try to find some way to reposition bologna and other troubled meats that were declining in popularity and sales. I met Drane at his home in Madison and went through the records he had kept on the birth of what would become much more than his solution to the company's meat problem. In 1985, when Drane began working on the project, his orders were to "figure out how to contemporize what we've got."

Drane's first move was to try to zero in not on what Americans felt about processed meat but on

what Americans felt about lunch. He organized focus-group sessions with the people most responsible for buying bologna—mothers—and as they talked, he realized the most pressing issue for them was time. Working moms strove to provide healthful food, of course, but they spoke with real passion and at length about the morning crush, that nightmarish dash to get breakfast on the table and lunch packed and kids out the door. He summed up their remarks for me like this: "It's awful. I am scrambling around. My kids are asking me for stuff. I'm trying to get myself ready to go to the office. I go to pack these lunches, and I don't know what I've got." What the moms revealed to him, Drane said, was "a gold mine of disappointments and problems."

He assembled a team of about 15 people with varied skills, from design to food science to advertising, to create something completely new—a convenient prepackaged lunch that would have as its main building block the company's sliced bologna and ham. They wanted to add bread, naturally, because who ate bologna without it? But this presented a problem: There was no way bread could stay fresh for the two months their product needed to sit in warehouses or in grocery coolers. Crackers, however, could—so they added a handful of cracker rounds to the package. Using cheese was the next obvious move, given its increased presence in processed foods. . .

Drane's team moved into a nearby hotel, where they set out to find the right mix of components and container. They gathered around tables where bagfuls of meat, cheese, crackers and all sorts of wrapping material had been dumped, and they let their imaginations run. After snipping and taping their way through a host of failures, the model they fell back on was the American TV dinner—and after some brainstorming about names (Lunch Kits? Go-Packs? Fun Mealz?), Lunchables were born.

The trays flew off the grocery-store shelves. Sales hit a phenomenal $218 million in the first 12 months, more than anyone was prepared for. . .

With production costs trimmed and profits coming in, the next question was how to expand the franchise, which they did by turning to one of the cardinal rules in processed food: When in doubt, add sugar. "Lunchables With Dessert is a logical extension," an Oscar Mayer official reported to Philip Morris executives in early 1991. The "target" remained the same as it was for regular Lunchables—"busy mothers" and "working women," ages 25 to 49—and the "enhanced taste" would attract shoppers who had grown bored with the current trays. A year later, the dessert Lunchable morphed into the Fun Pack, which would come with a Snickers bar, a package of M&M's or a Reese's Peanut Butter Cup, as well as a sugary drink. The Lunchables team started by using Kool-Aid and cola and then Capri Sun after Philip Morris added that drink to its stable of brands.

Eventually, a line of the trays, appropriately called Maxed Out, was released that had as many as nine grams of saturated fat, or nearly an entire day's recommended maximum for kids, with up to two-thirds of the max for sodium and 13 teaspoons of sugar.

When I asked Geoffrey Bible, former C.E.O. of Philip Morris, about this shift toward more salt, sugar and fat in meals for kids, he smiled and noted that even in its earliest incarnation, Lunchables was held up for criticism. "One article said something like, 'If you take Lunchables apart, the most healthy item in it is the napkin.'"

Well, they did have a good bit of fat, I offered. "You bet," he said. "Plus cookies."

The prevailing attitude among the company's food managers—through the 1990s, at least, before obesity became a more pressing concern—was one of supply and demand. "People could point to these things and say, 'They've got too much sugar, they've got too much salt,'" Bible said. "Well, that's what the consumer wants, and we're not putting a gun to their head to eat it. That's what they want. If we give them less, they'll buy less, and the competitor will get our market. So you're sort of trapped." (Bible would later press Kraft to reconsider its reliance on salt, sugar and fat.)

When it came to Lunchables, they did try to add more healthful ingredients. Back at the start, Drane experimented with fresh carrots but quickly gave up on that, since fresh components didn't work within the constraints of the processed-food system, which typically required weeks or months of transport and storage before the food arrived at the grocery store. Later, a low-fat version of the trays was developed, using meats and cheese and crackers that were formulated with less fat, but it tasted inferior, sold poorly and was quickly scrapped.

When I met with Kraft officials in 2011 to discuss their products and policies on nutrition, they had dropped the Maxed Out line and were trying to improve the nutritional profile of Lunchables through smaller, incremental changes that were less noticeable to consumers. Across the Lunchables line, they said they had reduced the salt, sugar and fat by about 10 percent, and new versions, featuring mandarin-orange and pineapple slices, were in development. These would be promoted as more healthful versions, with "fresh fruit," but their list of ingredients—containing upward of 70 items, with sucrose, corn syrup, high-fructose corn syrup and fruit concentrate all in the same tray—have been met with intense criticism from outside the industry.

One of the company's responses to criticism is that kids don't eat the Lunchables every day—on top of which, when it came to trying to feed them more healthful foods, kids themselves were unreliable. When their parents packed fresh carrots, apples and water, they couldn't be trusted to eat them. Once in school, they often trashed the healthful stuff in their brown bags to get right to the sweets.

This idea—that kids are in control—would become a key concept in the evolving marketing campaigns for the trays. In what would prove to be their greatest achievement of all, the Lunchables team would delve into adolescent psychology to discover that it wasn't the food in the trays that excited the kids; it was the feeling of power it brought to their lives. As Bob Eckert, then the C.E.O. of Kraft, put it in 1999: "Lunchables aren't about lunch. It's about kids being able to put together what they want to eat, anytime, anywhere."

Kraft's early Lunchables campaign targeted mothers. They might be too distracted by work to make a lunch, but they loved their kids enough to offer them this prepackaged gift. But as the focus swung toward kids, Saturday-morning cartoons started carrying an ad that offered a different message: "All day, you gotta do what they say," the ads said. "But lunchtime is all yours."

With this marketing strategy in place and pizza Lunchables—the crust in one compartment, the cheese, pepperoni and sauce in others—proving to be a runaway success, the entire world of fast food suddenly opened up for Kraft to pursue. They came out with a Mexican-themed Lunchables called Beef Taco Wraps; a Mini Burgers Lunchables; a Mini Hot Dog Lunchable, which also happened to provide a way for Oscar Mayer to sell its wieners. By 1999, pancakes—which included syrup, icing, Lifesavers candy and Tang, for a whopping 76 grams of sugar— and waffles were, for a time, part of the Lunchables franchise as well.

Annual sales kept climbing, past $500 million, past $800 million; at last count, including sales in Britain, they were approaching the $1 billion mark. Lunchables was more than a hit; it was now its own category. Eventually, more than 60 varieties of Lunchables and other brands of trays would show up in the grocery stores. In 2007, Kraft even tried a Lunchables Jr. for 3- to 5-year-olds. . .

Drane himself paused only briefly when I asked him if, looking back, he was proud of creating the trays. "Lots of things are trade-offs," he said. "And I do believe it's easy to rationalize anything. In the end, I wish that the nutritional profile of the thing could have been better, but I don't view the entire project as anything but a positive contribution to people's lives."

Today Bob Drane is still talking to kids about what they like to eat, but his approach has changed. He volunteers with a nonprofit organization that seeks to build better communications between school kids and their parents, and right in the mix of their problems, alongside the academic struggles, is childhood obesity. Drane has also prepared a précis on the food industry that he used with medical students at the University of Wisconsin. And while he does not name his Lunchables in this document, and cites numerous causes for the obesity epidemic, he holds the entire industry accountable. "What do University of Wisconsin M.B.A.'s learn about how to succeed in marketing?" his presentation to the med students asks. "Discover what consumers want to buy and give it to them with both barrels. Sell more, keep your job! How do marketers often translate these 'rules' into action on food? Our limbic brains love sugar, fat, salt. . . . So formulate products to deliver these. Perhaps add low-cost ingredients to boost profit margins. Then 'supersize' to sell more. . . . And advertise/promote to lock in 'heavy users.' Plenty of guilt to go around here!"

QUESTIONS

1. Research by the Oscar Mayer company showed that packing kids' lunches was difficult for working mothers—"a gold mine of disappointments and problems." Also recall, from Chapter 5, "Food and Identity," that a recent study found that mothers rarely serve a meal without at least one family member complaining about it. Did Lunchables solve a real problem that mothers had?
2. When prodded about how unhealthy kids' meals had become, the former executive Geoffrey Bible said, "Well, that's what the consumer wants, and we're not putting a gun to their head to eat it. That's what they want." Do you agree that Lunchables—convenient, popular with kids, and unhealthy—are what parents want? If someone is not being physically forced—with a gun to the head—to buy or eat a product, but she still buys or eats it, does that mean she wants it?
3. Michael Moss describes how Oscar Mayer marketed Lunchables directly to children. Should food companies market kids' foods directly to children? Is that ethical? Why or why not? Or should food companies only market kids' foods to parents?

MARION NESTLE

The Politics of Food Choice

In this excerpt from her influential book *Food Politics*, Marion Nestle summarizes how the food industry influences individual behavior and government regulation. The food industry shapes consumers' food preferences through marketing, and it shapes citizens' views about government regulation through alarmist emotional appeals. The food industry affects the political process through lobbying and relationships with government officials. She draws a parallel between the tactics of tobacco companies and the tactics of food companies, and she suggests that efforts to promote healthier food choices should be modeled after successful antismoking efforts.

The food industry uses lobbying, lawsuits, financial contributions, public relations, advertising, partnerships and alliances, philanthropy, threats, and biased information to convince Congress, federal agencies, nutrition and health professionals, and the public that the science relating diet to health is so confusing that they need not worry about diets: When it comes to diets, anything goes.[1]

Representatives of food companies and their trade associations repeatedly make the following claims:

- The keys to healthful diets are balance, variety, and moderation (especially when their products are included).
- All foods can be part of healthful diets (especially theirs).
- There is no such thing as a good or a bad food (except when their products are considered good).
- Dietary advice changes so often that we need not follow it (unless it favors their products).
- Research on diet and health is so uncertain that it is meaningless (except when it supports the health benefits of their products).

- Only a small percentage of the population would benefit from following population-based dietary advice (if that advice suggests restrictions on intake of their products).
- Diets are a matter of personal responsibility and freedom of choice (especially the freedom to choose their products).
- Advocacy for more healthful food choices is irrational (if it suggests eating less of their products).
- Government intervention in dietary choice is unnecessary, undesirable, and incompatible with democratic institutions (unless it protects and promotes their products).

Dr. Rhona Applebaum of the National Food Processors Association, for example, succinctly expresses such views when she says that diets should conform to "the three principles of sound nutritional advice: balance, variety, and moderation" and that societal measures to support more healthful food choices are unnecessary. Changing the environment of food choice is possible, she maintains, only

> if the federal government, in the role of "Big Brother," mandates what foods can or cannot be produced—which is not the role of government in a free market economy. Controlling, limiting, and outright banning of products deemed "unfit" does not work, and history attests to the failure of such extremist measures. . . . Food consumption is not supply driven, it is demand driven, and consumers are in the driver's seat . . . you cannot force people to comply with the Dietary Guidelines and it is wrong to try. It is an unworkable, totalitarian approach that brings with it all the evils associated with such a philosophy.[2]

With such statements, food industry officials appeal to emotion (in this case, fears of totalitarianism) to argue against something that no nutritionist, private or governmental, advocates. Nutritionists are simply trying to educate the public that some foods *are* better for health than others. The food industry fiercely opposes this idea and uses its substantial resources, political skills, and emotional appeals to discourage attempts to introduce "eat less" messages into public discussion of dietary issues and, instead, to encourage people to eat more.

These tactics on the part of food companies are, in one sense, a routine part of doing business; they are no different from those used by other large commercial interests, such as drug companies, or—as we shall see—tobacco companies. But sellers of food products do not attract the same kind of attention as purveyors of drugs or tobacco. They should, not only because of the health consequences of dietary choices, but also because of the ethical issues raised by industry marketing practices. Food marketing raises ethical dilemmas, but so does attempting to regulate or change people's food choices, deciding how government should protect health within the context of a free market economy, determining what kinds of policy changes might support more healthful food choices, and identifying the role of individual responsibility in making such choices. This chapter explores such dilemmas.

THE ENVIRONMENT OF FOOD CHOICE

We are fortunate to live in a free market economy that gives us an abundant—indeed an overabundant—food supply at low cost. What we choose to make of this supply is, of course, a matter of personal responsibility, as food company officials are quick to argue. But we do not make food choices in a vacuum. We select diets in a marketing environment in which billions of dollars are spent to convince us that nutrition advice is so confusing, and eating healthfully so impossibly difficult, that there is no point in bothering to eat less of one or another food product or category. We may believe that we make informed decisions about food choice, but we cannot do so if we are oblivious of the ways food companies influence our choices. Most of us, if we choose to do so, can recognize how food companies spend money on advertising, but it is far more difficult to know about the industry's behind-the-scenes efforts in Congress, federal agencies, courts, universities, and professional organizations to make diets seem a matter of personal choice rather than of deliberate manipulation. The emphasis on individual choice serves the interests of the food industry for one critical reason: if diet is a matter of individual free will, then the only appropriate remedy for poor diets is education, and nutritionists should be off teaching people to take personal responsibility for their own diet and health—not how to institute societal changes that might make it easier for everyone to do so.

That suggestions to change the social environment of food choice are threatening to industry is evident from the vehemence with which trade associations and the business press attack advice to restrict intake of one or another food group, to get "junk" food out of schools, to label foods more explicitly, or to tax sales of foods to generate funds for nutrition education. Business commentators equate such approaches with nothing less than fascism: "If [President] Bill Clinton really wants ideas for a healthy eating crusade, he must surely look to the only political regime that thoroughly made them part of national policy: Nazi Germany."[3] They could not be more sarcastic about societal approaches to dietary change: "This being America, of course, ordering Biggie Fries instead of the salad bar can't possibly be our own fault. . . . If all this sounds a bit preposterous, it only means you have an underdeveloped sense of victimhood. The parallels between Big Tobacco and Big Fat are too striking to be overlooked. . . . Come on, America. Get off that couch and sue."[4]

Sarcasm aside, if the business press finds parallels between the tobacco and food industries, it is because the parallels are impossible to avoid. Cigarette companies famously argue that smoking is a matter of individual choice and that it is wrong for government to interfere unduly in the private lives of citizens. They use science to sow confusion about the harm that cigarettes can cause. They set the standard in use of public relations, advertising, philanthropy, experts, political funding, alliances, lobbying, intimidation, and lawsuits to protect their sales. In efforts to expand markets, they promote cigarette smoking to children and adolescents; to minorities, women, and the poor; and to people in countries throughout the world, developing as well as industrialized.[5] The similarities between the actions of cigarette companies and food companies are no coincidence. Cigarette companies sometimes owned food companies.

No matter who owns them, food companies lobby government and agencies, and they become financially enmeshed with experts on nutrition and health. Although the food industry frames such tactics as promoting individual liberty and free will, its true objective is (not surprisingly) "trade and unrestricted profit."[6] With respect to cigarettes, most Americans by now are thoroughly aware of the marketing practices of tobacco companies; we learned about them through decades of antismoking campaigns. These campaigns succeeded in getting warning labels on cigarette packages, getting smoking-restricted areas in businesses and on airplanes, and even inspiring an attempt by the Food and Drug Administration (FDA) to regulate

tobacco as a drug. The parallel practices of food companies, however, have elicited nowhere near this level of protest.

The principal reasons for this difference must surely lie in the complexity of the messages about foods and their health effects. Although cigarettes and diet contribute to comparable levels of illness and death across the population, cigarettes constitute a single entity, in contrast to a food system that currently supplies 320,000 food products.[7] No nutritionist could ever suggest that eating an occasional candy bar or bag of potato chips might cause disease—it truly is the overall dietary pattern that counts, and it counts over a lifetime. Unlike the straightforward "don't smoke" advice, the dietary message can never be "don't eat." Instead, it has to be the more complicated and ambiguous "eat this instead of that," "eat this more often than that," and the overall prescription, "eat less."

THE ETHICS OF FOOD CHOICE

Ethical issues arise whenever actions that benefit one group harm another. Food choices have economic, political, social, and environmental consequences that place improvements to the health of individuals or populations in conflict with other considerations. Underlying the notion of food ethics is the assumption that following dietary guidelines improves health and well-being. If ethics is viewed as a matter of good conduct versus bad, then choosing a healthful diet—and advising people to do so—would seem to be virtuous actions.

Ethical or not, a message to eat less meat, dairy, and processed foods is not going to be popular among the producers of such foods. It will have only limited popularity with producers of fruits and vegetables because their scale of production is limited and they cannot easily add value to their products. The message will not be popular with cattle ranchers, meat packers, dairy producers, or milk bottlers; oil seed growers, processors, or transporters; grain producers (most grain is used to feed cattle); makers of soft drinks, candy bars, and snack foods; owners of fast-food outlets and franchise restaurants; media corporations and advertising agencies; manufacturers and marketers of television sets and computers (where advertising takes place); and, eventually, drug and health care industries likely to lose business if people stay healthier longer. The range of economic sectors that would be affected if people changed their diets, avoided obesity, and prevented chronic diseases surely rivals the range of industries that would be affected if people stopped smoking cigarettes.

TAKING ACTION: IMPROVING PUBLIC AND CORPORATE POLICIES

What should health professionals and concerned citizens do to improve the social and political environment in which people make food choices? And how can we make sure that the actions we take are both responsible and effective? Once again, the parallel with tobacco is instructive. In the 30 years or so since publication of the surgeon general's first report on smoking and health, cigarettes have become socially unacceptable—on health grounds—among many groups and in many locations. Many of the lessons learned from the "tobacco wars" apply just as well to food, especially the lesson that the industry will relentlessly counter even the slightest suggestion to use less of its products. That actions typical of antismoking campaigns are only rarely applied to nutrition issues is a tribute to how well the food industry has sown confusion about the research linking diet to health, about advice based on that research, and about dietary choices based on that advice. The result is the widely held idea that "eat less" need not apply to

categories of foods, to specific food products, or to food in general.

In this regard also, we have much to learn from the tobacco wars. Successful antismoking campaigns are based on four elements: a firm research base, a clear message, well-defined targets for intervention, and strategies that address the societal environment as well as the education of individual smokers. The research basis of antismoking messages is firmly established: Cigarettes cause lung cancer. The message is simple: don't smoke. The targets are well defined: antismoking efforts focus not only on individuals who smoke but also on the companies that produce cigarettes. The strategies include education but also encompass environmental measures, such as age thresholds for buying cigarettes, cigarette taxes, and bans on smoking in airplanes, restaurants, and workplaces.[5]

Could the four principal elements of antismoking campaign strategies—research, message, target, and tactics—be applied to dietary change? With regard to research, the evidence for the health benefits of hierarchical dietary patterns that emphasize fruits, vegetables, and grains is strong, consistent, and associated with prevention of as much illness as cessation of smoking. The message to follow *Pyramid*-like dietary patterns is more complicated than "don't smoke" but not impossible to understand. Just as "don't smoke" applies to everyone, so does the dietary message; everyone benefits from following a dietary pattern that contributes to prevention of so many diseases. Perhaps the most important lesson of all concerns tactics: antismoking campaigns succeeded when they began to focus on *environmental* issues rather than on the education of individuals. If we want to encourage people to eat better diets, we need to target societal means to counter food industry lobbying and marketing practices as well as the education of individuals.

Table 1 provides suggestions for actions that might improve the social environment of food choice in order to make it easier for people to eat better diets and be more active.

TABLE 1.   Modifications of public policies that would promote better food choices and more active lifestyles

Education

Mount a major, national campaign to promote "eat less, move more."

Teach teachers about nutrition and weight management.

In schools, ban commercials for foods of minimal nutritional value and teaching materials with corporate logos.

End the sale in schools of soft drinks, candy bars, and other foods of minimal nutritional value.

Require school meals to be consistent with *Dietary Guidelines.*

Require daily opportunities for physical education and sports in schools.

Food labeling and advertising

Require fast-food restaurants to provide nutrition information on packages and wrappers.

Require containers for soft drinks and snacks to carry information about calorie, fat, or sugar content.

Restrict television advertising of foods of minimal nutritional value; provide equal time for messages promoting "eat less, move more."

Require print food advertisements to disclose calories.

Prohibit misleading health claims in advertising and on package labels.

Health care and training

Require health care training programs to teach nutrition and methods for counseling patients about diet, activity, and health.

Sponsor research on environmental determinants of food choice.

Transportation and urban development

Provide incentives for communities to develop parks and other venues for physical activity.

Modify zoning requirements to encourage creation of sidewalks, pedestrian malls, and bicycle paths.

Taxes

Levy city, state, or federal taxes on soft drinks and other "junk" foods to fund "eat less, move more" campaigns.

Subsidize the costs of fruits and vegetables, perhaps by raising the costs of selected foods of minimal nutritional value.

NOTES

1. Parts of this chapter draw on material previously published as: Nestle M. Ethical dilemmas in choosing a healthful diet: Vote with your fork! Proceedings of the Nutrition Society (UK) 2000;59:619–629 (with permission), and Nestle M, Jacobson MF. Halting the Obesity Epidemic: A Public Health Policy Approach. Public Health Reports 2000;115:12–24 (courtesy of Michael Jacobson and Oxford University Press).

2. Applebaum RS. Commentary. Food Policy 1999;24:265–267.

3. Anderson D. Americans get fatter, but refuse to die. How naughty. Wall Street J June 8, 2000:A24.

4. Bernstein MF. A big fat target. Wall Street J August 28, 1997:A14.

5. Kluger R. Ashes to Ashes: America's Hundred-Year Cigarette War, the Public Health, and the Unabashed Triumph of Philip Morris. New York: Alfred A. Knopf, 1996. Advocacy Institute. Smoke & Mirrors: How the Tobacco Industry Buys & Lies Its Way to Power & Profits. Washington, DC: Advocacy Institute, 1998. Glantz SA Balbach ED. Tobacco War: Inside the

California Battles. Berkeley: University of California Press, 2000.

6. A manipulated dichotomy in global health policy (editorial). Lancet 2000;355:1023.

7. McGinnis JM, Foege WH. Actual causes of death in the United States. JAMA 1993;270:2207–2212. Gallo AE. Fewer food products introduced in last 3 years. FoodReview 1999;22(3):27–29.

QUESTIONS

1. Nestle takes objection to the emphasis on individual choice in public discussions about healthy eating: "The emphasis on individual choice serves the interests of the food industry for one critical reason: If diet is a matter of individual free will, then the only appropriate remedy for poor diets is education, and nutritionists should be off teaching people to take personal responsibility for their own diet and health—not how to institute societal changes that might make it easier for everyone to do so." What is Nestle saying in this passage? How might emphasizing that eating is an "individual choice" undermine environmental approaches to making eating healthier? Can we acknowledge that eating is an individual choice, in some sense, while still making the case for environmental changes and societal changes that make healthy eating easier?

2. In what ways are the "food wars" similar to the "tobacco wars," according to Nestle? What tactics does the food industry use to undermine efforts to promote healthy eating? How are these similar to tactics used in the past by the tobacco industry?

3. Nestle argues that the food industry is a powerful influence on what consumers think and choose, and on what government does. In Nestle's view, it is a problem that the food industry has this much influence. What do you think?

ERIC A. FINKELSTEIN AND LAURIE ZUCKERMAN

How the Economy Makes Us Fat

In this excerpt from their book *The Fattening of America: How the Economy Makes Us Fat, If It Matters, and What to Do About It*, the economist Eric Finkelstein and the writer Laurie Zuckerman give an economic explanation of why Americans consume more food than they used to. During recent decades, the price of food, and particularly unhealthy food, has dropped relative to the price of other goods, making unhealthy food a relatively cheap source of utility. Finkelstein and Zuckerman also suggest that the choices of overweight and obese people are typically *utility maximizing*, given the costs and benefits of healthy food, unhealthy food, and physical activity. They illustrate this point with a running discussion of Finkelstein's Uncle Al, an overweight corporate lawyer.

TABLE 2.   Foods-Equivalent to about 100 Calories

Foods	Calories
8 fluid ounces of Coca-Cola	162
10 teaspoons of sugar	150
2 slices of white bread	130
1 ounce of Cheerios	110
12 to 15 almonds	110
10 French fries	110
2 Oreo cookies	106
1 banana	105
4 Hershey's Kisses	100
3 ounces of fat-free vanilla ice cream	100
1 slice of French bread	100
1 tablespoon of peanut butter	95
1 tablespoon of ranch dressing	90
1 cup of skim milk	90
1 cup of blueberries	80

CHEAP FOOD GETS CHEAPER

Between the late 1970s and today, men have increased their daily food intake by about 180 calories (the equivalent of a pint of imported beer), and women have increased their daily food intake by about 360 calories (less than a four-ounce slice of chocolate cake). On average, according to the Centers for Disease Control and Prevention (CDC), men now consume 2,600 calories per day and women now consume 1,900 calories per day.[1] These increases are more than enough to create the rise in obesity rates shown above and, consistent with these findings, women have experienced greater weight gain than men. In fact, it is likely that the number of

calories consumed is even higher than the CDC data show. These numbers are based on food diaries by a random sample of adults. It's human nature to "fudge" calorie diaries because: (1) individuals eat less than usual when they know that others will see their data, and (2) due to laziness, embarrassment, or other reasons, individuals tend not to report all that they consume.

However you slice it, the plain fact is that Americans are consuming more calories than ever. So what is behind our increasing caloric consumption? The answer, in a word, is economics. During the past four decades, food costs, in terms of both money and preparation (time) costs, have been steadily dropping. Since 1960, the relative price of food compared with other goods has decreased by about 16 percent Since 1978, food prices have dropped 38 percent relative to the prices of other goods and services.[2] But what is even more relevant is the fact that high-calorie foods have become much cheaper compared with healthier alternatives such as fish, fruits, and vegetables.

Since 1983, prices of fresh fruits and vegetables, fish, and dairy products have increased by 190 percent, 144 percent, 100 percent, and 82 percent, respectively, whereas fats and oils, sugars and sweets, and carbonated beverages, for example, increased at much lower rates—by 70 percent, 66 percent, and 32 percent, respectively.[3] When compared to the general price for all foods and beverages, the prices of healthier foods have become relatively more expensive and the prices of unhealthy foods, those with lots of added sugars and added fats, have become cheaper.

So just what is the relationship between food consumption and food prices? Economics 101 teaches us that as the price of food becomes cheaper, people will eat more. So does that play out in the real world? Let's take a look at an example. If we compare trends in the relative price (compared to the consumer price index for food) and quantity of carbonated beverages, we will see that the large reduction in the relative price of carbonated beverages since 1978 has translated into a large increase in its consumption. For most people, an ice cold Coca-Cola used to be a treat reserved for special occasions. Now it's become part of our daily fare. I've even seen parents filling baby bottles with Coke at the free refill machines at our local Taco Bell (it's not just Britney Spears).

These low prices also translate into larger portions. Whereas the average-size Coke used to be 8 ounces, a 20-ounce bottle is now the norm. As a result, in 2004, the average American consumed 52 gallons of soft drinks, or an average of 16 ounces per day. This is 50 percent more than the amount consumed in 1980.[4,5] Today, soft drinks comprise about 7 percent of all calories consumed, making them the number one food consumed in the American diet.[6] We did some additional analysis and found that if the average American drank water instead of sugar-sweetened beverages, he would weigh about 15 pounds less than he does now.

A similar trend can be seen looking at fats and oils, common additives in high-calorie foods. Their prices dropped by about 16 percent during the past few decades. This price drop was accompanied by a 50 percent increase in consumption.

These findings illustrate, as we might reasonably expect, that price plays a major role in determining what and how much we eat. And for food producers, price is also a key component of decisions concerning which ingredients to use. So it logically follows that falling food prices, especially for fattening foods, are at least partly responsible for the rise in obesity rates.

This leads us to another question: Why have relative prices for high-calorie and high-fat foods decreased when compared to prices for healthy options? . . .

The answer lies largely in advances in food processing, preservation, and cooking technologies that have allowed more foods to be produced in a central location and then consumed quickly and cheaply. Innovations such as vacuum packing, improved preservatives, deep freezing, stretch-wrap films, irradiation, hydrogen peroxide sterilization, and microwaves, to

name a few, have significantly lowered the monetary and nonmonetary cost of food, including the time cost of acquiring, preparing, cooking, and cleaning up after food, as well as the financial cost of purchasing food.[7] Foods more dependent on technology are often those with the greatest amounts of added sugars and fats and therefore the highest in calories. It is exactly these foods that have seen the greatest drop in prices and preparation time and as a result, the greatest increases in consumption. . .

WHEN IS ENOUGH ENOUGH?

Brian Wansink, the author of *Mindless Eating: Why We Eat More Than We Think* (Bantam, 2006), believes that the two-thirds of Americans who are overweight or obese got that way, at least in part, because they didn't realize how much they were eating.[8]

"We don't have any idea what the normal amount to eat is, so we look around for clues or signals," he said. "When all you see is that big portions of food cost less than small ones, it can be confusing."

Wansink's studies on university campuses and in test kitchens for institutions like the United States Army have produced some interesting results. Here's one example: Moviegoers in a Chicago suburb were given free stale popcorn in a variety of sized buckets. What was left in the buckets was weighed at the end of the movie. The people with larger buckets ate 53 percent more than people with smaller buckets. And people didn't eat the popcorn because they liked it, he said. They were driven by hidden persuaders: the distraction of the movie, the sound of other people eating popcorn, and the Pavlovian popcorn trigger that is activated when we step into a movie theater.

Wansink focuses on the psychological aspects of food choices, of which clearly there are many. However, many of the results that people ascribe to food addiction or food psychology may simply be applications of basic economic principles. For example, it is well known that Uncle Al, like the rest of us, eats more when he orders the Shoney's buffet than when he orders off the menu. Some might chalk this up to

Uncle Al's inability to control his appetite. However, this is not the case. Once Uncle Al pays for the buffet, economic theory says he should continue eating if he gains any benefit at all from the food. This is because, unless he considers the long-term consequences of these additional bites of food on his weight and subsequent health, there is literally no cost to him for increased consumption. Although each additional bite may bring him less joy as he gets fuller and fuller, if the food tastes good, he might as well keep eating. Only when he is really stuffed, and an additional bite makes him worse off, should he stop eating.

This is not true when he orders off the menu. Once his plate is cleaned, for him to eat more food (barring stealing it off of my aunt's plate) requires him to purchase another meal. This cost, although perhaps only a few dollars, is enough for him to forgo additional consumption because by this time the value to him of additional food consumption has substantially decreased. Of course, he might be back for more (or dessert) when he has had some time to digest and the value of those additional bites begins to increase again.

This is economics, not psychology. Would Uncle Al eat free stale popcorn at a movie theatre? If it were better than nothing, you bet he would. And so would I. It *is* free, after all. . .

IS UNCLE AL OVERWEIGHT?

Is Uncle Al overweight? What? What a question! In Chapter 1, we clearly showed that based on BMI guidelines, Uncle Al would be classified as obese. We also documented some of the health problems that Uncle Al is experiencing, most of them, if not all of them, as a result of his extra weight and sedentary lifestyle. On top of diabetes, Uncle Al has developed hypertension (high blood pressure) and high cholesterol, and he suffers from aches and pains in his lower back.

So how could I even question whether Uncle Al is overweight? Didn't I already clearly indicate that he is?

Ahhh, but he's overweight based on government standards. What about the standards that Uncle Al sets for himself?

Let's consider a different question. Suppose at age 25, Uncle Al had the option of choosing to die at age 75 or at age 80. However, choosing age 80 would have required him to make a lifelong commitment to regular exercise and a restricted diet. I suspect he would have chosen age 75 and all the tasty fattening food and limited physical activity that accompanies this decision. Because I try very hard to avoid offending Uncle Al, I have not come out and asked him directly. But the truth is that I don't need to ask. Uncle Al has shown us his choice. He could have led a life that included a more restrictive diet and exercise regimen, but he chose not to.

Certainly, Uncle Al should care about the fact that his excess weight increases his risk of disease and premature death. In reality, I'm sure he does care. But the truth is that Uncle Al cares about lots of other things, too. He cares about being rich, for example. In fact, he spent much of his adult life working his ass off (or perhaps on) at the law firm to attain that goal. This left little time for exercise other than his occasional Sunday golf outings. Uncle Al also cares about fine dining. He and my aunt eat many of their meals at the country club, at restaurants, or order prepared meals to eat at home. These meals are much higher in added sugars, added fats, and calories than home-cooked meals. After all, that's why they taste so good.

So, for Uncle Al, and perhaps for the majority of overweight adults, it is not that they don't care about being overweight; it is that the change in behavior required to lose the weight and keep it off is just too great (and is getting greater all the time).

Uncle Al has at various times made efforts to reduce his weight and improve his health. And while these may have been effective at controlling his weight for a while, Uncle Al, like many of us, found that the effort required to fully offset the increase in weight was just too much. After all, Uncle Al's primary goal in life is not to be as skinny as my dad or to live as long as possible. He appears willing to live with some extra pounds and the adverse health risks that might come along with it in exchange for an increased quality of life, which by Uncle Al's definition includes many activities that are obesity promoting. Also, Uncle Al's generous health insurance gives him affordable access to new drugs and advanced medical technology, which is a nice cushion to fall back on when those pesky risk factors flare up.

So given these considerations, maybe Uncle Al is not overweight after all. In fact, perhaps he's at his optimum weight once he considers the costs and benefits of what is required to weigh less.

The story of Uncle Al may suggest that obesity is a consequence of gluttony. After all, one does not need all that money or excess. But consider the case of my overweight Cousin Carl. He's a minimum-wage kind of guy. He works long hours and eats out a lot, too. However, he needs to work the extra hours just to pay rent, and that leaves him with little time to exercise. Moreover, most of his dining occurs in fast-food restaurants because he can get a high-calorie meal for pennies on the dollar. Barring a lucky lottery ticket (or a nice inheritance from Uncle Al), I can't imagine him ever being rich, but he, too, is making choices that are leading to excess weight, albeit for very different reasons. So perhaps he's at his optimum weight as well.

And what about me? Focusing on the economics of obesity has renewed my interest in being healthy. Yet, I willingly spend 50-plus hours per week sitting in my office chair banging away on the computer and burning off almost no energy, even though I know it is doing nothing to improve my health.

People whose work is largely conducted while sitting behind a desk, such as secretaries, lawyers, teachers, and health economists, get very little physical activity during the day. Secretaries, for example, log an average of 4,327 steps, less than half of the often-recommended goal of 10,000 steps a day for optimal health.[9] Teachers get 4,726 steps, lawyers 5,062, and even police officers average only 5,336 steps per day (and who knows how many donuts)—all about the same as I get on days that I do not go out for a run. Letter carriers, by the way, average nearly 19,000 steps per day. Not too shabby.

I sometimes think how great it would be to quit my job and find a more active occupation, but I realize that would entail a huge financial sacrifice that I,

and especially the lovely Mrs. Finkelstein, am not prepared to make. What if I came home one day and said. "Hey honey, I've got great news, I quit my job today, but I got hired picking strawberries at Jean's Berry Patch (which, by the way, has great strawberries). I know I'm only making minimum wage, and we'll need to move out of our house in the next few months and sell your new minivan (and the automatic trash can), and God forbid, you might have to get a job, but just think of the health benefits. . . ." That's a conversation that we both hope never happens.

C'MON NOW, WE'RE ONLY UTILITY MAXIMIZING

Now let's put that same picture into economic terms. Economists would say that Uncle Al, Cousin Carl, and I are not making bad choices about diet and exercise. In fact, we are all utility maximizing. That means that given all the possible choices we could be making, we are choosing those options that make us best off (i.e., the ones that give us the most utility).

These choices concerning how much to eat, exercise, work, and so on are not necessarily made with perfect information or foresight, nor are they made without constraints. In fact, our choices are constrained in many ways, but perhaps the two most binding constraints are time and money.

For Uncle Al, time is the more important constraint. With unlimited time, he would gladly play more golf and get additional exercise, but once he made the choice to work at the law firm, that left scarce time for leisure activities, and exercise had to compete against all the other options available to him. For Cousin Carl, time remains a major constraint, but he also has a much tighter budget constraint than Uncle Al. It is this tight budget that encourages him to spend far less money on food, even though he knows this decision means he is not eating as healthily as he could be. Regardless, both Uncle Al and Cousin Carl are utility maximizers, as am I and most of the rest of us, no matter what our weight happens to be.

In economic terms, we all make choices to maximize our utility given our constraints. However, the factors that we derive utility from (i.e., our preferences) vary from person to person, as do our constraints. For example. Uncle Al loves to play golf. I hate golf, but I like to jog and play basketball. Whereas Uncle Al sometimes chooses to play golf in his free time, running is now my physical activity of choice. Although I like basketball more than running (i.e., I get greater utility from an hour of basketball than an hour of running), I choose running because I can get it done in 30 minutes, whereas basketball is a several-hour affair by the time I drive to the gym, wait for a game, play for a bit, and drive home. I used to choose basketball over running, but now that I have kids, I find it to be too costly in terms of the amount of time required and what I have to give up (i.e., time with my kids) in order to get a game in.

Then there is Cousin Carl, and perhaps lots of other individuals, who would prefer never to exercise at all. Whereas I get positive utility from exercise and Uncle Al clearly loves golf, physical activity may actually make some individuals worse off (i.e., lower their utility), all else being equal. This is not to say that they would never do it. For example, even though my sister admittedly hates to exercise, she still goes walking every morning because she hates being fat even more. That is the same reason she is always going on some crazy diet plan. Diet and exercise are two necessary evils in her efforts to remain thin. The same is true for many of us. It all depends on our valuations concerning exercise, weight, food preferences and other preferences, what trade-offs we are willing to make, and what constraints we face when making decisions that impact our weight and health.

Although I am unable to get confirmation from Cousin Carl or Uncle Al about these trade-offs, I do have data that reveals that, in fact, overweight and obese individuals are quite aware of their elevated risk of disease and premature death. My colleagues and I conducted a nationally representative telephone survey of 1,139 adults to assess whether those who are overweight or obese believe they are at greater risk of both morbidity and premature mortality.[10]

For four of the diseases known to be linked to excess weight (diabetes, cancer, heart disease, and stroke), both overweight and obese individuals reported risks of contracting these diseases that were greater than the risks reported from individuals who were in the normal BMI range. Greatest perceived risks were reported by obese individuals. In fact, obese individuals rated themselves more than twice as likely to get cancer and heart disease, roughly three times more likely to develop a stroke, and four times more likely to develop diabetes than individuals of normal weight. And these analyses included only individuals who were free of these diseases at the time of the survey.

Respondents to the survey who were in the normal BMI range predicted, on average, that they would live to about age 78. Overweight individuals, on average, rated their life expectancy at 75.5, 2.5 years less than normal-weight individuals. Obese adults predicted a life expectancy of 74 years, four years less than the predictions for the normal-weight group. Several published papers that use actual death data produce results for both overweight and obesity that are close to those predicted by the survey respondents.[11,12,13] In other words, overweight and obese individuals' predictions of a shorter life expectancy appear fairly accurate.

So why is this significant? It suggests that many individuals are making a *conscious* decision to engage in a lifestyle that is obesity promoting, even if they believe that it will result in poorer health and reduced life expectancy.

So are Uncle Al and Cousin Carl at their optimal weight? Could be. Was I at my optimum weight seven years ago when I weighed 194 pounds? I was. Am I at my optimum now, four marathons later and almost 20 pounds lighter? The answer is yes. What changed for me? The main change was my entry into obesity research and the belief that I would be more credible, especially when giving presentations, if I shed a few pounds. In other words, my perceived benefits of weight lost went up, so I lost some weight. This is Economics 101. Was I right? . . . Nonetheless,

I'll keep the sedentary office job and run marathons to stay in shape, rather than pick strawberries or carry letters for a living. . . .

NOW, LET'S TEAR THIS ARGUMENT APART (AND PUT IT BACK TOGETHER)

As economists are prone to do, the above discussion makes several assumptions. One of these assumptions is that Uncle Al, Cousin Carl, and the rest of us are rational decision makers; we are making the choices that make us best off from our own perspective (we are maximizing our utility) given our preferences and constraints. It does not assume that individuals have perfect information about these choices. However, the decision to acquire additional information is also a choice that individuals can make.

In other words, in its most basic form, utility maximization assumes that every time Uncle Al decides to take his wife out for a nice meal, work extra hours, or ride a golf cart instead of walking 18 holes, he is aware of how these behaviors will impact his future weight and health outcomes, and he is making the best choice for him once all of those factors are considered. If there is some additional information that Uncle Al might want to help him make an informed decision, utility maximization further assumes that he could go out and find that information if he chooses to do so.

For Uncle Al, who is a smart lawyer, this may not be so much of a stretch. I certainly don't know the health content of many of the foods I eat or how many calories I burn in various activities, but I could find out if I truly wanted to. But I'm a pretty smart guy, too. I mean, after all, I have a PhD. (*Note:* This is sarcasm.) What about the average consumer—are they able to acquire this information if they truly wanted to? At least for nutrition content for prepackaged food, the introduction of the Nutrition Facts panel in the early 1990s certainly made this

information easier to acquire. And although this information is not readily available for restaurant food, eating out is also a choice that consumers do not have to make.

I suspect that many non-economists will buy into the utility maximization argument in general, but not when it comes to food choices. Their skepticism may be due, in part, to the fact that information on the health content of many foods is hard to come by. The Nutrition Facts panel is available for prepackaged foods, but it is not easily digestible (pardon the pun).[14] Moreover, much of our consumption now occurs in restaurants, where there is often little or no information on the health content of the foods we consume. As a result, people are making food consumption decisions with limited understanding of the health content of these foods.

I agree that we may not know everything there is to know about our food consumption and even our physical activity levels, but a look in the mirror or a trip to the scale should be a pretty good indicator of the repercussions of the decisions. At that point, we can decide whether we care enough to attempt to make the difficult sacrifices required to reduce our weight. Some of these sacrifices would include educating ourselves about health information and the best strategies for weight loss and weight maintenance.

Moreover, if enough of us cared and created a demand for this information, restaurants and other food purveyors, seeking to attract our business, would do a better job of providing it . . .

There is a second concern about utility maximization for which Brian Wansink and other food psychologists would likely take me to task. I suspect they would probably disagree with the notion that Uncle Al has *full* control over all of the choices that impact his weight or that he is truly a forward-looking thinker while at the dinner table. Perhaps, as with smoking, Uncle Al has a food addiction that does not allow him to stop eating when he wants to. Or perhaps he is so short-sighted that he does not think about the long-term consequences of his food consumption decisions.

I have young children, and I know they don't consider the long-term consequences of many of their actions, but can the same really be said for Uncle Al? We do know he eats more at a buffet than he would at a sit-down restaurant. We also can guess that he probably would eat stale popcorn at a movie theater if it were free. Maybe, like an addict, he can't help himself. If not, then the utility maximization argument goes out the window and, as we discuss in the following chapter, Uncle Al may need some outside help to ensure he does not overeat.

Although I'm not discounting the notion that there are many psychological aspects related to food consumption, I'm skeptical that the rapid weight gain seen over the past three decades has much to do with food addictions. I'm sticking with the utility-maximization argument and our earlier conclusion that the rise in obesity rates is a result of our current obesity-promoting environment that has increased the costs of physical activity and lowered the costs of food consumption and of being obese.

Why? Because putting aside increases in food availability and falling prices for high-calorie foods, the reality is that I had to scratch my head for quite a while to think up an occupation, berry picking, which has not been automated to the point where people no longer get physical activity doing it. Given that, the choice to enter the workforce—which, for many of us, is not a choice if we want to eat and not be homeless—largely means that we are committed to 40-plus hours a week of inactivity. This stacks the deck against us in our efforts to remain thin.

I could have chosen to pick berries, but is that a realistic option? Combine that with increasingly low-cost, readily available, and tasty food options and the many new treatments for obesity-related risk factors and diseases, and the result is that, for many of us, weight gain seems to be the rational economic choice.

NOTES

1. Centers for Disease Control and Prevention. 2004. "Trends in intake of energy and macronutrients—United States, 1971–2000." *Morbidity and Mortality. Weekly Report* 53, no. 4:80–82, www.cdc.gov/mmwr/preview/mmwrhtml/mm5304a3.htm.

2. Author calculation from Council of Economic Advisors. 2005. *Economic Report of the President, 2005.* Washington, DC: U.S. Government Printing Office, http://a257.g.akamaitech.net/7/257/2422/17feb20051700/www.gpoaccess.gov/cop/2005/2005_erp.pdf.

3. Author calculation from "Consumer Price Index—all urban consumers." United States Bureau of Labor Statistics, http://data.bls.gov/PDQ/outside.jsp?survey=cu.

4. Economic Research Service. "Data sets—food availability." United States Department of Agriculture, www.ers.usda.gov/data/foodconsumption/Food AvailQueriable_aspx#midForm.

5. Putnam, J. J., J. E. Allshouse, and L.S. Kantor. 2002. "U.S. per capita food supply trends: more calories, refined carbohydrates, and fats." *Food Review* 25, no. 3:2–15.

6. Block, G. 2004. "Foods contributing to energy intake in the US: Data from NHANES III and NHANES 1999–2000." *Journal of Food Composition and Analysis* 17. no. 3–4: 439–447.

7. Cutler D.M.,E.L. Glaeser, and J.M. Shapiro. 2003. "Why have Americans become more obese?" National Bureau of Economic Research Working Paper, 9446.

8. Wansink, B. 2006. *Mindless Eating: Why We Eat More Than We Think.* New York: Bantam Books.

9. Stenson, J. 2007. "Is your job making you fat? Employment may be especially gainful for desk workers." MSNBC.com, February 6, www.msnbc.msn.com/id/16927021/.

10. Evans, W. D., J. M. Renaud, E. Finkelstein, D. B. Kamerow, and D. S. Brown. 2006. "Changing perceptions of the childhood obesity epidemic." *American Journal of Health Behavior* 30, no. 2 (March/April): 167–176.

11. The Pew Research Center for the People and the Press. 2004. "Survey experiment shows polls face growing resistance, but still representative." Washington, DC: Pew Research Center for the People and the Press, http://people-press.org/reports/pdf/211.pdf. Accessed on April 24, 2006.

12. Blumberg, S. J., J. V. Lake, and M. L. Cynamon. 2006. "Telephone coverage and health survey estimates: Evaluating the need for concern about wireless substitution." *American Journal of Public Health* 96, no. 5:926–931.

13. Curtin R., S. Presser, and E. Singer. 2005. "Changes in telephone survey nonresponse over the past quarter century." *Public Opinion Quarterly* 69, no. 1: 87–98.

14. Cowburn, G., and L. Stockley. 2005. "Consumer understanding and use of nutrition labeling: A systematic review." *Public Health Nutrition* 8, no.1: 21–28.

QUESTIONS

1. Finkelstein and Zuckerman suggest that people who overconsume are typically making utility-maximizing choices. Explain what they mean.
2. One objection to the claim that people who overconsume are typically making utility-maximizing choices is that people typically don't understand the health consequences of their consumption choices. How do Finkelstein and Zuckerman respond to this objection?
3. Another objection to the claim that people who overconsume are typically making utility-maximizing choices is that overconsuming isn't typically a choice at all. Does the work of Brian Wansink or David Kessler support that objection?
4. Finkelstein and Zuckerman discuss Wansink's popcorn experiment and offer this explanation of its result: "Although each additional bit may bring him less joy as he gets fuller and fuller, if the food tastes good, he might as well keep eating. Only when he is really stuffed, and an additional bit makes him worse off, should he stop eating." Does this explain why people with larger buckets ate more popcorn than people with smaller buckets?

DANIEL CALLAHAN

Obesity: Chasing an Elusive Epidemic

In this excerpt from a very controversial paper, Daniel Callahan argues that because obesity is a significant public health problem, but little progress is being made on reducing obesity rates, we should embrace new anti-obesity measures. Callahan proposes applying strong social pressure to individuals—what he calls "stigmatization lite"—in order to motivate them to adopt better dietary and exercise habits, and to accept strong antiobesity policies. Callahan discusses analogies and disanalogies between the stigmatization of obesity and the stigmatization of smoking, which he thinks was effective at reducing smoking rates and was widely embraced by the public health community.

Obesity may be the most difficult and elusive public health problem this country has ever encountered. Unlike the classical infectious diseases and plagues that killed millions in the past, it is not caused by deadly viruses or bacteria of a kind amenable to vaccines for prevention, nor are there many promising

Daniel Callahan, "Obesity: Chasing an Elusive Epidemic," in *Hastings Center Report*, 43, no. 1 (Hoboken, NJ: John Wiley and Sons, 2012), 34–40. © 2012 by The Hastings Center.

medical treatments so far. While diabetes, heart disease, and kidney failure can be caused by obesity, it is easier to treat those conditions than one of their causes. I call obesity elusive partly because of the disturbingly low success rate in treating it, but also because it requires changing the patterns, woven deeply into our social fabric, of food and beverage commerce, personal eating habits, and sedentary lifestyles . . .

Obesity is ordinarily defined as an excess proportion of bodily fat and technically defined in terms of body mass index (BMI) . . . Around 35 percent of Americans are obese, and 67 percent are either obese or overweight.[1] To put those figures in what might be called a visual context, a 2011 Gallup Health Survey found that the average American man now weighs 196 pounds, and the average woman 160—and both figures are 20 pounds higher than self-reported weights in 1990.[2] The survey also noted that men were, on average, 15 pounds over their ideal weight, and women were 22 pounds over.

PREVALENCE AND CAUSATION

But there is a disturbing twist in those findings: "the percentage of Americans who describe themselves as overweight [35 percent of men and 42 percent of women] has remained essentially unchanged over the past 20 years . . . while Americans are getting heavier, many may not recognize it or acknowledge it." They are also, the Gallup Survey reports, "notoriously poor judges of their children's weight as well." All of this helps "paint a picture of mass delusion in the United States about its rising weight."

The rapid upward trend of the prevalence of obesity in earlier decades has recently shown some small signs of leveling off, but with no evidence that its prevalence is declining in any group. The United States is hardly alone in having this problem. The World Health Organization has called obesity a "global epidemic," and another study projects an international potential of 2.16 billion overweight and 1.12 billion obese persons by 2030.[3] The United Kingdom and the United States have the worst figures, while Japan and Korea have some of the best. But almost every country is in trouble, including some developing nations with rising prosperity and emerging first-world habits. The common estimate is that about 17 percent of American children are obese—and many children who begin life obese are likely to remain so for the rest of their life.

The health impacts of obesity are notorious: bone and joint problems, heart disease, cancer, gall stones and liver problems, and diabetes. Obesity shortens lives (although, surprisingly, not by much), but the costs of the diseases it causes make it an expensive condition . . .

The causes of obesity include age (the body's metabolism slows with age); gender differences (more common in women); genetics (obesity tends to run in families); illness (hypothyroidism); cultural acceptance or indifference (poverty, race); sedentary habits (long commutes, sitting at a desk or work bench all day, watching TV, lack of exercise); poor diet (few fruits and vegetables, processed foods, overly large food portions at home and in restaurants, sugared beverages); and, too often neglected, all the luxuries we possess—automatic garage door openers, can openers, food blenders and mixers, escalators, elevators, golf carts, automobiles, and so on . . .

When all the data and trends are put together, it is only reasonable to conclude that little progress is being made. Educational efforts to reduce obesity have had little impact. Its prevalence is not decreasing, and the available treatments and weight loss strategies are successful for only a very small number of those targeted for such efforts. Most of the 67 percent who are overweight or obese will remain so for the rest of their lives, guaranteeing serious health problems as they get older . . .

The most promising directions, I believe, fall into three categories: strong and most likely somewhat coercive public health measures, mainly by government but also by the business community; childhood prevention programs; and social pressure on the overweight . . .

CHANGING INDIVIDUAL BEHAVIOR

A return to the discarded idea of changing individual behavior may be necessary. One way or another, the public—a majority of whom are, after all, overweight or obese, while the balance are at some risk of becoming so—must be persuaded of a number of points. Whether or not they recognize their own role in it, they need to understand that obesity is a national health problem, one that causes lethal diseases, shortens lives, and contributes substantially to rising health care costs. Not just their own welfare is at stake. They no less need to understand that, whatever they may think about the power and excess of government, it is inescapable in this case, as much as with national defense.

It will be no less necessary to find ways to bring strong social pressure to bear on individuals, going beyond anodyne education and low-key exhortation. It will be imperative, first, to persuade them that they ought to want a good diet and exercise for themselves and for their neighbor and, second, that excessive weight and outright obesity are not socially acceptable any longer. They need as well to be mobilized as citizens to support a more invasive role for government. Obesity is in great part a reflection of the kind of culture we have, one that is permissive about how people take care of their bodies and accepts many if not most of the features of our society that contribute to the problem. There has to be a popular uprising when so many aspects of our common lives, individually and institutionally, must be changed more or less simultaneously. Safe and slow incrementalism that strives never to stigmatize obesity has not and cannot do the necessary work.

STIGMATIZATION

When I was first drawn to think about obesity, I could not help thinking about the success of the antismoking campaign of recent decades. That campaign went simultaneously after the supply side (the tobacco industry) and the demand side (individual smokers). As a smoker, I was at first criticized for my nasty habit and eventually, along with all the others, sent outside to smoke, and my cigarette taxes were constantly raised. The force of being shamed and beat upon socially was as persuasive for me to stop smoking as the threats to my health. I was also helped by the fact that others around me were stopping as well. If they could do it, so could I. The campaign against smoking was a public health triumph, not eliminating smoking by any means but greatly reducing it, so that smokers now make up only about 20 percent of the population.[4] The campaign to stigmatize smoking was a great success, turning what had been considered simply a bad habit into reprehensible behavior.

Misled by the public health community's acceptance—and even enthusiastic embrace—of supply and demand measures against and outright stigmatization of smoking, I naively assumed that community would do the same against obesity. I had not realized that smoking was the exception—that the public health community generally opposes anything that looks like blaming the victim. This fact was surely evident in the struggle against HIV, as well as in other campaigns over the decades against the stigmatization of people with many other diseases. It has not been hard to find examples of stigmatization turning into outright discrimination, even (notoriously) in health care.[5]

Why is obesity said to be different from smoking? Three reasons are common: it is wrong to stigmatize people because of their health conditions; wrong to think it will work well, or at all, with obesity; and counterproductive with the obese because of evidence that it worsens rather than improves their condition. Ethically speaking, the social pressures on smokers focused on their behavior, not on them as persons. Stigmatizing the obese, by contrast, goes after their character and selfhood, it is said, not just their behavior. Stigmatization in their case also leads demonstrably to outright discrimination, in health care, education, and the job market more generally. The obese are said to be lazy, self-indulgent, lacking in discipline, awkward, unattractive, weak-willed and sloppy, insecure and shapeless, to mention only a few of the negative judgments among doctors and nurses.

As for government doing something about the discrimination, as of 2009 Michigan was the only state that prohibits weight discrimination in employment. There has been a wariness about using the American Disability Act against such discrimination out of fear that obesity might come to be seen as an outright disability (though for many it is disabling), not just a potentially unhealthy condition. And while there are many efforts under way to change the perceptions and judgments about the obese in the health community, there seems to be no evidence that a significant change is taking place.

While the public health community, and particularly those who take on obesity, have vigorously rejected deliberate efforts to stigmatize the obese, the fact of the matter is that they are already stigmatized, and notably among health care workers. As Governor Chris Christie of New Jersey found out when he was considered a possible presidential candidate, a number of jokes about his weight were made on TV and in other media, with some (possibly serious) concerns voiced about his health prospects. Yet it is hard to imagine that much progress can occur toward solutions for obesity unless we bring some form of social pressure to bear against it. If we are left with nothing but the need to change almost everything about the way we live, more or less simultaneously, progress seems improbable. How long will it take, for instance, to get rid of lengthy commutes to urban centers, to wean people from their TV and iPad screens, to get everyone and their children to eat healthy food and get regular exercise, and to get industry to stop inventing and selling us unhealthy junk food (and to get over its convenience and our liking for it)?

For any of those good goals to have real bite, it will be necessary to make just about everyone strongly want to avoid being overweight and obese. Education has not shown itself to be up to that task. Fear of illness has not, either. No technologies—surgery or pills—have made a major difference. Stigmatization, we have been told, is counterproductive. Moreover, it is a telling commentary on the difficult

road ahead that obesity experts have become willing (even if not happily) to settle for a success rate of 10 percent or less in finding ways to effectively help people lose weight and, most critically, to keep from putting it back on . . .

VARIETIES OF SOCIAL PRESSURE

Our best long-term possibility is to find ways of inducing a majority of the population to do what a minority now already do: working to stay thin in the first place and to lose weight early on if excess weight begins to emerge. That will take social pressure combined with vigorous government action. The social pressure will aim to push the public to accept strong interventions, just as it could induce them to change the way they eat, work, and exercise. While obesity is not in any ordinary medical sense a contagious disease, it is subtly contagious in a social sense. When it is as common as is now the case, those who are overweight hardly notice that others are the same: it is just the way ordinary people look. We need them to notice the others and to want something different for themselves—and those others will be similarly motivated.

But can there be social pressure that does not lead to outright discrimination—a kind of stigmatization lite? That will, I concede, be a difficult line to walk, but it is worth a try. I would couch the social pressure in the following terms, finding ways to induce people who are overweight or obese to put some uncomfortable questions to themselves:

- If you are overweight or obese, are you pleased with the way you look?
- Are you happy that your added weight has made many ordinary activities, such as walking up a long flight of stairs, harder?
- Would you prefer to lessen your risk of heart disease and diabetes?
- Are you aware that, once you gain a significant amount of weight, your chances of taking that weight back off and keeping it off are poor?

- Are you pleased when your obese children are called "fatty" or otherwise teased at school?
- Fair or not, do you know that many people look down upon those excessively overweight or obese, often in fact discriminating against them and making fun of them or calling them lazy and lacking in self-control?

That last question in effect aims to make people acutely aware of pervasive stigmatization, but then to invoke it as a danger to be avoided: don't let this happen to you! If you don't do something about yourself, that's what you are in for. Many of the other questions invoke vanity as a value, or the good opinion of one's neighbors, friends, or fellow employees, or the risk of illness. Use all of them together, carrots and sticks. That will not much help most of those who are already overweight or obese. But beyond marginal improvements, most of them are already lost. They should surely not be neglected, but the important work is to be done with those not yet in that condition . . .

None of the social pressure tactics will directly change the conditions of poverty that make so many people susceptible to obesity, or will necessarily induce the food and beverage industries to change their deleterious ways. But they can change the background pressures—creating a potent force for public opinion, making it easier to use government to bring forth necessary regulations and prohibitions, shaming delinquent industries, and leaning on the public to take the problem more seriously.

The need is for a bottom-up approach to create and sustain a truly effective antiobesity campaign that matches the necessary top-down structural efforts. One obvious target would be the large number of people who are unaware that they are overweight. They need, to use an old phrase, a shock of recognition. Only

a carefully calibrated effort of public social pressure is likely to awaken them to the reality of their condition. They have been lulled into obliviousness about their problem because they look no different from many others around them. They need to be leaned upon, nudged, and—when politically feasible—helped by regulations to understand that they are potentially in trouble. They should not want to be that way, nor should others.

What I am suggesting—empowering the victims, not blaming them, and that individual responsibility is necessary—has its risks. But if the individual and public health impact of being overweight and obese is dangerous, then it is hard to imagine any kind of strong and effective efforts that will not meet resistance. The failure of efforts to date to make much difference suggest that a change of strategy is necessary.

REFERENCES

1. Organisation of Economic Co-Operation and Development (OECD), *OECD Factbook 2011–2012: Economic, Environmental and Social Statistics* (Geneva, Switzerland: OECD, 2011), 233.

2. E. Mendes, "In U.S. Self-Reported Weight Up Nearly 20 Pounds Since 1990," *Gallup Wellbeing,* November 22, 2011.

3. T. Kelly et al., "Global Burden of Obesity in 2005 and Projections to 2030," *International Journal of Obesity* 33, no. 24 (2008): 1431–37.

4. R. Bayer, "Stigma and the Ethics of Public Health: Not Can We, But Should We?" *Social Science and Medicine* 69 (2008): 463–73.

5. R.M. Puhl and C.A. Heuer, "The Stigma of Obesity: A Review and Update," *Obesity* 12, no. 5 (2009): 941–64; R.A. Puhl and C.A. Heuer, "Obesity Stigma: Important Considerations for Public Health," *American Journal of Public Health* 100, no. 6 (2010): 1019–28.

QUESTIONS

1. What are differences between the stigmatization of obesity and the stigmatization of smoking, according to Callahan?
2. Callahan does not define stigma in his paper. What's your best guess at how Callahan would define stigma?

3. Is it possible to stigmatize a behavior (e.g., smoking) without stigmatizing the people who engage in that behavior (e.g., smokers)? Is it possible to stigmatize an attribute (e.g., being overweight) without stigmatizing the people who have that attribute (e.g., people who are overweight)? Is it possible to apply social pressure without leading to discrimination—what Callahan calls "stigmatization lite"? Callahan says stigmatization lite is "worth a try." What do you think?

4. Callahan seems to assume that people who are overweight or obese are not sufficiently motivated to maintain a normal weight: "it will be necessary to make just about everyone strongly want to avoid being overweight and obese." Is lack of motivation a primary cause of overweight and obese, in your view?

5. Callahan notes that many people who are overweight do not consider themselves overweight, and many parents of overweight children do not consider their children overweight. What is the right response to this, in your view?

DANIEL S. GOLDBERG AND REBECCA M. PUHL

Obesity Stigma

A Failed and Ethically Dubious Strategy

In this reply to Daniel Callahan's "Chasing Obesity: An Elusive Epidemic," Goldberg and Puhl argue against Callahan's proposal to apply social pressure to overweight and obese people. They argue that there is no evidence that stigmatization is effective at addressing obesity, but there is evidence that stigmatization is harmful to individuals and contributes to unhealthy behavior.

In his recent article, "Obesity: Chasing an Elusive Epidemic," Daniel Callahan laments the evidence suggesting that despite intensive devotion of resources, relatively little progress has been made in countering obesity in the United States. He recommends three categories of interventions: "strong and most likely coercive public health measures," "childhood prevention," and "social pressure on the overweight." Our response focuses on the third strategy, which is misguided on several fronts.

Daniel S. Goldberg and Rebecca M. Puhl, "Obesity Stigma: A Failed and Ethically Dubious Strategy," in *Hastings Center Report*, 43, no. 3 (Hoboken, NJ: John Wiley and Sons, 2013), 5–6. © 2013 by The Hastings Center.

Not only does weight stigmatization impose psychological and social harm, but it fails as an incentive for improving health behaviors and may instead reinforce obesity. Obese individuals are already highly stigmatized, despite their attempts to lose weight and despite the significant sociocultural and economic conditions that contribute to obesity, which is where our efforts should be focused. Even if obesity stigma were entirely effective, we submit that its use still violates ethical norms of social justice.

Callahan's argument in favor of "stigmatization lite" against overweight and obese persons begins by analogy, asserting that because such opprobrium helped reduce smoking incidence, it should similarly be used against obesity. Yet it is not clear to what extent the stigmatization of smoking was responsible for reduced incidence. Bell et al. argue that the "denormalization" of smoking may actually inhibit smoking cessation insofar as it increases patient non-disclosure.[1] While smoking incidence has decreased, the best evidence (which is from the Centers for Disease Control) suggests that taxation and other whole population measures are most responsible. Moreover, while absolute incidence has decreased, the social gradient in smoking has increased, and with it, the gradient in smoking-related disease. This means that smoking-related health inequities have expanded. Further, Bell et al. make clear that denormalization has contributed to this expansion in smoking-related inequities. Stigma therefore may increase health inequities, which alone renders it ethically problematic.

But even if stigma produced extremely salubrious consequences, we think it should not be deployed as a public health intervention. The intense harms stigma can impose and the way it can literally spoil identity provide a powerful argument against its usage regardless of the consequences.

That said, even the ultimate deontologist, Kant, acknowledged that consequences are germane to ethical analysis. Accordingly, when assessing the permissibility of stigmatizing overweight persons, the likelihood of salutary consequences is important. Callahan offers no evidence that stigmatization is an effective approach to address obesity and

acknowledges that obesity stigma actually tends to exacerbate obesity, but nevertheless contends that "social pressure" is necessary for amelioration of obesity. We do not understand this claim. To be clear, there is consistent evidence that individuals exposed to weight stigmatization are vulnerable to numerous adverse health consequences, including depression, anxiety, low self-esteem, suicidal ideation, and avoidance of health care. They also tend to eat in an unhealthy way, consuming lots of calories and indulging in binge-eating, and they do not engage in physical activity, which can reinforce weight gain and impair weight loss efforts. Furthermore, recent evidence shows that public health campaigns containing messages that stigmatize and shame obese persons actually induce *less* motivation and *lower* intentions to improve health behaviors among the American public compared to campaigns that instead encourage specific eating or exercise behaviors to help prevent or reduce obesity.[2]

Link and Phelan's influential formulation of stigma in a public health context consists of two central criteria: an out-group is marked or branded as different on the basis of a common demographic characteristic, and then the out-group is judged deviant or inferior on the basis of that characteristic.[3] These criteria demonstrate the crucial interplay between stigma, power, and inequities because without power and privilege the in-group literally could not mark itself as "in" and the out-group as "out." It is certainly true that obesity affects all segments of the population. But Callahan does not address the considerable evidence suggesting that living in deleterious social and economic conditions narrows choices, limits opportunities to improve weight-related health, and facilitates poor nutrition. This evidence suggests that interventions such as stigma that are targeted at changing individual behavior will be ineffective precisely because they fail to address the societal conditions that have contributed to obesity—conditions that are themselves intimately connected to historical pathways of power, privilege, and structural violence. Collective action on the social determinants of obesity represents a much more promising intervention strategy than stigmatization of obese persons and avoids many of the ethical problems that attend the latter.

Finally, Madison Powers and Ruth Faden's health sufficiency model of social justice suggests that we should prioritize interventions that break "densely-woven webs of disadvantage."[4] Note that stigma is a form of social disadvantage that is independently correlated with adverse health. Stigmatizing people contravenes Powers and Faden's model by intensifying such webs of disadvantage.

Obesity stigma has already been shown to be a failure. Yet even if it worked, it should not be tolerated as a public health strategy in a just social order. Callahan argues that despite its drawbacks, stigmatizing the obese "is worth a try." No, it is not.

NOTES

1. K. Bell et al., "Smoking, Stigma and Tobacco 'Denormalization': Further Reflections on the Use of Stigma as a Public Health Tool: A Commentary on *Social Science and Medicine*'s Stigma, Prejudice, Discrimination and Health Special Issue (67:3)," *Social Science and Medicine* 70, no. 6 (2010): 795–99.

2. R.M. Puhl, J.L. Peterson, and J. Luedicke, "Fighting Obesity or Obese Persons? Public Perceptions of Obesity-Related Health Messages," *International Journal of Obesity,* September 11, 2012, doi:10.1038/ijo.2012.156.

3. B.G. Link and J.C. Phelan, "Stigma and Its Public Health Implications," *Lancet* 367 (2006): 528–29.

4. Madison Powers and Ruth Faden, *Social Justice: The Moral Foundations of Public Health and Health Policy* (New York: Oxford University Press, 2006). DOI: 10.1002/hast.167

QUESTIONS

1. Goldberg and Puhl question whether the stigmatization of smoking caused a reduction in smoking rates. Instead of or along with stigmatization, what might have caused reductions in smoking rates?

2. Goldberg and Puhl note that there is no evidence that stigmatization is effective at reducing obesity, but there is evidence that stigmatization is harmful and counterproductive. What are some of the effects of stigmatization that they cite?

3. Goldberg and Puhl cite an influential definition of stigma: "an out-group is marked or branded as different on the basis of a common demographic characteristic, and then the out-group is judged deviant or inferior on the basis of that characteristic." Would applying social pressure to overweight people, in the way advocated by Callahan in "Chasing Obesity: An Elusive Epidemic," cause them to be stigmatized in this sense?

JULIE GUTHMAN

Can't Stomach It

How Michael Pollan et al. Made Me Want to Eat Cheetos

Julie Guthman discusses criticisms of the science of obesity. She also ethically critiques the "obesity epidemic" conversation as belittling toward fat people and stigmatizing, among other problems.

It has become common to speak of an "epidemic of obesity." Serious news sources routinely feature articles on obesity; some even suggest that the obesity epidemic is one of the greatest public health threats of our times, perhaps rivaling AIDS or avian flu. Obesity is commonly linked to other social problems, as well. It has been named as a cost to businesses in terms of worker productivity, a cause for poor pupil performance, a weight-load problem for the airlines due to increased fuel costs, and even a security threat in terms of military preparedness. Proposed and implemented social solutions have included snack taxes, corporate-sponsored exercise breaks, stronger food labeling laws, and, most troublingly, state-mandated student weigh-ins at public schools, with results included on report cards (as if fat kids and their parents need to be reminded).

Obesity further serves as a bonanza for social reformers who deploy the rhetoric of fat in support of their various projects, from farm-to-school programs to mixed-use housing and transportation centers; and for puritans who wish to use fatness as an example of the moral decrepitude to which we must just say no. Finally, the obesity epidemic, and its tendency to dignify obsessions that equate thinness and beauty,

is hugely profitable, contributing, by some estimates, to a one-hundred-billion-dollar-per-year weight-loss industry that distributes specialized products and services apart from the money made on bariatric and cosmetic surgery. Television shows like *The Biggest Loser,* sponsored by purveyors of diet foods, fitness centers, and pharmaceuticals, contribute to the false idea that diets work, thereby increasing the market for such goods and services. And if the daily e-mail spam I receive for Anatrim serves as any indication, the underground market in pharmaceuticals is cashing in, too.

Taken together, the above set of observations suggests that obesity has achieved the status of an infectious disease. Although obesity has not been deemed infectious—at least yet—the criteria employed by researcher Nancy Tomes to establish the existence of a germ panic equate obesity in degree, if not kind, to the problem of tuberculosis in the early twentieth century: a) the "disease" is deemed newsworthy; b) its incidence reflects other societal problems, giving activists and reformers an angle for addressing their specific concerns; and c) it has commercial potential to sell products or services, so that public concern is heightened by economic interests.[1] Tomes' study also discusses the central role that popular culture, in the form of news coverage, entertainment media, and popular nonfiction, plays in contributing to the hysteria that constitutes such a panic. These factors are all true of obesity. In particular, a rash of popular books has appeared on the so-called obesity epidemic. While these books take a variety of positions on the topic, virtually all claim to "expose the lies" and/or tell the "real" story about the epidemic and/or who is gaining by it. For example, J. Eric Oliver's *Fat Politics: The Real Story Behind America's Obesity Epidemic,* while voicing skepticism of the ways in which obesity has been framed, contributes to the frenzy through its tone.[2]

Lately, another group of writers has gotten in on the act. A more refined and measured group, their books turn on the theme of "what to eat"—the specific title of Marion Nestle's most recent volume.[3] Other books in this group include Peter Singer's *The Way We Eat: Why Our Food Choices Matter,* Anna Lappé's *Grub: Ideas for an Urban Organic Kitchen,* and Jane Goodall's *Harvest for Hope: A Guide to Mindful Eating.*[4] Of all these books, the sine qua non is Michael Pollan's *The Omnivore's Dilemma: A Natural History of Four Meals.*[5] It is like no other because not only does Pollan know his stuff, he can write his way out of a paper bag, and his book sales show it. Virtually all of these authors extol the virtues of the organic and the local while arguing for a commonsense, ecumenical approach to diet choices (no food faddism here). That makes them refreshing in relation to the usual weight loss books and painfully restrictive messages of latter-day health foodism. Or does it?

Many of these authors share a common rhetorical strategy. They refer to the statistics of rising obesity rates among Americans, the surfeit of calories taken in relative to those expended, and the inexorable road toward illness with concomitant rising healthcare costs (never tabulated against the healthcare costs of weight loss attempts). They then go on to discuss the ubiquity of fast, junky food (what Kelly Brownell calls the "toxic environment") in order to make their points about what constitutes "real" food.[6] But whereas most of the popular writers on fat attribute growing obesity to a variety of culprits—television

viewing, long drive-to-work times, supermarket product placement, working mothers, clothing designers (allowing baggy clothes), marketing to children, poverty, affluence, and modernity (i.e., everything under the sun)—Pollan is much more pointed in his analysis. As he puts it, "All these explanations are true, as far as they go. But it pays to go a little further, to search for the cause behind the causes. Which, very simply, is this: When food is abundant and cheap, people will eat more of it and get fat."[7] Pollan then points to an even more specific culprit: corn.

Pollan's excellent writing makes for a compelling story about how corn has become the foundation of the national diet. He traces this first to the transport of *Zea mays* from regions now known as central Mexico to points north, where it easily took hold in a variety of microclimatic conditions and outdid wheat in terms of its yield and ease of cultivation. But corn's strength turned to its weakness; it was prone to systematic overproduction in US agriculture, so that even historically, surpluses ended up to no good. Corn liquor, of course, was the beverage of choice (and necessity) in pre-Prohibition drinking binges. Since the 1970s, the overproduction of corn has been buttressed by a farm policy that subsidizes corn production, in part to appease the farm lobby and in part for geopolitical ends, with erstwhile Secretary of Agriculture Earl Butz having first encouraged planting "from fencerow to fencerow." Pollan reminds us that corn is omnipresent in a fast-food meal: the high fructose corn syrup that sweetens the soda; the feed of the steer that goes into the hamburger beef; often the oil that fries the potatoes; and as one of the many micro-ingredients that stabilizes the bun. Corn by-products, it turns out, are even used in the packaging and serving utensils. Processed food, Pollan argues, makes us "walking corn," and the "Alcohol Republic" has now given way to "the Republic of Fat."[8]

Pollan's critique of the cost-cutting measures of the fast-food giants, the nutritional impoverishment of processed food, and an agricultural subsidy system that encourages ecologically problematic monocropping, horrendous animal husbandry practices, and food-dumping in the name of "aid" (often at the expense of farmers in the global South) is spot on. In fact, I could think of no clearer path to a more ecological and socially just food system than the removal of those subsidies. Yet, in evoking obesity, Pollan turns our gaze, perhaps inadvertently, from an ethically suspect farm policy to the fat body. One of the questions I want to raise in this essay is whether it is necessary for fat people to bear the weight of this argument.

There is much to criticize in the public conversation about obesity. The evidentiary basis of an "epidemic" is fairly weak, as it relies on changes in average Body Mass Index (BMI), itself a contested, albeit convenient way to measure obesity. For example, as a weight to height ratio, BMI cannot differentiate between fat and lean body mass.[9] For that matter, discussions of an epidemic provide very little specificity as to dimensions of the growth in girth. To draw out two extremes of the problem statement, it is unclear whether a relatively small number of people have become extremely fat, or whether many people have put on a few pounds. Given the way the BMI is normalized and categorized, a small average weight gain among a large population can shift enormous numbers of people from one category into the next, say from "overweight" to "obese," and thereby deepen the impression of an epidemic.[10] Moreover, the relationship between food intake, exercise, and growing obesity is poorly understood. Michael Gard and Jan Wright's exhaustive review of obesity research shows that the mechanical notion that weight gain results from a surplus of calories in to calories out has not been borne out in the research; at best, caloric metabolism appears to explain less than half of individual variation in body size, with much of the residual remaining "black boxed."[11] Finally, claims that obesity is a primary cause of disease (or a disease itself) are filled with logical flaws, chief among them that obesity may be symptomatic of diseases of concern, such as Type II diabetes.[12] For all of these reasons, Gard and Wright argue that obesity research itself has become so entangled with moral discourses and aesthetic values that the "science of obesity" can no longer speak for itself.[13]

These popular renditions are also remarkably insensitive, and not necessarily just to those who feel themselves to be too fat.[14] Rather, these authors seem unaware of how obesity messages work as admonishment. According to Paul Campos, the people most personally affected by discussions of obesity are those who want to lose ten or fifteen pounds, despite the fact that those who are "overweight" by current standards have longer life spans than those who are "thin" or "normal."[15] In a course I taught, called the Politics of Obesity, I was not particularly surprised by the number of students who wrote in their journals (a required element of the class) of their hidden "fitness" or eating disorders. However, the number of entries that stated how the course itself had produced body anxiety and intensified concern over diet and exercise was shocking, given that a good deal of the material took a critical stance toward obesity talk. The philosopher Michel Foucault might have called this the "productive" power of obesity talk—that in naming a behavior as a problem, it intensifies anxiety around that problem.[16] In that way, swipes at obesity, especially coming from those who themselves have never been subject to such scrutiny or objectification, or the pain and frustration of weight loss, strikes me as naïve. Yet, entirely absent from the pages of the recent popular books is any authorial reflection on how obesity talk further stigmatizes those who are fat, or on how this social scolding might actually work at cross-purposes to health and well-being.

But there is something even more disturbing about these books and the claims they reproduce. To repeat Pollan's claim: "When food is abundant and cheap, people will eat more of it and get fat."[17] People eat corn because it's there. They are dupes. Jane Goodall makes a similar leap when she writes, "There is no mechanism that turns off the desire—instinct, really—to eat food when it is available."[18] Even Marion Nestle's concern with supermarket aisles suggests that people mechanically react to product placement. This raises an important question: why are Pollan, Goodall, and Nestle not fat? If junk food is so ubiquitous that it cannot be resisted, how is it that some people remain (or become) thin?

It appears, unfortunately, that these authors see themselves as morally superior to fat people in the sense that they characterize fat people as being short of subjectivity. Goodall makes the above assertion having just written of "sad," "overweight," "over-indulged" cats and dogs being "killed by kindness," seeming to equate fat people with family pets.[19] In the "documentary" *SuperSize Me,* virtually all shots of fat people are headless and certainly speechless, and usually the camera captures backsides only. Some might argue that having no personal identifiers protects fat people in the camera's eye, but headless-ness also invokes mindlessness. Moreover, such protection assumes that fat people are ashamed of their bodies and eating habits. Since thin people *are* consistently pictured with heads, it logically follows that they are not so ashamed. This presumption is precisely the problem that Kathleen LeBesco captures in *Revolting Bodies,* including her critique of the fat acceptance movement itself.[20] At best, fat people are seen as victims of food, bad genetic codes, or bad metabolism; at worst, they are slovenly, stupid, or without resolve. Perhaps, she argues, fat people exercise agency in their fatness. Meanwhile, she notes, many thin people can indulge in all manners of unhealthy behaviors without being called to account for their body size. What LeBesco makes clear, in other words, is that fat people are imbued with little subjectivity no matter what they do, while thin people are imbued with heightened subjectivity no matter what *they* do.

That, then, is the most pernicious aspect of the Pollan et al. analysis. If junk food is everywhere and people are all naturally drawn to it, those who resist it must have heightened powers. In the reality television show *The Biggest Loser,* where fat people compete to lose the most weight (about which much could be said), the contestants are treated paternalistically; the hard-body trainers are treated as super-subjects who readily and regularly bestow life wisdom on their charges. So when Pollan waxes poetic about his own rarefied, distinctive eating practices, he makes a similar move. The messianic quality and self-satisfaction is not accidental. In describing his ability to overcome King Corn, to conceive, procure, prepare, and (perhaps) serve his version of the perfect meal, Pollan affirms himself as a super-subject while relegating others to objects of education, intervention, or just plain scorn.

Even if it were true that obesity is the public-health threat it is purported to be, even if it could be proven that it results from fast-food consumption in a clear and identifiable way, and even if we didn't care about the stigmatization of obesity or treating fat people as objects, is Pollan's way the way out? At the end of a book whose biggest strength is a section that lays out the environmental history and political economy of corn, his answer, albeit oblique, is to eat like he does. The meal that he helped forage and hunt and cooked all by himself, as he puts it, "gave me the opportunity, so rare in modern life, to eat in full consciousness of everything involved in feeding myself: for once, I was able to pay the full karmic price of a meal."[21] Notwithstanding Pollan's arguably narrow understanding of a "full karmic price" (how, for example, does this rectify the exploitation of farm laborers?), my question is: To what kind of politics does this lead? Despite his early focus on corn subsidies, Pollan does not urge his readers to write to their congressional representative about the folly of such subsidies, to comment to the FDA about food additives, or even, for that matter, to sabotage fields where genetically engineered corn is grown.[22]

Indeed, no suggestion is made that we ought to alter the structural features of the food system, so that all might come to eat better. Pollan betrays himself in his admiration of Joel Salatin, a beyond-organic farmer who is hard-lined in his denunciation of state regulation, seeing it as an impediment to building a viable local food chain. Unfortunately, this antiregulatory approach to food politics has really taken hold, especially in my part of the country. I have read countless undergraduate papers at my university that begin with the premise that the global food system is anomic, and that "if people only knew where their food came from," food provisioning would somehow evolve to be more ecological, humane, and just. Many of my students have strong convictions that they should and can teach people how and what to eat, as if you could "change the world one meal at a time" without attention to policy.[23]

I worry that Michael Pollan reinforces this highly privileged and apolitical idea and reinforces the belief that some people—in this case thin people—clearly must have seen the light that the rest are blind to. Pollan is a damn good writer and a smart man, which makes *The Omnivore's Dilemma* a compelling read. But I can't stomach where it leads. In a funny way, it makes me crave some corn-based Cheetos.

NOTES

1. Nancy Tomes, "The Making of a Germ Panic, Then and Now," *American Journal of Public Health* 90, no.2 (2000): 191.

2. J. Eric Oliver, *Fat Politics: The Real Story Behind America's Obesity Epidemic* (New York: Oxford University, 2006).

3. Marion Nestle, *What to Eat* (New York: North Point Press, 2006).

4. Jane Goodall, Gary McAvoy, and Gail Hudson, *Harvest for Hope: A Guide to Mindful Eating* (New York: Warner Books, 2005); Anna Lappé and Bryant Terry, *Grub: Ideas for an Urban Organic Kitchen* (New York: Tarcher, 2006); Peter Singer and Jim Mason, *The Way We Eat: Why Our Food Choices Matter* (Emmaus, PA: Rodale Press, 2006). The coauthors' names were omitted from the main text because these books are clearly being sold on the relative fame of their primary authors.

5. Michael Pollan, *The Omnivore's Dilemma: A Natural History of Four Meals* (New York: Penguin, 2006).

6. Kelly D. Brownell, *Food Fight: The Inside Story of the Food Industry, America's Obesity Crisis, and What We Can Do About It* (New York: McGraw-Hill, 2004).

7. Pollan, *Omnivore's Dilemma*, 102.

8. Ibid., 101.

9. Glenn Gaesser, *Big Fat Lies: The Truth About Your Weight and Your Health* (New York: Burze Books, 2002), Paul Campos et al., "The Epidemiology of Overweight and Obesity: Public Health Crisis or Moral Panic?" *International Journal of Epidemiology* 35, no.1 (2006).

10. Bruce Ross, "Fat or Fiction? Weighing the Obesity Epidemic," in *The Obesity Epidemic: Science, Morality, and Ideology,* ed. Michael Gard and Jan Wright (London: Routledge, 2005).

11. Michael Gard and Jan Wright, *The Obesity Epidemic: Science, Morality, and Ideology* (London: Routledge, 2005). This point was deduced from a discussion on pp. 47–50, where the authors note that some researchers have claimed that genetic factors account for 50 to 90 percent of individual variation. Gard and Wright make the point that genetic factors are acting as a "black box" to defend the calories in–calories out model.

12. Oliver, *Fat Politics*.

13. Gard and Wright, *Obesity Epidemic*.

14. I cringed when Nestle, as a keynote speaker at the Ecological Farming Conference in January 2006, stated that the problem of obesity was "simple," using the very terminology that Gard and Wright refute (calories in–calories out). Most of this audience applauded wildly, for the obesity epidemic holds much marketing promise for those who stake their living in the production of organic fresh fruits and vegetables.

15. Paul Campos, *The Obesity Myth: Why America's Obsession with Weight Is Hazardous to Your Health* (New York: Gotham Press, 2004).

16. Michel Foucault, *History of Sexuality, an Introduction,* vol. I (New York: Vintage, 1985).

17. Pollan, *Omnivore's Dilemma*, 102.

18. Goodall et al, *Harvest for Hope*, 240.

19. Ibid.

20. Kathleen LeBesco, *Revolting Bodies? The Struggle to Redefine Fat Identity* (Amherst: University of Massachusetts, 2004).

21. Pollan, *Omnivore's Dilemma*, 9.

22. This is an activist strategy popular in Europe, intended presumably to incite public rancor about the unnecessary proliferation of genetic engineering, especially in light of the fact that the primary justification of such technologies is to improve productivity. In this way, such a strategy is surely germane to Pollan's point.

23. The quoted catchphrase is widely circulated in alternative-food-movement circles.

QUESTIONS

1. Is there really an "epidemic" of obesity, according to Guthman?

2. Guthman suggests that intense focus on the "obesity epidemic" serves to stigmatize and scold people who are overweight. How so? Is it possible to draw attention to a health problem such as obesity (assuming for the sake of argument that obesity is a health problem) without stigmatizing those who have this health problem? Are the specific ways that we talk about food consumption, weight, and health more stigmatizing than they need to be?

3. One point of the environmental account of obesity is to locate the causes of obesity in the environment (which is seen as pervaded with unhealthy foods that we're naturally disposed to overconsume), and not primarily in the individual. However, Guthman writes, "If junk food is everywhere and people are all naturally drawn to it, those who resist it must have heightened powers." In this way, the environmental account of obesity imbues thin people with heightened subjectivity and overweight people with little subjectivity, according to Guthman. What do you think?

13 } Paternalism and Public Health

This chapter discusses the ethics of paternalistic food policies and laws—that is, policies and laws that limit individual choice or liberty regarding food, in order to improve these individuals' welfare.

PATERNALISTIC FOOD POLICIES

We focus here on paternalistic policies and laws meant to promote healthy eating in order to reduce rates of diet-related illness, which we call *paternalistic healthy eating policies*. But there are other food policies and laws that are arguably paternalistic, for example:

- The fluoridation of tap water to prevent tooth decay
- Policies requiring the irradiation of food
- Laws prohibiting the sale of unpasteurized milk or "raw milk," because it can contain bacteria that makes people sick

In Chapter 12, "Overconsumption and Obesity," we examined the causes and consequences of overconsumption. There's disagreement about whether overconsumption is typically an informed and rational choice, or whether, instead, it is typically uninformed, irrational, or even involuntary behavior. As we'll discuss in this chapter, this disagreement bears on the ethics of paternalistic healthy eating policies. According to some ethicists, policies preventing informed and voluntary behavior are generally not justifiable, but policies preventing *un*informed and *in*voluntary behavior are. Similarly, some ethicists would support policies preventing irrational consumption, but not policies preventing rational consumption even if this consumption is overconsumption or otherwise unhealthy.

As we saw in Chapter 12, disagreement also exists about the health consequences of being overweight—is it less healthy or more healthy to be moderately overweight?—and about the severity of the health consequences of obesity. Nonetheless, there is a general consensus that poor diet, including overconsumption of unhealthy food and underconsumption of healthy food, increases the risk of diet-related illness such as heart disease, diabetes, and high blood pressure. Along with causing people to suffer, become disabled, and die prematurely, this diet-related illness is also expensive to treat. Thus, people's unhealthy diet causes suffering and death *and* contributes significantly to healthcare costs.

As discussed in Chapter 12, a variety of policies have been proposed to promote healthier eating. Many policies, but particularly those *limiting access* to unhealthy food, have been criticized as paternalistic and ethically problematic for that reason. Some examples include taxes on soda and other sugary drinks, limitations on where sugary drinks can be sold (e.g., banning them from vending machines in schools), and bans on the use of trans fat by restaurants. As a case study for this chapter, we use the New York City big soda ban.

THE NEW YORK CITY BIG SODA BAN

In 2012, New York City Mayor Michael Bloomberg proposed a novel approach to reducing New Yorkers' consumption of sugary drinks. He proposed what came to be known as the "soda ban," though its supporters referred to it as a "portion control policy." It prohibited the sale of containers of sodas and certain other sugary drinks larger than 16 ounces in restaurants, corner stores, delis, food carts, movie theatres, and some other food establishments in New York City. The ban was intended to reduce consumption of sugary drinks, in order to reduce the number of calories people consume and thereby reduce rates of overweight, obesity, and diet-related illness. The big soda ban was passed by the New York City Board of Health in September 2012 and was scheduled to go into effect in March 2013. However, the ban was overturned by a court the day before it was supposed to go into effect. This decision was appealed by the City of New York, but it was upheld in July 2013.

The big soda ban was criticized on multiple grounds. It was called arbitrary and discriminatory, because it did not apply to all food establishments, but exempted grocery stores and convenience stores. It was called undemocratic because it was passed by the Board of Health, which is appointed by the mayor and not democratically elected. These criticisms we won't discuss. The ban was also criticized as a "nanny state" law that would unjustifiably restrict consumer choice and limit personal freedom.

Question: Is the New York big soda ban unjustifiably paternalistic?

WHAT IS PATERNALISM?

What is paternalism? This is a surprisingly hard question to answer. As we'll see, philosophers define paternalism differently from one another. The philosophical terminology that's used to discuss paternalism can be very confusing: Philosophers use the same terms to mean different things, and they use different terms for the same thing.

Let's start with this working definition of paternalism: Paternalism is interfering with someone's choices or action, without her consent, with the intention of improving her welfare.[1]

Interfering with someone in order to protect another person, or to improve the welfare of another person, is not paternalism. If I grab Molly's arms to prevent her from hitting Maria, this is not paternalism. Actions that interfere with someone in order to improve someone else's welfare might be objectionable or, as in the Molly case, might not be. But, either way, they are not paternalistic.

Actions that improve someone's welfare, but without interfering with her choices or action, are also not paternalistic according to our definition. For example, if we give you $30,000 to pay off your student loans because we want to help you out, this is not paternalism. By simply giving you money, we are not interfering with your choices or actions in any way. Hence, according to our working definition, we do not act paternalistically.

To give another example, giving people coupons for fruits and vegetables, with the aim of increasing their consumption of fruits and vegetables and thereby improving their nutrition and health, is not a paternalistic policy. Giving people coupons does not interfere with their liberty or autonomy. Hence, according to our working definition, we do not act paternalistically. Similarly, laws requiring that calories be listed on restaurant menus are not paternalistic, because giving consumers additional information about their food choices does not interfere with their liberty or autonomy.

As you'll see in the reading "Nudge," by Richard H. Thaler and Cass R. Sunstein, not everyone accepts the preceding definition of paternalism. Sunstein and Thaler consider a policy paternalistic if "it attempts to influence choices of affected parties in a way that will make choosers better off," whether or not the policy interferes with individuals' choices or actions.

VARIETIES OF PATERNALISM

Soft Paternalism versus Hard Paternalism

Some ethicists recognize a distinction between paternalism that interferes with voluntary and informed action (hard paternalism), and paternalism that interferes with involuntary and uninformed actions (soft paternalism)[2]

Consider these three cases:

Poison: Lee is about to drink from a bottle of soda that, unbeknownst to him, has been spiked with cyanide. As he raises it to his lips, you grab the bottle out of his hands and dump out the soda, in order to prevent him from being poisoned.

Sleepwalking: Ever since he started taking sleeping pills, Lee has been sleepwalking regularly. Tonight, you find him standing in front of the open refrigerator, guzzling a bottle of soda. You think Lee will feel better in the morning if he doesn't consume a lot of sugar, so you wrestle the bottle out of his hands and lead him back to bed.

Diet: Lee wants to lose weight, and has started a diet. But now Lee is guzzling a 20-ounce bottle of soda with his lunch. "I know it has a lot of calories and is not on my diet," Lee says, "But I just want it." You think Lee will be better off if he sticks to his diet, so you wrestle the bottle out of his hand and dump out the soda.

In all three cases, you act paternalistically toward Lee. You interfere with his liberty, by preventing him from acting as he otherwise would, in order to improve his welfare. But there are important differences between the three cases. In "Poison," Lee's action is not informed: Lee does not know that the soda is poisoned. "Poison" is an instance of soft paternalism. In "Sleepwalking," Lee's action is not voluntary: Because he is sleepwalking, Lee does not have psychological control over his action. "Sleepwalking" is an instance of soft paternalism.

"Diet" is a more complicated case. Is Lee's action in "Diet" voluntary? Does Lee have the right kind of psychological control over this action for it to be voluntary? This depends on the underlying psychology of his behavior. It also depends on what *voluntary action* is—a question that philosophers discuss at great length.[3] Sarah Conly briefly discusses this issue in the selection "Coercive Paternalism." One possibility is that all *irrational* action is thereby involuntary. Or perhaps only certain kinds of irrational action are involuntary.

The deeper ethical issue, of course, is not whether we should classify irrational action of various sorts as voluntary action, but whether it is ethically justifiable to paternalistically interfere with irrational action of these various sorts. In the reading "Paternalism," Gerald Dworkin identifies two kinds of irrational action, and he argues that there's a stronger ethical case for intervening with the second:

- Action resulting from a failure of reasoning, when someone reaches an irrational conclusion about how she should act, because she attaches an unreasonable amount of weight to one factor or value. For example, someone who knows how dangerous it is not to wear seat belts, but judges that the inconvenience of fastening her seat belt outweighs these risks.
- Action resulting from weakness of will, when someone acts in a way that she judges she should not act. For example, someone judges that she should fasten her seat belt, but fails to do so.

Dworkin claims that there is a stronger case for paternalistic intervention in the second kind of case, when someone is acting contrary to her own judgment about how she should act. "Here we are really not—by assumption—imposing a good on another person," Dworkin explains. We are not contravening someone's own judgment about how she should act.

Is unhealthy eating typically action resulting from weakness of will? Or is it action that reflects a failure of reasoning—for example, attaching too much weight to convenience, or too little weight to health? Is it typically uninformed action? Or is it typically informed and perfectly rational action that reflects people's ends and values? Or does the psychology of unhealthy eating vary from person to person, from occasion to occasion, such that unhealthy eating is not *typically* one way or the other? How we answer these questions makes a difference to whether we think of the soda ban as a soft paternalistic measure or, alternately, as a hard paternalistic measure, and that might, in turn, make a difference to whether we think it is an ethically justifiable policy.

Weak Paternalism versus Strong Paternalism

In addition to a soft/hard distinction, some philosophers recognize a distinction between *weak paternalism* and *strong paternalism*. Weak paternalism interferes with the means someone is using to accomplish her ends, on the belief that these means will not be effective, but it does not challenge these ends. For example, suppose that Lee is trying to fix his motorcycle, but he's using the wrong kind of screwdriver for the job. Because you want to help him fix his motorcycle, but you think he'd be too proud to admit he's using the wrong screwdriver, you swap it out for the right screwdriver when he's not looking.

Strong paternalism aims to prevent someone from accomplishing her ends, on the belief that her ends are not the right ends. For example, you think that Lee shouldn't ride his motorcycle, even though he loves to, because it's too dangerous. So when he's not looking, you hide the tools he's been using to fix his motorcycle.

Some ethicists reject strong paternalism as ethically unjustifiable even while embracing weak paternalism. For example, Sarah Conly, in the selection "Coercive Paternalism," argues for paternalism "in cases where people's choices of instrumental means are confused, in a way that means they will not achieve their ultimate ends." She supports paternalism that helps people achieve their ultimate ends. But she does not argue for strong paternalism: "I do not argue that there are objectively good ends, or objectively rational ends, or ends objectively valuable in any way, which everyone should be made to pursue."

But the distinction between means, ends, and "ultimate ends" is far from clear. Suppose that you want to buy a large soda to share with your children, in order to give them a delicious treat after school. Is *buying a large soda* your means to accomplishing the end of *giving your children a delicious treat*? Could you accomplish this end via another means, such as buying a bag of potato chips or buying a bunch of grapes? Or should we say that *giving your children a delicious treat* is your means to accomplishing another end, such as *rewarding your children*? Could you accomplish the end of rewarding your children via another means besides giving them a delicious treat, such as *taking them someplace fun*? And what is your ultimate end in all this?

But if we can't distinguish between someone's ultimate ends (which we should help her achieve) and her means to those ends (which we can override, if they're ineffective means to her ultimate ends), then we won't be able to distinguish weak paternalism (which interferes with ineffective means, but does not interfere with ultimate ends) from strong paternalism (which interferes with ultimate ends).

Libertarian Paternalism

In the selection "Nudge," Richard H. Thaler and Cass R. Sunstein introduce another species of paternalism: *libertarian paternalism*, the attempt to change people's choices in ways that will improve their welfare but without blocking any choices or attaching significant costs to any choices.

SOME ETHICAL ARGUMENTS AGAINST GOVERNMENT PATERNALISM

The readings in this chapter present arguments for and against government paternalism of different forms. The classic argument against government paternalism was given by the nineteenth-century philosopher John Stuart Mill in his *On Liberty*. In the reading "Paternalism," Gerald Dworkin extracts two distinct arguments against paternalism from *On Liberty*. The first is a utilitarian argument relying upon the empirical claim that government paternalism typically fails to promote the individual's interests. Mill's second argument against paternalism appeals to the value of individual autonomy. In Mill's words, "it is the privilege . . . of a human being, arrived at the maturity of his faculties, to use and interpret experiences in his own way."[4] Even if paternalistic interference does promote the individual's interests, the individual has the privilege—the right—to be free of this interference.

A third argument against government paternalism is that it can violate the principle of state neutrality, the moral demand that the government remain neutral between different conceptions of the good. State neutrality is taken to require, for example, that the government should not favor one religion over another— either by prohibiting some religions or making their practice more difficult, or by directly encouraging other religions; this is a violation of state neutrality. In the reading "The Value in Sweet Drinks," Alva Nöe describes the New York big soda ban as a policy that presupposes a view of the good life—a view according to which improved health is more valuable than increased pleasure. But people have different conceptions of the good life, and governments cannot assume that they know what is good and what is bad, Nöe asserts. When the government bans the sale of Big Gulps because it believes that your life will be better if you drink less soda and become healthier, the government is assuming that certain views of the good life are correct and others are incorrect, which it shouldn't do.

The principle of state neutrality is contested among political philosophers, who disagree about whether governments are morally required to remain neutral between different conceptions of the good, and in what ways government must remain neutral. According to *perfectionism*, governments need not always remain neutral: It can be permissible for the government to promote or discourage certain activities or ways of life because of their inherent or intrinsic value; one of the legitimate functions of governments is to discourage citizens from pursuing disvaluable activities or ways of life.[5] The opposing point of view, here articulated by Jonathan Quong, is:

> The liberal state should not be in the business of deciding what constitutes a valuable or worthwhile life and trying to make sure that citizens live up to this ideal—that job should be left to citizens themselves. Instead, the liberal state should restrict itself to the task of providing a fair framework of rules and institutions within which citizens can pursue their own conception of what makes for a valuable life. On this view, the state should make no judgments about the goodness of citizens' lives. It should instead be concerned only with justice, with the just distribution of freedom, resources, and other advantages between citizens, ensuring that each is given a fair chance to develop and pursue his or her own conception of the good life.[6]

Among those theorists who embrace the principle of state neutrality (and reject perfectionism), there is disagreement about the form that state neutrality must take.[7] If policies have the effect of promoting one way of life over others, but are not rooted in the judgment that this way of life is better, do they violate neutrality? Or do policies only violate neutrality if they are based in the judgment that certain activities or ways of life are intrinsically better than others? Must all laws and policies remain neutral, or just some subset of laws and policies? For example, must noncoercive policies (such as educational campaigns) remain neutral, or just coercive policies (such as bans and taxes)?

Philosophers have raised other, related objections to paternalistic actions and paternalistic policies, for instance that they are degrading, demeaning, or fail to treat people as equals.[8]

The three arguments against paternalism just discussed do not apply equally to all forms of government paternalism. For example, one might be persuaded by the utilitarian argument against paternalism when applied to hard paternalism but not soft paternalism. That is, one might be persuaded that government paternalism typically does *not* make people better off when it interferes with informed and voluntary choice, but that it typically *does* make people better off when it interferes with involuntary or uninformed action. Similarly, one might be persuaded by the utilitarian argument against paternalism when applied to strong paternalism but not weak paternalism. That is, one might be persuaded that government paternalism typically does *not* make people better off when it prevents people from accomplishing their ultimate ends, on the belief that these aren't the right ends, but that it typically *does* make people better off when it interferes with the means someone is using to accomplish her ends, on the belief that these means will not be effective in accomplishing those ends.

So, too, one might think that the autonomy-based arguments and neutrality arguments against paternalism apply to some forms of paternalism but not others. For example, one might think that the neutrality argument applies to paternalistic policies that attempt to prevent people from accomplishing certain ends, on the belief that these are not the right ends (strong paternalism); because this paternalism is rooted in a judgment that certain ends are better than others, it violates state neutrality. But one might consistently think that the neutrality argument does not apply to paternalism that interferes with the means people take to accomplish their ends, on the belief that these ends will not be effective (weak paternalism). Because weak paternalism is not based on a judgment about the value of people's ultimate ends, it does not violate state neutrality, one might argue.

SOME ETHICAL ARGUMENTS FOR PATERNALISM

Let's consider three arguments *for* paternalism: first, a utilitarian argument that paternalism does more good than harm; second, the argument that paternalism can advance an individual's autonomy over the long run by restricting it in the short run; third, the argument that paternalism is justified if informed people would reasonably agree to it.[9]

An example of the first kind of argument is found in the selection "Coercive Paternalism," by Sarah Conly, who gives a utilitarian defense of paternalism. Conly argues that portion size regulation (such as the soda ban) is justifiable paternalism, and (in a passage not included here) argues that a government ban on the sale of cigarettes is also justifiable paternalism.[10] An example of the second kind of argument is given by Thomas Nys.[11] Nys argues that certain kinds of paternalistic interventions—ones that keep people safe and healthy—are justifiable because they ensure that people are able to exercise control over their lives. Arguments of this second sort appeal to positive conceptions of autonomy or freedom—autonomy or freedom as the ability to exercise control over one's behavior or one's life, or as the actual exercise of such control—and argue that restrictions of liberty can be justifiable in order to make people autonomous or free in these senses.

An example of the third kind of argument is given by Gerald Dworkin in his paper "Paternalism."[12] Dworkin argues that we can see paternalistic policies as "social insurance policies" that it is rational and prudent for individuals to accept. If fully rational individuals would consent to a paternalistic restriction of their liberty, for example a law requiring car passengers to wear seat belts, then it is morally justifiable to restrict their liberty in this way. Dworkin identifies three types of situations in which fully rational individuals would consent to paternalistic intervention: when a decision is far-reaching, potentially dangerous, and irreversible; when a decision is made under extreme psychological and sociological pressures; and when a decision involves dangers which are not sufficiently understood or correctly appreciated. An example of justified paternalism, according to Dworkin, is a law requiring people to wear seat belts.

IS THE SODA BAN UNJUSTIFIABLY PATERNALISTIC?

The New York City big soda ban would have prevented stores from selling large sodas, and thereby prevented individuals from purchasing them, with the aim of reducing individuals' soda consumption. Is it an unjustifiably paternalistic policy?

There are (at least) three different ways one might respond to the charge that the big soda ban is unjustifiably paternalistic:

1. **The soda ban is soft paternalism, which is justifiable.**

According to this response, the soda ban is paternalistic. However, drinking large amounts of sugary drinks is typically not a voluntary action; therefore, the soda ban interferes with involuntary action and is soft paternalism. Soft paternalism is an ethically justifiable form of paternalism.

2. **The soda ban is hard paternalism but weak paternalism, which is justifiable.**

According to this response, too, the ban is paternalistic. According to this response, unlike the previous one, drinking large sugary drinks is typically informed and voluntary action; so the soda ban is hard paternalism. But it is also weak paternalism: paternalism that interferes with the means people take to achieving their ends, on the belief that these are ineffective means. Drinking large sugary drinks, the argument goes, typically subverts the individual's long-term ends: Drinking large sugary drinks raises someone's risk of developing diet-related illness and dying sooner than she otherwise would, which undermines her achievement of her long-term ends— both the long-term end of being healthy and staying alive, and all the other ends that require health and continued life. As Sarah Conly writes, "We want longer lives and we want good health, both as ends in themselves and as means to doing everything else we want to do."[13]

Thus, the soda ban prevents us from doing something (drinking large sugary drinks) because doing it undermines our achievement of our long-term ends; it is an instance of weak paternalism. And according to this defense of the soda ban, weak paternalism is an ethically justifiable form of paternalism. Sarah Conly defends portion control regulations (of which the soda ban is one example) with this kind of argument.

3. **The soda ban is not, in fact, a paternalistic policy.**

Paternalism is interfering with someone's action or choice, without her consent, in order to improve her welfare. Some people embrace the soda ban, and would willingly accept having their beverage options restricted by it. Thus, we might conclude that the soda ban is not paternalistic *vis-à-vis them* because they agree with it (even though they have not actually voted for the soda ban, or formally given their consent). But the soda ban *is* paternalistic vis-à-vis other people who do not embrace it and do not willingly accept having their beverage options restricted. For the purposes of ethical evaluation, should we consider the soda ban a paternalistic policy or not? There is no easy answer to this question.

Paternalism is interfering with someone's action or choice *in order to increase her welfare.* Healthy eating policies typically aim to improve individuals' eating in order to reduce rates of overweight, obesity, and diet-related illness. But do these policies aim to reduce rates of overweight, obesity, and diet-related illness *in order to increase individuals' welfare?*

The rising healthcare costs associated with unhealthy eating and overweight/obesity, and the contribution of these costs to government budgets through government expenditures on healthcare, are often cited in support of healthy eating policies. This suggests that healthy eating policies might aim to reduce rates of overweight, obesity, and diet-related illness *in order to reduce health care costs imposed upon society.* Along with reducing healthcare costs, healthy eating policies may aim to reduce other social costs associated with overweight, obesity, and diet-related illness, including lower productivity, lost wages, and the inconvenience and suffering imposed upon the families of people who are sick.[14]

A further interpretation of healthy eating policies is that they aim to improve individuals' health in order to advance the common good. For our country to have a strong economy, strong military, and robust civic life, we need healthy workers, soldiers, and citizens, some argue. A thriving society requires a healthy population. Thus, we can see healthy eating policies not as policies aiming to improve each citizen's health in order directly to improve her well-being, but as policies aiming to improve each citizen's health in order to advance the common good.[15] This raises a rat's nest of questions about the aims of policies. Policymakers who implement a healthy eating policy could have different ideas about the ultimate aim of the policy, with some policymakers concerned to increase individuals' welfare by reducing their suffering and prolonging their lives, and other policymakers interested in reducing the government's healthcare expenditures, and others interested in increasing productivity. In this case, should the policy be considered paternalistic or not? This question has no obvious answer. (See Husak 2003, listed in the "Further Reading" section, for a longer discussion of this issue.)

Suffice it to say that *if* the ultimate aim of healthy eating policies is to improve individuals' eating *in order to reduce the societal costs of unhealthy eating* or *in order to promote the common good*, and not directly in order to benefit the individual herself, then these policies are not paternalistic policies and thus evade the objection that they are paternalistic and ethically problematic for that reason.

FURTHER ISSUES

1. *Protecting People from Themselves versus from the Food Industry*
One way to think about paternalism is that paternalism protects people from themselves. But some advocates see policies like the New York City soda ban as attempts to protect people

from the food industry, which intentionally formulates foods that "hook" consumers and aggressively markets them (see the reading "Lunchtime Is All Yours" in Chapter 12, "Overconsumption and Obesity"), manipulates consumers' preferences, and intentionally misleads consumers about the healthfulness of foods. Are government efforts to limit the sale of unhealthy food best thought of as protecting people from themselves or protecting them from the food industry? Are these efforts a way of curtailing or mitigating the power of the food industry to shape consumers' preferences and behaviors, and is that a justifiable aim for government policy?

2. *State Neutrality and Health*

Is the principle of state neutrality correct? Must governments remain neutral between different conceptions of the good life? Is it legitimate for the government to assume that a life in which people eat healthier and have a lower risk of diet-related illness is a better life, as compared to a life in which people eat less healthfully, have a higher risk of diet-related illness, and have a shorter life span? Is the primary task of governments to ensure conditions in which individuals can be self-determining and lead good lives of their own choosing (as *liberalism* would have it)? Or is the primary task of governments something else—for example, to help individuals have good lives according to a specific conception of the good, or to promote community well-being in conformity with the community's shared values (as *communitarianism* would have it)?

3. *Paternalism toward Children*

Paternalism toward children is not as ethically controversial as paternalism toward adults. Most people think that we should *of course* interfere with the choices or actions of children in order to make them better off. Do any of the arguments against government paternalism discussed herein apply to government paternalism toward children? The following proposed policies are meant to make children's diets healthier in order to protect their health. The first addresses hunger and food insecurity, whereas the others address overconsumption of unhealthy foods. Which are paternalistic? Which do you think are justifiable?

   a. Providing free breakfast and free lunch for low-income children
   b. Nutritional requirements for school lunches, including limiting the total calories and fat, and requiring a certain amount of fruits, vegetables, and whole grains
   c. Nutritional requirements for kids' meals at fast-food restaurants, including limits on total calories and fat
   d. Prohibiting the sale of sugary drinks in vending machines in schools
   e. Prohibiting the sale of home-baked goods at school bake sales (because these foods are too unhealthy)
   f. Prohibiting food advertising and marketing directed toward young children
   g. Prohibiting food advertising and marketing directed toward teenagers

FURTHER READING

Libertarian Paternalism

Loewenstein, George, and Peter Ubel. 2010. "Economics Behaving Badly" (op-ed), *New York Times*, July 14. http://www.nytimes.com/2010/07/15/opinion/15loewenstein.html?_r=0.

Sunstein, Cass R. 2014. *Why Nudge? The Politics of Libertarian Paternalism.* New Haven, CT: Yale University Press.

Thaler, Richard H., and Cass R. Sunstein. 2009. *Nudge: Improving Decisions about Health, Wealth, and Happiness.* New York: Penguin Books.

The Ethics of Paternalism in Public Health

Bayer, R., and J. D. Moreno. 1986. "Health Promotion: Ethical and Social Dilemmas of Government Policy," *Health Affairs* 5, no. 2 (May 1): 72–85. doi:10.1377/hlthaff.5.2.72.

Conly, Sarah. 2013a. *Against Autonomy: Justifying Coercive Paternalism.* Cambridge: Cambridge University Press.

———. 2013b. "Coercive Paternalism in Health Care: Against Freedom of Choice." *Public Health Ethics*, September 16. doi:10.1093/phe/pht025.

Dworkin, Gerald, 2014. "Paternalism," in Edward N. Zalta, ed., *Stanford Encyclopedia of Philosophy* (Summer ed.). http://plato.stanford.edu/archives/sum2014/entries/paternalism/.

Feinberg, Joel. 1986. *Harm to Self.* New York: Oxford University Press.

Husak, Doug. 2003. "Legal Paternalism," in Hugh LaFollette, *Oxford Handbook of Practical Ethics.* Oxford: Oxford University Press.

Pugh, Jonathan. 2014. "Coercive Paternalism and Back-Door Perfectionism," *Journal of Medical Ethics* 40, no. 5: 350–351.

State Neutrality

Quong, Jonathan. 2011. *Liberalism without Perfection.* Oxford: Oxford University Press.

Rawls, John. 2005. *Political Liberalism.* New York: Columbia University Press.

Sher, George. 1997. *Beyond Neutrality: Perfectionism and Politics.* Cambridge: Cambridge University Press.

NOTES

1. This is close to the definition given by Dworkin in Dworkin, Gerald, 2014. "Paternalism," in Edward N. Zalta, ed., *Stanford Encyclopedia of Philosophy* (Summer ed.). http://plato.stanford.edu/archives/sum2014/entries/paternalism/.

2. But note that Cass Sunstein, in a departure from this terminology, uses "soft paternalism" differently, to refer to paternalism that has no material costs and poses very low costs—including social and personal costs—to the people targeted by it.

3. Joel Feinberg, *Harm to Self* (New York: Oxford University Press, 1986), 98–142.

4. John Stuart Mill, *Utilitarianism and On Liberty* (Fontana Library Edition, ed. Mary Warnock, London, 1962), p. 186.

5. Jonathan Quong, *Liberalism without Perfection* (Oxford: Oxford University Press, 2011), see chap. 1, especially pp. 17–19.

6. Ibid., 1.

7. See "The Principle of Neutrality," in *Beyond Neutrality: Perfectionism and Politics*, ed. George Sher (Cambridge: Cambridge University Press, 1997), 20–44.

8. Sarah Conly, *Against Autonomy: Justifying Coercive Paternalism* (Cambridge: Cambridge University Press, 2013), chap. 1.

9. Gerald Dworkin, "Paternalism," in *Stanford Encyclopedia of Philosophy* (Summer 2014 ed.), ed. Edward N. Zalta. http://plato.stanford.edu/archives/sum2014/entries/paternalism/.

10. Sarah Conly, *Against Autonomy: Justifying Coercive Paternalism* (Cambridge: Cambridge University Press, 2013), see 149–181.

11. Thomas R. V. Nys, "Paternalism in Public Health Care," *Public Health Ethics* 1, no. 1 (April 1, 2008): 64–72. doi:10.1093/phe/phn002.

12. Gerald Dworkin, "Paternalism," *Monist* 56, no. 1 (1972): 64–84.

13. Conly, *Against Autonomy*, 164.

14. R. Bayer and J. D. Moreno, "Health Promotion: Ethical and Social Dilemmas of Government Policy," *Health Affairs* 5, no. 2 (May 1, 1986): 72–85. doi:10.1377/hlthaff.5.2.72; L. O. Gostin and K. G. Gostin, "A Broader Liberty: J. S. Mill, Paternalism and the Public's Health." *Public Health* 123, no. 3 (March 2009): 214–221. doi:10.1016/j.puhe.2008.12.024.

15. Beauchamp, Dan E. "Community: The Neglected Tradition of Public Health." *Hastings Center Report* 15, no. 6 (1985): 28–36; Gostin and Gostin, "A Broader Liberty."

GERALD DWORKIN

Paternalism

In this reading, the philosopher Gerald Dworkin gives examples of paternalistic policies and laws, and then discusses two arguments against paternalism found in John Stuart Mill's classic work, "On Liberty."

Neither one person, nor any number of persons, is warranted in saying to another human creature of ripe years, that he shall not do with his life for his own benefit what he chooses to do with it.

Mill

I do not want to go along with a volunteer basis. I think a fellow should be compelled to become better and not let him use his discretion whether he wants to get smarter, more healthy or more honest.

General Hershey

I take as my starting point the "one very simple principle" proclaimed by Mill in *On Liberty* . . . "That principle is, that the sole end for which mankind are warranted, individually or collectively, in interfering with the liberty of action of any of their number, is self-protection. That the only purpose for which power can be rightfully exercised over any member of a civilized community, against his will, is to prevent harm to others. He cannot rightfully be compelled to do or forbear because it will be better

Gerald Dworkin, "Paternalism," in *The Monist*, 56, no. 1 (January 1972), 64–84. © 1972 by *The Monist*. Published by, and reprinted with the permission of, Oxford University Press.

for him to do so, because it will make him happier, because, in the opinion of others, to do so would be wise, or even right."[1]

This principle is neither "one" nor "very simple." It is at least two principles; one asserting that self-protection or the prevention of harm to others is sometimes a sufficient warrant and the other claiming that the individual's own good is *never* a sufficient warrant for the exercise of compulsion either by the society as a whole or by its individual members. I assume that no one with the possible exception of extreme pacifists or anarchists questions the correctness of the first half of the principle. This essay is an examination of the negative claim embodied in Mill's principle—the objection to paternalistic interferences with a man's liberty.

By paternalism I shall understand roughly the interference with a person's liberty of action justified by reasons referring exclusively to the welfare, good, happiness, needs, interests or values of the person being coerced. One is always well-advised to illustrate one's definitions by examples but it is not easy to find "pure" examples of paternalistic interferences. For almost any piece of legislation is justified by several different kinds of reasons and even if historically a piece of legislation can be shown to have been introduced for purely paternalistic motives, it may be that advocates of the legislation with an anti-paternalistic outlook can find sufficient reasons justifying the legislation without appealing to the reasons which were originally adduced to support it. Thus, for example, it may be that the original legislation requiring motorcyclists to wear safety helmets was introduced for purely paternalistic reasons. But the Rhode Island Supreme Court recently upheld such legislation on the grounds that it was "not persuaded that the legislature is powerless to prohibit individuals from pursuing a course of conduct which could conceivably result in their becoming public charges," thus clearly introducing reasons of a quite different kind. Now I regard this decision as being based on reasoning of a very dubious nature but it illustrates the kind of problem one has in finding examples. The following is a list of the kinds of interferences I have in mind as being paternalistic.

1. Laws requiring motorcyclists to wear safety helmets when operating their machines.

2. Laws forbidding persons from swimming at a public beach when lifeguards are not on duty.
3. Laws making suicide a criminal offense.
4. Laws making it illegal for women and children to work at certain types of jobs.
5. Laws regulating certain kinds of sexual conduct, e.g. homosexuality among consenting adults in private.
6. Laws regulating the use of certain drugs which may have harmful consequences to the user but do not lead to anti-social conduct.
7. Laws requiring a license to engage in certain professions with those not receiving a license subject to fine or jail sentence if they do engage in the practice.
8. Laws compelling people to spend a specified fraction of their income on the purchase of retirement annuities. (Social Security)
9. Laws forbidding various forms of gambling (often justified on the grounds that the poor are more likely to throw away their money on such activities than the rich who can afford to).
10. Laws regulating the maximum rates of interest for loans.
11. Laws against duelling.

In addition to laws which attach criminal or civil penalties to certain kinds of action there are laws, rules, regulations, decrees, which make it either difficult or impossible for people to carry out their plans and which are also justified on paternalistic grounds. Examples of this are:

1. Laws regulating the types of contracts which will be upheld as valid by the courts, e.g. (an example of Mill's to which I shall return) no man may make a valid contract for perpetual involuntary servitude.
2. Not allowing as a defense to a charge of murder or assault the consent of the victim.
3. Requiring members of certain religious sects to have compulsory blood transfusions. This is made possible by not allowing the patient to have recourse to civil suits for assault and battery and by means of injunctions.
4. Civil commitment procedures when these are specifically justified on the basis of preventing

the person being committed from harming himself. (The D.C. Hospitalization of the Mentally Ill Act provides for involuntary hospitalization of a person who "is mentally ill, and because of that illness, is likely to injure *himself* or others if allowed to remain at liberty." The term injure in this context applies to unintentional as well as intentional injuries.)

5. Putting fluorides in the community water supply.

All of my examples are of existing restrictions on the liberty of individuals. Obviously one can think of interferences which have not yet been imposed. Thus one might ban the sale of cigarettes, or require that people wear safety-belts in automobiles (as opposed to merely having them installed) enforcing this by not allowing motorists to sue for injuries even when caused by other drivers if the motorist was not wearing a seat-belt at the time of the accident.

I shall not be concerned with activities which though defended on paternalistic grounds are not interferences with the liberty of persons, e.g. the giving of subsidies in kind rather than in cash on the grounds that the recipients would not spend the money on the goods which they really need, or not including a $1000 deductible provision in a basic protection automobile insurance plan on the ground that the people who would elect it could least afford it. Nor shall I be concerned with measures such as "truth-in-advertising" acts and the Pure Food and Drug legislation which are often attacked as paternalistic but which should not be considered so. In these cases all that is provided—it is true by the use of compulsion—is information which it is presumed that rational persons are interested in having in order to make wise decisions. There is no interference with the liberty of the consumer unless one wants to stretch a point beyond good sense and say that his liberty to apply for a loan without knowing the true rate of interest is diminished. It is true that sometimes there is sentiment for going further than providing information, for example when laws against usurious interest are passed preventing those who might wish to contract loans at high rates of

interest from doing so, and these measures may correctly be considered paternalistic . . .

* * *

I shall begin for dialectical purposes by discussing Mill's objections to paternalism and then go on to discuss more positive proposals.

An initial feature that strikes one is the absolute nature of Mill's prohibitions against paternalism. It is so unlike the carefully qualified admonitions of Mill and his fellow Utilitarians on other moral issues. He speaks of self-protection as the *sole* end warranting coercion, of the individual's own goals as *never* being a sufficient warrant. Contrast this with his discussion of the prohibition against lying in *Util*.

> Yet that even this, rule, sacred as it is, admits of possible exception, is acknowledged by all moralists, the chief of which is where the with-holding of some fact . . . would save an individual . . . from great and unmerited evil.[2]

The same tentativeness is present when he deals with justice.

> It is confessedly unjust to break faith with any one: to violate an engagement, either express or implied, or disappoint expectations raised by our own conduct, at least if we have raised these expectations knowingly and voluntarily. Like all the other obligations of justice already spoken of, this one is not regarded as absolute, but as capable of being overruled by a stronger obligation of justice on the other side.[3]

This anomaly calls for some explanation. The structure of Mill's argument is as follows:

1. Since restraint is an evil the burden of proof is on those who propose such restraint.
2. Since the conduct which is being considered is purely self-regarding, the normal appeal to the protection of the interests of others is not available.
3. Therefore we have to consider whether reasons involving reference to the individual's own good, happiness, welfare, or interests are sufficient to overcome the burden of justification.

4. We either cannot advance the interests of the individual by compulsion, or the attempt to do so involves evil which outweigh the good done.

5. Hence the promotion of the individual's own interests does not provide a sufficient warrant for the use of compulsion.

Clearly the operative premise here is (4). . .

As a Utilitarian Mill has to show, in Fitzjames Stephen's words, that:

> Self-protection apart, no good object can be attained by any compulsion which is not in itself a greater evil than the absence of the object which the compulsion obtains.[4]

To show this is impossible; one reason being that it isn't true. Preventing a man from selling himself into slavery (a paternalistic measure which Mill himself accepts as legitimate), or from taking heroin, or from driving a car without wearing seat-belts may constitute a lesser evil than allowing him to do any of these things. A consistent Utilitarian can only argue against paternalism on the grounds that it (as a matter of fact) does not maximize the good. It is always a contingent question that may be refuted by the evidence. But there is also a non-contingent argument which runs through *On Liberty*. When Mill states that "there is a part of the life of every person who has come to years of discretion, within which the individuality of that person ought to reign uncontrolled either by any other person or by the public collectively" he is saying something about what it means to be a person, an autonomous agent. It is because coercing a person for his own good denies this status as an independent entity that Mill objects to it so strongly and in such absolute terms. To be able to choose is a good that is independent of the wisdom of what is chosen. A man's "mode of laying out his existence is the best, not because it is the best in itself, but because it is his own mode."[5]

> It is the privilege and proper condition of a human being, arrived at the maturity of his faculties, to use and interpret experience in his own way.[6]. . .

What I have tried to show so far is that there are two strains of argument in Mill—one a straightforward Utilitarian mode of reasoning and one which relies not on the goods which free choice leads to but on the absolute value of the choice itself. The first cannot establish any absolute prohibition but at most a presumption and indeed a fairly weak one given some fairly plausible assumptions about human psychology; the second while a stronger line of argument seems to me to allow on its own grounds a wider range of paternalism then might be suspected. . . .

* * *

Extensions of paternalism are argued for by claiming that in various respects, chronologically mature individuals share the same deficiencies in knowledge, capacity to think rationally, and the ability to carry out decisions that children possess. Hence in interfering with such people we are in effect doing what they would do if they were fully rational . . . What I am looking for are certain kinds of conditions which make it plausible to suppose that rational men could reach agreement to limit their liberty even when other men's interests are not affected . . . Let me suggest types of situations in which it seems plausible to suppose that fully rational individuals would agree to having paternalistic restrictions imposed upon them. It is reasonable to suppose that there are "goods" such as health which any person would want to have in order to pursue his own good—no matter how that good is conceived. This is an argument that is used in connection with compulsory education for children but it seems to me that it can be extended to other goods which have this character. Then one could agree that the attainment of such goods should be promoted even when not recognized to be such, at the moment, by the individuals concerned.

An immediate difficulty that arises stems from the fact that men are always faced with competing goods and that there may be reasons why even a value such as health—or indeed life—may be overridden by competing values. [Consider two distinct types of situations in which someone acts in a non-rational fashion.] In one case he attaches incorrect weights to some of his values; in the other he neglects to act in accordance with his actual preferences and desires. Clearly there is a stronger and more persuasive argument for paternalism in the latter situation. Here we are really not—by assumption—imposing a good on another person . . . [In the former situation] part of what is involved in claiming [for example] that a man who doesn't fasten his seat-belts is attaching an irrational weight to the inconvenience of fastening them is that if he were to be involved in an accident and severely injured he would look back and admit that the inconvenience wasn't as bad as all that. So there is a sense in which if I could convince him of the consequences of his action he also would not wish to continue his present course of action . . .

[There is a sense in which paternalism imposes a good upon him.] But in another sense we are not imposing a good since what is being claimed—and what must be shown or at least argued for—is that an accurate accounting on his part would lead him to reject his current course of action. Now we all know that such cases exist, that we are prone to disregard dangers that are only possibilities, that immediate pleasures are often magnified and distorted . . .

A good deal depends on the nature of the deprivation—e.g. does it prevent the person from engaging in the activity completely or merely limit his participation—and how important to the nature of the activity is the absence of restriction when this is weighed against the role that the activity plays in the life of the person. In the case of automobile seat belts, for example, the restriction is trivial in nature, interferes not at all with the use or enjoyment of the activity, and does, I am assuming, considerably reduce a high risk of serious injury. Whereas, for example, making mountain climbing illegal prevents completely a person engaging in an activity which may play an important role in his life and his conception of the person he is.

NOTES

1. J. S. Mill, *Utilitarianism* and *On Liberty* (Fontana Library Edition, ed. by Mary Warnock, London, 1962), p. 135. All further quotes from Mill are from this edition unless otherwise noted.
2. Mill, *Utilitarianism* and *On Liberty*, p. 174.
3. *Ibid.,* p. 299.
4. J. F. Stephens, *Liberty, Equality, Fraternity* (New York: Henry Holt & Co., n.d.), p. 49.
5. Mill, *Utilitarianism* and *On Liberty*, p. 197.
6. *Ibid.,* p. 186.

QUESTIONS

1. Dworkin understands paternalism as "the interference with a person's liberty of action justified by reasons referring exclusively to the welfare, good, happiness, needs, interests or values of the person being coerced." According to this definition, whether a policy is paternalistic depends upon the reasons it is implemented. Suppose that a state legislature passes a soda tax in order to raise more tax revenue and reduce the state's budget deficit. Is this soda tax a paternalistic policy? Suppose that the state legislature passes the soda tax in order to reduce consumption of sugary drinks and reduce rates of diet-related illness, thereby reducing the state's expenditures on healthcare for Medicaid recipients. Is this soda tax a paternalistic policy? Suppose that the members of the state legislature vote in favor of the soda tax for different reasons: Some members want to raise tax revenue, some want to reduce Medicaid expenses, and some want to prevent the human suffering caused by overconsumption and diet-related illness. Is the soda tax a paternalistic policy?
2. Mill's first argument against paternalism is a utilitarian argument relying upon the empirical claim that paternalism fails to promote the individual's interests. This utilitarian argument, Dworkin points out, "may be refuted by the evidence" in particular cases. What does Dworkin mean?
3. Mill's second argument against paternalism relies on the value of individual autonomy. As quoted by Dworkin, Mill wrote that "it is the privilege . . . of a human being, arrived at the maturity of his faculties, to use and interpret experiences in his own way."* Explain, in your own words, why the value of individual autonomy might make paternalistic policies morally unjustifiable.

---

*John Stuart Mill, *Utilitarianism and On Liberty* (Fontana Library Edition, ed. Mary Warnock, London, 1962), p. 186.

RICHARD H. THALER AND CASS R. SUNSTEIN

Selections from *Nudge*

In this selection from their book *Nudge*, Richard H. Thaler and Cass R. Sunstein introduce their own species of paternalism, *libertarian paternalism*, and introduce *nudges*, features of choice environments that alter people's behavior without limiting options or significantly changing their economic incentives.

THE CAFETERIA

A friend of yours, Carolyn, is the director of food services for a large city school system. She is in charge of hundreds of schools, and hundreds of thousands of kids eat in her cafeterias every day. Carolyn has formal training in nutrition (a master's degree from the state university), and she is a creative type who likes to think about things in nontraditional ways.

One evening, over a good bottle of wine, she and her friend Adam, a statistically oriented management consultant who has worked with supermarket chains, hatched an interesting idea. Without changing any menus, they would run some experiments in her schools to determine whether the way the food is displayed and arranged might influence the choices kids make. Carolyn gave the directors of dozens of school cafeterias specific instructions on how to display the food choices. In some schools the desserts were placed first, in others last, in still others in a separate line. The location of various food items was varied from one school to another. In some schools the French fries, but in others the carrot sticks, were at eye level.

From his experience in designing supermarket floor plans, Adam suspected that the results would be dramatic. He was right. Simply by rearranging the cafeteria, Carolyn was able to increase or decrease the consumption of many food items by as much as 25 percent. Carolyn learned a big lesson: school children, like adults, can be greatly influenced by small changes in the context. The influence can be exercised for better or for worse. For example, Carolyn knows that she can increase consumption of healthy foods and decrease consumption of unhealthy ones.

With hundreds of schools to work with, and a team of graduate student volunteers recruited to collect and analyze the data, Carolyn believes that she now has considerable power to influence what kids eat. Carolyn is pondering what to do with her newfound power. Here are some suggestions she has received from her usually sincere but occasionally mischievous friends and coworkers:

1. Arrange the food to make the students best off, all things considered.
2. Choose the food order at random.
3. Try to arrange the food to get the kids to pick the same foods they would choose on their own.

4. Maximize the sales of the items from the suppliers that are willing to offer the largest bribes.

5. Maximize profits, period.

Option 1 has obvious appeal, yet it does seem a bit intrusive, even paternalistic. But the alternatives are worse! Option 2, arranging the food at random, could be considered fair-minded and principled, and it is in one sense neutral. But if the orders are randomized across schools, then the children at some schools will have less healthy diets than those at other schools. Is this desirable? Should Carolyn choose that kind of neutrality, if she can easily make most students better off, in part by improving their health?

Option 3 might seem to be an honorable attempt to avoid intrusion: try to mimic what the children would choose for themselves. Maybe that is really the neutral choice, and maybe Carolyn should neutrally follow people's wishes (at least where she is dealing with older students). But a little thought reveals that this is a difficult option to implement. Adam's experiment proves that what kids choose depends on the order in which the items are displayed. What, then, are the true preferences of the children? What does it mean to say that Carolyn should try to figure out what the students would choose "on their own"? In a cafeteria, it is impossible to avoid some way of organizing food.

Option 4 might appeal to a corrupt person in Carolyn's job, and manipulating the order of the food items would put yet another weapon in the arsenal of available methods to exploit power. But Carolyn is honorable and honest, so she does not give this option any thought. Like Options 2 and 3, Option 5 has some appeal, especially if Carolyn thinks that the best cafeteria is the one that makes the most money. But should Carolyn really try to maximize profits if the result is to make children less healthy, especially since she works for the school district?

Carolyn is what we will be calling a *choice architect*. A choice architect has the responsibility for organizing the context in which people make decisions.

Although Carolyn is a figment of our imagination, many real people turn out to be choice architects, most without realizing it. If you design the ballot voters use to choose candidates, you are a choice architect. If you are a doctor and must describe the alternative treatments available to a patient, you are a choice architect. If you design the form that new employees fill out to enroll in the company health care plan, you are a choice architect. If you are a parent, describing possible educational options to your son or daughter, you are a choice architect. If you are a salesperson, you are a choice architect (but you already knew that).

There are many parallels between choice architecture and more traditional forms of architecture. A crucial parallel is that there is no such thing as a "neutral" design. Consider the job of designing a new academic building. The architect is given some requirements. There must be room for 120 offices, 8 classrooms, 12 student meeting rooms, and so forth. The building must sit on a specified site. Hundreds of other constraints will be imposed—some legal, some aesthetic, some practical. In the end, the architect must come up with an actual building with doors, stairs, windows, and hallways. As good architects know, seemingly arbitrary decisions, such as where to locate the bathrooms, will have subtle influences on how the people who use the building interact. Every trip to the bathroom creates an opportunity to run into colleagues (for better or for worse). A good building is not merely attractive; it also "works."

As we shall see, small and apparently insignificant details can have major impacts on people's behavior. A good rule of thumb is to assume that "everything matters." In many cases, the power of these small details comes from focusing the attention of users in a particular direction. A wonderful example of this principle comes from, of all places, the men's rooms at Schiphol Airport in Amsterdam. There the authorities have etched the image of a black housefly into each urinal. It seems that men usually do not pay much attention to where they aim, which can create a bit of a mess, but if they see a target, attention and therefore accuracy are much increased. According to the man who came up with the idea, it works wonders. "It improves the aim," says Aad Kieboom. "If a man sees a fly, he aims at it." Kieboom, an economist, directs Schiphol's building expansion. His staff conducted fly-in-urinal trials and found that etchings reduce spillage by 80 percent.[1]

The insight that "everything matters" can be both paralyzing and empowering. Good architects realize that although they can't build the perfect building, they can make some design choices that will have beneficial effects. Open stairwells, for example, may produce more workplace interaction and more walking, and both of these are probably desirable. And just as a building architect must eventually build some particular building, a choice architect like Carolyn must choose a particular arrangement of the food options at lunch, and by so doing she can influence what people eat. She can nudge.*

LIBERTARIAN PATERNALISM

If, all things considered, you think that Carolyn should take the opportunity to nudge the kids toward food that is better for them, Option 1, then we welcome you to our new movement: *libertarian paternalism.* We are keenly aware that this term is not one that readers will find immediately endearing. Both words are somewhat off-putting, weighted down by stereotypes from popular culture and politics that make them unappealing to many. Even worse, the concepts seem to be contradictory. Why

combine two reviled and contradictory concepts? We argue that if the terms are properly understood, both concepts reflect common sense—and they are far more attractive together than alone. The problem with the terms is that they have been captured by dogmatists.

The libertarian aspect of our strategies lies in the straightforward insistence that, in general, people should be free to do what they like—and to opt out of undesirable arrangements if they want to do so. To borrow a phrase from the late Milton Friedman, libertarian paternalists urge that people should be "free to choose."[2] We strive to design policies that maintain or increase freedom of choice. When we use the term *libertarian* to modify the word *paternalism,* we simply mean liberty-preserving. And when we say liberty-preserving, we really mean it. Libertarian paternalists want to make it easy for people to go their own way; they do not want to burden those who want to exercise their freedom.

The paternalistic aspect lies in the claim that it is legitimate for choice architects to try to influence people's behavior in order to make their lives longer, healthier, and better. In other words, we argue for self-conscious efforts, by institutions in the private sector and also by government, to steer people's choices in directions that will improve their lives. In our understanding, a policy is "paternalistic" if it tries to influence choices in a way that will make choosers better off, *as judged by themselves.*[3] Drawing on some well-established findings in social science, we show that in many cases, individuals make pretty bad decisions—decisions they would not have made if they had paid full attention and possessed complete information, unlimited cognitive abilities, and complete self-control.

Libertarian paternalism is a relatively weak, soft, and nonintrusive type of paternalism because choices are not blocked, fenced off, or significantly burdened. If people want to smoke cigarettes, to eat a lot of candy, to choose an unsuitable health care plan, or to fail to save for retirement, libertarian paternalists will not force them to do otherwise—or even make things hard for them. Still, the approach we recommend does count as paternalistic, because private

---

*Please do not confuse *nudge* with *noodge.* As William Safire has explained in his "On Language" column in the *New York Times Magazine* (October 8, 2000), the "Yiddishism *noodge"* is "a noun meaning 'pest, annoying nag, persistent complainer.' . . . To *nudge* is 'to push mildly or poke gently in the ribs, especially with the elbow.' One who *nudges* in that manner—'to alert, remind, or mildly warn another'—is a far *geshrrei* from a *noodge* with his incessant, bothersome whining." *Nudge* rhymes with *judge,* while the *oo* sound in *noodge* is pronounced as in *book.*

and public choice architects are not merely trying to track or to implement people's anticipated choices. Rather, they are self-consciously attempting to move people in directions that will make their lives better. They nudge.

A nudge, as we will use the term, is any aspect of the choice architecture that alters people's behavior in a predictable way without forbidding any options or significantly changing their economic incentives. To count as a mere nudge, the intervention must be easy and cheap to avoid. Nudges are not mandates. Putting the fruit at eye level counts as a nudge. Banning junk food does not.

Many of the policies we recommend can and have been implemented by the private sector (with or without a nudge from the government). Employers, for example, are important choice architects in many of the examples we discuss in this book. In areas involving health care and retirement plans, we think that employers can give employees some helpful nudges. Private companies that want to make money, and to do good, can even benefit from environmental nudges, helping to reduce air pollution (and the emission of greenhouse gases). But as we shall show, the same points that justify libertarian paternalism on the part of private institutions apply to government as well.

HUMANS AND ECONS: WHY NUDGES CAN HELP

Those who reject paternalism often claim that human beings do a terrific job of making choices, and if not terrific, certainly better than anyone else would do (especially if that someone else works for the government). Whether or not they have ever studied economics, many people seem at least implicitly committed to the idea of *homo economicus,* or economic man—the notion that each of us thinks and chooses unfailingly well, and thus fits within the textbook picture of human beings offered by economists.

If you look at economics textbooks, you will learn that homo economicus can think like Albert Einstein, store as much memory as IBM's Big Blue, and exercise the willpower of Mahatma Gandhi. Really. But the folks that we know are not like that. Real people have trouble with long division if they don't have a calculator, sometimes forget their spouse's birthday, and have a hangover on New Year's Day. They are not homo economicus; they are homo sapiens. To keep our Latin usage to a minimum we will hereafter refer to these imaginary and real species as Econs and Humans.

Consider the issue of obesity. Rates of obesity in the United States are now approaching 20 percent, and more than 60 percent of Americans are considered either obese or overweight. There is overwhelming evidence that obesity increases risks of heart disease and diabetes, frequently leading to premature death. It would be quite fantastic to suggest that everyone is choosing the right diet, or a diet that is preferable to what might be produced with a few nudges.

Of course, sensible people care about the taste of food, not simply about health, and eating is a source of pleasure in and of itself. We do not claim that everyone who is overweight is necessarily failing to act rationally, but we do reject the claim that all or almost all Americans are choosing their diet optimally. What is true for diets is true for other risk-related behavior, including smoking and drinking, which produce more than five hundred thousand premature deaths each year. With respect to diet, smoking, and drinking, people's current choices cannot reasonably be claimed to be the best means of promoting their well-being. Indeed, many smokers, drinkers, and overeaters are willing to pay third parties to help them make better decisions.

But our basic source of information here is the emerging science of choice, consisting of careful research by social scientists over the past four decades. That research has raised serious questions about the rationality of many judgments and decisions that people make. To qualify as Econs, people are not required to make perfect forecasts (that would require omniscience), but they are required to make unbiased forecasts. That is, the forecasts can be wrong, but they can't be systematically wrong in a predictable direction. Unlike Econs, Humans predictably err. Take, for example, the "planning fallacy"—the systematic tendency toward unrealistic optimism about the time it takes to complete projects. It will come as no surprise to anyone who has ever hired a contractor to learn that everything takes longer than you think, even if you know about the planning fallacy.

Hundreds of studies confirm that human forecasts are flawed and biased. Human decision making is not so great either. Again to take just one example, consider what is called the "status quo bias," a fancy name for inertia. For a host of reasons, which we shall explore, people have a strong tendency to go along with the status quo or default option.

When you get a new cell phone, for example, you have a series of choices to make. The fancier the phone, the more of these choices you face, from the background to the ring sound to the number of times the phone rings before the caller is sent to voice mail. The manufacturer has picked one option as the default for each of these choices. Research shows that whatever the default choices are, many people stick with them, even when the stakes are much higher than choosing the noise your phone makes when it rings.

Two important lessons can be drawn from this research. First, never underestimate the power of inertia. Second, that power can be harnessed. If private companies or public officials think that one policy produces better outcomes, they can greatly influence the outcome by choosing it as the default. As we will show, setting default options, and other similar seemingly trivial menu-changing strategies, can have huge effects on outcomes, from increasing savings to improving health care to providing organs for lifesaving transplant operations.

The effects of well-chosen default options provide just one illustration of the gentle power of nudges. In accordance with our definition, a nudge is any factor that significantly alters the behavior of Humans, even though it would be ignored by Econs. Econs

respond primarily to incentives. If the government taxes candy, they will buy less candy, but they are not influenced by such "irrelevant" factors as the order in which options are displayed. Humans respond to incentives too, but they are also influenced by nudges.* By properly deploying both incentives and nudges, we can improve our ability to improve people's lives, and help solve many of society's major problems. And we can do so while still insisting on everyone's freedom to choose.

A FALSE ASSUMPTION AND TWO MISCONCEPTIONS

Many people who favor freedom of choice reject any kind of paternalism. They want the government to let citizens choose for themselves. The standard policy advice that stems from this way of thinking is to give people as many choices as possible, and then let them choose the one they like best (with as little government intervention or nudging as possible). The beauty of this way of thinking is that it offers a simple solution to many complex problems: Just Maximize (the number and variety of) Choices—full stop! The policy has been pushed in many domains, from education to prescription drug insurance plans. In some circles, Just Maximize Choices has become a policy mantra. Sometimes the only alternative to this mantra is thought to be a government mandate which is derided as "One Size Fits All."

---

*Alert readers will notice that incentives can come in different forms. If steps are taken to increase people's cognitive effort—as by placing fruit at eye level and candy in a more obscure place—it might be said that the "cost" of choosing candy is increased. Some of our nudges do, in a sense, impose cognitive (rather than material) costs, and in that sense alter incentives. Nudges count as such, and qualify as libertarian paternalism, only if any costs are low.

Those who favor Just Maximize Choices don't realize there is plenty of room between their policy and a single mandate. They oppose paternalism, or think they do, and they are skeptical about nudges. We believe that their skepticism is based on a false assumption and two misconceptions.

The false assumption is that almost all people, almost all of the time, make choices that are in their best interest or at the very least are better than the choices that would be made by someone else. We claim that this assumption is false—indeed, obviously false. In fact, we do not think that anyone believes it on reflection.

Suppose that a chess novice were to play against an experienced player. Predictably, the novice would lose precisely because he made inferior choices—choices that could easily be improved by some helpful hints. In many areas, ordinary consumers are novices, interacting in a world inhabited by experienced professionals trying to sell them things. More generally, how well people choose is an empirical question, one whose answer is likely to vary across domains. It seems reasonable to say that people make good choices in contexts in which they have experience, good information, and prompt feedback—say, choosing among ice cream flavors. People know whether they like chocolate, vanilla, coffee, licorice, or something else. They do less well in contexts in which they are inexperienced and poorly informed, and in which feedback is slow or infrequent—say, in choosing between fruit and ice cream (where the long-term effects are slow and feedback is poor) or in choosing among medical treatments or investment options. If you are given fifty prescription drug plans, with multiple and varying features, you might benefit from a little help. So long as people are not choosing perfectly, some changes in the choice architecture could make their lives go better (as judged by their own preferences, not those of some bureaucrat). As we will try to show, it is not only possible to design choice architecture to make people better off; in many cases it is easy to do so.

The first misconception is that it is possible to avoid influencing people's choices. In many situations, some organization or agent *must* make a choice that will affect the behavior of some other people. There is, in those situations, no way of avoiding nudging in some direction, and whether intended or not, these nudges will affect what people choose. As illustrated by the example of Carolyn's cafeterias, people's choices are pervasively influenced by the design elements selected by choice architects. It is true, of course, that some nudges are unintentional; employers may decide (say) whether to pay employees monthly or biweekly without intending to create any kind of nudge, but they might be surprised to discover that people save more if they get paid biweekly because twice a year they get three pay checks in one month. It is also true that private and public institutions can strive for one or another kind of neutrality—as, for example, by choosing randomly, or by trying to figure out what most people want. But unintentional nudges can have major effects, and in some contexts, these forms of neutrality are unattractive; we shall encounter many examples.

Some people will happily accept this point for private institutions but strenuously object to government efforts to influence choice with the goal of improving people's lives. They worry that governments cannot be trusted to be competent or benign. They fear that elected officials and bureaucrats will place their own interests first, or pay attention to the narrow goals of self-interested private groups. We share these concerns. In particular, we emphatically agree that for government, the risks of mistake, bias, and overreaching are real and sometimes serious. We favor nudges over commands, requirements, and prohibitions in part for that reason. But governments, no less than cafeterias (which governments frequently run), have to provide starting points of one or another kind. This is not avoidable. As we shall emphasize, they do so every day through the rules they set, in ways that inevitably affect some choices and outcomes. In this respect, the antinudge position is unhelpful—a literal nonstarter.

The second misconception is that paternalism always involves coercion. In the cafeteria example, the choice of the order in which to present food items does not force a particular diet on anyone, yet Carolyn, and others in her position, might select some arrangement of food on grounds that are paternalistic in the sense that we use the term. Would anyone object to putting the fruit and salad before the desserts at an elementary school cafeteria if the result were to induce kids to eat more apples and fewer Twinkles? Is this question fundamentally different if the customers are teenagers, or even adults? Since no coercion is involved, we think that some types of paternalism should be acceptable even to those who most embrace freedom of choice.

In domains as varied as savings, organ donations, marriage, and health care, we will offer specific suggestions in keeping with our general approach. And by insisting that choices remain unrestricted, we think that the risks of inept or even corrupt designs are reduced. Freedom to choose is the best safeguard against bad choice architecture.

CHOICE ARCHITECTURE IN ACTION

Choice architects can make major improvements to the lives of others by designing user-friendly environments. Many of the most successful companies have helped people, or succeeded in the marketplace, for exactly that reason. Sometimes the choice architecture is highly visible, and consumers and employers are much pleased by it. (The iPod and the iPhone are good examples because not only are they elegantly styled, but it is also easy for the user to get the devices to do what they want.) Sometimes the architecture is taken for granted and could benefit from some careful attention.

Consider an illustration from our own employer, the University of Chicago. The university, like many large employers, has an "open enrollment" period every November, when employees are allowed to revise the selections they have made about such benefits as health insurance and retirement savings. Employees are required to make their choices online. (Public computers are available for those who would otherwise not have Internet access.) Employees receive, by mail, a package of materials explaining the

choices they have and instructions on how to log on to make these choices. Employees also receive both paper and email reminders.

Because employees are human, some neglect to log on, so it is crucial to decide what the default options are for these busy and absent-minded employees. To simplify, suppose there are two alternatives to consider; those who make no active choice can be given the same choice they made the previous year, or their choice can be set back to "zero," Suppose that last year an employee, Janet, contributed one thousand dollars to her retirement plan. If Janet makes no active choice for the new year, one alternative would be to default her to a one thousand–dollar contribution; another would be to default her to zero contribution. Call these the "status quo" and "back to zero" options. How should the choice architect choose between these defaults?

Libertarian paternalists would like to set the default by asking what reflective employees in Janet's position would actually want. Although this principle may not always lead to a clear choice, it is certainly better than choosing the default at random, or making either "status quo" or "back to zero" the default for everything. For example, it is a good guess that most employees would not want to cancel their heavily subsidized health insurance. So for health insurance the status quo default (same plan as last year) seems strongly preferred to the back to zero default (which would mean going without health insurance).

Compare this to the employee's "flexible spending account," in which an employee sets aside money each month that can be used to pay for certain expenditures (such as uninsured medical or child care expenses). Money put into this account has to be spent each year or it is lost, and the predicted expenditures might vary greatly from one year to the next (for example, child care expenses go down when a child enters school). In this case, the zero default probably makes more sense than the status quo.

This problem is not merely hypothetical. We once had a meeting with three of the top administrative officers of the university to discuss similar issues, and the meeting happened to take place on the final day of the employees' open enrollment period. We mentioned this and asked whether the administrators had remembered to meet the deadline. One said that he was planning on doing it later that day and was glad for the reminder. Another admitted to having forgotten, and the third said that he was hoping that his wife had remembered to do it! The group then turned to the question of what the default should be for a supplementary salary reduction program (a tax-sheltered savings program). To that point, the default had been the "back to zero" option. But since contributions to this program could be stopped at any time, the group unanimously agreed that it would be better to switch to the status quo "same as last year" default. We are confident that many absent-minded professors will have more comfortable retirements as a result.

NOTES

1. See http://www.coathanger.com.au/archive/dibblys/loo.htm. The example is also discussed by Vicente (2006).
2. Friedman and Friedman (1980).
3. For a similar definition, see Van De Veer (1986).

REFERENCES

Friedman, Milton and Rose Friedman. Free to Choose: A Personal Statement. New York: Harcourt Brace Jovanovich, 1980.

Van De Veer, Donald. Paternalistic Intervention: The Moral Bounds on Benevolence. Princeton: Princeton University Press, 1986.

Vicente, Kim J. The Human Factor: Revolutionizing the Way People Live with Technology. New York: Routledge, 2006.

QUESTIONS

1. What is libertarian paternalism, according to Thaler and Sunstein? In what sense is it libertarian? In what sense is it paternalism?
2. Thaler and Sunstein argue that choice architecture—organizing the context in which people make decisions—is unavoidable. Why is it unavoidable?
3. A nudge is "any aspect of the choice architecture that alters people's behavior in a predictable way without forbidding any options or significantly changing their economic incentives." Nudges are "easy and cheap to avoid." What are some examples of nudges? Do you think the New York City big soda ban is a nudge?
4. What are "Econs," and how do they differ from "Humans"?
5. Thaler and Sunstein identify this "false assumption" behind opposition to paternalism: "almost all people, almost all of the time, make choices that are in their best interest or at the very least are better than the choices that would be made by someone else." Why do they think this assumption is false? What are some ways in which humans predictably make choices that are not in their best interests?
6. Thaler and Sunstein identify five strategies that Carolyn, the director of food services, might choose use in deciding how to arrange food items in the cafeteria line. The third strategy is "Try to arrange the food to get the kids to pick the same foods they would choose on their own." Why is this not a feasible strategy, according to Thaler and Sunstein? If you were the food services director, which strategy would you choose, and why?

CASS R. SUNSTEIN

Soft Paternalism and Its Discontents

In this excerpt from his book *Why Nudge?*, Cass R. Sunstein discusses three objections to nudging and other forms of soft paternalism. Note that Cass Sunstein uses "soft paternalism" to refer to paternalism that does not pose material costs and poses very low costs— including social and personal costs—on the people targeted by it. Note also that in this reading Sunstein refers to System 1 and System 2, two distinct systems in the human mind. As Sunstein explains elsewhere in his book *Why Nudge?*, System 1 is the fast, automatic, emotional system that is often driven by habits, whereas System 2 is the slow, deliberative, and reflective system.

The argument thus far has proceeded on the assumption that hard paternalism raises special problems and that soft paternalism is usually better along important dimensions. If paternalistic approaches impose small costs, or no material costs, on those who seek to go their own way, then such approaches are far less vulnerable to the objections I have discussed here. The central reason is that they preserve freedom of choice. . . .

At the same time, soft paternalism and nudging do run into three potentially special concerns, and they should be addressed independently. . .

OF EASY REVERSIBILITY

In imposing very low costs, or in failing to impose material costs, on choices, soft paternalism differs from mandates and bans. Because of the absence of such costs, soft paternalism appears to be *easily reversible*.

For example, graphic warnings do not override individual choice, and while they are not neutral and are meant to steer, people can ignore them if they want. We can easily imagine, and even find, graphic warnings that are meant to discourage texting while driving, smoking, abortion, premarital sex, and gambling. However powerful, such warnings can be ignored. Even if grocery stores put fruits and vegetables at the front and cigarettes and high-calorie foods at the back, people can always go to the back. A default rule in favor of automatic enrollment—in a savings or health insurance plan or a privacy policy—will greatly affect outcomes, and it may be decisive for many of us. But we can always opt out.

Does this mean that so long as soft paternalism or a nudge is involved, no one should worry about paternalism, or indeed about any abuse of authority or power? The answer is no. It is easy to identify an important problem with the idea of easy reversibility: the very biases and decisional inadequacies that I have traced here suggest that even when reversibility is easy in theory, it may prove difficult in practice. In part because of the power of System 1, soft paternalism may turn out to be decisive.

True, we can search for chocolate candy and cigarettes at the back of the store, and true, we might opt out of a website policy that authorizes a lot of tracking (perhaps with a simple click)—but because of the power of inertia, many of us are unlikely to do so. Graphic warnings, which appeal directly to System 1, may be exceedingly effective precisely because they target identifiable features of human cognition. The idea of easy reversibility might, in these circumstances, seem a bit of rhetoric, even a fraud—comforting, to be sure, but perhaps not a realistic response to those who are concerned about potential errors or bad faith on the part of soft paternalists and nudgers.

This objection has force. It would be wrong to suggest that because of easy reversibility, all risks are eliminated. Magazine subscribers who no longer enjoy the magazines to which they subscribe, but whose subscriptions are automatically renewed, often fail to take the trouble to discontinue them. (I speak from experience.) If people are defaulted into exploitative pension plans (with high fees and little diversification), or expensive health insurance programs that poorly fit their situations, it is not enough to say that they can go their own way if they choose to do so. If a website allows you to opt out of a privacy policy that allows it to track all of your movements on the Internet, you might well ignore the issue or say, "Yeah, whatever," and not alter the default.

In view of the fact that many people do not opt out even when it is simple to do so, a self-interested or malevolent government could easily use default rules to move people in its preferred directions. If we accept very strong assumptions about the likelihood of government mistake and about the virtues of private choice (uninfluenced by government), we might regard opt-out as an illusory safeguard and for that reason reject some forms of soft paternalism.

It remains true, however, that insofar as it maintains freedom of choice, soft paternalism is less intrusive and less dangerous than mandates and bans. This is so even if people will exercise that freedom less often than they would if inertia and procrastination were not powerful forces. While default rules matter, it is important to emphasize the empirical finding that

in the face of bad or harmful defaults, a number of people will in fact opt out. We know that if people are defaulted into a retirement plan that puts a lot of their money into savings while giving them too little right now, they will indeed reject the default.[1] If people are defaulted into a health insurance plan that works out very badly for them, many of them are going to switch. When people really dislike a default rule, they might well reject it. For that reason, liberty of choice is a real safeguard.

The freedom to opt out is no panacea. But it is exceedingly important.

WHAT MAKES LIFE WORTH LIVING? THE LEGITIMATE CLAIMS OF SYSTEM 1

Here is a way to understand one of the central claims made here. Often because of System 1, people err. We need to strengthen the hand of System 2 by promoting self-control, reducing unrealistic optimism, unshrouding attributes, counteracting biases, and eliminating an undue focus on the short term. Some forms of paternalism move people in the directions that they would go if they were fully rational. Paternalism, whether hard or soft, creates "as if" rationality. Indeed, that is a central point of good choice architecture.

It would be possible to object that if this approach is understood in a certain way, it ignores the legitimate claims of System 1.[2] More bluntly, it disregards what is most important in human life. People like to fall in love, even when it is pretty risky to do that. Many of our favorite foods are fattening. To be sure, most people care about their health, but unless they are fanatical, their health is not the only thing they care about. Many people like to drink and to smoke. Many of us care more about current consumption than consumption twenty years from now. When people enjoy their lives, it is because of System 1. The future matters, but the present matters too, and people reasonably and legitimately strike their own balance. As Mill wrote, "desires and impulses are as much a part of a perfect human being, as beliefs and restraints; and strong impulses are only perilous when not properly balanced."[3]

Isn't it System 1 that makes life worth living? Why should public officials, or anyone else, make people focus on something other than what they want to focus on, and promote choice architecture that devalues, denigrates, and undermines some of their most fundamental motivations and concerns? Indeed, might not System 2 be paralyzed if it lacks a sense of those concerns? How will it know what to do? . . .

The underlying questions are legitimate, and they suggest the problems with some imaginable nudges, not to mention hard paternalism. At the same time, they reflect a fundamental misunderstanding of the argument made here, and the approaches that it supports. To see why, we need to make a distinction between two different understandings of the kinds of biases and errors that choice architects might counteract.

I have mentioned Mr. Spock of the old *Star Trek* show, and the first view might be associated with him. (Aficionados might consider this the Vulcan view, after Mr. Spock's logic-dominated planet.) On that view, an understanding of bounded rationality and of cognitive biases suggests that System 2 needs to be put firmly in charge. To the extent that it is not, choice architecture should be established to move people to a situation of "as if" System 2 primacy. This view raises many puzzles, because some of the greatest pleasures of life appeal directly to System 1. No sensible private or public institution would be indifferent to the fact that for sufficient reasons, people take risks because that is what they like to do. They fall in love; they overeat; they stay up all night; they get drunk; they act on impulse; they run with apparently unpromising ideas; they experiment in a million and one different ways.

On a less ambitious view, bounded rationality and cognitive biases lead people to make what they themselves see as serious errors, or would see as serious errors after reflection, and choice architecture should be established to help make those errors less likely or less damaging. If inertia leads people not to take action that (they do or would agree, if properly informed) is in their interest, then inertia

might be enlisted to promote outcomes that (they do or would agree, if properly informed) are in their interest. If a problem of self-control is leading people to endanger their health, and if they do or would (if properly informed) want private and public institutions to help to solve that problem (and not to exploit it), then there is no cause for complaint if they do so.

We need not denigrate the legitimate claims of System 1 in order to accept these points. The real problem lies not in any question of high principle, but in identifying what people do or would want, and in deciding whether choice architects can be trusted. Perhaps choice architects do not know what people would want, if properly informed, and perhaps their own motivations are not pure. Perhaps the very idea of what people would want, if properly informed, raises difficult conceptual puzzles, at least in some cases, and creates unacceptable risks of overreaching by choice architects.

With respect to issues of this kind, there are limits to how much progress can be made in the abstract. We need to ask concrete questions about concrete problems. We could imagine forms of paternalism that would be objectionable because they would neglect what people really care about. Consider the Suffer Now, Celebrate When You're Almost Dead Pension Plan, automatically putting 51 percent of employee salaries into savings; or the Miserable Wellness Program, asking employees to commit to a grueling and unpleasant daily exercise regime; or the Joyless Cafeteria, keeping the tastiest foods relatively hidden. We could also imagine paternalistic approaches that are helpful rather than harmful. The challenge is to avoid the latter and promote the former.

THE PROBLEM OF IMPERMISSIBLE MOTIVATIONS

I have emphasized that soft paternalism does not impose material costs on choices. Even so, it is correct to object that this point is not conclusive, and that some forms of soft paternalism would go beyond the appropriate line. The most objectionable cases reflect not unacceptable paternalism but an altogether different problem: *impermissible motivations.* Indeed, many of the strongest intuitive objections to paternalism, even in its soft form, involve examples, real or imagined, in which government is acting on the basis of impermissible factors (potentially in violation of the Constitution itself). The objections are right, but the real problem has nothing to do with paternalism.[4]

We would not, for example, want to authorize government to default people into voting for incumbents by saying that unless they explicitly indicate otherwise, or actually show up at the ballot booth, they are presumed to vote for incumbents. Or suppose that government declared that for purposes of the census, citizens will be presumed to be Christian or Caucasian, unless they explicitly state otherwise. Some imaginable information campaigns would be unacceptable for the same reason, Suppose that government decided to inform people about all the misdeeds committed by members of a particular religious faith (say, Catholics or Jews). Or suppose that government decided to use vivid images to persuade people to choose products manufactured by its favorite interest groups.

In all of these cases, the problem does not lie with paternalism. The problem is the illegitimate or illicit ends that official paternalism, even if soft, is meant to produce. In a free and democratic society, government is not supposed to use the basic rules of voting to entrench itself, to favor certain racial and religious groups, to stigmatize members of a particular faith, or to tell people to buy the products that favored interest groups manufacture. When the government's ends are illicit, paternalism, designed to promote those ends, is illicit too.

We can imagine cases in which the illicit nature of the government's ends is clear; the examples given above are meant to be such cases. But we can also imagine cases about which people might disagree, Suppose, for example, that government were to engage in soft paternalism—say, through an aggressive educational campaign—designed to discourage

people from having sex outside of marriage. Some people might think that efforts of this kind would be illicit, because they would violate a commitment to a certain kind of neutrality. Perhaps those people are right; perhaps not. The central question is whether the government's ends are illicit. It is not about paternalism.

The examples of illicit ends are important because they identify some limits on even minimally intrusive forms of paternalism. But with respect to the issues under discussion here, they are uninformative, because they do not establish the central claim, which is that certain forms of paternalism are objectionable as such. If some people are strongly committed to that claim, it is not clear what might be said to dislodge that commitment. Is it really an insult to autonomy and dignity to provide graphic images of the harms associated with cigarette smoking? To take steps to promote a norm in favor of healthful eating or against texting while driving? For those who think so, the risk is that high-sounding abstractions are being enlisted to contest initiatives that insult no one's dignity and that reflect public commitments to both compassion and respect.

NOTES

1. *See* John Beshears et al., The Limitations of Defaults 8 (unpublished manuscript, 2010), http://www.nber.org/programs/ag/rrc/NB10-02,%20Beshears,%20Choi,%20Laibson,%20Madrian.pdf. *See also* Zachary Brown et al., *Testing the Effects of Defaults on the Thermostat Settings of OECD Employees,* 39 ENERGY ECONOMICS 128 (2013), which finds that in winter, OECD employees were often willing to change back a significant (two-degree C) reduction in the default thermostat setting—but that they were less likely to change a smaller reduction (one-degree C).

2. *See* Riccardo Rebonato, *Taking Liberties: A Critical Examination of Libertarian Paternalism* (2012).

3. John Stuart Mill, *On Liberty* 8 (Kathy Casey ed., 2002) (1859).

4. *See* Sarah Conly, *Against Autonomy: Justifying Coercive Paternalism* (2012), at 103–11, for a discussion of paternalism and perfectionism. Conly supports hard paternalism, but only as a means of promoting people's own

ends, and not in order to displace them. She rejects perfectionism. The paternalism defended here is similarly focused on means, not ends (with the qualifications I have explored); my discussion is thus compatible with Conly's rejection of perfectionism.

QUESTIONS

1. An advantage of nudging is that it does not limit liberty or reduce the choices available to people; nudging preserves individuals' freedom to opt out of the options they're nudged into. Nonetheless, Sunstein raises the concern that people will not always opt out of bad options, even when it is simple to do so. Why should we worry that people will stick with bad options?
2. Sunstein defends choice architecture that helps people avoid "what they themselves see as serious errors, or would see as serious errors after reflection." What are some examples of actions that you might engage in, that you yourself would see as serious errors? Would everyone see these actions as serious errors, were they to perform these actions?
3. Sunstein discusses the problem of "impermissible motivations"—when government policies have illegitimate ends. What are some examples of illegitimate ends of government action, according to Sunstein?

SARAH CONLY

Coercive Paternalism

In this excerpt from her book *Against Autonomy: Justifying Coercive Paternalism*, the philosopher Sarah Conly argues in favor of what she calls *coercive paternalism*, forcing people to act in certain ways in order to help them achieve their long-term ends. Coercive paternalism, Conly argues, is preferable to libertarian paternalism, an approach which neither respects choice nor achieves the best results. Conly identifies four criteria that paternalistic policies must meet in order to be justified. Portion size regulations, Conly argues, meet these four criteria and hence are justifiable instances of paternalism. One example of the portion size regulations Conly defends is the New York City soda ban, though Conly's book was written before the ban was proposed so Conly does not discuss the soda ban in particular.

PATERNALISM

We do things that are bad for us—we take risks we soon regret, we thwart our own desires, we undercut our own fulfillment. Should we be stopped?

On the one hand, we value our liberty, and resent being told what to do. On the other, we often regret bitterly the choices that have diminished the quality of our lives, and wish we could do it over and choose better. In such cases, we may well wish we had been stopped, given the costs of our actions. The question I address here is whether society—typically in the form of government legislation—should step in, and make people do what is good for them. I will argue that, in many more cases than we now allow, it should; that preserving our liberty of action is not worth the costs of exercising choice. I argue, then, against autonomy. "Autonomy" is something of a portmanteau word, including many distinct concepts, and certainly there are ways the word is used that denote things which are unobjectionable. What I argue against is what Joel Feinberg has called "[t]he kernel of the idea of autonomy . . . the right to make choices and decisions—what to put in my body, what contacts with my body to permit, where and how to move my body through public space, how to use my chattels and personal property, what personal information to disclose to others, what information to conceal, and more."[1] Whereas Feinberg argues that this ability to live according to the choices one has made is a core value that must be preserved, I will argue instead that it is something that has been overvalued. While in some cases autonomous action does no harm, in other cases it does, however "harm" is construed—as detrimental to happiness, detrimental to material survival, or even detrimental to the promotion of autonomous action. It is not worth our while to try to prevent all harmful action, of course, and so intervention is not always warranted. Other times, however, intervention is not only permissible but also obligatory, so that autonomous actions should be prevented.

We could, and I will argue we should, for example, make cigarettes illegal and generally reduce the number of unhealthy diet options . . . We need to limit people's freedom of action, their autonomy, in the interests of better living. Where such choices should be left to the chooser, and where intervention is permissible, will be a function of what is best described as a cost–benefit analysis, rather than a decision a priori that certain personal decisions should be sacrosanct.

I am arguing, then, for the permissibility of interference in personal lives, interference even in actions a person takes that will affect only himself . . . What I will argue for is a specific and controversial position: that we may, and indeed are sometimes morally obligated to, force people to refrain from certain actions and to engage in others. I will call this strong position Coercive Paternalism, and will show that it is indeed more acceptable, in some cases, than softer forms of paternalism that may seek to guide rather than constrain . . .

Libertarian Paternalism

An alternative to our present scenario has been articulated by Thaler and Sunstein in *Nudge*. They endorse what they call "libertarian paternalism." Their suggestion is that we help people do what is best for them by making the right choice easier for those with cognitive biases. If it is a question of pension plans, we make the most advantageous plan (for the employee) the default option: if you do nothing, you end up with (what is at least generally) the best choice. If you need help choosing healthy food, we put the healthy fruit at eye level, and the deep-fried salted fat on the bottom shelf, since people are more likely to choose whatever is at eye level. We give you a nudge in the direction that is best for you. However, while we change the "choice architecture," we don't actually eliminate options. You can still get those BBQ-flavor pork rinds by bending over, and you can still opt for the pension plan that makes it most likely that you will end up dependent and poor. As they see it, this preserves your autonomy, and thus allows us to have our cake (beneficial consequences) and eat it too (as we respect liberty of choice).

There are two important things to notice about this, though. First, Libertarian Paternalism is manipulative. That is, it does not suggest that we engage in free and open discussion in order to rationally persuade you to change your ways. Sunstein and Thaler are not opposed to free and open discussion, but they don't think engaging you in rational argument is enough to get you to choose efficiently, because of the cognitive deficits they have described. The point of the nudge is to push you in ways that bypass your reasoning. That is, they use your cognitive biases, like the tendency to go with the default option, to bring about good effects. There is a sense in which they then fail to respect people's decision-making ability. The assumption is that because our decision-making ability is limited we need to use nonrational means to seduce people into doing what is good for them, and are trying to get people to act through the use of nonrational means. It is true that for libertarian paternalism all options remain open, which means that some people could, in fact, resist this nonrational persuasion and rely on their own cognitive abilities to decide what they want to do. The assumption is, though, that most people won't do this but instead will fall in the direction in which they are nudged.

I don't think this is morally wrong, since I agree that we need to help people get where they really want to go. However, insofar as it is supposed to render the position more palatable to the classic liberal, it fails. Rather than regarding people as generally capable of making good choices, we outmaneuver them by appealing to their irrationality, just in more fruitful ways. We concede that people can't generally make good decisions when left to their own devices, and this runs against the basic premise of liberalism, which is that we are basically rational, prudent creatures who may thus, and should thus, direct themselves autonomously.

Second, libertarian paternalism is less likely to achieve its goal, benefit to those who choose, than is the more intrusive system of coercive paternalism. More freedom to choose means more people will choose badly. It is true that since a libertarian paternalist system allows individuals the ability to act contrary to the nudge, those for whom the default option, and so forth, are not good choices could bypass the nudge to hit upon a choice more appropriate to their own particular case, and thus would benefit from the freedom this system allows. Libertarian

paternalism might be the ideal choice if the manipulative nudges worked for those who would otherwise make foolish choices, while the remaining option to act differently allowed only those who are choosing the most rational means to their ends to deviate from the direction into which they are nudged . . .

However, when you allow people the option to choose contrary to the direction of the nudge, this freedom isn't preserved exclusively for those who are going to use it to do what is best for them. Some of those who ignore the nudge towards the fruit and go for the pork rinds will be wedging unhealthy, cholesterol-ridden bodies under the cafeteria table, because after years of such food they have a craving for fat and salt that no nudge will override, even while such a diet will give them shorter, more painful lives. Similarly, those who choose to smoke are really not likely to be those who have given it rational consideration and decided that it is truly worth it. Some people would refuse the pension plan because they have wild ideas about retirement (they want more to spend on lottery tickets) that will never yield the results they want. An irrational decision can be one accompanied by a very strong motivation. In other words, what libertarian paternalism does is not simply preserve the option of better choices for those who, for some reason, are different from the norm. It preserves options for those who have stronger motivations than others do, or for those who have stronger and crazier convictions than the norm. It preserves the option for error. The nudge will work for those whose motivation to the contrary isn't sufficiently strong, but some of us are too determinedly headed in the wrong direction to be prevented from taking our foolish actions by a simple nudge. The danger is, then, that libertarian paternalism may end up neither having its cake nor eating it—it doesn't really respect choice, in the sense of thinking that people should be left to their own devices in deciding what to do. And, while it would no doubt save many people from foolish actions by nudging them in a better direction, it will leave many others to suffer the consequences of their bad thinking. We may end up with neither of the valuable things libertarian paternalism hoped to promote.

Coercive Paternalism

. . . Coercive paternalism takes a different position. Rather than leaving us to sink or swim, as does liberalism, or engaging in mental manipulation, as does libertarian paternalism, the coercive paternalist will simply say some things are not allowed. I don't know that this is more respectful of people than manipulation is, but I don't see that it is less respectful. In either case, we are trying to control people on the grounds that their own decision making is not to be trusted. And, coercive paternalism is more likely to get us good results, because certain behaviors, like smoking, will be out of the question. . . . So instead of simply educating people about the dangers of smoking, as liberals do, or disincentivizing smoking by making it very expensive, I would recommend we get rid of cigarettes. . . . Coercive paternalism takes certain decisions out of our hands. It does this in order to help us do what we want to do, which is to lead longer and happier lives. We know that leaving people to fend for themselves is too often simply not successful in getting people to where they want to go. Instead of letting people languish in the misery caused by their own decisions, why not intervene, as we do with prescription drugs, as we do with seat belts, and help people out?

What exactly is the problem with coercion?

RESPECT

The initial answer is that to many, using coercion to stop people from doing what they have decided, however foolishly, that they want to do, seems somehow to devalue them, to degrade them; in short, to give them less than the respect they deserve. Stephen Darwall, for example, says that

> The objectionable character of paternalism of this sort is not that those who seek to benefit us against our wishes are likely to be wrong about what really benefits us . . . It is, rather, primarily a failure of respect, a failure to recognize the authority that persons have to

demand, within certain limits, that they be allowed to make their own choices for themselves.[2]

What adequate respect consists in—indeed, what respect itself consists in—is a difficult question, to say the least, and much ink has been spilt in its pursuit. At the least, though, to respect something seems to mean to recognize that thing's value, and to act in a way that is consistent with that value. When it comes to persons, we are all agreed that all persons have unique value, by reason of their personhood, regardless of the particular kinds of lives they live. Beyond this consensus, though, there are many questions: whether the value of persons lies in their rationality ability or their capacity for choice, or their capacity for moral thought, or some interrelationship of these; whether it is a function of their capacity for love, for sympathy, for sacrifice; whether it arises from their creativity and imagination, or even depends on their having been made in God's image, whatever that may mean. And, further, there is no very general agreement on what their valuable features, whatever they may be, call for in terms of behavior from others. Everyone seems to agree that certain behaviors are disrespectful: slavery, where one person is forever subordinated to the purposes of another, with no regard given to the way he himself wants to live his life, is a practice all parties agree is inconsistent with the respect due to a person, any person. For some, though, including Kant, the death penalty is a sign of respect, because it is an appropriate acknowledgement of the perpetrator's agency; for others, killing a human, whatever he may have done, is antithetical to respecting his value. . .

IS THIS CONTROVERSIAL?

While many people find this position objectionable, there may nonetheless be a question as to whether this view says anything controversial. Even Mill, the most influential opponent of forcing other people to do what you think is good for them, admitted exceptions in terms of what may be called long-term desires: as mentioned above, in the broken bridge example, Mill said that if you see someone stepping on to a bridge that you know to be unsound, you can stop him. The most significant condition is that he does not know the bridge is broken. You further assume that he doesn't want to fall through the bridge, and see that there is no opportunity to apprise him of the bridge's condition.[3] Some take this to mean that even on Mill's account, we are allowed to engage in coercive paternalism when what we are forcing you to do is what you would want to do if you were adequately informed. Forcing you to act in accordance with what your informed desire would direct is sometimes called Soft Paternalism, and many people see its legitimacy as obvious and uncontroversial precisely because they don't think it violates autonomy. Some argue that soft paternalism isn't even paternalism, because for an action to be paternalistic, it has to be contrary to your desires. Joel Feinberg, for example, says:

> It is not as clear that "soft paternalism" is paternalistic at all, in any clear sense. Certainly its motivating spirit seems closer to the liberalism of Mill than to the protectiveness of hard paternalism. Soft paternalism holds that the state has the right to prevent self-regarding conduct . . . *when but only when* that conduct is substantially nonvoluntary . . . [T]he soft paternalist points out that the law's concern should not be with the wisdom, prudence, or dangerousness of B's choice, but rather with whether or not the choice is truly his. Its concern should be to help implement B's real choice not to protect B from harm as such.[4]

Feinberg goes on to argue that decisions that are made in ignorance of the facts, and which will result in harm to the self, should be considered nonvoluntary, so that state intervention is permitted (although, confusingly, an equally ignorant decision which will harm someone else can be considered voluntary, and thus blameworthy, if the ignorance is due to negligence).[5] The paternalism I promote here is not a paternalism about ultimate ends; that is, I do not argue that there are objectively good ends, or objectively rational ends, or ends objectively valuable in any way, which everyone should be made to pursue. I am arguing for intervention in cases where people's

choices of instrumental means are confused, in a way that means they will not achieve their ultimate ends. If my subjective end is happiness, and I think playing the lottery will promote that, not because the suspense gives me some evanescent pleasure, but because I really think I have a reasonable chance of winning, I am mistaken about my means. Of course, Feinberg's definition is not universally accepted: many argue that an action can be voluntary even if mistaken in some respects, and others simply define paternalism in light of its constraints on behavior in light of present desires, without qualifying those desires. . . .[6]

What we need, in order to conclude that coercive paternalism is the appropriate strategy, is for it to meet these four criteria:

1. The activity to be prevented on paternalistic grounds really is one that is opposed to our long-term ends. . . . [W]e don't want to allow a "paternalistic" intervention just because an action, or its result, is, say, vulgar, or aesthetically unpleasing, or immoral, or silly, as long as it helps a person reach his own goals. Interference is justified on paternalistic grounds only when it reflects individuals' actual values, not the values we might like them to have.

2. Coercive measures actually have to be effective. Sometimes they aren't. As we know, Prohibition did not end alcohol consumption. It is foolish to introduce a legal constraint on an activity if that won't actually work to end or reduce that activity. And, we need the measure to be effective in two ways. In most cases, there will be an immediate goal (to stop someone using a substance, for example) and an ultimate goal to which that immediate goal is to lead (improving health). If a measure succeeds in the first, but not the second, then the measure is pointless. If, for example, we wanted to ban cupcakes to alleviate obesity, and succeeded in removing cupcakes from people's diets only to find that they had filled that gap with layer cake, then the cupcake ban would be foolish. We need efficacy throughout.

3. The benefits have to be greater than the costs. The benefits and costs are both material and psychological, with neither having absolute priority: a measure that greatly improves health, for example, could in fact be so psychological painful, over the long run, as not to be worth it.

4. The measure in question needs to be the most efficient way to prevent the activity. This criterion really implies criteria 2 and 3, but since many people dwell on the first three without noticing that a paternalist would also accept the fourth, I want to stress each individually. . . .

PORTION SIZE REGULATION

As far as I can tell, no state or municipality has actually tried to mandate smaller portion sizes in restaurants, or tried to reduce the size of single-serving packaged foods, like potato chips and cookies. It might, however, be a good idea. Obesity, the driving force behind the soda ban, is also the issue here. More and more researchers endorse the idea that an increase in the size of restaurant portions plays a significant role in this increasing obesity. Their reasoning includes various factors. For one thing, we eat out significantly more than we used to, so we consume more restaurant portions.[7] Portion sizes for all types of food, except pizza, increased markedly between 1978 and 1998,[8] and current portion sizes in fast food restaurants for French fries, hamburgers, and sodas are two to five times larger than the originals. Having larger sizes—larger than previously, and larger than the competitor's—is seen as making brands (like candy bars) and meals more desirable to the consumer. Fast food chains routinely tout the increased size of their offerings, and convenience stores push the size of their takeaway sodas ("Big Gulp") as a way to get people to stop in. Even Lean Cuisine and Weight Watchers advertise increased sizes in their meals.[9]

And, as anyone who's ever eaten can testify, we eat more when we have a bigger serving. It doesn't matter whether it is a serving we ourselves dish up

(which might perhaps correspond to hunger), or one we are given by someone else; numerous studies show that when portion sizes are larger, we eat more. This holds true of both restaurant servings and packaged foods—the bigger the bag of chips, the more we eat of them at one time.[10] Why this is something of a question: it may be that we've been trained to clean our plate, or it may have more biological roots. One factor is that as we eat bigger portions, we often don't feel more full than we do from smaller portions; signals that we are satiated are ignored.[11] So, we just keep eating until it's all gone. Lastly, these gargantuan portions at one meal aren't compensated for by Lilliputian ones at the next—despite the fact that we've consumed an entire day's worth of calories, we eat the next meal as if we'd previously had a salad and sparkling water.[12]

So, it seems plausible that increased portion size plays a significant role in our increased obesity. If this is so, then we may reasonably wonder whether there should be some sort of regulation of portion size. The federal government has its own system of "serving" sizes, but these bear little resemblance to portions actually served in restaurants. (Indeed, in packaged foods, federal serving sizes sometimes confuse us, rather than aiding us in making wise choices, since a package may state in large letters on the front that it contains only xxx calories per serving, and only mention in tiny letters on the back that that package, while clearly intended as a one-person portion, is actually three "servings.") Government "servings" could, though, be useful: they could be used as standards as to what portion sizes would be allowed in restaurants. This could, first and foremost, lessen how many calories people consume now. It could also stave off an even worse future, since it would eliminate the "size wars" between fast food chains that threaten to drive serving sizes up and up and up. Would the regulation of fast food portion sizes be a justified paternalistic policy?

1. *Would it promote a long-term goal?* As with all measures that decrease the chances of serious illness and premature death, the answer certainly appears to be yes. We want longer lives and we want good health, both as ends in themselves and as means to

doing everything else we want to do. Furthermore, despite its prevalence, obesity carries a social stigma. People who are fat are typically ashamed of it, presumably because they are indeed looked down upon by other people. Many people suffer acutely from the recognition of their failure to live up to the popular cultural standard of attractiveness. As if this loss of self-esteem and self-confidence were not bad enough, overweight women, at least, also suffer career setbacks stemming from their obesity, earning less and advancing more slowly than their thinner counterparts.[13] All things being equal, career advancement is considered desirable by most people, and failing to advance because of a feature irrelevant to job performance is painful to everyone.

2. *Is it effective?* Since there are as yet no regulations over portions, we cannot know this for certain. The facts adduced above, though, as to the overall effect on calorie intake of larger portion sizes, suggests that it would be, if restaurants were compliant, and the trans-fats experience here and abroad suggests that restaurants are willing to be compliant, at least where that costs them nothing.

3. *Are the benefits worth the costs?* The difficult question, of course, is what the costs to the individual would be if restaurant portion sizes were controlled. On the one hand, eating smaller portions can still satisfy our appetite, so losing supersizes wouldn't mean suffering hunger pangs. On the other hand, a lot of our eating has very little to do with satisfying hunger. We eat with others to enjoy a social occasion; we eat alone because we are bored; and first and foremost, we eat because we like the taste. We eat as much as we do out of the pure enjoyment of food. Fast food may not present a sophisticated, innovative, complex combination of flavors of the sort that entices restaurant reviewers, but that doesn't make it less appealing. Part of the reason public pleas to eat more salads and fruits fall on deaf ears is that to most people, they just don't taste as good. We love salt, we love sugar, we love fat.

Since we are not talking about eliminating fast food altogether, though, the question is how much more enjoyment people derive from eating larger, rather than smaller, portions. The mere fact that we continue to eat doesn't entail that we are continuing

to enjoy it—often we eat absentmindedly, simply because there is food in front of us, particularly if it is salty.[14] If we had to do something active to get those fries—to put a penny in the table-side dispenser to get each fry rather than paying up front for the whole serving—how many would we buy? And even if we do continue to enjoy as we eat our way through the supersized portion of fries, it seems likely that there will be diminishing marginal returns—we enjoy the fifty-second French fry a lot less than the first. It becomes less and less worth the cost. My guess is that a lot of the eating associated with larger portion sizes is passive eating, the sort we do because it is in front of us. This is presumably augmented by the fact that eating salt makes us crave more salt, something which no amount of fries is going to satisfy, since the last fry, whatever its number in the series, will still leave that salty taste in our mouths. For those few who really are suffering at not having the "rest" of their portion once portion sizes are reduced, a second trip to the counter is always an option. My guess is that most people won't want it, even as now they don't make second trips after finishing whatever portion size is in front of them. As long as portion sizes are within reasonable limits, when you're done you feel you've had enough, just because you're done.

A second issue is the emotional pain we may feel at knowing that our portions are now controlled; and not only controlled, but smaller than they once were. Some people feel this is a significant issue, that consumers will see the move to require smaller portions as unacceptably restrictive. This strikes me as odd, however. I have no control over restaurant portion size as it is now, without there being paternalistic restrictions in place. Yes, I can choose, in a fast food restaurant, to order small, medium, or large, but no one asks me exactly how much I would like; and in other restaurants I am given no choice whatsoever. The waiter brings the food and I discover what exactly I've got. We've never experienced freedom when it comes to portion size, because portion sizes have always been entirely up to the restaurant, so the only thing that changes with portion size regulation is that someone else—an outside agency, not a private business—is making the decision, and furthermore, is making it in order to benefit us, rather than to make a profit. That doesn't seem so daunting. And for what it is worth, we can still exercise our much vaunted freedom; we will be able to choose small, medium, or large orders, but what exactly we will get for that will be different. And if we really want more, we can always return to the counter and order a second portion. We're not so likely to want to, but we can if we want.

Not only does this not constitute a painful loss of control, it will also help us in those areas in which we have complete control—eating at home. Just as larger portion sizes have changed our perception of what constitutes a normal size for a serving, smaller portion sizes should do the same, eventually. This Aristotelian habituation means that portion size regulation in restaurants actually has a more far-reaching beneficial effect than it might at first seem, and we will end up choosing more rationally than before.

After the initial shock when our order of large fries turns out to have only 380 rather than 500 calories (the amounts in medium and large portions of McDonald's fries, respectively, according to the McDonald's website), it seems likely that we will adjust our expectations and won't feel disappointment at seeing a smaller small of fries, or a burger that is not too tall to fit into our mouth. We'll get at least very close to the same enjoyment, won't suffer from a lack of food portion freedom, and will be healthier and more conventionally attractive. Those who pine after the good old days, when you could eat more than your entire daily recommended dose of calories in one fast food meal, will eventually sound like any other set of old people who complain that things have gone downhill since their youth, when the matinee was 75 cents and a candy bar a nickel.

4. *Is it the most efficient way to get people to eat less fatty food?* This, of course, is a controversial question. The most popular approach to overcoming obesity now is education, and it is being pursued vigorously in especially one form, labeling. The basic idea is this: people don't want to be fat. They are fat because they eat more calories than they use in exercise, and they eat more than they should because they don't know how many calories they are consuming. Thus, there has been a lot of emphasis on letting people know how many calories fast foods

contain. This is why the Obama health care reform measure includes a requirement that calorie information should be posted in fast food restaurants. The question is whether pointing out the relevant facts will be successful in getting people to change their ways.

It doesn't seem likely. Increasing numbers of researchers in obesity admit that irrationality plays a significant role in our failure to make healthy choices. One problem with fast food may be that weight gain is incremental: no single two-patty burger with cheese is going to endanger your life. Presumably, if we knew we were going to follow our burger and fries with an immediate heart attack, instead of with a deep-fried apple turnover, none of us would eat it, no matter how strong our cravings, just as we won't drink antifreeze, no matter how thirsty. When this meal is only one out of a very long series, though, no one of which strikes the fatal blow, we find it easier to dismiss. Whatever the specific mechanisms may be, there is a growing recognition that poor reasoning plays a role in those who consistently choose what is bad for them. Recent studies tie poor dietary choices to particular cognitive biases of various sorts.[15] Here, as elsewhere, our poor reasoning leads us astray.

Human food consumption and dietary behaviors seem to invalidate conventional economic theory that assumes we each make rational, calculated decisions based on an analysis of the information presented to us. Were we real rational, economic creatures, it would follow, for example, that we eat ice cream sundaes and candy bars only after assessing the utility (including pleasure) that we may gain from that food against the future health consequences. Food consumption, however, is also governed by cravings, emotions, and environmental conditions that create irrational and often unhealthy dietary behaviors.[16]

Indeed, we have experience of food labeling, and it suggests that this just isn't sufficient to change people's eating habits. Labeling on packaged foods, including both calories (typically listed first!) and nutrients, has been around a long time, but as we've seen, people still consume enormous amounts of soda, as well as chips and other forms of high-fat, low nutrition snacks. Some people, of course, don't read labels, and won't read caloric information in restaurants, either. But even when they do, there is some evidence that it doesn't affect what they eat. New York City has had a law requiring that fast food restaurants display calories per portion since 2008, but a recent study suggests this has had no effect: while 57 percent of the people in the study noticed the information, only 9 percent said it influenced their choices, and information from customer receipts shows no difference in purchases before and after labeling.[17] These may be the same people who spend tens of billions of dollars per year on trying to lose weight through Nutrisystems, Weight Watchers, Jenny Craig, Herbalife, thousands of diet books, gym memberships, and machines that will magically jiggle the fat away. The individual eater obviously experiences some disconnect between the goal of losing weight and the choice to eat the 780-calorie Angus bacon and cheese burger with the 560-calorie order of fries and 1,100-calorie shake.

Yet, most people hesitate to try approaches that would actually address the effects of such irrationality. Most often we see recommendation for increased food labeling, and at most more regulation for children, both of advertising of unhealthy food geared to children and control of school food options—but this is a strange response to admitted irrationality. If we don't think clearly, giving us the facts on a food label will not produce a marked change. Perhaps reducing advertising geared towards children will reduce children's desire for unhealthy foods, and probably preventing their access to junk food at school will have some effect—but what about the rest of us? Given our failure to think well when it comes to choosing means to ends, it is not clear how additional education about calories will make us change our ways. Even if labeling has some effect, it seems likely that enforced portion sizes will have much more, without great cost. It's this that has prompted a number of obesity experts to doubt the efficacy of education alone in changing eating patterns.

> As public health advocates, we know all too well that teaching the world's population about the dangers of obesity and the need to avoid obesogenic foods that are inexpensive, tasty, and convenient will never work if food corporations are permitted to continue to spend massively to encourage the public to eat more of their products. Efforts to control obesity will have to enlist the public to focus on *behavior,* with a shift from a sole focus on citizens to a new one on the *behavior* of food corporations . . . We have come to believe that research studies concentrating on personal behavior and responsibility as causes of the obesity epidemic do little but offer cover to an industry seeking to downplay its own responsibility.[18]

Forcing corporations to downsize food servings is one reasonable approach to helping people who, left to their own autonomous choices, only make themselves worse off. Of course, we can imagine other options: enforced exercise classes, for example, or licenses to buy fattening food available only to those whose BMI is under 25. These seem a lot more burdensome on the individuals who must undergo them, though, as well as having implementation costs for society as a whole that seem much greater. Of the various options that might actually reduce obesity, reducing portion sizes seems practical, humane, and effective . . .

IS THIS HARD PATERNALISM?

In these circumstances, paternalistic intervention is plausible. However, some may argue that it is plausible here precisely because this isn't really hard paternalism; that is, this isn't paternalism of a sort that fails to respect people's autonomy. Indeed, in some cases—notably the New York trans-fats ban—one may ask whether it is paternalism at all. As was discussed before, the terms "hard" paternalism and "soft" paternalism are used in two ways. On the one hand, they are used, as I tend to use them here, to differentiate the *means* a paternalist may use, where hard paternalism forces people to behave in certain ways, and soft paternalism merely persuades or entices them. The terms are also used, we recall, to differentiate the *content* of the paternalistic measure: hard paternalism, in this sense, imposes actions that are not what the agent would voluntarily choose, whereas soft paternalistic methods simply make the agent act in a way that is in accordance with his real wishes, when, because of some significant impediment, he is able to do that. Using forceful methods to prevent someone from simply making a mistake—walking across the bridge he doesn't know is broken—for many people doesn't suggest any real interference with autonomy, since the person's choice to walk across the dangerous bridge isn't really voluntary.

One way of resolving this might be to say it depends on your definition of paternalism, and of hard paternalism, of which there are quite a few. This doesn't really capture the doctrinal issue, though. The question is what we can extrapolate from these examples as to when intervention is justified. It might be argued that these cases don't show much: in the case of the trans-fats ban, I've argued that one reason the ban is costless is that no one has a taste for trans-fats per se, and the pastries, crackers, etc. we do like are still available. So, eliminating it doesn't do anything that is contrary to what we want. In other cases (portion control, cigarettes) we do have a desire that is frustrated, in the sense that people want big stacks of French fries and cigarettes enough to seek them out and consume them, but even there I've argued that much of our jumbo eating is passive, and that while people want cigarettes, they generally want not to want them, and that they are not opposed to the idea of insurance per se. Thus, it may seem that we are not imposing upon people in any way contrary to their own expression of will. If that is true, then they don't provide evidence that it is acceptable to disrespect people's autonomy by preventing them from acting as their own decisions would direct them.

However, the fact that people don't derive a lot of satisfaction from their choices doesn't mean they aren't acting voluntarily when making those choices. Insofar as we are interfering with voluntary actions, we do impede people's autonomy. If we agree that it is rational to interfere with people's autonomous choices here, we may be able to extend that principle to other autonomous actions when the costs and benefits warrant. The question, then, is whether people's choices to smoke, and so forth, are voluntary, not whether it is one from which they will derive a lot of satisfaction, or even net satisfaction.

In Chapter 1 I used the reasoning of John Kleinig to argue that the fact that a choice is not entirely rational does not mean it isn't voluntary.[19] Richard Arneson makes the same point in discussing Joel Feinberg's categorization of acts involving any sort of deviation from pure rationality as involuntary—that this simply casts too wide a net.[20] Very few acts will qualify as voluntary if complete rationality is needed to make them voluntary. So, I will take it as a given here that an irrational choice may nonetheless be a voluntary one. On the other hand, some irrational choices surely aren't voluntary . . .

One argument that such actions are involuntary is that those who do these imprudent things are ignorant, in which case their actions don't count as voluntary. Ignorance is indeed a good excuse: I didn't voluntarily kill someone if I was ignorant of the fact that he was deathly allergic to nuts when I handed him the walnut brownie. I am not a murderer. (Of course, in some cases my ignorance might be culpable, if I should have known about his allergy—in such cases, responsibility is still thought to be mine, even though I intended no harm.) Ignorance doesn't generally seem to be a factor in the cases discussed above, though. It is true that there are those who argue, for example, that we don't know just how many calories fast foods contain.[21] I find this unlikely, in the main: while we don't know the specifics of the calorie content, it's hard to find anyone who doesn't know that a burger and French fries has way, way more calories than a salad, that a salad is good to eat if you want to avoid gaining (or to lose) weight. In my experience women are more aware of calorie content than are men, given the culture, but it's hard to imagine that at this point there are many people who are actually clueless . . .

The second way these actions might be involuntary is that our thinking is simply so confused that we don't know what we are doing, despite our possession of the facts. Goodin, who argued for the presence of cognitive bias in the choice to smoke, argued that its presence meant the actions in question were involuntary.[22] Part of Goodin's motivation seems to have been that he wanted to make cigarettes illegal, but not being a coercive paternalist, could only justify this by showing that the actions are involuntary. That is understandable, but it doesn't show that smoking is an involuntary act. As we saw in Chapter 1, the presence of irrationality in the form of cognitive bias doesn't make actions involuntary, as we understand that. It would take something greater than our accustomed poor thinking to say that an action is involuntary or that all our bad decisions could be categorized as involuntary ones. There is no evidence that there is more cognitive dysfunction involved in smoking than in general, though. It is true that, aside from the involvement of cognitive bias, smoking is addictive, and while this is irrelevant to the voluntariness of the actions of those who choose to smoke in the first place, it clearly affects the motivational structure of those who are already hooked. It's hard to say the drive to smoke is so overwhelming as to make the act involuntary, though; smokers do, after all, have enough control to pick the time and place, exiting the building, bus, airport, and so on, when they need to. Goodin says that we usually regard a state as involuntary if the only way to avoid it is to undergo a pain, but surely that depends on the degree of the pain—the bank teller who gives the robber the money under the threat of a slight pinch is not regarded as having had no choice. We wouldn't forgive someone who broke into stores to steal cigarettes as having acted involuntarily—we don't even excuse drug addicts who do this, and their addiction may be less manageable. So while being a smoker certainly places us under pressure, it's not sufficient pressure for us to regard the person who acts under it as having acted involuntarily. There are actions that are so irrational as to be involuntary, but even smoking, the most likely candidate, doesn't meet the criteria of involuntary action. The other choices discussed here don't even come close.

NOTES

1. Joel Feinberg, *Harm to Self: The Moral Limits of the Criminal Law* (Oxford University Press, 1986), p. 54.

2. Stephen Darwall, "The Value of Autonomy and Autonomy of the Will," *Ethics* 116.2 (January 2006), 263–284, at 268.

3. John Stuart Mill, *On Liberty* (in *Utilitarianism and On Liberty,* Meridian British Philosophers Series, ed. Mary Warnock [New York: World Publishing, 1971]), ch. 5, p. 229.

4. Feinberg, *Harm to Self,* p. 12.

5. Ibid., ch. 21, "Failures of Voluntariness."

6. For a critical discussion of Feinberg's theory of what it takes for an act be voluntary, see Richard Arneson, "Mill Versus Paternalism," *Ethics* 90.4 (July 1980), 470–489.

7. Lisa Young and Marion Nestle, "The Contribution of Expanding Portion Sizes to the US Obesity Epidemic," *American Journal of Clinical Nutrition* 92.2 (2002), 246–249.

8. Samara J. Nielsen, and Barry M. Popkin, "Patterns and Trends in Food Portion Sizes, 1977–1998," *Journal of the American Medical Association* 289.4 (2003), 450–453.

9. Young and Nestle, "Contribution of Expanding Portion Sizes"; see also B. J. Rolls, "The Supersizing of America: Portion Size and the Obesity Epidemic," *Nutrition Today* 38.2 (2000), 42–53.

10. B. J. Rolls, L. S. Roe, J. S. Meengs, and D. E. Wall, "Increasing the Portion Size of a Sandwich Increases Energy Intake," *Journal of the American Dietetic Association* 104 (2004), 367–372; N. Diliberti, P. L. Bordi, M. T. Conklin, L. S. Roe, and B. J. Rolls, "Increased Portion Size Leads to Increased Energy Intake in a Restaurant Meal," *Obesity Research* 12 (2004), 562–568; B. J. Rolls, L. S. Roe, T. V. E. Kral, J. S. Meengs, and D. E. Wall, "Increasing the Portion Size of a Packaged Snack Increases Energy Intake in Men and Women," *Appetite* 42 (2004), 63–69.

11. J. A. Elio-Martin, J. A. Ledikwe, and B. J. Rolls, "The Influence of Food Portion Size and Energy Density on Energy Intake: Implications of for Weight Management," *American Journal of Clinical Nutrition* 82.1 (2005), supplement 236S–241S.

12. Ibid.

13. Tinna Laufey Asgeirsdottir, "Do Body Weight and Gender Shape the Work Force? The Case of Iceland," *Economic and Human Biology* 9.2 (March 2011), 148–156; John Cawley, "The Impact of Obesity on Employment," *Journal of Human Resources* 39 (2004), 451–474; S. Morris, "The Impact of Obesity on Employment," *Labour Economics* 14 (2007), 413–433.

14. Aside from the fact that we can all attest to this, it has been studied and discussed extensively in Brian Wansink's *Mindless Eating: Why We Eat More Than We Think* (New York: Bantam Books, 2010).

15. R. Calitri, E. M. Pothos, K. Tapper, J. M. Brunstrom, and P. J. Rogers, "Cognitive Biases to Healthy and Unhealthy Food Words Predict Change in BMI," *Obesity* 18 (2010), 2282–2287; and K. Tapper, E. M. Pothos, and A. D. Lawrence, "Feast your Eyes: Hunger and Trait Reward Drive Predict Attentional Bias for Food Cues," *Emotion* 10 (2010), 949–954.

16. Cheryl L. Hayne, Patricia A. Moran, and Mary M. Ford, "Regulating Environments to Reduce Obesity," *Journal of Public Health Policy* 25.3–4 (2004), 391–407, at 392.

17. Brian Elbel, Joyce Gyamfi, and Rogan Kersh, "Child and Adolescent Fast Food Choices and the Influence of Caloric Labeling: A Natural Experiment," *International Journal of Obesity* 35.4 (April 2011), 493–500.

18. Anthony Robbins and Marion Nestle, "Call for Papers," *Journal of Public Health Policy* 32 (2011), 143–145.

19. Kleinig, *Paternalism.*

20. Arneson, "Mill Versus Paternalism," 470–489.

21. See Alex Rajezi, "A Liberal Approach to the Obesity Epidemic," *Public Affairs Quarterly* 22.3 (July 2008), 269–287.

22. Goodin, Robert, "Ethics of Smoking," *Ethics* 99:3 (April 1989), 574–624.

QUESTIONS

1. Conly discusses a common objection to paternalism: When we prevent people from acting on their decisions (what Conly calls coercing them), we fail to show them adequate respect. Conly writes that "to respect something seems to mean to recognize that thing's value, and to act in a way that is consistent with that value." Many philosophers maintain that the primary way in which we must respect people is to respect their autonomy. How might Conly respond to these philosophers?

2. Conly argues that libertarian paternalism is less effective than coercive paternalism and is manipulative. Explain both of these objections to libertarian paternalism.

3. Conly clarifies that she supports paternalism that helps people achieve their *ultimate ends.* Later, Conly gives four criteria for a justifiable paternalistic policy. One criterion is that it promotes a *long-term goal* of individuals. Is helping an individual achieve her ultimate ends the same thing as promoting her long-term goals? Could an individual's long-term goals conflict with her ultimate ends?

4. Conly argues that *portion* control regulations would promote a long-term goal of individuals: "We want longer lives and we want good health, both as ends in themselves and as means to doing everything else we want to do." Do you agree that people typically have, as long-term goals, maintaining good health and leading a longer life? How might Eric Finkelstein and Laurie Zuckerman (from Chapter 12) respond to Conly's claim that people typically have, as long-term goals, maintaining good health and leading a longer life? Recall that Finkelstein and Zuckerman assert that the choices of overweight people are typically utility-maximizing choices, given the benefits and costs of healthy eating, unhealthy eating, exercise, and poor health.

5. How might Conly respond to Finkelstein and Zuckerman's claim that the choices of overweight people are typically utility-maximizing choices? Which of the following long-term goals do you have?
   • Maintaining good health and leading a longer life
   • Being as healthy as possible and leading as long a life as possible
   • Striking the optimal balance between health, longevity, pleasure, and other values
   • Leading a life with as much pleasure as possible

6. Does the New York City big soda ban interfere with a voluntary choice to purchase sugary drinks larger than 16 ounces? How might Conly answer this question?

ALVA NOË

The Value in Sweet Drinks

In this blog post, philosopher Alva Nöe critiques the New York City big soda ban. The soda ban is based on the presumption that health is more important than pleasure, but this is a value judgment that not everyone shares.

New York City's ban on big sodas raises big issues.

Consider: modern political thought starts with the recognition that, as philosopher John Rawls put it, there are different, competing and incompatible conceptions of the good. We live in a pluralistic word.

Religious wars, political upheavals, the discovery and settlement of the New World—all this established the fact that there are wildly different conceptions of how to live, of what makes for a good life.

The great ambition, or maybe fantasy, of classical liberal thought is that it would be possible to set up a society in which radically different and incompatible conceptions of the good could flourish. The trick would be to come up with a constitution (or what Rawls called "a basic structure") that anyone, regardless of their world view and value system, could accept.

The rest is history. For the last two-hundred plus years we've been hashing out the limits of the liberal vision in our daily lives and in our domestic and international politics. And it isn't easy: there's lots of stuff that some people value (drinking alcohol, for example, or driving on the sabbath, or same-sex love, or free speech on some topics) that others find profoundly unacceptable.

This is what I had in mind, in my recent piece on the New York City soda ban, when I wrote that you can't go ahead and ban something, just because it's bad. I was appealing to the point that we aren't entitled—the mayor is not entitled—to take for granted that we know what is bad and what is good. These values are always up for grabs.

Now, in one sense this is a crazy point and I freely admit it. Soda-cup size is not fundamental; it's the sort of thing that governments can surely regulate without trampling on basic human rights or conceptions of the good. I wasn't trying to make a general "government, hands off" point.

But that's not the end of the story. What the mayor, and what some of the readers of this blog seem to have thought, is that the science of public health simply settles the matter.

Drinking large sodas makes you obese; being obese makes you more likely to get sick. Therefore, drinking soda in large quantities is bad. And therefore it is good to ban it, especially since government or, rather, society ends up bearing so much of the cost of taking care of sick people.

This is just a terrible argument. The same reasoning can be used to ban just about anything. Why not prohibit skateboards? Kitchen knives?

Alva Noë, "The Value in Sweet Drinks," from *NPR 13.7: Cosmos and Culture Blog* (September 2012). http://www.npr.org/sections/13.7/2012/09/24/161277720/the-value-in-sweet-drinks. Reprinted with permission of the author.

Automobiles? Use of these things is dangerous; if we banned their use, we'd prevent injury. We'd save money. We'd save lives.

What these examples bring out is the simple fact that a thing isn't bad just because, looked at in isolation, it poses a danger. Knives, cars and skateboards have a place in a good life, even if they are dangerous.

Now we come to large containers of soda. Do they have a place in anybody's conception of the good life?

I'll tell you this. They don't have any place in my conception of the good. I don't even drink soda. I grew up in the seventies and my parents didn't let me drink soda. I don't let my kids drink soda, except for special occasions. I don't even drink organic, locally-produced soda!

But to judge by behavior, there are lots of people who *do* value soda in large quantities. Am I, is Mayor Bloomberg, in a position to judge *for them* that they are wrong to value soda as they do?

And now we get to the nub:

There's no controversy about whether large quantities of soda belong in a healthy diet. Is there a link between extra-large sodas and the rise of obesity? I'm prepared to accept that there is.

But this leaves the big question unanswered. Does drinking large sodas (and here you can substitute your favorite vice: drinking alcohol, smoking tobacco or pot, eating high-fat foods, sweets) belong to anyone's legitimate conception of the good life *even though* it is dangerous?

No public health statistics will solve this for you. It is a question about value. In particular, it is a question about the value of *pleasure*.

Soda has no place in my conception of the good. But pleasure does. And it seems to me that the attack on soda and candy—an attack that is really just getting going, I fear—like the older and still ongoing attacks on drugs, tobacco and alcohol, is an attack on the value of pleasure. We've left the domain of public health, here. We are squarely in the domain of value.

There are many other issues at stake in the soda debate. For example, it might be said that consumers are actually the victims of Big Soda's manipulative super-sizing and that New York City is well within its rights to try to take measures to protect consumers. I'll return to this question next time.

QUESTIONS

1. Nöe writes: "Soda has no place in my conception of the good. But pleasure does. And it seems to me that the attack on soda and candy—an attack that is really just getting going, I fear—like the older and still ongoing attacks on drugs, tobacco and alcohol, is an attack on the value of pleasure." Do we drink large sodas because this gives us more pleasure than drinking smaller sodas? What might Brian Wansink ("The Mindless Margin," Chapter 12) say? What does Sarah Conly say about this?

2. Nöe thinks that the soda ban assumes a conception of the good that not everyone shares. Conly thinks that portion control policies (of which the soda ban is one example) help people to achieve their long-term goals. Do you agree more with Nöe or with Conly? Why?

Printed in the USA/Agawam, MA
September 23, 2020

761682.013